National Council of Teachers of Mathematics Principles and Standards for School Mathematics

Principles for School Mathematics

- EQUITY. Excellence in mathematics education requires equity—high expectations and strong support for all students.

- CURRICULUM. A curriculum is more than a collection of activities: it must be coherent, focused on important mathematics, and well articulated across the grades.

- TEACHING. Effective mathematics teaching requires understanding what students know and need to learn and then challenging and supporting them to learn it well.

- LEARNING. Students must learn mathematics with understanding, actively building new knowledge from experience and prior knowledge.

- ASSESSMENT. Assessment should support the learning of important mathematics and furnish useful information to both teachers and students.

- TECHNOLOGY. Technology is essential in teaching and learning mathematics; it influences the mathematics that is taught and enhances students' learning.

Standards for School Mathematics

NUMBER AND OPERATIONS

Instructional programs from prekindergarten through grade 12 should enable all students to—

- understand numbers, ways of representing numbers, relationships among numbers, and number systems;

- understand meanings of operations and how they relate to one another;

- compute fluently and make reasonable estimates.

ALGEBRA

Instructional programs from prekindergarten through grade 12 should enable all students to—

- understand patterns, relations, and functions;

- represent and analyze mathematical situations and structures using algebraic symbols;

- use mathematical models to represent and understand quantitative relationships;

- analyze change in various contexts.

GEOMETRY

Instructional programs from prekindergarten through grade 12 should enable all students to—

- analyze characteristics and properties of two- and three-dimensional geometric shapes and develop mathematical arguments about geometric relationships;

- specify locations and describe spatial relationships using coordinate geometry and other representational systems;

- apply transformations and use symmetry to analyze mathematical situations;

- use visualization, spatial reasoning, and geometric modeling to solve problems.

MEASUREMENT

Instructional programs from prekindergarten through grade 12 should enable all students to—

- understand measurable attributes of objects and the units, systems, and processes of measurement;

- apply appropriate techniques, tools, and formulas to determine measurements.

DATA ANALYSIS AND PROBABILITY

Instructional programs from prekindergarten through grade 12 should enable all students to—

- formulate questions that can be addressed with data and collect, organize, and display relevant data to answer them;
- select and use appropriate statistical methods to analyze data;
- develop and evaluate inferences and predictions that are based on data;
- understand and apply basic concepts of probability.

PROBLEM SOLVING

Instructional programs from prekindergarten through grade 12 should enable all students to—

- build new mathematical knowledge through problem solving;
- solve problems that arise in mathematics and in other contexts;
- apply and adapt a variety of appropriate strategies to solve problems;
- monitor and reflect on the process of mathematical problem solving.

REASONING AND PROOF

Instructional programs from prekindergarten through grade 12 should enable all students to—

- recognize reasoning and proof as fundamental aspects of mathematics;
- make and investigate mathematical conjectures;
- develop and evaluate mathematical arguments and proofs;
- select and use various types of reasoning and methods of proof.

COMMUNICATION

Instructional programs from prekindergarten through grade 12 should enable all students to—

- organize and consolidate their mathematical thinking through communication;
- communicate their mathematical thinking coherently and clearly to peers, teachers, and others;
- analyze and evaluate the mathematical thinking and strategies of others;
- use the language of mathematics to express mathematical ideas precisely.

CONNECTIONS

Instructional programs from prekindergarten through grade 12 should enable all students to—

- recognize and use connections among mathematical ideas;
- understand how mathematical ideas interconnect and build on one another to produce a coherent whole;
- recognize and apply mathematics in contexts outside of mathematics.

REPRESENTATION

Instructional programs from prekindergarten through grade 12 should enable all students to—

- create and use representations to organize, record, and communicate mathematical ideas;
- select, apply, and translate among mathematical representations to solve problems;
- use representations to model and interpret physical, social, and mathematical phenomena.

Sixth Edition

MATHEMATICS FOR ELEMENTARY TEACHERS
A Contemporary Approach

Gary L. Musser
Oregon State University

William F. Burger

Blake E. Peterson
Brigham Young University

John Wiley & Sons, Inc.

To:

Marge, my mother, for her continuing encouragement; Irene, my wife, for her constant support; Greg, my son, for being a great father; Maranda, my granddaughter, for her enthusiasm for learning; and Mary, Bill Burger's daughter, for the joyful times she shared with Bill.

G.L.M.

Shauna, my beautiful wife, for her unwavering love and encouragement; Quinn, Joelle, Taren, and Riley, my four children, for bringing me great joy and happiness as well as being my built-in laboratory; Dad, for the legacy of service and teaching he left behind; and Mom, for her continued, never-ending support.

B.E.P.

DEVELOPMENT EDITOR	Marian Provenzano
EDITORIAL ASSISTANTS	Lili Kalish, Stacy French
MARKETING MANAGER	Julie Lindstrom
SENIOR PRODUCTION EDITOR	Norine M. Pigliucci
SENIOR DESIGNER	Kevin Murphy
PHOTO EDITOR	Lisa Gee
SENIOR MEDIA EDITOR	Martin Batey
PRODUCTION MANAGEMENT SERVICES	mb editorial services
COVER AND INTERIOR DESIGN	Michael Jung

®Dynamic Geometry and *The Geometer's Sketchpad* are registered trademarks of Key Curriculum Press. ™*Sketchpad* and *JavaSketchpad* are trademarks of Key Curriculum Press.

This book was set in 10/12 Times New Roman by Progressive Information Technologies and printed and bound by Von Hoffmann Press. The cover was printed by Von Hoffmann Press.

This book is printed on acid-free paper. ∞

ISBN 0-471-16425-9

Printed in the United States of America

10 9 8 7 6 5 4 3 2 1

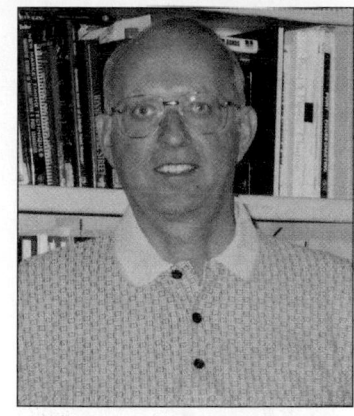

Gary L. Musser is currently Professor Emeritus from Oregon State University. He earned both his B.S. in Mathematics Education in 1961 and his M.S. in Mathematics in 1963 at the University of Michigan and his Ph.D. in Mathematics (Radical Theory) in 1970 at the University of Miami in Florida. He taught at the junior and senior high, junior college, college, and university levels for more than 30 years. He served his last 24 years teaching prospective teachers in the Department of Mathematics at Oregon State University. While at OSU, Dr. Musser developed the mathematics component of the elementary teacher program. Soon after Professor William F. Burger joined the OSU Department of Mathematics in a similar capacity, the two of them began to write the first edition of this book. Professor Burger passed away during the preparation of the second edition, and later Professor Blake E. Peterson was hired at OSU. Professor Peterson joined Professor Musser as a coauthor of the fifth edition.

Professor Musser has published 40 papers in many journals, including the *Pacific Journal of Mathematics*, *Canadian Journal of Mathematics*, *The Mathematics Association of America Monthly*, the NCTM's *The Mathematics Teacher*, the NCTM's *The Arithmetic Teacher*, *School Science and Mathematics*, *The Oregon Mathematics Teacher*, and *The Computing Teacher*. In addition, he is a coauthor of two other college mathematics books: *College Geometry—A Problem-Solving Approach with Applications* and *Mathematics in Life, Society, and the World*. He also coauthored the K–8 series *Mathematics in Action*. He has given more than 65 invited lectures/workshops at a variety of conferences, including NCTM and MAA conferences, and was awarded 15 federal, state, and local grants to improve the teaching of mathematics.

While Professor Musser was at OSU, he was awarded the university's prestigious College of Science Carter Award for Teaching. He is currently living in sunny Las Vegas, where he continues to write, do research, ponder the mysteries of the stock market, and enjoy his granddaughter, the sunshine of his life.

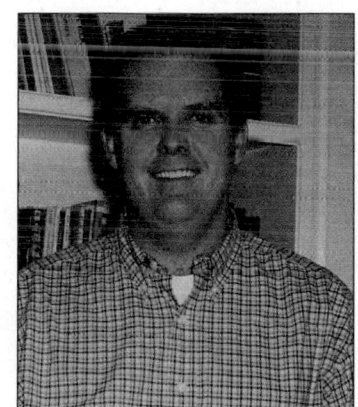

Blake E. Peterson is currently an Associate Professor in the Department of Mathematics Education at Brigham Young University. He was born and raised in Logan, Utah, where he graduated from Logan High School and Utah State University in secondary mathematics education. After graduation, he took his new wife, Shauna, to southern California, where he taught at Chino High School for two years. In addition to teaching general math and geometry, he coached basketball and football. In 1988, he began graduate school at Washington State University, where he later completed a M.S. and Ph.D. in pure mathematics.

After completing his Ph.D., Dr. Peterson was hired as a mathematics educator in the Department of Mathematics at Oregon State University in Corvallis, Oregon, where he taught for three years. It was at OSU that he met Gary Musser. He has since moved his wife and four children to Provo, Utah, to assume his position at Brigham Young University. As a professor, his first love is teaching, for which he has received a College Teaching Award in the College of Science. He has also designed the "Mathematics Teaching with Technology" and "Mathematics Teaching and the Classroom" courses at Brigham Young University.

Dr. Peterson has published papers in *Rocky Mountain Mathematics Journal*, *The American Mathematical Monthly*, *The Mathematical Gazette*, *Mathematics Teacher*, *Mathematics Magazine*, and *Mathematics Teaching in the Middle School*. His current research interests are the mathematical dialogue that occurs during teacher collaborations. In addition to teaching and writing, Dr. Peterson has done consulting for the College Board, is the president of the Utah Association of Mathematics Teacher Educators, is an associate editor of the journal *School, Science and Mathematics Education*, and is a board member of the Utah Council of Teachers of Mathematics.

Aside from his academic interests, Dr. Peterson enjoys spending time with his family, playing basketball, and working in the yard.

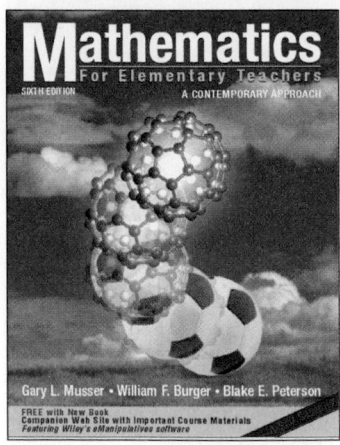

A Glowing Soccer Ball

Can a soccer ball glow? If it is a Carbon-60 molecule in the right setting, it can. In 1985, Richard Smalley, Harld Kroto, and Robert Curl discovered the third form of pure carbon called fullerenes. The other two forms of pure carbon are diamond and graphite. A fullerene, also called a Bucky Ball, consists of 60 carbon atoms arranged in the shape of a soccer ball. A unique feature of a fullerene, as compared to the other forms of pure carbon, is that it is more complex and the 60 atoms form a hollow sphere consisting of hexagons and pentagons on the surface. The name of fullerene, or Bucky Ball, comes from the name of the inventor of the geodesic dome, Buckminster Fuller.

So how does a Bucky Ball glow? In 1999, a group of researchers from University of California at Los Angeles and University of California at Santa Barbara added attachments to Bucky Balls that modified their electronic structure and caused them to emit white light. The surprising feature about this discovery is that up to this point, Bucky Balls were known for the ability to absorb light. There are other organic materials that can be easily engineered to emit green, orange, or yellow light, but white light has been quite difficult to generate. The fact that a molecule known for absorbing light has been engineered to emit white light makes this result even more astonishing.

Are there any practical applications for such a discovery? Whether it is dashboard displays in cars or cell phones, companies are always searching for ways of efficiently making their products useful in the light or dark. Several companies are researching ways of using organic materials for their products. It is not yet known if the glowing Bucky Ball will be an efficient way of meeting these needs.

Contents

Preface   ix

1 INTRODUCTION TO PROBLEM SOLVING   1
1.1   The Problem Solving Process and Strategies   3
1.2   Three Additional Strategies   15

2 SETS, WHOLE NUMBERS, AND NUMERATION   37
2.1   Sets As a Basis for Whole Numbers   39
2.2   Whole Numbers and Numeration   57
2.3   The Hindu–Arabic System   61
2.4   Relations and Functions   70

3 WHOLE NUMBERS: OPERATIONS AND PROPERTIES   93
3.1   Addition and Subtraction   95
3.2   Multiplication and Division   109
3.3   Ordering and Exponents   123

4 WHOLE-NUMBER COMPUTATION—MENTAL, ELECTRONIC AND WRITTEN   137
4.1   Mental Math, Estimation, and Calculators   139
4.2   Written Algorithms for Whole-Number Operations   153
4.3   Algorithms in Other Bases   171

5 NUMBER THEORY   183
5.1   Primes, Composites, and Tests for Divisibility   185
5.2   Counting Factors, Greatest Common Factor, and Least Common Multiple   197

6 FRACTIONS   215
6.1   The Set of Fractions   217
6.2   Fractions: Addition and Subtraction   230
6.3   Fractions: Multiplication and Division   241

7 DECIMALS, RATIO, PROPORTION, AND PERCENT   263
7.1   Decimals   265
7.2   Operations with Decimals   274
7.3   Ratio and Proportion   286
7.4   Percent   297

8 INTEGERS 317

8.1 Addition and Subtraction 319
8.2 Multiplication, Division, and Order 332

9 RATIONAL NUMBERS AND REAL NUMBERS, WITH AN INTRODUCTION TO ALGEBRA 353

9.1 The Rational Numbers 355
9.2 The Real Numbers 373
9.3 Functions and Their Graphs 390

10 STATISTICS 413

10.1 Organizing and Picturing Information 415
10.2 Analyzing Data 436
10.3 Misleading Graphs and Statistics 457

11 PROBABILITY 483

11.1 Probability and Simple Experiments 485
11.2 Probability and Complex Experiments 500
11.3 Simulation, Expected Value, Odds, and Conditional Probability 516
11.4 Additional Counting Techniques 530

12 GEOMETRIC SHAPES 547

12.1 Recognizing Geometric Shapes and Definitions 549
12.2 Analyzing Shapes 564
12.3 Properties of Geometric Shapes: Lines and Angles 576
12.4 Regular Polygons and Tessellations 586
12.5 Describing Three-Dimensional Shapes 597

13 MEASUREMENT 621

13.1 Measurement with Nonstandard and Standard Units 623
13.2 Length and Area 641
13.3 Surface Area 662
13.4 Volume 672

14 GEOMETRY USING TRIANGLE CONGRUENCE AND SIMILARITY 693

14.1 Congruence of Triangles 695
14.2 Similarity of Triangles 706
14.3 Basic Euclidean Constructions 718
14.4 Additional Euclidean Constructions 728
14.5 Geometric Problem Solving Using Triangle Congruence and Similarity 740

15 GEOMETRY USING COORDINATES 755

15.1 Distance and Slope in the Coordinate Plane 757
15.2 Equations and Coordinates 770
15.3 Geometric Problem Solving Using Coordinates 782

16 GEOMETRY USING TRANSFORMATIONS 797

16.1 Transformations 799
16.2 Congruence and Similarity Using Transformations 822
16.3 Geometric Problem Solving Using Transformations 839

EPILOGUE: AN ECLECTIC APPROACH TO GEOMETRY 855

TOPIC 1. ELEMENTARY LOGIC 858

TOPIC 2. CLOCK ARITHMETIC: A MATHEMATICAL SYSTEM 869

TOPIC 3. INTRODUCTION TO GRAPH THEORY 875

Answers to Exercise/Problem Sets-Part A, Chapter Tests, and Topics A1

Photograph Credits P1

Index I1

SPOTLIGHTS ON TECHNOLOGY

Chapter 1
eManipulatives
Counterfeit Coin
Tower of Hanoi
Spreadsheets
Consecutive Integer Sum
Sum of the Odds

Chapter 2
eManipulatives
Venn Diagrams
Multibase Blocks
Spreadsheets
Base Converter
Function Machines and Tables

Chapter 3
eManipulatives
Number Line

Chapter 4
eManipulatives
Base Blocks: Addition
Base Blocks: Subtraction
Spreadsheets
Scaffold Division
Calculator
Finding quotients and remainders

Chapter 5
eManipulatives
Sieve of Eratosthenes
Spreadsheets
Euclidean
Calculator
GCF
GCF using Euclidean algorithm

Chapter 6
eManipulatives
Equivalent Fractions
Comparing Fractions
Adding Fractions
Dividing Fractions
Calculator
Fraction equality
Converting improper fractions to mixed numbers
Cross-multiplication of fraction inequality
Adding fractions on a fraction calculator
Simplifying on a fraction calculator

Chapter 7
eManipulatives
Percent Gauge
Calculator
Converting fractions to percents
Solving percent problems
Finding discounts
Compound interest

Chapter 8
eManipulatives
Chips Plus
Chips Minus
Calculator
Integer computation on a scientific calculator
Negative Sign Key
Conversions from standard to scientific notation

Chapter 9
eManipulatives
Balance Beam Algebra
Function Grapher
Spreadsheets
Cubic
Calculator
Using a fraction calculator to find sums and differences of rational numbers
Using a fraction calculator to find products of rational numbers
Comparing fractions with negative numerators or denominators
Using calculators to find square roots
Using calculators to find roots of real numbers
Using exponent key to calculate real exponents

Chapter 10
eManipulatives
Histogram
Scatterplots
Spreadsheets
Circle Graph Budget
Standard Deviation
Calculator
Finding the mean of a data set
Finding the standard deviation

Chapter 11
eManipulatives
Simulation
Spreadsheets
Coin toss
Roll the dice
Calculator
Using factorial key to count permutations of n
Calculating $_nP_r$
Calculating $_nC_r$

Chapter 12
eManipulatives
Tessellations
Slicing Solids
Geometer's Sketchpad
Name That Quadrilateral
Triangle Angle Sum

Chapter 13
eManipulatives
Geoboard
Pythagorean Theorem
Geometer's Sketchpad
Rectangle Area
Same Base, Same Height, Same Area
Parallelogram Areas
Dynamic Pythagorean Theorem
Triangle Inequality

Chapter 14
eManipulatives
Congruence
Geometer's Sketchpad
Tree Height
Circumcircle
Midquad

Chapter 15
eManipulatives
Coordinate Geoboard
Geometer's Sketchpad
Slope
Perpendicular Lines

Chapter 16
eManipulatives
Translation Transformations
Geometer's Sketchpad
Size Transformation

Welcome to a world of mathematical understanding that we hope you will find stimulating, rewarding, enlightening, and fun. We salute you for choosing teaching as a profession and hope that your experiences with this book will help prepare you to be the best possible teacher of mathematics that you can be. We have presented this elementary mathematics material from a variety of perspectives so that you will be more able to address the broad range of learning styles that you will encounter in your future students. This book also encourages prospective teachers to gain an understanding of the underlying concepts of elementary mathematics while maintaining an appropriate level of mathematical precision.

We have also sought to present this material in a manner consistent with the recommendations in (1) *A Call for Change: Recommendations on the Mathematical Preparation of Teachers*; prepared by the Mathematical Association of America's Committee on the Mathematical Education of Teachers; (2) *The Mathematical Education of Teachers*; prepared by the Conference Board of the Mathematical Sciences; and (3) the National Council of Teachers of Mathematics' *Curriculum and Evaluation Standards for School Mathematics*, *Professional Standards for Teaching Mathematics*, and *Principles and Standards for School Mathematics*. In addition, we have received valuable advice from many of our colleagues around the United States through questionnaires, reviews, focus groups, and personal communications. We have taken great care to respect this advice and to ensure that the content of the book has mathematical integrity and is accessible and helpful to the variety of students who will use it. As always, we look forward to hearing from you about your experiences with this text.

GARY L. MUSSER
BLAKE E. PETERSON

Content Features

Number Systems Insofar as possible, number topics are covered sequentially to parallel their development in the school curriculum. Fractions and integers are each treated as extensions of whole numbers. Rational numbers are developed briskly as extensions of both the fractions (by adjoining their opposites) and the integers (by adjoining their reciprocals). The mathematical structure of an ordered field continues to serve to unify this presentation. The important applications of statistics and probability serve as a capstone to the study of number systems.

Approach to Geometry Geometry is organized from the point of view of the five-level van Hiele model of a child's development in geometry. After studying shapes and measurement, geometry is approached more formally through Euclidean congruence and similarity, coordinates, and transformations. The Epilogue provides an eclectic approach by solving geometry problems using a variety of techniques.

Underlying Themes

Problem Solving An extensive collection of problem-solving strategies is progressively developed; these strategies can be applied to a generous supply of problems in the exercise/problem sets. The depth of problem-solving coverage can be varied by the number of strategies selected throughout the book and by the problems assigned.

Deductive Reasoning The use of deduction is promoted throughout the book. The approach is gradual, with later chapters having more multistep problems. In particular, the last sections of Chapters 14, 15, and 16 and the Epilogue offer a rich source of interesting theorems and problems in geometry.

Technology The Math Explorer calculator, which has been upgraded to the TI-34 II, is used in many schools. These calculators are used to illustrate its capability to do long division with remainder, fraction calculations, and more. A graphing calculator is also illustrated at a few relevant junctures. The eManipulatives, which were on the CD in the fifth edition, have been expanded and integrated throughout the book. Many of these activities are electronic versions of the traditional manipulatives, while others expose students to some useful, modern software applications that are learning situations as well as problem-solving environments. In addition, dynamic Web site–centered activities are provided for students to solve problems using spreadsheets and dynamic geometry software. Webmodules are available on these latter two topics to encourage students to extend their knowledge.

Additional Topics

Since reviewers were split concerning where the following topics should appear in the text, they are placed near the end of the book to allow for maximum flexibility.

Topic 1, "Elementary Logic," may be used anywhere in a course.

Topic 2, "Clock Arithmetic: A Mathematical System," uses the concepts of opposite and reciprocal and hence may be most instructive after Chapter 6, "Fractions" and Chapter 8, "Integers" have been completed. This section also contains an introduction to modular arithmetic.

Topic 3, "Introduction to Graph Theory," develops the ideas of vertex-edge graphs or networks as a method to model and visualize certain problem situations. Because of the visual nature of the graphs, this topic may fit best at the end of Chapter 12. The topic, however, is independent enough to fit almost anywhere in the course.

Course Options

The material in this book has been organized to allow for a wide variety of courses. At Oregon State University, all preservice elementary teachers have been required to take 12 quarter-hours of mathematics. This book is used for the first 9 quarter-hours, a one-year sequence. Each week, students attend 3 one-hour lectures and a 1-hour lab in which materials from the *Student Resource Handbook* are covered. This book, together with *A Guide to Problem-Solving*, is also used in a 3 quarter-hour junior-level course in problem solving for elementary teachers. This course is devoted entirely to developing the students' facilities in applying Pólya's four-step process and the strategies introduced at the beginning of each chapter.

Since many schools have special mathematical requirements, the following are suggested chapters and topics to fit any particular course.

Basic course: Chapters 1–7.
Basic course with logic: Topic 1, Chapters 1–7.
Basic course with informal geometry: Chapters 1–7, 12.
Basic course with introduction to geometry and measurement: Chapters 1–7, 12, 13.

Pedagogical Features

The general organization of the book was motivated by the following mathematics learning cube:

The three dimensions of the cube—cognitive levels, representational levels, and mathematical content—are integrated throughout the textual material as well as in the problem sets and chapter tests. Problem sets are organized into exercises (to support knowledge, skill, and understanding) and problems (to support problem solving and applications).

We have developed new pedagogical features to implement and reinforce the goals discussed above and to address the many challenges in the course.

Summary of Changes in the Sixth Edition

• **Starting Points** have been added to the beginning of each section. These Starting Points can be used in a variety of ways. First, they can be used by an instructor at the beginning of class to have students engage in some novel thinking and/or discussion about forthcoming material. Second, they can be used in small groups where students discuss the query presented. Third, they can be used as an advanced organizer homework piece where a class begins with a discussion of what individual students have discovered.

• **Spotlights on Technology** appear throughout the book at points where use of technology enriches the presentation. The technology used includes activities from our expanded eManipulative activities, spreadsheet activities, Geometer's Sketchpad activities, and calculators including both TI-34 II and a graphing calculator. Many of these rich activities can be accessed through our Web site at John Wiley (*www.wiley.com/college/musser*).

Spotlight on Technology The rolling of two dice and recording the sum of the number of dots on their faces can be simulated using a spreadsheet. Refer to the dynamic spreadsheet *Roll the Dice,* in the Spreadsheet webmodule, which contains a dice-rolling spreadsheet for you to work with. Use the spreadsheet to simulate rolling two dice 200 times. How close are the results of this experiment to the theoretical probabilities in Table 11.2?

www.wiley.com/college/musser

Spotlight on Technology To better understand the properties of the various quadrilaterals, it is helpful to be able to see there properties in action. The Geometer's Sketchpad® webmodule activity, *Name That Quadrilateral,* displays seven different quadrilaterals in the shape of a square. However, each quadrilateral is constructed with different properties. Some have right angles, some have congruent sides, and some have parallel sides. By dragging each of the points on each of the quadrilaterals, you can determine the most general name of each quadrilateral. See if you can name all seven of the quadrilaterals.

www.wiley.com/college/musser

Spotlight on Technology The Chapter 4 eManipulative activity, *Base Blocks: Subtraction,* utilizes the comparison approach to model subtraction. By placing blue blocks and red blocks next to each other, you can compare, match up, and remove blocks until only the difference remains. The problem 35 − 18 is modeled by beginning with the blocks shown at the right. Perform 35 − 18, 321 − 43, and 234 − 158 on the eManipulative. What process of moving the blocks is analogous to "borrowing" in the standard subtraction algorithm?

www.wiley.com/college/musser

8. Using the Chapter 4 eManipulative activity, *Multi-base Blocks—Subtraction*, model the following subtraction problems using base ten blocks. Sketch how the base ten blocks would be used.

   a.   413   **b.**   625
      − 57   −138

- **eManipulative Activities** are integrated throughout the book in Spotlights in Technology as well as the problems and exercises. The activities, problem solving and exploratory in nature, are designed to develop concepts central to each chapter by allowing students to interact with virtual manipulatives. These virtual manipulatives are similar to physical manipulatives frequently used to teach mathematics (for elementary through secondary) and for pre-service students. Examples include the geoboard, base ten blocks, black and red chips, and pattern blocks. Many of the problems in the problem sets have been designed to take advantage of the technology. Icons are used to identify the technology used to solve each problem.
- **A Companion Web Site** has been developed to provide a rich bank of resources for both instructors and students. The expanded Web site contains the following material:
  - The eManipulative Activities
  - An Introduction to Spreadsheets
  - An Introduction to Geometer's Sketchpad
  - An Introduction to Logo
  - An Introduction to the TI-83 plus Graphing Calculator
  - Links to NCTM Standards
  - Problem Solving Guide
  - Using Children's Literature in Teaching Mathematics

All the technology sections that were at the end of the fifth edition book (LOGO, Dynamic Geometry Software, Graphing Calculators) are now available on our John Wiley Web site.

    Four new cumulative tests are available on the Web site covering material up to the end of Chapters 4, 9, 11, and 16.

- **Updated Contents**
  - **Chapter 8** now includes the chip model for multiplication.
  - **Chapter 10** has been updated with new data.
  - **Chapter 11** has been revised to moderate the pace of the coverage.
  - An **Introduction to Graph Theory** has been added as a topic near the end of the book.

- **Reflections from Research** marginal notes have been added and updated.
- **Student Page Snapshots** have been updated. Each chapter has a page from an elementary school textbook relevant to the material being studied.

Reflection from Research
Students who only view fractions like $\frac{3}{4}$ as "three out of 4 parts" struggle to handle fraction multiplication problems such as $\frac{2}{3}$ of $\frac{9}{10}$. Students who can more flexibly view $\frac{3}{4}$ as "three fourths of one whole or three units of one fourth" can better solve multiplication of two proper fractions (Mack, 2001).

Summary of Popular Features Continuing from the Fifth Edition

- **Problem solving strategies** are integrated throughout the book. Each chapter introduces a new Problem Solving Strategy; a comprehensive list is included at the beginning of each chapter. Following the chapter opening vignette, each chapter, beginning with Chapter 2, contains a relevant Initial Problem that introduces a new strategy.
- **Mathematical Structure** reveals the mathematical ideas of the book. Main Definitions, Theorems, and Properties in each section are highlighted by boxes for quick review.
- **Exercise / Problem Sets** are separated into Part A (all answers are provided in the back of the book and all solutions are provided in our supplement—*Hints and Solutions for Part A Problems*) and Part B (answers are only provided in the *Instructor's Resource Manual*). Also, exercises and problems are distinguished so that students can learn how they differ.
- **Problems for Writing/Discussion** are included at the end of each problem set as well as at the end of each chapter review.
- **NCTM Standards 2000** are called out in the margins at relevant points in the text. The inside front cover contains the essentials of the NCTM Principles and Standards for School Mathematics.
- **Historical vignettes** open each chapter and introduce ideas and concept central to each chapter.

- **Mathematical Morsels** end every section with an interesting historical tidbit. They are a reward for completing a section!
- **People in Mathematics** highlights many of the giants in mathematics throughout history as well as others who have contributed to mathematics in various ways.

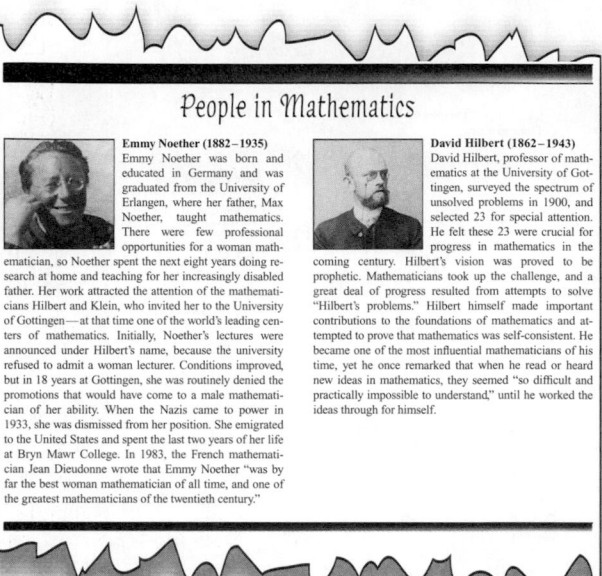

People in Mathematics

Emmy Noether (1882–1935)
Emmy Noether was born and educated in Germany and was graduated from the University of Erlangen, where her father, Max Noether, taught mathematics. There were few professional opportunities for a woman mathematician, so Noether spent the next eight years doing research at home and teaching for her increasingly disabled father. Her work attracted the attention of the mathematicians Hilbert and Klein, who invited her to the University of Gottingen—at that time one of the world's leading centers of mathematics. Initially, Noether's lectures were announced under Hilbert's name, because the university refused to admit a woman lecturer. Conditions improved, but in 18 years at Gottingen, she was routinely denied the promotions that would have come to a male mathematician of her ability. When the Nazis came to power in 1933, she was dismissed from her position. She emigrated to the United States and spent the last two years of her life at Bryn Mawr College. In 1983, the French mathematician Jean Dieudonne wrote that Emmy Noether "was by far the best woman mathematician of all time, and one of the greatest mathematicians of the twentieth century."

David Hilbert (1862–1943)
David Hilbert, professor of mathematics at the University of Gottingen, surveyed the spectrum of unsolved problems in 1900, and selected 23 for special attention. He felt these 23 were crucial for progress in mathematics in the coming century. Hilbert's vision was proved to be prophetic. Mathematicians took up the challenge, and a great deal of progress resulted from attempts to solve "Hilbert's problems." Hilbert himself made important contributions to the foundations of mathematics and attempted to prove that mathematics was self-consistent. He became one of the most influential mathematicians of his time, yet he once remarked that when he read or heard new ideas in mathematics, they seemed "so difficult and practically impossible to understand," until he worked the ideas through for himself.

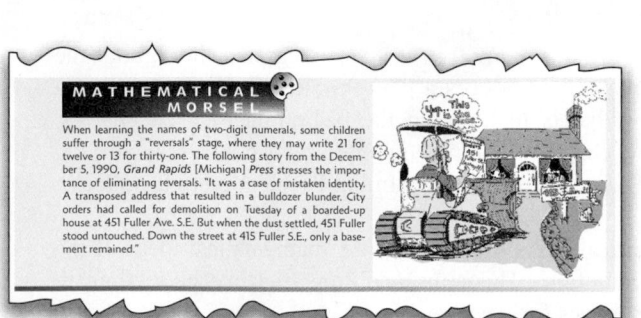

MATHEMATICAL MORSEL

When learning the names of two-digit numerals, some children suffer through a "reversals" stage, where they may write 21 for twelve or 13 for thirty-one. The following story from the December 5, 1990, *Grand Rapids* [Michigan] *Press* stresses the importance of eliminating reversals. "It was a case of mistaken identity. A transposed address that resulted in a bulldozer blunder. City orders had called for demolition on Tuesday of a boarded-up house at 451 Fuller Ave. S.E. But when the dust settled, 451 Fuller stood untouched. Down the street at 415 Fuller S.E., only a basement remained."

- **Chapter Review** is located at the end of each chapter together with a Chapter Test.
- **Epilogue,** following Chapter 16, provides a rich eclectic approach to geometry.
- **Logic and Clock Arithmetic** are discussed near the end of the book.

Companion Web Site/Supplements Package

Supplements for the Instructor

Instructor's Resource Manual This manual contains the following: (a) chapter-by-chapter discussion of the text material; (b) student "expectations" (objectives) for each chapter; (c) answers for all Part B exercises and problems; (d) answers for all the even-numbered problems in the Problem Solving Guide.

Computerized Test Bank The test bank contains true/false, multiple-choice, and open-ended questions.

eGrade This online assessment system contains a large bank of skill-building problems and solutions. Instructors can now automate the process of assigning, delivering, grading, and routing all kinds of homework, quizzes, and tests while providing students with immediate scoring and feedback on their work. Wiley eGrade "does the math" . . . and much more. For more information, visit www.wiley.com/college/egrade.

- **Instructor's Companion Web Site at www.wiley.com/college/musser**
- Instructors have access to all student Web site features
- PowerPoint Slides: more than 190 PowerPoints including figures from the text and several generic masters such as for dot paper, grids, and other formats
- Test Bank: contains true/false, multiple-choice, and free-response questions

Supplements for the Student

Student Resource Handbook This handbook is designed to enhance student learning as well as to begin to model effective classroom practices. Since many instructors are working with students to create a personalized journal, this edition of the handbook is three-hole-punched for easy customization.

—*Prepared by Karen Swenson and Marcia Swanson, two exceptional mathematics educators.*

   ISBN: 0471236799

FEATURES INCLUDE:
- **Warm Ups:** Short problem solving activities.
- **Hands On Activities:** Activities that help develop initial understandings at the concrete level.
- **Two Dimensional Manipulatives:** Cutouts are provided on cardstock.
- **Exercises:** Additional practice for building skills in concepts.
- **Mental Math:** Short activities to help develop better mental math skills.
- **Self-Test:** New 10-item tests in a variety of formats designed to assess student knowledge of key areas.
- **Solutions:** Solutions to all items in the handbook to enhance self-study.
- **Resource Articles:** Up-to-date references from journals for elementary teachers to help provide a connection to the classroom.
- **Directions in Education:** Specially written articles that provide insights into major issues of the day, including the Standards of the National Council of Teachers of Mathematics.

Hints and Solutions Manual for Part A Problems This manual can be used to help students develop problem solving proficiency in a self-study mode.

—*Developed by Lynn Trimpe, Roger Maurer, and Vikki Maurer of Linn-Benton Community College.*

   ISBN: 0471236780

FEATURES INCLUDE:
- **Hints:** These are provided to give students a start on all Part A problems in the text.
- **Additional Hints:** For more challenging problems, a second hint is provided.
- **Complete Solutions to Part A Problems:** Carefully written out solutions are provided to model one correct solution.

• Student Companion Web Site at www.wiley.com/college/musser

A Guide to Problem Solving This online resource contains more than 200 creative problems keyed to the strategies in the textbook.

—*Prepared by Don Miller, who was a professor of mathematics at St. Cloud State University.*

FEATURES INCLUDE:
- **Opening Problem:** An introductory problem to motivate the need for a strategy.
- **Solution/Discussion/Clues:** A worked-out solution of the opening problem together with a discussion of the strategy and some clues on when to select this strategy.
- **Practice Problems:** A second problem that uses the same strategy together with a worked-out solution and two practice problems.
- **Mixed Strategy Practice:** Four practice problems that can be solved using one or more of the strategies introduced to that point.

- **Additional Practice Problems and Additional Mixed Strategy Problems:** Sections that provide more practice for particular strategies as well as many problems for which students need to identify appropriate strategies.

eManipulative Activities Online eManipulatives are integrated in each chapter and are keyed to "Spotlight on Technology" exercises throughout the text. These activities are designed to develop concepts central to the chapter and many of the activities mirror physical manipulatives. The goal is to engage the learner in a way that will lead to a more indepth understanding of the concept.

—*Prepared by Lawrence O. Cannon, E. Robert Heal, and Richard Wellman of the Department of Mathematics and Statistics at Utah State University. This project is supported by the National Science Foundation.*

The Geometer's Sketchpad Activities and Tutorial The *Geometer's Sketchpad* Activities are keyed to "Spotlight on Technology" sections throughout the text. These dynamic activities allow you to work through selected problems using Java Sketchpad™ exercises, which were created from the Geometer's Sketchpad's award-winning learning environment. In addition, an online tutorial is designed to introduce students to *The Geometer's Sketchpad*®, an effective learning tool that helps future teachers broaden their mathematical understanding and the use of technology in the classroom.

—*Prepared by Armando Martinez-Cruz, California State University, Fullerton.*

Spreadsheet Activities and Tutorial "Spotlight on Technology" activities are keyed to specific online spreadsheet activities. A tutorial is designed to introduce students to the use of spreadsheets. Examples illustrate the use of spreadsheets and the tutorial contains exercises and problems.

—*Prepared by Keith Leatham, Portland State University.*

Children's Literature Tutorial This section consists of an introduction, suggestions on how to integrate children's literature into the classroom, and a list of book titles, which is annotated by math topic and includes questions, a checklist of how to evaluate books, and a general reference list.

—*Prepared by Joan Cohen Jones, Eastern Michigan University.*

Technology Section This section contains an Introduction to Programming in LOGO: Turtle Geometry and an Introduction to Graphing Calculators.

Links to National Council of Teachers of Mathematics and Other Helpful Math Sites.

ACKNOWLEDGMENTS

During the development of *Mathematics for Elementary Teachers*, Sixth Edition, we benefited from comments, suggestions, and evaluations from many of our colleagues. We would like to acknowledge the contributions made by the following people:

Reviewers

Scott Barnett, *Henry Ford Community College*
Dana S. Craig, *University of Central Oklahoma*
Gerald Grossman, *Oakland University*
Joan Cohen Jones, *Eastern Michigan University*
Marilyn L. Keir, *University of Utah*
Dottie King, *Indiana State University*
David E. Koslakiewicz, *University of Wisconsin, Milwaukee*
J. Lyn Miller, *Slippery Rock University*
Kathy C. Nickell, *College of DuPage*
Peggy Sacher, *University of Delaware*
Karen E. Spike, *University of North Carolina, Wilmington*
Debra S. Stokes, *East Carolina University*
Jeannine G. Vigerust, *New Mexico State University*
Brad Whitaker, *Point Loma Nazarene University*

CD Reviewers

Barbara Boschmans, *Northern Arizona University*
Thomas Hays, *Ohio State University, Newark*
Robert Edward Lewand, *Goucher College*
Linda Padilla, *Joliet Junior College*
Larry Smyrski, *Henry Ford Community College*

Questionnaire Respondents

Jane Baldwin, *Capital University*
Chuck Beals, *Hartnell College*
James Bierdan, *Rhode Island College*
Neil K. Bishop, *The University of Southern Mississippi-Gulf Coast*
Jonathan Bodrero, *Snow College*
Dianne Bolen, *Northeast Mississippi Community College*
Anne E. Brown, *Indiana University, South Bend*
R. Elaine Carbone, *Clarion University*
Dana S. Craig, *University of Central Oklahoma*
Jennifer Davis, *Ulster County Community College*
Dennis De Jong, *Dordt College*
Shobha Deshmukh, *College of Saint Benedict/St. John's University*
Sheila Doran, *Xavier University*
Francis Fennell, *Western Maryland College*
Joseph Ferrar, *Ohio State University*
Fay Fester, *The Pennsylvania State University*
Marie Franzosa, *Oregon State University*
Ginny Hamilton, *Shawnee State University*

Kathy E. Hays, *Anne Arundel Community College*
Holly M. Hoover, *Montana State University, Billings*
Wei-Shen Hsia, *University of Alabama*
Julie Keener, *Central Oregon Community College*
Jack Lombard, *Harold Washington College*
Ann Louis, *College of the Canyons*
Jeffery T. McLean, *University of St. Thomas*
Ken Monks, *University of Scranton*
Mike Mourer, *Johnston Community College*
Gary Nelson, *Central Community College, Columbus Campus*
Kathy C. Nickell, *College of DuPage*
Susan Patterson, *Erskine College (retired)*
Tammy Powell-Kopilak, *Dutchess Community College*
Christy Preis, *Arkansas State University, Mountain Home*
Stephen Prothero, *Williamette University*
Anne D. Roberts, *University of Utah*
Rebecca Seaberg, *Bethel College*
Marie Sheckels, *Mary Washington College*
William Speer, *University of Nevada, Las Vegas*
Karen E. Spike, *University of North Carolina, Wilmington*
Ruth Ann Stefanussen, *University of Utah*
Carol Steiner, *Kent State University*
Debra S. Stokes, *East Carolina University*
John L. Wisthoff, *Anne Arundel Community College (retired)*
Lohra Wolden, *Southern Utah University*

Focus Group Participants

Mara Alagic, *Wichita State University*
Robin L. Ayers, *Western Kentucky University*
Elaine Carbone, *Clarion University of Pennsylvania*
Janis Cimperman, *St. Cloud State University*
Richard DeCesare, *Southern Connecticut State University*
Maria Diamantis, *Southern Connecticut State University*
Jerrold W. Grossman, *Oakland University*
Richard H. Hudson, *University of South Carolina, Columbia*
Carol Kahle, *Shippensburg University*
Jane Keiser, *Miami University*
Catherine Carroll Kiaie, *Cardinal Stritch University*
Cynthia Y. Naples, *St. Edward's University*
Armando M. Martinez-Cruz, *California State University, Fullerton*
David L. Pagni, *Fullerton University*
Melanie Parker, *Clarion University of Pennsylvania*
Carol Phillips-Bey, *Cleveland State University*

In addition, we'd like to acknowledge the contributions made by colleagues from earlier editions.

Reviewers

Chuck Beals, *Hartnell College*
Peter Braunfeld, *University of Illinois*
Tom Briske, *Georgia State University*
Anne Brown, *Indiana University, South Bend*
Christine Browning, *Western Michigan University*
Tommy Bryan, *Baylor University*
Lucille Bullock, *University of Texas*
Thomas Butts, *University of Texas, Dallas*
Ann Dinkheller, *Xavier University*
John Dossey, *Illinois State University*
Carol Dyas, *University of Texas, San Antonio*
Donna Erwin, *Salt Lake Community College*
Sheryl Ettlich, *Southern Oregon State College*
Ruhama Even, *Michigan State University*
Iris B. Fetta, *Clemson University*
Majorie Fitting, *San Jose State University*
Susan Friel, *Math/Science Education Network, University of
  North Carolina*
Gerald Gannon, *California State University, Fullerton*
Virginia Ellen Hanks, *Western Kentucky University*
John G. Harvey, *University of Wisconsin, Madison*
Patricia L. Hayes, *Utah State University, Uintah
  Basin Branch Campus*
Alan Hoffer, *University of California, Irvine*
Barnabas Hughes, *California State University, Northridge*
Joe Kennedy, *Miami University*
Richard Kinson, *University of South Alabama*
John Koker, *University of Wisconsin*
Josephine Lane, *Eastern Kentucky University*
Louise Lataille, *Springfield College*
Roberts S. Matulis, *Millersville University*
Mercedes McGowen, *Harper College*
Flora Alice Metz, *Jackson State Community College*
Barbara Moses, *Bowling Green State University*
Maura Murray, *University of Massachusetts*
Kathy Nickell, *College of DuPage*
Dennis Parker, *The University of the Pacific*
James Riley, *Western Michigan University*
Eric Rowley, *Utah State University*
Lawrence Small, *L.A. Pierce College*
Joe K. Smith, *Northern Kentucky University*
J. Phillip Smith, *Southern Connecticut State University*
Judy Sowder, *San Diego State University*
Larry Sowder, *San Diego State University*
Karen Spike, *University of Northern Carolina, Wilmington*
Lynn Trimpe, *Linn–Benton Community College*
Bruce Vogeli, *Columbia University*
Kenneth C. Washinger, *Shippensburg University*
John Wilkins, *California State University, Dominguez Hills*

Questionnaire Respondents

Mary Alter, *University of Maryland*
Dr. J. Altinger, *Youngstown State University*

Jamie Whitehead Ashby, *Texarkana College*
Dr. Donald Balka, *Saint Mary's College*
Jim Ballard, *Montana State University*
Susan Baniak, *Otterbein College*
James Barnard, *Western Oregon State College*
Judy Bergman, *University of Houston, Clearlake*
James Bierden, *Rhode Island College*
Peter Braunfeld, *University of Illinois*
Harold Brockman, *Capital University*
Judith Brower, *North Idaho College*
Harmon Brown, *Harding University*
Christine Browning, *Western Michigan University*
Joyce W. Bryant, *St. Martin's College*
Randall Charles, *San Jose State University*
Deann Christianson, *University of the Pacific*
Lynn Cleary, *University of Maryland*
Judith Colburn, *Lindenwood College*
Sister Marie Condon, *Xavier University*
Lynda Cones, *Rend Lake College*
Sister Judith Costello, *Regis College*
H. Coulson, *California State University*
Greg Crow, *John Carroll University*
Henry A. Culbreth, *Southern Arkansas University, El Dorado*
Carl Cuneo, *Essex Community College*
Cynthia Davis, *Truckee Meadows Community College*
Gregory Davis, *University of Wisconsin, Green Bay*
Mary De Young, *Hop College*
Louise Deaton, *Johnson Community College*
Randall L. Drum, *Texas A&M University*
P. R. Dwarka, *Howard University*
Doris Edwards, *Northern State College*
Roger Engle, *Clarion University*
Kathy Ernie, *University of Wisconsin*
Ron Falkenstein, *Mott Community College*
Ann Farrell, *Wright State University*
Chris Ferris, *University of Akron*
Margaret Friar, *Grand Valley State College*
Cathey Funk, *Valencia Community College*
Dr. Amy Gaskins, *Northwest Missouri State University*
Judy Gibbs, *West Virginia University*
Daniel Green, *Olivet Nazarene University*
Anna Mae Greiner, *Eisenhower Middle School*
Julie Guelich, *Normandale Community College*
Virginia Hanks, *Western Kentucky University*
Dave Hansmire, *College of the Mainland*
Brother Joseph Harris, C.S.C., *St. Edward's University*
John Harvey, *University of Wisconsin*
Patricia Henry, *Weber State College*
Dr. Noal Herbertson, *California State University*
Ina Lee Herer, *Tri-State University*
Linda Hill, *Idaho State University*
Scott H. Hochwald, *University of North Florida*
Susan S. Hollar, *Kalamazoo Valley Community College*
Sandra Hsieh, *Pasadena City College*
Jo Johnson, *Southwestern College*
Patricia Johnson, *Ohio State University*

Pat Jones, *Methodist College*
Judy Kasabian, *El Camino College*
Vincent Kayes, *Mt. St. Mary College*
Joe Kennedy, *Miami University*
Susan Key, *Meridien Community College*
Mary Kilbridge, *Augustana College*
Mike Kilgallen, *Lincoln Christian College*
Judith Koenig, *California State University, Dominguez Hills*
Josephine Lane, *Eastern Kentucky University*
Don Larsen, *Buena Vista College*
Louise Lataille, *Westfield State College*
Vernon Leitch, *St. Cloud State University*
Steven C. Leth, *University of Northern Colorado*
Lawrence Levy, *University of Wisconsin*
Robert Lewis, *Linn-Benton Community College*
Lois Linnan, *Clarion University*
Betty Long, *Appalachian State University*
C. A. Lubinski, *Illinois State University*
Pamela Lundin, *Lakeland College*
Charles R. Luttrell, *Frederick Community College*
Carl Maneri, *Wright State University*
Nancy Maushak, *William Penn College*
Edith Maxwell, *West Georgia College*
George F. Mead, *McNeese State University*
Wilbur Mellema, *San Jose City College*
Diane Miller, *Middle Tennessee State University*
Clarence E. Miller, Jr. *Johns Hopkins University*
Bill Moody, *University of Delaware*
Kent Morris, *Cameron University*
Lisa Morrison, *Western Michigan University*
Barbara Moses, *Bowling Green State University*
Fran Moss, *Nicholls State University*
Katherine Muhs, *St. Norbert College*
Gale Nash, *Western State College of Colorado*
T. Neelor, *California State University*
Jerry Neft, *University of Dayton*
James A. Nickel, *University of Texas, Permian Basin*
Kathy Nickell, *College of DuPage*
Susan Novelli, *Kellogg Community College*
Jon O'Dell, *Richland Community College*
Jane Odell, *Richland College*
Bill W. Oldham, *Harding University*
Jim Paige, *Wayne State College*
Wing Park, *College of Lake County*
Shahla Peterman, *University of Missouri*
Gary D. Peterson, *Pacific Lutheran University*
Debra Pharo, *Northwestern Michigan College*
Robert Preller, *Illinois Central College*
Dr. William Price, *Niagara University*
Kim Prichard, *University of North Carolina*
Janice Rech, *University of Nebraska*
Tom Richard, *Bemidji State University*
Jan Rizzuti, *Central Washington University*
David Roland, *University of Mary Hardin–Baylor*
Frances Rosamond, *National University*
Richard Ross, *Southeast Community College*
Albert Roy, *Bristol Community College*
Bill Rudolph, *Iowa State University*

Bernadette Russell, *Plymouth State College*
Lee K. Sanders, *Miami University, Hamilton*
Ann Savonen, *Monroe County Community College*
Karen Sharp, *Mott Community College*
Melissa Shepard Loe, *University of St. Thomas*
Joseph Shields, *St. Mary's College, MN*
Lawrence Shirley, *Towson State University*
Keith Shuert, *Oakland Community College*
B. Signer, *St. John's University*
Rick Simon, *Idaho State University*
James Smart, *San Jose State University*
Ron Smit, *University of Portland*
Gayle Smith, *Lane Community College*
Larry Sowder, *San Diego State University*
Raymond E. Spaulding, *Radford University*
Sister Carol Speigel, BVM, *Clarke College*
Debbie Stokes, *East Carolina University*
Ruthi Sturdevant, *Lincoln University, MO*
Viji Sundar, *California State University, Stanislaus*
Ann Sweeney, *College of St. Catherine, MN*
Karen Swenson, *George Fox College*
Carla Tayeh, *Eastern Michigan University*
Janet Thomas, *Garrett Community College*
S. Thomas, *University of Oregon*
Mary Beth Ulrich, *Pikeville College*
Martha Van Cleave, *Linfield College*
Dr. Howard Wachtel, *Bowie State University*
Dr. Mary Wagner-Krankel, *St. Mary's University*
Barbara Walters, *Ashland Community College*
Bill Weber, *Eastern Arizona College*
Joyce Wellington, *Southeastern Community College*
Paula White, *Marshall University*
Heide G. Wiegel, *University of Georgia*
Jane Wilburne, *West Chester University*
Jerry Wilkerson, *Missouri Western State College*
Jack D. Wilkinson, *University of Northern Iowa*
Carole Williams, *Seminole Community College*
Delbert Williams, *University of Mary Hardin–Baylor*
Chris Wise, *University of Southwestern Louisiana*
Mary Wolfe, *University of Rio Grande*
Vernon E. Wolff, *Moorhead State University*
Maria Zack, *Point Loma Nazarene College*
Stanley J. Zehm, *Heritage College*
Makia Zimmer, *Bethany College*

Computer Test Bank Contributors for the Second Edition

Darrel Austin, *Anderson University*
Susan Baniak, *Otterbein College*
Deann Christianson, *University of the Pacific*
Gregory Davis, *University of Wisconsin*
Roger Engle, *Clarion University*
Mary Kilbrige, *Augustana College*
Carl Maneri, *Wright State University*
James A. Nickel, *University of Texas, Permian Basin*
Karen Sharp, *Mott Community College*
Sister Carol Spiegel, BVM, *Clarke College*
Barbara Walters, *Ashland Community College*

We would like to acknowledge the following people for their assistance in the preparation of the first five editions of this book: Ron Bagwell, Julie Borden, Sue Borden, Tommy Bryan, Juli Dixon, Christie Gilliland, Dale Green, Kathleen Seagraves Higdon, Hester Lewellen, Roger Maurer, David Metz, Naomi Munton, Tilda Runner, Karen Swenson, Donna Templeton, Lynn Trimpe, Rosemary Troxel, Virginia Usnick, and Kris Warloe.

We also want to give special thanks and acknowledgment to Marcia Swanson, Karen Swenson, Don Miller, Lynn Trimpe, Roger Mauer, and Vikki Mauer for their authorship of our written supplements; to Debra Pharo for her authorship of the Computerized Test Item File; and to Keith Leatham for the Spreadsheet webmodule and Armando Martinez-Cruz for The Geometer's Sketchpad webmodule, and Joan Cohen Jones for the Children's Literature webmodule. Finally, we'd like to acknowledge and thank Lawrence O. Cannon, E. Robert Heal, and Richard Wellman for the eManipulative activities.

We are very grateful to our developmental editor, Marian Provenzano, for her superb job, to our copy editor, Karen Osborne, for attending to details we missed, and to Martha Beyerlein, our production editor, for lighting the path as we went from manuscript to the final book. Other Wiley staff who helped bring this book, its supplements, and our Web site to fruition are: Julie Lindstrom, Marketing Manager; Helen McInnis, Project Manager; Martin Batey, Senior New Media Editor; Ann Berlin, Vice President, Production and Manufacturing; Jeanine Furino, Production Services Manager; Norine Pigliucci, Senior Production Manager; Kevin Murphy, Senior Designer; Lisa Gee, Associate Photo Researcher; Jennifer Battista, Supplements Editor; Lili Kalish and Stacy French, Editorial Assistants. They have been uniformly wonderful to work with—John Wiley would have been proud of them.

Finally, we welcome comments from colleagues and students. Please feel free to send suggestions to Gary at musser@math.orst.edu or glmusser@lvcm.com and Blake at peterson@mathed.byu.edu. Please include both of us in any communications.

G.L.M
B.E.P.

CHAPTER 1

Introduction to Problem Solving

George Pólya: The Father of Modern Problem Solving

George Pólya was born in Hungary in 1887. He received his Ph.D. at the University of Budapest. In 1940 he came to Brown University and then joined the faculty at Stanford University in 1942. In his studies, he became interested in the process of discovery, which led to his famous four-step process for solving problems:

1. Understand the problem.
2. Devise a plan.
3. Carry out the plan.
4. Look back.

He died in 1985, leaving mathematics with the important legacy of teaching problem solving. His "Ten Commandments for Teachers" are as follows:

1. Be interested in your subject.
2. Know your subject.
3. Try to read the faces of your students; try to see their expectations and difficulties, put yourself in their place.
4. Realize that the best way to learn anything is to discover it by yourself.
5. Give your students not only information, but also know-how, mental attitudes, the habit of methodical work.
6. Let them learn guessing.
7. Let them learn proving.
8. Look out for such features of the problem at hand as may be useful in solving the problems to come—try to disclose the general pattern that lies behind the present concrete situation.
9. Do not give away your whole secret at once—let the students guess before you tell it—let them find out by themselves as much as is feasible.
10. Suggest; do not force information down their throats.

George Pólya
Pólya wrote over 250 mathematical papers and three books that promote problem solving. His most famous book, *How to Solve It*, which has been translated into 15 languages, introduced his four-step approach together with heuristics, or strategies, which are helpful in solving problems. Other important works of Pólya are *Mathematical Discovery*, Volumes 1 and 2, and *Mathematics and Plausible Reasoning*, Volumes 1 and 2.

Problem Solving Strategies

1. Guess and Test
2. Use a Variable
3. Draw a Picture
4. Look for a Pattern
5. Make a List
6. Solve a Simpler Problem

Because problem solving is the main goal of mathematics, this chapter introduces the six strategies listed in the Problem-Solving Strategies box that are helpful in solving problems. Then, at the beginning of each chapter, an initial problem is posed that can be solved by using the strategy introduced in that chapter. As you move through this book, the Problem-Solving Strategies boxes at the beginning of each chapter expand, as should your ability to solve problems.

Initial Problem

Place the whole numbers 1 through 9 in the circles in the accompanying triangle so that the sum of the numbers on each side is 17.

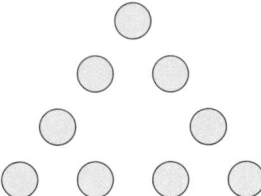

A solution to the preceding Initial Problem appears on page 30.

INTRODUCTION

Once, at an informal meeting, a social scientist asked of a mathematics professor, "What's the main goal of teaching mathematics?" The reply was, "Problem solving." In return, the mathematician asked, "What is the main goal of teaching the social sciences?" Once more the answer was "Problem solving." All successful engineers, scientists, social scientists, lawyers, accountants, doctors, business managers, and so on have to be good problem solvers. Although the problems that people encounter may be very diverse, there are common elements and an underlying structure that can help to facilitate problem solving. Because of the universal importance of problem solving, the main professional group in mathematics education, the National Council of Teachers of Mathematics (NCTM), recommended in its 1980 *An Agenda for Action* that "problem solving be the focus of school mathematics in the 1980s." The National Council of Teachers of Mathematics' 1989 *Curriculum and Evaluation Standards for School Mathematics* called for increased attention to the teaching of problem solving in K–8 mathematics. Areas of emphasis include word problems, applications, patterns and relationships, open-ended problems, and problem situations represented verbally, numerically, graphically, geometrically, or symbolically. The NCTM's 2000 *Principles and Standards for School Mathematics* identified problem solving as one of the processes by which all mathematics should be taught.

This chapter introduces a problem-solving process together with six strategies that will aid you in solving problems.

1.1   THE PROBLEM-SOLVING PROCESS AND STRATEGIES

Use any strategy you know to solve the problem below. As you solve the problem below, pay close attention to the thought processes and steps that you use. Write down these strategies and compare them to a classmate's. Are there any similarities in your approaches to solving the problem below?

> Lin's garden has an area of 782 square feet. The length of the garden is 5 less than three times its width. What are the dimensions of Lin's garden?

Pólya's Four Steps

In this book we often distinguish between "exercises" and "problems." Unfortunately, the distinction cannot be made precise. To solve an **exercise,** one applies a routine procedure to arrive at an answer. To solve a **problem,** one has to pause, reflect, and perhaps take some original step never taken before to arrive at a solution. This need for some sort of creative step on the solver's part, however minor, is what distinguishes a problem from an exercise. To a young child, finding 3 + 2 might be a problem, whereas it is a fact for you. For a child in the early grades, the question "How do you divide 96 pencils equally among 16 children?" might pose a problem, but for you it suggests the exercise "find 96 ÷ 16." These two examples illustrate how the distinction between an exercise and a problem can vary, since it depends on the state of mind of the person who is to solve it.

Doing exercises is a very valuable aid in learning mathematics. Exercises help you to learn concepts, properties, procedures, and so on, which you can then apply when solving problems. This chapter provides an introduction to the process of problem solving. The techniques that you learn in this chapter should help you to become a better problem solver and should show you how to help others develop their problem-solving skills.

A famous mathematician, George Pólya, devoted much of his teaching to helping students become better problem solvers. His major contribution is what has become known as **Pólya's four-step process** for solving problems.

Reflection from Research
Many children believe that the answer to a word problem can always be found by adding, subtracting, multiplying, or dividing two numbers. Little thought is given to understanding the context of the problem (Verschaffel, De Corte, & Vierstraete, 1999).

Pólya's 4 step
1. understand prob
2. Devise a plan
3. Carry out plan
4. LOOK Back

STEP 1   **Understand the Problem**

- Do you understand all the words?
- Can you restate the problem in your own words?
- Do you know what is given?
- Do you know what the goal is?
- Is there enough information?
- Is there extraneous information?
- Is this problem similar to another problem you have solved?

STEP 2   **Devise a Plan**

Can one of the following strategies (heuristics) be used? (A **strategy** is defined as an artful means to an end.)

1. Guess and test.
2. Use a variable.
3. Draw a picture.
4. Look for a pattern.
5. Make a list.
6. Solve a simpler problem.
7. Draw a diagram.
8. Use direct reasoning.
9. Use indirect reasoning.
10. Use properties of numbers.
11. Solve an equivalent problem.

12. Work backward.
13. Use cases.
14. Solve an equation.
15. Look for a formula.
16. Do a simulation.
17. Use a model.
18. Use dimensional analysis.
19. Identify subgoals.
20. Use coordinates.
21. Use symmetry.

The first six strategies are discussed in this chapter; the others are introduced in subsequent chapters.

STEP 3   **Carry Out the Plan**

- Implement the strategy or strategies that you have chosen until the problem is solved or until a new course of action is suggested.
- Give yourself a reasonable amount of time in which to solve the problem. If you are not successful, seek hints from others or put the problem aside for a while. (You may have a flash of insight when you least expect it!)
- Do not be afraid of starting over. Often, a fresh start and a new strategy will lead to success.

STEP 4   **Look Back**

- Is your solution correct? Does your answer satisfy the statement of the problem?
- Can you see an easier solution?
- Can you see how you can extend your solution to a more general case?

Reflection from Research
Correct answers are not a safe indicator of good thinking. Teachers must examine more than answers and must demand from students more than answers (Sowder, Threadgill-Sowder, Moyer, & Moyer, 1983).

Usually, a problem is stated in words, either orally or written. Then, to solve the problem, one translates the words into an equivalent problem using mathematical symbols, solves this equivalent problem, and then interprets the answer. This process is summarized in Figure 1.1.

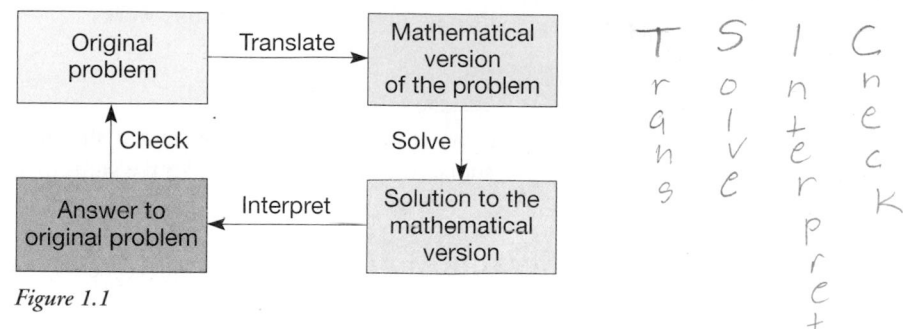

Figure 1.1

Reflection from Research
Researchers suggest that teachers think aloud when solving problems for the first time in front of the class. In so doing, teachers will be modeling successful problem-solving behaviors for their students (Schoenfeld, 1985).

Learning to utilize Pólya's four steps and the diagram in Figure 1.1 are first steps in becoming a good problem solver. In particular, the "Devise a Plan" step is very important. In this chapter and throughout the book, you will learn the strategies listed under the "Devise a Plan" step, which in turn help you decide how to proceed to solve problems. However, selecting an appropriate strategy is critical! As we worked with students who were successful problem solvers, we asked them to share "clues" that they observed in statements of problems that helped them select appropriate strategies. Their clues are listed after each corresponding strategy. Thus, in addition to learning *how* to use the various strategies herein, these clues can help you decide *when* to select an appropriate strategy or combination of strategies. Problem solving is as much an art as it is a science. Therefore, you will find that with experience you will develop a feeling for when to use one strategy over another by recognizing certain clues, perhaps subconsciously. Also, you will find that some problems may be solved in several ways using different strategies.

In summary, this initial material on problem solving is a foundation for your success in problem solving. Review this material on Pólya's four steps as well as the strategies and clues as you continue to develop your expertise in solving problems.

Problem-Solving Strategies

The remainder of this chapter is devoted to introducing several problem-solving strategies.

**NCTM Standards 2000
Problem Solving**
Instructional programs should enable all students to apply and adapt a variety of appropriate strategies to solve problems.

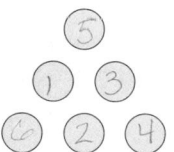

Figure 1.2

STRATEGY 1 *Guess and Test*

Problem

Place the digits 1, 2, 3, 4, 5, 6 in the circles in Figure 1.2 so that the sum of the three numbers on each side of the triangle is 12.

We will solve the problem in three ways to illustrate three different approaches to the Guess and Test strategy. As its name suggests, to use the Guess and Test strategy, you guess at a solution and test whether you are correct. If you are incorrect, you refine your guess and test again. This process is repeated until you obtain a solution.

STEP 1 Understand the Problem

Each number must be used exactly one time when arranging the numbers in the triangle. The sum of the three numbers on each side must be 12.

First Approach: Random Guess and Test

STEP 2 **Devise a Plan**

Tear off six pieces of paper and mark the numbers 1 through 6 on them and then try combinations until one works.

STEP 3 **Carry Out the Plan**

Arrange the pieces of paper in the shape of an equilateral triangle and check sums. Keep rearranging until three sums of 12 are found.

Second Approach: Systematic Guess and Test

STEP 2 **Devise a Plan**

Rather than randomly moving the numbers around, begin by placing the smallest numbers—namely, 1, 2, 3—in the corners. If that does not work, try increasing the numbers to 1, 2, 4, and so on.

STEP 3 **Carry Out the Plan**

With 1, 2, 3 in the corners, the side sums are too small; similarly with 1, 2, 4. Try 1, 2, 5 and 1, 2, 6. The side sums are still too small. Next try 2, 3, 4, then 2, 3, 5, and so on, until a solution is found. One also could begin with 4, 5, 6 in the corners, then try 3, 4, 5, and so on.

Third Approach: Inferential Guess and Test

STEP 2 **Devise a Plan**

Start by assuming that 1 must be in a corner and explore the consequences.

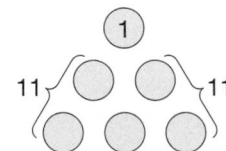

Figure 1.3

STEP 3 **Carry Out the Plan**

If 1 is placed in a corner, we must find two pairs out of the remaining five numbers whose sum is 11 (Figure 1.3). However, out of 2, 3, 4, 5, and 6, only $6 + 5 = 11$. Thus, we conclude that 1 cannot be in a corner. If 2 is in a corner, there must be two pairs left that add to 10 (Figure 1.4). But only $6 + 4 = 10$. Therefore, 2 cannot be in a corner. Finally, suppose that 3 is in a corner. Then we must satisfy Figure 1.5. However, only $5 + 4 = 9$ of the remaining numbers. Thus, if there is a solution, 4, 5, and 6 will have to be in the corners (Figure 1.6). By placing 1 between 5 and 6, 2 between 4 and 6, and 3 between 4 and 5, we have a solution.

Figure 1.4

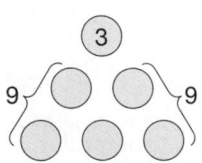

Figure 1.5

STEP 4 **Look Back**

Notice how we have solved this problem in three different ways using Guess and Test. Random Guess and Test is often used to get started, but it is easy to lose track of the various trials. Systematic Guess and Test is better because you develop a scheme to ensure that you have tested all possibilities. Generally, Inferential Guess and Test is superior to both of the previous methods because it usually saves time and provides more information regarding possible solutions.

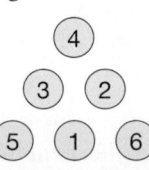

Figure 1.6

Additional Problems Where the Strategy "Guess and Test" Is Useful

1. In the following **cryptarithm**—that is, a collection of words where the letters represent numbers—*sun* and *fun* represent two three-digit numbers, and *swim* is their four-digit sum. Using all of the digits 0, 1, 2, 3, 6, 7, and 9 in place of the letters where no letter represents two different digits, determine the value of each letter.

$$\begin{array}{r} sun \\ +fun \\ \hline swim \end{array}$$

STEP 1 Understand the Problem

Each of the letters in *sun, fun,* and *swim* must be replaced with the numbers 0, 1, 2, 3, 6, 7, and 9, so that a correct sum results after each letter is replaced with its associated digit. When the letter n is replaced by one of the digits, then $n + n$ must be m or $10 + m$, where the 1 in the 10 is carried to the tens column. Since $1 + 1 = 2$, $3 + 3 = 6$, and $6 + 6 = 12$, there are three possibilities for n, namely, 1, 3, or 6. Now we can try various combinations in an attempt to obtain the correct sum.

STEP 2 Devise a Plan

Use Inferential Guess and Test. There are three choices for n. Observe that *sun* and *fun* are three-digit numbers and that *swim* is a four-digit number. Thus we have to carry when we add s and f. Therefore, the value for s in *swim* is 1. This limits the choices of n to 3 or 6.

STEP 3 Carry Out the Plan

Since $s = 1$ and $s + f$ leads to a two digit number, f must be 9. Thus there are two possibilities:

$$\text{(a)}\quad \begin{array}{r} 1\,u\,3 \\ +9\,u\,3 \\ \hline 1\,w\,i\,6 \end{array} \qquad \text{(b)}\quad \begin{array}{r} 1\,u\,6 \\ +9\,u\,6 \\ \hline 1\,w\,i\,2 \end{array}$$

In (a), if $u = 0$, 2, or 7, there is no value possible for i among the remaining digits. In (b), if $u = 3$, then $u + u$ plus the carry from $6 + 6$ yields $i = 7$. This leaves $w = 0$ for a solution.

STEP 4 Look Back

The reasoning used here shows that there is one and only one solution to this problem. When solving problems of this type, one could randomly substitute digits until a solution is found. However, Inferential Guess and Test simplifies the solution process by looking for unique aspects of the problem. Here the natural places to start are $n + n$, $u + u$, and the fact that $s + f$ yields a two-digit number.

2. Use four 4s and some of the symbols $+, \times, -, \div, (\,)$ to give expressions for the whole numbers from 0 through 9: for example, $5 = (4 \times 4 + 4) \div 4$.

3. For each shape in Figure 1.7, make one straight cut so that each of the two pieces of the shape can be rearranged to form a square.

Figure 1.7

(NOTE: Answers for these problems are given after the Solution of the Initial Problem near the end of this chapter.)

Clues

The Guess and Test strategy may be appropriate when

- There is a limited number of possible answers to test.
- You want to gain a better understanding of the problem.
- You have a good idea of what the answer is.
- You can systematically try possible answers.
- Your choices have been narrowed down by the use of other strategies.
- There is no other obvious strategy to try.

Review the preceding three problems to see how these clues may have helped you select the Guess and Test strategy to solve these problems.

NCTM Standards 2000
Algebra
Grades 3–5
All students should represent the idea of a variable as an unknown quantity using a letter or a symbol.

STRATEGY 2 Use a Variable

Observe how letters were used in place of numbers in the previous "sun + fun = swim" cryptarithm. Letters used in place of numbers are called **variables** or **unknowns.** The Use a Variable strategy, which is one of the most useful problem-solving strategies, is used extensively in algebra and in mathematics that involves algebra.

Problem

What is the greatest number that evenly divides the sum of any three consecutive whole numbers?

By trying several examples, you might guess that 3 is the greatest such number. However, it is necessary to use a variable to account for all possible instances of three consecutive numbers.

STEP 1 Understand the Problem

The whole numbers are 0, 1, 2, 3, . . . , so that consecutive whole numbers differ by 1. Thus an example of three consecutive whole numbers is the triple 3, 4, and 5. The sum of three consecutive whole numbers has a factor of 3 if 3 multiplied by another whole number produces the given sum. In the example of 3, 4, and 5, the sum is 12 and 3×4 equals 12. Thus $3 + 4 + 5$ has a factor of 3.

STEP 2 Devise a Plan

Since we can use a variable, say x, to represent any whole number, we can represent every triple of consecutive whole numbers as follows: $x, x + 1, x + 2$. Now we can proceed to see whether the sum has a factor of 3.

STEP 3 Carry Out the Plan

The sum of x, $x + 1$, and $x + 2$ is

$$x + (x + 1) + (x + 2) = 3x + 3 = 3(x + 1).$$

Thus $x + (x + 1) + (x + 2)$ is three times $x + 1$. Therefore, we have shown that the sum of any three consecutive whole numbers has a factor of 3. The case of $x = 0$ shows that 3 is the *greatest* such number.

STEP 4 Look Back

Is it also true that the sum of any five consecutive whole numbers has a factor of 5? Or, more generally, will the sum of any *n* consecutive whole numbers have a factor of *n*? Can you think of any other generalizations?

Spotlight On Technology Problems such as the previous one, which considers the sum of three consecutive integers, can be more easily understood by inputting a few values of *x* before doing the solution in general. Trying this for several values of *x* is simplified by using a spreadsheet. Refer to the dynamic spreadsheet, *Consecutive Integer Sum,* in the spreadsheet webmodule. Enter 5 to 10 values of *x* to see if the results of the spreadsheet are consistent with the findings above.

www.wiley.com/
college/musser

Additional Problems Where the Strategy "Use a Variable" Is Useful

1. Show that the sum of any five consecutive odd whole numbers has a factor of 5.

STEP 1 Understand the Problem

First, since any even number has a factor of 2, it can be expressed as $2m$, where *m* is a whole number. Since each odd number is one more than the preceding even number, any odd number can be written in the form $2m + 1$, where *m* is a whole number. Also, consecutive odd numbers differ by two.

STEP 2 Devise a Plan

To get information about the sum of *any* five consecutive odd numbers, a variable can be used. The next step is to represent the five numbers and add them to see whether 5 is a factor of the sum.

STEP 3 Carry Out the Plan

If $2m + 1$ is our first odd number, the next four are $2m + 3$, $2m + 5$, $2m + 7$, and $2m + 9$. Their sum is $(2m + 1) + (2m + 3) + (2m + 5) + (2m + 7) + (2m + 9) = 10m + 25$. Since $10m + 25 = 5(2m + 5)$, this sum has a factor of 5.

STEP 4 Look Back

Here are some similar statements that can be investigated:
  (i) The sum of any four consecutive odd numbers has a factor of 4.
 (ii) The sum of any seven consecutive odd numbers has a factor of 7.
(iii) The sum of any five consecutive even numbers has a factor of 5.
Test some of these. Then state a couple of generalizations.

2. A dog's weight is 10 kilograms plus half its weight. How much does the dog weigh?

3. The measure of the largest angle of a triangle is nine times the measure of the smallest angle. The measure of the third angle is equal to the difference of the largest and the smallest. What are the measures of the angles? (Recall that the sum of the measures of the angles in a triangle is 180°.)

Clues

The Use a Variable strategy may be appropriate when

- A phrase similar to "for any number" is present or implied.
- A problem suggests an equation.
- A proof or a general solution is required.
- A problem contains phrases such as "consecutive," "even," or "odd" whole numbers.
- There is a large number of cases.
- There is an unknown quantity related to known quantities.
- There is an infinite number of numbers involved.
- You are trying to develop a general formula.

Review the preceding three problems to see how these clues may have helped you select the Use a Variable strategy to solve these problems.

STRATEGY 3   Draw a Picture

Reflection from Research
Training children in the process of using pictures to solve problems results in more improved problem-solving performance than training students in any other strategy (Yancey, Thompson, & Yancey, 1989).

Often problems involve physical situations. In these situations, drawing a picture can help you better understand the problem so that you can formulate a plan to solve the problem. As you proceed to solve the following "pizza" problem, see whether you can visualize the solution *without* looking at any pictures first. Then work through the given solution using pictures to see how helpful they can be.

Problem

Can you cut a pizza into 11 pieces with four straight cuts?

STEP 1   Understand the Problem

Do the pieces have to be the same size and shape?

STEP 2   Devise a Plan

An obvious beginning would be to draw a picture showing how a pizza is usually cut and to count the pieces. If we do not get 11, we have to try something else (Figure 1.8). Unfortunately, we get only eight pieces this way.

NCTM Standards 2000
Algebra
Grades 3–5
All students should describe, extend, and make generalizations about geometric and numeric patterns.

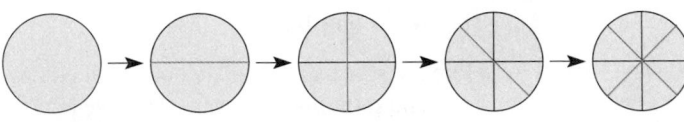

Figure 1.8

STEP 3   Carry Out the Plan

See Figure 1.9.

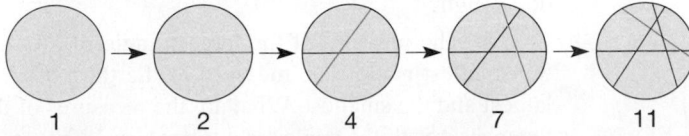

Figure 1.9

STEP 4 **STEP 4** **Look Back**

Were you concerned about cutting equal pieces when you started? That is normal. In the context of cutting a pizza, the focus is usually on trying to cut equal pieces rather than the number of pieces. Suppose that circular cuts were allowed. Does it matter whether the pizza is circular or is square? How many pieces can you get with five straight cuts? *n* straight cuts?

Not a tetromino

A tetromino

Figure 1.10

Additional Problems Where the Strategy "Draw a Picture" Is Useful

1. A **tetromino** is a shape made up of four squares where the squares must be joined along an entire side (Figure 1.10). How many different tetromino shapes are possible?

STEP 1 **Understand the Problem**

The solution of this problem is easier if we make a set of pictures of all possible arrangements of four squares of the same size.

STEP 2 **Devise a Plan**

Let's start with the longest and narrowest configuration and work toward the most compact.

STEP 3 **Carry Out the Plan**

Four in a row

Three in a row with one on top of (or below) the end square. (Note: The upper square can be at either end — these two are considered to be equivalent.)

Three in a row, with one on top of (or below) the center square.

Two in a row, with one above and one below the two.

Two in a row, with two above.

STEP 4 **Look Back**

Many similar problems can be posed using fewer or more squares. The problems become much more complex as the number of squares increases. Also, new problems can be posed using patterns of equilateral triangles.

2. If you have a chain saw with a bar 18 inches long, determine whether a 16-foot log, 8 inches in diameter, can be cut into 4-foot pieces by making only two cuts.

3. It takes 64 cubes to fill a cubical box that has no top. How many cubes are *not* touching a side or the bottom?

Clues

The Draw a Picture strategy may be appropriate when

- A physical situation is involved.
- Geometric figures or measurements are involved.
- You want to gain a better understanding of the problem.
- A visual representation of the problem is possible.

Review the preceding three problems to see how these clues may have helped you select the Draw a Picture strategy to solve these problems.

MATHEMATICAL MORSEL

There is a story about Sir Isaac Newton, coinventor of the calculus, who, as a youngster, was sent out to cut a hole in the barn door for the cats to go in and out. With great pride he admitted to cutting two holes, a larger one for the cat and a smaller one for the kittens.

 Section 1.1 EXERCISE / PROBLEM SET A

1. If the diagonals of a square are drawn in, how many triangles of all sizes are formed?

2. The distance around a standard tennis court is 228 feet. If the length of the court is 6 feet more than twice the width, find the dimensions of the tennis court.

3. A multiple of 11 I be,
   not odd, but even, you see.
   My digits, a pair,
   when multiplied there,
   make a cube and a square
   out of me. Who am I?

4. Show how 9 can be expressed as the sum of two consecutive numbers. Then decide whether every odd number can be expressed as the sum of two consecutive numbers. Explain your reasoning.

5. Using the symbols $+$, $-$, $\times$, and $\div$, fill in the following three blanks to make a true equation. (A symbol may be used more than once.)

$$6\_\_\_6\_\_\_6\_\_\_6 = 13$$

6. In the accompanying figure (called an **arithmogon**), the number that appears in a square is the sum of the numbers in the circles on each side of it. Determine what numbers belong in the circles.

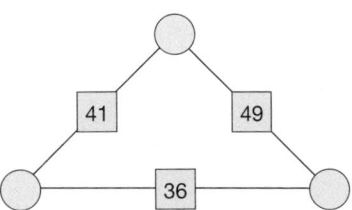

7. Place 10 stools along four walls of a room so that each of the four walls has the same number of stools.

8. Susan has 10 pockets and 44 dollar bills. She wants to arrange the money so that there are a different number of dollars in each pocket. Can she do it? Explain.

9. Arrange the numbers 1, 2, . . . , 9 in the accompanying triangle so that each side sums to 23.

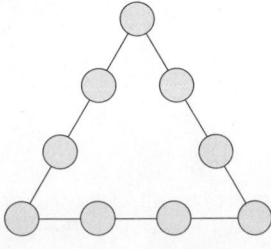

10. Place the digits 1 through 9 so that you can count from 1 to 9 by following the arrows in the diagram.

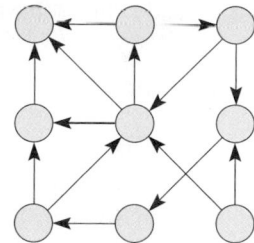

11. Scott and Greg were asked to add two whole numbers. Instead, Scott subtracted the two numbers and got 10, and Greg multiplied them and got 651. What was the correct sum?

12. Five friends were sitting on one side of a table. Gary sat next to Bill. Mike sat next to Tom. Howard sat in the third seat from Bill. Gary sat in the third seat from Mike. Who sat on the other side of Tom?

13. Using the numbers 9, 8, 7, 6, 5, and 4 once each, find the following:

   a. The largest possible sum:

   b. The smallest possible (positive) difference:

14. Using the numbers 1 through 8, place them in the following eight squares so that no two consecutive numbers are in touching squares (touching includes entire sides or simply one point).

15. Solve this cryptarithm, where each letter represents a digit and no digit represents two different letters:

$$\begin{array}{r} USSR \\ +USA \\ \hline PEACE \end{array}$$

16. On a balance scale, two spools and one thimble balance eight buttons. Also, one spool balances one thimble and one button. How many buttons will balance one spool?

17. Place the numbers 1 through 8 in the circles on the vertices of the accompanying cube so that the difference of any two connecting circles is greater than 1.

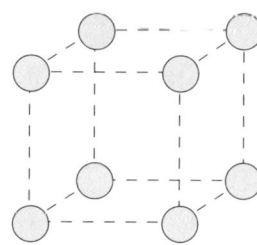

18. Think of a number. Add 10. Multiply by 4. Add 200. Divide by 4. Subtract your original number. Your result should be 60. Why?

19. The digits 1 through 9 can be used in decreasing order, with + and − signs, to produce 100 as shown: $98 − 76 + 54 + 3 + 21 = 100$. Find two other such combinations that will produce 100.

20. The Indian mathematician Ramanujan observed that the taxi number 1729 was very interesting because it was the smallest counting number that could be expressed as the sum of cubes in two different ways. Find a, b, c, and d such that $a^3 + b^3 = 1729$ and $c^3 + d^3 = 1729$.

 Section 1.1 EXERCISE / PROBLEM SET B

1. Carol bought some items at a variety store. All the items were the same price, and she bought as many items as the price of each item in cents. (For example, if the items cost 10 cents, she would have bought 10 of them.) Her bill was $2.25. How many items did Carol buy?

2. You can make one square with four toothpicks. Show how you can make two squares with seven toothpicks

(breaking toothpicks is not allowed), three squares with 10 toothpicks, and five squares with 12 toothpicks.

3. A textbook is opened and the product of the page numbers of the two facing pages is 6162. What are the numbers of the pages?

4. Place numbers 1 through 19 into the 19 circles so that any three numbers in a line through the center will give the same sum.

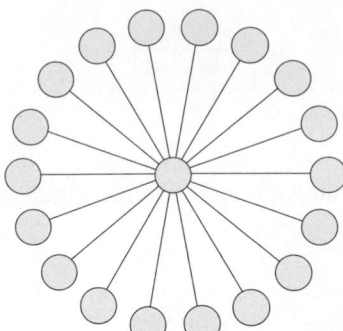

5. Using three of the symbols $+$, $-$, $\times$, and $\div$ *once* each, fill in the following three blanks to make a true equation. (Parentheses are allowed.)

$$6\_\_\_6\_\_\_6\_\_\_6 = 66$$

6. A water main for a street is being laid using a particular kind of pipe that comes in either 18-foot sections or 20-foot sections. The designer has determined that the water main would require 14 fewer sections of 20-foot pipe than if 18-foot sections were used. Find the total length of the water main.

7. Find the largest eight-digit number made up of the digits 1, 1, 2, 2, 3, 3, 4, and 4 such that the 1s are separated by one digit, the 2s by two digits, the 3s by three digits, and the 4s by four digits.

8. Mike said that when he opened his book, the product of the page numbers of the two facing pages was 7007. Without performing any calculations, prove that he was wrong.

9. The Smiths were about to start on an 18,000-mile automobile trip. They had their tires checked and found that each was good for only 12,000 miles. What is the smallest number of spares that they will need to take along with them to make the trip without having to buy a new tire?

10. Given: Six arrows arranged as follows:

Goal: By inverting two *adjacent* arrows at a time, rearrange to the following:

Can you find a minimum number of moves?

11. Two friends are shopping together when they encounter a special "3 for 2" shoe sale. If they purchase two pairs of shoes at the regular price, a third pair (of lower or equal value) will be free. Neither friend wants three pairs of shoes, but Pat would like to buy a $56 and a $39 pair while Chris is interested in a $45 pair. If they buy the shoes together to take advantage of the sale, what is the fairest share for each to pay?

12. Find digits A, B, C, and D that solve the following cryptarithm.

$$\begin{array}{r} \text{ABCD} \\ \times \quad\quad 4 \\ \hline \text{DCBA} \end{array}$$

13. Using a 5-minute and an 8-minute hourglass timer, how can you measure 1 minute?

14. If possible, find an odd number that can be expressed as the sum of four consecutive counting numbers. If impossible, explain why.

15. Think of a number. Multiply by 5. Add 8. Multiply by 4. Add 9. Multiply by 5. Subtract 105. Divide by 100. Subtract 1. How does your result compare with your original number? Explain.

16. In the following square array on the left, the corner numbers were given and the boldface numbers were found by adding the adjacent corner numbers. Following the same rules, find the corner numbers for the other square array.

6	**19**	13		—	**10**	—
8		**14**		**15**		**11**
2	**3**	1		—	**16**	—

17. Together, a baseball and a football weigh 1.25 pounds, the baseball and a soccer ball weigh 1.35 pounds, and the football and the soccer ball weigh 1.9 pounds. How much does each of the balls weigh?

18. Pick any two consecutive numbers. Add them. Then add 9 to the sum. Divide by 2. Subtract the smaller of the original numbers from the answer. What did you get? Repeat this process with two other consecutive numbers. Make a conjecture (educated guess) about the answer, and prove it.

19. An **additive magic square** has the same sum in each row, column, and diagonal. Find the error in this magic square and correct it.

47	56	34	22	83	7
24	67	44	26	13	75
29	52	3	99	18	48
17	49	89	4	53	37
97	6	3	11	74	28
35	19	46	87	8	54

20. Using the triangle in Problem 9 in Part A, determine whether you can make similar triangles using the digits 1, 2, . . . , 9, where the side sums are 18, 19, 20, 21, and 22.

PROBLEMS FOR WRITING/DISCUSSION

1. When college students hear the phrase "Use a variable," they usually think of algebra, which makes them think of using the letter x to represent the unknown. But first graders are often given problems like

$$\Box + 3 = 5$$

   Is this the same as $x + 3 = 5$? Do you think first graders can do simple algebra?

2. Some students feel "Guess and Test" is a waste of time; they just want to get an answer. Think of some reasons, other than those mentioned in the text, why "Guess and Test" is a good strategy to use.

3. Research has shown that some better math students tend *not* to draw pictures in their work. Yet future teachers are encouraged to draw pictures when solving problems. Is there a conflict here?

1.2 THREE ADDITIONAL STRATEGIES

STARTING POINT

Solve the problem below using Pólya's four steps and any other strategy. Describe how you used the four steps, focusing on any new insights that you gained as a result of *looking back*.

How many rectangles of all shapes and sizes are in the figure at the right?

NCTM Standard 2000
Algebra   Grades 6–8
All students should represent, analyze, and generalize a variety of patterns with tables, graphs, words, and, when possible, symbolic rules.

Figure 1.11

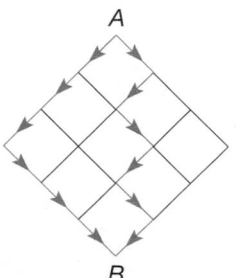

Figure 1.12

STRATEGY 4 *Look for a Pattern*

When using the Look for a Pattern strategy, one usually lists several specific instances of a problem and then looks to see whether a pattern emerges that suggests a solution to the entire problem. For example, consider the sums produced by adding consecutive odd numbers starting with 1: 1, $1 + 3 = 4 \,(= 2 \times 2)$, $1 + 3 + 5 = 9$ $(= 3 \times 3)$, $1 + 3 + 5 + 7 = 16 \,(= 4 \times 4)$, $1 + 3 + 5 + 7 + 9 = 25 \,(= 5 \times 5)$, and so on. Based on the pattern generated by these five examples, one might expect that such a sum will always be a perfect square.

www.wiley.com/
college/musser

Spotlight on Technology This problem of summing consecutive odd numbers can be further investigated to see if the pattern continues to hold by using a spreadsheet. Refer to the dynamic spreadsheet, *Sum of the Odds,* in the spreadsheet webmodule. Do you think that the pattern will continue to hold for the first 100 consecutive odd numbers? Test your hypothesis on the spreadsheet. Discuss why you think that this pattern holds or does not hold.

Problem

How many different downward paths are there from A to B in the grid in Figure 1.11? A path must travel on the lines.

STEP 1 **Understand the Problem**

What do we mean by different and downward? Figure 1.12 illustrates two paths. Notice that each such path will be 6 units long. *Different* means that they are not exactly the same; that is, some part or parts are different.

Figure 1.13

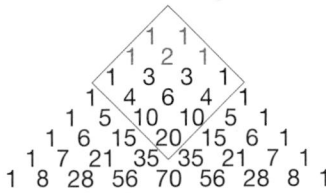

Figure 1.14

NCTM Standards 2000
Algebra
Grades Pre-K–2
All students should analyze how
both repeating and growing pat-
terns are generated.

Reflection from Research
In classrooms where problem
solving is valued, where instruction reflects the spirit of the
Standards (NCTM, 1989), and
where teachers have knowledge
of children's mathematical thinking, children perceive engaging in
mathematics as a problem-solving
endeavor in which communicating
mathematical thinking is important (Franke & Carey, 1997).

STEP 2   **Devise a Plan**

Let's look at each point of intersection in the grid and see how many different ways we can get to each point. Then perhaps we will notice a pattern
(Figure 1.13). For example, there is only one way to reach each of the points
on the two outside edges; there are two ways to reach the middle point in the
row of points labeled 1, 2, 1; and so on. Observe that the point labeled 2 in
Figure 1.13 can be found by adding the two 1s above it.

STEP 3   **Carry Out the Plan**

To see how many paths there are to any point, observe that you need only *add*
the number of paths required to arrive at the point or points immediately above.
To reach a point beneath the pair 1 and 2, the paths to 1 and 2 are extended
downward, resulting in $1 + 2 = 3$ paths to that point. The resulting number
pattern is shown in Figure 1.14. Notice, for example, that $4 + 6 = 10$ and $20 + 15 = 35$. (This pattern is part of what is called **Pascal's triangle.** It is used
again in Chapter 11.) The surrounded portion of this pattern applies to the
given problem; thus the answer to the problem is 20.

STEP 4   **Look Back**

Can you see how to solve a similar problem involving a larger square array, say
a 4×4 grid? How about a 10×10 grid? How about a rectangular grid?

A pattern of numbers arranged in a particular order is called a number **sequence,**
and the individual numbers in the sequence are called **terms** of the sequence. The
counting numbers, 1, 2, 3, 4, . . . , give rise to many sequences. (An **ellipsis,** the three
periods after the 4, means "and so on.") Several sequences of counting numbers follow.

SEQUENCE	NAME
2, 4, 6, 8, . . .	The **even** (counting) **numbers**
1, 3, 5, 7, . . .	The **odd** (counting) **numbers**
1, 4, 9, 16, . . .	The **square** (counting) **numbers**
$1, 3, 3^2, 3^3, . . .$	The **powers** of three
1, 1, 2, 3, 5, 8, . . .	The **Fibonacci sequence** (after the two 1s, each term is the sum of the two preceding terms)

Inductive reasoning is used to draw conclusions or make predictions about
a large collection of objects or numbers, based on a small representative subcollec-
tion. For example, inductive reasoning can be used to find the ones digit of the 400th
term of the sequence 8, 12, 16, 20, 24, ... By continuing this sequence for a few
more terms, 8, 12, 16, 20, 24, 28, 32, 36, 40, 44, 48, 52, 56, 60, . . . , one can observe
that the ones digit of every fifth term starting with the term 24 is a four. Thus, the
ones digit of the 400th term must be a four.

Additional Problems Where the Strategy "Look for a Pattern" Is Useful

1. Find the ones digit in 3^{99}.

STEP 1   **Understand the Problem**

The number 3^{99} is the product of 99 threes. Using the exponent key on one type
of scientific calculator yields the result $\boxed{1.717925065^{47}}$. This shows the first

Problem-Solving Strategy

Problem Solving
Find a Pattern

Finding a pattern can help you solve problems.

A fluffy chick grows from a single cell in a chicken egg. The cell divides into two cells. The two cells divide into four cells. The four cells divide into eight cells and so on. How many cells are there after eight divisions?

UNDERSTAND

What do you need to find?

You need to find the total number of cells after eight cell divisions.

PLAN

How can you solve the problem?

You can **find a pattern**. Look at the number of cells there are each time the cells divide.

Start
1 cell

1st Division
2 cells

SOLVE

Look at the numbers in the pattern.

2nd Division
4 cells

1   2   4   8   16

x 2   x 2   x 2   x 2

3rd Division
8 cells

The cell doubles each time there is a cell division. So the pattern for eight divisions will look like this.

4th Division
16 cells

1   2   4   8   16   32   64   128   **256**

After 8 cell divisions, there will be 256 cells.

LOOK BACK

Is there another way to describe the pattern above?

22

digit, but not the ones (last) digit, since the 47 indicates that there are 47 places to the right of the decimal. (See the discussion on scientific notation in Chapter 4 for further explanation.) Therefore, we will need to use another method.

STEP 2 Devise a Plan

Consider 3^1, 3^2, 3^3, 3^4, 3^5, 3^6, 3^7, 3^8. Perhaps the ones digits of these numbers form a pattern that can be used to predict the ones digit of 3^{99}.

NCTM Standards 2000
Problem Solving
Instructional programs should enable all students to build new mathematical knowledge through problem solving.

STEP 3 Carry Out the Plan

$3^1 = \mathbf{3}$, $3^2 = \mathbf{9}$, $3^3 = 27$, $3^4 = 81$, $3^5 = 243$, $3^6 = 729$, $3^7 = 2187$, $3^8 = 6561.$ The ones digits form the sequence 3, 9, 7, 1, 3, 9, 7, 1. Whenever the exponent of the 3 has a factor of 4, the ones digit is a 1. Since 100 has a factor of 4, 3^{100} must have a ones digit of 1. Therefore, the ones digit of 3^{99} must be 7, since 3^{99} precedes 3^{100} and 7 precedes 1 in the sequence 3, 9, 7, 1.

STEP 4 Look Back

Ones digits of other numbers involving exponents might be found in a similar fashion. Check this for several of the numbers from 4 to 9.

2. Which whole numbers, from 1 to 50, have an odd number of factors? For example, 15 has 1, 3, 5, and 15 as factors, and hence has an even number of factors: four.

3. In the next diagram, the left "H"-shaped array is called the 32-H and the right array is the 58-H.

0	1	2	3	4	5	6	7	8	9
10	11	12	13	14	15	16	17	18	19
20	21	22	23	24	25	26	27	28	29
30	31	32	33	34	35	36	37	38	39
40	41	42	43	44	45	46	47	48	49
50	51	52	53	54	55	56	57	58	59
60	61	62	63	64	65	66	67	68	69
70	71	72	73	74	75	76	77	78	79
80	81	82	83	84	85	86	87	88	89
90	91	92	93	94	95	96	97	98	99

a. Find the sums of the numbers in the 32-H. Do the same for the 58-H and the 74-H. What do you observe?

b. Find an H whose sum is 497.

c. Can you predict the sum in any H if you know the middle number? Explain.

Clues

The Look for a Pattern strategy may be appropriate when

- A list of data is given.
- A sequence of numbers is involved.

- Listing special cases helps you deal with complex problems.
- You are asked to make a prediction or generalization.
- Information can be expressed and viewed in an organized manner, such as in a table.

Review the preceding three problems to see how these clues may have helped you select the Look for a Pattern strategy to solve these problems.

STRATEGY 5   *Make a List*

Reflection from Research
Problem-solving ability develops with age, but the relative difficulty inherent in each problem is grade independent (Christou & Philippou, 1998).

The Make a List strategy is often combined with the Look for a Pattern strategy to suggest a solution to a problem. For example, here is a list of all the squares of the numbers 1 to 20 with their ones digits in boldface.

1,   4,   9,   16,   25,   36,   49,   64,   81,   100,
12**1**,   14**4**,   16**9**,   19**6**,   22**5**,   25**6**,   28**9**,   32**4**,   36**1**,   40**0**

The pattern in this list can be used to see that the ones digits of squares must be one of 0, 1, 4, 5, 6, or 9. This list suggests that a perfect square can never end in a 2, 3, 7, or 8.

Problem

The number 10 can be expressed as the sum of four odd numbers in three ways: (i) $10 = 7 + 1 + 1 + 1$, (ii) $10 = 5 + 3 + 1 + 1$, and (iii) $10 = 3 + 3 + 3 + 1$. In how many ways can 20 be expressed as the sum of eight odd numbers?

STEP 1   **Understand the Problem**

Recall that the odd numbers are the numbers 1, 3, 5, 7, 9, 11, 13, 15, 17, 19, ... Using the fact that 10 can be expressed as the sum of four odd numbers, we can form various combinations of those sums to obtain eight odd numbers whose sum is 20. But does this account for all possibilities?

STEP 2   **Devise a Plan**

Instead, let's make a list starting with the largest possible odd number in the sum and work our way down to the smallest.

STEP 3   **Carry Out the Plan**

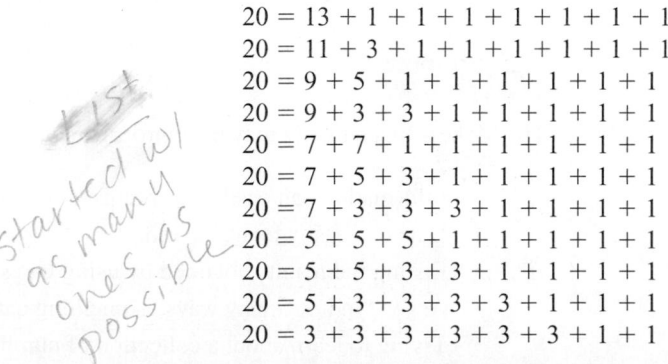

$$20 = 13 + 1 + 1 + 1 + 1 + 1 + 1 + 1$$
$$20 = 11 + 3 + 1 + 1 + 1 + 1 + 1 + 1$$
$$20 = 9 + 5 + 1 + 1 + 1 + 1 + 1 + 1$$
$$20 = 9 + 3 + 3 + 1 + 1 + 1 + 1 + 1$$
$$20 = 7 + 7 + 1 + 1 + 1 + 1 + 1 + 1$$
$$20 = 7 + 5 + 3 + 1 + 1 + 1 + 1 + 1$$
$$20 = 7 + 3 + 3 + 3 + 1 + 1 + 1 + 1$$
$$20 = 5 + 5 + 5 + 1 + 1 + 1 + 1 + 1$$
$$20 = 5 + 5 + 3 + 3 + 1 + 1 + 1 + 1$$
$$20 = 5 + 3 + 3 + 3 + 3 + 1 + 1 + 1$$
$$20 = 3 + 3 + 3 + 3 + 3 + 3 + 1 + 1$$

List — started w/ as many ones as possible

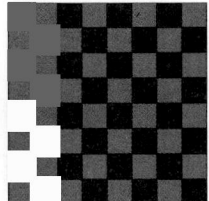

Figure 1.15

STEP 4 Look Back

Could you have used the three sums to 10 to help find these 11 sums to 20? Can you think of similar problems to solve? For example, an easier one would be to express 8 as the sum of four odd numbers, and a more difficult one would be to express 40 as the sum of 16 odd numbers. We could also consider sums of even numbers, expressing 20 as the sum of six even numbers.

Additional Problems Where the Strategy "Make a List" Is Useful

1. In a dart game, three darts are thrown. All hit the target (Figure 1.15). What scores are possible?

STEP 1 Understand the Problem

Assume that all three darts hit the board. Since there are four different numbers on the board, namely, 0, 1, 4, and 16, three of these numbers, with repetitions allowed, must be hit.

STEP 2 Devise a Plan

We should make a systematic list by beginning with the smallest (or largest) possible sum. In this way we will be more likely to find all sums.

STEP 3 Carry Out the Plan

$$
\begin{array}{lll}
0 + 0 + 0 = 0 & 0 + 0 + 1 = 1, & 0 + 1 + 1 = 2, \\
1 + 1 + 1 = 3, & 0 + 0 + 4 = 4, & 0 + 1 + 4 = 5, \\
1 + 1 + 4 = 6, & 0 + 4 + 4 = 8, & 1 + 4 + 4 = 9, \\
4 + 4 + 4 = 12, & \ldots, & 16 + 16 + 16 = 48
\end{array}
$$

STEP 4 Look Back

Several similar problems could be posed by changing the numbers on the dartboard, the number of rings, or the number of darts. Also, using geometric probability, one could ask how to design and label such a game to make it a fair skill game. That is, what points should be assigned to the various regions to reward one fairly for hitting that region?

2. How many squares, of all sizes, are there on an 8 × 8 checkerboard? (See Figure 1.16; the sides of the squares are on the lines.)

3. It takes 1230 numerical characters to number the pages of a book. How many pages does the book contain?

Figure 1.16

Clues

The Make a List strategy may be appropriate when

- Information can easily be organized and presented.
- Data can easily be generated.
- Listing the results obtained by using Guess and Test.
- Asked "in how many ways" something can be done.
- Trying to learn about a collection of numbers generated by a rule or formula.

Review the preceding three problems to see how these clues may have helped you select the Make a List strategy to solve these problems.

The problem-solving strategy illustrated next could have been employed in conjunction with the Make a List strategy in the preceding problem.

STRATEGY 6　Solve a Simpler Problem

Like the Make a List strategy, the Solve a Simpler Problem strategy is frequently used in conjunction with the Look for a Pattern strategy. The Solve a Simpler Problem strategy involves reducing the size of the problem at hand and making it more manageable to solve. The simpler problem is then generalized to the original problem.

Problem

In a group of nine coins, eight weigh the same and the ninth is heavier. Assume that the coins are identical in appearance. Using a pan balance, what is the smallest number of balancings needed to identify the heavy coin?

STEP 1　Understand the Problem

Coins may be placed on both pans. If one side of the balance is lower than the other, that side contains the heavier coin. If a coin is placed in each pan and the pans balance, the heavier coin is in the remaining seven. We could continue in this way, but if we missed the heavier coin each time we tried two more coins, the last coin would be the heavy one. This would require four balancings. Can we find the heavier coin in fewer balancings?

STEP 2　Devise a Plan

To find a more efficient method, let's examine the cases of three coins and five coins before moving to the case of nine coins.

STEP 3　Carry Out the Plan

Figure 1.17

Three coins: Put one coin on each pan (Figure 1.17). If the pans balance, the third coin is the heavier one. If they don't, the one in the lower pan is the heavier one. Thus, it only takes one balancing to find the heavier coin.

Figure 1.18

Five coins: Put two coins on each pan (Figure 1.18). If the pans balance, the fifth coin is the heavier one. If they don't, the heavier one is in the lower pan. Remove the two coins in the higher pan and put one of the two coins in the lower pan on the other pan. In this case, the lower pan will have the heavier coin. Thus, it takes at most two balancings to find the heavier coin.

Figure 1.19

Nine coins: At this point, patterns should have been identified that will make this solution easier. In the three-coin problem, it was seen that a heavy coin can be found in a group of three as easily as it can in a group of two. From the five-coin problem, we know that by balancing groups of coins together, we could quickly reduce the number of coins that needed to be examined. These ideas are combined in the nine-coin problem by breaking the nine coins into three groups of three and balancing two groups against each other (Figure 1.19). In this first balancing, the group with the heavy coin is identified. Once the heavy coin has been narrowed to three choices, then the three-coin balancing described above can be used.

The minimum number of balancings needed to locate the heavy coin out of a set of nine coins is two.

STEP 4 Look Back

In solving this problem by using simpler problems, no numerical patterns emerged. However, patterns in the balancing process that could be repeated with a larger number of coins did emerge.

Spotlight on Technology An excellent way to gain a better understanding of this problem is to actually have the opportunity of weighing coins or simulating the balancing of coins. This is possi-

www.wiley.com/
college/musser ble on the Chapter 1 eManipulative activity, *Counterfeit Coin.* Try the strategy described above on the eManipulative to see how it works.

Additional Problems Where the Strategy "Solve a Simpler Problem" Is Useful

1. Find the sum $\dfrac{1}{2} + \dfrac{1}{2^2} + \dfrac{1}{2^3} + \cdots + \dfrac{1}{2^{10}}$.

STEP 1 Understand the Problem

This problem can be solved directly by getting a common denominator, here 2^{10}, and finding the sum of the numerators.

STEP 2 Devise a Plan

Instead of doing a direct calculation, let's combine some previous strategies. Namely, make a list of the first few sums and look for a pattern.

STEP 3 Carry Out the Plan

$$\mathbf{\frac{1}{2}}, \frac{1}{2} + \frac{1}{4} = \mathbf{\frac{3}{4}}, \frac{1}{2} + \frac{1}{4} + \frac{1}{8} = \mathbf{\frac{7}{8}}, \frac{1}{2} + \frac{1}{4} + \frac{1}{8} + \frac{1}{16} = \mathbf{\frac{15}{16}}$$

The pattern of sums, $\dfrac{1}{2}, \dfrac{3}{4}, \dfrac{7}{8}, \dfrac{15}{16}$, suggests that the sum of the 10 fractions is $\dfrac{2^{10-1}}{2^{10}}$, or $\dfrac{1023}{1024}$.

STEP 4 Look Back

This method of combining the strategy of Solve a Simpler Problem with Make a List and Look for a Pattern is very useful. For example, what is the sum $\dfrac{1}{2} + \dfrac{1}{2^2} + \cdots + \dfrac{1}{2^{100}}$? Because of the large denominators, you wouldn't want to add these fractions directly.

2. Following the arrows in Figure 1.20, how many paths are there from *A* to *B*?

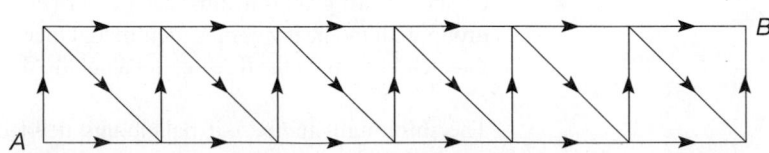

Figure 1.20

3. There are 20 people at a party. If each person shakes hands with each other person, how many handshakes will there be?

www.wiley.com/
college/musser

Spotlight on Technology Often the strategy of "Solving a Simpler Problem" is used to enable the problem solver to find a pattern. The patterns may be numerical or may be a process. This strategy can be utilized to solve the Chapter 1, eManipulative activity, *Tower of Hanoi.* Determine the fewest number of moves required when you start with two, three, and four disks. Describe a general process to move the disks in the fewest number of moves. What is the minimum number of moves that it should take to move six disks?

Clues

The Solve a Simpler Problem strategy may be appropriate when

- The problem involves complicated computations.
- The problem involves very large or very small numbers.
- A direct solution is too complex.
- You want to gain a better understanding of the problem.
- The problem involves a large array or diagram.

Review the preceding three problems to see how these clues may have helped you select the Solve a Simpler Problem strategy to solve these problems.

Recapitulation

When presenting the problems in this chapter, we took great care in organizing the solutions using Pólya's four-step approach. However, it is not necessary to label and display each of the four steps every time you work a problem. On the other hand, it is good to get into the habit of recalling the four steps as you plan and as you work through a problem. In this chapter we have introduced several useful problem-solving strategies. In each of the following chapters, a new problem-solving strategy is introduced. These strategies will be especially helpful when you are making a plan. As you are planning to solve a problem, think of the strategies as a collection of tools. Then an important part of solving a problem can be viewed as selecting an appropriate tool or strategy.

We end this chapter with a list of suggestions that students who have successfully completed a course on problem solving felt were helpful tips. Reread this list periodically as you progress through the book.

Reflection from Research
"The development of a disposition toward realistic mathematical modeling and interpreting of word problems should permeate the entire curriculum from the outset" (Verschaffel & DeCorte, 1997).

Suggestions from Successful Problem Solvers

- Accept the challenge of solving a problem.
- Rewrite the problem in your own words.
- Take time to explore, reflect, think. . . .
- Talk to yourself. Ask yourself lots of questions.
- If appropriate, try the problem using simple numbers.
- Many problems require an incubation period. If you get frustrated, do not hesitate to take a break—your subconscious may take over. But do return to try again.
- Look at the problem in a variety of ways.
- Run through your list of strategies to see whether one (or more) can help you get a start.

- Many problems can be solved in a variety of ways—you only need to find one solution to be successful.
- Do not be afraid to change your approach, strategy, and so on.
- Organization can be helpful in problem solving. Use the Pólya four-step approach with a variety of strategies.
- Experience in problem solving is very valuable. *Work lots of problems;* your confidence will grow.
- If you are not making much progress, do not hesitate to go back to make sure that you really understand the problem. This review process may happen two or three times in a problem since understanding usually grows as you work toward a solution.
- There is nothing like a breakthrough, a small *aha*!, as you solve a problem.
- Always, always look back. Try to see precisely what the key step was in your solution.
- Make up and solve problems of your own.
- Write up your solutions neatly and clearly enough so that you will be able to understand your solution if you reread it in 10 years.
- Develop good problem-solving helper skills when assisting others in solving problems. Do not give out solutions; instead, provide meaningful hints.
- By helping and giving hints to others, you will find that you will develop many new insights.
- Enjoy yourself! Solving a problem is a positive experience.

MATHEMATICAL MORSEL

Sophie Germain was born in Paris in 1776, the daughter of a silk merchant. At the age of 13, she found a book on the history of mathematics in her father's library. She became enthralled with the study of mathematics. Even though her parents disapproved of this pursuit, nothing daunted her—she studied at night wrapped in a blanket, because her parents had taken her clothing away from her to keep her from getting up. They also took away her heat and light. This only hardened her resolve until her father finally gave in and she, at last, was allowed to study to become a mathematician.

 Section 1.2 EXERCISE / PROBLEM SET A

Use any of the six problem-solving strategies introduced thus far to solve the following.

1. a. Complete this table and look for a pattern.

SUM	ANSWER
1	1
1 + 3	4
1 + 3 + 5	
1 + 3 + 5 + 7	
1 + 3 + 5 + 7 + 9	

b. How many odd whole numbers would have to be added to get a sum of 81? Check your guess by adding them.

c. How many odd whole numbers would have to be added to get a sum of 169? Check your guess by adding them.

d. How many odd whole numbers would have to be added to get a sum of 529? (You do not need to check.)

2. Find the missing term in each pattern.

   a. 256   128   64   ____   16   8

   b. $1\dfrac{1}{3}\ \dfrac{1}{9}$ _____ $\dfrac{1}{81}$

   c. 7, 9, 12, 16,

   d. 127, 863   12, 789 ____ 135   18

3. Sketch a figure that is next in each sequence.

   a.

   b.

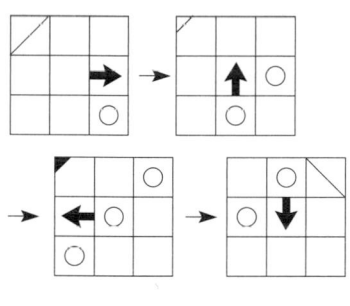

4. Consider the following differences. Use your calculator to verify that the statements are true.

$$6^2 - 5^2 = 11$$
$$56^2 - 45^2 = 1111$$
$$556^2 - 445^2 = 111,111$$

   a. Predict the next line in the sequence of differences. Use your calculator to check your answer.

   b. What do you think the eighth line will be?

5. Look for a pattern in the first two number grids. Then use the pattern you observed to fill in the missing numbers of the third grid.

21	7	3
3	1	3
7	7	1

72	36	2
8	4	2
9	9	1

60	6	
		5
2		

6. The **triangular numbers** are the whole numbers that are represented by certain triangular arrays of dots. The first five triangular numbers are shown.

1   2   3   4   5

   a. Complete the following table and look for a pattern.

NUMBER	NUMBER OF DOTS (TRIANGULAR NUMBERS)
1	1
2	3
3	
4	
5	
6	

   b. Make a sketch to represent the seventh triangular number.

   c. How many dots will be in the tenth triangular number?

   d. Is there a triangular number that has 91 dots in its shape? If so, which one?

   e. Is there a triangular number that has 150 dots in its shape? If so, which one?

   f. Write a formula for the number of dots in the nth triangular number.

   g. When the famous mathematician Carl Friedrich Gauss was in fourth grade, his teacher challenged him to add the first one hundred counting numbers. Find this sum.

$$1 + 2 + 3 + \cdots + 100$$

7. As mentioned in this section, the square numbers are the counting numbers 1, 4, 9, 16, 25, 36, ... Each square number can be represented by a square array of dots as shown in the following figure, where the second square number has four dots, and so on. The first four square numbers are shown.

   a. Find two triangular numbers (refer to Problem 6) whose sum equals the third square number.

   b. Find two triangular numbers whose sum equals the fifth square number.

c. What two triangular numbers have a sum that equals the 10th square number? the 20th square number? the nth square number?

d. Find a triangular number that is also a square number.

e. Find five pairs of square numbers whose difference is a triangular number.

8. Would you rather work for a month (30 days) and get paid 1 million dollars or be paid 1 cent the first day, 2 cents the second day, 4 cents the third day, 8 cents the fourth day, and so on? Explain.

9. Find the perimeters and then complete the table.

number of triangles	1	2	3	4	5	6	10	n
perimeter								40

10. The integers greater than 1 are arranged as shown.

$$
\begin{array}{cccc}
2 & 3 & 4 & 5 \\
9 & 8 & 7 & 6 \\
10 & 11 & 12 & 13 \\
17 & 16 & 15 & 14 \\
\end{array}
$$

a. In which column will 100 fall?

b. In which column will 1000 fall?

c. How about 1999?

d. How about 99,997?

11. How many cubes are in the 100th collection of cubes in this sequence?

12. The Fibonacci sequence is 1, 1, 2, 3, 5, 8, 13, 21, . . . , where each successive number beginning with 2 is the sum of the preceding two; for example, $13 = 5 + 8$, $21 = 8 + 13$, and so on. Observe the following pattern.

$$1^2 + 1^2 = 1 \times 2$$
$$1^2 + 1^2 + 2^2 = 2 \times 3$$
$$1^2 + 1^2 + 2^2 + 3^2 = 3 \times 5$$

Write out six more terms of the Fibonacci sequence and use the sequence to predict what $1^2 + 1^2 + 2^2 + 3^2 + \cdots + 144^2$ is without actually computing the sum. Then use your calculator to check your result.

13. Write out 16 terms of the Fibonacci sequence and observe the following pattern:

$$1 + 2 = 3$$
$$1 + 2 + 5 = 8$$
$$1 + 2 + 5 + 13 = 21$$

Use the pattern you observed to predict the sum

$$1 + 2 + 5 + 13 + \cdots + 610$$

without actually computing the sum. Then use your calculator to check your result.

14. Pascal's triangle is where each entry other than a 1 is obtained by adding the two entries in the row above it.

$$
\begin{array}{ccccccc}
 & & & 1 & & & \\
 & & 1 & & 1 & & \\
 & & 1 & 2 & 1 & & \\
 & 1 & 3 & & 3 & 1 & \\
1 & 4 & & 6 & & 4 & 1 \\
\end{array}
$$

a. Find the sums of the numbers on the diagonals in Pascal's triangle as are indicated in the following figure.

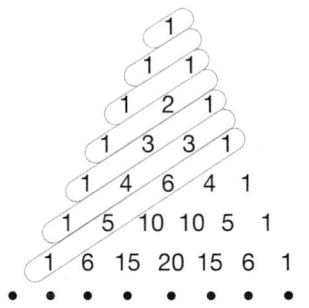

b. Predict the sums along the next three diagonals in Pascal's triangle without actually adding the entries. Check your answers by adding entries on your calculator.

15. Answer the following questions about Pascal's triangle (see Problem 14).

a. In the triangle shown here, one number, namely 3, and the six numbers immediately surrounding it are encircled. Find the sum of the encircled seven numbers.

```
                1
              1   1
            1   2   1
          1   3   3   1
        1   4   6   4   1
      1   5  10  10   5   1
    1   6  15  20  15   6   1
  •   •   •   •   •   •   •   •   •   •
```

b. Extend Pascal's triangle by adding a few rows. Then draw several more circles anywhere in the triangle like the one shown in part (a). Explain how the sums obtained by adding the seven numbers inside the circle are related to one of the numbers outside the circle.

16. Consider the following sequence of shapes. The sequence starts with one square. Then at each step squares are attached around the outside of the figure, one square per exposed edge in the figure.

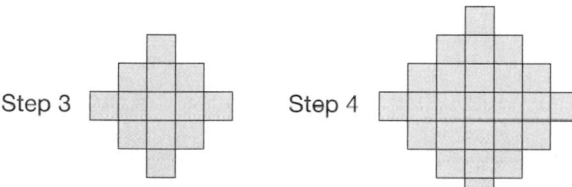

Step 1   Step 2

Step 3   Step 4

a. Draw the next two figures in the sequence.

b. Make a table listing the number of unit squares in the figure at each step. Look for a pattern in the number of unit squares. (*Hint:* Consider the number of squares attached at each step.)

c. Based on the pattern you observed, predict the number of squares in the figure at step 7. Draw the figure to check your answer.

d. How many squares would there be in the 10th figure? in the 20th figure? in the 50th figure?

17. In a dart game, only 4 points or 9 points can be scored on each dart. What is the largest score that it is *not* possible to obtain? (Assume that you have an unlimited number of darts.)

18. If the following four figures are referred to as stars, the first one is a three-pointed star and the second one is a six-pointed star. (*Note:* If this pattern of constructing a new equilateral triangle on each side of the existing equilateral triangle is continued indefinitely, the resulting figure is called the **Koch curve** or **Koch snowflake.**)

a. How many points are there in the third star?

b. How many points are there in the fourth star?

Section 1.2   EXERCISE / PROBLEM SET B

1. Find the missing term in each pattern.

   a. 10, 17, _____, 37, 50, 65

   b. $1, \dfrac{3}{2}, \underline{\hspace{1em}}, \dfrac{7}{8}, \dfrac{9}{16}$

   c. 243, 324, 405, _____, 567

   d. 234; _____; 23,481; 234,819; 2,348,200

b.

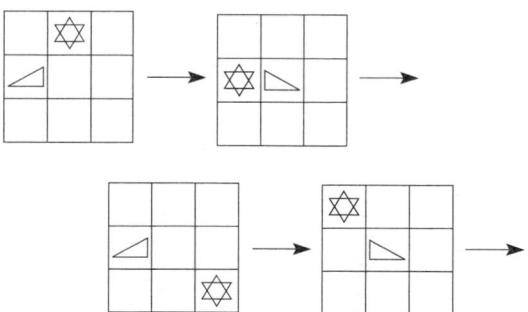

2. Sketch a figure that is next in each sequence.

   a.

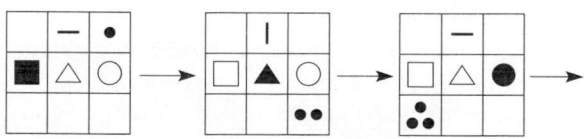

3. While only 19 years old, Carl Friedrich Gauss proved in 1796 that every positive integer is the sum of at the most three triangular numbers (see Problem 6 in Part A).

   a. Express each of the numbers 25 to 35 as a sum of no more than three triangular numbers.

   b. Express the numbers 74, 81, and 90 as sums of no more than three triangular numbers.

4. The **rectangular numbers** are whole numbers that are represented by certain rectangular arrays of dots. The first five rectangular numbers are shown.

   a. Complete the following table and look for a pattern.

NUMBER	NUMBER OF DOTS (RECTANGULAR NUMBERS)
1	2
2	6
3	
4	
5	
6	

   b. Make a sketch to represent the seventh rectangular number.

   c. How many dots will be in the tenth rectangular number?

   d. Is there a rectangular number that has 380 dots in its shape? If so, which one?

   e. Write a formula for the number of dots in the nth rectangular number.

   f. What is the connection between triangular numbers (see Problem 6 in Part A) and rectangular numbers?

5. The **pentagonal numbers** are whole numbers that are represented by pentagonal shapes. The first four pentagonal numbers are shown.

   a. Complete the following table and look for a pattern.

NUMBER	NUMBER OF DOTS (PENTAGONAL NUMBERS)
1	1
2	5
3	
4	
5	

   b. Make a sketch to represent the fifth pentagonal number.

   c. How many dots will be in the ninth pentagonal number?

   d. Is there a pentagonal number that has 200 dots in its shape? If so, which one?

   e. Write a formula for the number of dots in the nth pentagonal number.

6. Consider the following process.

   1. Choose a whole number.

   2. Add the squares of the digits of the number to get a new number.

   Repeat step 2 several times.

   a. Apply the procedure described to the numbers 12, 13, 19, 21, and 127.

   b. What pattern do you observe as you repeat the steps over and over?

   c. Check your answer for part (b) with a number of your choice.

7. How many triangles are in the picture?

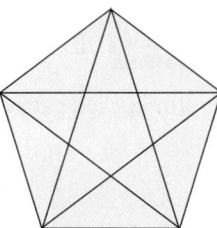

8. What is the smallest number that can be expressed as the sum of two squares in two different ways? (You may use one square twice.)

9. How many cubes are in the 10th collection of cubes in this sequence?

10. The 2 × 2 array of numbers $\begin{bmatrix} 4 & 5 \\ 5 & 6 \end{bmatrix}$ has a sum of

4 × 5, and the 3 × 3 array $\begin{bmatrix} 6 & 7 & 8 \\ 7 & 8 & 9 \\ 8 & 9 & 10 \end{bmatrix}$ has a sum

of 9 × 8.

a. What will be the sum of the similar 4 × 4 array starting with 7?

b. What will be the sum of a similar 100 × 100 array starting with 100?

11. The Fibonacci sequence was defined to be the sequence 1, 1, 2, 3, 5, 8, 13, 21, . . . , where each successive number is the sum of the preceding two. Observe the following pattern.

$$1 + 1 = 3 - 1$$
$$1 + 1 + 2 = 5 - 1$$
$$1 + 1 + 2 + 3 = 8 - 1$$
$$1 + 1 + 2 + 3 + 5 = 13 - 1$$

Write out six more terms of the Fibonacci sequence, and use the sequence to predict the answer to

$$1 + 1 + 2 + 3 + 5 + \cdots + 144$$

without actually computing the sum. Then use your calculator to check your result.

12. Write out 16 terms of the Fibonacci sequence.

a. Notice that the fourth term in the sequence (called F_4) is odd: $F_4 = 3$. The sixth term in the sequence (called F_6) is even: $F_6 = 8$. Look for a pattern in the terms of the sequence, and describe which terms are even and which are odd.

b. Which of the following terms of the Fibonacci sequence are even and which are odd:

F_{38}, F_{51}, F_{150}, F_{200}, F_{300}?

c. Look for a pattern in the terms of the sequence and describe which terms are divisible by 3.

d. Which of the following terms of the Fibonacci sequence are multiples of 3: F_{48}, F_{75}, F_{196}, F_{379}, F_{1000}?

13. Write out 16 terms of the Fibonacci sequence and observe the following pattern.

$$1 + 3 = 5 - 1$$
$$1 + 3 + 8 = 13 - 1$$
$$1 + 3 + 8 + 21 = 34 - 1$$

Use the pattern you observed to predict the answer to

$$1 + 3 + 8 + 21 + \cdots + 377$$

without actually computing the sum. Then use your calculator to check your result.

14. Answer the following for Pascal's triangle.

a. In the following triangle, six numbers surrounding a central number, 4, are circled. Compare the products of alternate numbers moving around the circle; that is, compare $3 \cdot 1 \cdot 10$ and $6 \cdot 1 \cdot 5$.

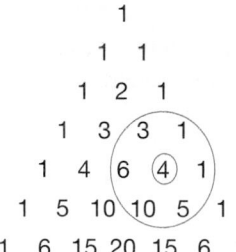

b. Extend Pascal's triangle by adding a few rows. Then draw several more circles like the one shown in part (a) anywhere in the triangle. Find the products as described in part (a). What patterns do you see in the products?

15. A certain type of gutter comes in 6-foot, 8-foot, and 10-foot sections. How many different lengths can be formed using three sections of gutter?

16. Consider the sequence of shapes shown in the following figure. The sequence starts with one triangle. Then at each step, triangles are attached to the outside of the preceding figure, one triangle per exposed edge.

Step 1   Step 2

Step 3   Step 4

a. Draw the next two figures in the sequence.

b. Make a table listing the number of triangles in the figure at each step. Look for a pattern in the number of triangles. (*Hint:* Consider the number of triangles added at each step.)

c. Based on the pattern you observed, predict the number of triangles in the figure at step 7. Draw the figure to check your answer.

d. How many triangles would there be in the 10th figure? in the 20th figure? in the 50th figure?

17. How many equilateral triangles of all sizes are there in the 3 × 3 × 3 equilateral triangle shown next?

18. Refer to the following figures to answer the questions. (NOTE: If this pattern is continued indefinitely, the resulting figure is called the **Sierpinski triangle** or the **Sierpinski gasket.**)

a. How many black triangles are there in the fourth figure?

b. How many white triangles are there in the fourth figure?

c. If the pattern is continued, how many black triangles are there in the *n*th figure?

d. If the pattern is continued, how many white triangles are there in the *n*th figure?

PROBLEMS FOR WRITING/DISCUSSION

1. Looking for a pattern can be frustrating if the pattern is not immediately obvious. Create your own sequence of numbers that follows a pattern but that has the capacity to stump some of your fellow students. Then write an explanation of how they might have been able to discover your pattern.

2. Many board games involve throwing two dice and summing of the numbers that come up to determine how many squares to move. Make a list of all the different sums that can appear. Then write down how many ways each different sum can be formed. For example, 11 can be formed in two ways: from a 5 on the first die and a 6 on the second OR a 6 on the first die and a 5 on the second. Which sum has the greatest number of combinations? What conclusion could you draw from that?

3. There is an old riddle about a frog at the bottom of a 20-foot well. If he climbs up 3 feet each day and slips back 2 feet each night, how many days will it take him to climb out of the well? The answer isn't 20. Try doing the problem with a well that is only 5 feet deep, and keep track of all the frog's moves. What strategy are you using?

END OF CHAPTER MATERIAL

Solution of Initial Problem

Place the whole numbers 1 through 9 in the circles in the accompanying triangle so that the sum of the numbers on each side is 17.

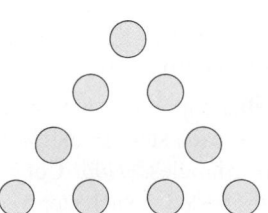

Strategy: Guess and Test

Having solved a simpler problem in this chapter, you might easily be able to conclude that 1, 2, and 3 must be in the corners. Then the remaining six numbers, 4, 5, 6, 7, 8, and 9, must pro-

duce three pairs of numbers whose sums are 12, 13, and 14. The only two possible solutions are as shown.

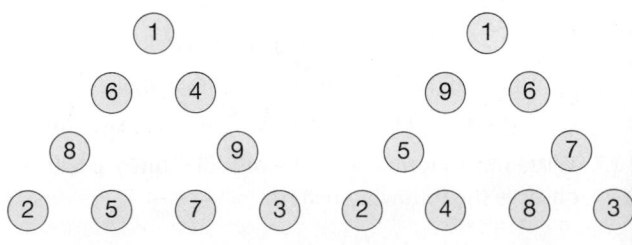

Solutions for Additional Problems

Guess and Test

1. $s = 1, u = 3, n = 6, f = 9, w = 0, i = 7, m = 2$

2. $0 = (4 - 4) + (4 - 4)$
$1 = (4 + 4) \div (4 + 4)$
$2 = (4 \div 4) + (4 \div 4)$
$3 = (4 + 4 + 4) \div 4$
$4 = 4 + 4 \times (4 - 4)$
$5 = (4 \times 4 + 4) \div 4$
$6 = ((4 + 4) \div 4) + 4$
$7 = 4 + 4 - (4 \div 4)$
$8 = ((4 \times 4) \div 4) + 4$
$9 = 4 + 4 + (4 \div 4)$

There are many other possible answers.

3.

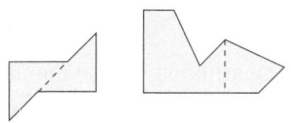

Use a Variable

1. $(2m + 1) + (2m + 3) + (2m + 5) + (2m + 7) + (2m + 9) = 10m + 25 = 5(2m + 5)$

2. 20 kilograms

3. 10°, 80°, 90°

Draw a Picture

1. 5

2. Yes; make one cut, then lay the logs side by side for the second cut.

3. 12

Look for a Pattern

1. 7

2. Square numbers

3. a. 224; 406; 518   **b.** 71
c. The sum is seven times the middle number.

Make a List

1. 48, 36, 33, 32, 24, 21, 20, 18, 17, 16, 12, 9, 8, 6, 5, 4, 3, 2, 1, 0

2. 204

3. 446

Solve a Simpler Problem

1. $\dfrac{1023}{1024}$

2. 377

3. 190

People in Mathematics

Carl Friedrich Gauss (1777–1885) Carl Friedrich Gauss, according to the historian E. T. Bell, "lives everywhere in mathematics." His contributions to geometry, number theory, and analysis were deep and wide-ranging. Yet he also made crucial contributions in applied mathematics. When the tiny planet Ceres was discovered in 1800, Gauss developed a technique for calculating its orbit, based on meager observations of its direction from Earth at several known times. Gauss contributed to the modern theory of electricity and magnetism, and with the physicist W. E. Weber constructed one of the first practical electric telegraphs. In 1807 he became director of the astronomical observatory at Gottingen, where he served until his death. At age 18, Gauss devised a method for constructing a 17-sided regular polygon, using only a compass and straightedge. Remarkably, he then derived a general rule that predicted which regular polygons are likewise constructible.

Sophie Germain (1776–1831) Sophie Germain, as a teenager in Paris, discovered mathematics by reading books from her father's library. At age 18, Germain wished to attend the prestigious Ecole Polytechnique in Paris, but women were not admitted. So she studied from classroom notes supplied by sympathetic male colleagues, and she began submitting written work using the pen name Antoine LeBlanc. This work won her high praise, and eventually she was able to reveal her true identity. Germain is noted for her theory of the vibration patterns of elastic plates and for her proof of Fermat's last theorem in some special cases. Of Sophie Germain, Carl Gauss wrote, "When a woman, because of her sex, encounters infinitely more obstacles than men . . . yet overcomes these fetters and penetrates that which is most hidden, she doubtless has the most noble courage, extraordinary talent, and superior genius."

CHAPTER REVIEW

Review the following terms and problems to determine which require learning or relearning—page numbers are provided for easy reference.

SECTION 1.1: The Problem-Solving Process and Strategies

VOCABULARY/NOTATION

Exercise 3	Random Guess and Test 6	Variable or unknown 8
Problem 3	Systematic Guess and Test 6	Tetromino 11
Pólya's four-step process 4	Inferential Guess and Test 6	
Strategy 4	Cryptarithm 7	

PROBLEMS

For each of the following, (i) determine a reasonable strategy to use to solve the problem, (ii) state a clue that suggested the strategy, and (iii) write out a solution using Pólya's four-step process.

1. Fill in the circles using the numbers 1 through 9 once each where the sum along each of the five rows totals 17.

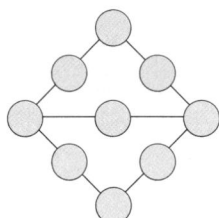

2. In the following arithmagon, the number that appears in a square is the product of the numbers in the circles on each side of it. Determine what numbers belong in the circles.

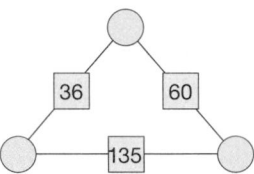

3. The floor of a square room is covered with square tiles. Walking diagonally across the room from corner to corner, Susan counted a total of 33 tiles on the two diagonals. What is the total number of tiles covering the floor of the room?

SECTION 1.2: Three Additional Strategies

VOCABULARY/NOTATION

Pascal's triangle 16	Ellipsis 16	Powers 16
Sequence 16	Even numbers 16	Fibonacci sequence 16
Terms 16	Odd numbers 16	Inductive reasoning 16
Counting numbers 16	Square numbers 16	

PROBLEMS

For each of the following, (i) determine a reasonable strategy to use to solve the problem, (ii) state a clue that suggested the strategy, and (iii) write out a solution using Pólya's four-step process.

1. Consider the following products. Use your calculator to verify that the statements are true.

$$1 \times (1) = 1^2$$
$$121 \times (1 + 2 + 1) = 22^2$$
$$12321 \times (1 + 2 + 3 + 2 + 1) = 333^2$$

Predict the next line in the sequence of products. Use your calculator to check your answer.

2. **a.** How many cubes of all sizes are in a $2 \times 2 \times 2$ cube composed of eight $1 \times 1 \times 1$ cubes?

   b. How many cubes of all sizes are in an $8 \times 8 \times 8$ cube composed of 512 $1 \times 1 \times 1$ cubes?

3. **a.** What is the smallest number of whole-number gram weights needed to weigh any whole-number amount from 1 to 12 grams on a scale allowing the weights to be placed on either or both sides?

   b. How about from 1 to 37 grams?

   c. What is the most you can weigh using six weights in this way?

PROBLEMS FOR WRITING/DISCUSSION

1. Describe reasoning that can be used to place the numbers 3, 4, 5, 6, 7, 8, 9, 10, 11 in the diagram to form a 3-by-3 magic square.

(NOTE: There seems to be more than one answer.)

2. In the movie *Die Hard with a Vengeance*, the hero was told that in order to stop an explosion from taking place he would have to place a plastic jug with exactly 4 gallons of water in it on a scale. The wrong weight would set off the big bang. Unfortunately, the villain had left the hero only two jugs, one that would hold exactly 3 gallons and one that would hold exactly 5 gallons. There was a fountain nearby with lots of water in it. Explain how to get exactly 4 gallons into the 5-gallon container. (No, there is no measuring cup.)

3. Show three different methods for solving the following problem: Find three consecutive counting numbers whose sum is 78.

4. Show why the following problem has no solution: Find three consecutive odd whole numbers whose sum is 102. (*Hint:* There is more than one way to demonstrate the answer.)

5. The following problem can be solved in more than one way. Find at least one way to solve it without algebra: Mary Kay wanted to buy some makeup. She spent $28 of her paycheck on foundations, $\frac{2}{3}$ of the rest for eye shadows, and $\frac{1}{2}$ of what was left after that for a lipstick. She had $12 left over. How much was her paycheck? (For the purposes of this problem, we'll ignore sales tax.)

6. Create a new problem similar to the preceding problem. Show a solution as well.

7. Try to discover a pattern in problems involving consecutive whole numbers. Focus on problems that involve finding three numbers that are either consecutive, consecutive even, or consecutive odd and that add up to some specific number. If you find the pattern, you will understand how teachers go about making up such problems.

8. Try to extend your pattern-finding skills to consecutive whole-number problems involving the sum of four consecutive (or consecutive odd or consecutive even) whole numbers. What pattern did you find?

9. Explain why the following problems are unsolvable. Then change each problem in such a way that it would be solvable.

   a. The sum of two numbers is 87. What are the numbers?

   b. The perimeter of a rectangular garden is 58 feet. The sum of the length and width is 29 feet. Find the length and width.

10. Mr. Nelson manages a shoe store in the mall. One day a man came into the store right after Mr. Nelson opened up and before he had a lot of change in the cash register. This man wanted to buy a pair of athletic shoes that cost $80, and he gave Mr. Nelson a $100 bill. Mr. Nelson did not have change for $100, so he ran next door and exchanged the $100 bill for five $20 bills from the cashier at The Gap. He then gave his customer the $20 in change, and the man left with the shoes.

    Later, the cashier at The Gap heard there were some counterfeit bills being passed in the mall. She went over to the shoe store, gave Mr. Nelson the $100 bill, and said she wanted five $20s. By now Mr. Nelson had change, so he took back the $100 bill and gave her five $20s.

    Shortly after that the police arrived and checked the $100 bill. Sure enough, it was counterfeit and the police confiscated it. Can you figure out how much money Mr. Nelson is out altogether? Be prepared to explain your reasoning!

CHAPTER TEST

Knowledge

1. List the four steps of Pólya's problem-solving process.

2. List the six problem-solving strategies you have learned in this chapter.

Skills

3. Identify the unneeded information in the following problem.

   Birgit took her $5 allowance to the bookstore to buy some back-to-school supplies. The pencils cost $.10, the erasers cost $.05 each, and the clips cost 2 for $.01. If she bought 100 items altogether at a total cost of $1, how many of each item did she buy?

4. Rewrite the following problem in your own words. If you add the square of Ruben's age to the age of Angelita, the sum is 62; but if you add the square of Angelita's age to the age of Ruben, the sum is 176. Can you say what the ages of Ruben and Angelita are?

5. Given the following problem and its numerical answer, write the solution in a complete sentence. Amanda leaves with a basket of hard-boiled eggs to sell. At her first stop she sold half her eggs plus half an egg. At her second stop she sold half her eggs plus half an egg. The same thing occurs at her third, fourth, and fifth stops. When she finishes, she has no eggs in her basket. How many eggs did she start with?
Answer: 31

Understanding

6. Explain the difference between an *exercise* and a *problem*.

7. List at least two characteristics of a problem that would suggest using the Guess and Test strategy.

8. List at least two characteristics of a problem that would suggest using the Use a Variable strategy.

Problem Solving / Application

For each of the following problems, read the problem carefully and solve it. Identify the strategy you used.

9. Can you rearrange the 16 numbers in this 4 × 4 array so that each row, each column, and each of the two diagonals total 10? How about a 2 × 2 array containing two 1s and two 2s? How about the corresponding 3 × 3 array?

1	1	1	1
2	2	2	2
3	3	3	3
4	4	4	4

10. In three years, Chad will be three times my *present* age. I will then be half as old as he. How old am I now?

11. There are six baseball teams in a tournament. The teams are lettered A through F. Each team plays each of the other teams twice. How many games are played altogether?

12. A fish is 30 inches long. The head is as long as the tail. If the head was twice as long and the tail was its present length, the body would be 18 inches long. How long is each portion of the fish?

13. The Orchard brothers always plant their apple trees in square arrays, like those illustrated. This year they planted 31 more apple trees in their square orchard than last year. If the orchard is still square, how many apple trees are there in the orchard this year?

14. Arrange 10 people so that there are five rows each containing 4 persons.

15. A milk crate holds 24 bottles and is shaped like the one shown below. The crate has four rows and six columns. Is it possible to put 18 bottles of milk in the crate so that each row and each column of the crate has an even number of bottles in it? If so, how? (*Hint:* One row has 6 bottles in it and the other three rows have 4 bottles in them.)

16. Otis has 12 coins in his pocket worth $1.10. If he only has nickels, dimes, and quarters, what are all of the possible coin combinations?

17. Show why 3 always divides evenly into the sum of any three consecutive whole numbers.

18. If 14 toothpicks are arranged to form a triangle so none of the toothpicks are broken or bent and all 14 toothpicks are used, how many different-shaped triangles can be formed?

19. Together a baseball and a football weigh 1.25 pounds, the baseball and a soccer ball weigh 1.35 pounds, and the football and the soccer ball weigh 1.6 pounds. How much does each of the balls weigh? Explain your reasoning.

References for Reflections from Research

CHRISTOU, C., & PHILIPPOU, G. (1998). The developmental nature of ability to solve one-step word problems. *Journal for Research in Mathematics Education, 29,* 436–442.

FRANKE, M. L., & CAREY, D. A. (1997). Young children's perceptions of mathematics in problem-solving environments. *Journal for Research in Mathematics Education, 28,* 8–25.

SCHOENFELD, A. H. (1985). *Mathematical problem solving.* Orlando, FL: Academic Press.

SILVER, E. A., & CAI, J. (1996). An analysis of arithmetic problem posing by middle school students. *Journal for Research in Mathematics Education, 27,* 521–539.

SOWDER, L., THREADGILL-SOWDER, J., MOYER, J., & MOYER, M. (1983). Format variables and learner characteristics in mathematical problem solving. (Final Tech. Rep., ERIC Document Reproduction Service No. Ed 238735.)

VERSCHAFFEL, L., & DE CORTE, E. (1997). Teaching realistic mathematical modeling in the elementary school: A teaching experiment with fifth graders. *Journal for Research in Mathematics Education, 28,* 577–601.

VERSCHAFFEL, L., DE CORTE, E., & VIERSTRAETE, H. (1999). Upper elementary school pupils' difficulties in modeling and solving nonstandard additive word problems involving ordinal numbers. *Journal for Research in Mathematics Education, 30,* 265–285.

YANCEY, A., THOMPSON, C., & YANCEY, J. (1989). Children must learn to draw diagrams. *Arithmetic Teacher, 36*(7), 15–19.

CHAPTER 2

Sets, Whole Numbers, and Numeration

FOCUS ON The Mayan Numeration System

Figure 1

he Maya people lived mainly in southeastern Mexico, including the Yucatan Peninsula, and in much of northwestern Central America, including Guatemala and parts of Honduras and El Salvador. Earliest archaeological evidence of the Maya civilization dates to 9000 B.C., with the principal epochs of the Maya cultural development occurring between 2000 B.C. and A.D. 1700.

Knowledge of arithmetic and calendrical and astronomical matters was more highly developed by the ancient Maya than by any other New World peoples. Their numeration system was simple, yet sophisticated. Their system utilized three basic numerals: a dot, •, to represent 1; a horizontal bar, —, to represent 5; and a conch shell, ⬭ to represent 0. They used these three symbols, in combination, to represent the numbers 0 through 19, as illustrated (Figure 1).

For numbers greater than 19, they initially used a base 20 system. That is, they grouped in twenties and displayed their numerals vertically. Three Mayan numerals are shown together with their values in our system and the place values initially used by the Mayans (Figure 2).

The sun, and hence the solar calendar, was very important to the Maya. They calculated that a year consisted of 365.2420 days. (Present calculations measure our year as 365.2422 days long.) At some point, the Maya decided to incorporate their chronological count into their mathematical system. Since 360 had convenient factors and was close to 365 days in their year and 400 in their numeration system, they changed their place values from 1, 20, 20^2, 20^3, and so on, to 1, 20, 20 · i18 (= 360), 20^2 · 18 (= 7200), 20^3 · 18 (= 144,000), and so on. Interestingly, the Maya could record all the days of their history simply by using the place values through 144,000. The Maya were also able to use larger numbers. One Mayan hieroglyphic text recorded a number equivalent to 1,841,641,600. Finally, the Maya, famous for their hieroglyphic writing, also used the 20 ideograms pictured here, called head variants, to represent the numbers 0 to 19 (Figure 3). The Mayan numeration system is studied in this chapter.

Figure 2

Figure 3

Venus Calendar According to the Mayans

Problem Solving Strategies

1. Guess and Test
2. Use a Variable
3. Draw a Picture
4. Look for a Pattern
5. Make a List
6. Solve a Simpler Problem
7. **Draw a Diagram**

Strategy
Draw a Diagram

Often there are problems where, although it is not necessary to draw an actual picture to represent the problem situation, a diagram that represents the essence of the problem is useful. For example, if we wish to determine the number of times two heads can turn up when we toss two coins, we could literally draw pictures of all possible arrangements of two coins turning up heads or tails. However, in practice, a simple tree diagram is used like the one shown next.

Outcomes when two
coins are tossed

Coin 1   Coin 2

This diagram shows that there is one way to obtain two heads out of four possible outcomes. Another type of diagram is helpful in solving the next problem.

Initial Problem

A survey was taken of 150 college freshmen. Forty of them were majoring in mathematics, 30 of them were majoring in English, 20 were majoring in science, 7 had a double major of mathematics and English, and none had a double (or triple) major with science. How many students had majors other than mathematics, English, or science?

Clues

The Draw a Diagram strategy may be appropriate when

- The problem involves sets, ratios, or probabilities.
- An actual picture can be drawn, but a diagram is more efficient.
- Relationships among quantities are represented.

A solution of the Initial Problem appears on page 85.

INTRODUCTION

Much of elementary school mathematics is devoted to the study of numbers. Children first learn to count using the **natural numbers** or **counting numbers** 1, 2, 3, . . . (the ellipsis, or three periods, means "and so on"). This chapter develops the ideas that lead to the concepts central to the system of **whole numbers** 0, 1, 2, 3, . . . (the counting numbers together with zero) and the symbols that are used to represent them. First, the notion of a one-to-one correspondence between two sets is shown to be the idea central to the formation of the concept of number. Then operations on sets are discussed. These operations form the foundation of addition, subtraction, multiplication, and division of whole numbers. Finally, the Hindu–Arabic numeration system, our system of symbols that represent numbers, is presented after its various attributes are introduced by considering other ancient numeration systems.

2.1   SETS AS A BASIS FOR WHOLE NUMBERS

After forming a group of students, use a diagram like the one at the right to place the names of each member of your group in the appropriate region. All members of the group will fit somewhere in the rectangle. Discuss the attributes of a person whose name is in the shaded region. Discuss the attributes of a person whose name is not in any of the circles.

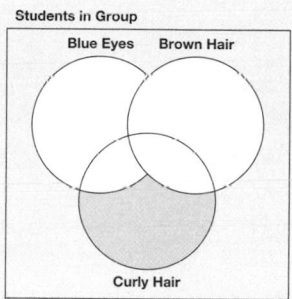

Sets

A collection of objects is called a **set** and the objects are called **elements** or **members** of the set. Sets can be defined in three common ways: (1) a verbal description, (2) a listing of the members separated by commas, with braces ("{" and "}") used to enclose the list of elements, and (3) **set-builder notation.** For example, the verbal description "the set of all states in the United States that border the Pacific Ocean" can be represented in the other two ways as follows:

1. *Listing:* {Alaska, California, Hawaii, Oregon, Washington}.
2. *Set-builder:* {$x \mid x$ is a U.S. state that borders the Pacific Ocean}. (This set-builder notation is read: "The set of all x such that x is a U.S. state that borders the Pacific Ocean.")

Sets are usually denoted by capital letters such as A, B, C, and so on. The symbols "∈" and "∉" are used to indicate that an object **is or is not an element of a set,** respectively. For example, if S represents the set of all U.S. states bordering the Pacific, then Alaska ∈ S and Michigan ∉ S. The set without elements is called the **empty set** (or **null set**) and is denoted by {} or the symbol ∅. The set of all U.S. states bordering Antarctica is the empty set.

Two sets A and B are **equal,** written $A = B$, if and only if they have precisely the same elements. Thus {$x \mid x$ is a state that borders Lake Michigan} = {Illinois, Indiana, Michigan, Wisconsin}. Notice that two sets, A and B, are equal if every element of A is in B, and vice versa. If A does not equal B, we write $A \neq B$.

There are two inherent rules regarding sets: (1) The same element is not listed more than once within a set, and (2) the order of the elements in a set is immaterial. Thus, by rule 1, the set $\{a, a, b\}$ would be written as $\{a, b\}$ and by rule 2. $\{a, b\} = \{b, a\}$, $\{x, y, z\} = \{y, z, x\}$, and so on.

The concept of a 1-1 correspondence, read "one-to-one correspondence," is needed to formalize the meaning of a whole number.

DEFINITION

One-to-One Correspondence

A **1-1 correspondence** between two sets A and B is a pairing of the elements of A with the elements of B so that each element of A corresponds to exactly one element of B, and vice versa. If there is a 1-1 correspondence between sets A and B, we write $A \sim B$ and say that A and B are **equivalent** or **match.**

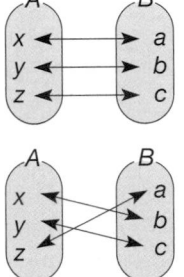

Figure 2.1 shows two 1-1 correspondences between two sets, A and B.

There are four other possible 1-1 correspondences between A and B. Notice that equal sets are always equivalent, since each element can be matched with itself, but that equivalent sets are not necessarily equal. For example, $\{1, 2\} \sim \{a, b\}$, but $\{1, 2\} \neq \{a, b\}$. The two sets $A = \{a, b\}$ and $B = \{a, b, c\}$ are not equivalent. However, they do satisfy the relationship defined next.

Figure 2.1

DEFINITION

Subset of a Set: $A \subseteq B$

Set A is said to be a **subset** of B, written $A \subseteq B$, if and only if every element of A is also an element of B.

The set consisting of New Hampshire is a subset of the set of all New England states and $\{a, b, c\} \subseteq \{a, b, c, d, e, f\}$. Since every element in a set A is in A, $A \subseteq A$ for all sets A. Also, $\{a, b, c\} \not\subseteq \{a, b, d\}$ because c is in the set $\{a, b, c\}$ but not in the set $\{a, b, d\}$. Using similar reasoning, you can argue that $\varnothing \subseteq A$ for any set A since it is impossible to find an element in $\varnothing$ that is not in A.

If $A \subseteq B$ and B has an element that is not in A, we write $A \subset B$ and say that A is a **proper subset** of B. Thus $\{a, b\} \subset \{a, b, c\}$, since $\{a, b\} \subseteq \{a, b, c\}$ and c is in the second set *but* not in the first.

Circles or other closed curves are used in **Venn diagrams** (named after the English logician John Venn) to illustrate relationships between sets. These circles are usually pictured within a rectangle, U, where the rectangle represents the **universal set** or **universe,** the set comprised of all elements being considered in a particular discussion. Figure 2.2 displays sets A and B inside a universal set U. Set A is comprised of everything inside circle A, and set B is comprised of everything inside circle B, including set A. Hence A is a *proper* subset of B since $x \in B$, but $x \notin A$. The idea of proper subset will be used later to help establish the meaning of the concept "less than" for whole numbers.

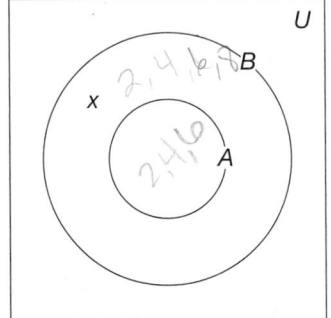

Figure 2.2

Operations on Sets

Two sets A and B that have no elements in common are called **disjoint sets.** The sets $\{a, b, c\}$ and $\{d, e, f\}$ are disjoint (Figure 2.3), whereas $\{x, y\}$ and $\{y, z\}$ are not disjoint, since y is an element in both sets.

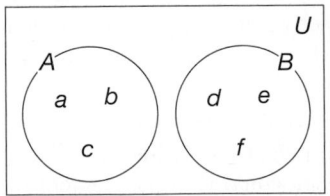

Figure 2.3

There are many ways to construct a new set from two or more sets. The following operations on sets will be very useful in clarifying our understanding of whole numbers and their operations.

DEFINITION

Union of Sets: $A \cup B$

The **union** of two sets A and B, written $A \cup B$, is the set that consists of all elements belonging either to A or to B (or to both).

Informally, $A \cup B$ is formed by putting all the elements of A and B together. The next example illustrates this definition.

Example 2.1   Find the union of the given pairs of sets.

a. $\{a, b\} \cup \{c, d, e\}$
b. $\{1, 2, 3, 4, 5\} \cup \varnothing$
c. $\{m, n, q\} \cup \{m, n, p\}$

Solution

a. $\{a, b\} \cup \{c, d, e\} = \{a, b, c, d, e\}$
b. $\{1, 2, 3, 4, 5\} \cup \varnothing = \{1, 2, 3, 4, 5\}$
c. $\{m, n, q\} \cup \{m, n, p\} = \{m, n, p, q\}$ ■

NOTE: The small solid square (■) is used to mark the end of an example or mathematical argument.

Notice that although m is a member of both sets in Example 2.1(c), it is listed only once in the union of the two sets. The union of sets A and B is displayed in a Venn diagram by shading the portion of the diagram that represents $A \cup B$ (Figure 2.4). The notion of set union is the basis for the addition of whole numbers, but only when disjoint sets are used. Notice how the sets in Example 2.1(a) can be used to show that $2 + 3 = 5$.

Another useful set operation is the intersection of sets.

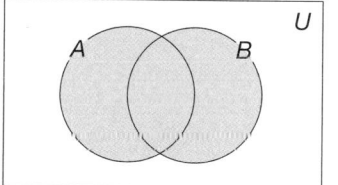

Figure 2.4   Shaded region is $A \cup B$

DEFINITION

Intersection of Sets: $A \cap B$

The **intersection** of sets A and B, written $A \cap B$, is the set of all elements common to sets A and B.

Thus $A \cap B$ is the set of elements shared by A and B. Example 2.2 illustrates this definition.

Example 2.2   Find the intersection of the given pairs of sets.

a. $\{a, b, c\} \cap \{b, d, f\}$ **b.** $\{a, b, c\} \cap \{a, b, c\}$
c. $\{a, b\} \cap \{c, d\}$

Solution

a. $\{a, b, c\} \cap \{b, d, f\} = \{b\}$ since b is the only element in both sets.
b. $\{a, b, c\} \cap \{a, b, c\} = \{a, b, c\}$ since a, b, c are in both sets.
c. $\{a, b\} \cap \{c, d\} = \varnothing$ since there are no elements common to the given two sets.   ■

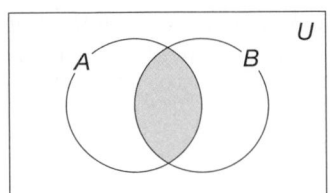

Figure 2.5 Shaded region is $A \cap B$.

Figure 2.5 displays $A \cap B$. Observe that two sets are disjoint if and only if their intersection is the empty set. Figure 2.3 shows a Venn diagram of two sets whose intersection is the empty set.

In many situations, instead of considering elements of a set A, it is more productive to consider all elements in the universal set *other than* those in A. This set is defined next.

DEFINITION

Complement of a Set: $\overline{A}$

The **complement** of a set A, written $\overline{A}$, is the set of all elements in the universe, U, that are *not* in A.

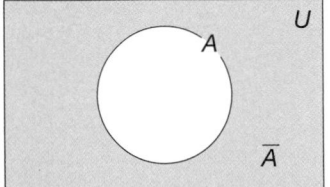

Figure 2.6 Shaded region is $\overline{A}$.

The set $\overline{A}$ is shaded in Figure 2.6.

Example 2.3 Find the following sets.

a. $\overline{A}$ where $U = \{a, b, c, d\}$ and $A = \{a\}$
b. $\overline{B}$ where $U = \{1, 2, 3, \ldots\}$ and $B = \{2, 4, 6, \ldots\}$
c. $\overline{A} \cup \overline{B}$ and $\overline{A} \cap \overline{B}$ where $U = \{1, 2, 3, 4, 5\}$, $A = \{1, 2, 3\}$, and $B = \{3, 4\}$

Solution

a. $\overline{A} = \{b, c, d\}$ **b.** $\overline{B} = \{1, 3, 5, \ldots\}$
c. $\overline{A} \cup \overline{B} = \{4, 5\} \cup \{1, 2, 5\} = \{1, 2, 4, 5\}$
$\overline{A} \cap \overline{B} = \overline{\{3\}} = \{1, 2, 4, 5\}$ ■

The next set operation forms the basis for subtraction.

DEFINITION

Difference of Sets: $A - B$

The **set difference** (or **relative complement**) of set B from set A, written $A - B$, is the set of all elements in A that are not in B.

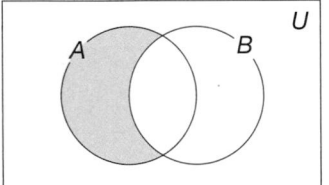

Figure 2.7 Shaded region is $A - B$.

In set-builder notation, $A - B = \{x \mid x \in A \text{ and } x \notin B\}$. Also, as can be seen in Figure 2.7, $A - B$ can be viewed as $A \cap \overline{B}$. Example 2.4 provides some examples of the difference of one set from another.

www.wiley.com/college/musser

Spotlight on Technology The regions $A \cap B$ and $A \cup B$ can each be found by shading the set A in one direction and the set B in another direction. The region with shading in both directions is $A \cap B$ and the entire shaded region is the set $A \cup B$. The Chapter 2 eManipulative activity, *Venn Diagrams*, uses this technique. Using the three-circle diagram on the eManipulative, find the region $(A \cup B) \cap C$. Draw a sketch of the shaded diagram you obtained. Then find the region $A \cup (B \cap C)$ and compare this diagram to your sketch. Are they the same or different? What conclusion can you draw regarding the placement of parentheses in cases such as these?

Date   Time

More about Venn Diagrams

1. The sixth graders at Lincoln Middle School were asked whether they write with their left hands or right hands. A small number of students reported that they write equally well with either hand.

   The survey results are shown in the Venn diagram at the right.

   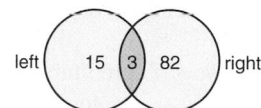

   left   15   3   82   right

   a. How many students were surveyed?   _____ students

   b. How many are *ambidextrous* (can write with either hand)? _____ students

   c. How many always write with their left hands?   _____ students

   d. How many always write with their right hands?   _____ students

   e. How many never write with their left hands?   _____ students

2. Mr. Carlson has 30 students in his sixth grade homeroom. After receiving their final test scores, he identified all students who scored 90% or above on each test. Mr. Carlson then drew this Venn diagram.

   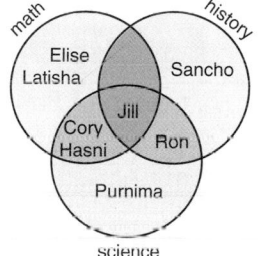

   math   history
   Elise Latisha   Sancho
   Jill
   Cory Hasni   Ron
   Purnima
   science

   a. Whose performance was best overall?   _____

   b. Who scored 90% or above on *at least 2* tests? _____

   c. Who scored 90% or above on *exactly 1* test? _____

   d. Who scored 90% or above in both math and science? _____

   e. Which two tests had the least overlap? _____

   f. What percent of the students in Mr. Carlson's homeroom had a score of 90% or above on *exactly 2* tests? _____

Use with Lesson 7.6.

271

43

Example 2.4   Find the difference of the given pairs of sets.

a. $\{a, b, c\} - \{b, d\}$
b. $\{a, b, c\} - \{e\}$
c. $\{a, b, c, d\} - \{b, c, d\}$

Solution

a. $\{a, b, c\} - \{b, d\} = \{a, c\}$
b. $\{a, b, c\} - \{e\} = \{a, b, c\}$
c. $\{a, b, c, d\} - \{b, c, d\} = \{a\}$ ■

In Example 2.4(c), the second set is a subset of the first. These sets can be used to show that $4 - 3 = 1$.

Another way of combining two sets to form a third set is called the Cartesian product. The Cartesian product, named after the French mathematician René Descartes, forms the basis of whole-number multiplication and is also useful in probability and geometry. To define the Cartesian product, we need to have the concept of ordered pair. An **ordered pair,** written (a, b), is a pair of elements where one of the elements is designated as first (a in this case) and the other is second (b here). The notion of an ordered pair differs from that of simply a set of two elements because of the preference in order. For example, $\{1, 2\} = \{2, 1\}$ as sets, because they have the same elements. But $(1, 2) \neq (2, 1)$ *as ordered pairs*, since the order of the elements is different. Two ordered pairs (a, b) and (c, d) are equal if and only if $a = c$ and $b = d$.

DEFINITION

Cartesian Product of Sets: $A \times B$

The **Cartesian product** of set A with set B, written $A \times B$ and read "A cross B," is the set of all ordered pairs (a, b), where $a \in A$ and $b \in B$.

In set-builder notation, $A \times B = \{(a, b) \mid a \in A \text{ and } b \in B\}$.

Example 2.5   Find the Cartesian product of the given pairs of sets.

a. $\{x, y, z\} \times \{m, n\}$ **b.** $\{7\} \times \{a, b, c\}$

Solution

a. $\{x, y, z\} \times \{m, n\} = \{(x, m), (x, n), (y, m), (y, n), (z, m), (z, n)\}$
b. $\{7\} \times \{a, b, c\} = \{(7, a), (7, b), (7, c)\}$ ■

Notice that when finding a Cartesian product, all possible pairs are formed where the first element comes from the first set and the second element comes from the second set. Also observe that in part (a) of Example 2.5, there are three elements in the first set, two in the second, and six in their Cartesian product, and that $3 \times 2 = 6$. Similarly, in part (b), these sets can be used to find the whole-number product $1 \times 3 = 3$.

Venn diagrams are often used to solve problems, as shown next.

Example 2.6   Thirty elementary teachers were asked which high school courses they appreciated: algebra or geometry. Seventeen appreciated algebra and 15 appreciated geometry; of these, 5 said that they appreciated both. How many appreciated neither?

(a)

(b)

(c)

(a)

(b)

(c)

(d)

Figure 2.8 (a)–(d)

Reflection from Research
While many students will agree that two infinite sets such as the set of counting numbers and the set of even numbers are equivalent, the same students will argue that the set of counting numbers is larger due to its inclusion of the odd numbers (Wheeler, 1987).

Solution Since there are two courses, we draw a Venn diagram with two over-lapping circles labeled A for algebra and G for geometry [Figure 2.8(a)]. Since 5 teachers appreciated both algebra and geometry, we place a 5 in the intersection of A and G [Figure 2.8(b)]. Seventeen must be in the A circle; thus 12 must be in the remaining part of A [Figure 2.8(c)]. Similarly, 10 must be in the G circle outside the intersection [Figure 2.8(d)]. Thus we have accounted for $12 + 5 + 10 = 27$ teachers. This leaves 3 of the 30 teachers who appreciated neither algebra nor geometry. ■

Finite and Infinite Sets

There are two broad categories of sets: finite and infinite. Informally, a set is **finite** if it is empty or can have its elements listed (where the list eventually ends), and a set is **infinite** if it goes on without end. A little more formally, a set is finite if (1) it is empty or (2) it can be put into a 1-1 correspondence with a set of the form $\{1, 2, 3, \ldots, n\}$, where n is a counting number. On the other hand, a set is infinite if it is *not* finite.

Example 2.7 Determine whether the following sets are finite or infinite.

a. $\{a, b, c\}$ **b.** $\{1, 2, 3, \ldots\}$ **c.** $\{2, 4, 6, \ldots, 20\}$

Solution

a. $\{a, b, c\}$ is finite since it can be matched with the set $\{1, 2, 3\}$.
b. $\{1, 2, 3, \ldots\}$ is an infinite set.
c. $\{2, 4, 6, \ldots, 20\}$ is a finite set since it can be matched with the set $\{1, 2, 3, \ldots, 10\}$. (Here, the ellipsis means to continue the pattern until the last element is reached.) ■

An interesting property of every infinite set is that it can be matched with a proper subset of itself. For example, consider the following 1-1 correspondence:

$$A = \{1, 2, 3, 4, \ldots, n, \ldots\}$$
$$\updownarrow \ \updownarrow \ \updownarrow \ \updownarrow \qquad \updownarrow$$
$$B = \{2, 4, 6, 8, \ldots, 2n, \ldots\}.$$

Note that $B \subset A$ and that each element in A is paired with exactly one element in B, and vice versa. Notice that matching n with $2n$ indicates that we never "run out" of elements from B to match with the elements from set A. Thus an alternative definition is that a set is infinite if it is equivalent to a proper subset of itself. In this case, a set is finite if it is not infinite.

MATHEMATICAL MORSEL

There are several theories concerning the rationale behind the shapes of the 10 digits in our Hindu–Arabic numeration system. One is that the number represented by each digit is given by the number of angles in the original digit. Count the "angles" in each digit below. (Here an "angle" is less than 180°.) Of course, zero is round, so it has no angles.

Section 2.1 EXERCISE / PROBLEM SET A

EXERCISES

1. Indicate the following sets by the listing method.
   a. Whole numbers between 5 and 9
   b. Even counting numbers less than 15
   c. Even counting numbers less than 151
   d. Whole numbers greater than 8
   e. Odd whole numbers less than 100
   f. Whole numbers less than 0

2. True or false?
   a. $7 \in \{6, 7, 8, 9\}$ b. $\frac{2}{3} \in \{1, 2, 3\}$
   c. $5 \notin \{2, 3, 4, 6\}$ d. $1 \notin \{0, 1, 2\}$
   e. $\{1, 2, 3\} \subseteq \{1, 2, 3\}$ f. $\{4, 3\} \subset \{2, 3, 4\}$
   g. $\{1, 2, 5\} \subset \{1, 2, 5\}$ h. $\varnothing \subseteq \{\}$
   i. $\{2\} \not\subseteq \{1, 2\}$ j. $\{1, 2\} \not\subseteq \{2\}$

3. List all the subsets of $\{a, b, c\}$.

4. List the proper subsets of $\{\bigcirc, \triangle\}$.

5. Find four 1-1 correspondences between A and B other than the two given in Figure 2.1.

6. Draw a Venn diagram like the following one for each part. Then shade each Venn diagram to represent each of the sets indicated.

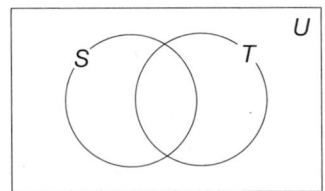

   a. $\overline{S}$ b. $\overline{S} \cap T$ c. $\overline{S} \cup T$

7. Draw Venn diagrams that represent sets A and B as described as follows:
   a. $A \subset B$ b. $A \cap B = \varnothing$ c. $A \cap B \neq \varnothing$

8. Let $A = \{a, b, c\}$, $B = \{b, c\}$, and $C = \{e\}$. Find each of the following.
   a. $A \cap B$ b. $B \cup C$ c. $A - B$

9. Let $W = \{$women who have won Nobel Prizes$\}$, $A = \{$Americans who have won Nobel Prizes$\}$, and $C = \{$winners of the Nobel Prize in chemistry$\}$. Describe the elements of the following sets.
   a. $W \cup A$ b. $W \cap A$ c. $A \cap C$

10. Given $A = \{0, 1, 2, 3, 4, 5\}$, $B = \{0, 2, 4, 6, 8, 10\}$, and $C = \{0, 4, 8\}$, find each of the following.

   a. $A \cup B$ b. $B \cup C$ c. $A \cap B$
   d. $B \cap C$ e. $B - C$ f. $(A \cup B) - C$

11. Let $M = $ the set of the months of the year, $J = \{$January, June, July$\}$, $S = \{$June, July, August$\}$, $W = \{$December, January, February$\}$. List the members of each of the following:
   a. $J \cup S$ b. $J \cap W$ c. $S \cap W$
   d. $J \cap (S \cup W)$ e. $M - (S \cup W)$ f. $J - S$

12. a. If $x \in X \cap Y$, is $x \in X \cup Y$? Justify your answer.
    b. If $x \in X \cup Y$, is $x \in X \cap Y$? Justify your answer.

13. A Venn diagram can be used to illustrate more than two sets. Shade the regions that represent each of the following sets. The Chapter 2 eManipulative activity, *Venn Diagrams*, may help in solving this problem.

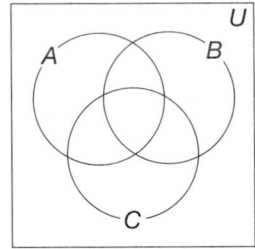

   a. $A \cap (B \cap C)$ b. $A - (B \cap C)$
   c. $A \cup (B - C)$

14. Represent the following shaded regions using the symbols A, B, C, $\cup$, $\cap$, and $-$. The Chapter 2 eManipulative activity, *Venn Diagrams,* can be used in solving this problem.

   a.

   b.

   c.
   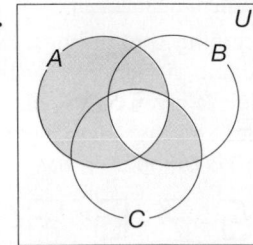

15. Let $A = \{3, 6, 9, 12, 15, 18, 21, 24, \ldots\}$ and $B = \{6, 12, 18, 24, \ldots\}$.

    a. Is $B \subseteq A$?   **b.** Find $A \cup B$.   **c.** Find $A \cap B$.

    d. In general, when $B \subseteq A$, what is true about $A \cup B$? about $A \cap B$?

16. In the drawing, C is the interior of the circle, T is the interior of the triangle, and R is the interior of the rectangle. Copy the drawing on a sheet of paper, then shade in each of the following regions.

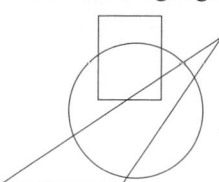

    a. $C \cup T$ **b.** $C \cap R$

    c. $(C \cap T) \cup R$ **d.** $(C \cup R) \cup T$

    e. $(C \cap R) \cap T$ **f.** $C \cap (R \cap T)$

17. Verify that $\overline{A \cup B} = \overline{A} \cap \overline{B}$ in two different ways as follows:

    a. Let $U = \{1, 2, 3, 4, 5, 6\}$, $A = \{2, 3, 5\}$, and $B = \{1, 4\}$. List the elements of the sets $\overline{A \cup B}$ and $\overline{A} \cap \overline{B}$. Do the two sets have the same members?

    b. Draw and shade a Venn diagram for each of the sets $\overline{A \cup B}$ and $\overline{A} \cap \overline{B}$. Do the two Venn diagrams look the same? NOTE: The equation $\overline{A \cup B} = \overline{A} \cap \overline{B}$ is one of two laws called **DeMorgan's laws.**

18. Find the following Cartesian products.

    a. $\{a\} \times \{b, c\}$ **b.** $\{5\} \times \{a, b, c\}$

    c. $\{a, b\} \times \{1, 2, 3\}$ **d.** $\{2, 3\} \times \{1, 4\}$

    e. $\{a, b, c\} \times \{5\}$ **f.** $\{1, 2, 3\} \times \{a, b\}$

19. Determine how many ordered pairs will be in the following sets.

    a. $\{1, 2, 3, 4\} \times \{a, b\}$

    b. $\{m, n, o\} \times \{1, 2, 3, 4\}$

20. If A has two members, how many members does B have when $A \times B$ has the following number of members? If an answer is not possible, explain why.

    a. 4   **b.** 8   **c.** 9

    d. 50   **e.** 0   **f.** 23

21. The Cartesian product, $A \times B$, is given in each of the following parts. Find A and B.

    a. $\{(a, 2), (a, 4), (a, 6)\}$

    b. $\{(a, b), (b, b), (b, a), (a, a)\}$

22. True or false?

    a. $\{(4, 5), (6, 7)\} = \{(6, 7), (4, 5)\}$

    b. $\{(a, b), (c, d)\} = \{(b, a), (c, d)\}$

    c. $\{(4, 5), (7, 6)\} = \{(7, 6), (5, 4)\}$

    d. $\{(a, c), (d, b)\} = \{a, c, d, b\}$

    e. $\{(c, d), (a, b)\} = \{(c, a), (d, b)\}$

23. Determine which of the following sets are finite. For those sets that are finite, how many elements are in the set?

    a. {cars on a typical elephant}

    b. $\{1, 2, 3, \ldots, 99\}$

    c. $\{0, 1, 2, 3, \ldots, 200\}$

    d. Set of points belonging to a line segment

    e. Set of points belonging to a circle

PROBLEMS

24. a. If X has five elements and Y has three elements. What is the greatest number of elements possible in $X \cap Y$? in $X \cup Y$?

    b. If X has x elements and Y has y elements with x greater than or equal to y, what is the greatest number of elements possible in $X \cap Y$? in $X \cup Y$?

25. How many different 1-1 correspondences are possible between $A = \{1, 2, 3, 4\}$ and $B = \{a, b, c, d\}$?

26. How many subsets does a set with the following number of members have?

    a. 0   **b.** 1   **c.** 2   **d.** 3   **e.** 5   **f.** n

27. If it is possible, give examples of the following. If it is not possible, explain why.

    a. Two sets that are not equal but are equivalent

    b. Two sets that are not equivalent but are equal

28. a. When does $D \cap E = D$?

    b. When does $D \cup E = D$?

    c. When does $D \cap E = D \cup E$?

29. Carmen has 8 skirts and 7 blouses. Show how the concept of Cartesian product can be used to determine how many different outfits she has.

30. How many matches are there if 32 participants enter a single-elimination tennis tournament (one loss eliminates a participant)?

31. Can you show a 1-1 correspondence between the points on base $\overline{AB}$ of the given triangle and the points on the two sides $\overline{AC}$ and $\overline{CB}$? Explain how you can or why you cannot.

32. Can you show a 1-1 correspondence between the points on chord $\overline{AB}$ and the points on arc $\overparen{ACB}$? Explain how you can or why you cannot.

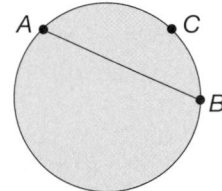

33. A poll of 100 registered voters designed to find out how voters kept up with current events revealed the following facts.

65 watched the news on television.

39 read the newspaper.

39 listened to radio news.

20 watched TV news and read the newspaper.

27 watched TV news and listened to radio news.

9 read the newspaper and listened to radio news.

6 watched TV news, read the newspaper, and listened to radio news.

a. How many of the 100 people surveyed kept up with current events by some means other than the three sources listed?

b. How many of the 100 people surveyed read the paper but did *not* watch TV news?

c. How many of the 100 people surveyed used only one of the three sources listed to keep up with current events?

34. At a convention of 375 butchers (B), bakers (A), and candlestick makers (C), there were

50 who were both B and A but not C

70 who were B but neither A nor C

60 who were A but neither B nor C

40 who were both A and C but not B

50 who were both B and C but not A

80 who were C but neither A nor B

How many at the convention were A, B, and C?

 Section 2.1 EXERCISE / PROBLEM SET B

EXERCISES

1. Represent the following sets using set-builder notation:

a. $\{0, 2, 4, \ldots, 12\}$ **b.** $\{1, 4, 9, 16, 25, \ldots\}$

c. $\{0, 1, 2\}$ **d.** $\varnothing$

2. Which of the following sets are equal to $\{4, 5, 6\}$?

a. $\{5, 6\}$ **b.** $\{5, 4, 6\}$

c. Whole numbers greater than 3

d. Whole numbers less than 7

e. Whole numbers greater than 3 or less than 7

f. Whole numbers greater than 3 and less than 8

g. $\{e, f, g\}$

h. $\{4, 5, 6, 5\}$

3. Write a set that is equivalent to, but not equal to the set $\{a, b, c, d, e, f\}$.

4. List all subsets of $\{\bigcirc, \triangle, \square\}$. Which are proper subsets?

5. How many proper subsets does $R = \{r, s, t, u, v\}$ have?

6. Show three different 1-1 correspondences between $\{1, 2, 3, 4\}$ and $\{x, y, z, w\}$.

7. Let $A = \{1, 2, 3, 4, 5\}$, $B = \{3, 4, 5\}$, and $C = \{4, 5, 6\}$. In the following insert $\in$, $\subset$, $\subseteq$, or $\not\subseteq$ to make a true statement.

a. 2___A **b.** B___A **c.** C___B

d. 6___C **e.** A___A **f.** $B \cap C$___A

8. Let $A = \{0, 10, 20, 30, \ldots\}$ and $B = \{5, 15, 25, 35, \ldots\}$. Decide which of the following are true and which are false. Explain your answers.

a. A equals B **b.** B is equivalent to A.

c. A is a proper subset of B.

d. B is equivalent to a proper subset of A.

e. There is a proper subset of B that is equivalent to a proper subset of A.

9. Let $R = \{a, b, c\}$, $S = \{c, d, e, f\}$, $T = \{x, y, z\}$. List the elements of the following sets.

a. $R \cup S$ **b.** $R \cap S$ **c.** $R \cup T$

d. $R \cap T$ **e.** $S \cup T$ **f.** $S \cap T$

10. Find each of the following differences.

   a. $\{h, i, j, k\} - \{k\}$

   b. $\{○, △, /, □\} - \{△, □\}$

   c. $\{3, 10, 13\} - \{\}$

   d. $\{0, 1, 2, \ldots\} - \{12, 13, 14, \ldots\}$

   e. {people} − {married people}

   f. {two-wheeled vehicles} − {two-wheeled vehicles that are not bicycles}

   g. $\{0, 2, 4, 6, \ldots, 20\} - \{12, 14, 16, 18, 20\}$

   h. $\{a, b, c, d\} - \{\}$

11. Draw a Venn diagram like the following for each part. Then shade each Venn diagram to represent each of the sets indicated.

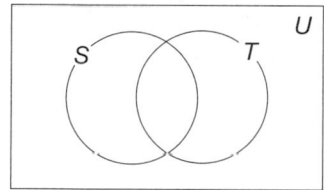

   a. $T - S$ **b.** $(S - T) \cup (T - S)$

   c. $(S - T) \cap (T - S)$

12. If A is the set of all sophomores in a school and B is the set of students who belong to the orchestra, describe the following sets in words.

   a. $A \cup B$ **b.** $A \cap B$ **c.** $A - B$ **d.** $B - A$

13. In each of the following cases, find $B - A$.

   a. $A \cap B = \emptyset$ **b.** $A - B$ **c.** $B \subseteq A$

14. Let $A = \{a, b, c, d, e\}$, $B = \{c, d, e, f, g\}$, and $C = \{a, e, f, h\}$. List the members of each set.

   a. $A \cup B$ **b.** $A \cap B$

   c. $(A \cup B) \cap C$ **d.** $A \cup (B \cap C)$

15. Let $A = \{50, 55, 60, 65, 70, 75, 80\}$
   $B = \{50, 60, 70, 80\}$
   $C = \{60, 70, 80\}$
   $D - \{55, 65\}$
   List the members of each set.

   a. $A \cup (B \cap C)$ **b.** $(A \cup B) \cap C$

   c. $(A \cap C) \cup (C \cap D)$ **d.** $(A \cap C) \cap (C \cup D)$

   e. $(B - C) \cap A$ **f.** $(A - D) \cap (B - C)$

16. A Venn diagram can be used to illustrate more than two sets. Shade the regions that represent each of the following sets. The Chapter 2 eManipulative activity, *Venn Diagrams*, may help in solving this problem.

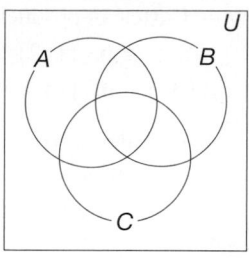

   a. $(A \cup B) \cap C$ **b.** $\overline{A} \cap (\overline{B} \cap \overline{C})$

   c. $(A \cup B) - (B \cap C)$

17. Represent the following shaded regions using the symbols $A, B, C, \cup, \cap,$ and $-$. The Chapter 2 eManipulative activity, *Venn Diagrams*, can be used in solving this problem.

   a.   **b.**

   c.

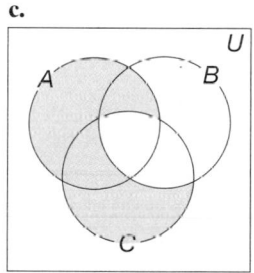

18. Use Venn diagrams to determine which, if any, of the following statements are true for all sets $A, B,$ and C:

   a. $A \cup (B \cup C) = (A \cup B) \cup C$

   b. $A \cup (B \cap C) = (A \cup B) \cap C$

   c. $A \cap (B \cap C) = (A \cap B) \cap C$

   d. $A \cap (B \cup C) = (A \cap B) \cup C$

19. Verify that $\overline{A \cap B} = \overline{A} \cup \overline{B}$ in two different ways as follows:

   a. Let $U = \{2, 4, 6, 8, 10, 12, 14, 16\}$, $A = \{2, 4, 8, 16\}$, and $B = \{4, 8, 12, 16\}$. List the elements of the sets $\overline{A \cap B}$ and $\overline{A} \cup \overline{B}$. Do the two sets have the same members?

   b. Draw and shade a Venn diagram for each of the sets $\overline{A \cap B} = \overline{A} \cup \overline{B}$. Do the two Venn diagrams look the same?

   NOTE: The equation $\overline{A \cap B} = \overline{A} \cup \overline{B}$ is one of the two laws called **DeMorgan's laws.**

20. Find the following Cartesian products.

a. $\{a, b, c\} \times \{1\}$ **b.** $\{1, 2\} \times \{p, q, r\}$

c. $\{p, q, r\} \times \{1, 2\}$ **d.** $\{a\} \times \{1\}$

21. Determine how many ordered pairs will be in $A \times B$ under the following conditions.

a. A has one member and B has four members.

b. A has two members and B has four members.

c. A has three members and B has seven members.

22. Find sets A and B so that $A \times B$ has the following number of members.

a. 1 **b.** 2 **c.** 3 **d.** 4

e. 5 **f.** 6 **g.** 7 **h.** 0

23. The Cartesian product, $X \times Y$, is given in each of the following parts. Find X and Y.

a. $\{(b, c), (c, c)\}$

b. $\{(2, 1), (2, 2), (2, 3), (5, 1), (5, 2), (5, 3)\}$

24. Show that the following sets are finite by giving the set of the form $\{1, 2, 3, \ldots, n\}$ that matches the given set.

a. $\{121, 122, 123, \ldots, 139\}$ **b.** $\{1, 3, 5, \ldots, 27\}$

25. Show that the following sets are infinite by matching each with a proper subset of itself.

a. $\{2, 4, 6, \ldots, n, \ldots\}$

b. $\{50, 51, 52, 53, \ldots, n, \ldots\}$

26. True or false?

a. The empty set is a subset of every set.

b. The set $\{105, 110, 115, 120, \ldots\}$ is an infinite set.

c. For all sets X and Y, either $X \subseteq Y$ or $Y \subseteq X$.

d. If A is an infinite set and $B \subseteq A$, then B also is an infinite set.

e. For all finite sets A and B, if $A \cap B = \varnothing$, then the number of elements in $A \cup B$ equals the number of elements in A plus the number of elements in B.

PROBLEMS

27. How many 1-1 correspondences are there between the following pairs of sets?

a. Two 2-member sets **b.** Two 4-member sets

c. Two 6-member sets

d. Two sets each having m members

28. Find sets (when possible) satisfying each of the following conditions.

a. Number of elements in A plus number of elements in B is greater than number of elements in $A \cup B$.

b. Number of elements in I plus number of elements in J is less than number of elements in $I \cup J$.

c. Number of elements in E plus number of elements in F equals number of elements in $E \cup F$.

d. Number of elements in G plus number of elements in K equals number of elements in $G \cap K$.

29. Your house can be painted in a choice of 7 exterior colors and 15 interior colors. Assuming that you choose only 1 color for the exterior and 1 color for the interior, how many different ways of painting your house are there?

30. a. Show a 1-1 correspondence between the points on the given circle and the triangle in which it is inscribed. Explain your procedure.

b. Show a 1-1 correspondence between the points on the given triangle and the circle that circumscribes it. Explain your procedure.

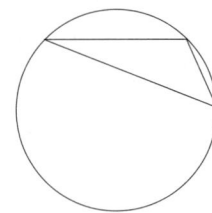

31. A schoolroom has 13 desks and 13 chairs. You want to arrange the desks and chairs so that each desk has a chair with it. How many such arrangements are there?

32. A university professor asked his class of 42 students when they had studied for his class the previous weekend. Their responses were as follows:

9 had studied on Friday.
18 had studied on Saturday.
30 had studied on Sunday.
3 had studied on both Friday and Saturday.
10 had studied on both Saturday and Sunday.
6 had studied on both Friday and Sunday.
2 had studied on Friday, Saturday, and Sunday.

Assuming that all 42 students responded and answered honestly, answer the following questions.

a. How many students studied on Sunday but not on either Friday or Saturday?

b. How many students did all of their studying on one day?

c. How many students did not study at all for this class last weekend?

33. At an automotive repair shop, 50 cars were inspected. Suppose that 23 cars needed new brakes and 34 cars needed new exhaust systems.

a. What is the least number of cars that could have needed both?

b. What is the greatest number of cars that could have needed both?

c. What is the greatest number of cars that could have needed neither?

34. If 70% of all students take science, 75% take social science, 80% take mathematics, and 85% take English, at least what percent take all four?

PROBLEMS FOR WRITING/DISCUSSION

1. If two sets are equal, does that mean they are equivalent? If two sets are equivalent, does that mean they are equal? Explain.

2. If A is a proper subset of B, and A has 23 elements, how many elements does B have? Explain.

3. A student says that $A - B$ means you start with all the elements of A and you take away all the elements of B. So $A \times B$ must mean you take all the elements of A and multiply them times all the elements of B. Do you agree with the student? How would you explain your reasoning?

2.2 WHOLE NUMBERS AND NUMERATION

Today our numeration system has the symbol "2" to represent the number of eyes a person has. The symbols "1" and "0" combine to represent the number of toes a person has, "10". The Roman numeration system used the symbol "X" to represent the number of toes and "C" to represent the number of years in a century.

Using only the three symbols at the right, devise your own numeration system and show how you can use your system to represent all of the quantities 0, 1, 2, 3, 4, . . . , 100.

NCTM Standards 2000
Number and Operations
Grades Pre-K–2
All students should develop understanding of the relative position and magnitude of whole numbers and of ordinal and cardinal numbers and their connections.

Numbers and Numerals

As mentioned earlier, the study of the set of whole numbers, $W = \{0, 1, 2, 3, 4, \ldots\}$, is the foundation of elementary school mathematics. But what precisely do we mean by the whole number 3? A **number** is an idea, or an abstraction, that represents a quantity. The symbols that we see, write, or touch when representing numbers are called **numerals.** There are three common uses of numbers. The most common use of whole numbers is to describe how many elements are in a finite set. When used in this manner, the number is referred to as a **cardinal number.** A second use is concerned with order. For example, you may be second in line, or your team may be fourth in the standings. Numbers used in this way are called **ordinal numbers.** Finally, **identification numbers** are used to name such things as telephone numbers, bank account numbers, and social security numbers. In this case, the numbers are used in a numeral sense in that only the symbols, rather than their values, are important. Before discussing our system of numeration or symbolization, the concept of cardinal number will be considered.

What is the number 3? What do you think of when you see the sets in Figure 2.9? First, there are no common elements. One set is made up of letters, one of shapes, one of Greek letters, and so on. Second, each set can be matched with every other set.

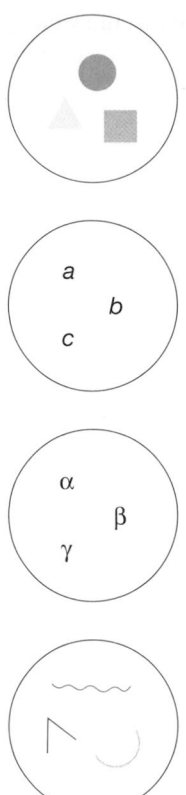

Figure 2.9

Reflection from Research
Students experience more success counting objects that can be moved around than they do counting pictured objects that cannot be moved (Wang, Resnick, & Boozer, 1971).

**NCTM Standards 2000
Number and Operations
Grades Pre-K–2**
All students should count with understanding and recognize "how many" in sets of objects.

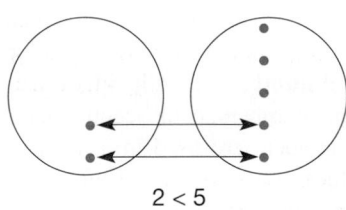

$2 < 5$

Figure 2.10

Now imagine all the infinitely many sets that can be matched with these sets. Even though the sets will be made up of various elements, they will all share the common attribute that they are equivalent to the set $\{a, b, c\}$. The common *idea* that is associated with all of these equivalent sets is the number 3. That is, *the number 3 is the attribute common to all sets that match the set* $\{a, b, c\}$. Similarly, the whole number 2 is the common idea associated with all sets equivalent to the set $\{a, b\}$. All other nonzero whole numbers can be conceptualized in a similar manner. Zero is the idea, or number, one imagines when asked: "How many elements are in the empty set?"

Although the preceding discussion regarding the concept of a whole number may seem routine for you, there are many pitfalls for children who are learning the concept of numerousness for the first time. Chronologically, children first learn how to *say* the counting chant "one, two, three, . . .". However, saying the chant and *understanding* the concept of number are not the same thing. Next, children must learn how to match the counting chant words they are saying with the objects they are counting. For example, to count the objects in the set $\{\triangle, \bigcirc, \square\}$, a child must correctly assign the words "one, two, three" to the objects in a 1-1 fashion. Actually, children first learning to count objects fail this task in two ways: (1) They fail to assign a word to each object, and hence their count is too small; or (2) they count one or more objects at least twice and end up with a number that is too large. To reach the final stage in understanding the concept of number, children must be able to observe several equivalent sets, as in Figure 2.9, and realize that, when they count each set, they arrive at the same word. Thus this word is used to name the attribute common to all such sets.

The symbol **$n(A)$** is used to represent the **number of elements in a finite set A.** More precisely, (1) $n(A) = m$ if $A \sim \{1, 2, \ldots, m\}$, where m is a counting number, and (2) $n(\varnothing) = 0$. Thus

$$n(\{a, b, c\}) = 3 \text{ since } \{a, b, c\} \sim \{1, 2, 3\}, \text{ and}$$
$$n(\{a, b, c, \ldots, z\}) = 26 \text{ since}$$
$$\{a, b, c, \ldots, z\} \sim \{1, 2, 3, \ldots, 26\},$$

and so on, for other finite sets.

Ordering Whole Numbers

Children may get their first introduction to ordering whole numbers through the counting chant "one, two, three, ..." For example, "two" is less than "five," since "two" comes before "five" in the counting chant.

A more meaningful way of comparing two whole numbers is to use 1-1 correspondences. We can say that 2 is less than 5, since any set with two elements matches a proper subset of any set with five elements (Figure 2.10).

The general set formulation of "less than" follows.

 DEFINITION

Ordering Whole Numbers

Let $a = n(A)$ and $b = n(B)$. Then $a < b$ (read "a **is less than** b") or $b > a$ (read "b **is greater than** a") if A is equivalent to a proper subset of B.

The "greater than" and "less than" signs can be combined with the equal sign to produce the following symbols: $a \leq b$ (a **is less than or equal to** b) and $b \geq a$ (b **is greater than or equal to** a).

Reflection from Research
Most counting mistakes made by young children can be attributed to not keeping track of objects that have already been counted and objects that still need to be counted (Fuson, 1988).

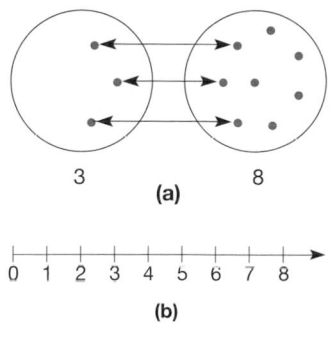

Figure 2.12

A third common way of ordering whole numbers is through the use of the whole-number "line" (Figure 2.11). Actually, the **whole-number line** is a sequence of equally spaced marks where the numbers represented by the marks begin on the left with 0 and increase by one each time we move one mark to the right.

Figure 2.11

Example 2.8 Determine the greater of the two numbers 3 and 8 in three different ways.

Solution

a. *Counting Chant:* One, two, *three*, four, five, six, seven, *eight*. Since "three" precedes "eight," eight is greater than three.
b. *Set Method:* Since a set with three elements can be matched with a proper subset of a set with eight elements, $3 < 8$ and $8 > 3$ [Figure 2.12(a)].
c. *Whole-Number Line:* Since 3 is to the left of 8 on the number line, 3 is less than 8 and 8 is greater than 3 [Figure 2.12(b)]. ■

Numeration Systems

Reflection from Research
Students as young as 4 and 5 can begin to develop estimation ability by judging if the number of objects in a set is more or less than a given number such as 5, 10, or 20 (Baroody & Gatzke, 1991).

To make numbers more useful, systems of symbols, or numerals, have been developed to represent numbers. In fact, throughout history, many different numeration systems have evolved. The following discussion reviews various ancient numeration systems with an eye toward identifying features of those systems that are incorporated in our present system, the Hindu–Arabic numeration system.

The Tally Numeration System The **tally numeration system** is composed of single strokes, one for each object being counted (Figure 2.13).

Figure 2.13

**NCTM Standards 2000
Number and Operations
Grades Pre-K–2**
All students should develop understanding of the relative position and magnitude of whole numbers and of ordinal and cardinal numbers and their connections.

The next six such tally numerals are

An advantage of this system is its simplicity; however, two disadvantages are that (1) large numbers require many individual symbols, and (2) it is difficult to read the numerals for such numbers. For example, what number is represented by these tally marks?

|||||||||||||||||||||||||||||||||||||||

The tally system was improved by the introduction of **grouping.** In this case, the fifth tally mark was placed across every four to make a group of five. Thus the last tally numeral can be written as follows:

卌 卌 卌 卌 卌 卌 卌||

Grouping makes it easier to recognize the number being represented; in this case, there are 37 tally marks.

The Egyptian Numeration System The **Egyptian numeration system,** which developed around 3400 B.C., involves grouping by ten. In addition, this system introduced new symbols for powers of 10 (Figure 2.14).

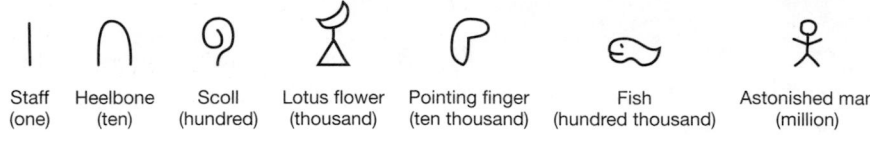

Staff	Heelbone	Scroll	Lotus flower	Pointing finger	Fish	Astonished man
(one)	(ten)	(hundred)	(thousand)	(ten thousand)	(hundred thousand)	(million)

Figure 2.14

Examples of some Egyptian numerals are shown in Figure 2.15. Notice how this system required far fewer symbols than the tally system once numbers greater than 10 were represented. This system is also an **additive system,** since the values for the various individual numerals are added together.

321   1034   1,120,013

Figure 2.15

Notice that the order in which the symbols are written is immaterial. A major disadvantage of this system is that computation is cumbersome. Figure 2.16 shows, in Egyptian numerals, the addition problem that we write as $764 + 598 = 1362$. Here 51 individual Egyptian numerals are needed to express this addition problem, whereas our system requires only 10 numerals!

Table 2.1

ROMAN NUMERAL	VALUE
I	1
V	5
X	10
L	50
C	100
D	500
M	1000

Table 2.2

ROMAN NUMERAL	VALUE
IV	4
IX	9
XL	40
XC	90
CD	400
CM	900

Figure 2.16

The Roman Numeration System The **Roman numeration system,** which developed between 500 B.C. and A.D. 100, also uses grouping, additivity, and many symbols. The basic Roman numerals are listed in Table 2.1.

Roman numerals are made up of combinations of these basic numerals, as illustrated next.

CCLXXXI (equals 281)   MCVIII (equals 1108)

Notice that the values of these Roman numerals are found by adding the values of the various basic numerals. For example, MCVIII means $1000 + 100 + 5 + 1 + 1 + 1$, or 1108. Thus the Roman system is an additive system.

Two new attributes that were introduced by the Roman system were a subtractive principle and a multiplicative principle. Both of these principles allow the system to use fewer symbols to represent numbers. The Roman numeration system is a **subtractive system** since it permits simplifications using combinations of basic Roman numerals: IV (I to the left of V means five minus one) for 4 rather than using IIII, IX (ten minus one) for 9 instead of VIIII, XL for 40, XC for 90, CD for 400, and CM for 900 (Table 2.2). Thus, when reading from left to right, if the values of the symbols in any pair of symbols increase, group the pair together. The value of this pair, then, is the value of the larger numeral less the value of the smaller.

To evaluate a complex Roman numeral, one looks to see whether any of these subtractive pairs are present, groups them together mentally, and then adds values from left to right. For example,

in   MCMXLIV

think · M   CM   XL   IV, which is $1000 + 900 + 40 + 4$.

Notice that without the subtractive principle, 14 individual Roman numerals would be required to represent 1944 instead of the 7 numerals used in MCMXLIV. Also, because of the subtractive principle, the Roman system is a **positional** system, since the position of a numeral can affect the value of the number being represented. For example, VI is six, whereas IV is four.

Example 2.9   Express the following Roman numerals in our numeration system:

a. MCCXLIV   **b.** MMCMXCIII   **c.** CCXLIX

Solution

a. *Think:* MCCC   XL   IV, or $1300 + 40 + 4 = 1344$
b. *Think:* MM   CM   XC   III, or $2000 + 900 + 90 + 3 = 2993$
c. *Think:* CC   XL   IX, or $200 + 40 + 9 = 249$ ■

The Roman numeration system also utilized a horizontal bar above a numeral to represent 1000 times the number. For example, $\overline{V}$ meant 5 times 1000, or 5000; $\overline{XI}$ meant 11,000; and so on. Thus the Roman system was also a **multiplicative system.** Although expressing numbers using the Roman system requires fewer symbols than the Egyptian system, it still requires many more symbols than our current system and is cumbersome for doing arithmetic. In fact, the Romans used an abacus to perform calculations instead of paper/pencil methods as we do (see the Focus On at the beginning of Chapter 3).

The Babylonian Numeration System The **Babylonian numeration system,** which evolved between 3000 and 2000 B.C., used only two numerals, a one and a ten (Figure 2.17). For numbers up to 59, the system was simply an additive system. For example, 37 was written using three tens and seven ones (Figure 2.18). However, even though the Babylonian numeration system was developed about the same time as the simpler Egyptian system, the Babylonians used the sophisticated notion of **place value,** where symbols represent different values depending on the place in which they were written. This is another example of a positional system where the position of the individual numerals affects values. Figure 2.19 displays three Babylonian numerals that illustrate this place-value attribute, which was based on 60. Notice the subtle spacing in the numbers to assist in understanding whether the ▼ symbol represents a 1 or a $1 \cdot 60$. Similarly, the symbol, ◄ ▼▼, is spaced slightly to the left to indicate that it represents a 12(60) instead of just a 12.

Unfortunately, in its earliest development, this system led to some confusion. For example, as illustrated in Figure 2.20, the numerals representing 74 $(= 1 \cdot 60 + 14)$ and 3614 $(= 1 \cdot 60 \cdot 60 + 0 \cdot 60 + 14)$ differed only in the spacing of symbols. Thus, there was a chance for misinterpretation. From 300 B.C. on, a separate symbol made up of two small triangles arranged one above the other was used to serve as a **placeholder** to indicate a vacant place (Figure 2.21). This removed some of the ambiguity. However, two Babylonian tens written next to each other could still be interpreted as 20, or 610, or even 3660. Although their placeholder acts much like our zero, the Babylonians did not recognize zero as a number.

NCTM Standards 2000
Number and Operations
Grades Pre-K–2
All students should develop a sense of whole numbers and represent and use them in flexible ways including relating, composing, and decomposing numbers.

One   Ten

Figure 2.17

$3(10) + 7 = 37$

Figure 2.18

$60 + 42 = 102$

$12(60) + 21 = 741$

$2(3600) + 11(60) + 34 = 7894$

Figure 2.19

Figure 2.20

Figure 2.21

Example 2.10 Express the following Babylonian numerals in our numeration system.

Solution

a.

2(60) + 11 = 131

b.

3600 + 0(60) + 1 = 3601

c.

21(60) + 15 = 1275 ■

one   five   zero

Figure 2.22

The Mayan Numeration System The **Mayan numeration system,** which developed between A.D. 300 and A.D. 900, was a vertical place-value system, and it introduced a symbol for **zero.** The system used only three elementary numerals (Figure 2.22). Several Mayan numerals are shown in Figure 2.23 together with their respective values. The symbol for twenty in Figure 2.23 illustrates the use of place value in that the "dot" represents one "twenty" and the ⬭ represents zero "ones." The various place values for this system are illustrated in Figure 2.24. The bottom section represents the number of ones (3 here), the second section from the bottom represents the number of 20s (0 here), the third section from the bottom represents the number of 18 · 20s (6 here), and the top section represents the number of 18 · 20 · 20s (1 here). Reading from top to bottom, the value of the number represented is $1(18 \cdot 20 \cdot 20) + 6(18 \cdot 20) + 0(20) + 3(1)$, or 9363. (See the Focus On at the beginning of this chapter for additional insight into this system.)

$18 \cdot 20^2$

$18 \cdot 20$

20

1

Figure 2.24

Six   Eleven   Eight   Nineteen   Twenty

Figure 2.23

Notice that in the Mayan numeration system, you must take great care in the way the numbers are spaced. For example, two horizontal bars could represent 5 + 5 as ═ or 5 · 20 + 5 as ▬, depending on how the two bars are spaced. Also notice that the place-value feature of this system is somewhat irregular. After the ones place comes the 20s place. Then comes the 18 · 20s place. Thereafter, though, the values of the places are increased by multiplying by 20 to obtain $18 \cdot 20^2$, $18 \cdot 20^3$, $18 \cdot 20^4$, and so on.

Example 2.11 Express the following Mayan numerals in our numeration system.

a.   b. •   c. ───

Solution

a.
$$\left.\rule{0pt}{10pt}\right\} 5 \cdot 20$$
$$\left.\rule{0pt}{10pt}\right\} + 18$$
$$\overline{\rule{0pt}{0pt}\qquad} 118$$

b.
$$\left.\rule{0pt}{10pt}\right\} 1 \cdot 18 \cdot 20$$
$$\left.\rule{0pt}{10pt}\right\} 6 \cdot 20$$
$$\left.\rule{0pt}{10pt}\right\} + \qquad 6$$
$$\overline{\rule{0pt}{0pt}\qquad} 486$$

c.
$$\left.\rule{0pt}{10pt}\right\} 5 \cdot 18 \cdot 20$$
$$\left.\rule{0pt}{10pt}\right\} 0$$
$$\left.\rule{0pt}{10pt}\right\} + \qquad 13$$
$$\overline{\rule{0pt}{0pt}\qquad} 1813$$

Table 2.3 summarizes the attributes of the number systems we have studied.

Table 2.3

SYSTEM	ADDITIVE	SUBTRACTIVE	MULTIPLICATIVE	POSITIONAL	PLACE VALUED	HAS A ZERO
Tally	Yes	No	No	No	No	No
Egyptian	Yes	No	No	No	No	No
Roman	Yes	Yes	Yes	Yes	No	No
Babylonian	Yes	No	Yes	Yes	Yes	No
Mayan	Yes	No	Yes	Yes	Yes	Yes

MATHEMATICAL MORSEL

When learning the names of two-digit numerals, some children suffer through a "reversals" stage, where they may write 21 for twelve or 13 for thirty-one. The following story from the December 5, 1990, *Grand Rapids* [Michigan] *Press* stresses the importance of eliminating reversals. "It was a case of mistaken identity. A transposed address that resulted in a bulldozer blunder. City orders had called for demolition on Tuesday of a boarded-up house at 451 Fuller Ave. S.E. But when the dust settled, 451 Fuller stood untouched. Down the street at 415 Fuller S.E., only a basement remained."

 Section 2.2 EXERCISE / PROBLEM SET A

EXERCISES

1. In the following paragraph, numbers are used in various ways. Specify whether each number is a cardinal number, an ordinal number, or an identification number. Linda dialed 314-781-9804 to place an order with a popular mail-order company. When the sales representative answered, Linda told her that her customer number was 13905. Linda then placed an order for 6 cotton T-shirts, stock number 7814, from page 28 of the catalog. For an extra $10 charge, Linda could have next-day delivery, but she chose the regular delivery system and was told her package would arrive November 20.

2. Define each of the following numbers in a way similar to the way in which the number three was defined in this section. (*Hint:* You may decide "impossible.")

    a. 7   **b.** 1   **c.** −3   **d.** 0

3. Explain how to count the elements of the set $\{a, b, c, d, e, f\}$.

4. Which number is larger, 5 or 8? Which numeral is larger?

5. Determine the greater of the two numbers 4 and 9 in three different ways.

6. Use the definition of "less than" given in this section to explain why there are exactly five whole numbers that are less than 5.

7. Change to Egyptian numerals.

   a. 9   **b.** 23   **c.** 453   **d.** 1231

8. Change to Roman numerals.

   a. 76   **b.** 49   **c.** 192   **d.** 1741

9. Change to Babylonian numerals.

   a. 47   **b.** 76   **c.** 347   **d.** 4192

10. Change to Mayan numerals.

    a. 17   **b.** 51   **c.** 275   **d.** 401

11. Change to numerals we use

    a.

    b.

    c.

    d. MCMXCI

    e. CMLXXVI

    f. MMMCCXLV

    g.

    h.

    i.

    j.

    k.

    l.

12. Perform each of the following numeral conversions.

    a. Roman numeral DCCCXXIV to a Babylonian numeral

    b. Mayan numeral to a Roman numeral

    c. Babylonian numeral to a Mayan numeral

13. Imagine representing 246 in the Mayan, Babylonian, and Egyptian numeration systems.

    a. In which system is the greatest number of symbols required?

    b. In which system is the smallest number of symbols required?

    c. Do your answers for parts (a) and (b) hold true for other numbers as well?

14. One system of numeration in Greece in about 300 B.C., called the Ionian system, was based on letters of the alphabet. The different symbols used for numbers less than 1000 are as follows:

    $$\alpha \ \beta \ \gamma \ \delta \ \epsilon \ \varsigma \ \xi \ \eta \ \theta \ \iota \ \kappa \ \lambda \ \mu \ \nu$$
    1 2 3 4 5 6 7 8 9 10 20 30 40 50
    $$\xi \ o \ \pi \ o \ \rho \ \sigma \ \tau \ \upsilon \ \phi \ \chi \ \psi \ \omega \ \lambda$$
    60 70 80 90 100 200 300 400 500 600 700 800 900

    To represent multiples of 1000 an accent mark was used. For example, $'\epsilon$ was used to represent 5000. The accent mark might be omitted if the size of the number being represented was clear without it.

    a. Express the following Ionian numerals in our numeration system.

    i. $\mu\beta$ **ii.** $\chi\kappa\epsilon$ **iii.** $'\gamma\phi\lambda\gamma$ **iv.** $'\pi'\theta\omega\alpha$

    b. Express each of the following numerals in the Ionian numeration system.

    i. 85   **ii.** 744   **iii.** 2153   **iv.** 21,534

    c. Was the Ionian system a place-value system?

PROBLEMS

15. Some children go through a reversal stage; that is, they confuse 13 and 31, 27 and 72, 59 and 95. What numerals would give Roman children similar difficulties? How about Egyptian children?

16. **a.** How many Egyptian numerals are needed to represent the following problems?

    i. $59 + 88$ **ii.** $150 - 99$

    iii. $7897 + 934$ **iv.** $9698 - 5389$

    b. State a general rule for determining the number of Egyptian numerals needed to represent an addition (or subtraction) problem written in our numeral system.

17. A newspaper advertisement introduced a new car as follows: IV Cams, XXXII Valves, CCLXXX Horsepower, coming December XXVI—the new 1999 Lincoln Mark VII. Write the Roman numeral that represents the year of the advertisement.

18. Linda pulled out one full page from the Sunday newspaper. If the left half was numbered A4 and the

right half was numbered A15, how many pages were in the A section of the newspaper?

19. Determine which of the following numbers is larger.

$$1993 \times (1 + 2 + 3 + 4 + \cdots + 1994)$$
$$1994 \times (1 + 2 + 3 + 4 + \cdots + 1993)$$

20. You have five coins that appear to be identical and a balance scale. One of these coins is counterfeit and either heavier or lighter than the other four. Explain how the counterfeit coin can be identified and whether it is lighter or heavier than the others with only three weighings on the balance scale.

(*Hint:* Solve a simpler problem—given just three coins, can you find the counterfeit in two weighings?)

Section 2.2 EXERCISE / PROBLEM SET B

EXERCISES

1. Write sentences that show the number 45 used in each of the following ways.

  a. As a cardinal number

  b. As an ordinal number

  c. As an identification number

2. Decide whether the word in parentheses is being used in the "number sense" (as an idea) or in the "numeral sense" (as a symbol for an idea).

  a. Camel is a five-letter word.   (camel)

  b. A camel is an animal with four legs.   (camel)

  c. Tim is an Anglo-Saxon name.   (Tim)

  d. Tim was an Anglo-Saxon.   (Tim)

3. Explain why each of the following sets can or cannot be used to count the number of elements in $\{a, b, c, d\}$.

  a. $\{4\}$ **b.** $\{0, 1, 2, 3\}$ **c.** $\{1, 2, 3, 4\}$

4. Place $<$ or $>$ in the blanks to make each statement true. Indicate how you would verify your choice.

  a. 3 _____ 7   **b.** 11 _____ 9

  c. 21 _____ 12

5. Use the set method as illustrated in Figure 2.10 to explain why $7 > 3$.

6. Some calculators can count. See whether yours can by pressing $\boxed{1}\boxed{+}\boxed{=}\boxed{=}\boxed{=}\boxed{=}$. What does your calculator display? If, in fact, your calculator has the constant feature, it can be very handy. Have your calculator

  a. count by 2s.   **b.** count by 4s.

  c. count by 5s.   **d.** count by 11s.

7. What is the largest number that you can enter on your calculator

  a. if you may use the same digit more than once?

  b. if you must use a different digit in each place?

8. Change to Roman numerals.

  a. 79   **b.** 3054

9. Change to Egyptian numerals.

  a. 2431   **b.** 10,352

10. Change to Mayan numerals.

  a. 926   **b.** 37,865

11. Change to Babylonian numerals.

  a. 117   **b.** 3521

12. Express each of the following numerals in our numeration system.

  a.   **b.**

  c. MCCXLVII   **d.**

13. Complete the following chart expressing the given numbers in the other numeration system.

	Babylonian	Egyptian	Roman	Mayan
a.				
b.			CXLIV	
c.				
d.				

14. After the credits for a film roll by, the Roman numeral MCMLXXXIX appears, representing the year in which the film was made. Express the year in our numeration system.

PROBLEMS

15. The following Chinese numerals are part of one of the oldest numeration systems known.

一 1   十 10

二 2   百 100

三 3   千 1000

四 4

五 5

六 6

七 7

八 8

九 9

The numerals are written vertically. Some examples follow.

十二   represents 12

二十   represents 20

三百六十七   represents 367

a. Express each of the following numerals in this Chinese numeration system: 80, 19, 52, 400, 603, 6031.

b. Is this system a positional system? an additive system? a multiplicative system?

16. Two hundred persons are positioned in 10 rows, each containing 20 persons. From each of the 20 columns thus formed, the shortest is selected, and the tallest of these 20 (short) persons is tagged A. These persons now return to their initial places. Next, the tallest person in each row is selected and from these 10 (tall) persons the shortest is tagged B. Which of the two tagged persons is the taller (if they are different people)?

17. Braille numerals are formed using dots in a two-dot by three-dot Braille cell. Numerals are preceded by a backwards "L" dot symbol. The following shows the basic elements for Braille numerals and two examples.

One billion, four hundred sixty-seven million, seventy thousand, two hundred seventy-nine.

Eight hundred four million, six hundred forty-seven thousand, seven hundred.

Express these Braille numerals in our numeration system.

a.

b.

18. The heights of five famous human-made structures are related as follows:

- The height of the Statue of Liberty is 65 feet more than half the height of the Great Pyramid at Giza.
- The height of the Eiffel Tower is 36 feet more than three times the height of Big Ben.
- The Great Pyramid at Giza is 164 feet taller than Big Ben.
- The Leaning Tower of Pisa is 137 feet shorter than Big Ben.
- The total of all of the heights is nearly half a mile. In fact, the sum of the five heights is 2264 feet.

Find the height of each of the five structures.

19. Can an 8 × 8 checkerboard with two opposite corner squares removed be exactly covered (without cutting) by thirty-one 2 × 1 dominoes? Give details.

PROBLEMS FOR WRITING/DISCUSSION

1. One of your students tells you that since zero means nothing, she doesn't have to use that symbol in writing Mayan numerals; she can just leave a space. Frame a response to the student that will refer back to our own number system.

2. Can you write a number on a piece of paper? Explain.

3. One of your students added these two Babylonian numbers and got the answer shown. Was he correct?

Frame a response to the student that will refer back to our own numeration system. (The ◀ and ▼ are meant to represent the stylus marks for 10 and 1.)

2.3 THE HINDU–ARABIC SYSTEM

In the land of Odd, they only use quarters, nickels, and pennies for their coins. Martina, who lives in Odd, likes to carry as few coins as possible. What is the minimum number of coins Martina could carry for each of the following amounts of money? How many of each coin would she have in each case?

68¢   39¢   83¢   97¢

If Martina always exchanges her money to have a minimum number of coins, what is the maximum number of nickels that she would have after an exchange? Why?

The Hindu–Arabic Numeration System

The **Hindu–Arabic numeration system** that we use today was developed about A.D. 800. The following list features the basic numerals and various attributes of this system.

1. *Digits, 0, 1, 2, 3, 4, 5, 6, 7, 8, 9:* These 10 symbols, or **digits,** can be used in combination to represent all possible numbers.

2. *Grouping by tens (decimal system):* Grouping into sets of 10 is a basic principle of this system, probably because we have 10 "digits" on our two hands. (The word *digit* literally means "finger" or "toe.") Ten ones are replaced by one ten, ten tens are replaced by one hundred, ten hundreds are replaced by one thousand, and so on. Figure 2.25 shows how grouping is helpful when representing a collection of objects. The number of objects grouped together is called the **base** of the system; thus our Hindu–Arabic system is a base ten system.

NOTE: Recall that an element is listed only once in a set. Although all the dots in Figure 2.25 look the same, they are assumed to be unique, individual elements here and in all such subsequent figures.

The following two models are often used to represent multidigit numbers.

a. Bundles of sticks can be any kind of sticks banded together with rubber bands. Each 10 loose sticks are bound together with a rubber band to represent 10, then 10 bundles of 10 are bound together to represent 100, and so on (Figure 2.26).

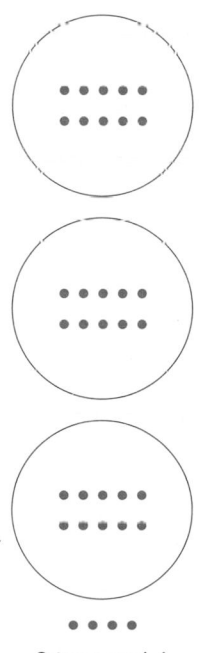

3 tens and 4

Figure 2.25

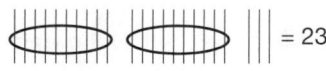

Figure 2.26

b. Base ten pieces (also called **Dienes blocks**) consist of individual cubes, called "units," "longs," made up of ten units, "flats," made up of ten longs, or one hundred units, and so on (Figure 2.27). Inexpensive two-dimensional sets of base ten pieces can be made using grid paper cutouts.

Unit	Long	Flat	Block

Figure 2.27

Reflection from Research
Results from research suggest that base ten blocks should be used in the development of students' place-value concepts (Fuson, 1990)

3. *Place value (hence positional):* Each of the various places in the numeral 6523, for example, has its own value.

thousand	hundred	ten	one
6	5	2	3

The 6 represents 6 thousands, the 5 represents 5 hundreds, the 2 represents 2 tens, and the 3 represents 3 ones due to the place-value attribute of the Hindu–Arabic system.

**NCTM Standards 2000
Number and Operations
Focus Area: Grades Pre-K–2**
All students should use multiple models to develop initial understandings of place value and the base-ten number system.

The following device is used to represent numbers written in place value. A **chip abacus** is a piece of paper or cardboard containing lines that form columns, on which chips or markers are used to represent unit values. Conceptually, this model is more abstract than the previous models because markers represent different values, depending on the columns in which the markers appear (Figure 2.28).

100	10	1
	••	

Twenty

100	10	1
••		

Two hundred

100	10	1
		••

Two

100	10	1
•••	••	•••• / ••

Three hundred twenty-six

Figure 2.28

4. *Additive and multiplicative.* The value of a Hindu–Arabic numeral is found by *multiplying* each place value by its corresponding digit and then *adding* all the resulting products.

Place values:	thousand	hundred	ten	one
Digits:	6	5	2	3
Numeral value:	$6 \times 1000 + 5 \times 100 + 2 \times 10 + 3 \times 1$			
Numeral:	6523			

Expressing a numeral as the sum of its digits times their respective place values is called the numeral's **expanded form** or **expanded notation.** The expanded form of 83,507 is

$$8 \times 10,000 + 3 \times 1000 + 5 \times 100 + 0 \times 10 + 7 \times 1.$$

Because $7 \times 1 = 7$, we can simply write 7 in place of 7×1 when expressing 83,507 in expanded form.

Example 2.12   Express the following numbers in expanded form.

a. 437   **b.** 3001

Solution

a. $437 = 4(100) + 3(10) + 7$
b. $3001 = 3(1000) + 0(100) + 0(10) + 1$ or $3(1000) + 1$ ■

Notice that our numeration system requires fewer symbols to represent numbers than did earlier systems. Also, the Hindu–Arabic system is far superior when performing computations. The computational aspects of the Hindu–Arabic system will be studied in Chapter 3.

Naming Hindu–Arabic Numerals

Reflection from Research
Children are able to recognize and read one- and two-digit numerals prior to being able to write them (Baroody, Gannon, Berent, & Ginsburg, 1983).

Associated with each Hindu–Arabic numeral is a word name. Some of the English names are as follows:

0 zero	10 ten
1 one	11 eleven
2 two	12 twelve
3 three	13 thirteen (three plus ten)
4 four	14 fourteen (four plus ten)
5 five	21 twenty-one (two tens plus one)
6 six	87 eighty-seven (eight tens plus seven)
7 seven	205 two hundred five (two hundreds plus five)
8 eight	1,374 one thousand three hundred seventy-four
9 nine	23,100 twenty-three thousand one hundred

Here are a few observations about the naming procedure.

1. The numbers 0, 1, . . . , 12 all have unique names.
2. The numbers 13, 14, . . . , 19 are the "teens," and are composed of a combination of earlier names, with the ones place named first. For example, "thirteen" is short for "three ten," which means "ten plus three," and so on.
3. The numbers 20, . . . , 99 are combinations of earlier names but *reversed* from the teens in that the tens place is named first. For example, 57 is "fifty-seven," which means "five tens plus seven," and so on. The method of naming the numbers from 20 to 90 is better than the way we name the teens, due to the left-to-right agreement with the way the numerals are written.
4. The numbers 100, . . . , 999 are combinations of hundreds and previous names. For example, 538 is read "five hundred thirty-eight," and so on.
5. In numerals containing more than three digits, groups of three digits are usually set off by commas. For example, the number

**NCTM Standards 2000
Number and Operations
Grades Pre-K–2**
All students should connect number words and numerals to the quantities they represent, using various physical models and representations.

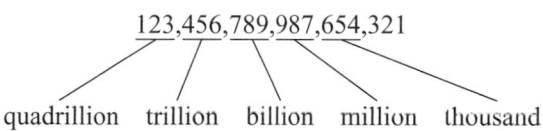

is read "one hundred twenty-three quadrillion four hundred fifty-six trillion seven hundred eighty-nine billion nine hundred eighty-seven million six hundred fifty-four thousand three hundred twenty-one." (Internationally, the commas are omitted and single spaces are used instead. Also, in some countries, commas are used in place of decimal points.) Notice that the word *and* does not appear in any of these names: it is reserved to separate the decimal portion of a numeral from the whole-number portion.

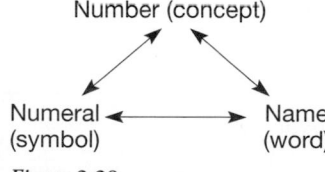

Figure 2.29

Figure 2.29 graphically displays the three distinct ideas that children need to learn in order to understand the Hindu–Arabic numeration system.

Nondecimal Numeration Systems

Our Hindu–Arabic system is based on grouping by ten. To understand our system better and to experience some of the difficulties children have when learning our numeration system, it is instructive to study similar systems, but with different place values. For example, suppose that a Hindu–Arabic-like system utilized one hand (five digits) instead of two (ten digits). Then, grouping would be done in groups of five. If sticks were used, bundles would be made up of five each (Figure 2.30). Here seventeen objects are represented by three bundles of five each with two left over. This can be expressed by the equation $17_{ten} = 32_{five}$, which is read "seventeen base ten equals three two base five." (Be careful not to read 32_{five} as "thirty-two," because thirty-two means "three tens and two," not "three fives and two.") The subscript words "ten" and "five" indicate that the grouping was done in tens and fives, respectively. For simplicity, the subscript "ten" will be omitted; hence 37 will always mean 37_{ten}. (With this agreement, the numeral 24_{five} could also be written 24_5 since the subscript "5" means the usual base ten 5.) The 10 digits 0, 1, 2, . . . , 9 are used in base ten; however, only the five digits 0, 1, 2, 3, 4 are necessary in base five. A few examples of base five numerals are illustrated in Figure 2.31.

Figure 2.30

Base Five Numeral	Base Five Block Representation	Base Ten Numeral
3_{five}		3
14_{five}		$1(5) + 4 = 9$
132_{five}		$1(25) + 3(5) + 2 = 42$
1004_{five}		$1(125) + 4 = 129$

Figure 2.31

Counting using base five names differs from counting in base ten. The first ten base five numerals appear in Figure 2.32. Interesting junctures in counting come after a number has a 4 in its ones column. For example, what is the next number (written in base five) after 24_{five}? after 34_{five}? after 44_{five}? after 444_{five}?

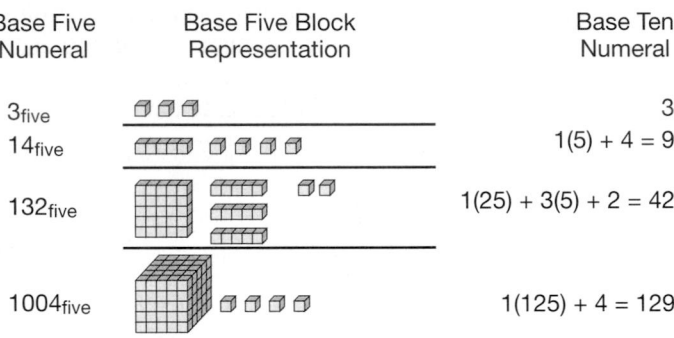

1_{five}	2_{five}	3_{five}	4_{five}	10_{five}
11_{five}	12_{five}	13_{five}	14_{five}	20_{five}

Figure 2.32

Figure 2.33 shows how to find the number after 24_{five} using multibase pieces.

Exchange these for a long

| 24_{five} | $24_{five} + 1_{five}$ | 30_{five} |

Figure 2.33

Converting numerals from base five to base ten can be done using (1) multibase pieces or (2) place values and expanded notation.

Example 2.13   Express 123_{five} in base ten.

Solution

a. *Using Base Five Pieces:* See Figure 2.34.

Base Five Pieces

$$123_{\text{five}} =$$

Base ten values $25 + 10 + 3 = 38$. Thus $123_{\text{five}} = 38$.

Figure 2.34

b. *Using Place Value and Expanded Notation*

Place values
in base ten $\longrightarrow$

$$
\begin{array}{c|c|c}
25 & 5 & 1
\end{array}
$$
$$123_{\text{five}} = \begin{array}{c|c|c} 1 & 2 & 3 \end{array} = 1(25) + 2(5) + 3(1) = 38$$ ■

Converting from base ten to base five also utilizes place value.

Spotlight on Technology The number 423_{five} can be converted to a base ten number by representing it using base five blocks. Using the Chapter 2 eManipulative activity, *Multibase Blocks,* select 4 flats, 2 longs, and 3 units of the base five blocks. The total number of units displayed is 4 flats at 25 units each, 2 longs at 5 units each, and 3 units for a total of $4 \cdot (25) + 2 \cdot (5) + 3 = 113$ units. Thus, $423_{\text{five}} - 113_{\text{ten}}$. Use the eManipulative to convert 221_{three} and 122_{four} to base ten numbers. Which is larger?

www.wiley.com/
college/musser

Example 2.14   Convert from base ten to base five.

a. 97   **b.** 341

Solution

a.
$$
\begin{array}{c|c|c}
25 & 5 & 1 \\
\hline
? & ? & ?
\end{array}
$$
$97 =$ $\longleftarrow$ Base five place values
expressed using base ten numerals

Think: How many 25s are in 97? There are three since $3 \cdot 25 = 75$ with 22 remaining. How many 5s in the remainder? There are four since $4 \cdot 5 = 20$. Finally, since $22 - 20 = 2$, there are two 1s.

$$97 = 3(25) + 4(5) + 2 = 342_{\text{five}}$$

b. A more systematic method can be used to convert 341 to its base five numeral. First, find the highest power of 5 that will divide into 341; that is, which is the greatest among 1, 5, 25, 125, 625, 3125, and so on, that will divide into 341? The answer in this case is 125. The rest of that procedure uses long division, each time dividing the remainder by the next smaller place value.

$$
\begin{array}{r}
2 \\
125\overline{)341} \\
250 \\
\hline
91
\end{array}
\qquad
\begin{array}{r}
3 \\
25\overline{)91} \\
75 \\
\hline
16
\end{array}
\qquad
\begin{array}{r}
3 \\
5\overline{)16} \\
15 \\
\hline
1
\end{array}
\quad 1
$$

Therefore, $341 = 2(125) + 3(25) + 3(5) + 1$, or 2331_{five}. More simply, $341 = 2331_{\text{five}}$, where 2, 3, and 3 are the quotients from left to right and 1 is the final remainder. ■

When expressing place values in various bases, **exponents** can provide a convenient shorthand notation. The symbol a^m represents the product of m factors of a. Thus $5^3 = 5 \cdot 5 \cdot 5$, $7^2 = 7 \cdot 7$, $3^4 = 3 \cdot 3 \cdot 3 \cdot 3$, and so on. Using this exponential notation, the first several place values of base five, in reverse order, are $1, 5, 5^2, 5^3, 5^4$. Although we have studied only base ten and base five thus far, these same place-value ideas can be used with any base greater than one. For example, in base two the place values, listed in reverse order, are $1, 2, 2^2, 2^3, 2^4, \ldots$; in base three the place values are $1, 3, 3^2, 3^3, 3^4, \ldots$. The next two examples illustrate numbers expressed in bases other than five and their relationship to base ten.

Example 2.15 Express the following numbers in base ten.

a. 11011_{two} **b.** 1234_{eight} **c.** $1ET_{\text{twelve}}$

(NOTE: Base twelve has twelve basic numerals: 0 through 9, T for ten, and E for eleven.)

Solution

a. $11011_{\text{two}} = \dfrac{2^4 \;|\; 2^3 \;|\; 2^2 \;|\; 2 \;|\; 1}{1 \;|\; 1 \;|\; 0 \;|\; 1 \;|\; 1} = 1(16) + 1(8) + 0(4) + 1(2) + 1(1) = 27$

b. $1234_{\text{eight}} = \dfrac{8^3 \;|\; 8^2 \;|\; 8 \;|\; 1}{1 \;|\; 2 \;|\; 3 \;|\; 4} = 1(8^3) + 2(8^2) + 3(8) + 4(1) = 512 + 128 + 24 + 4 = 668$

c. $1ET_{\text{twelve}} = \dfrac{12^{12} \;|\; 12 \;|\; 1}{1 \;|\; E \;|\; T} = 1(12^2) + E(12) + T(1) = 144 + 132 + 10 = 286$ ■

Converting from base ten to other bases is accomplished by using grouping just as we did in base five.

Example 2.16 Convert from base ten to the given base.

a. 53 to base two   **b.** 1982 to base twelve

Solution

a. $53 = \dfrac{2^5 \;|\; 2^4 \;|\; 2^3 \;|\; 2^2 \;|\; 2 \;|\; 1}{? \;|\; ? \;|\; ? \;|\; ? \;|\; ? \;|\; ?}$

Think: What is the largest power of 2 contained in 53?

Answer: $2^5 = 32$. Now we can find the remaining digits by dividing by decreasing powers of 2.

$$
\begin{array}{ccccccc}
& 1 & 1 & 0 & 1 & 0 & 1 \\
& 32\overline{)53} & 16\overline{)21} & 8\overline{)5} & 4\overline{)5} & 2\overline{)1} & \\
& \underline{32} & \underline{16} & \underline{0} & \underline{4} & \underline{0} & \\
& 21 & 5 & 5 & 1 & 1 &
\end{array}
$$

Therefore, $53 = 110101_{\text{two}}$.

b. $1982 = \dfrac{12^3 \,(= 1728) \;|\; 12^2 \,(= 144) \;|\; 12^1 \,(= 12) \;|\; 1}{? \;|\; ? \;|\; ? \;|\; ?}$

$$\begin{array}{c} 1 \\ 1728\overline{)1982} \\ 1728 \\ \hline 254 \end{array} \qquad \begin{array}{c} 1 \\ 144\overline{)254} \\ 144 \\ \hline 110 \end{array} \qquad \begin{array}{c} 9 \\ 12\overline{)110} \\ 108 \\ \hline 2 \end{array} \qquad \begin{array}{c} 2 \\ 1\overline{)2} \\ 2 \\ \hline 0 \end{array}$$

Therefore, $1982 = 1192_{\text{twelve}}$.   ■

 Spotlight on Technology Because this process of converting from a base ten number to another base follows the same series of steps regardless of the base that you are converting to, it lends www.wiley.com/ college/musser itself well to a spreadsheet. Although the construction of this spreadsheet is a bit advanced, it is very convenient for doing such conversions. Refer to the dynamic spreadsheet, *Base Converter,* in the spreadsheet webmodule. Convert the base ten numbers 2400 and 2408, which both have four digits, to a base seven number. What do you notice about the number of digits in the base seven representations of 2400 and 2408? Why is this?

MATHEMATICAL MORSEL

Consider the three cards shown here. Choose any number from 1 to 7 and note which cards your number is on. Then add the numbers in the upper right-hand corner of the cards containing your number. What did you find? This "magic" can be justified mathematically using the binary (base two) numeration system.

Section 2.3 EXERCISE / PROBLEM SET A

EXERCISES

1. Write each of the following numbers in expanded notation.
  a. 70   **b.** 300   **c.** 746
  d. 984   **e.** 60,006,060   **f.** 840,001

2. Write each of the following expressions in standard place-value form.
  a. $1(10^3) + 2(10^2) + 7(1)$
  b. $5(10^5) + 3(10^2)$
  c. $8(10^6) + 7(10^4) + 6(10^2) + 5(1)$
  d. $2(10^9) + 3(10^4) + 3(10^3) + 4(10)$
  e. $6(10^7) + 9(10^5)$

3. Write these numerals in words.
  a. 2,000,000,000
  b. 87,000,000,000,000
  c. 52,672,405,123,139
  d. 98,000,000,000,000,000

4. List three attributes of our Hindu–Arabic numeration system.

5. a. Group this entire set of x's (by circling them) in base 3.

XXX	XXX	XXX	XXX	XXX
XXX	XXX	XXX	XXX	XX
XXX	XXX	XXX	XXX	XX

  b. Write the base three numeral for the number of x's in the set.

 6. Write a base four numeral for the following set of base four pieces. Represent the blocks on the Chapter 2 eManipulative activity, *Multibase Blocks*, and make all possible trades first.

7. To express 651 with the smallest number of base eight pieces (blocks, flats, longs, and units), you need _____ blocks, _____ flats, _____ longs, and _____ units.

8. Represent each of the following numerals with multibase pieces. Where possible, use the Chapter 2 eManipulative activity, *Multibase Blocks*, to assist you.

   a. 134_{six}

   b. 1011_{two}

   c. 3211_{four}

9. Represent each of the following with bundling sticks and chips on a chip abacus.

   a. 24   b. 221_{four} c. 167_{eight}

10. a. Draw a sketch of 62 pennies and trade for nickels and quarters. Write the corresponding base five numeral.

    b. Write the base five numeral for 93 and 2173.

11. Write each of the following base seven numerals in expanded notation.

    a. 15_{seven} b. 123_{seven} c. 5046_{seven}

12. a. Write out the base five numerals in order from 1 to 100_{five}.

    b. Write out the base two numerals in order from 1 to 10000_{two}.

    c. Write out the base three numerals in order from 1 to 1000_{three}.

    d. In base six, write the next four numbers after 254_{six}.

   e. What base four numeral follows 303_{four}?

   f. What base nine numeral follows 888_{nine}?

13. Convert each base ten numeral into a numeral in the base requested.

    a. 395 in base eight

    b. 748 in base four

    c. 54 in base two

14. The base twelve numeration system has the following twelve symbols: 0, 1, 2, 3, 4, 5, 6, 7, 8, 9, T, E. Change each of the following numerals to base ten numerals.

    a. 142_{twelve} b. 234_{twelve} c. 503_{twelve}

    d. $T9_{twelve}$ e. $T0E_{twelve}$ f. $ETET_{twelve}$

15. Write each of the following numbers in base six and in base twelve.

    a. 74

    b. 128

    c. 210

    d. 2438

16. Convert the following base five numerals into base nine numerals.

    a. 12_{five}

    b. 204_{five}

    c. 1322_{five}

17. How many different symbols would be necessary for a base twenty-three system?

18. What is wrong with the numerals 85_{eight} and 24_{three}?

PROBLEMS

19. What bases make these equations true?

    a. 32 = 44 _____   b. 57_{eight} = 10 _____

    c. 31_{four} = 11 _____   d. $15_x = 30_y$

20. The set of even whole numbers is the set {0, 2, 4, 6, . . .}. What can be said about the ones digit of every even number in the following bases?

    a. 10   b. 4   c. 2   d. 5

21. Mike used 2989 digits to number the pages of a book. How many pages does the book have?

22. The sum of the digits in a two-digit number is 12. If the digits are reversed, the new number is 18 greater than the original number. What is the number?

23. To determine a friend's birth date, ask him or her to perform the following calculations and tell you the result: Multiply the number of the month in which you were born by 4 and add 13 to the result. Then multiply that answer by 25 and subtract 200. Add your birth date (day of month) to that answer and then multiply by 2. Subtract 40 from the result and then multiply by 50. Add the last two digits of your birth year to that answer and, finally, subtract 10,500.

    a. Try this sequence of operations with your own birth date. How does place value allow you to determine a birth date from the final answer? Try the sequence again with a different birth date.

    b. Use expanded notation to explain why this technique always works.

Section 2.3 EXERCISE / PROBLEM SET B

EXERCISES

1. Write each expression in place-value form.
   a. $3(1000) + 7(10) + 5$
   b. $7(10,000) + 6(100)$

2. State the place value of the digit 2 in each numeral.
   a. 6234   b. 5142   c. 2168

3. Words and their roots often suggest numbers. Using this idea, complete the following chart. (*Hint:* Look for a pattern.)

WORD	LATIN ROOT	MEANING OF ROOT	POWER OF 10
Billion	bi	2	9
Trillion	tri	3	(a)
Quadrillion	quater	(b)	15
(c)	quintus	5	18
Sextillion	sex	6	21
(d)	septem	7	(e)
Octillion	octo	8	27
Nonillion	novem	(f)	(g)
(h)	decem	10	33

   In following with this idea, on the premodern calendar the names for September, October, November, and December suggest the numbers of the months. What was September's number on the premodern calendar? What was October's number? November's? If December was the last month of the premodern calendar year, how many months made up a year?

4. To express 69 with the fewest pieces of base three blocks, flats, longs, and units, you need _____ blocks, _____ flats, _____ longs, and _____ units. The Chapter 2 eManipulative activity, *Multibase Blocks*, may help in the solution.

5. Write each of the following base three numerals in expanded notation.
   a. 22_{three} b. 212_{three} c. 12110_{three}

6. Write a base three numeral for the following set of base three pieces. Represent the blocks on the Chapter 2 eManipulative activity, *Multibase Blocks*, and make all possible trades first.

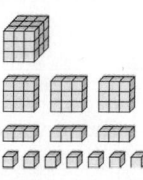

7. Represent each of the following with bundling sticks, multibase pieces, and chips on a chip abacus.
   a. 38   b. 52_{six} c. 1032_{four}

8. Suppose that you have 10 "longs" in a set of multibase pieces in each of the following bases. Make all possible exchanges and write the numeral the pieces represent in that base.
   a. Ten longs in base eight
   b. Ten longs in base six
   c. Ten longs in base three

9. a. Write out the first 20 base four numerals.
   b. How many base four numerals precede 2000_{four}?
   c. Write out the base six numerals in order from 1 to 100_{six}.

10. a. What is the largest six-digit base two number? What are the next three base two numbers that follow it? Give your answers in base two numeration.
    b. What is the largest three-digit base four number? What are the five base four numbers that follow it? Give your answers in base four numeration.

11. True or false?
    a. $7_{eight} - 7$ b. $30_{four} = 30$
    c. $8_{nine} = 8_{eleven}$ d. $30_{five} = 30_{six}$

12. If all the letters of the alphabet were used as our single-digit numerals, what would be the name of our base system? If a represented zero, b represented one, and so on, what would be the base ten numeral for the "alphabet" numeral zz?

13. Find the base ten numerals for each of the following.
    a. 342_{five} b. $TE0_{twelve}$ c. 101101_{two}

14. Convert each base ten numeral into its numeral in the base requested.
    a. 142 in base twelve   b. 72 in base two
    c. 231 in base eight

15. Convert these base two numerals into base eight numerals. Can you state a shortcut? [*Hint:* Look at part (d).]
    a. 1001_{two} b. 110110_{two}
    c. 10101010_{two} d. 101111_{two}

16. The hexadecimal numeration system, used in computer programming, is a base sixteen system that uses the symbols 0, 1, 2, 3, 4, 5, 6, 7, 8, 9, A, B, C, D, E, and F. Change each of the following hexadecimal numerals to base ten numerals.

    a. 213_{sixteen} **b.** $A4_{\text{sixteen}}$

    c. $1C2B_{\text{sixteen}}$ **d.** $420E_{\text{sixteen}}$

17. Write each of the following base ten numerals in base sixteen (hexadecimal) numerals.

    a. 375   **b.** 2941   **c.** 9520   **d.** 24,274

18. Find the missing base.

    a. $28 = 34$ _____   **b.** $28 = 26$ _____

    c. $23_{\text{twelve}} = 43$ _____

PROBLEMS

19. Under what conditions can this equation be true: $a_b = b_a$? Explain.

20. Propose new names for the numbers 11, 12, 13, . . . , 19 so that the naming scheme is consistent with the numbers 20 and above.

21. A certain number has four digits, the sum of which is 10. If you exchange the first and last digits, the new number will be 2997 larger. If you exchange the middle two digits of the original number, your new number will be 90 larger. This last enlarged number plus the original number equals 2558. What is the original number?

22. What number is twice the product of its two digits?

23. As described in the Mathematical Morsel, the three cards shown here can be used to read minds. Have a person think of a number from 1 to 7 (say, 6) and tell you what card(s) it is on (cards *A* and *B*).

You determine the person's number by adding the numbers in the upper right-hand corner ($4 + 2 = 6$).

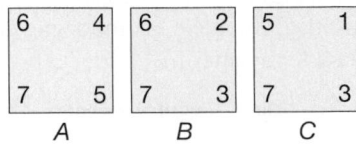

    a. How does this work?

    b. Prepare a set of four such magic cards for the numbers 1–15.

24. **a.** Assuming that you can put weights only on one pan, show that the gram weights 1, 2, 4, 8, and 16 are sufficient to weigh each whole-gram weight up to 31 grams using a pan balance. (*Hint:* Base two.)

    b. If weights can be used on either pan, what would be the fewest number of gram weights required to weigh 31 grams, and what would they weigh?

PROBLEMS FOR WRITING/DISCUSSION

1. Some students say that studying different number bases is a waste of time. Explain the value of studying base four, for example, in helping to understand our decimal system.

2. At a football game when you see the time on the clock is 2:00, what will the time be in one second?

(Hint for nonsports people: The clock is counting *down.*) Explain how this situation is similar to what happens in any base.

3. What is a real-world use for number bases 2 and 16?

2.4   RELATIONS AND FUNCTIONS

Describe a possible relationship between the two sets of numbers at the right. Include a description of how the numbers might be matched up. Describe a second relationship between the same sets. What are the similarities or differences between the two relationships?

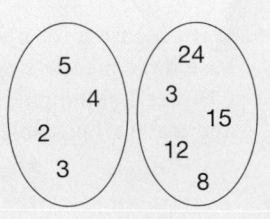

Relations and functions are central to mathematics. Relations are simply the description of relationships between two sets. Functions, which will be described later in this section, are specific types of relations.

Relations *No restriction*

Relationships between objects or numbers can be analyzed using ideas from set theory. For example, on the set $\{1, 2, 3, 4\}$, we can express the relationship "*a* is a divisor of *b*" by listing all the ordered pairs (a, b) for which the relationship is true, namely $\{(1, 1), (1, 2), (1, 3), (1, 4), (2, 2), (2, 4), (3, 3), (4, 4)\}$. In this section we study properties of relations.

Relations are used in mathematics to represent a relationship between two numbers or objects. For example, when we say, "3 is less than 7," "2 is a factor of 6," and "Triangle *ABC* is similar to triangle *DEF*," we are expressing relationships between pairs of numbers in the first two cases and triangles in the last case. More generally, the concept of relation can be applied to arbitrary sets. A set of ordered pairs can be used to show that certain pairs of objects are related. For example, the set $\{$(Hawaii, 50), (Alaska, 49), (New Mexico, 48)$\}$ lists the newest three states of the United States and their number of statehood. This relation can be verbally described as "_____ was state number _____ to join the United States"; for example, "Alaska was state number 49 to join the United States."

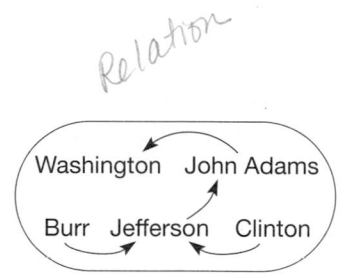

Figure 2.35

A diagrammatic way of denoting relationships is through the use of **arrow diagrams.** For example, in Figure 2.35, each arrow can be read "_____ was the vice-president under _____" where the arrow points to the president. When a relation can be described on a single set, an arrow diagram can be used on that set in two ways. For example, the relation "is a factor of" on the set $\{2, 4, 6, 8\}$ is represented in two equivalent ways in Figure 2.36, using one set in part (a) and two copies of a set in part (b). The advantage of using two sets in an arrow diagram is that relations between *two different* sets can be pictured, as in the case of the newest states (Figure 2.37).

Figure 2.36

Formally, a **relation** *R* from set *A* to set *B* is a subset of $A \times B$, the Cartesian product of *A* and *B*. If $A = B$, we say that *R* is a relation on *A*. In our example about the states, set *A* consists of the three newest states and *B* consists of the numbers 48, 49, and 50. In the preceding example, "is a factor of," the sets *A* and *B* were the same, namely, the set $\{2, 4, 6, 8\}$. This last relation is represented by the following set of ordered pairs.

$$R = \{(2, 2), (2, 4), (2, 6), (2, 8), (4, 4), (4, 8), (6, 6), (8, 8)\}$$

Notice that *R* is a subset of $\{2, 4, 6, 8\} \times \{2, 4, 6, 8\}$.

In the case of a relation *R* on a set *A*, that is, where $R \subseteq A \times A$, there are three useful properties that a relation may have.

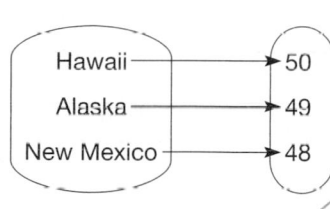

Figure 2.37

Reflexive Property A relation *R* on a set *A* is said to be **reflexive** if $(a, a) \in R$ for all $a \in A$. We say that *R* is reflexive if every element in *A* is related to itself. For example, the relation "is a factor of" on the set $A = \{2, 4, 6, 8\}$ is reflexive, since every number in *A* is a factor of itself. In general, in an arrow diagram, a relation is reflexive if every element in *A* has an arrow pointing to itself (Figure 2.38).

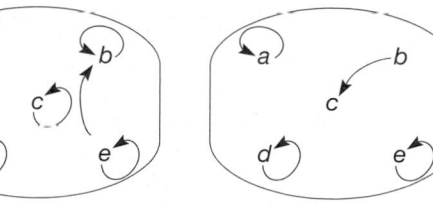

Figure 2.38

Symmetric Property A relation *R* on a set *A* is said to be **symmetric** if whenever $(a, b) \in R$, then $(b, a) \in R$ also; in words, if *a* is related to *b*, then *b* is related to *a*. Let *R* be the relation "is the opposite of" on the set $A = \{1, -1, 2, -2\}$.

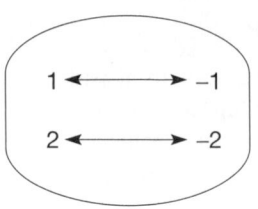

Figure 2.39

Then $R = \{(1, -1), (-1, 1), (2, -2), (-2, 2)\}$; that is, R has all possible ordered pairs (a, b) from $A \times A$ if a is the opposite of b. The arrow diagram of this relation is shown in Figure 2.39.

Notice that for a relation to be symmetric, whenever an arrow points in one direction, it must point in the opposite direction also. Thus the relation "is the opposite of" is symmetric on the set $\{1, -1, 2, -2\}$. The relation "is a factor of" on the set $\{2, 4, 6, 8\}$ is *not* symmetric, since 2 is a factor of 4, but 4 is not a factor of 2. Notice that this fact can be seen in Figure 2.36(a), since there is an arrow pointing from 2 to 4, but not conversely.

Transitive Property A relation R on a set A is **transitive** if whenever $(a, b) \in R$ and $(b, c) \in R$, then $(a, c) \in R$. In words, a relation is transitive if for all a, b, c in A, if a is related to b and b is related to c, then a is related to c. Consider the relation "is a factor of" on the set $\{2, 4, 6, 8, 12\}$. Notice that 2 is a factor of 4 and 4 is a factor of 8 *and* 2 is a factor of 8. Also, 2 is a factor of 4 and 4 is a factor of 12 *and* 2 is a factor of 12. The last case to consider, involving 2, 6, and 12, is also true. Thus "is a factor of" is a transitive relation on the set $\{2, 4, 6, 8, 12\}$. In an arrow diagram, a relation is transitive if whenever there is an "a to b" arrow and a "b to c" arrow, there is also an "a to c" arrow (Figure 2.40).

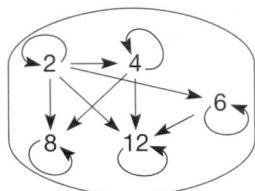

Figure 2.40

Now consider the relation "has the same ones digit as" on the set of numbers $\{1, 2, 3, \ldots, 40\}$. Clearly, every number has the same ones digit as itself; thus this relation is reflexive; it is also symmetric and transitive. Any relation on a set that is reflexive, symmetric, and transitive is called an **equivalence relation.** Thus the relation "has the same ones digit as" is an equivalence relation on the set $\{1, 2, 3, \ldots, 40\}$. There are many equivalence relations in mathematics. Some common ones are "is equal to" on any set of numbers and "is congruent to" and "is similar to" on sets of geometric shapes.

An important attribute of an equivalence relation R on a set A is that the relation imparts a subdivision, or partitioning, of the set A into a collection of nonempty, pairwise disjoint subsets (i.e., the intersection of any two subsets is $\varnothing$). For example, if the numbers that are related to each other in the preceding paragraph are collected into sets, the relation R on the set $\{1, 2, 3, \ldots, 40\}$ is represented by the following set of nonempty, pairwise disjoint subsets.

$$\{\{1, 11, 21, 31\}, \{2, 12, 22, 32\}, \ldots, \{10, 20, 30, 40\}\}$$

That is, all of the elements having the same ones digit are grouped together.

Formally, a **partition** of a set A is a collection of nonempty, pairwise disjoint subsets of A whose union is A. It can be shown that every equivalence relation on a set A gives rise to a unique partition of A *and*, conversely, that every partition of A yields a corresponding equivalence relation. The partition associated with the relation "has the same shape as" on a set of shapes is shown in Figure 2.41. Notice how all the squares are grouped together, since they have the "same shape."

Figure 2.41

Functions

As was mentioned earlier, functions are specific types of relations. The underlying concept of function is described in the following definition.

> ### DEFINITION
>
> *Function*
>
> A **function** is a relation that matches each element of a first set to an element of a second set in such a way that no element in the first set is assigned to two different elements in the second set.

The concept of a function is found throughout mathematics and society. Simple examples in society include (1) to each person is assigned his or her social security number, (2) to each item in a store is assigned a unique bar code number, and (3) to each house on a street is assigned a unique address.

Of the examples that we examined earlier in the section, the relation defined by "_____ is a factor of _____" is not a function because 2, being in the first set, is a factor of many numbers and would therefore be related to more than one number in the second set. The arrow diagram in Figure 2.36(b) also illustrates this point because the 2 in the first set has 4 arrows coming from it. The relation defined by "_____ was the vice-president under _____" is also not a function because George Clinton was the vice-president from 1805 to 1812 under two presidents, Thomas Jefferson and James Madison. The relation "_____ was state number _____ to join the United States," however, would be a function because each state is related to only one number.

The remainder of this section will list several other examples of functions followed by a description of notation and representations of functions. In Chapter 9, graphs of important types of functions that model applications in society will be studied.

1. Recall that a sequence is a list of numbers, called terms, arranged in order, where the first term is called the **initial term.** For example, the sequence of consecutive even counting numbers listed in *increasing order* is 2, 4, 6, 8, 10, ... Another way of showing this sequence is by using arrows:

$$1 \rightarrow 2, 2 \rightarrow 4, 3 \rightarrow 6, 4 \rightarrow 8, 5 \rightarrow 10, \ldots.$$

Here, the arrows assign to each counting number its double. Using a variable, this assignment can be represented as $n \rightarrow 2n$. Not only is this assignment an example of a function, a function is formed whenever each counting number is assigned to one and only one element.

Some special sequences can be classified by the way their terms are found. In the sequence 2, 4, 6, 8, . . . , each term after the first can be found by adding 2 to the preceding term. This type of sequence, in which successive terms differ by the same number, is called an arithmetic sequence. Using variables, an **arithmetic sequence** has the form

$$a, a + d, a + 2d, \ldots.$$

Here a is the initial term and d is the amount by which successive terms differ. The number d is called the **common difference** of the sequence.

In the sequence 1, 3, 9, 27, . . . , each term after the first can be found by multiplying the preceding term by 3. This is an example of a geometric sequence. By using variables, a **geometric sequence** has the form

$$a, ar, ar^2, ar^3, \ldots.$$

The number r, by which each successive term is multiplied, is called the **common ratio** of the sequence. Table 2.4 displays the terms for general arithmetic and geometric sequences.

Table 2.4

TERM	1	2	3	4	...	n	...
Arithmetic sequence	a	$a + d$	$a + 2d$	$a + 3d$	...	$a + (n-1)d$	...
Geometric sequence	a	ar	ar^2	ar^3	...	ar^{n-1}	...

Using this table, the 400th term of the arithmetic sequence 8, 12, 16, ... is found by observing that $a = 8$ and $d = 4$; thus the 400th term is $8 + (400 - 1)4 = 1604$. The 10th term of the geometric sequence 4, 8, 16, 32, ... is found by observing that $a = 4$ and $r = 2$; thus the 10th term is $4 \cdot 2^{10-1} = 2048$.

Example 2.17 Determine whether the following sequences are arithmetic, geometric, or neither. Then determine the common difference or ratio where applicable, and find the tenth term.

a. 5, 10, 20, 40, 80, ...   **b.** 7, 20, 33, 46, 59, ...   **c.** 2, 3, 6, 18, 108, 1944, ...

Solution

a. The sequence 5, 10, 20, 40, 80, ... can be written as 5, $5 \cdot 2$, $5 \cdot 2^2$, $5 \cdot 2^3$, $5 \cdot 2^4$, ... Thus it is a geometric sequence whose common ratio is 2. The 10th term is $5 \cdot 2^9 = 2560$.

b. The consecutive terms of the sequence 7, 20, 33, 46, 59, ... have a common difference of 13. Thus this is an arithmetic sequence whose 10th term is $7 + 9(13) = 124$.

c. The sequence 2, 3, 6, 18, 108, 1944, ... is formed by taking the product of two successive terms to find the next term. For example, $6 \cdot 18 = 108$. This sequence is neither arithmetic nor geometric. Using exponential notation, its terms are 2, 3, 2×3, 2×3^2, $2^2 \times 3^3$, $2^3 \times 3^5$, $2^5 \times 3^8$, $2^8 \times 3^{13}$, $2^{13} \times 3^{21}$, $2^{21} \times 3^{34}$ (the 10th term). ■

2	• •	1×2
6	• • • • • •	2×3
12	• • • • • • • • • • • •	3×4
20	• • • • • • • • • • • • • • • • • • • •	4×5

Figure 2.42

Figure 2.43

Table 2.6

NUMBER OF SPLITS	NUMBER OF AMOEBAS
1	2
2	4
3	8
4	16
.	.
.	.
.	.
n	2^n

2. Rectangular numbers are numbers that can be represented in arrays where the number of dots on the shorter side is one less than the number of dots on the longer side (Figure 2.42). The first six rectangular numbers are 2, 6, 12, 20, 30, and 42. The length of the shorter side of the nth array is n and the length of the longer side is $n + 1$. Thus the nth rectangular number is $n(n + 1)$, or $n^2 + n$.

3. Figure 2.43 displays a $3 \times 3 \times 3$ cube that is composed of three layers of nine unit cubes for a total of 27 of the unit cubes. Table 2.5 shows several instances where a larger cube is formed from unit cubes. In general, if there are n unit cubes along any side of a larger cube, the larger cube is made up of n^3 unit cubes.

Table 2.5

	1	2	3	4	5	6	
Number of unit cubes on a side	1	2	3	4	5	6	...
Number of unit cubes in the larger cube	1	8	27	64	125	216	...

4. Amoebas regenerate themselves by splitting into two amoebas. Table 2.6 shows the relationship between the number of splits and the number of amoebas after that split, starting with one amoeba. Notice how the number of amoebas grows rapidly. The rapid growth as described in this table is called **exponential growth.**

NCTM Standards 2000
Algebra
Grades 3–5
All students should represent and
analyze patterns and functions
using words, tables, and graphs.

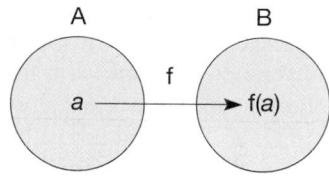

A   B

f

a ———→ f(a)

Figure 2.44

NCTM Standards 2000
Algebra
Grades 3–5
All students should identify and
describe situations with constant
or varying rates of change and
compare them.

NCTM Standards 2000
Algebra
Grades 6–8
All students should represent,
analyze, and generalize a variety of
patterns with tables, graphs, words,
and, when possible, symbolic rules.

Domain   Codomain
                1
1 ————→ 2
                3
2 ————→ 4
                5
3 ————→ 6
  •   •
  •   •
  •   •
Range is {2, 4, 6, . . .}

Figure 2.45

Domain   Codomain

a ————→ 1
e ————→ 2
i ————→ 3
o ————→ 4
u ————→ 5

Figure 2.46

Function Notation

A function, f, that assigns an element of set A to an element of set B is written $f: A \rightarrow B$. If $a \in A$, then the **function notation** for the element in B that is assigned to a is $f(a)$, read "*f of a*" or "*f at a*" (Figure 2.44). Consider how each of the preceding examples 1 to 4 satisfies the definition of a function.

1. *Even numbers:* Assigned to each counting number n is its double, namely $2n$; that is, $f(n) = 2n$.
2. *Rectangular numbers:* If there are n dots in the shorter side, there are $n + 1$ dots in the longer side. Since the number of dots in the nth rectangular number is $n(n + 1)$, we can write $f(n) = n(n + 1)$. So $f(n) = n(n + 1)$ is the function that produces rectangular numbers.
3. *Cube:* Assigned to each number n is its cube; that is, $f(n) = n^3$.
4. *Amoebas:* Assigned to each number of splits, n, is the number of amoebas, 2^n. Thus $f(n) = 2^n$.

NOTE: We are not required to use an f to represent a function and an n as the variable in $f(n)$. For example, the rectangular number function may be written $r(x) = x(x + 1)$ or $R(t) = t(t + 1)$. The function for the cube could be written $C(r) = r^3$. That is, a function may be represented by any upper- or lowercase letter. However, the variable is usually represented by a lowercase letter.

Example 2.18 Express the following relationships using function notation.

a. The cost of a taxi ride given that the rate is $1.75 plus 75 cents per quarter mile
b. The degree measure in Fahrenheit as a function of degrees Celsius, given that in Fahrenheit it is 32° more than 1.8 times the degrees measured in Celsius
c. The amount of muscle weight, in terms of body weight, given that for each 5 pounds of body weight, there are about 2 pounds of muscle
d. The value of a $1000 investment after t years at 7% interest, compounded annually, given that the amount will be 1.07^t times the initial principal

Solution

a. $C(m) = 1.75 + 4m(0.75)$, where m is the number of miles traveled
b. $F(c) = 1.8c + 32$, where c is degrees Celsius
c. $M(b) = \frac{2}{5} b$, where b is the body weight
d. $P(t) = 1000(1.07^t)$, where t is the number of years   ■

Representations of Functions

If f represents a function from set A to set B, set A is called the **domain** of f and set B is called the **codomain.** The doubling function, $f(n) = 2n$, can be defined to have the set of counting numbers as its domain and codomain. Notice that only the even numbers are used in the codomain in this function. The set of all elements in the codomain that the function pairs with an element of the domain is called the **range** of the function. The doubling function as already described has domain {1, 2, 3, . . .}, codomain {1, 2, 3, . . .}, and range {2, 4, 6, . . .} (Figure 2.45). Notice that the range must be a subset of the codomain. However, the codomain and range may be equal. For example, if $A = \{a, e, i, o, u\}$, $B = \{1, 2, 3, 4, 5\}$, and the function g assigns to each letter in A its alphabetical order among the five letters, then $g(a) = 1$, $g(e) = 2$, $g(i) = 3$, $g(o) = 4$, and $g(u) = 5$ (Figure 2.46). Here the range of g is B. The notation $g: A \rightarrow B$ is used to indicate the domain, A, and codomain, B, of the function g.

A function can assign more than one element from the domain to the same element in the codomain. For example, for sets A and B in the preceding paragraph, a letter could be assigned to 1 if it is in the first half of the alphabet and to 2 if it is in the second half. Thus a, e, and i would be assigned to 1 and o and u would be assigned to 2.

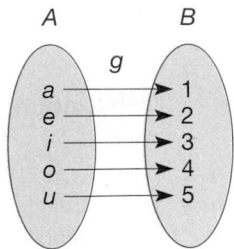

Figure 2.47

Functions as Arrow Diagrams Since functions are examples of relations, functions can be represented as arrow diagrams when sets A and B are finite sets with few elements. The arrow diagram associated with the function in Figure 2.46 is shown in Figure 2.47. To be a function, exactly one arrow must leave each element in the domain and point to one element in the codomain. However, not all elements in the codomain have to be hit by an arrow. For example, in the function shown in Figure 2.46, if B is changed to $\{1, 2, 3, 4, 5, \ldots\}$, the numbers 6, 7, 8, ... would not be hit by an arrow. Here the codomain of the function would be the set of counting numbers and the range would be the set $\{1, 2, 3, 4, 5\}$.

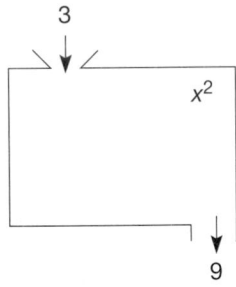

Figure 2.48

Functions as Tables The function in Figure 2.46, where B is the set $\{1, 2, 3, 4, 5\}$, also can be defined using a table (Figure 2.48). Notice how when one defines a function in this manner, it is implied that the codomain and range are the same, namely set B.

Functions as Machines A dynamic way of visualizing the concept of function is through the use of a machine. The "input" elements are the elements of the domain and the "output" elements are the elements of the range. The function machine in Figure 2.49 takes any number put into the machine, squares it, and then outputs the square. For example, if 3 is an input, its corresponding output is 9. In this case, 3 is an element of the domain and 9 is an element of the range.

Figure 2.49

Spotlight on Technology This dynamic view of functions as machines can be combined with functions as tables on a spreadsheet. The spreadsheet allows a user to input many different values www.wiley.com/ college/musser from the domain and see each of the corresponding outputs in the range in a table format. Refer to the dynamic spreadsheet, *Function Machines and Tables*, in the spreadsheet webmodule. This spreadsheet contains the input and output values for the function $f(x) = x^2 - 2x - 3$. Can you find two different values of x which produce the same output $f(x)$? Would such an example be inconsistent with the definition of a function? Why or why not?

Reflection from Research
Students tend to view a function as either a collection of points or ordered pairs; this limited view may actually hinder students' development of the concept of function (Adams, 1993).

Functions as Ordered Pairs The function in Figure 2.47 also can be expressed as the set of ordered pairs $\{(a, 1), (e, 2), (i, 3), (o, 4), (u, 5)\}$. This method of defining a function by listing its ordered pairs is practical if there is a small finite number of pairs that define the function. Functions having an infinite domain can be defined using this ordered-pair approach by using set-builder notation. For example, the squaring function $f: A \to B$, where $A = B$ is the set of whole numbers and $f(n) = n^2$, is $\{(a, b) \mid b = a^2, a$ any whole number$\}$, that is, the set of all ordered pairs of whole numbers, (a, b), where $b = a^2$.

Functions as Graphs The ordered pairs of a function can be represented as points on a two-dimensional coordinate system (graphing functions will be studied in depth in Section 9.3). Briefly, a horizontal line is usually used for elements in the domain of the function and a vertical line is used for the codomain. Then the ordered pair $(x, f(x))$ is plotted. Five of the ordered pairs associated with the squaring function, $f(x) = x^2$, where the domain of f is the set of whole numbers, are illustrated in Figure 2.50. Graphing is especially useful when a function consists of infinitely many ordered pairs.

Figure 2.50

Slide

Turn

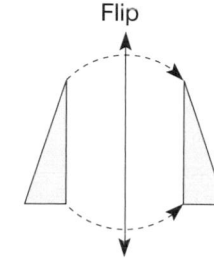

Flip

Figure 2.51

Reflection from Research
Students may be able to complete a task using one representation of a function but be unable to complete the same task when given a different representation of the function (Goldenberg, Harvey, Lewis, Umiker, West, & Zodhiates, 1988).

Functions as Formulas In Chapter 13 we derive formulas for finding areas of certain plane figures. For example, the formula for finding the area of a circle is $A = \pi r^2$, where r is the radius of the circle. To reinforce the fact that the area of a circle, A, is a function of the radius, we sometimes write this formula as $A(r) = \pi r^2$. Usually, formulas are used to define a function whenever the domain has infinitely many elements. In the formula $A(r) = \pi r^2$, we have that the domain of the area function is any number used to measure lengths, not simply the whole numbers: $A(1) = \pi$, $A(2) = 4\pi$, $A(0.5) = (0.5)^2\pi = 0.25\pi$, and so on.

Functions as Geometric Transformations Certain aspects of geometry can be studied more easily through the use of functions. For example, geometric shapes can be slid, turned, and flipped to produce other shapes (Figure 2.51). Such transformations can be viewed as functions that assign to each point in the plane a unique point in the plane. Geometric transformations of the plane are studied in Chapter 16.

Example 2.19 Identify the domain, codomain, and range of the following functions.

a. $a \rightarrow 1$
   $b \rightarrow 2$
        3

b.

x	y
1	11
2	21
3	31
4	41

c. $g: R \rightarrow S$, where $g(x) = x^2$, R and S are the counting numbers.

d.

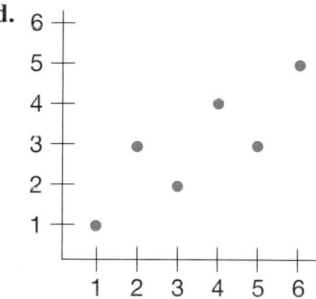

Solution

a. Domain: $\{a, b\}$, codomain: $\{1, 2, 3\}$, range: $\{1, 2\}$
b. Domain: $\{1, 2, 3, 4\}$, codomain: $\{11, 21, 31, 41\}$, range = codomain
c. Domain: $\{1, 2, 3, 4, \dots\}$, codomain = domain, range: $\{1, 4, 9, 16, \dots\}$
d. Domain: $\{1, 2, 3, 4, 5, 6\}$, codomain = domain, range: $\{1, 2, 3, 4, 5\}$ ■

MATHEMATICAL MORSEL

Suppose that a large sheet of paper one-thousandth of an inch thick is torn in half and the two pieces are put on a pile. Then these two pieces are torn in half and put together to form a pile of four pieces. If this process is continued a total of 50 times, the last pile will be over 17 million miles high!

"Yeah Houston.....
you're not going to
believe this ....."

Section 2.4   EXERCISE / PROBLEM SET A

EXERCISES

1. Express the following relations in arrow diagram form in their ordered-pair representation.

   a.

   b.

   c.

   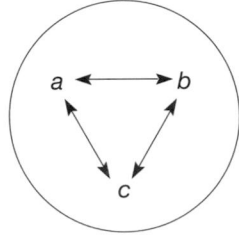

2. Make an arrow diagram for each relation.

   a.

   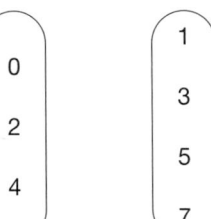

   Description: "is greater than"

   b.

   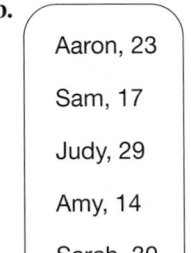

   Description: "is younger than"

c.

Broncos   San Francisco

Vikings   St. Louis

49ers   Oakland

Cowboys   Dallas

Rams   Denver

               Minnesota

Description: "is an NFL team representing"

d.

6	2
8	3
10	4
12	5
	6

Description: "has a factor of"

3. Determine whether the relations represented by the following sets of ordered pairs are reflexive, symmetric, or transitive. Which of them are equivalence relations?

   a. {(1, 1), (2, 1), (2, 2), (3, 1), (3, 2), (3, 3)}
   b. {(1, 2), (1, 3), (2, 3), (2, 1), (3, 2), (3, 1)}
   c. {(1, 1), (1, 3), (2, 2), (3, 2), (1, 2)}
   d. {(1, 1), (2, 2), (3, 3)}

4. Describe the partitions associated with the following equivalence relations.

   a. "Has the same surname as" on the collection of all people
   b. "Has the same tens digit as" on the set collection {1, 2, 3, 4, . . .}
   c. "Has the primary residence in the same state as" on the set of all people in the United States

5. Determine which of the reflexive, symmetric, and transitive properties are satisfied by the following relations. Which relations are equivalence relations?

a. "Less than" on the set $\{1, 2, 3, 4, \ldots\}$

b. "Has the same shape as" on the set of all triangles

c. "Is a factor of" on the set $\{1, 2, 3, 4, \ldots\}$

d. "Has the same number of factors as" on the set $\{1, 2, 3, 4, \ldots\}$

6. Which of the following arrow diagrams represent functions? If one does not represent a function, explain why not.

a.

b.

c.

d.
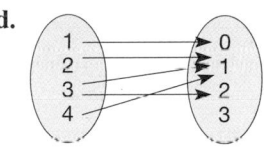

7. List the ordered pairs for these functions using the domain specified. Find the range for each function.

a. $C(t) = 2t^3 - 3t$, with domain $\{0, 2, 4\}$

b. $a(x) = x + 2$, with domain $\{1, 2, 9\}$

c. $P(n) = \left(\dfrac{n+1}{n}\right)^n$ with domain $\{1, 2, 3\}$

8. Which of the following relations, listed as ordered pairs, could belong to a function? For those that cannot, explain why not.

a. $\{(7, 4)\ (6, 3)\ (5, 2)\ (4, 1)\}$

b. $\{(\text{red}, 3)\ (\text{blue}, 4)\ (\text{green}, 5)\ (\text{yellow}, 6)\ (\text{black}, 5)\}$

c. $\{(1, 1)\ (1, 2)\ (3, 4)\ (4, 4)\}$

d. $\{(1, 1)\ (2, 1)\ (3, 1)\ (4, 1)\}$

e. $\{(a, b)\ (b, b)\ (d, e)\ (b, c)\ (d, f)\}$

9. Using the function machines, find all possible missing whole-number inputs or outputs.

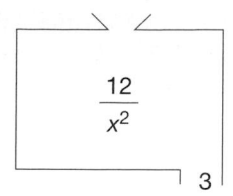

10. Which of the following relations describe a function? If one does not, explain why not.

a. Each U.S. citizen → his or her birthday

b. Each vehicle registered in Michigan → its license plate

c. Each college graduate → his or her degree

d. Each shopper in a grocery store → number of items purchased

11. The following functions are expressed in one of the following forms: a formula, an arrow diagram, a table, or a set of ordered pairs. Express each function in each of the other three forms.

a. $f(x) = x^3 - x$ for $x \in \{0, 1, 4\}$

b. $\{(1, 1), (4, 2), (9, 3)\}$

c.
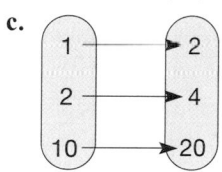

d.

x	f(x)
5	55
6	66
7	77

12. Inputs into a function are not always single numbers or single elements of the domain. For example, a function can be defined to accept as input the length and width of a rectangle and to output its perimeter.

$$P(l, w) = 2l + 2w$$
$$\text{or } P: (l, w) \rightarrow 2l + 2w$$

For each function defined, evaluate $f(2, 5), f(3, 3)$, and $f(1, 4)$.

a. $f(x, y) = x^2 + y^2$ **b.** $f: (a, b) \rightarrow 3a + 1$

c.
$$\frac{m + n}{2m + n}$$
(input (m, n))

d. $f: (x, y) \rightarrow x$ or y, whichever is larger

13. Determine whether the following sequences are arithmetic sequences, geometric sequences, or neither. Determine the common difference (ratio) and 200th term for the arithmetic (geometric) sequences.

a. 7, 12, 17, 22, 27, . . .

b. 14, 28, 56, 112, . . .

c. 4, 14, 24, 34, 44, . . .

d. 1, 11, 111, 1111, . . .

14. How many numbers are in this collection?

$$1, 4, 7, 10, 13, \ldots, 682$$

15. A 6% sales tax function applied to any price p can be described as follows: $f(p)$ is 0.06p rounded to the nearest cent, where half-cents are rounded up. For example, 0.06(1.25) = 0.075, so $f(1.25) = 0.08$, since 0.075 is rounded up to 0.08. Use the 6% sales tax function to find the correct tax on the following amounts.

a. $7.37   **b.** $9.25   **c.** $11.15   **d.** $76.85

PROBLEMS

16. Fractions are numbers of the form $\frac{a}{b}$, where a and b are whole numbers and $b \neq 0$. Fraction equality is defined as $\frac{a}{b} = \frac{c}{d}$ if and only if $ad = bc$. Determine whether fraction equality is an equivalence relation. If it is, describe the equivalence class that contains $\frac{1}{2}$.

17. a. The function $f(n) = \frac{9}{5}n + 32$ can be used to convert degrees Celsius to degrees Fahrenheit. Calculate $f(0), f(100), f(50),$ and $f(-40)$.

b. The function $g(m) = \frac{5}{9}(m - 32)$ can be used to convert degrees Fahrenheit to degrees Celsius. Calculate $g(32), g(212), g(104),$ and $g(-40)$.

c. Is there a temperature where the degrees Celsius equals the degrees Fahrenheit? If so, what is it?

18. Find the 458th number in the sequence 21, 29, 37, 45, ...

19. A fitness club charges an initiation fee of $85 plus $35 per month.

a. Write a formula for a function, $C(x)$, that gives the total cost for using the fitness club facilities after x months.

b. Calculate $C(18)$ using the formula you wrote in part (a). Explain in words what you have found.

c. When will the total amount spent by a club member first exceed $1000?

20. The second term of a certain geometric sequence is 1200 and the fifth term of the sequence is 150.

a. Find the common ratio, r, for this geometric sequence.

b. Write out the first six terms of the sequence.

21. Consider the following sequence of toothpick figures.

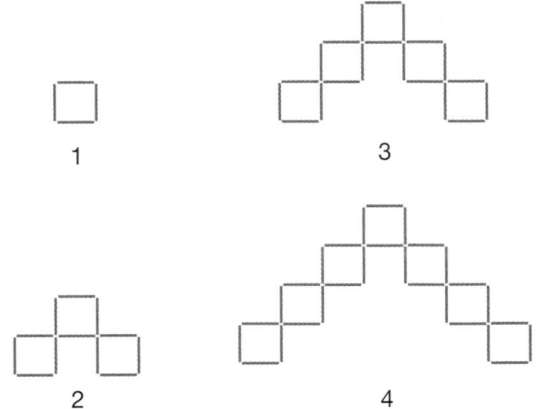

a. Let $T(n)$ be the function representing the total number of toothpicks in the nth figure. Complete the following table, which gives one representation of the function T.

n	$T(n)$
1	4
2	
3	
4	
5	
6	
7	
8	

b. What kind of sequence do the numbers in the second column form?

c. Represent the function T in another way by writing a formula for $T(n)$.

d. Find $T(20)$ and $T(150)$.

e. What are the domain and range of the function T?

22. Consider the following sequence of toothpick figures.

| 1 | 2 | 3 | 4 |

a. Let $T(n)$ be the function representing the total number of toothpicks in the nth figure. Complete the following table, which gives one representation of the function T.

n	$T(n)$
1	3
2	
3	
4	
5	
6	
7	
8	

b. Do the numbers in column 2 form a geometric or arithmetic sequence, or neither?

c. Represent the function T in another way by writing a formula for $T(n)$.

d. Find $T(15)$ and $T(100)$.

e. What are the domain and range of the function T?

23. Suppose that $100 is earning interest at an annual rate of 5%.

a. If the interest earned on the $100 is simple interest, the same amount of interest is earned each year. The interest is 5% of $100, or $5 per year. Complete a table like the one following to show the value of the account after 10 years.

NUMBER OF YEARS, n	ANNUAL INTEREST EARNED	VALUE OF ACCOUNT
0	0	100
1	5	105
2	5	110
3		
4		
5		
·		
·		
·		
10		

b. What kind of sequence, arithmetic or geometric, do the numbers in the third column form? What is the value of d or r? Write a function $A(n)$ that gives the value of the account after n years.

24. a. If the interest earned on the $100 is compound interest and is compounded annually, the amount of interest earned at the end of a year is 5% of the current balance. After the first year the interest is calculated using the original $100 plus any accumulated interest. Complete a table like the one following to show the value of the account after n years.

NUMBER OF YEARS, n	ANNUAL INTEREST EARNED	VALUE OF ACCOUNT
0	0	100
1	0.05(100) = 5	105
2	0.05(105) = 5.25	110.25
3		
4		
5		
·		
·		
·		
10		

b. What kind of sequence, arithmetic or geometric, do the numbers in the third column form? What is the value of d or r? Write a function $A(n)$ that gives the value of the account after n years.

c. Over a period of 10 years, how much more interest is earned when interest is compounded annually than when simple interest is earned? (NOTE: Generally, banks do pay compound interest rather than simple interest.)

25. A clown was shot out of a cannon at ground level. Her height above the ground at any time t was given by the function $h(t) = -16t^2 + 64t$. Find her height when $t = 1, 2,$ and 3. How many seconds of flight will she have?

26. Suppose that you want to find out my telephone number (it consists of seven digits) by asking me questions that I can only answer "yes" or "no." What method of interrogation leads to the correct answer after the smallest number of questions? (*Hint:* Use base two.)

Section 2.4 EXERCISE / PROBLEM SET B

EXERCISES

1. List all ordered pairs of each of the following relations on the sets listed. Which, if any, is an equivalence relation?

   a. Set: {1, 2, 3, 4, 5, 6}
      Relation: "Has the same number of factors as"

   b. Set: {2, 4, 6, 8, 10, 12}
      Relation: "Is a multiple of"

   c. Set: {1, 2, 3, 4, 5, 6, 7, 8}
      Relation: "Has more factors than"

2. Name the relations suggested by the following ordered pairs [e.g., (Hawaii, 50) has the name "is state number"].

   a. (Lincoln, 16)   b. (Atlanta, GA)
      (Madison, 4)   (Dover, DE)
      (Reagan, 40)   (Austin, TX)
      (McKinley, 25)   (Harrisburg, PA)

   c. (George III, England) d. (21, 441)
      (Philip, Spain)   (12, 144)
      (Louis XIV, France)   (38, 1444)
      (Alexander, Macedonia)   (53, 2809)

3. Determine whether the relations represented by the following diagrams are reflexive, symmetric, or transitive. Which of them are equivalence relations?

   a.   b.

   c.   d.
         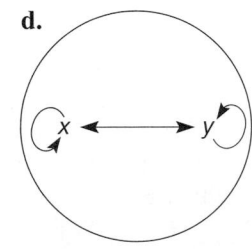

4. Determine which of the reflexive, symmetric, or transitive properties hold for these relations:

   a. {(1, 2), (1, 3), (1, 4), (2, 3), (2, 4), (3, 4)}

   b. {(1, 2), (2, 3), (1, 4), (2, 4), (4, 2), (2, 1), (4, 1), (3, 2)}

5. Determine whether the relations represented by the following arrow diagrams are reflexive, symmetric, or transitive. Which are equivalence relations?

   a.   b.

   c.   d.
         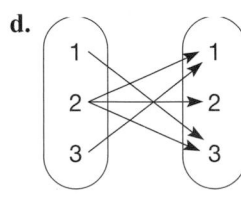

6. Which of the following arrow diagrams represent functions? If one does not represent a function, explain why not

   a.   b.

   c.   d.
        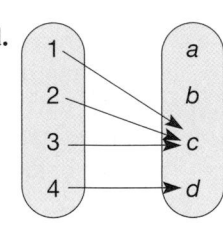

7. List the ordered pairs for these functions using the domains specified. Find the range for each function.

   a. $f(x) = 2x^2 + 4$, with domain: {0, 1, 2}

   b. $g(y) = (y + 2)^2$, with domain: {7, 2, 1}

   c. $h(t) = 2^t - 3$, with domain: {2, 3}

8. Which of the following relations, listed as ordered pairs, could belong to a function? For those that cannot, explain why not.

   a. {(Bob, m), (Sue, s), (Joe, s), (Jan, s), (Sue, m)}

   b. {(dog, 3), (horse, 7), (cat, 4)}, (mouse, 3), (bird, 7)}

c. $\{(a, x), (c, y), (x, a), (y, y), (b, z)\}$

d. $\{(1, x), (a, x), (\text{Joe}, y), (\text{Bob}, x)\}$

e. $\{(1, 2), (2, 3), (2, 1), (3, 3), (3, 1)\}$

9. Using the following function machines, find all possible missing whole-number inputs or outputs.

a. 3 10^x

b. 4 $x^2 + 2$

c. x^2 25

d. $x^3 - 1$ 26

10. Which of the following relations describe a function? If one does not, explain why not.

a. Each registered voter in California $\rightarrow$ his or her polling place

b. Each city in the United States $\rightarrow$ its zip code

c. Each type of plant $\rightarrow$ its genus

d. Each pet owner in the United States $\rightarrow$ his or her pet

11. The functions shown next are expressed in one of the following forms: a formula, an arrow diagram, a table, or a set of ordered pairs. Express each function in each of the three other forms.

a.
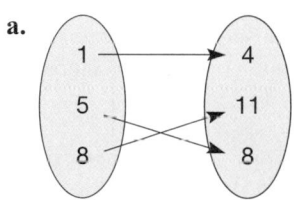

b.

x	$f(x)$
3	$\frac{1}{3}$
4	$\frac{1}{4}$
1	1
$\frac{1}{2}$	2

c. $\{(4, 12), (2, 6), (7, 21)\}$

d. $f(x) = x^2 - 2x + 1$ for $x \in \{2, 3, 4, 5\}$

12. Some functions expressed in terms of a formula use different formulas for different parts of the domain. Such a function is said to be defined piecewise. For example, suppose that f is a function with a domain of $\{1, 2, 3, \ldots\}$ and

$$f(x) = \begin{cases} 2x & \text{for } x \le 5 \\ x + 1 & \text{for } x > 5 \end{cases}$$

This notation means that if an element of the domain is 5 or less, the formula $2x$ is used. Otherwise, the formula $x + 1$ is used.

a. Evaluate each of the following: $f(3), f(10), f(25), f(5)$.

b. Sketch an example of what a function machine might look like for f.

13. Oregon's 1991 state income tax rate for single persons was expressed as follows, where i = taxable income.

TAX RATE (T_i)	TAXABLE INCOME (i)
$0.05i$	$i \le 2000$
$100 + 0.07(i - 2000)$	$2000 < i \le 5000$
$310 + 0.09(i - 5000)$	$i > 5000$

a. Calculate $T(4000)$, $T(1795)$, $T(26{,}450)$, and $T(2000)$.

b. Find the income tax on persons with taxable incomes of \$49,570 and \$3162.

c. A single person's tax calculated by this formula was \$1910.20. What was that person's taxable income?

14. The output of a function is not always a single number. It may be an ordered pair or a set of numbers. Several examples follow. Assume in each case that the domain is the set of natural numbers or ordered pairs of natural numbers, as appropriate.

a. $f: n \rightarrow \{\text{all factors of } n\}$. Find $f(7)$ and $f(12)$.

b. $f(n) = (n + 1, n - 1)$. Find $f(3)$ and $f(20)$.

c. $f: n \rightarrow \{\text{natural numbers greater than } n\}$. Find $f(6)$ and $f(950)$.

d. $f(n, m) = \{\text{natural numbers between } n \text{ and } m\}$. Find $f(2, 6)$ and $f(10, 11)$.

15. Determine whether the following sequences are arithmetic sequences, geometric sequences, or neither. Determine the common difference (ratio) and 200th term for the arithmetic (geometric) sequences.

a. 5, 50, 500, 5000, . . .   **b.** 8, 16, 32, 64, . . .

c. 12, 23, 34, 45, 56, . . .   **d.** 1, 12, 123, 1234, . . .

PROBLEMS

16. Find the 731st number in this collection: 2, 9, 16, 23, 30, ...

17. How many numbers are in this sequence? 16, 27, 38, 49, . . . , 1688

18. The volume of a cube whose sides have length s is given by the formula $V(s) = s^3$.

a. Find the volume of cubes whose sides have length 3; 5; 11.

b. Find the lengths of the sides of cubes whose volumes are 64; 216; 2744.

19. If the interest rate of a $1000 savings account is 5% and no additional money is deposited, the amount of money in the account at the end of t years is given by the function $a(t) = (1.05)^t \cdot 1000$.

a. Calculate how much will be in the account after 2 years; after 5 years; after 10 years.

b. What is the minimum number of years that it will take to more than double the account?

20. A rectangular parking area for a business will be enclosed by a fence. The fencing for the front of the lot, which faces the street, will cost $10 more per foot than the fencing for the other three sides. Use the dimensions shown to answer the following questions.

a. Write a formula for a function, $F(x)$, that gives the total cost of fencing for the lot if fencing for the three sides cost x per foot.

b. Calculate $F(11.50)$ using the formula you wrote in part (a). Explain in words what you have found.

c. Suppose that no more than $9000 can be spent on this fence. What is the most expensive fencing that can be used?

21. The third term of a certain geometric sequence is 36 and the seventh term of the sequence is 2916.

a. Find the common ratio, r, of the sequence.

b. Write out the first seven terms of the sequence.

22. Consider the following sequence of toothpick figures.

1   2

3   4

a. Let $T(n)$ be the function representing the total number of toothpicks in the nth figure. Complete the following table, which gives one representation of the function T.

n	$T(n)$
1	12
2	
3	
4	
5	
6	
7	
8	

b. What kind of sequence, arithmetic or geometric, do the numbers in the second column form? What is the value of d or r?

c. Represent the function T in another way by writing a formula for $T(n)$.

d. Find $T(25)$ and $T(200)$.

e. What are the domain and range of the function T?

23. The population of Mexico in 1990 was approximately 88,300,000 and was increasing at a rate of about 2.5% per year.

a. Complete a table like the one following to predict the population in subsequent years, assuming that the population continues to increase at the same rate.

YEAR	INCREASE IN POPULATION	POPULATION OF MEXICO
1990	0	88,300,000
1991	$0.025 \times 88,300,000 = 2,207,500$	90,507,500
1992	$0.025 \times 90,507,500 = 2,262,688$	92,770,188
1993		
1994		
1995		
1996		
1997		
1998		
1999		
2000		
2001		
2002		

b. What kind of sequence, geometric or arithmetic, do the figures in the third column form? What is the value of r or d?

c. Use the sequence you established to predict the population of Mexico in the year 2000 and in the year 2005. (NOTE: This means assuming that the growth rate remains the same, which may not be a valid assumption.)

d. Write a function, $P(n)$, that will give the estimated population of Mexico n years after 1990.

24. The 114th term of an arithmetic sequence is 341 and its 175th term is 524. What is its 4th term?

25. Write a 10-digit numeral such that the first digit tells the number of zeros in the numeral, the second digit tells the number of ones, the third digit tells the number of twos, and so on. For example, the numeral 9000000001 is not correct because there are not nine zeros and there is one 1.

26. Equations are equivalent if they have the same solution set. For example, $3x - 2 = 7$ and $2x + 4 = 10$ are equivalent since they both have $\{3\}$ as their solution set. Explain the connection between the notion of equivalent equations and equivalence classes.

PROBLEMS FOR WRITING/DISCUSSION

1. You are given the formula $C(m) = 1.75 + 4m(0.75)$ to represent the cost of a taxi ride (C) per mile traveled (m), given that the rate charged is $1.75 plus 75 cents per quarter mile. Explain where the 4 in the formula comes from.

2. Maria was sewing circular jewelry cases to give as Christmas presents. She wanted to put a binding around the edge of the circle. She thought about trying to measure around the outside of the circle with her tape measure to figure out how long the binding should be. Then she thought of a better way to figure it out. What did she do? How is that relevant to this section?

3. A student says the sequence 1, 11, 111, 1111, ... must be geometric because the successive differences, 10, 100, 1000, etc., are powers of 10. Do you agree? Explain.

END OF CHAPTER MATERIAL

Solution of Initial Problem

A survey was taken of 150 college freshmen. Forty of them were majoring in mathematics, 30 of them were majoring in English, 20 were majoring in science, 7 had a double major of mathematics and English, and none had a double (or triple) major with science. How many students had majors other than mathematics, English, or science?

Strategy: Draw a Diagram

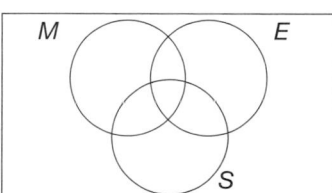

A Venn diagram with three circles, as shown here, is useful in this problem. There are to be 150 students within the rectangle, 40 in the mathematics circle, 30 in the English circle, 20 in the science circle, and 7 in the intersection of the mathematics and English circles but outside the science circle.

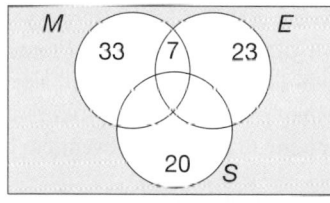

There are $33 + 7 + 23 + 20$, or 83, students accounted for, so there must be $150 - 83$, or 67, students outside the three circles. Those 67 students were the ones who did not major in mathematics, English, or science.

Additional Problems Where the Strategy "Draw a Diagram" Is Useful

1. A car may be purchased with the following options:
Radio: AM/FM, AM/FM Cassette, AM/FM Cassette/CD
Sunroof: Pop-up, Sliding
Transmission: Standard, Automatic
How many different cars can a customer select among these options?

2. One morning a taxi driver travels the following routes: North: 5 blocks; West: 3 blocks; North: 2 blocks; East: 5 blocks; and South: 2 blocks. How far is she from where she started?

3. For every 50 cars that arrive at a highway intersection, 25 turn right to go to Allentown, 10 go straight ahead to Boston, and the rest turn left to go to Canton. Half of the cars that arrive at Boston turn right to go to Denton, and one of every five that arrive at Allentown turns left to go to Denton. If 10,000 cars arrive at Denton one day, how many cars arrived at Canton?

People in Mathematics

Emmy Noether (1882–1935)
Emmy Noether was born and educated in Germany and was graduated from the University of Erlangen, where her father, Max Noether, taught mathematics. There were few professional opportunities for a woman mathematician, so Noether spent the next eight years doing research at home and teaching for her increasingly disabled father. Her work attracted the attention of the mathematicians Hilbert and Klein, who invited her to the University of Gottingen—at that time one of the world's leading centers of mathematics. Initially, Noether's lectures were announced under Hilbert's name, because the university refused to admit a woman lecturer. Conditions improved, but in 18 years at Gottingen, she was routinely denied the promotions that would have come to a male mathematician of her ability. When the Nazis came to power in 1933, she was dismissed from her position. She emigrated to the United States and spent the last two years of her life at Bryn Mawr College. In 1983, the French mathematician Jean Dieudonne wrote that Emmy Noether "was by far the best woman mathematician of all time, and one of the greatest mathematicians of the twentieth century."

David Hilbert (1862–1943)
David Hilbert, professor of mathematics at the University of Gottingen, surveyed the spectrum of unsolved problems in 1900, and selected 23 for special attention. He felt these 23 were crucial for progress in mathematics in the coming century. Hilbert's vision was proved to be prophetic. Mathematicians took up the challenge, and a great deal of progress resulted from attempts to solve "Hilbert's problems." Hilbert himself made important contributions to the foundations of mathematics and attempted to prove that mathematics was self-consistent. He became one of the most influential mathematicians of his time, yet he once remarked that when he read or heard new ideas in mathematics, they seemed "so difficult and practically impossible to understand," until he worked the ideas through for himself.

CHAPTER REVIEW

Review the following terms and problems to determine which require learning or relearning—page numbers are provided for easy reference.

SECTION 2.1: Sets As a Basis for Whole Numbers

VOCABULARY/NOTATION

Natural numbers   39
Counting numbers   39
Whole numbers   39
Set ({ . . . })   39
Is an element of (∈)   39
Member   39
Set-builder notation { . . . | . . . }   39
Is not an element of (∉)   39
Empty set (∅) or null set   39

Equal sets (=)   39
Is not equal to (≠)   39
1-1 correspondence   40
Equivalent sets (~)   40
Matching sets   40
Subset (⊆)   40
Proper subset (⊂)   40
Venn diagram   40
Universal set (U)   40

Disjoint sets   40
Union (∪)   41
Intersection (∩)   41
Complement ($\overline{A}$)   42
Set difference (−)   42
Ordered pair   44
Cartesian product (×)   44
Finite set   45
Infinite set   45

EXERCISES

1. Describe three different ways to define a set.

2. True or false?

    a. $1 \in \{a, b, 1\}$ **b.** $a \notin \{1, 2, 3\}$

    c. $\{x, y\} \subset \{x, y, z\}$ **d.** $\{a, b\} \subseteq \{a, b\}$

    e. $\varnothing = \{\}$ **f.** $\{a, b\} \sim \{c, d\}$

    g. $\{a, b\} = \{c, d\}$

    h. $\{1, 2, 3\} \cap \{2, 3, 4\} = \{1, 2, 3, 4\}$

    i. $\{2, 3\} \cup \{1, 3, 4\} = \{2, 3, 4\}$

    j. $\{1, 2\}$ and $\{2, 3\}$ are disjoint sets

    k. $\{4, 3, 5, 2\} - \{2, 3, 4\} = \{5\}$

    l. $\{a, 1\} \times \{b, 2\} = \{(a, b), (1, 2)\}$

3. What set is used to determine the number of elements in the set $\{a, b, c, d, e, f, g\}$?

4. Explain how you can distinguish between finite sets and infinite sets.

5. A poll at a party having 23 couples revealed that there were

    i. 25 people who liked both country-western and ballroom dancing.

    ii. 8 who liked only country-western dancing.

    iii. 6 who liked only ballroom dancing. How many did not like either type of dancing?

SECTION 2.2: Whole Numbers and Numeration

VOCABULARY/NOTATION

Number   51
Numeral   51
Cardinal number   51
Ordinal number   51
Identification number   52
Number of a set [$n(A)$]   52
Less than ($<$), greater than ($>$)   52
Less than or equal to ($\leq$)   52

Greater than or equal to ($\geq$)   52
Whole-number line   53
Tally numeration system   53
Grouping   53
Egyptian numeration system   54
Additive numeration system   54
Roman numeration system   54
Subtractive numeration system   54

Positional numeration system   55
Multiplicative numeration
   system   55
Babylonian numeration system   55
Place-value system   55
Placeholder   55
Mayan numeration system   56
Zero   56

EXERCISES

1. Is the expression "house number" literally correct? Explain.

2. Give an example of a situation where each of the following is useful:

    a. cardinal number

    b. ordinal number

    c. identification number

3. True or false?

    a. $n(\{a, b, c, d\}) = 4$ **b.** $7 \leq 7$

    c. $3 \geq 4$ **d.** $5 < 50$

    e. $|||$ is three in the tally system

    f. $\cap ||| = ||| \cap$ in the Egyptian system

    g. IV = VI in the Roman system

    h. ⠶ = ⠒⠒ in the Mayan system

4. Express each of the following in our system.

    a. ⟨∩| **b.** CXIV   **c.** ⦂⦂⦂

5. Express 37 in each of the following systems:

    a. Egyptian   **b.** Roman   **c.** Mayan

6. Using examples, distinguish between a positional numeration system and a place-value numeration system.

SECTION 2.3: The Hindu–Arabic System

VOCABULARY/NOTATION

Hindu–Arabic numeration
   system   61
Digits   61
Base   61

Bundles of sticks   61
Base ten pieces (Dienes blocks)   61
Chip abacus   61
Expanded form   61

Expanded notation   61
Exponents   66

EXERCISES

1. Explain how each of the following contributes to formulating the Hindu–Arabic numeration system.

  a. Digits

  b. Grouping by ten

  c. Place value

  d. Additive and multiplicative attributes

2. Explain how the names of 11, 12, . . . , 19 are inconsistent with the names of 21, 22, . . . , 29.

3. True or false?

  a. $100 = 212_{\text{five}}$ **b.** $172_{\text{nine}} = 146$

  c. $11111_{\text{two}} = 2222_{\text{three}}$ **d.** $18_{\text{twelve}} = 11_{\text{nineteen}}$

4. What is the value of learning different number bases?

SECTION 2.4: Relations and Functions

VOCABULARY/NOTATION

Arrow diagrams   71
Relation   71
Reflexive property   71
Symmetric property   71
Transitive property   72
Equivalence relation   72
Partition   72

Function ($f: A \rightarrow B$)   73
Initial term of a sequence   73
Arithmetic sequence   73
Common difference   73
Geometric sequence   73
Common ratio   73
Rectangular numbers   74

Exponential growth   74
Function notation [$f(a)$]   75
Domain   75
Codomain   75
Range   75

EXERCISES

1. Which, if any, of the following are equivalence relations? For those that aren't, which properties fail?

  a.   **b.**

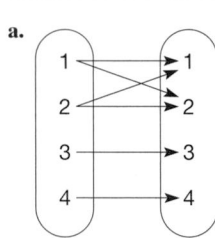

  c. $\{(1, 1), (1, 2), (2, 1), (2, 2), (2, 3), (3, 2), (3, 3)\}$

2. Using the relations on the set $S = \{1, 2, 3, 4, 5, 6, 7, 8, 9, 10, 11, 12\}$, determine all ordered pairs (a, b) that satisfy the equations. Which of the relations are reflexive, symmetric, or transitive?

  a. $a + b = 11$ **b.** $a - b = 4$

  c. $a \cdot b = 12$ **d.** $a/b = 2$

3. a. Give the first five terms of the following:

    i. The arithmetic sequence whose first two terms are 1, 7

    ii. The geometric sequence whose first two terms are 2, 8

  b. Determine the common difference and common ratio for the sequences in part (a).

4. True or false?

  a. There are 10 numbers in the geometric sequence 2, 6, 18, . . . , 39366.

  b. The 100th term of the sequence $\{3, 5, 7, 9, \ldots\}$ is 103.

  c. The domain and range of a function are the same set.

  d. If $f(n) = 3n$, then $f(2) = 9$.

5. Dawn, Jose, and Amad have Jones, Ortiz, and Rasheed, respectively, as their surnames. Express this information as a function in each of the following ways:

  a. As an arrow diagram

  b. As a table

  c. As order pairs

6. Draw a graph of the function $\{(1, 4), (2, 3), (3, 7), (4, 5), (5, 3)\}$ whose domain is $\{1, 2, 3, 4, 5\}$ and whose codomain is $\{1, 2, \ldots, 8\}$. What is the range of this function?

7. Give three examples of functions that are commonly presented as formulas.

PROBLEMS FOR WRITING/DISCUSSION

1. Of the numeration systems studied in this chapter, including our own, which ones had no zero? Explain how they compensated for this.

2. Explain why we say that computation is easier in a place-value system. Demonstrate using a two-digit multiplication problem in Roman numerals with the same example using Hindu–Arabic numerals.

3. If you take the arithmetic sequence given by the rule $3n - 1$ and turn it into ordered pairs (x, y) using the number of the first term as x and the actual term as y, the first three pairs would be $(1, 2)$, $(2, 5)$, and $(3, 8)$. If you graph those points in the coordinate plane, they seem to lie in a straight line. Will the next two pairs also lie on the same line? Explain.

4. If you take the terms of a geometric sequence, say $1/3, 1, 3, 9, \ldots$, and turn them into ordered pairs as you did for Problem 3, they will be represented by the points $(1, 1/3)$, $(2, 1)$, $(3, 3)$, $(4, 9)$. If you then graph those points, they also seem to lie in a straight line. Will the next few points also lie on the line? Explain.

5. Alonzo said that if a sequence begins $1, 3, \ldots$ the next term can be a 5 because it is going up by twos. Come up with three alternatives to 5. That is, find three sequences that begin 1, 3, but that do not have 5 as a third term. Explain how your sequences are formed.

6. While drawing Venn diagrams, Harvey notices that the picture of $\overline{A - B}$ looks like a photographic negative of the picture of $A - B$. That is, what is shaded in one picture is unshaded in the other, and vice versa. He asks if that would always be the case. How do you respond? (Include illustrations.)

7. Mary Lou says that the complement of $A - B$ must be $\overline{A} - \overline{B}$, but she's having trouble with the Venn diagrams. How would you help Mary Lou? (Include illustrations.)

8. The original abacuses (or abaci) had 10 beads per wire

and each wire represented a different place value. A later model, called a soroban, had on each wire one bead, which represented 5, above a middle bar, and four beads, each representing 1, below the middle bar. The beads that represented the number you wanted would be pulled to the middle bar. In the following (incomplete) picture, the number represented is 25.

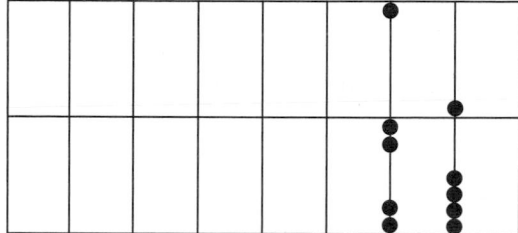

How would you represent the number 427? How would you represent the number 10 if there are only beads enough to represent 9 on the wire? Explain.

9. If there had been such a thing as a Mayan soroban, what is the fewest number of 5 and 1 beads that would have been needed on each wire? Take the number 427, convert it to a Mayan numeral, and illustrate what it would have looked like on a (completely imaginary) South American abacus.

10. Because our Hindu–Arabic numeration system is so streamlined, it is easy for us to write out the numerals for one million or one billion. What is less easy is comparing what the size of those numbers really is. The national debt and the federal budget are measured in trillions. But how big is a trillion compared to a million? How many days would one million seconds be? Then estimate how long you think a trillion seconds would be. Then figure out (in years) how long one trillion seconds would be. (Use 365 as the number of days in a year.)

CHAPTER TEST

Knowledge

1. True or false?
   a. If $A \sim B$, then $A = B$.
   b. If $A \subset B$, then $A \subseteq B$.
   c. $A \cap B \subseteq A \cup B$.
   d. $n(\{a, b\} \times \{x, y, z\}) = 6$.
   e. If $A \cap B = \varnothing$, then $n(A - B) < n(A)$.
   f. $\{2, 4, 6, \ldots, 2000000\} \sim \{4, 8, 12, \ldots\}$.
   g. The range of a function is a subset of the codomain of the function.
   h. VI = IV in the Roman numeration system.
   i. ∸ represents one hundred six in the Mayan numeration system.
   j. $123 = 321$ in the Hindu–Arabic numeration system.
   k. "If a is related to b, then b is related to a" is an example of the reflexive property.
   l. The ordered pair $(6, 24)$ satisfies the relation "is a factor of."

2. How many different symbols would be necessary for a base nineteen system?

3. Explain what it means for two sets to be disjoint.

4. List six different representations of a function.

Skill

5. For $A = \{a, b, c\}$, $B = \{b, c, d, e\}$, $C = \{d, e, f, g\}$, $D = \{e, f, g\}$, find each of the following.

   a. $A \cup B$ **b.** $A \cap C$

   c. $A \cap B$ **d.** $A \times D$

   e. $C - D$ **f.** $(B \cap D) \cup (A \cap C)$

6. Write the equivalent Hindu–Arabic base ten numeral for each of the following numerals.

   a. ∩∩∩|| (Egyptian)   **b.** CMXLIV (Roman)

   c. ⠶ (Mayan)   **d.**
   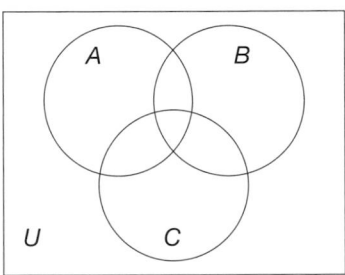

   e. 10101_{two} **f.** ET_{twelve}

7. Express the following in expanded form.

   a. 759   **b.** 7002   **c.** 1001001_{two}

8. Shade the region in the following Venn diagram to represent the set $A - \overline{(B \cup C)}$.

9. Rewrite the base ten number 157 in each of the following number systems that were described in this chapter.

   Babylonian:

   Roman:

   Egyptian:

   Mayan:

10. Write a base five numeral for the following set of base five blocks. (Make all possible trades first.)

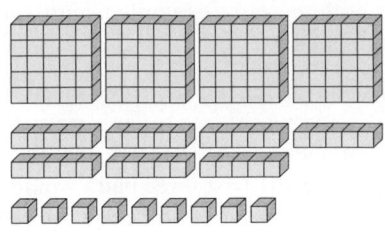

11. Represent the shaded region using the appropriate set notation.

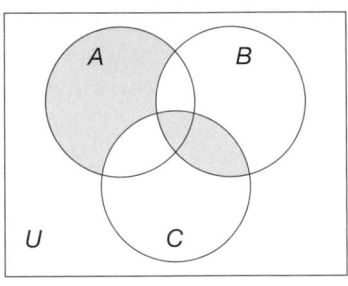

12. Express the following relations using ordered pairs, and determine which satisfy the symmetric property.

   a.

   b.

   c.
   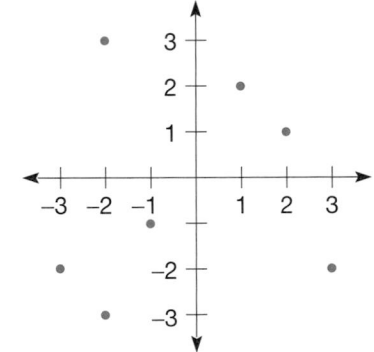

Understanding

13. Use the Roman and Hindu–Arabic systems to explain the difference between a *positional* numeration system and a *place-value* numeration system.

14. Determine conditions, if any, on nonempty sets A and B so that the following equalities will be true.

a. $A \cup B = B \cup A$ b. $A \cap B = B \cap A$

c. $A - B = B - A$ d. $A \times B = B \times A$

15. If (a, b) and (c, d) are in $A \times B$, name four elements in $B \times A$.

16. Show why the sequence that begins 2, 6, . . . could be either an arithmetic or a geometric sequence.

17. Explain two distinctive features of the Mayan number system as compared to the other three non-Hindu–Arabic number systems described in this chapter.

18. Given the universal set of $\{1, 2, 3, \ldots, 20\}$ and sets A, B, and C as described, place all of the numbers from the universal set in the appropriate location on the following Venn diagram.

$A = \{2, 4, 0, 1, 3, 5, 6\}$,
$B = \{10, 11, 12, 1, 2, 7, 6, 14\}$,
$C = \{18, 19, 6, 11, 16, 12, 9, 8\}$

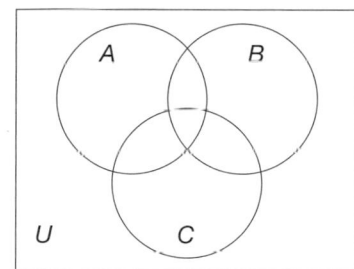

19. Let $A = \{x | x$ is a letter in the alphabet$\}$ and $B = \{10, 11, 12, \ldots, 40\}$. Is it possible to have 1-1 correspondence between sets A and B? If so, describe the correspondence. If not, explain why not.

20. Which of the following arrow diagrams represent functions from set A to set B? If one does not represent a function, explain why not.

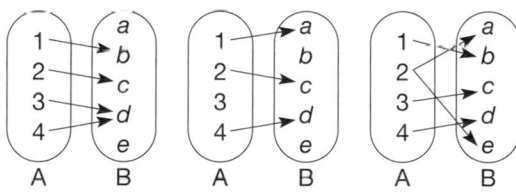

21. Represent the numeral 1212_{three} with base three blocks and chips on a chip abacus.

22. If the relation $\{(1, 2), (2, 1), (3, 4), (?, 4), (4, 2), (4, 3)\}$ on the set $\{1, 2, 3, 4\}$ is to be altered to have the properties listed, what other ordered pairs, if any, are needed?

a. Reflexive   b. Symmetric

c. Transitive   d. Reflexive and transitive

Problem Solving / Application

23. If $n(A) = 71$, $n(B) = 53$, $n(A \cap B) = 27$, what is $n(A \cup B)$?

24. Find the smallest values for a and b so that $21_b = 25_a$.

25. The 9th term of an arithmetic sequence is 59 and the 13th term is 87. What is the initial term of this sequence?

26. Joelle specializes in laying tiles in a certain tile pattern for square floors. This pattern is shown in the following diagrams. She buys her tiles from Taren's Floor Coverings at a rate of $4 a tile for gray tiles and $3 a tile for white tiles.

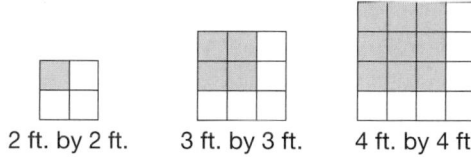

2 ft. by 2 ft.   3 ft. by 3 ft.   4 ft. by 4 ft.

a. Using these 1 foot-by-1 foot tiles from Taren's and the pattern shown, how much would it cost Joelle to buy tiles for an 8 foot-by-8 foot room?

b. To make it easier to give her customers quotes for materials, Joelle wants to find an equation that gives the cost, C, of materials as a function of the dimensions, n, of a square room. Find the equation that Joelle needs.

$$C(n) =$$

27. Find the 47th term and the nth term of the following sequence.

$$3, 7, 11, 15, 19, \ldots$$

28. The following set of ordered pairs represent a function.

$$\{(1, 2), (2, 4), (3, 8), (4, 16), (5, 32), (6, 64)\}$$

Represent this function as

a. an arrow diagram

b. a table

c. a graph

d. a formula

29. Your approximate ideal exercise heart rate is determined as follows: Subtract your age from 220 and multiply this by 0.75. Find a formula that expresses this exercise heart rate as related to one's age.

References for Reflections from Research

ADAMS, T. L. (1993). *The effects of graphing calculators and a model for conceptual change on community college students' concept of function,* Unpublished doctoral dissertation, University of Florida.

BAROODY, A. J., GANNON, K. E., BERENT, R., & GINSBURG, H. P. (1983). The development of basic formal math abilities. *Acta Paedologica, 1*, 133–151.

BAROODY, A. J., & GATZKE, M. R. (1991). The estimate of set size by potentially gifted kindergarten-age children. *Journal for Research in Mathematics Education, 22*, 59–68.

FUSON, K. C. (1990). *Children's counting and concepts of number.* New York: Springer-Verlag.

FUSON, K. C. (1990). Conceptual structures for multidigit numbers: Implications for learning and teaching multidigit addition, subtraction and place-value. *Cognition and Instruction, 7*, 343–403.

GOLDENBERG, E. P., HARVEY, W., LEWIS, P. G., UMIKER, R. J., WEST, J., & ZODHIATES, P. (1988). *Mathematical, technical, and pedagogical challenges in the graphical representation of functions* (Tech. Report No. 88-4). Cambridge, MA: Educational Technology Center, Harvard Graduate School of Education.

WANG, M. C., RESNICK, L. B., & BOOZER, R. F. (1971). The sequence of development of some early mathematics behaviors. *Child Development, 42*, 1767–1778.

WHEELER, M. M. (1987). Research into practice: Children's understanding of zero and infinity. *Arithmetic Teacher, 35*, 42–44.

CHAPTER 3

Whole Numbers: Operations and Properties

Calculation Devices Versus Written Algorithms: A Debate Through Time

The Hindu–Arabic numeration system can be traced back to 250 B.C. However, it was about A.D. 800 when a complete Hindu system was described in a book by the Persian mathematician al-Khowarizimi. Although the Hindu–Arabic numerals, as well as the Roman numeral system, were used to represent numbers, they were not used for computations, mainly because of the lack of inexpensive, convenient writing equipment such as paper and pencil. In fact, the Romans used a sophisticated abacus or "sand tray" made of a board with small pebbles (calculi) that slid in grooves as their calculator. Another form of the abacus was a wooden frame with beads sliding on thin rods, much like those used by the Chinese and Japanese.

From about A.D. 1100 to 1500 there was a great debate among Europeans regarding calculation. Those who advocated the use of Roman numerals along with the abacus were called the *abacists*. Those who advocated using the Hindu–Arabic numeration system together with written algorithms such as the ones we use today were called *algorists*. About 1500, the algorists won the argument and by the eighteenth century, there was no trace of the abacus in western Europe. However, parts of the world—notably, China, Japan, Russia, and some Arabian countries—continued to use a form of the abacus.

An algorithm vs. an abacus

It is interesting, though, that in the 1970s and 1980s, technology produced the inexpensive, hand-held calculator, which rendered many forms of written algorithms obsolete. Yet the debate continues regarding what role the calculator should play in arithmetic. Could it be that a debate will be renewed between algorists and the modern-day abacists (or "calculatorists")? Is it possible that we may someday return to being "abacists" by using our Hindu–Arabic system to record numbers while using calculators to perform all but simple mental calculations? Let's hope that it does not take us 400 years to decide the appropriate balance between written and electronic calculations!

Problem Solving Strategies

1. Guess and Test
2. Use a Variable
3. Draw a Picture
4. Look for a Pattern
5. Make a List
6. Solve a Simpler Problem
7. Draw a Diagram
8. Use Direct Reasoning

Strategy
Use Direct Reasoning

The Use Direct Reasoning strategy is used virtually all the time in conjunction with other strategies when solving problems. Direct reasoning is used to reach a valid conclusion from a series of statements. Often, statements involving direct reasoning are of the form "If A then B." Once this statement is shown to be true, statement B will hold whenever statement A does. (An expanded discussion of reasoning is contained in the Logic section near the end of the book.) In the following initial problem, no computations are required. That is, a solution can be obtained merely by using direct reasoning, and perhaps by drawing pictures.

Initial Problem

In a group of nine coins, eight weigh the same and the ninth is either heavier or lighter. Assume that the coins are identical in appearance. Using a pan balance, what is the smallest number of balancings needed to identify the heavy coin?

3 groups (pg 131)

Clue

The Use Direct Reasoning strategy may be appropriate when

- A proof is required.
- A statement of the form "If . . . , then . . ." is involved.
- You see a statement that you want to imply from a collection of known conditions.

A solution of the Initial Problem appears on page 131.

8. *Doubles ±1 and ±2*: This technique overlaps with the others. Many children use it effectively. For example, $7 + 8 = 7 + 7 + 1 = 14 + 1 = 15$, or $8 + 7 = 8 + 8 - 1 = 15$; $5 + 7 = 5 + 5 + 2 = 10 + 2 = 12$, and so on.

By using thinking strategies 6, 7, and 8, the remaining basic addition facts needed to complete the table in Figure 3.12 can be determined.

Example 3.2   Use thinking strategies in three different ways to find the sum of $9 + 7$.

Solution

a. $9 + 7 = 9 + (1 + 6) = (9 + 1) + 6 = 10 + 6 = 16$
b. $9 + 7 = (8 + 1) + 7 = 8 + (1 + 7) = 8 + 8 = 16$
c. $9 + 7 = (2 + 7) + 7 = 2 + (7 + 7) = 2 + 14 = 16$ ■

NCTM Standards 2000
Number and Operations
Grades Pre-K–2
All students should develop fluency with basic number combinations for addition and subtraction.

Thus far we have been adding single-digit numbers. However, thinking strategies can be applied to multidigit addition also. Figure 3.13 illustrates how multidigit addition is an extension of single-digit addition. The only difference is that instead of adding units each time, we might be adding longs, flats, and so on. Mentally combine similar pieces, and then exchange as necessary.

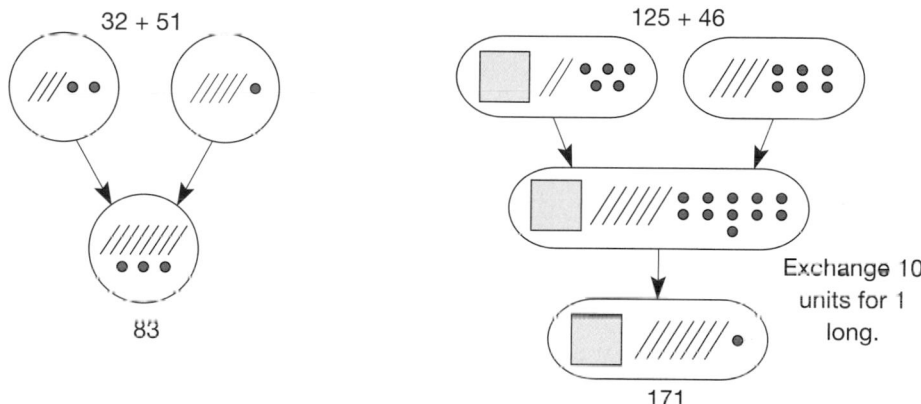

Figure 3.13

The next example illustrates how thinking strategies can be applied to multidigit numbers.

Example 3.3   Using thinking strategies, find the following sums.

a. $42 + 18$ b. $37 + (42 + 13)$ c. $51 + 39$

Solution

a. $42 + 18 = (40 + 2) + (10 + 8)$ *Addition*
$ = (40 + 10) + (2 + 8)$ *Commutativity and associativity*
$ = 50 + 10$ *Place value and combination to 10*
$ = 60$ *Addition*
b. $37 + (42 + 13) = 37 + (13 + 42)$
$ = (37 + 13) + 42$
$ = 50 + 42$
$ = 92$

c. $51 + 39 = (50 + 1) + 39$
$= 50 + (1 + 39)$
$= 50 + 40$
$= 90$

■

The use of other number bases can help you simulate how these thinking strategies are experienced by students when they learn base ten arithmetic. Perhaps the two most powerful thinking strategies, especially when used together, are associativity and combinations to the base (base ten above). For example, $7_{nine} + 6_{nine} = 7_{nine} + (2_{nine} + 4_{nine}) = (7_{nine} + 2_{nine}) + 4_{nine} = 14_{nine}$ (since the sum of 7_{nine} and 2_{nine} is one of the base in base nine), $4_{six} + 5_{six} = 3_{six} + 1_{six} + 5_{six} = 13_{six}$ (since $1_{six} + 5_{six}$ is one of the base in base six), and so on.

Example 3.4 Compute the following sums using thinking strategies.

a. $7_{eight} + 3_{eight}$ **b.** $5_{seven} + 4_{seven}$ **c.** $9_{twelve} + 9_{twelve}$

Solution

a. $7_{eight} + 3_{eight} = 7_{eight} + (1_{eight} + 2_{eight}) = (7_{eight} + 1_{eight}) + 2_{eight} = 12_{eight}$
b. $5_{seven} + 4_{seven} = 5_{seven} + (2_{seven} + 2_{seven}) = (5_{seven} + 2_{seven}) + 2_{seven} = 12_{seven}$
c. $9_{twelve} + 9_{twelve} = 9_{twelve} + (3_{twelve} + 6_{twelve}) = (9_{twelve} + 3_{twelve}) + 6_{twelve} = 16_{twelve}$

Notice how associativity and combinations to the base are used.

■

Subtraction

The Take-Away Approach There are two distinct approaches to subtraction. The take-away approach is often used to introduce children to the concept of subtraction. The problem "If you have 5 coins and spend 2, how many do you have left?" can be solved with a set model using the take-away approach. Also, the problem "If you walk 5 miles from home and turn back to walk 2 miles toward home, how many miles are you from home?" can be solved with a measurement model using the take-away approach (Figure 3.14).

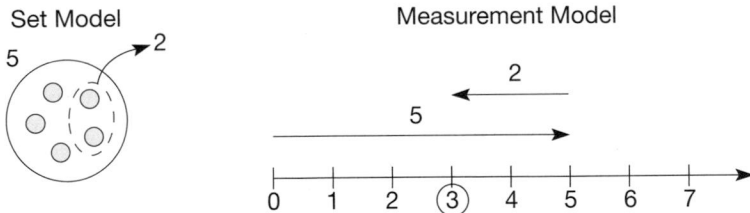

Figure 3.14

This approach can be stated using sets.

● DEFINITION

Subtraction of Whole Numbers: Take-Away Approach

Let a and b be any whole numbers and A and B be sets such that $a = n(A)$, $b = n(B)$, and $B \subseteq A$. Then

$$a - b = n(A - B).$$

NCTM Standards 2000
Number and Operations
Grades Pre-K–2
All students should understand
various meanings of addition and
subtraction of whole numbers and
the relationship between the two
operations.

The number "$a - b$" is called the **difference** and is read "a minus b," where a is called the **minuend** and b the **subtrahend.** To find $7 - 3$ using sets, think of a set with seven elements, say $\{a, b, c, d, e, f, g\}$. Then, using set difference, take away a subset of three elements, say $\{a, b, c\}$. The result is the set $\{d, e, f, g\}$, so $7 - 3 = 4$.

The Missing-Addend Approach The second method of subtraction, which is called the missing-addend approach, is often used when making change. For example, if an item costs 76 cents and 1 dollar is tendered, a clerk will often hand back the change by adding up and saying "76 plus *four* is 80, and *twenty* is a dollar" as four pennies and two dimes are returned. This method is illustrated in Figure 3.15.

Reflection from Research
Children frequently have difficulty
with missing-addend problems
when they are not related to word
problems. A common answer to
$5 + ? = 8$ is 13 (Kamii, 1985).

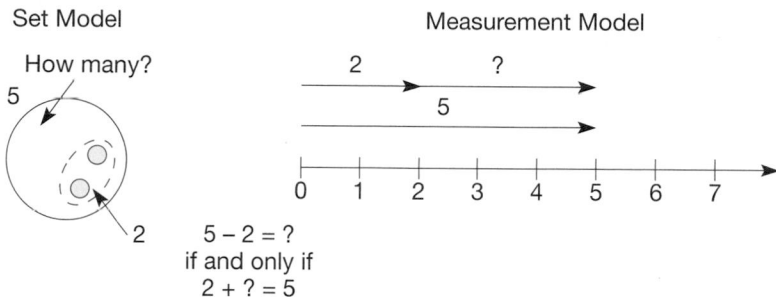

Figure 3.15

Since $2 + \mathbf{3} = 5$ in each case in Figure 3.15, we know that $5 - 2 = \mathbf{3}.$

◆ ALTERNATIVE DEFINITION

Subtraction of Whole Numbers: Missing-Addend Approach

Let a and b be any whole numbers. Then $a - b = c$ if and only if $a = b + c$ for some whole number c.

In this alternative definition of subtraction, c is called the **missing addend.** The missing-addend approach to subtraction is very useful for learning subtraction facts because it shows how to relate them to the addition facts via **four-fact families** (Figure 3.16).

Notice that this alternative definition of subtraction does *not* guarantee that there is an answer for every whole-number subtraction problem. For example, there is no whole number c such that $3 = 4 + c$, so the problem $3 - 4$ has no whole-number answer. Another way of expressing this idea is to say that the set of whole numbers is *not* closed under subtraction.

Finally, the reason for learning to add and subtract is to be able to solve problems. In particular, it is crucial to decide which operations to use in solving a problem. Consider the problem "If Larry has \$7 and Judy has \$3, how much more money does Larry have?" Neither the take-away approach nor the missing-addend approach can be applied literally, since Judy's \$3 is not a subset of Larry's \$7. However, Judy's three dollars can be matched with three of Larry's \$7, leaving a difference of 4 (Figure 3.17). This approach to subtraction is called the **comparison approach.** In this approach we begin with two distinct sets. Then we match the elements of the set having fewer elements with a subset of the larger set and apply either the take-away or missing-addend approach to find the difference. We can solve the preceding problem by rephrasing it in missing-addend format:

$$3 + c = 7 \text{ so } c = 7 - 3 = 4.$$

+	0 1 2 3 4 5 6 7 8 9
0	
1	
2	
3	
4	
5	8
6	
7	
8	
9	

Four fact family:
$5 + 3 = 8$
$3 + 5 = 8$
$8 - 5 = 3$
$8 - 3 = 5$

Figure 3.16

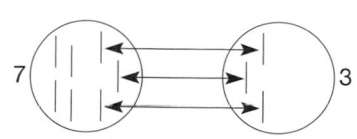

Figure 3.17

MATHEMATICAL MORSEL

Benjamin Franklin was known for his role in politics and as an inventor. One of his mathematical discoveries was an 8-by-8 square made up of the counting numbers from 1 to 64. Check out the following properties:

1. All rows and columns total 260.
2. All half-rows and half-columns total 130.
3. The four corners total 130
4. The sum of the corners in any 4-by-4 or 6-by-6 array is 130.
5. Every 2-by-2 array of four numbers total 130.

(NOTE: There are 49 of these 2-by-2 arrays!)

Section 3.1 EXERCISE / PROBLEM SET A

EXERCISES

1. **a.** Draw a figure similar to Figure 3.1 to find $4 + 3$.
   b. Find $3 + 5$ using a number line.

2. For which of the following pairs of sets is it true that $n(D) + n(E) = n(D \cup E)$?
   a. $D = \{1, 2, 3, 4\}, E = \{7, 8, 9, 10\}$
   b. $D = \{\ \}, E = \{1\}$
   c. $D = \{a, b, c, d\}, E = \{d, c, b, a\}$

3. Which of the following sets are closed under addition? Why or why not?
   a. $\{0, 10, 20, 30, \ldots\}$ **b.** $\{0\}$
   c. $\{0, 1, 2\}$ **d.** $\{1, 2\}$
   e. Whole numbers greater than 17
   f. $\{0, 3, 6, 9, \ldots\}$ **g.** $\{1\}$
   h. $\{1, 5, 9, 13, \ldots\}$ **i.** $\{8, 12, 16, 20, \ldots\}$
   j. Whole numbers less than 17

4. Identify the property or properties being illustrated.
   a. $1279 + 3847$ must be a whole number.
   b. $7 + 5 = 5 + 7$
   c. $53 + 47 = 50 + 50$
   d. $1 + 0 = 1$
   e. $1 + 0 = 0 + 1$
   f. $(53 + 48) + 7 = 60 + 48$

5. What property or properties justify that you get the same answer to the following problem whether you add "up" (starting with $9 + 8$) or "down" (starting with $3 + 8$)?

$$\begin{array}{r} 3 \\ 8 \\ +9 \\ \hline \end{array}$$

6. For the following figures, identify the problem being illustrated, the model, and the conceptual approach being used.
   a.

   b.

   c

7. Look for easy combinations of numbers to compute the following sums mentally. Show the groupings you used.
   a. $94 + 27 + 6 + 13$ **b.** $5 + 13 + 25 + 31 + 47$

8. **a.** State the difference of $8 - 3$ in terms of both definitions of subtraction given in this section.

b. Illustrate the missing-addend approach for $8 - 3$ using a measurement model and a set model.

c. Illustrate the take-away approach for $8 - 3$ using a set model and a measurement model.

d. Illustrate the comparison approach for $8 - 3$ using a set model.

9. Which of the following subtraction problems can be obtained immediately from an addition facts table?

a. $\begin{array}{r} 11 \\ -9 \\ \hline \end{array}$ **b.** $\begin{array}{r} 8 \\ -2 \\ \hline \end{array}$ **c.** $\begin{array}{r} 34 \\ -16 \\ \hline \end{array}$

d. $\begin{array}{r} 17 \\ -9 \\ \hline \end{array}$ **e.** $\begin{array}{r} 111 \\ -52 \\ \hline \end{array}$ **f.** $\begin{array}{r} 12 \\ -0 \\ \hline \end{array}$

10. Using different-shaped boxes for variables provides a transition to algebra as well as a means of stating problems. Try some whole numbers in the boxes to determine whether these properties hold.

a. Is subtraction closed?

$$\square - \triangle \overset{?}{=} \bigcirc$$

b. Is subtraction commutative?

$$\square - \triangle \overset{?}{=} \triangle - \square$$

c. Is subtraction associative?

$$(\square - \triangle) - \bigcirc \overset{?}{=} \square - (\triangle - \bigcirc)$$

d. Is there an identity element for subtraction?

$$\square - \triangle = \square \text{ and } \triangle - \square - \square$$

11. Each situation described next involves a subtraction problem. In each case, tell whether the problem situation is best represented by the take-away model, the missing-addend model, or the comparison approach, and why. Then write an appropriate equation to fit the situation.

a. An elementary teacher started the year with a budget of $200 to be spent on manipulatives. By the end of December, $120 had been spent. How much money remained in the budget?

b. Doreen planted 24 tomato plants in her garden and Justin planted 18 tomato plants in his garden. How many more plants did Doreen plant?

c. Tami is saving money for a trip to Hawaii over spring break. The package tour she is interested in costs $1795. From her part-time job she has saved $1240 so far. How much more money must she save?

12. a. Complete the following addition table in base five. Remember to use the thinking strategies.

+	0	1	2	3	4
0					
1					
2			(base five)		
3					
4					

b. For each of the following subtraction problems in base five, rewrite the problem using the missing-addend approach and find the answer in the table.

i. $13_{\text{five}} - 4_{\text{five}}$ **ii.** $11_{\text{five}} - 3_{\text{five}}$

iii. $12_{\text{five}} - 4_{\text{five}}$ **iv.** $10_{\text{five}} - 2_{\text{five}}$

13. Complete the following four-fact families in *base five*.

a. $3_{\text{five}} + 4_{\text{five}} = 12_{\text{five}}$

_____

_____

_____

b.

_____

$4_{\text{five}} + 1_{\text{five}} = 10_{\text{five}}$

_____

_____

c. _____

_____

$11_{\text{five}} - 4_{\text{five}} = 2_{\text{five}}$

_____

PROBLEMS

14. A given set contains the number 1. What other numbers must also be in the set if it is closed under addition?

15. The number 100 can be expressed using the nine digits 1, 2, ..., 9 with plus and minus signs as follows:

$$1 + 2 + 3 - 4 + 5 + 6 + 78 + 9 = 100$$

Find a sum of 100 using each of the nine digits and only three plus or minus signs.

16. Complete the following magic square in which the sum of each row, each column, and each diagonal is the

same. When completed, the magic square should contain each of the numbers 10 through 25 exactly once.

25			
		19	17
18	16		
	23		10

17. Magic squares are not the only magic figures. The following figure is a magic hexagon. What is "magic" about it?

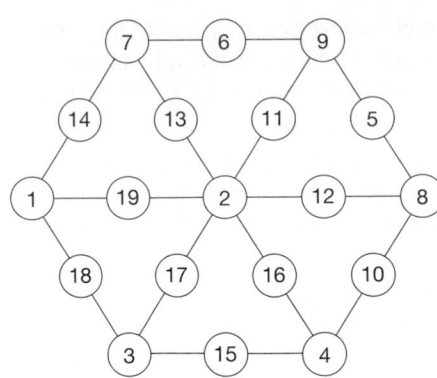

18. A **palindrome** is any number that reads the same backward and forward. For example, 262 and 37673 are palindromes. In the accompanying example, the process of reversing the digits and adding the two numbers has been repeated until a palindrome is obtained.

$$
\begin{array}{r}
67 \\
+\ 76 \\
\hline
143 \\
+341 \\
\hline
484
\end{array}
$$

a. Try this method with the following numbers.

    i. 39   **ii.** 87   **iii.** 32

b. Find a number for which the procedure takes more than three steps to obtain a palindrome.

19. Mr. Morgan has five daughters. They were all born the number of years apart as the youngest daughter is old. The oldest daughter is 16 years older than the youngest. What are the ages of Mr. Morgan's daughters?

20. Using the Chapter 3 eManipulative activity, *Number Puzzles* exercise 1, arrange the numbers 1, 2, 3, 4, 5, 6, 7, 8, 9 in the circles below so the sum of the numbers along each line of four is 17.

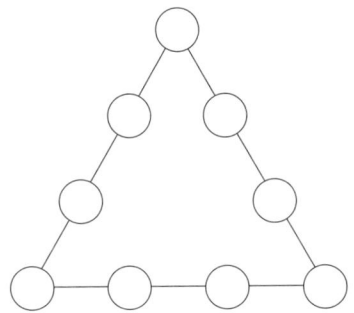

![Section 3.1] **Section 3.1**   **EXERCISE / PROBLEM SET B**

EXERCISES

1. Show that $2 + 6 = 8$ using two different types of models.

2. For which of the following pairs of sets is it true that $n(D) + n(E) = n(D \cup E)$?

  a. $D = \{a, c, e, g\}, E = \{b, d, f, g\}$

  b. $D = \{\ \}, E = \{\ \}$

  c. $D = \{1, 3, 5, 7\}, E = \{2, 4, 6\}$

3. Suppose that S is a set of whole numbers closed under addition. S contains 3, 27, and 72.

  a. List six other elements in S.

  b. Why must 24 be in S?

4. Each of the following is an example of one of the properties for addition of whole numbers. Fill in the blank to complete the statement, and identify the property.

  a. $5 + \underline{\hspace{1em}} = 5$

  b. $7 + 5 = \underline{\hspace{1em}} + 7$

  c. $(4 + 3) + 6 = 4 + (\underline{\hspace{1em}} + 6)$

  d. $(4 + 3) + 6 = \underline{\hspace{1em}} + (4 + 3)$

  e. $(4 + 3) + 6 = (3 + \underline{\hspace{1em}}) + 6$

  f. $2 + 9$ is a $\underline{\hspace{1em}}$ number.

5. Addition can be simplified using the associative property of addition. For example,

$$
\begin{aligned}
26 + 57 &= 26 + (4 + 53) = (26 + 4) + 53 \\
&= 30 + 53 = 83.
\end{aligned}
$$

Complete the following statements.

  a. $39 + 68 = 40 + \underline{\hspace{1em}} = \underline{\hspace{1em}}$

  b. $25 + 56 = 30 + \underline{\hspace{1em}} = \underline{\hspace{1em}}$

  c. $47 + 23 = 50 + \underline{\hspace{1em}} = \underline{\hspace{1em}}$

6. For the following figures, identify the problem being illustrated, the model, and the conceptual approach being used.

  a.

b.

How many?

c.

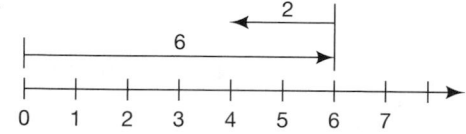

7. Without performing the addition, determine which sum (if either) is larger. What properties are you using?

$$\begin{array}{r} 3261 \\ 4287 \\ +5193 \\ \hline \end{array} \qquad \begin{array}{r} 4187 \\ 5291 \\ +3263 \\ \hline \end{array}$$

8. In the following figure, centimeter strips are used to illustrate $3 + 8 = 11$. What two subtraction problems are also being represented? What definition of subtraction is being demonstrated?

	10		1
	3		8

9. Rewrite each of the following subtraction problems as an addition problem.

a. $x - 156 = 279$ **b.** $279 - 156 = x$

c. $279 - x = 156$

10. For each of the following, determine whole numbers x, y, and z that make the statement true.

a. $x - 0 = 0 - x = x$

b. $x - y = y - x$

c. $(x - y) - z = x - (y - z)$

Which, if any, are true for all whole numbers x, y, and z?

11. Each situation described next involves a subtraction problem. In each case, tell whether the problem situation is best represented by the take-away approach, the missing-addend approach, or the comparison approach, and why. Then write an appropriate equation to fit the situation.

a. Robby has accumulated a collection of 362 sports cards. Chris has a collection of 200 cards. How many more cards than Chris does Robby have?

b. Jack is driving from St. Louis to Kansas City for a meeting, a total distance of 250 miles. After 2 hours he notices that he has traveled 114 miles. How far is he from Kansas City at that time?

c. An elementary school library consists of 1095 books. As of May 8, 105 books were checked out of the library. How many books were still available for checkout on May 8?

12. a. Complete the following addition table in base six. Remember to use the thinking strategies.

+	0	1	2	3	4	5
0						
1						
2				(base six)		
3						
4						
5						

b. For each of the following subtraction problems in base six, rewrite the problem using the missing–addend approach and find the answer in the table.

i. $13_{six} - 5_{six}$ **ii.** $5_{six} - 4_{six}$

iii. $12_{six} - 4_{six}$ **iv.** $10_{six} - 2_{six}$

13. Using the addition table for base six given in Exercise 12, write the following four-fact families in base six.

a. $2_{six} + 3_{six} = 5_{six}$ **b.** $11_{six} - 5_{six} = 2_{six}$

PROBLEMS

14. A given set contains the number 5. What other numbers must also be in the set if it is closed under addition?

15. The following figure can provide practice in addition and subtraction. The figure is completed by filling the upper two circles with the sums obtained by adding diagonally.

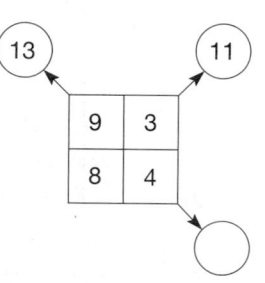

$9 + 4 = 13$ and $8 + 3 = 11$

The circle at the lower right is filled in one of two ways:

1. Adding the numbers in the upper circles:

$$13 + 11 = 24$$

2. Adding across the rows, adding down the columns, and then adding the results in each case:

$$12 + 12 = 24 \quad \text{and} \quad 17 + 7 = 24$$

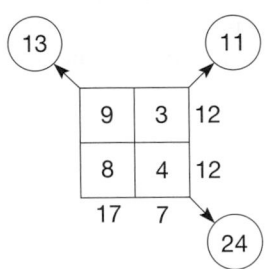

a. Fill in the missing numbers for the following figure.

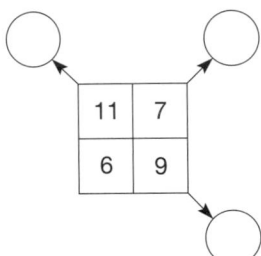

b. Fill in the missing numbers for the following figure.

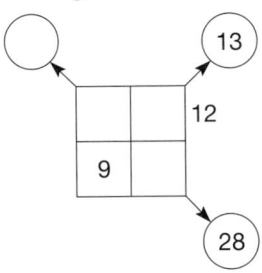

c. Use variables to show why the sum of the numbers in the upper two circles will always be the same as the sum of the two rows and the sum of the two columns.

16. Arrange numbers 1 to 10 around the outside of the circle shown so that the sum of any two adjacent numbers is the same as the sum of the two numbers on the other ends of the spokes. As an example, 6 and 9, 8 and 7 might be placed as shown, since $6 + 9 = 8 + 7$.

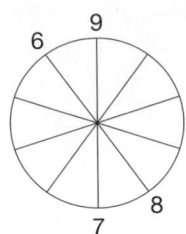

17. Place the numbers 1–16 in the cells of the following magic square so that the sum of each row, column, and diagonal is the same.

	2		
5			8
	7	6	
		15	1

18. Using the Chapter 3 eManipulative activity, *Number Puzzles* exercise 3, arrange the numbers 1, 2, 3, 4, 5, 6, 7, 8, 9 in the circles below so the sum of the numbers along each line of three is 15.

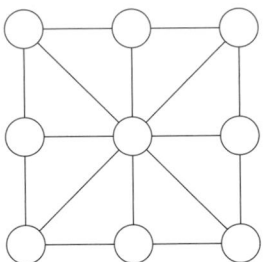

19. Shown here is a magic triangle discovered by the mental calculator Marathe. What is its magic?

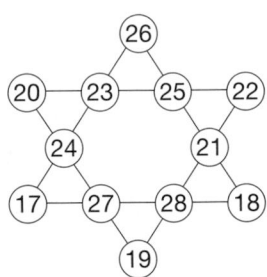

20. The property "If $a + c = b + c$, then $a = b$" is called the **additive cancellation property.** Is this property true for all whole numbers? If it is, how would you convince your students that it is always true? If not, give a counterexample.

PROBLEMS FOR WRITING/DISCUSSION

1. One of your students says, "When I added 27 and 36, I made the 27 a 30, then I added the 30 and the 36 and got 66, and then subtracted the 3 from the beginning and got 63." Another student says, "But when I added 27 and 36, I added the 20 and the 30 and got 50, then I knew 6 plus 6 was 12 so 6 plus 7 was 13, and then I

added 50 and 13 and got 63." Can you follow the students' reasoning here? How would you describe some of their techniques?

2. Karen says, "I think of closure as a bunch of numbers locked in a room, and the operation, like addition, comes along and links two of the numbers together. As long as the answer is inside the room, the set is closed, but if they have to go outside the room to get a new number for the answer, the set is not closed. Like if you have to open the door, then the set is not closed."

How would you respond to Karen's analogy? Use as an example the set {0, 1} and the operation of addition.

3. We know that $8 - 3 = 5$. This example seems to indicate that the whole numbers are closed under subtraction. But it is also possible to give an example that indicates that the whole numbers are not closed under subtraction. Demonstrate such an example, and explain why your example "wins" over the first example (that is, proves that the whole numbers are not closed under subtraction).

3.2   MULTIPLICATION AND DIVISION

STARTING POINT

The ways of thinking about the operations in the following two word problems are conceptually different. Discuss what the difference is and how it might impact the way students solve the problem.

Joshua has 12 cups of flour to make cookies. Each batch of cookies calls for 3 cups of flour. How many batches can Joshua make?

Emily made 8 loaves of bread to share with her 4 neighbors. If she gives the same amount of bread to each neighbor, how many loaves does each neighbor get?

Multiplication and Its Properties

There are many ways to view multiplication.

Reflection from Research
Children can solve a variety of multiplicative problems long before being formally introduced to multiplication and division (Mulligan & Mitchelmore, 1995).

Reflection from Research
When multiplication is represented by repeated addition, students have a great deal of difficulty keeping track of the two sets of numbers. For instance, when considering how many sets of three there are in fifteen, students need to keep track of counting up the threes and how many sets of three they count (Steffe, 1988).

Repeated-Addition Approach   Consider the following problems: There are five children, and each has three silver dollars. How many silver dollars do they have altogether? The silver dollars are about 1 inch wide. If the silver dollars are laid in a single row with each dollar touching the next, what is the length of the row? These problems can be modeled using the set model and the measurement model (Figure 3.18).

Figure 3.18

These models look similar to the ones that we used for addition, since we are merely adding repeatedly. They show that $3 + 3 + 3 + 3 + 3 = 15$, or that $5 \times 3 = 15$.

Reflection from Research
Multiplicative thinking is clearly distinguishable from additive thinking. Multiplicative thinking appears early (among 45% of second graders) and develops slowly (Clark & Kamii, 1996).

DEFINITION

Multiplication of Whole Numbers: Repeated-Addition Approach

Let a and b be any whole numbers where $a \neq 0$. Then

$$ab = \underbrace{b + b \cdots + b}_{a \text{ addends}}$$

If $a = 1$, then $ab = 1 \cdot b = b$; also $0 \cdot b = 0$ for all b.

Since multiplication combines two numbers to form a single number, it is a binary operation. The number **ab**, read "**a times b**," is called the **product** of a and b. The numbers a and b are called **factors** of ab. The product ab can also be written as "**a · b**" and "**a × b**". Notice that $0 \cdot b = 0$ for all b. That is, the product of zero and any whole number is zero.

Rectangular Array Approach   If the silver dollars in the preceding problem are arranged in a rectangular array, multiplication can be viewed in a slightly different way (Figure 3.19).

Reflection from Research
It is assumed that children automatically view two-dimensional rectangular arrays of squares as a row-by-column structure, but such structures must be personally constructed by each individual. This may affect how multiplication is introduced (Battista, Clements, Arnoff, Battista, & Van Auken Borrow, 1998).

Rectangular Array Approach
Set Model   Measurement Model

Figure 3.19

**NCTM Standards 2000
Number and Operations
Grades 3–5**
All students should understand various meanings of multiplication and division.

ALTERNATIVE DEFINITION

Multiplication of Whole Numbers: Rectangular Array Approach

Let a and b be any whole numbers. Then ab is the number of elements in a rectangular array having a rows and b columns.

Cartesian Product Approach   A third way of viewing multiplication is an abstraction of this array approach.

Reflection from Research
There appears to be a consistent progression through the basic intuitive models for multiplication and division. The progression is from direct counting to repeated addition or subtraction to multiplicative operations (Mulligan & Mitchelmore, 1997).

ALTERNATIVE DEFINITION

Multiplication of Whole Numbers: Cartesian Product Approach

Let a and b be any whole numbers. If $a = n(A)$ and $b = n(B)$, then

$$ab = n(A \times B).$$

For example, to compute $2 \cdot 3$, let $2 = n(\{a, b\})$ and $3 = n(\{x, y, z\})$. Then $2 \cdot 3$ is the number of ordered pairs in $\{a, b\} \times \{x, y, z\}$. Because $\{a, b\} \times \{x, y, z\} = \{(a, x), (a, y), (a, z), (b, x), (b, y), (b, z)\}$ has six ordered pairs, we conclude that

$2 \cdot 3 = 6$. Actually, by arranging the pairs in an appropriate row and column configuration, this approach can also be viewed as the array approach, as illustrated next (Figure 3.20).

	x	y	z
a	(a, x)	(a, y)	(a, z)
b	(b, x)	(b, y)	(b, z)

Figure 3.20

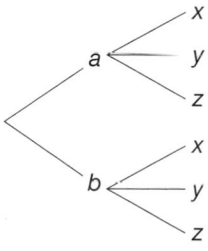

Figure 3.21

Tree Diagram Approach Another way of modeling this approach is through the use of a **tree diagram** (Figure 3.21). Tree diagrams are especially useful in the field of probability, which we study in Chapter 11.

Properties of Whole-Number Multiplication You have probably observed that whenever you multiplied any two whole numbers, your product was always a whole number. This fact is summarized by the following property.

PROPERTY

Closure Property for Multiplication of Whole Numbers

The product of two whole numbers is a whole number.

When two odd whole numbers are multiplied together, the product is odd; thus the set of odd numbers is closed under multiplication. Closure is a useful idea, since if we are multiplying two (or more) odd numbers and the product we calculate is even, we can conclude that our product is incorrect. The set $\{2, 5, 8, 11, 14, \ldots\}$ is not closed under multiplication, since $2 \cdot 5 = 10$ and 10 is not in the set.

The next property can be used to simplify learning the basic multiplication facts. For example, by the repeated-addition approach, 7×2 represents $2 + 2 + 2 + 2 + 2 + 2 + 2$, whereas 2×7 means $7 + 7$. Since $7 + 7$ was learned as an addition fact, viewing 7×2 as 2×7 makes this computation easier.

PROPERTY

Commutative Property for Whole-Number Multiplication

Let a and b be any whole numbers. Then

$$ab = ba.$$

Problem-Solving Strategy
Draw a Picture

The example in Figure 3.22 should convince you that the commutative property for multiplication is true.

Reflection from Research
If multiplication is viewed as computing area, children can see the commutative property relatively easily, but if multiplication is viewed as computing the price of a number of items, the commutative property is not obvious (Vergnaud, 1981).

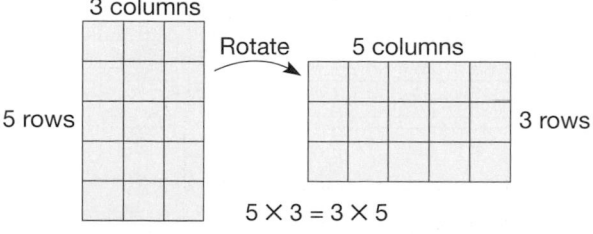

Figure 3.22

The product $5 \cdot (2 \cdot 13)$ is more easily found if it is viewed as $(5 \cdot 2) \cdot 13$. Regrouping to put the 5 and 2 together can be done because of the next property.

 PROPERTY

Associative Property for Whole-Number Multiplication

Let a, b, and c be any whole numbers. Then

$$a(bc) = (ab)c.$$

To illustrate the validity of the associative property for multiplication, consider the three-dimensional models in Figure 3.23.

Problem-Solving Strategy
Draw a Picture

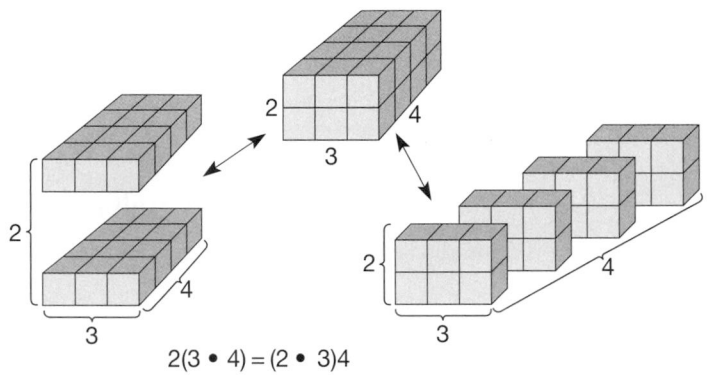

$$2(3 \cdot 4) = (2 \cdot 3)4$$

Figure 3.23

Reflection from Research
To further advance children's exploration of the properties of number systems, carefully designed situations that make mathematical properties relevant to the learner are necessary (Schliemann, Araujo, Cassundé, Macedo, & Nicéas, 1998).

The next property is an immediate consequence of each of our definitions of multiplication.

 PROPERTY

Identity Property for Whole-Number Multiplication

The number 1 is the unique whole-number such that for every whole number a,

$$a \cdot 1 = a = 1 \cdot a.$$

Because of this property, the number one is called the **multiplicative identity** or the **identity for multiplication.**

There is one other important property of the whole numbers. This property, distributivity, combines both multiplication and addition. Study the array model in Figure 3.24. This model shows that the *product of a sum*, $3(2 + 4)$, can be expressed as the *sum of products*, $(3 \cdot 2) + (3 \cdot 4)$. This relationship holds in general.

Problem-Solving Strategy
Draw a Picture

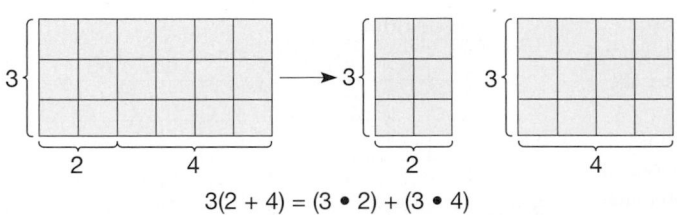

$$3(2 + 4) = (3 \cdot 2) + (3 \cdot 4)$$

Figure 3.24

NCTM Standards 2000
Number and Operations
Grades 3–5
All students should understand and use properties of operations such as the distributivity of multiplication over addition.

 PROPERTY

Distributive Property of Multiplication over Addition

Let a, b, and c be any whole numbers. Then

$$a(b + c) = ab + ac.$$

Because of commutativity, we can also write $(b + c)a = ba + ca$. Notice that the distributive property "distributes" the a to the b *and* the c.

Example 3.5 Rewrite each of the following expressions using the distributive property.

a. $3(4 + 5)$ **b.** $5 \cdot 7 + 5 \cdot 3$
c. $am + an$ **d.** $31 \cdot 76 + 29 \cdot 76$
e. $a(b + c + d)$

Solution

a. $3(4 + 5) = 3 \cdot 4 + 3 \cdot 5$ **b.** $5 \cdot 7 + 5 \cdot 3 = 5(7 + 3)$
c. $am + an = a(m + n)$ **d.** $31 \cdot 76 + 29 \cdot 76 = (31 + 29)76$
e. $a(b + c + d) = a(b + c) + ad = ab + ac + ad$ ■

Let's summarize the properties of whole-number addition and multiplication.

 PROPERTIES

Whole-Number Properties

PROPERTY	ADDITION	MULTIPLICATION
Closure	Yes	Yes
Commutativity	Yes	Yes
Associativity	Yes	Yes
Identity	Yes (zero)	Yes (one)
Distributivity of multiplication over addition		Yes

KNOW

In addition to these properties, we highlight the following property.

 PROPERTY

Multiplication Property of Zero

For every whole number, a,

$$a \cdot 0 = 0 \cdot a = 0.$$

Using the missing-addend approach to subtraction, we will show that $a(b - c) = ab - ac$ whenever $b - c$ is a whole number. In words, multiplication distributes over subtraction.

Let $\qquad b - c = n$

Then $\qquad b = c + n$ $\qquad$ *Missing addend*

$\qquad ab = a(c + n)$ $\qquad$ *Multiplication*

$\qquad ab = ac + an$ $\qquad$ *Distributivity*

Therefore, $\qquad ab - ac = an$ $\qquad$ *Missing addend from the first equation*

But $\qquad b - c = n$

So, substituting $b - c$ for n, we have

$$ab - ac = a(b - c).$$

◆ PROPERTY

Distributivity of Multiplication over Subtraction

Let a, b, and c be any whole numbers where $b \geq c$. Then

$$a(b - c) = ab - ac.$$

The following discussion shows how the properties are used to develop thinking strategies for learning the multiplication facts.

Thinking Strategies for Learning the Multiplication Facts The multiplication table in Figure 3.25 has $10 \times 10 = 100$ unfilled spaces.

1. *Commutativity*: As in the addition table, because of commutativity, only 55 facts in the unshaded region in Figure 3.26 have to be found.
2. *Multiplication by 0*: $a \cdot 0 = 0$ for all whole numbers a. Thus the first column is all zeros (Figure 3.27).
3. *Multiplication by 1*: $1 \cdot a = a \cdot 1 = a$. Thus the column labeled "1" is the same as the left-hand column outside the table (Figure 3.27).
4. *Multiplication by 2*: $2 \cdot a = a + a$, which are the doubles from addition (Figure 3.27).

We have filled in 27 facts using thinking strategies 1, 2, 3, and 4. Therefore, 28 facts remain to be found out of our original 55.

5. *Multiplication by 5*: The counting chant by fives, namely 5, 10, 15, 20, and so on, can be used to learn these facts (see the column and/or row headed by a 5 in Figure 3.28).
6. *Multiplication by 9*: The multiples of 9 are 9, 18, 27, 36, 45, 54, 63, 72, and 81 (Figure 3.28). Notice how the tens digit is one less than the number we are multiplying by 9. For example, the tens digit of $3 \cdot 9$ is 2 (one less than 3). Also, the sum of the digits of the multiples of 9 is 9. Thus $3 \cdot 9 = 27$ since $2 + 7 = 9$. The multiples of 5 and 9 eliminate 13 more facts, so 15 remain.
7. *Associativity and distributivity*: The remaining facts can be obtained using these two properties. For example, $8 \times 4 = 8 \times (2 \times 2) = (8 \times 2) \times 2 = 16 \times 2 = 32$ or $8 \times 4 = 8(2 + 2) = 8 \cdot 2 + 8 \cdot 2 = 16 + 16 = 32$.

In the next example we consider how knowledge of the basic facts and the properties can be applied to multiplying a single-digit number by a multidigit number.

Example 3.6 Compute the following products using thinking strategies.

a. 2×34 $\qquad$ **b.** $5(37 \cdot 2)$ $\qquad$ **c.** $7(25)$

Figure 3.25

Figure 3.26

55 facts

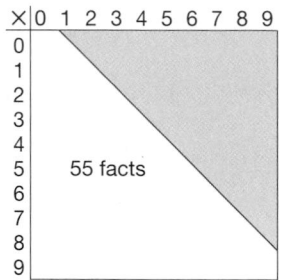

Figure 3.27

Figure 3.28

c. Exactly seven?

d. Exactly one?

e. Exactly six?

17. a. If $n^2 = 121$, what is n?

b. If $n^2 = 1,234,321$, what is n?

c. If $n^2 = 12,345,654,321$, what is n?

d. If $n^2 = 123,456,787,654,321$, what is n?

18. 12 is a factor of $10^2 - 2^2$, 27 is a factor of $20^2 - 7^2$, and 84 is a factor of $80^2 - 4^2$. Check to see whether these three statements are correct. Using a variable, prove why this works in general.

19. a. Verify that the property of less than and multiplication holds where $a = 3$, $b = 7$, and $c = 5$.

b. Show that the property does not hold if $c = 0$.

c. Give a formal proof of the property. (*Hint:* Use the fact that the product of two nonzero whole numbers is nonzero.)

d. State the corresponding property for division.

PROBLEMS FOR WRITING/DISCUSSION

1. If $7^3 \cdot 7^5 = 7^8$, and $3^5 \cdot 7^5 = 21^5$, then what does $7^3 \cdot 3^5$ equal? What rule could you formulate for such problems?

2. A student observes $0 + 0 = 0 \times 0$ and $2 + 2 = 2 \times 2$. Does that mean addition and multiplication are the same? Discuss.

3. Is it true that $(3^4)^2 = 3^{(4^2)}$? Explain. Find several examples where $(a^b)^c = a^{(b^c)}$.

END OF CHAPTER MATERIAL

Solution of Initial Problem

In a group of nine coins, eight weigh the same and the ninth is either heavier or lighter. Assume that the coins are identical in appearance. Using a pan balance, what is the smallest number of balancings needed to identify the counterfeit coin?

Strategy: Use Direct Reasoning

Three balancings are sufficient. Separate the coins into three groups of three coins each.

    A   *B*   *C*

Balance group A against group B. If they balance, we can deduce that the counterfeit coin is in group C. We then need to determine if the coin is heavier or lighter. Balance group C against group A. Based on whether group C goes up or down, we can deduce whether group C is light or heavy, respectively.

If the coins in group A do not balance the coins in group B, then we can conclude that either A is light or B is heavy (or vice versa). We now balance group A against group C. If they balance, we know that group B has the counterfeit coin. If group A and C do not balance, then group A has the counterfeit coin. We also know whether group A or B is light or heavy depending on which one went down on the first balancing.

In two balancings, we know which group of three coins contains the counterfeit one and whether the counterfeit coin is heavy or light. The third balancing will exactly identify the counterfeit coin.

From the group of three coins that has the counterfeit coin, select two coins and balance them against each other. This will determine which coin is the counterfeit one. Thus, the counterfeit coin can be found in three balancings.

Additional Problems Where the Strategy "Use Direct Reasoning" Is Useful

1. The sum of the digits of a three-digit palindrome is odd. Determine whether the middle digit is odd or is even.

2. Jose's room in a hotel was higher than Michael's but lower than Ralph's. Andre's room is on a floor between Ralph's and Jose's. If it weren't for Michael, Clyde's room would be the lowest. List the rooms from lowest to highest.

3. Given an 8-liter jug of water and empty 3-liter and 5-liter jugs, pour the water so that two of the jugs have 4 liters.

People in Mathematics

John Von Neumann (1903– 1957) John von Neumann was one of the most remarkable mathematicians of the twentieth century. His logical power was legendary. It is said that during and after World War II the U.S. government reached many scientific decisions simply by asking von Neumann for his opinion. Paul Halmos, his one-time assistant, said, "The most spectacular thing about Johnny was not his power as a mathematician, which was great, but his rapidity; he was very, very fast. And like the modern computer, which doesn't memorize logarithms, but computes them, Johnny didn't bother to memorize things. He computed them." Appropriately, von Neumann was one of the first to realize how a general-purpose computing machine—a computer—should be designed. In the 1950s he invented a "theory of automata," the basis for subsequent work in artificial intelligence.

Julia Bowman Robinson (1919– 1985) Julia Bowman Robinson spent her early years in Arizona, near Phoenix. She said that one of her earliest memories was of arranging pebbles in the shadow of a giant saguaro—"I've always had a basic liking for the natural numbers." In 1948, Robinson earned her doctorate in mathematics at Berkeley; she went on to contribute to the solution of "Hilbert's tenth problem." In 1975 she became the first woman mathematician elected to the prestigious National Academy of Sciences. Robinson also served as president of the American Mathematical Society, the main professional organization for research mathematicians. "Rather than being remembered as the first woman this or that, I would prefer to be remembered simply for the theorems I have proved and the problems I have solved."

CHAPTER REVIEW

Review the following terms and exercises to determine which require learning or relearning—page numbers are provided for easy reference.

SECTION 3.1: Addition and Subtraction

VOCABULARY/NOTATION

Plus 96	Associativity for addition 99	Minuend 103
Sum 96	Identity for addition 100	Subtrahend 103
Addend 96	Thinking strategies for addition	Missing-addend approach 103
Summand 96	facts 100	Missing addend 103
Binary operation 96	Take-away approach 102	Four-fact families 103
Closure for addition 97	Difference 103	Comparison approach 103
Commutativity for addition 97	Minus 103	

EXERCISES

1. Show how to find $5 + 4$ using
  a. a set model.   **b.** a measurement model.

2. Name the property of addition that is used to justify each of the following equations.
  a. $7 + (3 + 9) = (7 + 3) + 9$ **b.** $9 + 0 = 9$
  c. $13 + 27 = 27 + 13$
  d. $7 + 6$ is a whole number

3. Identify and use thinking strategies that can be used to find the following addition facts.
  a. $5 + 6$ **b.** $7 + 9$

4. Illustrate the following using $7 - 3$.
  a. The take-away approach
  b. The missing-addend approach

5. Show how the addition table for the facts 1 through 9 can be used to solve subtraction problems.

6. Which of the following properties hold for whole number subtraction?

   a. Closure   **b.** Commutative

   c. Associative   **d.** Identity

SECTION 3.2: Multiplication and Division

VOCABULARY / NOTATION

Repeated-addition approach   110
Product   110
Factor   110
Rectangular array approach   110
Cartesian product approach   110
Tree diagram approach   111
Closure for multiplication   111
Commutativity for
  multiplication   111
Associativity for
  multiplication   112

Identity for multiplication   112
Multiplicative identity   112
Distributive property   113
Multiplication property of
  zero   113
Distributivity of multiplication over
  subtraction   114
Thinking strategies for
  multiplication facts   114
Partitive division   115
Measurement division   115

Missing-factor approach   116
Dividend   116
Divisor   116
Quotient   116
Missing factor   116
Division property of zero   116
Division algorithm   117
Divisor   117
Quotient   117
Remainder   117
Repeated-subtraction approach   117

EXERCISES

1. Illustrate 3×5 using each of the following approaches.

   a. Repeated addition with the set model

   b. Repeated addition with the measurement model

   c. Rectangular array with the set model

   d. Rectangular array with the measurement model

2. Name the property of multiplication that is used to justify each of the following equations.

   a. $37 \times 1 = 37$

   b. $26 \times 5 = 5 \times 26$

   c. $2 \times (5 \times 17) = (2 \times 5) \times 17$

   d. 4×9 is a whole number

3. Show how the distributive property can be used to simplify these calculations.

   a. $7 \times 27 + 7 \times 13$ **b.** $8 \times 17 - 8 \times 7$

4. Use and name the thinking strategies that can be used to find the following addition facts.

   a. 6×7 **b.** 9×7

5. Show how $17 \div 3$ can be found using

   a. repeated subtraction with the set model.

   b. repeated subtraction with the measurement model.

6. Show how the multiplication table for the facts 1 through 9 can be used to solve division problems.

7. Calculate the following if possible. If impossible, explain why.

   a. $7 : 0$ **b.** $0 : 7$ **c.** $0 \div 0$

8. Apply the division algorithm and apply it to the calculation $39 \div 7$.

9. Which of the following properties hold for whole-number division?

   a. Closure   **b.** Commutative

   c. Associative   **d.** Identity

10. Label the following diagram and comment on its value.

SECTION 3.3: Ordering and Exponents

VOCABULARY / NOTATION

Less than   124
Less than or equal to   124
Greater than or equal to   124
Transitive property of less than   124

Property of less than and addition
  (subtraction)   124
Property of less than and
  multiplication (division)   125

Exponent   125
Power   125
Base   125
Theorem   126

EXERCISES

1. Describe how addition is used to define "less than" ("greater than").

2. For whole numbers a, b, and c, if $a < b$, what can be said about
   a. $a + c$ and $b + c$?   **b.** $a \times c$ and $b \times c$?

3. Rewrite 5^4 using the definition of exponent.

4. Rewrite the following using properties of exponents.
   a. $(7^3)^4$ **b.** $3^5 \times 7^5$ **c.** $5^7 \div 5^3$ **d.** $4^{12} \times 4^{13}$

5. Explain how to motivate the definition of zero as an exponent.

PROBLEMS FOR WRITING/DISCUSSION

1. Imagine that one of your students missed 27 points on a 100-point test and you need to calculate the final score. The common subtraction error here is $100 - 27 = 83$. Why? Invent a good technique for subtracting from 100 that will protect you from making this error.

2. In your checkbook your balance is $127.42 and you write a check for $39.64. Display at least two ways of subtracting this amount other than the standard subtraction algorithm.

3. Devise a proposal for the use of calculators in elementary classrooms. At what grade level do you think it's appropriate for students to use calculators? Could they use calculators for some kinds of problems but not others? What does it mean for a student to become "calculator dependent?" Be prepared to defend your position!

4. After looking at the solution to the Initial Problem in this chapter, consider how the problem would be changed if you had ten coins instead of nine. Then determine the fewest weighings it would take to determine the counterfeit.

5. If you take a deck of 52 playing cards and ask students in how many ways they can form a rectangular shape using all of the cards, they will find there are three. They can string all 52 cards out in one row (1×52), or put 26 cards two deep (2×26), or they can have a 4×13 rectangle. How many rectangles could you make if you used only 24 cards? How about 49 cards? Be sure to say what the size of the rectangles would be. What number less than 52 would give you the greatest number of rectangles?

6. An art dealer sent an employee to an art auction in Europe. The art dealer had worked out a code so that the employee could fax the expected prices of the two artworks on which he would be bidding, and then the art dealer could decide whether or not he could afford the pieces. The code involved allowing each digit to be represented by one letter. For example, if 7 was to be represented by H, then every H represented a 7. The fax that came through said

$$\begin{array}{r} \text{SEND} \\ + \text{ MORE} \\ \hline \text{MONEY} \end{array}$$

How much was each artwork expected to cost?

7. Suppose we were to define a new operation, not one of the ones we know, and call it ‡. Using this operation on numbers could be defined by this equation:

$$a ‡ b = 2a - b \qquad \text{Example: } 4 ‡ 5 = (2 \cdot 4) - 5$$
$$= 8 - 5 = 3.$$

If we choose a and b only from the whole numbers, explain whether or not this operation would be commutative or associative.

8. If we make up another operation, say Ω, and we give it a table using the letters A, B, C, D as the set on which this symbol is operating, determine whether this operation is commutative or associative.

Ω	A	B	C	D
A	B	B	B	B
B	B	C	D	A
C	B	A	C	D
D	B	D	A	C

Then create your own 4×4 table for a new operation @, operating on the same four numbers, A, B, C, D. Make sure your operation is commutative. Can you see something that would always be true in the table of a commutative operation?

9. What are the differences among these four problems? How would you explain the differences to students?

$$5 \div 0 \quad 0 \div 5 \quad 5 \div 5 \quad 0 \div 0$$

10. A student claims that if a set is closed with respect to multiplication, it must be closed with respect to addition. How do you respond?

CHAPTER TEST

Knowledge

1. True or false?

   a. $n(A \cup B) = n(A) + n(B)$ for all finite sets A and B.

   b. If $B \subseteq A$, then $n(A - B) = n(A) - n(B)$ for all finite sets A and B.

   c. Commutativity does not hold for subtraction of whole numbers.

   d. Distributivity of multiplication over subtraction does not hold in the set of whole numbers.

   e. The symbol m^a, where m and a are nonzero whole numbers, represents the product of m factors of a.

   f. If a is the divisor, b is the dividend, and c is the quotient, then $ab = c$.

   g. The statement "$a + b = c$ if and only if $c - b = a$" is an example of the take-away approach to subtraction.

   h. Factors are to multiplication as addends are to addition.

   i. If $n \neq 0$ and $b + n = a$, then $a < b$.

   j. If $n(A) = a$ and $n(B) = b$, then $A \times B$ contains exactly ab ordered pairs.

2. Complete the following table for the operations on the set of whole numbers. Write True in the box if the indicated property holds for the indicated operation on whole numbers and write False if the indicated property does not hold for the indicated operation on whole numbers.

	ADD	SUBTRACT	MULTIPLY	DIVIDE
Closure				
Commutative				
Associative				
Identity				

3. Identify the property of whole numbers being illustrated.

   a. $a \cdot (b \cdot c) = a \cdot (c \cdot b)$

   b. $(3 + 2) \cdot 1 = 3 + 2$

   c. $(4 + 7) + 8 = 4 + (7 + 8)$

   d. $(2 \cdot 3) \cdot 5 = 2 \cdot (3 \cdot 5)$

   e. $(6 - 5) \cdot 2 = 6 \cdot 2 - 5 \cdot 2$

   f. $m + (n + p) = m + (p + n)$

Skills

4. Find the following sums and products using thinking strategies. Show your work.

   a. $39 + 12$ **b.** $47 + 87$

   c. $5(73 \cdot 2)$ **d.** 12×33

5. Find the quotient and remainder when 321 is divided by 5.

6. Rewrite the following using a single exponent in each case.

   a. $3^7 \cdot 3^{12}$ **b.** $5^{31} \div 5^7$

   c. $(7^3)^5$ **d.** $4^5/2^8$

   e. $7^{12} \cdot 2^{12} \cdot 14^3$ **f.** $(12^8/12^5)^4 \cdot (3^6)^2$

7. Perform the following calculations by applying appropriate properties. Which properties are you using?

   a. $13 \cdot 97 + 13 \cdot 3$

   b. $(194 + 86) + 6$

   c. $7 \cdot 23 + 23 \cdot 3$

   d. $25(123 \cdot 8)$

8. Classify each of the following division problems as examples of either partitive or measurement division.

   a. Martina has 12 cookies to share between her three friends and herself. How many cookies will each person receive?

   b. Coach Massey had 56 boys sign up to play intramural basketball. If he puts 7 boys on each team, how many teams will he have?

   c. Eduardo is planning to tile around his bathtub. If he wants to tile 48 inches up the wall and the individual tiles are 4 inches wide, how many rows of tile will he need?

9. Each of the following situations involves a subtraction problem. In each case, tell whether the problem is best represented by the take-away approach or the missing-addend approach, and why. Then write an equation that could be used to answer the question.

   a. Ovais has 137 basketball cards and Quinn has 163 basketball cards. How many more cards does Quinn have?

   b. Regina set a goal of saving money for a $1500 down payment on a car. Since she started, she has been able to save $973. How much more money does she need to save in order to meet her goal?

   c. Riley was given $5 for his allowance. After he spent $1.43 on candy at the store, how much did he have left to put into savings for a new bike?

Understanding

10. Using the following table, find $A - B$.

+	A	B	C
A	C	A	B
B	A	B	C
C	B	C	A

11. a. Using the definition of an exponent, provide an explanation to show that $(7^3)^4 = 7^{12}$.

 b. Use the fact that $a^m \cdot a^n = a^{m+n}$ to explain why $(7^3)^4 = 7^{12}$.

12. Show why $3 \div 0$ is undefined.

13. Explain in detail why $a^m \cdot b^m = (a \cdot b)^m$.

14. Explain why $(a \cdot b)^c \ne a \cdot b^c$ for all $a, b, c, \in W$.

Problem Solving/Application

15. Which is the smallest set of whole numbers that contains 2 and 3 and is closed under addition and multiplication?

16. If the product of two numbers is even and their sum is odd, what can you say about the two numbers?

17. Illustrate the following approaches for 4×3 using the measurement model. Please include a written description to clarify the illustration.

 a. Repeated-addition approach

 b. Rectangular array approach

18. Use a set model to illustrate that the associative property for whole-number addition holds.

19. Illustrate the missing-addend approach for the subtraction problem $8 - 5$ by using

 a. the set model.

 b. the measurement model.

20. Use the rectangular array approach to illustrate that the commutative property for whole-number multiplication holds.

21. Find a whole number less than 100 that is both a perfect square and a perfect cube.

22. Find two examples where $a, b \in W$ and $a \cdot b = a + b$.

References for Reflections from Research

BATTISTA, M. T., CLEMENTS, D. H., ARNOFF, J., BATTISTA, K., & VAN AUKEN BORROW, C. (1998). Students' spatial structuring of 2D arrays of squares. *Journal for Research in Mathematics Education, 29*, 503–532.

CLARK, F. B., & KAMII, C. (1996). Identification of multiplicative thinking in children in grades 1–5. *Journal for Research in Mathematics Education, 27*, 41–51.

GRAEBER, A. O., & TIROSH, D. (1988, April). Extending multiplication and division to decimals: Insights fourth and fifth graders bring to task. R. Shavelson (Chair), *Understanding situations modeled by multiplication and division*. Symposium conducted at the 65th annual meeting of the American Educational Research Association, New Orleans.

KAMII, C. K. (1985). *Young children reinvent arithmetic— 2nd grade.* New York: Teachers College Press.

MULLIGAN, J., & MITCHELMORE, M. (1995). Children's intuitive models of multiplication and division. In B. Atweh & S. Flavel (Eds.), MERGA 18: GALTHA, *Proceedings for the 18th annual conference* (pp. 416–420). Darwin, Australia: Northern Territory University.

MULLIGAN, J. T., & MITCHELMORE, M. C. (1997). Young children's intuitive models of multiplication and division. *Journal for Research in Mathematics Education, 28*, 309–330.

SCHLIEMANN, A. D., ARAUJO, C., CASSUNDÉ, M. A., MACEDO, S., & NICÉAS, L. (1998). Use of multiplicative commutativity by school children and street sellers. *Journal for Research in Mathematics Education, 29*, 422–435.

STEFFE, L. (1988). Children's construction of number sequences and multiplying schemes. In J. Hiebert & M. Behr (Eds.), *Number concepts and operations in the middle grades* (pp. 119–140). Hillsdale, NJ: Erlbaum; Reston, VA: National Council of Teachers of Mathematics.

VERGNAUD, G. (1981). *L'Enfant, la mathématique et la réalité* [Children, mathematics and reality]. Bern, Switzerland: Peter Lang.

WIEGEL, H. G. (1998). Kindergarten students' organization of counting in joint counting tasks and the emergence of cooperation. *Journal for Research in Mathematics Education, 29*, 202–224.

CHAPTER 4

WHOLE-NUMBER Computation—Mental, Electronic, and Written

Computational Devices from the Abacus to the Computer

The abacus was one of the earliest computational devices. The Romans used a grooved board as an abacus, with stones in the grooves, which was shown in the Focus On in Chapter 3. The Chinese abacus, or suan-pan (Figure 1), and the Japanese abacus, or soroban (Figure 2), were composed of a frame together with beads on fixed rods.

In 1617, Napier invented lattice rods, called Napier's bones, which could be used to perform multiplication. To multiply, appropriate rods were selected, laid side by side, and then appropriate "columns" were added (Figure 3). This uses the lattice multiplication procedure that is studied in this chapter.

About 1594, Napier also invented logarithms. The most remarkable property of logarithms is that multiplication can be performed by adding the respective logarithms. The slide rule, used extensively by engineers and scientists through the 1960s, was designed using properties of logarithms (Figure 4).

In 1642, Pascal invented the first mechanical adding machine (Figure 5). In 1671, Leibniz developed his "reckoning machine," which could also multiply and divide (Figure 6). In 1812, Babbage built his Difference Engine, which was the first "computer" (Figure 7). By 1946, ENIAC (Electronic Numerical Integrator and Computer) was developed. It filled a room, weighed over 30 tons, and had nearly 20,000 vacuum tubes. Finally, vacuum tubes gave way to transistors, which gave way to integrated circuits, or "chips." Chips permitted the manufacture of microcomputers, such as the Apple computer in the late 1970s and the Apple Macintosh in the mid 1980s (Figure 8). Chip manufacture also allowed calculators to become more powerful to the point that the dividing line between calculator and computer has become blurred. The Texas Instruments TI-92 seen in Figure 9 is an example of this. Modern personal computers (Figure 10) are now 50 to 100 times faster than the ENIAC, much more reliable, and often cost less than $1,500.

Figure 1

Figure 2

Figure 3

Figure 4

Figure 5

Figure 6

Figure 7

Figure 8

Figure 9

Figure 10

Problem Solving Strategies

1. Guess and Test
2. Use a Variable
3. Draw a Picture
4. Look for a Pattern
5. Make a List
6. Solve a Simpler Problem
7. Draw a Diagram
8. Use Direct Reasoning
9. **Use Indirect Reasoning**

Strategy
Use Indirect Reasoning

Occasionally, in mathematics, there are problems that are not easily solved using direct reasoning. In such cases, indirect reasoning may be the best way to solve the problem. A simple way of viewing **indirect reasoning** is to consider an empty room with only two entrances, say A and B. If you want to use direct reasoning to prove that someone entered the room through A, you would watch entrance A. However, you could also prove that someone entered through A by watching entrance B. If a person got into the room and did not go through B, the person had to go through entrance A. In mathematics, to prove that a condition, say "A," is true, one assumes that the condition "not A" is true and shows the latter condition to be impossible.

Initial Problem

The whole numbers 1 through 9 can be used once, each being arranged in a 3×3 square array so that the sum of the numbers in each of the rows, columns, and diagonals is 15. Show that 1 cannot be in one of the corners.

```
        2  ┌────┬────┬────┐  5
           │    │    │    │     6
        1  ├────┼────┼────┤  7
           │    │    │    │
        3  ├────┼────┼────┤  8
           │    │    │    │
        4  └────┴────┴────┘  9
```

Clues

The Use Indirect Reasoning strategy may be appropriate when

- Direct reasoning seems too complex or does not lead to a solution.
- Assuming the negation of what you are trying to prove narrows the scope of the problem.
- A proof is required.

A solution of the Initial Problem appears on page 176.

INTRODUCTION

NCTM Standards 2000
Number and Operations
Grades 3–5
All students should select appropriate methods and tools for computing with whole numbers from
among mental computation, estimation, calculators, and paper and
pencil according to the context
and nature of the computation and
use the selected method or tool.

In the past, much of elementary school mathematics was devoted to learning written methods for doing addition, subtraction, multiplication, and division. Due to the availability of electronic calculators and computers, less emphasis is being placed on doing written calculations involving numbers with many digits. Instead, an emphasis is being placed on developing skills in the use of all three types of computations: mental, written, and electronic (calculators/computers). Then, depending on the size of the numbers involved, the number of operations to be performed, the accuracy desired in the answer, and the time required to do the calculations, the appropriate mode(s) of calculation will be selected and employed.

In this chapter you will study all three forms of computation: mental, electronic (calculators), and written.

4.1   MENTAL MATH, ESTIMATION, AND CALCULATORS

STARTING POINT

Compute each of the following mentally and write a sentence describing your thoughts. After a discussion with classmates, determine some common strategies.

$$32 \cdot 26 \quad 23 \cdot 32 \qquad (16 \times 9) \times 25 \qquad 25 + (39 + 105)$$
$$49 + 27 \qquad\qquad 152 - 87 \quad 46 \times 99 \qquad 252 \div 12$$

Mental Math

The availability and widespread use of calculators and computers have permanently changed the way we compute. Consequently, there is an increasing need to develop students' skills in estimating answers when checking the reasonableness of results obtained electronically. Computational estimation, in turn, requires a good working knowledge of mental math. Thus this section begins with several techniques for doing calculations mentally.

In Chapter 3 we saw how the thinking strategies for learning the basic arithmetic facts could be extended to multidigit numbers, as illustrated next.

Example 4.1   Calculate the following mentally.
a. $15 + (27 + 25)$ **b.** $21 \cdot 17 - 13 \cdot 21$ **c.** $(8 \times 7) \times 25$
d. $98 + 59$ **e.** $87 + 29$ **f.** $168 \div 3$

Solution

a. $15 + (27 + 25) = (27 + 25) + 15 = 27 + (25 + 15) = 27 + 40 = 67$. Notice how commutativity and associativity play a key role here.
b. $21 \cdot 17 - 13 \cdot 21 = 21 \cdot 17 - 21 \cdot 13 = 21(17 - 13) = 21 \cdot 4 = 84$. Observe how commutativity and distributivity are useful here.
c. $(8 \times 7) \times 25 = (7 \times 8) \times 25 = 7 \times (8 \times 25) = 7 \times 200 = 1400$. Here commutativity is used first; then associativity is used to group the 8 and 25 since their product is 200.
d. $98 + 59 = 98 + (2 + 57) = (98 + 2) + 57 = 157$. Associativity is used here to form 100.
e. $87 + 29 = 80 + 20 + 7 + 9 = 100 + 16 = 116$ using associativity and commutativity.
f. $168 \div 3 = (150 \div 3) + (18 \div 3) = 50 + 6 = 56$.   ■

Observe that part (f) makes use of **right distributivity of division over addition;** that is, whenever the three quotients are whole numbers, $(a + b) \div c = (a \div c) + (b \div c)$. Right distributivity of division over subtraction also holds.

The calculations in Example 4.1 illustrate the following important mental techniques.

Properties Commutativity, associativity, and distributivity play an important role in simplifying calculations so that they can be performed mentally. Notice how useful these properties were in parts (a), (b), (c), (d), and (e) of Example 4.1. Also, the solution in part (f) uses right distributivity.

Compatible Numbers **Compatible numbers** are numbers whose sums, differences, products, or quotients are easy to calculate mentally. Examples of compatible numbers are 86 and 14 under addition (since $86 + 14 = 100$), 25 and 8 under multiplication (since $25 \times 8 = 200$), and 600 and 30 under division (since $600 \div 30 = 20$). In part (a) of Example 4.1, adding 15 to 25 produces a number, namely 40, that is easy to add to 27. Notice that numbers are compatible with *respect to an operation.* For example, 86 and 14 are compatible with respect to addition but not with respect to multiplication.

Example 4.2 Calculate the following mentally using properties and/or compatible numbers.

a. $(4 \times 13) \times 25$ **b.** $1710 \div 9$ **c.** 86×15

Solution

a. $(4 \times 13) \times 25 = 13 \times (4 \times 25) = 1300$
b. $1710 \div 9 = (1800 - 90) \div 9 = (1800 \div 9) - (90 \div 9) = 200 - 10 = 190$
c. $86 \times 15 = (86 \times 10) + (86 \times 5) = 860 + 430 = 1290$ (Notice that 86×5 is half of 86×10.) ■

Compensation The sum $43 + (38 + 17)$ can be viewed as $38 + 60 = 98$ using commutativity, associativity, and the fact that 43 and 17 are compatible numbers. Finding the answer to $43 + (36 + 19)$ is not as easy. However, by reformulating the sum $36 + 19$ mentally as $37 + 18$, we obtain the sum $(43 + 37) + 18 = 80 + 18 = 98$. This process of reformulating a sum, difference, product, or quotient to one that is more readily obtained mentally is called **compensation.** Some specific techniques using compensation are introduced next.

In the computations of Example 4.1(d), 98 was *increased* by 2 to 100 and then 59 was *decreased* by 2 to 57 (a compensation was made) to maintain the same sum. This technique, **additive compensation,** is an application of associativity. Similarly, additive compensation is used when $98 + 59$ is rewritten as $97 + 60$ or $100 + 57$. The problem $47 - 29$ can be thought of as $48 - 30 \ (= 18)$. This use of compensation in subtraction is called the **equal additions method** since the same number (here 1) is added to both 47 and 29 to maintain the same difference. This compensation is performed to make the subtraction easier by subtracting 30 from 48. The product 48×5 can be found using **multiplicative compensation** as follows: $48 \times 5 = 24 \times 10 = 240$. Here, again, associativity can be used to justify this method.

Left-to-Right Methods To add 342 and 136, first add the hundreds $(300 + 100)$, then the tens $(40 + 30)$, and then the ones $(2 + 6)$, to obtain 478. To add 158 and 279, one can think as follows: $100 + 200 = 300$, $300 + 50 + 70 = 420$, $420 + 8 + 9 = 437$. Alternatively, $158 + 279$ can be found as follows: $158 + 200 = 358$,

$358 + 70 = 428$, $428 + 9 = 437$. Subtraction from left to right can be done in a similar manner. Research has found that people who are excellent mental calculators utilize this left-to-right method to reduce memory load, instead of mentally picturing the usual right-to-left written method. The multiplication problem 3×123 can be thought of mentally as $3 \times 100 + 3 \times 20 + 3 \times 3$ using distributivity. Also, 4×253 can be thought of mentally as $800 + 200 + 12 = 1012$ or as $4 \times 250 + 4 \times 3 = 1000 + 12 = 1012$.

Multiplying Powers of 10 These special numbers can be multiplied mentally in either standard or exponential form. For example, $100 \times 1000 = 100,000$, $10^4 \times 10^5 = 10^9$, $20 \times 300 = 6000$, and $12,000 \times 110,000 = 12 \times 11 \times 10^7 = 1,320,000,000$.

Multiplying by Special Factors Numbers such as 5, 25, and 99 are regarded as special factors because they are convenient to use mentally. For example, since $5 = 10 \div 2$, we have $38 \times 5 = 38 \times 10 \div 2 = 380 \div 2 = 190$. Also, since $25 = 100 \div 4$, $36 \times 25 = 3600 \div 4 = 900$. The product 46×99 can be thought of as $46(100 - 1) = 4600 - 46 = 4554$. Also, dividing by 5 can be viewed as dividing by 10, then multiplying by 2. Thus $460 \div 5 = (460 \div 10) \times 2 = 46 \times 2 = 92$.

Example 4.3   Calculate mentally using the indicated method.

a. $197 + 248$ using additive compensation
b. 125×44 using multiplicative compensation
c. $273 - 139$ using the equal additions method
d. $321 + 437$ using a left-to-right method
e. 3×432 using a left-to-right method
f. 456×25 using the multiplying by a special factor method

Solution

a. $197 + 248 = 197 + 3 + 245 = 200 + 245 = 445$
b. $125 \times 44 = 125 \times 4 \times 11 = 500 \times 11 = 5500$
c. $273 - 139 = 274 - 140 = 134$
d. $321 + 437 = 758$ [*Think*: $(300 + 400) + (20 + 30) + (1 + 7)$]
e. $3 \times 432 = 1296$ [*Think*: $(3 \times 400) + (3 \times 30) + (3 \times 2)$]
f. $456 \times 25 = 114 \times 100 = 11,400$ (*Think*: $25 \times 4 = 100$. Thus $456 \times 25 = 114 \times 4 \times 25 = 114 \times 100 = 11,400$.)   ■

NCTM Standards 2000 Number and Operations Grades 3–5
All students should develop and use strategies to estimate the results of whole-number computations and to judge the reasonableness of such results.

Reflection from Research
Students can develop a better understanding of number through activities involving estimation (Leutzinger, Rathmell, & Urbatsch, 1986).

Computational Estimation

The process of estimation takes on various forms. The number of beans in a jar may be estimated using no mathematics, simply a "guesstimate." Also, one may estimate how long a trip will be, based simply on experience. **Computational estimation** is the process of finding an approximate answer (an estimate) to a computation, often using mental math. With the use of calculators becoming more commonplace, computational estimation is an essential skill. Next we consider various types of computational estimation.

Front-End Estimation Three types of front-end estimation will be demonstrated.
Range Estimation   Often it is sufficient to know an interval or **range**—that is, a low value and a high value—that will contain an answer. The following example shows how ranges can be obtained in addition and multiplication.

Example 4.4 Find a range for answers to these computations by using only the leading digits.

a. 257
     +576

b. 294
     × 53

Solution

a.

Sum	Low Estimate	High Estimate
257	200	300
+576	+500	+600
	700	900

Reflection from Research
In comparing student understanding of measurement versus estimation, students displayed orientation to and the authority of the ruler (the tool and the teacher) and little orientation to the idea or characterization of estimation as a concept (Forrester & Pike, 1998).

Thus a range for the answer is from 700 to 900. Notice that you have to look at only the digits having the largest place values (2 + 5 = 7, or 700) to arrive at the low estimate, and these digits each increased by one (3 + 6 = 9, or 900) to find the high estimate.

b.

Product	Low Estimate	High Estimate
294	200	300
× 53	× 50	× 60
	10,000	18,000

Due to the nature of multiplication, this method gives a wide range, here 10,000 to 18,000. Even so, this method will catch many errors. ■

One-Column/Two-Column Front-End We can estimate the sum 498 + 251 using the **one-column front-end estimation method** as follows: To estimate 498 + 251, think 400 + 200 = 600 (the estimate). Notice that this is simply the low end of the range estimate. The one-column front-end estimate always provides low estimates in addition problems as well as in multiplication problems. In the case of 376 + 53 + 417, the one-column estimate is 300 + 400 = 700, since there are no hundreds in 53. The two-column front-end estimate also provides a low estimate for sums and products. However, this estimate is closer to the exact answer than one obtained from using only one column. For example, in the case of 372 + 53 + 417, the **two-column front-end estimation method** yields 370 + 50 + 410 = 830, which is closer to the exact answer 842 than the 700 obtained using the one-column method.

Front-End with Adjustment This method enhances the one-column front-end estimation method. For example, to find 498 + 251, think 400 + 200 = 600 and 98 + 51 is about 150. Thus the estimate is 600 + 150 = 750. Unlike one-column or two-column front-end estimates, this technique may produce either a low estimate or a high estimate, as in this example.

Keep in mind that one estimates to obtain a "rough" answer, so all of the preceding forms of front-end estimation belong in one's estimation repertoire.

Example 4.5 Estimate using the method indicated.

a. 503 × 813 using one-column front-end
b. 1200 × 35 using range estimation
c. 4376 − 1889 using two-column front-end
d. 3257 + 874 using front-end adjustment

Solution

a. To estimate 503 × 813 using the one-column front-end method, think 500 × 800 = 400,000. Using words, think "5 hundreds times 8 hundreds is 400,000."

b. To estimate a range for 1200×35, think $1200 \times 30 = 36,000$ and $1200 \times 40 = 48,000$. Thus a range for the answer is from 36,000 to 48,000. One also could use $1000 \times 30 = 30,000$ and $2000 \times 40 = 80,000$. However, this yields a wider range.

c. To estimate $4376 - 1889$ using the two-column front-end method, think $4300 - 1800 = 2500$. You also can think $43 - 18 = 25$ and then append two zeros after the 25 to obtain 2500.

d. To estimate $3257 + 874$ using front-end with adjustment, think 3000, but since $257 + 874$ is about 1000, adjust to 4000. ■

Rounding Rounding is perhaps the best-known computational estimation technique. The purpose of rounding is to replace complicated numbers with simpler numbers. Here, again, since the objective is to obtain an estimate, any of several rounding techniques may be used. However, some may be more appropriate than others, depending on the word problem situation. For example, if you are estimating how much money to take along on a trip, you would round up to be sure that you had enough. When calculating the amount of gas needed for a trip, one would round the miles per gallon estimate down to ensure that there would be enough money for gas. Unlike the previous estimation techniques, rounding is often applied to an answer as well as to the individual numbers before a computation is performed.

Several different methods of rounding are illustrated next. What is common, however, is that each method rounds to a particular place. You are asked to formulate rules for the following methods in the problem set.

Figure 4.1

Round Up (Down) The number 473 **rounded up** to the nearest tens place is 480 since 473 is between 470 and 480 and 480 is *above* 473 (Figure 4.1). The number 473 **rounded down** to the nearest tens place is 470. Rounding down is also called truncating (**truncate** means "to cut off"). The number 1276 truncated to the hundreds place is 1200.

Round a 5 Up The most common rounding technique used in schools is the round a 5 up method. This method can be motivated using a number line. Suppose that we wish to round 475 to the nearest ten (Figure 4.2).

Figure 4.2

Since 475 is midway between 470 and 480, we have to make an agreement concerning whether we round 475 to 470 or to 480. The **round a 5 up** method always rounds such numbers up, so 475 rounds to 480. In the case of the numbers 471 to 474, since they are all nearer 470 than 480, they are rounded to 470 when rounding to the nearest ten. The numbers 476 to 479 are rounded to 480.

One disadvantage of this method is that estimates obtained when several 5s are involved tend to be on the high side. For example, the "round a 5 up" to the nearest ten estimate applied to the addends of the sum $35 + 45 + 55 + 65$ yields $40 + 50 + 60 + 70 = 220$, which is 20 more than the exact sum 200.

Round to the Nearest Even Rounding to the nearest even can be used to avoid errors of accumulation in rounding. For example, if $475 + 545 (= 1020)$ is estimated by rounding up to the tens place or rounding a 5 up, the answer is $480 + 550 = 1030$. By rounding down, the estimate is $470 + 540 = 1010$. Since 475 is between 480 and 470 and the 8 in the tens place is even, and 545 is between 550 and 540 and the 4 is even, **rounding to the nearest even** method yields $480 + 540 = 1020$.

Example 4.6   Estimate using the indicated method. (The symbol "≈" means "is approximately.")

a. Estimate $2173 + 4359$ by rounding down to the nearest hundreds place.
b. Estimate $3250 - 1850$ by rounding to the nearest even hundreds place.
c. Estimate $575 - 398$ by rounding a 5 up to the nearest tens place.

Solution

a. $2173 + 4359 \approx 2100 + 4300 = 6400$
b. $3250 - 1850 \approx 3200 - 1800 = 1400$
c. $575 - 398 \approx 580 - 400 = 180$ ■

Round to Compatible Numbers   Another rounding technique can be applied to estimate products such as 26×37. A reasonable estimate of 26×37 is $25 \times 40 = 1000$. The numbers 25 and 40 were selected since they are estimates of 26 and 37, respectively, and are compatible with respect to multiplication. (Notice that the rounding up technique would have yielded the considerably higher estimate of $30 \times 40 = 1200$, whereas the exact answer is 962.) This **round to compatible numbers** technique allows one to round either up or down to compatible numbers to simplify calculations, rather than rounding to specified places. For example, a reasonable estimate of 57×98 is $57 \times 100 \; (= 5700)$. Here, only the 98 needed to be rounded to obtain an estimate mentally. The division problem $2716 \div 75$ can be estimated mentally by considering $2800 \div 70 \; (= 40)$. Here 2716 was rounded up to 2800 and 75 was rounded down to 70 because $2800 \div 70$ easily leads to a quotient since 2800 and 70 are compatible numbers with respect to division.

Example 4.7   Estimate by rounding to compatible numbers in two different ways.

a. 43×21 **b.** $256 \div 33$

Reflection from Research
Good estimators use three computational processes. They make the number easier to manage (possibly by rounding), change the structure of the problem itself to make it easier to carry out, and compensate by making adjustments in their estimation after the problem is carried out (Reys, Rybolt, Bestgen, & Wyatt, 1982.)

Solution

a. $43 \times 21 \approx 40 \times 21 = 840$ **b.** $256 \div 33 \approx 240 \div 30 = 8$
     $43 \times 21 \approx 43 \times 20 = 860$ $256 \div 33 \approx 280 \div 40 = 7$
     (The exact answer is 903.)   (The exact answer is 7 with remainder 25.)   ■

Rounding is a most useful and flexible technique. It is important to realize that the main reasons to round are (1) to simplify calculations while obtaining reasonable answers and (2) to report numerical results that can be easily understood. Any of the methods illustrated here may be used to estimate.

The ideas involving mental math and estimation in this section were observed in children who were facile in working with numbers. The following suggestions should help develop number sense in all children.

1. Learn the basic facts using thinking strategies, and extend the strategies to multidigit numbers.
2. Master the concept of place value.
3. Master the basic addition and multiplication properties of whole numbers.
4. Develop a habit of using the front-end and left-to-right methods.
5. Practice mental calculations often, daily if possible.
6. Accept approximate answers when exact answers are not needed.
7. Estimate prior to doing exact computations.
8. Be flexible by using a variety of mental math and estimation techniques.

Reflection from Research
Students in classrooms where calculators are used tend to have more positive attitudes about mathematics than students in classrooms where calculators are not used (Reys & Reys, 1987.)

Figure 4.3

Using a Calculator

Although a basic calculator that costs less than $10 is sufficient for most elementary school students, there are features on $15 to $30 calculators that simplify many complicated calculations. The TI-34 II, manufactured by Texas Instruments, is shown in Figure 4.3. The TI-34 II, which is designed especially for elementary and middle schools, performs fraction as well as the usual decimal calculations, can perform long division with remainders directly, and has the functions of a scientific calculator. One nice feature of the TI-34 II is that it has two lines of display, which allows the student to see the input *and* output at the same time.

The ON key turns the calculator on. The DEL key is an abbreviation for "delete" and allows the user to delete one character at a time from the right if the cursor is at the end of an expression or delete the character under the cursor. Pressing the CLEAR key will clear the current entry. The previous entry can be retrieved by pressing the ▲ key.

Three types of logic are available in calculators: arithmetic, algebraic, and reverse Polish notation. Reverse Polish notation is considerably more complicated and not as common as the other two, so we will only discuss arithmetic and algebraic logic.

(NOTE: For ease of reading, we will write numerals without the usual squares around them to indicate that they are keys.)

Arithmetic Logic In arithmetic logic, the calculator performs operations in the order they are entered. For example, if 3 ⊞ 4 ⊠ 5 ⊟ is entered, the calculations are performed as follows: $(3 + 4) \times 5 = 7 \times 5 = 35$. That is, the operations are performed from left to right as they are entered.

Algebraic Logic If your calculator has algebraic logic and the expression 3 ⊞ 4 ⊠ 5 ⊟ is entered, the result is different; here the calculator evaluates expressions according to the usual mathematical convention for **order of operations.**

Within the innermost parentheses

> *First*: Calculate exponentials.
> *Second*: Perform multiplications and divisions from left to right.
> *Third*: Perform additions and subtractions from left to right.

Repeat until all calculations have been performed. For 3 ⊞ 4 ⊠ 5 ⊟,

$$3 + (4 \times 5) = 3 + 20 = 23,$$

since multiplication takes precedence over addition. If a calculator has parentheses, they can be inserted to be sure that the desired operation is performed first. In a calculator using algebraic logic, the calculation $13 - 5 \times 4 \div 2 + 7$ will result in $13 - 10 + 7 = 10$. If one wishes to calculate $13 - 5$ first, parentheses must be inserted. Thus $(13 - 5) \times 4 \div 2 + 7 = 23$.

Example 4.8 Using the order of operations associated with algebraic logic, mentally calculate the following.

a. $(4 + 2 \times 5) \div 7 + 3$
b. $8 \div 2^2 + 3 \times 2^2$
c. $17 - 4(5 - 2)$
d. $40 \div 5 \times 2^3 - 2 \times 3$

Solution

a. $(4 + 2 \times 5) \div 7 + 3 = (4 + 10) \div 7 + 3$
$$= (14 \div 7) + 3$$
$$= 2 + 3 = 5$$

b. $8 \div 2^2 + 3 \times 2^2 = (8 \div 4) + (3 \times 4)$
$$= 2 + 12 = 14$$
c. $17 - 4(5 - 2) = 17 - (4 \times 3)$
$$= 17 - 12 = 5$$
d. $40 \div 5 \times 2^3 - 2 \times 3 = [(40 \div 5) \times 2^3] - (2 \times 3)$
$$= 8 \times 8 - 2 \times 3$$
$$= 64 - 6 = 58 \qquad\blacksquare$$

Now let's consider some features that make a calculator helpful both as a computational and a pedagogical device. Several keystroke sequences will be displayed to simulate the variety of calculator operating systems available.

Parentheses As mentioned earlier when we were discussing algebraic logic, one must always be attentive to the order of operations when several operations are present. For example, the product $2 \times (3 + 4)$ can be found in two ways. First, by using commutativity, the following keystrokes will yield the correct answer:

$$3 \boxplus 4 \boxminus \boxtimes 2 \boxminus \boxed{\qquad 14}.$$

Alternatively, the parentheses keys may be used as follows:

$$2 \boxtimes \boxed{(} 3 \boxplus 4 \boxed{)} \boxminus \boxed{\qquad 14}.$$

Parentheses are needed, since pressing the keys $2 \boxtimes 3 \boxplus 4 \boxminus$ on a calculator with algebraic logic will result in the answer 10. Distributivity may be used to simplify calculations. For example, $753 \cdot 8 + 753 \cdot 9$ can be found using $753 \boxtimes \boxed{(} 8 \boxplus 9 \boxed{)}$ $\boxminus$ instead of $753 \boxtimes 8 \boxplus 753 \boxtimes 9 \boxminus$.

Constant Functions In Chapter 3, multiplication was viewed as repeated addition; in particular, $5 \times 3 = 3 + 3 + 3 + 3 + 3 = 15$. Repeated operations are carried out in different ways depending on the model of calculator. For example, the following keystroke sequence is used to calculate 5×3 on one calculator that has a built-in constant function:

$$3 \boxplus \boxminus \boxminus \boxminus \boxminus \boxed{\qquad 15}.$$

Numbers raised to a whole-number power can be found using a similar technique. For example, 3^5 can be calculated by replacing the $\boxplus$ with a $\boxtimes$ in the preceding examples. A constant function can also be used to do repeated subtraction to find a quotient and a remainder in a division problem. For example, the following sequence can be used to find $35 \div 8$:

$$35 \boxminus 8 \boxminus \boxminus \boxminus \boxminus \boxed{\qquad 3}.$$

The remainder (3 here) is the first number displayed that is less than the divisor (8 here), and the number of times the equal sign was pressed is the quotient (4 here).

Because of the two lines of display, the T1-34 II can handle most of these examples by typing in the entire expression. For example, representing 5×3 as repeated addition is entered into the TI-34 II as

$$3 \boxplus 3 \boxplus 3 \boxplus 3 \boxplus 3 \boxminus.$$

The entire expression of $3 + 3 + 3 + 3 + 3$ appears on the first line of display and the result $\boxed{\qquad 15}$ appears on the second line of display.

Exponent Keys There are three common types of exponent keys: $\boxed{x^2}$, $\boxed{y^x}$, and $\boxed{\wedge}$. The x^2 key is used to find squares in one of two ways:

$$3 \boxed{x^2} \boxminus \boxed{\qquad 9} \quad \text{or} \quad 3 \boxed{x^2} \boxed{\qquad 9}.$$

The $\boxed{y^x}$ and $\boxed{\wedge}$ keys are used to find more general powers and have similar keystrokes. For example, 7^3 may be found as follows:

$$7 \boxed{y^x} 3 \boxed{=} \boxed{343} \quad \text{or} \quad 7 \boxed{\wedge} 3 \boxed{343}.$$

Memory Functions Many calculators have a memory function designated by the keys $\boxed{M+}$, $\boxed{M-}$, $\boxed{MR}$, or $\boxed{STO}$ $\boxed{RCL}$, $\boxed{SUM}$. Your calculator's display will probably show an "M" to remind you that there is a nonzero number in the memory. The problem $5 \times 9 + 7 \times 8$ may be found as follows using the memory keys:

$$5 \boxed{\times} 9 \boxed{=} \boxed{M+} 7 \boxed{\times} 8 \boxed{=} \boxed{M+} \boxed{MR} \boxed{101} \text{ or}$$

$$5 \boxed{\times} 9 \boxed{=} \boxed{SUM} 7 \boxed{\times} 8 \boxed{=} \boxed{SUM} \boxed{RCL} \boxed{101}.$$

It is a good practice to clear the memory for each new problem using the all clear key.

The TI-34 II has five memory locations—A, B, C, D, and E—which can be accessed by pressing the $\boxed{STO\Rightarrow}$ key and then using the right arrow key, $\boxed{\Rightarrow}$, to select the desired variable. The following keystrokes are used to evaluate the expression above.

$$5 \boxed{\times} 9 \boxed{STO\Rightarrow} \boxed{=} \text{ and } 7 \boxed{\times} 8 \boxed{STO\Rightarrow} \boxed{\Rightarrow} \boxed{=}$$

The above keys will store the value 45 in the memory location A and the value 56 in the memory location B. The values A and B can then be added together as follows.

$$\boxed{MEMVAR} \boxed{=} \boxed{+} \boxed{MEMVAR} \boxed{\Rightarrow} \boxed{=} \boxed{=}$$

This will show $A + B$ on the first line of the calculator display and $\boxed{101}$ on the second line of the display.

Additional special keys will be introduced throughout the book as the need arises.

Scientific Notation Input and output of a calculator are limited by the number of places in the display (generally 8, 10, or 12). Two basic responses are given when a number is too large to fit in the display. Simple calculators either provide a partial answer with an "E" (for "error"), or the word "ERROR" is displayed. Many scientific calculators automatically express the answer in **scientific notation** (that is, as the product of a decimal number greater than or equal to 1 but less than 10, and the appropriate power of 10). For example, on the TI-34 II, the product of 123,456,789 and 987 is displayed $\boxed{1.218518507 \times 10^{11}}$. (NOTE: Scientific notation is discussed in more detail in Chapter 9 after decimals and negative numbers have been studied.) If an exact answer is needed, the use of the calculator can be combined with paper and pencil and distributivity as follows:

$$\begin{aligned} 123{,}456{,}789 \times 987 &= 123{,}456{,}789 \times 900 + 123{,}456{,}789 \times \\ &\quad 80 + 123{,}456{,}789 \times 7 \\ &= 111{,}111{,}110{,}100 + 9{,}876{,}543{,}120 \\ &\quad + 864{,}197{,}523. \end{aligned}$$

Now we can obtain the product by adding:

$$\begin{array}{r} 111{,}111{,}110{,}100 \\ 9{,}876{,}543{,}120 \\ + \quad\ 864{,}197{,}523 \\ \hline 121{,}851{,}850{,}743. \end{array}$$

Calculations with numbers having three or more digits will probably be performed on a calculator (or computer) to save time and increase accuracy. Even so, it is prudent to estimate your answer when using your calculator.

MATHEMATICAL MORSEL

In his fascinating book *The Great Mental Calculators*, author Steven ß. Smith discusses various ways that the great mental calculators did their calculations. In his research, he found that all auditory calculators (people who are given problems verbally and perform computations mentally) except one did their multiplications from left to right to minimize their short-term memory load.

Section 4.1   EXERCISE / PROBLEM SET A

EXERCISES

1. Calculate mentally using properties.

   a. $(37 + 25) + 43$ **b.** $47 \cdot 15 + 47 \cdot 85$

   c. $(4 \times 13) \times 25$ **d.** $26 \cdot 24 - 21 \cdot 24$

2. Find each of these differences mentally using equal additions. Write out the steps that you thought through.

   a. $43 - 17$ **b.** $62 - 39$

   c. $132 - 96$ **d.** $250 - 167$

3. Calculate mentally left to right.

   a. $123 + 456$ **b.** $342 + 561$

   c. $587 - 372$ **d.** $467 - 134$

4. Calculate mentally using the indicated method.

   a. $198 + 387$ (additive compensation)

   b. 84×5 (multiplicative compensation)

   c. 99×53 (special factor)

   d. $4125 \div 25$ (special factor)

5. Calculate mentally.

   a. $58,000 \times 5,000,000$

   b. $7 \times 10^5 \times 21,000$

   c. $13,000 \times 7,000,000$

   d. $4 \times 10^5 \times 3 \times 10^6 \times 7 \times 10^3$

   e. $5 \times 10^3 \times 7 \times 10^7 \times 4 \times 10^5$

   f. $17,000,000 \times 6,000,000,000$

6. Estimate each of the following using the four front-end methods: (i) range, (ii) one-column, (iii) two-column, and (iv) with adjustment.

   a.   3741
          +1252

   b.   1591
             346
             589
          + 163

   c.   2347
              58
             192
          +5783

7. Find a range estimate for these products.

   a. 37×24 **b.** 157×231 **c.** 491×8

8. Estimate using compatible number estimation.

   a. 63×97 **b.** 51×212 **c.** $3112 \div 62$

   d. 103×87 **e.** 62×58 **f.** $4254 \div 68$

9. Round as specified.

   a. 373 to the nearest tens place

   b. 650 using round a 5 up method to the hundreds place

   c. 1123 up to the tens place

   d. 457 to the nearest tens place

   e. 3457 to the nearest thousands place

10. **Cluster estimation** is used to estimate sums and products when several numbers cluster near one number. For example, the addends in $789 + 810 + 792$ cluster around 800. Thus $3 \times 800 = 2400$ is a good estimate of the sum. Estimate the following using cluster estimation.

   a. $347 + 362 + 354 + 336$

   b. $61 \times 62 \times 58$

   c. $489 \times 475 \times 523 \times 498$

   d. $782 + 791 + 834 + 812 + 777$

11. The sum $26 + 38 + 55$ can be found mentally as follows: $26 + 30 = 56, 56 + 8 = 64, 64 + 50 = 114, 114 + 5 = 119$. Find the following sums mentally using this technique.

   a. $32 + 29 + 56$ **b.** $54 + 28 + 67$

   c. $19 + 66 + 49$ **d.** $62 + 84 + 27 + 81$

12. Before granting an operating license, a scientist has to estimate the amount of pollutants that should be allowed to be discharged from an industrial

chimney. Should she overestimate or underestimate? Explain.

13. Estimate the following values and check with a calculator.

   a. 656×74 is between _____ 000 and _____ 000.

   b. 491×3172 is between _____ 00000 and _____ 00000.

   c. 143^2 is between _____ 0000 and _____ 0000.

14. Often subtraction can be done more easily in steps. For example, $43 - 37$ can be found as follows: $43 - 37 = (43 - 30) - 7 = 13 - 7 = 6$. Find the following differences using this technique.

   a. $52 - 35$ **b.** $173 - 96$

   c. $241 - 159$ **d.** $83 - 55$

15. In division you can sometimes simplify the problem by multiplying or dividing both the divisor and dividend by the same number. This is called **division compensation.** For example,

   $72 \div 12 = (72 \div 2) \div (12 \div 2) = 36 \div 6 = 6$ and
   $145 \div 5 = (145 \times 2) \div (5 \times 2) = 290 \div 10 = 29$

   Calculate the following mentally using this technique.

   a. $84 \div 14$ **b.** $234 \div 26$

   c. $120 \div 15$ **d.** $168 \div 14$

16. The **halving and doubling** method can be used to multiply two numbers when one factor is a power of 2 For example, to find 8×17, find 4×34 or $2 \times 68 - 136$. Find the following products using this method.

   a. 16×21 **b.** 4×72

   c. 8×123 **d.** 16×211

17. Guess what whole numbers can be used to fill in the blanks. Use your calculator to check.

   a. _____$^6 = 4096$ **b.** _____$^4 = 28,561$

18. Some products can be found most easily using a combination of mental math and a calculator. For example, the product $20 \times 47 \times 139 \times 5$ can be found by calculating 47×139 on a calculator and then multiplying your result by 100 mentally ($20 \times 5 = 100$). Calculate the following using a combination of mental math and a calculator.

   a. $17 \times 25 \times 817 \times 4$ **b.** $98 \times 2 \times 673 \times 5$

   c. $674 \times 50 \times 889 \times 4$ **d.** $783 \times 8 \times 79 \times 125$

19. Guess which is larger. Check with your calculator.

   a. 5^4 or 4^5?   **b.** 7^3 or 3^7?

   c. 7^4 or 4^7?   **d.** 6^3 or 3^6?

20. Compute the quotient and remainder (a whole number) for the following problems on a calculator without using repeated subtraction. Describe the procedure you used.

   a. $8\overline{)103}$ **b.** $17\overline{)543}$

   c. $123\overline{)849}$ **d.** $894\overline{)107,214}$

21. $1233 = 12^2 + 33^2$ and $8833 = 88^2 + 33^2$. How about 10,100 and 5,882,353? (*Hint*: Think 558 2353.)

22. Determine whether the following equation is true for $n = 1, 2,$ or 3.

   $$1^n + 6^n + 8^n = 2^n + 4^n + 9^n$$

23. Notice that $153 = 1^3 + 5^3 + 3^3$. Determine which of the following numbers have the same property.

   a. 370   **b.** 371   **c.** 407

24. Determine whether the following equation is true when n is 1, 2, or 3.

   $$1^n + 4^n + 5^n + 5^n + 6^n + 9^n =$$
   $$2^n + 3^n + 3^n + 7^n + 7^n + 8^n$$

PROBLEMS

25. Place a multiplication sign or signs so that the product in each problem is correct; for example, in $1\ 2\ 3\ 4\ 5\ 6 = 41,472$, the multiplication sign should be between the 2 and the 3 since $12 \times 3456 = 41,472$.

   a. $1\ 3\ 5\ 7\ 9\ 0 = 122,130$

   b. $6\ 6\ 6\ 6\ 6\ 6 = 439,956$

   c. $7\ 8\ 9\ 3\ 4\ 5\ 6 = 3,307,824$

   d. $1\ 2\ 3\ 4\ 5\ 6\ 7 = 370,845$

26. Develop a method for finding a range for subtraction problems for three-digit numbers.

27. Find $13,333,333^2$.

28. Calculate $99 \cdot 36$ and $99 \cdot 23$ and look for a pattern. Then predict $99 \cdot 57$ and $99 \cdot 63$ mentally and check with a calculator.

29. **a.** Calculate $25^2, 35^2, 45^2,$ and 55^2 and look for a pattern. Then find $65^2, 75^2,$ and 95^2 mentally and check your answers.

   b. Using a variable, prove that your result holds for squaring numbers that have a 5 as their ones digit.

30. George Bidder was a calculating prodigy in England during the nineteenth century. As a nine-year-old, he was asked: If the moon were 123,256 miles from the Earth and sound traveled at the rate of 4 miles a minute, how long would it be before inhabitants of the moon could hear the battle of Waterloo? His answer—21 days, 9 hours, 34 minutes—was given in 1 minute. Was he correct? Try to do this calculation in less than 1 minute using a calculator. (NOTE: The moon is about 240,000 miles from Earth and sound travels about 12.5 miles per second.)

31. Found in a newspaper article: What is

241,573,142,393,627,673,576,957,439,048 ×
45,994,811,347,886,846,310,221,728,895,223,
034,301,839?

The answer is 71 consecutive 1s—one of the biggest numbers a computer has ever factored. This factorization bested the previous high, the factorization of a 69-digit number. Find a mistake here, and suggest a correction.

32. Some mental calculators use the following fact: $(a + b)(a - b) = a^2 - b^2$. For example, $43 \times 37 = (40 + 3)(40 - 3) = 40^2 - 3^2 = 1600 - 9 = 1591$. Apply this technique to find the following products mentally.

  a. 54×46

  b. 81×79

  c. 122×118

  d. 1210×1190

33. Fermat claimed that

$$100,895,598,169 = 898,423 \times 112,303.$$

Check this on your calculator.

34. Show how to find $439,268 \times 6852$ using a calculator that displays only eight digits.

35. Insert parentheses (if necessary) to obtain the following results.

  a. $76 \times 54 + 97 = 11,476$

  b. $4 \times 13^2 = 2704$

  c. $13 + 59^2 \times 47 = 163,620$

  d. $79 - 43 \div 2 + 17^2 = 307$

36. a. Find a shortcut.

$$24 \times 26 = 624$$
$$62 \times 68 = 4216$$
$$73 \times 77 = 5621$$
$$41 \times 49 = 2009$$
$$86 \times 84 = 7224$$
$$57 \times 53 = \underline{}$$

  b. Prove that your result works in general.

  c. How is this problem related to Problem 29?

37. Develop a set of rules for the round a 5 up method.

38. There are eight consecutive odd numbers that when multiplied together yield 34,459,425. What are they?

39. Jill goes to get some water. She has a 5-liter pail and a 3-liter pail and is supposed to bring exactly 1 liter back. How can she do this?

Section 4.1   EXERCISE / PROBLEM SET B

EXERCISES

1. Calculate mentally using properties.

  a. $52 \cdot 14 - 52 \cdot 4$ **b.** $(5 \times 37) \times 20$

  c. $(56 + 37) + 44$ **d.** $23 \cdot 4 + 23 \cdot 5 + 7 \cdot 9$

2. Find each of these differences mentally using equal additions. Write out the steps that you thought through.

  a. $56 - 29$ **b.** $83 - 37$

  c. $214 - 86$ **d.** $542 - 279$

3. Calculate mentally using the left-to-right method.

  a. $246 + 352$ **b.** $49 + 252$

  c. $842 - 521$ **d.** $751 - 647$

4. Calculate mentally using the method indicated.

  a. $359 + 596$ (additive compensation)

  b. 76×25 (multiplicative compensation)

  c. 4×37 (halving and doubling)

  d. 37×98 (special factor)

  e. $1240 \div 5$ (special factor)

5. Calculate mentally.

  a. $32,000 \times 400$ **b.** $6000 \times 12,000$

  c. $4000 \times 5000 \times 70$ **d.** $5 \times 10^4 \times 30 \times 10^5$

  e. $12,000 \times 4 \times 10^7$ **f.** $23,000,000 \times 5,000,000$

6. Estimate each of the following using the four front-end methods: (i) one-column, (ii) range, (iii) two-column, and (iv) with adjustment.

a.	**b.**	**c.**
4652	2659	15923
+8134	3752	672
	79	2341
	+ 143	+ 251

7. Find a range estimate for these products.

a. 57×1924 **b.** 1349×45 **c.** $547 \times 73{,}951$

8. Estimate using compatible number estimation.

a. 84×49 **b.** $5527 \div 82$

c. $2315 \div 59$ **d.** 78×81

e. 207×73 **f.** $6401 \div 93$

9. Round as specified.

a. 257 down to the nearest tens place

b. 650 to the nearest even hundreds place

c. 593 to the nearest tens place

d. 4157 to the nearest hundreds place

e. 7126 to the nearest thousands place

10. Estimate using cluster estimation.

a. $547 + 562 + 554 + 556$ **b.** $31 \times 32 \times 35 \times 28$

c. $189 + 175 + 193 + 173$ **d.** $562 \times 591 \times 634$

11. Five of the following six numbers were rounded to the nearest thousand, then added to produce an estimated sum of 87,000. Which number was not included?

5228   14,286   7782   19,628   9168   39,228

12. In determining an evacuation zone, a scientist must estimate the distance that lava from an erupting volcano will flow. Should she overestimate or underestimate? Explain.

13. Estimate the following values and check with a calculator.

a. 324×56 is between _____ 000 and _____ 000.

b. 5714×13 is between _____ 000 and _____ 000.

c. 256^3 is between _____ 000000 and _____ 000000.

14. One student calculated $84 - 28$ as $84 - 30 = 54$ and $54 + 2 = 56$; thus $84 - 28 = 56$. Another student calculated $84 - 28$ as $84 - 30 = 54$ and $54 - 2 = 52$; thus $84 - 28 = 52$. Determine which of these two methods is valid. Explain why students might have trouble with this method.

15. Find the quotient and remainder using a calculator. Check your answers.

a. $18{,}114 \div 37$ **b.** $381{,}271 \div 147$

c. $9{,}346{,}870 \div 1349$ **d.** $817{,}293 \div 749$

16. Here are four ways to estimate 26×12:

$$26 \times 10 = 260 \qquad 30 \times 12 = 360$$
$$25 \times 12 = 300 \qquad 30 \times 10 = 300$$

Estimate the following in four ways.

a. 31×23 **b.** 35×46

c. 48×27 **d.** 76×12

17. Guess what whole numbers can be used to fill in the blanks. Use your calculator to check.

a. _____$^4 = 6561$

b. _____$^5 = 16{,}807$

18. True or false? $493{,}827{,}156^2 = 246{,}913{,}578 \times 987{,}654{,}312$.

19. Notice how by starting with 55 and continuing to raise the digits to the third power and adding, 55 reoccurs in three steps.

$$55 \longrightarrow 5^3 + 5^3 = 250 \longrightarrow 2^3 + 5^3$$
$$= 133 \longrightarrow 1^3 + 3^3 + 3^3 = 55$$

Check to see whether this phenomenon is also true for these three numbers:

a. 136   **b.** 160   **c.** 919

20. What is interesting about the quotient obtained by dividing 987,654,312 by 8? (Do this mentally.)

21. It is easy to show that $3^2 + 4^2 = 5^2$, and $5^2 + 12^2 = 13^2$. However, in 1966 two mathematicians claimed the following:

$$27^5 + 84^5 + 110^5 + 133^5 = 144^5.$$

True or false?

22. Check to see that $1634 = 1^4 + 6^4 + 3^4 + 4^4$. Then determine which of the following four numbers satisfy the same property.

a. 8208   **b.** 9474   **c.** 1138   **d.** 2178

23. Verify the following patterns.

$$3^2 + 4^2 = 5^2$$
$$10^2 + 11^2 + 12^2 = 13^2 + 14^2$$
$$21^2 + 22^2 + 23^2 + 24^2 = 25^2 + 26^2 + 27^2$$

24. For which of the values $n = 1, 2, 3, 4$ is the following true?

$$1^n + 5^n + 8^n + 12^n + 18^n + 19^n =$$
$$2^n + 3^n + 9^n + 13^n + 16^n + 20^n$$

PROBLEMS

25. Using distributivity, show that $(a - b)^2 = a^2 - 2ab + b^2$. How can this idea be used to compute the following squares mentally? (*Hint*: $99 = 100 - 1$.)

   a. 99^2 **b.** 999^2 **c.** 9999^2

26. Fill in the empty squares to produce true equations.

$$
\begin{array}{ccccccc}
\boxed{3} & \times & \boxed{5} & \times & \boxed{} & = & \boxed{135} \\
\times & & \times & & \times & & \times \\
\boxed{} & \times & \boxed{} & \times & \boxed{} & = & \boxed{56} \\
\times & & \times & & \times & & \times \\
\boxed{} & \times & \boxed{8} & \times & \boxed{1} & = & \boxed{48} \\
= & & = & & = & & = \\
\boxed{126} & \times & \boxed{160} & \times & \boxed{18} & = & \boxed{}
\end{array}
$$

27. Discuss the similarities/differences of using (i) special factors and (ii) multiplicative compensation when calculating 36×5 mentally.

 28. Find $166,666,666^2$.

 29. Megan tried to multiply 712,000 by 864,000 on her calculator and got an error message. Explain how she can use her calculator (and a little thought) to find the exact product.

 30. What is the product of 777,777,777 and 999,999,999?

 31. Explain how you could calculate 342×143 even if the 3 and 4 keys did not work.

 32. Find the missing products by completing the pattern. Check your answers with a calculator.

$$
\begin{aligned}
11 \times 11 &= 121 \\
111 \times 111 &= 12321 \\
1111 \times 1111 &= \underline{} \\
11111 \times 11111 &= \underline{} \\
111111 \times 111111 &= \underline{}
\end{aligned}
$$

 33. Use your calculator to find the following products.

$$12 \times 11 \qquad 24 \times 11 \qquad 35 \times 11$$

Look at the middle digit of each product and at the first and last digits. Write a rule that you can use to multiply by 11. Now try these problems using your rule and check your answers with your calculator.

$$54 \times 11 \qquad 62 \times 11 \qquad 36 \times 11$$

Adapt your rule to handle

$$37 \times 11 \qquad 59 \times 11 \qquad 76 \times 11.$$

34. When asked to multiply 987,654,321 by 123,456,789, one mental calculator replied, "I saw in a flash that $987,654,321 \times 81 = 80,000,000,001$, so I multiplied 123,456,789 by 80,000,000,001 and divided by 81." Determine whether his reasoning was correct. If it was, see whether you can find the answer using your calculator.

35. a. Find a pattern for multiplying the following pairs.

$$32 \times 72 = 2304 \qquad 43 \times 63 = 2709$$
$$73 \times 33 = 2409$$

Try finding these products mentally.

$$17 \times 97 \qquad 56 \times 56 \qquad 42 \times 62$$

   b. Prove why your method works.

36. Have you always wanted to be a calculating genius? Amaze yourself with the following problems.

   a. To multiply 4,109,589,041,096 by 83, simply put the 3 in front of it and the 8 at the end of it. Now check your answer.

   b. After you have patted yourself on the back, see whether you can find a fast way to multiply

$$7,894,736,842,105,263,158 \text{ by } 86.$$

(NOTE: This works only in special cases.)

37. Develop a set of rules for the round to the nearest even method.

38. Find the ones digits.

   a. 2^{10}

   b. 432^{10}

   c. 3^6

   d. 293^6

39. A magician had his subject hide an odd number of coins in one hand and an even number of coins in another. He then told the subject to multiply the number of coins in the right hand by 2 and the number of coins in the left hand by 3 and to announce the sum of these two numbers. The magician immediately then correctly stated which hand had the odd number of coins. How did he do it?

PROBLEMS FOR WRITING/DISCUSSION

1. If your student is multiplying 3472 times 259 and she gets 89,248 as an answer, how can you, by using estimation, know right away that there must be a mistake somewhere? What is the error?

2. A student tells you that multiplying by 5 is a lot like dividing by 2. For example, $48 \times 5 = 240$, but it is easier just to go $48 \div 2 = 24$ and then affix a zero at the end. Will this method always work? Explain.

3. Another student says dividing by 5 is the same as multiplying by 2 and "dropping" a zero. Can you figure out what this student is saying? Does this work? Explain.

4.2   WRITTEN ALGORITHMS FOR WHOLE-NUMBER OPERATIONS

STARTING POINT

When a class of students was given the problem $\begin{array}{r} 48 \\ +35 \\ \hline \end{array}$, the following three responses were typical of what the students did.

Nick	Trevor	Courtney

Nick
$$\begin{array}{r} 48 \\ +\ 35 \\ \hline 70 \\ 13 \\ \hline 83 \end{array}$$
I combined 40 and 30 to get 70
$8 + 5 = 13$
70 and 13 is 83

Trevor
$$\begin{array}{r} 1 \\ 48 \\ +35 \\ \hline 83 \end{array}$$
$8+5$ is 13
Carry the 1
write down 3
$4+3+1-8$
write down 8

Courtney
$$\begin{array}{r} 48 \\ +35 \\ \hline 83 \end{array}$$
48 plus 30 is 78.
Now I add the 5
and get 83.

Which of these methods demonstrates the best (least) understanding of place value? Which method is the best? Justify.

Section 4.1 was devoted to mental and calculator computation. This section presents the common written algorithms as well as some alternative ones that have historical interest and can be used to help students better understand how their algorithms work.

NCTM Standards 2000
Number and Operations
Grades Pre-K–2
All students should develop and use strategies for whole-number computations, with a focus on addition and subtraction.

Algorithms for the Addition of Whole Numbers

An **algorithm** is a systematic, step-by-step procedure used to find an answer, usually to a computation. The common written algorithm for addition involves two main procedures: (1) adding single digits (thus using the basic facts) and (2) carrying (regrouping or exchanging).

A development of our **standard addition algorithm** is used in Figure 4.4 to find the sum $134 + 325$.

Base Ten Pieces	Chip Abacus	Place–Value Representations
(1)	(2)	(3) (4)

Figure 4.4

Observe how the left-to-right sequence in Figure 4.4 becomes progressively more abstract. When one views the base ten pieces (1), the hundreds, tens, and ones are distinguishable due to their sizes and the number of each type of piece. In the chip abacus (2), the chips all look the same. However, representations are distinguished by the number of chips in each column and by the column containing the chips (i.e., place value). In the place-value representation (3), the numbers are distinguished by the digits and the place values of their respective columns. Representation (4) is the common "add in columns" algorithm. The place-value method can be justified using expanded form and properties of whole-number addition as follows.

$$
\begin{aligned}
134 + 325 &= (1 \cdot 10^2 + 3 \cdot 10 + 4) && \text{\textit{Expanded form}}\\
&\quad + (3 \cdot 10^2 + 2 \cdot 10 + 5)\\
&= (1 \cdot 10^2 + 3 \cdot 10^2) && \text{\textit{Associativity and}}\\
&\quad + (3 \cdot 10 + 2 \cdot 10) + (4 + 5) && \text{\textit{commutativity}}\\
&= (1 + 3)10^2 + (3 + 2)10 + (4 + 5) && \text{\textit{Distributivity}}\\
&= 4 \cdot 10^2 + 5 \cdot 10 + 9 && \text{\textit{Addition}}\\
&= 459 && \text{\textit{Simplified form}}
\end{aligned}
$$

Note that $134 + 325$ can be found working from left to right (add the hundreds first, etc.) or from right to left (add the ones first, etc.).

An addition problem when regrouping is required is illustrated in Figure 4.5 to find the sum $37 + 46$.

Figure 4.5

www.wiley.com/
college/musser

Spotlight on Technology Using base ten blocks in the Chapter 4 eManipulative activity, *Base Blocks: Addition*, perform the operation $355 + 456$. (This can be done by selecting ⬚clear⬚ and then ⬚base = 10⬚. Represent each number, 355 and 456, with the blocks and then combine.) What part of the base block manipulation is analogous to the "carrying" process in the standard addition algorithm?

The procedure illustrated in the place-value representation can be refined in a series of steps to lead to our standard carrying algorithm for addition. Intermediate algorithms that lead to our standard addition algorithm are illustrated next.

(a) INTERMEDIATE ALGORITHM 1

$$
\begin{array}{r}
568\\
+394\\
\hline
12\\
150\\
\underline{800}\\
962
\end{array}
$$

    sum of ones
    sum of tens
    sum of hundreds
    final sum

(b) INTERMEDIATE ALGORITHM 2

$$
\begin{array}{r}
568\\
+394\\
\hline
12\\
15\\
\underline{8}\\
962
\end{array}
$$

(c) STANDARD ALGORITHM

$$
\begin{array}{r}
\overset{1\ 1}{568}\\
+394\\
\hline
962
\end{array}
$$

The preceding intermediate algorithms are easier to understand than the standard algorithm. However, they are less efficient and generally require more time and space.

Throughout history many other algorithms have been used for addition. One of these, the **lattice method for addition,** is illustrated next.

LATTICE METHOD

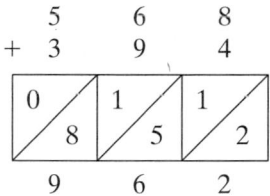

First add down the columns. Then add down the diagonals.

Notice how the lattice method is very much like intermediate algorithm 2. Other interesting algorithms are contained in the problem sets.

Algorithms for the Subtraction of Whole Numbers

The common algorithm for subtraction involves two main procedures: (1) subtracting numbers that are determined by the addition facts table and (2) exchanging or regrouping (the reverse of the carrying process for addition). Although this exchanging procedure is commonly called "borrowing," we choose to avoid this term because the numbers that are borrowed are not paid back. Hence the word *borrow* does not represent to children the actual underlying process of exchanging.

A development of our **standard subtraction algorithm** is used in Figure 4.6 to find the difference $357 - 123$.

Concrete Models

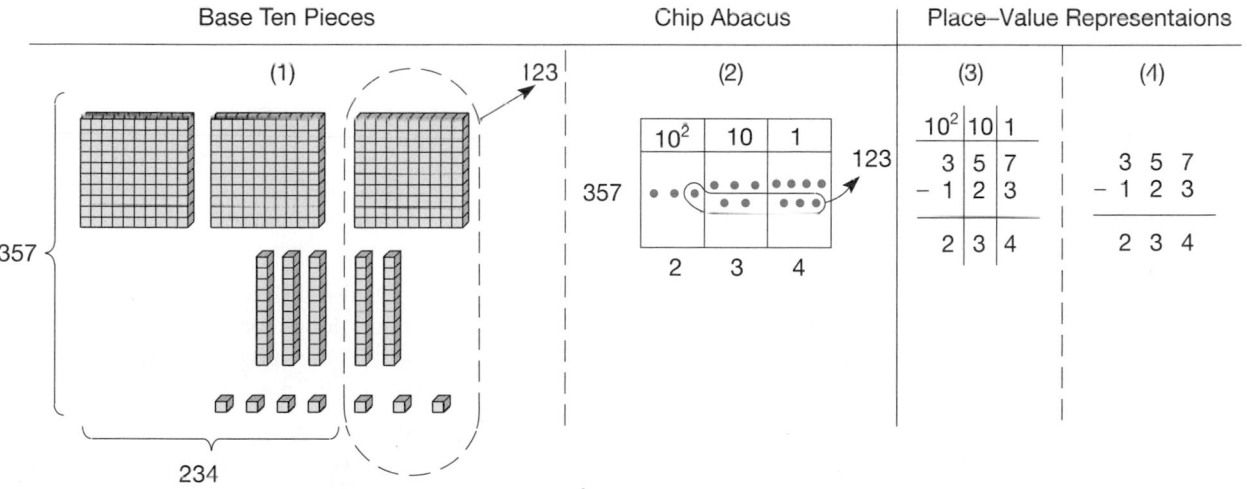

Figure 4.6

Notice that in the example in Figure 4.6, the answer will be the same whether we subtract from left to right or from right to left. The problem $423 - 157$ cannot be done in the same way, since we cannot subtract 7 from 3 directly. In such cases, we need to make exchanges in order to use this subtraction algorithm. This is illustrated in Figure 4.7.

Figure 4.7

This place-value procedure is finally shortened to produce our standard subtraction algorithm.

$$
\begin{array}{cc}
 & \text{make} & \overset{3\ 11\ 13}{\cancel{4}\ \cancel{2}\ \cancel{3}} \\
423 & \text{exchanges} & \cancel{4}\,\cancel{2}\,\cancel{3} \\
-157 & \longrightarrow & \underline{1\ 5\ 7} \\
 & & 2\ 6\ 6
\end{array}
$$

One nontraditional algorithm that is especially effective in any base is called the **subtract-from-the-base algorithm.** This algorithm is illustrated in Figure 4.8 using base ten pieces to find $323 - 64$. In (1), observe that the 4 is subtracted from the 10 (instead of finding $13 - 4$, as in the standard algorithm). The difference, $10 - 4 = 6$, is then combined with the 3 units in (2) to form 9 units. Then the 6 longs are sub-

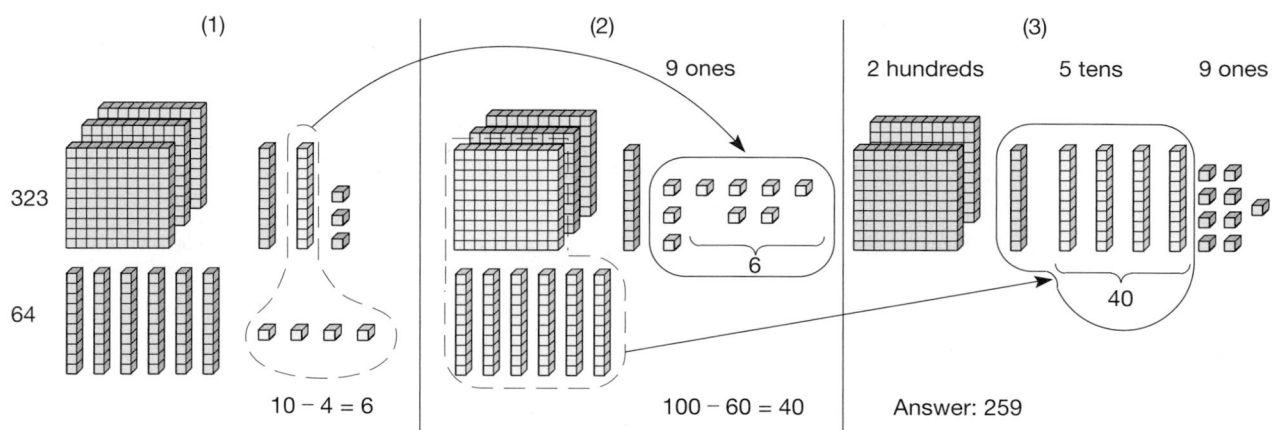

Figure 4.8

tracted from 1 flat (instead of finding $11 - 6$). The difference, $10 - 6 = 4$ longs, is then combined with the 1 long in (3) to obtain 5 longs (or 50). Thus, since two flats remain, $323 - 64 = 259$. The following illustrates this process symbolically.

$$
\begin{array}{ccccc}
 & & \overset{1\ \ 10}{} & \overset{2\ 10\ 10}{} & \overset{2\ 10\ 10}{} \\
323 & & 3\ \cancel{2}\ 3 & \cancel{3}\ \cancel{2}\ 3 & \cancel{3}\ \cancel{2}\ 3 \\
-\ 64 & \rightarrow & -\ 6\ 4 & \rightarrow & -\ 6\ 4 & \rightarrow & -\ 6\ 4 \\
\hline
 & & 9 & 5\ 9 & 2\ 5\ 9 \\
 & & \underline{(10-4)+3} & \underline{(10-6)+1} &
\end{array}
$$

Reflection from Research
Having students create their own computational algorithms for large number addition and subtraction is a worthwhile activity (Cobb, Yackel, & Wood, 1988).

The advantage of this algorithm is that we only need to know the addition facts and *differences from 10* (as opposed to differences from all the teens). As you will see later in this chapter, this method can be used in any base (hence the name *subtract-from-the-base*). After a little practice, you may find this algorithm to be easier and faster than our usual algorithm for subtraction.

STUDENT PAGE SNAPSHOT

Whole Numbers

Partial-Differences Method

1. Subtract from left to right, one column at a time.

2. Always subtract the smaller number from the larger number.

   - If the smaller number is on the bottom, the difference is **added** to the answer.
   - If the smaller number is on the top, the difference is **subtracted** from the answer.

EXAMPLE $746 - 263 = ?$

$$
\begin{array}{r}
7\ 4\ 6 \\
-\ 2\ 6\ 3 \\
\hline
\end{array}
$$

Subtract the 100s.	$700 - 200 \rightarrow$	+ 5 0 0
Subtract the 10s.	$60 - 40 \rightarrow$	− 2 0
Subtract the 1s.	$6 - 3 \rightarrow$	+ 3
Find the total.	$500 - 20 + 3 \rightarrow$	4 8 3

(The smaller number is on top, so include a minus sign.)

$746 - 263 = 483$

Same-Change Rule

Here is the **same-change rule** for subtraction problems:

- If you add the same number to both numbers in the problem, the answer is the same.
- If you subtract the same number from both numbers in the problem, the answer is the same.

Use this rule to change the second number in the problem to a number that has zero in the ones place.

EXAMPLES $92 - 36 = ?$

One way: Add 4.

$$
\begin{array}{r}
9\ 2 \quad \text{(add 4)} \\
-\ 3\ 6 \quad \text{(add 4)} \\
\end{array}
\qquad
\begin{array}{r}
9\ 6 \\
-\ 4\ 0 \\
\hline
5\ 6 \\
\end{array}
$$

Another way: Subtract 6.

$$
\begin{array}{r}
9\ 2 \quad \text{(subtract 6)} \\
-\ 3\ 6 \quad \text{(subtract 6)} \\
\end{array}
\qquad
\begin{array}{r}
8\ 6 \\
-\ 3\ 0 \\
\hline
5\ 6 \\
\end{array}
$$

CHECK YOUR UNDERSTANDING

Subtract.

1. $714 - 192$ 2. $174 - 36$ 3. $483 - 164$ 4. $857 - 409$

Check your answers on page 277.

SRB 14 fourteen

Spotlight on Technology The Chapter 4 eManipulative activity, *Base Blocks: Subtraction,* utilizes the comparison approach to model subtraction. By placing blue blocks and red blocks next to each other, you can compare, match up, and remove blocks until only the difference remains. The problem $35 - 18$ is modeled by beginning with the blocks shown at the right. Perform $35 - 18$, $321 - 43$, and $234 - 158$ on the eManipulative. What process of moving the blocks is analogous to "borrowing" in the standard subtraction algorithm?

www.wiley.com/college/musser

Algorithms for the Multiplication of Whole Numbers

The standard multiplication algorithm involves the multiplication facts, distributivity, and a thorough understanding of place value. A development of our **standard multiplication algorithm** is used in Figure 4.9 to find the product 3×213.

Concrete Model	Place Value Representations

Figure 4.9

Next, the product of a two-digit number times a two-digit number is found. Calculate 34×12.

$$
\begin{aligned}
34 \times 12 &= 34(10 + 2) && \textit{Expanded form} \\
&= 34 \cdot 10 + 34 \cdot 2 && \textit{Distributivity} \\
&= (30 + 4)10 + (30 + 4)2 && \textit{Expanded form} \\
&= 30 \cdot 10 + 4 \cdot 10 + 30 \cdot 2 + 4 \cdot 2 && \textit{Distributivity} \\
&= 300 + 40 + 60 + 8 && \textit{Multiplication} \\
&= 408 && \textit{Addition}
\end{aligned}
$$

The product 34×12 also can be represented pictorially (Figure 4.10).

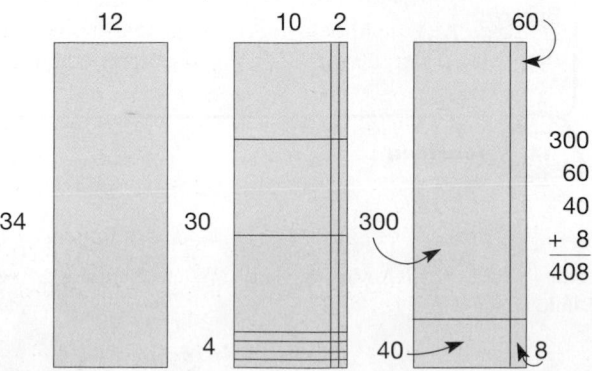

Figure 4.10

The following vertical intermediate multiplication algorithms can be used to lead to our standard multiplication algorithm.

(a) INTERMEDIATE ALGORITHM 1	**(b)** INTERMEDIATE ALGORITHM 2	**(c)** STANDARD ALGORITHM

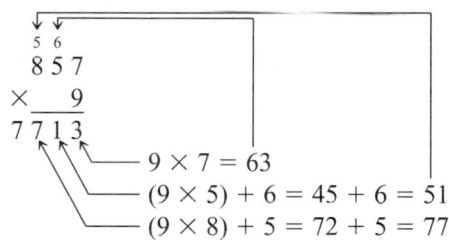

One final complexity in the standard multiplication algorithm is illustrated next. Calculate 857×9.

(a) INTERMEDIATE ALGORITHM

$$
\begin{array}{r}
857 \\
\times \quad 9 \\
\hline
63 \longleftarrow 9 \times 7 \\
450 \longleftarrow 9 \times 50 \\
7200 \longleftarrow 9 \times 800 \\
\hline
7713
\end{array}
$$

(b) STANDARD ALGORITHM

$$
\begin{array}{r}
\overset{5\ 6}{8\ 5\ 7} \\
\times \qquad 9 \\
\hline
7\ 7\ 1\ 3
\end{array}
$$

$9 \times 7 = 63$

$(9 \times 5) + 6 = 45 + 6 = 51$

$(9 \times 8) + 5 = 72 + 5 = 77$

Notice the complexity involved in explaining the standard algorithm!

The **lattice method for multiplication** is an example of an extremely simple multiplication algorithm that is no longer used, perhaps because we do not use paper with lattice markings on it and it is too time-consuming to draw such lines.

To calculate 35×4967, begin with a blank lattice and find products of the digits in intersecting rows and columns. The 18 in the completed lattice was obtained by multiplying its row value, 3, by its column value, 6 (Figure 4.11). The other values are filled in similarly. Then the numbers are added down the diagonals as in lattice addition. The answer, read counterclockwise from left to right, is 173,845.

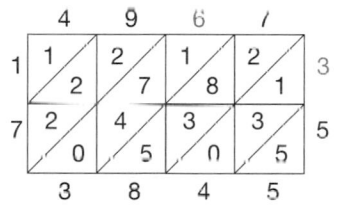

Figure 4.11

Algorithms for the Division of Whole Numbers

The long-division algorithm is the most complicated procedure in the elementary mathematics curriculum. Because of calculators, the importance of written long division using multidigit numbers has greatly diminished. However, the long-division algorithm involving one- and perhaps two-digit divisors continues to have common applications. The main idea behind the long-division algorithm is the division algorithm, which was given in Section 3.2. It states that if a and b are any whole numbers with $b \neq 0$, there exist unique whole numbers q and r such that $a = bq + r$, where $0 \leq r < b$. For example, if $a = 17$ and $b = 5$, then $q = 3$ and $r = 2$ since $17 = 5 \cdot 3 + 2$. The purpose of the long division algorithm is to find the quotient, q, and remainder, r, for any given divisor, b, and dividend, a.

To gain an understanding of the division algorithm, we will use base ten blocks and a fundamental definition of division. Find the quotient and remainder of 461 divided by 3. This can be thought of as 461 divided into groups of size 3. As you read this example, notice how the manipulation of the base ten blocks parallels the written algorithm. The following illustrates **long division using base ten blocks.**

Thought One

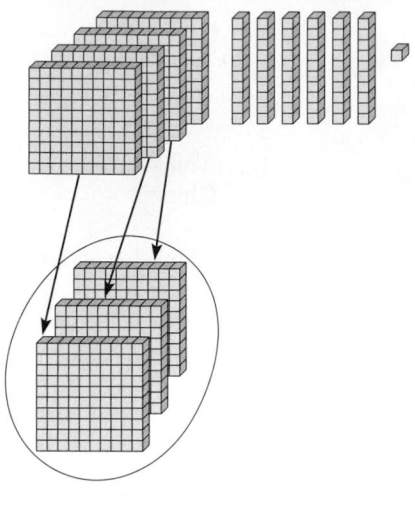

$$\begin{array}{r} 1 \\ 3\overline{)461} \\ \underline{3} \\ 1 \end{array}$$

Think: One group of three flats leaves one flat left over.

Thought Two

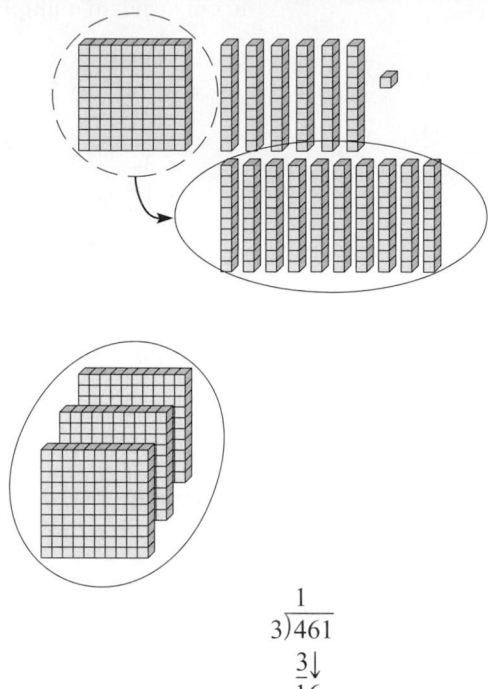

$$\begin{array}{r} 1 \\ 3\overline{)461} \\ \underline{3}{\downarrow} \\ 16 \end{array}$$

Think: Convert the one leftover flat to 10 longs and add it to the existing 6 longs to make 16 longs.

Thought Three

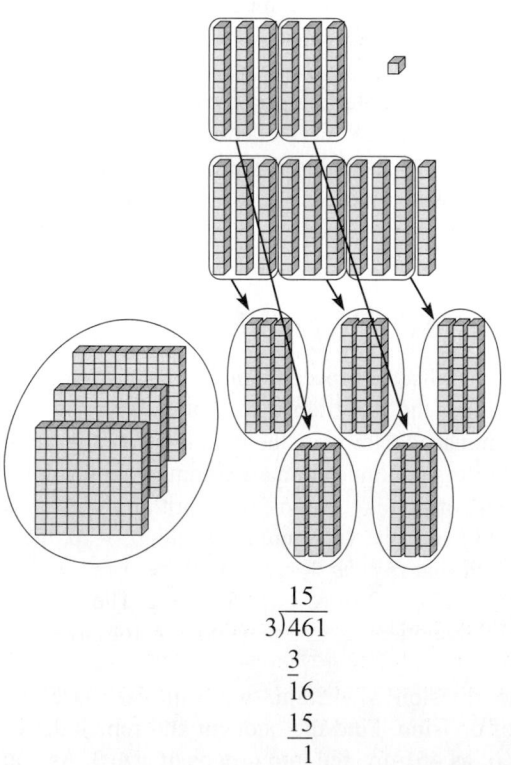

$$\begin{array}{r} 15 \\ 3\overline{)461} \\ \underline{3} \\ 16 \\ \underline{15} \\ 1 \end{array}$$

Think: Five groups of 3 longs leaves 1 long left over.

Thought Four

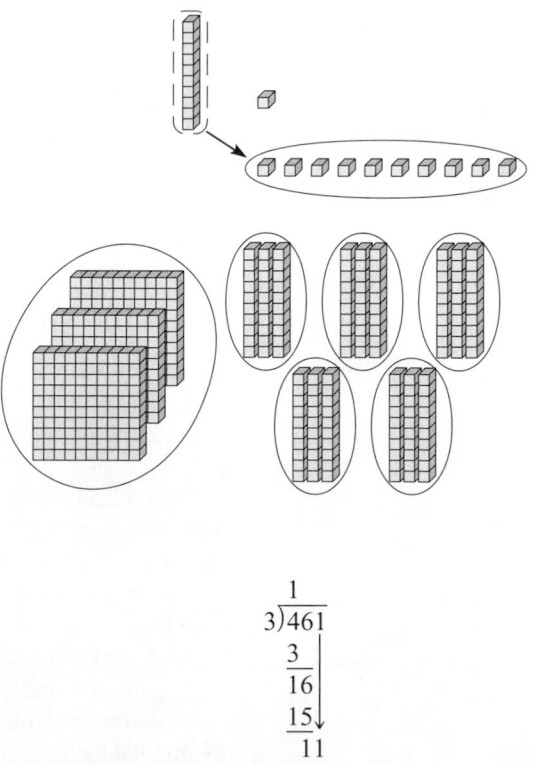

$$\begin{array}{r} 1 \\ 3\overline{)461} \\ \underline{3}| \\ 16 \\ \underline{15}{\downarrow} \\ 11 \end{array}$$

Think: Convert the one leftover long into 10 units and add it to the existing 1 unit to make 11 units.

Thought Five

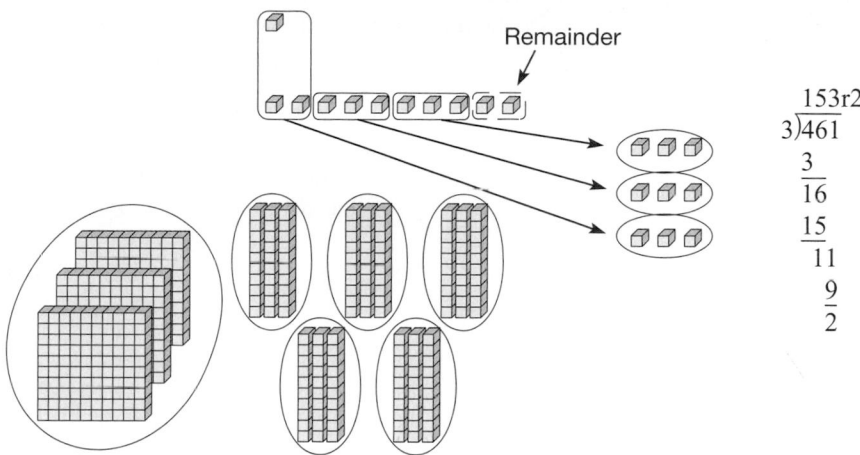

Think: Three groups of 3 units each leaves 2 units left over. Since there is one group of flats (hundreds), five groups of longs (tens), and three groups of units (ones) with 2 left over, the quotient is 153 with a remainder of 2.

We will arrive at the final form of the long-division algorithm by working through various levels of complexity to illustrate how one can gain an understanding of the algorithm by progressing in small steps.

Find the quotient and remainder for 5739 ÷ 31.

The **scaffold method** is a good one to use first.

$$
\begin{array}{r}
31\overline{)5739} \\
-3100 \\ \hline
2639 \\
-1550 \\ \hline
1089 \\
-930 \\ \hline
159 \\
155 \\ \hline
4
\end{array}
$$

	100(31)
	50(31)
	30(31)
+	5(31)
	185(31)

How many 31s in 5739? *Guess:* 100

How many 31s in 2639? *Guess:* 50

How many 31s in 1089? *Guess:* 30

How many 31s in 159? *Guess:* 5

Since 4 < 31, we stop and add 100 + 50 + 30 + 5. Therefore, the quotient is 185 and remainder is 4.

Check: 31 · 185 + 4 = 5735 + 4 = 5739.

As just shown, various multiples of 31 are subtracted successively from 5739 (or the resulting difference) until a remainder less than 31 is found. The key to this method is how well one can estimate the appropriate multiples of 31. In the scaffold method, it is better to estimate too low rather than too high, as in the case of the 50. However, 80 would have been the optimal guess at that point. Thus, although the quotient and remainder can be obtained using this method, it can be an inefficient application of the Guess and Test strategy.

Spotlight on Technology The scaffold method can be performed using a spreadsheet. Refer to the dynamic spreadsheet, *Scaffold Division*, in the spreadsheet webmodule. Using this scaffold method spreadsheet, perform the divisions 899 ÷ 13 and 5697 ÷ 23. What are the advantages and disadvantages of the scaffold method?

www.wiley.com/college/musser

The next example illustrates how division by a single digit can be done more efficiently.

Find the quotient and remainder for 3159 ÷ 7.

INTERMEDIATE ALGORITHM

$$
\begin{array}{r}
451 \\
\hline
1 \\
50 \\
400 \\
\hline
\end{array}
$$

Start here:
$$
\begin{array}{r}
7\overline{)3159} \\
-2800 \\
\hline
359 \\
-350 \\
\hline
9 \\
-7 \\
\hline
2
\end{array}
$$

Think: How many 7s
in 3100? 400
Think: How many 7s
in 350? 50
Think: How many 7s
in 9? 1

Therefore, the quotient is the sum 400 + 50 + 1, or 451, and the remainder is 2.
Check: 7 · 451 + 2 = 3157 + 2 = 3159.

Now consider division by a two-digit divisor, Find the quotient and remainder for 1976 ÷ 32.

INTERMEDIATE ALGORITHM

$$
\begin{array}{r}
61 \\
\hline
1 \\
60 \\
32\overline{)1976} \\
-1920 \\
\hline
56 \\
-32 \\
\hline
24
\end{array}
$$

Think: How many
32s in 1976? 60
Think: How many
32s in 56? 1

Therefore, the quotient is 61 and the remainder is 24.
Check: 32 · 61 + 24 = 1952 + 24 = 1976.

Next we will employ rounding to help estimate the appropriate quotients. Find the quotient and remainder of 4238 ÷ 56.

$$
\begin{array}{r}
5 \\
70 \\
56\overline{)4238} \\
-3920 \\
\hline
318 \\
-280 \\
\hline
38
\end{array}
$$

Think: How many 60s in 4200? 70
70 × 56 = 3920
Think: How many 60s in 310? 5
5 × 56 = 280

Therefore, the quotient is 70 + 5 = 75 and the remainder is 38.
Check: 56 · 75 + 38 = 4200 + 38 = 4238.

Observe how we rounded the divisor up to 60 and the dividend *down* to 4200 in the first step. This up/down rounding assures us that the quotient at each step will not be too large.

This algorithm can be simplified further to our **standard algorithm for division** by reducing the "think" steps to divisions with single-digit divisors. For example, in place of "How many 60s in 4200?" one could ask equivalently "How many 6s in 420?" Even easier, "How many 6s in 42?" Notice also that in general, the *divisor should be rounded up and the dividend should be rounded down.*

Example 4.9   Find the quotient and remainder for $4238 \div 56$.

Solution

$$
\begin{array}{r}
75 \\
56\overline{)4238} \\
392 \\
\hline
\end{array}
$$

$\left\{ \begin{array}{l} \textit{Think:} \text{ How many 6s in 42? 7} \\ \text{Put the 7 above the 3 since we are actually} \\ \text{finding } 4230 \div 56. \\ \text{The 392 is } 7 \cdot 56. \end{array} \right.$

$$
\begin{array}{r}
318 \\
-280 \\
\hline
38 \\
\end{array}
$$

$\left\{ \begin{array}{l} \textit{Think:} \text{ How many 6s in 31? 5} \\ \text{Put the 5 above the 8 since we are finding } 318 \div 56. \\ \text{The 280 is } 5 \cdot 56. \end{array} \right.$

■

Figure 4.12

Spotlight on Technology   The quotient and remainder for $4238 \div 56$ can be found using a calculator. The TI-34 II does long division with remainder directly using 4238 [2nd] [INT÷] 56 [=]. The result for this problem is shown in Figure 4.12 as it appears on the second line of the calculator's display. To find the quotient and remainder using a standard calculator, press these keys: 4238 [÷] 56 [=]. Your display should read 75.678571 (perhaps with fewer or more decimal places). Thus the whole-number quotient is 75. From the relationship $a = bq + r$, we see that $r = a - bq$ is the remainder. In this case $r = 4238 - 56 \cdot 75$, or 38.

As the preceding calculator example illustrates, calculators virtually eliminate the need for becoming skilled in performing involved long divisions and other tedious calculations.

In this section, each of the four basic operations was illustrated by different algorithms. The problem set contains examples of many other algorithms. Even today, other countries use algorithms different from our "standard" algorithms. Also, students may even invent "new" algorithms. Since computational algorithms are aids for simplifying calculations, it is important to understand that *all correct algorithms are acceptable.* Clearly, computation in the future will rely less and less on written calculations and more and more on mental and electronic calculations.

MATHEMATICAL MORSEL

Have someone write down a three-digit number using three different digits hidden from your view. Then have the person form all of the other five three-digit numbers that can be obtained by rearranging his or her three digits. Add these six numbers together with a seventh number, which is any other one of the six. The person tells you the sum, and then you, in turn, tell him or her the seventh number.

Here is how. Add the thousands digit of the sum to the remaining three-digit number (if the sum was 2347, you form $347 + 2 = 349$). Then take the remainder upon division of this new number by nine ($349 \div 9$ leaves a remainder of 7). Multiply the remainder by 111 ($7 \times 111 = 777$) and add this to the previous number ($349 + 777 = 1126$). Finally, add the thousands digit (if there is one) to the remaining number (1126 yields $126 + 1 = 127$, the seventh number!).

Section 4.2   EXERCISE / PROBLEM SET A

EXERCISES

1. The physical models of base ten blocks and the chip abacus have been used to demonstrate addition. Using bundling sticks, sketch the solution to the following addition problems.

   a. $15 + 32$ **b.** $63 + 79$

2. Give a reason or reasons for each of the following steps to justify the addition process.

$$
\begin{aligned}
17 + 21 &= (1 \cdot 10 + 7) + (2 \cdot 10 + 1) \\
&= (1 \cdot 10 + 2 \cdot 10) + (7 + 1) \\
&= (1 + 2) \cdot 10 + (7 + 1) \\
&= 3 \cdot 10 + 8 \\
&= 38
\end{aligned}
$$

3. There are many ways of providing intermediate steps between the models for computing sums (base ten blocks, chip abacus, etc.) and the algorithm for addition. One of these is to represent numbers in their expanded forms. Consider the following examples:

$$
\begin{aligned}
246 &= 2 \text{ hundreds} + 4 \text{ tens} + 6 \\
+352 &= 3 \text{ hundreds} + 5 \text{ tens} + 2 \\
&= 5 \text{ hundreds} + 9 \text{ tens} + 8 \\
&= 598
\end{aligned}
$$

$$
\begin{aligned}
547 &= 5(10)^2 + 4(10) + 7 \\
+296 &= 2(10)^2 + 9(10) + 6 \\
&\left.\begin{aligned}
&7(10)^2 + 13(10) + 13 \\
&7(10)^2 + 14(10) + 3 \\
&8(10)^2 + 4(10) + 3
\end{aligned}\right\} \text{regrouping} \\
&= 843
\end{aligned}
$$

Use this expanded form of the addition algorithm to compute the following sums.

   a. 351 **b.** 478 **c.** 1965
   $+635$ $+269$ $+\ 857$

4. An alternative algorithm for addition, called **scratch addition,** is shown next. Using it, students can do more complicated additions by doing a series of single-digit additions. This method is sometimes more effective with students having trouble with the standard algorithm. For example, to compute $78 + 56 + 38$:

   7 8   Add the number in the units place starting
   5 6̸   at the top. When the sum is ten or more,
   3 8⁴   scratch a line through the last number added
   ‾‾‾‾   and write down the unit. The scratch repre-
          sents 10.

   ²
   7 8   Continue adding units (adding 4 and 8).
   5 6̸   Write the last number of units below the
   3 8̸⁴ line. Count the number of scratches, and
   ‾‾‾‾   write above the second column.
       2

   ²
   7 8   Repeat the procedure for each column.
   5̸ 6̸
   3⁴ 8̸⁴
   ‾‾‾‾‾
   1 7 2

   Compute the following additions using the scratch algorithm.

   a. 734   **b.** 1364
           468   7257
         + 27   +4813

5. Compute the following sums using the lattice method.

   a. 482   **b.** 567
          $+269$ $+765$

6. Give an advantage and a disadvantage of each of the following methods for addition.

   a. Intermediate algorithm   **b.** Lattice

7. Sketch solutions to the following problems, using bundling sticks.

   a. 57   **b.** 44   **c.** 34
         -37 -22 -29

8. Using the Chapter 4 eManipulative activity, *Multibase Blocks—Addition*, model the following addition problems using base ten blocks. Sketch how the base ten blocks would be used.

   a. 347   **b.** 258
         $+\ 86$ $+149$

9. 9342 is usually thought of as 9 thousands, 3 hundreds, 4 tens, and 2 ones, but in subtracting 6457 from 9342 using the customary algorithm, we regroup and think of 9342 as

   _____ thousands, _____ hundreds, _____ tens, and _____ ones.

10. Order these computations from easiest to hardest.

    a. 809   **b.** 8   **c.** 82
          -306 -3 -67

11. To perform some subtractions, it is necessary to reverse the rename and regroup process of addition. Perform the following subtraction in expanded form and follow regrouping steps.

$$
\begin{array}{r} 732 \\ -378 \end{array} \qquad \begin{array}{r} 700 + 30 + 2 \\ -(300 + 70 + 8) \end{array} \quad \text{or}
$$

$$
\begin{array}{r} 700 + 20 + 12 \\ -(300 + 70 + 8) \end{array} \quad \text{or} \quad \begin{array}{r} 600 + 120 + 12 \\ -(300 + 70 + 8) \\ \hline 300 + 50 + 4 \ = 354 \end{array}
$$

Use expanded form with regrouping as necessary to perform the following subtractions.

a. $652 - 175$

b. $923 - 147$

c. $8257 - 6439$

12. Subtraction by **adding the complement** goes as follows:

$$
\begin{array}{r} 619 \\ -476 \end{array} \qquad \begin{array}{r} 619 \\ +523 \\ \hline \cancel{1}142 \\ +\quad 1 \\ \hline 143 \end{array}
$$

The complement of 476 is 523 since $476 + 523 = 999$. (The sum in each place is 9.) Cross out the leading digit. Add 1. Answer = 143

a. Find the following differences using this algorithm.

$$
\begin{array}{r} 537 \\ -179 \end{array} \qquad \begin{array}{r} 86{,}124 \\ -38{,}759 \end{array} \qquad \begin{array}{r} 6{,}002{,}005 \\ -4{,}187{,}269 \end{array}
$$

b. Explain how the method works with three-digit numbers.

13. Without performing the addition, tell which sum, if either, is greater.

$$
\begin{array}{r} 23{,}456 \\ 23{,}400 \\ 23{,}000 \\ +20{,}002 \\ \hline \end{array} \qquad \begin{array}{r} 20{,}002 \\ 32 \\ 432 \\ +65{,}432 \\ \hline \end{array}
$$

14. Add the following numbers. Then turn this page upside down and add it again. What did you find? What feature of the numerals 1, 6, 8, 9 accounts for this?

$$
\begin{array}{r} 986 \\ 818 \\ 969 \\ 989 \\ 696 \\ 616 \end{array}
$$

15. Show how to find 34×28 on this grid paper.

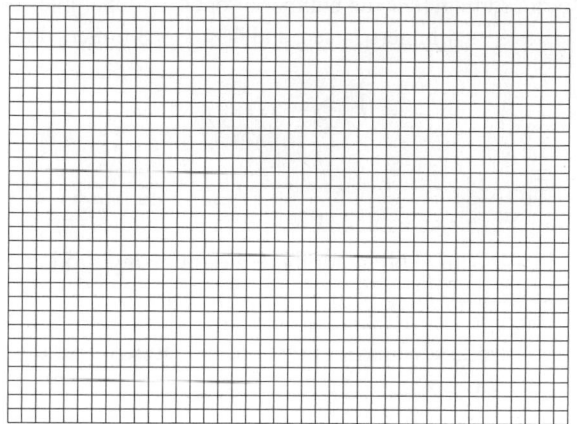

16. Justify each step in the following proof that $72 \times 10 = 720$.

$$
\begin{aligned}
72 \times 10 &= (70 + 2) \times 10 \\
&= 70 \times 10 + 2 \times 10 \\
&= (7 \times 10) \times 10 + 2 \times 10 \\
&- 7 \times (10 \times 10) + 2 \times 10 \\
&= 7 \times 100 + 2 \times 10 \\
&= 700 + 20 \\
&= 720
\end{aligned}
$$

17. Solve the following problems using the lattice method for multiplication and an intermediate algorithm.

a. 23×62 **b.** 17×45

18. Study the pattern in the following left-to-right multiplication.

$$
\begin{array}{r} 731 \\ 238 \\ \hline 1462 \\ 2193 \\ 5848 \\ \hline 173978 \end{array} \quad \begin{array}{l} \\ \\ (2 \cdot 731) \\ (3 \cdot 731) \\ (8 \cdot 731) \\ \\ \end{array}
$$

Use this algorithm to do the following computations.

a. 75×47 **b.** 364×421 **c.** 768×891

19. The use of finger numbers and systems of finger computation has been widespread through the years. One such system for multiplication uses the finger positions shown for computing the products of numbers from 6 through 10.

6   7   8   9   10

The two numbers to be multiplied are each represented on a different hand. The sum of the raised fingers is the number of tens, and the product of the closed fingers is the number of ones. For example, $1 + 3 = 4$ fingers raised, and $4 \times 2 = 8$ fingers down.

6×8

Use this method to compute the following products.

a. 7×8 **b.** 6×7 **c.** 6×10

20. A third-grade teacher prepared her students for division this way:

$$20 \div 4$$

$$
\begin{array}{r}
20 \\
-\ 4\ \checkmark \\
\hline
16 \\
-\ 4\ \checkmark \\
\hline
12 \\
-\ 4\ \checkmark \quad 20 \div 4 = 5 \\
\hline
8 \\
-\ 4\ \checkmark \\
\hline
4 \\
-\ 4\ \checkmark \\
\hline
0
\end{array}
$$

How would her students find $42 \div 6$?

21. Without using the divide key, use a calculator to find the quotient and remainder for each of the following problems.

a. $3\overline{)39}$

b. $8\overline{)89}$

c. $6\overline{)75}$

22. When performing the division problem $2137 \div 14$ using the standard algorithm, the first few steps look like what is shown here. The next step is to "bring down" the 3. Explain how that process of "bringing down" the 3 is modeled using base ten blocks.

$$
\begin{array}{r}
1 \\
14\overline{)2137} \\
14 \\
\hline
7
\end{array}
$$

PROBLEMS

23. Larry, Curly, and Moe each add incorrectly as follows.

Larry:
$$
\begin{array}{r}
29 \\
+83 \\
\hline
1012
\end{array}
$$

Curly:
$$
\begin{array}{r}
\overset{2}{} \\
29 \\
+83 \\
\hline
121
\end{array}
$$

Moe:
$$
\begin{array}{r}
29 \\
+83 \\
\hline
102
\end{array}
$$

How would you explain their mistakes to each of them?

24. Use the digits 1 to 9 to make an addition problem and answer. Use each digit only once.

$$
+\ \begin{array}{ccc}
\square & \square & \square \\
\square & \square & \square \\
\hline
\square & \square & \square
\end{array}
$$

25. Place the digits 2, 3, 4, 6, 7, 8 in the boxes to obtain the following sums.

a. The greatest sum **b.** The least sum

$$
+\ \begin{array}{ccc}
\square & \square & \square \\
\square & \square & \square
\end{array}
$$

26. Arrange the digits 1, 2, 3, 4, 5, 6, 7 such that they add up to 100. (For example, $12 + 34 + 56 + 7 = 109$.)

27. Given the following addition problem, replace seven digits with 0s so that the sum of the numbers is 1111.

$$
\begin{array}{r}
999 \\
777 \\
555 \\
333 \\
111 \\
\hline
\end{array}
$$

b. Do the same problem by replacing (i) eight digits with 0s, (ii) nine digits with 0s, (iii) ten digits with 0s.

28. Consider the following array:

1	2	3	4	5	6	7	8	9	10
11	12	13	14	15	16	17	18	19	20
㉑	㉒	23	24	25	㉖	㉗	28	29	30
31	32	33	34	35	㊱	㊲	38	39	40
㊶	42	43	44	45	46	47	48	49	50
㊿	52	53	54	55	56	57	58	59	60

Compare the pair 26, 37 with the pair 36, 27.

a. Add: $26 + 37 =$ ____. $\quad 36 + 27 =$ ____.
What do you notice about the answers?

Notice that to do subtraction in base five using the subtract-from-the-base algorithm, you only need to know two addition combinations to five, namely $1_{\text{five}} + 4_{\text{five}} = 10_{\text{five}}$ and $2_{\text{five}} + 3_{\text{five}} = 10_{\text{five}}$. These two, in turn, lead to the four subtraction facts you need to know, namely $10_{\text{five}} - 4_{\text{five}} = 1_{\text{five}}$, $10_{\text{five}} - 1_{\text{five}} = 4_{\text{five}}$, $10_{\text{five}} - 3_{\text{five}} = 2_{\text{five}}$, and $10_{\text{five}} - 2_{\text{five}} = 3_{\text{five}}$.

Multiplication To perform multiplication efficiently, one must know the multiplication facts. The multiplication facts for base five are displayed in Figure 4.17. The entries in this multiplication table can be visualized by referring to the number line shown in Figure 4.18. The number line includes a representation of $4_{\text{five}} \times 3_{\text{five}} = 22_{\text{five}}$ using the repeated-addition approach. (All numerals in the multiplication table and number line are written in base five with subscripts omitted.)

×	0	1	2	3	4
0	0	0	0	0	0
1	0	1	2	3	4
2	0	2	4	11	13
3	0	3	11	14	22
4	0	4	13	22	31

Figure 4.17

Figure 4.18

Example 4.12　Calculate $43_{\text{five}} \times 123_{\text{five}}$ using the following methods.

Solution

a. Lattice Method

b. Intermediate Algorithm

$$
\begin{array}{rl}
123_{\text{five}} & \\
\times\ 43_{\text{five}} & \\
\hline
14 & 3 \cdot 3 \\
110 & 3 \cdot 20 \\
300 & 3 \cdot 100 \\
220 & 40 \cdot 3 \\
1300 & 40 \cdot 20 \\
4000 & 40 \cdot 100 \\
\hline
11444_{\text{five}} &
\end{array}
$$

c. Standard Algorithm

$$
\begin{array}{r}
123_{\text{five}} \\
\times 43_{\text{five}} \\
\hline
424 \\
1102 \\
\hline
11444_{\text{five}}
\end{array}
$$

Notice how efficient the lattice method is. Also, instead of using the multiplication table, you could find single-digit products using repeated addition and thinking strategies. For example, you could find $4_{\text{five}} \times 2_{\text{five}}$ as follows.

$$4_{\text{five}} \times 2_{\text{five}} = 2_{\text{five}} \times 4_{\text{five}} = 4_{\text{five}} + 4_{\text{five}} = 4_{\text{five}} + (1 + 3)_{\text{five}}$$
$$= (4 + 1)_{\text{five}} + 3_{\text{five}} = 13_{\text{five}}$$

Although this may look like it would take a lot of time, it would go quickly mentally, especially if you imagine base five pieces.

Division Doing long division in other bases points out the difficulties of learning this algorithm and, especially, the need to become proficient at approximating multiples of numbers.

Example 4.13 Find the quotient and remainder for $1443_{\text{five}} \div 34_{\text{five}}$ using the following methods.

Solution

a. Scaffold Method

$$
\begin{array}{r}
34_{\text{five}}\overline{)1443_{\text{five}}} \\
-1230 \qquad 20_{\text{five}} \\
\hline
213 \\
-212 \qquad\ 3_{\text{five}} \\
\hline
1 \qquad\ 23_{\text{five}}
\end{array}
$$

Quotient: 23_{five}
Remainder: 1_{five}

b. Standard Long-Division Algorithm

$$
\begin{array}{r}
23_{\text{five}} \\
34_{\text{five}}\overline{)1443_{\text{five}}} \\
-123 \qquad (2_{\text{five}} \times 34_{\text{five}}) \\
\hline
213 \\
-212 \qquad (3_{\text{five}} \times 34_{\text{five}}) \\
\hline
1
\end{array}
$$

In the scaffold method, the first estimate, namely 20_{five}, was selected because $2_{\text{five}} \times 3_{\text{five}}$ is 11_{five}, which is less than 14_{five}. ■

In summary, doing computations in other number bases can provide insights into how computational difficulties arise, whereas our own familiarity and competence with our algorithms in base ten tend to mask the trouble spots that children face.

MATHEMATICAL MORSEL

George Parker Bidder (1806–1878), who lived in Devonshire, England, was blessed with an incredible memory as well as being a calculating prodigy. When he was 10 he was read a number backward and he immediately gave the number back in its correct form. An hour later, he repeated the original number, which was

2,563,721,987,653,461,598,746,231,905,607,541,128, 975,231.

Furthermore, his brother memorized the entire Bible and could give the chapter and verse of any quoted text. Also, one of Bidder's sons could multiply 15-digit numbers in his head.

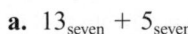 **Section 4.3** EXERCISE / PROBLEM SET A

EXERCISES

1. Create a base seven number line and illustrate the following operations.

   a. $13_{\text{seven}} + 5_{\text{seven}}$ **b.** $21_{\text{seven}} - 4_{\text{seven}}$

   c. $6_{\text{seven}} \times 3_{\text{seven}}$ **d.** $24_{\text{seven}} + 16_{\text{seven}}$

2. Use bundling sticks, chips, or multibase pieces for the appropriate base to illustrate the following problems.

   a. $41_{\text{six}} + 33_{\text{six}}$ **b.** $555_{\text{seven}} + 66_{\text{seven}}$

   c. $3030_{\text{four}} + 322_{\text{four}}$

3. Solve each of the following base four addition problems. The Chapter 4 eManipulative activity, *Multibase Blocks—Addition*, can be used in the solution process.

   a. $1_{\text{four}} + 2_{\text{four}}$ **b.** $11_{\text{four}} + 23_{\text{four}}$

   c. $212_{\text{four}} + 113_{\text{four}}$ **d.** $2023_{\text{four}} + 3330_{\text{four}}$

4. Use an intermediate algorithm to compute the following sums.

   a. $78_{\text{nine}} + 65_{\text{nine}}$ **b.** $TE_{\text{twelve}} + EE_{\text{twelve}}$

5. Use the standard algorithm to compute the following sums.

   a. $213_{\text{five}} + 433_{\text{five}}$ **b.** $716_{\text{eight}} + 657_{\text{eight}}$

6. Use bundling sticks, chips, or multibase pieces for the appropriate base to illustrate the following problems.

   a. $41_{\text{six}} - 33_{\text{six}}$ **b.** $555_{\text{seven}} - 66_{\text{seven}}$

   c. $3030_{\text{four}} - 102_{\text{four}}$

7. Solve each of the following base four subtraction problems using both the standard algorithm and the subtract-from-the-base algorithm. The Chapter 4 eManipulative activity, *Multibase Blocks—Subtraction*, can be used in the solution process.

   a. $31_{\text{four}} - 12_{\text{four}}$ **b.** $123_{\text{four}} - 32_{\text{four}}$

   c. $1102_{\text{four}} - 333_{\text{four}}$

8. Find $10201_{\text{three}} - 2122_{\text{three}}$ using "adding the complement." What is the complement of a base three number?

9. Solve the following problems using the lattice method, an intermediate algorithm, and the standard algorithm.

   a. $\begin{array}{r} 31_{\text{four}} \\ \times\ 2_{\text{four}} \\ \hline \end{array}$ **b.** $\begin{array}{r} 43_{\text{five}} \\ \times\ 3_{\text{five}} \\ \hline \end{array}$ **c.** $\begin{array}{r} 22_{\text{four}} \\ \times\ 3_{\text{four}} \\ \hline \end{array}$

10. Use the scaffold method of division to compute the following numbers. (*Hint:* Write out a multiplication table in the appropriate base to help you out.)

   a. $22_{\text{six}} \div 2_{\text{six}}$ **b.** $4044_{\text{seven}} \div 51_{\text{seven}}$

   c. $13002_{\text{four}} \div 33_{\text{four}}$

11. Solve the following problems using the missing-factor definition of division. (*Hint:* Use a multiplication table for the appropriate base.)

   a. $21_{\text{four}} \div 3_{\text{four}}$ **b.** $23_{\text{six}} \div 3_{\text{six}}$

   c. $24_{\text{eight}} \div 5_{\text{eight}}$

12. Sketch how to use base seven blocks to illustrate the operation $534_{\text{seven}} \div 4_{\text{seven}}$.

PROBLEMS

13. $345\ \underline{\quad} + 122\ \underline{\quad} = 511\ \underline{\quad}$ is an addition problem done in base $\underline{\quad}$.

14. Jane has $10 more than Bill, Bill has $17 more than Tricia, and Tricia has $21 more than Steve. If the total amount of all their money is $115, how much money does each have?

15. Without using a calculator, determine which of the five numbers is a perfect square. There is exactly one.

$$39{,}037{,}066{,}087$$
$$39{,}037{,}066{,}084$$
$$39{,}037{,}066{,}082$$
$$38{,}336{,}073{,}623$$
$$38{,}414{,}432{,}028$$

16. What single number can be added separately to 100 and 164 to make them both perfect square numbers?

Section 4.3   EXERCISE / PROBLEM SET B

EXERCISES

1. Create a base six number line to illustrate the following operations.

   a. $23_{\text{six}} + 4_{\text{six}}$ **b.** $12_{\text{six}} - 5_{\text{six}}$

   c. $4_{\text{six}} \times 5_{\text{six}}$ **d.** $32_{\text{six}} - 14_{\text{six}}$

2. Use bundling sticks, chips, or multibase pieces for the appropriate base to illustrate the following problems.

   a. $32_{\text{four}} + 33_{\text{four}}$ **b.** $54_{\text{eight}} + 55_{\text{eight}}$

   c. $265_{\text{nine}} + 566_{\text{nine}}$

3. Write out a base six addition table. Use your table to compute the following sums.

   a. $32_{\text{six}} + 23_{\text{six}}$ **b.** $45_{\text{six}} + 34_{\text{six}}$

   c. $145_{\text{six}} + 541_{\text{six}}$ **d.** $355_{\text{six}} + 211_{\text{six}}$

4. Use the lattice method to compute the following sums.

   a. $46_{\text{seven}} + 13_{\text{seven}}$ **b.** $13_{\text{four}} + 23_{\text{four}}$

5. Use the standard algorithm to compute the following sums.

   a. $79_{\text{twelve}} + 85_{\text{twelve}}$ **b.** $T1_{\text{eleven}} + 99_{\text{eleven}}$

6. Use bundling sticks, chips, or multibase pieces for the appropriate base to illustrate the following problems.

   a. $123_{\text{five}} - 24_{\text{five}}$ **b.** $253_{\text{eight}} - 76_{\text{eight}}$

   c. $1001_{\text{two}} - 110_{\text{two}}$

7. Solve the following problems using both the standard algorithm and the subtract-from-the-base algorithm.

   a. $45_{\text{seven}} - 36_{\text{seven}}$ **b.** $99_{\text{twelve}} - 7T_{\text{twelve}}$

   c. $100_{\text{eight}} - 77_{\text{eight}}$

8. Find $1001010_{two} - 111001_{two}$ by "adding the complement."

9. Solve the following problems using the lattice method, an intermediate algorithm, and the standard algorithm.

a. $\begin{array}{r} 11011_{two} \\ \times\ 1101_{two} \\ \hline \end{array}$
b. $\begin{array}{r} 43_{twelve} \\ \times 23_{twelve} \\ \hline \end{array}$
c. $\begin{array}{r} 66_{seven} \\ \times 66_{seven} \\ \hline \end{array}$

10. Use the scaffold method of division to compute the following numbers. (*Hint:* Write out a multiplication table in the appropriate base to help you out.)

a. $14_{five} \div 3_{five}$
b. $2134_{six} \div 14_{six}$
c. $61245_{seven} \div 354_{seven}$

11. Solve the following problems using the missing-factor definition of division. (*Hint:* Use a multiplication table for the appropriate base.)

a. $42_{seven} \div 5_{seven}$
b. $62_{nine} \div 7_{nine}$
c. $92_{twelve} \div E_{twelve}$

12. Sketch how to use base four blocks to illustrate the operation $3021_{four} \div 11_{four}$.

PROBLEMS

13. $320 \_\_\_\_ - 42 \_\_\_\_ = 256 \_\_\_\_$ is a correct subtraction problem in what base?

14. Betty has three times as much money as her brother Tom. If each of them spends $1.50 to see a movie, Betty will have nine times as much money left over as Tom. How much money does each have before going to the movie?

15. To stimulate his son in the pursuit of mathematics, a math professor offered to pay his son $8 for every equation correctly solved and to fine him $5 for every incorrect solution. At the end of 26 problems, neither owed any money to the other. How many did the boy solve correctly?

16. Prove: If n is a whole number and n^2 is odd, then n is odd. (*Hint:* Use indirect reasoning. Either n is even or it is odd. Assume that n is even and reach a contradiction.)

PROBLEMS FOR WRITING/DISCUSSION

1. What is wrong with the following problem in base four? Explain.

$$\begin{array}{r} 1022_{four} \\ +\ 413_{four} \\ \hline \end{array}$$

2. Write out the steps you would go through to mentally subtract 234_{five} from 421_{five} using the standard subtraction algorithm.

3. Doing a division problem in base five takes a great deal of concentration on your part. What similar problem would you ask your students to do that would be as difficult as this? What can you, as a teacher, do to make this difficult problem easier for your students?

END OF CHAPTER MATERIAL

Solution of Initial Problem

The whole numbers 1 through 9 can be used once, each arranged in a 3×3 square array so that the sum of the numbers in each of the rows, columns, and diagonals is 15. Show that 1 cannot be in one of the corners.

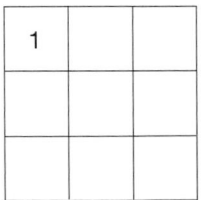

Strategy: Use Indirect Reasoning

Suppose that 1 could be in a corner as shown in the following figure. Each row, column, and diagonal containing 1 must have a sum of 15. This means that there must be three pairs of numbers among 2 through 9 whose sum is 14. Hence the sum of all three pairs is 42. However, the largest six numbers—9, 8, 7, 6, 5, and 4—have a sum of 39, so that it is impossible to find three pairs whose sum is 14. Therefore, it is impossible to have 1 in a corner.

Additional Problems Where the Strategy "Use Indirect Reasoning" Is Useful

1. If x represents a whole number and $x^2 + 2x + 1$ is even, prove that x cannot be even.

2. If n is a whole number and n^4 is even, then n is even.

3. For whole numbers x and y, if $x^2 + y^2$ is a square, then x and y cannot both be odd.

People in Mathematics

Grace Brewster Murray Hopper (1906–1992) Grace Brewster Murray Hopper recalled that as a young girl, she disassembled one of her family's alarm clocks. When she was unable to reassemble the parts, she dismantled another clock to see how those parts fit together. This process continued until she had seven clocks in pieces. This attitude of exploration foreshadowed her innovations in computer programming. Trained in mathematics, Hopper worked with some of the first computers and invented the business language COBOL. After World War II she was active in the Navy, where her experience in computing and programming began. In 1985 she was promoted to the rank of rear admiral. Known for her common sense and spirit of invention, she kept a clock on her desk that ran (and kept time) counterclockwise. Whenever someone argued that a job must be done in the traditional manner, she just pointed to the clock. Also, to encourage risk taking, she once said, "I do have a maxim—I teach it to all youngsters: A ship in port is safe, but that's not what ships are built for."

John Kemeny (1926–1992) John Kemeny created BASIC with Tom Kurtz while both were teaching in the mathematics department at Dartmouth in the mid-1960s. The idea was to design a language much friendlier than anything then available. Today, BASIC continues to be a widely used computer language, and Kemeny made Dartmouth a leader in the educational uses of computers. Kemeny's first faculty position was in philosophy. "The only good job offer I got was from the Princeton philosophy department," he said, explaining that his degree was in logic, and he studied philosophy as a hobby in college. Kemeny had the distinction of having served as Einstein's mathematical assistant while still a young graduate student at Princeton. Einstein's assistants were always mathematicians. Contrary to popular belief, Einstein did need help in mathematics. He was very good at it, but he was not an up-to-date research mathematician.

CHAPTER REVIEW

Review the following terms and exercises to determine which require learning or relearning—page numbers are provided for easy reference.

SECTION 4.1: Mental Math, Estimation, and Calculators

VOCABULARY/NOTATION

Right distributivity   140
Compatible numbers   140
Compensation   140
Additive compensation   140
Equal additions method   140
Multiplicative compensation   140
Left-to-right methods   140
Powers of 10   141
Special factors   141
Computational estimation   141
Front-end estimation   141

Range   141
Range estimation   141
One-column front-end estimation method   142
Two-column front-end estimation method   142
Front-end with adjustment   142
Round up/down   143
Truncate   143
Round a 5 up   143
Round to the nearest even   143

Round to compatible numbers   144
Arithmetic logic   145
Algebraic logic   145
Order of operations   145
Parentheses   145
Constant function   146
Exponent keys   146
Memory functions   147
Scientific notation   147

EXERCISES

1. Calculate the following mentally, and name the property(ies) you used.

   a. $97 + 78$

   b. $267 \div 3$

   c. $(16 \times 7) \times 25$

   d. $16 \times 9 - 6 \times 9$

   e. 92×15

   f. 17×99

   g. $720 \div 5$

   h. $81 - 39$

2. Estimate using the techniques given.

   a. Range: $157 + 371$

   b. One-column front-end: 847×989

   c. Front-end with adjustment: $753 + 639$

   d. Compatible numbers: 23×56

3. Round as indicated.

   a. Up to the nearest 100: 47,943

   b. To the nearest 10: 4751

   c. Down to the nearest 10: 576

4. Insert parentheses (wherever necessary) to produce the indicated results.

   a. $3 + 7 \times 5 = 38$

   b. $7 \times 5 - 2 + 3 = 24$

   c. $15 + 48 \div 3 \times 4 = 19$

5. Fill in the following without using a calculator.

   a. $5\ \boxed{+}\ 2\ \boxed{\times}\ 3\ \boxed{=}\ \boxed{}$

   b. $8\ \boxed{-}\ 6\ \boxed{\div}\ 3\ \boxed{=}\ \boxed{}$

   c. $2\ \boxed{\times}\ \boxed{(}\ 3\ \boxed{+}\ 2\ \boxed{)}\ \boxed{=}\ \boxed{}$

   d. $2\ \boxed{y^x}\ 3\ \boxed{=}\ \boxed{}$

   e. $3\ \boxed{\text{STO}}\ 7\ \boxed{+}\ \boxed{\text{RCL}}\ \boxed{=}\ \boxed{}$

   f. $3\ \boxed{\times}\ 5\ \boxed{=}\ \boxed{\text{STO}}\ 8\ \boxed{\div}\ 2\ \boxed{=}\ \boxed{+}\ \boxed{\text{RCL}}\ \boxed{=}$
   $\boxed{}$

SECTION 4.2: Written Algorithms for Whole-Number Operations

VOCABULARY/NOTATION

Algorithm   153
Standard addition algorithm   153
Lattice method for addition   155
Standard subtraction algorithm   155
Subtract-from-the-base
   algorithm   156

Standard multiplication
   algorithm   157
Lattice method for
   multiplication   159
Long division using base ten
   blocks   159

Scaffold method for division   161
Standard algorithm for division
   162

EXERCISES

1. Find $837 + 145$ using

   a. the lattice method.

   b. an intermediate algorithm.

   c. the standard algorithm.

2. Find $451 - 279$ using

   a. the standard algorithm.

   b. a nonstandard algorithm.

3. Find 72×43 using

   a. an intermediate algorithm.

   b. the standard algorithm.

   c. the lattice method.

4. Find $253 \div 27$ using

   a. the scaffold method.

   b. an intermediate algorithm.

   c. the standard algorithm.

   d. a calculator.

SECTION 4.3: Algorithms in Other Bases

VOCABULARY/NOTATION

Bases other than ten   171

EXERCISES

1. Find $413_{six} + 254_{six}$ using
   a. the lattice method.
   b. an intermediate algorithm.
   c. the standard algorithm.

2. Find $234_{seven} - 65_{seven}$ using
   a. the standard algorithm.
   b. a nonstandard algorithm.

3. Find $21_{four} \times 32_{four}$ using
   a. an intermediate algorithm.
   b. the standard algorithm.
   c. the lattice method.

4. Find $213_{five} \div 41_{five}$ using
   a. repeated subtraction
   b. the scaffold method.
   c. the standard algorithm.

PROBLEMS FOR WRITING/DISCUSSION

1. One place in real life where people use estimation and their knowledge of number relationships is in tipping a waiter or waitress at a restaurant. The typical percent for tipping is 15%. Suppose the bill for you and your friends is $47.31. How would you go about estimating the amount you should leave for a tip? Can you come up with more than one way?

2. Teachers often require their students to add numbers according to the usual addition algorithm, that is, adding from right to left, whereas many children, especially those who understand place value, choose to add from left to right. Is there room for flexibility here, or do you think that letting the students add any way they want will lead to confusion in the classroom?

3. Some problems can be solved by your knowledge of patterns when the arithmetic is beyond the scope of your calculator. For example, can you find the units digit of the number represented by 10^{351}? How about the units digit of 5^{351}? 2^{351}? 7^{351}? Explain your reasoning.

4. In Exercise 18 in Exercise/Problem Set 4.2 Part B, the "Russian peasant algorithm" was introduced. Far from being a method for peasants, this was the way mathematicians multiplied numbers until the introduction of the new "standard algorithm." In the example given there, 27 times 51, the answer is found by adding the numbers left in the "doubling" column. Each of those numbers is a multiple of 51. Find out what multiple of 51 each of the remaining numbers is. Determine why this method produces the correct answer. Two ideas that may help are the distributive property and the base two numeration system.

5. As an added example, use the Russian peasant algorithm to multiply 375 times 47. Which number do you want to put in the "halving" column? Why? Does $47 = 111101_{two}$ or 101111_{two}? How is that related to the multiplication problem?

6. In the "People in Mathematics" section at the end of this chapter, there is a short biography of Grace Hopper in which she is quoted as saying, "A ship in port is safe, but that's not what ships are built for." How would you explain that saying to students? How does it relate to learning?

7. In Exercise 19 in Exercise/Problem Set 4.2 Part A, "finger multiplication" was introduced. Determine what are the smallest and largest products you can find with this system. Take turns demonstrating to one another 6×6, 7×7, and 8×9. Did you have a teacher who told you you shouldn't count on your fingers? What would be his or her reaction to this method? What is your position on this issue?

8. In a unit on estimation a student is asked to estimate the answer to 99×37. The student is very anxious about getting the right answer, so she multiplies the numbers on a calculator, then rounds off the answer and gets 4000. How would you respond to this student?

9. How could you use something you learned in algebra to do mental multiplication problems if the numbers being multiplied are equally distant from some "nice" number? For example, devise a quick method for multiplying 47 times 53 by writing it as $(50 - 3)$ $(50 + 3)$. Can you do this mentally? Make up three similar problems.

10. The following two estimations are known as **Fermi problems,** which request estimates *without* seeking any exact numbers from reference materials. See what your team can come up with. Be prepared to defend your estimate.
    a. Estimate the number of hot dogs sold at all of the major league baseball games played in the United States in one year.
    b. Estimate the number of days of playing time there are on all the musical compact discs sold in your state in one month.

CHAPTER TEST

Knowledge

1. True or false?

   a. An algorithm is a technique that is used exclusively for doing algebra.

   b. Intermediate algorithms are helpful because they require less writing than their corresponding standard algorithms.

   c. There is only one computational algorithm for each of the four operations: addition, subtraction, multiplication, and division.

   d. Approximating answers to computations by rounding is useful because it increases the *speed* of computation.

Skill

2. Compute each of the following using an intermediate algorithm.

   a. $376 + 594$ **b.** 56×73

3. Compute the following using the lattice method.

   a. $568 + 493$ **b.** 37×196

4. Compute the following mentally. Then, explain how you did it.

   a. $54 + 93 + 16 + 47$ **b.** $9223 - 1998$

   c. $3497 - 1362$ **d.** 25×52

5. Find $7496 \div 32$ using the standard division algorithm, and check your results using a calculator.

6. Estimate the following using (i) one-column front-end, (ii) range estimation, (iii) front-end with adjustment, and (iv) rounding to the nearest 100.

   a. $546 + 971 + 837 + 320$ **b.** 731×589

Understanding

7. Compute 32×21 using expanded form; that is, continue the following.

   $$32 \times 21 = (30 + 2)(20 + 1) = \ldots$$

8. In the standard multiplication algorithm, why do we "shift over one to the left" as illustrated in the 642 in the following problem?

   $$\begin{array}{r} 321 \\ \times\ 23 \\ \hline 963 \\ +642 \\ \hline \end{array}$$

9. To check an addition problem where one has "added down the column," one can "add up the column." Which properties guarantee that the sum should be the same in both directions?

10. Sketch how a chip abacus could be used to perform the following operation.

    $$374 + 267$$

11. Use an appropriate intermediate algorithm to compute the following quotient and remainder.

    $$7261 \div 43$$

12. Sketch how base ten blocks could be used to find the quotient and remainder of the following.

    $$538 \div 4$$

13. Sketch how base four blocks could be used to find the following difference.

    $$32_{\text{four}} - 13_{\text{four}}$$

14. Sketch how a chip abacus could be used to find the following sum.

    $$278_{\text{nine}} + 37_{\text{nine}}$$

15. Sketch how base ten blocks could be used to model the following operations and explain how the manipulations of the blocks relate to the standard algorithm.

    a. $357 + 46$

    b. $253 - 68$

    c. $789 \div 5$

16. Compute 492×37 using an intermediate algorithm and a standard algorithm. Explain how the distributive property is used in each of these algorithms.

17. State some of the advantages and disadvantages of the standard algorithm versus the lattice algorithm for multiplication.

18. State some of the advantages and disadvantages of the standard subtraction algorithm versus the subtract-from-the-base algorithm.

19. Show how to find 17×23 on the following grid paper and explain how the solution on the grid paper can be related to the intermediate algorithm for multiplication.

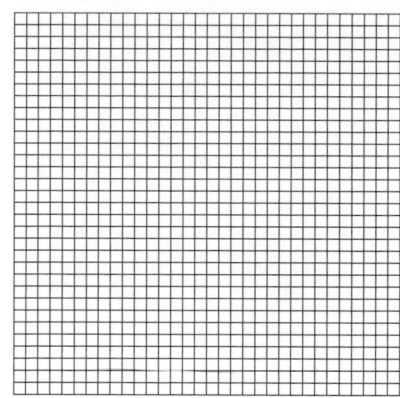

21. Find values for a, b, and c in the lattice multiplication problem shown. Also find the product.

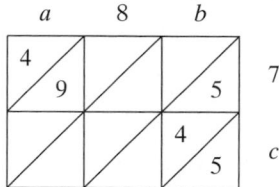

22. Find digits represented by A, B, C, and D so that the following operation is correct.

$$
\begin{array}{r}
\text{ABA} \\
+\text{BAB} \\
\hline
\text{CDDC}
\end{array}
$$

Problem Solving/Application

20. If each different letter represents a different digit, find the number "HE" such that $(HE)^2 = SHE$. (NOTE: "HE" means $10 \cdot H + E$ due to place value.)

References for Reflections from Research

CARPENTER, T. P., FRANKE, M. L., JACOBS, V. R., FENNEMA, E., & EMPSON, S. B. (1997). A longitudinal study of invention and understanding in children's multi-digit addition and subtraction. *Journal for Research in Mathematics Education, 29*, 3–20.

COBB, P., YACKEL, E., & WOOD, T. (1988). Curriculum and teacher development: Psychological and anthropological perspectives. In E. Fennema, T. P. Carpenter, & S. J. Lamon (Eds.), *Integrating research on teaching and learning mathematics* (pp. 92–130). Madison, WI: Wisconsin Center for Education Research.

FORRESTER, M. A., & PIKE, C. D. (1998). Learning to estimate in the mathematics classroom: A conversation-analytic approach. *Journal for Research in Mathematics Education, 29*, 334–356.

FUSON, K. C., SMITH, S. T., & LO CICERO, A. M. (1997). Supporting Latino first graders' ten-structured thinking in urban classrooms. *Journal for Research in Mathematics Education, 28*, 738–766.

LEUTZINGER, L. R., RATHMELL, E. C., & URBATSCH, T. D. (1986). Developing estimation skills in the primary grades. In H. L. Shoen (Ed.), *Estimation and mental computation* (pp. 82–92). Reston, VA: National Council of Teachers of Mathematics.

REYS, R. E., & REYS, B. J. (1987). Calculators in the classroom: How can we make it happen? *Arithmetic Teacher, 34*(6), 12–14.

REYS, R. E., RYBOLT, J. E., BESTGEN, B. J., & WYATT, J. W. (1982). Processes used by good computational estimators. *Journal for Research in Mathematics Education, 13*, 183–201.

CHAPTER 5

Number Theory

FOCUS ON *Famous Unsolved Problems*

umber theory provides a rich source of intriguing problems. Interestingly, there are many problems in number theory that are easily understood but still have never been solved. Most of these problems are statements or conjectures that have never been proven right or wrong. The most famous "unsolved" problem, known as Fermat's Last Theorem, states "There are no nonzero whole numbers a, b, c, where $a^n + b^n = c^n$, for n a whole number greater than two."

The following list contains several such problems that are still unsolved. If you can solve any of them, you will surely become famous, at least among mathematicians.

Pierre de Fermat

1. *Goldbach's conjecture. Every even number greater than 4 can be expressed as the sum of two odd primes.* For example, $6 = 3 + 3$, $8 = 3 + 5$, $10 = 5 + 5$, $12 = 5 + 7$, and so on. It is interesting to note that if Goldbach's conjecture is true, then every odd number greater than 7 can be written as the sum of three odd primes.

2. *Twin prime conjecture. There is an infinite number of pairs of primes whose difference is two.* For example, $(3, 5)$, $(5, 7)$, and $(11, 13)$ are such prime pairs. Notice that 3, 5, and 7 are three prime numbers where $5 - 3 = 2$ and $7 - 5 = 2$. It can easily be shown that this is the only such triple of primes.

3. *Odd perfect number conjecture. There is no odd perfect number; that is, there is no odd number that is the sum of its proper factors.* For example, $6 = 1 + 2 + 3$; hence 6 is a perfect number. It has been shown that the even perfect numbers are all of the form $2^{p-1}(2^p - 1)$, where $2^p - 1$ is a prime.

4. *Ulam's conjecture. If a nonzero whole number is even, divide it by 2. If a nonzero whole number is odd, multiply it by 3 and add 1. If this process is applied repeatedly to each answer, eventually you will arrive at 1.* For example, the number 7 yields this sequence of numbers: 7, 22, 11, 34, 17, 52, 26, 13, 40, 20, 10, 5, 16, 8, 4, 2, 1. Interestingly, there is a whole number less than 30 that requires at least 100 steps before it arrives at 1. It can be seen that 2^n requires n steps to arrive at 1. Hence one can find numbers with as many steps (finitely many) as one wishes.

Fermat left a marginal note in a book saying that he did not have room to write up a proof of what is now called Fermat's Last Theorem. However, it remained an unsolved problem for over 350 years since mathematicians were unable to prove it. In 1993, Andrew Wiles, an English mathematician on the Princeton faculty, presented a "proof" at a conference at Cambridge University. However, there was a hole in his proof. Happily, Wiles and Richard Taylor produced a valid proof in 1995 which followed from work done by Serre, Mazur, and Ribet beginning in 1985.

The material in this chapter includes a discussion of many of the concepts in these unsolved problems.

Problem Solving Strategies

1. Guess and Test
2. Use a Variable
3. Draw a Picture
4. Look for a Pattern
5. Make a List
6. Solve a Simpler Problem
7. Draw a Diagram
8. Use Direct Reasoning
9. Use Indirect Reasoning
10. Use Properties of Numbers

Strategy
Use Properties of Numbers

Understanding the intrinsic nature of numbers is often helpful in solving problems. For example, knowing that the sum of two even numbers is even and that an odd number squared is odd may simplify checking some computations. The solution of the initial problem will seem to be impossible to a naive problem solver who attempts to solve it using, say, the Guess and Test strategy. On the other hand, the solution is immediate for one who understands the concept of divisibility of numbers.

Initial Problem

A major fast-food chain held a contest to promote sales. With each purchase a customer was given a card with a whole number less than 100 on it. A $100 prize was given to any person who presented cards whose numbers totaled 100. The following are several typical cards. Can you find a winning combination?

$$\boxed{3} \quad \boxed{9} \quad \boxed{12} \quad \boxed{15} \quad \boxed{18} \quad \boxed{27} \quad \boxed{51} \quad \boxed{72} \quad \boxed{84}$$

Can you suggest how the contest could be structured so that there would be at most 1000 winners throughout the country?

Clues

The Use Properties of Numbers strategy may be appropriate when

- Special types of numbers, such as odds, evens, primes, and so on, are involved.
- A problem can be simplified by using certain properties.
- A problem involves lots of computation.

A solution of the Initial Problem appears on page 211.

INTRODUCTION

Number theory is a branch of mathematics that is devoted primarily to the study of the set of counting numbers. In this chapter, those aspects of the counting numbers that are useful in simplifying computations, especially those with fractions (Chapter 6), are studied. The topics central to the elementary curriculum that are covered in this chapter include primes, composites, and divisibility tests as well as the notions of greatest common factor and least common multiple.

5.1   PRIMES, COMPOSITES, AND TESTS FOR DIVISIBILITY

On a piece of paper, sketch all of the possible rectangles that can be made up of exactly 12 squares. An example of a rectangle consisting of 6 squares is shown at the right.

Repeat these sketches for 13 squares. Why can more rectangles be made with 12 squares than with 13 squares? How are the dimensions of the rectangles related to the number of squares?

Primes and Composites

Prime numbers are building blocks for the counting numbers 1, 2, 3, 4, ...

**NCTM Standards 2000
Number and Operations
Grades 6–8**
All students should use factors, multiples, prime factorization, and relatively prime numbers to solve problems.

    DEFINITION

Prime and Composite Numbers

A counting number with exactly two different factors is called a **prime number,** or a **prime.** A counting number with more than two factors is called a **composite number,** or a **composite.**

For example, 2, 3, 5, 7, 11 are primes, since they have only themselves and 1 as factors: 4, 6, 8, 9, 10 are composites, since they each have more than two factors; 1 is neither prime nor composite, since 1 is its only factor.

An algorithm used to find primes is called the **Sieve of Eratosthenes** (Figure 5.1).

```
1    ②   ③   4̸   ⑤   6̸   ⑦   8̸   9̸   1̸0̸
⑪   1̸2̸  ⑬   1̸4̸  1̸5̸  1̸6̸  ⑰   1̸8̸  ⑲   2̸0̸
2̸1̸  2̸2̸  ㉓   2̸4̸  2̸5̸  2̸6̸  2̸7̸  2̸8̸  ㉙   3̸0̸
㉛   3̸2̸  3̸3̸  3̸4̸  3̸5̸  3̸6̸  ㊲   3̸8̸  3̸9̸  4̸0̸
㊶   4̸2̸  ㊸   4̸4̸  4̸5̸  4̸6̸  ㊼   4̸8̸  4̸9̸  5̸0̸
 ·    ·    ·    ·    ·    ·    ·    ·    ·    ·
 ·    ·    ·    ·    ·    ·    ·    ·    ·    ·
```

Figure 5.1

The directions for using this procedure are as follows: Skip the number 1. Circle 2 and cross out every second number after 2. Circle 3 and cross out every third number after 3 (even if it had been crossed out before). Continue this procedure with 5, 7, and each succeeding number that is not crossed out. The circled numbers will be the primes and the crossed-out numbers will be the composites, since prime factors cause them to be crossed out. Again, notice that 1 is neither prime nor composite.

Spotlight on Technology The Chapter 5 eManipulative activity, *Sieve of Eratosthenes*, is an electronic version of the sieve process described above. Using the Sieve of Eratosthenes on the eManipu- lative, select the "Remove Multiples" option. When the number 2 is selected, the multiples of 2 up to 200 are automatically removed one at a time. When the number 3 is selected, the multiples of 3 up to 200 are removed. If you continue selecting the next several primes, 5, 7, and so forth, at what point are there no more multiples to remove? Why is that the turning point?

www.wiley.com/
college/musser

Composite numbers have more than two factors and can be expressed as the prod- uct of two smaller numbers. Figure 5.2 shows how a composite can be expressed as the product of smaller numbers using **factor trees.**

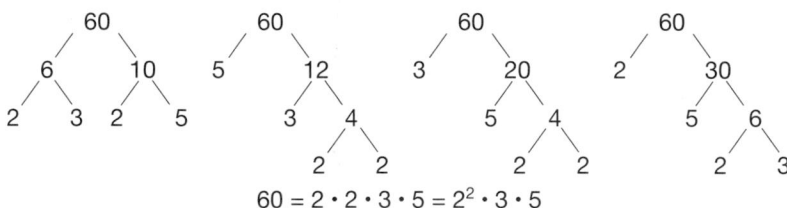

$$60 = 2 \cdot 2 \cdot 3 \cdot 5 = 2^2 \cdot 3 \cdot 5$$

Figure 5.2

Notice that 60 was expressed as the product of two factors in several different ways. However, when we kept factoring until we reached primes, each method led us to the same **prime factorization,** namely $60 = 2 \cdot 2 \cdot 3 \cdot 5$. This example illustrates the following important results.

 THEOREM

Fundamental Theorem of Arithmetic
Each composite number can be expressed as the product of primes in exactly one way (except for the order of the factors).

Example 5.1   Express each number as the product of primes.
a. 84   **b.** 180   **c.** 324

Solution

a. $84 = 4 \times 21 = 2 \cdot 2 \cdot 3 \cdot 7 = 2^2 \cdot 3 \cdot 7$
b. $180 = 10 \times 18 = 2 \cdot 5 \cdot 2 \cdot 3 \cdot 3 = 2^2 \cdot 3^2 \cdot 5$
c. $324 = 4 \times 81 = 2 \cdot 2 \cdot 3 \cdot 3 \cdot 3 \cdot 3 = 2^2 \cdot 3^4$ ■

Next, we will study shortcuts that will help us find prime factors. When division yields a zero remainder, as in the case of $15 \div 3$, for example, we say that 15 is divisible by 3, 3 is a divisor of 15, or 3 divides 15. In general, we have the following definition.

 DEFINITION

Divides

Let a and b be any whole numbers with $a \neq 0$. We say that a **divides** b, and write $a \mid b$, if and only if there is a whole number x such that $ax = b$. The symbol $a \nmid b$ means that a **does not divide** b.

(a)

Does not make an entire column.

(b)

Figure 5.3

In words, a divides b if and only if a is a factor of b. When a divides b, we can also say that a is a **divisor** of b, a is a **factor** of b, b is a **multiple** of a, and b **is divisible by** a.

We can also say that $a \mid b$ if b objects can be arranged in a rectangular array with a rows. For example, $4 \mid 12$ because 12 dots can be placed in a rectangular array with 4 rows, as shown in Figure 5.3(a). On the other hand, $5 \nmid 12$ because if 12 dots are placed in an array with 5 rows, a rectangular array cannot be formed [Figure 5.3(b)].

Example 5.2 Determine whether the following are true or false. Explain.

a. $3 \mid 12$. **b.** 8 is a divisor of 96.
c. 216 is a multiple of 6. **d.** 51 is divisible by 17.
e. 7 divides 34. **f.** $(2^2 \cdot 3) \mid (2^3 \cdot 3^2 \cdot 5)$.

Solution

a. True. $3 \mid 12$, since $3 \cdot 4 = 12$.
b. True. 8 is a divisor of 96, since $8 \cdot 12 = 96$.
c. True. 216 is a multiple of 6, since $6 \cdot 36 = 216$.
d. True. 51 is divisible by 17, since $17 \cdot 3 = 51$.
e. False. $7 \nmid 34$, since there is no whole number x such that $7x = 34$.
f. True. $(2^2 \cdot 3) \mid (2^3 \cdot 3^2 \cdot 5)$, since $(2^2 \cdot 3)(2 \cdot 3 \cdot 5) = (2^3 \cdot 3^2 \cdot 5)$. ■

Reflection from Research
When students are allowed to use calculators to generate data and are encouraged to examine the data for patterns, they often discover divisibility rules on their own (Bezuszka, 1985).

Tests for Divisibility

Some simple tests can be employed to help determine the factors of numbers. For example, which of the numbers 27, 45, 38, 70, and 111, 110 are divisible by 2, 5, or 10? If your answers were found simply by looking at the ones digits, you were applying tests for divisibility. The tests for divisibility by 2, 5, and 10 are stated next.

 THEOREM

Tests for Divisibility by 2, 5, and 10
A number is divisible by 2 if and only if its ones digit is 0, 2, 4, 6, or 8.
A number is divisible by 5 if and only if its ones digit is 0 or 5.
A number is divisible by 10 if and only if its ones digit is 0.

Now notice that $3 \mid 27$ and $3 \mid 9$. It is also true that $3 \mid (27 + 9)$ and that $3 \mid (27 - 9)$. This is an instance of the following theorem.

THEOREM

Let a, m, n, and k be whole numbers where $a \neq 0$.
a. If $a \mid m$ and $a \mid n$, then $a \mid (m + n)$.
b. If $a \mid m$ and $a \mid n$, then $a \mid (m - n)$ for $m \geq n$.
c. If $a \mid m$, then $a \mid km$.

Proof

a. If $a \mid m$, then $ax = m$ for some whole number x.

If $a \mid n$, then $ay = n$ for some whole number y.

Therefore, adding the respective sides of the two equations, we have $ax + ay = m + n$, or

$$a(x + y) = m + n.$$

Since $x + y$ is a whole number, this last equation implies that $a \mid (m + n)$. Part (b) can be proved simply by replacing the plus signs with minus signs in this discussion. The proof of (c) follows from the definition of divides. ■

Part (a) in the preceding theorem can also be illustrated using the rectangular array description of *divides*. In Figure 5.4, $3 \mid 9$ is represented by a rectangle with 3 rows of 3 blue dots. $3 \mid 12$ is represented by a rectangle of 3 rows of 4 black dots. By placing the 9 blue dots and the 12 black dots together, there are $(9 + 12)$ dots arranged in 3 rows, so $3 \mid (9 + 12)$.

$3\mid9$ $\qquad\qquad$ $3\mid12$ $\qquad\qquad\qquad$ $3\mid(9+12)$

Figure 5.4

Using this result, we can verify the tests for divisibility by 2, 5, and 10. The main idea of the proof of the test for 2 is now given for an arbitrary three-digit number (the same idea holds for any number of digits).

Let $r = a \cdot 10^2 + b \cdot 10 + c$ be any three-digit number.

Observe that $a \cdot 10^2 + b \cdot 10 = 10(a \cdot 10 + b)$.

Since $2 \mid 10$, it follows that $2 \mid 10(a \cdot 10 + b)$ or $2 \mid (a \cdot 10^2 + b \cdot 10)$ for any digits a and b.

Thus if $2 \mid c$ (where c is the ones digit), then $2 \mid [10(a \cdot 10 + b) + c]$.

Thus $2 \mid (a \cdot 10^2 + b \cdot 10 + c)$, or $2 \mid r$.

Conversely, let $2 \mid (a \cdot 10^2 + b \cdot 10 + c)$. Since $2 \mid (a \cdot 10^2 + b \cdot 10)$, it follows that $2 \mid [(a \cdot 10^2 + b \cdot 10 + c) - (a \cdot 10^2 + b \cdot 10)]$ or $2 \mid c$.

Therefore, we have shown that 2 divides a number if and only if 2 divides the number's ones digit. One can apply similar reasoning to see why the tests for divisibility for 5 and 10 hold.

The next two tests for divisibility can be verified using arguments similar to the test for 2. Their verifications are left for the problem set.

 THEOREM

Tests for Divisibility by 4 and 8

A number is divisible by 4 if and only if the number represented by its last two digits is divisible by 4.

A number is divisible by 8 if and only if the number represented by its last three digits is divisible by 8.

Notice that the test for 4 involves two digits and $2^2 = 4$. Also, the test for 8 requires that one consider the last three digits and $2^3 = 8$.

Example 5.3 Determine whether the following are true or false. Explain.
a. 4 | 1432   **b.** 8 | 4204
c. 4 | 2,345,678   **d.** 8 | 98,765,432

Solution

a. True. 4 | 1432, since 4 | 32.
b. False. 8 ∤ 4204, since 8 ∤ 204.
c. False. 4 ∤ 2,345,678, since 4 ∤ 78.
d. True. 8 | 98,765,432, since 8 | 432.   ■

The next two tests for divisibility provide a simple way to test for factors of 3 or 9.

THEOREM

Tests for Divisibility by 3 and 9
A number is divisible by 3 if and only if the sum of its digits is divisible by 3.
A number is divisible by 9 if and only if the sum of its digits is divisible by 9.

Example 5.4 Determine whether the following are true or false. Explain.
a. 3 | 12,345   **b.** 9 | 12,345   **c.** 9 | 6543

Solution

a. True. 3 | 12,345, since $1 + 2 + 3 + 4 + 5 = 15$ and 3 | 15.
b. False. 9 ∤ 12,345, since $1 + 2 + 3 + 4 + 5 = 15$ and 9 ∤ 15.
c. True. 9 | 6543, since 9 | (6 + 5 + 4 + 3).   ■

The following justification of the test for divisibility by 3 in the case of a three-digit number can be extended to prove that this test holds for any whole number.

Let $r = a \cdot 10^2 + b \cdot 10 + c$ be any three-digit number. We will show that if $3 \,|\, (a + b + c)$, then $3 \,|\, r$. Rewrite r as follows:

$$r = a \cdot (99 + 1) + b \cdot (9 + 1) + c$$
$$= a \cdot 99 + a \cdot 1 + b \cdot 9 + b \cdot 1 + c$$
$$= a \cdot 99 + b \cdot 9 + a + b + c$$
$$= (a \cdot 11 + b)9 + a + b + c.$$

Since 3 | 9, it follows that $3 \,|\, (a \cdot 11 + b)9$. Thus if $3 \,|\, (a + b + c)$, where $a + b + c$ is the sum of the digits of r, then $3 \,|\, r$ since $3 \,|\, [(a \cdot 11 + b)9 + (a + b + c)]$. On the other hand, if $3 \,|\, r$, then $3 \,|\, (a + b + c)$, since $3 \,|\, [r - (a \cdot 11 + b)9]$ and $r - (a \cdot 11 + b)9 = a + b + c$.

The test for divisibility by 9 can be justified in a similar manner.
The following is a test for divisibility by 11.

THEOREM

Test for Divisibility by 11
A number is divisible by 11 if and only if 11 divides the difference of the sum of the digits whose place values are odd powers of 10 and the sum of the digits whose place values are even powers of 10.

Example 5.5   Determine whether the following are true or false. Explain.
a. 11 | 5346   **b.** 11 | 909,381   **c.** 11 | 16,543

Solution

a. True. 11 | 5346, since $(5 + 4) - (3 + 6) = 0$ and 11 | 0.
b. True. 11 | 909,381, since $(9 + 9 + 8) - (0 + 3 + 1) = 22$ and 11 | 22.
c. False. 11 ∤ 16,543, since $(6 + 4) - (1 + 5 + 3) = 1$ and 11 ∤ 1.

The justification of this test for divisibility by 11 is left for Problem 42 in Part A of the Exercise/Problem Set. Also, a test for divisibility by 7 is given in Exercise 12 in Part B of the Exercise/Problem Set.

One can test for divisibility by 6 by applying the tests for 2 and 3.

THEOREM

Test for Divisibility by 6

A number is divisible by 6 if and only if both of the tests for divisibility by 2 and 3 hold.

This technique of applying two tests simultaneously can be used in other cases also. For example, the test for 10 can be thought of as applying the tests for 2 and 5 simultaneously. By the test for 2, the ones digit must be 0, 2, 4, 6, or 8, *and* by the test for 5 the ones digit must be 0 or 5. Thus a number is divisible by 10 if and only if its ones digit is zero. Testing for divisibility by applying two tests can be done in general.

THEOREM

A number is divisible by the product, *ab*, of two nonzero whole numbers *a* and *b* if it is divisible by both *a* and *b*, and *a* and *b* have only the number 1 as a common factor.

According to this theorem, a test for divisibility by 36 would be to test for 4 and test for 9, since 4 and 9 both divide 36 and 4 and 9 have only 1 as a common factor. However, the test "a number is divisible by 24 if and only if it is divisible by 4 and 6" is *not* valid, since 4 and 6 have a common factor of 2. For example, 4 | 36 and 6 | 36, but 24 ∤ 36. The next example shows how to use tests for divisibility to find the prime factorization of a number.

Example 5.6   Find the prime factorization of 5148.

Solution

First, since the sum of the digits of 5148 is 18 (which is a multiple of 9), we know that $5148 = 9 \cdot 572$. Next, since 4 | 72, we know that 4 | 572. Thus $5148 = 9 \cdot 572 = 9 \cdot 4 \cdot 143 = 3^2 \cdot 2^2 \cdot 143$. Finally, since in 143, $1 + 3 - 4 = 0$ is divisible by 11, the number 143 is divisible by 11, so $5148 = 2^2 \cdot 3^2 \cdot 11 \cdot 13$.

We can also use divisibility tests to help decide whether a particular counting number is prime. For example, we can determine whether 137 is prime or composite by checking to see if it has any prime factors less than 137. None of 2, 3, or 5 divides 137.

How about 7? 11? 13? How many prime factors must be considered before we know whether 137 is a prime? Consider the following example.

Example 5.7   Determine whether 137 is a prime.

Solution

First, by the tests for divisibility, none of 2, 3, or 5 is a factor of 137. Next try 7, 11, 13, and so on.

$$7 \times 19 < 137 \text{ and } 7 \times 20 > 137, \text{ so } 7 \nmid 137$$
$$11 \times 12 < 137 \text{ and } 11 \times 13 > 137, \text{ so } 11 \nmid 137$$
$$13 \times 10 < 137 \text{ and } 13 \times 11 > 137, \text{ so } 13 \nmid 137$$
$$17 \times 8 < 137 \text{ and } 17 \times 9 > 137, \text{ so } 17 \nmid 137$$

column 1

column 2

Notice that the numbers in column 1 form an increasing list of primes and the numbers in column 2 are decreasing. Also, the numbers in the two columns "cross over" between 11 and 13. Thus, if there is a prime factor of 137, it will appear in column 1 first and reappear later as a factor of a number in column 2. Thus, as soon as the crossover is reached, there is no need to look any further for prime factors. Since the crossover point was passed in testing 137 and no prime factor of 137 was found, we conclude that 137 is prime.   ■

Example 5.7 suggests that to determine whether a number n is prime, we need only search for prime factors p, where $p^2 \leq n$. Recall that $y = \sqrt{x}$ (read "the **square root** of x") means that $y^2 = x$ where $y \geq 0$. For example, $\sqrt{25} = 5$ since $5^2 = 25$. Not all whole numbers have whole-number square roots. For example, using a calculator, $\sqrt{27} \approx 5.196$, since $5.196^2 \approx 27$. (A more complete discussion of the square root is contained in Chapter 9.) Thus the search for prime factors of a number n by considering only those primes p where $p^2 \leq n$ can be simplified even further by using the $\boxed{\sqrt{x}}$ key on a calculator and checking only those primes p where $p \leq \sqrt{n}$.

> ### ● THEOREM
>
> #### Prime Factor Test
> To test for prime factors of a number n, one need only search for prime factors p of n, where $p^2 \leq n$ (or $p \leq \sqrt{n}$).

Example 5.8   Determine whether the following numbers are prime or composite.
a. 299   **b.** 401

Solution

a. Only the prime factors 2 through 17 need to be checked, since $17^2 < 299 < 19^2$ (check this on your calculator). None of 2, 3, 5, 7, or 11 is a factor, but since $299 = 13 \cdot 23$, the number 299 is composite.
b. Only primes 2 through 19 need to be checked, since $\sqrt{401} \approx 20$. Since none of the primes 2 through 19 are factors of 401, we know that 401 is a prime. (The tests for divisibility show that 2, 3, 5, and 11 are not factors of 401. A calculator, tests for divisibility, or long division can be used to check 7, 13, 17, and 19.)   ■

MATHEMATICAL MORSEL

Finding large primes is a favorite pastime of some mathematicians. Before the advent of calculators and computers, this was certainly a time-consuming endeavor. Three anecdotes about large primes follow.

- Euler once announced that 1,000,009 was prime. However, he later found that it was the product of 293 and 3413. At the time of this discovery, Euler was 70 and blind.

- Fermat was once asked whether 100,895,598,169 was prime. He replied shortly that it had two factors, 898,423 and 112,303.

- For more than 200 years the Mersenne number $2^{67} - 1$ was thought to be prime. In 1903, Frank Nelson Cole, in a speech to the American Mathematical Society, went to the blackboard and without uttering a word, raised 2 to the power 67 (by hand, using our usual multiplication algorithm!) and subtracted 1. He then multiplied 193,707,721 by 761,838,257,287 (also by hand). The two numbers agreed! When asked how long it took him to crack the number, he said, "Three years of Sundays."

Section 5.1 EXERCISE / PROBLEM SET A

EXERCISES

1. Using the Chapter 5 eManipulative activity, *Sieve of Eratosthenes*, find all primes less than 100.

2. Find a factor tree for each of the following numbers.
   a. 36 **b.** 54 **c.** 102 **d.** 1000

3. A factor tree is not the only way to find the prime factorization of a composite number. Another method is to divide the number first by 2 as many times as possible, then by 3, then by 5, and so on, until all possible divisions by prime numbers have been performed. For example, to find the prime factorization of 108, you might organize your work as follows to conclude that $108 = 2^2 \times 3^3$.

$$
\begin{array}{r|r}
 & 3 \\
3 & 9 \\
3 & 27 \\
2 & 54 \\
2 & 108 \\
\end{array}
$$

   Use this method to find the prime factorization of the following numbers.
   a. 216 **b.** 2940 **c.** 825 **d.** 198,198

4. Determine which of the following are true. If true, illustrate it with a rectangular array. If false, explain.
   a. 3 | 9
   b. 12 | 6
   c. 3 is a divisor of 21.
   d. 6 is a factor of 3.

   e. 4 is a factor of 16.
   f. 0 | 5
   g. 11 | 11
   h. 48 is a multiple of 16.

5. Decide whether the following are true or false using only divisibility ideas given in this section (do not use long division or a calculator). Give a reason for your answers.
   a. 6 | 80
   b. 15 | 10,000
   c. 4 | 15,000
   d. 12 | 32,304

6. If 21 divides m, what else must divide m?

7. **a.** Show that 8 | 123,152 using the test for divisibility by 8.
   b. Show that 8 | 123,152 by finding x such that $8x = 123,152$.
   c. Is the x that you found in part (b) a divisor of 123,152? Prove it.

8. Which of the following are multiples of 3? of 4? of 9?
   a. 123,452 **b.** 1,114,500

9. True or false? Explain.
   a. If a counting number is divisible by 9, it must be divisible by 3.
   b. If a counting number is divisible by 3 and 11, it must be divisible by 33.

10. If the variables represent counting numbers, determine whether each of the following is true or false.

    a. If $x \nmid y$ and $x \nmid z$, then $x \nmid (y + z)$.

    b. If $2 \mid a$ and $3 \mid a$, then $6 \mid a$.

11. Which of the following numbers are composite? Why?

    a. 12   **b.** 123   **c.** 1234   **d.** 12,345

12. Use the test for divisibility by 11 to determine which of the following numbers are divisible by 11.

    a. 2838   **b.** 71,992   **c.** 172,425

PROBLEMS

13. a. Write 36 in prime factorization form.

    b. List the divisors of 36.

    c. Write each divisor of 36 in prime factorization form.

    d. What relationship exists between your answer to part (a) and each of your answers to part (c)?

    e. Let $n = 13^2 \times 29^5$. If m divides n, what can you conclude about the prime factorization of m?

14. Justify the tests for divisibility by 5 and 10 for any three-digit number by reasoning by analogy from the test for divisibility by 2.

15. The symbol 4! is called four **factorial** and means $4 \times 3 \times 2 \times 1$; thus $4! = 24$. Which of the following statements are true?

    a. $6 \mid 6!$ **b.** $5 \mid 6!$ **c.** $11 \mid 6!$

    d. $30 \mid 30!$ **e.** $40 \mid 30!$ **f.** $30 \mid (30! + 1)$

    [Do not multiply out parts (d) to (f).]

16. a. Does $8 \mid 7!$?   **b.** Does $7 \mid 6!$?

    c. For what counting numbers n will n divide $(n - 1)!$?

17. There is one composite number in this set: 331, 3331, 33,331, 333,331, 3,333,331, 33,333,331, 333,333,331. Which one is it? (*Hint*: It has a factor less than 30.)

18. Show that the formula $p(n) = n^2 + n + 17$ yields primes for $n = 0, 1, 2,$ and 3. Find the smallest whole number n for which $p(n) = n^2 + n + 17$ is not a prime.

19. a. Compute $n^2 + n + 41$, where $n = 0, 1, 2, \ldots, 10$, and determine which of these numbers is prime.

    b. On another piece of paper, continue the following spiral pattern until you reach 151. What do you notice about the main upper left to lower right diagonal?

```
           etc.
53   52    51    50    ↑
     43    42    49    |
     44    41    48    |
     45    46    47    ↓
                  ────────→
```

20. In his book *The Canterbury Puzzles* (1907), Dudeney mentioned that 11 was the only number consisting entirely of ones that was known to be prime. In 1918, Oscar Hoppe proved that the number 1,111,111,111,111,111,111 (19 ones) was prime. Later it was shown that the number made up of 23 ones was also prime. Now see how many of these "repunit" numbers up to 19 ones you can factor.

21. Which of the following numbers can be written as the sum of two primes, and why?

$$7, 17, 27, 37, 47, \ldots$$

22. One of Fermat's theorems states that every prime of the form $4x + 1$ is the sum of two square numbers in one and only one way. For example, $13 = 4(3) + 1$, and $13 = 4 + 9$, where 4 and 9 are square numbers.

    a. List the primes less than 100 that are of the form $4x + 1$, where x is a whole number.

    b. Express each of these primes as the sum of two square numbers.

23. The primes 2 and 3 are consecutive whole numbers. Is there another such pair of consecutive primes? Justify your answer.

24. Two primes that differ by 2 are called **twin primes.** For example, 5 and 7, 11 and 13, 29 and 31 are twin primes. Using the Chapter 5 eManipulative activity, *Sieve of Eratosthenes*, to display all primes less than 200, find all twin primes less than 200.

25. One result that mathematicians have been unable to prove true or false is called Goldbach's conjecture. It claims that each even number greater than 2 can be expressed as the sum of two primes. For example.

$$4 = 2 + 2, \quad 6 = 3 + 3, \quad 8 = 3 + 5,$$
$$10 = 5 + 5, \quad 12 = 5 + 7.$$

    a. Verify that Goldbach's conjecture holds for even numbers through 40.

    b. Assuming that Goldbach's conjecture is true, show how each odd whole number greater than 6 is the sum of three primes.

26. For the numbers greater than 5 and less than 50, are there at least two primes between every number and its double? If not, for which number does this not hold?

27. Find two whole numbers with the smallest possible difference between them that when multiplied together will produce 1,234,567,890.

28. Find the largest counting number that divides every number in the following sets.
    a. $\{1 \cdot 2 \cdot 3, 2 \cdot 3 \cdot 4, 3 \cdot 4 \cdot 5, \ldots\}$
    b. $\{1 \cdot 3 \cdot 5, 2 \cdot 4 \cdot 6, 3 \cdot 5 \cdot 7, \ldots\}$

    Can you explain your answer in each case?

29. Find the smallest counting number that is divisible by the numbers 2 through 10.

30. What is the smallest counting number divisible by 2, 4, 5, 6, and 12?

31. Fill in the blank. The sum of three consecutive counting numbers always has a divisor (other than 1) of _____. Prove.

32. Choose any two numbers, say 5 and 7. Form a sequence of numbers as follows: 5, 7, 12, 19, and so on, where each new term is the sum of the two preceding numbers until you have 10 numbers. Add the 10 numbers. Is the seventh number a factor of the sum? Repeat several times, starting with a different pair of numbers each time. What do you notice? Prove that your observation is always true.

33. a. $5! = 5 \cdot 4 \cdot 3 \cdot 2 \cdot 1$ is divisible by 2, 3, 4, and 5. Prove that $5! + 2$, $5! + 3$, $5! + 4$, and $5! + 5$ are all composite.
    b. Find 1000 consecutive numbers that are composite.

34. The customer said to the cashier. "I have 5 apples at 27 cents each and 2 pounds of potatoes at 78 cents per pound. I also have 3 cantaloupes and 6 lemons, but I don't remember the price for each." The cashier said, "That will be $3.52." The customer said, "You must have made a mistake." The cashier checked and the customer was correct. How did the customer catch the mistake?

35. There is a three-digit number with the following property: If you subtract 7 from it, the difference is divisible by 7; if you subtract 8 from it, the difference is divisible by 8; and if you subtract 9 from it, the difference is divisible by 9. What is the number?

36. Paula and Ricardo are serving cupcakes at a school party. If they arrange the cupcakes in groups of 2, 3, 4, 5, or 6, they always have exactly one cupcake left over. What is the smallest number of cupcakes they could have?

37. Prove that all six-place numbers of the form *abcabc* (e.g., 416,416) are divisible by 13. What other two numbers are always factors of a number of this form?

38. a. Prove that all four-digit palindromes are divisible by 11.
    b. Is this also true for every palindrome with an even number of digits? Prove or disprove.

39. The annual sales for certain calculators were $2567 one year and $4267 the next. Assuming that the price of the calculators was the same each of the two years, how many calculators were sold in each of the two years?

40. Observe that 7 divides 2149. Also check to see that 7 divides 149,002. Try this pattern on another four-digit number using 7. If it works again, try a third. If that one also works, formulate a conjecture based on your three examples and prove it. (*Hint*: 7 | 1001.)

41. How long does this list continue to yield primes?
$$17 + 2 = 19$$
$$19 + 4 = 23$$
$$23 + 6 = 29$$
$$29 + 8 = 37$$

42. Justify the test for divisibility by 11 for four-digit numbers by completing the following: Let $a \cdot 10^3 + b \cdot 10^2 + c \cdot 10 + d$ be any four-digit number. Then
$$a \cdot 10^3 + b \cdot 10^2 + c \cdot 10 + d$$
$$= a(1001 - 1) + b(99 + 1) + c(11 - 1) + d$$
$$= \cdots.$$

43. If p is a prime greater than 5, then the number 111 … 1, consisting of $p - 1$ ones, is divisible by p. For example, 7 | 111,111, since $7 \times 15873 = 111,111$. Verify the initial sentence for the next three primes.

44. a. Find the largest n such that $3^n \mid 24!$.
    b. Find the smallest n such that $3^6 \mid n!$.
    c. Find the largest n such that $12^n \mid 24!$.

45. Do Problem 18 using a spreadsheet to create a table of values, n and $p(n)$, for $n = 1, 2, \ldots 20$. Once the smallest value of n is found, evaluate $p(n + 1)$ and $p(n + 2)$. Are they prime or composite?

Section 5.1 EXERCISE / PROBLEM SET B

EXERCISES

1. An efficient way to find all the primes up to 100 is to arrange the numbers from 1 to 100 in six columns. As with the Sieve of Eratosthenes, cross out the multiples of 2, 3, 5, and 7. What pattern do you notice?

(*Hint*: Look at the columns and diagonals.)

1	2	3	4	5	6
7	8	9	10	11	12
13	14	15	16	17	18
19	20	21	22	23	24
25	26	27	28	29	30
31	32	33	34	35	36
37	38	39	40	41	42
43	44	45	46	47	48
49	50	51	52	53	54
55	56	57	58	59	60
61	62	63	64	65	66
67	68	69	70	71	72
73	74	75	76	77	78
79	80	81	82	83	84
85	86	87	88	89	90
91	92	93	94	95	96
97	98	99	100		

2. Find a factor tree for each of the following numbers.
   a. 192   **b.** 380   **c.** 1593   **d.** 3741

3. Factor each of the following numbers into primes.
   a. 39   **b.** 1131   **c.** 55
   d. 935   **e.** 3289   **f.** 5889

4. Use the definition of *divides* to show that each of the following is true. (*Hint*: Find *x* that satisfies the definition of *divides*.)
   a. $7 \mid 49$
   b. $21 \mid 210$
   c. $3 \mid (9 \times 18)$
   d. $2 \mid (2^2 \times 5 \times 7)$
   e. $6 \mid (2^4 \times 3^2 \times 7^3 \times 13^5)$
   f. $100,000 \mid (2^7 \times 3^9 \times 5^{11} \times 17^8)$
   g. $6000 \mid (2^{21} \times 3^{17} \times 5^{89} \times 29^{37})$
   h. $22 \mid (121 \times 4)$
   i. $p^3 q^5 r \mid (p^5 q^{13} r^7 s^2 t^{27})$ **j.** $7 \mid (5 \times 21 + 14)$

5. Decide whether the following are true or false using only divisibility ideas given in this section (do not use long division or a calculator). Give a reason for your answers.
   a. $24 \mid 325,608$ **b.** $45 \mid 13,075$
   c. $40 \mid 1,732,800$ **d.** $36 \mid 677,916$

6. If 24 divides *b*, what else must divide *b*?

7. a. Prove in two different ways that 2 divides 114.
   b. Prove in two different ways that $3 \mid 336$.

8. Which of the following are multiples of 3? of 4? of 9?
   a. 2,199,456   **b.** 31,020,417

9. True or false? Explain.
   a. If a counting number is divisible by 6 and 8, it must be divisible by 48.
   b. If a counting number is divisible by 4, it must be divisible by 8.

10. If the variables represent counting numbers, determine whether each of the following is true or false.
   a. If $2 \mid a$ and $6 \mid a$, then $12 \mid a$.
   b. $6 \mid xy$, then $6 \mid x$ or $6 \mid y$.

11. Which of the following numbers are composite? Why?
   a. 123,456   **b.** 1,234,567   **c.** 123,456,789

12. A test for divisibility by 7 is illustrated as follows. Does 7 divide 17,276?

   Test:

17276	
− 12	Subtract 2×6 from 1727
1715	
− 10	Subtract 2×5 from 171
161	
− 2	Subtract 2×1 from 16
14	

   Since $7 \mid 14$, we also have $7 \mid 17,276$. Use this test to see whether the following numbers are divisible by 7.
   a. 8659   **b.** 46,187   **c.** 864,197,523

PROBLEMS

13. A calculator may be used to test for divisibility of one number by another, where *n* and *d* represent counting numbers.
   a. If $n \div d$ gives the answer 176, is it necessarily true that $d \mid n$?
   b. If $n \div d$ gives the answer 56.3, is it possible that $d \mid n$?

14. Justify the test for divisibility by 9 for any four-digit number. (*Hint*: Reason by analogy from the test for divisibility by 3.)

15. Justify the tests for divisibility by 4 and 8.

16. Find the first composite number in this list.

    $3! - 2! + 1! = 5$ Prime
    $4! - 3! + 2! - 1! = 19$ Prime
    $5! - 4! + 3! - 2! + 1! = 101$ Prime

    Continue this pattern. (*Hint*: The first composite comes within the first 10 such numbers.)

17. In 1845, the French mathematician Bertrand made the following conjecture: Between any whole number greater than 1 and its double there is at least one prime. In 1911, the Russian mathematician Tchebyshev proved the conjecture true. Using the Chapter 5 eManipulative activity, *Sieve of Eratosthenes*, to display all primes less than 200, find three primes between each of the following numbers and its double.

    a. 30   **b.** 50   **c.** 100

18. The numbers 2, 3, 5, 7, 11, and 13 are not factors of 211. Can we conclude that 211 is prime without checking for more factors? Why or why not?

19. It is claimed that the formula $n^2 - n + 41$ yields a prime for all whole-number values for n. Decide whether this statement is true or false.

20. In 1644, the French mathematician Mersenne asserted that $2^n - 1$ was prime only when $n = 2, 3, 5, 7, 13,$ 17, 19, 31, 67, 127, and 257. As it turned out, when $n = 67$ and $n = 257$, $2^n - 1$ was a composite, and $2^n - 1$ was also prime when $n = 89$ and $n = 107$. Show that Mersenne's assertion was correct concerning $n = 3, 5, 7,$ and 13.

21. It is claimed that every prime greater than 3 is either one more or one less than a multiple of 6. Investigate. If it seems true, prove it. If it does not, find a counterexample.

22. Is it possible for the sum of two odd prime numbers to be a prime number? Why or why not?

23. Mathematician D. H. Lehmer found that there are 209 consecutive composites between 20,831,323 and 20,831,533. Pick two numbers at random between 20,831,323 and 20,831,533 and prove that they are composite.

24. **Prime triples** are consecutive primes whose difference is 2. One such triple is 3, 5, 7. Find more or prove that there cannot be any more.

25. A seventh-grade student named Arthur Hamann made the following conjecture: Every even number is the difference of two primes. Express the following even numbers as the difference of two primes.

    a. 12   **b.** 20   **c.** 28

26. The numbers 1, 7, 13, 31, 37, 43, 61, 67, and 73 form a 3×3 additive magic square. (An **additive magic square** has the same sum in all three rows, three columns, and two main diagonals.) Find it.

27. Can you find whole numbers a and b such that $3^a = 5^b$? Why or why not?

28. I'm a two-digit number less than 40. I'm divisible by only one prime number. The sum of my digits is a prime, and the difference between my digits is another prime. What numbers could I be?

29. What is the smallest counting number divisible by 2, 4, 6, 8, 10, 12, and 14?

30. What is the smallest counting number divisible by the numbers 1, 2, 3, 4, . . . 24, 25? (*Hint*: Give your answer in prime factorization form.)

31. The sum of five consecutive counting numbers has a divisor (other than 1) of _____. Prove.

32. Take any number with an even number of digits. Reverse the digits and add the two numbers. Does 11 divide your result? If yes, try to explain why.

33. Take a number. Reverse its digits and subtract the smaller of the two numbers from the larger. Determine what number always divides such differences for the following types of numbers.

    a. A two-digit number   **b.** A three-digit number
    c. A four-digit number

34. Choose any three digits. Arrange them three ways to form three numbers. *Claim*: The sum of your three numbers has a factor of 3. True or false?

    $$\begin{array}{r} Example: \quad 371 \\ 137 \\ +713 \\ \hline 1221 \end{array}$$

    and $1221 = 3 \times 407$

35. Someone spilled ink on a bill for 36 sweatshirts. If only the first and last digits were covered and the other three digits were, in order, 8, 3, 9 as in ?83.9?, how much did each cost?

36. Determine how many zeros are at the end of the numerals for the following numbers in base ten.
    a. 10!   **b.** 100!   **c.** 1000!

37. Find the smallest number n with the following property: If n is divided by 3, the quotient is the number obtained by moving the last digit (ones digit) of n to become the first digit. All of the remaining digits are shifted one to the right.

38. A man and his grandson have the same birthday. If for six consecutive birthdays the man is a whole number of times as old as his grandson, how old is each at the sixth birthday?

39. Let m be any odd whole number. Then m is a divisor of the sum of any m consecutive whole numbers. True or false? If true, prove. If false, provide a counterexample.

40. A merchant marked down some pads of paper from $2 and sold the entire lot. If the gross received from the sale was $603.77, how many pads did she sell?

41. How many prime numbers less than 100 can be written using the digits 1, 2, 3, 4, 5 if

a. no digit is used more than once?

b. a digit may be used twice?

42. Which of the numbers in the set

$$\{9, 99, 999, 9999, \ldots\}$$

are divisible by 7?

43. Two digits of this number were erased: 273*49*5. However, we know that 9 and 11 divide the number. What is it?

44. This problem appeared on a Russian mathematics exam: Show that all the numbers in the sequence 100001, 10000100001, 1000010000100001, ... are composite. Show that 11 divides the first, third, fifth numbers in this sequence, and so on, and that 111 divides the second. An American engineer claimed that the fourth number was the product of

21401   and   4672725574038601.

Was he correct?

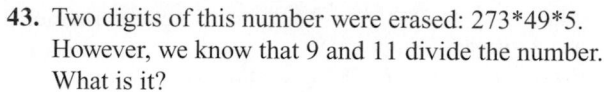

45. The Fibonacci sequence, 1, 1, 2, 3, 5, 8, 13, . . . , is formed by adding any two consecutive numbers to find the next term. Prove or disprove: The sum of any ten consecutive Fibonacci numbers is a multiple of 11.

46. Do Part A Problem 19(a) using a spreadsheet to create a table of values, n and $p(n)$, for $n = 1, 2, \ldots 20$.

PROBLEMS FOR WRITING/DISCUSSION

1. You know that $a \mid b$ means "a divides b" and $b \mid a$ means "b divided by a." Discuss the differences between these two expressions.

2. It is true that if $2 \mid 36$ and $9 \mid 36$, then $18 \mid 36$, since $18 = 2 \times 9$. So wouldn't it also be true that since

$4 \mid 36$ and $6 \mid 36$, then $24 \mid 36$ since $24 = 4 \times 6$? Why or why not?

3. We know that $a(b - c)$ equals $ab - ac$. Is it also true that $a \mid (b - c)$ means $a \mid b$ and $a \mid c$? Explain.

5.2 COUNTING FACTORS, GREATEST COMMON FACTOR, AND LEAST COMMON MULTIPLE

STARTING POINT

The numbers from 1 to 20 are listed below along with all of their factors. Which numbers have exactly 2 factors? How are these numbers related? Which numbers have exactly 3 factors? What patterns do you notice among these numbers? How are numbers with exactly 4, 5, or 6 factors related? Use your conclusions to predict how many factors the numbers 24, 25, 26, and 27 have. Check your predictions.

NUMBER	FACTORS	NUMBER	FACTORS	NUMBER	FACTORS	NUMBER	FACTORS
1	1	6	1, 2, 3, 6	11	1, 11	16	1, 2, 4, 8, 16
2	1, 2	7	1, 7	12	1, 2, 3, 4, 6, 12	17	1, 17
3	1, 3	8	1, 2, 4, 8	13	1, 13	18	1, 2, 3, 6, 9, 18
4	1, 2, 4	9	1, 3, 9	14	1, 2, 7, 14	19	1, 19
5	1, 5	10	1, 2, 5, 10	15	1, 3, 5, 15	20	1, 2, 4, 5, 10, 20

Problem-Solving Strategy
Look for a Pattern

Counting Factors

In addition to finding prime factors, it is sometimes useful to be able to find how many factors (not just prime factors) a number has. The fundamental theorem of arithmetic is helpful in this regard. For example, to find all the factors of 12, consider

EXPO-NENT OF 2	EXPO-NENT OF 3	FACTOR
0	0	$2^0 \cdot 3^0 = 1$
1	0	$2^1 \cdot 3^0 = 2$
2	0	$2^2 \cdot 3^0 = 4$
0	1	$2^0 \cdot 3^1 = 3$
1	1	$2^1 \cdot 3^1 = 6$
2	1	$2^2 \cdot 3^1 = 12$

its prime factorization $12 = 2^2 \cdot 3^1$. All factors of 12 must be made up of products of at most 2 twos and 1 three. All such combinations are contained in the table to the left. Therefore, 12 has six factors, namely, 1, 2, 3, 4, 6, and 12.

The technique used in this table can be used with any whole number that is expressed as the product of primes with their respective exponents. To find the number of factors of $2^3 \cdot 5^2$, a similar list could be constructed. The exponents of 2 would range from 0 to 3 (four possibilities), and the exponents of 5 would range from 0 to 2 (three possibilities). In all there would be $4 \cdot 3$ combinations, or 12 factors of $2^3 \cdot 5^2$, as shown in the following table.

EXPONENTS OF 5	0	1	2
0	$2^0 5^0$	$2^0 5^1$	$2^0 5^2$
1	$2^1 5^0$	$2^1 5^1$	$2^1 5^2$
2	$2^2 5^0$	$2^2 5^1$	$2^2 5^2$
3	$2^3 5^0$	$2^3 5^1$	$2^3 5^2$

This method for finding the number of factors of any number can be summarized as follows.

THEOREM

Suppose that a counting number n is expressed as a product of *distinct* primes with their respective exponents, say $n = (p_1^{n_1})(p_2^{n_2}) \cdots (p_m^{n_m})$. Then the number of factors of n is the product $(n_1 + 1) \cdot (n_2 + 1) \cdots (n_m + 1)$.

Example 5.9   Find the number of factors.
a. 144   **b.** $2^3 \cdot 5^7 \cdot 7^4$ **c.** $9^5 \cdot 11^2$

Solution

a. $144 = 2^4 \cdot 3^2$. So, the number of factors of 144 is $(4 + 1)(2 + 1) = 15$.
b. $2^3 \cdot 5^7 \cdot 7^4$ has $(3 + 1)(7 + 1)(4 + 1) = 160$ factors.
c. $9^5 \cdot 11^2 = 3^{10} \cdot 11^2$ has $(10 + 1)(2 + 1) = 33$ factors. (NOTE: 9^5 had to be rewritten as 3^{10}, since 9 was not prime.) ■

Notice that the number of factors does not depend on the prime factors, but rather on their respective exponents.

Greatest Common Factor

The concept of greatest common factor is useful when simplifying fractions.

DEFINITION

Greatest Common Factor

The **greatest common factor (GCF)** of two (or more) nonzero whole numbers is the largest whole number that is a factor of both (all) of the numbers. The GCF of a and b is written **GCF(a, b)**.

There are two elementary ways to find the greatest common factor of two numbers: the set intersection method and the prime factorization method. The GCF(24, 36) is found next using these two methods.

Set Intersection Method

STEP 1

Find all factors of 24 and 36. Since $24 = 2^3 \cdot 3$, there are $4 \cdot 2 = 8$ factors of 24, and since $36 = 2^2 \cdot 3^2$, there are $3 \cdot 3 = 9$ factors of 36. The set of factors of 24 is $\{1, 2, 3, 4, 6, 8, 12, 24\}$, and the set of factors of 36 is $\{1, 2, 3, 4, 6, 9, 12, 18, 36\}$.

STEP 2

Find all common factors of 24 and 36 by taking the intersection of the two sets in step 1.
$$\{1, 2, 3, 4, 6, 8, 12, 24\} \cap \{1, 2, 3, 4, 6, 9, 12, 18, 36\} = \{1, 2, 3, 4, 6, 12\}$$

STEP 3

Find the largest number in the set of common factors in step 2. The largest number in $\{1, 2, 3, 4, 6, 12\}$ is 12. Therefore, 12 is the GCF of 24 and 36. (NOTE: The set intersection method can also be used to find the GCF of more than two numbers in a similar manner.)

Prime Factorization Method

STEP 1

Express the numbers 24 and 36 in their prime factor exponential form: $24 = 2^3 \cdot 3$ and $36 = 2^2 \cdot 3^2$.

STEP 2

The GCF will be the number $2^m 3^n$ where m is the smaller of the exponents of the 2s and n is the smaller of the exponents of the 3s. For $2^3 \cdot 3$ and $2^2 \cdot 3^2$, m is the smaller of 3 and 2, and n is the smaller of 1 and 2. Therefore, the GCF of $2^3 \cdot 3^1$ and $2^2 \cdot 3^2$ is $2^2 \cdot 3^1 = 12$. Review this method so that you see why it always yields the largest number that is a factor of both of the given numbers.

Example 5.10　Find GCF(42, 24) in two ways.

Solution

Set Intersection Method
$42 = 2 \cdot 3 \cdot 7$, so 42 has $2 \cdot 2 \cdot 2 = 8$ factors.
$24 = 2^3 \cdot 3$, so 24 has $4 \cdot 2 = 8$ factors.
Factors of 42 are 1, 2, 3, 6, 7, 14, 21, 42.
Factors of 24 are 1, 2, 3, 4, 6, 8, 12, 24.
Common factors are 1, 2, 3, 6.
GCF(42, 24) = 6.

Prime Factorization Method
$42 = 2 \cdot 3 \cdot 7$ and $24 = 2^3 \cdot 3$.
GCF(42, 24) = $2 \cdot 3 = 6$.

Notice that only the common primes (2 and 3) are used, since the exponent on the 7 is zero in the prime factorization of 24. ■

Earlier in this chapter we obtained the following result: If $a \mid m$, $a \mid n$, and $m \geq n$, then $a \mid (m - n)$. In words, if a number divides each of two numbers, then it divides their difference. Hence, if c is a common factor of a and b, where $a \geq b$, then c is also a common factor of b and $a - b$. Since every common factor of a and b is also a common factor of b and $a - b$, the pairs (a, b) and $(a - b, b)$ have the same common factors. So GCF(a, b) and GCF$(a - b, b)$ must also be the same.

THEOREM

If a and b are whole numbers, with $a \geq b$, then

$$\text{GCF}(a, b) = \text{GCF}(a - b, b).$$

The usefulness of this result is illustrated in the next example.

Example 5.11   Find the GCF(546, 390).

Solution

$$
\begin{aligned}
\text{GCF}(546, 390) &= \text{GCF}(546 - 390, 390) \\
&= \text{GCF}(156, 390) \\
&= \text{GCF}(390 - 156, 156) \\
&= \text{GCF}(234, 156) \\
&= \text{GCF}(78, 156) \\
&= \text{GCF}(78, 78) \\
&= 78
\end{aligned}
$$

■

Spotlight on Technology   Using a calculator, we can find the GCF(546, 390) as follows:

$$
\begin{array}{c}
546 \;\boxed{-}\; 390 \;\boxed{=}\; 156 \\
390 \;\boxed{-}\; 156 \;\boxed{=}\; 234 \\
234 \;\boxed{-}\; 156 \;\boxed{=}\; 78 \\
156 \;\boxed{-}\; 78 \;\boxed{=}\; 78
\end{array}
$$

Therefore, since the last two numbers in the last line are equal, then the GCF(546, 390) = 78. Notice that this procedure may be shortened by storing 156 in the calculator's memory.

This calculator method can be refined for very large numbers or in exceptional cases. For example, to find GCF(1417, 26), 26 must be subtracted many times to produce a number that is less than (or equal to) 26. Since division can be viewed as repeated subtraction, long division can be used to shorten this process as follows:

$$
\begin{array}{r}
54 \text{ R } 13 \\
26\overline{)1417}
\end{array}
$$

Here 26 was "subtracted" from 1417 a total of 54 times to produce a remainder of 13. Thus GCF(1417, 26) = GCF(13, 26). Next, divide 13 into 26.

$$
\begin{array}{r}
2 \text{ R } 0 \\
13\overline{)26}
\end{array}
$$

Thus GCF(13, 26) = 13, so GCF(1417, 26) = 13. Each step of this method can be justified by the following theorem.

THEOREM

If a and b are whole numbers with $a \geq b$ and $a = bq + r$, where $r < b$, then

$$\text{GCF}(a, b) = \text{GCF}(r, b).$$

Thus, to find the GCF of any two numbers, this theorem can be applied repeatedly until a remainder of zero is obtained. The final divisor that leads to the zero remainder is the GCF of the two numbers. This method is called the **Euclidean algorithm.**

Example 5.12   Find the GCF(840, 3432).

Solution

$$
\begin{array}{r}
4 \text{ R } 72 \\
840\overline{)3432}
\end{array}
$$

$$
\begin{array}{r}
11 \text{ R } 48 \\
72\overline{)840}
\end{array}
$$

$$
\begin{array}{r}
1 \text{ R } 24 \\
48\overline{)72}
\end{array}
$$

$$
\begin{array}{r}
2 \text{ R } 0 \\
24\overline{)48}
\end{array}
$$

Therefore, GCF(840, 3432) = 24.   ■

www.wiley.com/
college/musser

Spotlight on Technology The Euclidean algorithm is the same process of dividing and finding the remainder over and over again, searching for the last nonzero remainder. Because of the iterative process, spreadsheets are a good technological tool for implementing the Euclidean algorithm. Refer to the dynamic spreadsheet, *Euclidean*, in the spreadsheet webmodule. Using this spreadsheet, find two numbers that take at least 10 steps to find the GCF. (*Hint:* the numbers are not necessarily large, but they can be found by thinking of doing the algorithm backward.)

Spotlight on Technology A calculator also can be used to calculate the GCF(3432, 840) using the Euclidean algorithm.

$$
\begin{array}{r}
3432 \div 840 = \boxed{4.085714286} \\
3432 - 4 \times 840 = \boxed{72.} \\
840 \div 72 = \boxed{11.66666667} \\
840 - 11 \times 72 = \boxed{48.} \\
72 \div 48 = \boxed{1.5} \\
72 - 1 \times 48 = \boxed{24.} \\
48 \div 24 = \boxed{2.}
\end{array}
$$

Reflection from Research
Possibly because students often confuse factors and multiples, the greatest common factor and the least common multiple are difficult topics for students to grasp (Graviss & Greaver, 1992).

Therefore, 24 is the GCF(3432, 840). Notice how this method parallels the one in Example 5.12.

Least Common Multiple

The least common multiple is useful when adding or subtracting fractions.

> ### DEFINITION
>
> *Least Common Multiple*
>
> The **least common multiple (LCM)** of two (or more) nonzero whole numbers is the smallest nonzero whole number that is a multiple of each (all) of the numbers. The LCM of a and b is written **LCM(a, b).**

For the GCF, there are three elementary ways to find the least common multiple of two numbers: the set intersection method, the prime factorization method, and the build-up method. The LCM(24, 36) is found next using these three methods.

Set Intersection Method

STEP 1

List the first several nonzero multiples of 24 and 36. The set of nonzero multiples of 24 is $\{24, 48, 72, 96, 120, 144, \ldots\}$, and the set of nonzero multiples of 36 is $\{36, 72, 108, 144, \ldots\}$. (NOTE: The set of multiples of any nonzero whole number is an infinite set.)

STEP 2

Find the first several common multiples of 24 and 36 by taking the intersection of the two sets in step 1:
$$\{24, 48, 72, 96, 120, 144, \ldots\} \cap \{36, 72, 108, 144, \ldots\} = \{72, 144, \ldots\}.$$

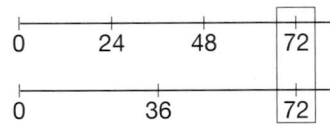

Figure 5.5

STEP 3

Find the smallest number in the set of common multiples in step 2. The smallest number in $\{72, 144, \ldots\}$ is 72. Therefore, 72 is the LCM of 24 and 36 (Figure 5.5).

Prime Factorization Method

STEP 1

Express the numbers 24 and 36 in their prime factor exponential form: $24 = 2^3 \cdot 3$ and $36 = 2^2 \cdot 3^2$.

STEP 2

The LCM will be the number $2^r 3^s$, where r is the larger of the exponents of the twos and s is the larger of the exponents of the threes. For $2^3 \cdot 3^1$ and $2^2 \cdot 3^2$, r is the larger of 3 and 2 and s is the larger of 1 and 2. That is, the LCM of $2^3 \cdot 3^1$ and $2^2 \cdot 3^2$ is $2^3 \cdot 3^2$, or 72. Review this procedure to see why it always yields the smallest number that is a multiple of both of the given numbers.

Build-up Method

STEP 1

As in the prime factorization method, express the numbers 24 and 36 in their prime factor exponential form: $24 = 2^3 \cdot 3$ and $36 = 2^2 \cdot 3^2$.

STEP 2

Select the prime factorization of one of the numbers and build the LCM from that as follows. Beginning with $24 = 2^3 \cdot 3$, compare it to the prime factorization of $36 = 2^2 \cdot 3^2$. Because $2^2 \cdot 3^2$ has more threes than $2^3 \cdot 3^1$, build up the $2^3 \cdot 3^1$ to have the same number of threes as $2^2 \cdot 3^2$, making the LCM $2^3 \cdot 3^2$. If there are more than two numbers for which the LCM is to be found, continue to compare and build with each subsequent number.

Example 5.13   Find the LCM(42, 24) in three ways.

Solution

Set Intersection Method
Multiples of 42 are 42, 84, 126, 168, ...
Multiples of 24 are 24, 48, 72, 96, 120, 144, 168, ...
Common multiples are 168, ...
LCM(42, 24) = 168.

Prime Factorization Method
$42 = 2 \cdot 3 \cdot 7$ and $24 = 2^3 \cdot 3$.
LCM(42, 24) = $2^3 \cdot 3 \cdot 7 = 168$.

Build-up Method
$42 = 2 \cdot 3 \cdot 7$ and $24 = 2^3 \cdot 3$. Beginning with $24 = 2^3 \cdot 3$, compare to $2 \cdot 3 \cdot 7$ and build $2^3 \cdot 3$ up to $2^3 \cdot 3 \cdot 7$.
LCM(42, 24) = $2^3 \cdot 3 \cdot 7 = 168$.

Notice that *all* primes from either number are used when forming the least common multiple.   ■

These methods can also be applied to find the GCF and LCM of several numbers.

Example 5.14   Find the (a) GCF and (b) LCM of the three numbers $2^5 \cdot 3^2 \cdot 5^7$, $2^4 \cdot 3^4 \cdot 5^3 \cdot 7$, and $2 \cdot 3^6 \cdot 5^4 \cdot 13^2$.

Solution

a. The GCF is $2^1 \cdot 3^2 \cdot 5^3$ (use the common primes and the smallest respective exponents).
b. Using the build-up method, begin with $2^5 \cdot 3^2 \cdot 5^7$. Then compare it to $2^4 \cdot 3^4 \cdot 5^3 \cdot 7$ and build up the LCM to $2^5 \cdot 3^4 \cdot 5^7 \cdot 7$. Now compare with $2 \cdot 3^6 \cdot 5^4 \cdot 13^2$ and build up $2^5 \cdot 3^4 \cdot 5^7 \cdot 7$ to $2^5 \cdot 3^6 \cdot 5^7 \cdot 7 \cdot 13^2$.   ■

If you are trying to find the GCF of several numbers that are not in prime-factored exponential form, as in Example 5.14, you may want to use a computer program. By considering examples in exponential notation, one can observe that the GCF of a, b, and c can be found by finding GCF(a, b) first and then GCF(GCF(a, b), c). This idea can be extended to as many numbers as you wish. Thus one can use the Euclidean algorithm by finding GCFs of numbers, two at a time. For example, to find GCF(24, 36, 160), find GCF(24, 36), which is 12, and then find GCF(12, 160), which is 4.

Multiples and Least Common Multiples

Quick Review

Count by

1. fives from 5 to 30.
2. threes from 3 to 18.
3. fours from 4 to 24.
4. sixes from 6 to 36.
5. eights from 8 to 40.

VOCABULARY

common multiple

least common multiple (LCM)

MATERIALS

red and yellow counters

▶ **Explore**

A multiple is the product of two or more nonzero whole numbers.

When a number is a multiple of 2 or more numbers in a set, it is a **common multiple**.

The least number that is a common multiple is the **least common multiple**, or **LCM**.

Activity

You can make a model to find the least common multiple of 3 and 5.

 STEP 1

Place 3 red counters in a row. Place 5 yellow counters in a row directly below.

 STEP 2

Continue placing groups of 3 red counters and groups of 5 yellow counters until both rows have the same number of counters. At that point, the number of counters in each row is the least common multiple, or LCM, of 3 and 5.

There are 15 counters in each row. So, the least common multiple of 3 and 5 is 15.

Try It

Use counters to find the least common multiple for each set of numbers.

a. 2, 7   **b.** 4, 5   **c.** 4, 8

d. 3, 4   **e.** 2, 3, 6   **f.** 2, 3, 9

What should you do next to find the LCM of 2 and 7?

260

Finally, there is a very useful connection between the GCF and LCM of two numbers, as illustrated in the next example.

Example 5.15 Find the GCF and LCM of a and b, for the numbers $a = 2^5 \cdot 3^7 \cdot 5^2 \cdot 7$ and $b = 2^3 \cdot 3^2 \cdot 5^6 \cdot 11$.

Solution

Notice in the following solution that the products of the factors of a and b, which are in bold type, make up the GCF, and the products of the remaining factors, which are circled, make up the LCM.

$$\text{GCF} = 2^3 \cdot 3^2 \cdot 5^2$$
$$a = \textcircled{2^5} \cdot \textcircled{3^7} \cdot \mathbf{5^2} \cdot \textcircled{7} \qquad b = \mathbf{2^3 \cdot 3^2} \cdot \textcircled{5^6} \cdot \textcircled{11}$$
$$\text{LCM} = 2^5 \cdot 3^7 \cdot 5^6 \cdot 7 \cdot 11$$

Hence

$$\begin{aligned}
\text{GCF}\,(a, b) \times \text{LCM}\,(a, b) &= (2^3 \cdot 3^2 \cdot 5^2)(2^5 \cdot 3^7 \cdot 5^6 \cdot 7 \cdot 11) \\
&= (2^5 \cdot 3^7 \cdot 5^2 \cdot 7) \cdot (2^3 \cdot 3^2 \cdot 5^6 \cdot 11) \\
&= a \times b.
\end{aligned}$$

Example 5.15 illustrates that *all* of the prime factors and their exponents from the original number are accounted for in the GCF and LCM. This relationship is stated next.

THEOREM

Let a and b be any two whole numbers. Then

$$\text{GCF}(a, b) \times \text{LCM}(a, b) = ab.$$

Also, $\text{LCM}(a, b) = \dfrac{ab}{\text{GCF}(a,b)}$ is a consequence of this theorem. So if the GCF of two numbers is known, the LCM can be found using the GCF.

Example 5.16 Find the LCM(36, 56).

Solution

$\text{GCF}(36, 56) = 4$. Therefore, $\text{LCM} = \dfrac{36 \cdot 56}{4} = 9 \cdot 56 = 504$. ■

This technique applies only to the case of finding the GCF and LCM of *two* numbers.

We end this chapter with an important result regarding the primes by proving that there is an infinite number of primes.

THEOREM

There is an infinite number of primes.

Problem-Solving Strategy
Use Indirect Reasoning

Proof Either there is a finite number of primes or there is an infinite number of primes. We will use indirect reasoning. Let us *assume* that there is only a *finite* number of primes, say 2, 3, 5, 7, 11, . . . , p, where p is the greatest prime. Let $N = (2 \cdot 3 \cdot 5 \cdot 7 \cdot 11 \cdots p) + 1$. This number, N, must be 1, prime, or composite. Clearly, N is greater than 1. Also, N is greater than any prime. But then, if N is composite, it must have a prime factor. Yet whenever N is divided by a prime, the remainder is always 1 (think about this)! Therefore, N is neither 1, nor a prime, nor a composite. But that is impossible. Using indirect reasoning, we conclude that there must be an infinite number of primes. ■

There are also infinitely many composite numbers (for example, the even numbers greater than 2).

MATHEMATICAL MORSEL

On June 1, 1999, the record was broken again. For the third time in 2 years, a new largest prime was found. The previous records of $2^{2976221} - 1$ and $2^{3021377} - 1$ were set on August 24, 1997, and January 27, 1998, respectively. The newest prime, $2^{6972593} - 1$, has 2,098,960 digits and, if written out in a typical newsprint size, would fill 64 pages of a newspaper. Why search for such large primes? One reason is that it requires trillions of calculations and hence can be used to test computer speed and reliability. Also, it is important in writing messages in code. Besides, as a computer expert put it: "It's like Mount Everest. Why do people climb mountains?"

Section 5.2 EXERCISE / PROBLEM SET A

EXERCISES

1. How many factors does each of the following numbers have?

   a. $2^2 \times 3$ **b.** $3^3 \times 5^2$ **c.** $5^2 \times 7^3 \times 11^4$

2. **a.** Factor 36 into primes.

   b. Factor each divisor of 36 into primes.

   c. What relationship exists between the prime factors in part (b) and the prime factors in part (a)?

   d. Let $x = 7^4 \times 17^2$. If n is a divisor of x, what can you say about the prime factorization of n?

3. Which are larger, divisors of 18 or multiples of 18? Are there any exceptions?

4. Use the prime factorization method to find the GCFs.

   a. GCF(8, 18) **b.** GCF(36, 42) **c.** GCF(24, 66)

5. Using a calculator method, find the following.

   a. GCF(138, 102) **b.** GCF(484, 363)

   c. GCF(297, 204) **d.** GCF(222, 2222)

6. Use any method to find the following GCFs.

   a. GCF(12, 60, 90) **b.** GCF(15, 35, 42)

   c. GCF(55, 75, 245) **d.** GCF(28, 98, 154)

   e. GCF(1105, 1729, 3289)

   f. GCF(1421, 1827, 2523)

7. Use the (i) prime factorization method and the (ii) build-up method to find the following LCMs.

   a. LCM(6, 8) **b.** LCM(4, 10)

   c. LCM(7, 9) **d.** LCM(2, 3, 5)

   e. LCM(8, 10) **f.** LCM(8, 12, 18)

8. Another method of finding the LCM of two or more numbers is shown. Find the LCM(27, 36, 45, 60).

2	27	36	45	60
2	27	18	45	30
3	27	9	45	15
3	9	3	15	5
3	3	1	5	5
5	1	1	5	5
	1	1	1	1

Divide all even numbers by 2. If not divisible by 2, bring down, Repeat until none are divisible by 2.

Proceed to the next prime number and repeat the process

Continue until the last row is all 1s.

LCM = $2^2 \cdot 3^3 \cdot 5$ (see the left column)

Use this method to find the following LCMs.

   a. LCM(21, 24, 63, 70)   **b.** LCM(20, 36, 42, 33)

   c. LCM(15, 35, 42, 80)

9. Using the Euclidean algorithm, find the following GCFs.

   a. GCF(24, 54)   **b.** GCF(39, 91)

   c. GCF(72, 160)   **d.** GCF(5291, 11951)

10. The factors of a number that are less than the number itself are called **proper factors.** The Pythagoreans classified numbers as deficient, abundant, or perfect, depending on the sum of their proper factors.

   a. A number is **deficient** if the sum of its proper factors is less than the number. For example, the proper factors of 4 are 1 and 2. Since $1 + 2 = 3 < 4$, 4 is a deficient number. What other numbers less than 25 are deficient?

   b. A number is **abundant** if the sum of its proper factors is greater than the number. Which numbers less than 25 are abundant?

   c. A number is **perfect** if the sum of its proper factors is equal to the number. Which number less than 25 is perfect?

11. Two counting numbers are **relatively prime** if the greatest common factor of the two numbers is 1. Which of the following pairs of numbers are relatively prime?

   a. 4 and 9

   b. 24 and 123

   c. 12 and 45

12. A pair of whole numbers is called **amicable** if each is the sum of the proper divisors of the other. For example, 284 and 220 are amicable, since the proper divisors of 220 are 1, 2, 4, 5, 10, 11, 20, 22, 44, 55, 110, which sum to 284, whose proper divisors are 1, 2, 4, 71, 142, which sum to 220. Determine which of the following pairs are amicable.

   a. 1184 and 1210

   b. 1254 and 1832

   c. 2620 and 2924

   d. If 17,296 is one of a pair of amicable numbers, what is the other one? Be sure to check your work.

PROBLEMS

13. In the following problems, you are given three pieces of information. Use them to answer the question.

   a. GCF$(a, b) = 2 \times 3$, LCM$(a, b) = 2^2 \times 3^3 \times 5$, $b = 2^2 \times 3 \times 5$. What is a?

   b. GCF$(a, b) = 2^2 \times 7 \times 11$,
   LCM$(a, b) = 2^5 \times 3^2 \times 5 \times 7^3 \times 11^2$,
   $b = 2^5 \times 3^2 \times 5 \times 7 \times 11$.
   What is a?

14. What is the smallest whole number having exactly the following number of divisors?

   a. 1   **b.** 2   **c.** 3   **d.** 4

   e. 5   **f.** 6   **g.** 7   **h.** 8

15. Find six examples of whole numbers that have the following number of factors. Then try to characterize the set of numbers you found in each case.

   a. 2   **b.** 3   **c.** 4   **d.** 5

16. Euclid (300 B.C.) proved that $2^{n-1}(2^n - 1)$ produced a perfect number [see Exercise 10(c)] whenever $2^n - 1$ is prime, where $n = 1, 2, 3, \ldots$. Find the first four

such perfect numbers. (NOTE: Some 2000 years later, Euler proved that this formula produces all even perfect numbers.)

17. Find all whole numbers x such that GCF(24, x) = 1 and $1 \le x \le 24$.

18. Following recess, the 1000 students of a school lined up and entered the school as follows: The first student opened all of the 1000 lockers in the school. The second student closed all lockers with even numbers. The third student "changed" all lockers that were numbered with multiples of 3 by closing those that were open and opening those that were closed. The fourth student changed each locker whose number was a multiple of 4, and so on. After all 1000 students had entered the building in this fashion, which lockers were left open?

19. George made enough money by selling candy bars at 15 cents each to buy several cans of pop at 48 cents each. If he had no money left over, what is the fewest number of candy bars he could have sold?

20. Three chickens and one duck sold for as much as two geese, whereas one chicken, two ducks, and three geese were sold together for $25. What was the price of each bird in an exact number of dollars?

3	61	19	37
43	31	5	—
—	—	—	29
—	—	23	—

21. Which, if any, of the numbers in the set {10, 20, 40, 80, 160, . . .} is a perfect square?

22. What is the largest three-digit prime all of whose digits are prime?

23. Take any four-digit palindrome whose digits are all nonzero and not all the same. Form a new palindrome by interchanging the unlike digits. Add these two numbers.

$$\begin{array}{r} \text{Example:} \quad 8{,}448 \\ +4{,}884 \\ \hline 13{,}332 \end{array}$$

  a. Find a whole number greater than 1 that divides *every* such sum.

  b. Find the *largest* such whole number.

24. Fill in the following 4 × 4 additive magic square, which is comprised entirely of primes.

25. What is the least number of cards that could satisfy the following three conditions?

  If all the cards are put in two equal piles, there is one card left over.
  If all the cards are put in three equal piles, there is one card left over.
  If all the cards are put in five equal piles, there is one card left over.

26. Show that the number 343 is divisible by 7. Then prove or disprove: Any three-digit number of the form $100a + 10b + a$, where $a + b = 7$, is divisible by 7.

27. In the set {18, 96, 54, 27, 42}, find the pair(s) of numbers with the greatest GCF and the pair(s) with the smallest LCM.

Section 5.2   EXERCISE / PROBLEM SET B

EXERCISES

1. How many factors does each of the following numbers have?

  a. $2^2 \times 3^2$ **b.** $7^3 \times 11^3$

  c. $7^{11} \times 19^6 \times 79^{23}$ **d.** 12^4

2. a. Factor 120 into primes.

  b. Factor each divisor of 120 into primes.

  c. What relationship exists between the prime factors in part (b) and the prime factors in part (a)?

  d. Let $x = 11^5 \times 13^3$. If n is a divisor of x, what can you say about the prime factorization of n?

3. a. Which is larger, GCF(12, 18) or LCM(12, 18)?

  b. Let a and b represent two nonzero whole numbers. Which is larger, GCF(a, b) or LCM(a, b)?

4. Use the prime factorization method to find the following GCFs.

  a. GCF(18, 36, 54)   **b.** GCF(16, 51)

  c. GCF(136, 153)

5. Using a calculator method, find the following.

  a. GCF(276, 54)   **b.** GCF(111, 111111)

  c. GCF(399, 102)   **d.** GCF(12345, 54323)

6. Use any method to find the following GCFs.

  a. GCF(38, 68)   **b.** GCF(60, 126)

  c. GCF(56, 120)   **d.** GCF(42, 385)

  e. GCF(117, 195)   **f.** GCF(338, 507)

7. Use the (1) prime factorization method and the (2) build-up method to find the following LCMs.

  a. LCM(15, 21)   **b.** LCM(14, 35)

  c. LCM(75, 100)   **d.** LCM(66, 88)

  e. LCM(130, 182)   **f.** LCM(410, 1024)

8. Find the following LCMs using any method.

  a. LCM(21, 51)   **b.** LCM(111, 39)

  c. LCM(125, 225)

9. Using the Euclidean algorithm and your calculator, find the GCF for each pair of numbers.

  a. 2244 and 418   **b.** 963 and 657

  c. 7286 and 1684

10. Identify the following numbers as deficient, abundant, or perfect. [See Exercise 10(a)]

  a. 36   **b.** 28   **c.** 60   **d.** 51

11. a. Show that 83,154,367 and 4 are relatively prime.

  b. Show that 165,342,985 and 13 are relatively prime.

  c. Show that 165,342,985 and 33 are relatively prime.

12. Two numbers are said to be **betrothed** if the sum of all proper factors greater than 1 of one number equals the other, and vice versa. For example, 48 and 75 are betrothed, since

$$48 = 3 + 5 + 15 + 25,$$
proper factors of 75 except for 1,

and

$$75 = 2 + 3 + 4 + 6 + 8 + 12 + 16 + 24,$$
proper factors of 48 except for 1.

Determine which of the following pairs are betrothed.

  a. (140, 195)   **b.** (1575, 1648)   **c.** (2024, 2295)

PROBLEMS

13. a. Complete the following table by listing the factors for the given numbers. Include 1 and the number itself as factors.

  b. What kind of numbers have only two factors?

  c. What kind of numbers have an odd number of factors?

NUMBER	FACTORS	NUMBER OF FACTORS
1	1	1
2	1, 2	2
3		
4		
5		
6		
7		
8		
9		
10		
11		
12		
13		
14		
15		
16		

14. Let the letters p, q, and r represent different primes. Then p^2qr^3 has 24 divisors. So would p^{23}. Use p, q, and r to describe all whole numbers having exactly the following number of divisors.

  a. 2   **b.** 3   **c.** 4   **d.** 5   **e.** 6   **f.** 12

15. Let a and b represent whole numbers. State the conditions on a and b that make the following statements true.

  a. $GCF(a, b) = a$ **b.** $LCM(a, b) = a$
  c. $GCF(a, b) = a \times b$ **d.** $LCM(a, b) = a \times b$

16. If $GCF(x, y) = 1$, what is $GCF(x^2, y^2)$? Justify your answer.

17. It is claimed that every perfect number greater than 6 is the sum of consecutive odd cubes beginning with 1.

For example, $28 = 1^3 + 3^3$. Determine whether the preceding statement is true for the perfect numbers 496 and 8128.

18. Plato supposedly guessed (and may have proved) that there are only four relatively prime whole numbers that satisfy both of the following equations simultaneously.

$$x^2 + y^2 = z^2 \quad \text{and} \quad x^3 + y^3 + z^3 = w^3$$

If $x = 3$ and $y = 4$ are two of the numbers, what are z and w?

19. Tilda's car gets 34 miles per gallon and Naomi's gets 8 miles per gallon. When traveling from Washington, D.C., to Philadelphia, they both used a whole number of gallons of gasoline. How far is it from Philadelphia to Washington, D.C.?

20. Three neighborhood dogs barked consistently last night. Spot, Patches, and Lady began with a simultaneous bark at 11 P.M. Then Spot barked every 4 minutes, Patches every 3 minutes, and Lady every 5 minutes. Why did Mr. Jones suddenly awaken at midnight?

21. The numbers 2, 5, and 9 are factors of my locker number and there are 12 factors in all. What is my locker number, and why?

22. Which number less than 70 has the greatest number of factors?

23. The theory of biorhythm states that there are three "cycles" to your life:

The physical cycle: 23 days long
The emotional cycle: 28 days long
The intellectual cycle: 33 days long

If your cycles are together one day, in how many days will they be together again?

24. Show that the number 494 is divisible by 13. Then prove or disprove: Any three-digit number of the form $100a + 10b + a$, where $a + b = 13$, is divisible by 13.

25. A **Smith number** is a counting number the sum of whose digits is equal to the sum of all the digits of its prime factors. Prove that 4,937,775 (which was discovered by Harold Smith) is a Smith number.

26. **a.** Draw a 2 × 3 rectangular array of squares. If one diagonal is drawn in, how many squares will the diagonal go through?

b. Repeat for a 4 × 6 rectangular array.

c. Generalize this problem to an $m \times n$ array of squares.

27. Ramanujan observed that 1729 was the smallest number that was the sum of two cubes in two ways. Express 1729 as the sum of two cubes in two ways.

PROBLEMS FOR WRITING/DISCUSSION

1. Although most people associate Euclid's name most closely with geometry, he is also given credit for three of the ideas about number theory that are contained in this section. He was the first person to prove there are an infinite number of prime numbers. State the other two ideas in this section for which we give Euclid credit, and show an example of each (*Hint*: One of the ideas is described in the Part A Problems.)

2. A student is confused by all the letters abbreviating the math concepts in this section. There are LCM and GCF, and the one that says "greatest" is a smaller number than the one that says "least." How would you explain this to your student?

3. A student says she saw some other abbreviations in another book: LCD and GCD. What do they mean, and how are they related to LCM and GCF?

END OF CHAPTER MATERIAL

Solution of Initial Problem

A major fast-food chain held a contest to promote sales. With each purchase a customer was given a card with a whole number less than 100 on it. A $100 prize was given to any person who presented cards whose numbers totaled 100. The following are several typical cards. Can you find a winning combination?

| 3 | 9 | 12 | 15 | 18 | 27 | 51 | 72 | 84 |

Can you suggest how the contest could be structured so that there would be at most 1000 winners throughout the country?

Strategy: Use Properties of Numbers

Perhaps you noticed something interesting about the numbers that were on sample cards—they are all multiples of 3. From work in this chapter, we know that the sum of two (hence any number of) multiples of 3 is a multiple of 3. Therefore, any combination of the given numbers will produce a sum that is a multiple of 3. Since 100 is not a multiple of 3, it is impossible

to win with the given numbers. Although there are several ways to control the number of winners, a simple way is to include only 1000 cards with the number 1 on them.

Additional Problems Where the Strategy "Use Properties of Numbers" Is Useful

1. How old is Mary?

   • She is younger than 75 years old.
   • Her age is an odd number.
   • The sum of the digits of her age is 8.
   • Her age is a prime number.
   • She has three great-grandchildren.

2. A folding machine folds letters at a rate of 45 per minute and a stamping machine stamps folded letters at a rate of 60 per minute. What is the fewest number of each machine required so that all machines are kept busy?

3. Find infinitely many natural numbers each of which has exactly 91 factors.

People in Mathematics

Srinivasa Ramanujan (1887–1920) Srinivasa Ramanujan developed a passion for mathematics when he was a young man in India. Working from numerical examples, he arrived at astounding results in number theory. Yet he had little formal training beyond high school and had only vague notions of the principles of mathematical proof. In 1913 he sent some of his results to the English mathematician George Hardy, who was astounded at the raw genius of the work. Hardy arranged for the poverty-stricken young man to come to England. Hardy became his mentor and teacher but later remarked, "I learned from him much more than he learned from me." After several years in England, Ramanujan's health declined. He went home to India in 1919 and died of tuberculosis the following year. On one occasion, Ramanujan was ill in bed. Hardy went to visit, arriving in taxicab number 1729. He remarked to Ramanujan that the number seemed rather dull, and he hoped it wasn't a bad omen. "No," said Ramanujan, "it is a very interesting number; it is the smallest number expressible as a sum of cubes in two different ways."

Constance Bowman Reid (1917–) Constance Bowman Reid, Julia Bowman Robinson's older sister, became a high school English and journalism teacher. She gave up teaching after marriage to become a free-lance writer. Reid became fascinated with number theory as a result of discussions with her mathematician sister Julia. Her first popular exposition of mathematics appeared in *Scientific American* in 1952; it was an article about finding perfect numbers using a computer. When it was published, one of the readers complained that *Scientific American* articles should be written by recognized authorities, not by housewives! Reid has written the popular books *From Zero to Infinity*, *A Long Way from Euclid*, and *Introduction to Higher Mathematics*. In recent years, she has written highly regarded biographies of the mathematicians Hilbert, Courant, and Neyman.

CHAPTER REVIEW

Review the following terms and exercises to determine which require learning or relearning—page numbers are provided for easy reference.

SECTION 5.1: Primes, Composites, and Tests for Divisibility

VOCABULARY/NOTATION

Prime number   185
Composite number   185
Sieve of Eratosthenes   185
Factor tree   186

Prime factorization   186
Divides ($a \mid b$)   186
Does not divide ($a \nmid b$)   186
Divisor   187

Factor   187
Multiple   187
Is divisible by   187
Square root   191

EXERCISES

1. Find the prime factorization of 17,017.

2. Find all the composite numbers between 90 and 100 inclusive.

3. True or false?

   a. 51 is a prime number.

   b. 101 is a composite number.

   c. 7 | 91.

   d. 24 is a divisor of 36.

   e. 21 is a factor of 63.

   f. 123 is a multiple of 3.

   g. 81 is divisible by 27.

   h. $\sqrt{169} = 13$.

4. Using tests for divisibility, determine whether 2, 3, 4, 5, 6, 8, 9, 10, or 11 are factors of 3,963,960.

5. Invent a test for divisibility by 25.

SECTION 5.2: Counting Factors, Greatest Common Factor, and Least Common Multiple

VOCABULARY/NOTATION

Greatest common factor   Euclidean algorithm   201   Least common multiple
   [GCF (a, b)]   198   [LCM (a, b)]   202

EXERCISES

1. How many factors does $3^5 \cdot 7^3$ have?

2. Find GCF(144, 108) using the prime factorization method.

3. Find GCF(54, 189) using the Euclidean algorithm.

4. Find LCM(144, 108).

5. Given that there is an infinite number of primes, show that there is an infinite number of composite numbers.

6. Explain how the four numbers 81, 135, GCF(81, 135), and LCM(81, 135) are related.

PROBLEMS FOR WRITING/DISCUSSION

1. Suppose a student said that the sum of the digits of the number 354 is 12 and therefore 354 is divisible by any number that divides into 12, like 2, 3, 4, and 6. Would you agree with the student? Explain.

2. If you were looking for the two numbers closest together whose product is 68,370, how would you start? Would you start with the two numbers that are farthest apart, or would there be an easier way? Find the two numbers. Also, find the two numbers closest together whose product is 68,121.

3. A number is divisible by 5 if its ones digit is a 5. Thus, the number 357 is divisible by 7 since the last digit is a 7. Is this correct reasoning? Discuss.

4. If a student wanted to find out if 47 was a prime number, would she have to divide it by every number from 1 to 47? Explain what numbers she would have to check and how she should go about it.

5. It is possible to use a Venn diagram to help find the GCF and LCM of two numbers. For example, to find the GCF and LCM of the numbers 48 and 66, you would find the prime factorization of each and organize the factors in such a way that the common factors went into the overlap of the two circles representing 48 and 66. This is demonstrated in the following picture, which shows that the GCF is 6. Using this picture, how could you also find the LCM? Use this technique to represent and find the GCF and LCM of 56 and 91.

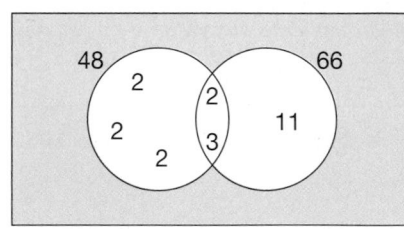

6. Try the method from Problem 5 with three numbers. For example, find the LCM and GCF of 24, 36, and 57. What works and what does not work?

7. Write out all the numbers from 1 to 100 in a six-column array, beginning as follows:

1	2	3	4	5	6
7	8	9	10	11	12, etc.

Proceed as in the Sieve of Eratosthenes given in Section 5.1. That is, circle every prime number and then draw a line through all the multiples of that number, starting with 2, then 3, etc. What do you notice about the multiples of 5? of 7? Once you have crossed out all the multiples of 7, have you found all the primes from 1 to 100? How do you know?

8. What would go wrong with the fundamental theorem of arithmetic if we allowed the number 1 to be called a prime number? Explain and give an example.

9. How would you create a test for divisibility by 12? Write it out, and give an example.

10. In mathematics, what is the difference between a "conjecture" and a "theorem"? (*Hint:* See the Focus On at the beginning of the chapter.) Was your answer to the preceding problem a conjecture or a theorem? If it was a conjecture, how could you turn it into a theorem?

CHAPTER TEST

Knowledge

1. True or false?

   a. Every prime number is odd.

   b. The Sieve of Eratosthenes is used to find primes.

   c. A number is divisible by 6 if it is divisible by 2 and 3.

   d. A number is divisible by 8 if it is divisible by 4 and 2.

   e. If $a \neq b$, then $GCF(a, b) < LCM(a, b)$.

   f. The number of factors of n can be determined by the exponents in its prime factorization.

   g. The prime factorization of a and b can be used to find the GCF and LCM of a and b.

   h. The larger a number, the more prime factors it has.

   i. The number 12 is a multiple of 36.

   j. Every counting number has more multiples than factors.

2. Write a complete sentence that conveys the meaning of and correctly uses each of the following terms or phrases.

   a. divided into   b. divided by   c. divides

Skill

3. Find the prime factorization of each of the following numbers.

   a. 120   b. 10,800   c. 819

4. Test the following for divisibility by 2, 3, 4, 5, 6, 8, 9, 10, and 11.

   a. 11,223,344   b. 6,543,210   c. $2^3 \cdot 3^4 \cdot 5^6$

5. Determine the number of factors for each of the following numbers.

   a. 360   b. 216   c. 900

6. Find the GCF and LCM of each of the following pairs of numbers.

   a. 144, 120   b. 147, 70

   c. $2^3 \cdot 3^5 \cdot 5^7, 2^7 \cdot 3^4 \cdot 5^3$ d. 2419, 2173

   e. 45, 175, 42, 60

7. Use the Euclidean algorithm to find $GCF(6273, 1025)$.

8. Find the $LCM(18, 24)$ by using the (i) set intersection method, (ii) prime factorization method, and (iii) build-up method.

Understanding

9. Explain how the Sieve of Eratosthenes can be used to find composite numbers.

10. Is it possible to find nonzero whole numbers x and y such that $7^x = 11^y$? Why or why not?

11. Show that the sum of any four consecutive counting numbers must have a factor of 2.

12. a. Show why the following statement is not true. "If $4 \mid m$ and $6 \mid m$ then $24 \mid m$."

    b. Devise a divisibility test for 18.

13. Given that $a \cdot b = 270$ and $GCF(a, b) = 3$, find $LCM(a, b)$.

14. Use rectangular arrays to illustrate why $4 \mid 8$ but $3 \nmid 8$.

15. If $n = 2 \cdot 3 \cdot 2 \cdot 7 \cdot 2 \cdot 3$ and $m = 2 \cdot 2^2 \cdot 3^2 \cdot 7$, how are m and n related? Justify your answer.

Problem-Solving/Application

16. Find the smallest number that has factors of 2, 3, 4, 5, 6, 7, 8, 9, and 10.

17. The primes 2 and 5 differ by 3. Prove that this is the only pair of primes whose difference is 3.

18. If $a = 2^2 \cdot 3^3$ and the $LCM(a, b)$ is 1080, what is the (a) smallest and (b) the largest that b can be?

19. Find the longest string of consecutive composite numbers between 1 and 50. What are those numbers?

20. Identify all of the numbers between 1 and 20 that have an odd number of divisors. How are these numbers related?

21. What is the maximum value of n that makes the statement $2^n \mid 15 \cdot 14 \cdot 13 \cdot 12 \cdots 3 \cdot 2 \cdot 1$ true?

22. Find two pairs of numbers a and b such that $GCF(a, b) = 15$ and $LCM(a, b) = 180$.

23. When Alpesh sorts his marbles, he notices that if he puts them into groups of 5, he has 1 left over. When he puts them in groups of 7, he also has 1 left over, but in groups of size 6, he has none left over. What is the smallest number of marbles that he could have?

References for Reflections from Research

BEZUSZKA, S. J. (1985). A test for divisibility by primes. *Arithmetic Teacher*, *33*(2), 36–38.

GRAVISS, T., & GREAVER, J. (1992). Extending the number line to make connections with number theory. *Mathematics Teacher*, *85*, 418–420.

FOCUS ON *Fractions: A Historical Sketch*

The first extensive treatment of fractions known to us appears in the Ahmes (or Rhind) Papyrus (1600 B.C.), which contains the work of Egyptian mathematicians. The Egyptians expressed ratios in unit fractions (that is, fractions in which the numerator is 1). For example, the ratio $2:43$ was expressed as $\frac{1}{42} + \frac{1}{86} + \frac{1}{129} + \frac{1}{301}$, rather than our modern fraction $\frac{2}{43}$. Of course, the Egyptians used hieroglyphics to represent these unit fractions; for example,

$$\frac{1}{5} = \text{⟨⟩}||||| \qquad \frac{1}{10} = \text{⟨⟩}\cap \qquad \frac{1}{21} = \text{⟨⟩}\cap\cap|$$

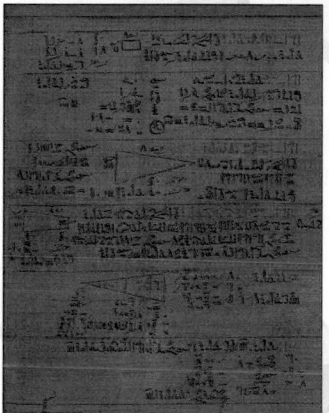

The Rhind Papyrus

Our present way of expressing fractions is probably due to the Hindus. Brahmagupta (circa A.D. 630) wrote the symbol $\frac{2}{3}$ (with no bar) to represent "two-thirds." The Arabs introduced the "bar" to separate the two parts of a fraction, but this first attempt did not catch on. Later, due to typesetting constraints, the bar was omitted and, at times, the fraction "two-thirds" was written as 2/3.

The name *fraction* came from the Latin word *frangere*, which means "to break." The term *common fraction* was used to refer to fractions employed in trade as opposed to the special collection of fractions used by astronomers. The notion of an improper fraction, such as $\frac{3}{2}$, is a fairly recent development, perhaps arising first in the sixteenth century. The names *numerator* and *denominator* also came to us from Latin writers.

Adding and subtracting fractions was generally done by using the product of the denominators as the common denominator. It was not until the seventeenth century that the "least" common denominator method was used extensively. Although the multiplication of fractions as we know it has been unchanged for centuries, the division of fractions was carried out in two different ways, neither of which is the method currently used.

Although the Hindu and Arab writers were aware of the "invert the divisor and multiply" algorithm for division, this method dropped out of sight for 300 to 400 years, only to reappear and then come into favor in the seventeenth century.

Method 1 (Common Denominator)

$$\frac{2}{3} \div \frac{3}{4} = \frac{8}{12} \div \frac{9}{12} = \frac{8}{9}$$

Method 2 (Cross-Multiplication)

$$\frac{2}{3} \diagup\!\!\!\!\diagdown \frac{3}{4} = \frac{8}{9}$$

Problem Solving Strategies

1. Guess and Test
2. Use a Variable
3. Draw a Picture
4. Look for a Pattern
5. Make a List
6. Solve a Simpler Problem
7. Draw a Diagram
8. Use Direct Reasoning
9. Use Indirect Reasoning
10. Use Properties of Numbers
11. **Solve an Equivalent Problem**

Strategy
Solve an Equivalent Problem

One's point of view or interpretation of a problem can often change a seemingly difficult problem into one that is easily solvable. One way to solve the next problem is by drawing a picture or, perhaps, by actually finding some representative blocks to try various combinations. On the other hand, another approach is to see whether the problem can be restated in an equivalent form, say, using numbers. Then if the equivalent problem can be solved, the solution can be interpreted to yield an answer to the original problem.

Initial Problem

A child has a set of 10 cubical blocks. The lengths of the edges are 1 cm, 2 cm, 3 cm, . . . , 10 cm. Using all the cubes, can the child build two towers of the same height by stacking one cube upon another? Why or why not?

Clues

The Solve an Equivalent Problem strategy may be appropriate when

- You can find an equivalent problem that is easier to solve.
- A problem is related to another problem you have solved previously.
- A problem can be represented in a more familiar setting.
- A geometric problem can be represented algebraically, or vice versa.
- Physical problems can easily be represented with numbers or symbols.

A solution of the Initial Problem appears on page 257.

INTRODUCTION

Chapters 2 to 5 have been devoted to the study of the system of whole numbers. Understanding the system of whole numbers is necessary to ensure success in mathematics later. This chapter is devoted to the study of fractions. Fractions were invented because it was not convenient to describe many problem situations using only whole numbers. As you study this chapter, note the importance that the whole numbers play in helping to make fraction concepts easy to understand.

6.1   THE SET OF FRACTIONS

STARTING POINT

For each of the following visual representations of fractions, there is a corresponding incorrect symbolic expression. Discuss what aspects of the visual representation might lead a student to the *incorrect* expression.

THE CONCEPT OF A FRACTION

There are many times when whole numbers do not fully describe a mathematical situation. For example, using whole numbers, try to answer the following questions, which refer to Figure 6.1: (1) How much pizza is left? (2) How much of the stick is shaded? (3) How much paint is left in the can?

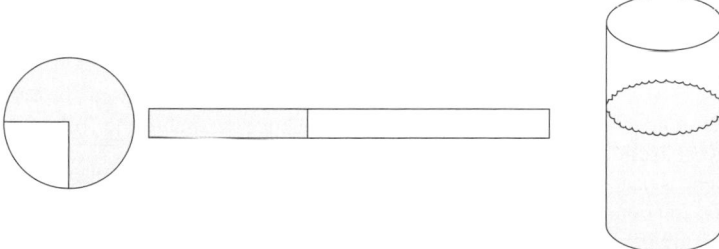

Figure 6.1

Reflection from Research
Students often have an informal understanding of fractions before they receive instruction on fractions in school. This informal knowledge should be built upon when giving meaning to formal fraction symbols and operations (Mack, 1990).

Although it is not easy to provide whole-number answers to the preceding questions, the situations in Figure 6.1 can be conveniently described using fractions. Reconsider the preceding questions in light of the subdivisions added in Figure 6.2. Typical answers to these questions are (1) "Three-fourths of the pizza is left," (2) "Four-tenths of the stick is shaded," (3) "The paint can is three-fifths full."

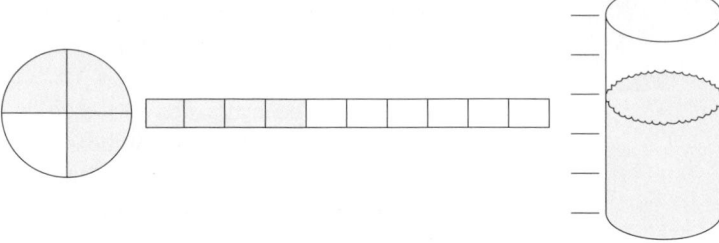

Figure 6.2

The term *fraction* is used in two distinct ways in elementary mathematics. Initially, fractions are used as numerals to indicate the number of parts of a whole to be considered. In Figure 6.2, the pizza was cut into 4 equivalent pieces, and 3 remain. In this case we use the fraction $\frac{3}{4}$ to represent the 3 out of 4 equivalent pieces (i.e., equivalent in size). The use of a fraction as a numeral in this way is commonly called the "part-to-whole" model. Succinctly, if a and b are whole numbers, where $b \neq 0$, then the fraction $\frac{a}{b}$ or a/b, represents a of b equivalent parts; a is called the **numerator** and b is called the **denominator.** The term *equivalent parts* means equivalent in some attribute, such as length, area, volume, number, or weight, depending on the composition of the whole and appropriate parts. In Figure 6.2, since 4 of 10 equivalent parts of the stick are shaded, the fraction $\frac{4}{10}$ describes the shaded part when it is compared to the whole stick. Also, the fraction $\frac{3}{5}$ describes the filled portion of the paint can in Figure 6.2. The fraction $\frac{7}{2}$ would mean that an object was divided into 2 equivalent parts and 7 such parts are designated.

As with whole numbers, a fraction also has an *abstract* meaning as a number. What do you think of when you look at the relative amounts represented by the shaded regions in Figure 6.3?

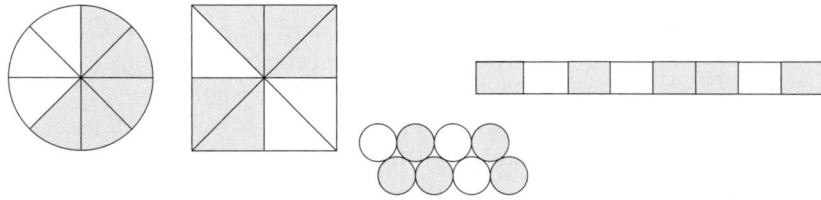

Figure 6.3

Although the various diagrams are different in size and shape, they share a common attribute—namely, that 5 of 8 equivalent parts are shaded. That is, the same *relative amount* is shaded. This attribute can be represented by the fraction $\frac{5}{8}$. Thus, in addition to representing parts of a whole, a fraction is viewed as a number representing a relative amount. Hence we make the following definition.

● DEFINITION

Fractions

A **fraction** is a number that can be represented by an ordered pair of whole numbers $\frac{a}{b}$ (or a/b), where $b \neq 0$. In set notation, the **set of fractions** is

$$F = \left\{ \frac{a}{b} \,\middle|\, a \text{ and } b \text{ are whole numbers, } b \neq 0 \right\}.$$

Before proceeding with the computational aspects of fractions as numbers, it is instructive to comment further on the complexity of this topic—namely, viewing

Figure 6.5

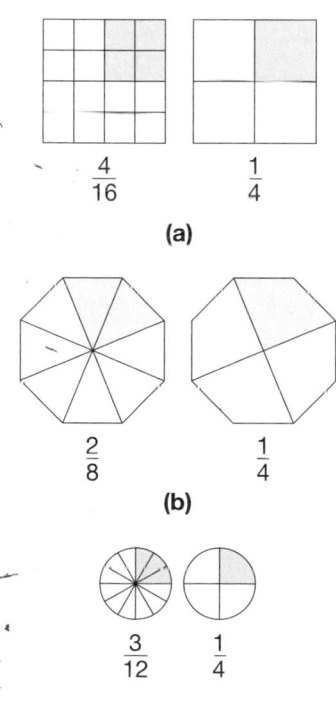

Figure 6.6

fractions as numerals and as numbers. Recall that the whole number three was the attribute common to all sets that match the set $\{a, b, c\}$. Thus if a child who understands the concept of a whole number is shown a set of three objects, the child will answer the question "How many objects?" with the word "three" regardless of the size, shape, color, and so on of the objects themselves. That is, it is the "numerousness" of the set on which the child is focusing.

With fractions, there are two attributes that the child must observe. First, when considering a fraction *as a number*, the focus is on relative amount. For example, in Figure 6.4, the relative amount represented by the various shaded regions is described by the fraction $\frac{1}{4}$ (which is considered as a number). Notice that $\frac{1}{4}$ describes the relative amount shaded without regard to size, shape, arrangement, orientation, number of equivalent parts, and so on; thus it is the "numerousness" of a fraction on which we are focusing.

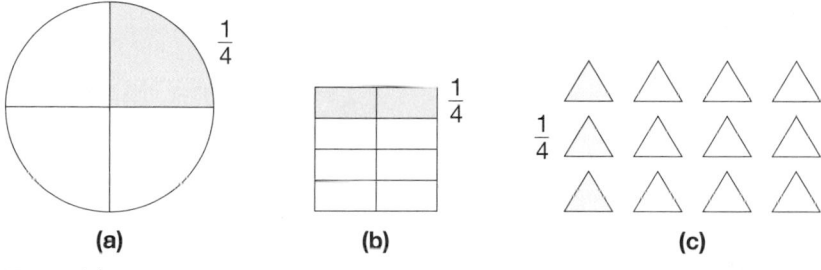

Figure 6.4

Second, when considering a fraction *as a numeral* representing a part-to-whole relationship, many numerals can be used for the relationship. For example, the three diagrams in Figure 6.4 can be labeled differently (Figure 6.5).

In Figures 6.5(b) and (c), the shaded regions have been renamed using the fractions $\frac{2}{8}$ and $\frac{3}{12}$, respectively, to call attention to the different subdivisions. The notion of fraction as a numeral displaying a part-to-whole relationship can be merged with the concept of fraction as a number. That is, the fraction (number) $\frac{1}{4}$ can also be thought of and represented by any of the fractions $\frac{2}{8}, \frac{3}{12}, \frac{4}{16}$, and so on. Figure 6.6 brings this into sharper focus.

In each of the pairs of diagrams in Figure 6.6, the same relative amount is shaded, although the subdivisions into equivalent parts and the sizes of the diagrams are different. As suggested by the shaded regions, the fractions $\frac{4}{16}, \frac{2}{8}$, and $\frac{3}{12}$ all represent the same relative amount as $\frac{1}{4}$.

Two fractions that represent the same relative amount are said to be **equivalent fractions.**

Spotlight on Technology Being able to find equivalent fractions is a key concept when dealing with operations on fractions. The Chapter 6 eManipulative activity, *Fraction Concepts—Equivalent Fractions*, provides a visual, interactive way of finding equivalent fractions. After finding some pairs of equivalent fractions using the eManipulative, answer the following question: "Based on the picture, how do you know when you have subdivided the whole into a correct number of pieces to have an equivalent fraction?"

www.wiley.com/
college/musser

The diagrams in Figure 6.6 were different shapes and sizes. **Fraction strips,** which can be constructed out of paper or cardboard, can be used to visualize fractional parts (Figure 6.7). The advantage of this model is that the unit strips are the same size—only the shading and number of subdivisions vary.

It is useful to have a simple test to determine whether fractions such as $\frac{2}{8}, \frac{3}{12}$, and $\frac{4}{16}$ represent the same relative amount without having to draw a picture of each represen-

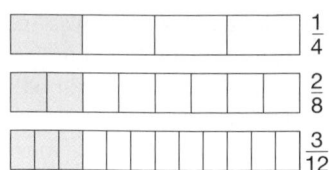

Figure 6.7

tation. Two approaches can be taken. First, observe that $\frac{2}{8} = \frac{1 \cdot 2}{4 \cdot 2}$, $\frac{3}{12} = \frac{1 \cdot 3}{4 \cdot 3}$, and $\frac{4}{16} = \frac{1 \cdot 4}{4 \cdot 4}$. These equations illustrate the fact that $\frac{2}{8}$ can be obtained from $\frac{1}{4}$ by equally subdividing each portion of a representation of $\frac{1}{4}$ by 2 [Figure 6.6(b)]. A similar argument can be applied to the equations $\frac{3}{12} = \frac{1 \cdot 3}{4 \cdot 3}$ [Figure 6.6(c)] and $\frac{4}{16} = \frac{1 \cdot 4}{4 \cdot 4}$ [Figure 6.6(a)]. Thus it appears that any fraction of the form $\frac{1 \cdot n}{4 \cdot n}$, where n is a counting number, represents the same relative amount as $\frac{1}{4}$, or that $\frac{an}{bn} = \frac{a}{b}$, in general. When $\frac{an}{bn}$ is replaced with $\frac{a}{b}$, where $n \neq 1$, we say that $\frac{an}{bn}$ has been **simplified.**

To determine whether $\frac{3}{12}$ and $\frac{4}{16}$ are equal, we can simplify each of them: $\frac{3}{12} = \frac{1}{4}$ and $\frac{4}{16} = \frac{1}{4}$. Since they both equal $\frac{1}{4}$, we can write $\frac{3}{12} = \frac{4}{16}$. Alternatively, we can view view $\frac{3}{12}$ and $\frac{4}{16}$ as $\frac{3 \cdot 16}{12 \cdot 16}$ and $\frac{4 \cdot 12}{16 \cdot 12}$ instead. Since the numerators $3 \cdot 16 = 48$ and $4 \cdot 12 = 48$ are equal and the denominators are the same, namely $12 \cdot 16$, the two fractions $\frac{3}{12}$ and $\frac{4}{16}$ must be equal. As the next diagram suggests, the numbers $3 \cdot 16$ and $4 \cdot 12$ are called the cross-products of the fractions $\frac{3}{12}$ and $\frac{4}{16}$.

$$\frac{3}{12} \bowtie \frac{4}{16}$$

The technique, which can be used for any pair of fractions, leads to the following definition of fraction equality.

DEFINITION

Fraction Equality

Let $\frac{a}{b}$ and $\frac{c}{d}$ be any fractions. Then $\frac{a}{b} = \frac{c}{d}$ if and only if $ad = bc$.

In words, two fractions are **equal fractions** if and only if their **cross-products,** that is, products ad and bc obtained by **cross-multiplication,** are equal. The first method described for determining whether two fractions are equal is an immediate consequence of this definition, since $a(bn) = b(an)$ by associativity and commutativity. This is summarized next.

Reflection from Research
Students need extensive exposure to graphical and conceptual representations of the concept of unit prior to being introduced to algebraic symbols (Lamon, 1996).

THEOREM

Let $\frac{a}{b}$ be any fraction and n a nonzero whole number. Then

$$\frac{a}{b} = \frac{an}{bn} = \frac{na}{nb}.$$

It is important to note that this theorem can be used in two ways: (1) to replace the fraction $\frac{a}{b}$ with $\frac{an}{bn}$ and (2) to replace the fraction $\frac{an}{bn}$ with $\frac{a}{b}$. Occasionally, the term *reducing* is used to describe the process in (2). However, the term *reducing* can be misleading, since fractions are not reduced in size (the relative amount they represent) but only in complexity (the numerators and denominators are smaller).

Example 6.1 Verify the following equations using the definition of fraction equality or the preceding theorem.

a. $\dfrac{5}{6} = \dfrac{25}{30}$ **b.** $\dfrac{27}{36} = \dfrac{54}{72}$ **c.** $\dfrac{16}{48} = \dfrac{1}{3}$

Solution

a. $\dfrac{5}{6} = \dfrac{5 \cdot 5}{6 \cdot 5} = \dfrac{25}{30}$ by the preceding theorem.

b. $\dfrac{54}{72} = \dfrac{27 \cdot 2}{36 \cdot 2} = \dfrac{27}{36}$ by simplifying. Alternatively, $\dfrac{27}{36} = \dfrac{3 \cdot 9}{4 \cdot 9} = \dfrac{3}{4}$ and

$\dfrac{54}{72} = \dfrac{3 \cdot 18}{4 \cdot 18} = \dfrac{3}{4}$, so $\dfrac{27}{36} = \dfrac{54}{72}$.

c. $\dfrac{16}{48} = \dfrac{1}{3}$, since their cross-products, $16 \cdot 3$ and $48 \cdot 1$, are equal. ■

Spotlight on Technology Fraction equality can readily be checked on a calculator using an alternative version of cross-multiplication—namely, $\dfrac{a}{b} = \dfrac{c}{d}$ if and only if $\dfrac{ad}{b} = c$. Thus the equality $\dfrac{20}{36} = \dfrac{30}{54}$ can be checked by pressing 20 $\boxed{\times}$ 54 $\boxed{\div}$ 36 $\boxed{=}$ $\boxed{ 30}$. Since 30 obtained in this way equals the numerator of $\dfrac{30}{54}$, the two fractions are equal.

Since $\dfrac{a}{b} = \dfrac{an}{bn}$ for $n = 1, 2, 3, \ldots$, every fraction has an infinite number of representations (numerals). For example,

$$\frac{1}{2} = \frac{2}{4} = \frac{3}{6} = \frac{4}{8} = \frac{5}{10} = \frac{6}{12} = \cdots$$

are different numerals for the number $\frac{1}{2}$. In fact, another way to view a fraction as a number is to think of the idea that is common to all of its various representations. That is, the fraction $\frac{2}{3}$, as a *number*, is the idea that one associates with the set of all fractions, as *numerals*, that are equivalent to $\frac{2}{3}$, namely $\frac{2}{3}, \frac{4}{6}, \frac{6}{9}, \frac{8}{12}, \ldots$. Notice that the term *equal* refers to fractions as numbers, while the term *equivalent* refers to fractions as numerals.

Every whole number is a fraction and hence has an infinite number of fraction representations. For example,

$$1 = \frac{1}{1} = \frac{2}{2} = \frac{3}{3} = \cdots, 2 = \frac{2}{1} = \frac{4}{2} = \frac{6}{3} = \cdots, 0 = \frac{0}{1} = \frac{0}{2} = \cdots,$$

and so on. Thus the set of fractions extends the set of whole numbers.

A fraction is written in its **simplest form** or **lowest terms** when its numerator and denominator have no common prime factors.

Example 6.2 Find the simplest form of the following fractions.

a. $\dfrac{12}{18}$ **b.** $\dfrac{36}{56}$ **c.** $\dfrac{9}{31}$ **d.** $(2^3 \cdot 3^5 \cdot 5^7)/(2^6 \cdot 3^4 \cdot 7)$

Solution

a. $\dfrac{12}{18} = \dfrac{2 \cdot 6}{3 \cdot 6} = \dfrac{2}{3}$

b. $\dfrac{36}{56} = \dfrac{18 \cdot 2}{28 \cdot 2} = \dfrac{18}{28} = \dfrac{9 \cdot 2}{14 \cdot 2} = \dfrac{9}{14}$ or $\dfrac{36}{56} = \dfrac{2 \cdot 2 \cdot 3 \cdot 3}{2 \cdot 2 \cdot 2 \cdot 7} = \dfrac{3 \cdot 3}{2 \cdot 7} = \dfrac{9}{14}$

c. $\dfrac{9}{31}$ is in simplest form, since 9 and 31 have only 1 as a common factor.

d. To write $(2^3 \cdot 3^5 \cdot 5^7)/(2^6 \cdot 3^4 \cdot 7)$ in simplest form, first find the GCF of $2^3 \cdot 3^5 \cdot 5^7$ and $2^6 \cdot 3^4 \cdot 7$:

$$\text{GCF}(2^3 \cdot 3^5 \cdot 5^7,\ 2^6 \cdot 3^4 \cdot 7) = 2^3 \cdot 3^4.$$

Then

$$\frac{2^3 \cdot 3^5 \cdot 5^7}{2^6 \cdot 3^4 \cdot 7} = \frac{(3 \cdot 5^7)(2^3 \cdot 3^4)}{(2^3 \cdot 7)(2^3 \cdot 3^4)} = \frac{3 \cdot 5^7}{2^3 \cdot 7}. \qquad ■$$

Reflection from Research
When dealing with improper fractions, like $\dfrac{12}{11}$, students struggle to focus on the whole, $\dfrac{11}{11}$, and not the number of parts, 12 (Tzur, 1999).

Fractions with numerators greater than or equal to their denominators fall into two categories. The fractions $\frac{1}{1}, \frac{2}{2}, \frac{3}{3}, \frac{4}{4}, \ldots$, in which the numerators and denominators are equal, represent the whole number 1. Fractions where the numerators are greater than the denominators are called **improper fractions.** For example, $\frac{7}{2}, \frac{8}{5}$, and $\frac{117}{35}$ are improper fractions. Figure 6.8 illustrates a model for $\frac{7}{2}$ because seven halves are shaded where one shaded circle represents one unit. The diagram in Figure 6.8 illustrates that $\frac{7}{2}$ can also be viewed as 3 wholes plus $\frac{1}{2}$, or $3\frac{1}{2}$. A combination of a whole number with a fraction juxtaposed to its right is called a **mixed number.** Mixed numbers will be studied in Section 6.2.

Figure 6.8

Spotlight on Technology The TI-34 II calculator can be used to convert improper fractions to mixed numbers. For example, to convert $\dfrac{1234}{378}$ to a mixed number in its simplest form on a fraction calculator, press 1234 $\boxed{/}$ 378 $\boxed{\text{2nd}}$ $\boxed{\text{A}^{b}\!/_{c}\,◁▷^{d}\!/_{e}}$ $\boxed{=}$ $\boxed{3\cup100/378}$ (If the fraction mode is set as A ∪ $^{b}\!/_{c}$, the $\boxed{\text{A}^{b}\!/_{c}\,◁▷^{d}\!/_{e}}$ button will not need to be used.) Pressing $\boxed{\text{SIMP}}$ $\boxed{=}$ yields the result $3\dfrac{50}{189}$, which is in simplest form. For calculators without the fraction function, 1234 $\boxed{÷}$ 378 = $\boxed{3.2645502}$ shows the whole-number part, namely 3, together with a decimal fraction. The calculation 1234 $\boxed{-}$ 3 $\boxed{×}$ 378 $\boxed{=}$ $\boxed{100}$ gives the numerator of the fraction part; thus $\dfrac{1234}{378} = 3\dfrac{100}{378}$, which is $3\dfrac{50}{189}$ in simplest form.

Ordering Fractions

$\frac{2}{4} < \frac{3}{4}$ since less is shaded in $\frac{2}{4}$.

Figure 6.9

The concepts of less than and greater than in fractions are extensions of the respective whole-number concepts. Fraction strips can be used to order fractions (Figure 6.9).

Next consider the three pairs of fractions on the **fraction number line** in Figure 6.10.

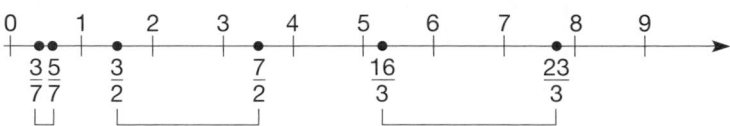

Figure 6.10

Reflection from Research

Young children have a very difficult time believing that a fraction such as one-eighth is smaller than one-fifth because the number eight is larger than five (Post, Wachsmuth, Lesh, & Behr, 1985).

As it was in the case of whole numbers, the smaller of two fractions is to the left of the larger fraction on the fraction number line. Also, the three examples in Figure 6.10 suggest the following definition, where fractions having common denominators can be compared simply by comparing their numerators (which are whole numbers).

DEFINITION

Less Than for Fractions

Let $\dfrac{a}{c}$ and $\dfrac{b}{c}$ be any fractions. Then $\dfrac{a}{c} < \dfrac{b}{c}$ if and only if $a < b$.

NOTE: Although the definition is stated for "less than," a corresponding statement holds for "**greater than.**" Similar statements hold for "**less than or equal to**" and "**greater than or equal to.**"

For example, $\frac{3}{7} < \frac{5}{7}$, since $3 < 5$; $\frac{4}{13} < \frac{10}{13}$, since $4 < 10$; and so on. The numbers $\frac{2}{7}$ and $\frac{4}{13}$ can be compared by getting a common denominator.

$$\frac{2}{7} = \frac{2 \cdot 13}{7 \cdot 13} = \frac{26}{91} \quad \text{and} \quad \frac{4}{13} = \frac{4 \cdot 7}{13 \cdot 7} = \frac{28}{91}$$

Since $\frac{26}{91} < \frac{28}{91}$, we conclude that $\frac{2}{7} < \frac{4}{13}$.

This last example suggests a convenient shortcut for comparing any two fractions. To compare $\frac{2}{7}$ and $\frac{4}{13}$, we compared $\frac{26}{91}$ and $\frac{28}{91}$ and, eventually, 26 and 28. But $26 = 2 \cdot 13$ and $28 = 7 \cdot 4$. In general, this example suggests the following theorem.

THEOREM

Cross-Multiplication of Fraction Inequality

Let $\dfrac{a}{b}$ and $\dfrac{c}{d}$ be any fractions. Then $\dfrac{a}{b} < \dfrac{c}{d}$ if and only if $ad < bc$.

Notice that this theorem reduces the ordering of fractions to the ordering of whole numbers. Also, since $\frac{a}{b} < \frac{c}{d}$ if and only if $\frac{c}{d} > \frac{a}{b}$, we can observe that $\frac{c}{d} > \frac{a}{b}$ if and only if $bc > ad$.

Example 6.3   Arrange in order.
a. $\frac{7}{8}$ and $\frac{9}{11}$ **b.** $\frac{17}{32}$ and $\frac{19}{40}$

Solution

a. $\frac{7}{8} < \frac{9}{11}$ if and only if $7 \cdot 11 < 8 \cdot 9$. But $77 > 72$; therefore, $\frac{7}{8} > \frac{9}{11}$.
b. $17 \cdot 40 = 680$ and $32 \cdot 19 = 608$. Since $32 \cdot 19 < 17 \cdot 40$, we have $\frac{19}{40} < \frac{17}{32}$. ■

www.wiley.com/
college/musser

Spotlight on Technology When comparing two fractions to see which is larger, one method is to find a common denominator. Another is to plot the fractions on a number line. The Chapter 6 eManipulative activity, *Fraction Concepts—Comparing Fractions*, uses both of these approaches to visualize the ordering of fractions. This activity will have you plot two fractions, $\frac{a}{b}$ and $\frac{c}{d}$, on a number line. Do a few examples and plot the fraction $\frac{a + c}{b + d}$ on the number line as well. How does the fraction $\frac{a + c}{b + d}$ compare to $\frac{a}{b}$ and $\frac{c}{d}$? Does this relationship appear to hold for all fractions $\frac{a}{b}$ and $\frac{c}{d}$?

Often fractions can be ordered mentally using your "fraction sense." For example, fractions like $\frac{4}{5}, \frac{7}{8}, \frac{11}{12}$, and so on are close to 1, fractions like $\frac{1}{15}, \frac{1}{14}, \frac{1}{10}$, and so on are close to 0, and fractions like $\frac{6}{14}, \frac{8}{15}, \frac{11}{20}$, and so on are close to $\frac{1}{2}$. Thus $\frac{4}{7} < \frac{12}{13}$, since $\frac{4}{7} \approx \frac{1}{2}$ and $\frac{12}{13} \approx 1$. Also, $\frac{1}{11} < \frac{7}{13}$, since $\frac{1}{11} \approx 0$ and $\frac{7}{13} \approx \frac{1}{2}$.

Keep in mind that this procedure is just a shortcut for finding common denominators and comparing the numerators.

Spotlight on Technology Cross-multiplication of fraction inequality can also be adapted to a calculator as follows: $\frac{a}{b} < \frac{c}{d}$ if and only if $\frac{ad}{b} < c$ (or $\frac{a}{b} > \frac{c}{d}$ if and only if $\frac{ad}{b} > c$). To order $\frac{17}{32}$ and $\frac{19}{40}$ using a fraction calculator, press 17 $\boxed{/}$ 32 $\boxed{\times}$ 40 $\boxed{=}$ $\boxed{21 \cup 3/32}$, or $21\frac{1}{4}$. Since $21\frac{1}{4} > 19$, we conclude that $\frac{17}{32} > \frac{19}{40}$. On a decimal calculator, the following sequence leads to a similar result: 17 $\boxed{\times}$ 40 $\boxed{\div}$ 32 $\boxed{=}$ $\boxed{21.25}$. Since 21.25 is greater than 19, $\frac{17}{32} > \frac{19}{40}$. Ordering fractions using decimal equivalents, which is shown next, will be covered in Chapter 7. In this case, 17 $\boxed{\div}$ 32 $\boxed{=}$ $\boxed{0.53125}$ and 19 $\boxed{\div}$ 40 $\boxed{=}$ $\boxed{0.475}$. Therefore, $\frac{19}{40} < \frac{17}{32}$, since $0.475 < 0.53125$. Finally, one could have ordered these two fractions mentally by observing that $\frac{19}{40}$ is less than $\frac{1}{2} (= \frac{20}{40})$, whereas $\frac{17}{32}$ is greater than $\frac{1}{2} (= \frac{16}{32})$.

On the whole-number line, there are gaps between the whole numbers (Figure 6.11).

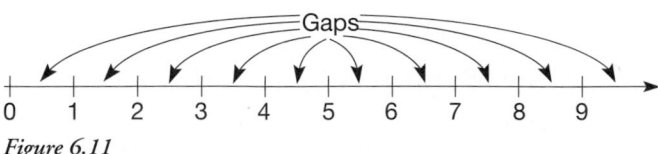

Figure 6.11

However, when fractions are introduced to make up the fraction number line, many new fractions appear in these gaps (Figure 6.12).

Figure 6.12

Unlike the case with whole numbers, it can be shown that there is a fraction between any two fractions. For example, consider $\frac{3}{4}$ and $\frac{5}{6}$. Since $\frac{3}{4} = \frac{18}{24}$ and $\frac{5}{6} = \frac{20}{24}$, we have that $\frac{19}{24}$ is between $\frac{3}{4}$ and $\frac{5}{6}$. Now consider $\frac{18}{24}$ and $\frac{19}{24}$. These equal $\frac{36}{48}$ and $\frac{38}{38}$, respectively; thus $\frac{37}{48}$ is between $\frac{3}{4}$ and $\frac{5}{6}$ also. Continuing in this manner, one can show that there are infinitely many fractions between $\frac{3}{4}$ and $\frac{5}{6}$. From this it follows that there are *infinitely* many fractions between any two different fractions.

Example 6.4   Find a fraction between these pairs of fractions.
a. $\frac{7}{11}$ and $\frac{8}{11}$ **b.** $\frac{9}{13}$ and $\frac{12}{17}$

Solution

a. $\frac{7}{11} = \frac{14}{22}$ and $\frac{8}{11} = \frac{16}{22}$. Hence $\frac{15}{22}$ is between $\frac{7}{11}$ and $\frac{8}{11}$.

b. $\frac{9}{13} = \frac{9 \cdot 17}{13 \cdot 17} = \frac{153}{13 \cdot 17}$ and $\frac{12}{17} = \frac{12 \cdot 13}{17 \cdot 13} = \frac{156}{17 \cdot 13}$. Hence both $\frac{154}{13 \cdot 17}$ and $\frac{155}{13 \cdot 17}$ are between $\frac{9}{13}$ and $\frac{12}{17}$. ■

Sometimes students incorrectly add numerators and denominators to find the sum of two fractions. It is interesting, though, that this simple technique does provide an easy way to find a fraction between two given fractions. For example, for fractions $\frac{2}{3}$ and $\frac{3}{4}$, the number $\frac{5}{7}$ satisfies $\frac{2}{3} < \frac{5}{7} < \frac{3}{4}$ since $2 \cdot 7 < 3 \cdot 5$ and $5 \cdot 4 < 7 \cdot 3$. This idea is generalized next.

THEOREM

Let $\frac{a}{b}$ and $\frac{c}{d}$ be any fractions, where $\frac{a}{b} < \frac{c}{d}$. Then

$$\frac{a}{b} < \frac{a + c}{b + d} < \frac{c}{d}.$$

Proof   Let $\frac{a}{b} < \frac{c}{d}$. Then we have $ad < bc$. From this inequality, it follows that $ad + ab < bc + ab$, or $a(b + d) < b(a + c)$. By cross-multiplication of fraction inequality, this last inequality implies $\frac{a}{b} < \frac{a + c}{b + d}$, which is "half" of what we are to prove. The other half can be proved in a similar fashion. ■

To find a fraction between $\frac{9}{13}$ and $\frac{12}{17}$ using this theorem, add the numerators and denominators to obtain $\frac{21}{30}$. This theorem shows that there is a fraction between any two fractions. The fact that there is a fraction between any two fractions is called the **density property** of fractions.

MATHEMATICAL MORSEL

Although decimals are prevalent in our monetary system, the stock market used fractions involving sixteenths, eighths, fourths, and halves until 2001. It has been suggested that this tradition was based on the Spanish milled dollar coin and its fractional parts that were used in our American colonies. Its fractional parts were called "bits" and each bit had a value of $12\frac{1}{2}$ cents (thus a quarter is known as "two bits"). Some also believe that this fraction system evolved from the British shilling and pence. A shilling was one-fourth of a dollar and a sixpence was one-eighth of a dollar, or $12\frac{1}{2}$ cents.

Section 6.1 EXERCISE / PROBLEM SET A

EXERCISES

1. In this section fractions were represented using equivalent parts. Another representation uses a set model. In the following set of objects, four out of the total of five objects are triangles.

We could say that $\frac{4}{5}$ of the objects are triangles. This interpretation of fractions compares part of a set with all of the set. Draw pictures to represent the following fractions.

 a. $\frac{3}{5}$ **b.** $\frac{3}{7}$ **c.** $\frac{1}{3}$

2. Fractions can also be represented on the number line by selecting a unit length and subdividing the interval into equal parts. For example, to locate the fraction $\frac{2}{5}$, subdivide the interval from 0 to 1 into five parts and mark off two. Represent the following fractions on a number line.

 a. $\frac{4}{5}$ **b.** $\frac{2}{3}$ **c.** $\frac{3}{8}$ **d.** $\frac{7}{10}$

3. Does the following picture represent $\frac{3}{4}$? Explain.

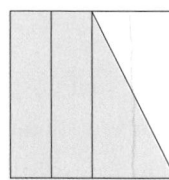

4. Fill in the blank with the correct fraction.

 a. 10 cents is _____ of a dollar.

 b. 15 minutes is _____ of an hour.

 c. If you sleep eight hours each night, you spend _____ of a day sleeping.

 d. Using the information in part (c), what part of a year do you sleep?

5. Use the area model illustrated on the Chapter 6 eManupulative activity, *Fraction Concepts— Equivalent Fractions*, to show that $\frac{5}{8} = \frac{15}{24}$.

6. Determine whether the following pairs are equal by writing each in simplest form.

 a. $\frac{5}{8}$ and $\frac{625}{1000}$ **b.** $\frac{11}{18}$ and $\frac{275}{450}$

 c. $\frac{24}{36}$ and $\frac{50}{72}$ **d.** $\frac{14}{98}$ and $\frac{8}{56}$

7. Determine which of the following pairs are equal.

 a. $\frac{349}{568}, \frac{569}{928}$ **b.** $\frac{734}{957}, \frac{468}{614}$

 c. $\frac{156}{558}, \frac{52}{186}$ **d.** $\frac{882}{552}, \frac{147}{92}$

8. Rewrite in simplest form.

 a. $\frac{21}{28}$ **b.** $\frac{49}{56}$ **c.** $\frac{108}{156}$ **d.** $\frac{220}{100}$

9. Rewrite as a mixed number in simplest form.

 a. $\frac{525}{96}$ **b.** $\frac{1234}{432}$

10. **a.** Arrange each of the following from smallest to largest.

 i. $\frac{11}{17}, \frac{13}{17}, \frac{12}{17}$ **ii.** $\frac{1}{5}, \frac{1}{6}, \frac{1}{7}$

 b. What patterns do you observe?

11. Order the following sets of fractions from smaller to larger and find a fraction between each pair

 a. $\frac{17}{23}, \frac{51}{68}$ **b.** $\frac{43}{567}, \frac{50}{687}$ **c.** $\frac{214}{897}, \frac{597}{2511}$ **d.** $\frac{93}{2811}, \frac{3}{87}$

12. According to Bureau of the Census data, in 2000 in the United States there were about

 105,000,000 households
 55,000,000 married-couple households
 4,000,000 family households with a male householder
 13,000,000 family households with a female householder
 32,000,000 households consisting of one person

 (NOTE: Figures have been rounded to simplify calculations.)

 a. What fraction of U.S. households in 2000 were headed by a married couple? To what fraction with a denominator of 100 is this fraction closest?

 b. What fraction of U.S. households in 2000 consisted of individuals living alone? To what fraction with a denominator of 100 is this closest?

 c. What fraction of U.S. family households with one head of household were headed by a woman in 2000? To what fraction with a denominator of 100 is this fraction closest?

PROBLEMS

13. What is mathematically inaccurate about the following sales "pitches"?

a. "Save $\frac{1}{2}, \frac{1}{3}, \frac{1}{4}$, and even more!"

b. "You'll pay only a fraction of the list price!"

14. In 1991, Illinois was generating approximately 13,100,000 tons of waste per year, and of that amount, 786,000 tons were being recycled. In 1991, Texas was generating approximately 18,000,000 tons of waste, and of that amount, 1,440,000 tons were being recycled. Which state had the higher recycling rate? (SOURCE: *1991 Environmental Almanac.*)

15. The shaded regions in the figures represent the fractions $\frac{1}{2}$ and $\frac{1}{3}$, respectively.

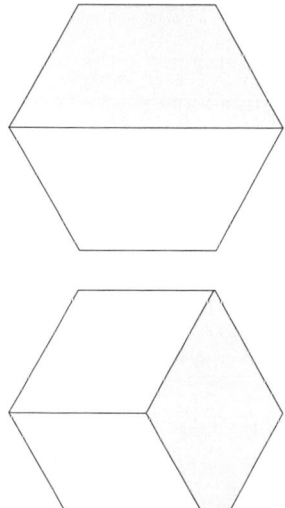

Trace the outline of a figure like those shown and shade in portions that represent the following fractions.

a. $\frac{1}{2}$ (different from the one shown)

b. $\frac{1}{3}$ (different from the one shown)

c. $\frac{1}{4}$ **d.** $\frac{1}{6}$ **e.** $\frac{1}{12}$ **f.** $\frac{1}{24}$

16. A student simplifies $\frac{286}{583}$ by "canceling" the 8s, obtaining $\frac{26}{53}$, which equals $\frac{286}{583}$. He uses the same method with $\frac{28,886}{58,883}$, simplifying it to $\frac{26}{53}$ also. Does this always work with similar fractions? Why or why not?

17. I am a proper fraction. The sum of my numerator and denominator is a one-digit square. Their product is a cube. What fraction am I?

18. True or false? Explain.

a. The greater the numerator, the greater the fraction.

b. The greater the denominator, the smaller the fraction.

c. If the denominator is fixed, the greater the numerator, the greater the fraction.

d. If the numerator is fixed, the greater the denominator, the smaller the fraction.

19. The fraction $\frac{12}{18}$ is simplified on a fraction calculator and the result is $\frac{2}{3}$. Explain how this result can be used to find the GCF(12, 18). Use this method to find the following.

a. GCF(72, 168)

b. GCF(234, 442)

20. Determine whether the following are correct or incorrect. Explain.

a. $\dfrac{a\not{b} + c}{\not{b}} = a + c$ **b.** $\dfrac{a + b}{a + c} = \dfrac{b}{c}$

c. $\dfrac{\not{d}b + \not{d}c}{\not{d}d} = \dfrac{b + c}{d}$

21. Three-fifths of a class of 25 students are girls. How many are girls?

22. The Independent party received one-eleventh of the 6,186,279 votes cast. How many votes did the party receive?

23. Seven-eighths of the 328 adults attending a school bazaar were relatives of the students. How many attendees were not relatives?

24. The school library contains about 5280 books. If five-twelfths of the books are for the primary grades, how many such books are there in the library?

25. Talia walks to school at point B from her house at point A, a distance of six blocks. For variety she likes to try different routes each day. How many different paths can she take if she always moves closer to B? One route is shown.

26. If you place a 1 in front of the number 5, the new number is 3 times as large as the original number.

    a. Find another number (not necessarily a one-digit number) such that when you place a 1 in front of it, the result is 3 times as large as the original number.

    b. Find a number such that when you place a 1 in front of it, the result is 5 times as large as the original number. Is there more than one such number?

    c. Find a number such that, when you place a 2 in front of it, the result is 6 times as large as the

original number. Can you find more than one such number?

    d. Find a number such that, when you place a 3 in front of it, the result is 5 times as large as the original number. Can you find more than one such number?

27. After using the Chapter 6 eManipulative activity, *Fraction Concepts—Comparing Fractions*, identify two fractions between $\frac{4}{7}$ and $\frac{1}{2}$.

Section 6.1   EXERCISE / PROBLEM SET B

EXERCISES

1. What fraction is represented by the shaded portion of each diagram?

    a.

    b.

    c. ⊢—————⊢——⟶
         0   1

    d. ⊢————————⊢—⟶
         0   1   2   3

2. Illustrate $\frac{4}{7}$ using the following models.

    a. Set model   **b.** Area model

    c. Number-line model

3. Using the diagram, represent each of the following as a fraction of all the dots.

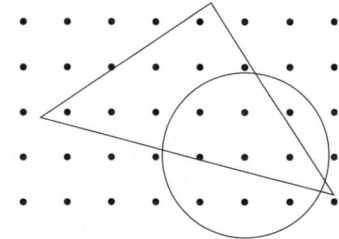

    a. The part of the collection of dots inside the circle

    b. The part of the collection of dots inside both the circle and the triangle

    c. The part of the collection of dots inside the triangle but outside the circle

4. True or false? Explain.

    a. 5 days is $\frac{1}{6}$ of a month.

    b. 4 days is $\frac{4}{7}$ of a week.

    c. 1 month is $\frac{1}{12}$ of a year.

5. Use the area model illustrated on the Chapter 6 eManupulative activity, *Fraction Concepts— Equivalent Fractions*, to show that $\frac{3}{2} = \frac{9}{6}$.

6. Decide which of the following are true. Do this mentally.

    a. $\frac{7}{6} = \frac{29}{24}$ **b.** $\frac{3}{12} = \frac{20}{84}$ **c.** $\frac{7}{9} = \frac{63}{81}$ **d.** $\frac{7}{12} = \frac{105}{180}$

7. Determine which of the following pairs are equal.

    a. $\frac{693}{858}, \frac{42}{52}$ **b.** $\frac{873}{954}, \frac{184}{212}$ **c.** $\frac{48}{84}, \frac{756}{1263}$ **d.** $\frac{468}{891}, \frac{156}{297}$

8. Rewrite in simplest form.

    a. $\frac{189}{153}$ **b.** $\frac{294}{63}$ **c.** $\frac{480}{672}$ **d.** $\frac{3335}{230}$

9. Rewrite as a mixed number in simplest form.

    a. $\frac{2332}{444}$ **b.** $\frac{8976}{144}$

10. Arrange each of the following from smallest to largest.

    a. $\frac{4}{7}, \frac{7}{13}, \frac{14}{25}$ **b.** $\frac{3}{11}, \frac{7}{23}, \frac{2}{9}, \frac{5}{18}$

11. Determine whether the following pairs are equal. If they are not, order them and find a fraction between them.

    a. $\frac{231}{654}$ and $\frac{308}{872}$ **b.** $\frac{1516}{2312}$ and $\frac{2653}{2890}$

    c. $\frac{516}{892}$ and $\frac{1376}{2376}$

12. According to Bureau of the Census data on living arrangements of children under 18 (not counting persons under 18 who maintained households), in 2000 in the United States there were about

72,000,000 children under 18
50,000,000 children under 18 living with
         two parents
19,000,000 children under 18 living with one parent
16,000,000 children under 18 living with
         mother only
3,000,000 children under 18 living with
         father only
2,000,000 children under 18 living with relatives
         other than parents

(NOTE: Figures have been rounded to simplify calculations.)

a. In 2000 what fraction of children under 18 in the United States lived with two parents? To what fraction with a denominator of 100 is this fraction closest?

b. In 2000 what fraction of children under 18 in the United States lived with only one parent? To what fraction with a denominator of 100 is this closest?

c. In 2000, of those children under 18 who lived with one parent, what fraction were living with their mother? To what fraction with a denominator of 100 is this fraction closest?

d. In 2000, what fraction of children under 18 were living with relatives other than their parents? To what fraction with a denominator of 100 is this fraction closest?

PROBLEMS

13. Frank ate 12 pieces of pizza and Dave ate 15 pieces. "I ate $\frac{1}{4}$ more," said Dave. "I ate $\frac{1}{5}$ less," said Frank. Who was right?

14. Mrs. Wills and Mr. Roberts gave the same test to their fourth-grade classes. In Mrs. Wills's class, 28 out of 36 students passed the test. In Mr. Roberts's class, 26 out of 32 students passed the test. Which class had the higher passing rate?

15. The shaded regions in the following figures represent the fractions $\frac{1}{2}$ and $\frac{1}{6}$, respectively.

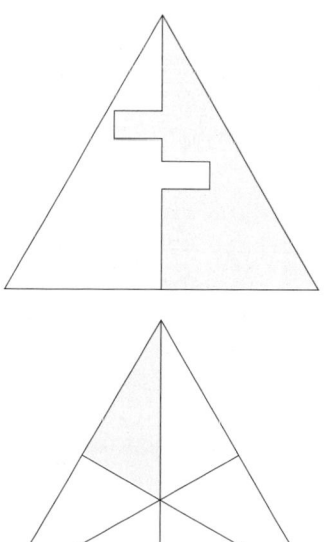

Trace outlines of figures like the ones shown and shade in portions that represent the following fractions.

a. $\frac{1}{2}$ (different from the one shown)

b. $\frac{1}{3}$ **c.** $\frac{1}{4}$ **d.** $\frac{1}{8}$ **e.** $\frac{1}{9}$

16. A popular math trick shows that a fraction like $\frac{16}{64}$ can be simplified by "canceling" the 6s and obtaining $\frac{1}{4}$. There are many other fractions for which this technique yields a correct answer.

a. Apply this technique to each of the following fractions and verify that the results are correct.

   i. $\frac{16}{64}$ **ii.** $\frac{19}{95}$ **iii.** $\frac{26}{65}$ **iv.** $\frac{199}{995}$ **v.** $\frac{26666}{66665}$

b. Using the pattern established in parts (iv) and (v) of part (a), write three more examples of fractions for which this method of simplification works.

17. Find a fraction less than $\frac{1}{12}$. Find another fraction less than the fraction you found. Can you continue this process? Is there a "smallest" fraction greater than 0? Explain.

18. What is wrong with the following argument?

Therefore, $\frac{1}{4} > \frac{1}{2}$, since the area of the shaded square is greater than the area of the shaded rectangle.

19. Use a method like the one in Problem 19(a) of Part A, find the following.

    a. LCM(224, 336)　　**b.** LCM(861, 1599)

20. If the same number is added to the numerator and denominator of a proper fraction, is the new fraction greater than, less than, or equal to the original fraction? Justify your answer. (Be sure to look at a variety of fractions.)

21. Find 999 fractions between $\frac{1}{3}$ and $\frac{1}{2}$ such that the difference between pairs of numbers next to each other is the same. (*Hint*: Find convenient equivalent fractions for $\frac{1}{3}$ and $\frac{1}{2}$.)

22. About one-fifth of a federal budget goes for defense. If the total budget is $400 billion, how much is spent on defense?

23. The U.S. Postal Service delivers about 170 billion pieces of mail each year. If approximately 90 billion of these are first class, what fraction describes the other classes of mail delivered?

24. Tuition in public universities is about two-ninths of tuition at private universities. If the average tuition at private universities is about $12,600 per year, what should you expect to pay at a public university?

25. A hiker traveled at an average rate of 2 kilometers per hour (km/h) going up to a lookout and traveled at an average rate of 5 km/h coming back down. If the entire trip (not counting a lunch stop at the lookout) took approximately 3 hours and 15 minutes, what is the total distance the hiker walked? Round your answer to the nearest tenth of a kilometer.

26. Five women participated in a 10-kilometer (10 K) Volkswalk, but started at different times. At a certain time in the walk the following descriptions were true.

    1. Rose was at the halfway point (5 K).

    2. Kelly was 2 K ahead of Cathy.

    3. Janet was 3 K ahead of Ann.

    4. Rose was 1 K behind Cathy.

    5. Ann was 3.5 K behind Kelly.

    a. Determine the order of the women at that point in time. That is, who was nearest the finish line, who was second closest, and so on?

    b. How far from the finish line was Janet at that time?

PROBLEMS FOR WRITING/DISCUSSION

1. You have a student who says she knows how to divide a circle into pieces to illustrate what $\frac{2}{3}$ means, but how can she divide up a circle to show $\frac{3}{2}$?

2. A student says that if $ab = cd$, then $\frac{a}{b} = \frac{c}{d}$. What is your response?

3. Another student says he cannot find a number between $\frac{3}{4}$ and $\frac{3}{5}$ because these two numbers are "right together." What is your response?

6.2　FRACTIONS: ADDITION AND SUBTRACTION

STARTING POINT

Some students initially view the addition of fractions as adding the numerators and adding the denominators as follows: $\dfrac{6}{7} + \dfrac{1}{2} = \dfrac{7}{9}$.

Using this example, discuss why such a method for addition is unreasonable.

$\dfrac{6}{7}$

$\dfrac{1}{2}$

Addition and Its Properties

Addition of fractions is an extension of whole-number addition and can be motivated using models. To find the sum of $\frac{1}{5}$ and $\frac{3}{5}$, consider the following measurement models: the region model and number-line model in Figure 6.13.

**NCTM Standards 2000
Number and Operations
Grades 3–5**
All students should use visual models, benchmarks, and equivalent forms to add and subtract commonly used fractions and decimals.

Region Model   **Number–Line Model**

Figure 6.13

Reflection from Research
Manipulative materials such as colored chips, Cuisenaire rods, and circular and rectangular pieces play a crucial role in developing students' conceptual understanding of operations with fractions (Behr, Lesh, Post, & Silver, 1983).

Figure 6.14

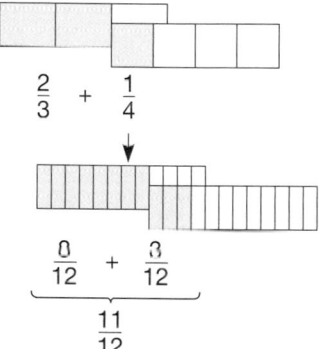

Figure 6.15

The idea illustrated in Figure 6.13 can be applied to any pair of fractions that have the same denominator. Figure 6.14 shows how fraction strips, which are a blend of these two models, can be used to find the sum of $\frac{1}{5}$ and $\frac{3}{5}$. That is, the sum of two fractions with the same denominator can be found by adding the numerators, as stated next.

DEFINITION

Addition of Fractions with Common Denominators

Let $\frac{a}{b}$ and $\frac{c}{b}$ be any fractions. Then

$$\frac{a}{b} + \frac{c}{b} = \frac{a+c}{b}.$$

Figure 6.15 illustrates how to add fractions when the denominators are not the same. Similarly, to find the sum $\frac{2}{7} + \frac{3}{5}$, use the equality of fractions to express the fractions with common denominators as follows:

$$\frac{2}{7} + \frac{3}{5} = \frac{2 \cdot 5}{7 \cdot 5} + \frac{3 \cdot 7}{5 \cdot 7}$$

$$= \frac{10}{35} + \frac{21}{35}$$

$$= \frac{31}{35}.$$

This procedure can be generalized as follows.

THEOREM

Addition of Fractions with Unlike Denominators

Let $\frac{a}{b}$ and $\frac{c}{d}$ be any fractions. Then

$$\frac{a}{b} + \frac{c}{d} = \frac{ad + bc}{bd}.$$

Proof

$$\frac{a}{b} + \frac{c}{d} = \frac{ad}{bd} + \frac{bc}{bd} \qquad \textit{Equality of fractions}$$

$$= \frac{ad + bc}{bd} \qquad \textit{Addition with common denominators}$$ ■

In words, to add fractions with unlike denominators, find equivalent fractions with common denominators. Then the sum will be represented by the sum of the numerators over the common denominator.

Example 6.5 Find the following sums and simplify.

a. $\frac{3}{7} + \frac{2}{7}$ **b.** $\frac{5}{9} + \frac{3}{4}$ **c.** $\frac{17}{15} + \frac{5}{12}$

Solution

a. $\dfrac{3}{7} + \dfrac{2}{7} = \dfrac{3+2}{7} = \dfrac{5}{7}$

b. $\dfrac{5}{9} + \dfrac{3}{4} = \dfrac{5 \cdot 4}{9 \cdot 4} + \dfrac{9 \cdot 3}{9 \cdot 4} = \dfrac{20}{36} + \dfrac{27}{36} = \dfrac{47}{36}$

c. $\dfrac{17}{15} + \dfrac{5}{12} = \dfrac{17 \cdot 12 + 15 \cdot 5}{15 \cdot 12} = \dfrac{204 + 75}{180} = \dfrac{279}{180} = \dfrac{31}{20}$ ▪

Spotlight on Technology Using the Chapter 6 eManipulative activity, *Fraction Concepts—Adding Fractions,* do at least five examples of adding fractions. For each operation $\dfrac{a}{b} + \dfrac{c}{d}$, determine if the sum has a denomintor of *bd* or something else. By looking at *b* and *d,* tell when the denominator of the sum will be *bd* and when it will be something else.

www.wiley.com/college/musser

In Example 6.5(c), an alternative method can be used. Rather than using $15 \cdot 12$ as the common denominator, the least common multiple of 12 and 15 can be used. The LCM(15, 12) = $2^2 \cdot 3 \cdot 5 = 60$. Therefore,

$$\frac{17}{15} + \frac{5}{12} = \frac{17 \cdot 4}{15 \cdot 4} + \frac{5 \cdot 5}{12 \cdot 5} = \frac{68}{60} + \frac{25}{60} = \frac{93}{60} = \frac{31}{20}.$$

Although using the LCM of the denominators (called the **least common denominator** and abbreviated LCD) simplifies paper-and-pencil calculations, using this method does not necessarily result in an answer in simplest form as in the previous case. For example, to find $\frac{3}{10} + \frac{8}{15}$, use 30 as the common denominator since LCM(10, 15) = 30. Thus $\frac{3}{10} + \frac{8}{15} = \frac{9}{30} + \frac{16}{30} = \frac{25}{30}$, which is not in simplest form.

Calculators and computers can also be used to calculate the sums of fractions. A common four-function calculator can be used to find sums, as in the following example.

Spotlight on Technology A fraction calculator can be used to find sums as follows: To calculate $\frac{23}{48} + \frac{38}{51}$, press. 23 $\boxed{/}$ 48 $\boxed{+}$ 38 $\boxed{/}$ 51 $\boxed{=}$ 1∪183/816. This mixed number can be simplified by pressing $\boxed{\text{SIMP}}$ $\boxed{=}$ to obtain 1∪61/272. The sum $\frac{237}{496} + \frac{384}{517}$ may not fit on a common fraction calculator display. In this case, the common denominator approach to addition can be used instead, namely $\dfrac{a}{b} + \dfrac{c}{d} = \dfrac{ad + bc}{bd}$. Here

$$
\begin{aligned}
ad &= 237 \times 517 & &= 122529 \\
bc &= 496 \times 384 & &= 190464 \\
ad + bc &= 122529 + 190464 & &= 312993 \\
bd &= 496 \times 517 & &= 256432.
\end{aligned}
$$

Therefore, the sum is $\frac{312993}{256432}$. Notice that the latter method may be done on any four-function calculator.

The following properties of fraction addition can be used to simplify computations. For simplicity, all properties are stated using common denominators, since any two fractions can be expressed with the same denominator.

 PROPERTY

Closure Property for Fraction Addition

The sum of two fractions is a fraction.

This follows from the equation $\dfrac{a}{c} + \dfrac{b}{c} = \dfrac{a + b}{c}$, since $a + b$ and c are both whole numbers and $c \neq 0$.

 PROPERTY

Commutative Property for Fraction Addition

Let $\dfrac{a}{b}$ and $\dfrac{c}{d}$ be any fractions. Then

$$\frac{a}{b} + \frac{c}{b} = \frac{c}{b} + \frac{a}{b}.$$

Problem-Solving Strategy
Draw a Picture

Figure 6.16

Figure 6.16 provides a visual justification using fraction strips. The following is a formal proof of this commutativity.

$$\frac{a}{b} + \frac{c}{b} = \frac{a + c}{b} \qquad \textit{Addition of fractions}$$

$$= \frac{c + a}{b} \qquad \textit{Commutative property of whole-number addition}$$

$$= \frac{c}{b} + \frac{a}{b} \qquad \textit{Addition of fractions}$$

 PROPERTY

Associative Property for Fraction Addition

Let $\dfrac{a}{b}, \dfrac{c}{b}$, and $\dfrac{e}{b}$ be any fractions. Then

$$\left[\frac{a}{b} + \frac{c}{b}\right] + \frac{e}{b} = \frac{a}{b} + \left[\frac{c}{b} + \frac{e}{b}\right].$$

The associative property for fraction addition is easily justified using the associative property for whole-number addition.

PROPERTY

Additive Identity Property for Fraction Addition

Let $\dfrac{a}{b}$ be any fraction. There is a unique fraction, $\dfrac{0}{b}$, such that

$$\frac{a}{b} + \frac{0}{b} = \frac{a}{b} = \frac{0}{b} + \frac{a}{b}.$$

The following equations show how this additive identity property can be justified using the corresponding property in whole numbers.

$$\frac{a}{b} + \frac{0}{b} = \frac{a + 0}{b} \qquad \textit{Addition of fractions}$$

$$= \frac{a}{b} \qquad \textit{Additive identity property of whole-number addition}$$

The fraction $\frac{0}{b}$ is also written as $\frac{0}{1}$ or 0. It is shown in the problem set that this is the only fraction that serves as an additive identity.

The preceding properties can be used to simplify computations.

Example 6.6 Compute: $\frac{3}{5} + \left[\frac{4}{7} + \frac{2}{5}\right]$.

Solution

$$\frac{3}{5} + \left[\frac{4}{7} + \frac{2}{5}\right] = \frac{3}{5} + \left[\frac{2}{5} + \frac{4}{7}\right] \qquad \textit{Commutativity}$$

$$= \left[\frac{3}{5} + \frac{2}{5}\right] + \frac{4}{7} \qquad \textit{Associativity}$$

$$= 1 + \frac{4}{7} \qquad \textit{Addition} \qquad ■$$

The number $1 + \frac{4}{7}$ can be expressed as the mixed number $1\frac{4}{7}$. As in Example 6.6, any mixed number can be expressed as a sum. For example, $3\frac{2}{5} = 3 + \frac{2}{5}$. Also, any mixed number can be changed to an improper fraction, and vice versa, as shown in the next example.

Example 6.7
a. Express $3\frac{2}{5}$ as an improper fraction.
b. Express $\frac{36}{7}$ as a mixed number.

Solution

a. $3\frac{2}{5} = 3 + \frac{2}{5} = \frac{15}{5} + \frac{2}{5} = \frac{17}{5}$

$$\left[\text{Shortcut: } 3\frac{2}{5} = \frac{5 \cdot 3 + 2}{5} = \frac{17}{5}\right]$$

b. $\dfrac{36}{7} = \dfrac{35}{7} + \dfrac{1}{7} = 5 + \dfrac{1}{7} = 5\dfrac{1}{7}$ ■

Subtraction

Problem-Solving Strategy
Draw a Picture

Subtraction of fractions can be viewed in two ways as we did with whole-number subtraction—either as (1) take-away or (2) using the missing-addend approach.

Example 6.8 Find $\dfrac{4}{7} - \dfrac{1}{7}$.

Solution

From Figure 6.17, $\dfrac{4}{7} - \dfrac{1}{7} = \dfrac{3}{7}$. ■

This example suggests the following definition.

Figure 6.17

DEFINITION

Subtraction of Fractions with Common Denominators

Let $\dfrac{a}{b}$ and $\dfrac{c}{b}$ be any fractions with $a \geq c$. Then

$$\frac{a}{b} - \frac{c}{b} = \frac{a-c}{b}.$$

Now consider the subtraction of fractions using the missing-addend approach. For example, to find $\dfrac{4}{7} - \dfrac{1}{7}$, find a fraction $\dfrac{n}{7}$ such that $\dfrac{4}{7} = \dfrac{1}{7} + \dfrac{n}{7}$. The following argument shows that the missing-addend approach leads to the take-away approach.

If $\dfrac{a}{b} - \dfrac{c}{b} = \dfrac{n}{b}$, and the missing-addend approach holds, then $\dfrac{a}{b} = \dfrac{c}{b} + \dfrac{n}{b}$ or $\dfrac{a}{b} = \dfrac{c+n}{b}$. This implies that $a = c + n$ or $a - c = n$.

That is, $\dfrac{a}{b} - \dfrac{c}{b} = \dfrac{a-c}{b}$.

Also, it can be shown that the missing-addend approach is a consequence of the take-away approach.

If fractions have different denominators, subtraction is done by first finding common denominators, then subtracting as before.

Suppose that $\dfrac{a}{b} \geq \dfrac{c}{d}$. Then $\dfrac{a}{b} - \dfrac{c}{d} = \dfrac{ad}{bd} - \dfrac{bc}{bd} = \dfrac{ad - bc}{bd}$.

Therefore, fractions with unlike denominators may be subtracted as follows.

 THEOREM

Subtraction of Fractions with Unlike Denominators

Let $\dfrac{a}{b}$ and $\dfrac{c}{d}$ be any fractions, where $\dfrac{a}{b} \geq \dfrac{c}{d}$. Then

$$\frac{a}{b} - \frac{c}{d} = \frac{ad - bc}{bd}.$$

Example 6.9   Find the following differences.

a. $\dfrac{4}{7} - \dfrac{3}{8}$ **b.** $\dfrac{25}{12} - \dfrac{7}{18}$ **c.** $\dfrac{7}{10} - \dfrac{8}{15}$

Solution

NCTM Standards 2000
Number and Operations
Grades 3–5
All students should develop and use strategies to estimate computations involving fractions and decimals in situations relevant to students' experience.

a. $\dfrac{4}{7} - \dfrac{3}{8} = \dfrac{4 \cdot 8}{7 \cdot 8} - \dfrac{7 \cdot 3}{7 \cdot 8} = \dfrac{32 - 21}{56} = \dfrac{11}{56}$

b. $\dfrac{25}{12} - \dfrac{7}{18}$. NOTE: LCM(12, 18) = 36.

$\dfrac{25}{12} - \dfrac{7}{18} = \dfrac{25 \cdot 3}{12 \cdot 3} - \dfrac{7 \cdot 2}{18 \cdot 2} = \dfrac{75 - 14}{36} = \dfrac{61}{36}$

c. $\dfrac{7}{10} - \dfrac{8}{15} = \dfrac{21}{30} - \dfrac{16}{30} = \dfrac{5}{30} = \dfrac{1}{6}$ ■

Mental Math and Estimation for Addition and Subtraction

Mental math and estimation techniques similar to those used with whole numbers can be used with fractions.

Example 6.10 Calculate mentally.

a. $\left(\dfrac{1}{5} + \dfrac{3}{4}\right) + \dfrac{4}{5}$ 　　b. $3\dfrac{4}{5} + 2\dfrac{2}{5}$ 　　c. $40 - 8\dfrac{3}{7}$

Solution

a. $\left(\dfrac{1}{5} + \dfrac{3}{4}\right) + \dfrac{4}{5} = \dfrac{4}{5} + \left(\dfrac{1}{5} + \dfrac{3}{4}\right) = \left(\dfrac{4}{5} + \dfrac{1}{5}\right) + \dfrac{3}{4} = 1\dfrac{3}{4}$

Commutativity and associativity were used to be able to add $\dfrac{4}{5}$ and $\dfrac{1}{5}$, since they are compatible fractions (their sum is 1).

b. $3\dfrac{4}{5} + 2\dfrac{2}{5} = 4 + 2\dfrac{1}{5} = 6\dfrac{1}{5}$

This is an example of additive compensation, where $3\dfrac{4}{5}$ was increased by $\dfrac{1}{5}$ to 4 and consequently $2\dfrac{2}{5}$ was decreased by $\dfrac{1}{5}$ to $2\dfrac{1}{5}$.

c. $40 - 8\dfrac{3}{7} = 40\dfrac{4}{7} - 9 = 31\dfrac{4}{7}$

Here $\dfrac{4}{7}$ was added to both 40 and $8\dfrac{3}{7}$ $\left(\text{since } 8\dfrac{3}{7} + \dfrac{4}{7} = 9\right)$, an example of the equal-additions method of subtraction. This problem could also be viewed as $39\dfrac{7}{7} - 8\dfrac{3}{7} = 31\dfrac{4}{7}$. ■

NCTM Standards 2000
Number and Operations
Grades 6–8
All students should develop and use strategies to estimate the results of rational-number computations and judge the reasonableness of the results.

Example 6.11 Estimate using the indicated techniques.

a. $3\dfrac{3}{7} + 6\dfrac{2}{5}$ using range estimation 　$9-11$

b. $15\dfrac{1}{4} + 7\dfrac{3}{5}$ using front-end with adjustment

c. $3\dfrac{5}{6} + 5\dfrac{1}{8} + 8\dfrac{3}{8}$ rounding to the nearest $\frac{1}{2}$ or whole

Solution

a. $3\dfrac{3}{7} + 6\dfrac{2}{5}$ is between $3 + 6 = 9$ and $4 + 7 = 11$.

b. $15\dfrac{1}{4} + 7\dfrac{3}{5} \approx 23$, since $15 + 7 = 22$ and $\dfrac{1}{4} + \dfrac{3}{5} \approx 1$.

c. $3\dfrac{5}{6} + 5\dfrac{1}{8} + 8\dfrac{3}{8} \approx 4 + 5 + 8\dfrac{1}{2} = 17\dfrac{1}{2}$. ■

MATHEMATICAL MORSEL

Around 2900 B.C. the Great Pyramid of Giza was constructed. It covered 13 acres and contained over 2,000,000 stone blocks averaging 2.5 tons each. Some chamber roofs are made of 54-ton granite blocks, 27 feet long and 4 feet thick, hauled from a quarry 600 miles away and set into place 200 feet above the ground. The relative error in the lengths of the sides of the square base was $\frac{1}{14,000}$ and in the right angles was $\frac{1}{27,000}$. This construction was estimated to have required 100,000 laborers working for about 30 years.

Section 6.2 EXERCISE / PROBLEM SET A

EXERCISES

1. Illustrate the problem $\frac{2}{5} + \frac{1}{3}$ using the following models.

   a. A region model **b.** A number-line model

2. Using rectangles or circles as the whole, illustrate the following problems. The Chapter 6 eManipulative activity, *Fraction Concepts—Adding Fractions*, will help you understand this process.

   a. $\frac{2}{3} + \frac{1}{6}$ **b.** $\frac{1}{4} + \frac{3}{8}$ **c.** $\frac{3}{4} + \frac{2}{3}$

3. Find the following sums and express your answer in simplest form.

   a. $\frac{1}{8} + \frac{5}{8}$ **b.** $\frac{1}{4} + \frac{1}{2}$ **c.** $\frac{3}{7} + \frac{1}{3}$

   d. $\frac{8}{9} + \frac{1}{12} + \frac{3}{16}$ **e.** $\frac{8}{13} + \frac{4}{51}$ **f.** $\frac{9}{22} + \frac{89}{121}$

   g. $\frac{61}{100} + \frac{7}{1000}$ **h.** $\frac{7}{10} + \frac{20}{100}$ **i.** $\frac{143}{1000} + \frac{759}{100,000}$

4. Change the following mixed numbers to improper fractions.

   a. $3\frac{5}{6}$ **b.** $2\frac{7}{8}$ **c.** $5\frac{1}{5}$ **d.** $7\frac{1}{9}$

5. On a number line, demonstrate the following problems using the take-away approach.

   a. $\frac{7}{10} - \frac{3}{10}$ **b.** $\frac{5}{12} - \frac{1}{12}$ **c.** $\frac{2}{3} - \frac{1}{4}$

6. Perform the following subtractions.

   a. $\frac{9}{11} - \frac{5}{11}$ **b.** $\frac{3}{7} - \frac{2}{9}$ **c.** $\frac{4}{5} - \frac{3}{4}$

   d. $\frac{13}{18} - \frac{8}{27}$ **e.** $\frac{21}{51} - \frac{7}{39}$ **f.** $\frac{11}{100} - \frac{99}{1000}$

7. Find the sum and difference (first minus second) for the following pairs of mixed numbers. Answers should be written as mixed numbers.

   a. $2\frac{2}{3}, 1\frac{1}{4}$ **b.** $7\frac{5}{7}, 5\frac{2}{3}$ **c.** $22\frac{1}{6}, 15\frac{11}{12}$

8. Use the properties of fraction addition to calculate each of the following sums mentally.

   a. $(\frac{3}{7} + \frac{1}{9}) + \frac{4}{7}$ **b.** $1\frac{9}{13} + \frac{5}{6} + \frac{4}{13}$

   c. $(2\frac{2}{5} + 3\frac{3}{8}) + (1\frac{4}{5} + 2\frac{3}{8})$

9. Find each of these differences mentally using the equal-additions method. Write out the steps that you thought through.

   a. $8\frac{2}{7} - 2\frac{6}{7}$ **b.** $9\frac{1}{8} - 2\frac{5}{8}$

   c. $11\frac{3}{7} - 6\frac{5}{7}$ **d.** $8\frac{1}{6} - 3\frac{5}{6}$

10. Estimate each of the following using (i) range and (ii) front-end with adjustment estimation.

    a. $6\frac{7}{11} + 7\frac{3}{9}$ **b.** $7\frac{4}{6} + 6\frac{6}{7}$ **c.** $8\frac{2}{11} + 2\frac{7}{11} + 5\frac{2}{9}$

11. Estimate each of the following using "rounding to the nearest whole number or $\frac{1}{2}$."

    a. $9\frac{7}{9} + 3\frac{6}{13}$ **b.** $9\frac{5}{8} + 5\frac{4}{9}$ **c.** $7\frac{2}{11} + 5\frac{3}{13} + 2\frac{7}{12}$

12. Estimate using cluster estimation: $5\frac{1}{3} + 4\frac{4}{5} + 5\frac{6}{7}$.

13. An alternative definition of "less than" for fractions is as follows:

    $\frac{a}{b} < \frac{c}{d}$ if and only if
    $\frac{a}{b} + \frac{m}{n} = \frac{c}{d}$ for a
    nonzero $\frac{m}{n}$

    Use this definition to confirm the following statements.

    a. $\frac{3}{7} < \frac{5}{7}$ **b.** $\frac{1}{3} < \frac{1}{2}$

14. Calculate using a fraction calculator.

    a. $\frac{3}{4} + \frac{7}{10}$ **b.** $\frac{8}{9} - \frac{3}{5}$

15. To find the sum $\frac{2}{5} + \frac{3}{4}$ on a scientific calculator, press
    $2 \boxed{\div} 5 \boxed{+} 3 \boxed{\div} 4 \boxed{=} \boxed{1.15}$. The whole-
    number part of the sum is 1. Subtract it: $\boxed{-} 1 \boxed{=}$
    $\boxed{0.15}$. This represents the fraction part of the
    answer in decimal form. Since the denominator of

the sum should be $5 \times 4 = 20$, multiply by 20: $\boxed{\times}$
$20 \boxed{=} \boxed{3}$. This is the numerator of the fraction
part of the sum. Thus $\frac{2}{5} + \frac{3}{4} = 1\frac{3}{20}$. Find the simplest
form of the sums/differences using this method.

a. $\frac{3}{7} + \frac{5}{8}$ **b.** $\frac{3}{5} - \frac{4}{7}$

PROBLEMS

16. Sally, her brother, and another partner own a pizza
    restaurant. If Sally owns $\frac{1}{3}$ and her brother owns $\frac{1}{4}$ of
    the restaurant, what part does the third partner own?

17. John spent a quarter of his life as a boy growing up,
    one-sixth of his life in college, and one-half of his
    life as a teacher. He spent his last six years in retire-
    ment. How old was he when he died?

18. Rafael ate one-fourth of a pizza and Rocco ate
    one-third of it. What fraction of the pizza did they eat?

19. Greg plants two-fifths of his garden in potatoes and
    one-sixth in carrots. What fraction of the garden
    remains for his other crops?

20. About eleven-twelfths of a golf course is in fair-
    ways, one-eighteenth in greens, and the rest in tees.
    What part of the golf course is in tees?

21. David is having trouble when subtracting mixed
    numbers. What might be causing his difficulty?
    How might you help David?

$$3\frac{2}{5} = 2\frac{12}{5}$$
$$-\frac{3}{5} = \frac{3}{5}$$
$$2\frac{9}{5} = 3\frac{4}{5}$$

22. **a.** The divisors (other than 1) of 6 are 2, 3, and 6.
    Compute $\frac{1}{2} + \frac{1}{3} + \frac{1}{6}$.
    b. The divisors (other than 1) of 28 are 2, 4, 7, 14,
    and 28. Compute $\frac{1}{2} + \frac{1}{4} + \frac{1}{7} + \frac{1}{14} + \frac{1}{28}$.
    c. Will this result be true for 496? What other num-
    bers will have this property?

23. Determine whether $\dfrac{1 + 3}{5 + 7} = \dfrac{1 + 3 + 5}{7 + 9 + 11}$. Is
    $\dfrac{1 + 3 + 5 + 7}{9 + 11 + 13 + 15}$ also the same fraction? Find
    two other such fractions. Prove why this works.
    (*Hint*: $1 + 3 = 2^2$, $1 + 3 + 5 = 3^2$, etc.)

24. Find this sum: $\dfrac{1}{2} + \dfrac{1}{2^2} = \dfrac{1}{2^3} + \cdots + \dfrac{1}{2^{100}}$.

25. In the first 10 games of the baseball season, Jim has
    15 hits in 50 times at bat. The fraction of his times at

bat that were hits is $\frac{15}{20}$. In the next game he is at bat 6
times and gets 3 hits.

a. What fraction of at-bats are hits in this game?

b. How many hits does he now have this season?

c. How many at-bats does he now have this season?

d. What is his record of hits/at-bats this season?

e. In this setting "baseball addition" can be defined as

$$\frac{a}{b} \oplus \frac{c}{d} = \frac{a + c}{b + d}.$$

(Use $\oplus$ to distinguish from ordinary $+$.)

Using this definition, do you get an equivalent
answer when fractions are replaced by equivalent
fractions?

26. Fractions whose numerators are 1 are called **unitary
    fractions.** Do you think that it is possible to add uni-
    tary fractions with different odd denominators to
    obtain 1? For example, $\frac{1}{2} + \frac{1}{3} + \frac{1}{6} = 1$, but 2 and
    6 are even. How about the following sum?

$$\frac{1}{3} + \frac{1}{5} + \frac{1}{7} + \frac{1}{9} + \frac{1}{15} + \frac{1}{21} + \frac{1}{27} +$$
$$\frac{1}{35} + \frac{1}{63} + \frac{1}{105} + \frac{1}{135}$$

27. The Egyptians were said to use only unitary fractions
    with the exception of $\frac{2}{3}$. It is known that every unitary
    fraction can be expressed as the sum of two unitary
    fractions in more than one way. Represent the follow-
    ing fractions as the sum of two different unitary frac-
    tions. (NOTE: $\frac{1}{2} = \frac{1}{4} + \frac{1}{4}$, but $\frac{1}{2} = \frac{1}{3} + \frac{1}{6}$ is requested.)

    a. $\frac{1}{5}$ **b.** $\frac{1}{7}$ **c.** $\frac{1}{17}$

28. At a round-robin tennis tournament, each of eight
    players plays every other player once. How many
    matches are there?

29. New lockers are being installed in a school and will
    be numbered from 0001 to 1000. Stick-on digits will
    be used to number the lockers. A custodian must cal-
    culate the number of packages of numbers to order.
    How many 0s will be needed to complete the task?
    How many 9s?

PROBLEMS FOR WRITING/DISCUSSION

1. A student asks you which is easier, adding fractions or multiplying fractions. How would you answer?

2. A student tells you that it's easy to determine which of two fractions is larger: If the numerator is larger, then that fraction is larger; if the denominator is larger, then that fraction is smaller. Do you agree with the student? How would you explore this issue?

3. You asked a student to determine whether certain fractions were closer to 0, to $\frac{1}{2}$, or to 1. He answered that since fractions were always small, they would all be close to 0. How would you respond?

4. A student asks why he needs to find a common denominator when adding fractions. How do you respond?

6.3 FRACTIONS: MULTIPLICATION AND DIVISION

STARTING POINT

Write a word problem for each of the following expressions. Each word problem should have the corresponding expression as part of its solution.

$$\text{(a) } 3 \div \frac{1}{2} \qquad \text{(b) } \frac{1}{3} \div 4 \qquad \text{(c) } \frac{5}{8} \div \frac{1}{4}$$

An example of a word problem for the expression $4 \times \frac{2}{3}$ is the following.

Darius had 4 pies for his birthday party. By the end of his party, two-thirds of each pie had been eaten. How much pie had been eaten altogether?

Reflection from Research

Until students understand operations with fractions, they often have misconceptions that multiplication always results in a larger answer and division in a smaller (Greer, 1988).

Multiplication and Its Properties

Extending the repeated-addition approach of whole-number multiplication to fraction multiplication is an interesting challenge. Consider the following cases.

CASE 1: A Whole Number Times a Fraction

$$3 \times \frac{1}{4} = \frac{1}{4} + \frac{1}{4} + \frac{1}{4} = \frac{3}{4}$$
$$6 \times \frac{1}{2} = \frac{1}{2} + \frac{1}{2} + \frac{1}{2} + \frac{1}{2} + \frac{1}{2} + \frac{1}{2} = 3$$

Here repeated addition works well since the first factor is a whole number.

CASE 2: A Fraction Times a Whole Number

$$\frac{1}{2} \times 6$$

Reflection from Research

Students who only view fractions like $\frac{3}{4}$ as "three out of 4 parts" struggle to handle fraction multiplication problems such as $\frac{2}{3}$ of $\frac{9}{10}$. Students who can more flexibly view $\frac{3}{4}$ as "three fourths of one whole or three units of one fourth" can better solve multiplication of two proper fractions (Mack, 2001).

Here, we cannot apply the repeated-addition approach directly, since that would literally say to add 6 one-half times. But if multiplication is to be commutative, then $\frac{1}{2} \times 6$ would have to be equal to $6 \times \frac{1}{2}$, or 3, as in case 1. Thus a way of interpreting $\frac{1}{2} \times 6$ would be to view the $\frac{1}{2}$ as taking "one-half of 6" or "one of two equal parts of 6," namely 3. Similarly, $\frac{1}{4} \times 3$ could be modeled by finding "one-fourth of 3" on the fraction number line to obtain $\frac{3}{4}$ (Figure 6.18).

Figure 6.19

Figure 6.18

In the following final case, it is impossible to use the repeated-addition approach, so we apply the new technique of case 2.

CASE 3: A Fraction of a Fraction

$$\frac{1}{3} \times \frac{5}{7} \quad \text{means} \quad \frac{1}{3} \text{ of } \frac{5}{7}$$

First picture $\frac{5}{7}$. Then take one of the three equivalent parts of $\frac{5}{7}$ (Figure 6.19).

After subdividing the region in Figure 6.19 horizontally into seven equivalent parts and vertically into three equal parts, the shaded region consists of 5 of the 21 smallest rectangles (each small rectangle represents $\frac{1}{21}$). Therefore,

$$\frac{1}{3} \times \frac{5}{7} = \frac{5}{21}$$

Similarly, $\frac{2}{3} \times \frac{5}{7}$ would comprise 10 of the smallest rectangles, so

$$\frac{2}{3} \times \frac{5}{7} = \frac{10}{21}.$$

This discussion should make the following definition of fraction multiplication seem reasonable.

DEFINITION

Multiplication of Fractions

Let $\dfrac{a}{b}$ and $\dfrac{c}{d}$ be any fractions. Then

$$\frac{a}{b} \cdot \frac{c}{d} = \frac{ac}{bd}.$$

Example 6.12 Compute the following products and express the answers in simplest form.

a. $\frac{2}{3} \cdot \frac{5}{13}$ **b.** $\frac{3}{4} \cdot \frac{28}{15}$ **c.** $2\frac{1}{3} \cdot 7\frac{2}{5}$

Solution

a. $\dfrac{2}{3} \cdot \dfrac{5}{13} = \dfrac{2 \cdot 5}{3 \cdot 13} = \dfrac{10}{39}$

b. $\dfrac{3}{4} \cdot \dfrac{28}{15} = \dfrac{3 \cdot 28}{4 \cdot 15} = \dfrac{84}{60} = \dfrac{21 \cdot 4}{15 \cdot 4} = \dfrac{21}{15} = \dfrac{7 \cdot 3}{5 \cdot 3} = \dfrac{7}{5}$

c. $2\dfrac{1}{3} \cdot 7\dfrac{2}{5} = \dfrac{7}{3} \cdot \dfrac{37}{5} = \dfrac{259}{15}$, or $17\dfrac{4}{15}$ ■

Two mixed numbers were multiplied in Example 6.12(c). Children may *incorrectly* multiply mixed numbers as follows:

$$2\tfrac{2}{3} \cdot 3\tfrac{1}{2} = (2 \cdot 3) + (\tfrac{2}{3} \cdot \tfrac{1}{2})$$
$$= 6\tfrac{1}{3}.$$

However, Figure 6.20 shows that multiplying mixed numbers is more complex.

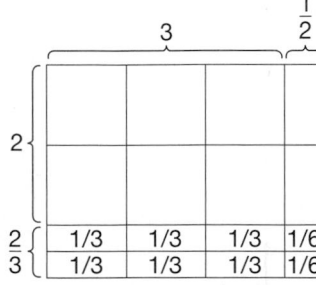

$$2\tfrac{2}{3} \times 3\tfrac{1}{2} = (2 \times 3) + \left(2 \times \tfrac{1}{2}\right) +$$
$$\left(\tfrac{2}{3} \times 3\right) + \left(\tfrac{2}{3} \times \tfrac{1}{2}\right) =$$
$$6 + 1 + 2 + \tfrac{1}{3} = 9\tfrac{1}{3}$$

Figure 6.20

Multiplication of Fractions and Whole Numbers

For this lesson, the yellow hexagon is one whole. Mr. Moreno's class uses diagrams and pattern blocks to show multiplication of fractions. Here are several ways to show $\frac{1}{2} \times 4$ and $4 \times \frac{1}{2}$:

Here is Frank's diagram:

Brandon uses pattern blocks
to show that $\frac{1}{2}$ of $4 = 2$.
Here is one way.

Here is another way Brandon shows that $\frac{1}{2}$ of $4 = 2$.

Arti thinks that $\frac{1}{2} \times 4$ is the same as $4 \times \frac{1}{2}$. Here is her diagram for $4 \times \frac{1}{2}$. Is she correct?

$$\frac{1}{2} + \frac{1}{2} + \frac{1}{2} + \frac{1}{2} = 4 \times \frac{1}{2} = 2$$

1. **A.** Use pattern blocks to show $3 \times \frac{1}{2}$.
   B. Use pattern blocks to show $\frac{1}{2}$ of 3.
   C. Is the product of $\frac{1}{2}$ and 3 larger or smaller than 3?

2. **A.** Use pattern blocks to show 2 groups of $\frac{3}{4}$.
   B. Use pattern blocks to show $\frac{3}{4}$ of 2.
   C. Is the product of $\frac{3}{4}$ and 2 larger or smaller than 2?

From *Math Trailblazers*, Grade 5 Student Guide p. 335, by the *TIMS PROJECT*. Copyright © 1997 by Kendall/Hunt Publishing Company. Reprinted with permission.

In Example 6.12(b), the product was easy to find but the process of simplification required several steps.

Spotlight on Technology When using a fraction calculator, the answers are usually not given in simplest form. For example, on the TI-34 II, Example 6.12(b) is obtained:

$$3 \boxed{/} 4 \boxed{\times} 28 \boxed{/} 15 \boxed{=} \boxed{1 \cup 24/60}$$

This mixed number is simplified one step at a time by pressing the simplify key repeatedly as follows:

$$\boxed{\text{SIMP}} \boxed{=} \boxed{1 \cup 12/30} \boxed{\text{SIMP}} \boxed{=} \boxed{1 \cup 6/15} \boxed{\text{SIMP}} \boxed{=} \boxed{1 \cup 2/5}.$$

The display of the original result on the TI-34 II may be the improper fraction $\boxed{84/60}$, depending on how the $\boxed{\text{FracMode}}$ has been set.

The next example shows how one can simplify first (a good habit to cultivate) and then multiply.

Example 6.13 Compute and simplify: $\frac{3}{4} \cdot \frac{28}{15}$.

Solution

Instead, simplify, and then compute.

$$\frac{3}{4} \cdot \frac{28}{15} = \frac{3 \cdot 28}{4 \cdot 15} = \frac{3 \cdot 28}{15 \cdot 4} = \frac{3}{15} \cdot \frac{28}{4} = \frac{1}{5} \cdot \frac{7}{1} = \frac{7}{5}.$$

Another way to calculate this product is

$$\frac{3}{4} \cdot \frac{28}{15} = \frac{3 \cdot 2 \cdot 2 \cdot 7}{2 \cdot 2 \cdot 3 \cdot 5} = \frac{7}{5}.$$ ■

The equation $\frac{a}{b} \cdot \frac{c}{d} = \frac{a}{d} \cdot \frac{c}{b}$ is a simplification of the essence of the procedure in Example 6.13. That is, we simply interchange the two denominators to expedite the simplification process. This can be justified as follows:

$$\frac{a}{b} \cdot \frac{c}{d} = \frac{ac}{bd} \qquad \textit{Multiplication of fractions}$$

$$= \frac{ac}{bd} \qquad \textit{Commutativity for whole-number multiplication}$$

$$= \frac{a}{d} \cdot \frac{c}{b}. \qquad \textit{Multiplication of fractions}$$

You may have seen the following even shorter method.

Example 6.14 Compute and simplify.

a. $\frac{18}{13} \cdot \frac{39}{72}$ **b.** $\frac{50}{15} \cdot \frac{39}{55}$

Solution

a. $\dfrac{18}{13} \cdot \dfrac{39}{72} = \dfrac{18}{\cancel{13}_{1}} \cdot \dfrac{\cancel{39}^{3}}{72} = \dfrac{\cancel{18}_{1}}{\cancel{13}_{1}} \cdot \dfrac{\cancel{39}^{3}}{\cancel{72}_{4}} = \dfrac{3}{4}$

b. $\dfrac{50}{15} \cdot \dfrac{39}{55} = \dfrac{\cancel{50}^{10}}{\cancel{15}_{3}} \cdot \dfrac{39}{55} = \dfrac{\cancel{10}^{2}}{3} \cdot \dfrac{39}{\cancel{55}_{11}} = \dfrac{2}{\cancel{3}_{1}} \cdot \dfrac{\cancel{39}^{13}}{11} = \dfrac{26}{11}$ ■

The definition of fraction multiplication together with the corresponding properties for whole-number multiplication can be used to verify properties of fraction multiplication. A verification of the multiplicative identity property for fraction multiplication is shown next.

$$\frac{a}{b} \cdot 1 = \frac{a}{b} \cdot \frac{1}{1} \qquad \textit{Recall that } 1 = \frac{1}{1} = \frac{2}{2} = \frac{3}{3} = \cdots$$

$$= \frac{a \cdot 1}{b \cdot 1} \qquad \textit{Fraction multiplication}$$

$$= \frac{a}{b} \qquad \textit{Identity for whole-number multiplication}$$

It is shown in the problem set that 1 is the only multiplicative identity.

The properties of fraction multiplication are summarized next. Notice that fraction multiplication has an additional property, different from any whole-number properties—namely, the multiplicative inverse property.

 PROPERTY

Properties of Fraction Multiplication

Let $\dfrac{a}{b}, \dfrac{c}{d},$ and $\dfrac{e}{f}$ be any fractions.

Closure Property for Fraction Multiplication
The product of two fractions is a fraction.

Commutative Property for Fraction Multiplication

$$\frac{a}{b} \cdot \frac{c}{d} = \frac{c}{d} \cdot \frac{a}{b}$$

Associative Property for Fraction Multiplication

$$\left(\frac{a}{b} \cdot \frac{c}{d}\right) \cdot \frac{e}{f} = \frac{a}{b} \cdot \left(\frac{c}{d} \cdot \frac{e}{f}\right)$$

Multiplicative Identity Property for Fraction Multiplication

$$\frac{a}{b} \cdot 1 = \frac{a}{b} = 1 \cdot \frac{a}{b}. \quad \left(1 = \frac{m}{m}, m \neq 0\right)$$

Multiplicative Inverse Property for Fraction Multiplication
For every nonzero fraction $\dfrac{a}{b}$, there is a unique fraction $\dfrac{b}{a}$ such that

$$\frac{a}{b} \cdot \frac{b}{a} = 1.$$

When $\dfrac{a}{b} \neq 0, \dfrac{b}{a}$ is called the **multiplicative inverse** or **reciprocal** of $\dfrac{a}{b}$. The multiplicative inverse property is useful for solving equations involving fractions.

Example 6.15 Solve: $\frac{3}{7}x = \frac{5}{8}$.

Solution

$$\frac{3}{7}x = \frac{5}{8}$$

$$\frac{7}{3}\left(\frac{3}{7}x\right) = \frac{7}{3} \cdot \frac{5}{8} \qquad \textit{Multiplication}$$

$$\left(\frac{7}{3} \cdot \frac{3}{7}\right)x = \frac{7}{3} \cdot \frac{5}{8} \qquad \textit{Associative property}$$

$$1 \cdot x = \frac{35}{24} \qquad \textit{Multiplicative inverse property}$$

$$x = \frac{35}{24} \qquad \textit{Multiplicative identity property}$$

Finally, as with whole numbers, distributivity holds for fractions. This property can be verified using distributivity in the whole numbers.

PROPERTY

Distributive Property of Fraction Multiplication over Addition

Let $\frac{a}{b}, \frac{c}{d}$, and $\frac{e}{f}$ be any fractions. Then

$$\frac{a}{b}\left(\frac{c}{d} + \frac{e}{f}\right) = \frac{a}{b} \times \frac{c}{d} + \frac{a}{b} \times \frac{e}{f}.$$

Distributivity of multiplication over subtraction also holds; that is,

$$\frac{a}{b}\left(\frac{c}{d} - \frac{e}{f}\right) = \frac{a}{b} \times \frac{c}{d} - \frac{a}{b} \times \frac{e}{f}.$$

Division

Division of fractions is a difficult concept for many children (and adults), in part because of the lack of simple concrete models. We will view division of fractions as an extension of whole-number division. Several other approaches will be used in this section and in the problem set. These approaches provide a *meaningful way* of learning fraction division. Such approaches are a departure from simply memorizing the rote procedure of "invert and multiply," which offers no insight into fraction division.

By using common denominators, division of fractions can be viewed as an extension of whole-number division. For example, $\frac{6}{7} \div \frac{2}{7}$ is just a measurement division problem where we ask the question, "How many groups of size $\frac{2}{7}$ are in $\frac{6}{7}$?" The answer to this question is the equivalent measurement division problem of $6 \div 2$, where the question is asked, "How many groups of size 2 are in 6?" Since there are *three* 2s in 6, there are *three* $\frac{2}{7}$s in $\frac{6}{7}$. Figure 6.21 illustrates this visually. In general, the division of fractions in which the divisor is not a whole number can be viewed as a measurement division problem. On the other hand, if the division problem has a divisor that is a whole number, then it should be viewed as a partitive division problem.

Figure 6.21

Example 6.16   Find the following quotients.

a. $\frac{12}{13} \div \frac{4}{13}$ **b.** $\frac{6}{17} \div \frac{3}{17}$ **c.** $\frac{16}{19} \div \frac{2}{19}$

Solution

a. $\frac{12}{13} \div \frac{4}{13} = 3$, since there are three $\frac{4}{13}$ in $\frac{12}{13}$.

b. $\frac{6}{17} \div \frac{3}{17} = 2$, since there are two $\frac{3}{17}$ in $\frac{6}{17}$.

c. $\frac{16}{19} \div \frac{2}{19} = 8$, since there are eight $\frac{2}{19}$ in $\frac{16}{19}$.

Notice that the answers to all three of these problems can be found simply by dividing the numerators in the correct order.   ■

In the case of $\frac{12}{13} \div \frac{5}{13}$, we ask ourselves, "How many $\frac{5}{13}$ make $\frac{12}{13}$?" But this is the same as asking, "How many 5s (including fractional parts) are in 12?" The answer is 2 and $\frac{2}{5}$ fives or $\frac{12}{5}$ fives. Thus $\frac{12}{13} \div \frac{5}{13} = \frac{12}{5}$. Generalizing this idea fraction division is defined as follows.

DEFINITION

Division of Fraction with Common Denominators

Let $\frac{a}{b}$ and $\frac{c}{b}$ be any fractions with $c \neq 0$. Then

$$\frac{a}{b} \div \frac{c}{b} = \frac{a}{c}.$$

To divide fractions with different denominators, we can rewrite the fractions so that they have the same denominator. Thus we see that

$$\frac{a}{b} \div \frac{c}{d} = \frac{ad}{bd} \div \frac{bc}{bd} = \frac{ad}{bc} \left(= \frac{a}{b} \times \frac{d}{c} \right)$$

using division with common denominators. For example,

$$\frac{3}{7} \div \frac{5}{9} = \frac{27}{63} \div \frac{35}{63} = \frac{27}{35}.$$

Notice that the quotient $\frac{a}{b} \div \frac{c}{d}$ is equal to the product $\frac{a}{b} \times \frac{d}{c}$, since they are both equal to $\frac{ab}{bc}$. Thus a procedure for dividing fractions is to invert the divisor and multiply.

Another interpretation of division of fractions using the missing-factor approach refers directly to multiplication of fractions.

Example 6.17   Find: $\frac{21}{40} \div \frac{7}{8}$.

Solution

Let $\frac{21}{40} \div \frac{7}{8} = \frac{e}{f}$. If the missing-factor approach holds, then $\frac{21}{40} = \frac{7}{8} \times \frac{e}{f}$. Then $\frac{7 \times e}{8 \times f} = \frac{21}{40}$ and we can take $e = 3$ and $f = 5$. Therefore, $\frac{e}{f} = \frac{3}{5}$, or $\frac{21}{40} \div \frac{7}{8} = \frac{3}{5}$.   ■

In Example 6.17 we have the convenient situation where one set of numerators and denominators divides evenly into the other set. Thus a short way of doing this problem is

$$\frac{21}{40} \div \frac{7}{8} = \frac{21 \div 7}{40 \div 8} = \frac{3}{5},$$

since $21 \div 7 = 3$ and $40 \div 8 = 5$. This "divide-the-numerators-and-denominators approach" can be adapted to a more general case, as the following example shows.

Example 6.18   Find: $\frac{21}{40} \div \frac{6}{11}$.

Solution

$$\begin{aligned}
\frac{21}{40} \div \frac{6}{11} &= \frac{21 \times 6 \times 11}{40 \times 6 \times 11} \div \frac{6}{11} \\
&= \frac{(21 \times 6 \times 11) \div 6}{(40 \times 6 \times 11) \div 11} \\
&= \frac{21 \times 11}{40 \times 6} \\
&= \frac{231}{240} = \frac{21}{40} \times \frac{11}{6}
\end{aligned}$$

■

Notice that this approach leads us to conclude that $\frac{21}{40} \div \frac{6}{11} = \frac{21}{40} \times \frac{11}{6}$. Generalizing from these examples and results using the common-denominator approach, we are led to the following familiar "invert-the-divisor-and-multiply" procedure.

Reflection from Research
Teachers are better at interpreting student incorrect responses to division of fractions if they understand "students' tendencies to attribute observed properties of division with natural numbers to fractions or properties of other operations on fractions to division of fractions" (Tirosh, 2000).

THEOREM

Division of Fractions with Unlike Denominators—Invert the Divisor and Multiply

Let $\dfrac{a}{b}$ and $\dfrac{c}{d}$ be any fractions with $c \neq 0$. Then

$$\frac{a}{b} \div \frac{c}{d} = \frac{a}{b} \times \frac{d}{c}.$$

A more visual way to understand why you "invert and multiply" in order to divide fractions is described next. Consider the problem $3 \div \frac{1}{2}$. Viewing it as a measurement division problem, we ask "How many groups of size $\frac{1}{2}$ are in 3?" Let each rectangle in Figure 6.22 represent *one whole*. Since each of the rectangles can be broken into *two* halves and there are three rectangles, there are $3 \times 2 = 6$ one-halfs in 3. Thus we see that $3 \div \frac{1}{2} = 3 \times 2 = 6$.

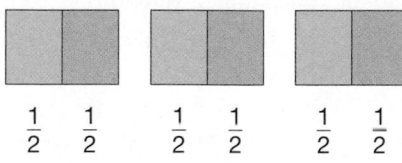

$$\frac{1}{2} \quad \frac{1}{2} \qquad \frac{1}{2} \quad \frac{1}{2} \qquad \frac{1}{2} \quad \frac{1}{2}$$

Figure 6.22

The problem $4 \div \frac{2}{3}$ should also be approached as a measurement division problem for which the question is asked, "How many groups of size $\frac{2}{3}$ are in 4?" In order to answer this question, we must first determine how many groups of size $\frac{2}{3}$ are in *one whole.* Let each rectangle in Figure 6.23 represent one whole and divide each of them into three equal parts.

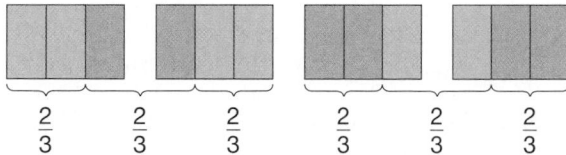

$$\underbrace{}_{\frac{2}{3}}\quad\underbrace{}_{\frac{2}{3}}\quad\underbrace{}_{\frac{2}{3}}\quad\underbrace{}_{\frac{2}{3}}\quad\underbrace{}_{\frac{2}{3}}\quad\underbrace{}_{\frac{2}{3}}$$

Figure 6.23

As shown in Figure 6.23, there is *one* group of size $\frac{2}{3}$ in the rectangle and *one-half* of a group of size $\frac{2}{3}$ in the rectangle. Therefore, each rectangle has $1\frac{1}{2}$ groups of size $\frac{2}{3}$ in it. In this case there are 4 rectangles, so there are $4 \times 1\frac{1}{2} = 6$ groups of size $\frac{2}{3}$ in 4. Since $1\frac{1}{2}$ can be rewritten as $\frac{3}{2}$, the expression $4 \times 1\frac{1}{2}$ is equivalent to $4 \times \frac{3}{2}$. Thus, $4 \div \frac{2}{3} = 4 \times \frac{3}{2} = 6$.

Spotlight on Technology The way that fraction division was viewed in the previous paragraph can be illustrated dynamically by using the Chapter 6 eManipulative activity, *Fraction Concepts—Dividing Fractions.* After trying a few examples, answer the follow-
www.wiley.com/college/musser
ing question: "When dividing 1 by $\dfrac{3}{5}$, it can be seen that there are $1\dfrac{2}{3}$ groups of size $\dfrac{3}{5}$ in 1. Why aren't there $1\dfrac{2}{5}$ groups of size $\dfrac{3}{5}$ in 1?"

In a similar way, this visual approach can be extended to handle problems with a dividend that is not a whole number.

Example 6.19 Find the following quotients using the most convenient division method.

a. $\frac{17}{11} \div \frac{4}{11}$ **b.** $\frac{3}{4} \div \frac{5}{7}$ **c.** $\frac{6}{25} \div \frac{2}{5}$ **d.** $\frac{5}{19} \div \frac{13}{11}$

Solution

a. $\dfrac{17}{11} \div \dfrac{4}{11} = \dfrac{17}{4}$, using the common-denominator approach.

b. $\dfrac{3}{4} \div \dfrac{5}{7} = \dfrac{3}{4} \times \dfrac{7}{5} = \dfrac{21}{20}$, using the invert-the-divisor-and-multiply approach.

c. $\dfrac{6}{25} \div \dfrac{2}{5} = \dfrac{6 \div 2}{25 \div 5} = \dfrac{3}{5}$, using the divide-numerators-and-denominators approach.

d. $\dfrac{5}{19} \div \dfrac{13}{11} = \dfrac{5}{19} \times \dfrac{11}{13} = \dfrac{55}{247}$, using the invert-the-divisor-and-multiply approach. ■

In summary, there are three equivalent ways to view the division of fractions:

1. The common-denominator approach.
2. The divide-the-numerators-and-denominators approach
3. The invert-the-divisor-and-multiply approach

Now, through the division of fractions, we can perform the division of any whole numbers without having to use remainders. (Of course, we still cannot divide by zero.) That is, if a and b are whole numbers and $b \neq 0$, then $a \div b = \dfrac{a}{1} \div \dfrac{b}{1} = \dfrac{a}{1} \times \dfrac{1}{b} = \dfrac{a}{b}$. This approach is summarized next.

> **For all whole numbers a and b, $b \neq 0$,**
> $$a \div b = \frac{a}{b}.$$

Example 6.20 Find $17 \div 6$ using fractions.

Solution

$$17 \div 6 = \tfrac{17}{6} = 2\tfrac{5}{6}$$ ■

There are many situations in which the answer $2\frac{5}{6}$ is more useful than 2 with a remainder of 5. For example, suppose that 17 acres of land were to be divided among 6 families. Each family would receive $2\frac{5}{6}$ acres, rather than each receiving 2 acres with 5 acres remaining unassigned.

Expressing a division problem as a fraction is a useful idea. For example, **complex fractions** such as $\dfrac{\frac{1}{2}}{\frac{3}{5}}$ may be written in place of $\frac{1}{2} \div \frac{3}{5}$. Although fractions are comprised of whole numbers in elementary school mathematics, numbers other than whole numbers are used in numerators and denominators of "fractions" later. For example, the "fraction" $\dfrac{\sqrt{2}}{\pi}$ is simply a symbolic way of writing the quotient $\sqrt{2} \div \pi$ (numbers such as $\sqrt{2}$ and π are discussed in Chapter 9).

Complex fractions are used to divide fractions, as shown next.

Example 6.21 Find $\frac{1}{2} \div \frac{3}{5}$ using a complex fraction.

Solution

$$\frac{1}{2} \div \frac{3}{5} = \frac{\frac{1}{2}}{\frac{3}{5}} \cdot \frac{\frac{5}{3}}{\frac{5}{3}} = \frac{\frac{1}{2} \cdot \frac{5}{3}}{1} = \frac{5}{6}$$

Notice that the multiplicative inverse of the denominator $\frac{3}{5}$ was used to form a complex fraction form of one. ■

Mental Math and Estimation for Multiplication and Division

Mental math and estimation techniques similar to those used with whole numbers can be used with fractions.

Example 6.22 Calculate mentally.

a. $(25 \times 16) \times \dfrac{1}{4}$ **b.** $3\dfrac{1}{8} \times 24$ **c.** $\dfrac{4}{5} \times 15$

Solution

a. $(25 \times 16) \times \frac{1}{4} = 25 \times \left(16 \times \frac{1}{4}\right) = 25 \times 4 = 100.$

Associativity was used to group 16 and $\frac{1}{4}$ together, since they are compatible numbers. Also, 25 and 4 are compatible with respect to multiplication.

b. $3\frac{1}{8} \times 24 = \left(3 + \frac{1}{8}\right) \times 24 = 3 \times 24 + \frac{1}{8} \times 24 = 72 + 3 = 75$

Distributivity can often be used when multiplying mixed numbers, as illustrated here.

c. $\frac{4}{5} \times 15 = \left(4 \times \frac{1}{5}\right) \times 15 = 4 \times \left(\frac{1}{5} \times 15\right) = 4 \times 3 = 12$

The calculation also can be written as $\frac{4}{5} \times 15 = 4 \times \frac{15}{5} = 4 \times 3 = 12$. This product also can be found as follows: $\frac{4}{5} \times 15 = \left(\frac{4}{5} \times 5\right) \times 3 = 4 \times 3 = 12$ ■

Example 6.23 Estimate using the indicated techniques.

a. $5\frac{1}{8} \times 7\frac{5}{6}$ using range estimation

b. $4\frac{3}{8} \times 9\frac{1}{16}$ rounding to the nearest $\frac{1}{2}$ or whole

Solution

a. $5\frac{1}{8} \times 7\frac{5}{6}$ is between $5 \times 7 = 35$ and $6 \times 8 = 48$.

b. $4\frac{3}{8} \times 9\frac{1}{16} \approx 4\frac{1}{2} \times 9 = 36 + 4\frac{1}{2} = 40\frac{1}{2}$

MATHEMATICAL MORSEL

The Hindu mathematician Bhaskara (1119–1185) wrote an arithmetic text called the *Lilavat* (named after his wife). The following is one of the problems contained in this text. "A necklace was broken during an amorous struggle. One-third of the pearls fell to the ground, one-fifth stayed on the couch, one-sixth were found by the girl, and one-tenth were recovered by her lover; six pearls remained on the string. Say of how many pearls the necklace was composed."

Section 6.3 EXERCISE / PROBLEM SET A

EXERCISES

1. Illustrate the following products using the rectangular area model.

   a. $\frac{1}{3} \times \frac{2}{5}$ **b.** $\frac{3}{8} \times \frac{5}{6}$ **c.** $\frac{2}{3} \times \frac{7}{10}$

2. What multiplication problems are represented by each of the following area models? What are the products?

   a.

   b.

   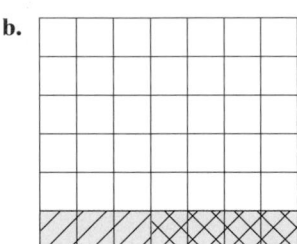

3. Find reciprocals for the following numbers.

   a. $\frac{11}{21}$ **b.** $\frac{9}{3}$

   c. $13\frac{4}{9}$ **d.** 108

4. **a.** Insert the appropriate equality or inequality symbol in the following statement:

   $$\frac{3}{4} \underline{\quad} \frac{3}{2}$$

   b. Find the reciprocals of $\frac{3}{4}$ and $\frac{3}{2}$ and complete the following statement, inserting either $<$ or $>$ in the center blank.

   reciprocal of $\frac{3}{4}$ _____ reciprocal of $\frac{3}{2}$

   c. What do you notice about ordering reciprocals?

5. Use the common-denominator method to divide the following fractions.

   a. $\frac{15}{17} \div \frac{3}{17}$ **b.** $\frac{4}{7} \div \frac{3}{7}$ **c.** $\frac{33}{51} \div \frac{39}{51}$

6. Use the fact that the numerators and denominators divide evenly to simplify the following quotients.

   a. $\frac{15}{16} \div \frac{3}{4}$ **b.** $\frac{21}{27} \div \frac{7}{9}$ **c.** $\frac{39}{56} \div \frac{3}{8}$

   d. $\frac{17}{24} \div \frac{17}{12}$

7. Perform the following operations and express your answers in simplest form.

   a. $\frac{4}{7} \times \frac{3}{8}$ **b.** $\frac{6}{25} \times \frac{5}{9} \times \frac{3}{2}$

   c. $\frac{2}{5} \times \frac{9}{13} + \frac{2}{5} \times \frac{4}{13}$ **d.** $\frac{11}{12} \times \frac{5}{13} + \frac{5}{13} \times \frac{7}{12}$

   e. $\frac{4}{7} \times \frac{3}{14}$ **f.** $\frac{2}{9} \times \frac{4}{3} \times \frac{5}{7}$

   g. $\frac{7}{15} \times 3\frac{1}{2} \times \frac{3}{5}$ **h.** $\frac{1}{3} \times \frac{5}{4} + \frac{1}{4} \times \frac{5}{6}$

   i. $\frac{1}{3} \times (\frac{5}{4} - \frac{1}{4}) \times \frac{5}{6}$ **j.** $\frac{1}{3} + \frac{5}{4}(\frac{1}{4} \div \frac{5}{6})$

8. Find the following products and quotients.

   a. $5\frac{1}{3} \times 2\frac{1}{6}$ **b.** $3\frac{7}{8} \times 2\frac{3}{4}$ **c.** $3\frac{3}{4} \times 2\frac{2}{5}$

   d. $8\frac{1}{3} \div 2\frac{1}{10}$ **e.** $6\frac{1}{4} \div 1\frac{2}{3}$ **f.** $16\frac{2}{3} \div 2\frac{7}{9}$

9. Calculate mentally using properties.

   a. $15 \times \frac{3}{7} + 6 \times \frac{3}{7}$ **b.** $35 \times \frac{6}{7} - 35 \times \frac{3}{7}$

   c. $(\frac{3}{7} + \frac{1}{9}) + \frac{4}{7}$ **d.** $3\frac{5}{9} \times 54$

10. Suppose that the following unit square represents the whole number 1. ☐ We can use squares like this one to represent division problems like $3 \div \frac{1}{2}$, by asking how many $\frac{1}{2}$s are in 3. ▱▱▱ $3 \div \frac{1}{2} = 6$, since there are six one-half squares in the three squares. Draw similar figures and calculate the quotients for the following division problems.

    a. $4 \div \frac{1}{3}$ **b.** $2\frac{1}{2} \div \frac{1}{4}$ **c.** $3 \div \frac{3}{4}$

11. Estimate using compatible numbers.

    a. $29\frac{1}{3} \times 4\frac{2}{3}$ **b.** $57\frac{1}{5} \div 7\frac{4}{5}$ **c.** $70\frac{3}{5} \div 8\frac{5}{8}$

    d. $31\frac{1}{4} \times 5\frac{3}{4}$

12. Estimate using cluster estimation.

    a. $12\frac{1}{4} \times 11\frac{5}{6}$

    b. $5\frac{1}{10} \times 4\frac{8}{9} \times 5\frac{4}{11}$

13. Another way to find a fraction between two given fractions $\frac{a}{b}$ and $\frac{c}{d}$ is to find the average of the two fractions. For example, the average of $\frac{1}{2}$ and $\frac{2}{3}$ is $\frac{1}{2}(\frac{1}{2} + \frac{2}{3}) = \frac{7}{12}$. Use this method to find a fraction between each of the given pairs.

    a. $\frac{7}{8}, \frac{8}{9}$ **b.** $\frac{7}{12}, \frac{11}{16}$

14. Change each of the following complex fractions into ordinary fractions.

    a. $\dfrac{\frac{7}{9}}{\frac{13}{14}}$ **b.** $\dfrac{\frac{2}{3}}{\frac{3}{2}}$

15. Identify which of the properties of fractions could be applied to simplify each of the following computations.

    a. $\frac{2}{7} + (\frac{5}{7} + \frac{2}{9})$ **b.** $(\frac{3}{5} \times \frac{2}{11}) + (\frac{2}{5} \times \frac{2}{11})$

    c. $(\frac{8}{5} \times \frac{3}{13}) \times \frac{13}{3}$

16. The introduction of fractions allows us to solve equations of the form $ax = b$ by dividing whole numbers. For example, $5x = 16$ has as its solution $x = \frac{16}{5}$ (which is 16 divided by 5). Solve each of the following equations and check your results.

    a. $31x = 15$ **b.** $67x = 56$ **c.** $102x = 231$

17. We usually think of the distributive property for fractions as "multiplication of fractions distributes over addition of fractions." Which of the following variations of the distributive property for fractions holds for arbitrary fractions?

    a. Addition over subtraction

    b. Division over multiplication

18. Calculate using a fraction calculator.

    a. $\frac{7}{6} \times \frac{4}{5}$

    b. $\frac{4}{5} \div \frac{2}{7}$

PROBLEMS

19. You buy a family-size box of laundry detergent that contains 40 cups. If your washing machine calls for $1\frac{1}{4}$ cups per wash load, how many loads of wash can you do?

20. In 1999, only $\frac{9}{22}$ of the oil refined in the United States was produced in the United States. If the United States produced 5,925,000 barrels per day in 1999, how much oil was being refined at that time? (Source: *U.S. Energy Information Administration*)

21. All but $\frac{1}{16}$ of the students enrolled at a particular elementary school participated in "Family Fun Night" activities. If a total of 405 students were involved in the evening's activities, how many students attend the school?

22. The directions for Weed-Do-In weed killer recommend mixing $2\frac{1}{2}$ ounces of the concentrate with 1 gallon of water. The bottle of Weed-Do-In contains 32 ounces of concentrate.

    a. How many gallons of mixture can be made from the bottle of concentrate?

    b. Since the weed killer is rather expensive, one gardener decided to stretch his dollar by mixing only $1\frac{3}{4}$ ounces of concentrate with a gallon of water. How many more gallons of mixture can be made this way?

23. A number of employees of a company enrolled in a fitness program on January 2. By March 2, $\frac{4}{5}$ of them were still participating. Of those, $\frac{5}{6}$ were still participating on May 2 and of those, $\frac{9}{10}$ were still participating on July 2. Determine the number of employees who originally enrolled in the program if 36 of the original participants were still active on July 2.

24. Each morning Tammy walks to school. At one-third of the way she passes a grocery store, and halfway to school she passes a bicycle shop. At the grocery store, her watch says 7:40 and at the bicycle shop it says 7:45. When does Tammy reach her school?

25. A recipe that makes 3 dozen peanut butter cookies calls for $1\frac{1}{4}$ cups of flour.

    a. How much flour would you need if you doubled the recipe?

    b. How much flour would you need for half the recipe?

    c. How much flour would you need to make 5 dozen cookies?

26. A softball team had three pitchers: Gale, Ruth, and Sandy. Gale started in $\frac{3}{8}$ of the games played in one season. Sandy started in one more game than Gale, and Ruth started in half as many games as Sandy. In how many of the season's games did each pitcher start?

27. A piece of office equipment purchased for $60,000 depreciates in value each year. Suppose that each year the value of the equipment is $\frac{1}{20}$ less than its value the preceding year.

    a. Calculate the value of the equipment after 2 years.

    b. When will the piece of equipment first have a value less than $40,000?

28. If a nonzero number is divided by one more than itself, the result is one-fifth. If a second nonzero number is divided by one more than itself, the answer is one-fifth of the number itself. What is the product of the two numbers?

29. Carpenters divide fractions by 2 in the following way:

$$\frac{11}{16} \div 2 = \frac{11}{16 \times 2} = \frac{11}{32}$$

(doubling the denominator)

   a. How would they find $\frac{11}{16} \div 5$?

   b. Does $\dfrac{a}{b} \div n = \dfrac{a}{b \times n}$ always?

   c. Find a quick mental method for finding $5\frac{3}{8} \div 2$. Do the same for $10\frac{9}{16} \div 2$.

30. **a.** Following are examples of student work in multiplying fractions. In each case, identify the error and answer the given problem as the student would.

Sam: $\frac{1}{2} \times \frac{2}{3} = \frac{3}{6} \times \frac{4}{6} = \frac{12}{6} = 2$

$\frac{3}{4} \times \frac{1}{8} = \frac{6}{8} \times \frac{1}{8} = \frac{6}{8} = \frac{3}{4}$ $\quad \frac{3}{4} \times \frac{1}{6} = ?$

Sandy: $\frac{3}{8} \times \frac{5}{6} = \frac{3}{8} \times \frac{6}{5} = \frac{18}{40} = \frac{9}{20}$

$\frac{2}{5} \times \frac{2}{3} = \frac{2}{5} \times \frac{3}{2} = \frac{6}{10} = \frac{3}{5}$ $\quad \frac{5}{6} \times \frac{3}{8} = ?$

   b. Each student is confusing the multiplication algorithm with another algorithm. Which one?

31. Mr. Chen wanted to buy all the grocer's apples for a church picnic. When he asked how many apples the store had, the grocer replied, "If you added $\frac{1}{4}$, $\frac{1}{5}$, and $\frac{1}{6}$ of them, it would make 37." How many apples were in the store?

32. Seven years ago my son was one-third my age at that time. Seven years from now he will be one-half my age at that time. How old is my son?

Section 6.3 EXERCISE / PROBLEM SET B

EXERCISES

1. Illustrate the following products using the rectangular area model.

   a. $\frac{1}{4} \times \frac{3}{5}$ $\quad$ **b.** $\frac{4}{7} \times \frac{2}{3}$ $\quad$ **c.** $\frac{3}{4} \times \frac{5}{6}$

2. What multiplication problems are represented by each of the following area models? What are the products?

   a.

   b.

   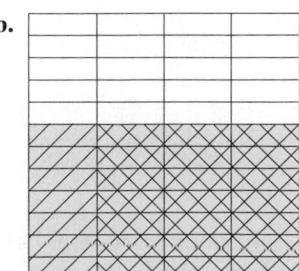

3. **a.** What is the reciprocal of the reciprocal of $\frac{4}{13}$?

   b. What is the reciprocal of the multiplicative inverse of $\frac{4}{13}$?

4. **a.** Order the following numbers from smallest to largest.

$$\frac{5}{8} \quad \frac{3}{16} \quad \frac{7}{5} \quad \frac{9}{10}$$

   b. Find the reciprocals of the given numbers and order them from smallest to largest.

   c. What do you observe about these two orders?

5. The missing-factor approach can be applied to fraction division, as illustrated.

$$\frac{4}{7} \div \frac{2}{5} = \boxed{} \quad \text{so} \quad \frac{2}{5} \times \boxed{} = \frac{4}{7}$$

Since we want $\frac{4}{7}$ to be the result, we insert that in the box. Then if we put in the reciprocal of $\frac{2}{5}$, we have

$$\frac{2}{5} \times \boxed{\frac{5}{2} \times \frac{4}{7}} = \frac{4}{7} \text{ so}$$

$$\frac{4}{7} \div \frac{2}{5} = \boxed{\frac{5}{2} \times \frac{4}{7}} = \frac{20}{14} = \frac{10}{7}$$

Use this approach to do the following division problems.

   a. $\frac{3}{5} \div \frac{2}{7}$ $\quad$ **b.** $\frac{13}{6} \div \frac{3}{7}$ $\quad$ **c.** $\frac{12}{13} \div \frac{6}{5}$

6. Find the following quotients using the most convenient of the three methods for division. Express your answer in simplest form.

   a. $\frac{5}{7} \div \frac{4}{9}$ $\quad$ **b.** $\frac{33}{14} \div \frac{11}{7}$ $\quad$ **c.** $\frac{5}{13} \div \frac{3}{13}$ $\quad$ **d.** $\frac{3}{11} \div \frac{8}{22}$

7. Perform the following operations and express your answer in simplest form.

a. $\frac{3}{5} \times \frac{4}{9}$ **b.** $\frac{2}{7} \times \frac{21}{10}$

c. $\frac{7}{100} \times \frac{11}{10,000}$ **d.** $\frac{4}{9} \times \frac{8}{11} + \frac{7}{9} \times \frac{8}{11}$

e. $\frac{3}{5} \times \frac{2}{3} + \frac{4}{7}$ **f.** $\frac{3}{5} + \frac{2}{3} \times \frac{4}{7}$

g. $\frac{3}{5} \times (\frac{2}{3} + \frac{4}{7})$ **h.** $7\frac{2}{5} \times 5\frac{4}{7}$

i. $8\frac{1}{4} \times 3\frac{4}{5}$ **j.** $\frac{9}{11} \div \frac{2}{3}$

k. $4\frac{3}{7} \div 3\frac{8}{11}$ **l.** $\frac{17}{100} \div \frac{9}{10,000}$

8. Calculate the following and express as mixed numbers in simplest form.

a. $11\frac{3}{5} \div 9\frac{8}{9}$ **b.** $7\frac{5}{8} \times 13\frac{2}{3}$ **c.** $11\frac{3}{5} \times 9\frac{8}{9}$

d. $7\frac{5}{8} \div 13\frac{2}{3}$

9. Calculate mentally using properties.

a. $52 \cdot \frac{7}{8} - 52 \cdot \frac{3}{8}$

b. $(\frac{2}{5} + \frac{5}{8}) + \frac{3}{5}$

c. $36 \times 2\frac{3}{4}$

d. $23 \cdot \frac{3}{7} + 7 + 23 \cdot \frac{4}{7}$

10. a. Does $2\frac{3}{4} + 5\frac{7}{8} = 2\frac{7}{8} + 5\frac{3}{4}$? Explain.

b. Does $2\frac{3}{4} \times 5\frac{7}{8} = 2\frac{7}{8} \times 5\frac{3}{4}$? Explain.

11. Estimate using compatible numbers.

a. $19\frac{1}{3} \times 5\frac{3}{5}$ **b.** $77\frac{1}{5} \div 23\frac{4}{5}$ **c.** $54\frac{3}{5} \div 7\frac{5}{8}$

d. $25\frac{2}{3} \times 3\frac{3}{4}$

12. Estimate using cluster estimation.

a. $5\frac{2}{3} \times 6\frac{1}{8}$

b. $3\frac{1}{10} \times 2\frac{8}{9} \times 3\frac{2}{11}$

13. Find a fraction between $\frac{2}{7}$ and $\frac{3}{8}$ in two different ways.

14. Change each of the following complex fractions into ordinary fractions.

a. $\dfrac{\frac{2}{3}}{\frac{2}{3}}$ **b.** $\dfrac{1\frac{4}{7}}{3\frac{7}{8}}$

15. Here is a shortcut for multiplying by 25:

$$25 \times 36 = \frac{100}{4} \times 36 = 100 \times \frac{36}{4} = 900.$$

Use this idea to find the following products mentally.

a. 25×44 **b.** 25×120 **c.** 25×488

d. 1248×25

Now make up your own shortcuts for multiplying by 50 and 75, and use them to compute the following products mentally.

e. 50×246 **f.** $84,602 \times 50$ **g.** 75×848

h. 420×75

16. Solve the following equations involving fractions.

a. $\frac{2}{5}x = \frac{3}{7}$ **b.** $\frac{1}{6}x = \frac{5}{12}$ **c.** $\frac{2}{9}x = \frac{7}{9}$

d. $\frac{5}{3}x = \frac{1}{10}$

17. Which of the following variations of the distributive property for fractions holds for arbitrary fractions?

a. Multiplication over subtraction

b. Subtraction over addition

18. Calculate using a fraction calculator.

a. $2 \times \frac{3}{8}$ **b.** $12 \div \frac{2}{3}$

PROBLEMS

19. According to the Container Recycling Institute, 57 billion aluminum cans were recycled in the United States in 1999. That amount was about $\frac{5}{11}$ of the total number of aluminum cans sold in the United States in 1999. How many aluminum cans were sold in the United States in 1999?

20. Kids belonging to a Boys and Girls Club collected cans and bottles to raise money by returning them for the deposit. If 54 more cans than bottles were collected and the number of bottles was $\frac{5}{11}$ of the total number of beverage containers collected, how many bottles were collected?

21. Mrs. Martin bought $20\frac{1}{4}$ yards of material to make 4 bridesmaid dresses and 1 dress for the flower girl.

The flower girl's dress needs only half as much material as a bridesmaid dress. How much material is needed for a bridesmaid dress? For the flower girl's dress?

22. In a cost-saving measure, Chuck's company reduced all salaries by $\frac{1}{8}$ of their present salaries. If Chuck's monthly salary was $2400, what will he now receive? If his new salary is $2800, what was his old salary?

23. If you place one full container of flour on one pan of a balance scale and a similar container $\frac{3}{4}$ full and a $\frac{1}{3}$- pound weight on the other pan, the pans balance. How much does the full container of flour weigh?

24. A young man spent $\frac{1}{4}$ of his allowance on a movie. He spent $\frac{11}{18}$ of the remainder on after-school snacks. Then from the money remaining, he spent \$3.00 on a magazine, which left him $\frac{1}{24}$ of his original allowance to put into savings. How much of his allowance did he save?

25. An airline passenger fell asleep halfway to her destination. When she awoke, the distance remaining was half the distance traveled while she slept. How much of the entire trip was she asleep?

26. A recipe calls for $\frac{2}{3}$ of a cup of sugar. You find that you only have $\frac{1}{2}$ a cup of sugar left. What fraction of the recipe can you make?

27. The following students are having difficulty with division of fractions. Determine what procedure they are using, and answer their final question as they would.

Abigail: $\frac{4}{6} \div \frac{2}{6} = \frac{2}{6}$

$\frac{6}{10} \div \frac{2}{10} = \frac{3}{10}$

$\frac{8}{12} \div \frac{2}{12} =$

Harold: $\frac{2}{3} \div \frac{3}{8} = \frac{3}{2} \times \frac{3}{8} = \frac{9}{16}$

$\frac{3}{4} \div \frac{5}{6} = \frac{4}{3} \times \frac{5}{6} = \frac{20}{18}$

$\frac{5}{8} \div \frac{3}{4} =$

28. **a.** A chicken and a half lays an egg and a half in a day and a half. How many eggs do 12 chickens lay in 12 days?

   b. How long will it take 3 chickens to lay 2 dozen eggs?

   c. How many chickens will it take to lay 36 eggs in 6 days?

29. Fill in the empty squares with different fractions to produce equations.

$$\boxed{1\tfrac{1}{2}} \times \boxed{1\tfrac{1}{3}} \times \boxed{} = \boxed{5\tfrac{1}{3}}$$
$$\times \qquad \times \qquad \times \qquad \times$$
$$\boxed{} \times \boxed{} \times \boxed{} = \boxed{2\tfrac{3}{16}}$$
$$\times \qquad \times \qquad \times \qquad \times$$
$$\boxed{} \times \boxed{\tfrac{2}{3}} \times \boxed{4} = \boxed{1\tfrac{1}{3}}$$
$$\| \qquad \| \qquad \| \qquad \|$$
$$\boxed{1\tfrac{7}{8}} \times \boxed{3\tfrac{1}{9}} \times \boxed{2\tfrac{2}{3}} = \boxed{}$$

30. If the sum of two numbers is 18 and their product is 40, find the following without finding the two numbers.

   a. The sum of the reciprocals of the two numbers

   b. The sum of the squares of the two numbers [*Hint*: What is $(x + y)^2$?]

31. Observe the following pattern:

$$3 + 1\tfrac{1}{2} = 3 \times 1\tfrac{1}{2}$$
$$4 + 1\tfrac{1}{3} = 4 \times 1\tfrac{1}{3}$$
$$5 + 1\tfrac{1}{4} = 5 \times 1\tfrac{1}{4}$$

   a. Write the next two equations in the list.

   b. Determine whether this pattern will always hold true. If so, explain why.

32. Using the alternative definition of "less than," prove the following statements. Assume that the product of two fractions is a fraction in part (c).

   a. If $\frac{a}{b} < \frac{c}{d}$ and $\frac{c}{d} < \frac{e}{f}$, then $\frac{a}{b} < \frac{e}{f}$.

   b. If $\frac{a}{b} < \frac{c}{d}$, then $\frac{a}{b} + \frac{e}{f} < \frac{c}{d} + \frac{e}{f}$.

   c. If $\frac{a}{b} < \frac{c}{d}$, then $\frac{a}{b} \times \frac{e}{f} < \frac{c}{d} \times \frac{e}{f}$ for any nonzero $\frac{e}{f}$.

33. How many guests were present at a dinner if every two guests shared a bowl of rice, every three guests shared a bowl of broth, every four guests shared a bowl of fowl, and 65 bowls were used altogether?

PROBLEMS FOR WRITING/DISCUSSION

1. One of your students asks you if you can draw a picture to explain what $\frac{3}{4}$ of $\frac{5}{7}$ means. What would you draw?

2. Another student asks if you can illustrate what $8 \div \frac{3}{4}$ means. What would you draw?

3. A student noticed that $9 \div 6 = \frac{3}{2}$ whereas $6 \div 9 = \frac{2}{3}$. She wonders if turning a division problem around will always give answers that are reciprocals. How would you respond?

END OF CHAPTER MATERIAL

Solution of Initial Problem

A child has a set of 10 cubical blocks. The lengths of the edges are 1 cm, 2 cm, 3 cm, ..., 10 cm. Using all the cubes, can the child build two towers of the same height by stacking one cube upon another? Why or why not?

Strategy: Solve an Equivalent Problem

This problem can be restated as an equivalent problem: Can the numbers 1 through 10 be put into two sets whose sums are equal? Answer—No! If the sums are *equal* in each set and if these two sums are added together, the resulting sum would be even. However, the sum of 1 through 10 is 55, an odd number!

Additional Problems Where the Strategy "Solve an Equivalent Problem" Is Useful

1. How many numbers are in the set $\{11, 18, 25, \ldots, 396\}$?
2. Which is larger: 2^{30} or 3^{20}?
3. Find eight fractions equally spaced between 0 and $\frac{1}{3}$ on the number line.

People in Mathematics

Evelyn Boyd Granville (1924–) Evelyn Boyd Granville was a mathematician in the Mercury and Apollo space programs, specializing in orbit and trajectory computations and computer techniques. She says that if she had foreseen the space program and her role in it, she would have been an astronomer. Granville grew up in Washington, D.C., at a time when the public schools were racially segregated. She was fortunate to attend a black high school with high standards and was encouraged to apply to the best colleges. In 1949 she graduated from Yale with a Ph.D. in mathematics, one of two black women to receive doctorates in mathematics that year and the first ever to do so. Following her work with the space program, she joined the mathematics faculty at California State University. She has written (with Jason Frand) the text *Theory and Application of Mathematics for Teachers*. "I never encountered any problems in combining career and private life. Black women have always had to work."

Paul Erdos (1913–1996) Paul Erdos was one of the most prolific mathematicians of the modern era. Erdos (pronounced "air-dish") authored or coauthored approximately 900 research papers. He was called an "itinerant mathematician" because of his penchant for traveling to mathematical conferences around the world. His achievements in number theory are legendary. At one mathematical conference, he was dozing during a lecture of no particular interest to him. When the speaker mentioned a problem in number theory, Erdos perked up and asked him to explain the problem again. The lecture then proceeded, and a few minutes later Erdos interrupted to announce that he had the solution! Erdos was also known for posing problems and offering monetary awards for their solution, from $25 to $10,000. He also was known for the many mathematical prodigies he discovered and "fed" problems to.

CHAPTER REVIEW

Review the following terms and exercises to determine which require learning or relearning—page numbers are provided for easy reference.

SECTION 6.1: The Set of Fractions

VOCABULARY/NOTATION

Numerator   218
Denominator   218
Fraction (*a*/*b*)   218
Set of fractions (*F*)   218
Equivalent fractions   219
Fraction strips   219
Simplified   220

Equal fractions   220
Cross-product   220
Cross-multiplication   220
Simplest form   221
Lowest terms   221
Improper fraction   222
Mixed number   222

Fraction number line   223
Less than (<)   223
Greater than (>)   223
Less than or equal to (≤)   223
Greater than or equal to (≥)   223
Density property   225

EXERCISES

1. Explain why a child might think that $\frac{1}{4}$ is greater than $\frac{1}{2}$.

2. Draw a sketch to show why $\frac{3}{4} = \frac{6}{8}$.

3. Explain the difference between an improper fraction and a mixed number.

4. Determine whether the following are equal. If not, determine the smaller of the two.

   a. $\frac{24}{56}, \frac{8}{19}$ b. $\frac{12}{28}, \frac{15}{35}$

5. Express each fraction in Exercise 4 in simplest form.

6. Illustrate the density property using $\frac{2}{5}$ and $\frac{5}{12}$.

SECTION 6.2: Fractions: Addition and Subtraction

VOCABULARY/NOTATION

Least common denominator
  (LCD)   232

EXERCISES

1. Use fraction strips to find the following.

   a. $\frac{1}{6} + \frac{5}{12}$ b. $\frac{7}{8} - \frac{3}{4}$

2. Find the following sum/difference, and express your answers in simplest form.

   a. $\frac{12}{27} + \frac{13}{15}$ b. $\frac{17}{25} - \frac{7}{15}$

3. Name the property of addition that is used to justify each of the following equations.

   a. $\frac{3}{7} + \frac{2}{7} = \frac{2}{7} + \frac{3}{7}$ b. $\frac{4}{15} + \frac{0}{15} = \frac{4}{15}$

   c. $\frac{2}{5} + \left(\frac{3}{5} + \frac{4}{7}\right) = \left(\frac{2}{5} + \frac{3}{5}\right) + \frac{4}{7}$

   d. $\frac{2}{5} + \frac{3}{7}$ is a fraction

4. Which of the following properties hold for fraction subtraction?

   a. Closure   b. Commutative   c. Associative
   d. Identity

5. Calculate mentally, and state your method.

   a. $5\frac{3}{8} + 3\frac{7}{8}$ b. $31 - 4\frac{7}{8}$ c. $\left(\frac{2}{7} + \frac{3}{5}\right) + \frac{5}{7}$

6. Estimate using the techniques given.

   a. Range: $5\frac{2}{3} + 7\frac{1}{6}$

   b. Rounding to the nearest $\frac{1}{2}$: $17\frac{1}{8} + 24\frac{2}{5}$

   c. Front-end with adjustment: $9\frac{3}{4} + 7\frac{2}{3} + 5\frac{1}{6}$

SECTION 6.3: Fractions: Multiplication and Division

VOCABULARY/NOTATION

Multiplicative inverse   245   Reciprocal   245   Complex fraction   250

EXERCISES

1. Use a model to find $\dfrac{2}{3} \times \dfrac{4}{5}$.

2. Find the following product/quotient, and express your answers in simplest form.

  a. $\dfrac{16}{25} \times \dfrac{15}{36}$ **b.** $\dfrac{17}{19} \div \dfrac{34}{57}$

3. Name the property of multiplication that is used to justify each of the following equations.

  a. $\dfrac{6}{7} \times \dfrac{7}{6} = 1$ **b.** $\dfrac{7}{5}\left(\dfrac{3}{4} \times \dfrac{5}{7}\right) = \left(\dfrac{7}{5} \times \dfrac{3}{4}\right)\dfrac{5}{7}$

  c. $\dfrac{5}{9} \times \dfrac{6}{6} = \dfrac{5}{9}$ **d.** $\dfrac{2}{5} \times \dfrac{3}{7}$ is a fraction.

  e. $\dfrac{3}{8}\left(\dfrac{8}{3} \times \dfrac{4}{7}\right) = \left(\dfrac{3}{8} \times \dfrac{8}{3}\right)\dfrac{4}{7}$

4. State the distributive property of fraction multiplication over addition and give an example to illustrate its usefulness.

5. Find $\dfrac{12}{25} \div \dfrac{1}{5}$ in two ways.

6. Which of the following properties hold for fraction division?

  a. Closure   **b.** Commutative   **c.** Associative

  d. Identity

7. Calculate mentally and state your method.

  a. $\dfrac{2}{3} \times (5 \times 9)$ **b.** $25 \times 2\dfrac{2}{5}$

8. Estimate using the techniques given.

  a. Range: $5\dfrac{2}{3} \times 7\dfrac{1}{6}$

  b. Rounding to the nearest $\dfrac{1}{2}$: $3\dfrac{3}{5} \times 4\dfrac{1}{7}$

PROBLEMS FOR WRITING/DISCUSSION

1. How would you respond to a student who says that fractions don't change in value if you multiply the top and bottom by the same number or add the same number to the top and bottom?

2. A student suggests that when working with fractions it is always a good idea to get common denominators. It doesn't matter if you're adding, subtracting, multiplying, or dividing. How do you respond?

3. In algebra, when you write 5 next to y, as in $5y$, there is a "secret" operation. How is that the same or different from writing 3 next to $\dfrac{1}{4}$ as in $3\dfrac{1}{4}$? How would you explain to a student what $2\dfrac{3}{5}x$ means?

4. A student told you that his previous teacher said $\dfrac{34}{9}$ is an "improper" fraction. So to make it "proper," you change it to $3\dfrac{7}{9}$. How do you react to this statement?

5. A student says that dividing always makes numbers smaller, for example, $10 \div 5 = 2$ and 2 is smaller than 10. So how could $6 \div \dfrac{1}{2} = 12$? Can you help this student make sense of this problem?

6. Can you think of an example where you could add fractions like 87/100 and 16/20 and get 103/120 as the right answer?

7. How would you explain to a student why

$\dfrac{5}{6} \times \dfrac{7}{10} \times \dfrac{3}{14}$ can be rewritten as

$\dfrac{5}{10} \times \dfrac{7}{14} \times \dfrac{3}{6}$? That is, when can you move the numerators and denominators around like this?

8. Marilyn said her family made two square pizzas at home, one 8″ on a side and the other 12″ on a side. She ate 1/4 of the small pizza and 1/6 of the larger pizza. So Marilyn says she ate 5/12 of the pizza. Do you agree? Explain.

9. When we compare fractions of two pizzas, as in the last problem, why do we consider area and not volume? Didn't Marilyn eat a three-dimensional pizza? How would you explain this?

10. Billy Joe asks "Since 0/3 = 0/4, how could you draw different pictures to represent 0/3 and 0/4?" How would you respond?

CHAPTER TEST

Knowledge

1. True or false?

   a. Every whole number is a fraction.

   b. The fraction $\frac{17}{51}$ is in simplest form.

   c. The fractions $\frac{2}{12}$ and $\frac{15}{20}$ are equivalent.

   d. Improper fractions are always greater than 1.

   e. There is a fraction less than $\frac{2}{1,000,000}$ and greater than $\frac{1}{1,000,000}$.

   f. The sum of $\frac{5}{7}$ and $\frac{3}{8}$ is $\frac{8}{15}$.

   g. The difference $\frac{4}{7} - \frac{5}{6}$ does not exist in the set of fractions.

   h. The quotient $\frac{6}{11} \div \frac{7}{13}$ is the same as the product $\frac{11}{6} \cdot \frac{7}{13}$.

2. Select two possible meanings of the fraction $\frac{3}{4}$ and explain each.

3. Identify a property of an operation that holds in the set of fractions but does not hold for the same operation on whole numbers.

Skill

4. Write the following fractions in simplest form.

   a. $\frac{12}{18}$ b. $\frac{34}{36}$ c. $\frac{34}{85}$ d. $\frac{123,123}{567,567}$

5. Write the following mixed numbers as improper fractions, and vice versa.

   a. $3\frac{5}{11}$ b. $\frac{91}{16}$ c. $5\frac{2}{7}$ d. $\frac{123}{11}$

6. Determine the smaller of each of the following pairs of fractions.

   a. $\frac{3}{4}, \frac{10}{13}$ b. $\frac{7}{2}, \frac{7}{3}$ c. $\frac{16}{92}, \frac{18}{94}$

7. Perform the following operations and write your answer in simplest form.

   a. $\frac{4}{9} + \frac{5}{12}$ b. $\frac{7}{15} - \frac{8}{25}$ c. $\frac{4}{5} \cdot \frac{15}{16}$ d. $\frac{8}{7} \div \frac{7}{8}$

8. Use properties of fractions to perform the following computations in the easiest way. Write answers in simplest form.

   a. $\frac{5}{2} \cdot (\frac{3}{4} \cdot \frac{2}{5})$ b. $\frac{4}{7} \cdot \frac{3}{5} + \frac{4}{5} \cdot \frac{3}{5}$

   c. $(\frac{13}{17} + \frac{5}{11}) + \frac{4}{17}$ d. $\frac{3}{8} \cdot \frac{5}{7} - \frac{4}{9} \cdot \frac{3}{8}$

9. Estimate the following and describe your method of estimation.

   a. $35\frac{4}{5} \div 9\frac{2}{7}$ b. $3\frac{5}{8} \times 14\frac{2}{3}$

   c. $3\frac{4}{9} + 13\frac{1}{5} + \frac{3}{13}$

Understanding

10. Using a carton of 12 eggs as a model, explain how the fractions $\frac{6}{12}$ and $\frac{12}{24}$ are distinguishable.

11. Show how the statement "$\frac{a}{c} < \frac{b}{c}$ if and only if $a < b$" can be used to verify the statement "$\frac{a}{b} < \frac{c}{d}$ if and only if $ad < bc$," where b and d are nonzero.

12. Verify the distributive property of fraction multiplication over subtraction using the distributive property of whole-number multiplication over subtraction.

13. Make a drawing that would show why $\frac{2}{3} > \frac{3}{5}$.

14. Use rectangles to explain the process of adding $\frac{1}{4} + \frac{2}{3}$.

15. Use the area model to illustrate $\frac{3}{5} \times \frac{3}{4}$.

16. Write a word problem for each of the following.

    a. $2 \times \frac{3}{4}$ b. $2 \div \frac{1}{3}$ c. $\frac{2}{5} \div 3$

17. If is one whole, then shade the following regions:

    a. $\frac{1}{4}$ b. $\frac{2}{3}$ of $\frac{1}{4}$

Problem Solving/Application

18. Notice that $\frac{2}{3} < \frac{3}{4} < \frac{4}{5}$. Show that this sequence continues indefinitely—namely, that

$$\frac{n}{n+1} < \frac{n+1}{n+2} \text{ when } n \geq 0.$$

19. An auditorium contains 315 occupied seats and was $\frac{7}{9}$ filled. How many empty seats were there?

20. Upon his death, Mr. Freespender left $\frac{1}{2}$ of his estate to his wife, $\frac{1}{8}$ to each of his two children, $\frac{1}{16}$ to each of his three grandchildren, and the remaining \$15,000 to his favorite university. What was the value of his entire estate?

21. Find three fractions that are greater than $\frac{2}{5}$ and less than $\frac{3}{7}$.

22. Inga was making a cake that called for 4 cups of flour. However, she could only find a two-thirds measuring cup. How many two-thirds measuring cups of flour will she need to make her cake?

References for Reflections from Research

BANA. J., FARREL, B., & McINTOSH, A. (1995). Error patterns in mental computation in years 3–9. In B. Atweh & S. Flavel (Eds.), MERGA 18: GALTHA, *Proceedings of the 18th annual conference* (pp. 51–56). Darwin, Australia: Northern Territory University.

BEHR, M. J., LESH, R., POST, T. R., & SILVER, E. A. (1983). Rational number concepts. In R. Lesh & M. Landau (Eds.). *Acquisition of mathematics concepts and processes* (pp. 91–126). New York: Academic Press.

GREER, B. (1988). Nonconservation of multiplication and division: Analysis of a symptom. *Journal of Mathematical Behavior, 7,* 281–298.

KOUBA, V. L., BROWN, C. A., CARPENTER, T. R., LINDQUIST, M. M., SILVER, E. A., & SWAFFORD, J. O. (1988). Results of the fourth NAEP assessment of mathematics: Number, operations, and word problems. *Arithmetic Teacher, 35*(8), 14–19.

LAMON, S. (1996). The development of unitizing: Its role in children's partitioning strategies. *Journal for Research in Mathematics Education, 27,* 170–193.

MACK, N. K. (1990). Learning fractions with understanding: Building on informal knowledge. *Journal for Research in Mathematics Education, 21,* 16–32.

MACK, N. K. (2001). Building on informal knowledge through instruction in a complex content domain: Partitioning, units, and understanding multiplication of fractions. *Journal for Research in Mathematics Education, 32,* 267–295.

POST, T. R., WACHSMUTH, I., LESH, R., & BEHR, M. J. (1985). Order and equivalence of rational numbers: A congnitive analysis. *Journal for Research in Mathematics Education, 16,* 18–36.

SOWDER, J., & SCHAPPELLE, B. (1994). Number sense making, *Arithmetic Teacher, 41*(2), 342–345.

TIROSH, D. (2000). Enhancing prospective teachers' knowledge of children's conceptions: The case of division of fractions. *Journal for Research in Mathematics Education, 31,* 5–25.

TZUR, R. (1999). An integrated study of children's construction of improper fractions and the teacher's role in promoting that learning. *Journal for Research in Mathematics Education, 30,* 390–416.

CHAPTER 7

Decimals, Ratio, Proportion, and Percent

FOCUS ON *The Golden Ratio*

he **golden ratio,** also called the **divine proportion,** was known to the Pythagoreans in 500 B.C. and has many interesting applications in geometry. The golden ratio may be found using the Fibonacci sequence, 1, 1, 2, 3, 5, 8, . . . , a_n, . . . , where a_n is obtained by adding the previous two numbers. That is, $1 + 1 = 2$, $1 + 2 = 3$, $2 + 3 = 5$, and so on. If the quotient of each consecutive pair of numbers, $\dfrac{a_n}{a_{n-1}}$, is formed, the numbers produce a new sequence. The first several terms of this new sequence are 1, 2, 1.5, 1.66 . . . , 1.6, 1.625, 1.61538 . . . , 1.61904 . . . , ... These numbers approach a decimal 1.61803 . . . , which is the golden ratio, ϕ. Technically, $\phi = \dfrac{1 + \sqrt{5}}{2}$. (Square roots are discussed in Chapter 9.)

The Parthenon

Here are a few of the remarkable properties associated with the golden ratio.

1. *Aesthetics.* In a golden rectangle, the ratio of the length to the width is the golden ratio, ϕ. Golden rectangles were deemed by the Greeks to be especially pleasing to the eye. The Parthenon at Athens can be surrounded by such a rectangle (Figure 1). Along these lines, notice how index cards are usually dimensioned 3×5 and 5×8, two pairs of numbers in the Fibonacci sequence whose quotients approximate ϕ.

Figure 1

2. *Geometric fallacy.* If one cuts out the square in Figure 2 and rearranges it into the rectangle, a surprising result regarding the areas is obtained. (Check this!) Notice that the numbers 5, 8, 13, and 21 occur. If these numbers from the Fibonacci sequence are replaced by 8, 13, 21, and 34, respectively, an even more surprising result occurs. These surprises continue when using the Fibonacci sequence. However, if the four numbers are replaced with 1, ϕ, $\phi + 1$, and $2\phi + 1$, respectively, all is in harmony.

3. *Surprising places.* Part of Pascal's triangle is shown in Figure 3. However, if carefully rearranged, the Fibonacci sequence reappears (Figure 4).

Figure 2

These are but a few of the many interesting relationships that arise from the golden ratio and its counterpart, the Fibonacci sequence.

Figure 3

Figure 4

Strategy
Work Backward

Problem Solving Strategies

1. Guess and Test
2. Use a Variable
3. Draw a Picture
4. Look for a Pattern
5. Make a List
6. Solve a Simpler Problem
7. Draw a Diagram
8. Use Direct Reasoning
9. Use Indirect Reasoning
10. Use Properties of Numbers
11. Solve an Equivalent Problem
12. **Work Backward**

Normally, when you begin to solve a problem, you probably start at the beginning of the problem and proceed "forward" until you arrive at an answer by applying appropriate strategies. At times, though, rather than start at the beginning of a problem statement, it is more productive to begin at the end of the problem statement and work backward. The following problem can be solved quite easily by this strategy.

Initial Problem

A street vendor had a basket of apples. Feeling generous one day, he gave away one-half of his apples plus one to the first stranger he met, one-half of his remaining apples plus one to the next stranger he met, and one-half of his remaining apples plus one to the third stranger he met. If the vendor had one left for himself, with how many apples did he start?

Clues

The Work Backward strategy may be appropriate when

- The final result is clear and the initial portion of a problem is obscure.
- A problem proceeds from being complex initially to being simple at the end.
- A direct approach involves a complicated equation.
- A problem involves a sequence of reversible actions.

A solution of the Initial Problem appears on page 311.

INTRODUCTION

In Chapter 6, the set of fractions was introduced to permit us to deal with parts of a whole. In this chapter we introduce decimals, which are a convenient numeration system for fractions, and percents, which are representations of fractions convenient for commerce. Then the concepts of ratio and proportion are developed because of their importance in applications throughout mathematics.

7.1 DECIMALS

STARTING POINT

The numbers .1, .10, and .100 are all equal but can be represented differently. Use base ten blocks to represent .1, .10, and .100 and demonstrate that they are, in fact, equal.

NCTM Standards 2000
Number and Operations
Grades 3–5
All students should understand the place-value structure of the base ten number system and be able to represent and compare whole numbers and decimals.

Reflection from Research
Students often have misconceptions regarding decimals. Some students see the decimal point as something that separates two whole numbers (Greer, 1987).

Decimals

Decimals are used to represent fractions in our usual base ten place-value notation. The method used to express decimals is shown in Figure 7.1.

Figure 7.1

In the figure the number 3457.968 shows that the **decimal point** is placed between the ones column and the tenths column to show where the whole-number portion ends and where the decimal (or fractional) portion begins. Decimals are read as if they were written as fractions and the decimal point is read "and." The number 3457.968 is written in its **expanded form** as

$$3(1000) + 4(100) + 5(10) + 7(1) + 9\left(\frac{1}{10}\right) + 6\left(\frac{1}{100}\right) + 8\left(\frac{1}{1000}\right)$$

From this form one can see that $3457.968 = 3457\frac{968}{1000}$ and so is read "three thousand four hundred fifty-seven *and* nine hundred sixty-eight thousandths." Note that the word *and* should only be used to indicate where the decimal point is located.

Figure 7.2 shows how a **hundreds square** can be used to represent tenths and hundredths. Notice that the large square represents 1, one vertical strip represents 0.1, and each one of the smallest squares represents 0.01.

A number line can also be used to picture decimals. The number line in Figure 7.3 shows the location of various decimals between 0 and 1.

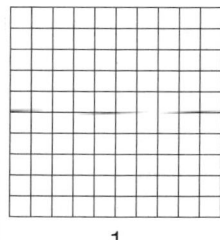

1

Figure 7.2 (Continued on next page)

1

0.4 or 4 tenths

0.07 or 7 hundredths

Figure 7.2

Figure 7.3

Example 7.1   Rewrite each of these numbers in decimal form, and state the decimal name.

a. $\frac{7}{100}$ **b.** $\frac{123}{10,000}$ **c.** $1\frac{7}{8}$

Solution

a. $\frac{7}{100} = 0.07$, read "seven hundredths"

b. $\frac{123}{10,000} = \frac{100}{10,000} + \frac{20}{10,000} + \frac{3}{10,000} = \frac{1}{100} + \frac{2}{1000} + \frac{3}{10,000} = 0.0123$, read "one hundred twenty-three ten thousandths"

c. $1\frac{7}{8} = 1 + \frac{7}{8} = 1 + \frac{7 \cdot 5 \cdot 5 \cdot 5}{2 \cdot 2 \cdot 2 \cdot 5 \cdot 5 \cdot 5} = 1 + \frac{875}{1000} =$

$1 + \frac{800}{1000} + \frac{70}{1000} + \frac{5}{1000} = 1 + \frac{8}{10} + \frac{7}{100} + \frac{5}{1000} = 1.875$,   read   "one   and eight hundred seventy-five thousandths"   ■

All of the fractions in Example 7.1 have denominators whose only prime factors are 2 or 5. Such fractions can always be expressed in decimal form, since they have equivalent fractional forms whose denominators are powers of 10. This idea is illustrated in Example 7.2.

Example 7.2   Express as decimals.

a. $\frac{3}{2^4}$ **b.** $\frac{7}{2^3 \cdot 5}$ **c.** $\frac{43}{1250}$

Solution

a. $\frac{3}{2^4} = \frac{3 \cdot 5^4}{2^4 \cdot 5^4} = \frac{1875}{10,000} = 0.1875$ **b.** $\frac{7}{2^3 \cdot 5} = \frac{7 \cdot 5^2}{2^3 \cdot 5^3} = \frac{175}{1000} = 0.175$

c. $\frac{43}{1250} = \frac{43}{2 \cdot 5^4} = \frac{43 \cdot 2^3}{2^4 \cdot 5^4} = \frac{344}{10,000} = 0.0344$ ■

Reflection from Research
Students should be encouraged to express decimal fractions with meaningful language (rather than using "point"). It is sometimes helpful to have students break fractions down into compositions of tenths; for instance, 0.35 would be read three tenths plus five hundredths rather than 35 hundredths (Resnick, Nesher, Leonard, Magone, Omanson, & Peled, 1989).

The decimals we have been studying thus far are called **terminating decimals,** since they can be represented using a finite number of nonzero digits to the right of the decimal point. We will study nonterminating decimals later in this chapter. The following result should be clear, based on the work we have done in Example 7.2.

> **● THEOREM**
>
> ### Fractions with Terminating Decimal Representations
>
> Let $\frac{a}{b}$ be a fraction in simplest form. Then $\frac{a}{b}$ has a terminating decimal representation if and only if b contains only 2s and/or 5s in its prime factorization.

Ordering Decimals

Terminating decimals can be compared using a hundreds square, using a number line, by comparing them in their fraction form, or by comparing place values one at a time from left to right just as we compare whole numbers.

Example 7.3   Determine the larger of each of the following pairs of numbers in the four ways mentioned in the preceding paragraph.
a. 0.7, 0.23   **b.** 0.135, 0.14

Solution

a. Hundreds Square: See Figure 7.4. Since more is shaded in the 0.7 square, we conclude that $0.7 > 0.23$.

Number Line: See Figure 7.5. Since 0.7 is to the right of 0.23, we have $0.7 > 0.23$.

Fraction Method: First, $0.7 = \frac{7}{10}$, $0.23 = \frac{23}{100}$. Now $\frac{7}{10} = \frac{70}{100}$ and $\frac{70}{100} > \frac{23}{100}$ since $70 > 23$. Therefore, $0.7 > 0.23$.

Place-Value Method: $0.7 > 0.23$, since $7 > 2$. The reasoning behind this method is that since $7 > 2$, we have $0.7 > 0.2$. Furthermore, in a terminating decimal, the digits that appear after the 2 cannot contribute enough to make a decimal as large as 0.3 yet have 2 in its tenths place. This technique holds for all terminating decimals.

b. Hundreds Square: The number 0.135 is one tenth plus three hundredths plus five thousandths. Since $\frac{5}{1000} = \frac{1}{200} = \frac{1}{2} \cdot \frac{1}{100}$, $13\frac{1}{2}$ squares on a hundreds square must be shaded to represent 0.135. The number 0.14 is represented by 14 squares on a hundreds square. See Figure 7.6. Since an extra half of a square is shaded in 0.14, we have $0.14 > 0.135$.

0.7

0.23

Figure 7.4

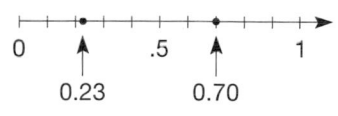

0   .5   1
0.23   0.70

Figure 7.5

0.135   0.14

Figure 7.6

0   .5   1
0.135 0.140

Figure 7.7

Number Line: See Figure 7.7. Since 0.14 is to the right of 0.135 on the number line, $0.14 > 0.135$.

Fraction Method: $0.135 = \frac{135}{1000}$ and $014. = \frac{14}{100} = \frac{140}{1000}$. Since $140 > 135$, we have $0.14 > 0.135$. Many times children will write $0.135 > 0.14$ because they know $135 > 14$ and believe that this situation is the same. It is not! Here we are comparing *decimals*, not whole numbers. A decimal comparison can be turned into a whole-number comparison by getting common denominators or, equivalently, by having the same number of decimal places. For example, $0.14 > 0.135$ since $\frac{140}{1000} > \frac{135}{1000}$, or $0.140 > 0.135$.

Place-Value Method: $0.14 > 0.135$, since (1) the tenths are equal (both are 1), but (2) the hundredths place in 0.14, namely 4, is greater than the hundredths place in 0.135, namely 3.

■

NCTM Standards 2000
Number and Operations
Grades 3–5
All students should use models, benchmarks, and equivalent forms to judge the size of fractions.

Mental Math and Estimation

The operations of addition, subtraction, multiplication, and division involving decimals are similar to the corresponding operations with whole numbers. In particular, place value plays a key role. For example, to find the sum $3.2 + 5.7$ mentally, one may add the whole-number parts, $3 + 5 = 8$, and then the tenths, $0.2 + 0.7 = 0.9$, to obtain 8.9. Observe that the whole-number parts were added first, then the tenths—that is, the addition took place from left to right. In the case of finding the sum $7.6 + 2.5$, one could add the tenths first, $0.6 + 0.5 = 1.1$, then combine this sum with $7 + 2 = 9$ to obtain the sum $9 + 1.1 = 10.1$. Thus, as with whole numbers, decimals may be added from left to right or right to left.

Before developing algorithms for operations involving decimals, some mental math and estimation techniques similar to those that were used with whole numbers and fractions will be extended to decimal calculations.

Example 7.4 Use compatible (decimal) numbers, properties, and/or compensation to calculate the following mentally.

a. $1.7 + (3.2 + 4.3)$ **b.** $(0.5 \times 6.7) \times 4$ **c.** 6×8.5
d. $3.76 + 1.98$ **e.** $7.32 - 4.94$ **f.** $17 \times 0.25 + 0.25 \times 23$

Solution

a. $1.7 + (3.2 + 4.3) = (1.7 + 4.3) + 3.2 = 6 + 3.2 = 9.2$. Here 1.7 and 4.3 are compatible numbers with respect to addition, since their sum is 6.
b. $(0.5 \times 6.7) \times 4 = 6.7 \times (0.5 \times 4) = 6.7 \times 2 = 13.4$. Since $0.5 \times 4 = 2$, it is more convenient to use commutativity and associativity to find 0.5×4 rather than to find 0.5×6.7 first.
c. Using distributivity, $6 \times 8.5 = 6(8 + 0.5) = 6 \times 8 + 6 \times 0.5 = 48 + 3 = 51$.
d. $3.76 + 1.98 = 3.74 + 2 = 5.74$ using additive compensation.
e. $7.32 - 4.94 = 7.38 - 5 = 2.38$ by equal additions.
f. $17 \times 0.25 + 0.25 \times 23 = 17 \times 0.25 + 23 \times 0.25 = (17 + 23) \times 0.25 = 40 \times 0.25 = 10$ using distributivity and the fact that 40 and 0.25 are compatible numbers with respect to multiplication. ■

Reflection from Research
Students often have difficulty understanding the equivalence between a decimal fraction and a common fraction (for instance, that 0.4 is equal to 2/5). Research has found that this understanding can be enhanced by teaching the two concurrently by using both a decimal fraction and a common fraction to describe the same situation (Owens, 1990).

Since common decimals have fraction representations, the **fraction equivalents** shown in Table 7.1 can often be used to simplify decimal calculations.

Example 7.5 Find these products using fraction equivalents.

a. 68×0.5 **b.** 0.25×48 **c.** 0.2×375
d. 0.05×280 **e.** 56×0.125 **f.** 0.75×72

Solution

a. $68 \times 0.5 = 68 \times \frac{1}{2} = 34$ **b.** $0.25 \times 48 = \frac{1}{4} \times 48 = 12$
c. $0.2 \times 375 = \frac{1}{5} \times 375 = 75$ **d.** $0.05 \times 280 = \frac{1}{20} \times 280 = \frac{1}{2} \times 28 = 14$
e. $56 \times 0.125 = 56 \times \frac{1}{8} = 7$
f. $0.75 \times 72 = \frac{3}{4} \times 72 = 3 \times \frac{1}{4} \times 72 = 3 \times 18 = 54$ ■

Table 7.1

DECIMAL	FRACTION
0.05	$\frac{1}{20}$
0.1	$\frac{1}{10}$
0.125	$\frac{1}{8}$
0.2	$\frac{1}{5}$
0.25	$\frac{1}{4}$
0.375	$\frac{3}{8}$
0.4	$\frac{2}{5}$
0.5	$\frac{1}{2}$
0.6	$\frac{3}{5}$
0.625	$\frac{5}{8}$
0.75	$\frac{3}{4}$
0.8	$\frac{4}{5}$
0.875	$\frac{7}{8}$

Multiplying and dividing decimals by powers of 10 can be performed mentally in a fashion similar to the way we multiplied and divided whole numbers by powers of 10.

Example 7.6   Find the following products and quotients by converting to fractions.

a. 3.75×10^4 **b.** 62.013×10^5 **c.** $127.9 \div 10$ **d.** $0.53 \div 10^4$

Solution

justify

a. $3.75 \times 10^4 = \frac{375}{100} \times \frac{10,000}{1} = 37,500$

b. $62.013 \times 10^5 = \frac{62013}{1000} \times \frac{100,000}{1} = 6,201,300$

c. $127.9 \div 10 = \frac{1279}{10} \div 10 = \frac{1279}{10} \times \frac{1}{10} = 12.79$

d. $0.53 \div 10^4 = \frac{53}{100} \div 10^4 = \frac{53}{100} \times \frac{1}{10,000} = 0.000053$ ■

mult (right)
divide (left)

Notice that in Example 7.6(a), multiplying by 10^4 was equivalent to moving the decimal point of 3.75 four places to the right to obtain 37,500. Similarly, in part (b), because of the 5 in 10^5, moving the decimal point five places to the right in 62.013 results in the correct answer, 6,201,300. When dividing by a power of 10, the decimal point is moved to the left an appropriate number of places. These ideas are summarized next.

> ### THEOREM
>
> #### Multiplying/Dividing Decimals by Powers of 10
>
> Let n be any decimal number and m represent any nonzero whole number. *Multiplying* a number n by 10^m is equivalent to forming a new number by moving the decimal point of n to the right m places. *Dividing* a number n by 10^m is equivalent to forming a new number by moving the decimal point of n to the left m places.

Multiplying/dividing by powers of 10 can be used with multiplicative compensation to multiply some decimals mentally. For example, to find the product $0.003 \times 41,000$, one can multiply 0.003 by 1000 (yielding 3) and then divide 41,000 by 1000 (yielding 41) to obtain the product $3 \times 41 = 123$.

Previous work with whole-number and fraction computational estimation can also be applied to estimate the results of decimal operations.

Example 7.7   Estimate each of the following using the indicated estimation techniques.
a. $\$1.57 + \$4.36 + \$8.78$ using (i) range, (ii) front-end with adjustment, and (iii) rounding techniques
b. 39.37×5.5 using (i) range and (ii) rounding techniques

Solution

a. Range: A low estimate for the range is $\$1 + \$4 + \$8 = \$13$, and a high estimate is $\$2 + \$5 + \$9 = \$16$. Thus a range estimate of the sum is $\$13$ to $\$16$.

know for Quiz

Front-end: The one-column front-end estimate is simply the low estimate of the range, namely $13. The sum of 0.57, 0.36, and 0.78 is about $1.50, so a good estimate is $14.50.

Rounding: Rounding to the nearest whole or half yields an estimate of $\$1.50 + \$4.50 + \$9.00 = \$15.00$.

b. Range: A low estimate is $30 \times 5 = 150$, and a high estimate is $40 \times 6 = 240$. Hence a range estimate is 150 to 240.

Rounding: One choice for estimating this product is to round 39.37×5.5 to 40×6 to obtain 240. A better estimate would be to round to $40 \times 5.5 = 220$. ▉

Decimals can be rounded to any specified place as was done with whole numbers.

Example 7.8 Round 56.94352 to the nearest

a. tenth   **b.** hundredth
c. thousandth   **d.** ten thousandth

Solution

a. First, $56.9 < 56.94352 < 57.0$. Since 56.94352 is closer to 56.9 than to 57.0, we round to 56.9 (Figure 7.8).

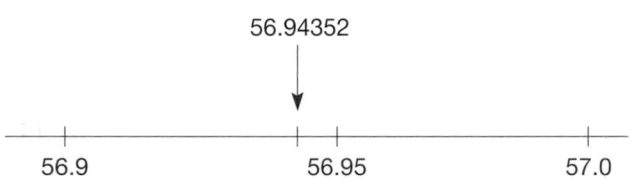

Figure 7.8

b. $56.94 < 56.94352 < 56.95$ and 56.94352 is closer to 56.94 (since $352 < 500$), so we round to 56.94.
c. $56.943 < 56.94352 < 56.944$ and 56.94352 is closer to 56.944, since $52 > 50$. Thus we round up to 56.944.
d. $56.9435 < 56.94352 < 56.9436$. Since $56.94352 < 56.94355$, and 56.94355 is the halfway point between 56.94350 and 56.94360, we round down to 56.9435. ▉

For decimals ending in a 5, we can use the "round a 5 up" method, as is usually done in elementary school. For example, 1.835, rounded to hundredths, would round to 1.84.
Perhaps the most useful estimation technique for decimals is rounding to numbers that will, in turn, yield compatible whole numbers or fractions.

Example 7.9 Estimate.

a. 203.4×47.8 **b.** $31 \div 1.93$ **c.** 75×0.24
d. $124 \div 0.74$ **e.** $0.0021 \times 44{,}123$ **f.** $3847.6 \div 51.3$

Solution

a. $203.4 \times 47.8 \approx 200 \times 50 = 10{,}000$
b. $31 \div 1.93 \approx 30 \div 2 = 15$
c. $75 \times 0.24 \approx 75 \times \frac{1}{4} \approx 76 \times \frac{1}{4} = 19$. (Note that 76 and $\frac{1}{4}$ are compatible, since 76 has a factor of 4.)
d. $124 \div 0.74 \approx 124 \div \frac{3}{4} = 124 \times \frac{4}{3} \approx 123 \times \frac{4}{3} = 164$. (123 and $\frac{3}{4}$, hence $\frac{4}{3}$, are compatible, since 123 has a factor of 3.)
e. $0.0021 \times 44{,}123 = 0.21 \times 441.23 \approx \frac{1}{5} \times 450 = 90$. (Here multiplicative compensation was used by *multiplying* 0.0021 by 100 and *dividing* 44,123 by 100.)
f. $3847.6 \div 51.3 \approx 38.476 \div 0.513 \approx 38 \div \frac{1}{2} = 76$; alternatively, $3847.6 \div 51.3 \approx 3500 \div 50 = 70$ ▉

MATHEMATICAL MORSEL

Decimal notation has evolved over the years without universal agreement. Consider the following list of decimal expressions for the fraction $\frac{3142}{1000}$.

NOTATION	DATE INTRODUCED
3 142	1522, Adam Riese (German)
3|142 } 3,142	1579, François Vieta (French)
0|1|2|3 / 3|1|4|2	1585, Simon Stevin (Dutch)
3 · 142	1614, John Napier (Scottish)

Today, Americans use a version of Napier's "decimal point" notation (3.142, where the point is on the line), the English retain the original version (3 · 142, where the point is in the middle of the line), and the French and Germans retain Vieta's "decimal comma" notation (3,142). Hence the issue of establishing a universal decimal notation remains unresolved to this day.

Section 7.1   EXERCISE / PROBLEM SET A

EXERCISES

1. Write each of the following sums in decimal form.

  a. $7(10) + 5 + 6(\frac{1}{10}) + 3(\frac{1}{1000})$

  b. $6(\frac{1}{10})^2 + 3(\frac{1}{10})^3$

  c. $3(10)^2 + 6 + 4(\frac{1}{10})^2 + 2(\frac{1}{10})^3$

2. Write each of the following decimals (i) in its expanded form and (ii) as a fraction.

  a. 0.45   **b.** 3.183   **c.** 24.2005

3. Write the following expressions as decimal numbers.

  a. Seven hundred forty-six thousand

  b. Seven hundred forty-six thousandths

  c. Seven hundred forty-six million

4. Write the following numbers in words.

  a. 0.013   **b.** 68,485.532

  c. 0.0082   **d.** 859.080509

5. Determine, without converting to decimals, which of the following fractions has a terminating decimal representation.

  a. $\frac{21}{45}$ **b.** $\frac{62}{125}$ **c.** $\frac{63}{90}$

  d. $\frac{326}{400}$ **e.** $\frac{39}{60}$ **f.** $\frac{54}{130}$

6. Decide whether the following fractions terminate in their decimal form. If a fraction terminates, tell in how many places and explain how you can tell from the fraction form.

  a. $\frac{4}{3}$ **b.** $\frac{7}{8}$ **c.** $\frac{1}{15}$ **d.** $\frac{3}{16}$

7. Arrange the following numbers in order from smallest to largest.

  a. 0.58, 0.085, 0.85

  b. 781.345, 781.354, 780.9999

  c. 4.9, 4.09, 4.99, 4.099

  d. 8.01002, 8.010019, 8.0019929

  e. 0.5, 0.505, 0.5005, 0.55

8. One method of comparing two fractions is to find their decimal representations by calculator and compare them. For example, divide the numerator by the denominator.

$$\frac{7}{12} = \boxed{0.58333333} \qquad \frac{9}{16} = \boxed{0.56250000}$$

Thus $\frac{9}{16} < \frac{7}{12}$. Use this method to compare the following fractions.

  a. $\frac{5}{9}$ and $\frac{19}{34}$ **b.** $\frac{38}{52}$ and $\frac{18}{25}$

9. A student reads the number 3147 as "three thousand one hundred and forty-seven." What is wrong with this reading?

10. Calculate mentally. Describe your method.

   a. $18.43 - 9.96$ b. $1.3 \times 5.9 + 64.1 \times 1.3$

   c. $4.6 + (5.8 + 2.4)$ d. $(0.25 \times 17) \times 8$

   e. $51.24 \div 10^3$ f. $21.28 + 17.79$

   g. $8(9.5)$ h. 0.15×10^5

11. It is possible to write any decimal as a number between 1 and 10 (including 1) times a power of 10. This scientific notation is particularly useful in expressing large numbers. For example,

$$6321 = 6.321 \times 10^3 \qquad \text{and}$$
$$760{,}000{,}000 = 7.6 \times 10^8.$$

   Write each of the following in scientific notation.

   a. 59   b. 4326

   c. 97,000   d. 1,000,000

   e. 64,020,000   f. 71,000,000,000

12. Find each of the following products and quotients.

   a. $(6.75)(1{,}000{,}000)$ b. $19.514 \div 100{,}000$

   c. $(2.96 \times 10^{16})(10^{12})$ d. $\dfrac{2.96 \times 10^{16}}{10^{12}}$

13. The nearest star (other than the sun) is Alpha Centauri, which is the brightest star in the constellation Centaurus.

   a. Alpha Centauri is 41,600,000,000,000,000 meters from our sun. Express this distance in scientific notation.

   b. Although it appears to the naked eye to be one star, Alpha Centauri is actually a double star. The two stars that comprise it are about 3,500,000,000 meters apart. Express this distance in scientific notation.

14. Calculate by using fraction equivalents.

   a. 0.25×44 b. 0.75×80

   c. 35×0.4 d. 0.2×65

   e. 65×0.8 f. 380×0.05

15. Estimate, using the indicated techniques.

   a. $4.75 + 5.91 + 7.36$; range and rounding to the nearest whole number

   b. 74.5×6.1; range and rounding

   c. $3.18 + 4.39 + 2.73$; front-end with adjustment

   d. 4.3×9.7; rounding to the nearest whole number

16. Estimate by rounding to compatible numbers and fraction equivalents.

   a. $47.1 \div 2.9$ b. 0.23×88

   c. 126×0.21 d. $56{,}324 \times 0.25$

   e. $14{,}897 \div 750$ f. 0.59×474

17. Round the following.

   a. 97.26 to the nearest tenth

   b. 345.51 to the nearest ten

   c. 345.00 to the nearest ten

   d. 0.01826 to the nearest thousandth

   e. 0.01826 to the nearest ten thousandth

   f. 0.498 to the nearest tenth

   g. 0.498 to the nearest hundredth

PROBLEMS

18. The numbers shown next can be used to form an additive magic square:

   10.48, 15.72, 20.96, 26.2, 31.44,
       36.68, 41.92, 47.16, 52.4.

   Use your calculator to determine where to place the numbers in the nine cells of the magic square.

19. Suppose that classified employees went on strike for 22 working days. One of the employees, Kathy, made $9.74 per hour before the strike. Under the old contract, she worked 240 six-hour days per year. If the new contract is for the same number of days per year, what increase in her hourly wage must Kathy receive to make up for the wages she lost during the strike in one year?

Section 7.1 EXERCISE / PROBLEM SET B

EXERCISES

1. Write each of the following sums in decimal form.
   a. $5(\frac{1}{10})^2 + 7(10) + 3(\frac{1}{10})^5$
   b. $8(\frac{1}{10}) + 3(10)^3 + 9(\frac{1}{10})^2$
   c. $5(\frac{1}{10})^3 + 2(\frac{1}{10})^2 + (\frac{1}{10})^6$

2. Write each of the following decimals (i) in its expanded form and (ii) as a fraction.
   a. 0.525   **b.** 34.007   **c.** 5.0102

3. Write the following expressions as decimal numerals.
   a. Seven hundred forty-six millionths
   b. Seven hundred forty-six thousand and seven hundred forty-six millionths
   c. Seven hundred forty-six million and seven hundred forty-six thousandths

4. Write the following numbers in words.
   a. 0.000000078   **b.** 7,589.12345
   c. 187,213.02003   **d.** 1,001,002,003.00100002

5. Determine which of the following fractions have terminating decimal representations.
   a. $\dfrac{2^4 \cdot 11^{16} \cdot 17^{19}}{5^{12}}$ **b.** $\dfrac{2^3 \cdot 3^{11} \cdot 7^9 \cdot 11^{16}}{7^{13} \cdot 11^9 \cdot 5^7}$
   c. $\dfrac{2^3 \cdot 3^9 \cdot 11^{17}}{2^8 \cdot 3^4 \cdot 5^7}$

6. Decide whether the following fractions terminate in their decimal form. If a fraction terminates, tell in how many places and explain how you can tell from the fraction form.
   a. $\dfrac{1}{11}$ **b.** $\dfrac{17}{625}$ **c.** $\dfrac{3}{12,800}$ **d.** $\dfrac{17}{2^{19} \times 5^{23}}$

7. Order each of the following from smallest to largest by changing each fraction to a decimal.
   a. $\frac{5}{7}, \frac{4}{5}, \frac{10}{13}$ **b.** $\frac{4}{11}, \frac{3}{7}, \frac{2}{5}$ **c.** $\frac{5}{9}, \frac{7}{13}, \frac{11}{18}$ **d.** $\frac{3}{5}, \frac{11}{18}, \frac{17}{29}$

8. Order each of the following from smallest to largest as simply as possible by using any combinations of the three following methods. (i) common denominators, (ii) cross-multiplication, and (iii) converting to a decimal.
   a. $\frac{5}{8}, \frac{1}{2}, \frac{17}{23}$ **b.** $\frac{13}{16}, \frac{2}{3}, \frac{3}{4}$ **c.** $\frac{8}{5}, \frac{26}{15}, \frac{50}{31}$

9. According to state law, the amount of radon released from wastes cannot exceed a 0.033 working level. A study of two locations reported a 0.0095 working level at one location and 0.0039 at a second location. Does either of these locations fail to meet state standards?

10. Calculate mentally.
    a. $7 \times 3.4 + 6.6 \times 7$ **b.** $26.53 - 8.95$
    c. $0.491 \div 10^2$ **d.** $5.89 + 6.27$
    e. $(5.7 + 4.8) + 3.2$ **f.** 67.32×10^3
    g. $0.5 \times (639 \times 2)$ **h.** 6.5×12

11. Write each of the following numbers in scientific notation.
    a. 860   **b.** 4520
    c. 26,000,000   **d.** 315,000
    e. 1,084,000,000   **f.** 54,000,000,000,000

12. Find each of the following products and quotients. Express your answers in scientific notation.
    a. 12.6416×100 **b.** $\dfrac{7.8752}{10,000,000}$
    c. $(8.25 \times 10^{20})(10^7)$ **d.** $\dfrac{8.25 \times 10^{20}}{10^7}$

13. **a.** The longest human life on record was more than 113 years, or about 3,574,000,000 seconds. Express this number of seconds in scientific notation.
    b. Some tortoises have been known to live more than 150 years, or about 4,730,000,000 seconds. Express this number of seconds in scientific notation.
    c. The oldest living plant is probably a bristlecone pine tree in Nevada; it is about 4900 years old. Its age in seconds would be about 1.545×10^{11} seconds. Express this number of seconds in standard form and write a name for it.

14. Calculate using fraction equivalents.
    a. 230×0.1 **b.** 36×0.25 **c.** 82×0.5
    d. 125×0.8 **e.** 175×0.2 **f.** 0.6×35

15. Estimate, using the indicated techniques.
    a. 34.7×3.9; range and rounding to the nearest whole number
    b. $15.71 + 3.23 + 21.95$; two-column front-end
    c. 13.7×6.1; one-column front-end and range
    d. $3.61 + 4.91 + 1.3$; front-end with adjustment

16. Estimate by rounding to compatible numbers and fraction equivalents.

    a. $123.9 \div 5.3$ **b.** 87.4×7.9

    c. $402 \div 1.25$ **d.** $34,546 \times 0.004$

    e. $0.0024 \times 470,000$ **f.** $3591 \div 0.61$

17. Round the following as specified.

    a. 321.0864 to the nearest hundredth

    b. 12.16231 to the nearest thousandth

    c. 4.009055 to the nearest thousandth

    d. 1.9984 to the nearest tenth

    e. 1.9984 to the nearest hundredth

PROBLEMS

18. Determine whether each of the following is an additive magic square. If not, change one entry so that your resulting square is magic.

a.

2.4	5.4	1.2
1.8	3	4.2
4.8	1.4	3.6

b.

0.438	0.073	0.584
0.511	0.365	0.219
0.146	0.657	0.292

19. Solve the following cryptarithm where $D = 5$.

$$
\begin{array}{r}
\text{DONALD} \\
+\text{GERALD} \\
\hline
\text{ROBERT}
\end{array}
$$

PROBLEMS FOR WRITING/DISCUSSION

1. Joseph says to read the number 357.8 as "three hundred and fifty seven and eight tenths." After being corrected, he says "Why can't I do that? Everybody knows what I mean." What would be your response?

2. Decimals are just fractions whose denominators are powers of 10. Change these decimals to fractions and add them by finding a common denominator. In what way(s) is this easier than adding fractions such as $\frac{2}{7}, \frac{5}{6},$ and $\frac{3}{4}$?

$$0.6 + 0.783 + 0.29$$

3. A student says the fraction $\frac{42}{150}$ should be a repeating decimal because the factors of the denominator include a 3 as well as 2s and 5s. But on her calculator $42 \div 150$ seems to terminate. How would you explain this?

7.2   OPERATIONS WITH DECIMALS

STARTING POINT

Many young students have the misconception that in any multiplication problem, the product is always larger than either of the factors—multiplication makes bigger. What is a problem or situation where "multiplication makes bigger" does not hold?

Similarly, many students believe that in a division problem, the quotient is always smaller than the dividend—division makes smaller. What is a problem or situation where this does not hold? Discuss where the misconception "multiplication makes bigger, division makes smaller" might come from.

Algorithms for Operations with Decimals

Algorithms for adding, subtracting, multiplying, and dividing decimals are simple extensions of the corresponding whole-number algorithms.

ADDITION

Example 7.10   Add:
a. $3.56 + 7.95$ **b.** $0.0094 + 80.183$

Solution

We will find these sums in two ways: using fractions and using a decimal algorithm.

Fraction Approach

a. $3.56 + 7.95 = \dfrac{356}{100} + \dfrac{795}{100}$

$= \dfrac{1151}{100}$

$= 11.51$

b. $0.0094 + 80.183 = \dfrac{94}{10{,}000} + \dfrac{80{,}183}{1000}$

$= \dfrac{94}{10{,}000} + \dfrac{801{,}830}{10{,}000}$

$= \dfrac{801{,}924}{10{,}000}$

$= 80.1924$ ▪

Decimal Approach   As with whole-number addition, arrange the digits in columns according to their corresponding place values and add the numbers in each column, regrouping when necessary (Figure 7.9).

This decimal algorithm can be stated more simply as "align the decimal points, add the numbers in columns as if they were whole numbers, and insert a decimal point in the answer immediately beneath the decimal points in the numbers being added." This algorithm can easily be justified by writing the two summands in their expanded form and applying the various properties for fraction addition and/or multiplication.

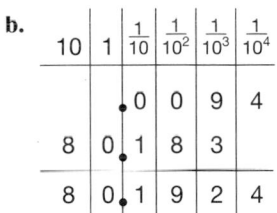

Figure 7.9

SUBTRACTION

Example 7.11   Subtract:
a. $14.793 - 8.95$ **b.** $7.56 - 0.0008$

Solution   Here we could again use the fraction approach as we did with addition. However, the usual subtraction algorithm is more efficient.

a.
Step 1: Align Decimal Points	Step 2: Subtract as if Whole Numbers	Step 3: Insert Decimal Point in Answer
14.793 − 8.95	14793 − 8950 5843	14.793 − 8.95 5.843

(NOTE: Step 2 is performed mentally—there is no need to rewrite the numbers without the decimal points.)

b. Rewrite 7.56 as 7.5600.

$$\begin{array}{r} 7.5600 \\ - \ 0.0008 \\ \hline 7.5592 \end{array}$$

▪

Now let's consider how to multiply decimals.

MULTIPLICATION

Example 7.12   Multiply 437.09×3.8.

Solution

Refer to fraction multiplication.

$$437.09 \times 3.8 = \frac{43{,}709}{100} \times \frac{38}{10} = \frac{43{,}709 \times 38}{100 \times 10}$$
$$= \frac{1{,}660{,}942}{1000} = 1660.942$$

■

Observe that when multiplying the two fractions in Example 7.12, we multiplied 43,709 and 38 (the original numbers "without the decimal points"). Thus the procedure illustrated in Example 7.12 suggests the following algorithm for multiplication.
Multiply the numbers "without the decimal points":

$$\begin{array}{r} 43{,}709 \\ \times 38 \\ \hline 1{,}660{,}942 \end{array}$$

Insert a decimal point in the answer as follows: The number of digits to the right of the decimal point in the answer is the sum of the number of digits to the right of the decimal points in the numbers being multiplied.

$$\begin{array}{r} 437.09 \\ \times 3.8 \\ \hline 1660.942 \end{array}$$

(2 digits to the right of the decimal point)
(1 digit to the right of the decimal point)
(2 + 1 digits to the right of the decimal point)

Reflection from Research
Students tend to assume that adding a zero to the end of a decimal fraction is the same as adding a zero to the end of a whole number. The most common error on a test item for which students were to write the number ten times bigger than 437.56 was 437.560 (Hiebert & Wearne, 1986).

Notice that there are three decimal places in the answer, since the product of the two denominators (100 and 10) is 10^3. This procedure can be justified by writing the decimals in expanded form and applying appropriate properties.
An alternative way to place the decimal point in the answer of a decimal multiplication problem is to do an approximate calculation. For example, 437.09×3.8 is approximately 400×4 or 1600. Hence the answer should be in the thousands—namely, 1660.942, not 16,609.42 or 16.60942, and so on.

Example 7.13   Compute: 57.98×1.371 using a calculator.

Solution First, the answer should be a little less than 60×1.4, or 84. Using a calculator we find $57.98 \; \boxed{\times} \; 1.371 \; \boxed{=} \; 79.49058$. Notice that the answer is close to the estimate of 84.

■

DIVISION

Example 7.14   Divide $154.63 \div 4.7$.

Solution

First let's estimate the answer: $155 \div 5 = 31$, so the answer should be approximately 31. Next, we divide using fractions.

$$154.63 \div 4.7 = \frac{15{,}463}{100} \div \frac{47}{10} = \frac{15{,}463}{100} \div \frac{470}{100}$$
$$= \frac{15{,}463}{470} = 32.9$$

■

Objective: Divide decimals by decimals.

 3·9

Explore Dividing Decimals by Decimals

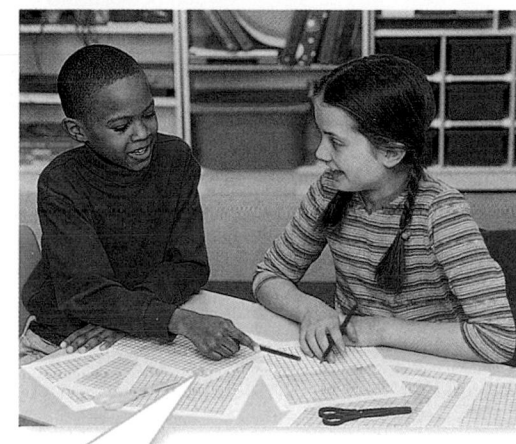

Learn

Math Word

power of 10
a number obtained by raising 10 to an exponent

Examples: $10^1 = 10$,
$10^2 = 10 \times 10 = 100$

You can use graph paper to explore dividing decimals by decimals.

Work Together

▶ Use models to find 7.5 ÷ 1.5.

You Will Need
• graph paper
• scissors

• Represent 7.5 by shading 10-by-10 grids.

• Cut off the unshaded part.

• Cut apart the 10-by-10 grids to make equal groups of 1.5.

• Count the number of groups. How many are there?

▶ Use models to divide.

| 5.2 ÷ 1.3 | 7.5 ÷ 2.5 | 5.6 ÷ 0.8 | 4 ÷ 0.4 |

Reflection from Research
Division of decimals tends to be quite difficult for students, especially when the division problem requires students to add zeros as place holders in either the dividend or the quotient (Trafton & Zawojewski, 1984).

Notice that in the fraction method, we replaced our original problem in decimals with an equivalent problem involving whole numbers:

$$154.63 \div 4.7 \rightarrow 15{,}463 \div 470.$$

Similarly, the problem $1546.3 \div 47$ also has the answer 32.9 by the missing-factor approach. Thus, as this example suggests, any decimal division problem can be replaced with an equivalent one having a whole-number divisor. This technique is usually used when performing the long-division algorithm with decimals, as illustrated next.

Example 7.15 Compute: $4.7\overline{)154.63}$.

Solution

Replace with an equivalent problem where the divisor is a whole number.

$$47\overline{)1546.3}$$

Note: Both the divisor and dividend have been multiplied by 10. Now divide as if it is whole-number division. The decimal point in the dividend is temporarily omitted.

$$
\begin{array}{r}
329 \\
47\overline{)15463} \\
-141 \\
\hline
136 \\
-94 \\
\hline
423 \\
-423 \\
\hline
0
\end{array}
$$

Replace the decimal point in the dividend, and place a decimal point in the quotient directly above the decimal point in the dividend. This can be justified using division of fractions.

$$
\begin{array}{r}
32.9 \\
47\overline{)1546.3}
\end{array}
$$

Check: $4.7 \times 32.9 = 154.63$. ■

The "moving the decimal points" step to obtain a whole-number divisor in Example 7.15 can be justified as follows:

> Let a and b be decimals.
> If $a \div b = c$, then $a = bc$.
> Then $a \cdot 10^n = bc \cdot 10^n = (b \cdot 10^n) c$ for any n.
> Thus $(a \cdot 10^n) \div (b \cdot 10^n) = c$.

This last equation shows we can multiply both a and b (the dividend and divisor) by the same power of 10 to make the divisor a whole number. This technique is similar to equal-additions subtraction except that division and multiplication are involved here.

Classifying Repeating Decimals

In Example 7.2 we observed that fractions in simplest form whose denominators are of the form $2^m \cdot 5^n$ have terminating decimal representations. Fractions of this type can also be converted into decimals using a calculator or the long-division algorithm for decimals.

Example 7.16   Express $\frac{7}{40}$ in decimal form **(a)** using a calculator and **(b)** using the long-division algorithm.

Solution

a. $7 \boxed{\div} 40 \boxed{=} \boxed{0.175}$

b.
$$
\begin{array}{r}
0.175 \\
40\overline{)7.000} \\
-4\ 0 \\
\hline
3\ 00 \\
-2\ 80 \\
\hline
200 \\
-200 \\
\hline
0
\end{array}
$$

Therefore, $\frac{7}{40} = 0.175$.   ■

Now, let's express $\frac{1}{3}$ as a decimal. Using a calculator, we obtain

$$1 \boxed{\div} 3 \boxed{=} \boxed{0.333333333}.$$

This display shows $\frac{1}{3}$ as a terminating decimal, since the calculator can display only finitely many decimal places. However, the long-division method adds some additional insight to this situation.

$$
\begin{array}{r}
0.333\ldots \\
3\overline{)1.000} \\
-\ 9 \\
\hline
10 \\
-\ 9 \\
\hline
10 \\
-\ 9 \\
\hline
1
\end{array}
$$

Using long division, we see that the decimal in the quotient will never terminate, since every remainder is 1. Similarly, the decimal for $\frac{1}{11}$ is 0.0909. . . . Instead of writing dots, a horizontal bar may be placed above the **repetend,** the first string of repeating digits. Thus

$$\frac{1}{3} = 0.\overline{3}., \qquad \frac{1}{11} = 0.\overline{09}.,$$

$$\frac{2}{7} = 0.\overline{285714}, \qquad \frac{2}{9} = 0.\overline{2},$$

$$\text{and} \quad \frac{40}{99} = 0.\overline{40}.$$

(Use your calculator or the long-division algorithm to check that these are correct.) Decimals having a repetend are called **repeating decimals.** (NOTE: Terminating decimals are those repeating decimals whose repetend is zero.) The number of digits in the repetend is called the **period** of the decimal. For example, the period of $\frac{1}{11}$ is 2. To gain additional insight into why certain decimals repeat, consider the next example.

Example 7.17 Express $\frac{6}{7}$ as a decimal.

Solution

$$
\begin{array}{r}
0.857142 \\
7\overline{)6.000000} \\
-56 \\
\hline
40 \\
-35 \\
\hline
50 \\
-49 \\
\hline
10 \\
-7 \\
\hline
30 \\
-28 \\
\hline
20 \\
-14 \\
\hline
6
\end{array}
$$

Problem-Solving Strategy
Look for a Pattern

When dividing by 7, there are seven possible remainders—0, 1, 2, 3, 4, 5, 6. Thus, when dividing by 7, either a 0 will appear as a remainder (and the decimal terminates) or one of the other nonzero remainders must eventually *reappear* as a remainder. At that point, the decimal will begin to repeat. Notice that the remainder 6 appears for a second time, so the decimal will begin to repeat at that point. Therefore, $\frac{6}{7} = 0.\overline{857142}$. Similarly, $\frac{1}{13}$ will begin repeating no later than the 13th remainder, $\frac{7}{23}$ will begin repeating by the 23rd remainder, and so on. ■

By considering several examples where the denominator has factors other than 2 or 5, the following statement will be apparent.

 THEOREM

Fractions with Repeating, Nonterminating Decimal Representations

Let $\frac{a}{b}$ be a fraction written in simplest form. Then $\frac{a}{b}$ has a repeating decimal representation that does not terminate if and only if b has a prime factor other than 2 or 5.

Earlier we saw that it was easy to express any terminating decimal as a fraction. But suppose that a number has a repeating, nonterminating decimal representation. Can we find a fractional representation for that number?

Example 7.18 Express $0.\overline{34}$ its fractional form.

Solution

Let $n = 0.\overline{34}$. Thus $100n = 34.\overline{34}$.

$$
\begin{array}{rl}
\text{Then} & 100n = 34.343434\ldots \\
- & n = .343434\ldots \\
\hline
\text{so} & 99n = 34 \\
\text{or} & n = \dfrac{34}{99}.
\end{array}
$$

■

This procedure can be applied to any repeating decimal that does not terminate, except that instead of multiplying n by 100 each time, you must multiply n by 10^m, where m is the number of digits in the repetend. For example, to express $17.\overline{531}$ in its fractional form, let $n = 17.\overline{531}$ and multiply both n and $17.\overline{531}$ by 10^3, since the repetend $.\overline{531}$ has three digits. Then $10^3 n - n = 17,531.\overline{531} - 17.\overline{531} = 17,514.$ From this we find that $n = \frac{17,514}{999}$.

Finally, we can state the following important result that links fractions and repeating decimals.

THEOREM

Every fraction has a repeating decimal representation, and every repeating decimal has a fraction representation.

The following diagram provides a visual summary of this theorem.

Fractions ⟷ Repeating Decimals

Terminating   Nonterminating
(decimals whose   (decimals whose
repetend is zero) repetend is not zero)

MATHEMATICAL MORSEL

Debugging is a term used to describe the process of checking a computer program for errors and then correcting the errors. According to legend, the process of debugging was adopted by Grace Hopper, who designed the computer language COBOL. When one of her programs was not running as it should, it was found that one of the computer components had malfunctioned and that a real bug found among the components was the culprit. Since then, if a program did not run as it was designed to, it was said to have a "bug" in it. Thus it had to be "debugged."

Section 7.2 EXERCISE / PROBLEM SET A

EXERCISES

1. a. Perform the following operations using the decimal algorithms of this section.

   i. $38.52 + 9.251$ **ii.** $534.51 - 48.67$

   b. Change the decimals in part (a) to fractions, perform the computations, and express the answers as decimals.

2. a. Perform the following operations using the algorithms of this section.

   i. 5.23×0.034 **ii.** $8.272 \div 1.76$

b. Change the decimals in part (a) to fractions, perform the computations, and express the answers as decimals.

3. Find answers on your calculator *without* using the decimal-point key. (*Hint*: Locate the decimal point by doing approximate calculations.)

   a. 48.62×52.7 **b.** $1695.76 \div 45.1$

   c. 147.21×39.7 **d.** $123,658.57 \div 17.9$

4. Mentally determine which of the following division problems have the same quotient.

a. $56\overline{)1680}$ **b.** $0.056\overline{)0.168}$ **c.** $0.56\overline{)0.168}$

5. Perform the following calculations.

a. $2.16 \times \frac{1}{3}$ **b.** $2\frac{1}{5} \times 1.55$ **c.** $16.4 \div \frac{4}{9}$

6. Using the properties of numbers and exponents, it is possible to do multiplication in scientific notation. For example,

$$\begin{aligned} 3100 \times 460 &= (3.1 \times 10^3) \times (4.6 \times 10^2) \\ &= (3.1 \times 4.6) \times (10^3 \times 10^2) \\ &= 14.26 \times 10^5 \\ &= 1.426 \times 10^1 \times 10^5 \\ &= 1.426 \times 10^6. \end{aligned}$$

Find the following products, and express answers in scientific notation.

a. $(6.2 \times 10^1) \times (5.9 \times 10^4)$

b. $(7.1 \times 10^2) \times (8.3 \times 10^6)$

7. Quotients in scientific notation can be found as follows:

$$\begin{aligned} \frac{5.27 \times 10^2}{8.5 \times 10^2} &= \frac{5.27}{8.5} \times \frac{10^6}{10^2} \\ &= 0.62 \times 10^4 \\ &= 0.62 \times 10 \times 10^3 \\ &= 6.2 \times 10^3. \end{aligned}$$

Find the following quotients, and express the answers in scientific notation.

a. $\dfrac{1.612 \times 10^5}{3.1 \times 10^2}$ **b.** $\dfrac{8.019 \times 10^9}{9.9 \times 10^5}$

8. A scientific calculator can be used to perform calculations with numbers written in scientific notation. The $\boxed{\text{SCI}}$ key or $\boxed{\text{EE}}$ key is used as shown in the following multiplication example:

$(3.41 \times 10^{12})(4.95 \times 10^8)$.

$3.41 \boxed{\text{SCI}} \; 12 \boxed{\times} \; 4.95 \boxed{\text{SCI}} \; 8 \boxed{=} \boxed{1.68795 \; 21}$

So the product is 1.68795×10^{21}.

Try this example on your calculator. The sequence of steps and the appearance of the result may differ slightly from what was shown. Consult your manual if necessary. Use your calculator to find the following products and quotients. Express your answers in scientific notation.

a. $(7.19 \times 10^6)(1.4 \times 10^8)$ **b.** $\dfrac{6.4 \times 10^{24}}{5.0 \times 10^{10}}$

9. The Earth's oceans have a total volume of approximately 1,286,000,000 cubic kilometers. The volume of fresh water on the Earth is approximately 35,000,000 cubic kilometers.

a. Express each of these volumes in scientific notation.

b. The volume of salt water in the oceans is about how many times greater than the volume of fresh water on the Earth?

10. Write each of the following using a bar over the repetend.

a. $0.7777\ldots$ **b.** $0.47121212\ldots$

c. $0.181818\ldots$ **d.** 0.35

e. $0.14141414\ldots$ **f.** $0.45315961596\ldots$

11. Write out the first 12 decimal places of each of the following.

a. $0.3\overline{174}$ **b.** $0.31\overline{74}$ **c.** $0.317\overline{4}$

12. Express each of the following repeating decimals as a fraction in simplest form.

a. $0.\overline{16}$ **b.** $0.\overline{387}$ **c.** $0.7\overline{25}$

PROBLEMS

13. The star Deneb is approximately 1.5×10^{19} meters from Earth. A light year, the distance that light travels in one year, is about 9.46×10^{15} meters. What is the distance from Earth to Deneb measured in light years?

14. Is the decimal expansion of 151/7,018,923,456,413 terminating or nonterminating? How can you tell without computing the decimal expansion?

15. Give an example of a fraction whose decimal expansion terminates in the following numbers of places.

a. 3   **b.** 4   **c.** 8   **d.** 17

16. From the fact that $0.\overline{1} = \frac{1}{9}$, mentally convert the following decimals into fractions.

a. $0.\overline{3}$ **b.** $0.\overline{5}$ **c.** $0.\overline{7}$ **d.** $2.\overline{8}$ **e.** $5.\overline{9}$

17. From the fact that $0.\overline{01} = \frac{1}{99}$, mentally convert the following decimals into fractions.

a. $0.\overline{03}$ **b.** $0.\overline{05}$ **c.** $0.\overline{07}$

d. $0.\overline{37}$ **e.** $0.\overline{64}$ **f.** $5.\overline{97}$

18. From the fact that $0.\overline{001} = \frac{1}{999}$, mentally convert the following decimals into fractions.

a. $0.\overline{003}$ **b.** $0.\overline{005}$ **c.** $0.\overline{007}$

d. $0.\overline{019}$ **e.** $0.\overline{827}$ **f.** $3.\overline{217}$

19. a. Use the pattern you have discovered in Problems 16 to 18 to convert the following decimals into fractions. Do mentally.

i. $0.\overline{23}$ **ii.** $0.0\overline{10}$ **iii.** $0.\overline{769}$
iv. $0.\overline{9}$ **v.** $0.5\overline{7}$ **vi.** $0.1\overline{827}$

b. Verify your answers by using the method taught in the text for converting repeating decimals into fractions using a calculator.

20. a. Give an example of a fraction whose decimal representation has a repetend containing exactly five digits.

b. Characterize all fractions whose decimal representations are of the form $0.\overline{abcde}$, where a, b, c, d, and e are arbitrary digits 0 through 9 and not all five digits are the same.

21. a. What is the 11th digit to the right of the decimal in the decimal expansion of $\frac{1}{13}$?

b. What is the 33rd digit of $\frac{1}{13}$?

c. What is the 2731st digit of $\frac{1}{13}$?

d. What is the 11,000,000th digit of $\frac{1}{13}$?

22. From the observation that $100 \times \frac{1}{71} = \frac{100}{71} = 1\frac{29}{71}$, what conclusion can you draw about the relationship between the decimal expansions of $\frac{1}{71}$ and $\frac{29}{71}$?

23. It may require some ingenuity to calculate the following number on an inexpensive four-function calculator. Explain why, and show how one can, in fact, calculate it.

$$\frac{364 \times 363 \times 362 \times 361 \times 360 \times 359}{365 \times 365 \times 365 \times 365 \times 365 \times 365}$$

24. Gary cashed a check from Joan for $29.35. Then he bought two magazines for $1.95 each, a book for $5.95, and a tape for $5.98. He had $21.45 left.

How much money did he have before cashing the check?

25. Each year a car depreciates to about 0.8 of its value the year before. What was the original value of a car that is worth $16,000 at the end of 3 years?

26. A regional telephone company advertises calls for $.11 a minute. How much will an hour and 21 minute call cost?

27. Juanita's family's car odometer read 32,576.7 at the beginning of the trip and 35,701.2 at the end. If $98.60 worth of gasoline at $1.01 per gallon was purchased during the trip, how many miles per gallon (to the nearest mile) did they average?

28. In 2001, the exchange rate for the Japanese yen was 120 yen per U.S. dollar. How many dollars should one receive in exchange for 10,000 yen (round to the nearest hundredth)?

29. A typical textbook measures 8 inches by 10 inches. There are exactly 2.54 centimeters per inch. What are the dimensions of a textbook in centimeters?

30. Inflation causes prices to increase about .03 per year. If a textbook costs $89 in 2002, what would you expect the book to cost in 2006 (round to the nearest dollar)?

31. Sport utility vehicles advertise the following engine capacities: a 2.4-liter 4-cylinder, a 3.5-liter V-6, a 4.9-liter V-8, and a 6.8-liter V-10. Compare the capacities of these engines in terms of liters per cylinder.

32. Three nickels, one penny, and one dime are placed as shown. You may move only one coin at a time, to an adjacent empty square. Move the coins so that the penny and the dime have exchanged places and the lower middle square is empty. Try to find the minimum number of such moves.

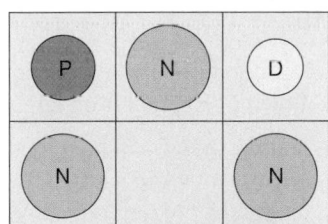

Section 7.2 EXERCISE / PROBLEM SET B

EXERCISES

1. Perform the following operations using the decimal algorithms of this section.

a. $7.482 + 94.3$ **b.** $100.63 - 72.495$

c. $0.08 + 0.1234$ **d.** $24 - 2.099$

2. Perform the following operations using the decimal algorithms of this section.

a. 16.4×2.8 **b.** 0.065×1.92

c. $44.4 \div 0.3$ **d.** $129.168 \div 4.14$

3. Find answers on your calculator *without* using the decimal-point key. (*Hint*: Locate the decimal point by doing approximate calculations.)

a. 473.92×49.12 **b.** $479,658.307 \div 374.9$

c. 97.77×2382.3 **d.** $537,978.4146 \div 1379.4$

4. Mentally determine which of the following division problems have the same quotient.

   a. $5.6\overline{)16.8}$ **b.** $0.056\overline{)1.68}$ **c.** $0.56\overline{)16.8}$

5. Perform the following calculations.

   a. $\frac{1}{4} + 0.373$ **b.** $5.21 + 3\frac{2}{5}$ **c.** $0.923 - \frac{1}{8}$

6. Perform the following operations, and express answers in scientific notation.

   a. $(2.3 \times 10^2) \times (3.5 \times 10^4)$

   b. $(7.3 \times 10^3) \times (8.6 \times 10^6)$

   c. $\dfrac{9.02 \times 10^5}{2.2 \times 10^3}$ **d.** $\dfrac{5.561 \times 10^7}{6.7 \times 10^2}$

7. Find the following quotients, and express the answers in scientific notation.

   a. $\dfrac{1.357 \times 10^{27}}{2.3 \times 10^3}$ **b.** $\dfrac{4.894689 \times 10^{23}}{5.19 \times 10^{18}}$

8. Use your calculator to find the following products and quotients. Express your answers in scientific notation.

   a. $(1.2 \times 10^{10})(3.4 \times 10^{12})(8.5 \times 10^{17})$

   b. $\dfrac{(4.56 \times 10^9)(7.0 \times 10^{21})}{(1.2 \times 10^6)(2.8 \times 10^{10})}$

   c. $(3.6 \times 10^{18})^3$

9. At a height of 8.488 kilometers, the highest mountain in the world is Mount Everest in the Himalayas. The deepest part of the oceans is the Marianas Trench in

the Pacific Ocean, with a depth of 11.034 kilometers. What is the vertical distance from the top of the highest mountain in the world to the deepest part of the oceans?

10. Determine whether the following are equal. If not, which is smaller, and why?

    $$0.25\overline{25} \qquad 0.2\overline{525}$$

11. Write out the first 12 decimal places of each of the following.

    a. $0.3\overline{174}$ **b.** $0.3\overline{174}$ **c.** $0.1\overline{159123}$

12. Express each of the following decimals as fractions.

    a. $0.\overline{5}$ **b.** $0.\overline{78}$ **c.** $0.1\overline{23}$

    d. $0.12\overline{4}$ **e.** $0.01\overline{78}$ **f.** $0.123\overline{456}$

13. The amount of gold in the Earth's crust is about 120,000,000,000,000 kilograms.

    a. Express this amount of gold in scientific notation.

    b. The market value of gold in December 2001 was about $9800 per kilogram. What was the total market value of all the gold in the Earth's crust at that time?

    c. The total U.S. national debt in December 2001 was about 6×10^{12}. How many times would the value of the gold pay off the national debt?

    d. If there were about 280,000,000 people in the United States in December 2001, how much do each of us owe on the national debt?

PROBLEMS

14. Without doing any written work or using a calculator, order the following numbers from largest to smallest.

    $$x = 0.00000456789 \div 0.00000987654$$
    $$y = 0.00000456789 \times 0.00000987654$$
    $$z = 0.00000456789 + 0.00000987654$$

15. Look for a pattern in each of the following sequences of decimal numbers. For each one, write what you think the next two terms would be.

    a. $11.5, 14.7, 17.9, 21.1, \ldots$

    b. $24, 33.6, 47.04, 65.856, \ldots$

    c. $0.5, 0.05, 0.055, 0.0055, 0.00555, \ldots$

    d. $0.5, 0.6, 1.0, 1.9, 3.5, 6.0, \ldots$

    e. $1.0, 0.5, 0.\overline{6}, 0.75, 0.8, \ldots$

16. In Chapter 3 a palindrome was defined to be a number such as 343 that reads the same forward and

backward. A process of reversing the digits of any number and adding until a palindrome is obtained was described. The same technique works for decimal numbers, as shown next.

$$
\begin{array}{ll}
\quad 7.95 & \\
+59.7 & \textit{Step 1} \\
\hline
\ 67.65 & \\
+56.76 & \textit{Step 2} \\
\hline
124.41 & \\
+14.421 & \textit{Step 3} \\
\hline
138.831 & \textit{A palindrome}
\end{array}
$$

   a. Determine the number of steps required to obtain a palindrome from each of the following numbers.

   i. 16.58 **ii.** 217.8

   iii. 1.0097 **iv.** 9.63

   b. Find a decimal number that requires exactly four steps to give a palindrome.

17. a. Express each of the following as fractions.

    i. $0.\overline{1}$ **ii.** $0.\overline{01}$

    iii. $0.\overline{001}$ **iv.** $0.\overline{0001}$

  b. What fraction would you expect to be given by 0.000000001?

  c. What would you expect the decimal expansion of $\frac{1}{90}$ to be?

18. Change $0.\overline{9}$ to a fraction. Can you explain your result?

19. Consider the decimals: $a_1 = 0.9$, $a_2 = 0.99$, $a_3 = 0.999$, $a_4 = 0.9999$, ..., $a_n = 0.999 \ldots 9$ (with n digits of 9).

  a. Give an argument that $0 < a_n < a_{n+1} < 1$ for each n.

  b. Show that there is a term a_n in the sequence such that

$$1 - a_n < \frac{1}{10^{100}}.$$

    (Find a value of n that works.)

  c. Give an argument that the sequence of terms gets arbitrarily close to 1. That is, for any distance d, no matter how small, there is a term a_n in the sequence such that $1 - d < a_n < 1$.

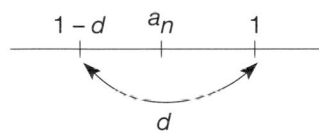

  d. Use parts (a) to (c) to explain why $0.\overline{9} = 1$.

20. a. Write $\frac{1}{7}, \frac{2}{7}, \frac{3}{7}, \frac{4}{7}, \frac{5}{7}$, and $\frac{6}{7}$ in their decimal expansion form. What do the repetends for each expansion have in common?

  b. Write $\frac{1}{13}, \frac{2}{13}, \frac{3}{13}, \ldots, \frac{11}{13}$, and $\frac{12}{13}$ in decimal expansion form. What observations can you make about the repetends in these expansions?

21. Characterize all fractions a/b, $a < b$, whose decimal expansions consist of n random digits to the right of the decimal followed by a five-digit repetend. For example, suppose that $n = 7$; then $0.213567\overline{451139}$ would be the decimal expansion of such a fraction.

22. If $\frac{9}{13} = 0.\overline{3913043478260869565217}$, what is the 999th digit to the right of the decimal?

23. Name the digit in the 4321st place of each of the following decimals.

  a. $0.\overline{142857}$ **b.** $0.1234567891011121314\ldots$

24. What happened to the other $\frac{1}{4}$?

16.5	$16\frac{1}{2}$	
×12.5	× $12\frac{1}{2}$	
8.25	32	
33	160	
165	$8\frac{1}{4}$	(one half of $16\frac{1}{2}$)
206.25	$6\frac{1}{4}$	(one half of $12\frac{1}{2}$)
	$206\frac{1}{2}$	

25. The weight in grams, to the nearest hundredth, of a particular sample of toxic waste was 28.67 grams.

  a. What is the minimum amount the sample could have weighed? (Write out your answer to the ten-thousandths place.)

  b. What is the maximum amount? (Write out your answer to the ten-thousandths place.)

26. A map shows a scale of 1 in. = 73.6 mi.

  a. How many miles would 3.5 in. represent?

  b. How many inches would represent 576 miles (round to the nearest tenth)?

27. If you invest $7500 in a mutual fund at $34.53 per share, how much profit would you make if the price per share increases to $46.17?

28. A casino promises a payoff on its slot machines of 93 cents on the dollar. If you insert 188 quarters one at a time, how much would you expect to win?

29. Your family takes a five-day trip logging the following miles and times: (503 mi, 9 hr), (480 mi, 8.5 hr), (465 mi, 7.75 hr), (450 mi, 8.75 hr), and (490 mi, 9.75 hr). What was the average speed (to the nearest mile per hour) of the trip?

30. The total value of any sum of money that earns interest at 9% per year doubles about every 8 years. What amount of money invested now at 9% per year will accumulate to about $120,000 in about 40 years (assuming no taxes are paid on the earnings and no money is withdrawn)?

31. An absentminded bank teller switched the dollars and cents when he cashed a check for Mr. Spencer, giving him dollars instead of cents, and cents instead of dollars. After buying a 5-cent newspaper, Mr. Spencer discovered that he had left exactly twice as much as his original check. What was the amount of the check?

PROBLEMS FOR WRITING/DISCUSSION

1. Mary Lou says that 50 times 4.68 is the same as 0.50 times 468, so she can just take half of 468, which is 234. Can she do this? How could she find 500 times 8.52 in a similar way? Explain.

2. When changing $7.\overline{452}$ to a fraction. Henry set $n = 7.\overline{452}$, then multiplied both sides by 100, but

when he went to subtract he got another repeating decimal. How could you help?

3. Barry said that to find $\frac{1}{3}$ of a number, he just had to multiply by 0.3, so that $\frac{1}{3}$ of 54, for example, would equal 16.2. Do you agree with Barry? Explain.

7.3   RATIO AND PROPORTION

STARTING POINT

For his construction project, José needed to cut some boards into two pieces A and B so that piece A is $\frac{1}{3}$ as big as piece B. For this situation, discuss the following questions:

1. Piece A is how much of the board?
2. Piece B is _____ times as big as piece A?
3. What is the ratio of piece A to piece B?

Repeat for the following two situations:
Piece A is $\frac{3}{4}$ as big as piece B
Piece A is $\frac{2}{5}$ as big as piece B

Ratio

The concept of ratio occurs in many places in mathematics and in everyday life, as the next example illustrates.

Example 7.19
a. In Washington School, the ratio of students to teachers is $17:1$, read "17 to 1."
b. In Smithville, the ratio of girls to boys is $3:2$.
c. A paint mixture calls for a $5:3$ ratio of blue paint to red paint.
d. The ratio of centimeters to inches is $2.54:1$.   ■

In this chapter the numbers used in ratios will be whole numbers, fractions, or decimals representing fractions. Ratios involving real numbers are studied in Chapter 9.

In English, the word *per* means "for every" and indicates a ratio. For example, rates such as miles per gallon (gasoline mileage), kilometers per hour (speed), dollars per hour (wages), cents per ounce (unit price), people per square mile (population density), and percent are all ratios.

 DEFINITION

Ratio

A **ratio** is an ordered pair of numbers, written $a:b$, with $b \neq 0$.

Unlike fractions, there are instances of ratios in which b could be zero. For example, the ratio of men to women on a starting major league baseball team could be reported as $9:0$. However, since such applications are rare, the definition of the ratio $a:b$ excludes cases in which $b = 0$.

G G G
　B B

Figure 7.10

Reflection from Research
Children understand the effects of changes to parts on an uncounted whole before they start school, and this understanding is not utilized for up to 2 years in school (Irwin, 1996).

Ratios allow us to compare the relative sizes of two quantities. This comparison can be represented by the ratio symbol $a{:}b$ or as the quotient $\frac{a}{b}$. Quotients occur quite naturally when we interpret ratios. In Example 7.19(a), there are $\frac{1}{17}$ as many teachers as students in Washington School. In part (b) there are $\frac{3}{2}$ as many girls as boys in Smithville. We could also say that there are $\frac{2}{3}$ as many boys as girls, or that the ratio of boys to girls is $2{:}3$. This is illustrated in Figure 7.10.

Notice that there are several ratios that we can form when comparing the population of boys and girls in Smithville, namely $2{:}3$ (boys to girls), $3{:}2$ (girls to boys), $2{:}5$ (boys to children), $5{:}3$ (children to girls), and so on. Some ratios give a **part-to-part** comparison, as in Example 7.19(c). In mixing the paint, we would use 5 units of blue paint and 3 units of red paint. (A unit could be any size—milliliter, teaspoon, cup, and so on.) Ratios can also represent the comparison of **part-to-whole** or **whole-to-part**. In Example 7.19(b) the ratio of boys (part) to children (whole) is $2{:}5$. Notice that the part-to-whole ratio, $2{:}5$, is the same concept as the fraction of the children that are boys, namely $\frac{2}{5}$. The comparison of all the children to the boys can be expressed in a whole-to-part ratio as $5{:}2$, or as the fraction $\frac{5}{2}$.

In Example 7.19(b), the ratio of girls to boys indicates only the *relative* sizes of the populations of girls and boys in Smithville. There could be 30 girls and 20 boys, 300 girls and 200 boys, or some other pair of numbers whose ratio is equivalent. It is important to note that ratios always represent relative, rather than absolute, amounts. In many applications, it is useful to know which ratios represent the same relative amounts. Consider the following example.

Example 7.20　In class 1 the ratio of girls to boys is $8{:}6$. In class 2 the ratio is $4{:}3$. Suppose that each class has 28 students. Do these ratios represent the same relative amounts?

Solution　Notice that the classes can be grouped in different ways (Figure 7.11).

Class 1:　GGGG　　GGGG │ GGGG　　GGGG
　　　　　　BBB　　　BBB │　BBB　　　BBB　　Ratio 8:6

Class 2:　GGGG │ GGGG │ GGGG │ GGGG
　　　　　　BBB │　BBB │　BBB │　BBB　　Ratio 4:3

Figure 7.11

The subdivisions shown in Figure 7.11 do not change the relative number of girls to boys in the groups. We see that in both classes there are 4 girls for every 3 boys. Hence we say that, as ordered pairs, the ratios $4{:}3$ and $8{:}6$ are equivalent, since they represent the same relative amount. They are equivalent to the ratio $16{:}12$. ■

From Example 7.20 it should be clear that the ratios $a{:}b$ and $ar{:}br$, where $r \neq 0$, represent the same relative amounts. Using an argument similar to the one used with fractions, we can show that the ratios $a{:}b$ and $c{:}d$ represent the same relative amounts if and only if $ad = bc$. Thus we have the following definition.

 DEFINITION

Equality of Ratios

Let $\dfrac{a}{b}$ and $\dfrac{c}{d}$ be any two ratios. Then $\dfrac{a}{b} = \dfrac{c}{d}$ if and only if $ad = bc$.

Just as with fractions, this definition can be used to show that if n is a nonzero number, then $\dfrac{an}{bn} = \dfrac{a}{b}$, or $an:bn = a:b$. In the equation $\dfrac{a}{b} = \dfrac{c}{d}$, a and d are called the **extremes,** since a and d are at the "extremes" of the equation $a:b = c:d$, while b and c are called the **means.** Thus the equality of ratios states that two ratios are equal if and only if the product of the means equals the product of the extremes.

Proportion

The concept of proportion is useful in solving problems involving ratios.

 DEFINITION

Proportion

A **proportion** is a statement that two given ratios are equal.

The equation $\dfrac{10}{12} = \dfrac{5}{6}$ is a proportion since $\dfrac{10}{12} = \dfrac{5 \cdot 2}{6 \cdot 2} = \dfrac{5}{6}$. Also, the equation $\frac{14}{21} = \frac{22}{33}$ is an example of a proportion, since $14 \cdot 33 = 21 \cdot 22$. In general, $\dfrac{a}{b} = \dfrac{c}{d}$ is a proportion if and only if $ad = bc$. The next example shows how proportions are used to solve everyday problems.

Example 7.21   Adams School orders 3 cartons of chocolate milk for every 7 students. If there are 581 students in the school, how many cartons of chocolate milk should be ordered?

Solution   Set up a proportion using the ratio of cartons to students. Let n be the unknown number of cartons. Then

$$\frac{3 \ (\text{cartons})}{7 \ (\text{students})} = \frac{n \ (\text{cartons})}{581 \ (\text{students})}.$$

Using the cross-multiplication property of ratios, we have that

$$3 \times 581 = 7 \times n,$$

so

$$n = \frac{3 \times 581}{7} = 249.$$

The school should order 249 cartons of chocolate milk.   ■

In Example 7.21, the number of cartons of milk was compared with the number of students. Ratios involving different units (here cartons to students) are called **rates.** Commonly used rates include miles per gallon, cents per ounce, and so on.

When solving proportions like the one in Example 7.21, it is important to set up the ratios in a consistent way according to the units associated with the numbers. In our solution, the ratios $3:7$ and $n:581$ represented ratios of *cartons of chocolate milk* to *students in the school.* The following proportion could also have been used.

Reflection from Research
Sixth-grade students "seem able to generalize the arithmetic that they know well, but they have difficulty generalizing the arithmetic with which they are less familiar. In particular, middle school students would benefit from more experiences with a rich variety of multiplicative situations, including proportionality, inverse variation and exponentiation" (Swafford & Langrall, 2000).

**NCTM Standards 2000
Number and Operations
Grades 6–8**
All students should develop, analyze, and explain methods for solving problems involving proportions such as scaling and finding equivalent ratios.

Reflection from Research
When asked to solve a variety of ratio and proportion tasks, students recognize the need for noninteger numbers and will develop understanding of multiplicative concepts in addition to ratio and proportion concepts (Lo & Watanabe, 1997).

$$\frac{3\left(\begin{array}{c}\text{cartons of chocolate}\\\text{milk in the ratio}\end{array}\right)}{n\left(\begin{array}{c}\text{cartons of chocolate}\\\text{milk in school}\end{array}\right)} = \frac{7\left(\begin{array}{c}\text{students}\\\text{in the ratio}\end{array}\right)}{581\left(\begin{array}{c}\text{students}\\\text{in school}\end{array}\right)}$$

Here the numerators show the original ratio. (Notice that the proportion $\frac{3}{n} = \frac{581}{7}$ would *not* correctly represent the problem, since the units in the numerators and denominators would not correspond.)

In general, the following proportions are equivalent (i.e., have the same solutions). This can be justified by cross-multiplication.

$$\frac{a}{b} = \frac{c}{d} \qquad \frac{a}{c} = \frac{b}{d} \qquad \frac{b}{a} = \frac{d}{c} \qquad \frac{c}{a} = \frac{d}{b}$$

Thus there are several possible correct proportions that can be established when equating ratios.

Example 7.22 A recipe calls for 1 cup of mix, 1 cup of milk, the whites from 4 eggs, and 3 teaspoons of oil. If this recipe serves 6 people, how many eggs are needed to make enough for 15 people?

Solution When solving proportions, it is useful to list the various pieces of information as follows:

	ORIGINAL RECIPE	NEW RECIPE
Number of eggs	4	x
Number of people	6	15

Thus $\frac{4}{6} = \frac{x}{15}$. This proportion can be solved in two ways.

CROSS-MULTIPLICATION	EQUIVALENT RATIOS
$\frac{4}{6} = \frac{x}{15}$	$\frac{4}{6} = \frac{x}{15}$
$4 \cdot 15 = 6x$	$\frac{4}{6} = \frac{2 \cdot 2}{2 \cdot 3} = \frac{2}{3} = \frac{2 \cdot 5}{3 \cdot 5} = \frac{10}{15} = \frac{x}{15}$
$60 = 6x$	Thus $x = 10$.
$10 = x$	

Notice that the table in Example 7.22 showing the number of eggs and people can be used to set up three other equivalent proportions:

$$\frac{4}{x} = \frac{6}{15} \qquad \frac{x}{4} = \frac{15}{6} \qquad \frac{6}{4} = \frac{15}{x}.$$

Example 7.23 If your car averages 29 miles per gallon, how many gallons should you expect to buy for a 609-mile trip?

Solution

	AVERAGE	TRIP
Miles	29	609
Gallons	1	x

Therefore, $\dfrac{29}{1} = \dfrac{609}{x}$, or $\dfrac{x}{1} = \dfrac{609}{29}$. Thus $x = 21$. ■

Example 7.24   In a scale drawing, 0.5 centimeter represents 35 miles.
a. How many miles will 4 centimeters represent?
b. How many centimeters will represent 420 miles?

Solution

a.

	SCALE	ACTUAL
Centimeters	0.5	4
Miles	35	x

Thus, $\dfrac{0.5}{35} = \dfrac{4}{x}$. Solving, we obtain $x = \dfrac{35 \cdot 4}{0.5}$, or $x = 280$.

b.

	SCALE	ACTUAL
Centimeters	0.5	y
Miles	35	420

Thus, $\dfrac{0.5}{35} = \dfrac{y}{420}$, or $\dfrac{0.5 \times 420}{35} = y$. Therefore, $y = \dfrac{210}{35} = 6$ centimeters. ■

Example 7.24 could have been solved mentally by using the following mental technique called **scaling up/scaling down;** that is, by multiplying/dividing each number in a ratio by the same number. In Example 7.24(a) we can scale up as follows:

$$0.5 \text{ centimeter} : 35 \text{ miles} = 1 \text{ centimeter} : 70 \text{ miles}$$
$$= 2 \text{ centimeters} : 140 \text{ miles}$$
$$= 4 \text{ centimeters} : 280 \text{ miles}.$$

Similarly, the number of centimeters representing 420 miles in Example 7.24(b) could have been found mentally by scaling up as follows:

$$35 \text{ miles} : 0.5 \text{ centimeter} = 70 \text{ miles} : 1 \text{ centimeter}$$
$$= 6 \times 70 \text{ miles} : 6 \times 1 \text{ centimeters}.$$

Thus, 420 miles is represented by 6 centimeters.

In Example 7.22, to solve the proportion $4:6 = x:15$, the ratio $4:6$ was scaled down to $2:3$, then $2:3$ was scaled up to $10:15$. Thus $x = 10$.

Example 7.25 Two neighbors were trying to decide whether their property taxes were fair. The assessed value of one house was $175,800 and its tax bill was $2777.64. The other house had a tax bill of $3502.85 and was assessed at $189,300. Were the two houses taxed at the same rate?

Solution Since the ratio of property taxes to assessed values should be the same, the following equation should be a proportion:

$$\frac{2777.64}{175,800} = \frac{3502.85}{189,300}$$

Equivalently, we should have $2777.64 \times 189,300 = 175,800 \times 3502.85$. Using a calculator, $2777.64 \times 189,300 = 525,807,252$ and $3502.85 \times 175,800 = 615,801,030$. Thus, the two houses are not taxed the same, since $525,807,252 \neq 615,801,030$.

An alternative solution to this problem would be to determine the tax rate per $1000 for each house.

$$\text{First house: } \frac{2777.64}{175,800} = \frac{r}{1000} \text{ yields } r = \$15.80 \text{ per } \$1000.$$

$$\text{Second house: } \frac{3502.85}{189,3000} = \frac{r}{1000} \text{ yields } r = \$18.50 \text{ per } \$1000.$$

Thus, it is likely that two digits of one of the tax rates were accidentally interchanged when calculating one of the bills. ■

MATHEMATICAL MORSEL

The famous mathematician Pythagoras founded a school that bore his name. As lore has it, to lure a young student to study at this school, he agreed to pay the student a penny for every theorem the student mastered. The student, motivated by the penny-a-theorem offer, studied intently and accumulated a huge sum of pennies. However, he so enjoyed the geometry that he begged Pythagoras for more theorems to prove. Pythagoras agreed to provide him with more theorems, but for a price—namely, a penny a theorem. Soon, Pythagoras had all his pennies back, in addition to a sterling student.

Section 7.3 EXERCISE / PROBLEM SET A

EXERCISES

1. The ratio of girls to boys in a particular classroom is $6:5$.

   a. What is the ratio of boys to girls?

   b. What fraction of the total number of students are boys?

   c. How many boys are in the class?

   d. How many boys are in the class if there are 33 students?

2. Explain how each of the following rates satisfies the definition of ratio. Give an example of how each is used.

   a. 250 miles/11.6 gallons

   b. 25 dollars/3.5 hours

   c. 1 dollar (American)/0.65 dollar (Canadian)

   d. 2.5 dollars/0.96 pound

3. Write a fraction in the simplest form that is equivalent to each ratio.

   a. 16 to 64   **b.** 30 to 75   **c.** 82.5 to 16.5

4. Determine whether the given ratios are equal.
   a. $3:4$ and $15:22$ **b.** $11:6$ and $66:36$

5. When blood cholesterol levels are tested, sometimes a cardiac risk ratio is calculated.

   Cardiac risk ratio =
   $$\frac{\text{total cholesterol level}}{\text{high-density lipoprotein level (HDL)}}$$

   For women, a ratio between 3.0 and 4.5 is desirable. A woman's blood test yields an HDL cholesterol level of 60 mg/dL and a total cholesterol level of 225 mg/dL. What is her cardiac risk ratio, expressed as a one-place decimal? Is her ratio in the normal range?

6. Solve each proportion for n.

   a. $\dfrac{n}{70} = \dfrac{6}{21}$ **b.** $\dfrac{n}{84} = \dfrac{3}{14}$

   c. $\dfrac{7}{n} = \dfrac{42}{48}$ **d.** $\dfrac{12}{n} = \dfrac{18}{45}$

7. Solve each proportion for x. Round each answer to two decimal places.

   a. $16:125 = x:5$ **b.** $\dfrac{9}{7} = \dfrac{10.8}{x}$

   c. $\dfrac{35.2}{19.6} = \dfrac{5}{3x}$ **d.** $\dfrac{x}{4-x} = \dfrac{3}{4}$

   e. $\dfrac{3\frac{1}{4}}{2\frac{1}{4}} = \dfrac{x}{1\frac{1}{2}}$ **f.** $\dfrac{2x}{x+10} = \dfrac{0.04}{1.85}$

8. Solve these proportions mentally by scaling up or scaling down.

   a. 24 miles for 2 gallons is equal to _____ miles for 16 gallons.

   b. $13.50 for 1 day is equal to _____ for 6 days.

   c. 300 miles in 12 hours is equal to _____ miles in 8 hours. (*Hint:* Scale down to 4 hours, then scale up to 8 hours.)

   d. 20 inches in 15 hours is equal to 16 inches in _____ hours.

   e. 32 cents for 8 ounces is equal to _____ cents for 12 ounces.

9. Write three other proportions for each given proportion.
   $$\frac{36 \text{ cents}}{18 \text{ ounces}} = \frac{42 \text{ cents}}{21 \text{ ounces}}$$

10. If you are traveling 100 kilometers per hour, how fast are you traveling in mph? For this exercise, use 50 mph = 80 kph (kilometers per hour). (The exact metric equivalent is 80.4672 kph.)

11. Which of the following is the better buy?

    a. 67 cents for 58 ounces or 17 cents for 15 ounces

    b. 29 ounces for 13 cents or 56 ounces for 27 cents

    c. 17 ounces for 23 cents, 25 ounces for 34 cents, or 73 ounces for 96 cents

━━━━━━━━━━━━━━━━━━━━━━━━━━━━━━

PROBLEMS

12. Grape juice concentrate is mixed with water in a ratio of 1 part concentrate to 3 parts water. How much grape juice can be made from a 10-ounce can of concentrate?

13. A crew clears brush from $\frac{1}{2}$ acre of land in 3 days. How long will it take the same crew to clear the entire plot of $2\frac{3}{4}$ acres?

14. A recipe for peach cobbler calls for 6 small peaches for 4 servings. If a large quantity is to be prepared to serve 10 people, about how many peaches would be needed?

15. Dan used a 128-ounce bottle of liquid laundry detergent over a period of $6\frac{1}{2}$ weeks. About how many ounces of liquid laundry detergent will he probably purchase in a year's time if this use of detergent is typical?

16. If a 92-year-old man has averaged 8 hours per 24-hour day sleeping, how many years of his life has he been asleep?

17. A man who weighs 175 pounds on Earth would weigh 28 pounds on the moon. How much would his 30-pound dog weigh on the moon?

18. Suppose that you drive an average of 4460 miles every half-year in your car. At the end of $2\frac{3}{4}$ years, how far will your car have gone?

19. Becky is climbing a hill that has a 17° slope. For every 5 feet she gains in altitude, she travels about 16.37 horizontal feet. If at the end of her uphill climb she has traveled 1 mile horizontally, how much altitude has she gained?

20. The *Spruce Goose*, a wooden flying boat built for Howard Hughes, had the world's largest wingspan, 319 ft 11 in. according to the *Guinness Book of World Records*. It flew only once in 1947, for a distance of about 1000 yards. Shelly wants to build a scale model of the 218 ft 8 in–long *Spruce Goose*. If her model will be 20 inches long, what will its wingspan be (to the nearest inch)?

21. Jefferson School has 1400 students. The teacher–pupil ratio is $1:35$.

    a. How many additional teachers will have to be hired to reduce the ratio to $1:20$?

    b. If the teacher–pupil ratio remains at $1:35$ and if the cost to the district for one teacher is $33,000 per year, how much will be spent per pupil per year?

    c. Answer part (b) for a ratio of $1:20$.

22. An **astronomical unit (AU)** is a measure of distance used by astronomers. In October 1985 the relative distance from Earth to Mars in comparison with the distance from Earth to Pluto was $1:12.37$.

    a. If Pluto was 30.67 AU from Earth in October 1985, how many astronomical units from Earth was Mars?

    b. Earth is always about 1 AU from the sun (in fact, this is the basis of this unit of measure). In October 1985, Pluto was about 2.85231×10^9 miles from Earth. About how many miles is Earth from the sun?

    c. In October 1985 about how many miles was Mars from Earth?

23. According to the "big-bang" hypothesis, the universe was formed approximately 10^{10} years ago. The analogy of a 24-hour day is often used to put the passage of this amount of time into perspective. Imagine that the universe was formed at midnight 24 hours ago and answer the following questions.

    a. To how many years of actual time does 1 hour correspond?

    b. To how many years of actual time does 1 minute correspond?

    c. To how many years of actual time does 1 second correspond?

    d. The Earth was formed, according to the hypothesis, approximately 5 billion years ago. To what time in the 24-hour day does this correspond?

    e. Earliest known humanlike remains have been determined by radioactive dating to be approximately 2.6 million years old. At what time of the 24-hour day did the creatures who left these remains die?

    f. Intensive agriculture and the growth of modern civilization may have begun as early as 10,000 years ago. To what time of the 24-hour day does this correspond?

24. Cary was going to meet Jane at the airport. If he traveled 60 mph, he would arrive 1 hour early, and if he traveled 30 mph, he would arrive 1 hour late. How far was the airport? (*Recall:* Distance $=$ rate $\cdot$ time.)

25. Seven children each had a different number of pennies. The ratio of each child's total to the next poorer was a whole number. Altogether they had $28.79. How much did each have?

26. Two baseball batters, Eric and Morgan, each get 31 hits in 69 at-bats. In the next week, Eric slumps to 1 hit in 27 at-bats and Morgan bats 4 for 36 (1 out of 9). Without doing any calculations, which batter do you think has the higher average? Check your answer by calculating the two averages (the number of hits divided by the number of times at bat).

27. A woman has equal numbers of pennies, nickels, and dimes. If the total value of the coins is $12.96, how many dimes does she have?

28. A man walked into a store to buy a hat. The hat he selected cost $20. He said to his father, "If you will lend me as much money as I have in my pocket, I will buy that $20 hat." The father agreed. Then they did it again with a $20 pair of slacks and again with a $20 pair of shoes. The man was finally out of money. How much did he have when he walked into the store?

29. What is the largest sum of money in U.S. coins that you could have without being able to give change for a nickel, dime, quarter, half-dollar, or dollar?

30. Beginning with 100, each of two persons, in turn, subtracts a single-digit number. The player who ends at zero is the loser. Can you explain how to play so that one player always wins?

31. How can you cook something for exactly 15 minutes if all you have are a 7-minute and an 11-minute egg timer?

32. Twelve posts stand equidistant along a race track. Starting at the first post, a runner reaches the eighth post in 8 seconds. If she runs at a constant velocity, how many seconds are needed to reach the twelfth post?

Section 7.3 EXERCISE / PROBLEM SET B

EXERCISES

1. Write a ratio based on each of the following.
 a. Two-fifths of Ted's garden is planted in tomatoes.
 b. The certificate of deposit you purchased earns $6.18 interest on every $100 you deposit.
 c. Three out of every four voters surveyed favor ballot measure 5.
 d. There are five times as many boys as girls in Mr. Wright's physics class.
 e. There are half as many sixth graders in Fremont School as eighth graders.
 f. Nine of every 16 students in the hot-lunch line are girls.

2. Explain how each of the following rates satisfies the definition of ratio. Give an example of how each is used.
 a. 1580 people/square mile
 b. 450 people/year
 c. 360 kilowatt-hours/4 months
 d. 355 calories/6 ounces

3. Write a fraction in the simplest form that is equivalent to each ratio.
 a. 17 to 119   **b.** 26 to 91   **c.** 97.5 to 66.3

4. Determine whether the given ratios are equal.
 a. 5:8 and 15:25   **b.** 7:12 and 36:60

5. In one analysis of people of the world, it was reported that of every 1000 people of the world the following numbers speak the indicated language as their native tongue.

> 165 speak Mandarin
> 86 speak English
> 83 speak Hindi/Urdu
> 64 speak Spanish
> 58 speak Russian
> 37 speak Arabic

 a. Find the ratio of Spanish speakers to Russian speakers.
 b. Find the ratio of Arabic speakers to English speakers.
 c. The ratio of which two groups is nearly 2:1?
 d. Find the ratio of persons who speak Mandarin, English, or Hindi/Urdu to the total group of 1000 people.

 e. What fraction of persons in the group of 1000 world citizens are *not* accounted for in this list? These persons speak one of the more than 200 other languages spoken in the world today.

6. Solve for the unknown in each of the following proportions.

 a. $\dfrac{\frac{3}{5}}{6} = \dfrac{D}{25}$ **b.** $\dfrac{B}{8} = \dfrac{2\frac{1}{4}}{18}$ **c.** $\dfrac{X}{100} = \dfrac{4.8}{1.5}$

 d. $\dfrac{57.4}{39.6} = \dfrac{7.4}{P}$ (to one decimal place)

7. Solve each proportion for x. Round your answers to two decimal places where decimal answers do not terminate.

 a. $\dfrac{7}{5} = \dfrac{x}{40}$ **b.** $\dfrac{12}{35} = \dfrac{40}{x}$

 c. $2 : 9 = x : 3$ **d.** $\dfrac{3}{4} : 8 = 9 : x$

 e. $\dfrac{15}{32} = \dfrac{x}{x+2}$ **f.** $\dfrac{3x}{4} = \dfrac{12-x}{6}$

8. Solve these proportions mentally by scaling up or scaling down.
 a. 26 miles for 6 hours is equal to _____ miles for 24 hours.
 b. 84 ounces for each 6 square inches is equal to _____ ounces for each 15 square inches.
 c. 40 inches in 12 hours is equal to _____ inches in 9 hours.
 d. $27.50 for 1.5 days is equal to _____ for 6 days.
 e. 750 people for each 12 square miles is equal to _____ people for each 16 square miles.

9. Write three other proportions for each given proportion.

$$\dfrac{35 \text{ miles}}{2 \text{ hours}} = \dfrac{87.5 \text{ miles}}{5 \text{ hours}}$$

10. If you are traveling 55 mph, how fast are you traveling in kph?

11. Determine which of the following is the better buy.
 a. 60 ounces for 29 cents or 84 ounces for 47 cents
 b. $45 for 10 yards of material or $79 for 15 yards
 c. 18 ounces for 40 cents, 20 ounces for 50 cents, or 30 ounces for 75 cents (*Hint*: How much does $1 purchase in each case?)

PROBLEMS

12. Three car batteries are advertised with warranties as follows.

    Model *XA*: 40-month warranty, $34.95
    Model *XL*: 50-month warranty, $39.95
    Model *XT*: 60-month warranty, $49.95

Considering only the warranties and the prices, which model of car battery is the best buy?

13. Cari walked 3.4 kilometers in 45 minutes. At that rate, how long will it take her to walk 11.2 kilometers? Round to the nearest minute.

14. A family uses 5 gallons of milk every 3 weeks. At that rate, how many gallons of milk will they need to purchase in a year's time?

15. A couple was assessed property taxes of $1938.90 on a home valued at $168,600. What might Frank expect to pay in property taxes on a home he hopes to purchase in the same neighborhood if it has a value of $181,300? Round to the nearest dollar.

16. By reading just a few pages at night before falling asleep, Randy finished a 248-page book in $4\frac{1}{2}$ weeks. He just started a new book of 676 pages. About how long should it take him to finish the new book if he reads at the same rate?

17. a. If 1 inch on a map represents 35 miles, how many miles are represented by 3 inches? 10 inches? *n* inches?

    b. Los Angeles is about 1000 miles from Portland. About how many inches apart would Portland and Los Angeles be on this map?

18. A farmer calculates that out of every 100 seeds of corn he plants, he harvests 84 ears of corn. If he wants to harvest 7200 ears of corn, how many seeds must he plant?

19. A map is drawn to scale such that $\frac{1}{8}$ inch represents 65 feet. If the shortest route from your house to the grocery store measures $23\frac{7}{16}$ inches, how many miles is it to the grocery store?

20. a. If $1\frac{3}{4}$ cups of flour are required to make 28 cookies, how many cups are required for 88 cookies?

    b. If your car gets 32 miles per gallon, how many gallons do you use on a 160-mile trip?

    c. If your mechanic suggests 3 parts antifreeze to 4 parts water, and if your radiator is 14 liters, how many liters of antifreeze should you use?

d. If 11 ounces of roast beef cost $1.86, how much does roast beef cost per pound?

21. Two professional drag racers are speeding down a $\frac{1}{4}$-mile track. If the lead driver is traveling 1.738 feet for every 1.670 feet that the trailing car travels, and if the trailing car is going 198 miles per hour, how fast in miles per hour is the lead car traveling?

22. In 1994, the Internal Revenue Service audited 107 of every 10,000 individual returns.

    a. In a community in which 12,500 people filed returns, how many returns might be expected to be audited?

    b. In 1996, 163 returns per 10,000 were audited. How many more of the 12,500 returns would be expected to be audited for 1996 than for 1994?

23. a. A baseball pitcher has pitched a total of 25 innings so far during the season and has allowed 18 runs. At this rate, how many runs, to the nearest hundredth, would he allow in nine innings? This number is called the pitcher's **earned run average**, or ERA.

    b. Randy Johnson of the Arizona Diamondbacks had an ERA of 2.64 in 2000. At that rate, how many runs would he be expected to allow in 100 innings pitched? Round your answer to the nearest whole number.

24. Many tires come with $\frac{13}{32}$ inch of tread on them. The first $\frac{2}{32}$ inch wears off quickly (say, during the first 1000 miles). From then on the tire wears uniformly (and more slowly). A tire is considered "worn out" when only $\frac{2}{32}$ inch of tread is left.

    a. How many 32nds of an inch of usable tread does a tire have after 1000 miles?

    b. A tire has traveled 20,000 miles and has $\frac{5}{32}$ inch of tread remaining. At this rate, how many total miles should the tire last before it is considered worn out?

25. In classroom *A*, there are 12 boys and 15 girls. In classroom *B*, there are 8 boys and 6 girls. In classroom *C*, there are 4 boys and 5 girls.

    a. Which two classrooms have the same boys-to-girls ratio?

    b. On one occasion classroom *A* joined classroom *B*. What was the resulting boys-to-girls ratio?

    c. On another occasion classroom *C* joined classroom *B*. What was the resulting ratio of boys to girls?

    d. Are your answers to parts (b) and (c) equivalent? What does this tell you about adding ratios?

26. An old picture frame has dimensions 33 inches by 24 inches. What one length must be cut from each dimension so that the ratio of the shorter side to the longer side is $\frac{2}{3}$?

27. The Greek musical scale, which very closely resembles the 12-note tempered scale used today, is based on ratios of frequencies. To hear the first and fifth tones of the scale is equivalent to hearing the ratio $\frac{3}{2}$, which is the ratio of their frequencies.

CDEFGABCDEFGABCDEFGABCDEFGABC

a. If the frequency of middle C is 256 vibrations per second, find the frequencies of each of the other notes given. For example, since G is a fifth above middle C, it follows that G:256 = 3:2 or G = 384 vibrations/second. (NOTE: Proceeding beyond B would give sharps, below F, flats.)

b. Two notes are an octave apart if the frequency of one is double the frequency of the other. For example, the frequency of C above middle C is 512 vibrations per second. Using the values found in part (a), find the frequencies of the corresponding notes in the octave above middle C (in the following range).

256512
C   DEFGABC

c. The aesthetic effect of a chord depends on the ratio of its frequencies. Find the following ratios of seconds.

D:C   E:D   A:G

What simple ratio are these equivalent to?

d. Find the following ratio of fourths.

F:C   G:D   A:E

What simple ratio are these equivalent to?

28. Ferne, Donna, and Susan have just finished playing three games. There was only one loser in each game. Ferne lost the first game, Donna lost the second game, and Susan lost the third game. After each game, the loser was required to double the money of the other two. After three rounds, each woman had $24. How much did each have at the start?

29. A ball, when dropped from any height, bounces $\frac{1}{3}$ of the original height. If the ball is dropped, bounces back up, and continues to bounce up and down so that it has traveled 106 feet when it strikes the ground for the fourth time, what is the original height from which it was dropped?

30. Mary had a basket of hard-boiled eggs to sell. She first sold half her eggs plus half an egg. Next she sold half her eggs and half an egg. The same thing occurred on her third, fourth, and fifth times. When she finished, she had no eggs in her basket. How many did she have when she started?

31. Joleen had a higher batting average than Maureen for the first half of the season, and Joleen also had a higher batting average than Maureen for the second half of the season. Does it follow that Joleen had a better batting average than Maureen for the entire season? Why or why not?

32. A box contains three different varieties of apples. What is the smallest number of apples that must be taken to be sure of getting at least 2 of one kind? How about at least 3 of one kind? How about at least 10 of a kind? How about at least n of a kind?

33. Ms. Price has three times as many girls as boys in her class. Ms. Lippy has twice as many girls as boys. Ms. Price has 60 students in her class and Ms. Lippy has 135 students. If the classes were combined into one, what would be the ratio of girls to boys?

PROBLEMS FOR WRITING/DISCUSSION

1. When a new student heard that the ratio of boys to girls in his new class would be 5:4, he thought that meant there would be just 5 boys. What other possibilities are there?

2. Melvina was planning a long trip by car. She knew she could average about 180 miles in 4 hours, but she was trying to figure out how much farther she could get each day if she and her friend (who drives about the same speed) shared the driving and they drove for 10 hours per day. She figured they could travel an extra 450 miles, so altogether they could do 630 miles a day. Is she on track? How would you explain this?

3. Marvin is trying to find the height of a tree in the school yard. He is using the proportion

$$\frac{\text{Marvin's height}}{\text{Marvin's shadow length}} = \frac{\text{tree's height}}{\text{tree's shadow length}}$$

His height is 4 feet. His shadow length is 15 inches. The length of the tree's shadow is 12 feet. Marvin used the proportion $\frac{4}{15} = \frac{\text{tree}}{12}$. But that gave the tree's height as being shorter than Marvin's! What went wrong?

7.4 PERCENT

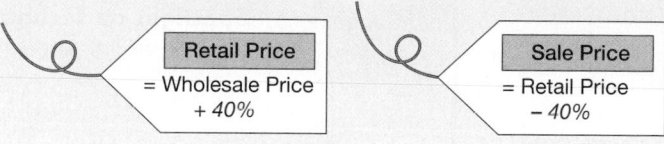

STARTING POINT

If the wholesale price of a jacket is marked up 40% to obtain the retail price and the retail price is then marked down 40% to a sale price, are the wholesale price and the sale price the same? If not, explain why not and determine which is larger.

Retail Price
= Wholesale Price
+ 40%

Sale Price
= Retail Price
− 40%

Converting Percents

Percents provide another common way of representing fractions. The word **percent** has a Latin origin that means "per hundred." Thus 25 percent means 25 per hundred, $\frac{25}{100}$, or 0.25. The symbol "%" is used to represent percent. So 420% means $\frac{420}{100}$, 4.20, or 420 per hundred. In general, $n\%$ represents the ratio $\frac{n}{100}$.

Since percents are alternative representations of fractions and decimals, it is important to be able to convert among all three forms, as suggested in Figure 7.12. Since we have studied converting fractions to decimals, and vice versa, there are only four cases of conversion left to consider in Figure 7.12.

Figure 7.12

$\frac{31}{100} = 31\%$

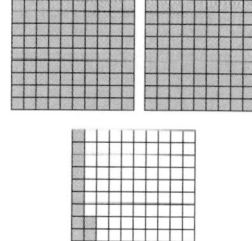

$\frac{213}{100} = 213\%$

$\frac{.5}{100} = 0.5\%$

Figure 7.13

CASE 1: Percents to Fractions
Use the definition of *percent*. For example, $63\% = \frac{63}{100}$ by the meaning of *percent*.

CASE 2: Percents to Decimals
Since we know how to convert fractions to decimals, we can use this skill to convert percents to fractions and then to decimals. For example, $63\% = \frac{63}{100} = 0.63$ and $27\% = \frac{27}{100} = 0.27$. These two examples suggest the following shortcut, which eliminates the conversion to a fraction step. Namely, to convert a percent directly to a decimal, "drop the % symbol and move the number's decimal point two places to the *left*." Thus $31\% = 0.31$, $213\% = 2.13$, $0.5\% = .005$, and so on. These examples can also be seen visually in Figure 7.13 on a 10-by-10 grid, where 31% is represented by shading 31 out of 100 squares, 213% is represented by shading 213 squares (2 full grids and 13 squares on a third grid), and 0.5% is represented by shading half of 1 square on the grid.

CASE 3: Decimals to Percents
Here we merely reverse the shortcut in case 2. For example, $0.83 = 83\%$, $5.1 = 510\%$, and $0.0001 = 0.01\%$ where the percents are obtained from the decimals by "moving the decimal point two places to the *right* and writing the % symbol on the *right* side."

NCTM Standards 2000
Number and Operations
Grades 3–5
All students should recognize and generate equivalent forms of commonly used fractions, decimals, and percents.

CASE 4: Fractions to Percents

Some fractions that have terminating decimals can be converted to percents by expressing the fraction with a denominator of 100. For example, $\frac{17}{100} = 17\%$, $\frac{2}{5} = \frac{4}{100} = \frac{40}{100} = 40\%$, $\frac{3}{25} = \frac{12}{100} = 12\%$, and so on. Also, fractions can be converted to decimals (using a calculator or long division), and then case 3 can be applied.

Spotlight on Technology A calculator is useful when converting fractions to percents. For example,

$$3 \;\boxed{\div}\; 13 \;\boxed{=}\; \boxed{0.23076923}$$

shows that $\frac{3}{13} \approx 0.23$ or 23%. Also,

$$5 \;\boxed{\div}\; 9 \;\boxed{=}\; \boxed{0.555555556}$$

shows that $\frac{5}{9} \approx 56\%$.

Example 7.26 Write each of the following in all three forms: decimal, percent, fraction (in simplest form).
  a. 32% **b.** 0.24 **c.** 450% **d.** $\frac{1}{16}$

Solution

a. $32\% = 0.32 = \frac{8}{25}$ **b.** $0.24 = 24\% = \frac{6}{25}$ **c.** $450\% = 4.5 = 4\frac{1}{2}$

d. $\dfrac{1}{16} = \dfrac{1}{2^4} = \dfrac{1 \cdot 5^4}{2^4 \cdot 5^4} = \dfrac{625}{10,000} = 0.0625 = 6.25\%$ ■

NCTM Standards 2000
Number and Operations
Grades 6–8
All students should work flexibly with fractions, decimals, and percents to solve problems.

Mental Math and Estimation Using Fraction Equivalents

Since many commonly used percents have convenient fraction equivalents, it is often easier to find the percent of a number mentally, using fractions (Table 7.2). Also, as was the case with proportions, percentages of numbers can be estimated by choosing compatible fractions.

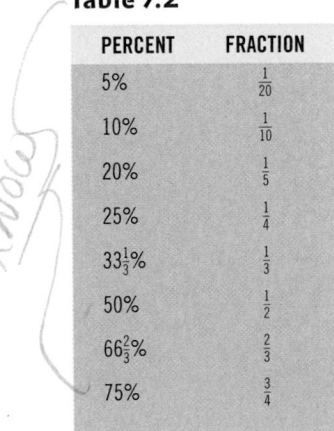

Table 7.2

PERCENT	FRACTION
5%	$\frac{1}{20}$
10%	$\frac{1}{10}$
20%	$\frac{1}{5}$
25%	$\frac{1}{4}$
$33\frac{1}{3}\%$	$\frac{1}{3}$
50%	$\frac{1}{2}$
$66\frac{2}{3}\%$	$\frac{2}{3}$
75%	$\frac{3}{4}$

Example 7.27 Find the following percents mentally, using fraction equivalents.
  a. 25% × 44 **b.** 75% × 24 **c.** 50% × 76
  d. $33\frac{1}{3}\%$ × 93 **e.** 38% × 50 **f.** 84% × 25

Solution

a. $25\% \times 44 = \frac{1}{4} \times 44 = 11$ **b.** $75\% \times 24 = \frac{3}{4} \times 24 = 18$
c. $50\% \times 76 = \frac{1}{2} \times 76 = 38$ **d.** $33\frac{1}{3}\% \times 93 = \frac{1}{3} \times 93 = 31$
e. $38\% \times 50 = 38 \times 50\% = 38 \times \frac{1}{2} = 19$
f. $84\% \times 25 = 84 \times 25\% = 84 \times \frac{1}{4} = 21$ ■

Example 7.28 Estimate the following percents mentally, using fraction equivalents.
  a. 48% × 73 **b.** 32% × 95 **c.** 24% × 71
  d. 123% × 54 **e.** 0.45% × 57 **f.** 59% × 81

Solution

a. $48\% \times 73 \approx 50\% \times 72 = 36$. (Since 50% > 48%, 73 was rounded down to 72 to compensate.)

b. $32\% \times 95 \approx 33\frac{1}{3} \times 93 = \frac{1}{3} \times 93 = 31$. (Since $33\frac{1}{3}\% > 32\%$, 95 was rounded down to 93, which is a multiple of 3.)

c. $24\% \times 71 \approx \frac{1}{4} \times 72 = \frac{1}{4} \times 8 \times 9 = 18$

d. $123\% \times 54 \approx 125\% \times 54 \approx \frac{5}{4} \times 56 = 5 \times 14 = 70$; alternatively,

   $123\% \times 54 = 123 \times 54\% \approx 130 \times 50\% = 130 \times \frac{1}{2} = 65$

e. $0.45\% \times 57 \approx 0.5\% \times 50 = 0.5 \times 50\% = 0.25$

f. $59\% \times 81 \approx 60\% \times 81 \approx \frac{3}{5} \times 80 = 3 \times 16 = 48$ ■

Solving Percent Problems

The following questions illustrate three common types of problems involving percents.

1. A car was purchased for $13,000 with a 20% down payment. How much was the down payment?   *2600*

2. One hundred sixty-two seniors, 90% of the senior class, are going on the class trip. How many seniors are there?   *14*

3. Susan scored 48 points on a 60-point test. What percent did she get correct?   *80*

There are three approaches to solving percent problems such as the preceding three problems. The first of the three approaches is the grid approach and relies on the 10-by-10 grids introduced earlier in this section. This approach is more concrete and aids in understanding the underlying concept of percents. The more common approaches, proportions and equations, are more powerful and can be used to solve a broader range of problems.

Know Grid Method

Grid Approach Since *percent* means "per hundred," solving problems to find a missing percent can be visualized by using the 10-by-10 grids introduced earlier in the section.

Example 7.29   Answer the preceding three problems using the grid approach.

Solution

$13,000

$130

Figure 7.14

a. A car was purchased for $13,000 with a 20% down payment. How much was the down payment?

Let the grid in Figure 7.14 represent the total cost of the car, or $13,000. Since the down payment was 20%, shade 20 out of 100 squares. The solution can be found by reasoning that since 100 squares represent $13,000, then 1 square represents $\frac{13,000}{100} = \$130$ and therefore 20 squares represent the down payment of $20 \times \$130 = \$2600$.

162 students

1.8 students

Figure 7.15

b. One hundred sixty-two seniors, 90% of the senior class, are going on the class trip. How many seniors are there?

Let the grid in Figure 7.15 represent the total class size. Since 90% of the students will go on the class trip, shade 90 of the 100 squares. The reasoning used to solve this problem is that since 90 squares represent 162 students, then 1 square represents $\frac{162}{90} = 1.8$ students. Thus 100 squares, the whole class, is $100 \cdot 1.8 = 180$ students.

60 points

0.6 points

Figure 7.16

c. Susan scored 48 points on a 60-point test. What percent did she get correct?

Let the grid in Figure 7.16 represent all 60 points on the test. In this case, the percent is not given, so determining how many squares should be shaded to represent Susan's score of 48 points becomes the focus of the problem. Reasoning with the grid, it can be seen that since 100 squares represent 60 points, then 1 square represents 0.6 points. Thus 10 squares is 6 points and 80 squares is Susan's 6 × 8 = 48 point score. Thus she got 80% correct. ■

Proportion Approach Since percents can be written as a ratio, solving percent problems may be done using proportions. For problems involving percents between 0 and 100, it may be helpful to think of a fuel gauge that varies from empty (0%) to full (100%) (Figure 7.17). The next example shows how this visual device leads to solving a proportion.

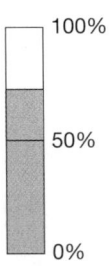

Figure 7.17

Example 7.30 Answer the preceding three problems using the proportion approach.

Solution

a. A car was purchased for $13,000 with a 20% down payment. How much was the down payment (Figure 7.18)?

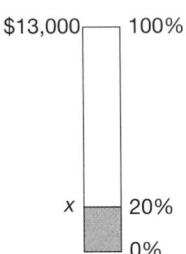

Figure 7.18

	DOLLARS	PERCENT
Down payment	x	20
Purchase price	13,000	100

Thus $\dfrac{x}{13,000} = \dfrac{20}{100}$, or $x = \dfrac{13,000}{5} = \$2600$.

b. One hundred sixty-two seniors, 90% of the senior class, are going on the class trip. How many seniors are there (Figure 7.19)?

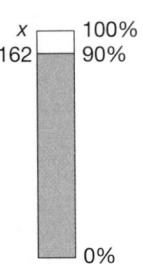

Figure 7.19

	SENIORS	PERCENT
Class trip	162	90
Class total	x	100

Thus $\dfrac{162}{x} = \dfrac{90}{100}$, or $x = 162\left(\dfrac{10}{9}\right) = 180$.

c. Susan scored 48 points on a 60-point test. What percent did she get correct (Figure 7.20)?

Figure 7.20

	TEST	PERCENT
Score	48	x
Total	60	100

Thus $\dfrac{48}{60} = \dfrac{x}{100}$, or $x = 100 \cdot \dfrac{4}{5} = 80$. ■

Spotlight on Technology An electronic version of this fuel gauge model can be found as a Chapter 7 eManipulative activity, *Percent Gauge*. The model also relies on the proportion above. To solve

www.wiley.com/ college/musser Example 7.30(a) using the eManipulative, enter $13,000 for n and 20 for p. The amount displayed for a is the solution to the question. The percent gauge can be further utilized by dragging the sliders. If you wanted to know what percent a down payment of $4420 is, you could move the a slider until $4420 is displayed and read the corresponding value for p. Similarly, if you wanted to find the amount needed to make a down payment of 23%, you could move the p slider accordingly. Use the percent gauge to double-check parts (b) and (c) of Example 7.30.

Notice how (a), (b), and (c) lead to the following generalization:

$$\frac{\text{Part}}{\text{Whole}} = \frac{\text{percent}}{100}.$$

In other examples, if the "part" is larger than the "whole," the percent is larger than 100%.

Equation Approach An equation can be used to represent each of the problems in Example 7.30 as follows:

(a) $20\% \cdot 13{,}000 = x$
(b) $90\% \cdot x = 162$
(c) $x\% \cdot 60 = 48.$

In fact, many percent problems can be solved easily by expressing the problem in an equation in one of the three preceding forms and then by solving the equation. The following equations illustrate these three forms, where x represents an unknown and $p, n,$ and a are fixed numbers.

TRANSLATION OF PROBLEM	EQUATION
(a) $p\%$ of n is x	$\left(\dfrac{p}{100}\right)n = x$
(b) $p\%$ of x is a	$\left(\dfrac{p}{100}\right)x = a$
(c) $x\%$ of n is a	$\left(\dfrac{x}{100}\right)n = a$

Once we have obtained one of these three equations, the solution, x, can be found. In equation (a), we multiply $\dfrac{p}{100}$ and n. In equations (b) and (c) we solve for the missing factor x.

Example 7.31 Solve the problems in Example 7.30 using the equation approach.

Solution

a. $20\% \cdot 13{,}000 = 0.20(13{,}000) = \$2600$
b. $90\% \cdot x = 162$ or $0.9x = 162.$ Thus, by the missing-factor approach, $x = 162 \div (0.9),$ or $x = 180.$ *Check:* $90\%(180) = 162.$
c. $x\% \cdot 60 = 48,$ or $\dfrac{x}{100}(60) = 48.$ By the missing-factor approach,

$$\frac{x}{100} = \frac{48}{60} = \frac{8}{10}, \text{ or } x = 80. \qquad \textit{Check: } 80\%(60) = 48. \qquad ■$$

Spotlight on Technology A calculator can also be used to solve percent problems once the correct equations or proportions are set up. (Problems can be done using fewer keystrokes if your calculator has a percent key.) The following key sequences can be used to solve the equations arising from Example 7.31.

a. $20\% \times 13000 = x$.

$$20 \boxed{\%} \boxed{\times} 13000 \boxed{=} \boxed{2600}$$

NOTE: With some calculators, the 13000 must be keyed in before the 20%. Also, the $\boxed{=}$ may not be needed in this case.

b. $90\% \times x = 162$ (or $x = 162 \div 90\%$):

$$162 \boxed{\div} 90 \boxed{\%} \boxed{=} \boxed{180}$$

NOTE: Some calculators do not require the $\boxed{=}$ here.

c. $x\% \times 60 = 48$ (or $\dfrac{x}{100} = 48 \div 60$):

$$48 \boxed{\div} 60 \boxed{\times} 100 \boxed{=} \boxed{80}$$

As mentioned earlier, the proportion and equation approaches are more powerful because they can be used with a broader range of problems. For example, in Example 7.30(a), if the car costs $13,297 instead of $13,000 and the down payment was 22.5% instead of 20%, then the proportion and equation approaches could be used in an identical manner. However, the visualization aspect of the grid approach becomes less effective because the problems no longer deal with whole numbers.

We end this section on percent with several applications.

Example 7.32 Rachelle bought a dress whose original price was $125 but was discounted 10%. What was the discounted price? Also, what is a quick way to mark down several items 10% using a calculator?

Reflection from Research
When presented with algebraic relationships expressed in words (e.g., There are 3 times as many girls as boys), many students translate this relationship as $3g = b$ rather than $3b = g$ (Lopez-Real, 1995).

Solution The original price is $125. The discount is $(10\%)(125)$, or $12.50. The new price is $125 - \$12.50 = \$112.50$. In general, if the original price was n, the discount would be $(10\%)n$. Then the new price would be $n - (10\%)n = n - (0.1)n = 0.9n$. ■

Spotlight on Technology If many prices were to be discounted 10%, the new prices could be found by multiplying the old price by 0.9, or 90%. If your calculator has a percent key, the solution to the original problem would be

$$125 \boxed{\times} 90 \boxed{\%} \boxed{112.50}.$$

(NOTE: It is not necessary to use the percent key; we could simply multiply by 0.9.)

Example 7.33 A television set is put on sale at 28% off the regular price. The sale price is $379. What was the regular price?

Solution The sale price is 72% of the regular price (since $100\% - 28\% = 72\%$). Let P be the regular price. Then, in proportion form,

$$\frac{72}{100} = \frac{370}{P} \left(\frac{\text{sale price}}{\text{regular price}} \right)$$

$$72 \times P = 379 \times 100 = 37,900$$

$$P = \frac{37,900}{72} = \$526.39, \text{ rounding to the nearest cent.}$$

Check: $(0.72)(526.39) = 379$, rounding to the nearest dollar.   ■

Example 7.34   Suppose that Irene's credit-card balance is $576. If the monthly interest rate is 1.5% (i.e., 18% per year), what will this debt be at the end of 5 months if she makes no payments to reduce her balance?

Solution The amount of interest accrued by the end of the first month is 1.5% × 576, or $8.64, so the balance at the end of the first month is $576 + $8.64, or $584.64. The interest at the end of the second month would be (1.5%)(584.64), or $8.77 (rounding to the nearest cent), so the balance at the end of the second month would be $593.41. Continuing in this manner, the balance at the end of the fifth month would be $620.52. Can you see why this is called compound interest?   ■

Spotlight on Technology A much faster way to solve this problem is to use the technique illustrated in Example 7.32. The balance at the end of a month can be found by multiplying the balance from the end of the previous month by 1.015 (this is equal to 100% + 1.5%). Then, using your calculator, the computation for the balance after five months would be

$$576(1.015)(1.015)(1.015)(1.015)(1.015) = 576(1.015)^5 = 620.52.$$

If your calculator has a constant function, your number of key presses would be reduced considerably. Here is a sequence of steps that works on many calculators.

1.015 $\boxed{\times}$ $\boxed{=}$ $\boxed{=}$ $\boxed{=}$ $\boxed{=}$ $\boxed{\times}$ 576 $\boxed{=}$ $\boxed{620.5155862}$

(On some calculators you may have to press the $\boxed{\times}$ key twice after entering 1.015 to implement the constant function to repeat multiplication.) Better yet, if your calculator has a $\boxed{y^x}$ (or $\boxed{x^y}$ or $\boxed{\wedge}$) key, the following keystrokes can be used.

1.015 $\boxed{y^x}$ 5 $\boxed{\times}$ 576 $\boxed{=}$ $\boxed{620.5155862}$

The balance at the end of a year is

1.015 $\boxed{y^x}$ 12 $\boxed{\times}$ 576 $\boxed{=}$ $\boxed{688.6760668}$,

or $688.68.

Example 7.34 illustrates a problem involving interest. Most of us encounter interest through savings, loans, credit cards, and so on. With a calculator that has an exponential key, such as $\boxed{y^x}$ or $\boxed{x^y}$, calculations that formerly were too time-consuming for the average consumer are now merely a short sequence of keystrokes. However, it is important that one understand how to set up a problem so that the calculator can be correctly used. Our last two examples illustrate how a calculator with an exponential key can be used to show the effect of compound interest.

Example 7.35   Parents want to establish a college fund for their 8-year-old daughter. The father received a bonus of $10,000. The $10,000 is deposited in a tax-deferred account guaranteed to yield at least $7\frac{3}{4}$% compounded quarterly. How much will be available from this account when the child is 18?

Solution

There are several aspects to this problem. First, one needs to understand what *compounded quarterly* means. *Compounded quarterly* means that earned interest is added to the principal amount every 3 months. Since the annual rate is $7\frac{3}{4}\%$, the quarterly rate is $\frac{1}{4}(7\frac{3}{4}\%) = 1.9375\%$. Following the ideas in Example 7.34, the principal, which is $10,000, will amount to $10,000(1.019375) = \$10,193.75$ at the end of the first quarter.

Next, one needs to determine the number of quarters (of a year) that the $10,000 will earn interest. Since the child is 8 and the money is needed when she is 18, this account will grow for 10 years (or 40 quarters). Again, following Example 7.34, after 40 quarters the $10,000 will amount to $10,000(1.019375)^{40} \approx \$21,545.63$. If the interest rate had simply been $7\frac{3}{4}\%$ per year not compounded, the $10,000 would have earned $10,000(7\frac{3}{4}\%) = \$775$ per year for each of the 10 years, or would have amounted to $\$10,000 + 10(\$775) = \$17,750$. Thus, the compounding quarterly amounted to an extra $3795.63. ■

Our last example shows you how to determine how much to save now for a specific amount at a future date.

Example 7.36 You project that you will need $20,000 before taxes in 15 years. If you find a tax-deferred investment that guarantees you 10% interest, compounded semiannually, how much should you set aside now?

Solution As you may have observed while working through Examples 7.34 and 7.35, if P is the amount of your initial principal, r is the interest rate for a given period, and n is the number of payment periods for the given rate, then your final amount, A, will be given by the equation $A = P(1 + r)^n$. In this example, $A = \$20,000$, $r = \frac{1}{2}$ (10%), since *semiannual* means "every half-year", and $n = 2 \times 15$, since there are $2 \times 15 = 30$ half-years in 15 years. Thus

$$20{,}000 = P[1 + \tfrac{1}{2}(0.10)]^{30} \quad \text{or} \quad P = \frac{20{,}000}{[1 + \tfrac{1}{2}(0.10)]^{30}}.$$

■

 Spotlight on Technology A calculator can be used to find the dollar value for P.

$$20000 \; \boxed{\div} \; \boxed{(} \; 1.05 \; \boxed{y^x} \; 30 \; \boxed{)} \; \boxed{=} \; \boxed{4627.548973}$$

Thus $4627.55 needs to be set aside now at 10% interest compounded semiannually to have $20,000 available in 15 years.

MATHEMATICAL MORSEL

Two students were finalists in a free-throw shooting contest. In the two parts of the contest, the challenger had to shoot 25 free-throws in the first part, then 50 in the second part, while the champion shot 50 free-throws first and 25 second. In the first part, Vivian made 20 of 25, or 80%, and Joan made 26 of 50, or 52%. Then Vivian made 9 of 50, or 18%, and Joan made 4 of 25, or 16%. Since Vivian had a higher percentage in both parts, she declared herself to be the winner. However, Joan cried "Foul!" and claimed the totals should be counted. In that case, Vivian made 29 of 75 and Joan made 30 of 75. Who should win? This mathematical oddity can arise when data involving ratios are combined (Simpson's paradox).

Section 7.4 EXERCISE / PROBLEM SET A

EXERCISES

1. Fill in this chart.

FRACTION	DECIMAL	PERCENT
		50%
	0.35	
$\frac{1}{4}$		
$\frac{1}{8}$		
	0.0125	
		125%
	0.75	

2. a. Mentally calculate each of the following.

  i. 10% of 50   **ii.** 10% of 68.7

  iii. 10% of 4.58   **iv.** 10% of 32.900

  b. Mentally calculate each of the following. Use the fact that 5% is half of 10%

  i. 5% of 240   **ii.** 5% of 18.6

  iii. 5% of 12,000   **iv.** 5% of 62.56

  c. Mentally calculate each of the following. Use the fact that 15% is 10% + 5%.

  i. 15% of 90   **ii.** 15% of 50,400

  iii. 15% of 7.2   **iv.** 15% of 0.066

3. Complete the following statements mentally.

  a. 126 is 50% of _____.   **b.** 36 is 25% of _____.

  c. 154 is $66\frac{2}{3}$% of _____.   **d.** 78 is 40% of _____.

  e. 50 is 125% of _____.   **f.** 240 is 300% of _____.

4. Solve mentally.

  a. 56 is _____% of 100.   **b.** 38 is _____% of 50.

  c. 17 is _____% of 25.   **d.** 7.5 is _____% of 20.

  e. 75 is _____% of 50.   **f.** 40 is _____% of 30.

5. Mentally find the following percents using fraction equivalents.

  a. 50% of 64   **b.** 25% of 148   **c.** 75% of 244

  d. $33\frac{1}{3}$% of 210   **e.** 20% of 610   **f.** 60% of 450

6. Estimate.

  a. 39% of 72   **b.** 58.7% of 31

  c. 123% of 59   **d.** 0.48% of 207

  e. 18% of 76   **f.** 9.3% of 315

  g. 0.97% of 63 **h.** 412% of 185

7. As discussed in this section, percent problems can be solved using three different methods: (i) grids, (ii) proportions, and (iii) equations. For each of the following problems (i) set up a grid with appropriate shading, (ii) set up a proportion similar to the one below, and (iii) set up an equation Select one of these methods to solve the problem.

$$\frac{\text{Part}}{\text{Whole}} = \frac{\text{percent}}{100}$$

Finally, enter the proportion that you have determined into the Chapter 7 eManipulative activity, *Percent Gauge*, and check your solution.

  a. 42 is what percent of 75?

  b. 17% of 964 is what number?

  c. 156.6 is 37% of what number?

  d. $8\frac{3}{4}$ is what percent of $12\frac{1}{3}$?

  e. 225% of what number is $12\frac{1}{3}$?

8. Answer the following and round to one decimal place.

  a. Find 24% of 140.

  b. Find $3\frac{1}{2}$% of 78.

  c. Find 32.7% of 252.

  d. What percent of 23 is 11.2?

  e. What percent of 1.47 is 0.816?

  f. 21 is 17% of what number?

  g. What percent of $\frac{1}{4}$ is $\frac{1}{12}$?

  h. 512 is 240% of what number?

  i. 140% of a number is 0.65. Find the number.

  j. Find $\frac{1}{2}$% of 24.6.

9. Use your calculator to find the following percents.

  a. 63% of 90 is _____.

  b. 27.5% of 420 is _____.

  c. 31.3% of 1200 is _____.

  d. 147 is 42% of _____.

  e. 3648 is 128% of _____.

  f. 0.5% of _____ is 78.4.

  g. 3.5% is _____ is 154.

  h. 36.3 is _____% of 165.

  i. 7.5 is _____% of 1250.

  j. 87.5 is _____% of 125.

  k. 221 is _____% of 34.

10. It is common practice to leave a 15% tip when eating in a restaurant. Mentally estimate the amount of tip to leave for each of the following check amounts.

  a. $11.00   **b.** $14.87   **c.** $35.06   **d.** $23.78

PROBLEMS

11. A 4200-pound automobile contains 357 pounds of rubber. What percent of the car's total weight is rubber? Set up a proportion to solve this problem in the Chapter 7 eManipulative activity, *Percent Gauge.* Describe the setup and the solution.

12. The senior class consists of 2780 students. If 70% of the students will graduate, how many students will graduate? Set up a proportion to solve this problem in the Chapter 7 eManipulative activity, *Percent Gauge.* Describe the setup and the solution.

13. An investor earned $208.76 in interest in one year on an account that paid 4.25% simple interest.

   a. What was the value of the account at the end of that year?

   b. How much more interest would the account have earned at a rate of 5.33%?

14. Suppose that you have borrowed $100 at the daily interest rate of 0.04839%. How much would you save by paying the entire $100.00 15 days before it is due?

15. A basketball team played 35 games. They lost 2 games. What percent of the games played did they lose? What percent did they win?

16. In 1997, total individual charitable contributions increased by 73% from 1990 contributions.

   a. If a total of 9.90×10^{10} was donated to charity in 1997. what amount was donated to charity in 1990?

   b. The average charitable contribution increased from $1958 to $3041 over the same period. What was the percent increase in average charitable contributions from 1990 to 1997?

17. The following pie chart shows the sources of U.S. energy production in 1999 in quadrillion BTUs.

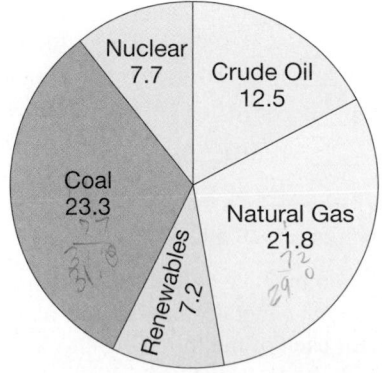

a. How much energy was produced, from all sources, in the United States in 1999?

b. What percent of the energy produced in the United States in 1999 came from each of the sources? Round your answers to the nearest tenth of a percent.

18. A clothing store advertised a coat at a 15% discount. The original price was $115.00, and the sale price was $100. Was the price consistent with the ad? Explain.

19. Rosemary sold a car and made a profit of $850, which was 17% of the selling price. What was the selling price?

20. Complete the following. Try to solve them mentally before using written or calculator methods.

   a. 30% of 50 is 6% of _____.

   b. 40% of 60 is 5% of _____.

   c. 30% of 80 is _____% of 160.

21. A car lot is advertising an 8% discount on a particular automobile. You pay $4485.00 for the car. What was the original price of the car?

22. a. The continents of Asia, Africa, and Europe together have an area of 8.5×10^{13} square meters. What percent of the surface area of the Earth do these three continents comprise if the total surface area of the Earth is about 5.2×10^{14} square meters?

   b. The Pacific Ocean has an area of about 1.81×10^{14} square meters. What percent of the surface of the Earth is covered by the Pacific Ocean?

   c. If all of the oceans are taken together, they make up about 70% of the surface of the Earth. How many square meters of the Earth's surface are covered by ocean?

   d. What percent of the landmass of the Earth is contained in Texas, with an area of about 6.92×10^{11} square meters?

23. The nutritional information on a box of cereal indicates that one serving provides 3 grams of protein, or 4% of U.S. recommended daily allowances (RDA). One serving with milk provides 7 grams, or 15% U.S. RDA. Is the information provided consistent? Explain.

24. A pair of slacks was made of material that was expected to shrink 10%. If the manufacturer makes the 32-inch inseam of the slacks 10% longer, what will the inseam measure after shrinkage?

25. Which results in a higher price: a 10% markup followed by a 10% discount, or a 10% discount followed by a 10% markup?

26. Joseph has 64% as many baseball cards as Cathy. Martin has 50% as many cards as Joseph. Martin has _____% as many cards as Cathy.

27. Your optimal exercise heart rate for cardiovascular benefits is calculated as follows: Subtract your age from 220. Then find 70% of this difference and 80% of this difference. The optimal rate is between the latter two numbers. Find the optimal heart rate range for a 50-year-old.

28. In an advertisement for a surround-sound decoder, it was stated that "our unit provides six outputs of audio information—that's 40% more than the competition." Explain why the person writing this ad does not understand the mathematics involved.

29. A heart doctor in Florida offers patients discounts for adopting good health habits. He offers 10% off if a patient stops smoking and another 5% off if a patient lowers her blood pressure or cholesterol a certain percentage. If you qualify for both discounts, would you rather the doctor (i) add them together and take 15% off your bill, or (ii) take 10% off first and then take 5% off the resulting discounted amount? Explain.

30. The population in one country increased by 4.2% during 1999, increased by 2.8% in 2000, and then decreased by 2.1% in 2001. What was the net percent change in population over the three-year period? Round your answer to the nearest tenth of a percent.

31. Monica has a daisy with nine petals. She asks Jerry to play the following game: They will take turns picking either one petal or two petals that are next to each other. The player who picks the last petal wins. Does the first player always win? Can the first player ever win? Discuss.

32. A clothing store was preparing for its semiannual 20% off sale. When it came to marking down the items, the salespeople wondered if they should (i) deduct the 20% from the selling price and then add the 6% sales tax, or (ii) add the 6% tax and then deduct the 20% from the total. Which way is correct, and why?

33. Elaine wants to deposit her summer earnings of $12,000 in a savings account to save for retirement. The bank pays 7% interest per year compounded semiannually (every 6 months). How much will her tax-deferred account be worth at the end of 3 years?

34. Assuming an inflation rate of 11%, how much would a woman earning $35,000 per year today need to earn five years from now to have the same buying power? Round your answer to the nearest thousand.

35. A couple wants to increase their savings for their daughter's college education. How much money must they invest now at 8.25% compounded annually in order to have accumulated $20,000 at the end of 10 years?

36. The consumer price index (CPI) is used by the government to relate prices to inflation. In July 2001, the CPI was 177.5, which means that prices were 77.5% higher than prices for the 1982–1984 period. If the CPI in July 2000 was 172.8, what was the percent increase from July 2000 to July 2001?

37. The city of Taxaphobia imposed a progressive income tax rate; that is, the more you earn, the higher the rate you pay. The rate they chose is equal to the number of thousands of dollars you earn. For example, a person who earns $13,000 pays 13% of her earnings in taxes. If you could name your own salary less than $100,000, what would you want to earn? Explain.

38. Wages were found to have risen to 108% from the previous year. If the current average wage is $9.99, what was the average wage last year?

39. A man's age at death was $\frac{1}{29}$ of the year of his birth. How old was he in 1949?

40. Your rectangular garden, which has whole-number dimensions, has an area of 72 square feet. However, you have absentmindedly forgotten the actual dimensions. If you want to fence the garden, what possible lengths of fence might be needed?

41. The pilot of a small plane must make a round trip between points *A* and *B,* which are 300 miles apart. The plane has an airspeed of 150 mph, and the pilot wants to make the trip in the minimum length of time. This morning there is a tailwind of 50 mph blowing from *A* to *B* and therefore a headwind of 50 mph from *B* to *A*. However, the weather forecast is for no wind tomorrow. Should the pilot make the trip today and take advantage of the tailwind in one direction or should the pilot wait until tomorrow, assuming that there will be no wind at all? That is, on which day will travel time be shorter?

Section 7.4 EXERCISE / PROBLEM SET B

EXERCISES

1. Fill in this chart.

FRACTION	DECIMAL	PERCENT
——	——	66.66%
——	0.003	——
$\frac{1}{40}$	——	——
——	0.05	——
——	——	1.6%
$\frac{1}{100}$	——	——
——	0.00001	——
——	——	0.0085%

2. Mentally complete the following sets of information.

a. A school's enrollment of seventh-, eighth-, and ninth-graders is 1000 students. 40% are seventh-graders = _____ of 1000 students. 35% are eighth-graders = _____ of 1000 students. _____% are ninth-graders = _____ of 1000 students.

b. 10% interest rate: 10 cents on every _____; $1.50 on every _____; $4.00 on every _____.

c. 6% sales tax: $ _____ on $1.00; $ _____ on $6.00; $_____ on $0.50; $_____ on $7.50.

3. Mentally complete the following statements.

a. 196 is 200% of _____.

b. 25% of 244 is _____.

c. 39 is _____% of 78.

d. 731 is 50% of _____.

e. 40 is _____% of 32.

f. 40% of 355 is _____.

g. $166\frac{2}{3}$% of 300 is _____.

h. 4.2 is _____% of 4200.

i. 210 is 60% of _____.

4. Find mentally.

a. 10% of 16 **b.** 1% of 1000

c. 20% of 150 **d.** 200% of 75

e. 15% of 40 **f.** 10% of 440

g. 15% of 50 **h.** 300% of 120

5. Find mentally, using fraction equivalents.

a. 50% of 180 **b.** 25% of 440

c. 75% of 320 **d.** $33\frac{1}{3}$% of 210

e. 40% of 250 **f.** $12\frac{1}{2}$% of 400

g. $66\frac{2}{3}$% of 660 **h.** 20% of 120

6. Estimate.

a. 21% of 34 **b.** 42% of 61

c. 24% of 57 **d.** 211% of 82

e. 16% of 42 **f.** 11.2% of 431

g. 48% of 26 **h.** 39.4% of 147

7. Write a percent problem for each proportion and then solve it using either grids or equations. Check your solution by inputting the original proportion into the Chapter 7 eManipulative activity, *Percent Gauge*.

a. $\dfrac{67}{95} = \dfrac{x}{100}$ **b.** $\dfrac{18.4}{x} = \dfrac{112}{100}$

c. $\dfrac{x}{3.5} = \dfrac{16\frac{2}{3}}{100}$ **d.** $\dfrac{2.8}{0.46} = \dfrac{x}{100}$

e. $\dfrac{4200}{x} = \dfrac{0.05}{100}$

8. Find each missing number in the following percent problems. Round to the nearest tenth.

a. 48% of what number is 178?

b. 14.36 is what percent of 35?

c. What percent of 2.4 is 5.2?

d. $83\frac{1}{3}$% of 420 is what number?

e. 6 is $\frac{1}{4}$% of what number?

f. What percent of $16\frac{3}{4}$ is $12\frac{2}{3}$?

9. Calculate, using a percent key.

a. 34% of 90

b. 126% of 72

c. 30% of what number is 57?

d. 50 is what percent of 80?

e. $90 marked up 13%

f. $120 discounted 12%

10. Compute each of the following to the nearest cent.

a. 65% of $298.54

b. 52.7% of $211.53

c. 35.2% of $2874.65

d. 49.5% of $632.09

PROBLEMS

11. A mathematics test had 80 questions, each worth the same value. Wendy was correct on 55 of the questions. Using the Chapter 7 eManipulative activity, *Percent Gauge*, determine what percent of the questions Wendy got correct. Describe how you used the eManipulative to find the solution.

12. A retailer sells a shirt for $21.95. If the retailer marked up the shirt about 70%, what was his cost for the shirt? Use the Chapter 7 eManipulative activity, *Percent Gauge*, to find the solution and describe how the eManipulative was used to accomplish this.

13. In 1995, 87,000 taxpayers reported incomes of more than $1,000,000. In 1997, the number of taxpayers reporting incomes of more than $1,000,000 had increased to 144,000. By what percent did the number of taxpayers earning more than $1,000,000 increase between 1995 and 1997? Round your answer to the nearest whole number.

14. Frank's salary is $240 per week. He saves $28 a week. What percent of his salary does he save?

15. It is common practice to pay salespeople extra money, called a **commission,** on the amount of sales. Bill is paid $315.00 a week, plus 6% commission on sales. Find his total earnings if his sales are $575.

16. The following pie chart (or circle chart) shows a student's relative expenditures. If the student's resources are $8000.00, how much is spent on each item?

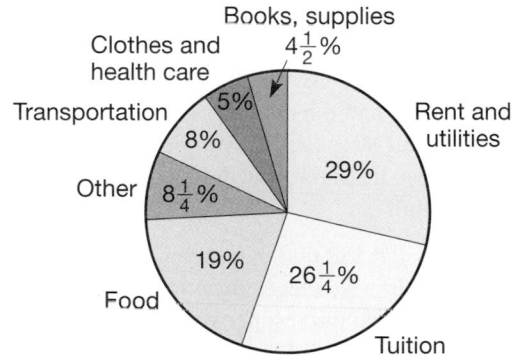

17. In a class of 36 students, 13 were absent on Friday. What percent of the class was absent?

18. A volleyball team wins 105 games, which is 70% of the games played. How many games were played?

19. The mass of all the bodies in our solar system, excluding the sun, is about 2.67×10^{27} kg. The mass of Jupiter is about 1.9×10^{27} kg.

   a. What percent of the total mass of the solar system, excluding the sun, does Jupiter contain?

   b. The four largest planets together (Jupiter, Saturn, Neptune, and Uranus) account for nearly all of the mass of the solar system, excluding the sun. If the masses of Saturn, Neptune, and Uranus are 5.7×10^{26} kg, 1.03×10^{26} kg, and 8.69×10^{25} kg, respectively, what percent of the total mass of the solar system, excluding the sun, do these four planets contain?

20. Henry got a raise of $80, which was 5% of his salary. What was his salary? Calculate mentally.

21. A CD store is advertising all CDs at up to 35% off. What would be the price range for CDs originally priced at $12.00?

22. Shown in the following table are data on the number of registered motor vehicles in the United States and fuel consumption in the United States in 1990 and 1998.

	VEHICLE REGISTRATIONS (MILLIONS)	MOTOR FUEL CONSUMPTION (THOUSANDS OF BARRELS PER DAY)
1990	188.8	8532
1998	211.6	10,104

   a. By what percent did the number of vehicle registrations increase between 1990 and 1998?

   b. By what percent did the consumption of motor fuel increase between 1990 and 1998?

   c. Are these increases proportional? Explain.

23. A refrigerator and range were purchased and a 5% sales tax was added to the purchase price. If the total bill was $834.75, how much did the refrigerator and range cost?

24. Susan has $20.00. Sharon has $25.00. Susan claims that she has 20% less than Sharon. Sharon replies. "No. I have 25% more than you." Who is right?

25. Following is one tax table from a recent income tax form.

IF YOUR TAXABLE INCOME IS:	YOUR TAX IS:
Not over $500	4.2% of taxable income
Over $500 but not over $1000	$21.00 + 5.3% of excess over $500
Over $1000 but not over $2000	$47.50 + 6.5% of excess over $1000
Over $2000 but not over $3000	$112.50 + 7.6% of excess over $2000
Over $3000 but not over $4000	$188.50 + 8.7% of excess over $3000
Over $4000 but not over $5000	$275.50 + 9.8% of excess over $4000
Over $5000	$373.50 + 10.8% of excess over $5000

a. Given the following taxable income figures, compute the tax owed (to the nearest cent).
(i) $3560, (ii) $8945, (iii) $2990.

b. If your tax was $324.99, what was your taxable income?

26. The price of coffee was 50 cents a pound 10 years ago. If the current price of coffee is $4.25 a pound, what percent increase in price does this represent?

27. A bookstore had a spring sale. All items were reduced by 20%. After the sale, prices were marked up at 20% over sale price. How do prices after the sale differ from prices before the sale?

28. A department store marked down all of its summer clothing 25%. The following week the remaining items were marked down again 15% off the sale price. When Jorge bought two tank tops on sale, he presented a coupon that gave him an additional 20% off. What percent of the original price did Jorge save?

29. A fishing crew is paid 43% of the value of their catch.

a. If they catch $10,500 worth of fish, what is the crew paid?

b. If the crew is paid $75,000 for a year's work, what was the total catch worth?

c. Suppose that the owner has the following expenses for a year:

ITEM	EXPENSE
Insurance	$12,000
Fuel	20,000
Maintenance	7,500
Miscellaneous	5,000

How much does he need to make to pay all his expenses and the crew?

d. If the fish are selling to the processors for an average of 22 cents/pound, how many pounds of fish does the owner need to sell to pay his expenses in part (c)?

30. Alan has thrown 24 passes and completed 37.5% of them. How many consecutive passes will Alan have to complete if he wants to have a completion average above 58%?

31. Beaker A has a quantity of water and beaker B has an equal quantity of wine. A milliliter of A is placed in B and B is mixed thoroughly. Then a milliliter of the mixture in B is placed in A and mixed. Which is greater, the percentage of wine in A or the percentage of water in B? Explain.

32. A girl bought some pencils, erasers, and paper clips at the stationery store. The pencils cost 10 cents each, the erasers cost 5 cents each, and the clips cost 2 for 1 cent. If she bought 100 items altogether at a total cost of $1, how many of each item did she buy?

33. If you add the square of Tom's age to the age of Carol, the sum is 62; but if you add the square of Carol's age to the age of Tom, the result is 176. Determine the ages of Tom and Carol.

34. Suppose that you have 5 chains each consisting of 3 links. If a single chain of 15 links is to be formed by cutting and welding, what is the fewest number of cuts that need to be made?

35. A pollster found that 36.723672% of her sample voted Republican. What is the smallest number of people that could have been in the sample?

36. Think of any whole number. Add 20. Multiply by 10. Find 20% of your last result. Find 50% of the last number. Subtract the number you started with. What is your result? Repeat. Did you get a similar result? If yes, prove that this procedure will always lead to a certain result.

37. Eric deposited $32,000 in a savings account to save for his children's college education. The bank pays 8% tax-deferred interest per year compounded quarterly. How much will his account be worth at the end of 18 years?

38. Jim wants to deposit money in an account to save for a new stereo system in two years. He wants to have $4000 available at that time. The following rates are available to him:

1. 6.2% simple interest

2. 6.1% compounded annually

3. 5.58% compounded semiannually

4. 5.75% compounded quarterly

a. Which account(s) should he choose if he wants to invest the smallest amount of money now?

b. How much money must he invest to accumulate $4000 in two years' time?

39. Suppose that you have $1000 in a savings account that pays 4.8% interest per year. Suppose, also, that you owe $500 at 1.5% per month interest.

a. If you pay the interest on your loan for one month so that you can collect one month's interest on

$500 in your savings account, what is your net gain or loss?

b. If you pay the loan back with $500 from your savings account rather than pay one month's interest on the loan, what is your net gain or loss?

c. What strategy do you recommend?

40. One-fourth of the world's population is Chinese and one-fifth of the rest is Indian. What percent of the world's population is Indian?

41. A **cevian** is a line segment that joins a vertex of a triangle and a point on the opposite side. How many triangles are formed if eight cevians are drawn from one vertex of a triangle?

PROBLEMS FOR WRITING/DISCUSSION

1. A student says that if the sale price of a shirt during a 60% off sale is $27.88, then you can find the amount of money you *saved* by multiplying $27.88 times $\frac{60}{40}$ or 1.5. What would you respond?

2. Yoko says that if a car dealer pays General Motors $17,888 for a new car and he then tries to sell it for 20% over cost and it doesn't sell, he can later sell it

for 20% off and he'll still come out even. Do you agree? Explain.

3. Jerry says that if a store has a sale for 35% off and the sale price of a stairmaster is $137, then you can figure out what the original price was by taking 35% of $137 and then adding it back onto the $137. So the original price should be $184.95. But that answer doesn't check. Explain what mistake Jerry is making.

END OF CHAPTER MATERIAL

Solution of Initial Problem

A street vendor had a basket of apples. Feeling generous one day, he gave away one-half of his apples plus one to the first stranger he met, one-half of his remaining apples plus one to the next stranger he met, and one-half of his remaining apples plus one to the third stranger he met. If the vendor had one left for himself, with how many apples did he start?

Strategy: Work Backward

The vendor ended up with 1 apple. In the previous step, he gave away half of his apples plus 1 more. Thus he must have had 4 apples since the one he had plus the one he gave away was 2, and 2 is half of 4. Repeating this procedure, $4 + 1 = 5$ and $2 \cdot 5 = 10$; thus he must have had 10 apples when he met the second stranger. Repeating this procedure once more, $10 + 1 = 11$ and $2 \cdot 11 = 22$. Thus he had 22 apples when he met the first stranger.

Check:

    Start with 22.
    Give away one-half (11) plus one, or 12.

10 remain.
Give away one-half (5) plus one, or 6.
4 remain.
Give away one-half (2) plus one, or 3.
1 remains.

Additional Problems Where the Strategy "Work Backward" Is Useful

1. On a class trip to the world's tallest building, the class rode up several floors, then rode down 18 floors, rode up 59 floors, rode down 87 floors, and ended up on the first floor. How many floors did they ride up initially?

2. At a sports card trading show, one trader gave 3 cards for 5. Then she traded 7 cards for 2. Finally, she bought 4 and traded 2 for 9. If she ended up with 473 cards, how many did she bring to the show?

3. Try the following "magic" trick: Multiply a number by 6. Then add 9. Double this result. Divide by 3. Subtract 6. Then divide by 4. If the answer is 13, what was your original number?

People in Mathematics

David Blackwell (1919–) When David Blackwell entered college at age 16, his ambition was to earn a bachelor's degree and become an elementary teacher. Six years later, he had a doctorate in mathematics and was nominated for a fellowship at the Institute for Advanced Study at Princeton. The position included an honorary membership in the faculty at nearby Princeton University, but the university objected to the appointment of a black man as a faculty member. The director of the institute insisted on appointing Blackwell, and eventually won out. From Princeton, Blackwell went on to teach for 10 years at Howard University, then at Berkeley. He has made important contributions to statistics, probability, game theory, and set theory. "Why do you want to share something beautiful with someone else? It's because of the pleasure he will get, and in transmitting it you will appreciate its beauty all over again. My high school geometry teacher really got me interested in mathematics. I hear it suggested from time to time that geometry might be dropped from the curriculum. I would really hate to see that happen. It is a beautiful subject."

Sonya Kovalevskaya (1850– 1891) As a young woman, Sonya Kovalevskaya hoped to study in Berlin under the great mathematician Karl Weierstrass. But women were barred from attending the university. She approached Weierstrass directly. Skeptical, he assigned her a set of difficult problems. When Kovalevskaya a returned the following week with solutions, he agreed to teach her privately and was influential in seeing that she was granted her degree—even though she never officially attended the university. Kovalevskaya is known for her work in differential equations and for her mathematical theory of the rotation of solid bodies. In addition, she was editor of a mathematical journal, wrote two plays (with Swedish writer Anne Charlotte Leffler), a novella, and memoirs of her childhood. Of her literary and mathematical talents, she wrote, "The poet has to perceive that which others do not perceive, to look deeper than others look. And the mathematician must do the same thing."

CHAPTER REVIEW

Review the following terms and exercises to determine which require learning or relearning—page numbers are provided for easy reference.

SECTION 7.1: Decimals

VOCABULARY/NOTATION

Decimal 265	Expanded form 265	Terminating decimal 266
Decimal point 265	Hundreds square 265	Fraction equivalents 268

EXERCISES

1. Write 37.149 in expanded form.

2. Write 2.3798 in its word name.

3. Determine which of the following fractions have a terminating decimal representation.

　　a. $\dfrac{7}{2^3}$　　**b.** $\dfrac{5^3}{3^2 \cdot 2^5}$　　**c.** $\dfrac{17}{2^{13}}$

4. Explain how to determine the smaller of 0.24 and 0.3 using the following techniques.

　　a. A hundreds square

　　b. The number line

　　c. Fractions

　　d. Place value

5. Calculate mentally and explain what techniques you used.

  a. $(0.25 \times 12.3) \times 8$

  b. $1.3 \times 2.4 + 2.4 \times 2.7$

  c. $15.73 + 2.99$

  d. $27.51 - 19.98$

6. Estimate using the techniques given.

  a. Range: $2.51 \times 3.29 \times 8.07$

  b. Front-end with adjustment: $2.51 + 3.29 + 8.2$

  c. Rounding to the nearest tenth: $8.549 - 2.352$

  d. Rounding to compatible numbers: $421.7 \div 52.937$

SECTION 7.2: Operations with Decimals

VOCABULARY/NOTATION

Repetend $(.\overline{abcd})$ 279   Repeating decimal   279   Period   279

EXERCISES

1. Calculate the following using (i) a standard algorithm and (ii) a calculator.

  a. $16.179 + 4.83$

  b. $84.25 - 47.761$

  c. 41.5×3.7

  d. $154.611 \div 4.19$

  a. $\dfrac{5}{13}$

  b. $\dfrac{132}{333}$

  c. $\dfrac{46}{92}$

2. Determine which of the following fractions have repeating decimals. For those that do, express them as a decimal with a bar over their repetend.

3. Find the fraction representation in simplest form for each of the following decimals.

  a. $3.\overline{674}$ **b.** $24.1\overline{32}$

SECTION 7.3: Ratio and Proportion

VOCABULARY/NOTATION

Ratio   286   Whole-to-part   287   Proportion   288
Part-to-part   287   Extremes   288   Rates   288
Part-to-whole   287   Means   288   Scaling up/scaling down   290

EXERCISES

1. How do the concepts ratio and proportion differ?

2. Determine whether the following are proportions. Explain your method.

  a. $\dfrac{7}{13} = \dfrac{9}{15}$ **b.** $\dfrac{12}{15} = \dfrac{20}{25}$

3. Describe two ways to determine whether $\dfrac{a}{b} = \dfrac{c}{d}$ is a proportion.

4. Which is the better buy? Explain.

  a. 58 cents for 24 oz or 47 cents for 16 oz

  b. 7 pounds for \$3.45 or 11 pounds for \$5.11

5. Solve: If $3\frac{1}{4}$ cups of sugar are used to make a batch of candy for 30 people, how many cups are required for 40 people?

SECTION 7.4: Percent

VOCABULARY/NOTATION

Percent   297   Proportion approach   300   Equation approach   301
Grid approach   299

EXERCISES

1. Write each of the following in all three forms: decimal, percent, and fraction (in simplest form).

   a. 56%   **b.** 0.48   **c.** $\frac{1}{8}$

2. Calculate mentally using fraction equivalents.

   a. $48 \times 25\%$

   b. $33\frac{1}{3}\% \times 72$

   c. $72 \times 75\%$

   d. $20\% \times 55$

3. Estimate using fraction equivalents.

   a. $23\% \times 81$ **b.** $49\% \times 199$

   c. $32\% \times 59$ **d.** $67\% \times 310$

4. Solve:

   a. A car was purchased for $17,120 including a 7% sales tax. What was the price of the car before tax?

   b. A soccer player has been successful 60% of the times she kicks toward goal. If she has taken 80 kicks, what percent will she have if she kicks 11 out of the next 20?

PROBLEMS FOR WRITING/DISCUSSION

1. Mary Lou said she knows that when fractions are written as decimals they either repeat or terminate. So 12/17 must not be a fraction because when she divided 12 by 17 on her calculator, she got a decimal that did not repeat or terminate. How would you react to this?

2. A student in your class says that if the ratio of oil to vinegar in a salad dressing is $3:4$, that means that 75% of the salad dressing is oil. Another student says less than 50% is oil. Can you explain this?

3. A student tells you that 6.45 is greater than 6.5 because 45 is greater than 5. How would you explain?

4. Can you use lattice multiplication for decimals? For example, how would you multiply 3.24 times 1.7?

5. Caroline is rounding decimals to the nearest hundredth. She takes 19.67472 and she changes it to 19.6747, then 19.675, then 19.68. Her teacher says the answer is 19.67. Caroline says, "I thought I was supposed to round up when the next digit is 5 or more." Can you help explain this problem?

6. Looking at the same problem that Caroline had, Amir comes up with the answer 19.66. When his teacher asks him how he got that answer, he says, "because of the 4, I had to round down." What is Amir's misconception?

7. There is a new student in your class whose family has just moved to your district from Germany. When he writes out the number for π, he writes 3,14 instead of 3.14, and when you tell him he's wrong, he gets upset. The next day he brings a note from home saying that 3,14 is correct. What is going on here? How would you explain?

8. Merilee said her calculator changed $\frac{2}{3}$ to .6666667, so obviously it does not repeat. Therefore it must be a terminating decimal. How would you respond to Merilee?

9. How do you calculate a 15% tip in a restaurant? Explain your method. What do you think is the best way to do it mentally?

10. Hair stylists tell you that human hair typically grows $\frac{1}{2}$ inch per month. How would you translate that into miles per hour? How would you explain your method to students?

CHAPTER TEST

Knowledge

1. True or false?

   a. The decimal 0.034 is read "thirty-four hundredths."

   b. The expanded form of 0.0271 is $\frac{2}{100} + \frac{7}{1000} + \frac{1}{10,000}$.

   c. The fraction $\frac{27}{125}$ has a terminating decimal representation.

   d. The repetend of $0.03\overline{74}$ is "374."

   e. The fraction $\frac{27}{225}$ has a repeating, nonterminating decimal representation.

   f. Forty percent equals two-fifths.

   g. The ratios $m:n$ and $p:q$ are equal if and only if $mq = np$.

   h. If $p\%$ of n is x, then $\frac{100x}{n}$.

2. Write the following in expanded form.

   a. 32.198   **b.** .000342

3. What does the "cent" part of the word *percent* mean?

4. In a bag of 23 Christmas candies there were 14 green candies and 9 red candies. Express the following types of ratios.

   a. Part to part

   b. Part to whole

Skill

5. Compute the following problems without a calculator. Find approximate answers first.

   a. $3.71 + 13.809$

   b. $14.3 - 7.961$

   c. 7.3×11.41

   d. $6.5 \div 0.013$

6. Determine which number in the following pairs is larger using (i) the fraction representation, and (ii) the decimal representation.

   a. 0.103 and 0.4

   b. 0.0997 and 0.1

7. Express each of the following fractions in its decimal form.

   a. $\frac{2}{7}$ **b.** $\frac{5}{8}$ **c.** $\frac{7}{48}$ **d.** $\frac{4}{9}$

8. Without converting, determine whether the following fractions will have a terminating or nonterminating decimal representation.

   a. $\frac{9}{16}$ **b.** $\frac{17}{78}$ **c.** $\frac{2^3}{2^7 \cdot 5^3}$

9. Express each of the following decimals in its simplest fraction form.

   a. $0.\overline{36}$ **b.** $0.3\overline{6}$ **c.** 0.3636

10. Express each of the following in all three forms: decimal, fraction, and percent.

   a. 52%   **b.** 1.25   **c.** $\frac{17}{25}$

11. The ratio of boys to girls is 3:2 and there are 30 boys and girls altogether. How many boys are there?

12. Estimate the following and describe your method.

   a. 53×0.48

   b. $1469.2 \div 26.57$

   c. $33 \div 0.76$

   d. 442.78×18.7

13. Arrange the following from smallest to largest.

$$\frac{1}{3}, \quad 0.3, \quad 3\%, \quad \frac{2}{7}$$

Understanding

14. Without performing any calculations, explain why $\frac{1}{123456789}$ must have a repeating, nonterminating decimal representation.

15. Suppose that the percent key and the decimal point key on your calculator are both broken. Explain how you could still use your calculator to solve problems like "Find 37% of 58."

16. Write a word problem involving percents that would have the following proportion or equation as part of its solution.

   a. $80\% \cdot x = 48$

   b. $\dfrac{x}{100} = \dfrac{35}{140}$

17. When adding 1.3 and 0.2, the sum has 1 digit to the right of the decimal. When multiplying 1.3 and 0.2, the product has 2 digits to the right of the decimal. Explain why the product has 2 digits to the right of the decimal and not just 1.

Problem-Solving/Application

18. What is the 100th digit in $0.\overline{564793}$?

19. If the cost of a new car is $12,000 (plus 5% sales tax) and a down payment of 20% (including the tax) is required, how much money will a customer need to drive out in a new car?

20. A television set was to be sold at a 13% discount, which amounted to $78. How much would the set sell for after the discount?

21. A photograph measuring 3 inches by $2\frac{1}{2}$ inches is to be enlarged so that the smaller side, when enlarged, will be 8 inches. How long will the enlarged longer side be?

22. Find three numbers between 5.375 and 5.3751.

23. Dr. Fjeldsted has 91 students in his first-quarter calculus class. If the ratio of math majors to non-math majors is 4 to 9, how many math majors are in the class?

24. In a furniture store advertisement it was stated "our store offers six new sofa styles—that's 40% more than the competition." Explain why the person writing this advertisement does not understand the mathematics involved.

25. A refrigerator was on sale at the appliance store for 20% off. Marcus received a coupon from the store for an additional 30% off any current price in the store. If he uses the coupon to buy the refrigerator, the price would be $487.20 before taxes. What was the original price?

References for Reflections from Research

BELL, A. (1986). Diagnostic teaching 2. Developing conflict–discussion lessons. *Mathematics Teacher*, *116*, 26–29.

GREER, B. (1987). Nonconservation of multiplication and division involving decimals. *Journal for Research in Mathematics Education*, *18*, 37–45.

HIEBERT, J., & WEARNE, D. (1987). Procedure over concept: The acquisition of decimal number knowledge. In J. Hiebert (Ed.), *Conceptual and procedural knowledge: The case of mathematics* (pp. 199–233). Hillsdale, NJ: Erlbaum.

IRWIN, K. (1996). Children's understanding of the principles of covariation and compensation in part-whole relationships. *Journal for Research in Mathematics Education*, *27*, 25–40.

LO, J., & WATANABE, T. (1997). Developing ratio and proportion schemes: A story of a fifth grader. *Journal for Research in Mathematics Education*, *28*, 216–236.

LOPEZ-REAL, F. (1995). How important is the reversal error in algebra? In B. Atweh & S. Flavel (Eds.), MERGA 18: GALTHA, *Proceedings of the 18th annual conference* (pp. 390–396). Darwin, Australia: Northern Territory University.

OWENS, D. T. (1990). Thinking on rational number concepts. A teaching experiment. Final Report to Social Sciences and Humanities Research Council of Canada Grant #410-88-0678.

RESNICK, L. B., NESHER, P., LEONARD, F., MAGONE, M., OMANSON, S., & PELED, I. (1989). Conceptual bases of arithmetic errors: The case of decimal fractions. *Journal for Research in Mathematics Education*, *20*, 8–27.

SWAFFORD, J. O., & LANGRALL, C. W. (2000). Grade 6 students' preinstructional use of equations to describe and represent problem situations. *Journal for Research in Mathematics Education*, *31*, 89–110.

TRAFTON, P. R., & ZAWOJEWSKI, J. S. (1984). Teaching rational number division: A special problem. *Arithmetic Teacher*, *31*(6), 20–22.

FOCUS ON *A Brief History of Negative Numbers*

N o trace of the recognition of negative numbers can be found in any of the early writings of the Egyptians, Babylonians, Hindus, Chinese, or Greeks. Even so, computations involving subtraction, such as $(10 - 6) \cdot (5 - 2)$, were performed correctly where rules for multiplying negatives were applied. The first mention of negative numbers can be traced to the Chinese in 200 B.C.

In the fourth century in his text *Arithmetica*, Diophantus spoke of the equation $4x + 20 = 4$ as "absurd," since x would have to be -4! The Hindu Brahmagupta (circa A.D. 630) spoke of "negative" and "affirmative" quantities, although these numbers always appeared as subtrahends. Around 1300, the Chinese mathematician Chu Shi-Ku gave the "rule of signs" in his algebra text. Also, in his text *Ars Magna* (1545) the Italian mathematician Cardano recognized negative roots and clearly stated rules of negatives.

Various notations have been used to designate negative numbers. The Hindus placed a dot or small circle over or beside a number to denote that it was negative; for example, 6́ or 6̊ represented -6. The Chinese used red to denote positive and black to denote negative integers, and indicated negative numbers by drawing a slash through a portion of the numeral; for example, $-10,200$ was written 10 ✗ ✗ 00. Cardano used the symbol m: (probably for "minus") for negative; for example, -3 was written m:3.

In this chapter we use black chips and red chips to motivate the concepts underlying positive ("in the black") and negative ("in the red") numbers much as the Chinese may have done, although with the colors reversed.

Both zeros and negative terms occur in this page from Chu Shih-Chieh's book on algebra, *Precious Mirror of the Four Elements*, published in 1303. Each box, consisting of a group of squares containing signs, represents a "matrix" form of writing an algebraic expression. The frequent occurrence of the sign "0" for zero may be clearly seen. (In these cases it means that terms corresponding to those squares do not occur in the equation.) The diagonal lines slashed through some of the numbers in the squares indicate that they are negative terms. (The number "one" is one vertical line, the number "two" is two vertical lines, etc.)

Problem Solving Strategies

1. Guess and Test
2. Use a Variable
3. Draw a Picture
4. Look for a Pattern
5. Make a List
6. Solve a Simpler Problem
7. Draw a Diagram
8. Use Direct Reasoning
9. Use Indirect Reasoning
10. Use Properties of Numbers
11. Solve an Equivalent Problem
12. Work Backward
13. Use Cases

Strategy
Use Cases

Many problems can be solved more easily by breaking the problem into various cases. For example, consider the following statement: The square of any whole number n is a multiple of 4 or one more than a multiple of 4. To prove this, we need only consider two cases: n is even or n is odd. If n is even, then $n = 2x$ and $n^2 = 4x^2$, which is a multiple of 4. If n is odd, then $n = 2x + 1$ and $n^2 = 4x^2 + 4x + 1$, which is one more than a multiple of 4. The following problem can be solved easily by considering various cases for a, b, and c.

Initial Problem

Prove or disprove: 2 is a factor of $(a - b)(b - c)(c - a)$ for any integers a, b, c. (*Hint*: Try a few examples first.)

$a = 8$, $b = 5$, $c = 1$.
$(a - b)(b - c)(c - a) = -84$.
$2 \mid -84$.

Clues

The Use Cases strategy may be appropriate when

- A problem can be separated into several distinct cases.
- A problem involves distinct collections of numbers such as odds and evens, primes and composites, and positives and negatives.
- Investigations in specific cases can be generalized.

A solution of the Initial Problem appears on page 347.

INTRODUCTION

Whole numbers and fractions are useful in solving many problems and applications in society. However, there are many situations where negative numbers are useful. For example, negative numbers are very helpful in describing temperature below zero, elevation below sea level, losses in the stock market, and an overdrawn checking account. In this chapter we study the integers, the set of numbers that consists of the whole numbers, together with the negative numbers that are the opposites of the nonzero whole numbers. The four basic operations of the integers are introduced together with order relationships.

8.1   ADDITION AND SUBTRACTION

In the above introduction, temperature, elevation, stocks, and banking are presented as situations where positive and negative numbers are used. Using one of these scenarios, write a word problem for each of the following expressions.

$$-30 + 14 \qquad -30 - 14 \qquad -30 + (-14)$$

Integers and the Integer Number Line

Reflection from Research
An understanding of integers is crucial to an understanding of future work in algebra (Sheffield & Cruikshank, 1996).

Reflection from Research
It is important to introduce children to negative numbers using manipulatives (Thompson, 1988).

The introduction to this chapter lists several situations in which negative numbers are useful. There are other situations in mathematics in which negative numbers are needed. For example, the subtraction problem $4 - 7$ has no answer when using whole numbers. Also, the equation $x + 7 = 4$ has no whole-number solution. To remedy these situations, we introduce a new set of numbers, the integers. Our approach here will be to introduce the integers using a physical model. This model is related to a procedure that was used in accounting. Numerals written in black ink represent amounts above zero ("in the black" is positive) and in red ink represent accounts below zero ("in the red" is negative). We will use the integers to represent these situations.

+5
Five black chips

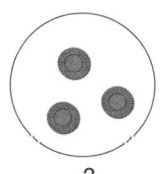

−3
Three red chips
Figure 8.1

 DEFINITION

Integers

The set of **integers** is the set

$$I = \{. \, . \, . \, , -3, -2, -1, 0, 1, 2, 3, \, . \, . \, .\}.$$

The numbers $1, 2, 3, \ldots$ are called **positive integers** and the numbers $-1, -2, -3, \ldots$ are called **negative integers.** Zero is neither a positive nor a negative integer.

In a set model, chips can be used to represent integers. However, *two* colors of chips must be used, one color to represent positive integers (black) and a second to represent negative integers (red) (Figure 8.1). One black chip represents a credit of 1 and one red chip represents a debit of 1. Thus *one black chip and one red chip cancel each other*, or "make a zero" [Figure 8.2(a)]. Using this concept, each integer can be represented by chips in many different ways [Figure 8.2(b)].

(a)

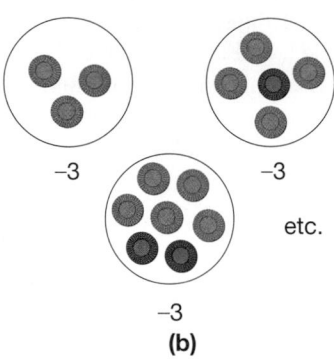

−3   −3

etc.

−3

(b)

Figure 8.2

4 and −4 are
opposites of each other.

Figure 8.4

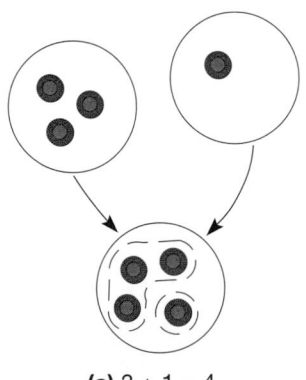

(a) 3 + 1 = 4

Figure 8.6a

An extension from the examples in Figure 8.2 is that each integer has infinitely many representations using chips. (Recall that every fraction also has an infinite number of representations.)

Another way to represent the integers is to use a measurement model, the **integer number line** (Figure 8.3). The integers are equally spaced and arranged sym-

Figure 8.3

metrically to the right and left of zero on the number line. This symmetry leads to a useful concept associated with positive and negative numbers. This concept, the opposite of a number, can be defined using either the measurement model or the set model of integers. The **opposite** of the integer a, written $-a$ or $(-a)$, is defined as follows:

Set Model The opposite of a is the integer that is represented by the same number of chips as a, but of the opposite color (Figure 8.4).

Measurement Model The opposite of a is the integer that is its mirror image about 0 on the integer number line (Figure 8.5).

Figure 8.5

The opposite of a positive integer is negative, and the opposite of a negative integer is positive. Also, the opposite of zero is zero. The concept of opposite will be seen to be very useful later in this section when we study subtraction.

Addition and Its Properties

Consider the following situation. In a football game, a running back made 12 running attempts and was credited with the following yardage for each attempt: 12, 7, −6, 8, 13, −1, 17, −5, 32, 16, 14, −7. What was his total yardage for the game? Integer addition can be used to answer this question. The definition of addition of integers can be motivated using both the set model and the measurement model.

Set Model Addition means to put together or form the union of two disjoint sets (Figure 8.6).

www.wiley.com/
college/musser

Spotlight on Technology The set model using black and red chips is illustrated in the Chapter 8 eManipulative activity, *Chips Plus*. After trying a few examples, answer the following question: "In general, when will the sum of two integers be negative?"

Measurement Model Addition means to put directed arrows end to end starting at zero. Note that positive integers are represented by arrows pointing to the right and negative integers by arrows pointing to the left (Figure 8.7).

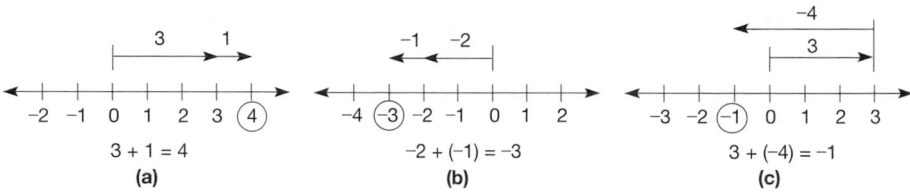

$3 + 1 = 4$	$-2 + (-1) = -3$	$3 + (-4) = -1$
(a)	(b)	(c)

Figure 8.7a   *Figure 8.7b*   *Figure 8.7c*

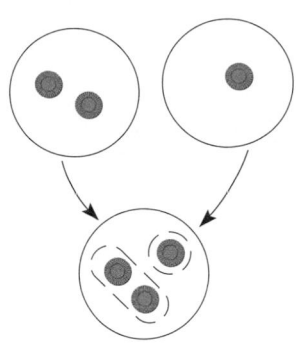

(b) $(-2) + (-1) = -3$

Figure 8.6b

The examples in Figures 8.6 and 8.7 lead to the following definition of integer addition.

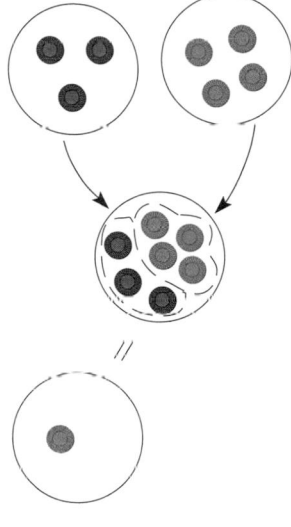

(c) $3 + (-4) = -1$

Figure 8.6c

DEFINITION

Addition of Integers

Let a and b be any integers.

1. *Adding zero*: $a + 0 = 0 + a = a$.
2. *Adding two positives*: If a and b are positive, they are added as whole numbers.
3. *Adding two negatives*: If a and b are positive (hence $-a$ and $-b$ are negative), then $(-a) + (-b) = -(a + b)$, where $a + b$ is the whole-number sum of a and b.
4. *Adding a positive and a negative*:
   a. If a and b are positive and $a \geq b$, then $a + (-b) = a - b$, where $a - b$ is the whole-number difference of a and b.
   b. If a and b are positive and $a < b$, then $a + (-b) = -(b - a)$, where $b - a$ is the whole-number difference of a and b.

These rules for addition are abstractions of what most people do when they add integers—namely, compute mentally using whole numbers and then determine whether the answer is positive, negative, or zero.

Example 8.1   Calculate the following using the definition of integer addition.
a. $3 + 0$ **b.** $3 + 4$ **c.** $(-3) + (-4)$
d. $7 + (-3)$ **e.** $3 + (-7)$ **f.** $5 + (-5)$

Solution

a. *Adding zero*: $3 + 0 = 3$
b. *Adding two positives*: $3 + 4 = 7$
c. *Adding two negatives*: $(-3) + (-4) = -(3 + 4) = -7$
d. *Adding a positive and a negative*: $7 + (-3) = 7 - 3 = 4$
e. *Adding a positive and a negative*: $3 + (-7) = -(7 - 3) = -4$
f. *Adding a number and its opposite*: $5 + (-5) = 0$ ■

The problems in Example 8.1 have interpretations in the physical world. For example, $(-3) + (-4)$ can be thought of as the temperature dropping 3 degrees one

PRACTICE

LESSON
22

Using Negative Numbers

In many real-life situations we need to describe things using numbers that are less than 0. In this lesson you'll review how to identify and name these negative numbers.

◆ Can you think of times when it might be useful to use numbers less than 0?

Suppose the temperature is 10°C and it goes down 15°C. What will the temperature be?

Temperature: 10°C   Goes Down 15°C   Temperature: 5° below 0°

We can then write this problem in this way: 10 − 15 = (−5)

−5 is read "negative 5."

We often call a temperature of 5° below 0°C a temperature of −5°C.

You can show negative numbers on a number line.

$$-10\ -9\ -8\ -7\ -6\ -5\ -4\ -3\ -2\ -1\quad 0\quad 1\quad 2\quad 3\quad 4\quad 5\quad 6\quad 7\quad 8\quad 9\quad 10$$

Write the missing items.

	Temperature Before Change	Temperature Change	Temperature After Change
1	15°C	up 5°	▨
2	10°C	down 15°	▨
3	−5°C (5° below 0°C)	down 5°	▨
4	−10°C	up 2°	▨
5	−5°C	up 5°	▨

hour and 4 degrees the next for a total of 7 degrees. In football, $3 + (-7)$ represents a gain of 3 and a loss of 7 for a net loss of 4 yards.

The integer models and the rules for the addition of integers can be used to justify the following properties of integers.

 PROPERTIES

Properties of Integer Addition

Let a, b, and c be any integers.

Closure Property for Integer Addition

$$a + b \text{ is an integer.}$$

Commutative Property for Integer Addition

$$a + b = b + a$$

Associative Property for Integer Addition

$$(a + b) + c = a + (b + c)$$

Identity Property for Integer Addition

0 is the unique integer such that $a + 0 = a = 0 + a$ for all a.

Additive Inverse Property for Integer Addition

For each integer a there is a unique integer, written $-a$, such that $a + (-a) = 0$. The integer $-a$ is called the **additive inverse** of a.

In words, this property states that any number plus its additive inverse is zero. A useful result that is a consequence of the additive inverse property is **additive cancellation.**

THEOREM

Additive Cancellation for Integers

Let a, b, and c be any integers. If $a + c = b + c$, then $a = b$.

Proof Let $a + c = b + c$. Then

$$(a + c) + (-c) = (b + c) + (-c) \qquad \textit{Addition}$$

$$a + [c + (-c)] = b + [c + (-c)] \qquad \textit{Associativity}$$

$$a + 0 = b + 0 \qquad \textit{Additive inverse}$$

$$a = b \qquad \textit{Additive identity}$$

Thus, if $a + c = b + c$, then $a = b$.   ■

Observe that $-a$ need not be negative. For example, the opposite of -7, written $-(-7)$, is 7, a positive number. In general, if a is positive, then $-a$ is negative; if a is negative, then $-a$ is positive; and if a is zero, then $-a$ is zero. As shown in Figure 8.8, using colored chips or a number line, it can be seen that $-(-a) = a$ for any integer a. (NOTE: The three small dots are used to allow for enough chips to represent any integer a, not necessarily just -3 and 3 as suggested by the black and red chips.)

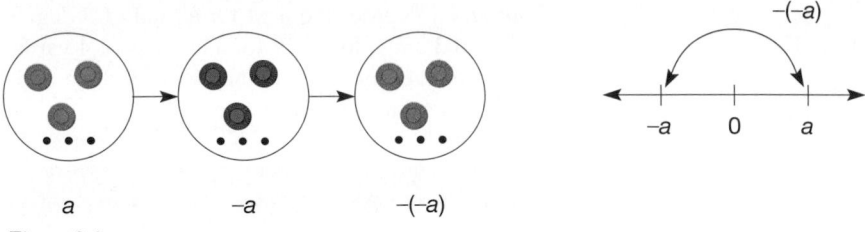

Figure 8.8

THEOREM

Let a be any integer. Then $-(-a) = a$.

Proof Notice that $a + (-a) = 0$ and $-(-a) + (-a) = 0$.
Therefore, $a + (-a) = -(-a) + (-a)$.
Finally, $a = -(-a)$, since the $(-a)$s can be canceled by additive cancellation. ■

Properties of integer addition, together with thinking strategies, are helpful in doing computations. For example,

$$3 + (-10) = 3 + [(-3) + (-7)]$$
$$= [3 + (-3)] + (-7) = 0 + (-7) = -7$$

and

$$(-7) + 21 = (-7) + (7 + 14)$$
$$= [(-7) + 7] + 14 = 0 + 14 = 14.$$

Problem-Solving Strategy
Look for a Pattern.

Each preceding step can be justified using a property or the definition of integer addition. When one does the preceding problem mentally, not all the steps need to be carried out. However, it is important to understand how the properties are being applied.

Subtraction

Subtraction of integers can be viewed in several ways.

Pattern

THE FIRST COLUMN	$4 - 2 = 2$	
REMAINS 4.	$4 - 1 = 3$	*1 MORE*
THE SECOND COLUMN	$4 - 0 = 4$	*1 MORE*
DECREASES BY 1 EACH	$4 - (-1) = 5$	*1 MORE*
TIME.	$4 - (-2) = 6$	*1 MORE*

Take-Away

Example 8.2 Calculate the following differences.

a. $6 - 2$
b. $-4 - (-1)$
c. $-2 - (-3)$
d. $2 - 5$

Solution See Figure 8.9. ■

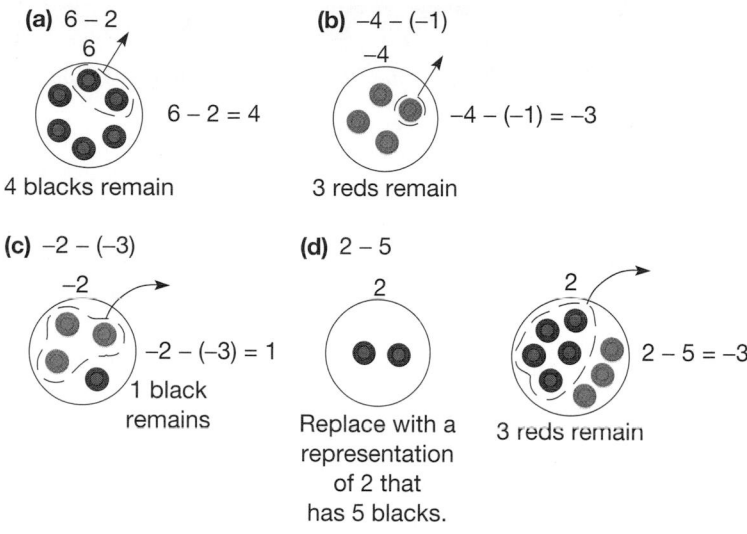

Figure 8.9

Adding the Opposite Let's reexamine the problem in Example 8.2(d). The difference $2 - 5$ can be found in yet another way using the chip model (Figure 8.10).

Figure 8.10

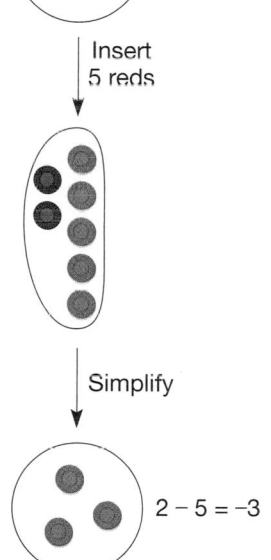

Figure 8.11

This second method can be simplified. The process of inserting 5 blacks and 5 reds and then removing 5 blacks can be accomplished more simply by inserting 5 reds, since we would just turn around and take the 5 blacks away once they were inserted.

Simplified Second Method Find $2 - 5$. The simplified method in Figure 8.11 finds $2 - 5$ by finding $2 + (-5)$. Thus the method of subtraction replaces a subtraction problem with an equivalent addition problem—namely, adding the opposite.

www.wiley.com/
college/musser

Spotlight on Technology The set model using black and red chips for subtraction is illustrated in the Chapter 8 eManipulative activity, *Chips Minus*. A key idea in using the chips to model integer operations is that adding 1 black chip and 1 red chip to a set does not change the value of the set because it is the same as adding 0. In fact, a pair of chips where one is black and the other is red is often referred to as a **zero pair.** After doing a few examples of integer subtraction on the eManipulative explain why the concept of a zero pair is important.

> ### DEFINITION
>
> **Subtraction of Integers: Adding the Opposite**
>
> Let a and b be any integers. Then
>
> $$a - b = a + (-b).$$

Adding the opposite is perhaps the most efficient method for subtracting integers because it replaces any subtraction problem with an equivalent addition problem.

Example 8.3   Find the following differences by adding the opposite.

a. $(-8) - 3$ **b.** $4 - (-5)$

Solution

a. $(-8) - 3 = (-8) + (-3) = -11$ **b.** $4 - (-5) = 4 + [-(-5)] = 4 + 5 = 9$ ■

Missing Addend Recall that another approach to subtraction, the missing-addend approach, was used in whole-number subtraction. For example,

$$7 - 3 = n \quad \text{if and only if} \quad 7 = 3 + n.$$

In this way, subtraction can be done by referring to addition. This method can also be extended to integer subtraction.

Example 8.4   Find $7 - (-3)$.

Solution $7 - (-3) = n$ if and only if $7 = -3 + n$. But $-3 + 10 = 7$. Therefore, $7 - (-3) = 10$. ■

Using variables, we can state the following.

> ### ALTERNATIVE DEFINITION
>
> **Subtraction of Integers: Missing-Addend Approach**
>
> Let a, b, and c be any integers. Then $a - b = c$ if and only if $a = b + c$.

In summary, there are three equivalent ways to view subtraction in the integers.

1. Take-away
2. Adding the opposite
3. Missing addend

Notice that both the take-away and the missing-addend approaches are extensions of whole-number subtraction. The adding-the-opposite approach is new because the additive inverse property is a property the integers have but the whole numbers do not. As one should expect, all of these methods yield the same answer. The following argument shows that adding the opposite is a consequence of the missing-addend approach.

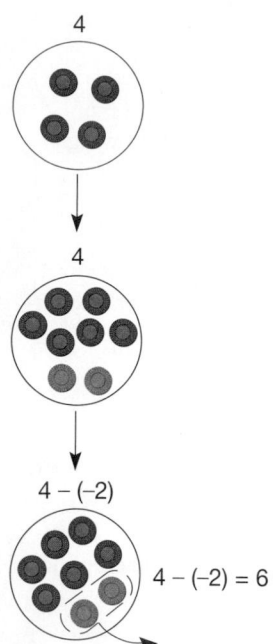

Figure 8.12

Let $a - b = c$.
Then $a = b + c$ by the missing-addend approach.
Hence $a + (-b) = b + c + (-b) = c$, or
$$a + (-b) = c.$$
Therefore, $a - b = a + (-b)$.

It can also be shown that the missing-addend approach follows from adding the opposite.

Example 8.5   Find $4 - (-2)$ using all three methods of subtraction.

Solution

a. **Take-Away:** See Figure 8.12
b. **Adding the Opposite:** $4 - (-2) = 4 + [-(-2)] = 4 + 2 = 6$.
c. **Missing Addend:** $4 - (-2) = c$ if and only if $4 = (-2) + c$. But $4 = -2 + 6$. Therefore, $c = 6$.   ■

Spotlight on Technology Using a scientific calculator to do integer computation requires an understanding of the difference between subtracting a number and a negative number. On a calculator the subtraction key is $\boxed{-}$ and the negative key is $\boxed{(-)}$. The number -9 is found by pressing $\boxed{(-)}$ 9 $\boxed{-9}$. To calculate $(-18) - (-3)$, press these keys: $\boxed{(-)}$ 18 $\boxed{-}$ $\boxed{(-)}$ 3 $\boxed{=}$ $\boxed{-15}$. (NOTE: On some calculators there is a change-of-sign key $\boxed{+/-}$ instead of a negative key $\boxed{(-)}$. In those cases a -9 is entered as 9 $\boxed{+/-}$.)

As you may have noticed, the "$-$" symbol has three different meanings. Therefore, it should be read in a way that distinguishes among its uses. First, the symbol "-7" is read "negative 7" (*negative* means "less than zero"). Second, since it also represents the opposite or additive inverse of 7, "-7" can be read "the opposite of 7" or "the additive inverse of 7." Remember that "opposite" and "additive inverse" are not synonymous with "negative integers." For example, the opposite or additive inverse of -5 is 5 and 5 is a positive integer. In general, the symbol "$-a$" should be read "the opposite of a" or "the additive inverse of a." It is confusing to children to call it "negative a" since $-a$ may be positive, zero, or negative, depending on the value of a. Third, "$a - b$" is usually read "a minus b" to indicate subtraction.

MATHEMATICAL MORSEL

Often, very surprising results in mathematics spring from simple problems. One such result is the following: Take any collection of seven integers, say a, b, c, d, e, f, and g. Form all consecutive sums from the left; $a, a + b, a + b + c, \ldots, a + b + \cdots + g; b, b + c, b + c + d, \ldots, b + c + \cdots + g$; and so on. Then one of these sums must have a factor of 7. For example, in $\{2, -3, 5, -1, 3, -4, -5\}$, the consecutive sum $(-1) + 3 + (-4) + (-5)$ is $7(-1)$ and hence has a factor of 7. It is interesting that the preceding result holds for any collection of integers, not just 7. That is, if one takes any collection of n integers, there is always a consecutive sum of these integers that has a factor of n.

Section 8.1 EXERCISE / PROBLEM SET A

EXERCISES

1. Which of the following are integers? If they are, identify as positive, negative, or neither.

   a. 25   **b.** -7 **c.** 0

2. Represent the opposites of each of the numbers represented by the following models, where B = black chip and R = red chip.

   a. *BBBBR*   **b.** *RBBRRRRR*

   c.

   d.

3. Use the set model and number-line model to represent each of the following integers.

   a. 3   **b.** -5 **c.** 0

4. Write the opposite of each integer.

   a. 3   **b.** -4 **c.** 0

   d. -168 **e.** 56   **f.** -1235

5. Given I = integers, $N = \{-1, -2, -3, -4, . . .\}$, $P = \{1, 2, 3, 4, . . .\}$, W = whole numbers, list the members of the following sets.

   a. $N \cup W$ **b.** $N \cup P$ **c.** $N \cap P$

6. Dixie had a balance of $115 in her checking account at the beginning of the month. She deposited $384 in the account and then wrote checks for $153, $86, $196, $34, and $79. Then she made a deposit of $123. If at any time during the month the account is overdrawn, a $10 service charge is deducted. At the end of the month, what was Dixie's balance?

7. Show how you could find the following sums (i) using a number-line model and (ii) using black and red chips. Look at the Chapter 8 eManipulative activity, *Chips Plus*, to gain a better understanding of how to use the black and red chips.

   a. $5 + (-3)$ **b.** $(-3) + (-2)$

8. Use thinking strategies to compute the following sums. Identify your strategy.

   a. $-14 + 6$ **b.** $17 + (-3)$

9. Identify the property illustrated by the following equations.

   a. $3 + [6 + (-3)] = 3 + (-3 + 6)$

   b. $[3 + (-3)] + 6 = 0 + 6$

10. Apply the properties and thinking strategies to compute the following sums mentally.

   a. $-126 + (635 + 126)$

   b. $84 + (-67) + (-34)$

11. The Chapter 8 eManipulative activity, *Chips Minus*, demonstrates how to use black and red chips to model integer subtraction. After doing a few examples on the eManipulative, sketch how the chip model could be used to do the following problems.

   a. $3 - 7$ **b.** $4 - (-5)$

12. Calculate.

   a. $3 - 7$ **b.** $8 - (-4)$

   c. $(-2) + 3$ **d.** $(-7) - (-8)$

13. Find the following using your calculator and the $\boxed{(-)}$ key. Check mentally.

   a. $-27 + 53$

   b. $(-51) - (-46)$

   c. $123 - (-247)$

   d. $-56 - 72$

14. The existence of additive inverses in the set of integers enables us to solve equations of the form $x + b = c$. For example, to solve $x + 15 = 8$, add (-15) to both sides; $x + 15 + (-15) = 8 + (-15)$ or $x = -7$. Solve the following equations using this technique.

   a. $x + 21 = 16$ **b.** $(-5) + x = 7$

   c. $65 + x = -13$ **d.** $x - 6 = -5$

   e. $x - (-8) = 17$ **f.** $x - 53 = -45$

15. True or false?

   a. Every whole number is an integer.

   b. The set of additive inverses of the whole numbers is equal to the set of integers.

   c. Every integer is a whole number.

   d. The set of additive inverses of the negative integers is a proper subset of the whole numbers.

16. Write out in words (use *minus*, *negative*, *opposite*).

   a. $5 - 2$

   b. -6 (two possible answers)

   c. -3 **d.** $-(-5)$

   e. $10 - [-(-2)]$

   f. $-p$ (two possible answers)

17. The **absolute value** of an integer a, written $|a|$, is defined to be the distance from a to zero on the integer number line. For example, $|3| = 3$, $|0| = 0$, and $|-7| = 7$. Evaluate the following absolute values.

   a. $|5|$ **b.** $|-17|$ **c.** $|5 - 7|$

   d. $|5| - |7|$ **e.** $-|7 - 5|$ **f.** $|-(7 - 5)|$

18. Fill in each empty square so that the number in the square will be the sum of the pair of numbers beneath the square.

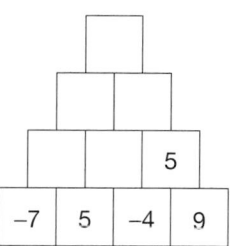

PROBLEMS

19. Which of the following properties hold for integer subtraction? If the property holds, give an example. If it does not hold, disprove it by a counterexample.

   a. Closure   **b.** Commutative

   c. Associative   **d.** Identity

20. Assume that the adding-the-opposite approach is true, and prove that the missing-addend approach is a consequence of it. (*Hint*: Assume that $a - b = c$, and show that $a = b + c$ using the adding-the-opposite approach.)

21. a. If possible, for each of the following statements find a pair of integers a and b that satisfy the equation or inequality.

    i. $|a + b| = |a| + |b|$

    ii. $|a + b| < |a| + |b|$

    iii. $|a + b| > |a| + |b|$

    iv. $|a + b| \le |a| + |b|$

  b. Which of these conditions will hold for all pairs of integers?

22. Complete the magic square using the following integers.

$$10, 7, 4, 1, -5, -8, -11, -14$$

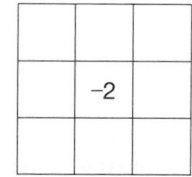

23. a. Let A be a set that is closed under subtraction. If 4 and 9 are elements of A, show that each of the following are also elements of A.

    i. 5   **ii.** -5 **iii.** 0

    iv. 13   **v.** 1   **vi.** -3

  b. List all members of A.

  c. Repeat part (b) if 4 and 8 are given as elements of A.

  d. Make a generalization about your findings.

24. Fill in each empty square so that the number in a square will be the sum of the pair of numbers beneath the square.

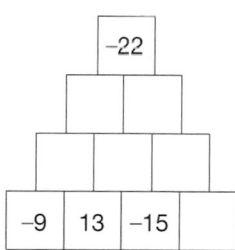

25. A student suggests the following algorithm for calculating $72 - 38$.

$$
\begin{array}{r}
72 \\
-38 \\
\hline
-6 \\
40 \\
\hline
34
\end{array}
$$

Two minus eight equals negative six.

Seventy minus thirty equals forty.

Forty plus negative six equals thirty-four, which therefore is the result.

As a teacher, what is your response? Does this procedure always work? Explain.

26. A **squared rectangle** is a rectangle whose interior can be divided into two or more squares. One example of a squared rectangle follows. The number written inside a square gives the length of a side of that square. Determine the dimensions of the unlabeled squares.

Section 8.1 EXERCISE / PROBLEM SET B

EXERCISES

1. Which of the following are integers? Identify those that are as positive, negative, or neither.

   a. $\frac{3}{4}$ **b.** 556   **c.** $-252/5$

2. Identify each of the integers represented by the following models, where B = black chip and R = red chip.

   a. *BBBRR*   **b.** *BRRRRBRR*

   c.

   d.

3. Use the set model and number-line model to represent each of the following integers.

   a. -3 **b.** 6

4. What is the opposite or additive inverse of each of the following (a and b represent integers)?

   a. a **b.** $-b$ **c.** $a + b$ **d.** $a - b$

5. Given I = integers, $N = \{-1, -2, -3, -4, . . .\}$, $P = \{1, 2, 3, 4, . . .\}$, W = whole numbers, list the members of the following sets.

   a. $N \cap I$ **b.** $P \cap I$ **c.** $I \cap W$

6. Write an addition statement for each of the following sentences and then find the answer.

   a. In a series of downs, a football team gained 7 yards, lost 4 yards, lost 2 yards, and gained 8 yards. What was the total gain or loss?

   b. In a week, a given stock gained 5 points, dropped 12 points, dropped 3 points, gained 18 points, and dropped 10 points. What was the net change in the stock's worth?

   c. A visitor in an Atlantic City casino won $300, lost $250, and then won $150. Find the gambler's overall gain or loss.

7. Show how you could find the following sums (i) using a number-line model and (ii) using black and red chips. Look at the Chapter 8 eManipulative activity, *Chips Plus*, to gain a better understanding of how to use the black and red chips.

   a. $4 + (-7)$ **b.** $(-3) + (-5)$

8. Use thinking strategies to compute the following sums. Identify your strategy.

   a. $14 + (-6)$ **b.** $21 + (-41)$

9. Identify the property illustrated by the following equations.

   a. $3 + [(-3) + 6] = [3 + (-3)] + 6$

   b. $0 + 6 = 6$

10. Apply the properties and thinking strategies to compute the following sums mentally.

    a. $-165 + 3217 + 65$

    b. $173 + (-43) + (-97)$

11. The Chapter 8 eManipulative activity, *Chips Minus*, demonstrates how to use black and red chips to model integer subtraction. After doing a few examples on the eManipulative, sketch how the chip model could be used to do the following problems.

    a. $(-3) - (-6)$ **b.** $0 - (-4)$

12. Calculate the following sums and differences.

   a. $13 - 27$ **b.** $38 - (-14)$

   c. $(-21) + 35$ **d.** $-26 - (-32)$

13. Find the following using your calculator and the $\boxed{(-)}$ key. Check mentally.

   a. $-119 + 351 + (-463)$

   b. $-98 - (-42)$

   c. $632 - (-354)$

   d. $-752 - (-549) + (-352)$

14. For each of the following equations, find the integer that satisfies the equation.

   a. $-x = 5$ **b.** $x + (-3) = -10$

   c. $x - (-5) = -8$ **d.** $6 - x = -3$

   e. $-5 - x = -2$ **f.** $x = -x$

15. If p and q are arbitrary negative integers, which of the following is true?

   a. $-p$ is negative.

   b. $p - q = q - p$

   c. $-(p + q) = q - p$

   d. $-p$ is positive.

16. Is $-x$ positive or negative if x is

   a. positive?   **b.** negative?   **c.** zero?

17. An alternate definition of absolute value is

$$|a| = \begin{cases} a \text{ if } a \text{ is positive or zero} \\ -a \text{ if } a \text{ is negative.} \end{cases}$$

   (NOTE: $-a$ is the opposite of a.) Using this definition, calculate the following values.

   a. $|-3|$ **b.** $|7|$

   c. $|x|$ if $x < 0$ **d.** $|-x|$ if $-x > 0$

   e. $-|x|$ if $x < 0$ **f.** $-|-x|$ if $-x > 0$

18. Fill in each empty square so that the number in the square will be the sum of the pair of numbers beneath the square.

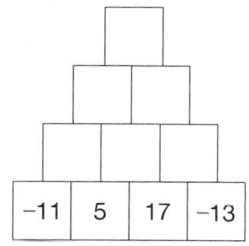

−11	5	17	−13

PROBLEMS

19. Under what conditions is the following equation true?

$$(a - b) - c = (a - c) - b$$

   a. Never

   b. Always

   c. Only when $b = c$

   d. Only when $b = c = 0$

20. On a given day, the following Fahrenheit temperature extremes were recorded. Find the range between the high and low temperature in each location.

CITY	HIGH	LOW
Philadelphia	65	37
Cheyenne	35	−9
Bismarck	−2	−13

21. A student claims that if $a \neq 0$, then $|a| = -a$ is never true, since absolute value is always positive. Explain why the student is wrong. What two concepts is the student confusing?

22. Switch two numbers to produce an additive magic square.

140	−56	−42	−28
−14	70	56	28
42	14	0	84
98	112	126	−70

23. If a is an element of $\{-3, -2, -1, 0, 1, 2\}$ and b is an element of $\{-5, -4, -3, -2, -1, 0, 1\}$, find the smallest and largest values for the following expressions.

   a. $a + b$

   b. $b - a$

   c. $|a + b|$

24. Fill in each empty square so that a number in a square will be the sum of the pair of numbers beneath the square.

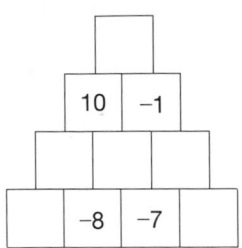

25. a. Demonstrate a 1-1 correspondence between the sets given.

    i. Positive integers and negative integers

    ii. Positive integers and whole numbers

    iii. Whole numbers and integers

b. What does part (iii) tell you about the number of whole numbers compared to the number of integers?

26. A **squared square** is a square whose interior can be subdivided into two or more squares. One example of a squared square follows. The number written inside a square gives the length of a side of that square. Determine the dimensions of the unlabeled squares.

PROBLEMS FOR WRITING/DISCUSSION

1. Using the black and red chip model, how would you explain to students why you were inserting 5 black and 5 red chips to the circle in order to subtract 8 from 3?

2. Some people learn this rule for adding two numbers whose signs are different: "Subtract the numbers and take the sign of the larger." Explain why this rule might lead to some confusion for students when doing the problem "4 + (−6)."

3. In the additive inverse property there is the phrase "there is a unique integer." How would you explain the meaning of that phrase to students?

8.2   MULTIPLICATION, DIVISION, AND ORDER

STARTING POINT

Recall that for positive exponents, the following properties hold:

$$7^4 = 7 \cdot 7 \cdot 7 \cdot 7 \qquad 7^0 = 1 \qquad 7^5 \div 7^3 = 7^{5-3} = 7^2 \qquad 7^5 \cdot 7^3 = 7^{5+3} = 7^8$$

It is important that the properties of negative exponents are consistent with the properties of exponents above. If the properties were consistent, what would 7^{-2} be equal to? Justify your conclusion. (*Hint:* Consider $7^3 \div 7^5$ or $7^2 \cdot 7^{-2}$.)

Reflection from Research

If students understand multiplication as repeated addition, then a positive times a negative, such as 7×-6, can be taught as "seven negative 6s" (Bley & Thornton, 1989).

Multiplication and Its Properties

Integer multiplication can be viewed as extending whole-number multiplication. Recall that the first model for whole-number multiplication was repeated addition, as illustrated here:

$$3 \times 4 = 4 + 4 + 4 = 12.$$

Now suppose that you were selling tickets and you accepted three bad checks worth $4 each. A natural way to think of your situation would be $3 \times (-4) = (-4) + (-4) + (-4) = -12$ (Figure 8.13).

Figure 8.13

Rules for integer multiplication can be motivated using the following pattern.

THE FIRST COLUMN REMAINS 3 THROUGHOUT.
THE SECOND COLUMN IS DECREASING BY 1 EACH TIME.

$3 \times 4 = 12$ *3 LESS*
$3 \times 3 = 9$ *3 LESS*
$3 \times 2 = 6$ *3 LESS*
$3 \times 1 = 3$ *ETC.*
$3 \times 0 = 0$
$3 \times (-1) = ?$
$3 \times (-2) = ?$
$3 \times (-3) = ?$
$3 \times (-4) = ?$

This pattern extended suggests that $3 \times (-1) = -3$, $3 \times (-2) = -6$, $3 \times (-3) = -9$, and so on. A similar pattern can be used to suggest what the product of two negative integers should be, as follows.

THE FIRST COLUMN REMAINS (−3).

$(-3) \times 3 = -9$
$(-3) \times 2 = -6$ *3 MORE*
$(-3) \times 1 = -3$ *3 MORE*
$(-3) \times 0 = 0$ *3 MORE*

THE SECOND COLUMN DECREASES BY 1 EACH TIME.

$(-3) \times (-1) = ?$ *ETC.*
$(-3) \times (-2) = ?$
$(-3) \times (-3) = ?$

Problem-Solving Strategy
Look for a Pattern.

This pattern suggests that $(-3)(-1) = 3$, $(-3)(-2) = 6$, $(-3)(-3) = 9$, and so on.

Integer multiplication can also be modeled using black and red chips. Since 4×3 can be thought of as "combine 4 groups of 3 black chips," the operation $4 \times \quad 3$ can be thought of as "combine 4 groups of 3 red chips" (see Figure 8.14).

Notice that the sign on the second number in the operation determines the color of chips being used. Since the first number in 4×-3 is positive, we *combined* 4 groups of -3. How would the situation of -4×3 be handled? In this case the first number (4) is negative, which indicates that we should "*take away* 4 groups of 3 black chips" rather than combine. When the first number is positive, the groups are *combined* into a new set that has a value of 0. When the first number is negative, the groups are *taken away* from a set that has a value of 0. In order to take something away from a set with a value of 0, we must add some chips with a value of 0 to the set. This is done by adding an equal number of red and black chips to the set. After taking away 4 groups of 3 black chips, the resulting set has 12 red chips or a value of -12 (Figure 8.15).

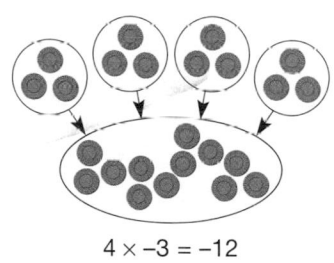

$4 \times -3 = -12$

Figure 8.14

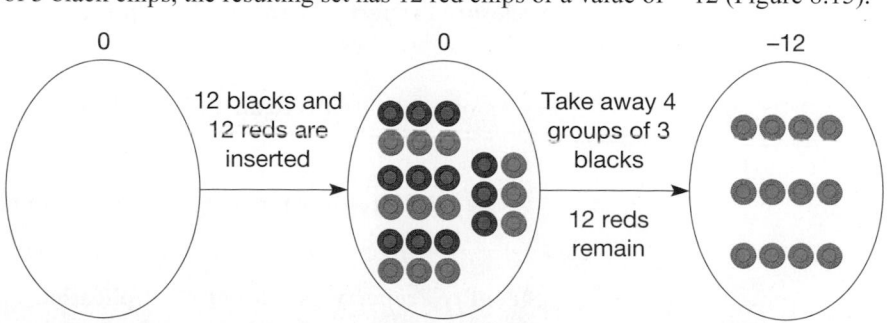

0   0   −12

12 blacks and 12 reds are inserted

Take away 4 groups of 3 blacks

12 reds remain

Figure 8.15

The number-line model, the patterns, and the black and red chips model all lead to the following definition.

DEFINITION

Multiplication of Integers

Let a and b be any integers.

1. *Multiplying by 0*: $a \cdot 0 = 0 = 0 \cdot a$.
2. *Multiplying two positives*: If a and b are positive, they are multiplied as whole numbers.
3. *Multiplying a positive and a negative*: If a is positive and b is positive (thus $-b$ is negative), then
$$a(-b) = -(ab),$$
where ab is the whole-number product of a and b. That is, the product of a positive and a negative is negative.

4. *Multiplying two negatives*: If a and b are positive, then
$$(-a)(-b) = ab,$$
where ab is the whole-number product of a and b. That is, the product of two negatives is positive.

Example 8.6   Calculate the following using the definition of integer multiplication.
a. $5 \cdot 0$ **b.** $5 \cdot 8$ **c.** $5(-8)$ **d.** $(-5)(-8)$

Solution

a. *Multiplying by zero*: $5 \cdot 0 = 0$
b. *Multiplying two positives*: $5 \cdot 8 = 40$
c. *Multiplying a positive and a negative*: $5(-8) = -(5 \cdot 8) = -40$
d. *Multiplying two negatives*: $(-5)(-8) = 5 \cdot 8 = 40$ ■

The definition of multiplication of integers can be used to justify the following properties.

PROPERTIES

Properties of Integer Multiplication

Let a, b, and c be any integers.
Closure Property for Integer Multiplication

$$ab \text{ is an integer.}$$

Commutative Property for Integer Multiplication

$$ab = ba$$

Associative Property for Integer Multiplication

$$(ab)c = a(bc)$$

Identity Property for Integer Multiplication
1 is the unique integer such that $a \cdot 1 = a = 1 \cdot a$ for all a.

As in the system of whole numbers, our final property, the distributive property, connects addition and multiplication.

PROPERTY

Distributivity of Multiplication over Addition of Integers

Let a, b, and c be any integers. Then

$$a(b + c) = ab + ac.$$

Using the preceding properties of addition and multiplication of integers, some important results that are useful in computations can be justified.

THEOREM

Let a be any integer. Then

$$a(-1) = -a.$$

Proof   First, $a \cdot 0 = 0$ by definition.

$$
\begin{aligned}
\text{But } a \cdot 0 &= a[1 + (-1)] && \textit{Additive inverse}\\
&= a(1) + a(-1) && \textit{Distributivity}\\
&= a + a(-1). && \textit{Multiplicative identity}
\end{aligned}
$$

Therefore, $a + a(-1) = 0$.

Then $\quad a + a(-1) = a + (-a)$.   *Additive inverse*

Finally, $a(-1) = -a$ *Additive cancellation*   ■

Stating the preceding result in words, we have "the product of negative one and any integer is the opposite (or additive inverse) of that integer." Notice that, on the integer number line, multiplication by -1 is equivalent geometrically to reflecting an integer about the origin (Figure 8.16).

Figure 8.16

THEOREM

Let a and b be any integers. Then

$$(-a)b = -(ab).$$

Proof

$$
\begin{aligned}
(-a)b &= [(-1)a]b && \textit{(-1)a = -a}\\
&= (-1)(ab) && \textit{Associativity for multiplication}\\
&= -(ab) && \textit{(-1)a = -a}
\end{aligned}
$$

Using commutativity with this result gives $a(-b) = -(ab)$.   ■

THEOREM

Let a and b be any integers. Then

$$(-a)(-b) = ab \text{ for all integers } a, b.$$

Proof

$$
\begin{aligned}
(-a)(-b) &= [(-1)a][(-1)b] & &(-1)a = -a \\
&= [(-1)(-1)](ab) & &\text{Associativity and commutativity} \\
&= 1ab & &\text{Definition of integer multiplication} \\
&= ab & &\text{Multiplicative identity} \quad ■
\end{aligned}
$$

NOTE: The three preceding results encompass more than just statements about multiplying by negative numbers. For example, $(-a)(-b) = ab$ is read "the opposite of a times the opposite of b is ab." The numbers a and b may be positive, negative, or zero; hence $(-a)$ and $(-b)$ also may be negative, positive, or zero. Thus there is a subtle but important difference between these results and parts 3 and 4 of the definition of multiplication of integers.

Example 8.7 Calculate the following products.
a. $3(-1)$ **b.** $(-3)5$ **c.** $(-3)(-4)$ **d.** $(-1)(-7)$ **e.** $(-x)(-y)(-z)$

Solution

a. $3(-1) = -3$, since $a(-1) = -a$.
b. $(-3)5 = -(3 \cdot 5) = -15$, since $(-a)b = -(ab)$.
c. $(-3)(-4) = (3 \cdot 4) = 12$, since $(-a)(-b) = ab$.
d. $(-1)(-7)$ can be found in two ways: $(-1)(-7) = -(-7) = 7$, since $(-1)a = -a$, and $(-1)(-7) = 1 \cdot 7 = 7$, since $(-a)(-b) = ab$.
e. $(-x)(-y)(-z) = xy(-z)$, since $(-a)(-b) = ab$; and $xy(-z) = -(xyz)$, since $a(-b) = -(ab)$. ■

Finally, the next property will be useful in integer division.

 PROPERTY

Multiplicative Cancellation Property

Let a, b, c be any integers with $c \neq 0$. If $ac = bc$, then $a = b$.

Notice that the condition $c \neq 0$ is necessary, since $3 \cdot 0 = 2 \cdot 0$, but $3 \neq 2$.

The multiplicative cancellation property is truly a *property* of the integers (and whole numbers and counting numbers) because it cannot be proven from any of our previous properties. However, in a system where nonzero numbers have multiplicative inverses (such as the fractions), it is a theorem. The following property is equivalent to the multiplicative cancellation property.

 PROPERTY

Zero Divisors Property

Let a and b be integers. Then $ab = 0$ if and only if $a = 0$ or $b = 0$ or a and b both equal zero.

Division

Recall that to find $6 \div 3$ in the whole numbers, we sought the whole number c, where $6 = 3 \cdot c$. Division of integers can be viewed as an extension of whole-number division using the missing-factor approach.

 DEFINITION

Division of Integers

Let a and b be any integers, where $b \neq 0$. Then $a \div b = c$ if and only if $a = b \cdot c$ for a unique integer c.

Example 8.8 Find the following quotients (if possible).
a. $12 \div (-3)$
b. $(-15) \div (-5)$
c. $(-8) \div 2$
d. $7 \div (-2)$

Solution

a. $12 \div (-3) = c$ if and only if $12 = (-3) \cdot c$. From multiplication, $12 = (-3)(-4)$. Since $(-3) \cdot c = (-3)(-4)$, by multiplicative cancellation, $c = -4$.
b. $(-15) \div (-5) = c$ if and only if $-15 = (-5) \cdot c$. From multiplication, $-15 = (-5) \cdot 3$. Since $(-5) \cdot c = (-5) \cdot 3$, by multiplicative cancellation, $c = 3$.
c. $(-8) \div 2 = c$ if and only if $(-8) = 2 \cdot c$. Thus $c = -4$, since $2(-4) = -8$.
d. $7 \div (-2) = c$ if and only if $7 = (-2) \cdot c$. There is no such integer c. Therefore, $7 \div (-2)$ is undefined in the integers. ■

Considering the results of this example, the following generalizations can be made about the division of integers: Assume that b divides a; that is, that b is a factor of a.

1. *Dividing by 1:* $a \div 1 = a$.
2. *Dividing two positives (negatives):* If a and b are both positive (or both negative), then $a \div b$ is positive.
3. *Dividing a positive and a negative:* If one of a or b is positive and the other is negative, then $a \div b$ is *negative*.
4. *Dividing zero by a nonzero integer:* $0 \div b = 0$, where $b \neq 0$, since $0 = b \cdot 0$. As with whole numbers, division by zero is undefined for integers.

Example 8.9 Calculate.
a. $0 \div 5$
b. $40 \div 5$
c. $40 \div (-5)$
d. $(-40) \div (-5)$

Solution

a. *Dividing into zero:* $0 \div 5 = 0$
b. *Dividing two positives:* $40 \div 5 = 8$
c. *Dividing a positive and negative:* $40 \div (-5) = -8$ and $(-40) \div 5 = -8$
d. *Dividing two negatives:* $(-40) \div (-5) = 8$ ■

Spotlight on Technology The negative-sign key can be used to find $-306 \times (-76) \div 12$ as follows:

$$\boxed{(-)}\;306\;\boxed{\times}\;\boxed{(-)}\;76\;\boxed{\div}\;12\;\boxed{=}\;\boxed{1938}$$

However, this calculation can be performed without the negative-sign key by observing that there are an even number (two) of negative integers multiplied together. Thus the product is positive. In the case of an odd number of negative factors, the product is negative.

Negative Exponents and Scientific Notation

When studying whole numbers, exponents were introduced as a shortcut for multiplication. As the following pattern suggests, there is a way to extend our current definition of exponents to include integer exponents.

Problem-Solving Strategy
Look for a Pattern.

$$a^3 = a \cdot a \cdot a$$
$$a^2 = a \cdot a \qquad \Big) \div a$$
$$a^1 = a \qquad \Big) \div a$$
$$a^0 = 1 \qquad \Big) \div a$$
$$a^{-1} = \frac{1}{a} \qquad \Big) \div a$$
$$a^{-2} = \frac{1}{a^2} \qquad \Big) \div a$$
$$a^{-3} = \frac{1}{a^3} \qquad \Big) \div a$$
$$\vdots$$
$$\text{etc.}$$

This pattern leads to the next definition.

 DEFINITION

Negative Integer Exponent

Let a be any nonzero number and n be a positive integer. Then

$$a^{-n} = \frac{1}{a^n}.$$

For example, $7^{-3} = \frac{1}{7^3}$, $2^{-5} = \frac{1}{2^5}$, $3^{-10} = \frac{1}{3^{10}}$, and so on. Also, $\frac{1}{4^{-3}} = \frac{1}{1/4^3} = 4^3$.

The last sentence indicates how the definition leads to the statement $a^{-n} = \frac{1}{a^n}$ *for all integers n.*

It can be shown that the theorems on whole-number exponents given in Section 3.3 can be extended to integer exponents. That is, for any nonzero numbers a and b, and integers m and n, we have

$$a^m \cdot a^n = a^{m+n}$$

$$a^m \cdot b^m = (ab)^m$$

$$(a^m)^n = a^{nm}$$

$$\frac{a^m}{a^n} = a^{m-n}.$$

NCTM Standards 2000
Number and Operations
Grades 6–8
All students should develop an understanding of large numbers and recognize and appropriately use exponential, scientific, and calculator notations.

In Section 4.1 scientific notation was discussed in the context of using a scientific calculator. Numbers are said to be in **scientific notation** when expressed in the form $a \times 10^n$, where $1 \leq a < 10$ and n is any integer. The number a is called the **mantissa** and n the **characteristic** of $a \times 10^n$. The following table provides some examples of numbers written in scientific notation.

	SCIENTIFIC NOTATION	STANDARD NOTATION
Diameter of Jupiter	1.438×10^8 meters	143,800,000 meters
Total amount of gold in Earth's crust	1.2×10^{16} kilograms	12,000,000,000,000,000 kilograms
Mass of a human egg	1.5×10^{-9} kilogram	0.0000000015 kilogram
Diameter of a proton	1×10^{-11} meter	0.00000000001 meter

Example 8.10 Convert as indicated.
a. 38,500,000 to scientific notation
b. 7.2×10^{-14} to standard notation
c. 4.135×10^{11} to standard notation
d. 0.0000961 to scientific notation

Solution

a. $38,500,000 = 3.85 \times 10^7$
b. $7.2 \times 10^{-14} = 0.000000000000072$
c. $4.135 \times 10^{11} = 413,500,000,000$
d. $0.0000961 = 9.61 \times 10^{-5}$ ■

Spotlight on Technology Conversions from standard notation to scientific notation can be performed on most scientific calculators. For example, the following keystrokes convert 38,500,000 to scientific notation.

$$38500000 \boxed{\text{2nd}} \boxed{\text{Sci}} \boxed{3.85^{07}}$$

The raised "07" represents 10^7. Since the number of digits displayed by calculators differs, one needs to keep these limitations in mind when converting between scientific and standard notations.

Scientific notation is used to solve problems involving very large and very small numbers, especially in science and engineering.

Example 8.11 The diameter of Jupiter is about 1.438×10^8 meters, and the diameter of Earth is about 1.27×10^7 meters. What is the ratio of the diameter of Jupiter to the diameter of Earth?

Solution

$$\frac{1.438 \times 10^8}{1.27 \times 10^7} = \frac{1.438}{1.27} \times \frac{10^8}{10^7} \approx 1.13 \times 10 = 11.3$$ ■

When performing calculations involving numbers written in scientific notation, it is customary to express the answer in scientific notation. For example, the product $(5.4 \times 10^7)(3.5 \times 10^6)$ is written as follows:

$$(5.4 \times 10^7)(3.5 \times 10^6) = 18.9 \times 10^{13} = 1.89 \times 10^{14}.$$

NCTM Standards 2000
Number and Operations
Grades 6–8
All students should develop meaning for integers and represent and compare quantities with them.

Ordering Integers

The concepts of **less than** and **greater than** in the integers are defined to be extensions of ordering in the whole numbers. In the following, ordering is viewed in two equivalent ways, the number-line approach and the addition approach. Let a and b be any integers.

Number-Line Approach The integer a *is less than* the integer b, written $a < b$, if a is to the left of b on the integer number line. Thus, by viewing the number line, one can see that $-3 < 2$ (Figure 8.17). Also, $-4 < -1$, $-2 < 3$, and so on.

$-3 < 2$

Figure 8.17

Addition Approach The integer a *is less than* the integer b, written $a < b$, if and only if there is a *positive* integer p such that $a + p = b$. Thus $-5 < -3$, since $-5 + 2 = -3$, and $-7 < 2$, since $-7 + 9 = 2$. Equivalently, $a < b$ if and only if $b - a$ is positive (since $b - a = p$). For example, $-27 < -13$, since $-13 - (-27) = 14$, which is positive.

The integer a **is greater than** the integer b, written $a > b$, if and only if $b < a$. Thus, the discussion of greater than is analogous to that of less than. Similar definitions can be made for $\leq$ and $\geq$.

Example 8.12 Order the following integers from the smallest to largest using the number-line approach.

$$2, 11, -7, 0, 5, -8, -13.$$

Solution

See Figure 8.18.

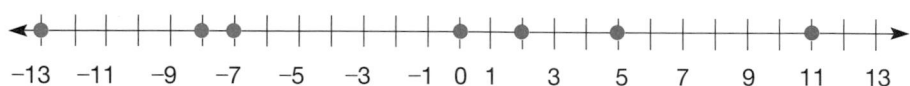

$-13 < -8 < -7 < 0 < 2 < 5 < 11$

Figure 8.18

■

Example 8.13 Determine the smallest integer in the set $\{3, 0, -5, 9, -8\}$ using the addition approach.

Solution

$-8 < -5$, since $(-8) + 3 = -5$. Also, since any negative integer is less than 0 or any positive integer, -8 must be the smallest.

■

The following results involving ordering, addition, and multiplication extend similar ones for whole numbers.

 PROPERTY

Properties of Ordering Integers

Let a, b, and c be any integers, p a positive integer, and n a negative integer.

Transitive Property for Less Than

$$\text{If } a < b \text{ and } b < c, \text{ then } a < c.$$

Property of Less Than and Addition

$$\text{If } a < b, \text{ then } a + c < b + c.$$

Property of Less Than and Multiplication by a Positive

$$\text{If } a < b, \text{ then } ap < bp.$$

Property of Less Than and Multiplication by a Negative

$$\text{If } a < b, \text{ then } an > bn.$$

The first three properties for ordering integers are extensions of similar statements in the whole numbers. However, the fourth property deserves special attention because it involves multiplying both sides of an inequality by a *negative* integer. For example, $2 < 5$ but $2(-3) > 5(-3)$. [Note that 2 *is less than* 5 but that $2(-3)$ *is greater than* $5(-3)$.] Similar properties hold where $<$ is replaced by $\le$, $>$, and $\ge$. The last two properties, which involve multiplication and ordering, are illustrated in Example 8.14 using the number-line approach.

Example 8.14

a. $-2 < 3$ and $4 > 0$; thus $(-2) \cdot 4 < 3 \cdot 4$ by the property of less than and multiplication by a positive (Figure 8.19).

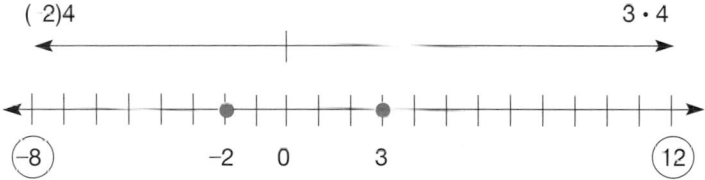

Figure 8.19

b. $-2 < 3$ and $-4 < 0$; thus $(-2)(-4) > 3(-4)$ by the property of less than and multiplication by a negative (Figure 8.20).

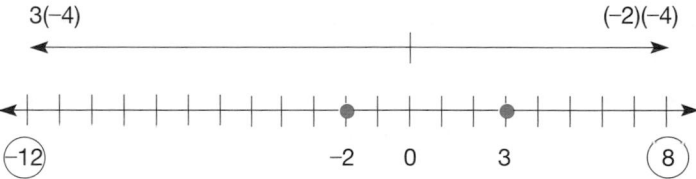

Figure 8.20

Notice how -2 was to the left of 3, *but* $(-2)(-4)$ is to the *right* of $(3)(-4)$. ■

To see why the property of less than and multiplication by a negative is true, recall that multiplying an integer a by -1 is geometrically the same as reflecting a across the origin on the integer number line. Using this idea in all cases leads to the following general result.

If $a < b$, then $(-1)a > (-1)b$ (Figure 8.21).

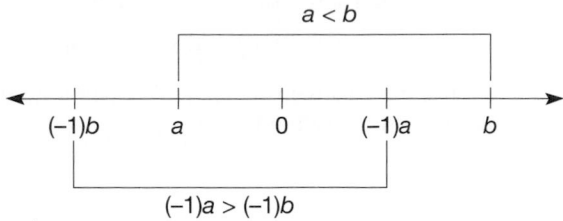

Figure 8.21

To justify the statement "if $a < b$ and $n < 0$, then $an > bn$," suppose that $a < b$ and $n < 0$. Since n is negative, we can express n as $(-1)p$, where p is positive. Then $ap < bp$ by the property of less than and multiplication by a positive. But if $ap < bp$, then $(-1)ap > (-1)bp$, or $a[(-1)p] > b[(-1)p]$, which, in turn, yields $an > bn$. Informally, this result says that "multiplying an inequality by a negative number 'reverses' the inequality."

MATHEMATICAL MORSEL

In January 1999, a 16-year-old high school student from Cork County, Ireland, named Sarah Flannery, caused quite a stir in the technology world. She devised an advanced mathematical code used to encrypt information sent electronically. Her algorithm uses the properties of 2×2 matrices and is said to be up to 30 times faster than the previous algorithm, Rivest, Shamir, and Adlemann (RSA), which was created by three students at Massachusetts Institute of Technology in 1977. She named her algorithm the Cayley-Purser algorithm, after nineteenth-century mathematician Arthur Cayley and Michael Purser, a Trinity College professor who gave her the initial ideas and inspired her. Because such an advancement can have a significant impact in the computer and banking industries, Sarah had computer firms offering her consulting jobs and prestigious universities inviting her to sign up when she graduated.

Section 8.2 EXERCISE / PROBLEM SET A

EXERCISES

1. Write one addition and one multiplication equation represented by each number-line model.

   a.

   b.

   c.

2. **a.** Extend the following patterns by writing the next three equations.

   i. $6 \times 3 = 18$ **ii.** $9 \times 3 = 27$
   $6 \times 2 = 12$ $9 \times 2 = 18$
   $6 \times 1 = 6$ $9 \times 1 = 9$
   $6 \times 0 = 0$ $9 \times 0 = 0$

b. What rule of multiplication of negative numbers is suggested by the equations you have written?

3. Find the following products.

   a. $6(-5)$ **b.** $(-2)(-16)$

   c. $-(-3)(-5)$ **d.** $-3(-7-6)$

4. Represent the following products using black and red chips and give the results.

   a. $3 \times (-2)$

   b. $(-3) \times (-4)$

5. The uniqueness of additive inverses and other properties of integers enable us to give another justification that $(-3)4 = -12$. By definition, the additive inverse of $3(4)$ is $-(3 \cdot 4)$. Provide reasons for each of the following equations.

$$(-3)(4) + 3 \cdot 4 = (-3 + 3) \cdot 4$$
$$= 0 \cdot 4$$
$$= 0$$

   Thus we have shown that $(-3)4$ is also the additive inverse of $3 \cdot 4$ and hence is equal to $-(3 \cdot 4)$.

6. Extend the meaning of a whole-number exponent.

$$a^n = \underbrace{a \cdot a \cdot a \cdots a}_{n \text{ factors}},$$

   where a is any integer. Use this definition to find the following values.

   a. 2^4 **b.** $(-3)^3$ **c.** $(-2)^4$

   d. $(-5)^2$ **e.** $(-3)^5$ **f.** $(-2)^6$

7. If a is an integer and $a \neq 0$, which of the following expressions are always positive and which are always negative?

   a. a **b.** $-a$ **c.** a^2

   d. $(-a)^2$ **e.** $(-a)^2$ **f.** a^3

8. Provide reasons for each of the following steps.

$$a(b - c) = a[b + (-c)]$$
$$= ab + a(-c)$$
$$= ab + [-(ac)]$$
$$= ab - ac$$

   Which property have you justified?

9. Find each quotient.

   a. $-18 \div 3$ **b.** $-45 \div (-9)$

   c. $75 \div (-5)$ **d.** $(-5 + 5) \div (-2)$

   e. $[144 \div (-12)] \div (-3)$

   f. $144 \div [-12 \div (-3)]$

10. Make use of the $\boxed{(-)}$ key on a calculator to calculate each of the following problems.

   a. -36×72 **b.** $-51 \times (-38)$

   c. $-128 \times (-765)$ **d.** $-658 \div 14$

   e. $3588 \div (-23)$ **f.** $-108,697 \div (-73)$

11. Consider the statement $(x + y) \div z = (x \div z) + (y \div z)$. Is this a true statement in the integers for the following values of x, y, and z?

   a. $x = 16, y = -12, z = 4$

   b. $x = -20, y = 36, z = -4$

   c. $x = -42, y = -18, z = -6$

   d. $x = -12, y = -8, z = 3$

12. Write each of the following as a fraction without exponents.

   a. 10^{-2} **b.** 4^{-3} **c.** 2^{-6} **d.** 5^{-3}

13. **a.** Simplify $4^{-2} \cdot 4^6$ by expressing it in terms of whole-number exponents and simplifying.

   b. Simplify $4^{-2} \cdot 4^6$ by applying $a^m \cdot a^n = a^{m+n}$.

   c. Repeat parts (a) and (b) to simplify $5^{-4} \cdot 5^{-2}$.

   d. Does it appear that the property $a^m \cdot a^n = a^{m+n}$ still applies for integer exponents?

14. **a.** Simplify $\dfrac{3^{-2}}{3^5}$ by expressing it in terms of whole-number exponents and simplifying.

   b. Simplify the expression in part (a) by applying

$$\frac{a^m}{a^n} = a^{m-n}.$$

   c. Repeat parts (a) and (b) to simplify $\dfrac{6^3}{6^{-7}}$.

   d. Does it appear that the property $\dfrac{a^m}{a^n} = a^{m-n}$ still applies for integer exponents?

15. Use the definition of integer exponents and properties of exponents to find a numerical value for the following expressions.

   a. $3^{-2} \cdot 3^5$ **b.** $\dfrac{6^{-3}}{6^{-4}}$ **c.** $(3^{-4})^{-2}$

16. Each of the following numbers is written in scientific notation. Rewrite each in standard decimal form.

   a. 3.7×10^{-5} **b.** 2.45×10^{-8}

17. Express each of the following numbers in scientific notation.

   a. 0.0004 **b.** 0.0000016 **c.** 0.000000000495

   d. $0.00000000000000000008071$

18. You can use a scientific calculator to perform arithmetic operations with numbers written in scientific notation. If the exponent is negative, use your $\boxed{+/-}$ or $\boxed{\text{CHS}}$ or $\boxed{(-)}$ key to change the sign.

For example, see the following multiplication problem.

$$(1.6 \times 10^{-4})(2.7 \times 10^{-8})$$

1.6 $\boxed{\text{SCI}}$ 4 $\boxed{+/-}$ $\boxed{\times}$ 2.7 $\boxed{\text{SCI}}$ 8 $\boxed{+/-}$ $\boxed{=}$

$$\boxed{4.32 - 12}$$

(NOTE: The sequence of steps or appearance of the answer in the display window may be slightly different on your calculator.)

Use your calculator to evaluate each of the following. Express your results in scientific notation.

a. $(7.6 \times 10^{10})(9.5 \times 10^{-36})$

b. $(2.4 \times 10^{-6})(3.45 \times 10^{-20})$

c. $\dfrac{1.2 \times 10^{-15}}{4.8 \times 10^{-6}}$

d. $\dfrac{(7.5 \times 10^{-12})(8 \times 10^{-17})}{(1.5 \times 10^{9})}$

e. $\dfrac{480,000,000}{0.0000006}$

f. $\dfrac{0.000000000000123}{0.0000006}$

19. Show that each of the following is true by using the number-line approach.

a. $-3 < 2$ **b.** $-6 < -2$ **c.** $-3 > -12$

20. Write each of the following lists of integers in increasing order from left to right.

a. $-5, 5, 2, -2, 0$ **b.** $12, -6, -8, 3, -5$

c. $-2, -3, -5, -8, -11$

d. $23, -36, 45, -72, -108$

21. Complete the following statements by inserting $<$, $=$, or $>$ in the blanks to produce true statements.

a. If $x < 4$, then $x + 2$ ___ 6.

b. If $x > -2$, then $x - 6$ ___ -8.

PROBLEMS

22. Fill in each empty square so that a number in a square is the product of the two numbers beneath it.

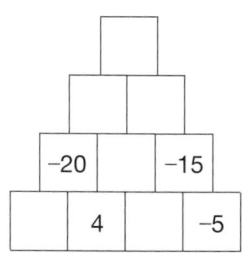

23. a. Which of the following integers when substituted for x make the given inequality true: $-6, -10, -8, -7$?

$$3x + 5 < -16$$

b. Is there a largest integer value for x that makes the inequality true?

c. Is there a smallest integer value for x that makes the inequality true?

24. a. The rules of integer addition can be summarized in a table as follows:

+	+	−
+	+	?
−		

Positive + positive = positive (+ sign)
Positive + negative = positive or negative or zero (? sign)
Complete the table.

b. Make a similar table for

   i. subtraction.

   ii. multiplication.

   iii. division (when possible).

25. a. If possible, find an integer x to satisfy the following conditions.

   i. $|x| > x$ **ii.** $|x| = x$

   iii. $|x| < x$ **iv.** $|x| \geq x$

b. Which, if any, of the conditions in part (a) will hold for all integers?

26. A student suggests that she can show $(-1)(-1) = 1$ using the fact that $-(-1) = 1$. Is her reasoning correct? If yes, what result will she apply? If not, why not?

27. A student does not believe that $-10 < -5$. He argues that a debt of \$10 is greater than a debt of \$5. How would you convince him that the inequality is true?

28. In a multiplicative magic square, the product of the integers in each row, each column, and each diagonal is the same number. Complete the multiplication magic square given.

-2		
3	-4	-18

29. If $0 < x < y$ where x and y are integers, prove that $x^2 < y^2$.

30. There are 6.022×10^{23} atoms in 12.01 grams of carbon. Find the mass of one atom of carbon. Express your answer in scientific notation.

31. Hair on the human body can grow as fast as 0.0000000043 meter per second.

   a. At this rate, how much would a strand of hair grow in one month of 30 days? Express your answer in scientific notation.

   b. About how long would it take for a strand of hair to grow to be 1 meter in length?

32. A farmer goes to market and buys 100 animals at a total cost of $1000. If cows cost $50 each, sheep cost $10 each, and rabbits cost 50 cents each, how many of each kind does he buy?

33. Prove or disprove: The square of any whole number is a multiple of 3 or one more than a multiple of 3.

34. A shopper asked for 50 cents worth of apples. The shopper was surprised when she received five more than the previous week. Then she noticed that the price had dropped 10 cents per dozen. What was the new price per dozen?

35. Assume that if $ac = bc$ and $c \neq 0$, then $a = b$. Prove that if $ab = 0$, then $a = 0$ or $b = 0$. (*Hint*: Assume that $b \neq 0$. Then $ab = 0 = 0 \cdot b$ . . . .)

Section 8.2   EXERCISE / PROBLEM SET B

EXERCISES

1. Illustrate the following products on an integer number line.

   a. $2 \times (-5)$ **b.** $3 \times (-4)$

   c. $5 \times (-2)$

2. Extend the following patterns by writing the next three equations. What rule of multiplication of negative numbers is suggested by the equations you have written?

   a. $-5 \times 3 = -15$ **b.** $-8 \times 3 = -24$
   $\quad -5 \times 2 = -10$ $\quad -8 \times 2 = -16$
   $\quad -5 \times 1 = -5$ $\quad -8 \times 1 = -8$
   $\quad -5 \times 0 = 0$ $\quad -8 \times 0 = 0$

3. Find the following products.

   a. $(-2)(-5)(-3)$
   b. $(-10)(7)(-6)$
   c. $5[(-2)(13) + 5(-4)]$
   d. $-23[(-2)(6) + (-3)(-4)]$

4. Represent the following products using black and red chips and give the results.

   a. $(-3) \times 4$ **b.** $(2) \times (-4)$
   c. $(-2) \times (-1)$

5. The following argument shows another justification for $(-3)(-4) = 12$. Provide reasons for each of the following equations.

$(-3)(-4) + (-3) \cdot 4 = (-3)(-4 + 4)$
$\qquad\qquad\qquad\qquad = (-3) \cdot 0$
$\qquad\qquad\qquad\qquad = 0$

Therefore, $(-3)(-4)$ is the additive inverse of $(-3)4 = -12$. But the additive inverse of -12 is 12, so $(-3)(-4) = 12$.

6. Are the following numbers positive or negative?

   a. $(-2)^5$ **b.** $(-2)^8$ **c.** $(-5)^3$
   d. $(-5)^{16}$ **e.** $(-1)^{20}$ **f.** $(-1)^{33}$
   g. a^n if $a < 0$ and n is even
   h. a^n if $a < 0$ and n is odd

7. If a is an integer and $a \neq 0$, which expressions are always positive and which are always negative?

   a. a^3 **b.** $(-a)^3$ **c.** $-(a^3)$
   d. a^4 **e.** $(-a)^4$ **f.** $-(a^4)$

8. Expand each of the following products.

   a. $-6(x + 2)$ **b.** $-5(x - 11)$
   c. $-3(x - y)$ **d.** $x(a - b)$
   e. $-x(a - b)$ **f.** $(x - 3)(x + 2)$

9. Solve the following equations using the missing-factor approach.

   a. $-3x = -9$ **b.** $-15x = 1290$
   c. $11x = -374$ **d.** $-9x = -8163$

10. Compute using a calculator.
    a. $(-36)(52)$ b. $(-83)(-98)$
    c. $(127)(-31)(-57)$ d. $(-39)(-92)(-68)$
    e. $-899 \div 29$ f. $-5904 \div (-48)$
    g. $7308 \div (-126)$
    h. $[-1848 \div (-56)] \div (-33)$

11. Consider the statement $x \div (y + z) = (x \div y) + (x \div z)$. Is this statement true for the following values of x, y, and z?
    a. $x = 12, y = -2, z = -4$
    b. $x = 18, y = 2, z = -3$

12. Write each of the following as a fraction without exponents.
    a. 4^{-2} b. 2^{-5} c. 7^{-3}

13. a. Simplify $(3^2)^{-3}$ by expressing it in terms of whole-number exponents and simplifying.
    b. Simplify $(3^2)^{-3}$ by applying $(a^m)^n = a^{mn}$.
    c. Repeat parts (a) and (b) to simplify $(5^{-3})^{-2}$.
    d. Does it appear that the property $(a^m)^n = a^{mn}$ still applies for integer exponents?

14. a. Simplify $(2^{-3})(4^{-3})$ by expressing it in terms of whole-number exponents and simplifying.
    b. Simplify $(2^{-3})(4^{-3})$ by applying $(a^m)(b^m) = (ab)^m$.
    c. Repeat parts (a) and (b) to simplify $(3^{-4})(5^{-4})$.
    d. Does it appear that the property $(a^m)(b^m) = (ab)^m$ still applies for integer exponents?

15. Apply the properties of exponents to express the following values in a simpler form.
    a. $\dfrac{5^{-2} \cdot 5^3}{5^{-4}}$ b. $\dfrac{(3^{-2})^{-5}}{3^{-6}}$
    c. $\dfrac{8^3}{2^3 \cdot 4^{-2}}$ d. $\dfrac{2^6 \cdot 3^2}{(3^{-3})^{-2} \cdot 4^5}$

16. Each of the following numbers is written in scientific notation. Rewrite each in standard decimal form.
    a. 9.0×10^{-6} b. 1.26×10^{-13}

17. Express each of the following numbers in scientific notation.
    a. 0.000000691 b. 0.0000000000003048

18. Use your calculator to evaluate each of the following. Express your answers in scientific notation.
    a. $(9.62 \times 10^{-12})(2.8 \times 10^{-9})$ b. $\dfrac{3.74 \times 10^{-6}}{8.5 \times 10^{-30}}$
    c. $(4.35 \times 10^{-40})(7.8 \times 10^{19})$
    d. $\dfrac{(1.38 \times 10^{12})(4.5 \times 10^{-16})}{1.15 \times 10^{10}}$
    e. $(62{,}000)(0.00000000000033)$
    f. $\dfrac{0.000000000000000232}{0.000000145}$

19. Show that each of the following inequalities is true by using the addition approach.
    a. $-7 < -3$ b. $-6 < 5$ c. $-17 > -23$

20. Fill in the blanks with the appropriate symbol—$<$, $>$, or $=$ >—to produce true statements.
    a. -4 ___ 9 b. 3 ___ -2 c. -4 ___ -5
    d. 0 ___ -2 e. $3 + (-5)$ ___ $2 \times (-3)$
    f. $(-12) \div (-2)$ ___ $-2 - (-3)$
    g. $15 - (-6)$ ___ $(-3) \times (-7)$
    h. $5 + (-5)$ ___ $(-3) \times (-6)$

21. Complete the following statements by inserting $<$, $=$, or $>$ in the blanks to produce true statements.
    a. If $x < -3$, then $4x$ ___ -12.
    b. If $x > -6$, then $-2x$ ___ 12.

PROBLEMS

22. Fill in each empty square so that a number in a square is the product of the two numbers beneath it.

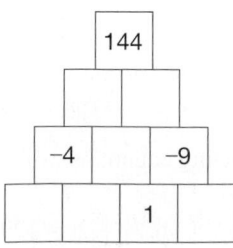

23. a. Which of the following integers when substituted

for x make the given inequality true: $-4, -3, -2, -1$?
$$5x - 3 \geq -18$$

b. Is there a largest integer value for x that makes the inequality true?

c. Is there a smallest integer value for x that makes the inequality true?

24. a. Is there a largest whole number? integer? negative integer? positive integer? If yes, what is it?

b. Is there a smallest whole number? integer? negative integer? positive integer? If yes, what is it?

25. Use absolute-value notation to write the following two parts of the definition of integer multiplication.
    a. If p is positive and q is negative, then $pq =$ ___.
    b. If p is negative and q is negative, then $pq =$ ___.

26. Use the absolute-value notation to express the answers for these division problems.
    a. If p is positive and q is negative, then $p \div q =$ ___.
    b. If both of p and q are negative, then $p \div q =$ ___.

27. If $x < y$, where x and y are integers, is it always true that $x^2 < y^2$? Prove or give a counterexample.

28. If $x < y$, where x and y are integers, is it always true that $z - y < z - x$, if z is an integer? Prove or give a counterexample.

29. The mass of one electron is 9.11×10^{-28} grams. A uranium atom contains 92 electrons. Find the total mass of the electrons in a uranium atom. Express your answer in scientific notation.

30. A rare gas named "krypton" glows orange when heated by an electric current. The wavelength of the light it emits is about 605.8 nanometers, and this wavelength is used to define the exact length of a meter. If one nanometer is 0.000000001 meter, what is the wavelength of krypton in meters? Express your answer in scientific notation.

31. The mass of one molecule of hemoglobin can be described as 0.11 attogram.
    a. If 1 attogram $= 10^{-21}$ kilogram, what is the mass in kilograms of one molecule of hemoglobin?
    b. The mass of a molecule of hemoglobin can be specified in terms of other units, too. For example, the mass of a molecule of hemoglobin might be given as 68,000 daltons. Determine the number of kilograms in 1 dalton.

32. Red blood corpuscles in the human body are constantly disintegrating and being replaced. About 73,000 of them disintegrate and are replaced every 3.16×10^{-2} second.
    a. How many red blood corpuscles break down in 1 second? Express your answer in scientific notation.
    b. There are approximately 25,000,000,000,000 red blood corpuscles in the blood of an adult male at any given time. About how long does it take for all of these red blood corpuscles to break down and be replaced?

33. Prove or disprove: If $x^2 + y^2 = z^2$ for whole numbers x, y, and z, either x or y is a multiple of 3.

34. A woman born in the first half of the nineteenth century (1800 to 1849) was X years old in the year X^2. In what year was she born?

35. Assume that the statement "If $ab = 0$, then $a = 0$ or $b = 0$" is true. Prove the multiplication cancellation property. [*Hint:* If $ac = bc$, where $c \neq 0$, then $ac - bc = 0$, or $(a - b)c = 0$. Since $(a - b)c = 0$, what can you conclude based on the statement assumed here?]

PROBLEMS FOR WRITING/DISCUSSION

1. In an example, the answer to $(-x)(-y)(-z)$ is given as $-xyz$. You have a student who asks, "How do you know the answer is negative if you don't know what x, y, and z are?" How do you respond?

2. A student asks if 3 can equal 0. He is looking at the equation $3x = 0$, and he explains that since that means $3 = 0$ or $x = 0$, then 3 and x must both equal zero. How would you explain?

3. Maurice says that $a^2 + b^2 = (a + b)(a + b)$. Is this always true, never true, or sometimes true? Explain.

END OF CHAPTER MATERIAL

Solution of Initial Problem

Prove or disprove: 2 is a factor of $(a - b)(b - c)(c - a)$ for any integers a, b, c.

Strategy: Use Cases

Note that if x and y are integers with $x \neq 0$, then $x \mid y$ means $x = y$ for some integer n.

CASE 1: Assume that at least two of a, b, or c are even (say, a and b are even). Then $a = 2m, b = 2n$, and $a - b = 2m - 2n = 2(m - n)$. Thus $2 \mid (a - b)$, so $2 \mid (a - b)(b - c)(c - a)$.

CASE 2: Assume that at least two of a, b, or c are odd (say, a and b are odd). Then $a = 2m + 1, b = 2n + 1$, and $a - b = (2m + 1) - (2n + 1) = 2(m - n)$. Thus $2 \mid (a - b)$, so $2 \mid (a - b)(b - c)(c - a)$.

Since either at least two of a, b, or c are even or at least two are odd, we have covered all cases.

Additional Problems Where the Strategy "Use Cases" Is Useful

1. If the sum of three consecutive numbers is even, prove that two of the numbers must be odd.

2. If m and n are integers, under what circumstances will $m^2 - n^2$ be positive?

3. Show that the square of any whole number is either a multiple of 5, one more than a multiple of 5, or one less than a multiple of 5.

People in Mathematics

Grace Chisholm Young (1868–1944) Grace Chisholm Young, who was born in England, became the first woman to receive a doctoral degree in Germany. She married William Young, a mathematician who had been her tutor in England. A curious collaboration developed between the two. Both had done important mathematical research independently, but together they produced 220 mathematical papers, several books, and six children. Their joint papers were usually published under Will's name alone because of prejudice against women mathematicians. In a letter to Grace, Will wrote, "Our papers ought to be published under our joint names, but if this were done neither of us get the benefit of it." Their daughter Cecily describes their collaboration: "My mother had decision and initiative and the stamina to carry an undertaking to its conclusion. If not for [her skill] my father's genius would probably have been abortive, and would not have eclipsed hers and the name she had already made for herself."

Martin Gardner (1914–) Martin Gardner wrote the lively and thoughtful "Mathematical Games" column in *Scientific American* magazine for more than 20 years. Readers were served an eclectic blend of diversions—logical puzzles, number problems, card tricks, game theory, and much more. Perhaps more than anyone else in our time, Gardner has succeeded in popularizing mathematics, which he calls "a kind of game that we play with the universe." There are now 14 book collections of his *Scientific American* features, and he has written more than 50 books in all. He wrote, "A good mathematical puzzle, paradox, or magic trick can stimulate a child's imagination much faster than a practical application (especially if the application is remote from the child's experience), and if the game is chosen carefully, it can lead almost effortlessly into significant mathematical ideas."

CHAPTER REVIEW

Review the following terms and exercises to determine which require learning or relearning—page numbers are provided for easy reference.

SECTION 8.1: Addition and Subtraction

VOCABULARY/NOTATION

Integers 319
Positive integers 319
Negative integers 319
Integer number line 320

Opposite 320
Additive inverse 320
Additive cancellation 323
Take-away 324

Adding the opposite 325
Zero pair 325
Missing-addend approach 326

EXERCISES

1. Explain how to represent integers in two ways using the following:

   a. A set model

   b. A measurement model

2. Show how to find $7 + (-4)$ using (a) colored chips and (b) the integer number line.

3. Name the property of addition of integers that is used to justify each of the following equations.

   a. $(-7) + 0 = -7$ b. $(-3) + 3 = 0$

   c. $4 + (-5) = (-5) + 4$

d. $(7 + 4) + (-4) = 7 + [4 + (-4)]$

e. $(-9) + 7$ is an integer

4. Show how to find $3 - (-2)$ using each of the following approaches.

   a. Take-away   b. Adding the opposite

   c. Missing addend

5. Which of the following properties hold for integer subtraction?

   a. Closure   b. Commutative

   c. Associative   d. Identity

SECTION 8.2: Multiplication, Division, and Order

VOCABULARY/NOTATION

Scientific notation   339   Characteristic   339   Less than, greater than   340
Mantissa   339

EXERCISES

1. Explain how you can provide motivation for the following.

   a. $5(-2) = -10$ b. $(-5)(-2) = 10$

2. Name the property of multiplication of integers that is used to justify each of the following equations.

   a. $(-3)(-4) = (-4)(-3)$

   b. $(-5)[2(-7)] = [(-5)(2)](-7)$

   c. $(-5)(-7)$ is an integer

   d. $(-8) \times 1 = -8$

   e. If $(-3)n = (-3)7$, then $n = 7$.

3. Explain how $(-a)(-b) = ab$ is a generalization of $(-3)(-4) = 3 \times 4$.

4. If $3n = 0$, what can you conclude? What property can you cite for justification?

5. Explain how integer division is related to integer multiplication.

6. Which of the following properties hold for integer division?

   a. Closure

   b. Commutative

   c. Associative

   d. Identity

7. Without doing the indicated calculations, determine whether the answers are positive, negative, or zero. Explain your reasoning.

   a. $(-3)(-7)(-5) \div (-15)$

   b. $(-27) \div 3 \times (-4) \div (-3)$

   c. $35(-4) \div 5 \times 0 \times (-2)$

8. Explain how you can motivate the fact that $7^{-4} = \dfrac{1}{7^4}$.

9. Convert as indicated.

   a. 0.000079 to scientific notation

   b. 3×10^{-4} to standard notation

   c. 458.127 to scientific notation

   d. 2.39×10^7 to standard notation

10. Explain how to determine the smaller of -17 and -21 using the following techniques.

    a. The number-line approach

    b. The addition approach

11. Complete the following, and name the property you used as a justification.

    a. If $(-3) < 4$, then $(-3)(-2)$ ____ $4(-2)$.

    b. If $-5 < 7$ and $7 < 9$, then -5 ____ 9.

    c. If $-3 < 7$, then $(-3)2$ ____ $7 \cdot 2$.

    d. If $-4 < 5$, then $(-4) + 3$ ____ $5 + 3$.

PROBLEMS FOR WRITING/DISCUSSION

1. Suppose you were working out the following problem with a student. What would be your explanation for each step? For each step write out how you would read it (when would you say "minus" and when "negative," for example) and what reason you would give for each change.

$$-3 - (-2) = -3 + 2$$
$$= -1$$

2. Students often get confused when working a problem like $-5 - 7$. A common mistake is to rewrite the problem as $(-5) + (+7) = 2$. Why might the student be making this mistake? How would you explain the right way to do it?

3. Students know that when there is a negative sign in front of a number, it means that the number is negative. "-3" means "negative 3." Therefore, many students assume that "$-n$" is also a negative number. How would you explain to students that "$-n$" is sometimes positive and sometimes negative (and sometimes neither)?

4. Joe and Misha are using their calculators to do the problem -7^2. Joe types the negative sign, the seven, the exponent character ^, and then 2. He gets the answer -49. Misha's calculator won't allow him to type the negative sign first, so he types 7, then the negative sign, then the exponent character ^, then 2. His calculator says the answer is 49. What's going on here?

5. Mary Lou is trying to find 2^{42} using her calculator. She tells you that her calculator says the answer is 4.398 to the 12th power, which equals 52,367,603.57. Where did she go wrong?

6. Roger tells you that 3^7 means 3 multiplied times itself 7 times, so 3^{-7} must mean 3 multiplied times itself -7 times. He wants to know how to do that. How would you explain?

7. List all the real-life applications of negative numbers you can think of.

8. Students can model $4(-3)$ with successive additions by writing $(-3) + (-3) + (-3) + (-3)$. How would you explain how to multiply $(-4)(-3)$?

9. A student performing the subtraction problem $4 - (-3)$ says, "A negative times a negative is a positive, so this problem means $4 + 3$." How would you respond?

10. One student says that since $7x > -28$, then $x < -4$, because when you have a negative, you reverse the inequality. What do you say?

CHAPTER TEST

Knowledge

1. True or false?

   a. The sum of any two negative integers is negative.

   b. The product of any two negative integers is negative.

   c. The difference of any two negative integers is negative.

   d. The result of any positive integer subtracted from any negative integer is negative.

   e. If $a < b$, then $ac < bc$ for integers a, b, and nonzero integer c.

   f. The opposite of an integer is negative.

   g. If $c = 0$ and $ac = bc$, then $a = b$.

   h. The sum of an integer and its additive inverse is zero.

2. What does the notation a^{-n} mean, where a is not zero and n is a positive integer?

3. Which of the following is a property of the integers but not of the whole numbers? (circle all that apply)

   a. Additive identity

   b. Additive inverse

   c. Closure for subtraction

4. Identify three different approaches to the subtraction of integers.

Skill

5. Compute each of the following problems without using a calculator.

   a. $37 + (-43)$ b. $(-7)(-6)$

   c. $45 - (-3)$ d. $16 \div (-2)$

   e. $(-13) - 17$ f. $(-24) \div (-8)$

   g. $(-13)(4)$ h. $[-24 - (-27)] \times (-4)$

6. Evaluate each of the following expressions in two ways to check the fact that $a(b + c)$ and $ab + ac$ are equal.

a. $a = 3, b = -4, c = 2$
b. $a = -3, b = -5, c = -2$

7. Express the following in scientific notation.
   a. $(9.7 \times 10^8)(8.5 \times 10^3)$
   b. $(5.5 \times 10^{-7}) \div (9.1 \times 10^{-2})$

8. Solve for n in the following expression.

$$\frac{(2^5)^{-2} \cdot 2^3}{2^{-3}} = 2^n$$

Understanding

9. Name the property or properties that can be used to simplify these computations.
   a. $(-37 + 91) + (-91)$ **b.** $[(-2)17] \cdot 5$
   c. $(-31)17 + (-31)83$ **d.** $(-7)13 + 13(17)$

10. Compute using each of the three approaches: (i) take-away, (ii) adding the opposite, and (iii) missing addend.
    a. $8 - (-5)$ **b.** $(-2) - (-7)$

11. If a and b are negative and c is positive, determine whether the following are positive or negative.
    a. $(-a)(-c)$ **b.** $(-a)(b)$
    c. $(c - b)(c - a)$ **d.** $a(b - c)$

12. Illustrate the following operations using a (i) number line, and (ii) black and red chips.
    a. $8 + -3$ **b.** $-2 + 4$ **c.** $3 + -5$

13. Illustrate with black and red chips the operation $-2 - 3$ using the (i) take-away and the (ii) missing-addend approaches.

14. **a.** Building from the fact that $3 \times 4 = 12$, use patterns to illustrate why $-2 \times 4 = -8$.
    b. Building from the fact established in part (a), use patterns to illustrate why $-2 \times -4 = 8$.

15. Explain whether or not $a(b \cdot c)$ is equal to $(a \cdot b) \times (a \cdot c)$.

Problem Solving/Application

16. If $30 \le a \le 60$ and $-60 \le b \le -30$, where a and b are integers, find the largest and smallest possible *integer* values for the following expressions.
    a. $a + b$
    b. $a - b$
    c. ab
    d. $a \div b$

17. Complete this *additive* magic square of integers using 9, -12, 3, -6, 6, -3, 12, -9.

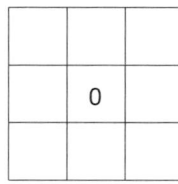

18. Complete this *multiplicative* magic square of integers.

		-64
32	128	
	-4	

19. Find all values of a and b such that $a - b = b - a$.

20. On Hideki's history exams he gets 4 points for each problem answered correctly, he loses 2 points for each incorrect answer, and he gets 0 points for each question left blank. On a 25-question test, Hideki received a score of 70.
    a. What is the largest number of questions that he could have answered correctly?
    b. What is the fewest number of questions that he could have answered correctly?
    c. What is the largest number of questions that he could have left blank?

References for Reflections from Research

BLEY, N. S., & THORNTON, C. A. (1989). *Teaching mathematics to the learning disabled* (2nd ed.). Austin, TX: PRO-ED.

SHEFFIELD, L. J., & CRUIKSHANK, D. E. (1996). *Teaching and learning elementary and middle school mathematics* (3rd ed.). Upper Saddle River, NJ: Prentice Hall.

THOMPSON, F. M. (1998). Algebraic instruction for the younger child. In A. Coxford (Ed.), *The ideas of algebra, K-12* (pp. 8–19). Reston, VA: National Council of Teachers of Mathematics.

THOMPSON, P. W., & DREYFUS, T. (1988). Integers as transformations. *Journal of Research in Mathematics Education, 19*, 115–133.

CHAPTER 9

Rational Numbers and Real Numbers, with an Introduction to Algebra

FOCUS ON The Pythagoreans and Irrational Numbers

Pythagoras (circa 570 B.C.) was one of the most famous of all Greek mathematicians. After his studies and travels, he founded a school in southern Italy. This school, an academy of philosophy, mathematics, and natural science, developed into a closely knit brotherhood with secret rites and observances. The society was dispersed, but the brotherhood continued to exist for at least two centuries after the death of Pythagoras.

Much of the work of the Pythagoreans was done in whole numbers, but they also believed that *all* measurements could be done with fractions. However, the hypotenuse of the unit right triangle caused them some alarm, since they could not find a fraction to measure it and still fit the Pythagorean theorem. One feeble attempt was to say that $c = \frac{7}{5}$. Then $c^2 = \frac{49}{25}$ (or *almost* 2).

Hippasus is attributed with the discovery of incommensurable ratios, that is, numbers not expressible as the ratio of two whole numbers. This discovery caused a scandal among the Pythagoreans, since their theory did not allow for such a number. Legend has it that Hippasus, a Pythagorean, was drowned because he shared the secret of incommensurables with others outside the society. Actually, according to Aristotle, the Pythagoreans gave the first proof (using an indirect proof) that there is no fraction whose square is 2. However, they still would not accept the existence of a number whose square is 2.

By 300 B.C. many other irrational numbers were known, such as $\sqrt{3}, \sqrt{5}, \sqrt{6}$, and $\sqrt{8}$. Eudoxus, a Greek mathematician, developed a geometric method for handling irrationals. This treatment was presented in Euclid's *Elements*. (See the Focus On section for Chapter 14.)

In the first century A.D. the Hindus began to treat irrationals like other numbers, replacing expressions such as $5\sqrt{2} + 4\sqrt{2}$ with $9\sqrt{2}$, and so on. Finally, in the late nineteenth century, irrationals were fully accepted as numbers.

Irrationals cannot be expressed exactly as decimals. For example, $\pi = 3.141592654$ ... has been calculated to over one billion places, but it has no exact decimal representation. This may seem strange to you at first, but if you have difficulty grasping the concept of an irrational number, keep in mind that many famous mathematicians throughout history had similar difficulties.

Pythagoras

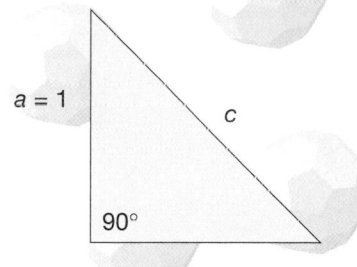

Pythagorean theorem: $a^2 + b^2 = c^2$

3000 B.C.	Babylonians and Egyptians
500 B.C.	Pythagoreans
300 B.C.	Greeks
A.D. 100	Hindus
A.D. 1880	Acceptance of irrationals

Problem Solving Strategies

1. Guess and Test
2. Use a Variable
3. Draw a Picture
4. Look for a Pattern
5. Make a List
6. Solve a Simpler Problem
7. Draw a Diagram
8. Use Direct Reasoning
9. Use Indirect Reasoning
10. Use Properties of Numbers
11. Solve an Equivalent Problem
12. Work Backward
13. Use Cases
14. **Solve an Equation**

Strategy
Solve an Equation

Often, when applying the Use a Variable strategy to solve a problem, the representation of the problem will be an equation. The following problem yields such an equation. Techniques for solving simple equations are given in Section 9.2.

Initial Problem

A man's boyhood lasted for $\frac{1}{6}$ of his life, he played soccer for the next $\frac{1}{12}$ of his life, and he married after $\frac{1}{7}$ more of his life. A daughter was born 5 years after his marriage, and the daughter lived $\frac{1}{2}$ as many years as her father did. If the man died 4 years after his daughter did, how old was the man when he died?

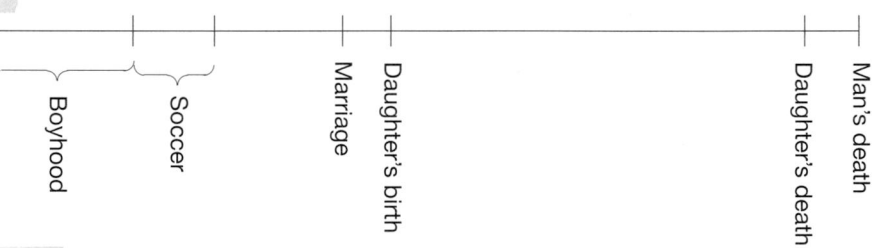

Clues

The Solve an Equation strategy may be appropriate when

- A variable has been introduced.
- The words *is*, *is equal to*, or *equals* appear in a problem.
- The stated conditions can easily be represented with an equation.

A solution of the Initial Problem appears on page 406.

INTRODUCTION

In this book we have introduced number systems much the same as they are developed in the school curriculum. The counting numbers came first. Then zero was included to form the whole numbers. Because of the need to deal with parts of a whole, fractions were introduced. Since there was a need to have numbers to represent amounts less than zero, the set of integers was introduced. The relationships among these sets are illustrated in Figure 9.1, where each arrow represents "is a subset of." For example, the set of counting numbers is a subset of the set of whole numbers, and so on. Recall that as number systems, both the fractions and integers extend the system of whole numbers.

**NCTM Standards 2000
Number and Operations
Grades 6–8**
All students should understand the meaning and effects of arithmetic operations with fractions, decimals, and integers.

Figure 9.1

It is the objective of this chapter to introduce our final number systems, first the rational numbers and then the real numbers. Both of these are extensions of our existing number systems. The set of rational numbers is composed of the fractions and their opposites, and the real numbers include all of the rational numbers together with additional numbers such as π and $\sqrt{2}$. Finally, we use the real numbers to solve equations and inequalities, and we graph functions.

9.1 THE RATIONAL NUMBERS

STARTING POINT

The fraction $\frac{2}{3}$ can be thought of as the number $0.\overline{6}$, which lies on the number line between 0 and 1. It can also be thought of as one whole broken into 3 parts where 2 of those parts are of interest.

How are the symbols $-\frac{2}{3}$ and $\frac{-2}{3}$ related to each other or to either of the meanings described to the right.

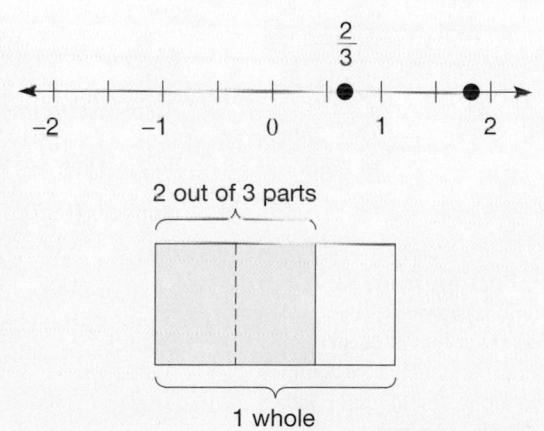

Rational Numbers: An Extension of Fractions and Integers

There are many reasons for needing numbers that have both reciprocals, as fractions do, and opposites, as integers do. For example, the fraction $\frac{2}{3}$ satisfies the equation $3x = 2$, since $3(\frac{2}{3}) = 2$, and -3 satisfies the equation $x + 3 = 0$, since $-3 + 3 = 0$. However, there is neither a fraction nor an integer that satisfies the equation $3x = -2$. To find such a number, we need the set of rational numbers.

There are various ways to introduce a set of numbers that extends both the fractions and the integers. Using models, one could merge the shaded-region model for fractions with the black and red chip model for integers. The resulting model would represent rational numbers by shading parts of wholes—models with black shaded parts to represent positive rational numbers and with red shaded parts to represent negative rational numbers.

For the sake of efficiency and mathematical clarity, we will introduce the rational numbers abstractly by focusing on the two properties we wish to extend; namely, that every nonzero number has a reciprocal and that every number has an opposite. There are two directions we can take. First, we could take all the fractions together with their opposites. This would give us a new collection of numbers, namely the fractions and numbers such as $-\frac{2}{3}, -\frac{5}{7}, -\frac{11}{2}$. A second approach would be to take the integers and form all possible "fractions" where the numerators are *integers* and the denominators are *nonzero integers*. We adopt this second approach, in which a rational number will be defined to be a *ratio* of integers. The set of rational numbers defined in this way will include the opposites of the fractions.

 DEFINITION

Rational Numbers

The set of **rational numbers** is the set

$$Q = \left\{ \frac{a}{b} \mid a \text{ and } b \text{ are integers}, b \neq 0 \right\}.$$

Examples of rational numbers are $\frac{2}{3}, \frac{-5}{7}, \frac{4}{-9}, \frac{0}{1}$, and $\frac{-7}{-9}$. Mixed numbers such as $-3\frac{1}{4} = \frac{-13}{4}$, $-5\frac{2}{7} = \frac{-37}{7}$ and $2\frac{1}{3} = \frac{7}{3}$ are also rational numbers, since they can be expressed in the form $\frac{a}{b}$, where a and b are integers, $b \neq 0$. Notice that every fraction is a rational number; for example, in the case when $a \geq 0$ and $b > 0$ in $\frac{a}{b}$. Also, every integer is a rational number; for example, in the case when $b = 1$ in $\frac{a}{b}$. Thus we can extend our diagram in Figure 9.1 to include the set of rational numbers (Figure 9.2).

Reflection from Research

Rational number programs which report success in deeper understanding have a common feature of "highlighting rather than glossing over the difference between rational and whole numbers" (Moss & Case, 1999).

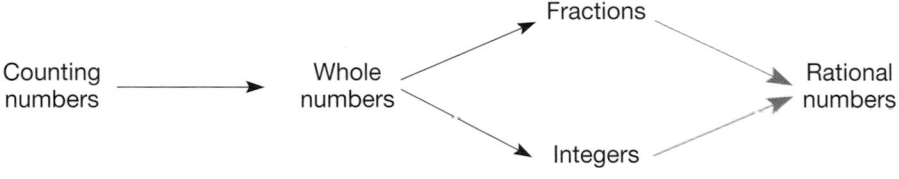

Figure 9.2

Equality of rational numbers and the four basic operations are defined as natural extensions of their counterparts for fractions and integers.

 DEFINITION

Equality of Rational Numbers

Let $\frac{a}{b}$ and $\frac{c}{d}$ be any rational numbers. Then $\frac{a}{b} = \frac{c}{d}$ if and only if $ad = bc$.

The equality-of-rational-numbers definition is used to find equivalent representations of rational numbers (1) to simplify rational numbers and (2) to obtain common denominators to facilitate addition, subtraction, and comparing rational numbers.

As with fractions, each rational number has an infinite number of representations. That is, by the definition of equality of rational numbers, $\frac{1}{2} = \frac{2}{4} = \frac{3}{6} = \cdots = \frac{-1}{-2} = \frac{-2}{-4} = \frac{-3}{-6} = \cdots$. The rational number $\frac{1}{2}$ can then be viewed as the idea represented by all of its various representations. Similarly, the number $\frac{-2}{3}$ should come to mind when any of the representations $\frac{-2}{3}, \frac{2}{-3}, \frac{-4}{6}, \frac{4}{-6}, \frac{-6}{9}, \frac{6}{-9}, \cdots$ are considered.

By using the definition of equality of rational numbers, it can be shown that the following theorem holds for rational numbers.

THEOREM

Let $\frac{a}{b}$ be any rational number and n any nonzero integer. Then

$$\frac{a}{b} = \frac{an}{bn} = \frac{na}{nb}.$$

A rational number $\frac{a}{b}$ is said to be in **simplest form** or in **lowest terms** if a and b have no common prime factors and b is *positive*. For example, $\frac{2}{3}, \frac{5}{7}$, and $\frac{3}{10}$ are in simplest form, whereas $\frac{5}{-7}, \frac{4}{6}$, and $\frac{-3}{81}$ are not because of the -7 in $\frac{5}{-7}$, and because $\frac{4}{6} = \frac{2}{3}$ and $\frac{-3}{81} = \frac{-1}{27}$.

Example 9.1 Determine whether the following pairs are equal. Then express them in simplest form.

a. $\dfrac{5}{-7}, \dfrac{-5}{7}$ b. $\dfrac{-20}{-12}, \dfrac{5}{3}$ c. $\dfrac{16}{-30}, \dfrac{-8}{15}$ d. $\dfrac{-15}{36}, \dfrac{20}{-48}$

Solution

a. $\dfrac{5}{-7} = \dfrac{-5}{7}$, since $5 \cdot 7 = (-7)(-5)$. The simplest form is $\dfrac{-5}{7}$.

b. $\dfrac{-20}{-12} = \dfrac{(-4)\,5}{(-4)\,3} = \dfrac{5}{3}$ due to simplification. The simplest form is $\dfrac{5}{3}$.

c. $\dfrac{16}{-30} = \dfrac{-8}{15}$, since $16 \cdot 15 = 240$ and $(-30)(-8) = 240$. The simplest form is $\dfrac{-8}{15}$.

d. $\dfrac{-15}{36} = \dfrac{20}{-48}$, since $(-15)(-48) = 720 = 36 \times 20$. The simplest form is $\dfrac{-5}{12}$. ■

Addition and Its Properties

Addition of rational numbers is defined as an extension of fraction addition.

DEFINITION

Addition of Rational Numbers

Let $\dfrac{a}{b}$ and $\dfrac{c}{d}$ be any rational numbers. Then

$$\frac{a}{b} + \frac{c}{d} = \frac{ad + bc}{bd}.$$

It follows from this definition that $\dfrac{a}{b} + \dfrac{c}{b} = \dfrac{a + c}{b}$ also.

Example 9.2 Find these sums.

a. $\dfrac{3}{7} + \dfrac{-5}{7}$ b. $\dfrac{-2}{5} + \dfrac{4}{-7}$ c. $\dfrac{-2}{5} + \dfrac{0}{5}$ d. $\dfrac{5}{6} + \dfrac{-5}{6}$

Solution

a. $\dfrac{3}{7} + \dfrac{-5}{7} = \dfrac{3 + (-5)}{7} = \dfrac{-2}{7}$

b. $\dfrac{-2}{5} + \dfrac{4}{-7} = \dfrac{(-2)(-7) + 5 \cdot 4}{5(-7)} = \dfrac{14 + 20}{-35} = \dfrac{34}{-35} = \dfrac{-34}{35}$

c. $\dfrac{-2}{5} + \dfrac{0}{5} = \dfrac{-2 + 0}{5} = \dfrac{-2}{5}$

d. $\dfrac{5}{6} + \dfrac{-5}{6} = \dfrac{5 + (-5)}{6} = \dfrac{0}{6}$ ■

Example 9.2(c) suggests that just as with the integers, the rationals have an additive identity. Also, Example 9.2(d) suggests that there is an additive inverse for each rational number. These two observations will be substantiated in the rest of this paragraph.

$$\frac{a}{b} + \frac{0}{b} = \frac{a + 0}{b} \qquad \textit{Addition of rational numbers}$$

$$= \frac{a}{b} \qquad \textit{Identity property for integer addition}$$

Thus $\dfrac{0}{b}$ is an identity for addition of rational numbers; moreover, it can be shown to be unique. For this reason, we write $\dfrac{0}{b}$ as 0, where b can represent any nonzero integer.

Next, let's consider additive inverses.

$$\frac{a}{b} + \frac{-a}{b} = \frac{a + (-a)}{b} \qquad \textit{Addition of rational numbers}$$

$$= \frac{0}{b} \qquad \textit{Additive inverse property for integer addition}$$

Thus the rational number $\dfrac{-a}{b}$ is an additive inverse of $\dfrac{a}{b}$. Moreover, it can be shown that each rational number has a unique additive inverse.

Notice that $\dfrac{-a}{b} = \dfrac{a}{-b}$, since $(-a)(-b) = ab = ba$. Therefore, $\dfrac{a}{-b}$ is the additive inverse of $\dfrac{a}{b}$ also. The symbol $-\dfrac{a}{b}$ is used to represent this additive inverse. We summarize this in the following result.

THEOREM

Let $\dfrac{a}{b}$ be any rational number. Then

$$-\frac{a}{b} = \frac{-a}{b} = \frac{a}{-b}.$$

We can represent the rational numbers on a line that extends both the fraction number line and the integer number line. Since every fraction and every integer is a rational number, we can begin to form the rational number line from the combination of the fraction number line and the integer number line (Figure 9.3).

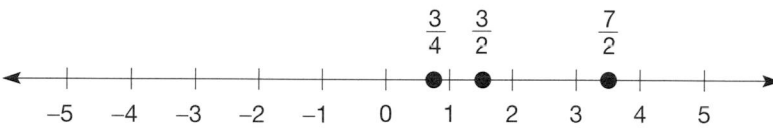

Figure 9.3

Just as in the case of fractions, we cannot label the entire fraction portion of the line, since there are infinitely many fractions between each pair of fractions. Furthermore, this line does not represent the rational numbers, since the additive inverses of the fractions are not yet represented. The additive inverses of the nonzero fractions, called the negative rational numbers, can be located by reflecting each nonzero fraction across zero (Figure 9.4). In particular, $-\frac{2}{3}, -\frac{5}{7}, -\frac{13}{4}$, and so on, are examples of negative rational numbers. In general, $\dfrac{a}{b}$ is a **positive rational number** if a and b are both positive or both negative integers, and $\dfrac{a}{b}$ is a **negative rational number** if one of a or b is positive and the other is negative.

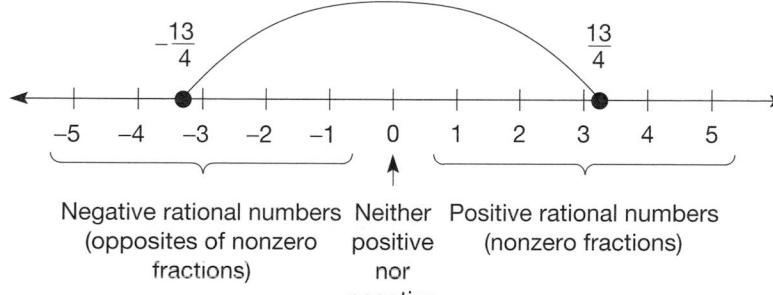

Figure 9.4

Next we list all the properties of rational-number addition. These properties can be verified using similar properties of integers.

PROPERTIES

Rational-Number Addition

Let $\dfrac{a}{b}, \dfrac{c}{d}$, and $\dfrac{e}{f}$ be any rational numbers.

Closure Property for Rational-Number Addition

$$\frac{a}{b} + \frac{c}{d} \text{ is a rational number.}$$

Commutative Property for Rational-Number Addition

$$\frac{a}{b} + \frac{c}{d} = \frac{c}{d} + \frac{a}{b}$$

Associative Property for Rational-Number Addition

$$\left(\frac{a}{b} + \frac{c}{d}\right) + \frac{e}{f} = \frac{a}{b} + \left(\frac{c}{d} + \frac{e}{f}\right)$$

Identity Property for Rational-Number Addition

$$\frac{a}{b} + 0 = \frac{a}{b} = 0 + \frac{a}{b} \qquad \left(0 = \frac{0}{m}, m \neq 0\right)$$

Additive Inverse Property for Rational-Number Addition

For every rational number $\dfrac{a}{b}$ there exists a unique rational number $-\dfrac{a}{b}$ such that

$$\frac{a}{b} + \left(-\frac{a}{b}\right) = 0 = \left(-\frac{a}{b}\right) + \frac{a}{b}.$$

**NCTM Standards 2000
Number and Operations
Grades 6–8**
All students should use the associative and commutative properties of addition and multiplication and the distributive property of multiplication over addition to simplify computations with integers, fractions, and decimals.

Example 9.3 Apply properties of rational-number addition to calculate the following sums. Try to do them mentally before looking at the solutions.

a. $\left(\dfrac{3}{4} + \dfrac{5}{6}\right) + \dfrac{1}{4}$ **b.** $\left(\dfrac{5}{7} + \dfrac{3}{8}\right) + \dfrac{-6}{16}$

Solution

a.
$$\left(\frac{3}{4} + \frac{5}{6}\right) + \frac{1}{4} = \frac{1}{4} + \left(\frac{3}{4} + \frac{5}{6}\right) \qquad \textit{Commutativity}$$

$$= \left(\frac{1}{4} + \frac{3}{4}\right) + \frac{5}{6} \qquad \textit{Associativity}$$

$$= 1 + \frac{5}{6} \qquad \textit{Addition}$$

$$= 1\frac{5}{6} \quad \text{or} \quad \frac{11}{6} \qquad \textit{Addition}$$

b.
$$\left(\frac{5}{7} + \frac{3}{8}\right) + \frac{-6}{16} = \frac{5}{7} + \left(\frac{3}{8} + \frac{-6}{16}\right) \qquad \textit{Associativity}$$

$$= \frac{5}{7} + 0 \qquad \textit{Additive inverse}$$

$$= \frac{5}{7} \qquad \textit{Additive identity}$$

The following two consequences of the rational-number properties are extensions of corresponding integer results. Their verifications are left for the Problem Set (Problems 29 in Part A and 26 in Part B).

THEOREM

Additive Cancellation for Rational Numbers

Let $\dfrac{a}{b}, \dfrac{c}{d},$ and $\dfrac{e}{f}$ be any rational numbers.

$$\text{If } \frac{a}{b} + \frac{e}{f} = \frac{c}{d} + \frac{e}{f}, \text{ then } \frac{a}{b} = \frac{c}{d}.$$

THEOREM

Opposite of the Opposite for Rational Numbers

Let $\dfrac{a}{b}$ be any rational number. Then

$$-\left(-\frac{a}{b}\right) = \frac{a}{b}.$$

Subtraction

Since there is an additive inverse for each rational number, subtraction can be defined as an extension of integer subtraction.

DEFINITION

Subtraction of Rational Numbers: Adding the Opposite

Let $\dfrac{a}{b}$ and $\dfrac{c}{d}$ be any rational numbers. Then

$$\frac{a}{b} - \frac{c}{d} = \frac{a}{b} + \left(-\frac{c}{d}\right).$$

The following discussion shows that this definition is also an extension of fraction subtraction.

Common Denominators

$$\frac{a}{b} - \frac{c}{b} = \frac{a}{b} + \left(-\frac{c}{b}\right) = \frac{a}{b} + \left(\frac{-c}{b}\right) = \frac{a + (-c)}{b} = \frac{a - c}{b}$$

That is,

$$\frac{a}{b} - \frac{c}{b} = \frac{a - c}{b}.$$

Thus rational numbers with common denominators can be subtracted as is done with fractions that have common denominators, namely by subtracting numerators.

Unlike Denominators

$$\frac{a}{b} - \frac{c}{d} = \frac{ad}{bd} - \frac{bc}{bd} = \frac{ad - bc}{bd} \qquad \textit{Using common denominators}$$

Example 9.4 Calculate the following differences and express the answers in simplest form.

a. $\dfrac{3}{10} - \dfrac{4}{5}$ **b.** $\dfrac{8}{27} - \dfrac{-1}{12}$

Solution

a. $\dfrac{3}{10} - \dfrac{4}{5} = \dfrac{3}{10} - \dfrac{8}{10} = \dfrac{3-8}{10} = \dfrac{-5}{10} = \dfrac{-1}{2}$

b. $\dfrac{8}{27} - \left(\dfrac{-1}{12} \right) = \dfrac{32}{108} - \left(\dfrac{-9}{108} \right) = \dfrac{32}{108} + \left[-\left(\dfrac{-9}{108} \right) \right] = \dfrac{41}{108}$ ▪

The fact that the missing-addend approach to subtraction is equivalent to the adding-the-opposite approach is discussed in the Problem Set (Problem 26 in Part A).

 Spotlight on Technology A fraction calculator can be used to find sums and differences of rational numbers just as we did with fractions, except that the $\boxed{(-)}$ key may have to be used. For example $\dfrac{5}{27} - \left(\dfrac{-7}{15} \right)$ can be found as follows: $5 \boxed{/} 27 \boxed{-} \boxed{(-)} 7 \boxed{/} 15 \boxed{=} \boxed{88/135}$. On some calculators, there is a change-of-sign key $\boxed{+/-}$ instead of a negative key $\boxed{(-)}$. In those cases, a -7 is entered as $7 \boxed{+/-}$. Notice that the keystrokes $7 \boxed{/} \boxed{(-)} 15$ would also be correct because $\dfrac{-7}{15} = \dfrac{7}{-15}$. Using a decimal calculator, the numerator, $5 \cdot 15 + 27 \cdot 7$, and the denominator, $27 \cdot 15$, can be calculated. The result, $\dfrac{264}{405}$, can be simplified to $\dfrac{88}{135}$.

Multiplication and Its Properties

Multiplication of rational numbers is defined as an extension of fraction multiplication as follows.

> ### DEFINITION
>
> *Multiplication of Rational Numbers*
>
> Let $\dfrac{a}{b}$ and $\dfrac{c}{d}$ be any rational numbers. Then
>
> $$\frac{a}{b} \cdot \frac{c}{d} = \frac{ac}{bd}.$$

 Spotlight on Technology A fraction calculator can be used to find products of rational numbers. For example, $\dfrac{-24}{35} \cdot \dfrac{-15}{16}$ can be found as follows: $\boxed{(-)} 24 \boxed{/} 35 \boxed{\times} \boxed{(-)} 15 \boxed{/} 16 \boxed{=} \boxed{360/560}$, which simplifies to $\dfrac{9}{14}$. Also, this product can be found as follows using a decimal calculator. $24 \boxed{\times} 15 \boxed{=} \boxed{360}$ (the numerator) and $35 \boxed{\times} 16 \boxed{=} \boxed{560}$ (the denominator); the product is 360/560 (since the product of two negative numbers is positive, the two $\boxed{(-)}$ keys were omitted).

Reasoning by analogy to fraction multiplication, the following properties can be verified using the definition of rational-number multiplication and the corresponding properties of integer multiplication.

 PROPERTIES

Rational-Number Multiplication

Let $\dfrac{a}{b}, \dfrac{c}{d}$, and $\dfrac{e}{f}$ be any rational numbers.

Closure Property for Rational-Number Multiplication

$$\frac{a}{b} \cdot \frac{c}{d} = \frac{ac}{bd} \text{ is a rational number.}$$

Commutative Property for Rational-Number Multiplication

$$\frac{a}{b} \cdot \frac{c}{d} = \frac{c}{d} \cdot \frac{a}{b}$$

Associative Property for Rational-Number Multiplication

$$\left(\frac{a}{b} \cdot \frac{c}{d}\right)\frac{e}{f} = \frac{a}{b}\left(\frac{c}{d} \cdot \frac{e}{f}\right)$$

Identity Property for Rational-Number Multiplication

$$\frac{a}{b} \cdot 1 = \frac{a}{b} = 1 \cdot \frac{a}{b} \qquad \left(1 = \frac{m}{m}, m \neq 0\right)$$

Multiplicative Inverse Property for Rational-Number Multiplication

For every nonzero rational number $\dfrac{a}{b}$ there exists a unique rational number $\dfrac{b}{a}$

such that $\dfrac{a}{b} \cdot \dfrac{b}{a} = 1.$

Recall that the multiplicative inverse of a number is also called the **reciprocal** of the number. Notice that the reciprocal of the reciprocal of any nonzero rational number is the original number.

It can be shown that distributivity also holds in the set of rational numbers. The verification of this fact takes precisely the same form as it did in the set of fractions and will be left for the Problem Set (Problem 27 in Part A).

PROPERTY

Distributive Property of Multiplication over Addition of Rational Numbers

Let $\dfrac{a}{b}, \dfrac{c}{d}$, and $\dfrac{e}{f}$ be any rational numbers. Then

$$\frac{a}{b}\left(\frac{c}{d} + \frac{e}{f}\right) = \frac{a}{b} \cdot \frac{c}{d} + \frac{a}{b} \cdot \frac{e}{f}.$$

The distributive property of multiplication over subtraction also holds.

Example 9.5 Use properties of rational numbers to compute the following problems (mentally if possible).

a. $\dfrac{2}{3} \cdot \dfrac{5}{7} + \dfrac{2}{3} \cdot \dfrac{2}{7}$ **b.** $\dfrac{-3}{5}\left(\dfrac{13}{37} \cdot \dfrac{10}{3}\right)$ **c.** $\dfrac{4}{5} \cdot \dfrac{7}{8} - \dfrac{1}{4} \cdot \dfrac{4}{5}$

Solution

a. $\dfrac{2}{3} \cdot \dfrac{5}{7} + \dfrac{2}{3} \cdot \dfrac{2}{7} = \dfrac{2}{3}\left(\dfrac{5}{7} + \dfrac{2}{7}\right) = \dfrac{2}{3}\left(\dfrac{7}{7}\right) = \dfrac{2}{3}$

b. $\dfrac{-3}{5}\left(\dfrac{13}{37} \cdot \dfrac{10}{3}\right) = \left(\dfrac{13}{37} \cdot \dfrac{10}{3}\right)\left(\dfrac{-3}{5}\right) = \dfrac{13}{37}\left(\dfrac{10}{3} \cdot \dfrac{-3}{5}\right) = \dfrac{-26}{37}$

NOTE: Just as with fractions, we could simplify before multiplying as follows.

$$\dfrac{-3}{5}\left(\dfrac{13}{37} \cdot \dfrac{10}{3}\right) = \dfrac{\overset{-1}{\cancel{-3}}}{\cancel{5}}\left(\dfrac{13}{37} \cdot \dfrac{\overset{2}{\cancel{10}}}{\cancel{3}}\right) = \dfrac{-26}{37}$$

c. $\dfrac{4}{5} \cdot \dfrac{7}{8} - \dfrac{1}{4} \cdot \dfrac{4}{5} = \dfrac{4}{5} \cdot \dfrac{7}{8} - \dfrac{4}{5} \cdot \dfrac{1}{4} = \dfrac{4}{5}\left(\dfrac{7}{8} - \dfrac{1}{4}\right) = \dfrac{4}{5} \cdot \dfrac{5}{8} = \dfrac{1}{2}$ ■

Division

Division of rational numbers is the natural extension of fraction division, namely, "invert the divisor and multiply" or "multiply by the reciprocal of the divisor."

DEFINITION

Division of Rational Numbers

Let $\dfrac{a}{b}$ and $\dfrac{c}{d}$ be any rational numbers where $\dfrac{c}{d}$ is nonzero. Then

$$\dfrac{a}{b} \div \dfrac{c}{d} = \dfrac{a}{b} \times \dfrac{d}{c}.$$

The common-denominator approach to fraction division also holds for rational-number division, as illustrated next.

$$\dfrac{a}{b} \div \dfrac{c}{b} = \dfrac{a}{b} \times \dfrac{b}{c} = \dfrac{a}{c}, \text{ that is, } \dfrac{a}{b} \div \dfrac{c}{b} = \dfrac{a}{c}$$

Also, since $a \div b$ can be represented as $\dfrac{a}{b}$, the numerator and denominator of the quotient of two rationals can also be found by dividing numerators and denominators in order from left to right. That is,

$$\dfrac{a}{b} \div \dfrac{c}{d} = \dfrac{a}{b} \times \dfrac{d}{c} = \dfrac{a}{c} \times \dfrac{d}{b} = \dfrac{a}{c} \div \dfrac{b}{d} = \dfrac{a \div c}{b \div d};$$

in summary, $\dfrac{a}{b} \div \dfrac{c}{d} = \dfrac{a \div c}{b \div d}$. When c is a divisor of a, the rational number $\dfrac{a}{c}$ equals the integer $a \div c$ and, if d is a divisor of b, $\dfrac{b}{d}$ equals $b \div d$.

Thus, just as with fractions, there are three equivalent ways to divide rational numbers.

THEOREM

Three Methods of Rational-Number Division

Let $\dfrac{a}{b}$ and $\dfrac{c}{d}$ be any rational numbers where $\dfrac{c}{d}$ is nonzero. Then the following are equivalent.

1. $\dfrac{a}{b} \div \dfrac{c}{d} = \dfrac{a}{b} \times \dfrac{d}{c}$

2. $\dfrac{a}{b} \div \dfrac{c}{b} = \dfrac{a}{c}$

3. $\dfrac{a}{b} \div \dfrac{c}{d} = \dfrac{a \div c}{b \div d}$

Example 9.6 Express the following quotients in simplest form using the most appropriate of the three methods of rational-number division.

a. $\dfrac{12}{-25} \div \dfrac{4}{5}$ **b.** $\dfrac{13}{17} \div \dfrac{-4}{9}$ **c.** $\dfrac{-18}{23} \div \dfrac{-6}{23}$

Solution

a. $\dfrac{12}{-25} \div \dfrac{4}{5} = \dfrac{12 \div 4}{-25 \div 5} = \dfrac{3}{-5} = \dfrac{-3}{5}$ by dividing the numerators and denominators using method (3) of the previous theorem, since $4\,|\,12$ and $5\,|\,25$.

b. $\dfrac{13}{17} \div \dfrac{-4}{9} = \dfrac{13}{17} \times \dfrac{-9}{4} = \dfrac{-117}{68}$ by multiplying by the reciprocal using method (1).

c. $\dfrac{-18}{23} \div \dfrac{-6}{23} = \dfrac{-18}{-6} = 3$ by the common-denominator approach using method (2), since the denominators are equal. ■

Figure 9.5 shows how rational numbers are extensions of the fractions and the integers.

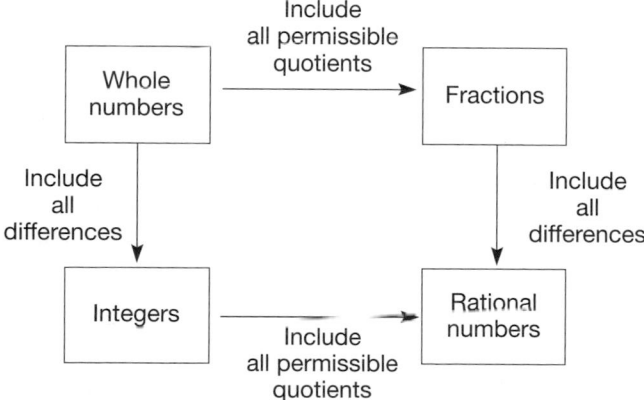

Figure 9.5

Ordering Rational Numbers

There are three equivalent ways to order rationals in much the same way as the fractions were ordered.

Number-Line Approach $\frac{a}{b} < \frac{c}{d}$ $\left(\text{or } \frac{c}{d} > \frac{a}{b}\right)$ if and only if $\frac{a}{b}$ is to the left of $\frac{c}{d}$ on the rational-number line.

Common-Positive-Denominator Approach $\frac{a}{b} < \frac{c}{b}$ if and only if $a < c$ and $b > 0$. Look at some examples where $a < c$ and $b < 0$. What can be said about $\frac{a}{b}$ and $\frac{c}{b}$ in these cases? In particular, consider the pair $\frac{3}{-5}$ and $\frac{4}{-5}$ to see why a positive denominator is required in this approach.

Addition Approach $\frac{a}{b} < \frac{c}{d}$ if and only if there is a *positive* rational number $\frac{p}{q}$ such that $\frac{a}{b} + \frac{p}{q} = \frac{c}{d}$. An equivalent form of the addition approach is $\frac{a}{b} < \frac{c}{d}$ if and only if $\frac{c}{d} - \frac{a}{b}$ is positive.

Example 9.7   Order the following pairs of numbers using one of the three approaches to ordering.

a. $\frac{-3}{7}, \frac{5}{2}$ **b.** $\frac{-7}{13}, \frac{-2}{13}$ **c.** $\frac{-5}{7}, \frac{-3}{4}$

Solution

a. Using the number line, all negatives are to the left of all positives, hence $\frac{-3}{7} < \frac{5}{2}$.

b. Since $-7 < -2$, we have $\frac{-7}{13} < \frac{-2}{13}$ by the common-positive-denominator approach.

c. $\frac{-5}{7} - \left(\frac{-3}{4}\right) = \frac{-5}{7} + \frac{3}{4} = \frac{-20}{28} + \frac{21}{28} = \frac{1}{28}$, which is positive.

Therefore, $\frac{-3}{4} < \frac{-5}{7}$ by the addition approach. Alternately, using the common-positive-denominator approach, $\frac{-3}{4} = \frac{-21}{28} < \frac{-20}{28} = \frac{-5}{7}$.   ■

As was done with fractions, the common-positive-denominator approach to ordering can be used to develop a shortcut for determining which of two rationals is smaller.

Suppose that $\frac{a}{b} < \frac{c}{d}$, where $b > 0$ and $d > 0$.

Then $\frac{ad}{bd} < \frac{bc}{bd}$. Since $bd > 0$, we conclude that $ad < bc$.

Similarly, if $ad < bc$, where $b > 0$ and $d > 0$, then $\frac{ad}{bd} < \frac{bc}{bd}$, so $\frac{a}{b} < \frac{c}{d}$.

We can summarize this as follows.

> ### THEOREM

> #### Cross-Multiplication of Rational-Number Inequality
>
> Let $\dfrac{a}{b}$ and $\dfrac{c}{d}$ be any rational numbers, where $b > 0$ and $d > 0$. Then
>
> $$\frac{a}{b} < \frac{c}{d} \text{ if and only if } ad < bc.$$

Cross-multiplication of inequality can be applied immediately when the two rational numbers involved are in simplest form, since their denominators will be positive.

Spotlight on Technology To compare $\dfrac{-37}{56}$ and $\dfrac{63}{-95}$, first rewrite both numbers with a positive denominator: $\dfrac{-37}{56}$ and $\dfrac{-63}{95}$.
Now $(-37)95 = -3515$, and $(-63)(56) = -3528$, and $-3528 < -3515$. Therefore, $\dfrac{-63}{95} < \dfrac{-37}{56}$. Of course, one could also compare the two numbers using their decimal representations: $\dfrac{-37}{56} \approx -0.6607$, $\dfrac{63}{-95} \approx -0.6632$, and $-0.6632 < -0.6607$. Therefore, $\dfrac{63}{-95} < \dfrac{-37}{56}$. One could also use the fact that $\dfrac{a}{b} < \dfrac{c}{d}$ if and only if $\dfrac{ad}{b} < c \left(\dfrac{a}{b} > \dfrac{c}{d} \text{ if and only if } \dfrac{ad}{b} > c \right)$, where $b, d > 0$, as we did with fractions.

The following relationships involving order, addition, and multiplication are extensions of similar ones involving fractions and integers. The verification of these is left for the Problem Set (Problems 28 Part A and 29–31 Part B).

> ### PROPERTIES

> #### Ordering Rational Numbers
>
> **Transitive Property for Less Than**
> **Property of Less Than and Addition**
> **Property of Less Than and Multiplication by a Positive**
> **Property of Less Than and Multiplication by a Negative**
> **Density Property**

Similar properties hold for $>$, $\leq$, and $\geq$. Applications of these properties are given in Section 9.2.

MATHEMATICAL MORSEL

To approximate $\sqrt{2}$, the Greeks built the "ladder" of numbers. The fourth rung "12, 17" is obtained from the third rung as follows: $12 = 5 + 7$, and $17 = 12 + 5$. In general, the nth rung, obtained by the $(n-1)$st rung "a,b," is "$a + b$, $2a + b$." The ratio of the number in the second column to the number in the first column (like 7/5 in rung 3) approaches $\sqrt{2}$.

Column 1	Column 2	Ratio	Rung
1	1	$1 : 1 = 1$	1
2	3	$3 : 2 = 1.5$	2
5	7	$7 : 5 = 1.4$	3
12	17	$17 : 12 = 1.41\overline{6}$	4
29	41	$41 : 29 = 1.413\cdots$	5
.	.	.	.
.	.	.	.
.	.	.	.
a	b	$b : a$	$n - 1$
$a + b$	$2a + b$	$(2a + b) : (a + b)$	n
.	.	.	.
.	.	.	.
.	.	.	.

Section 9.1 EXERCISE / PROBLEM SET A

EXERCISES

1. Explain how the following numbers satisfy the definition of a rational number.
   a. $-\frac{2}{3}$ b. $-5\frac{1}{6}$ c. 10

2. Which of the following are equal to -3?
$$\frac{-3}{1}, \frac{3}{1}, \frac{3}{-1}, -\frac{3}{1}, \frac{-3}{-1}, -\frac{-3}{1}, -\frac{-3}{-1}$$

3. Determine which of the following pairs of rational numbers are equal (try to do mentally first).
   a. $\frac{-3}{5}$ and $\frac{63}{-105}$ b. $\frac{-18}{-24}$ and $\frac{45}{60}$

4. Rewrite each of the following rational numbers in simplest form.
   a. $\frac{5}{-7}$ b. $\frac{21}{-35}$ c. $\frac{-8}{-20}$ d. $\frac{-144}{180}$

5. Add the following rational numbers. Express your answers in simplest form.
   a. $\frac{4}{9} + \frac{-5}{9}$ b. $\frac{-5}{12} + \frac{11}{-12}$
   c. $\frac{-2}{5} + \frac{13}{20}$ d. $\frac{-7}{8} + \frac{1}{12} + \frac{2}{3}$

6. Apply the properties of rational-number addition to calculate the following sums. Do mentally, if possible.
   a. $\frac{5}{7} + \left(\frac{9}{7} + \frac{5}{8}\right)$ b. $\left(\frac{5}{9} + \frac{3}{5}\right) + \frac{4}{9}$

7. Find the additive inverses of each of the following numbers.
   a. -2 b. $\frac{5}{3}$

8. Perform the following subtractions. Express your answers in simplest form.
   a. $\frac{5}{6} - \frac{1}{6}$ b. $\frac{3}{4} - \frac{-5}{4}$
   c. $\frac{-4}{7} - \frac{-9}{7}$ d. $\frac{-7}{12} - \frac{5}{18}$

9. Perform each of the following multiplications. Express your answers in simplest form.
   a. $\frac{2}{3} \cdot \frac{7}{9}$ b. $\frac{-5}{6} \cdot \frac{7}{3}$
   c. $\frac{-3}{10} \cdot \frac{-25}{27}$ d. $\frac{-2}{5} \cdot \frac{-15}{24}$

10. Use the properties of rational numbers to compute the following (mentally, if possible).

a. $-\dfrac{3}{5} \cdot \left(\dfrac{11}{17} \cdot \dfrac{5}{3}\right)$ **b.** $\left(-\dfrac{3}{7} \cdot \dfrac{10}{12}\right) \cdot \dfrac{6}{10}$

c. $\dfrac{2}{3} \cdot \left(\dfrac{3}{2} + \dfrac{5}{7}\right)$ **d.** $\dfrac{5}{9} \cdot \dfrac{2}{7} + \dfrac{2}{7} \cdot \dfrac{4}{9}$

11. Find the following quotients using the most appropriate of the three methods of rational-number division.

a. $\dfrac{-40}{27} \div \dfrac{-10}{9}$ **b.** $\dfrac{-1}{4} \div \dfrac{3}{2}$

c. $\dfrac{-3}{8} \div \dfrac{5}{6}$ **d.** $\dfrac{21}{25} \div \dfrac{-3}{5}$

12. Calculate and express in simplest form.

a. $\dfrac{25}{33} + \dfrac{-23}{39}$ **b.** $\dfrac{47}{49} - \dfrac{19}{-35}$

13. Order the following pairs of rational numbers using any of the approaches.

a. $\dfrac{-9}{11}, \dfrac{-3}{11}$ **b.** $\dfrac{-1}{3}, \dfrac{2}{5}$

c. $\dfrac{-5}{6}, \dfrac{-9}{10}$ **d.** $\dfrac{-10}{9}, \dfrac{-9}{8}$

14. Using a calculator and cross-multiplication of inequality, order the following pairs of rational numbers.

a. $\dfrac{-232}{356}, \dfrac{152}{201}$ **b.** $\dfrac{-761}{532}, \dfrac{-500}{345}$

15. Let W = the set of whole numbers

F = the set of (nonnegative) fractions

I = the set of integers

N = the set of negative integers

Q = the set of rational numbers.

List all the sets that have the following properties.

a. -5 is an element of the set.

b. $-\dfrac{3}{4}$ is an element of the set.

c. The set is closed under addition.

d. The set is closed under subtraction.

e. The set is closed under multiplication.

16. State the property that justifies each statement.

a. $\dfrac{-2}{3} + \left(\dfrac{1}{6} + \dfrac{3}{4}\right) = \left(\dfrac{-2}{3} + \dfrac{1}{6}\right) + \dfrac{3}{4}$

b. $\left(\dfrac{5}{6} \cdot \dfrac{7}{8}\right) \cdot \dfrac{-8}{3} = \left(\dfrac{7}{8} \cdot \dfrac{5}{6}\right) \cdot \dfrac{-8}{3}$

c. $\dfrac{1}{4}\left(\dfrac{8}{3} + \dfrac{-5}{4}\right) = \dfrac{1}{4}\left(\dfrac{8}{3}\right) + \dfrac{1}{4}\left(\dfrac{-5}{4}\right)$

d. $\dfrac{4}{9} + \dfrac{3}{5} < \dfrac{5}{9} + \dfrac{3}{5}$, since $\dfrac{4}{9} < \dfrac{5}{9}$

17. The property of less than and addition for ordering rational numbers can be used to solve simple inequalities. For example,

$$x + \dfrac{3}{5} < \dfrac{-7}{10}$$

$$x + \dfrac{3}{5} + \left(-\dfrac{3}{5}\right) < \dfrac{-7}{10} + \left(\dfrac{3}{5}\right)$$

$$x < -\dfrac{13}{10}.$$

Solve the following inequalities.

a. $x + \dfrac{1}{2} < -\dfrac{5}{6}$ **b.** $x - \dfrac{2}{3} < \dfrac{-3}{4}$

18. Some inequalities with rational numbers can be solved by applying the property of less than and multiplication by a positive for ordering rational numbers. For example,

$$\dfrac{2}{3}x < \dfrac{5}{6}$$

$$\left(\dfrac{3}{2}\right)\left(\dfrac{2}{3}x\right) < \left(\dfrac{3}{2}\right)\left(-\dfrac{5}{6}\right)$$

$$x < \dfrac{5}{4}.$$

Solve the following inequalities.

a. $\dfrac{5}{4}x < \dfrac{15}{8}$ **b.** $\dfrac{3}{2}x < -\dfrac{9}{8}$

19. When the property of less than and multiplication by a negative for ordering rational numbers is applied to solve inequalities, we need to be careful to change the inequality sign. For example,

$$-\dfrac{2}{3}x < \dfrac{5}{-6}$$

$$\left(-\dfrac{3}{2}\right)\left(-\dfrac{2}{3}x\right) > \left(-\dfrac{3}{2}\right)\left(-\dfrac{5}{6}\right)$$

$$x > \dfrac{5}{4}.$$

Solve each of the following inequalities.

a. $-\dfrac{3}{4}x < -\dfrac{15}{16}$ **b.** $-\dfrac{3}{5}x < \dfrac{9}{10}$

20. Calculate the following in two ways: (i) exactly as written and (ii) calculating an answer using all positive numbers and then determining whether the answer is positive or negative.

    a. $(-37)(-43)(-57)$ **b.** $\dfrac{(-55)(-49)}{-35}$

21. Calculate and express in simplest form.

    a. $\dfrac{13}{27} + \dfrac{-21}{31}$ **b.** $\dfrac{-15}{22} - \dfrac{-31}{48}$

22. Order the following pairs of numbers, and find a number between each pair.

    a. $\dfrac{-37}{76}, \dfrac{-43}{88}$ **b.** $\dfrac{59}{-97}, \dfrac{-68}{113}$

23. The set of rational numbers also has the density property. Recall some of the methods we used for fractions, and find three rational numbers between each pair of given numbers.

    a. $\dfrac{-3}{4}$ and $\dfrac{-1}{2}$ **b.** $\dfrac{-5}{6}$ and $\dfrac{-7}{8}$

PROBLEMS

24. Using the definition of equality of rational numbers, prove that $\dfrac{a}{b} = \dfrac{an}{bn}$, where n is any nonzero integer.

25. Using the corresponding properties of integers and reasoning by analogy from fraction properties, prove the following properties of rational-number multiplication.

    a. Closure   **b.** Commutativity

    c. Associativity   **d.** Identity

    e. Inverse

26. a. Complete the following statement for the missing-addend approach to subtraction.

$$\frac{a}{b} - \frac{c}{d} = \frac{e}{f} \text{ if and only if } \underline{\quad\quad}.$$

    b. Assuming the adding-the-opposite approach, prove that the missing-addend approach is true.

    c. Assume that the missing-addend approach is true, and prove that the adding-the-opposite approach is true.

27. Verify the distributive property of multiplication over addition for rational numbers: If $\dfrac{a}{b}, \dfrac{c}{d}$, and $\dfrac{e}{f}$ are rational numbers, then

$$\frac{a}{b}\left(\frac{c}{d} + \frac{e}{f}\right) = \frac{a}{b} \cdot \frac{c}{d} + \frac{a}{b} \cdot \frac{e}{f}.$$

28. Verify the following statement.

$$\text{If } \frac{a}{b} < \frac{c}{d}, \text{ then } \frac{a}{b} + \frac{e}{f} < \frac{c}{d} + \frac{e}{f}.$$

29. Prove that additive cancellation holds for the rational numbers.

$$\text{If } \frac{a}{b} + \frac{e}{f} = \frac{c}{d} + \frac{e}{f}, \text{ then } \frac{a}{b} = \frac{c}{d}.$$

30. Using a 5-minute and an 8-minute hourglass timer, how can you measure 6 minutes?

Section 9.1 EXERCISE / PROBLEM SET B

EXERCISES

1. Explain how the following numbers satisfy the definition of a rational number.

    a. $\frac{7}{3}$ **b.** $7\frac{1}{8}$ **c.** -3

2. Which of the following are equal to $\dfrac{5}{6}$?

$$-\frac{5}{6}, \frac{-5}{6}, \frac{5}{-6}, \frac{-5}{-6}, -\frac{-5}{6}, \frac{5}{-6}$$

3. Determine whether the following statements are true or false.

    a. $\dfrac{-32}{22} = \dfrac{48}{-33}$ **b.** $\dfrac{-75}{-65} = \dfrac{21}{18}$

4. Rewrite each of the following rational numbers in simplest form.

    a. $\dfrac{4}{-6}$ **b.** $\dfrac{-60}{-84}$ **c.** $\dfrac{64}{-144}$ **d.** $\dfrac{96}{-108}$

5. Add the following rational numbers. Express your answers in simplest form.

    a. $\dfrac{3}{10} + \dfrac{-8}{10}$ **b.** $\dfrac{-5}{4} + \dfrac{1}{9}$

    c. $\dfrac{-5}{6} + \dfrac{5}{12} + \dfrac{-1}{4}$ **d.** $\dfrac{-3}{8} + \dfrac{5}{12}$

6. Apply the properties of rational-number addition to calculate the following sums. Do mentally, if possible.

a. $\left(\dfrac{3}{11} + \dfrac{-18}{66}\right) + \dfrac{17}{23}$ b. $\left(\dfrac{3}{17} + \dfrac{6}{29}\right) + \dfrac{3}{-17}$

7. Find the additive inverses of each of the following numbers.

a. $\dfrac{2}{-7}$ b. $-\dfrac{5}{16}$

8. Perform the following subtractions. Express your answers in simplest form.

a. $\dfrac{8}{9} - \dfrac{2}{9}$ b. $\dfrac{-3}{7} - \dfrac{3}{4}$

c. $\dfrac{2}{9} - \dfrac{-7}{12}$ d. $\dfrac{-13}{24} + \dfrac{-11}{24}$

9. Multiply the following rational numbers. Express your answers in simplest form.

a. $\dfrac{3}{5} \cdot \dfrac{-10}{21}$ b. $\dfrac{-6}{11} \cdot \dfrac{-33}{18}$

c. $\dfrac{5}{12} \cdot \dfrac{48}{-15} \cdot \dfrac{-9}{8}$ d. $\dfrac{-6}{11} \cdot \dfrac{-22}{21} \cdot \dfrac{7}{-12}$

10. Apply the properties of rational numbers to compute the following (mentally, if possible).

a. $\dfrac{2}{9} + \left(\dfrac{3}{5} + \dfrac{7}{9}\right)$ b. $\dfrac{3}{7}\left(\dfrac{-11}{21}\right) + \left(\dfrac{3}{7}\right)\left(\dfrac{-11}{21}\right)$

c. $\dfrac{3}{7} + \left(\dfrac{5}{6} + \dfrac{-3}{7}\right)$ d. $\left(\dfrac{-9}{7} \cdot \dfrac{23}{-27}\right) \cdot \left(\dfrac{7}{9}\right)$

11. Find the following quotients. Express your answer in simplest form.

a. $\dfrac{-8}{9} \div \dfrac{2}{9}$ b. $\dfrac{12}{15} \div \dfrac{-4}{3}$

c. $\dfrac{-10}{9} \div \dfrac{-5}{4}$ d. $\dfrac{-13}{24} \div \dfrac{-39}{-48}$

12. Calculate and express in simplest form.

a. $\dfrac{67}{42} \times \dfrac{51}{59}$ b. $\dfrac{213}{76} \div \dfrac{-99}{68}$

13. Put the appropriate symbol, $<$, $=$, or $>$, between each pair of rational numbers to make a true statement.

a. $-\dfrac{5}{6} \underline{\hspace{1cm}} -\dfrac{11}{12}$ b. $-\dfrac{1}{3} \underline{\hspace{1cm}} \dfrac{5}{4}$

c. $\dfrac{-12}{15} \underline{\hspace{1cm}} \dfrac{36}{-45}$ d. $-\dfrac{3}{12} \underline{\hspace{1cm}} \dfrac{-4}{20}$

14. Using a calculator and cross-multiplication of inequality, order the following pairs of rational numbers.

a. $\dfrac{475}{652}, \dfrac{-308}{-421}$ b. $\dfrac{372}{487}, \dfrac{-261}{-319}$

15. Let W = the set of whole numbers
F = the set of (nonnegative) fractions
I = the set of integers
N = the set of negative integers
Q = the set of rational numbers.

List all the sets that have the following properties.

a. The set is closed under division.
b. The set has an additive identity.
c. The set has a multiplicative identity.
d. The set has additive inverses for each element.
e. The set has multiplicative inverses for each nonzero element.

16. State the property that justifies each statement.

a. $-\dfrac{2}{3}\left(\dfrac{3}{2} \cdot \dfrac{3}{5}\right) = \left(-\dfrac{2}{3} \cdot \dfrac{3}{2}\right) \cdot \dfrac{3}{5}$

b. $\dfrac{-7}{9}\left(\dfrac{3}{2} + \dfrac{-4}{5}\right) = \dfrac{-7}{9}\left(\dfrac{-4}{5} + \dfrac{3}{2}\right)$

c. $\left(\dfrac{-3}{5}\right) + \left(\dfrac{-5}{6}\right) < \left(\dfrac{-1}{5}\right) + \left(\dfrac{-5}{6}\right)$,

since $\dfrac{-3}{5} < \dfrac{-1}{5}$

d. $\dfrac{5}{11} \cdot \left(\dfrac{-1}{3}\right) > \dfrac{6}{11} \cdot \left(\dfrac{-1}{3}\right)$, since $\dfrac{5}{11} < \dfrac{6}{11}$

17. Solve the following inequalities.

a. $x - \dfrac{6}{5} < \dfrac{-12}{7}$ b. $x + \left(\dfrac{-3}{7}\right) > \dfrac{-4}{5}$

18. Solve the following inequalities.

a. $\dfrac{1}{6}x < \dfrac{-5}{12}$ b. $\dfrac{2}{5}x < -\dfrac{7}{8}$

19. Solve the following inequalities.

a. $-\dfrac{1}{3}x < -\dfrac{5}{6}$ b. $\dfrac{-3}{7}x > \dfrac{8}{5}$

20. Calculate the following in two ways: (i) exactly as written and (ii) calculating an answer using all positive numbers and then determining whether the answer is positive or negative.

a. $\dfrac{(-1111)(-23)(49)}{-77}$ b. $(-43)^2(-36)^3$

21. Calculate and express in simplest form.

a. $\dfrac{-65}{72} \times \dfrac{7}{48}$ b. $\dfrac{43}{57} \div \dfrac{37}{72}$

22. Order the following pairs of numbers and find a number between each pair.

a. $\dfrac{-113}{217}, \dfrac{-163}{314}$ b. $\dfrac{-812}{779}, \dfrac{545}{-522}$

23. Find three rational numbers between each pair of given numbers.

a. $\dfrac{-5}{4}$ and $\dfrac{-6}{5}$ b. $\dfrac{-1}{10}$ and $\dfrac{-1}{11}$

PROBLEMS

24. The closure property for rational-number addition can be verified as follows:

$$\frac{a}{b} + \frac{c}{d} = \frac{ad + bc}{bd} \text{ by definition of addition.}$$

$ab + bc$ and bd are both integers by closure properties of integer addition and multiplication and $bd \neq 0$. Therefore, by the definition of rational number,

$$\frac{ad + bc}{bd} \text{ is a rational number.}$$

In a similar way, verify the following properties of rational-number addition.

a. Commutative   b. Associative

25. Which of the following properties hold for subtraction of rational numbers? Verify the property or give a counterexample.

a. Closure   b. Commutative   c. Associative
d. Identity   e. Inverse

26. Using additive cancellation, prove $-\left(-\dfrac{a}{b}\right) = \dfrac{a}{b}$.

27. The positive rational numbers can be defined as those a/b where $ab > 0$. Determine whether the following are true or false. If true, prove; if false, give a counterexample.

a. The sum of two positive rationals is a positive rational.

b. The difference of two positive rationals is a positive rational.

c. The product of two positive rationals is a positive rational.

d. The quotient of two positive rationals is a positive rational.

28. Given: $\dfrac{a}{b} \cdot \left(\dfrac{c}{d} + \dfrac{e}{f}\right) = \dfrac{a}{b} \cdot \dfrac{c}{d} + \dfrac{a}{b} \cdot \dfrac{e}{f}$

Prove: $\dfrac{a}{b} \cdot \left(\dfrac{c}{d} - \dfrac{e}{f}\right) = \dfrac{a}{b} \cdot \dfrac{c}{d} - \dfrac{a}{b} \cdot \dfrac{e}{f}$

29. Prove: If $\dfrac{a}{b} < \dfrac{c}{d}$ and $\dfrac{c}{d} < \dfrac{e}{f}$, then $\dfrac{a}{b} < \dfrac{e}{f}$.

30. Prove each of the following statements.

a. If $\dfrac{a}{b} < \dfrac{c}{d}$ and $\dfrac{e}{f} > 0$, then $\dfrac{a}{b} \cdot \dfrac{e}{f} < \dfrac{c}{d} \cdot \dfrac{e}{f}$.

b. If $\dfrac{a}{b} < \dfrac{c}{d}$ and $\dfrac{e}{f} < 0$, then $\dfrac{a}{b} \cdot \dfrac{e}{f} > \dfrac{c}{d} \cdot \dfrac{e}{f}$.

31. Prove: If $\dfrac{a}{b} < \dfrac{c}{d}$, then there is an $\dfrac{e}{f}$ such that $\dfrac{a}{b} < \dfrac{e}{f} < \dfrac{c}{d}$.

32. José discovered what he thought was a method for generating a **Pythagorean triple**, that is, three whole numbers a, b, c such that $a^2 + b^2 = c^2$. Here are his rules: Take any odd number (say, 11). Square it (121). Subtract 1 and divide by 2 (60). Add 1 (61). (NOTE: $11^2 + 60^2 = 121 + 3600 = 3721 = 61^2$.) Try another example. Prove that José's method always works by using a variable.

PROBLEMS FOR WRITING/DISCUSSION

1. Maria multiplied $\dfrac{15}{7}$ and $\dfrac{14}{9}$ to obtain $\dfrac{210}{63}$. She says the answer in simplest form is $\dfrac{10}{3}$. Karl says the answer in simplest form is $3\dfrac{1}{3}$. Who is correct (or are they both correct)? Explain.

2. On another problem. Maria got an answer of $\dfrac{-3}{4}$, Billy got an answer of $\dfrac{3}{-4}$, and Karl got an answer of $\dfrac{-3}{-4}$.

Karl said, "We all have the same answer." How would you respond?

3. Explain how you know why the sum of two rational numbers, say $\dfrac{3}{7}$ and $\dfrac{2}{5}$, will be a rational number. In other words, explain why the closure property holds for rational number addition.

9.2 THE REAL NUMBERS

In Chapter 6, it was stated that fractions could be written as terminating or repeating decimals. The same is true for rational numbers. (Remember that terminating decimals are those decimals that repeat zero.) What are some examples of nonterminating, nonrepeating decimal numbers?

$$-\frac{3}{8} = -0.375$$

$$\frac{13}{5} = 4.333333\ldots$$

$$-\frac{5}{7} = -0.\overline{714285}714285$$

Real Numbers: An Extension of Rational Numbers

Every repeating decimal (this includes terminating decimals because of the repeating zero) can be written as a rational number $\frac{a}{b}$ where a and b are integers. Therefore, numbers with decimal representations that do not repeat are not rational numbers. What type of numbers are such decimals? Let's approach this question from another point of view.

The equation $x - 3 = 0$ has a whole-number solution, namely 3. However, the equation $x + 3 = 0$ does not have a *whole*-number solution. But the equation $x + 3 = 0$ does have an *integer* solution, namely -3. Now consider the equation $3x = 2$. This equation has neither a whole-number nor an integer solution. But the *fraction* $\frac{2}{3}$ is a solution of $3x = 2$. What about the equation $-3x = 2$? We must move to the set of *rationals* to find its solution, namely $-\frac{2}{3}$. Since solving equations plays an important role in mathematics, we want to have a number system that will allow us to solve many types of equations. Mathematicians encountered great difficulty when attempting to solve the equation $x^2 = 2$ using rational numbers. Because of its historical significance, we give a proof to show that it is actually *impossible* to find a rational number whose square is 2.

THEOREM

There is no rational number whose square is 2.

Problem-Solving Strategy
Use Indirect Reasoning

Proof Use indirect reasoning. Suppose that there is a rational number $\frac{a}{b}$ such that $\left(\frac{a}{b}\right)^2 = 2$. Then we have the following.

$$\left(\frac{a}{b}\right)^2 = 2$$

$$\frac{a^2}{b^2} = 2$$

$$a^2 = 2b^2$$

Now the argument will become a little subtle. By the Fundamental Theorem of Arithmetic, the numbers a^2 and $2b^2$ have the same prime factorization. Because squares have prime factors that occur in pairs, a^2 must have an *even* number of prime factors in its prime factorization. Similarly, b^2 has an even number of prime factors in its prime factorization. But 2 is a prime also, so $2 \cdot b^2$ has an *odd* number of prime factors in its prime factorization. (Note that b^2 contributes an even number of prime factors, and the factor 2 produces one more, hence an odd number of prime factors.) Recapping, we have (i) $a^2 = 2b^2$, (ii) a^2 has an even number of prime factors in its prime factorization, and (iii) $2b^2$ has an odd number of prime factors in its prime factorization. According to the Fundamental Theorem of Arithmetic, it is impossible for a number to have an even number of prime factors *and* an odd number of prime factors in its prime factorization. Thus there is *no* rational number whose square is 2. ■

Using similar reasoning, it can be shown that for every prime p there is no rational number, $\frac{a}{b}$, whose square is p. We leave that verification for the problem set.

Using a calculator, one can show that the square of the rational number 1.414213562 is very close to 2. However, we have proved that *no* rational number squared is exactly 2. Consequently, we have a need for a new system of numbers that will include infinite nonrepeating decimals, such as 0.020020002 . . . , as well as numbers that are solutions to equations such as $x^2 = p$, where p is a prime.

 DEFINITION

Real Numbers

The set of **real numbers,** R, is the set of all numbers that have an infinite decimal representation.

Thus the real numbers contain all the rationals (which are the infinite *repeating* decimals, positive, negative, or zero) together with a new set of numbers called, appropriately, the irrational numbers. The set of **irrational numbers** is the set of numbers that have infinite *nonrepeating* decimal representations. Figure 9.6 shows the different types of decimals. Since irrational numbers have infinite nonrepeating decimal representations, rational-number approximations (using finite decimals) have to be used to perform approximate computations in some cases.

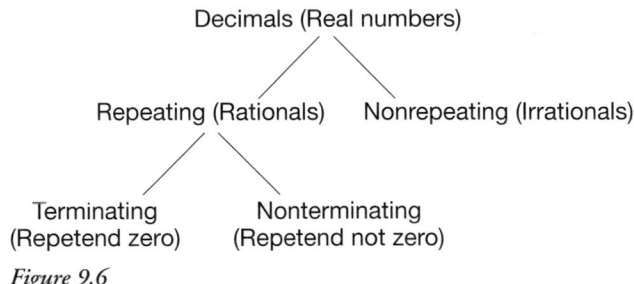

Figure 9.6

Example 9.8 Determine whether the following decimals represent rational or irrational numbers.
a. 0.273   **b.** 3.14159 . . .   **c.** $-15.7\overline{6}$

Solution

a. 0.273 is a rational number, since it is a terminating decimal.
b. 3.14159 . . . should be considered to be irrational, since the three dots indicate an infinite decimal and there is no repetend indicated.
c. $-15.7\overline{6}$ is rational, since it is a repeating decimal. ■

Now we can extend our diagram in Figure 9.2 to include the real numbers (Figure 9.7).

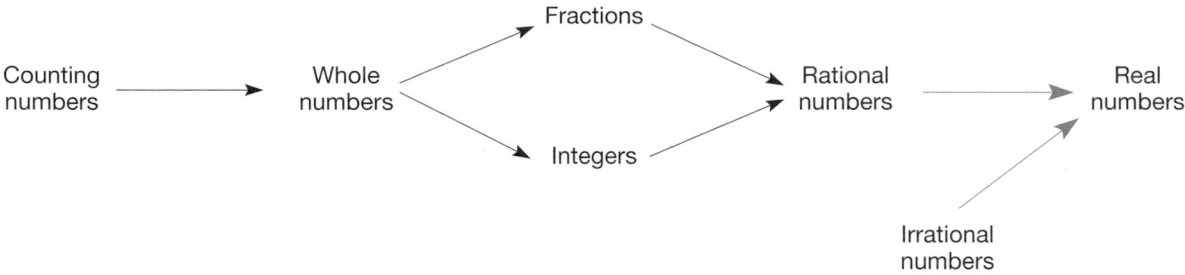

Figure 9.7

In terms of a number line, the points representing real numbers completely fill in the gaps in the rational number line. In fact, the points in the gaps represent irrational numbers (Figure 9.8).

Figure 9.8

Figure 9.9

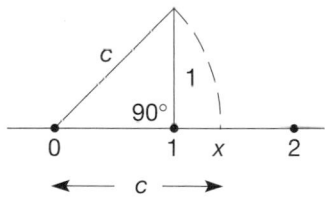

Figure 9.10

**NCTM Standards 2000
Number and Operations
Grades 6–8**
All students should understand and use the inverse relationships of addition and subtraction, multiplication and division, and squaring and finding square roots to simplify computations and solve problems.

Let's take this geometric representation of the real numbers one step further. The Pythagorean theorem from geometry states that in a right triangle whose sides have lengths a and b and whose hypotenuse has length c, the equation $a^2 + b^2 = c^2$ holds (Figure 9.9).

Now consider the construction in Figure 9.10. The length c is found by using the Pythagorean theorem:

$$1^2 + 1^2 = c^2 \qquad \text{or} \qquad c^2 = 2.$$

Moreover, the length of the segment from 0 to x is c also, since the dashed arc in Figure 9.10 is a portion of a circle. Thus $x = c$ where $c^2 = 2$. Since we know the number whose square is 2 is not rational, c must have an infinite *nonrepeating* decimal representation. To represent c with numerals other than an infinite nonrepeating decimal, we need the concept of square root.

Since both $(-3)^2$ and 3^2 equal 9, -3 and 3 are called *square roots* of 9. The symbol $\sqrt{a}$ represents the *nonnegative* square root of a, called the **principal square root.** For example, $\sqrt{4} = 2$, $\sqrt{25} = 5$, $\sqrt{144} = 12$, and so on. We can also write symbols such as $\sqrt{2}$, $\sqrt{3}$, and $\sqrt{17}$. These numbers are not rational, so they have infinite nonrepeating decimal representations. Thus it is necessary to leave them written as $\sqrt{2}, \sqrt{3}, \sqrt{17}$, and so on. According to the definition, though, we know that $(\sqrt{2})^2 = 2$, $(\sqrt{3})^2 = 3$, and $(\sqrt{17})^2 = 17$.

> ### DEFINITION
>
> **Square Root**
>
> Let a be a nonnegative real number. Then the **square root** of a (i.e., the principal square root of a), written $\sqrt{a}$, is defined as
>
> $$\sqrt{a} = b \qquad \text{where } b^2 = a \quad \text{and} \quad b \geq 0.$$

Spotlight on Technology Calculators can be used to find square roots. First, a $\boxed{\sqrt{}}$ key can be used. For example, to find $\sqrt{3}$ press $\boxed{\sqrt{}}$ 3 $\boxed{=}$ $\boxed{1.732050808}$ or simply 3 $\boxed{\sqrt{}}$. (Some calculators have "$\sqrt{}$" as a second function.) The $\boxed{\sqrt[x]{y}}$ key may also be used where x is 2 for square root. To find $\sqrt{3}$ using $\boxed{\sqrt[x]{y}}$, press 2 $\boxed{\sqrt[x]{y}}$ 3 $\boxed{=}$ $\boxed{1.732050808}$. Notice that this entered in the same way that it would be read, namely "the second root of three." Some calculators, however, use the following syntax: 3 $\boxed{\sqrt[x]{y}}$ 2, where the y is entered first. NOTE: The calculator displayed number is an *approximation* to $\sqrt{3}$.

One can observe that there are infinitely many irrational numbers, namely $\sqrt{p}$, where p is a prime. However, the fact that there are many more irrationals will be developed in the problem set. The number pi (π), of circle fame, was proved to be irrational around 1870; π is the ratio of the circumference to the diameter in any circle.

Using the decimal representation of real numbers, addition, multiplication, subtraction, and division of real numbers can be defined as extensions of similar operations in the rationals. The following properties hold (although it is beyond the scope of this book to prove them).

> ### PROPERTIES
>
> **Real-Number Operations**
>
> | ADDITION | MULTIPLICATION |
> |:---:|:---:|
> | Closure | Closure |
> | Commutativity | Commutativity |
> | Associativity | Associativity |
> | Identity (0) | Identity (1) |
> | Inverse ($-a$) | Inverse $\left(\dfrac{1}{a} \text{ for } a \neq 0\right)$ |
>
> **Distributivity of Multiplication over Addition**

Also, subtraction is defined by $a - b = a + (-b)$, and division is defined by $a \div b = a \cdot \dfrac{1}{b}$, where $b \neq 0$. "Less than" and "greater than" can be defined as extensions of ordering in the rationals, namely $a < b$ if and only if $a + p = b$ for some positive real number p. The following order properties also hold. Similar properties hold for $>$, $\leq$, and $\geq$.

Ordering Real Numbers

Transitive Property of Less Than
Property of Less Than and Addition
Property of Less Than and Multiplication by a Positive
Property of Less Than and Multiplication by a Negative
Density Property

You may have observed that the system of real numbers satisfies all of the properties that we have identified for the system of rational numbers. The main property that distinguishes the two systems is that the real numbers are "complete" in the sense that this is the set of numbers that finally fills up the entire number line. Even though the rational numbers are dense, there are still infinitely many gaps in the rational-number line, namely, the points that represent the irrationals. Together, the rationals and irrationals comprise the entire real number line.

Rational Exponents

Now that we have the set of real numbers, we can extend our study of exponents to rational exponents. We begin by generalizing the definition of square root to more general types of roots. For example, since $(-2)^3 = -8$, -2 is called the cube root of -8. Because of negative numbers, the definition must be stated in two parts.

⬡ DEFINITION

nth Root

Let a be a real number and n be a positive integer.

1. If $a \geq 0$, then $\sqrt[n]{a} = b$ if and only if $b^n = a$ and $b \geq 0$.
2. If $a < 0$ and n is odd, then $\sqrt[n]{a} = b$ if and only if $b^n = a$.

Example 9.9   Where possible, write the following values in simplest form by applying the previous two definitions.
a. $\sqrt[4]{81}$
b. $\sqrt[5]{-32}$
c. $\sqrt[6]{-64}$

Solution

a. $\sqrt[4]{81} = b$ if and only if $b^4 = 81$. Since $3^4 = 81$, we have $\sqrt[4]{81} = 3$.
b. $\sqrt[5]{-32} = b$ if and only if $b^5 = -32$. Since $(-2)^5 = -32$, we have $\sqrt[5]{-32} = -2$.
c. It is tempting to begin to apply the definition and write $\sqrt[6]{-64} = b$ if and only if $b^6 = -64$. However, since b^6 must always be positive or zero, there is no real number b such that $\sqrt[6]{-64} = b$.   ■

The number a in $\sqrt[n]{a}$ is called the **radicand** and n is called the **index.** The symbol $\sqrt[n]{a}$ is read **the *n*th root of *a*** and is called a **radical.** Notice that $\sqrt[n]{a}$ has not been defined for the case when n is even and a is negative. The reason is that $b^n \geq 0$ for any real number b and n an even positive integer. For example, there is no real number b such that $b = \sqrt{-1}$, for if there were, then b^2 would equal -1. This is impossible since, by the property of less than and multiplication by a positive (or negative), it can be shown that the square of any nonzero real number is positive.

Spotlight on Technology Roots of real numbers can be calculated by using the $\sqrt[x]{y}$ key. For example, to find $\sqrt[5]{30}$, enter it into the calculator just as it is read: the fifth root of thirty, or 5 $\sqrt[x]{y}$ 30. $=$ 1.9743505. (NOTE: Some calculators require that you press the second function key, 2nd, to get to the $\sqrt[x]{y}$ function.) Also, as a good mental check, since $2^5 = 32$, a good estimate of $\sqrt[5]{30}$ is a number somewhat less than 2. Hence, the calculator display of 1.9743505 is a reasonable approximation for $\sqrt[5]{30}$.

Using the concept of radicals, we can now proceed to define rational exponents. What would be a good definition of $3^{1/2}$? If the usual additive property of exponents is to hold, then $3^{1/2} \cdot 3^{1/2} = 3^{1/2 + 1/2} = 3^1 = 3$. But $\sqrt{3} \cdot \sqrt{3} = 3$. Thus $3^{1/2}$ should represent $\sqrt{3}$. Similarly, $5^{1/3} = \sqrt[3]{5}$, $2^{1/7} = \sqrt[7]{2}$, and so on. We summarize this idea in the next definition.

DEFINITION

Unit Fraction Exponent

Let a be any real number and n any positive integer. Then

$$a^{1/n} = \sqrt[n]{a}$$

where

1. n is arbitrary when $a \geq 0$, and
2. n must be odd when $a < 0$.

For example, $(-8)^{1/3} = \sqrt[3]{-8} = -2$, and $81^{1/4} = \sqrt[4]{81} = 3$.

The combination of this last definition with the definitions for integer exponents leads us to this final definition of **rational exponent.** For example, taking into account the previous definition and our earlier work with exponents, a natural way to think of $27^{2/3}$ would be $(27^{1/3})^2$. For the sake of simplicity, we restrict our definition to rational exponents of nonnegative real numbers.

DEFINITION

Rational Exponents

Let a be a nonnegative number and $\dfrac{m}{n}$ be a rational number in simplest form. Then $a^{m/n} = (a^{1/n})^m = (a^m)^{1/n}$.

Example 9.10 Express the following values without exponents.
a. $9^{3/2}$ **b.** $16^{5/4}$ **c.** $125^{-4/3}$

Solution

a. $9^{3/2} = (9^{1/2})^3 = 3^3 = 27$
b. $16^{5/4} = (16^{1/4})^5 = 2^5 = 32$

c. $125^{-4/3} = (125^{1/3})^{-4} = 5^{-4} = \dfrac{1}{5^4} = \dfrac{1}{625}$ ■

The following properties hold for rational exponents.

PROPERTIES

Rational Exponents

Let a, b represent positive real numbers and m, n positive rational exponents. Then

$$a^m a^n = a^{m+n}$$
$$a^m b^m = (ab)^m$$
$$(a^m)^n = a^{mn}$$
$$a^m \div a^n = a^{m-n}.$$

Real-number exponents are defined using more advanced mathematics, and they have the same properties as rational exponents.

 Spotlight on Technology An exponent key such as $\boxed{^\wedge}$ or $\boxed{y^x}$ can be used to calculate real exponents. For example, to calculate $3^{\sqrt{2}}$, press 3 $\boxed{^\wedge}$ $\boxed{\sqrt{}}$ 2 $\boxed{=}$ $\boxed{4.7288044}$.

Introduction to Algebra

Reflection from Research
Sixth-grade students with no formal instruction in algebra are "generally able to solve problems involving specific cases and showed remarkable ability to generalize the problem situations and to write equations using variables. However, they rarely used their equations to solve related problems" (Swafford & Langrall, 2000).

Solving equations and inequalities is one of the most important processes in mathematics. Traditionally, this topic has represented a substantial portion of an entire course in introductory algebra. An **equation** is a sentence involving numbers, or symbols representing numbers, where the verb is *equals* ($=$). There are various types of equations:

$$3 + 4 = 7 \qquad \textit{True equation}$$
$$3 + 4 = 9 \qquad \textit{False equation}$$
$$x + 4 = 9 \qquad \textit{Conditional equation}$$
$$2x + 5x = 7x \qquad \textit{Identity}$$

An **inequality** is a sentence whose verb is one of the following: $<, \leq, >, \geq,$ or $\neq$. Examples of conditional equations and inequalities follow.

NCTM Standards 2000
Algebra
Grades 6–8
All students should develop an initial conceptual understanding of different uses of variables.

EQUATIONS	INEQUALITIES
$x + 3 = 7$	$2x + 4 < -17$
$\dfrac{1}{3}x + \dfrac{2}{5} = \dfrac{2}{7}x - \dfrac{4}{13}$	$(\sqrt{2})x - \dfrac{2}{5} \leq 8x - \dfrac{1}{\sqrt{3}}$

The following treatment will be limited to solving equations of the form $ax + b = cx + d$, where a, b, c, d, and x are real numbers, as well as inequalities of the form $ax + b \leq cx + d$. The symbol x is a **variable.** We will permit variables to represent real numbers. When a particular number replaces a variable to produce a true equation (or inequality), that number is called a **solution.** The set of all solutions for a given equation (inequality) is called the **solution set** of the equation (inequality). For example, the solution set of the equation $x + 3 = 7$ is $\{4\}$, of $x + 4 < 7$ is $\{x \mid x < 3\}$, and so on. To **solve** an equation or inequality means to find its solution set.

Solving Equations Before we solve equations of the form $ax + b = cx + d$, the next example shows three different ways to solve equations of the form $ax + b = c$.

Example 9.11 Solve the equation $3x + 4 = 19$.

Solution

Guess and Test As the name of this method suggests, one guesses values for the variable and substitutes to see if a true equation results.

Try $x = 1: 3(1) + 4 = 7 \neq 19$.
Try $x = 4: 3(4) + 4 = 16 \neq 19$.
Try $x = 5: 3(5) + 4 = 19$. Therefore, 5 is a solution of the equation.

Problem-Solving Strategy
Draw a Diagram

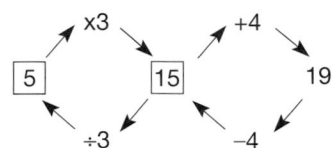

Cover Up In this method we cover up the term with the variable: $\square + 4 = 19$. To make a true equation, the $\square$ must be 15. Thus $3x = 15$. Since $3 \cdot 5 = 15$, x must be 5.

Work Backward The left side of the equation shows that x was *multiplied* by 3 and then 4 was *added* to obtain 19. Thus if we *subtract* 4 from 19 and *divide* by 3, we can work backward to the value of x. Here $19 - 4 = 15$ and $15 \div 3 = 5$, so $x = 5$. The diagram to the left summarizes this. ■

Next we develop a systematic approach for solving more complex equations and inequalities, which we call the **balancing method.** Consider equations of the form $ax + b = cx + d$, where x is a variable and a, b, c, and d are fixed real numbers. Here, a and c are called **coefficients** of the variable x; they are numbers multiplied by a variable. We begin with an elementary form and proceed to more complex forms.

Problem-Solving Strategy
Draw a Picture

Form 1

$$x + a = b$$
Solve: $x + 4 = 7$.

Concrete/Pictorial Representation	Abstract Representation

$$x + 4 = 7$$

Reflection from Research
The use of objects and containers as analogues for variables helped students solve linear equations. The analogue positively influenced not only students' achievement, but also their attitude toward the topic (Quinlan, 1995).

There are four coins and some more hidden from view behind the square. Altogether they balance seven coins. How many coins are hidden?

(NOTE: Throughout this section we are assuming that the coins are identical.)

Add (-4) to both sides

$$x + 4 + (-4) = 7(-4)$$
$$x + 0 = 3$$
$$x = 3$$

Remove four coins from each side. There are three coins hidden.

Form 2

$$ax + b = c$$

Solve: $3x + 6 = 12$.

Concrete/Pictorial Representation	Abstract Representation

$$3x + 6 = 12$$

Objective: Solve addition equations.

10·8 Explore Addition Equations

Algebra & functions

Learn

You can use counters and cups to solve equations.

Work Together

You Will Need
• counters
• cups

▶ You can use counters and cups to solve the equation $d + 9 = 24$.
  • Use a sheet of paper to represent each side of the equation.
  • Use counters to represent the numbers and a cup to stand for the variable, d.

d +   9

=   24

  • Take 9 counters away from each side of the equation.
    Note: If you add or subtract the same number from both sides of an equation, the equation will still be true.
  • The variable d is equal to the number of counters left on the right side of the equal sign.
  • Record your work.
▶ Use counters and cups to solve each equation. Record your work.

     $9 + x = 23$ $3 + t = 12$ $y + 9 = 14$ $t + 7 = 19$

 Cluster B

Remove six coins from each side.

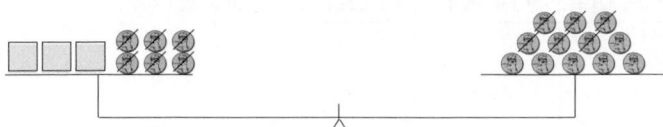

Add (-6) to both sides (equivalently, subtract 6 from both sides).

$$3x + 6 + (-6) = 12 + (-6)$$
$$3x = 6$$

Divide the coins into three equal piles (one pile for each square). Each square hides two coins.

Multiply both sides by $\frac{1}{3}$ (equivalently, divide both sides by 3).

$$\left(\frac{1}{3}\right)3x = \left(\frac{1}{3}\right)6$$
$$\left(\frac{1}{3} \cdot 3\right)x = 2$$
$$1 \cdot x = 2$$
$$x = 2$$

Form 3

$$ax + b = cx + d$$
Solve: $4x + 5 = 2x + 13$.

Concrete/Pictorial Representation	**Abstract Representation**
	$4x + 5 = 2x + 13$

Remove five coins from each pan. (We could have removed the coins behind two squares from each pan also.)

Add (-5) to both sides (equivalently, subtract 5 from both sides).

$$4x + 5 + (-5) = 2x + 13 + (-5)$$
$$4x = 2x + 8$$

Remove all the coins behind two squares from each pan. Remember, all squares hide the same number of coins.

Add $(-2x)$ to both sides (equivalently, subtract $2x$ from both sides).

$$4x = 2x + 8$$
$$-2x + 4x = -2x + 2x + 8$$
$$2x = 8$$

Divide the coins into two equal piles (one for each square). Each square hides four coins

Multiply both sides by $\frac{1}{2}$ (equivalently, divide both sides by 2).

$$2x = 8$$
$$\frac{1}{2}(2x) = \frac{1}{2} \cdot 8$$
$$x = 4$$

(NOTE: In the preceding three examples, all the coefficients of x were chosen to be positive. However, the same techniques we have applied hold for negative coefficients also.)

Spotlight on Technology The Chapter 9 eManipulative activity, *Balance Beam Algebra*, models the solution of algebraic equations using a balance beam. Use the eManipulative to solve the equation

www.wiley.com/college/musser $2(x + 3) = 10$. When students solve such a problem, they often write $2(x + 3) = 2x + 3$ because they forget to use the distributive property properly. How does the balance beam model help students avoid making this mistake?

The previous examples show that to solve equations of the form $ax + b = cx + d$, you should add the appropriate values to each side to obtain another equation of the form $mx = n$. Then multiply both sides by $\dfrac{1}{m}$ (or, equivalently, divide by m) to yield the solution $x = \dfrac{n}{m}$.

Example 9.12 Solve these equations.

a. $5x + 11 = 7x + 5$ **b.** $\dfrac{2}{3}x + \dfrac{5}{7} = \dfrac{9}{4}x - \dfrac{2}{11}$

Solution

a.
$$5x + 11 = 7x + 5$$
$$(-5x) + 5x + 11 = (-5x) + 7x + 5$$
$$11 = 2x + 5$$
$$11 + (-5) = 2x + 5 + (-5)$$
$$6 = 2x$$
$$\frac{1}{2} \cdot 6 = \frac{1}{2} \cdot 2x$$
$$3 = x$$

To check, substitute 3 for x into the initial equation:

Check: $5 \cdot 3 + 11 = \mathbf{26}$,   and $7 \cdot 3 + 5 = \mathbf{26}$

b. This solution incorporates some shortcuts.

$$\frac{2}{3}x + \frac{5}{7} = \frac{9}{4}x - \frac{2}{11}$$
$$\frac{2}{3}x = \frac{9}{4}x - \frac{2}{11} - \frac{5}{7}$$
$$\frac{2}{3}x - \frac{9}{4}x = -\frac{69}{77}$$
$$\frac{-19}{12}x = \frac{-69}{77}$$
$$x = \left(-\frac{12}{19}\right)\left(-\frac{69}{77}\right) = \frac{828}{1463}$$

Check: $\dfrac{2}{3} \cdot \dfrac{828}{1463} + \dfrac{5}{7} = \dfrac{552}{1463} + \dfrac{5}{7} = \dfrac{\mathbf{1597}}{\mathbf{1463}}$ and

$\dfrac{9}{4} \cdot \dfrac{828}{1463} - \dfrac{2}{11} = \dfrac{1863}{1463} - \dfrac{2}{11} = \dfrac{\mathbf{1579}}{\mathbf{1463}}$ ■

In the solution of Example 9.12(a), the same term was added to both sides of the equation or both sides were multiplied by the same number until an equation of the form $x = a$ (or $a = x$) resulted. In the solution of Example 9.12(b), terms were moved from one side to the other, changing signs when addition was involved and inverting when multiplication was involved. This method is called **transposing.**

Solving Inequalities Inequalities can be solved in much the same manner using the following properties of order.

> *Property of less than and addition*: If $a < b$, then $a + c < b + c$.
> *Property of less than and multiplication by a positive*: If $a < b$ and $c > 0$, then $ac < bc$.
> *Property of less than and multiplication by a negative*: If $a < b$ and $c < 0$, then $ac > bc$.

Notice that in the third property, the property of less than and multiplication by a negative, the inequality $a < b$ "reverses" to the inequality $ac > bc$, since c is negative. Also, similar corresponding properties hold for "greater than," "less than or equal to," and "greater than or equal to."

Example 9.13 Solve these inequalities.

a. $3x - 4 < x + 12$ **b.** $\frac{1}{3}x - 7 > \frac{3}{5}x + 3$

Solution

a.

$$3x - 4 < x + 12$$ *Property of less than and addition*

$$3x + (-4) + 4 < x + 12 + 4$$

$$3x < x + 16$$ *Property of less than and addition*

$$(-x) + 3x < (-x) + x + 16$$

$$2x < 16$$

$$\frac{1}{2}(2x) < \frac{1}{2}(16)$$ *Property of less than and multiplication by a positive*

$$x < 8$$

b.

$$\frac{1}{3}x - 7 > \frac{3}{5}x + 3$$

$$\frac{1}{3}x - 7 + 7 > \frac{3}{5}x + 3 + 7$$ *Property of greater than and addition*

$$\frac{1}{3}x > \frac{3}{5}x + 10$$

$$-\frac{3}{5}x + \frac{1}{3}x > -\frac{3}{5}x + \frac{3}{5}x + 10$$ *Property of greater than and addition*

$$-\frac{4}{15}x > 10$$

$$\left(-\frac{15}{4}\right)\left(-\frac{4}{15}x\right) < \left(\frac{15}{4}\right)10$$ *Property of greater than and multiplication by a negative*

$$x < \frac{-75}{2} = -37.5$$ ■

Solutions of equations can be checked by substituting the solutions back into the initial equation. In Example 9.12(a), the substitution of 3 into the equation $5x + 11 = 7x + 5$ yields $5 \cdot 3 + 11 = 7 \cdot 3 + 5$, or $26 = 26$. Thus 3 is a solution of this equation. The process of checking inequalities is more involved. Usually, there are infinitely many numbers in the solution set of an inequality. Since there are infinitely many numbers to check, it is reasonable to check only a few (perhaps two or three) well-chosen numbers. For example, let's consider Example 9.13(b). The solution set for the inequality $\frac{1}{3}x - 7 > \frac{3}{5}x + 3$ is $\{x \mid x < -37.5\}$ (Figure 9.11).

-37.5 0

Figure 9.11

To check the solution, substitute into the inequality one "convenient" number from the solution set and one outside the solution set. Here -45 (in the solution set) and 0 (not in the solution set) are two convenient values.

1. In $\frac{1}{3}x - 7 > \frac{3}{5}x + 3$, substitute 0 for x: $\frac{1}{3} \cdot 0 - 7 > \frac{3}{5} \cdot 0 + 3$, or $-7 > 3$, which is false. Therefore, 0 does *not* belong to the solution set.
2. To test -45: $\frac{1}{3}(-45) - 7 > \frac{3}{5}(-45) + 3$, or $-22 > -24$ which is true. Therefore, -45 does belong to the solution set.

You may want to check several other numbers. Although this method is not a complete check, it should add to your confidence that your solution set is correct.

Algebra has important uses in addition to solving equations and inequalities. For example, the problem-solving strategy Use a Variable is another application of algebra that is very useful.

Example 9.14　Prove that the sum of any five consecutive whole numbers has a factor of 5.

Solution　Let x, $x + 1$, $x + 2$, $x + 3$, $x + 4$ represent any five consecutive whole numbers.

Then

$$x + (x + 1) + (x + 2) + (x + 3) + (x + 4) = 5x + 10 = 5(x + 2),$$

which has a factor of 5.　■

MATHEMATICAL MORSEL

Throughout history there have been many interesting approximations of π as well as many ways of computing them. The value of pi to seven decimal places can easily be remembered using the mnemonic "May I have a large container of coffee?", where the number of letters in each word yields 3.1415926.

1. Found in an Egyptian papyrus:

$$\pi \approx \left(2 \times \frac{8}{9}\right)^2.$$

2. Due to Archimedes: $\pi \approx \frac{22}{7}$, $\pi \approx \frac{355}{113}$.

3. Due to Wallis:

$$\pi = 2 \cdot \frac{2}{1} \cdot \frac{2}{3} \cdot \frac{4}{3} \cdot \frac{4}{5} \cdot \frac{6}{5} \cdot \frac{6}{7} \cdot \frac{8}{7} \cdots$$

4. Due to Gregory:

$$\pi = 4\left(1 - \frac{1}{3} + \frac{1}{5} - \frac{1}{7} + \cdots\right).$$

5. Due to Euler and Bernoulli:

$$\pi^2 = 6\left(\frac{1}{1^2} + \frac{1}{2^2} - \frac{1}{3^2} + \cdots\right).$$

6. In 1989, Gregory V. and David V. Chudnovsky calculated π to 1,011,196,691 places.

Section 9.2 EXERCISE / PROBLEM SET A

EXERCISES

1. Which of the following numbers are rational, and which are irrational? Assume that the decimal patterns continue.

   a. 6.233233323333 . . .   **b.** $\sqrt{49}$ **c.** $\sqrt{61}$

   d. −5.235723572357 . . .

   e. 7.121231234 . . .

   f. $\sqrt{37}$ **g.** $\sqrt{64}$ **h.** 4.233233233 . . .

2. The number π is given as an example of an irrational number. Often the value $\frac{22}{7}$ is used for π. Does $\pi = \frac{22}{7}$? Why or why not?

3. Arrange the following real numbers in increasing order.

   0.56   0.5̄6̄   0.5̄6̄6̄   0.56565556 . . .
   0.566̄   0.56656665 . . .
   0.565566555666 . . .

4. Find an irrational number between $0.\overline{37}$ and $0.\overline{38}$.

5. Find four irrational numbers between 3 and 4.

6. **a.** Which property of real numbers justifies the following statement?

   $$2\sqrt{3} + 5\sqrt{3} = (2 + 5)\sqrt{3} = 7\sqrt{3}$$

   b. Can this property be used to simplify $5\pi + 3\pi$? Explain.

   c. Can this property be used to simplify $2\sqrt{3} + 7\sqrt{5}$? Explain.

7. Compute the following pairs of expressions.

   a. $\sqrt{4} \times \sqrt{9}, \sqrt{4 \times 9}$

   b. $\sqrt{4} \times \sqrt{25}, \sqrt{4 \times 25}$

   c. $\sqrt{9} \times \sqrt{16}, \sqrt{9 \times 16}$

   d. $\sqrt{9} \times \sqrt{25}, \sqrt{9 \times 25}$

   e. What conclusion do you draw about $\sqrt{a}$ and $\sqrt{b}$ and $\sqrt{a \times b}$? (NOTE: a and b must be nonnegative.)

8. Estimate the following values; then check with a calculator.

   a. $\sqrt{361}$ **b.** $\sqrt{729}$

9. The result $\sqrt{a} \times \sqrt{b} = \sqrt{a \times b}$ may be used to simplify square roots. For example, $\sqrt{20} = \sqrt{4 \times 5} = \sqrt{4} \times \sqrt{5} = 2\sqrt{5}$. Simplify the following so that the radical is as small a whole number as possible.

   a. $\sqrt{20} \times \sqrt{5}$

   b. $\sqrt{11} \times \sqrt{44}$

10. Construct the lengths $\sqrt{2}, \sqrt{3}, \sqrt{4}, \sqrt{5}, \ldots$ as follows.

    a. First construct a right triangle with both legs of length 1. What is the length of the hypotenuse?

    b. This hypotenuse is a leg of the next right triangle. The other leg has length 1. What is the length of the hypotenuse of this triangle?

    c. Continue drawing right triangles, using the hypotenuse of the preceding triangle as a leg of the next triangle until you have constructed one with length $\sqrt{7}$.

11. Use the Pythagorean theorem to find the length of the indicated side of the following right triangles. (NOTE: The square-like symbol indicates the 90° angle.)

    a.

    b.

    c.

    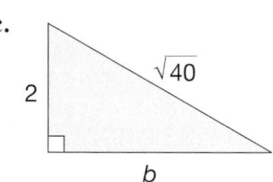

12. Since the square roots of some numbers are irrational, their decimal representations do not repeat. Approximations of these decimal representations can be made by a process of squeezing. For example, from Figure 9.9, we see that $1 < \sqrt{2} < 2$. To improve this approximation, find two numbers between 1 and 2 that "squeeze" $\sqrt{2}$. Since $(1.4)^2 = 1.96$ and $(1.5)^2 = 2.25$, $1.4 < \sqrt{2} < 1.5$. To obtain a closer approximation, we could continue the squeezing process by choosing numbers close to 1.4 (since 1.96 is closer to 2 than 2.25). Since $(1.41)^2 = 1.9981$ and $(1.42)^2 = 2.0164$, $1.41 < \sqrt{2} < 1.42$, or $\sqrt{2} \approx 1.41$. Use the squeezing process to approximate square roots of the following to the nearest hundredth.

    a. 7   **b.** 15.6   **c.** 0.036

13. Using a calculator with a square-root key, enter the number 2. Press the square-root key several times consecutively. What do you observe about the numbers displayed? Continue to press the square-root key until no new numbers appear in the display. What is this number?

14. Using the square-root key on your calculator, find the square roots of the following numbers. Then order the given number and its square root in increasing order. What do you observe?

a. 0.3   **b.** 0.5

15. Express the following values without exponents.

a. $25^{1/2}$ **b.** $32^{1/5}$ **c.** $9^{5/2}$

d. $(-27)^{4/3}$ **e.** $16^{3/4}$ **f.** $25^{-3/2}$

16. Write the following radicals in simplest form if they are real numbers.

a. $\sqrt[3]{-27}$ **b.** $\sqrt[4]{-16}$ **c.** $\sqrt[5]{32}$

17. Calculate the following to three decimal places.

a. $625^{0.5}$ **b.** $37^{0.37}$ **c.** $11111^{1.7}$ **d.** $7^{8.23}$

18. Determine the larger of each pair.

a. π, $\frac{22}{7}$ **b.** $\sqrt[3]{37}$, 1.35^4

19. Solve the following equations using any method.

a. $x + 15 = 7$ **b.** $x + (-21) = -16$

c. $x + \frac{11}{9} = \frac{2}{3}$ **d.** $x + 2\sqrt{2} = 5\sqrt{2}$

20. Solve the following equations using each of the three methods of Example 9.11.

a. $2x - 5 = 13$ **b.** $3x + 7 = 22$

c. $-5x + 13 = -12$ **d.** $\frac{2}{3}x + \frac{1}{6} = \frac{11}{22}$

e. $-\frac{3}{5}x - \frac{1}{4} = \frac{9}{20}$ **f.** $3x + \pi = 7\pi$

21. Solve these inequalities.

a. $3x - 6 < 6x + 5$ **b.** $2x + 3 \geq 5x - 9$

c. $\frac{2}{3}x - \frac{1}{4} > \frac{1}{9}x + \frac{3}{4}$ **d.** $\frac{6}{5}x \quad \frac{1}{3} \leq \frac{3}{10}x + \frac{2}{5}$

PROBLEMS

22. Prove that $\sqrt{3}$ is not rational. (*Hint*: Reason by analogy from the proof that there is no rational number whose square is 2.)

23. Show why, when reasoning by analogy from the proof that $\sqrt{2}$ is irrational, an indirect proof does not lead to a contradiction when you try to show that $\sqrt{9}$ is irrational.

24. Prove that $\sqrt[3]{2}$ is irrational.

25. a. Show that $5\sqrt{3}$ is an irrational number. (*Hint*: Assume that it is rational, say a/b, isolate $\sqrt{3}$, and show that a contradiction occurs.)

b. Using a similar argument, show that the product of any nonzero rational number with an irrational number is an irrational number.

26. a. Prove that $1 + \sqrt{3}$ is an irrational number.

b. Show, similarly, that $m + n\sqrt{3}$ is an irrational number for all rational numbers m and n ($n \neq 0$).

27. Show that the following are irrational numbers.

a. $6\sqrt{2}$ **b.** $2 + \sqrt{3}$ **c.** $5 + 2\sqrt{3}$

28. A student says to his teacher, "You proved to us that $\sqrt{a} \cdot \sqrt{b} = \sqrt{ab}$. Reasoning by analogy, we get $\sqrt{a} + \sqrt{b} = \sqrt{a + b}$. Therefore, $\sqrt{9} + \sqrt{16} = \sqrt{25}$ or $3 + 4 = 5$. Right?" Comment!

29. A student says to her teacher, "You proved that $\sqrt{a} \cdot \sqrt{b} = \sqrt{ab}$. Therefore,

$$-1 = (\sqrt{-1})^2 = \sqrt{-1}\sqrt{-1} = \sqrt{(-1)(-1)} = \sqrt{1} = 1,$$

so that $-1 = 1$." What do you say?

30. Recall that a Pythagorean triple is a set of three nonzero whole numbers (a, b, c) where $a^2 + b^2 = c^2$. For example, $(3, 4, 5)$ is a Pythagorean triple. Show that there are infinitely many Pythagorean triples.

31. A **primitive Pythagorean triple** is a Pythagorean triple whose members have only 1 as a common prime factor. For example, $(3, 4, 5)$ is primitive, whereas $(6, 8, 10)$ is not. It has been shown that all primitive Pythagorean triples are given by the three equations:

$$a = 2uv \qquad b = u^2 - v^2 \qquad c = u^2 + v^2,$$

where u and v are relatively prime, one of u or v is even and the other is odd, and $u > v$. Generate five primitive triples using these equations.

32. You have three consecutive integers less than 20. Add two of them together, divide by the third, and the answer is the smallest of the three integers. What are the numbers?

33. Can a rational number plus its reciprocal ever be an integer? If yes, say precisely when.

34. If you are given two straight pieces of wire, is it possible to cut one of them into two pieces so that the length of one of the three pieces is the average of the lengths of the other two? Explain.

35. Messrs. Carter, Farrell, Milne, and Smith serve the little town of Milford as architect, banker, druggist, and grocer, though not necessarily respectively. The druggist earns exactly twice as much as the grocer, the architect earns exactly twice as much as the druggist, and the banker earns exactly twice as much as the architect. Although Carter is older than anyone who makes more money than Farrell, Farrell does not make twice as much as Carter. Smith earns exactly $3776 more than Milne. Who is the druggist?

36. At a contest, two persons were asked their ages. Then, to test their arithmetical powers, they were asked to add the two ages together. One gave 44 as the answer and the other gave 1280. The first had subtracted one age from the other, while the second person had multiplied them together. What were their ages?

Section 9.2 EXERCISE / PROBLEM SET B

EXERCISES

1. Which of the following numbers are rational, and which are irrational?
   a. $2.375375\ldots$ **b.** $3.0120123\ldots$ **c.** $\sqrt{169}$
   d. 2π **e.** $3.\overline{12}$ **f.** $\sqrt{7}$
   g. $\dfrac{35}{0.72}$ **h.** $5.626626662\ldots$

2. The number $\sqrt{2}$ is often given as 1.414. Doesn't this show that $\sqrt{2}$ is rational, since it has a terminating decimal representation? Discuss.

3. Arrange the following real numbers in increasing order.

   $0.876 \qquad 0.8\overline{76} \qquad 0.\overline{876} \qquad 0.876787677876\ldots$

   $0.\overline{8766} \qquad 0.8766876667\ldots$

   $0.8767876677887666\ldots$

4. Find an irrational number between $0.\overline{5777}$ and $0.\overline{5778}$.

5. Find three irrational numbers between 2 and 3.

6. Simplify the following square roots.
   a. $\sqrt{40}$ **b.** $\sqrt{80}$ **c.** $\sqrt{180}$

7. Compute and simplify the following expressions.
   a. $\sqrt{18} \times \sqrt{2}$ **b.** $\sqrt{27} \times \sqrt{3}$
   c. $\sqrt{60} \times \sqrt{12}$ **d.** $5\sqrt{2} - 9\sqrt{2}$
   e. $\sqrt{18} \times \sqrt{32}$ **f.** $\sqrt{20} - \sqrt{5} + \sqrt{45}$

 8. Estimate the following values; then check with a calculator.
   a. $\sqrt{3136}$ **b.** $\sqrt{5041}$

9. Simplify the following so that the radical is as small a whole number as possible.
   a. $\sqrt{16} \times \sqrt{48}$ **b.** $\sqrt{12} \times \sqrt{216}$

10. Use the Pythagorean theorem to find the lengths of the given segments drawn on the following square lattices.

a.   **b.**

1 unit

c.

11. Use the Pythagorean theorem to find the missing lengths in the following diagrams.

a.

b.
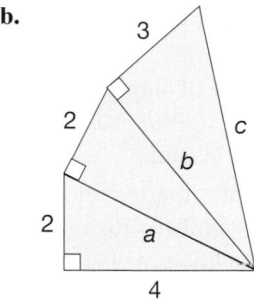

12. Find $\sqrt{13}$ using the following method: Make a guess, say r_1. Then find $13 \div r_1 = s_1$. Then find the average of r_1 and s_1 by computing $(r_1 + s_1)/2 = r_2$. Now find $13 \div r_2 = s_2$. Continue this procedure until r_n and s_n differ by less than 0.00001.

 13. On your calculator, enter a positive number less than 1. Repeatedly press the square-root key. The displayed numbers should be increasing. Will they ever reach 1?

14. Using the square key on your calculator, find the squares of the following numbers. Then order the given number and its square in increasing order. What do you observe?
   a. 0.71   **b.** 0.98

15. Express the following values without exponents.

   a. $36^{1/2}$ **b.** $9^{3/2}$ **c.** $27^{2/3}$

   d. $(-32)^{3/5}$ **e.** $(81)^{3/4}$ **f.** $(-243)^{6/5}$

16. Write the following radicals in simplest form if they are real numbers.

   a. $\sqrt[5]{-32}$ **b.** $\sqrt[3]{-216}$ **c.** $\sqrt[6]{-64}$

17. Use a scientific calculator to calculate approximations of the following values. (They will require several steps and/or the use of the memory.)

   a. $(\sqrt{2})^{4/3}$ **b.** $\sqrt{3}^{\sqrt{2}}$ **c.** $\sqrt{17}^{\sqrt{17}}$ **d.** $391^{0.31}$

18. Determine the larger of each pair.

   a. $\sqrt[5]{7^2}, \sqrt[13]{7^5}$ **b.** $\pi^{\sqrt{2}}, (\sqrt{2})^{\pi}$

19. Solve the following equations.

   a. $3x + \sqrt{6} = 2x - 3\sqrt{6}$ **b.** $x - \sqrt{2} = 9\sqrt{3}$

   c. $5x - \sqrt{3} = 4\sqrt{3}$ **d.** $2\pi x - 6 = 5\pi x + 9$

20. Solve the following equations using three methods.

   a. $x + 9 = -5$ **b.** $x - (-\frac{3}{4}) = \frac{5}{6}$

   c. $3x - 4 = 9$ **d.** $\frac{1}{2}x + 1 = \frac{5}{2}$

   e. $6 = 3x - 9$ **f.** $-2 = (\frac{-5}{12})x + 3$

21. Solve the following inequalities.

   a. $x - \frac{2}{3} > \frac{5}{6}$ **b.** $-2x + 4 \le 11$

   c. $3x + 5 \ge 6x - 7$ **d.** $\frac{3}{2}x - 2 < \frac{5}{6}x + \frac{1}{3}$

PROBLEMS

22. True or false? $\sqrt{p}$ is irrational for any prime p. If true, prove. If false, give a counterexample.

23. Prove that $\sqrt{6}$ is irrational. (*Hint*: You should use an indirect proof as we did for $\sqrt{2}$; however, this case requires a little additional reasoning.)

24. Prove that $\sqrt{p^7 q^5}$ is not rational where p and q are primes.

25. Prove or disprove: $\sqrt[n]{2}$ is irrational for any whole number $n \ge 2$.

26. Let p represent any prime. Determine whether the following are rational or irrational, and prove your assertion.

   a. $\sqrt[3]{p}$ **b.** $\sqrt[3]{p^2}$

27. **a.** Let r be a nonzero rational number and p and q be two irrational numbers. Determine whether the following expressions are rational or irrational. Prove your assertion in each case.

   (i) $r + p$ **(ii)** $r \cdot p$ **(iii)** $p + q$ **(iv)** $p \cdot q$

   b. What if $r = 0$? Would this change your answers in part (a)? Explain.

28. Give an example that shows that each of the following can occur.

   a. The sum of two irrational numbers may be an irrational number.

   b. The sum of two irrational numbers may be a rational number.

   c. The product of two irrational numbers may be an irrational number.

   d. The product of two irrational numbers may be a rational number.

29. Is the set of irrational numbers

   a. closed under addition?

   b. closed under subtraction?

   c. closed under multiplication?

   d. closed under division?

30. Take *any* two real numbers whose sum is 1 (fractions, decimals, integers, etc. are appropriate). Square the larger and add the smaller. Then square the smaller and add the larger.

   a. What will be true?

   b. Prove your assertion.

31. The tempered musical scale, first employed by Johann Sebastian Bach, divides the octave into 12 equally spaced intervals:

   $$C\ C^{\#}\ D\ D^{\#}\ E\ F\ F^{\#}\ G\ G^{\#}\ A\ A^{\#}\ B\ C^{oct}.$$

   The fact that the intervals are equally spaced means that the ratios of the frequencies between any adjacent notes are the same. For example,

   $$C^{\#}:C = k \quad \text{and} \quad D:C^{\#} = k.$$

   From this we see that $C^{\#} = k \cdot C$ and $D = k \cdot C^{\#} = k(k \cdot C) = k^2 C$. Continuing this pattern, we can show that $C^{oct} = k^{12} \cdot C$ (verify this). It is also true that two notes are an octave apart if the frequency of one is double the other. Thus $C^{oct} = 2 \cdot C$. Therefore, $k^{12} = 2$ or $k = \sqrt[12]{2}$. In tuning instruments, the frequency of A above middle C is 440 cycles per second. From this we can find the other frequencies of the octave:

   $$A^{\#} = \sqrt[12]{2} \cdot 440 = 466.16$$
   $$G^{\#} = 440/(\sqrt[12]{2}) = 415.31.$$

a. Find the remaining frequencies to the nearest hundredth of a cycle.

b. In the Greek scale, a fifth (C to G, F to C) had a ratio of $\frac{3}{2}$. How does the tempered scale compare?

c. Also in the Greek scale, a fourth (C to F, D to G) had a ratio of $\frac{4}{3}$. How close is the tempered scale to this ratio?

32. Two towns A and B are 3 miles apart. It is proposed to build a new school to serve 200 students in town A and 100 students in town B. How far from A should the school be built if the total distance traveled by all 300 students is to be as small as possible?

33. *Calendar calculus:*

a. Mark any 4 × 4 array of dates on a calendar.

		1	2	3	4	5
6	7	8	9	10	11	12
13	14	15	16	17	18	19
20	21	22	23	24	25	26
27	28	29	30	31		

b. Circle any numeral in the 4 × 4 array, say 15. Then cross out all other numerals in the same row and column as 15.

c. Circle any numeral not crossed out, say 21. Then cross out all other numerals in the same row and column as 21.

d. Continue until there are four circled numbers. Their sum should be 76 (this is true for this particular 4 × 4 array).

Try this with another 4 × 4 calendar array. Are all such sums the same there? Does this work for 3 × 3 calendar arrays? How about $n \times n$ arrays if we make bigger calendars?

34. Two numbers are reciprocals of each other. One number is 9 times as large as the other. Find the two numbers.

35. The following problem was given as a challenge to Fibonacci: Three men are to share a pile of money in the fractions $\frac{1}{2}, \frac{1}{3}, \frac{1}{6}$. Each man takes some money from the pile until there is nothing left. The first man returns one-half of what he took, the second returns one-third, and the third one-sixth. When the returned amount is divided equally among the men, it is found that they each have what they are entitled to. How much money was in the original pile, and how much did each man take from the original pile?

36. Chad was the same age as Shelly, and Holly was 4 years older than both of them. Chad's dad was 20 when Chad was born, and the average age of the four of them is 39. How old is Chad?

PROBLEMS FOR WRITING/DISCUSSION

1. Gerny says that 5 and -5 are both square roots of 25. So $\sqrt{25} = \pm 5$. Do you agree with Gerny? Explain.

2. A student who is trying to graph $\sqrt{4}, \sqrt{5}, \sqrt{6}, \sqrt{7}$, and $\sqrt{8}$ on the number line reasons that since $\sqrt{4} = 2$, the other numbers must go up by ones. So $\sqrt{5} = 3$, $\sqrt{6} - 4, \sqrt{7} = 5$, and $\sqrt{8} = 6$. What might be the student's mistake in thinking?

3. Suppose you have assigned your students the task of writing some problems that can be solved using the Pythagorean theorem. One of your students comes up to you and says she does not like decimals, so could you please give her a list of all the possible answers that would be only whole numbers. How would you respond?

9.3   FUNCTIONS AND THEIR GRAPHS

STARTING POINT   Tanika and Marcelle each went for a bike ride down a different road. The graphs below represent each girl's bicycle speed as she traveled along her respective road. Describe the possible roads and/or bike-riding scenarios that would correspond to these graphs.

The Cartesian Coordinate System

The concept of a function was introduced in Section 2.4. Here we see how functions can be displayed using graphs on a coordinate system. This section has several goals: to emphasize the importance of functions by showing how they represent many types of physical situations, to help develop skills in graphing functions, and to help you learn how to use a graph to develop a better understanding of the corresponding function.

Suppose that we choose two perpendicular real number lines l and m in the plane and use their point of intersection, O, as a reference point called the **origin** [Figure 9.12(a)]. To locate a point P relative to point O, we use the directed real-number distances x and y that indicate the position of P left/right of and above/below the origin O, respectively. If P is to the right of line m, then x is positive [Figure 9.12(b)].

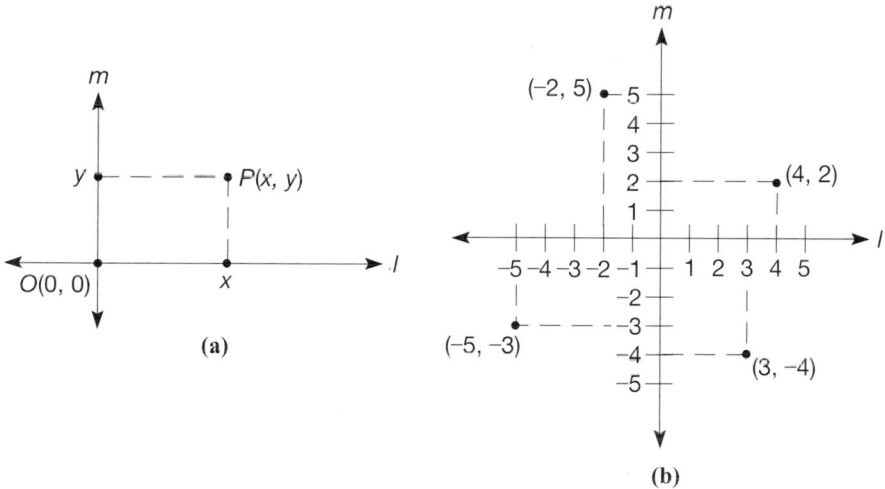

Figure 9.12

If P is to the left of line m, then x is negative. If P is on line m, then x is zero. Similarly, y is positive, negative, or zero, respectively, according to whether P is above, below, or on line l. The pair of real numbers x and y are called the **coordinates** of point P. We identify a point simply by giving its coordinates in an ordered pair (x, y). That is, by "the point (x, y)" we mean the point whose coordinates are x and y, respectively. In an ordered pair of coordinates, the first number is called the *x*-coordinate, and the second is the *y*-coordinate. Figure 9.13 shows the various possible cases for the coordinates of points in the plane.

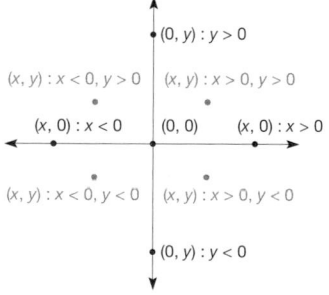

Figure 9.13

NCTM Standards 2000
Geometry
Grades 3–5
All students should make and use coordinate systems to specify locations and to describe paths.

We say that lines l and m determine a **coordinate system** for the plane. Customarily, the horizontal line l is called the *x*-axis, and the vertical line m is called the *y*-axis for the coordinate system. Observe in Figure 9.14 that l and m have been relabeled as the x-axis and y-axis and that they divide the plane into four dis-

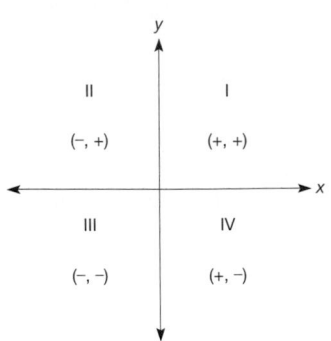

Figure 9.14

joint regions, called **quadrants.** (The axes are not part of any of the quadrants.) The points in quadrants I and IV have positive x-coordinates, while the points in quadrants II and III have negative x-coordinates. Similarly, the points in quadrants I and II have positive y-coordinates, while the points in quadrants III and IV have negative y-coordinates (Figure 9.14).

The following example provides a simple application of coordinates in mapmaking.

Example 9.15   Plot the points with the following coordinates.

$P_1\ (-7, 5),\ P_2\ (-5, 5),\ P_3\ (-4, 3),\ P_4\ (0, 3),\ P_5\ (3, 4),\ P_6\ (6, 4),\ P_7\ (7, 3),$
$P_8\ (5, -1),\ P_9\ (6, -2),\ P_{10}\ (6, -7),\ P_{11}\ (-8, -7),\ P_{12}\ (-8, -3)$

Connect the points, in succession, P_1 to P_2, P_2 to P_3, . . . , P_{12} to P_1 with line segments to form a polygon (Figure 9.15).

Solution

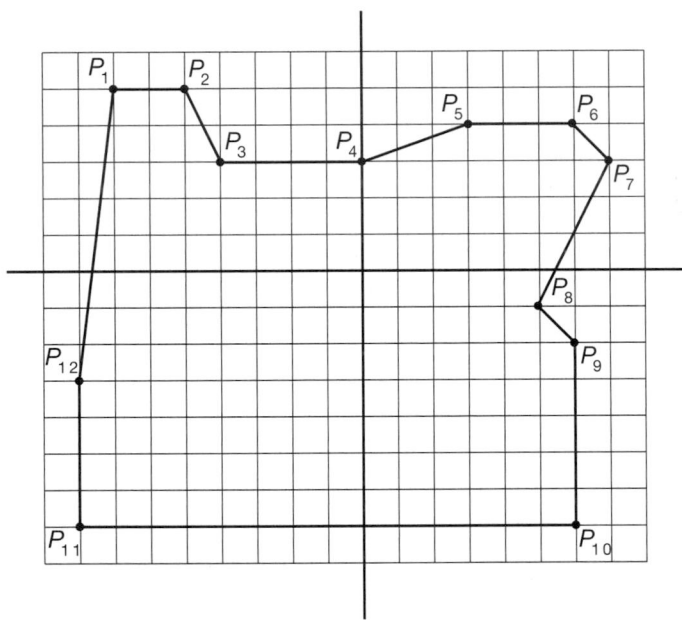

Figure 9.15   ■

Notice that the polygon in Figure 9.15 is a simplified map of Oregon. Cartographers use computers to store maps of regions in coordinate form. They can then print maps in a variety of sizes. In the Problem Set we will investigate altering the size of a two-dimensional figure using coordinates.

Graphs of Linear Functions

As the name suggests, **linear functions** are functions whose graphs are lines. The next example involves a linear function and its graph.

Example 9.16   A salesperson is given a monthly salary of $1200 plus a 5% commission on sales. Graph the salesperson's total earnings as a function of sales.

Solution Let s represent the dollar amount of the salesperson's monthly sales. The total earnings can be represented as a function of sales, s, as follows: $E(s) = 1200 + (0.05)s$. Several values of this function are shown in Table 9.1. Using these values, we can plot the function $E(s)$ (Figure 9.16). The mark on the vertical axis below 1200 is used to indicate that this portion of the graph is not the same scale as on the rest of the axis.

NCTM Standards 2000
Algebra
Grades 6–8
All students should use symbolic algebra to represent situations and to solve problems, especially those that involve linear relationships.

Table 9.1

SALES, s	Earnings, $E(s)$
1000	1250
2000	1300
3000	1350
4000	1400
5000	1450

Reflection from Research
Having students describe a possible relationship to real-world phenomena modeled by a graph may encourage students' understanding of the purpose of graphs (Narode, 1986).

NCTM Standards 2000
Algebra
Grades 6–8
All students should explore relationships between symbolic expressions and graphs of lines, paying particular attention to the meaning of intercept and slope.

NCTM Standards 2000
Algebra
Grades 3–5
All students should investigate how a change in one variable relates to the change in a second variable.

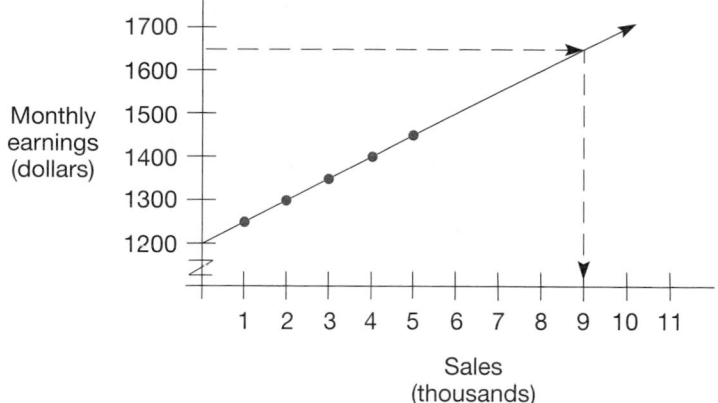

Figure 9.16

Notice that the points representing the pairs of values lie on a line. Thus, by extending the line, which is the graph of the function, we can see what salaries will result from various sales. For example, to earn $1650, Figure 9.17 shows that the salesperson must have sales of $9000.

A *linear function* has the algebraic form $f(x) = ax + b$, where a and b are constants. In the function $E(s) = (0.05)s + 1200$, the value of a is 0.05 and of b is 1200.

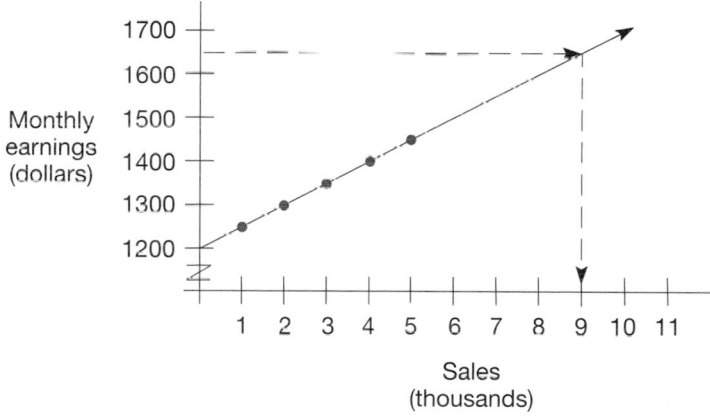

Figure 9.17

Graphs of Quadratic Functions

A **quadratic function** is a function of the form $f(x) = ax^2 + bx + c$, where a, b, and c are constants and $a \neq 0$. The next example presents a problem involving a quadratic function.

Example 9.17 A ball is tossed up vertically at a velocity of 50 feet per second from a point 5 feet above the ground. It is known from physics that the height of the ball above the ground, in feet, is given by the position function $p(t) = -16t^2 + 50t + 5$, where t is the time in seconds. At what time, t, is the ball at its highest point?

Solution Table 9.2 lists several values for t with the corresponding function values from $p(t) = -16t^2 + 50t + 5$. Figure 9.18 shows a graph of the points in the table. Unfortunately, it is unclear from the graph of these four points what the highest point will be. One way of getting a better view of this situation would be to plot several

Table 9.2

t	$p(t)$
0	5
1	39
2	41
3	11

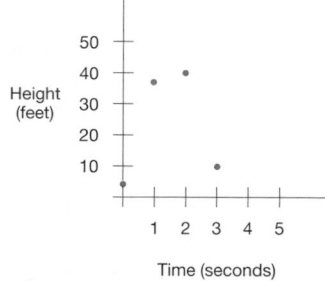

Figure 9.18

Reflection from Research

The emergence of the graphing calculator has caused an emphasis to be placed on the graphical representation of functions (Adams, 1993).

X=1.5578947 Y=44.062161

Figure 9.19

more points between 1 and 2, say $t = 1.1, 1.2, 1.3, \ldots, 1.9$. However, this can be tedious. Instead, Figure 9.19 shows how a graphics calculator can be used to get an estimate of this point.

By moving the cursor (the "□") to what appears to be the highest point on the graph, the calculator's display screen shows that the value $t = 1.5578947$ corresponds to that point. It can be shown *mathematically* that $t = \frac{25}{16} = 1.5625$ seconds is the exact time when the ball is at its highest point, 44.0625 feet. ▪

www.wiley.com/
college/musser

Spotlight on Technology Quadratic functions can be further explored by using the Chapter 9 eManipulative activity, *Function Grapher*. Enter the general function $f(x) = ax^2 + bx + c$ by typing the following key strokes:

$$\boxed{\text{Reset}}\ a\ \boxed{*}\ x\ \boxed{\square^\square}\ 2\ \boxed{\rightarrow}\ +\ b\ \boxed{*}\ x\ +\ c$$

Once the function has been entered, click the graph button and the graph of the quadratic equation will appear. By selecting the Parameters and either *a*, *b*, or *c*, you will be able to change the values of *a*, *b*, and *c* by moving the slider. What role do *a* and *c* play in the shape of the graph of $f(x) = ax^2 + bx + c$?

Graphs of Exponential Functions

Amoebas have the interesting property that they split in two over time intervals. Therefore, the number of amoebas is a function of the number of splits. Table 9.3 lists the first several ordered pairs of this function, and Figure 9.20 shows the corresponding graph.

Table 9.3

NUMBER OF SPLITS	NUMBER OF AMOEBAS
0	1
1	2 $(= 2^1)$
2	4 $(= 2^2)$
3	8 $(= 2^3)$
4	16 $(= 2^4)$
5	32 $(= 2^5)$

NCTM Standards 2000
Algebra
Grades 6–8
All students should model and solve contextualized problems using various representations, such as graphs and equations.

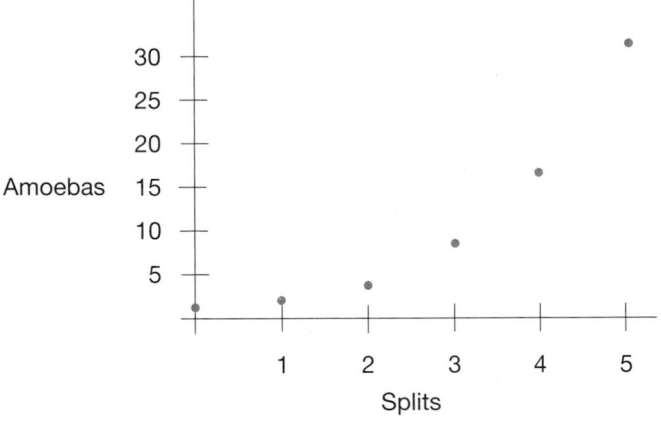

Figure 9.20

This functional relationship can be represented as the formula $f(x) = 2^x$, where $x = 0, 1, 2, \ldots$. This is an example of an **exponential function,** since, in the function rule, the variable appears as the exponent.

Exponential growth also appears in the study of compound interest. In Section 8.3 it was shown that for an initial principal of P_0, an interest rate of r, compounded annually, and time t, in years, the amount of principal is given by the equation $P(t) = P_0(1 + r)^t$. In particular, if $100 is deposited at 6% interest, the value of the investment after t years is given by $P(t) = 100 (1.06)^t$. Figure 9.21 shows a portion of the graph of this function.

Example 9.18 How long does it take to double your money when the interest rate is 6% compounded annually? (Assume that your money is in a tax-deferred account so that you don't have to pay taxes until the money is withdrawn.)

Solution If a horizontal line is drawn through $200 in Figure 9.21, it will intersect the graph of the function approximately above the 12. Thus it takes about 12 years to double the $100 investment. (A more precise estimate that can be obtained from the formula is 11.9 years.)

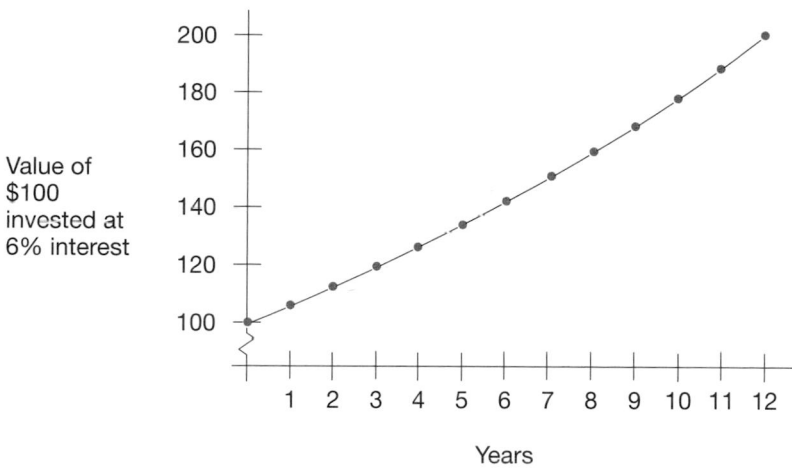

Figure 9.21

■

Interestingly, it takes only seven more years to add another $100 to the account and five more to add the next $100. This acceleration in accumulating principal illustrates the power of compounding, in particular, and of exponential growth, in general.

A similar phenomenon, decay, occurs in nature. Radioactive materials decay at an exponential rate. For example, the half-life of uranium-238 is 4.5 billion years. The formula for calculating the amount of ^{238}U after t billion years is $U(t) = (0.86)^t$. Figure 9.22 shows part of the graph of this function.

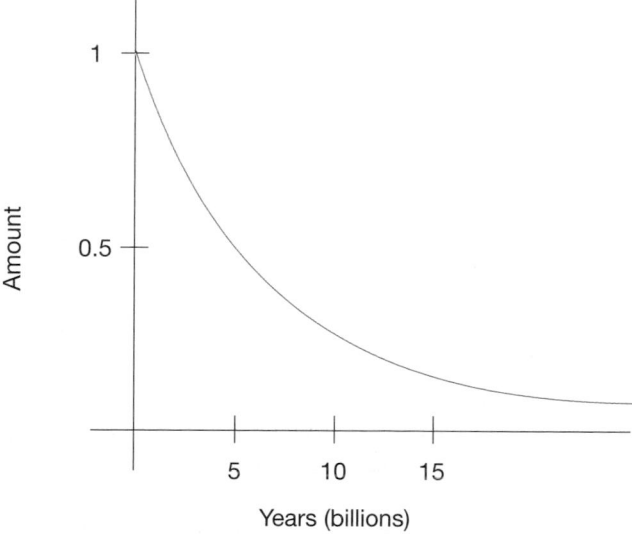

Figure 9.22

This graph shows that although uranium decays rapidly at first, relatively speaking, it lingers around a long time.

Graphs of Other Common Functions

Cubic Functions The following example illustrates a cubic function.

Example 9.19 A box is to be constructed from a piece of cardboard 20 cm-by-20 cm square by cutting out square corners and folding up the resulting sides (Figure 9.23). Estimate the maximum volume of a box that can be formed in this way.

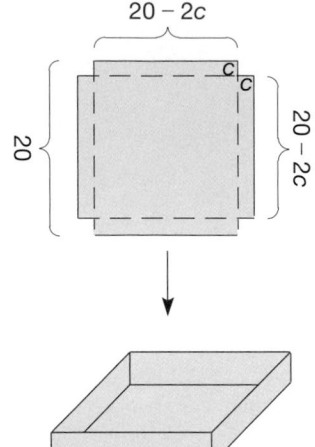

Figure 9.23

Solution When a corner of dimensions 1 cm-by-1 cm is cut out, a box of dimensions 1 cm-by-18 cm by 18 cm is formed. Its volume is $1 \times 18 \times 18 = 324$. In general, if the corner is c by c, the volume of the resulting box is given by $V(c) = c(20 - 2c)(20 - 2c)$. Table 9.4 shows several sizes of corners together with the resulting box volumes. Using these values, we can sketch the graph of the function $V(c)$ (Figure 9.24).

The five points in the table are shown in the graph in Figure 9.24. From the graph it appears that when the corner measures about 3.5 by 3.5, the maximum volume is achieved, $V(3.5) = (3.5)(13)(13) \approx 592$ cm^3. It can be shown mathematically that the value $c = 3\frac{1}{3}$ actually leads to the maximum volume of about 593.

Table 9.4

CORNERS	VOLUME
1 cm by 1 cm	324 cm^3
2 cm by 2 cm	512 cm^3
3 cm by 3 cm	588 cm^3
4 cm by 4 cm	576 cm^3
5 cm by 5 cm	500 cm^3

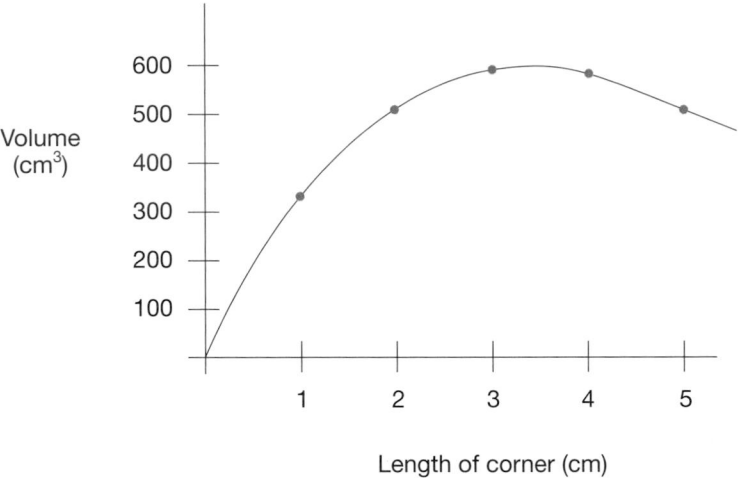

Figure 9.24

The function $V(c) = c(20 - 2c)(20 - 2c)$ can be rewritten as $V(c) = 4c^3 - 80c^2 + 400c$, a **cubic function.** Actually, the graph in Figure 9.24 looks similar to the quadratic function pictured earlier in this section. However, if the function $V(c) = 4c^3 - 80c^2 + 400c$ were allowed to take on all real-number values, its graph would take the shape as shown from a graphics calculator in Figure 9.25. (This shape is characteristic of all cubic functions.)

However, in Example 9.19, only a portion of this graph is shown, since the values of c are limited to $0 < c < 10$, the only lengths that produce corners that lead to a box.

Figure 9.25

Spotlight on Technology Spreadsheets can be used to graph a wide variety of functions, including those discussed in this section. One advantage of using a spreadsheet for graphing is www.wiley.com/college/musser that the table of function values is displayed right next to the graph itself, which makes it easier to see the connections between the two different representations. Refer to the dynamic spreadsheet, *Cubic*, in the spreadsheet webmodule. Use the spreadsheet to graph $f(x) = ax^3 + bx^2 + cx + d$. Set $a = c = d = 1$ and enter different values for b. What is the impact of the coefficient b on the shape of the graph of $f(x)$?

Table 9.5

AMOUNT (CENTS)	TAX (CENTS)
0–15	0
16–35	1
36–55	2
56–75	3
76–95	4
96–115	5

Step Functions The sales tax or the amount of postage are examples of step functions. Table 9.5 shows a typical sales tax, in cents, for sales up to $1.15. The graph in Figure 9.26 displays this information.

The open circles indicate that those points are *not* part of the graph. Otherwise, the endpoints are included in a segment. Notice that although the steps in this function are pictured as line segments, they could actually be pictured as a series of dots, one for each cent in the amount. A similar graph, which can be drawn for postage stamp rates, must use a line segment, since the weights of envelopes vary continuously. A function such as the one pictured in Figure 9.26 is called a **step function**, since its values are pictured in a series of line segments, or steps.

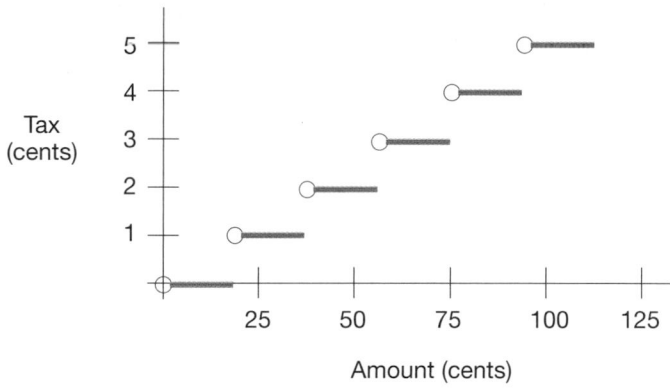

Figure 9.26

Graphs and Their Functions Thus far we have studied several special types of functions: linear, quadratic, exponential, cubic, and step. Rather than starting with a function and constructing the graph, this subsection will develop your graphical sense by first displaying a graph and then analyzing it to predict what type of function would produce the graph.

Example 9.20　Water is poured at a constant rate into the three containers shown in Figure 9.27. Which graph corresponds to which container?

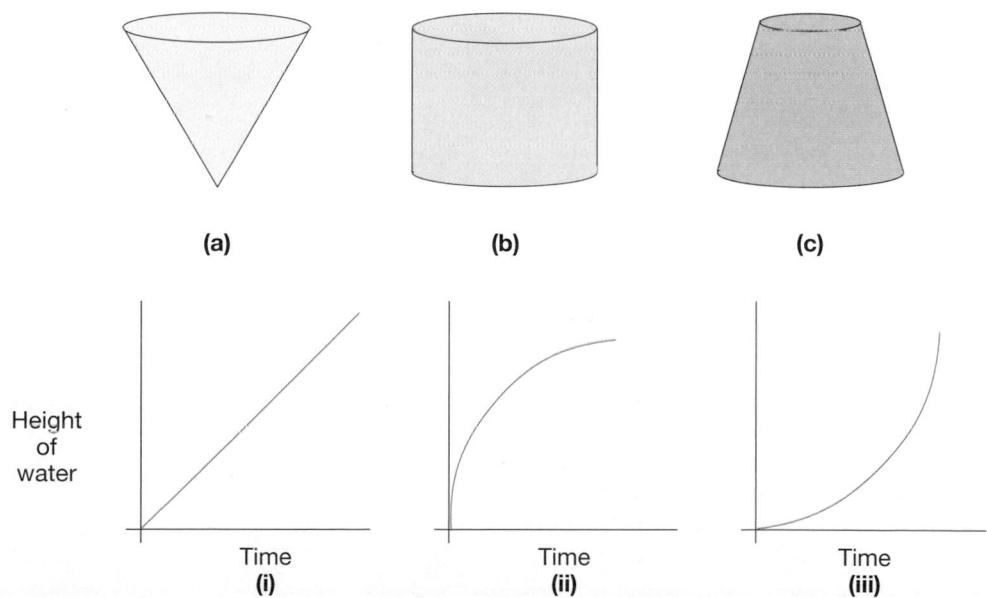

Figure 9.27

Solution Since the bottom of the figure in (a) is the narrowest, if water is poured into it at a constant rate, its height will rise faster initially and will slow in time. Graph (ii) is steeper initially to indicate that water is rising faster. Then it levels off slowly as the container is being filled. Thus graph (ii) best represents the height of water in container (a) as it is being filled. Container (b) should fill at a constant rate; thus graph (i) best represents its situation. Since the bottom of (c) is larger than its top, the water's height will rise more slowly at first, as in (iii). ■

Finally, since a function assigns to each element in its domain only one element in its codomain, there is a simple visual test to see whether a graph represents a function. The **vertical line test** states that a graph can represent a function if every vertical line that can be drawn intersects the graph in at most one point. Review the graphs of functions in this section to see that they pass this test by moving a vertical pencil across the graph as suggested in Figure 9.28.

Figure 9.28

MATHEMATICAL MORSEL

Functions are used to try to predict the price action of the stock market. Since the action is the result of the psychological frame of mind of millions of individuals, price movements do not seem to conform to a nice smooth curve. One stock market theory, the Elliott wave theory, postulates that prices move in waves, 5 up and 3 down. Interestingly, when these waves are broken into smaller subdivisions, numbers of the Fibonacci sequence, such as 3, 5, 8, 13, 21, 34, and 55, arise naturally. Another interesting mathematical relationship associated with this theory is the concept of self-similarity. That is, when a smaller wave is enlarged, its structure is supposed to look exactly like the larger wave containing it. If the stock market behaved exactly as Elliott had postulated it should, everyone would become rich by playing the market. Unfortunately, it is not that easy.

Section 9.3 EXERCISE / PROBLEM SET A

EXERCISES

1. Plot the following points on graph paper.

   a. $(3, 2), (-3, 2), (-3, -2), (3, -2)$

   b. $(0, 5), (5, 0), (3, -6), (-2, 1)$

   c. $(-1, -3), (-2, -3), (-3, -4), (-5, -2)$

   d. $(2, -4), (-2, 5), (-2, -3), (1, -2)$

2. In which of the four quadrants will a point have the following characteristics?

   a. Negative y-coordinate

   b. Positive x-coordinate and negative y-coordinate

   c. Negative x-coordinate and negative y-coordinate

3. On a coordinate system, shade the region consisting of all points that satisfy both of the following conditions:

   $$-3 \leq x \leq 2 \quad \text{and} \quad 2 \leq y \leq 4.$$

4. Determine which of the following graphs represent functions. (*Hint*: Use the vertical line test.) For those that are functions, specify the domain and range.

   a.

   b.

   c.

   d.

   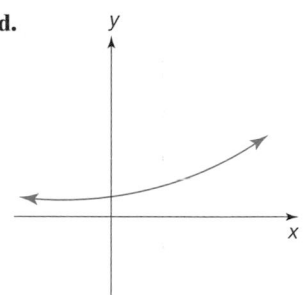

5. Consider the function f whose graph is shown next

   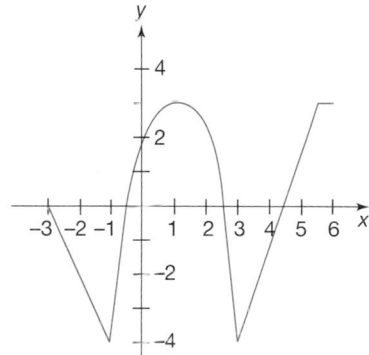

   a. Find the following: (i) $f(1)$, (ii) $f(-1)$, and (iii) $f(4.5)$.

   b. Specify the domain and range of the function.

   c. For which value(s) of x is $f(x) = 2$?

6. As you stand on a beach and look out toward the ocean, the distance that you can see is a function of the height of your eyes above sea level. The following formula and graph represent this relationship, where h is the height of your eyes in *feet* and d is the distance you can see *in miles*.

   $$d(h) = 1.2\sqrt{h}$$

   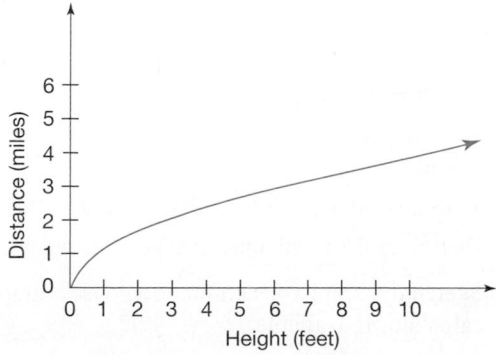

a. Use the formula to calculate the approximate values of $d(4)$ and $d(5.5)$. Use the graph to check your answers.

b. A child's eyes are about 3 feet 3 inches from the ground. How far can she see out to the horizon?

c. Specify the domain and range of the function.

7. Make a table of at least five values for each of the following linear functions, and sketch the graph of each function. How does the coefficient of the x affect the graph? How does the constant term affect the graph?

a. $f(x) = 2x + 3$　　**b.** $m(x) = 40 - 5x$

c. $g(x) = 7.2x - 4.5$

8. Make a table of at least five values for each of the following functions and sketch their graphs.

a. $h(x) = \frac{1}{2}x^2 + x$　　**b.** $r(x) = 3^x$

c. $s(x) = 2 - x^3$

9. The **greatest integer function** of x, denoted $f(x) = [\![x]\!]$, is defined to be the greatest integer that is less than or equal to x. For example, $[\![3.5]\!] = 3$, $[\![-3.9]\!] = -4$, and $[\![17]\!] = 17$.

a. Evaluate the following.

　i. $[\![2.4]\!]$　　　**ii.** $[\![7.98]\!]$

　iii. $[\![-4.2]\!]$　　**iv.** $[\![0.3]\!]$

b. Sketch the graph of $f(x) = [\![x]\!]$ for $-3 \le x \le 3$.

10. a. Sketch the graph of each of the following linear functions. Compare your graphs. A graphics calculator would be helpful.

　i. $f(x) = 2x - 3$　　**ii.** $f(x) = \frac{1}{2}x - 3$

　iii. $f(x) = 4x - 3$　　**iv.** $f(x) = \frac{2}{3}x - 3$

b. How is the graph of the line affected by the coefficient of x?

c. How would a negative coefficient of x affect the graph of the line? Try graphing the following functions to test your conjecture.

　i. $f(x) = (-2)x - 3$　　**ii.** $f(x) = (-\frac{3}{4})x - 3$

11. Use the Chapter 9 eManipulative activity, *Function Grapher*, to graph the function $f(x) = ax + 2$ (enter ax as $a * x$). Move the slider for a back and forth to answer the following questions.

a. What happens to the shape of the graph as a gets larger?

b. What does the graph look like when $a = 0$?

c. How does the graph change when a is negative?

12. a. Sketch the graph of each function. Use a graphics calculator if available.

　i. $f(x) = x^2$　　　**ii.** $f(x) = x^2 + 2$

　iii. $f(x) = x^2 - 2$　　**iv.** $f(x) = (x - 2)^2$

　v. $f(x) = (x + 2)^2$

b. Taking the graph in part (i) as a standard, what effect does the constant 2 have on the graph in each of the other parts of part (a)?

c. Use the pattern you observed in part (a) to sketch graphs of $f(x) = x^2 + 4$ and $f(x) = (x - 3)^2$. Use a graphics calculator to check your prediction.

13. Use the Chapter 9 eManipulative activity, *Function Grapher*, to graph the function $f(x) = (x - b)^2 + c$. Move the slider for b and c back and forth to answer the following questions.

a. How does b affect the position of the graph?

b. How does c affect the position of the graph?

14. a. Sketch the graph of each of the following exponential functions. Use a graphics calculator if available. Compare your graphs.

　i. $f(x) = 2^x$　　**ii.** $f(x) = 5^x$

　iii. $f(x) = (\frac{1}{2})^x$　　**iv.** $f(x) = (\frac{3}{4})^x$

b. How is the shape of the graph of each function affected by the value of the base of the function?

c. Use the pattern you observed in part (a) to predict the shapes of the graphs of $f(x) = 10^x$ and $f(x) = (0.95)^x$. Check your prediction by sketching their graphs.

15. Use the Chapter 9 eManipulative activity, *Function Grapher*, to graph the function $f(x) = a^x$. Move the slider for a back and forth to answer the following questions.

a. What happens to the shape of the graph as a gets larger?

b. What does the graph look like when $a = 1$?

c. How does the graph look different when $0 < a < 1$?

16. On July 1, 2001, the first-class postal rates changed to the following:

34 cents for the first ounce or less
57 cents for over 1 oz and up to 2 oz
80 cents for over 2 oz and up to 3 oz
$1.03 for over 3 oz and up to 4 oz
$1.26 for over 4 oz and up to 5 oz
$1.49 for over 5 oz and up to 6 oz
$1.72 for over 6 oz and up to 7 oz
$1.95 for over 7 oz and up to 8 oz
$2.18 for over 8 oz and up to 9 oz
$2.41 for over 9 oz and up to 10 oz
$2.64 for over 10 oz and up to 11 oz
$2.87 for over 11 oz and up to 12 oz
$3.10 for over 12 oz and up to 13 oz

a. If $P(w)$ gives the rate for a parcel weighing w ounces, find each of the following.

   i. $P(0.5)$ **ii.** $P(5.5)$

  iii. $P(11.9)$ **iv.** $P(12.1)$

b. Specify the domain and range for P based on the previous list.

c. Sketch the graph of the first-class rates as a function of weight.

d. Suppose that you have 15 pieces weighing $\frac{3}{4}$ oz each that you wish to mail first class to the same destination. Explain why it is cheaper to package them together in one bundle than to mail them separately.

17. Sketch the graph of each of the following step functions.

a. $f(x) = [\![x + 1]\!]$ for $0 \le x \le 4$

b. $f(x) = [\![2 - x]\!]$ for $- \le x \le 3$

c. $f(x) = 5 - [\![x]\!]$ for $0 \le x < 5$

d. $f(x) = 6 \left[\!\!\left[\dfrac{x}{2}\right]\!\!\right]$ for $2 \le x \le 6$

18. Which type of function best fits each of the following graphs: linear, quadratic, cubic, exponential, or step?

a.

b.

c.

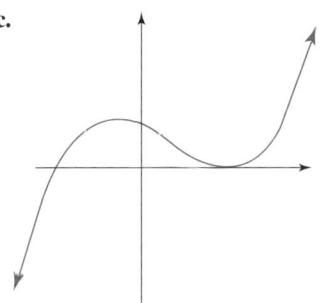

PROBLEMS

19. The following graph shows the relationship between the length of the shadow of a 100-meter-tall building and the number of hours that have passed since noon.

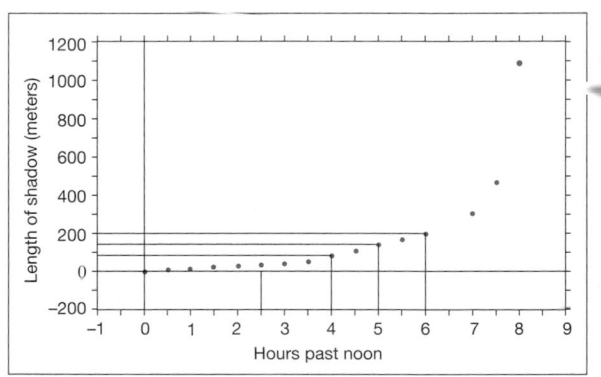

a. If L represents the length of the shadow and n represents the number of hours since noon, why is L a function of n? What type of function does the graph appear to represent?

b. Use the graph to approximate $L(5)$, $L(8)$, and $L(2.5)$ to the nearest 50.

c. After how many hours is the shadow 100 meters long? When is it twice as long?

d. Why do you think the graph stops at $n = 8$?

20. A man standing at a window 55 feet above the ground leans out and throws a ball straight up into the air with a speed of 70 feet per second. The height, s, of the ball above the ground, as a function of the number of seconds elapsed, t, is given as

$$s(t) = -16t^2 + 70t + 55.$$

a. Sketch a graph of the function for $0 \le t \le 6$. If available, use a graphics calculator.

b. Use your graph to determine when the ball is about 90 feet above the ground. (NOTE: There are two times when this occurs. Use the formula as a check.)

c. About when does the ball hit the ground?

d. About how high does the ball go before it starts back down?

21. The population of the world is growing exponentially. A formula that can be used to make rough predictions of world population based on the population in 1990 and 2001 is given as

$$P(t) = 5.284e^{.0139t},$$

where $P(t)$ is the world population in billions, t is the number of years since 1990, and e is an irrational number approximately equal to 2.718. (NOTE: Scientific calculators have a key to calculate e.)

a. Sketch the graph of the function P. A graphics calculator will be helpful.

b. Use the formula to predict the world population in 2006.

c. Use your graph to predict when the world population will reach 8 billion.

d. Use your graph to estimate the current doubling time for the world population. That is, about how many years are required for the 1990 population to double?

22. A bicyclist pedals at a constant rate along a route that is essentially flat but has one hill, as shown in the next figure.

Which of the following graphs best describes what happens to the speed of the cyclist as she travels along the route?

a.

b.

c.

23. Three people on the first floor of a building wish to take the elevator up to the top floor. The maximum weight that the elevator can carry is 300 pounds. Also, one of the three people must be in the elevator to operate it. If the people weigh 130, 160, and 210 pounds, how can they get to the top floor?

 Section 9.3 EXERCISE / PROBLEM SET B

EXERCISES

1. Plot the following points on graph paper. Indicate in which quadrant or on which axis the point lies.

   a. $(-3, 0)$ **b.** $(6, 4)$ **c.** $(-2, 3)$

   d. $(0, 5)$ **e.** $(-1, -4)$ **f.** $(3, -2)$

2. In which of the four quadrants will a point have the following characteristics?

   a. Negative x-coordinate and positive y-coordinate

   b. Positive x-coordinate and positive y-coordinate

   c. Positive x-coordinate

3. A region in the coordinate plane is shaded where each mark on the axes represents one unit. Describe this region algebraically. That is, describe the values of the coordinates of the region using equations and/or inequalities.

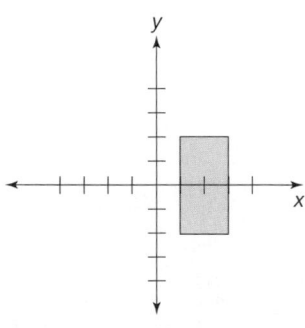

4. Determine which of the following graphs represent functions. That is, in which cases is y a function of x? For those that are functions, specify the domain and range.

a.

b.

c.

d.

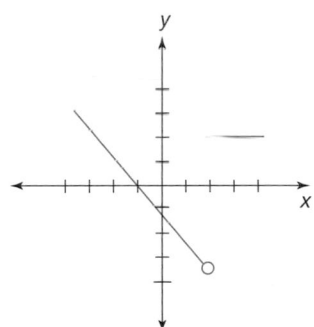

5. Consider the function f whose graph follows.

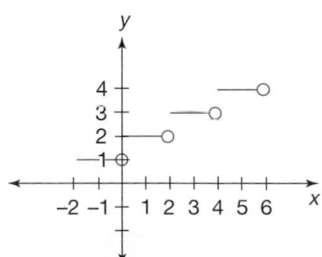

a. Use the graph to find the following: (i) $f(-1)$.
(ii) $f(2)$, and (iii) $f(3.75)$.

b. Specify the domain and range of f.

c. For what value(s) of x is $f(x) = 3$? For what value(s) of x is $f(x) = 1.5$?

d. What type of function is f?

6. The following graph shows the relationship between the diameter of a circular cake, d, and the area of the top of the cake, A.

$$A(d) \approx 0.7854d^2$$

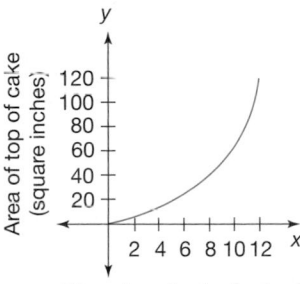

Diameter of cake (inches)

a. Which type of function is A?

b. Find $A(4)$ and $A(12)$ from the graph. Check your estimate using the formula.

c. Sketch the graph of $A(d) = 0.7854d^2$ for values of d between -5 and 5. A graphics calculator would be helpful.

d. Why are no points in the second quadrant included in the original graph?

7. Make a table of at least five values for each of the following linear functions and sketch their graphs.

a. $f(x) = 3x - 2$ **b.** $g(x) = -\frac{3}{4}x + 9$

c. $h(x) = 120x + 25$

8. Make a table of at least five values for each of the following functions and sketch their graphs.

a. $f(x) = x^2 - 4x$ **b.** $f(x) = \left(\frac{1}{2}\right)^x$

c. $f(x) = \frac{2}{3}x^3 - 4$

9. a. Evaluate the following.

    i. $[\![3.999]\!]$ **ii.** $[\![-17.1]\!]$

    iii. $[\![-4]\!]$ **iv.** $[\![-0.0001]\!]$

b. Sketch the graph of $f(x) = [\![-2x]\!]$ for $-3 \le x \le 3$.

10. a. Sketch the graph of each of the following linear equations. Use a graphics calculator if available. Compare your graphs.

    i. $f(x) = x + 2$ **ii.** $f(x) = x - 4$

    iii. $f(x) = x + 6.5$ **iv.** $f(x) = x$

b. How is the graph of the line affected by the value of the constant term of the function?

11. Use the Chapter 9 eManipulative activity, *Function Grapher*, to graph the function $f(x) = x + b$. Move the slider for b back and forth to answer the following questions.

a. What does the graph look like when $b = 0$?

b. How does the value of b affect the graph of $f(x) = x + b$?

12. a. Sketch a graph of each of the following quadratic equations. Use a graphics calculator if available.

    i. $f(x) = x^2$ **ii.** $f(x) = 2x^2$

    iii. $f(x) = \frac{1}{2}x^2$ **iv.** $f(x) = -3x^2$

b. What role does the coefficient of x^2 play in determining the shape of the graph?

c. Use the pattern you observed in part (a) and in Exercise 10 to predict the shape of the graphs of $f(x) = 5x^2$ and $f(x) = \frac{1}{3}x^2 + 2$.

13. Use the Chapter 9 eManipulative activity, *Function Grapher*, to graph the function $f(x) = ax^2$ (enter ax as $a * x$). Move the slider for a back and forth to answer the following questions.

a. What happens to the shape of the graph as a gets larger?

b. What does the graph look like when $a = 0$?

c. How does the graph change when a is negative?

14. a. Draw graphs of each of the following pairs of exponential functions. Compare the graphs you obtain. Use a graphics calculator if available.

    i. $f(x) = (\frac{1}{3})^x$ and $f(x) = 3^{-x}$

    ii. $f(x) = (\frac{2}{5})^x$ and $f(x) = 2.5^{-x}$

    iii. $f(x) = 10^x$ and $f(x) = (0.1)^{-x}$

b. What interesting observation can be made about the pairs in part (a)?

15. Use the Chapter 9 eManipulative activity, *Function Grapher*, graph the function $f(x) = 2^{(cx)}$ (enter cx as $c \times x$). Move the slider for c back and forth to answer the following questions.

a. What happens to the shape of the graph as c gets larger?

b. What does the graph look like when $c = 0$?

c. How does the graph change when c is negative?

16. The Institute for Aerobics Research recommends an optimal heart rate for exercisers who want to get the maximum benefit from their workouts. The rate is a function of the age of the exerciser and should be between 65% and 80% of the difference between 220 and the person's age. That is, if a is the age in years, then the minimum heart rate for 1 minute is

$$r(a) = 0.65(220 - a)$$

and the maximum is

$$R(a) = 0.8(220 - a).$$

a. Sketch the graphs of the functions r and R on the same set of axes.

b. A woman 30 years old begins a new exercise program. To benefit from the program, into what range should her heart rate fall?

c. How are the recommended heart rates affected as the age of the exerciser increases? How does your graph display this information?

17. Sketch the graph of each of the following step functions.

a. $f(x) = [\![x + 3]\!]$ for $0 \leq x \leq 5$

b. $f(x) = [\![4 - x]\!]$ for $-2 \leq x \leq 2$

c. $f(x) = 4 - [\![2 - x]\!]$ for $0 \leq x \leq 4$

d. $f(x) = 10 \left[\!\left[\frac{x}{4}\right]\!\right]$ for $-4 \leq x \leq 8$

18. Which type of function best fits each of the following graphs: linear, quadratic, cubic, exponential, or step?

a.

b.

c.

d.

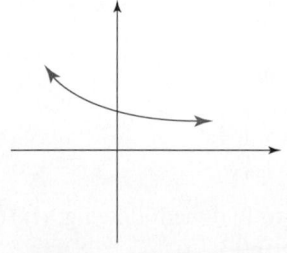

PROBLEMS

19. The length of time that passes between the time you see a flash of lightning and the time you hear the clap of thunder is related directly to your distance from the lightning. The following graph displays this relationship.

a. If D represents your distance from the lightning and t represents the elapsed time between the lightning and thunder, is D a function of t? Explain.

b. Use the graph to determine the approximate value of $D(8)$. Describe in words what this $D(8)$ means.

c. Write a formula for $D(t)$.

20. If interest is compounded, the value of an investment increases exponentially. The following formula gives the value, V, of an investment of $250 after t years, where the interest rate is 6.25% and interest is compounded continuously:

$$V(t) = 250e^{0.0625t}.$$

a. Sketch the graph of V. A graphics calculator will be helpful here.

b. Use the formula and your calculator to calculate the value of the $250 investment after 5 years.

c. Use your graph and your calculator to predict when the investment will be worth $700.

d. Use your graph to estimate the doubling time for this investment. That is, how long does it take to accumulate a total of $500?

21. A man is inflating a spherical balloon by blowing air into the balloon at a constant rate. Which of the following graphs best represents the radius of the balloon as a function of time?

i.

ii.

iii.

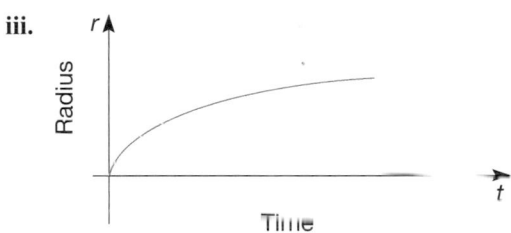

22. In an effort to boost sales, an employer offers each sales associate a $20 bonus for every $500 of sales. However, no credit is given for amounts less than a multiple of $500.

a. Two sales associates have sales totaling $758 and $1625. Calculate the amount of bonus each earned.

b. One sales associate was paid a bonus of $80. Give a range for the dollar amount of merchandise that he or she sold.

c. Make a table of values, and sketch the graph of the bonus paid by the employer as a function of the dollar value of the merchandise.

d. Write a function $B(n)$ that gives the bonus earned by an employee in terms of n, the number of dollars of merchandise sold. (*Hint*: Use the greatest integer function.)

23. The following table displays the number of cricket chirps per minute at various temperatures. Show how cricket chirps can thus be used to measure the temperature by expressing T as a function of n;

that is, find a formula for $T(n)$. Also graph your function.

cricket chirps per minute, n	20	40	60	80	100
temperature, $T(°F)$		45	50	55	60	65

24. What fraction of the square region is shaded? Assume that the pattern of shading continues forever.

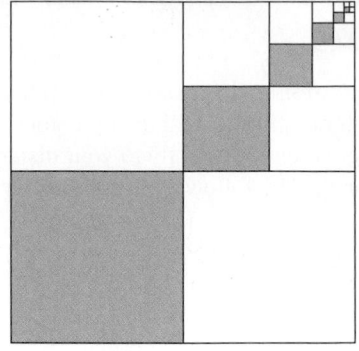

PROBLEMS FOR WRITING/DISCUSSION

1. Millicent was making a table of values to graph a function. The table looked like this:

x	1	2	3	4	5
y	3	7	11	15	19

She noticed that the y values formed an arithmetic sequence and her graph was a straight line. She wondered if every arithmetic sequence made a straight line graph. How would you respond?

2. Millicent's next table of values showed y's that seemed to form a geometric sequence.

x	1	2	3	4	5
y	2	6	18	54	162

Millicent wondered what kind of graph this would make. How would you respond to this question?

3. Millicent graphed the functions she had been working on in Problems 1 and 2. She noticed that both of the graphs seemed to be moving upward as she looked from left to right. She wondered what changes in the sequences would make the graphs go downward instead. How would you explain?

END OF CHAPTER MATERIAL

Solution of Initial Problem

A man's boyhood lasted for $\frac{1}{6}$ of his life, he played soccer for the next $\frac{1}{12}$ of his life, and he married after $\frac{1}{7}$ more of his life. A daughter was born 5 years after his marriage, and the daughter lived $\frac{1}{2}$ as many years as her father did. If the man died 4 years after his daughter did, how old was the man when he died?

Strategy: Solve an Equation

Let a represent the age of the father when he died. Then his boyhood was $\frac{1}{6}a$, he played soccer $\frac{1}{12}a$, and he married $\frac{1}{7}a$ years later. His daughter was born 5 years after his marriage. She lived $\frac{1}{2}$ as many years as her father, and he died 4 years after her, as shown in the following diagram.

The diagram leads to the following equation.

$$\frac{1}{6}a + \frac{1}{12}a + \frac{1}{7}a + 5 + \frac{1}{2}a + 4 = a$$

Solving this equation, we obtain

$$\frac{25}{28}a + 9 = a$$
$$9 = \frac{3}{28}a$$
$$84 = a.$$

Therefore, the father lived to be 84 years old. Check this solution back in the story to convince yourself that it is correct.

Additional Problems Where the Strategy "Solve an Equation" Is Useful

1. A saver opened a savings account and increased the account by one-third at the beginning of each year. At the end of the third year, she buys a $10,000 car and still has $54,000. If interest earned is not considered, how much did she have at the end of the first year?

2. Albert Einstein was once asked how many students he had had. He replied, "One-half of them study only arithmetic, one-third of them study only geometry, one-seventh of them study only chemistry, and there are 20 who study nothing at all." How many students did he have?

3. In an insect collection, centipedes had 100 legs and spiders had 8 legs. There were 824 legs altogether and 49 more spiders than centipedes. How many centipedes were there?

People in Mathematics

Paul Cohen (1934–   ) Paul Cohen has won two of the most prestigious awards in mathematics: the Fields medal and the Bocher Prize. In 1963, he solved the so-called continuum hypothesis, the first problem in David Hilbert's famous list of 23 unsolved problems. As a youngster in Brooklyn, Cohen was intensely curious about math and science. Children were not allowed in the main section of the public library, but he would sneak in to browse the math section. At age 9 he proved the converse of the Pythagorean theorem, and by age 11 his older sister was bringing him math books from the college library. A major influence was his attendance at Stuyvesant High School, a competitive math-science school in Manhattan. "When my proof [of the continuum hypothesis] was first presented, some people thought it was wrong. Then it was thought to be extremely complicated. Then it was thought to be easy. But of course it is easy in the sense that there is a clear philosophical idea."

Rozsa Peter (1905–1977) Rozsa Peter was a pioneer in the field of mathematical logic, writing two books and more than 50 papers on the subject. She was also known as a consummate teacher who engaged her students in the joint discovery of mathematics. She served for 10 years at a teacher's college in Budapest, where she wrote mathematics textbooks and proposed reforms in mathematics education. She fought against elitism and urged mathematicians to visit primary schools to communicate the spirit of their work. Her popularized account of mathematics, *Playing with Infinity*, was published in 1945 and has been translated into 12 languages. Peter wrote that she would like others to see that "mathematics and the arts are not so different from each other. I love mathematics not only for its technical applications, but principally because it is beautiful."

CHAPTER REVIEW

Review the following terms and exercises to determine which require learning or relearning—page numbers are provided for easy reference.

SECTION 9.1: The Rational Numbers

VOCABULARY/NOTATION

Rational number   356
Equality of rational numbers   356
Simplest form (lowest terms)   357
Addition of rational numbers   358

Positive rational number   359
Negative rational number   359
Subtraction of rational numbers   361

Multiplication of rational numbers   362
Reciprocal   363
Division of rational numbers   364

EXERCISES

1. Explain what the statement "the set of rational numbers is an extension of the fractions and integers" means.

2. Explain how the definition of the rational numbers differs from the definition of fractions.

3. Explain how the simplest form of a rational number differs from the simplest form of a fraction.

4. Explain the difference between $-\dfrac{3}{4}$ and $\dfrac{-3}{4}$.

5. True or false?

   a. $\dfrac{3}{-4} = \dfrac{-6}{8}$

   b. $\dfrac{12}{18} = \dfrac{-16}{-24}$

   c. $\dfrac{-3}{5} + \dfrac{2}{7} = \dfrac{31}{35}$

   d. $\dfrac{5}{9} - \dfrac{-1}{6} = \dfrac{13}{18}$

   e. $\dfrac{-5}{7} = \dfrac{5}{-7}$

   f. $\dfrac{2}{-5} \times \dfrac{-3}{7} = \dfrac{6}{35}$

   g. $-\left(-\dfrac{2}{3}\right) = \dfrac{2}{3}$

   h. $\dfrac{8}{90} \div \dfrac{2}{9} = \dfrac{8}{2}$

   i. $\dfrac{5}{7} \div \dfrac{4}{3} = \dfrac{7}{5} \times \dfrac{4}{3}$

   j. $\dfrac{-3}{4} \times \dfrac{-4}{3} = 1$

   k. $\dfrac{-2}{3} < \dfrac{-3}{7}$

   l. $\dfrac{15}{-9} > \dfrac{-13}{4}$

6. Name the property that is used to justify each of the following equations.

   a. $\dfrac{2}{7} + \dfrac{5}{8} = \dfrac{5}{8} + \dfrac{2}{7}$

   b. $\dfrac{3}{4} \times \left(\dfrac{-5}{7} \times \dfrac{6}{11}\right) = \left(\dfrac{3}{4} \times \dfrac{-5}{7}\right) \times \dfrac{6}{11}$

   c. $\dfrac{4}{13} \times 1 = \dfrac{4}{13}$

   d. $\dfrac{-5}{6}\left(\dfrac{4}{7} + \dfrac{3}{8}\right) = \dfrac{-5}{6}\left(\dfrac{4}{7}\right) + \dfrac{-5}{6}\left(\dfrac{3}{8}\right)$

   e. $\dfrac{2}{3} + \left(\dfrac{-2}{3} + \dfrac{5}{7}\right) = \left(\dfrac{2}{3} + \dfrac{-2}{3}\right) + \dfrac{5}{7}$

   f. $\dfrac{5}{-8} \times \dfrac{8}{-5} = 1$

   g. $\dfrac{-2}{3} + \dfrac{5}{-7}$ is a rational number.

   h. $\dfrac{10}{12} + \dfrac{-5}{6} = 0$

   i. $\dfrac{2}{7} + 0 = \dfrac{2}{7}$

   j. $\dfrac{-4}{-5} \times \dfrac{-2}{7}$ is a rational number.

   k. $\dfrac{2}{-3} \times \dfrac{-5}{7} = \dfrac{-5}{7} \times \dfrac{2}{-3}$

   l. If $\dfrac{1}{2} + \dfrac{-2}{3} = x + \dfrac{-2}{3}$, then $\dfrac{1}{2} = x$.

7. Show how to determine if $\dfrac{-3}{7} < \dfrac{-5}{11}$ using

   a. the rational number line.

   b. common positive denominators.

   c. addition.

   d. cross-multiplication.

8. Complete the following, and name the property that is used as a justification.

   a. If $\dfrac{-2}{3} < \dfrac{3}{4}$ and $\dfrac{3}{4} < \dfrac{7}{5}$, then _____ < _____.

   b. If $\dfrac{-3}{5} < \dfrac{-6}{11}$, then $\left(\dfrac{-3}{5}\right)\dfrac{2}{3}$ _____ $\left(\dfrac{-6}{11}\right)\dfrac{2}{3}$.

   c. If $\dfrac{-4}{7} < \dfrac{7}{4}$, then $\dfrac{-4}{7} + \dfrac{5}{8} < \dfrac{7}{4} +$ _____.

   d. If $\dfrac{-3}{4} > \dfrac{11}{3}$, then $\left(\dfrac{-3}{4}\right)\left(\dfrac{-5}{7}\right)$ _____ $\dfrac{11}{3}\left(\dfrac{-5}{7}\right)$.

   e. There is a rational number _____ any two (unequal) rational numbers.

SECTION 9.2: The Real Numbers

VOCABULARY/NOTATION

Real numbers   374
Irrational numbers   374
Principal square root   375
Square root ($\sqrt{\ }$)   376
Radicand   377
Index   377
nth root ($\sqrt[n]{\ }$)   377

Radical   377
Rational exponent   378
Equation   379
Inequality   379
Variable   379
Solution   379
Solution set   379

Solve   379
Guess and Test method   379
Cover-up method   380
Work Backward method   380
Balancing method   380
Coefficients   380
Transposing   384

EXERCISES

1. Explain how the set of real numbers extends the set of rational numbers.

2. Explain how the rational numbers and irrational numbers differ.

3. Which new property for addition and multiplication, if any, holds for real numbers that doesn't hold for the rational numbers?

4. Which new property for ordering holds for the real numbers that doesn't hold for the rational numbers?

5. True or false?
   a. $\sqrt{144} = 12$ b. $\sqrt{27} = 3\sqrt{3}$
   c. $\sqrt[4]{16} = 2$ d. $\sqrt[3]{27} = 3$

e. $25^{1/2} = 5$ f. $36^{3/2} = 54$

g. $(-8)^{5/3} = -32$ h. $4^{-3/2} = -\dfrac{1}{8}$

6. State four properties of rational-number exponents.

7. Solve the equation $-3x + 4 = 17$ using each of the following methods.
   a. Guess and Test b. Cover-up
   c. Work Backward d. Balancing

8. Solve.
   a. $\dfrac{-1}{6}x + \dfrac{2}{7} = \dfrac{4}{3}x - \dfrac{5}{14}$ b. $\dfrac{1}{3}x - \dfrac{4}{5} < \dfrac{-2}{5}x + \dfrac{1}{6}$

SECTION 9.3: Functions and Their Graphs

VOCABULARY/NOTATION

Origin   391
Coordinates   391
x-coordinate   391
y-coordinate   391
Coordinate system   391

x-axis   391
y-axis   391
Quadrants   392
Linear function   392
Quadratic function   393

Exponential function   394
Cubic function   396
Step function   397
Vertical line test   398

EXERCISES

1. Sketch graphs of the following functions for the given values of x and identify their type from the following choices: linear, quadratic, exponential, and cubic.
   a. $x^3 + 5x + 7$ for $x = 1, 2, 3, 4$
   b. $2000(1.05)^x$ for $x = 1, 2, 3, 4, 5$
   c. $(x - 2)(x + 3)$ for $x = -4, -3, -2, -1, 0, 1, 2, 3, 4$

   d. $\dfrac{3}{4}x - \dfrac{5}{3}$ for $x = -2, -1, 0, 1, 2$

2. Sketch a portion of a step function.

3. Sketch a graph that does not represent a function and show how you can use the vertical line test to verify your assertion.

PROBLEMS FOR WRITING/DISCUSSION

1. Show why the problem $\dfrac{6}{7} \div \dfrac{3}{14}$ gives the same answer as $\dfrac{6}{3} \div \dfrac{7}{14}$. Is one problem easier than the other?

2. Miranda says, "You say I can't do $\sqrt{-4}$, but my last year's teacher said I couldn't subtract $3 - 5$, and then you showed us negative numbers. Will my next year's teacher let me do $\sqrt{-4}$?" What would you say?

3. Juan is trying to find $32^{(3/5)}$. He says it can be done in two ways, but he gets two different answers. If he takes the fifth root first, then he gets $2^3 = 8$. But if he

raises 32 to the third power first, then he gets $(32768)^5$, which his calculator says is $3.778 \cdot 10^{22}$. How would you discuss this with Juan?

4. Claudia says that when you see $3^4 \times 5^6$ or $7^9 \times 2^9$, there is nothing you can do because the bases of the exponents are unequal. Do you agree? How would you explain your reasoning?

5. Erik says that $3.25 > 3.5$ because $25 > 5$, and $6.2 < 6.04$ because $2 < 4$. Discuss.

6. Chuck asks you how it could be that $0.99999999 \ldots$ would equal 1 as it says in his book. Doesn't 0.9 equal $\dfrac{9}{10}$? And $\dfrac{9}{10}$ is not equal to 1, right? Discuss.

7. Fatima wants you to show her some numbers other than π that are real but not rational. What would you show her?

8. Carol Ann was using the Pythagorean theorem to find one leg of a right triangle with hypotenuse 7 and leg 4. She came to the equation $x^2 + 4^2 = 7^2$, and she said, "Oh, I can make it $x + 4 = 7$, so $x = 3$." How would you explain her error?

9. Consider the problem $125^{-4/3}$. This problem can be done in six different ways. Try to find all six ways.

10. Glending tells you that if the bases of exponents are the same, then the exponents can be added, so $3^4 + 3^7 = 3^{11}$. Discuss.

CHAPTER TEST

Knowledge

1. True or false?

   a. The fractions together with the integers comprise the rational numbers.

   b. Every rational number is a real number.

   c. The square root of any positive rational number is irrational.

   d. 7^{-3} means $(-7)(-7)(-7)$.

   e. $25^{5/2}$ means $(\sqrt{25})^5$.

   f. If a, b, and c are real numbers and $a < b$, then $ac < bc$.

   g. If $(-3)x + 7 = 13$, then $x = -2$.

   h. If F is a function, the graph of F can be intersected at most once by any horizontal line.

2. Which of the following properties holds for (i) rational numbers, (ii) irrational numbers, (iii) real numbers?

   a. Associative property of multiplication

   b. Commutative property of addition

   c. Closure property of subtraction

   d. Closure property of multiplication

   e. Additive inverse

Skill

3. Compute the following problems and express the answers in simplest form.

   a. $\dfrac{-5}{3} + \dfrac{4}{7}$ b. $\dfrac{-3}{11} \div \dfrac{5}{2}$ c. $\dfrac{3}{(-4)} - \dfrac{(-5)}{7}$

4. Which properties can be used to simplify these computations?

   a. $\dfrac{2}{3} + \left(\dfrac{5}{7} + \dfrac{-2}{3} \right)$ b. $\dfrac{3}{4} \cdot \dfrac{5}{11} + \dfrac{5}{11} \cdot \dfrac{1}{4}$

5. Solve for x.

   a. $\left(\dfrac{-3}{5} \right)x + \dfrac{4}{7} < \dfrac{8}{5}$ b. $\dfrac{5}{4}x - \dfrac{3}{7} = \dfrac{2}{3}x + \dfrac{5}{8}$

6. Express the following values without using exponents.

   a. $(3^{10})^{3/5}$ b. $8^{7/3}$ c. $81^{-5/4}$

7. Sketch the graph of each of the following functions.

   a. $f(x) = 3x + 4$ b. $g(x) = x^2 - 3$

   c. $h(x) = 1.5^x$

8. List the following numbers in increasing order and underline the numbers that are irrational.

   $$\sqrt{2}, \dfrac{7}{5}, 1.\overline{41}, 1.41411411\ldots, 14.1\%, 1.41\overline{42}$$

9. Simplify

   a. $(-32)^{\frac{4}{5}}$ b. $\sqrt{108}$ c. $\sqrt{245}$

   d. $\dfrac{3 - (3 - 7) + -4}{3 + -2(5 + -2)}$

Understanding

10. Using the fact that $\dfrac{a}{b} \cdot \dfrac{c}{d} = \dfrac{ac}{bd}$, show that $\dfrac{-3}{7} = \dfrac{3}{-7}$. (*Hint*: Make a clever choice for $\dfrac{c}{d}$.)

11. Cross-multiplication of inequality states: If $b > 0$ and $d > 0$, then $\dfrac{a}{b} < \dfrac{c}{d}$ if and only if $ad < bc$. Would this property still hold if $b < 0$ and $d > 0$? Why or why not?

12. By definition $a^{-m} = \dfrac{1}{a^m}$, where m is a positive integer. Using this definition, carefully explain why $\dfrac{1}{5^{-7}} = 5^7$.

13. Sketch pictures of a balancing scale that would represent the solution of the equation $2x + 3 = 9$.

14. Determine if $\sqrt{17} = 4.12310562$. Explain.

15. Identify the following graphs as either linear, quadratic, exponential, cubic, step, or other.

a.

b.

c.

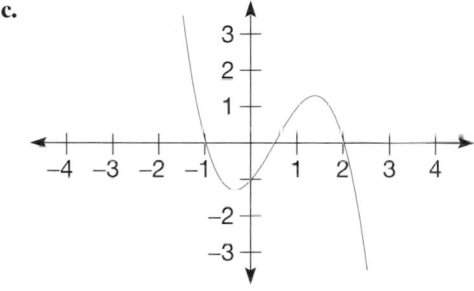

Problem Solving/Application

16. Extending the argument used to show that $\sqrt{2}$ is not rational, show that $\sqrt{8}$ is not rational.

17. Four-sevenths of a school's faculty are women. Four-fifths of the male faculty members are married, and 9 of the male faculty members are unmarried. How many faculty members are there?

18. Some students *incorrectly* simplify fractions as follows: $\dfrac{3+4}{5+4} = \dfrac{3}{5}$. Determine all possible values for x such that $\dfrac{a+x}{b+x} = \dfrac{a}{b}$, that is, find all values for x for which this *incorrect* process works.

19. For the function $f(t) = (0.5)^t$, its value when $t = 0$ is $f(0) = (0.5)^0 = 1$. For what value of t is $f(t) = 0.125$?

20. Find an irrational number between $.\overline{45}$ and $.\overline{46}$.

21. Find three examples where the following mathematical statement is false.

$$\sqrt{a^2 + b^2} = a + b$$

22. Some corresponding temperatures in Celsius and Fahrenheit are given in the following table. Find an equation for the Fahrenheit temperature as a function of the Celsius temperature.

Celsuis	0	5	15	25	35	100
Fahrenheit	32	41	59	77	95	212

References for Reflections from Research

ADAMS, T. L. (1993). *The effects of graphing calculators and a model for conceptual change on community college students' concept of function*. Unpublished doctoral dissertation. University of Florida.

Moss, J., & CASE, R. (1999). Developing children's understanding of the rational numbers: A new model and an experimental curriculum. *Journal for Research in Mathematics Education, 30*, 122–147.

NARODE, R. (1986). *Qualitative graphing: A construction in mathematics*. (ERIC Document Reproduction Service No. 289 745.)

QUINLAN, C. (1995). Analyzing teaching/learning strategies for algebra. In B. Atweh & S. Flavel (Eds.), MERGA 18: GALTHA, *Proceedings of the 18th annual conference* (pp. 459–464). Darwin, Australia: Northern Territory University.

SWAFFORD, J. O., & LANGRALL, C. W. (2000). Grade 6 students' preinstructional use of equations to describe and represent problem situations. *Journal for Research in Mathematics Education, 31*, 89–110.

FOCUS ON *Statistics in the Everyday World*

Statistics influence our daily lives in many ways: in presidential elections, weather forecasting, television programming, and advertising, to name a few. H. G. Wells once said, "Statistical thinking will one day be as necessary as the ability to read and write." The accompanying graphs from *USA Today* are testimony to Wells's statement.

One of the real challenges in interpreting everyday statistically based information is to keep alert to "misinformation" derived through the judicious misuse of statistics. Several examples of such misinformation follow.

1. An advertisement stated that "over 95% of our cars registered in the past 11 years are still on the road." This is an interesting statistic, but what if most of these cars were sold within the past two or three years? The implication in the ad was that the cars are durable. However, no additional statistics were provided from which the readers could draw conclusions.

2. The advertisement of another company claimed that only 1% of the more than half million people who used their product were unsatisfied and applied for their double-your-money-back guarantee. The implication is that 99% of their customers are happy, when it could be that many customers were unhappy, but only 1% chose to apply for the refund.

3. In an effort to boost its image, a company claimed that its sales had increased by 50% while its competitor's had increased by only 20%. No mention was made of earnings or of the absolute magnitude of the increases. After all, if one's sales are $100, it is easier to push them to $150 than it is to increase, say, $1 billion of sales by 20%.

4. A stockbroker who lets an account balance drop by 25% says to a client, "We'll easily be able to make a 25% recovery in your account." Unfortunately, a $33\frac{1}{3}\%$ increase is required to reach the break-even point.

Additional creative ways to influence you through the misuse of statistics via graphs are presented in this chapter.

Copyright 1993, USA TODAY. Reprinted with permission.

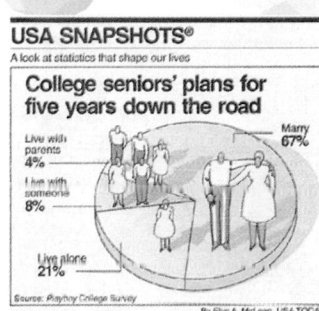

Copyright 1993, USA TODAY. Reprinted with permission.

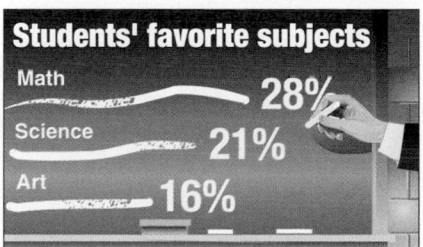

Source: Peter D. Hart Research Associates for the National Science Foundation and Bayer

Copyright 1993, USA TODAY. Reprinted with permission.

Four graphs from USA Today

413

Strategy
Look for a Formula

Problem Solving Strategies

1. Guess and Test
2. Use a Variable
3. Draw a Picture
4. Look for a Pattern
5. Make a List
6. Solve a Simpler Problem
7. Draw a Diagram
8. Use Direct Reasoning
9. Use Indirect Reasoning
10. Use Properties of Numbers
11. Solve an Equivalent Problem
12. Work Backward
13. Use Cases
14. Solve an Equation
15. Look for a Formula

The strategy Look for a Formula is especially appropriate in problems involving number patterns. Often it extends and refines the strategy Look for a Pattern and gives more general information. For example, in the number sequence 1, 4, 7, 10, 13, . . . we observe many patterns. If we wanted to know the 100th term in the sequence, we could eventually generate it by using patterns. However, with some additional investigation, we can establish that the formula $T = 3n - 2$ gives the value of the nth term in the sequence, for $n = 1, 2, 3,$ and so on. Hence the 100th term can be found directly to be $3 \cdot 100 - 2 = 298$. We will make use of the Look for a Formula strategy in this chapter and subsequent chapters. For example, in Chapter 13 we look for formulas for various measurement aspects of geometrical figures.

Initial Problem

A servant was asked to perform a job that would take 30 days. The servant would be paid 1000 gold coins. The servant replied, "I will happily complete the job, but I would rather be paid 1 copper coin on the first day, 2 copper coins on the second day, 4 on the third day, and so on, with the payment of copper coins doubling each day." The king agreed to the servant's method of payment. If a gold coin is worth 1000 copper coins, did the king make the right decision? How much was the servant paid?

Clues

The Look for a Formula strategy may be appropriate when

- A problem suggests a pattern that can be generalized.
- Ideas such as percent, rate, distance, area, volume, or other measurable attributes are involved.
- Applications in science, business, and so on are involved.
- Solving problems involving such topics as statistics, probability, and so on.

A solution of the Initial Problem appears on page 476.

INTRODUCTION

NCTM Standards 2000
Data Analysis and
Probability
Grades 6–8
All students should select, create,
and use appropriate graphical
representations of data including
histograms, box plots, and
scatterplots.

After World War II, W. Edwards Deming, an American statistician, was sent to Japan to aid in its reconstruction. Deming worked with the Japanese to establish quality control in their manufacturing system. If a problem arose, they would (1) formulate questions, (2) design a study, (3) collect data, (4) organize and analyze the data, (5) present the data, and finally (6) interpret the data to identify the cause of the problem. It is interesting to note that the most prestigious award given for quality manufacturing in Japan is the Deming Award. In the past several years, many of his techniques have also been adapted by American manufacturers. In Section 10.1, ways of organizing and presenting data are studied. Then, in Section 10.2, data are analyzed and interpreted. Finally in Section 10.3, misuses of statistics are presented.

10.1   ORGANIZING AND PICTURING INFORMATION

A survey was conducted at two major universities where 10 randomly selected students were asked how far their parents lived from campus. Looking at this data, what conclusions can you draw about the differences and similarities of the student populations at the two universities? How could you represent or organize the data to make those differences and/or similarities clearer?

UNIVERSITY A	UNIVERSITY B
600	80
50	200
710	10
320	70
10	1500
750	30
520	310
2000	40
640	90
60	740

Organizing Information

Line Plots Suppose that 30 fourth graders took a science test and made the following scores: 22, 23, 14, 45, 39, 11, 9, 46, 22, 25, 6, 28, 33, 36, 16, 39, 49, 17, 22, 32, 34, 22, 18, 21, 27, 34, 26, 41, 28, 25. What can we conclude about the students' performance? At the outset, we can say very little, since the data are so disorganized. First, let us put them in increasing order (Table 10.1).

Table 10.1   Science Test Scores

6, 9, 11, 14, 16, 17, 18, 21, 22, 22, 22, 22, 23, 25, 25, 26, 27, 28, 28, 32, 33, 34, 34, 36, 39, 39, 41, 45, 46, 49

Reflection from Research
Graphing provides students opportunities to use their sorting and classifying skills (Shaw, 1984).

From the table we can make the general observation that the scores range from 6 to 49 and seem rather spread out. With the **line plot** or **dot plot** in Figure 10.1, we can graph the scores and obtain a more visual representation of the data.

NCTM Standards 2000
Data Analysis and
Probability
Grades 3–5
All students should represent data
using tables and graphs such as
line plots, bar graphs, and line
graphs.

Reflection from Research
Stem and leaf plots maintain the
data so that individual elements
can be identified and are useful
for ordering data. These characteristics may make stem and leaf
plots preferable over bar or line
graphs (Landwehr, Swift, &
Watkins, 1987).

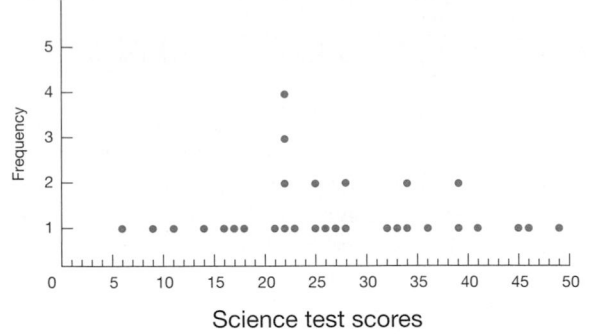

Figure 10.1

Table 10.2

STEMS	LEAVES
0	9 6
1	4 1 6 7 8
2	2 3 2 5 8 2 2 1 7 6 8 5
3	9 3 6 9 2 4 4
4	5 6 9 1

Table 10.3

STEMS	LEAVES
0	6 9
1	1 4 6 7 8
2	1 2 2 2 2 3 5 5 6 7 8 8
3	2 3 4 4 6 9 9
4	1 5 6 9

Table 10.4

STEMS	LEAVES
9	4
10	5 7 8 8
11	
12	0 1 2 2 3

Each dot corresponds to one score. The **frequency** of a number is the number of times it occurs in a collection of data. From the line plot, we see that five scores occurred more than once and that the score 22 had the greatest frequency.

Stem and Leaf Plots One popular method of organizing data is to use a **stem and leaf plot.** To illustrate this method, refer to the list of the science test scores:

22, 23, 14, 45, 39, 11, 9, 46, 22, 25, 6, 28, 33, 36, 16,
39, 49, 17, 22, 32, 34, 22, 18, 21, 27, 34, 26, 41, 28, 25

A stem and leaf plot for the scores appears in Table 10.2. The stems are the tens digits of the science test scores, and the leaves are the ones digits. For example, 0 | 6 represents a score of 6, and 1|4 represents a score of 14.

Notice that the leaves are recorded in the order in which they appear in the list of science test scores, not in increasing order. We can refine the stem and leaf plot by listing the leaves in increasing order, as in Table 10.3.

Example 10.1 Make a stem and leaf plot for the following children's heights, in centimeters: 94, 105, 107, 108, 108, 120, 121, 122, 122, 123

Solution Use the numbers in the hundreds and tens places as the stems and the ones digits as the leaves (Table 10.4). For example, 10 | 5 represents 105 cm. ▮

From the stem and leaf plot in Table 10.4, we see that no data occur between 108 and 120. A large empty interval such as this is called a **gap** in the data. We also see that several values of the data lie close together—namely, those with stems "10" and "12." Several values of the data that lie in close proximity form a **cluster.** Thus one gap and two clusters are evident in Table 10.4. The presence or absence of gaps and clusters is often revealed in stem and leaf plots as well as in line plots. *Gap* and *cluster* are imprecise terms describing general breaks or groupings in data and may be interpreted differently by different people. However, such phenomena often reveal useful information. For example, clusters of data separated by gaps in reading test scores for a class can help in the formation of reading groups.

Suppose that a second class of fourth graders took the same science test as the class represented in Table 10.3 and had the following scores:

5, 7, 12, 13, 14, 22, 25, 26, 27, 28, 28, 29, 31, 32, 33,
34, 34, 35, 36, 37, 38, 39, 42, 43, 45, 46, 47, 48, 49, 49

Using a **back-to-back stem and leaf plot,** we can compare the two classes by listing the leaves for the classes on either side of the stem (Table 10.5). Notice that the

NCTM Standards 2000
Data Analysis and
Probability
Grades Pre-K–2
All students should pose questions
and gather data about themselves
and their surroundings.

Table 10.5

CLASS 1		CLASS 2
9 6	0	5 7
8 7 6 4 1	1	2 3 4
8 8 7 6 5 5 3 2 2 2 2 1	2	2 5 6 7 8 8 9
9 9 6 4 4 3 2	3	1 2 3 4 4 5 6 7 8 9
9 6 5 1	4	2 3 5 6 7 8 9 9

leaves increase as they move away from the stems. By comparing the corresponding leaves for the two classes in Table 10.5, we see that class 2 seems to have performed better than class 1. For example, there are fewer scores in the 10s and 20s in class 2 and more scores in the 30s and 40s.

Histograms Another common method of representing data is to group it in intervals and plot the frequencies of the data in each interval. For example, in Table 10.3, we see that the interval from 20 to 29 had more scores than any other, and that relatively few scores fell in the extreme intervals 0–9 and 40–49. To make this visually apparent, we can make a **histogram,** which shows the number of scores that occur in each interval (Figure 10.2). We determine the height of each rectangular bar of the histogram by using the frequency of the scores in the intervals. Bars are centered above the midpoints of the intervals. The vertical axis of the histogram shows the frequency of the scores in each of the intervals on the horizontal axis. Here we see that a cluster of scores occurs in the interval from 20 to 29 and that there are relatively few extremely high or low scores.

Science test scores

Figure 10.2

Notice that if we turn the stem and leaf plot in Table 10.3 counterclockwise through one-quarter of a turn, we will have a diagram resembling the histogram in Figure 10.2. An advantage of a stem and leaf plot is that each value of the data can be retrieved. With a histogram, only approximate data can be retrieved.

Total School Expenditures

Figure 10.3 Source: U.S. National Center for Educational Statistics.

www.wiley.com/
college/musser

Spotlight on Technology The Chapter 10 eManipulative activity, *Histogram*, makes constructing and adjusting histograms much simpler than doing it by hand. Enter the data from Table 10.5 for class 2 into the *Histogram* eManipulative activity. Once the data are entered, you can move the slider to change the cell width of the histogram. As the cell width gets smaller, what happens to the number of bars? Why? When the cell width gets smaller, there are also some gaps between some of the bars. Why are those gaps present for some cell widths and not for others?

Charts and Graphs

Bar Graphs A bar graph is useful for making direct visual comparisons over a period of time. The **bar graph** in Figure 10.3 shows the total school expenditures in the United States over a six-year period. The entries along the horizontal axis are years and the vertical axis represents billions of dollars, so the label of 300 on that axis actually means $300,000,000,000. The mark on the vertical axis is used to indicate that this part of the scale is not consistent with the rest of the scale. This is a common practice to conserve space.

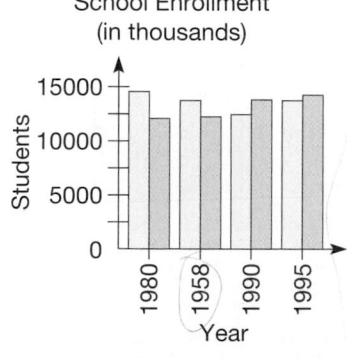

School Enrollment
(in thousands)

Grades 9-12 □ College ▣

Figure 10.4 Source: U.S. National Center for Educational Statistics.

Multiple-bar graphs can be used to show comparisons of data. In Figure 10.4 the nationwide enrollments in grades 9–12 and college are shown for the years 1980, 1985, 1990, and 1995. We see that there was a larger enrollment in grades 9–12 for the years 1980 and 1985 but the college enrollment surpassed it in 1990 and 1995.

A histogram and a bar graph are very similar and yet are different in subtle ways. Both types of graphs use rectangles or bars to illustrate the frequency or magnitude of some type of category. Histograms are typically drawn with the categories along the horizontal or *x*-axis and the frequency or magnitude along the vertical or *y*-axis. This orientation will result with the bars being drawn vertically. Bar graphs, on the other hand, can be drawn either with the bars vertical (categories on the *x*-axis) or horizontal (categories on the *y*-axis). The major distinction between a histogram and a bar graph is the type of data used for the categories. If the categories represent numbers that are continuous and could be regrouped in different intervals, then a histogram should be used. If, however, the categories represent discrete values, then a bar graph should be used. Because the intervals on the categories of a histogram cover all possible values of data, the bars on the graph are drawn with no spaces between them.

The graph in Figure 10.2 is a histogram because the categories on the *x*-axis represent a continuous set of numbers that cover all possible values and could be regrouped into different intervals, as shown in Figure 10.5. The graph in Figure 10.4 is a bar graph because there are gaps in the data used for categories along the *x*-axis. There are no data for the years between 1980 and 1985, between 1985 and 1990, and between 1990 and 1995. As a result, there must be a gap between the bars representing the enrollments for 1980, 1985, 1990, and 1995. The graph shown in Figure 10.3 is not as clear-cut as to whether it should be a histogram or a bar graph. Because every year from 1992 to 1997 is represented, a case could be made for using a histogram. However, because the nature of the data is more discrete, we chose to use a bar graph.

In Figure 10.4, high school and college enrollment were compared against each other using a double-bar graph. In that case, all the data were of the same type, but there are cases when two different types of data are of interest. In such cases, a double-bar graph with two different axes can be constructed. The graph in Figure 10.6 compares the per student expenditure against the average SAT scores for each state.

Notice that the vertical axis on the left represents the per-pupil expenditure and the vertical axis on the right has a very different scale because it represents the average SAT score for a given state. Based on this graph, one might conclude that spending more money on schools does not yield better student achievement. While this

Figure 10.5

Figure 10.6

Name _____ Date _____

Ms. Carter's Class

Ms. Carter's class used the information in the data table to make a graph. Use the graph to answer questions on the following page.

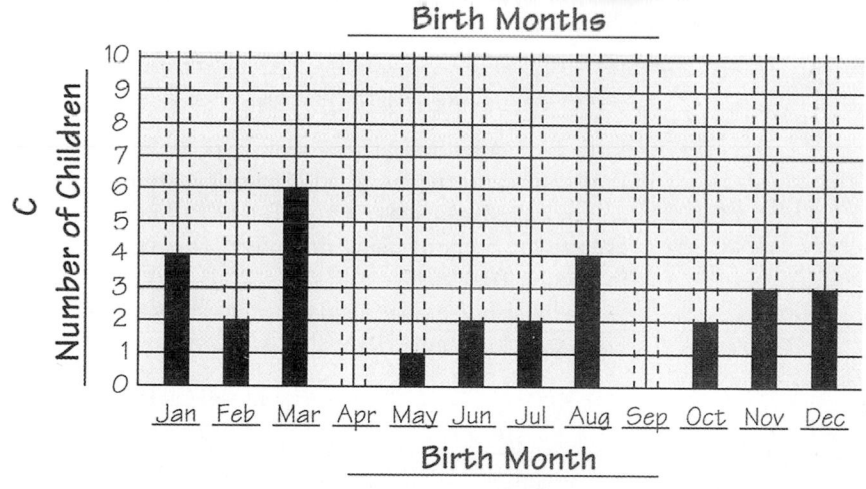

From *Math Trailblazers*, Grade 2 Student Guide, p. 2, by the *TIMS PROJECT*. Copyright © 1997 by Kendall/Hunt Publishing Company. Reprinted with permission.

419

graph has been constructed correctly, there is a key piece of information that is missing. Do the same percentage of students take the test in all of the states? If only the best high school students take it in one state and all of the college-bound students take it in another state, then a comparison between those states' average SAT scores would be invalid. Such is the case with this data. For example, most of the universities in the state of Utah require incoming students to take the ACT college entrance exam instead of the SAT exam. Thus, only those top students who are intending to go to a school out of the state of Utah would take the SAT. In fact, a careful examination of the states with the top SAT scores reveals that most of them have a small percentage of students taking the exam, while most of those with lower average SAT score have two or three times the percentage of students taking the exam. Other examples of misleading statistics will be discussed further in Section 10.3.

Line Graphs A **line graph** is useful for plotting data over a period of time to indicate trends. Figure 10.7 gives an example.

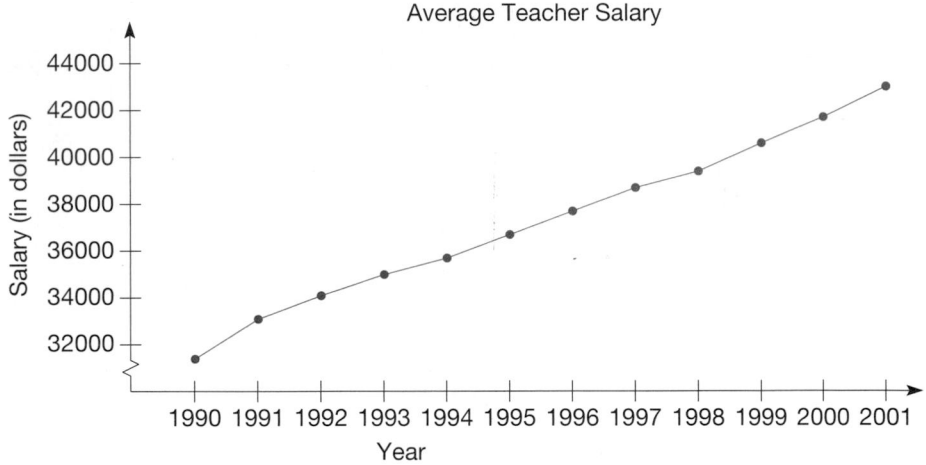

Figure 10.7 *Source*: National Education Association.

Once again the vertical scale has been compressed to conserve space and to help accentuate the trend. The convention of compressing the vertical axis is common and can have a significant influence on the appearance of the graph, even to the point of being deceptive. This issue will be discussed in further detail in Section 10.3.

Multiple-line graphs can be used to show trends and comparisons simultaneously. For example, Figure 10.8 shows the milk production each month for the years

Figure 10.8 *Source*: Hoard's Dairyman Magazine.

1996–1998 (the December 1998 value is an approximation). Notice that the production falls off every February, builds to its peak every May, and then slows down for the remainder of the year. In 1997 and 1998 the production was consistently greater than that of 1996. Production in 1998 was greater than in 1997 except for the months of July and August, in which it was slightly less than the previous year. Notice that the break in the vertical axis does not affect the analysis of comparisons and trends.

Line graphs also can be used to display two different pieces of information simultaneously. For example, the graph in Figure 10.9 shows world fertilizer use and grain area per person from 1950 to 1985. By graphing this information together, it is noticeable that as fertilizer use was increased, the amount of area devoted to grain production was decreased.

Figure 10.10

Figure 10.11

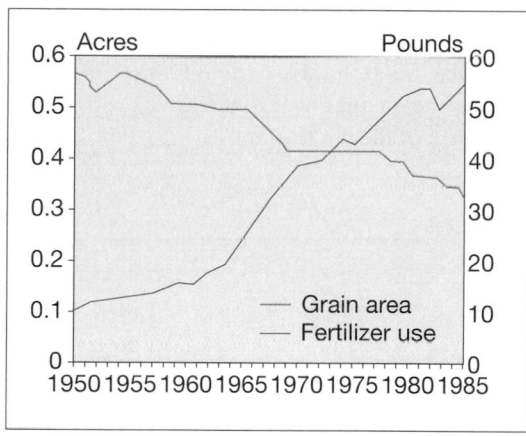

Figure 10.9 World fertilizer use and grain area per person, 1950–1986. *Source*: U.S. Department of Agriculture.

Changes in Meat Consumption per Person, 1971 and 1998 (in percentages)

Figure 10.12 *Source*: U.S. Department of Agriculture, 1999.

Circle Graphs The next type of graph we will consider is a **circle graph** or **pie chart.** Circle graphs are used for comparing parts of a whole. Figure 10.10 shows the percentages of people working in a certain community.

In making a circle graph, the area of a sector is proportional to the fraction or percentage that it represents. The central angle in the sector is equal to the given percentage of 360°. For example, in Figure 10.10 the central angle for the teachers' sector is 12% of 360°, or 43.2° (Figure 10.11).

Multiple-circle graphs can be used to show trends. For example, Figure 10.12 shows the changes in meat consumption between the two years 1971 and 1998. One can see that the relative amount of red meat consumed per person has declined and the relative amounts of both poultry and seafood have increased.

Example 10.2 In the 2000 Summer Olympics in Sydney, Australia, the highest medal count was held by the United States, as shown in the table below. Construct a circle graph to illustrate the different distribution of medals.

	GOLD	SILVER	BRONZE	TOTAL
UNITED STATES	39	25	33	97

Solution Since 39 out of the 97 medals won by the United States were gold, the portion of the circle graph representing the gold medals should be determined by a $\frac{39}{97} \cdot 360° = 145°$ angle. Similarly, the regions for silver and bronze should be deter-

United States

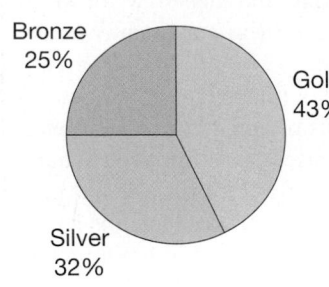

Figure 10.13

mined by a $\frac{25}{97} \cdot 360° = 93°$ angle and a $\frac{33}{97} \cdot 360° = 122°$ angle, respectively.

Using these angles and a protractor, construct three sectors in a circle with these angle measures to represent gold, silver, and bronze as shown in Figure 10.13.

Notice that the sum of the percentages is exactly 100% and the sum of the angles determining the sectors of the circle is 360°. ▪

Spotlight on Technology Circle graphs can be constructed very easily if the work is left to a spreadsheet. Refer to the dynamic spreadsheet, *Circle Graph Budget*, in the spreadsheet webmodule, www.wiley.com/college/musser which contains a monthly budget spreadsheet for you to work with. Enter the following values into the monthly budget categories: housing—$250, transportation—$200, food—$150, utilities—$125, entertainment—$50, savings—$75. Suppose the savings were increased by $100 a month. How does that change the appearance of the circle graph?

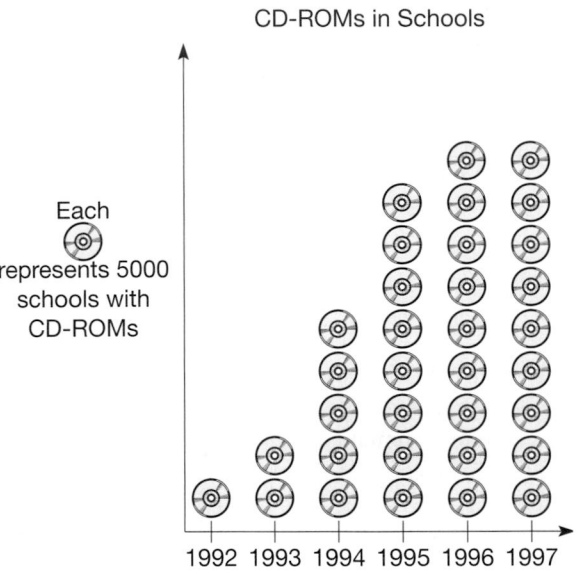

Figure 10.14 *Source*: Quality Education Data.

Figure 10.15 *Source*: Quality Education Data.

Pictographs Many common types of charts and graphs are used for picturing data. A **pictograph,** like the one in Figure 10.14, uses a picture, or icon, to symbolize the quantities being represented. From a pictograph we can observe the change in a quantity over time. We can also make comparisons between similar situations. For example, in Figure 10.15 we can compare the numbers of schools with CD-ROMs in their computers in American elementary, middle, and high schools in 1997. Notice that Figures 10.14 and 10.15 are equivalent to line plots, with pictures of CDs instead of dots.

Pictorial Embellishments With the continually increasing graphics capabilities of computers in a TV-intensive society, **pictorial embellishments** are commonly used with graphs in an attempt to make them more visually appealing. A pictorial embellishment is the addition of some type of picture or art to the basic graphs described thus far in this section. Although pictorial embellishments do make graphs more eye-catching, they also can have the effect of being visually deceptive, as we will discuss in Section 10.3.

A look at statistics that shape the nation

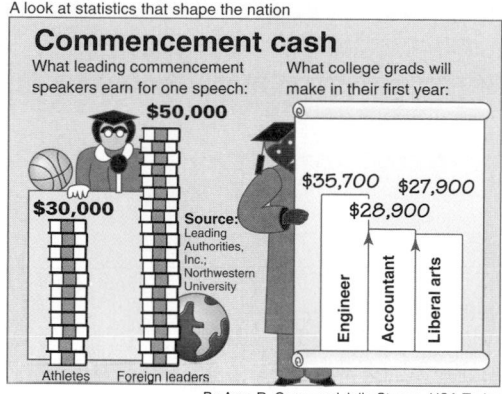

By Arne R. Carey and Julie Stacey, *USA Today.*

Figure 10.16

Figure 10.17

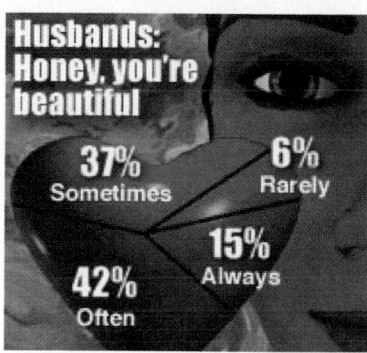

Source: Harris Poll for Clairol, "Honey, you're beautiful."

Figure 10.18

Figure 10.16 provides an example of a pictorial embellishment of a pictograph on the left and a bar graph on the right. Figures 10.17 and 10.18 show pictorial embellishments of a line graph and a circle graph, respectively. In all of these cases, the graphs could have easily been presented without the embellishments but, as most publishers have learned, you probably wouldn't look at it.

Scatterplots Sometimes data are grouped into pairs of numbers that may or may not have a relation to each other. For example, data points might be records of dates and temperature, selling price of a house and its appraised value, employment and interest rates, or education and income. Such pairs of numbers can be plotted as points on a portion of the (x, y)-plane, forming what is called a **scatterplot.** For example, Table 10.6 lists significant earthquakes of the 1960s.

**NCTM Standards 2000
Data Analysis and
Probability
Grades 6–8**
All students should make conjectures about possible relationships between two characteristics of a sample on the basis of scatterplots of the data and approximate lines of fit.

Table 10.6 Significant Earthquakes of the 1960s

DATE	PLACE	DEATHS	MAGNITUDES
Feb. 29, 1960	Morocco	12,000	5.8
May 21–30, 1960	Chile	5,000	8.3
Sept. 1, 1962	Iran	12,230	7.1
July 26, 1963	Yugoslavia	1,100	6.0
Mar. 27, 1964	Alaska	131	8.4
Aug. 19, 1966	Turkey	2,520	6.9
Aug. 31, 1968	Iran	12,000	7.4

To investigate the possible relationship between the magnitude of an earthquake and the number of deaths resulting from the trembler, we make a scatterplot of the data in the table.

Here the magnitude scale is placed along the horizontal axis and the number-of-deaths scale is placed along the vertical axis. For each earthquake we place a dot at the intersection of the appropriate horizontal and vertical lines. For instance, the dot representing the July 1963 earthquake in Yugoslavia is on the vertical line for magnitude 6 and is on an imagined horizontal line for 1100 deaths; that is, just a little above the horizontal line for 1000 deaths (Figure 10.19).

When we look at Figure 10.19, the scatterplot of the earthquake data, there does not appear to be any particular pattern other than that the magnitude of all the earthquakes is above 5. Can you explain why there does not seem to be a relationship between the magnitude of the earthquake and the number of deaths it causes? In the case of other

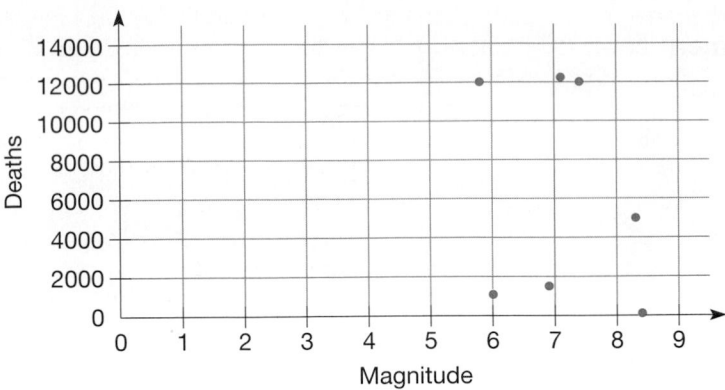

Figure 10.19

data, it often happens that you can see a pattern. Many times it seems that the data points are approximately on a line, as in the next example.

Example 10.3 Suppose that 10 people are interviewed and asked about their income level and educational attainments (Table 10.7).

Table 10.7 Educational Level vs. Income

PERSON	EDUCATIONAL LEVEL	INCOME (1000s)	DATA POINTS
1	12	22	(12, 22)
2	16	63	(16, 63)
3	18	48	(18, 48)
4	10	14	(10, 14)
5	14	2	(14, 2)
6	14	34	(14, 34)
7	13	31	(13, 31)
8	11	97	(11, 97)
9	21	92	(21, 92)
10	16	44	(16, 44)

(a)

(b)

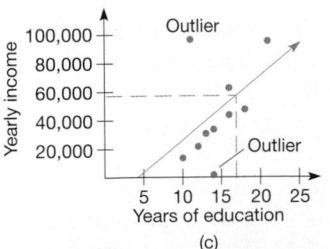

(c)

Figure 10.20

Plot this information in a scatterplot and draw a line that these data seem to approximate or fit.

Solution To visualize this information, we plot it on a graph with years of Education on the horizontal axis and yearly income on the vertical axis [Figure 10.20(a)].

There are two exceptional points in these data, called **outliers.** One is a person with an 11th-grade education who makes $97,000 a year. The interview revealed that this person owned his own successful tulip bulb import business. The other outlier was a person with two years of college (14 years of education) who made only $2000 annually. This unfortunate was an unemployed homeless person. Ignoring the outliers, we notice that these points lie roughly on the straight line. If there is a specific line that best fits some pairs of data, as shown in Figure 10.20(b), this line is called the **regression line.** The presence of a regression line indicates a possible relationship between educational level and yearly income, in which higher income levels correspond to higher educational levels. We call such a mutual relationship a **correlation.** This does not imply that one is the cause of the other, only that they are related. In many problems, you can use a straightedge and "eyeball" a best-fitting line, as we did in this example.

A regression line is very useful. If you know the value of one of the variables, say the educational level, then you can use the regression line to estimate a likely value for the other variable, the income level. For example, if we were to interview another person whose educational level was 17 years (one year of graduate school), then we could give an educated guess as to what this person's income level might be using the regression line. To make this estimate, you trace a vertical line from 17 on the horizontal axis up to the regression line; then you trace a horizontal line left until it intersects the income axis. The process is shown by the dashed lines in Figure 10.20(c). In this case, we use the regression line to project that this person's income level is likely to be close to $58,000. ■

Spotlight on Technology Scatterplots can be easily constructed by using the Chapter 10 eManipulative activity, *Scatterplots*. The dynamic nature of the eManipulative activity allows you to see how the regression line changes when a data point is added or moved.

www.wiley.com/college/musser

Enter the data for Example 10.3 on the eManipulative by first adjusting the scale to be $8 < x < 22$ and $0 < y < 100$. As the data points from Table 10.7 are entered into the scatterplot, the regression will automatically be plotted to fit the data. Predict what would happen to the regression line if the two outliers were removed. Check your prediction.

From the preceding examples, we see that there are many useful methods of organizing and picturing data but that each method has limitations and can be misleading. Table 10.8 gives a summary of our observations about charts and graphs. Notice that although *individual* circle graphs are not designed to show trends, multiple-circle graphs may be used for that purpose, as illustrated in Figure 10.12.

Table 10.8

GRAPHS	GOOD FOR PICTURING	NOT AS GOOD FOR PICTURING
Bar	Totals and trends	Relative amounts
Line	Trends and comparisons of several quantities simultaneously	Relative amounts
Circle	Relative amounts	Trends
Pictograph	Totals, trends, and comparisons	Relative amounts
Scatterplot	Ordered pairs, correlations, trends	Relative amounts

NCTM Standards 2000 Data Analysis and Probability Grades 3–5
All students should compare different representations of the same data and evaluate how well each representation shows important aspects of the data.

MATHEMATICAL MORSEL

There is statistical evidence to indicate that some people postpone death so that they can witness an important birthday or anniversary. For example, there is a dip in U.S. deaths before U.S. presidential elections. Also, Presidents Jefferson and Adams died on the 4th of July, 50 years after signing the Declaration of Independence. This extending-death phenomenon is further reinforced by Jefferson's doctor, who quoted Jefferson on his deathbed as asking, "Is it the Fourth?" The doctor replied, "It soon will be." These were the last words spoken by Thomas Jefferson.

Section 10.1 EXERCISE / PROBLEM SET A

EXERCISES

1. A class of 30 students made the following scores on a 100-point test:

63, 76, 82, 85, 65, 95, 98, 92, 76,
80, 72, 76, 80, 78, 72, 69, 92, 72,
74, 85, 58, 86, 76, 74, 67, 78, 88,
93, 80, 70

  a. Arrange the scores in increasing order.

  b. What is the lowest score? the highest score?

  c. What score occurs most often?

  d. Make a line plot to represent these data.

  e. Make a frequency table, grouping the data in increments of 10 (91–100, 81–90, etc.).

  f. From the information in the frequency table, make a histogram.

  g. Which interval has the most scores?

  h. Using the Chapter 10 eManipulative activity, *Histogram*, construct a histogram of the above data. By moving the slider, group the data in increments of 5 and 8. Sketch each histogram.

  i. For each grouping in part (h), which interval has the largest number of scores? How do the two intervals compare?

2. Make a stem and leaf plot for the following weights of children in kilograms. Use two-digit stems.

17.0, 18.1, 19.2, 20.2, 21.1, 15.8, 22.0,
16.1, 15.9, 18.2, 18.5, 22.0, 16.3, 20.3,
20.9, 18.5, 22.1, 21.4, 17.5, 19.4, 21.8,
16.4, 20.9, 18.5, 20.6

3. Consider the following stem and leaf plot, where the stems are the tens digits of the data.

```
2 | 0 0 1 1 7
3 | 1 3 5 5 5
4 | 2 3 3 3 5 8 9
5 | 4 7
```

  a. Construct the line plot for the data.

  b. Construct the histogram for the data grouped by tens.

4. a. Make a back-to-back stem and leaf plot for the following test scores.

Class 1: 57, 62, 76, 80, 93, 87, 76, 86,
75, 60, 59, 86, 72, 80, 93, 79, 58, 86,
93, 81

Class 2: 68, 79, 75, 87, 92, 90, 83, 77,
95, 67, 84, 92, 85, 77, 66, 87, 92, 82,
90, 85

  b. Which class seems to have performed better?

5. The following pictograph represents the mining production in a given state.

Mining Production

 = $10 million

Bauxite

Sand and gravel

Petroleum and natural gas

  a. About how many dollars worth of bauxite was mined?

  b. About how many dollars worth of sand and gravel was mined?

  c. About how many dollars worth of petroleum and natural gas were mined?

6. The following are data on public school enrollments during the twentieth century.

1900	15,503,110	1910	17,813,852
1920	21,578,316	1930	25,678,015
1940	25,433,542	1950	25,111,427
1960	36,086,771	1970	45,909,088
1980	40,984,093	1990	41,216,000

  a. Choose an appropriate icon, a reasonable amount for it to represent, and draw a pictograph.

  b. In which decades were there increases in enrollment?

  c. What other types of graphs could we use to represent these data?

7. The given bar graphs represent the average monthly precipitation in Portland, Oregon, and New York City.

Portland, Oregon

New York City

a. Which city receives more precipitation, on the average, in January?

b. In how many months are there less than 2 inches precipitation in Portland? in New York City?

c. In which month does the greatest amount of precipitation occur in Portland? the least?

d. In which month does the greatest amount of precipitation occur in New York City? the least?

e. Which city has the greater annual precipitation?

8. Given are several gasoline vehicles and their fuel consumption averages.

Buick	27 mpg
BMW	28 mpg
Honda Civic	35 mpg
Geo	46 mpg
Neon	38 mpg
Land Rover	16 mpg

a. Draw a bar graph to represent these data.

b. Which model gets the least miles per gallon? the most?

c. _____ gets about three times as many miles per gallon as _____.

d. What is the cost of fuel for 80,000 miles of driving at $1.29 per gallon for each car?

e. Could a histogram be used in this case? Why or why not?

9. The populations of the world's nine largest urban areas in 1990 and their populations in 2000 are given in the following table.

World's Largest Urban Areas

	POPULATION (MILLIONS)	
	1990	2000
Tokyo/Yokohama	27.25	29.97
Mexico City	20.90	27.87
Sao Paulo	18.70	25.35
Seoul	16.80	21.98
New York	14.60	14.65
Bombay	12.10	15.46
Calcutta	11.90	14.09
Rio de Janeiro	11.70	14.17
Buenos Aires	11.70	12.91

Source: World Almanac, 1995.

a. Draw a double-bar graph of the data with two bars for each urban area.

b. Which urban area has the largest percentage growth?

c. Which area has the smallest percentage gain in population?

10. Public education expenditures in the United States, as a percentage of gross national product, are given in the following table.

YEAR	EXPENDITURE (%)
1940	3.6
1950	3.5
1960	4.8
1970	7.1
1980	6.7
1990	7.2

a. Make a line graph illustrating the data.

b. Make another line graph illustrating the data, but with a vertical scale unit interval twice as long as that of part (a) and the same otherwise.

c. Which of your graphs would be used to lobby for more funds for education? Which graph would be used to oppose budget increases?

11. The circle graphs here represent the revenues and expenditures of a state government. Use them to answer the following questions.

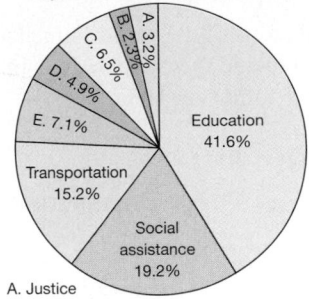

Expenditures by Function

A. 3.2%
B. 2.3%
C. 6.5%
D. 4.9%
E. 7.1%
Education 41.6%
Transportation 15.2%
Social assistance 19.2%

A. Justice
B. Natural resources
C. Business, community and consumer affairs
D. Health and rehabilitation
E. General government

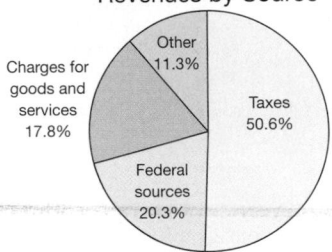

Revenues by Source

Other 11.3%
Charges for goods and services 17.8%
Taxes 50.6%
Federal sources 20.3%

a. What is the largest source of revenue?

b. What percent of the revenue comes from federal sources?

c. Find the central angle of the sector "charges for goods and services."

d. What category of expenditures is smallest?

e. Which four categories, when combined, have the same expenditures as education?

f. Find the central angles of the sectors for "business, community, and consumer affairs" and "general government."

12. The following circle graph shows how a state spends its revenue of $4,500,000,000. Find out how much was spent on each category.

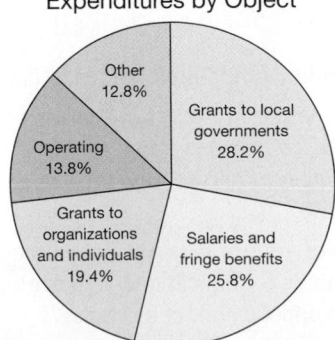

Expenditures by Object

Other 12.8%
Grants to local governments 28.2%
Operating 13.8%
Grants to organizations and individuals 19.4%
Salaries and fringe benefits 25.8%

Complete the following for Problems 13 and 14.

a. Make a scatterplot for the data.

b. Identify any outliers in the scatterplot.

c. Use the Chapter 10 eManipulative activity, *Scatterplot*, to construct a scatterplot and regression line. Sketch the regression line on the scatterplot constructed in part (a).

13. The college admissions office uses high school grade point average (GPA) as one of its selection criteria for admitting new students. At the end of the year, 10 students are selected at random from the freshman class and a comparison is made between their high school grade point averages and their grade point averages at the end of their freshman year in college.

HIGH SCHOOL GPA	FRESHMAN GPA
2.8	2.5
3.2	2.6
3.4	3.1
3.7	3.2
3.5	3.3
3.8	3.3
3.9	3.6
4.0	3.8
3.6	3.9
3.8	4.0

14. Students taking a speed reading course produced the following gains in their reading speeds:

WEEKS IN PROGRAM	SPEED GAIN (WORDS PER MINUTE)
2	50
4	100
4	140
5	130
6	170
6	140
7	180
8	230

Complete the following for Problems 15 and 16.

a. Make a scatterplot for the data.

b. Sketch the regression line. As a line that best fits this data, the line should have a balance of data points that are above it and below it.

c. Use the Chapter 10 eManipulative activity, *Scatterplot*, to construct a scatterplot and regression line. Describe how your regression line from part (b) compares to the one generated by the eManipulative.

15. A golf course professional collected the following data on the average scores for eight golfers and their average weekly practice time.

PRACTICE TIME (HOURS)	AVERAGE SCORE
6	79
3	83
4	92
6	78
3	84
2	94
5	80
6	82

16. A company that assembles electronic parts uses several methods for screening potential new employees. One of these is an aptitude test requiring good eye–hand coordination. The personnel director selects eight employees at random and compares their test results with their average weekly output.

APTITUDE TEST RESULTS	WEEKLY OUTPUT (DOZENS OF UNITS)
6	30
9	49
5	32
8	42
7	39
5	28
8	41
16	52

17. A doctor conducted a study to investigate the relationship between weight and diastolic blood pressure of males between 40 and 50 years of age. The scatterplot and regression line indicate the relationship.

a. Predict the diastolic blood pressure of a 45-year-old man who weighs 160 pounds.

b. Predict the diastolic blood pressure of a 42-year-old man who weighs 180 pounds.

PROBLEMS

18. The projected enrollment (in thousands) of public and private schools in the United States in 2000 is given in the table.

TYPE OF SCHOOL	PUBLIC	PRIVATE
Elementary	33,903	4640
Secondary	13,537	1366
College	11,626	3263

Source: U.S. National Center for Educational Statistics.

a. What is an appropriate type of graph for displaying the data? Explain.

b. Make a graph of the data using your chosen type.

19. The federal budget is derived from several sources, as listed in the table.

Federal Budget Revenue, 1998

SOURCE	PERCENT
Individual income taxes	53
Social insurance receipts	31
Corporate taxes	12
Excise taxes	3
Estate and gift taxes	1
	100

Source: U.S. Internal Revenue Service.

a. What is an appropriate type of graph for displaying the data? Explain.

b. Make a graph of the data using your chosen type.

20. Given in the table is the average cost of tuition and fees at an American four-year college.

U.S. College Tuition and Fees

	PUBLIC	PRIVATE
1989	1846	9451
1990	2035	10,348
1991	2159	11,379
1992	2410	12,192
1993	2604	13,055
1994	2820	13,874
1995	2977	14,537
1996	3151	15,605
1997	3321	16,531

Source: U.S. National Center for Educational Statistics.

a. What is an appropriate type of graph for displaying the data? Explain.

b. Make a graph of the data using your chosen type.

c. For the nine-year period, which college costs increased at the greater rate—public or private?

21. The table below represents the percent of persons in each category who participated in television viewing or newspaper reading in the week prior to the survey in the spring of 2000.

Media Audiences, 2000

GROUP OF PEOPLE	TELEVISION VIEWING	NEWSPAPER READING
Not high school graduate	94.8	60
High school graduate	94.5	78.8
Attended college	93.6	83.7
College graduate	91.1	89.7

Source: Mediamark Research Inc.

a. What is an appropriate type of graph for displaying the data? Explain.

b. Make a graph of the data using your chosen type.

22. The table gives the number (in thousands) of cellular telephone subscribers.

a. What is an appropriate type of graph for displaying the data? Explain.

b. Make a graph of the data using your chosen type.

Cell Phone Subscibers

YEAR	NUMBER OF CELLULAR TELEPHONE SUBSCRIBERS (×1000)
1993	16,009
1994	24,134
1995	33,786
1996	44,043
1997	55,312
1998	69,209
1999	86,047

Source: Cellular Telecommunications Industry Association.

23. Given in the following table are revenues for public elementary and secondary schools from federal, state, and local sources.

Source of School Funds by Percent, 1920–1990

SCHOOL YEAR	FEDERAL	STATE	LOCAL
1920	0.3	16.5	83.2
1930	0.4	16.9	82.7
1940	1.8	30.3	68.0
1950	2.9	39.8	57.3
1960	4.4	39.1	56.5
1970	8.0	39.9	52.1
1980	9.8	46.8	43.4
1990	6.1	47.2	46.6

Source: National Center for Education Statistics.

a. What is an appropriate type of graph for displaying the data? Explain.

b. Make a graph of the data using your chosen type.

c. What trends does your graph display?

24. A company compared the commuting distance and number of absences for a group of employees, with the following data:

COMMUTING DISTANCE (MI.)	NUMBER OF ABSENCES (YR.)
8	4
21	5
8	5
8	3
2	2
15	5
17	7
11	4

a. Make a scatterplot of the data.

b. Estimate the regression line.

c. Predict the number of absences (per year) for an employee with a commute of 15 miles.

25. A report from the Bureau of Labor Statistics listed the 1993 median weekly earnings (for both men and women) of full-time workers in selected occupational categories. Predict the median weekly salary for a woman if the median weekly salary for a man is $450.

MEDIAN WEEKLY EARNINGS OCCUPATION	MEN	WOMEN
Managerial and prof. specialty	791	580
Technical, sales, admin. support	534	376
Service occupations	350	259
Precision production	511	344
Operators, fabricators, laborers	399	288
Transportation	456	358
Handlers, equip. cleaners	319	286
Farming, forestry, fishing	274	242

26. a. Check to see whether the first equation is true.

$$4^2 + 5^2 + 6^2 = 2^2 + 3^2 + 8^2$$
$$42^2 + 53^2 + 68^2 = 24^2 + 35^2 + 86^2$$

b. The numbers on each side of the first equation were rearranged to form the resulting second equation. Is the second equation true?

c. Determine whether similar equations always hold.

27. Find all four-digit squares whose digits are all even.

Section 10.1   EXERCISE / PROBLEM SET B

EXERCISES

1. The following are test scores out of 100 for one student throughout the school year in math class.

64, 73, 45, 74, 83, 71, 56, 82, 76, 85, 83, 87, 92, 84, 95, 92, 96, 92, 91

a. Express these scores in a line plot.

b. Express these scores in a histogram.

 c. Use the Chapter 10 eManipulative activity, *Histogram*, to construct a histogram. By moving the slider, group the data in an increment of 3. Sketch the histogram.

2. Consider the following data, representing interest rates in percent.

12.50, 12.45, 12.25, 12.80, 12.50, 12.15, 12.80, 12.40, 12.50, 12.85

a. Make a stem and leaf plot using two-digit stems.

b. Make a stem and leaf plot using three-digit stems.

c. Which stem and leaf plot is more informative?

3. Consider the following stem and leaf plot, where the stems are the tens digits of the data.

4	0 1 1 1 2 7 9
5	2 4 5 6 7 8 8 8 9
6	3 3 3 3 3 4 5 7 9
7	9
8	1 1 2 7 8 9

a. Construct the line plot for the data.

b. Construct the histogram for the data grouped by tens.

4. a. Make a back-to-back stem and leaf plot for the following test scores.

Class 1: 65, 76, 78, 54, 86, 93, 45, 90, 86, 77, 65, 41, 77, 94, 56, 89, 76

Class 2: 74, 46, 87, 98, 43, 67, 78, 46, 75, 85, 84, 76, 65, 82, 79, 31, 92

b. Which class seems to have performed better?

5. Given are data for American automobile factory sales.

YEAR	NUMBER OF PASSENGER CARS (THOUSANDS)
1900	4
1910	181
1920	1,906
1930	2,787
1940	3,717
1950	6,666
1960	6,675
1970	6,547
1980	6,400
1990	6,050
1999	6,982

a. What problem would you encounter in trying to make a pictograph?

b. Construct a line graph representing these data.

6. Germany won 14 gold, 17 silver, and 26 bronze medals in the 2000 Summer Olympics. Using these data and the data from Example 10.2, construct a pictograph to show how the United States and Germany compared in each of the categories: gold, silver, and bronze.

7. The following bar graph represents the Dow-Jones Industrial Average for the month of September 2001. Use it to answer the following questions.

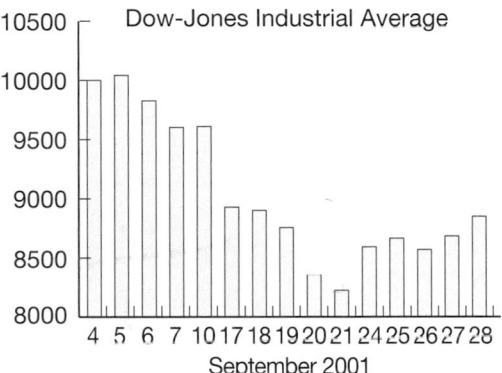

Dow-Jones Industrial Average

September 2001

a. Does it appear that the average on September 5 was more than eight times the average on September 21? Is this true?
b. Does it appear that the average more than doubled from September 21 to September 24? Is this true?
c. Why is this graph misleading?

8. Given are several cars and some braking data.

MAKE OF CAR	BRAKING FROM 70 MPH TO 0 MPH (FT)
Chrysler	188
Lincoln	178
Cadillac	214
Oldsmobile	200
Buick	197
Ford	197

a. Draw a bar graph to represent these data.
b. Describe how one could read your graph to choose the safest car.

9. The following chart lists the four leading death rates per 100,000 population for three years in the United States.
a. Display these data in a triple-bar graph where each cause of death is represented by the three years.

b. Based on your graphs, in which causes are we making progress?

CAUSE OF DEATH	1970	1980	1990
Cardiovascular diseases	945	878	863
Cancer	163	184	203
Accidents	56	47	37
Pulmonary diseases	15	25	35

Source: Statistical Abstract of the United States.

c. Does your graph suggest where most of our research resources should be targeted? Explain.

10. Following is one tax table from a recent state income tax form.

IF YOUR TAXABLE INCOME IS:	YOUR TAX IS:
Not over $500	4.2% of taxable income
At or over $500 but not over $1000	$21.00 + 5.3% of excess over $500
Over $1000 but not over $2000	$47.50 + 6.5% of excess over $1000
Over $2000 but not over $3000	$112.50 + 7.6% of excess over $2000
Over $3000 but not over $4000	$188.50 + 8.7% of excess over $3000
Over $4000 but not over $5000	$275.50 + 9.8% of excess over $4000
Over $5000	$373.50 + 10.8% of excess over $5000

a. Compute the tax when taxable income is $0, $500, $1000, $2000, $3000, $4000, $5000, $6000.
b. Use these data to construct a line graph of tax versus income.

11. Roger has totaled his expenses for the last school year and represented his findings in a circle graph.

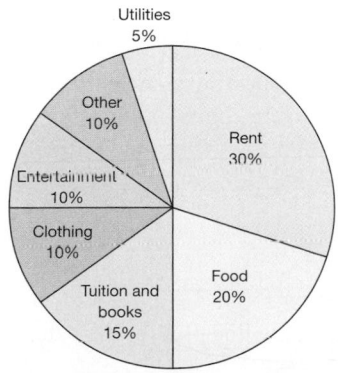

a. What is the central angle of the rent sector?

b. for the food sector?

c. for tuition and books?

d. If his total expenses were $6000, what amount was spent on rent? on entertainment? on clothing?

12. Of a total population of 135,525,000 people 25 years of age and over, 39,357,000 had completed less than four years of high school, 51,426,000 had completed four years of high school, 20,692,000 had completed one to three years of college, and 24,050,000 had completed four or more years of college.

a. To construct a circle graph, find the percentage (to nearest percent) and central angle (to nearest degree) for each of the following categories.

   i. Less than four years of high school

   ii. Four years of high school

   iii. One to three years of college

   iv. Four or more years of college

b. Construct the circle graph.

Complete the following for Problems 13 and 14.

a. Make a scatterplot for the data.

b. Identify any outliers in the scatterplot.

c. Use the Chapter 10 eManipulative activity, *Scatterplot*, to construct a scatterplot and regression line. Sketch the regression line on the scatterplot constructed in part (a).

d. Using the eManipulative, remove the outlier identified in part (b). Describe how the removal of the outlier affected the location of the regression line.

13. A female student thinks that people of similar heights tend to date each other. She measures herself, her roommates, and several others in the dormitory. Then she has them find out the heights of the last man each of the women dated. The heights are given in inches.

FEMALE	MALE
64	70
62	71
66	73
65	68
64	72
70	71
61	66
66	69

14. A high school career counselor does a 10-year follow-up study of graduates. Among the data she collects is a list of the number of years of education beyond high school and incomes earned by the graduates. The following table shows the data for 10 randomly selected graduates.

YEARS OF EDUCATION BEYOND HIGH SCHOOL	INCOME (1000S)
2	27
5	33
0	22
2	25
7	48
4	35
0	28
6	32
4	22
5	30

Complete the following for Problems 15 and 16.

a. Make a scatterplot for the data.

b. Sketch the regression line. As a line that best fits these data, the line should have a balance of data points that are above it and below it.

c. Use the Chapter 10 eManipulative activity, *Scatterplot*, to construct a scatterplot and regression line. Describe how your regression line from part (b) compares to the one generated by the eManipulative.

15. An Alaska naturalist made aerial surveys of a certain wooded area on 10 different days, noting the wind velocity and the number of black bears sighted.

WIND VELOCITY (MPH)	BLACK BEARS SIGHTED
2.1	93
16.7	60
21.1	30
15.9	63
4.9	82
11.8	76
23.6	43
4.0	89
21.5	49
24.4	36

16. A high school math teacher has students maintain records on their study time and then compares their average nightly study time to the scores received on an exam. A random sample of the students showed these comparisons:

STUDY TIME (NEAREST 5 MIN)	EXAM SCORE
15	58
25	72
50	85
20	75
25	68
30	88
40	80
15	74
25	78
30	70
45	94
35	75

17. In a study on obesity involving 12 women, the lean body mass (in kilograms) was compared to the resting metabolic rate. The scatterplot and regression line indicate the data and relationship.

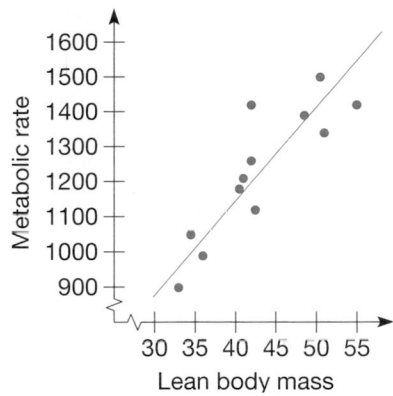

a. Predict the resting metabolic rate for a woman with a lean body mass of 40 kilograms.

b. Predict the resting metabolic rate for a woman with a lean body mass of 50 kilograms.

PROBLEMS

18. Given is the volume of all types of mail handled by the U.S. Postal Service in 1999.

Volume of Mail Handled 1999

TYPE	PIECES (MILLIONS)
First class	101.9
Priority	1.2
Periodicals (2nd Class)	10.3
Standard A (3rd Class)	85.7
Standard B (4th Class)	1.1
Other	0.5

Source: U.S. Postal Service.

a. What is an appropriate type of graph for displaying the data? Explain.

b. Make a graph of the data using your chosen type.

19. Projections of the population of the United States, by race and Hispanic origin, are given in the following table.

a. What is an appropriate type of graph for displaying the data? Explain.

b. Make a graph of the data using your chosen type.

U.S. Population Projections 2010–2020 (Millions)

	2010	2015	2020
White	242	249	257
Black	40	42	45
Hispanic	44	49	55
Other	18	20	23

Source: U.S. Census Bureau.

20. The federal budget is spent on several categories, as listed in the following table.

Federal Budget Expenses, 2000

EXPENSE CATEGORY	PERCENT
Human resources	65
National defense	17
Net interest	13
Physical resources	5
	100

Source: U.S. Office of Management and Budget.

a. What is an appropriate type of graph for displaying the data? Explain.

b. Make a graph of the data using your chosen type.

21. The growth of the U.S. population age 65 and over is given in the following table.

YEAR	PERCENT OF POPULATION AGE 65 AND OVER
1900	4.1
1910	4.3
1920	4.7
1930	5.5
1940	6.9
1950	8.1
1960	9.2
1970	9.8
1980	11.3
1990	12.5
2000	12.7*
2010	13.3*
2020	17.3*
2030	21.2*

Source: U.S. Bureau of the Census.
*Percentages from 2000 on are projections.

a. What is an appropriate type of graph for displaying the data? Explain.

b. Make a graph of the data using your chosen type.

22. The table gives the projected numbers of DVD player shipments worldwide for the years 2001–2004.

Worldwide DVD Player Shipments

YEAR	NUMBER OF DVD PLAYERS (MILLIONS)
2001	28
2002	39
2003	50
2004	61

Source: Cahners In-State Group.

a. What is an appropriate type of graph for displaying the data? Explain.

b. Make a graph of the data using your chosen type.

23. The following table gives the percentages of various types of solid waste in the United States in 1998.

TYPE	PERCENT OF TOTAL
Paper	38.2
Glass	5.7
Metals	7.6
Plastics	10.2
Rubber and leather	3.1
Textiles	3.9
Wood	5.4
Food wastes	10.0
Yard wastes	12.6
Other	3.3

Source: Franklin Associates, Ltd.

a. What is an appropriate type of graph for displaying the data?

b. Make a graph of the data using your chosen type.

24. A local bank compared the number of car loans and new home mortgages it processed each month for a year.

MONTH	CAR LOANS	MORTGAGES
Jan	45	6
Feb	36	6
Mar	48	10
Apr	62	14
May	60	15
Jun	72	18
Jul	76	14
Aug	84	15
Sep	67	12
Oct	60	10
Nov	53	9
Dec	68	11

a. Make a scatterplot of the data.

b. Estimate the regression line.

c. Predict the number of new home mortgages in a month that has 50 car loans.

25. During the last two decades corporations have invested in new plants and equipment as corporate profits have continued to increase. Predict the expenditures for new plants and equipment if corporate profits were $250 billion.

	CORPORATE PROFITS (BILLIONS)	EXPENDITURES FOR PLANTS AND EQUIPMENT (BILLIONS)
1970	69	106
1975	121	163
1980	192	318
1985	223	455
1990	293	592
1993	442	650

Source: 1995 *Information Please* almanac.

26. What is the 100th term in each sequence?

  a. 1, 4, 7, 10, 13, 16, . . .

  b. 1, 3, 6, 10, 15, 21, 28, . . .

  c. $\frac{1}{2} - \frac{1}{3}, \frac{1}{3} - \frac{1}{4}, \frac{1}{4} - \frac{1}{5}, \ldots$

27. What is the smallest number that ends in a 4 and is multiplied by 4 by moving the last digit (a 4) to be the first digit? (*Hint*: It is a six-digit number.)

PROBLEMS FOR WRITING/DISCUSSION

1. Your student, Rosa, asked everybody in the class how many pets they had (including dogs, cats, hamsters, guinea pigs, fish, etc.) and found the following statistics.

# PETS	# STUDENTS WITH THAT NUMBER OF PETS
0	6
1	7
2	3
3	5
4 or more	9

Rosa wanted to make a circle graph of the data, so she made the angles match the numbers in the chart by multiplying by 10. She got 60°, 70°, 30°, 50°, and 90°. There seemed to be some space left over, but Rosa said she just must have measured the angles wrong with her protractor. How could you help her?

2. Michael collected data on the favorite colors of everybody in the class. He then drew a line graph of the data, but Rosa said he should have drawn a circle graph. Which student was correct, and why?

3. Michael asked Rosa if he could have just drawn a bar graph or histogram to represent the data in Problem 2. Rosa said a bar graph would be OK, but not a histogram. Do you agree? Explain.

4. The following is a list of student midterm grades and their corresponding final exam grades.

(Midterm, Final Exam): (124, 250), (120, 176), (60, 148), (153, 283), (79, 240), (135, 241), (170, 255), (145, 281), (114, 210), (120, 272), (210, 299), (94, 220), (126, 233), (116, 249), (128, 285), (137, 272), (84, 207), (68, 202), (38, 209), (156, 213), (77, 270), (138, 275), (200, 275), (166, 266), (123, 260), (172, 263), (205, 292)

Suppose that a student has a midterm score of 180 points. What is our best guess for this student's final exam score? How sure are we that this is a good prediction?

10.2 ANALYZING DATA

STARTING POINT

Two girls are arguing over who is on the taller basketball team. The table lists the heights in inches of the players on the two teams. Identify ways that you could help these girls settle their disagreement about the heights of their respective teams. Some might say that the taller team is the team with the two tallest players on it. Describe another way to determine which team is the taller one by taking all players into account.

TEAM 1	TEAM 2
64	69
72	61
65	70
63	69
75	62
65	71
74	63
67	70
64	63
66	67

NCTM Standards 2000
Data Analysis and
Probability
Grades 6–8
All students should find, use, and
interpret measures of center and
spread, including mean and
interquartile range.

Measuring Central Tendency

Suppose that two fifth-grade classes take a reading test, yielding the following scores. Scores are given in year–month equivalent form. For example, a score of 5.3 means that the student is reading at the fifth-year, third-month level, where years mean years in school.

Class 1: 5.3, 4.9, 5.2, 5.4, 5.6, 5.1, 5.8, 5.3, 4.9, 6.1, 6.2, 5.7, 5.4, 6.9, 4.3, 5.2, 5.6,
5.9, 5.3, 5.8

Class 2: 4.7, 5.0, 5.5, 4.1, 6.8, 5.0, 4.7, 5.6, 4.9, 6.3, 7.8, 3.6, 8.4, 5.4, 4.7, 4.4, 5.6,
3.7, 6.2, 7.5

How did the two classes compare on the reading test? This question is complicated, since there are many ways to compare the classes. To answer it, we need several new concepts.

Since we wish to compare the classes as a whole, we need to take the overall performances into account rather than individual scores. Numbers that give some indication of the overall "average" of some data are called **measures of central tendency.** The three measures of central tendency that we study in this chapter are the mode, median, and mean.

Mode, Median, Mean To compare these two classes, we first begin by putting the scores from the two classes in increasing order.

Class 1: 4.3, 4.9, 4.9, 5.1, 5.2, 5.2, 5.3, 5.3, 5.3, 5.4, 5.4, 5.6, 5.6, 5.7, 5.8, 5.8, 5.9,
6.1, 6.2, 6.9

Class 2: 3.6, 3.7, 4.1, 4.4, 4.7, 4.7, 4.7, 4.9, 5.0, 5.0, 5.4, 5.5, 5.6, 5.6, 6.2, 6.3, 6.8,
7.5, 7.8, 8.4

The most frequently occurring score in class 1 is 5.3 (it occurs three times), while in class 2 it is 4.7 (it also occurs three times). Each of the numbers 5.3 and 4.7 is called the mode score for its respective list of scores.

DEFINITION

Mode

In a list of numbers, the number that occurs most frequently is called the **mode.** There can be more than one mode, for example, if several numbers occur most frequently. If each number appears equally often, there is no mode.

The mode for a class gives us some very rough information about the general performance of the class. It is unaffected by all the other scores. On the basis of the mode scores *only*, it appears that class 1 scored higher than class 2.

The median score for a class is the "middle score" or "halfway" point in a list of the scores that is arranged in increasing (or decreasing) order. The median of the data set 7, 11, 13, 17, 23 is 13. For the data set 7, 11, 13, 17, there is no middle score; thus the median is taken to be the average of 11 and 13 (the two middle scores), or 12. The following precise definition states how to find the median of any data set.

NCTM Standards 2000
Data Analysis and
Probability
Grades 3–5
All students should use measures
of center, focusing on the median,
and understand what each does or
does not indicate about the data
set.

 DEFINITION

Median

Suppose that $x_1, x_2, x_3, \ldots, x_n$ is a collection of numbers in increasing order; that is, $x_1 \le x_2 \le x_3 \le \cdots \le x_n$. If n is odd, the **median** of the numbers is the middle score in the list; that is, the median is the number with subscript $\dfrac{n+1}{2}$. If n is even, the **median** is the arithmetic average of the two middle scores; that is, the median is one-half of the sum of the two numbers with subscripts $\dfrac{n}{2}$ and $\dfrac{n}{2} + 1$.

Since there is an even number of scores (20) in each class, we average the tenth and eleventh scores. The median for class 1 is 5.4. For class 2, the median is 5.2 (verify). On the basis of the median scores *only*, it appears that class 1 scored higher than class 2. Notice that the median does not take into account the magnitude of any scores except the score (or scores) in the middle. Hence it is not affected by extreme scores. Also, the median is not necessarily a member of the original set of scores if there are an even number of scores.

Example 10.4   Find the mode and median for each collection of numbers.
a. 1, 2, 3, 3, 4, 6, 9   **b.** 1, 1, 2, 3, 4, 5, 10
c. 0, 1, 2, 3, 4, 4, 5, 5   **d.** 1, 2, 3, 4

Solution

a. The mode is 3, since it occurs more often than any other number. The median is also 3, since it is the middle score in this ordered list of numbers.

b. The mode is 1 and the median is 3.

c. There are two modes, 4 and 5. Here we have an even number of scores. Hence we average the two middle scores to compute the median. The median is $\dfrac{3+4}{2} = 3.5$. Note that the median is not one of the scores in this case.

d. The median is $\dfrac{2+3}{2} = 2.5$. There is no mode, since each number occurs equally often.   ▪

Reflection from Research
It is worthwhile to demonstrate the
need for other measures of central
tendency by pointing out the main
weakness of the mean—the extent
to which its value can be affected
by extreme scores (Brohan &
Moreland, 1981).

From Example 10.4 we observe that the mode can be equal to, less than, or greater than the median [see parts (a), (b), and (c), respectively].

A third, and perhaps the most useful, measure of central tendency is the mean, also called the **arithmetic average.**

Reflection from Research
A difficult concept for students is
that the mean is not necessarily a
member of the data set (Brown &
Silver, 1989).

 DEFINITION

Mean

Suppose that $x_1, x_2, \ldots, x_n$ is a collection of numbers. The **mean** of the collection is

$$\frac{x_1 + x_2 + \cdots + x_n}{n}.$$

The mean for each class is obtained by summing all the scores and dividing the sum by the total number of scores. For our two fifth-grade classes, we can compute the means as in Table 10.9.

Table 10.9

CLASS	SUM OF SCORES	MEAN
1	109.9	$\dfrac{109.9}{20} = 5.495$
2	109.9	$\dfrac{109.9}{20} = 5.495$

On the basis of the mean scores, the classes performed equivalently. That is, the "average student" in each class scored 5.495 on the reading test. This means that if all the students had equal scores (and the class total was the same), each student would have a score of 5.495. The mean takes every score into account and hence is affected by extremely high or low scores. Among the mean, median, and mode, any one of the three can be the largest or smallest measure of central tendency.

Spotlight on Technology The mean of a data set can be found using the T1-34 II calculator. For example, to find the mean of 5, 5, 13, 15, and 17, first press $\boxed{\text{2nd}}$ $\boxed{\text{STAT}}$ $\boxed{\text{ENTER}}$. This will put the calculator in statistics mode with one variable. Both values of 5 can be entered separately or entered once with a frequency of 2. Enter the data as follows:

$$\boxed{\text{DATA}} \ 5 \ \boxed{\blacktriangledown} \ 2 \ \boxed{\blacktriangledown} \ 13 \ \boxed{\blacktriangledown} \ \boxed{\blacktriangledown} \ 15 \ \boxed{\blacktriangledown} \ \boxed{\blacktriangledown} \ 17 \ \boxed{\text{ENTER}}$$

Once the data is entered, the mean is computed by pressing $\boxed{\text{STATVAR}}$ and then pressing the right arrow once so that $\bar{x}$ is underlined. Since $\bar{x}$ is the symbol commonly used to represent the mean, the second line of the display is $\boxed{11}$, which is the mean of the five numbers above.

NCTM Standards 2000
Data Analysis and
Probability
Grades 6–8
All students should discuss and understand the correspondence between data sets and their graphical representations, especially histograms, stem-and-leaf plots, box plots, and scatterplots.

Box and Whisker Plots A popular application of the median is a **box and whisker plot** or simply a **box plot.** To construct a box and whisker plot, we first find the lowest score, the median, the highest score, and two additional statistics, namely the lower and upper quartiles. We define the lower and upper quartiles using the median. To find the lower and upper quartiles, arrange the scores in increasing order. With an even number of scores, say $2n$, the **lower quartile** is the median of the n smallest scores. The **upper quartile** is the median of the n largest scores. With an odd number of scores, say $2n + 1$, the lower quartile is the median of the n smallest scores, and the upper quartile is the median of the n largest scores.

We will use the reading test scores from class 1 as an illustration:

$$4.3, 4.9, 4.9, 5.1, 5.2, 5.2, 5.3, 5.3, 5.3, 5.4,$$
$$5.4, 5.6, 5.6, 5.7, 5.8, 5.8, 5.9, 6.1, 6.2, 6.9$$

Lowest score $= 4.3$
Lower quartile $=$ median of 10 lowest scores $= 5.2$
Median $= 5.4$
Upper quartile $=$ median of 10 highest scores $= 5.8$
Highest score $= 6.9$

NCTM Standards 2000
Data Analysis and
Probability
Grades 3–5
All students should describe the
shape and important features of
a set of data and compare related
data sets, with an emphasis on
how the data are distributed.

Next, we plot these five statistics on a number line, then make a box from the lower quartile to the upper quartile, indicating the median with a line crossing the box. Finally, we connect the lowest score to the lower quartile with a line segment, one "whisker," and the upper quartile to the highest score with another line segment, the other whisker (Figure 10.21). The box represents about 50% of the scores, and each whisker represents about 25%.

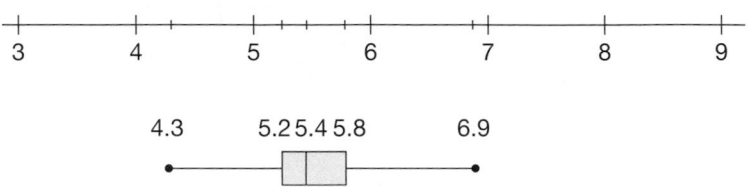

Figure 10.21

The difference between the upper and lower quartiles is called the **interquartile range (IQR).** This statistic is useful for identifying extremely small or large values of the data, called outliers. An **outlier** is commonly defined as any value of the data that lies more than 1.5 IQR units below the lower quartile or more than 1.5 IQR units above the upper quartile. For the class scores, IQR = 5.8 − 5.2 = 0.6, so that 1.5 IQR units = (1.5)(0.6) = 0.9. Hence any score below 5.2 − 0.9 = 4.3 or above 5.8 + 0.9 = 6.7 is an outlier. Thus 6.9 is an outlier for these data; that is, it is an unusually large value given the relative closeness of the rest of the data. Later in this section, we will see an explanation of outliers using z-scores. Often outliers are indicated using an asterisk. In the case of the earlier reading test scores, 6.9 was identified to be an outlier. This is indicated in Figure 10.22. When there are outliers, the whiskers end at the value farthest away from the box that is still within 1.5 IQR units from the end.

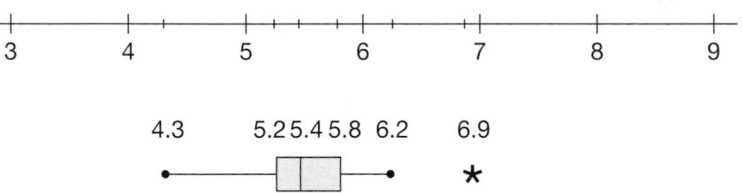

Figure 10.22

We can visually compare the performances of class 1 and class 2 on the reading test by comparing their box and whisker plots. The reading scores from class 2 are 3.6, 3.7, 4.1, 4.4, 4.7, 4.7, 4.7, 4.9, 5.0, 5.0, 5.4, 5.5, 5.6, 5.6, 6.2, 6.3, 6.8, 7.5, 7.8, and 8.4. Thus we have

Lowest score = 3.6
Lower quartile = 4.7
Median = 5.2
Upper quartile = 6.25
Highest score = 8.4
1.5 IQR = 2.325.

The box and whisker plots for both classes appear with outliers in Figure 10.23.

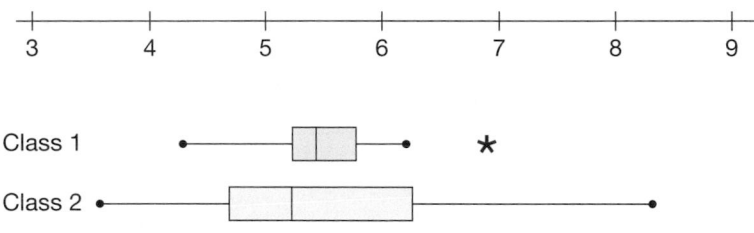

Figure 10.23

From the two box and whisker plots, we see that the scores for class 2 are considerably more widely spread; the box is wider, and the distances to the extreme scores are greater.

Example 10.5 Teacher salary averages for 1997 are given in Table 10.10. Construct a stem and leaf plot as well as box and whisker plots for the data. How do the salaries compare?

Table 10.10 Teacher Salary Averages in 1997 ($\times$ $1000)

STATE	ELEMENTARY TEACHERS	SECONDARY TEACHERS	STATE	ELEMENTARY TEACHERS	SECONDARY TEACHERS
AL	32.5	32.5	MT	29.6	30.7
AK	50.6	50.6	NE	31.8	31.8
AZ	33.3	33.3	NV	37.0	37.8
AR	29.5	31.3	NH	36.0	36.0
CA	42.5	44.5	NJ	48.7	51.6
CO	36.1	36.5	NM	29.4	30.4
CT	50.0	51.6	NY	47.0	49.3
DE	41.3	41.6	NC	31.0	31.4
DC	45.5	46.3	ND	27.9	27.4
FL	33.9	33.9	OH	38.3	39.4
GA	35.1	36.3	OK	30.1	30.6
HI	35.8	35.8	OR	40.6	41.5
ID	31.8	31.9	PA	46.6	47.7
IL	40.4	46.2	RI	43.0	43.1
IN	39.0	38.7	SC	32.6	33.4
IA	32.3	34.1	SD	26.9	26.6
KS	35.7	35.7	TN	33.9	35.2
KY	33.5	35.1	TX	32.3	33.8
LA	29.0	29.0	UT	32.0	32.0
ME	33.3	34.5	VT	37.9	36.5
MD	40.3	42.3	VA	34.7	37.3
MA	42.7	42.7	WA	37.8	37.9
MI	48.2	48.2	WV	32.9	33.7
MN	38.5	38.0	WI	38.7	39.9
MS	28.1	27.3	WY	31.8	31.6
MO	32.5	33.9			

Source: National Education Association.

Solution The stem and leaf plot is given in Table 10.11, where the statistics for constructing the box and whisker plots are shown in boldface type.

Table 10.11

ELEMENTARY TEACHERS	STEM	SECONDARY TEACHERS
9	26.	**6**
9	27.	3 4
1	28.	
6 5 4 0	29.	0
1	30.	4 6 7
8 8 8 0	31.	3 4 6 8 9
9 6 5 5 3 3 **0**	32.	**0** 5
9 9 5 3 3	33.	3 4 7 8 9 9
7	34.	1 5
8 7 **1**	35.	1 2 7 **8**
1 0	36.	0 3 5 5
9 8 0	37.	3 8 9
7 5 3	38.	0 7
0	39.	4 9
6 **4** 3	40.	
3	41.	5 **6**
7 5	42.	3 7
0	43.	1
	44.	5
5	45.	
6	46.	2 3
0	47.	7
7 2	48.	2
	49.	3
6 0	50.	6
	51.	6 **6**

Thus we have the following quartile statistics for constructing the box and whisker plots (Table 10.12). Using the statistics in Table 10.12, we can construct the box and whisker plots (Figure 10.24).

Since the box and whisker plot for the secondary teachers lies to the right of that of the elementary teachers, we see that secondary teachers were generally paid more.

Table 10.12

	ELEMENTARY TEACHERS	SECONDARY TEACHERS
Lowest data value	26.9	26.6
Lower quartile	32	32
Median	35.1	35.8
Upper quartile	40.4	41.6
Highest data value	50.6	51.6
Interquartile range	8.4	9.6
1.5 IQR	12.6	14.4
Outliers	$< 32 - 12.6 = 19.4$	$< 32 - 14.4 = 17.6$
	$> 40.4 + 12.6 = 53.0$	$> 41.6 + 14.4 = 56.0$

Figure 10.24

Notice how the box and whisker plots of Figure 10.24 give us a *direct visual comparison* of the statistics in Table 10.12. In the next section we will investigate methods of actually measuring the spread of data.

Percentiles When constructing box and whisker plots, we used medians and quartiles. Medians essentially divide the data so that 50% of the data are equal to or below the median. Similarly, quartiles divide the data into fourths. In other words, one-fourth of the data points are equal to or below the lower quartile and the other three-fourths of the data points are above it. The upper quartile is equal to or above three-fourths of the data and below the remaining one-fourth of the data. If we were to divide the data into 100 equal parts, **percentiles** could be used to mark the dividing points in the data. For example, the first percentile would separate the bottom 1% of the data from the top 99% and the 37th percentile would separate the bottom 37% of the data from the upper 63%. Formally, a number is in the **nth percentile** of some data if it is greater than or equal to n% of the data.

Percentiles are frequently used in connection with scores on large standardized tests like the ACT and SAT or when talking about the height and weight of babies. The doctor may say that your baby is in the 70th percentile for height and the 45th percentile for weight. This would mean that the baby is taller than 70% and heavier than 45% of the babies of the same age. Percentiles will be discussed later in this section.

Measuring Dispersion

Statistics that give an indication of how the data are "spread out" or distributed are called **measures of dispersion.** The **range** of the scores is simply the difference of the largest and smallest scores. For the class 1 scores at the beginning of this section, the range is $6.9 - 4.3 = 2.6$. For class 2, the range of the scores is $8.4 - 3.6 = 4.8$. The range gives us limited information about the distribution of scores, since it takes only the extremes into account, ignoring the intervening scores.

Variance and Standard Deviation Perhaps the most common measures of dispersion are the variance and the standard deviation.

● DEFINITION

Variance

The **variance** of a collection of numbers is the arithmetic average of the squared differences between each number and the mean of the collection of numbers. Symbolically, for the numbers, $x_1, x_2, \ldots, x_n$, with mean $\bar{x}$, the variance is

$$\frac{(x - \bar{x})^2 + (x_2 - \bar{x})^2 + \cdots + (x_n - \bar{x})^2}{n}.$$

To find the variance of a set of numbers, use the following procedure.

1. Find the mean, $\bar{x}$.
2. For each number x, find the difference between the number and the mean, namely $x - \bar{x}$.
3. Square all the differences in step 2, namely $(x - \bar{x})^2$.
4. Find the arithmetic average of all the squares in step 3. This average is the variance.

Example 10.6   Find the variance for the numbers 5, 7, 7, 8, 10, 11.

Solution

The mean, $\bar{x} = \dfrac{5 + 7 + 7 + 8 + 10 + 11}{6} = 8$.

	STEP 1 $\bar{x}$	STEP 2 $x - \bar{x}$	STEP 3 $(x - \bar{x})^2$
5	8	−3	9
7	8	−1	1
7	8	−1	1
8	8	0	0
10	8	2	4
11	8	3	9

Step 4: $\dfrac{9 + 1 + 1 + 0 + 4 + 9}{6} = 4$, the variance. ■

● DEFINITION

Standard Deviation

The **standard deviation** is the square root of the variance.

Example 10.7   Find the standard deviation for the data in Example 10.6.

Solution   The standard deviation is the square root of the variance, 4. Hence the standard deviation is 2. ■

In general, the greater the standard deviation, the more the scores are spread out.

 Spotlight on Technology   Finding the standard deviation for a collection of data is a straightforward task when using a calculator that possesses the appropriate statistical keys. Usually, a calculator must be set in its statistics or standard deviation mode. Then, after the data are entered one at a time, the mean and standard deviation can be found simply by pressing appropriate keys. For example, assuming that the calculator is in its statistics mode, enter the data 3, 4, 7, 8, 9 using the $\boxed{\Sigma +}$ key as follows:

$$3 \; \boxed{\Sigma +} \; 4 \; \boxed{\Sigma +} \; 7 \; \boxed{\Sigma +} \; 8 \; \boxed{\Sigma +} \; 9 \; \boxed{\Sigma +}$$

Pressing the $\boxed{n}$ key yields the number 5, which is the number of data entered. Pressing $\boxed{\bar{x}}$ yields 6.2, the mean of our data. Pressing $\boxed{\sigma_n}$ yields 2.315167381, the standard deviation. Squaring this result yields the variance, 5.36.

NOTE: When the key representing standard deviation is pressed in the preceding example, a number greater than 2.315167381 appears on some calculators. This difference is due to two different interpretations of standard deviation. If *all n* of the data for some experiment are used in calculating the standard deviation, then $\boxed{\sigma_n}$ is the correct choice. However, if only *n* pieces of data from a large collection of numbers (more than *n*) are used, the variance is calculated with an $n - 1$ in the denominator. Some calculators have a $\boxed{\sigma_{n-1}}$ key to distinguish this case. Computing the standard deviation on the TI-34 II is identical to computing the mean described earlier in this section except in the final step we select *Sx* or *σx*.

Spotlight on Technology When computing the standard deviation of a set of data, changing one number can dramatically impact the standard deviation. To see how this occurs, a spreadsheet can be constructed that does all of the computation for each set of data.

www.wiley.com/
college/musser

Refer to the dynamic spreadsheet, *Standard Deviation*, in the spreadsheet webmodule to work with. Using this spreadsheet, find two sets of data where the standard deviation of one set is twice the standard deviation of the other. What process did you use to find these sets of data?

Let us return to our comparison of the two fifth-grade classes on their reading test. Table 10.13 gives the variance and standard deviation for each class, rounded to two decimal places.

Table 10.13

CLASS	VARIANCE	STANDARD DEVIATION
1	0.29	0.54
2	1.67	1.29

Comparing the classes on the basis of the standard deviation shows that the scores in class 2 were more widely distributed than were the scores in class 1, since the greater the standard deviation, the larger the spread of scores. Hence class 2 is more heterogeneous in reading ability than is class 1. This finding may mean that more reading groups are needed in class 2 than in class 1 if students are grouped by ability. Although it is difficult to give a general rule of thumb about interpreting the standard deviation, it does allow us to compare several sets of data to see which set is more homogeneous. In summary, comparing the two classes on the basis of the mean scores, the classes performed equivalently on the reading. However, on the basis of the standard deviation, class 2 is more heterogeneous than class 1.

In addition to obtaining information about the entire class, we can use the mean and standard deviation to compare an individual student's performances on different tests relative to the class as a whole. Example 10.8 illustrates how we might do this.

Example 10.8 Adrienne made the following scores on two achievement tests. On which test did she perform better relative to the class?

	TEST 1	TEST 2
Adrienne	45	40
Mean	30	25
Standard deviation	10	15

Solution Comparing Adrienne's scores only to the means seems to suggest that she performed equally well on both tests, since her score is 15 points higher than the mean in each case. However, using the standard deviation as a unit of distance, we see that she was 1.5 (15 divided by 10) standard deviations above the mean on test 1 and only 1 (15 divided by 15) standard deviation above the mean on test 2. Hence she performed better on test 1, relative to the whole class. ■

We are able to make comparisons as in Example 10.8 more easily if we use z-scores.

DEFINITION

z-score

The ***z-score***, z, for a particular score, x, is $z = \dfrac{x - \bar{x}}{s}$,

where $\bar{x}$ is the mean of all the scores and s is the standard deviation.

The z-score of a number indicates how many standard deviations the number is away from the mean. Numbers above the mean have positive z-scores, and numbers below the mean have negative z-scores.

Example 10.9 Compute Adrienne's z-score for tests 1 and 2 in Example 10.8.

Solution For test 1, her z-score is $\dfrac{45 - 30}{10} = 1.5$, and for test 2, her z-score is $\dfrac{40 - 25}{15} = 1$. ■

Notice that Adrienne's z-score tells us how far her score was above the mean, measured in multiples of the standard deviation. Example 10.10 illustrates several other features of z-scores.

Example 10.10 Find the z-scores for the data 1, 1, 2, 3, 4, 9, 12, 18.

Solution We first find the mean, $\bar{x}$, and the standard deviation, s.

$$\bar{x} = \frac{1 + 1 + 2 + 3 + 4 + 9 + 12 + 18}{8} = \frac{50}{8} = 6.25$$

$$s = 5.78 \text{ to two places (verify)}$$

Hence we can find the z-scores for each number in the set of data (Table 10.14). ■

Table 10.14

SCORE	z-SCORE
1	$\dfrac{1 - 6.25}{5.78} = -0.91$
2	$\dfrac{2 - 6.25}{5.78} = -0.74$
3	$\dfrac{3 - 6.25}{5.78} = -0.56$
4	$\dfrac{4 - 6.25}{5.78} = -0.39$
9	$\dfrac{9 - 6.25}{5.78} = 0.48$
12	$\dfrac{12 - 6.25}{5.78} = 0.99$
18	$\dfrac{18 - 6.25}{5.78} = 2.03$

The computations in Table 10.14 suggest the following observations.

CASE 1: If $x > \bar{x}$, then $x - \bar{x} > 0$, so $z = \dfrac{x - \bar{x}}{s} > 0$.

Conclusion: x is greater than the mean if and only if the z-score of x is positive.

CASE 2: If $x = \bar{x}$, then $z = \dfrac{x - \bar{x}}{s} = \dfrac{\bar{x} - \bar{x}}{s} = 0$.

Conclusion: The z-score of the mean is 0.

CASE 3: If $x < \bar{x}$, then $x - \bar{x} < 0$, so $z = \dfrac{x - \bar{x}}{s} < 0$.

Conclusion: x is less than the mean if and only if the z-score of x is negative.

We will use z-scores to provide even more defined information later in this section.

Distributions

Large amounts of data are commonly organized in increasing order and pictured in relative frequency form in a histogram. The **relative frequency** that a number occurs is the percentage of the total amount of data that the number represents. For example, in a collection of 100 numbers, if the number 14 appears 6 times, the relative frequency of 14 is 6%. A graph of the data versus the relative frequency of each number in the data is called a **distribution.** Two hypothetical distributions are discussed in Example 10.11.

Example 10.11   For the data in Figures 10.25 and 10.26, identify the mode and describe any observable symmetry of the data.

Solution The distribution in Figure 10.25 has two modes, 34 and 36 kilograms. The modes are indicated by the "peaks" of the histogram. The distribution is also symmetrical, since there is a vertical line that would serve as a "mirror" line of symmetry, namely a line through 35 on the horizontal axis. The distribution in Figure 10.26 has only one mode (4 hours) and is not symmetrical.

Figure 10.25

Figure 10.26

In Figure 10.25 students' weights were rounded to the nearest 2 kilograms, producing 12 possible values from 24 to 46. Suppose, instead, that very accurate weights were obtained for the students, say to the nearest gram (one one-thousandth of a kilogram). Suppose, also, that a smooth curve was used to connect the midpoints of the "steps" of the histogram. One possibility is shown in Figure 10.27. The curve shows a symmetrical "bell-shaped" distribution with one mode.

Figure 10.27

Distributions of physical measurements such as heights and weights for one sex, for large groups of data, frequently are smooth bell-shaped curves, such as the curve in Figure 10.27. There is a geometrical, or visual, way to interpret the median, mean, and mode for such smooth distributions. The vertical line through the median cuts the region between the curve and the horizontal axis into two regions of equal area (Figure 10.28). (NOTE: This characterization of the median does not always hold for histograms because they are not "smooth.")

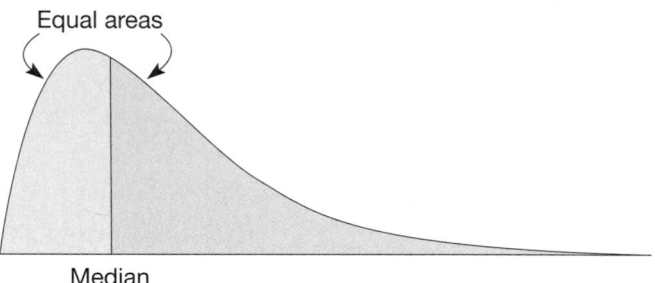

Figure 10.28

The mean is the point on the horizontal axis where the distribution would balance (Figure 10.29). This characterization of the mean holds for all distributions, histograms as well as smooth curves. Since the mode is the most frequently occurring value of the data, the highest point or points of the graph occur above the mode(s).

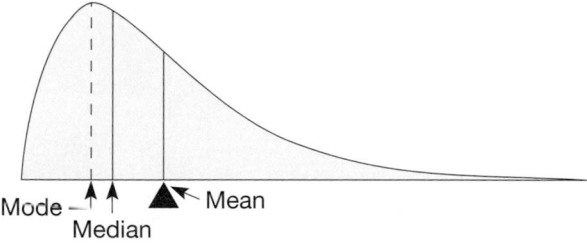

Figure 10.29

A special type of smooth, bell-shaped distribution is the **normal distribution.** The normal distribution is symmetrical, with the mean, median, and mode all being equal. Figure 10.30 shows the general shape of the normal distribution. (The technical definition of the normal distribution is more complicated than we can go into here.) An interesting feature of the normal distribution is that it is completely determined by the mean, $\bar{x}$, and the standard deviation, s. The "peak" is always directly above the mean. The standard deviation determines the shape, in the following way. The larger the standard deviation, the lower and flatter is the curve. That is, if two normal distributions are represented using the same horizontal and vertical scales, the one with the larger standard deviation will be lower and flatter (Figure 10.31).

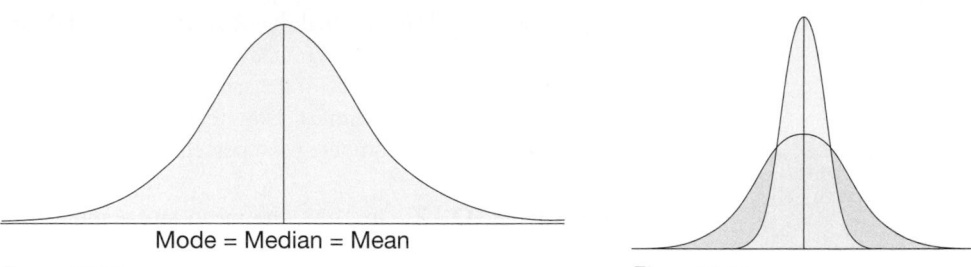

Mode = Median = Mean

Figure 10.30   *Figure 10.31*

The distribution of the weights in Figure 10.25 is essentially normal, so we could determine everything about the curve from the mean and the standard deviation as follows:

1. About 68% of the data are between $\bar{x} - s$ and $\bar{x} + s$.
2. About 95% of the data are between $\bar{x} - 2s$ and $\bar{x} + 2s$.
3. About 99.7% of the data are between $\bar{x} - 3s$ and $\bar{x} + 3s$ (Figure 10.32).

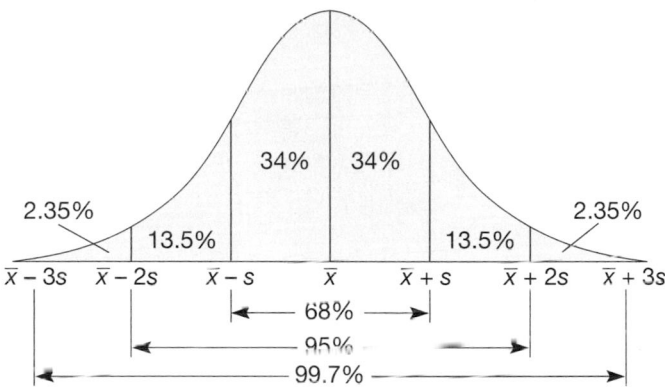

Figure 10.32

We can picture our results about z-scores for normal distributions in Figure 10.33. From Figures 10.32 and 10.33, we see the following:

1. About 68% of the scores are within one z-score of the mean.
2. About 95% of the scores are within two z-scores of the mean.
3. About 99.7% of the scores are within three z-scores of the mean.

z-scores of 2 or more in a normal distribution are very high (higher than 97.5% of all other scores—50% below the mean plus 47.5% up to $z = 2$). Also, z-scores of 3 or more are extremely high. On the other hand, z-scores of -2 or less from a normal distribution are lower than 97.5% of all scores.

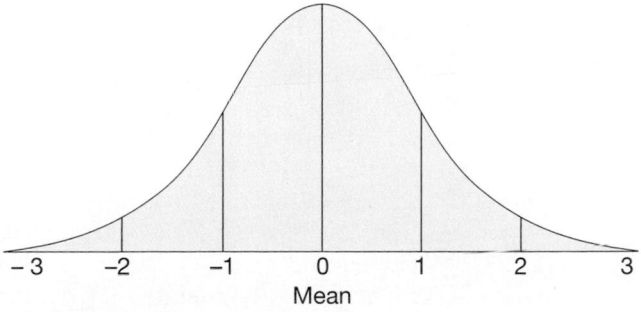

Figure 10.33

A z-score of 2 in a normal distribution is very high; in fact, it is about the 97.5 percentile. By comparing the graphs in Figures 10.32 and 10.33, it can be seen that a z-score of 2 is above 97.5% of the scores. On the other hand, a z-score of -1 is between the 15th and 16th percentiles. Now that we see this connection between z-scores and percentile, we could compute what percentile a score on the SAT would be in.

Example 10.12 In 1998, the mean and standard deviation for the math portion of the SAT were 512 and 112 respectively. If Quinn scored 686 on the math portion, what percentile was he in?

Solution Since Quinn scored a 686, his z-score would be computed using the mean of 512 and standard deviation of 112 for that year. This would give him a z-score of

$$z = \frac{686 - 512}{112} \approx 1.55357.$$

We can now refer to the percentiles and z-scores in Table 10.15 to see that Quinn's score on the math SAT in 1998 was about the 94th percentile and, therefore, it was higher than 94% of the other scores.

Table 10.15

PERCENTILE	z-SCORE	PERCENTILE	z-SCORE	PERCENTILE	z-SCORE
1	−2.326	34	−0.412	67	0.44
2	−2.054	35	−0.385	68	0.468
3	−1.881	36	−0.358	69	0.496
4	−1.751	37	−0.332	70	0.524
5	−1.645	38	−0.305	71	0.553
6	−1.555	39	−0.279	72	0.583
7	−1.476	40	−0.253	73	0.613
8	−1.405	41	−0.228	74	0.643
9	−1.341	42	−0.202	75	0.674
10	−1.282	43	−0.176	76	0.706
11	−1.227	44	−0.151	77	0.739
12	−1.175	45	−0.126	78	0.772
13	−1.126	46	−0.1	79	0.806
14	−1.08	47	−0.075	80	0.842
15	−1.036	48	−0.05	81	0.878
16	−0.994	49	−0.025	82	0.915
17	−0.954	50	0	83	0.954
18	−0.915	51	0.025	84	0.994
19	−0.878	52	0.05	85	1.036
20	−0.842	53	0.075	86	1.08
21	−0.806	54	0.1	87	1.126
22	−0.772	55	0.126	88	1.175
23	−0.739	56	0.151	89	1.227
24	−0.706	57	0.176	90	1.282
25	−0.674	58	0.202	91	1.341
26	−0.643	59	0.228	92	1.405
27	−0.613	60	0.253	93	1.476
28	−0.583	61	0.279	94	1.555
29	−0.553	62	0.305	95	1.645
30	−0.524	63	0.332	96	1.751
31	−0.496	64	0.358	97	1.881
32	−0.468	65	0.385	98	2.054
33	−0.44	66	0.412	99	2.326

Tabulated values of *z*-scores for a normal distribution can be used to explain the relatively unlikely occurrence of outliers. For example, for data from a normal distribution, small outliers have *z*-scores less than -2.6 and are smaller than 99.5% of the data. Similarly, large outliers from a normal distribution have *z*-scores greater than 2.6 and are larger than 99.5% of the data. Thus outliers represent very rare observations. The normal distribution is a very commonly occurring distribution for many large collections of data. Hence the mean, standard deviation, and *z*-scores are especially important statistics.

MATHEMATICAL MORSEL

Did it rain a lot or didn't it? Sometimes the answer to that question depends on how you want to measure it. For example, during October 1994 in Portland, Oregon, the most commonly occurring daily precipitation total (the mode) was 0 inches. In the same month the median daily precipitation total was 0 inches. These measures would seem to indicate that it was a dry month. But was it? The mean daily precipitation in October of 1994 was 0.27 inches. By most standards, this measure would indicate that it did rain a lot. How could this happen? How could two measures say it was dry and another measure indicate that it was wet? Here's how. On 21 of the days in that October, there was no measurable rain and yet on three of the 10 days that it did rain, it rained 2.33, 2.44, and 2.44 inches.

OCTOBER 1994

DAY OF MONTH	1	2	3	4	5	6	7	8	9	10	
DAILY PRECIPITATION	0	0	0	0	0	0	0	0	0	0	
DAY OF MONTH	11	12	13	14	15	16	17	18	19	20	
DAILY PRECIPITATION	0	0	.12	.13	0	0	T	0	T	.03	
DAY OF MONTH	21	22	23	24	25	26	27	28	29	30	31
DAILY PRECIPITATION	.13	0	T	0	.09	2.33	2.44	.24	0	.46	2.44

 Section 10.2 EXERCISE / PROBLEM SET A

EXERCISES

1. Calculate the mean, median, and mode for each collection of data.

   a. 8, 9, 9, 10, 11, 12

   b. 17, 2, 10, 29, 14, 13

   c. 4.2, 3.8, 9.7, -4.8, 0, -10.0

   d. 29, 42, -65, -73, 48, 17, 0, 0, -36

2. Calculate the mean, median, and mode for each collection of data.

   a. 1, 2, 3, 4, 5, 5

   b. 2, 4, 6, 8, 10

   c. 12, 14, 10, 9, 7, 13, 16, 19, 15, 10, 2

   d. -20, 9, 5, -8, 5, -1, 0

3. Scores for Mrs. McClellan's class on mathematics and reading tests are given in the following table. Which student is the "average" student for the group?

STUDENT	MATHEMATICS TEST SCORE	READING TEST SCORE
Rob	73	87
Doug	83	58
Myron	62	90
Alan	89	70
Ed	96	98

4. All the students in a school were weighed. Their average weight was 31.4 kilograms, and their total weight was 18,337.6 kilograms. How many students are in the school?

5. Which of the following situations are possible regarding the mean, median, and mode for a set of data? Give examples.

   a. Mean = median = mode

   b. Mean < median = mode

6. Make a box and whisker plot for the following heights of children, in centimeters.

   120, 121, 121, 124, 126, 128, 132,
   134, 140, 142, 147, 150, 152, 160

7. a.   Make box and whisker plots on the same number line for the following test scores.

   Class 1: 57, 58, 59, 60, 62, 72, 75,
            76, 76, 79, 80, 80, 81, 86,
            86, 86, 87, 93, 93, 93
   Class 2: 66, 67, 68, 75, 77, 77, 79,
            82, 83, 84, 85, 85, 87, 87,
            90, 90, 92, 92, 92, 95

   b. Which class performed better on the test? Explain.

8. Compute the variance and standard deviation for each collection of data.

   a. 4, 4, 4, 4, 4

   b. −4, −3, −2, −1, 0, 1, 2, 3, 4

   c. 14.6, −18.7, 29.3, 15.4, −17.5

9. Compute the variance and standard deviation for each collection of data. What do you observe?

   a. 1, 2, 3, 4, 5

   b. 3, 6, 9, 12, 15

   c. 5, 10, 15, 20, 25

   d. −6, −12, −18, −24, −30

    e. Use the spreadsheet, *Standard Deviation*, from the spreadsheet webmodule to find the standard deviation for the sets of data 3, 8, 13, 18, 23 and 31, 36, 41, 46, 51. Describe how the data and results in part (c) compare to these sets of data and their standard deviations.

10. Compute the mean, median, mode, variance, and standard deviation for the distribution represented by this histogram.

11. Compute the *z*-scores for the following test scores.

STUDENT	SCORE	STUDENT	SCORE
Larry	59	Lou	62
Curly	43	Jerry	65
Moe	71	Dean	75
Bud	89		

12. Given in the table are projected changes in the U.S. population for the period 1986–2010. For example, the population of Alaska is expected to increase 38.7%. Make a box and whisker plot for states east of the Mississippi River (in boldface) and beneath it a box and whisker plot for states west of the Mississippi River. What trends, if any, do your box and whisker plots reveal?

Projected Population Changes (1986–2010)

STATE	PERCENT CHANGE	STATE	PERCENT CHANGE	STATE	PERCENT CHANGE
AK	38.7	LA	1.0	**OH**	−3.3
AL	13.2	**MA**	7.1	OK	6.2
AR	10.3	**MD**	25.2	OR	10.5
AZ	51.4	**ME**	11.1	**PA**	−6.4
CA	34.4	**MI**	−0.6	**RI**	10.9
CO	23.6	MN	8.1	**SC**	22.9
CT	10.4	MO	8.6	SD	1.9
DE	23.3	**MS**	14.6	**TN**	13.8
FL	43.8	MT	−3.1	TX	30.3
GA	42.3	**NC**	26.5	UT	27.8
HI	41.2	ND	−10.4	**VA**	25.9
IA	−17.4	NE	−4.3	**VT**	12.0
ID	7.4	**NH**	37.5	WA	17.4
IL	−0.5	**NJ**	16.0	**WI**	−4.1
IN	−1.8	NM	45.0	**WV**	−16.5
KS	4.2	NV	46.7	WY	−4.1
KY	−0.5	**NY**	2.1		

Source: U.S. Bureau of the Census.

13. Twenty-seven major league baseball players have hit more than 400 home runs in their careers as of 1998.

PLAYER	HOME RUNS
Hank Aaron	755
Babe Ruth	714
Willie Mays	660
Frank Robinson	586
Harmon Killebrew	573
Reggie Jackson	563
Mike Schmidt	548
Mickey Mantle	536
Jimmie Foxx	534
Willie McCovey	521
Ted Williams	521
Ernie Banks	512
Eddie Mathews	512
Mel Ott	511
Eddie Murray	504
Lou Gehrig	493
Stan Musial	475
Willie Stargell	475
Dave Winfield	465
Mark McGwire	457
Carl Yastrzemski	452
Dave Kingman	442
Andre Dawson	438
Billy Williams	426
Darrell Evans	414
Barry Bonds	411
Duke Snider	407

Source: The Baseball Encyclopedia.

a. Make a stem and leaf plot and a box and whisker plot of the data.

b. Outliers between 1.5 and 3.0 IQR are called **mild outliers,** and those greater than 3.0 IQR are called **extreme outliers.** What outliers, mild or extreme, occur?

14. a. What percentile is the median score?

   b. In a normal distribution, what percentile has a z-score of 1? 2? -1? -2?

15. On the verbal portion of the SAT in 1998 the mean was 505 and the standard deviation was 111. If Marcella had a score of 630 on the exam, what percent of all of the students who took the exam had a score lower than hers?

16. Vince's 1998 ACT reading score was below 33% of all of the scores. If the mean and standard deviation for all ACT reading scores in 1998 were 21.3 and 6.1 respectively, what was Vince's score?

17. If the average (mean) mid-twenties male weighs 169 pounds and a weight of 150 is in the 31st percentile, what is the standard deviation of the weights in this age group?

PROBLEMS

18. The class average on a reading test was 27.5 out of 40 possible points. The 19 girls in the class scored 532 points. How many total points did the 11 boys score?

19. When 100 students took a test, the average score was 77.1. Two more students took the test. The sum of their scores was 125. What is the new average?

20. The mean score for a set of 35 mathematics tests was 41.6, with a standard deviation of 4.2. What was the sum of all the scores?

21. Here are Mr. Emery's class scores for two tests. On which test did Lora do better relative to the entire class?

STUDENT	TEST 1 SCORE	TEST 2 SCORE
Lora	85	89
Verne	72	93
Harvey	89	96
Lorna	75	65
Jim	79	79
Betty	86	60

22. At a shoe store, which statistic would be most helpful to the manager when reordering shoes: mean, median, or mode? Explain.

23. a. On the same axes, draw a graph of two normal distributions with the same means but different variances. Which graph has a higher "peak"?

b. On the same axes, draw a graph of two normal distributions with different means but equal variances. Which graph is farther to the right?

24. Reading test scores for Smithville had an average of 69.2. Nationally, the average was 60.3 with a standard deviation of 7.82. In Miss Brown's class, the average was 75.9.

a. What is the z-score for Smithville's average score?

b. What is the z-score for Miss Brown's class average?

c. Assume that the distribution of all scores was a normal distribution. Approximately what percent of students in the country scored lower than Miss Brown's average?

25. A dirt biker must circle a 5-mile track twice. His average speed must be 60 mph. On his first lap, he averaged 30 mph. How fast must he travel on his second lap in order to qualify?

26. A $3 \times 3 \times 3$ cube was painted on all faces, then cut apart into 27 little $1 \times 1 \times 1$ cubes.

a. How many $1 \times 1 \times 1$ cubes had no faces painted? one face painted? two faces painted? three faces painted? four or more faces painted?

b. Answer the same questions for a $4 \times 4 \times 4$ and a $5 \times 5 \times 5$ cube.

c. Answer the same questions for an $n \times n \times n$ cube, where n is any whole number greater than 1.

 Section 10.2 EXERCISE / PROBLEM SET B

EXERCISES

1. Calculate the mean, median, and mode for each collection of data. Give exact answers.

a. $-10, -9, -8, -7, 0, 0, 7, 8, 9, 10$

b. $-5, -3, -1, 0, 3, 6$

c. $-6.5, -6.3, -6.1, 6.0, 6.3, 6.6$

d. $3 + \sqrt{2}, 4 + \sqrt{2}, 5 + \sqrt{2}, 6 + \sqrt{2}, 7 + \sqrt{2}$

2. Calculate the mean, median, and mode for each collection of data. Give exact answers.

a. $\sqrt{2}, 3\sqrt{2}, -8\sqrt{2}, 4\sqrt{2}, 3\sqrt{2}, 0$

b. $-2\pi, 4\pi, 0, 6\pi, 10\pi, 4\pi$

c. $-3 + \pi, -8 + \pi, -15 + \pi, \pi, 4 + \pi, 4 + \pi, 18 + \pi$

d. $\sqrt{2} + \pi, 2\sqrt{2} + \pi, \pi, -3\sqrt{2} + \pi, \sqrt{3} + \pi, \sqrt{3} + \pi$

3. Jamie made the following grades during fall term at State University. What was his grade point average? (A = 4 points, B = 3 points, C = 2, D = 1, F = 0.)

COURSE	CREDITS	GRADE
English	2	B
Chemistry	3	C
Mathematics	4	A
History	3	B
French	3	C

4. Twenty-seven students averaged 70 on their midterm. Could 21 of them have scored above 90? Explain.

5. Which of the following situations are possible regarding the mean, median, and mode for a set of data? Give examples.

a. Mean < median < mode

b. Mean = median < mode

6. a. From the box and whisker plot for 80 test scores, find the lowest score, the highest score, the lower quartile, the upper quartile, and the median.

b. Approximately how many scores are between the lowest score and the lower quartile? between the lower quartile and the upper quartile? between the lower quartile and the highest score?

7. a. Consider the following double stem and leaf plot (Table 10.5).

CLASS 1		CLASS 2
9 6	0	5 7
8 7 6 4 1	1	2 3 4
8 8 7 6 5 5 3 2 2 2 2 1	2	2 5 6 7 8 8 9
9 9 6 4 4 3 2	3	1 2 3 4 4 5 6 7
9 6 5 1	4	2 3 5 6 7 8 9

Construct a box and whisker plot for each class on the same number line for the test scores.

b. Which class performed better? Explain.

c. From the following box and whisker plots, which class performed the best? Explain.

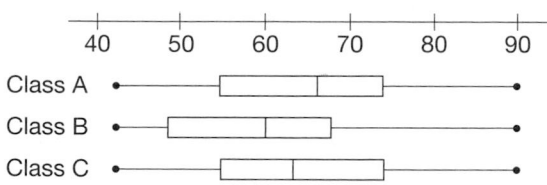

8. Compute the variance and standard deviation for each collection of data.

  a. 5, 5, 5, 5, 5, 5, 5

  b. 8.7, 3.8, 9.2, 14.7, 26.3

  c. 1, 3, 5, 7, 9, 11

  d. $-13.8, -12.3, -9.7, -15.4, -19.7$

9. Use the spreadsheet, *Standard Deviation*, from the spreadsheet webmodule to compute the standard deviations described below.

  a. Compute the variance and standard deviation for the data 2, 4, 6, 8, and 10.

  b. Add 0.7 to each element of the data in part (a) and compute the variance and standard deviation.

  c. Subtract 0.5 from each data value in part (a) and compute the variance and standard deviation.

  d. Given that the variance and standard deviation of the set of data a, b, c, and d is 16 and 4, respectively, what are the variance and standard deviation of the set $a + x$, $b + x$, $c + x$, $d + x$, where x is any real number?

10. Compute the mean, median, mode, variance, and standard deviation for the data in the following table.

NUMBER	FREQUENCY
15	2
18	3
19	4
20	1

11. Compute the *z*-scores for the following data.

  8, 10, 4, 3, 6, 9, 2, 1, 15, 20

12. Given in the table are school expenditures per student by state in 1997.

School Expenditures, 1997 (×100)

STATE	EXPENDITURES PER STUDENT	STATE	EXPENDITURES PER STUDENT
AL	55	MT	60
AK	104	NE	56
AZ	48	NV	54
AR	45	NH	66
CA	53	NJ	103
CO	56	NM	55
CT	88	NT	96
DE	81	NC	56
DC	82	ND	50
FL	60	OH	61
GA	65	OK	45
III	61	OR	66
ID	48	PA	77
IL	60	RI	80
IN	64	SC	54
IA	55	SD	50
KS	66	TN	53
KY	60	TX	60
LA	61	UT	38
ME	68	VT	76
MD	71	VA	64
MA	76	WA	61
MI	73	WV	68
MN	65	WI	70
MS	44	WY	65
MO	54		

Source: National Education Association.

  a. Make a stem and leaf plot of the data, using one-digit stems.

  b. What gaps or clusters occur?

  c. Which, if any, data values are outliers (using IQR units)? What explanation is there for the occurrence of outliers in these data?

  d. Make a box and whisker plot for states east of the Mississippi River (see Exercise 12 in Part A), and beneath it a box and whisker plot for states west of the Mississippi River. What trends, if any, do your box and whisker plots reveal?

13. Twenty baseball pitchers have won 300 or more games in their careers, as of 1998.

PITCHER	VICTORIES	PITCHER	VICTORIES
Cy Young	511	John Clarkson	326
Walter Johnson	416	Don Sutton	324
Grover Alexander	373	Nolan Ryan	324
Christy Mathewson	373	Phil Niekro	318
Warren Spahn	363	Gaylord Perry	314
James Galvin	361	Tom Seaver	311
Charles Nichols	361	Charles Radbourne	311
Tim Keefe	342	Mickey Welch	308
Steve Carlton	329	"Lefty" Grove	300
Eddie Plank	327	Early Wynn	300

Source: The Baseball Encyclopedia.

a. Make a stem and leaf plot and a box and whisker plot of the data.

b. What outliers, mild or extreme, occur?

14. Assume a certain distribution with mean 65 and standard deviation 10. Find the 50th percentile score. Find the 16th percentile and the 84th percentile scores.

15. Sabino took the ACT in 1997 and received a composite score of 22. If the mean and standard deviation for that year were, respectively, 21.0 and 4.7, what percent of all of the students who took the exam scored better than him?

16. Dorian's score of 572 on the verbal portion of the 1996 SAT exam placed him in the 73rd percentile. If the mean on this exam was 505, what was the standard deviation?

17. Using the information from Part A, Exercise 17, determine what percent of the males age 20–29 weigh less than 200 pounds.

PROBLEMS

18. The average height of a class of students is 134.7 cm. The sum of all the heights is 3771.6 cm. There are 17 boys in the class. How many girls are in the class?

19. The average score on a reading test for 58 students was 87.3. Twelve more students took the test. The average of the 12 students was 90.7. What was the average for all students?

20. Suppose that the variance for a set of data is zero. What can you say about the data?

21. a. Give two sets of data with the same means but different variances.

b. Give two sets of data with the same variances but different means.

22. Amy's z-score on her reading test was 1.27. The class average was 60, the median was 58.5, and the variance was 6.2. What was Amy's "raw" score (i.e., her score before converting to z-scores)?

23. a. Can two different numbers in a distribution have the same z-score?

b. Can all of the z-scores for a distribution be equal?

24. a. For the distribution given here by the histogram, find the median according to the following definition: The median is the number through which a vertical line divides the area under the graph into two equal areas. (Recall that the area of a rectangle is the product of the length of the base and the height.)

b. Find the median according to the definition in Section 10.1. Are the two "medians" equal?

25. The **unbiased standard deviation,** s_{n-1}, is computed in exactly the same way as the standard deviation, s, except that instead of dividing by n, we divide by $n - 1$. That is, s_{n-1} is equal to

$$\sqrt{\frac{(x_1 - x)^2 + (x_2 - x)^2 + \cdots + (x_n - x)^2}{n - 1}}$$

where $x_1, \ldots, x_n$ are the data and $\bar{x}$ is the mean. The unbiased standard deviation of a sample is a better estimate of the true standard deviation for a normal distribution.

a. Compute s_{n-1} and s for the following data: 1, 2, 3, 4, 5.

b. True or false? $s_{n-1} \geq s$ for all sets of data. Explain.

26. Amy deposited $1000 in the bank at 8% annual interest. If she leaves her money on deposit for 10 years, how much will she have at the end of 10 years?

27. Prove or disprove: If a three-digit number whose digits are all the same is divided by the sum of its digits, the result is 37.

PROBLEMS FOR WRITING/DISCUSSION

1. Spike looks at the data 5, 6, 7, 5, 8, 8, 9, 4, 9 and tells you that the median is 8. Do you agree? If not, how can you explain his misconception?

2. Chris gathered data about how tall the students were in grades 3, 4, and 5 in her school. She made a stem and leaf chart for each grade level and found that in each grade there was a cluster that occurred in the forties (inches). She decided that fourth, fifth, and sixth graders in her school were all about the same height. What would you say to Chris?

3. Over the summer the third-grade classroom was painted lavender. Amber took a poll of her third-grade classmates in September to see how they liked the new color. They were asked to respond on a five-point scale with 1 meaning they really did not like the new color, 3 being neutral, and 5 meaning they really liked it. Amber announced the results as follows: The median was 5, but the mean was 3.9, so it seemed people were pretty neutral about it. How would you respond?

10.3　MISLEADING GRAPHS AND STATISTICS

STARTING POINT　Mayor Marcus is running for a second term as mayor against the challenger, Councilwoman Claudia. One of the hot topics is crime prevention. Each of the graphs displays crime statistics for the four years of Mayor Marcus's current term. What are the differences between the two graphs? Depending on which candidate you are, which graph would you chose to make your point?

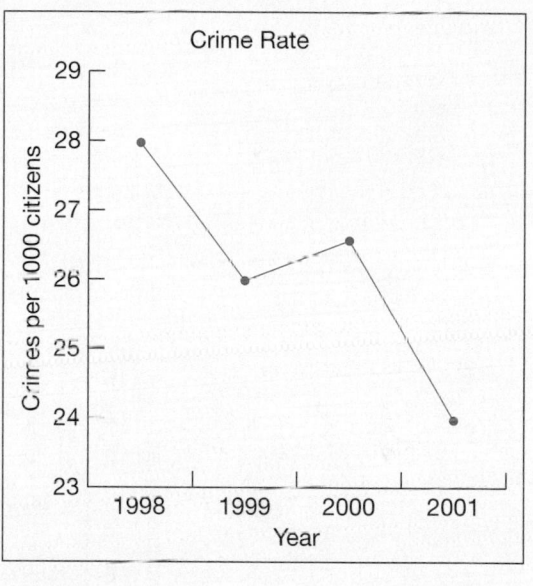

Clearly presenting statistical data is a challenging task. When presenting quantitative information in a graphical form, determining what to emphasize from the data and how to construct the actual graphs must both be considered. If some aspect of the graph is distorted, a misleading graph can easily result. Distortion may be benign and unintentional, but at other times it is intentional with the purpose to deceive or misdirect the reader. In this section we will look at ways in which the elements of a graph can be manipulated to create different impressions of the data. We will also look at how sampling can affect the quality of the data.

First we consider variations on the basic kinds of graphs. We particularly wish to consider ways that the graph may subtly mislead so that you can determine when you are being misled. This knowledge can point out honest ways to put your viewpoint in the most favorable light. We will also consider graphs that have been enhanced with pictorial embellishments. These graphs are more interesting and can reinforce your message, but they also can be misleading. Finally, we will look at how data are gathered through sampling and how bias can be introduced by the size and type of samples used.

Reflection from Research
Graphing gives the child an opportunity to compare, count, add, subtract, sequence, and classify data. A tactile and visual representation of amounts facilitates children's understanding of comparative values (Choate & Okey, 1981).

Scaling and Axis Manipulation

If someone wants the differences among the bars of a histogram or bar chart to look more dramatic, a chart is often displayed with part of the vertical axis missing. Puffed Oats, a children's cereal, is advertised as wholesome since it has less sugar than the other children's cereals even though it has 9 grams of sugar. The high-sugar-content cereals chosen to be compared to Puffed Oats had the following grams of sugar per serving: 15, 14, 13, 11. The bar graph in Figure 10.34 shows the grams of sugar in each variety of cereal.

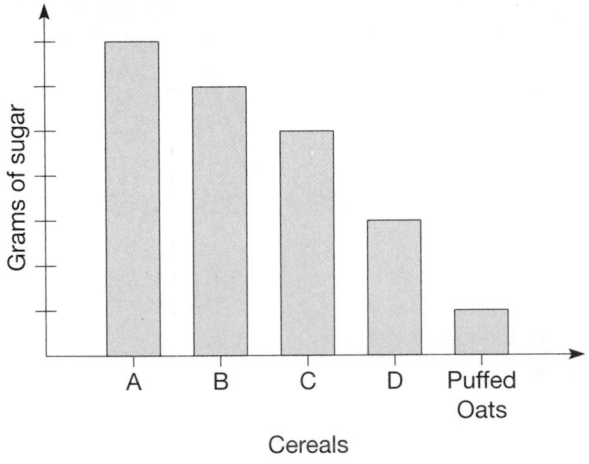

Figure 10.34

The scale of the vertical axis is intentionally not shown, and indeed begins at 8 instead of 0. A less misleading graph would look like the one in Figure 10.35

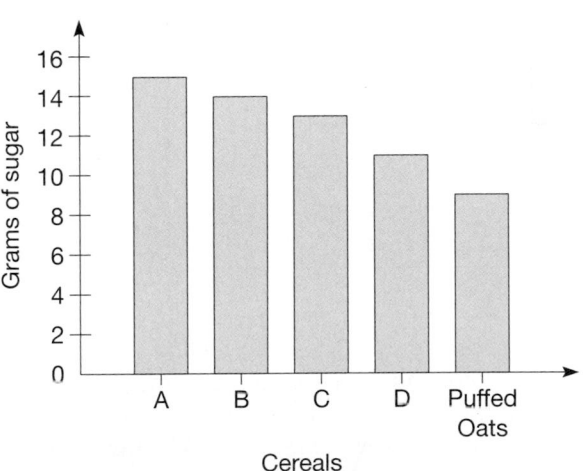

Figure 10.35

Notice that the Puffed Oats company did not choose to compare the sugar content of their cereal with either cornflakes (2 grams per serving) or shredded wheat (0 grams per serving).

Example 10.13   The prices of three brands of baked beans are as follows:

Brand X—79¢, Brand Y—89¢, Brand Z—99¢

Draw a bar graph so the Brand X looks like a much better buy than the other two brands.

Solution Brand X can be made to look much cheaper than the other two brands by starting the price scale at 75¢, as shown in Figure 10.36.

Figure 10.36

Notice that although the values from 0 to 75 have been left off the *y*-axis, there is no marking on the axis indicating the removal of these numbers, making it more difficult to notice the scaling of the vertical axis. ■

Another technique to distort the nature of some data is to reverse the axes and reverse the orientation of an axis. Figure 10.37 is a bar graph that shows declining profits of a company.

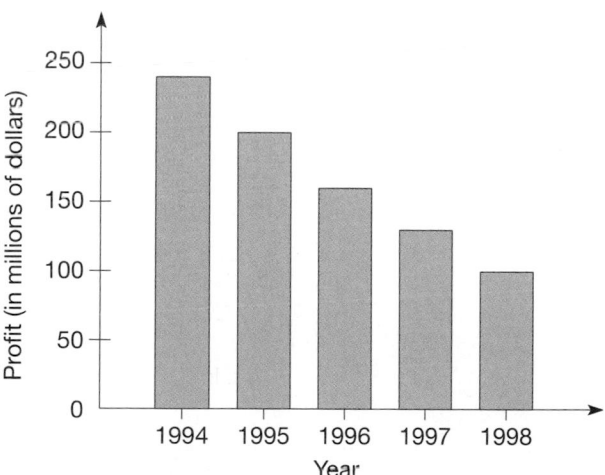

Figure 10.37

In Figure 10.38 the same data are displayed in a horizontal bar graph in which the years are in the reverse order.

The graph in Figure 10.38 displays the same information but has less of a negative connotation because it does not have the "feel" of a decreasing trend.

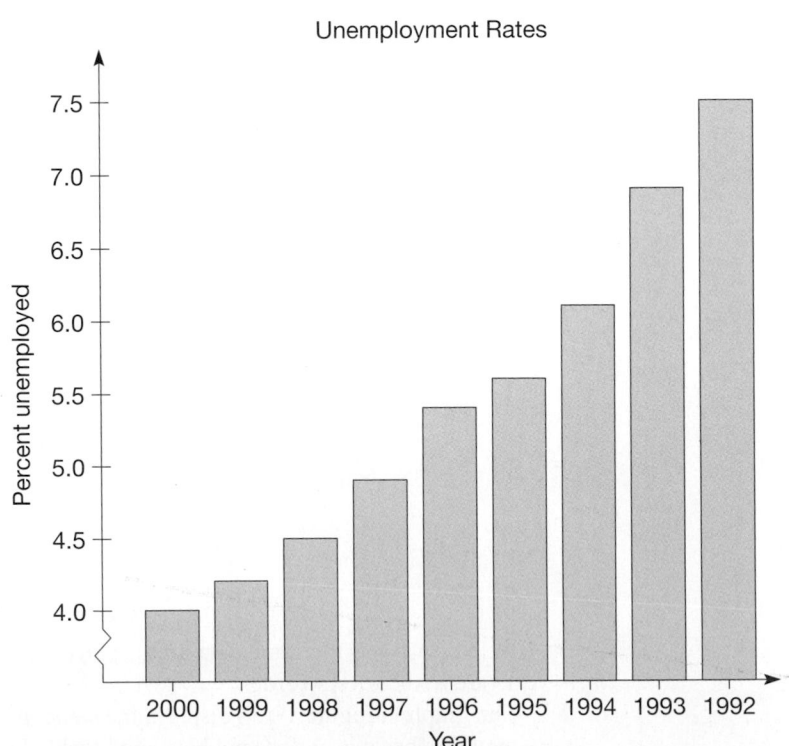

Figure 10.38

Table 10.16

YEAR	PERCENT OF THE LABOR FORCE THAT IS UNEMPLOYED
1992	7.5
1993	6.9
1994	6.1
1995	5.6
1996	5.4
1997	4.9
1998	4.5
1999	4.2
2000	4.0

Source: U.S. Bureau of Labor Statistics.

Example 10.14 The unemployment rates for the United States from 1992 to 2000 are displayed in Table 10.16.

If a political candidate wanted to mislead the voters into believing that the incumbent senator or member of Congress had not been successful in reducing the unemployment rate, how could he construct a bar graph to mislead readers intentionally?

Solution Since the categories along the *x*-axis of a bar graph do not necessarily need to be in any specific order, the years can be shown in reverse chronological order. By showing the years in decreasing order, the graph in Figure 10.39 can be used to lead citizens to think that the unemployment rate is increasing. This reverse trend is further accentuated by (i) starting the graph at 4.5, and (ii) making the graph narrow.

Unemployment Rates

Figure 10.39 Source: U.S. Bureau of Labor Statistics.

Line Graphs and Cropping

What we have seen regarding bar graphs also applies to line graphs. Recall the data of average teacher salaries displayed in the line graph in Figure 10.7. That graph makes it appear as if the increase was fairly significant. Suppose, however, that the teachers' union wants to make a case for better teacher pay. This increase may be made less dramatic by extending the scale of the vertical axis and using larger increments, as in Figure 10.40.

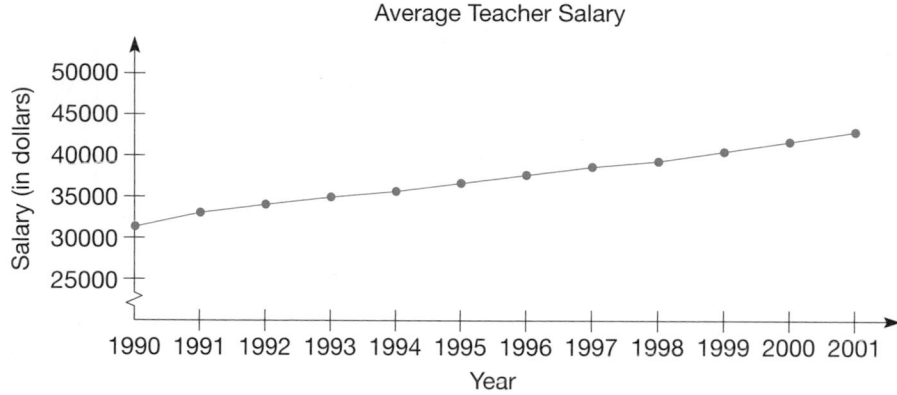

Figure 10.40 *Source*: National Education Association.

Example 10.15 Draw two line graphs of the unemployment data (see Table 10.16) from Example 10.14 that give different impressions of the situation.

Solution

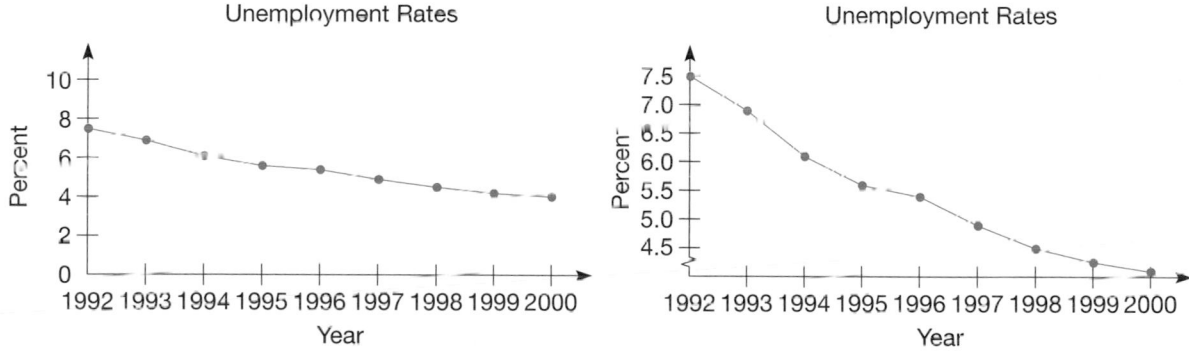

Figure 10.41 *Source*: U.S. Bureau of Labor Statistics.

The graph on the left in Figure 10.41 suggests that the rate of unemployment is decreasing slowly, whereas the graph on the right gives the impression that unemployment is decreasing more rapidly. ■

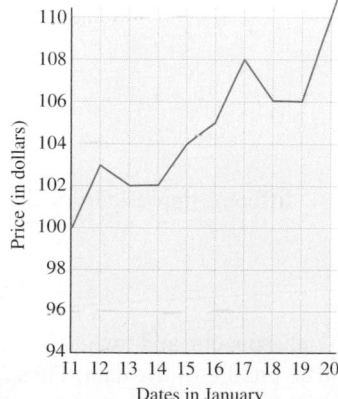

Figure 10.42

Figure 10.42 shows the values of a stock from January 11 through January 20.

The stock appears to be a good buy because it is on an upward trend. Notice that the graph is rising above the edge of the vertical scale. Graphs that do this or even go to the edge of the scale make the trend appear more dramatic.

This kind of scale manipulation is part of a larger phenomenon called cropping. **Cropping** refers to the choice of the window that the graph uses to view the data. Suppose we wish to present the price of a certain company's stock. We may choose which time period and vertical axis to display. In other words, when we show a picture we have to choose a window in which to frame it. Figure 10.43 shows the value of the stock over the previous five months; the stock price is plotted every 10 days.

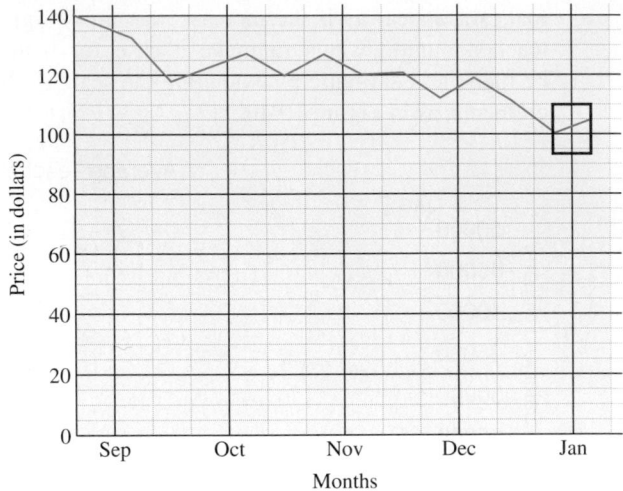

Figure 10.43

The data from Figure 10.42 are now contained in the box of Figure 10.43. Thus, this graph gives a very different perception regarding the value of the stock. This different perception is caused by the change in the vertical scale as well as the horizontal scale.

The downward trend in Figure 10.43 would be more apparent if we choose the vertical scale to be between 100 and 140. The data from Figure 10.43 are shown in Figure 10.44.

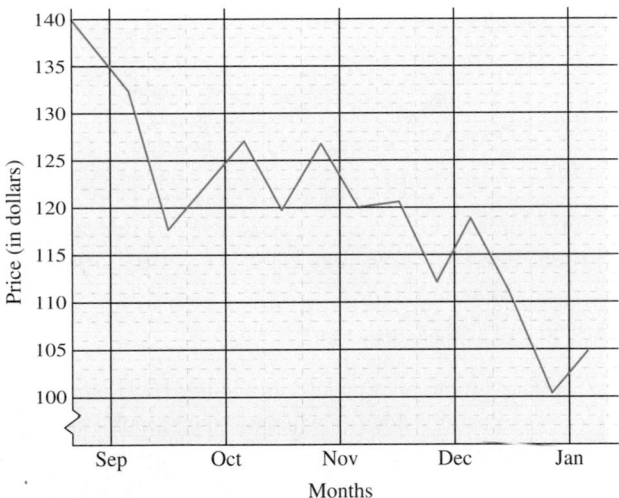

Figure 10.44

Notice how by changing the vertical axis, we get a very different impression of the price trend of the company's stock.

Three-Dimensional Effects

Three-dimensional effects, which are often found in newspapers and magazines, make a graph more attractive but can also obscure the true picture of the data. These graphs are difficult to draw unless you have computer graphing software.

The data for average teacher salary shown in Figure 10.40 are shown using a bar graph with three-dimensional effects in Figure 10.45.

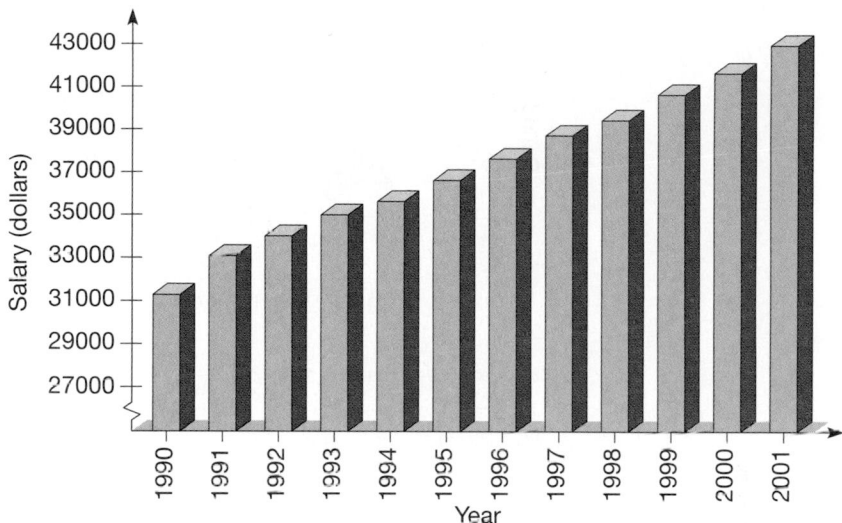

Figure 10.45 *Source*: National Education Association.

The perspective of the graph makes it difficult to see exact values. For example, the average salary in 1997 was $38,700, but to glance at the graph it could be estimated to be as much as $40,000.

Line charts with three-dimensional effects may also reduce the amount of visible information, as shown in Figure 10.46.

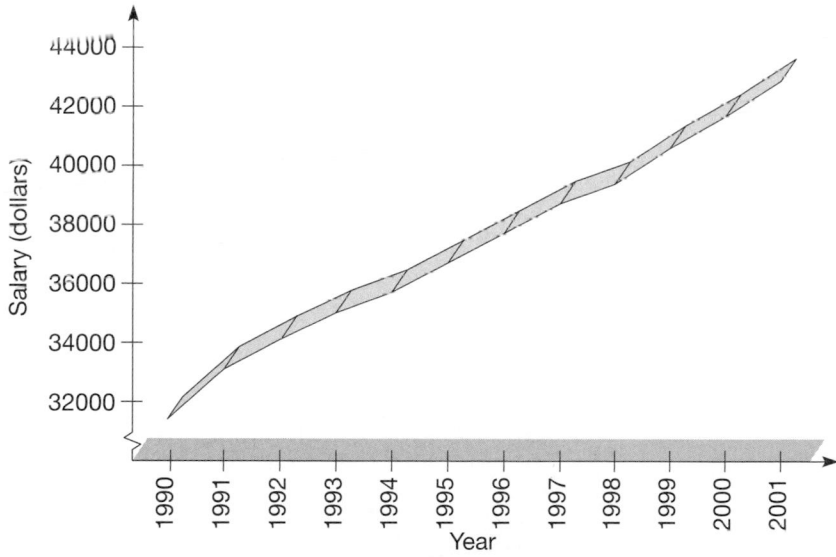

Figure 10.46 *Source*: National Education Association.

The upward trend is still apparent, but the exact values are very difficult to read. This is a graph of the same data as shown in Figures 10.45 and 10.40.

Objects, either two dimensional or three dimensional, that are used to represent quantities in pictographs can also be a point of deception. Consider the pictographs of milk cartons showing the increased consumption of skim milk from 1980 to 1995 [Figure 10.47(a)]

Pounds of Skim Milk Consumed per Capita

(a)

Pounds of Skim Milk Consumed per Capita

(b)

Figure 10.47

The amount of skim milk consumed per capita in 1995 (53.8 pounds per year) is twice as much as that consumed in 1980 (26.9 pounds per year). At first glance, it might seem appropriate to make one carton twice as tall as the other. However, looking at the pictures of the two cartons in Figure 10.47(a), we get the impression that the taller one is much more than twice the volume of the other. In addition to making the height of the larger twice the height of the smaller, the larger carton's width and depth have been doubled. Thus, the carton on the right in Figure 10.47(a) represents a volume that is $2 \times 2 \times 2 = 8$ times as large as the one on the left. The pictograph in Figure 10.47(b) shows how a 3-D pictograph could be constructed without deception.

Circle Graphs

Circle graphs allow for visual comparisons of the relative sizes of fractional parts. The graph in Figure 10.48 shows the relative sizes of the vitamin content in a serving of cornflakes and milk. Four vitamins are present—B_1, B_2, A, and C. We can conclude that most of the vitamin content is B_1 and B_2, that less vitamin A is present, and that the vitamin C content is the least. However, the graph is deceptive, in that it gives no indication whatsoever of the actual amount of these four vitamins, either by weight (say in grams) or by percentage of minimum daily requirement. Thus, although the

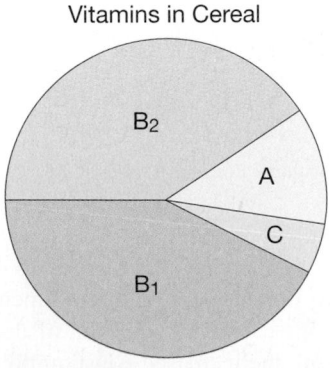

Vitamins in Cereal

Figure 10.48

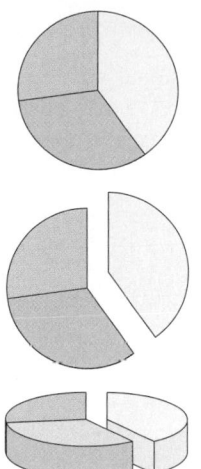

Figure 10.49

NCTM Standard
Draw inferences from charts, tables, and graphs that summarize data from real-world situations.

circle graph is excellent for picturing relative amounts, it does not necessarily indicate absolute amounts.

Circle graphs or pie charts can also be manipulated to reinforce a particular message or even to mislead. It is very common to take a sector of the "pie" and **explode** it (that is, move it slightly away from the center; Figure 10.49).

This gives the sector more emphasis and may make it seem larger than it is. Making it three-dimensional and exploding the sector makes the largest sector seem even larger still. The graph in Figure 10.50 is a good example of the dominant effect of the exploded sector representing the share of stocks owned by individuals.

Copyright 1994, USA TODAY. Reprinted with permission.

Figure 10.50

A third way in which circle graphs can be deceptive is illustrated in the following example.

Example 10.16 Figure 10.51 shows what looks like a circle graph embedded in a picture of a hamburger. It conceals a misleading piece of distortion. Can you spot it?

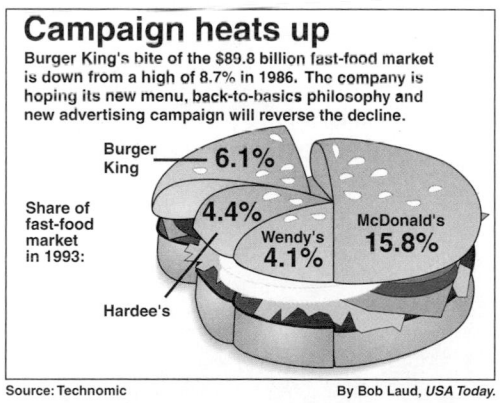

Copyright 1994, USA TODAY. Reprinted with permission.

Figure 10.51

Solution The percentages do not add up to 100%. There are only a total of 30.4%. The impression is given that McDonald's and the other chains have a much larger share of the market than they actually do. This graph also provides an example of a pictorial embellishment, which we will now discuss as another source of misleading graphs. ■

Deceptive Pictorial Embellishments

Pictorial embellishments in both two-dimensional and three-dimensional situations can also lead to confusion and be deceptive. Figure 10.52 displays a bar chart, embedded into a gasoline pump nozzle, which compares the price of gas in Tokyo, Japan; Caracas, Venezuela; and the average price in the United States.

Copyright 1994, USA TODAY. Reprinted with permission.

Figure 10.52

The chart has a visual appeal but is drawn in a misleading way. The length of the bar corresponding to Tokyo is 1 inch in the original graph, which is to represent a price of $4.58 per gallon. Thus 1 inch of bar represents $4.58. The length of the bar for the United States was 1/4 inch in the original graph so that an inch represents only $1.11 × 4 = $4.44. The length for Caracas was 1/16 inch in the original graph, giving a scale of $0.21 × 16 = $3.36 per inch. These discrepancies, while slight, make the differences appear more pronounced.

Figure 10.53 gives a variation on a bar chart by curving the bars. The point of the graphic is that Barbie dolls may be considered to be as much ambassadors of the United States as the representatives of the government. Curving the bars makes them appear to be closer to the same length because the lower edge of the "U.S. embassies" bar is compared to the upper edge of the "Barbie doll sales" bar.

Copyright 1993, USA TODAY. Reprinted with permission.

Figure 10.53

Example 10.17 The three-dimensional bar chart in Figure 10.54 compares the average size of a city in the National Football Conference with the average size of a city in the American Football Conference. What is misleading about it?

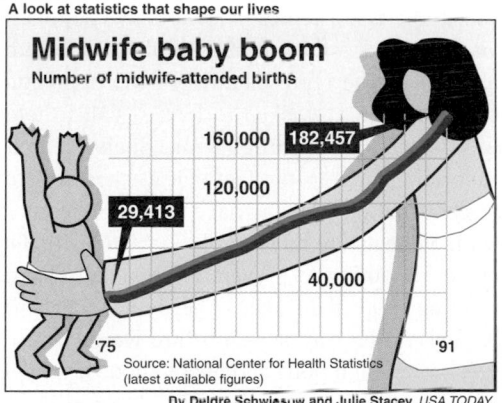

Copyright 1993, USA TODAY. Reprinted with permission.

Figure 10.54

Solution The population sizes are labeled at the top of the skyscrapers and the skyscrapers appear as bars in a bar chart. However, they are not drawn to scale. Since the NFC skyscraper is $1\frac{5}{16}$ inch tall in the original graph, a vertical inch represents 4.22 million people ($5.54/1\frac{5}{16} = 4.22$). However, a vertical inch on the AFC skyscraper in the original graph represents 5.19 million people since it is 27/32 inches tall [$4.38/(27/32) = 5.19$]. There is more deception afoot in this pictorial embellishment. The NFC building is wider than the AFC building, and the perspective gives the larger building a more imposing presence. ■

Any graph may be embedded in a picture to make it more eyecatching and provide emphasis so that you interpret the graph in a desired way. Figure 10.55 shows a line graph of the number of babies delivered by midwives. This shows a strong increasing trend.

A look at statistics that shape our lives

Midwife baby boom
Number of midwife-attended births

160,000   182,457

120,000

29,413

40,000

'75   '91

Source: National Center for Health Statistics
(latest available figures)

By Deidre Schwiesow and Julie Stacey, *USA TODAY.*

Copyright 1994, USA TODAY. Reprinted with permission.

Figure 10.55

By making the line of the graph the arm of the midwife, the eye is directed upward from the infant at the left of the graph up the arm to the midwife. This exaggerates the increasing nature of the graph.

NCTM Standards 2000
Data Analysis and
Probability
Grades 6–8
All students should use
observations about differences
between two or more samples
to make conjectures about the
populations from which the
samples were taken.

Reflection from Research
Students need help as they
transition from understanding
the colloquial term, *sample*, as a
piece of cheese on a toothpick in
a supermarket to the statistical
meaning of *sample* where
variation and representation
are important (Watson &
Moritz, 2000).

Samples and Bias

All of the examples of misleading statistics that we have looked at thus far have dealt with the way in which the data were presented. However, this assumes that the data were accurate to begin with, which may not be the case, depending on how the data were gathered. One of the most common uses of statistics is gathering and analyzing information about specific groups of people or objects. In the following, we will look at how this information is gathered and analyzed and how bias can enter this process.

As President William Jefferson Clinton was facing the possibility of impeachment during the summer and fall of 1998, one of the interesting controversies of the process was conflict between public opinion polls and the opinions of the members of the House of Representatives. A question that naturally arises regarding the public opinion polls is, "How is such information gathered?" Do the pollsters contact *every* voter in the United States? If they only contact a subset of the voters, how is that subset selected? Is the information collected from voters in the East or in the West, Republicans or Democrats, young voters or older voters? How all of these questions are addressed will determine the quality of the data collected.

The entire group in question is called the **population,** and the subset of the population that is actually observed, questioned, or analyzed is called a **sample.** If a sample is carefully chosen, we may assume that it is representative of the population and shares the main characteristics of the group. The results we obtain from the sample, such as means or percentages, can then be used as estimates for values we would find in the population. However, a great deal of care should be taken in selecting a sample.

Example 10.18 Suppose you wish to determine voter opinion regarding the ballot measure to fund the proposed new library. To determine this, you survey potential voters among the pedestrians on Main Street during the lunch hour. What is the population and what is the sample?

Solution The population consists of people who are going to vote in the upcoming election. The sample consists of those interviewed on the street who say they will be voting in the election. ■

If a sample is not representative of the population, we will draw an erroneous conclusion. A **bias** is a flaw in the sampling procedure that makes it more likely that the sample will not be representative of the population. As an example, suppose a late-night news program wished to have a call-in telephone poll on a gun control issue with a 50-cent cost of participation. Such a telephone poll has many sources of bias. An important source is the fact that it takes an effort and some expense to participate. This means that people who have strong opinions about gun control and are willing to part with 50 cents are more likely to participate. Other sources of bias include the fact that there is nothing to prevent nonresidents from participating or to prevent people from voting more than once. There are other forms of bias that can also affect the result, such as the way questions are worded. In this section, we will discuss how to analyze surveys and polls and how to choose samples that are free of bias.

Example 10.19 Suppose you wish to determine voter opinion regarding the elimination of the capital gains tax (a profit made on an investment is called a capital gain). To determine this, you survey potential voters near Wall Street in New York City. Identify a source of bias in this poll.

Solution One source of bias in choosing this sample is that many people involved in trading stocks work on Wall Street and their income could be enhanced by the elimination of the capital gains tax. The percentage of people in this sample that favor elimination is likely to be much higher than that of the population as a whole. ■

The population and sample need not always consist of people, as we see in the next example.

Example 10.20 To test the reliability of a lot (a unit of production) of automobile components produced at a certain factory, the first 30 components of a lot of 1000 are tested for defects. Describe the population, the sample, and any potential sources of bias.

Solution The population is the lot of 1000 automobile components that are produced at the factory. The sample is the set of the first 30 produced from the lot. Bias results from the fact that the first 30 are chosen. It is possible that these 30 were made with special care or that they were made at the start of the process when defects are more likely. ■

A summary of the common errors that occur when surveys are conducted is provided in Table 10.17.

Table 10.17 Common Sources of Bias Surveys

TYPE OF ERROR	DESCRIPTION
Faulty sampling	The chosen sample is not representative.
Faulty questions	Questions worded so as to influence the answers.
Faulty interviewing	Failure to interview all of the chosen sample. Misreading the questions. Misinterpreting the answers.
Lack of understanding or knowledge	The person being interviewed does not understand what is being asked or does not have the information needed
False answers	The person being interviewed intentionally gives incorrect information.

MATHEMATICAL MORSEL

Several presidential election polls went statistically awry in this century. A spectacular failure was the 1935 *Literary Digest* poll predicting that Alfred Landon would defeat Franklin Roosevelt in the 1936 election. So devastated was the *Literary Digest* by its false prediction that it subsequently ceased publication. The *Literary Digest* poll used voluntary responses from a preselected sample—but only 23% of the people in the sample responded. Evidently, the majority of those who did were more enthusiastic about their candidate (Landon) than were the majority of the entire sample. Thus the sampling error was so large that a false prediction resulted. A study by J. H. Powell showed that if the data were analyzed and weighted according to how the respondents represented the general population, they would have picked Roosevelt.

The Dewey–Truman 1948 Gallup poll also used a biased sample. Interviewers were allowed to select individuals based on certain quotas (e.g., sex, race, and age). However, the people selected tended to be more prosperous than average, which produced a sample biased toward Republican candidates. Also, the poll was conducted three weeks before the election, when Truman was gaining support and Dewey was slipping.

Nowadays, sampling procedures are done with extreme care to produce representative samples of public opinion.

Section 10.3 EXERCISE / PROBLEM SET A

EXERCISES

1. The world record time for the mile run is given in the following table:

   a. Draw a line graph of this data using 3:30.0 as the baseline for the graph.

   b. What effect does having 3:30.0 as the baseline have on the impression made by the graph?

YEAR	WORLD RECORD FOR MILE RUN	
1950	4:01.4	(4 min 1.4 sec)
1955	3:58.0	
1960	3:54.5	
1965	3:53.6	
1970	3:51.1	
1975	3:49.4	
1980	3:48.8	
1985	3:46.3	
1990	3:46.3	
1995	3:44.4	
2000	3:43.1	

2. Since 1900, the death rate related to certain causes (other than old age) in the United States has fallen, while it has risen for several other causes. For major cardiovascular disease, the death rate per 100,000 population was as follows:

1950	1980	1990	1998
510.8	434.5	368.3	347.6

   Source: National Center for Health Statistics.

   a. Draw a bar graph for this data using the same distance between each of the bars.

   b. Draw a line graph for the data having the years as the baseline with the usual spacing.

   c. Which graphing approach do you prefer? Why?

   Use the following for Problems 3 and 4.

   The following pictorial embellishment of a circle graph was taken from the May 17, 1993, issue of *Fortune* magazine. In it, the ovals that represent the "nest eggs" have lengths that are in proportion to the total amounts in the pension accounts. This tends to exaggerate the amounts they represent. That is, the area of the third oval is actually *four* times the area of the first oval although the amount it represents is only *two* times as great.

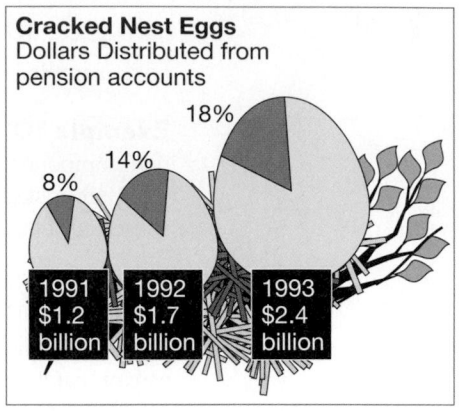

Cracked Nest Eggs
Dollars Distributed from pension accounts

18%

14%

8%

| 1991 $1.2 billion | 1992 $1.7 billion | 1993 $2.4 billion |

Credit: *Keehan for Fortune*
Source: Fidelity Investments © 1993 Time Inc. All rights reserved.

3. Create a set of three pie charts based on the data from the pictograph. Make all the circles the same size. How does making the circles the same size affect the impression about the amounts involved?

4. Create a segmented bar chart based on the data from the pictograph. Make each of the bars proportional in height to the amounts in the pension accounts.

5. The following graphs represent the average wages of employees in a given company.

   i.

   (a)

   ii.

   (b)

a. Do these graphs represent the same data?

b. What is the difference between these graphs?

c. Which graph would you use if you were the leader of a labor union seeking increased wages?

d. Which graph would you use if you were seeking to impress prospective employees with wages?

6. Health-care costs became a major issue in the last decade for both employers and employees. The following graph shows changes that occurred during this period.

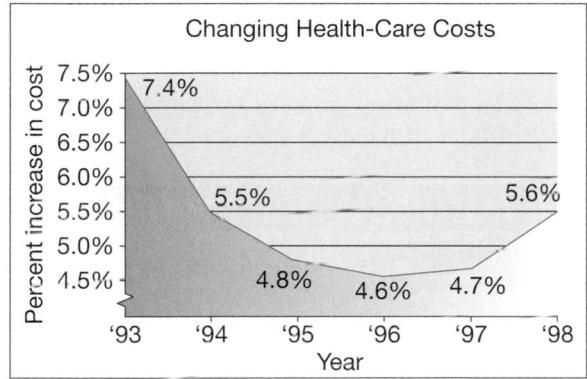

Redo the graph, showing percentage of change without shortening the vertical scale.

7. Create a 3-D bar chart for the following data.

YEAR	NEW CAR SALES (× 1000)
1992	8,213
1994	8,991
1996	8,527
1998	8,142

8. Use the following pie chart for Meat Consumption per Person, 1998, to create an "exploded" 3-D pie chart to emphasize the amount of red meat consumed per person.

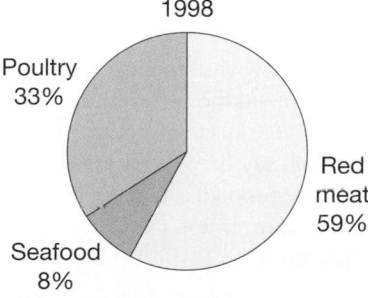

9. Using perspective with pie charts can be deceiving.

52 weeks ending June 13, 1992, in millions of units

52 weeks ending Dec. 11, 1993, in millions of units

Source: Company reports, Nielson Marketing Research, *Investors Business Daily*.

a. Use the data from these two pie charts to draw two new pie charts in the usual manner.

b. How do the pie charts you drew compare to the original ones?

c. Do the comparative pieces seem the same as before?

10. Identify three ways in which bar graphs can be deceptive.

11. a. Which of the following pictographs would be correct to show that sales have doubled from the left figure to the right figure?

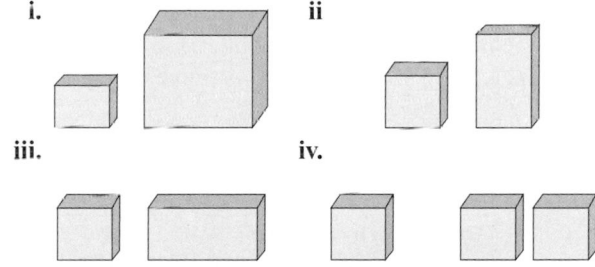

b. What is misleading about the other(s)?

In Problems 12 and 13 identify the population being studied and the sample that is actually observed.

12. A light bulb company says that its light bulbs last 2000 hours. To test this, a package of 8 bulbs is purchased and the bulbs are kept lit until they burn out. Five of the bulbs burn out before 2000 hours.

13. The registrar's office is interested in the percentage of full-time students who commute on a regular basis. One hundred students are randomly selected and briefly interviewed; 75 of these students commute on a regular basis.

PROBLEMS

14. Pictographs are often drawn incorrectly even if there is no intent to distort the data. Suppose we want to show that the number of women in the work force today is twice what it was at some time in the past. One way this could be done is to have two pictures of women representing the number of women in the work force and draw the one for today twice as tall as the one for the past, similar to what was done with the milk cartons in Figure 10.47. The problem is that most people tend to respond to graphics by comparing areas; we are also used to interpreting depth and perspective in drawings depicting three-dimensional objects.

Suppose we want to compare the revenue of two companies. Suppose company A had revenues of $5,000,000 last year and company B had $10,000,000.

a. If we want to use the area of circles to represent the revenues of the companies, what should be the radius of the circle for company B if the radius of the circle for company A is 1 inch? Explain.

b. If we want to use the volume of spheres to represent the revenues of the companies, what should be the radius of the sphere for company B if the radius of the sphere for company A is 1 inch? Explain.

15. One indicator of how well the economy is doing is the number of "Help Wanted" ads that appear in the newspapers. Redo the following graph so that the increase in 1994 appears even more dramatic than it is.

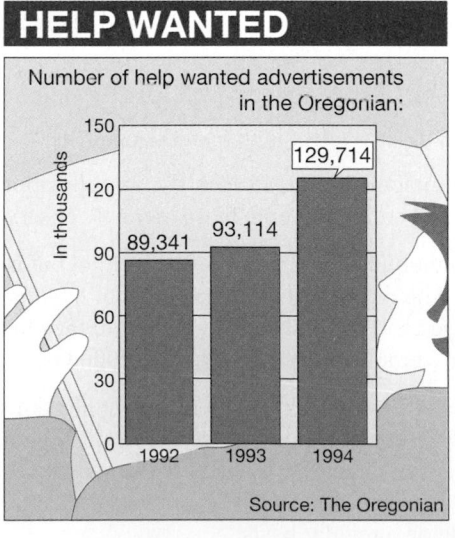

16. Prepare a vertical bar chart for the data on the federal tax burden per capita in such a way that the amount actually appears to be decreasing.

The Federal Tax Burden per Capita

FISCAL YEARS 1990–1995					
1990	1991	1992	1993	1994	1995
$4,026	$4,064	$4,153	$4,382	$4,701	$5,049 (cst)

17. Redraw the graph on the increases in the federal tax burden per capita, 1990–1995, to emphasize the changes and make the increases appear more dramatic.

18. Redo the following graph so that agriculture prices from 1988 to 1996 don't appear to change so much.

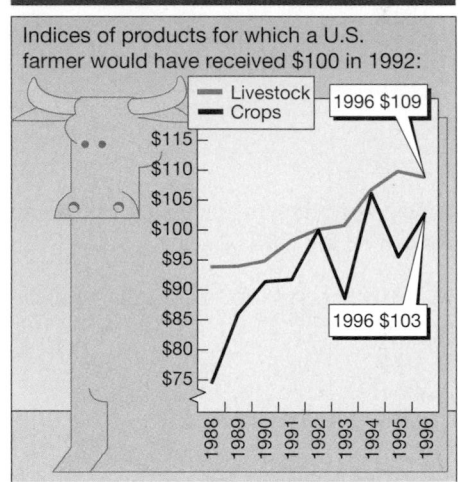

In Problems 19 and 20 identify the population being studied, the sample actually observed, and discuss any sources of bias.

19. A biologist wants to estimate the number of fish in a lake. As part of the study, 250 fish are caught, tagged, and released back into the lake. Later, 500 fish are caught and examined; 18 of these fish are found to be tagged and the rest are untagged.

20. A drug company wishes to claim that 9 out of 10 doctors recommend the active ingredients in their product. They commission a study of 20 doctors. If at least 18 doctors say they recommend the active ingredients in the product, the company will feel free to make this claim. If not, the company will commission another study.

Section 10.3 EXERCISE / PROBLEM SET B

EXERCISES

1. Harness Racing Records for the Mile

TROTTERS		PACERS	
1921	1:57.8	1904	1:56
1922	1:57	1938	1:55
1922	1:56.8	1955	1:54.8
1937	1:56.6	1960	1:54.6
1937	1:56	1966	1:54
1938	1:55.2	1966	1:53.6
1969	1:54.8	1971	1:52
1980	1:54.6	1980	1:49.2
1982	1:54	1989	1:48.4
1987	1:52.2	1993	1:46.2

Source: 1995 *Information Please* almanac.

a. Draw a line graph of the data on Trotters using 1:40.0 as the baseline for the graph.

b. What effect does having 1:40.0 as the baseline have on the impression made by the graph?

2. Redraw the bar graph from Figure 10.37 with horizontal bars, but this time reverse the order of the bars from how they appear in Figure 10.38.

a. What is the visual impression regarding profits in this graph?

b. Which graph would you use? Why?

For Problems 3 and 4 refer to the graph used for Exercise 3 in Part A.

3. Create a proportional bar graph based on the data from the pictograph. In a proportional bar chart, all bars are the same height. How does making the bars all the same height affect the impression about the amount of funds distributed?

4. Create a set of three pie charts based on the data in the pictograph. Make the area of each circle proportional to the amount in the pension fund. That is, the area of the circle for 1993 should be twice the area of the circle for 1991.

5. A circle graph with equal-sized sectors is shown in (i). The same graph is shown in (ii), but drawn as if three-dimensional and in perspective.

i.

ii.

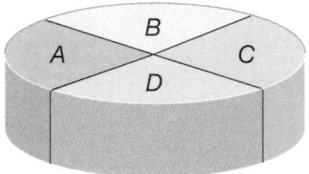

Explain how the perspective version is deceptive.

6. From 1985 to 1998, the minimum wages based on 1998 dollars is shown in the following graph. Redo the graph with a full vertical scale.

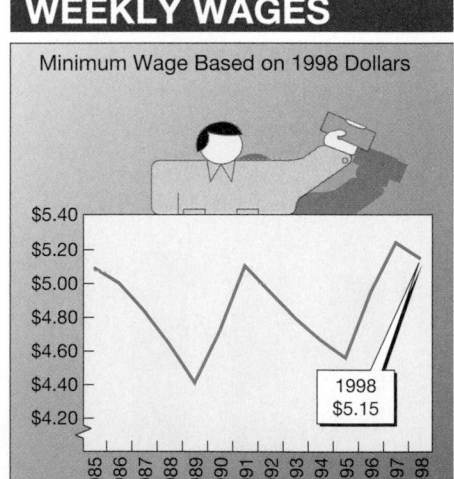

7. Create a 3-D line chart for the following data on the projected number of landfills in the United States.

YEARS	LANDFILLS
1985	6000
1990	3300
1995	2600
2000	1500
2005	1100

8. Use the pie chart from Exercise 8, Part A, to create an "exploded" 3-D pie chart to emphasize the amount of poultry consumed per person. Rotate the pie chart further to emphasize the poultry.

9. The following graphs appeared together in an environmental publication. Estimate values from each graph, combine them into a single set of numbers, and produce a single bar graph.

Smog Levels Above Standards, Selected U.S. Cities
Average Number of Days

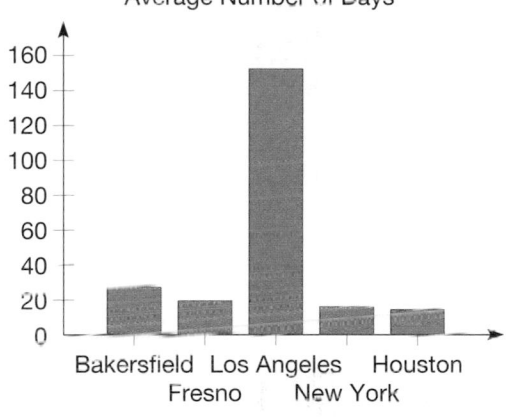

Smog Levels Above Standards, Selected Canadian Cities
Average Number of Days

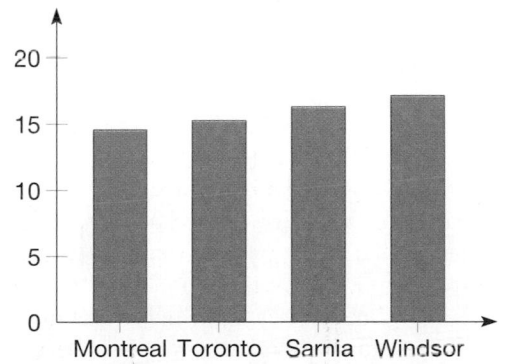

10. Identify three ways in which circle graphs can be deceptive.

11. Record sales of a certain singing group tripled from March to June. Is the following graph an accurate representation of the increase in sales? Why or why not?

Record Sales

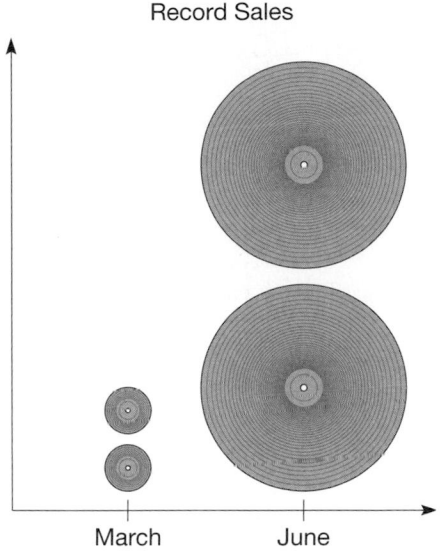

In Problems 12 and 13 identify the population being studied and the sample that is actually observed.

12. A chest of 1000 gold coins is to be presented to the king. The royal minter believes the king will not notice if only one of the coins is counterfeit. The king is suspicious and has 20 coins taken from the top of the chest and tested to see if they are pure gold.

13. The mathematics department is concerned about the amount of time students regularly set aside for studying. A questionnaire is distributed in three classes having a total of 82 students.

PROBLEMS

Use the following graph for Problems 14 and 15.

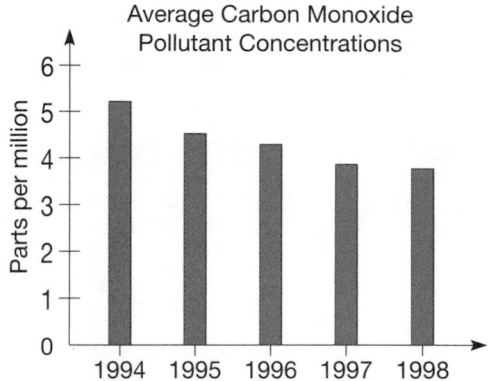

Source: U.S. Environmental Protection Agency

14. Redraw the graph on Average Carbon Monoxide Pollutant Concentration to emphasize the changes and make the decreases less dramatic.

15. Redraw the graph on Average Carbon Monoxide Pollutant Concentration to emphasize the changes and make the increases more dramatic.

16. Gun control has been a major political issue for many years. The following graph shows the number of robberies committed with firearms from 1992 to 1998.

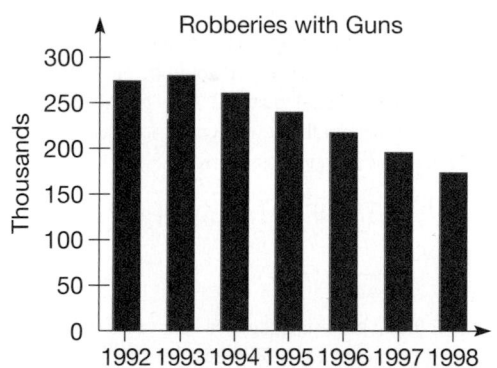

Source: U.S. Federal Bureau of Investigation

a. Redo the graph so the decrease appears even greater.

b. Redo the graph so the decrease is not so obvious.

17. During the 1980s and early 1990s, many changes occurred with respect to the work force, including downsizing and hiring of temporary employees. As a result, job security became a significant concern. The following graph shows the changes in attitude among workers.

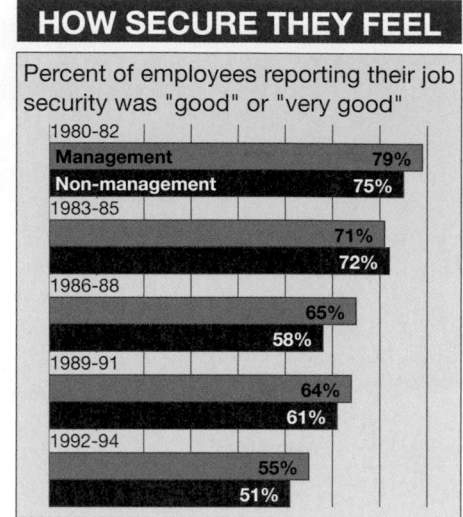

Redo the graph so that

a. the downward trend is obvious.

b. the trend is apparently even worse than it is.

In Problems 18 and 19 identify the population being studied, the sample actually observed, and discuss any sources of bias.

18. A college professor is up for promotion. Teaching performance, as judged through student evaluations, is a significant factor in the decision. The professor is asked to choose one of his classes for student evaluations. The day of the evaluations he passes out questionnaires and then remains in the room to answer any questions about the form and filling it out.

19. There are two candidates for student body president of a college. Candidate Johnson believes that the student body resources should be used to enhance the social atmosphere of the college and that the number one priority should be dances, concerts, and other social events. Candidate Jackson believes that sports should be the number one priority and wants to subsidize student sporting events and enlarge the recreation facility. A poll is taken by the student newspaper. One interviewer goes to a coffeehouse near the college one evening and asks students which candidate they prefer. Another interviewer goes to the gym and asks students which candidate they prefer.

PROBLEMS FOR WRITING/DISCUSSION

1. Discuss the misleading attributes of the following graph and what could be done to the graph to make it more mathematically accurate.

2. If only part of a vertical axis on a graph is shown (see Figures 10.36, 10.39, and 10.40), does it necessarily mean

that the graph was constructed with the intent to deceive? Discuss some legitimate reasons for cropping a graph.

3. Identify any misleading features of the following graph and discuss what could be done to correct them.

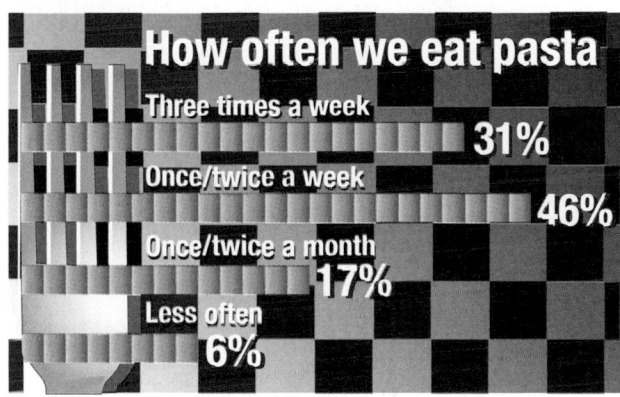

END OF CHAPTER MATERIAL

Solution of Initial Problem

A servant was asked to perform a job that would take 30 days. The servant would be paid 1000 gold coins. The servant replied, "I will happily complete the job, but I would rather be paid 1 copper coin on the first day, 2 copper coins on the second day, 4 on the third day, and so on, with the payment of copper coins doubling each day." The king agreed to the servant's method of payment. If a gold coin is worth 1000 copper coins, did the king make the right decision? How much was the servant paid?

Strategy: Look for a Formula

Make a table.

DAY	PAYMENT (COPPER COINS)	TOTAL PAYMENT TO DATE
1	$1 = 2^0$	1
2	$2 = 2^1$	$1 + 2 = 3$
3	$4 = 2^2$	$1 + 2 + 4 = 7$
4	$8 = 2^3$	$1 + 2 + 4 + 8 = 15$
5	$16 = 2^4$	$1 + 2 + 4 + 8 + 16 = 31$
.	.	.
.	.	.
.	.	.
n	2^{n-1}	$1 + 2 + 4 + 8 + \cdots + 2^{n-1} = S$

From our table we see on the nth day, where n is a whole number from 1 to 30, the servant is paid 2^{n-1} copper coins. His total payment through n days is $1 + 2 + 4 + \cdots + 2^{n-1}$ copper coins. Hence we wish to find a formula for $1 + 2 + \cdots + 2^{n-1}$. From the table it appears that this sum is 2^{n-1}. (Check this for $n = 1, 2, 3, 4, 5$.) Notice that this formula allows us to make a quick calculation of the value of S for any whole number n. In particular, for $n = 30$, $S = 2^{30} - 1$, so the servant would be paid $2^{30} - 1$ copper coins altogether. Using a calculator, $2^{30} - 1 = 1,073,741,823$. Hence the servant is paid the equivalent of 1,073,741.823 gold coins. The king made a very costly error!

Additional Problems Where the Strategy "Look for a Formula" Is Useful

1. Hector's parents suggest the following allowance arrangements for a 30-week period: a penny a day for the first week, 3 cents a day for the second week, 5 cents a day for the third week, and so on, or $2 a week. Which deal should he take?

2. Jack's beanstalk increases its height by $\frac{1}{2}$ the first day, $\frac{1}{3}$ the second day, $\frac{1}{4}$ the third day, and so on. What is the smallest number of days it would take to become at least 100 times as tall as its original height?

3. How many different (nonzero) angles are formed in a fan of rays like the one pictured on the left, but one having 100 rays?

People in Mathematics

Mina Rees (1902–1997) Mina Rees graduated from Hunter College, a women's school where mathematics was one of the most popular majors. "I wanted to be in the mathematics department, not because of its practical uses at all; it was because it was such fun!" Ironically, much of her recognition in mathematics has been for practical results. During World War II, she served on the National Defense Research Committee, working on wartime applications of mathematics. Later, she was director of mathematical sciences in the Office of Naval Research. Rees also taught for many years at Hunter College and the City College of New York, where she served as president. After her retirement, she was active in the applications of research to social problems. "I have always found that mathematics was an advantage when I was dean or president of a college. If your habit is to organize things a certain way, the way a mathematician does, then you are apt to have an organization that is easier to present and explain."

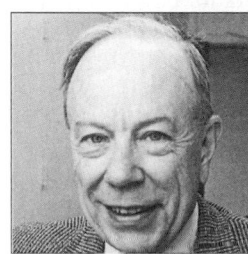

Andrew Gleason (1921–) Andrew Gleason says that he has always had a knack for solving problems. As a young man, he worked in cryptanalysis during World War II. The work involved problems in statistics and probability, and Gleason—despite having only a bachelor's degree—found that he understood the problems better than many experienced mathematicians. After the war, he made his mark in the mathematical world when he contributed to the solution of Hilbert's famous Fifth Problem. Today, Gleason is a longtime professor of mathematics at Harvard. "[As part of the School Mathematics Project] I worked with a group of kids who had just finished the first grade. One day I produced some squared paper and said, 'Here's how you multiply.' I drew a 3 × 4 rectangle and said, 'This is 3 times 4; we count the squares and get 12. So 3 × 4 is 12.' Then I did another, 4 × 5. Then I gave each kid some paper and said, 'You do some.' They were very soon doing two-digit problems."

CHAPTER REVIEW

Review the following terms and exercises to determine which require learning or relearning—page numbers are provided for easy reference.

SECTION 10.1: Organizing and Picturing Information

VOCABULARY/NOTATION

Line plot (or dot plot)   415
Frequency   416
Stem and leaf plot   416
Gap   416
Cluster   416
Back-to-back stem and leaf plot   416

Histogram   417
Bar graph   417
Line graph   420
Circle graph   421
Pie chart   421
Pictograph   422

Pictorial embellishments   422
Scatterplot   423
Outlier   424
Regression line   424
Correlation   424

EXERCISES

1. Construct a back-to-back stem and leaf plot for the following two data sets:

   Class 1: 72, 74, 76, 74, 23, 78, 37, 79, 80, 23, 81, 90, 82, 39, 94, 96, 41, 94, 94

   Class 2: 17, 99, 25, 97, 29, 40, 39, 97, 40, 95, 92, 89, 40, 49, 40, 85, 52, 80, 52, 51

2. Construct a histogram for the data for class 1 in Exercise 1 using intervals $0-9$, $10-19$, . . . , $90-100$.

3. Draw a multiple-bar graph to represent the following two data sets.

YEAR	1988	1990	1992	1994	1996
SALARIES OF BEGINNING ELEMENTARY TEACHERS (IN THOUSANDS OF DOLLARS)	18.9	19.1	19.4	19.7	20.6
SALARIES OF BEGINNING SECONDARY TEACHERS (IN THOUSANDS OF DOLLARS)	19.6	20.3	20.9	21.8	22.5

4. Draw a double-line graph representing the data sets in Exercise 3.

5. Draw a circle graph to display the following data: Fruit, 30%; Vegetable, 40%; Meat, 10%; Milk, 10%; Others, 10%.

6. The manager of a sporting goods store notes that high levels of rainfall have a negative effect on sales of beach equipment and apparel. Sales in thousands of dollars and summer rainfall in inches measured for various years are recorded in the following table.

RAIN (IN INCHES)	SALES (IN THOUSANDS OF DOLLARS)
10	300
22	120
20	160
2	360
21	180
5	320
18	340

Make a scatterplot of these data. Identify any outliers. Sketch a regression line. If the predicted rainfall for the coming summer is 15 inches, what is the best prediction for sales? If the sales in one year were $260,000, what is the best guess for rainfall that summer?

SECTION 10.2: Analyzing Data

VOCABULARY/NOTATION

Measures of central tendency   437
Mode   437
Median   438
Arithmetic average   438
Mean   438
Box and whisker plot   439
Lower quartile   439

Upper quartile   439
Interquartile range (IQR)   440
Outlier   440
Percentile   443
nth percentile   443
Measures of dispersion   443
Range   443

Variance   443
Standard deviation   444
z-score   446
Relative frequency   447
Distribution   447
Normal distribution   449

EXERCISES

1. Determine the mode, median, and mean of the data set: 1, 2, 3, 5, 9, 9, 13, 14, 14, 14.

2. Construct the box and whisker plot for the data in Exercise 1.

3. Find the range, variance, and standard deviation of the data set in Exercise 1.

4. Find the z-scores for 2, 5, and 14 for the data set in Exercise 1.

5. What is the usefulness of the z-score of a number?

6. In a normal distribution, approximately what percent of the data are within 1 standard deviation of the mean?

7. On a test whose scores form a normal distribution, approximately how many of the scores have a z-score between -2 and 2?

8. Find the percentile of 2, 5, and 14 for the data set in Exercise 1.

SECTION 10.3: Misleading Graphs and Statistics

VOCABULARY/NOTATION

Scaling   458
Cropping   461
Three-dimensional effects   462

Explode   465
Deceptive pictorial
   embellishments   466

Population   468
Sample   468
Bias   468

EXERCISES

1. From April 1993 to April 1994, the average weekly wages in manufacturing in Oregon went through many changes, as shown in the following graph. Redo the graph with a full vertical scale.

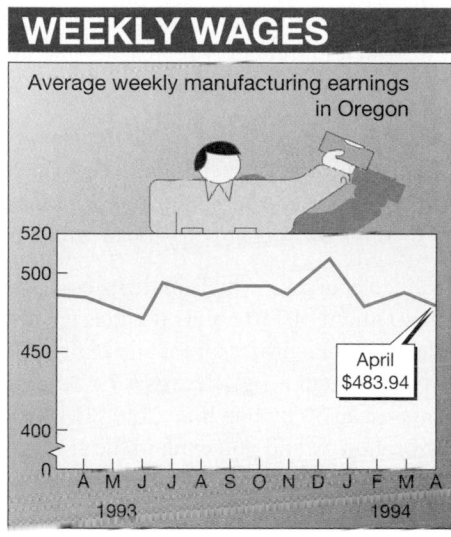

2. Health-care reform has become a major political issue. The following graph shows health-care spending as a percentage of the gross domestic product (GDP). The GDP is the value of all goods and services produced in the national economy.

a. Redo the graph so the increase appears even greater.

b. Redo the graph so the increase is not so dramatic.

3. Use the data in Problem 1 of Section 10.3 Problems for Writing/Discussion to construct a circle graph. Construct a second circle graph of this same data with the sector representing "the kids" exploded.

4. On the first page of this chapter evaluate the graph about "college seniors' plans." Discuss what aspects of the pictorial embellishment might be misleading.

5. We wish to determine the opinion of the voters in a certain town with regard to allowing in-line skating in the town square. A survey is taken of adult passersby near the local high school one late afternoon. What is the population in this case? What is the sample? What sources of bias might there be in the sampling procedure?

6. In the following scenario, identify and discuss any sources of bias in the sampling method.

   A Minnesota-based toothpaste company claims that 90% of dentists prefer the formula in its toothpaste to any other. To prove this, they conduct a study. They send questionnaires to 100 dentists in the Minneapolis–St. Paul area asking if they prefer this formula to others.

PROBLEMS FOR WRITING/DISCUSSION

1. Five houses sold for $90,000, $100,000, $105,000, $120,000, and $224,000. Would the mean or the median be the better representative of house prices in this neighborhood? Explain.

2. Could the mode ever be the most representative average of a set of data? Explain your reasoning and give an example.

3. If you want to compare two sets of data, would you use two box and whisker plots or a double stem and leaf? What are the advantages of each?

4. Suppose you need to find out how many miles per day are driven by the typical 30-year-old driver in your state. How would you go about compiling these statistics? What information would you need, and how would you go about finding it? Discuss.

5. In a normal distribution of test scores are the median and mean equal? What does it mean if the median is greater than the mean?

6. Statistics are used for keeping track of trends. We try to explain/rationalize these trends and, from inferences, predict future events. Suppose you learned that the number of births to teenage mothers in the United States had been tabulated in 1990, 1995, and 2000, and each time the number had increased dramatically. You wish to predict the number of births to teen mothers in the year 2005. What would you need to know?

7. One of the students in your class was absent the day of the test. The teacher announced that the class average for the 24 students who took the test was 75%. After the other student returned and took the test, the teacher announced that the class average had increased to 76%. Explain how you can calculate what the absentee student got on her test.

8. Sketch two pictographs, one of which accurately illustrates that Miata sales tripled in 1999, and the other of which inaccurately represents that information. Explain the difference.

9. A nineteenth-century British prime minister, Benjamin Disraeli, is said to have exclaimed, "There are lies, damned lies, and statistics." Can you explain what he meant by this? Do you agree? Why or why not?

10. In a college course in which students could accumulate a maximum of 750 points per quarter, a student complained to the professor that he really deserved a B− even though his grade was a 79. After all, he only missed an 80 by one little point. If you were the professor, how would you explain the student's error?

CHAPTER TEST

Knowledge

1. True or false?

   a. The mode of a collection of data is the middle score.

   b. The range is the last number minus the first number in a collection of data.

   c. A z-score is the number of standard deviations away from the median.

   d. The median is always greater than the mean.

   e. A circle graph is effective in displaying relative amounts.

   f. Pictographs can be used to mislead by displaying two dimensions when only one of the dimensions represents the data.

   g. Every large group of data has a normal distribution.

   h. In a normal distribution, more than half of the data are contained within 1 standard deviation from the mean.

   i. When determining the opinion of a voting population, the larger the sample the better.

   j. A score in the 37th percentile is greater than 63% of all of the scores.

   k. When the vertical axis of a bar graph is cropped or compressed, it is done to mislead the reader.

2. Identify three measures of central tendency and two measures of dispersion.

3. Identify the kinds of information that bar graphs and line graphs are good for picturing and circle graphs are not. Conversely, identify the kinds of information that circle graphs are good for picturing but bar and line graphs are not.

Skill

4. If a portion of a circle graph is to represent 30%, what will be the measure of the corresponding central angle?

5. Find the mean, median, mode, and range of the following data: 5, 7, 3, 8, 10, 3.

6. If a collection of data has a mean of 17 and a standard deviation of 3, what numbers would have z-scores of -2, -1, 1, and 2?

7. Calculate the standard deviation for the following data: 15, 1, 9, 13, 17, 8, 3.

8. On a football team with a mean weight of 220 pounds and a standard deviation of the weights being 35 pounds, what percentile is a 170-pound receiver or a 290-pound lineman?

9. Using the following scores, construct a box and whisker plot.

   97, 54, 81, 80, 69, 94, 86, 79, 82, 64, 84, 72, 78

10. Use the data in the following golf ball advertisement to produce a new bar graph in which the length of each bar is proportional to the combined distances it represents.

ULTRA® DISTANCE	
	591.2 yds
DUNLOP® DOH IV	
	584.2 yds
MAXFLI® MO	
	571.2 yds
TITLEIST® HVC	
	568.3 yds
TOP FLITE® Tour 80	
	565.9 yds
TOP FLITE® MAGNA	
	564.3 yds
Combined yardage with a driver, #5 iron, and #9 iron	

11. A statistics professor gives an 80-point test to his class, with the following scores:

   35, 44, 48, 55, 56, 57, 60, 61, 62, 62, 63, 64, 67, 70, 71, 71, 75

   To provide an example of how histograms might be constructed, she is considering two options.

   a. Grouping the data into subintervals of length 10, beginning with 71–80, 61–70, etc.

   b. Grouping the data into subintervals of length 8, beginning with 73–80, 65–72, etc.

   Draw the histogram for each option.

12. A sociologist working for a large school system is interested in demographic information on the families having children in the schools served by the system. Two hundred students are randomly selected from the school system's database and a questionnaire is sent to the home address in care of the parents or guardian. Identify the population being studied and the sample that was actually observed.

Understanding

13. If possible, give a single list of data such that the mean equals the mode and the mode is less than the median. If impossible, explain why.

14. If possible, give a collection of data for which the standard deviation is zero and the mean is nonzero. If impossible, explain why.

15. Give a reason justifying the use of each histogram constructed in Problem 11. Why might the professor use the first one? Why might she use the second one?

16. Explain how pictographs can be deceptive.

17. Give an example of two sets of data with the same means and different standard deviations.

18. Explain how line graphs can be deceptive.

19. What type of graph would be best for displaying the data in the following table? Justify your answer and construct the graph.

High School Graduates Enrolled in College

YEAR	MALE	FEMALE
1990	57.8	62.0
1991	57.6	67.1
1992	59.6	63.8
1993	59.7	65.4
1994	60.6	63.2
1995	62.6	61.4
1996	60.1	69.7

Source: U.S. National Center for Educational Statistics.

20. Redraw the following graph of the increases in the federal tax burden per capita, 1990–1995, to deemphasize the changes. Manipulate the horizontal and/or vertical axes so that the increases appear less dramatic.

The Federal Tax Burden per Capita, Fiscal Years 1990–1995

1990	1991	1992	1993	1994	1995
$4,026	$4,064	$4,163	$4,382	$4,701	$5,049 (est)

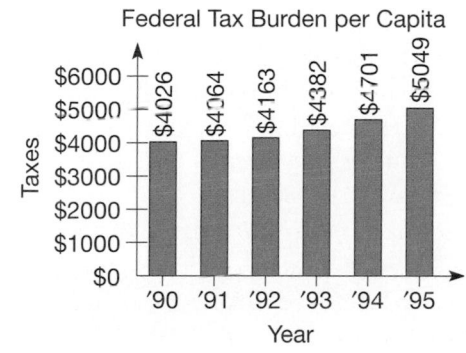

Problem-Solving/Application

21. In a distribution, the number 7 has a *z*-score of -2 and the number 19 has a *z*-score of 1. What is the mean of the distribution?

22. If the mean of the numbers 1, 3, *x*, 7, 11 is 9, what is *x*?

23. On which test did Ms. Brown's students perform the best compared to the national averages? Explain.

	MS. BROWN'S CLASS AVERAGE	NATIONAL AVERAGE	AVERAGE DEVIATION
Reading	77.9	75.2	12.3
Mathematics	75.2	74.1	14.2
Science	74.3	70.3	13.6
Social studies	71.7	69.3	10.9

24. Identify any possible sources of bias in the sampling procedure in the following scenario.

   A soft-drink company produces a lemon-lime drink that it says people prefer by a margin of two-to-one over its main competitor, a cola. To prove this claim, it sets up a booth in a large shopping mall where customers are allowed to try both drinks. The customers are filmed for a possible television commercial. They are asked which drink they prefer.

25. On the first page of this chapter evaluate the graph about "dominating college lacrosse." Discuss what aspects of the graph might be misleading.

References for Reflections from Research

BOHAN, H., & MORELAND, M. J. (1981). Developing some statistical concepts in the elementary school. In A. P. Shulte & J. R. Smart (Eds.), *Teaching Statistics and Probability* (pp. 60–63). Reston, VA: National Council of Teachers of Mathematics.

BROWN, C. A., & SILVER, E. A. (1989). Data organization and interpretation. In M. M. Lindquist (Ed.), *Results from the fourth mathematics assessment of the National Assessment of Education Progress*. Reston, VA: National Council of Teachers of Mathematics.

CHOATE, L. D., & OKEY, J. K. (1981). Graphically speaking: Primary level graphing experiences. In A. P. Shulte & J. R. Smart (Eds.), *Teaching statistics and probability* (pp. 33–40). Reston, VA: National Council of Teachers of Mathematics.

LANDWEHR, J. M., SWIFT, J., & WATKINS, A. E. (1987). *Exploring surveys and information from samples: Quantitative literacy series*. Palo Alto, CA: Dale Seymour.

SHAW, J. M. (1984). Making graphs. *Arithmetic Teacher*, *31*(5), 7–11.

WATSON, J. M., & MORITZ, J. B. (2000). Developing concepts of sampling. *Journal for Research in Mathematics Education*, *31*, 44–70.

CHAPTER 11

Probability

FOCUS ON Probability in the Everyday World

I t is generally agreed that the science of probability began in the sixteenth century from the so-called *problem of the points*. The problem is to determine the division of the stakes of two equally skilled players when a game of chance is interrupted before either player has obtained the required number of points in order to win. However, real progress on this subject began in 1654 when Chevalier de Mere, an experienced gambler whose theoretical understanding of the problem did not match his observations, approached the mathematician Blaise Pascal for assistance. Pascal communicated with Fermat about the problem and, remarkably, each solved the problem by different means. Thus, in this correspondence, Pascal and Fermat laid the foundations of probability.

Blaise Pascal

Now, probability is recognized in many aspects of our lives. For example, when you were conceived, you could have had any of 8,388,608 different sets of characteristics based on 23 pairs of chromosomes. In school, if you guess at random on a 10-item true/false test, there is only about a 17% probability that you will answer 7 or more questions correctly. In the manufacturing process, quality control is becoming the buzzword. Thus it is important to know the probability that certain parts will fail when deciding to revamp a production process or offer a warranty. In investments, advisers assign probabilities to future prices in an effort to decide among various investment opportunities. Another important use of probability is in actuarial science, which is used to determine insurance premiums. Probability also continues to play a role in games of chance such as dice and cards.

One very popular application of probability is the famous "birthday problem." Simply stated, in a group of people, what is the probability of two people having the same month and day of birth? Surprisingly, the probability of such matching birth dates is about 0.5 when there are 23 people and almost 0.9 when there are 40 people. An interesting application of this problem is the birthdays of the 39 American presidents through Reagan. Presidents Polk and Harding were both born on November 2 and Presidents Andrew Johnson and Wilson were both born on December 29. The surprising solution of this problem will be possible using the concepts developed in this chapter.

Problem Solving Strategies

1. Guess and Test
2. Use a Variable
3. Draw a Picture
4. Look for a Pattern
5. Make a List
6. Solve a Simpler Problem
7. Draw a Diagram
8. Use Direct Reasoning
9. Use Indirect Reasoning
10. Use Properties of Numbers
11. Solve an Equivalent Problem
12. Work Backward
13. Use Cases
14. Solve an Equation
15. Look for a Formula
16. **Do a Simulation**

Strategy
Do A Simulation

A simulation is a representation of an experiment using some appropriate objects (slips of paper, dice, etc.) or perhaps a computer program. The purpose of a simulation is to run many replications of an experiment that may be difficult or impossible to perform. As you will see, to solve the following Initial Problem, it is easier to simulate the problem than to perform the actual experiment many times by questioning five strangers repeatedly.

Initial Problem

At a party, a friend bets you that at least two people in a group of five strangers will have the same astrological sign. Should you take the bet? Why or why not?

Clues

The Do a Simulation strategy may be appropriate when

- A problem involves a complicated probability experiment.
- An actual experiment is too difficult or impossible to perform.
- A problem has a repeatable process that can be done experimentally.
- Finding the actual answer requires techniques not previously developed.

A solution of the Initial Problem appears on page 540.

INTRODUCTION

In this chapter we discuss the fundamental concepts and principles of probability. Probability is the branch of mathematics that enables us to predict the likelihood of uncertain occurrences. There are many applications and uses of probability in the sciences (meteorology and medicine, for example), in sports and games, and in business, to name a few areas. Because of its widespread usefulness, the study of probability is an essential component of a comprehensive mathematics curriculum. In the first section of this chapter we develop the main concepts of probability. In the second section some counting procedures are introduced that lead to more sophisticated methods for computing probabilities. In the third section, simulations are developed and several applications of probability are presented. Finally, in the last section, additional counting methods referred to as permutations and combinations are discussed. These methods are used to determine probabilities on large sets.

11.1   PROBABILITY AND SIMPLE EXPERIMENTS

A red cube, a white cube, and a blue cube are placed in a box. One cube is randomly drawn, its color is recorded, and it is returned to the box. A second cube is drawn and its color recorded. What are the chances (probability) of drawing a red cube? (*Hint:* Drawing a red cube could be done on the first draw, the second draw, or both draws.)

Simple Experiments

Probability is the mathematics of chance. Example 11.1 illustrates how probability is commonly used and reported.

Reflection from Research
When teachers use contexts (e.g., a lottery) for teaching probability concepts, many elementary students have difficulty learning the mathematical concepts because their personal experiences interfere (e.g., "It's impossible to win the lottery because no one in my family has ever won.") (Taylor & Biddulph, 1994).

Example 11.1
a. The probability of precipitation today is 80%.
   Interpretation: On days in the past with atmospheric conditions like today's, it rained at some time on 80% of the days.

b. The odds that a patient improves using drug X are 60 : 40.
   Interpretation: In a group of 100 patients who have had the same symptoms as the patient being treated, 60 of them improved when administered drug X, and 40 did not.

c. The chances of winning the lottery game "Find the Winning Ticket" are 1 in 150,000.
   Interpretation: If 150,000 lottery tickets are printed, only one of the tickets is the winning ticket. If more tickets are printed, the fraction of winning tickets is approximately $\frac{1}{150,000}$.   ■

Probability tells us the relative frequency with which we expect an event to occur. Thus it can be reported as a fraction, decimal, percent, or ratio. The greater the probability, the more likely the event is to occur. Conversely, the smaller the probability, the less likely the event is to occur.

To study probability in a mathematically precise way, we need special terminology and notation. An **experiment** is the act of making an observation or taking a measurement. An **outcome** is one of the possible things that can occur as a result of an experiment. The set of all the possible outcomes is called the **sample space.** Finally, an **event** is any subset of the sample space.

Since a sample space is a set, it is commonly represented in set notation with the letter *S*. Similarly, because an event is a subset, in set notation, it is frequently represented with letters like *A*, *B*, *C*, or the generic letter *E* for event. These concepts are illustrated in Example 11.2.

Example 11.2

a. Experiment: Toss a fair coin and record whether the top side is heads or tails.

Sample Space: There are two possible outcomes when tossing a coin, heads or tails. Hence the sample space is $S = \{H, T\}$, where H and T are abbreviations for heads and tails, respectively.

Event: Since an event is simply a subset of the sample space, we will first consider all the subsets of the sample space *S*. The subsets are $\{\}, \{H\}, \{T\}, \{H, T\}$. It is not always the case that we can describe in words an event associated with each subset, but in this case we can. The events are as follows:

$$A = \text{getting a heads} = \{H\}$$
$$B = \text{getting a tails} = \{T\}$$
$$C = \text{getting either a heads or a tails} = \{H, T\}$$
$$D = \text{getting neither a heads nor a tails} = \{\}$$

Figure 11.1

Reflection from Research
When presented with a regular, six-sided die or a bag with six identical balls numbered one to six, many children feel the die is "fairer" (Truran, 1995).

b. Experiment: Roll a standard six-sided die with one, two, three, four, five, and six dots on the six faces (Figure 11.1). Record the number of dots showing on the top face.

Sample Space: There are six outcomes:—1, 2, 3, 4, 5, 6—where numerals represent the number of dots. Thus the sample space is $S = \{1, 2, 3, 4, 5, 6\}$.

Event: For this experiment, there are many more events than for the previous example of tossing a single coin. In fact, there are $2^6 = 64$ possible events. Each event is a subset of *S*. Some of the events are:

$$A = \text{getting a prime number of dots} = \{2, 3, 5\}$$
$$B = \text{getting an even number of dots} = \{2, 4, 6\}$$
$$C = \text{getting more than 4 dots} = \{5, 6\}$$

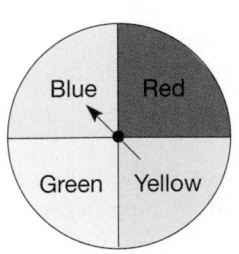

Figure 11.2

c. Experiment: Spin a spinner as shown in Figure 11.2 once and record the color of the indicated region.

Sample Space: There are 4 different colored regions (outcomes) on this spinner, so the sample space is $S = \{R, Y, G, B\}$. It is important to note that the regions on the spinner are the same size. If they were not the same size, we would have to approach the sample space differently.

Event: Some of the possible events for this experiment are:

$$A = \text{pointing to the red region} = \{R\}$$
$$B = \text{pointing to a blue or green region} = \{B, G\}$$
$$C = \text{pointing to a region with a primary color} = \{R, Y, B\}$$

STUDENT PAGE SNAPSHOT

 Enrichment

> More of the spinner is red. I am more likely to spin red.

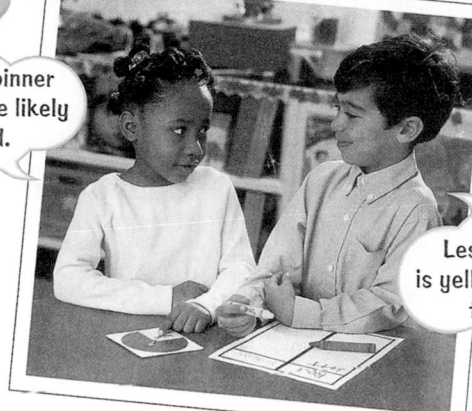

> Less of the spinner is yellow. I am less likely to spin yellow.

Circle more likely or less likely. Tell how you decided.

1. The spinner will land on yellow.

   more likely

(less likely)

The spinner will land on blue.

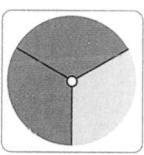   more likely

less likely

2. The spinner will land on green.

   more likely

less likely

The spinner will land on red.

   more likely

less likely

3. The spinner will land on blue.

   more likely

less likely

The spinner will land on green.

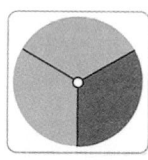   more likely

less likely

512 five hundred twelve

McGraw-Hill, MCGRAW-HILL MATHEMATICS "Enrichment," Grade 1, p. 512. Copyright © 2002 by The McGraw-Hill Companies. Reproduced with permission of the publisher.

487

d. Experiment: A single card is drawn from a standard deck of playing cards. The suit and type of card are recorded.

Sample Space: There are 4 suits [diamonds (♦), hearts (♥), spades (♠), and clubs (♣)] and 13 cards (2, 3, 4, 5, 6, 7, 8, 9, 10, jack, queen, king, and ace) in each suit for a total of 52 possible outcomes.

$$
\begin{aligned}
S = \{ & 2♦, 3♦, 4♦, 5♦, 6♦, 7♦, 8♦, 9♦, 10♦, J♦, Q♦, K♦, A♦, \\
& 2♥, 3♥, 4♥, 5♥, 6♥, 7♥, 8♥, 9♥, 10♥, J♥, Q♥, K♥, A♥, \\
& 2♠, 3♠, 4♠, 5♠, 6♠, 7♠, 8♠, 9♠, 10♠, J♠, Q♠, K♠, A♠, \\
& 2♣, 3♣, 4♣, 5♣, 6♣, 7♣, 8♣, 9♣, 10♣, J♣, Q♣, K♣, A♣ \}
\end{aligned}
$$

Event: This sample space of 52 elements has $2^{52} = 4{,}503{,}599{,}627{,}370{,}496$ different subsets (events). Some of the events are:

$$
\begin{aligned}
A = \text{drawing a diamond} = \{ & 2♦, 3♦, 4♦, 5♦, 6♦, 7♦, 8♦, 9♦, \\
& 10♦, J♦, Q♦, K♦, A♦ \} \\
B = \text{drawing a face card} = \{ & J♦, Q♦, K♦, J♥, Q♥, K♥, J♠, Q♠, K♠, \\
& J♣, Q♣, K♣ \} \\
C = \text{drawing a diamond or face card} = \{ & 2♦, 3♦, 4♦, 5♦, 6♦, 7♦, 8♦, \\
& 9♦, 10♦, J♦, Q♦, K♦, A♦, J♥, Q♥, K♥, \\
& J♠, Q♠, K♠, J♣, Q♣, K♣ \} \\
D = \text{drawing a diamond face card} = \{ & J♦, Q♦, K♦ \}
\end{aligned}
$$

Notice that $D = A \cap B$ and $C = A \cup B$. ■

NCTM Standards 2000
Data Analysis and
Probability
Grades 3–5
All students should describe events as likely or unlikely and discuss the degree of likelihood using such words as *certain*, *equally likely*, and *impossible*.

Computing Probabilities in Simple Experiments

The probability of an event, E, is the fraction (decimal, percent, or ratio) indicating the relative frequency with which event E should occur in a given sample space S. Two events are **equally likely** if they occur with equal relative frequency (i.e., equally often).

● DEFINITION

Probability of an Event with Equally Likely Outcomes

Suppose that all of the outcomes in the nonempty sample space S of an experiment are equally likely to occur. Let E be an event, $n(E)$ be the number of outcomes in E, and $n(S)$ the number of outcomes in S. Then the **probability of event E**, denoted $P(E)$, is

$$
P(E) = \frac{\text{number of elements in } E}{\text{number of elements in } S},
$$

or in symbols

$$
P(E) = \frac{n(E)}{n(S)}.
$$

Using this definition, we can compute the probabilities of some of the events described in Example 11.2.

Example 11.3

a. What is the probability of getting tails when tossing a fair coin?

b. For the experiment of rolling a standard six-sided die and recording the number of dots on the top face, what is the probability of getting a prime number?

c. On the spinner found in Figure 11.2, what is the probability of pointing to a primary color?

d. For the experiment of drawing a card from a standard deck of playing cards, what is the probability of getting a diamond? What is the probability of getting a diamond face card?

Solution

a. While the probability of getting tails might seem like common sense, we will discuss it in terms of the definition in order to lay the groundwork for more complicated probabilities. The sample space for this experiment is $S = \{H, T\}$, where each of the outcomes is equally likely. The event of getting tails corresponds to the subset $B = \{T\}$. Thus the probability of getting tails is

$$P(B) = \frac{n(B)}{n(S)} = \frac{1}{2}.$$

b. Since all of the outcomes in the sample space $S = \{1, 2, 3, 4, 5, 6\}$ are equally likely and the event of getting a prime number is subset $A = \{2, 3, 5\}$, the probability of getting a prime is

$$P(A) = \frac{n(A)}{n(S)} = \frac{3}{6} = \frac{1}{2}.$$

c. Since each region is exactly the same size, each color has an equally likely chance of being selected. The event of pointing to a primary color is subset $C = \{R, Y, B\}$ and $S = \{R, Y, G, B\}$, so the probability of pointing to a primary color is

$$P(C) = \frac{n(C)}{n(S)} = \frac{3}{4}.$$

d. Since each card in the deck has an equally likely chance of being drawn, we can again use the previous definition. The event of getting a diamond is represented by subset A, which consists of 13 cards, and the event of getting a diamond face card is subset $D = \{J\blacklozenge, Q\blacklozenge, K\blacklozenge\}$. Thus the probability of drawing a diamond is

$$P(A) = \frac{n(A)}{n(S)} = \frac{13}{52} = \frac{1}{4}$$

and the probability of a diamond face card is

$$P(D) = \frac{n(D)}{n(S)} = \frac{3}{52}. \qquad ■$$

NCTM Standards 2000
Data Analysis and
Probability
Grades 3–5
All students should understand
that the measure of the likelihood
of an event can be represented by
a number from 0 to 1.

These examples provide a sense of the types of numbers that probabilities can take on. By using the fact that $\emptyset \subseteq E \subseteq S$, we can determine the range for $P(E)$. In particular, $\emptyset \subseteq E \subseteq S$, so

$$0 = n(\emptyset) \leq n(E) \leq n(S);$$

hence

$$\frac{0}{n(S)} \leq \frac{n(E)}{n(S)} \leq \frac{n(S)}{n(S)}$$

so that

$$0 \leq P(E) \leq 1.$$

Reflection from Research
When discussing the terms
certain, possible, and impossible,
it was found that children had
difficulty generating examples
of certain and would often
suggest a new category: almost
certain (Nugent, 1990).

The last inequality tells us that the probability of an event must be between 0 and 1, inclusive. If $P(E) = 0$, the event E contains no outcomes (hence E is an **impossible**

event); if $P(E) = 1$, the event E equals the entire sample space S (hence E is a **certain event**).

For each of the examples considered thus far, we see that the probability is simply a ratio of the number of objects or outcomes of interest compared to the total number of objects or outcomes under consideration. The objects or outcomes of interest make up the event. Thus, a more general description of probability is

$$P(\text{event}) = \frac{\text{the number of objects or outcomes of interest}}{\text{the total number of objects or outcomes under consideration}}.$$

The primary use of a sample space is to make sure that you have accounted for all possible outcomes. The examples done thus far could likely be done without listing a sample space, but they prepare us for using a sample space to compute the probabilities in the next few examples.

Each of the experiments that we have investigated thus far involve doing an action with one object once: tossing a coin, rolling a die, spinning a spinner, drawing a card. Computing probabilities becomes more difficult when multiple actions or objects are involved. Examples of using multiple objects such as tossing three coins and rolling two dice follow.

Example 11.4 When tossing three coins—a penny, a nickel, and a dime—what is the probability of getting exactly two heads (Figure 11.3)?

Solution While it may seem that since there are three coins and two of them need to be heads, we might simply say that it is the probability of two out of three. This reasoning, however, does not take into consideration all of the possible outcomes. To do this, we will fall back on the idea of a sample space and event. The sample space for this experiment is

$$S = \{\overbrace{HHH}^{\text{3 heads}}, \overbrace{HHT, HTH, THH}^{\text{2 heads}}, \underbrace{HTT, THT, TTH}_{\text{1 head}}, \underbrace{TTT}_{\text{0 heads}}\}$$

where the first letter in each three-letter sequence represents the outcome of the penny, the second letter is the nickel, and the last letter is the dime. The event of getting exactly two heads is $A = \{HHT, HTH, THH\}$. Thus the probability of getting exactly two heads is

$$P(A) = \frac{n(A)}{n(S)} = \frac{3}{8}. \qquad ■$$

This probability is based on *ideal* occurrences and is referred to as a **theoretical probability**. Another way to approach this problem is by actually tossing three coins many times and recording the results. Computing probability in this way by determining the ratio of the frequency of an event to the total number of repetitions is called **experimental probability**. Table 11.1 gives the observed results of tossing a penny, nickel, and dime 500 times.

From Table 11.1, the outcomes of the event of getting exactly two heads occurred as follows: HHT, 67 times; HTH, 56 times; and THH, 64 times. Thus the experimental probability of getting exactly two heads is

$$\frac{67 + 56 + 64}{500} = \frac{187}{500} = .374,$$

Reflection from Research
Ongoing experiences with experimental activities with continuous and discrete probability generators (like dice, coins, and spinners) seemed to be successful in enabling most student to recognize that no one outcome was certain in probability situations (Jones et al., 1999).

T H H

Figure 11.3

Reflection from Research
Many mathematics educators recommend performing dozens of trials (e.g., rolling a die 100 times). However, many elementary children have not developed the attention span needed to sustain their interest for such lengths of time (Taylor & Biddulph, 1994).

Table 11.1

OUTCOME	FREQUENCY
HHH	71
HHT	67
HTH	56
THH	64
TTH	53
THT	61
HTT	66
TTT	62
Total	500

which is comparable to the theoretical probability of

$$P(E) = \frac{n(E)}{n(S)} = \frac{3}{8} = .375.$$

Experimental probability has the advantage of being established via observations. The obvious disadvantage is that it depends on a particular set of repetitions of an experiment and may not generalize to other repetitions of the same type of experiment. In either case, however, the probability was found by determining a ratio. From this point on, all probabilities will be computed theoretically unless otherwise indicated.

Spotlight on Technology Tossing three coins 500 times would be a tedious task. Using a spreadsheet to accomplish this would only require the push of a button. Refer to the dynamic spreadsheet, *Coin Toss*, in the Spreadsheet webmodule, which contains a coin toss spreadsheet for you to work with. Using this spreadsheet, perform five different experiments of 100 tosses. In any case did the experimental probability match the theoretical? What was the closest match? What was the worst match?

www.wiley.com/ college/musser

Reflection from Research

A common error experienced by children considering probability with respect to sums of numbers from two dice is that they mistakenly believe that the sums are equally likely (Fischbein & Gazit, 1984).

Example 11.5   The experiment of tossing two fair, six-sided dice is performed and the sum of the dots on the two faces is recorded. Let *A* be the event of getting a total of 7 dots, *B* be the event of getting 8 dots, and *C* be the event of getting at least 4 dots. What is the probability of each of these events?

Solution   In determining the sample space for this experiment, one might consider listing only the sums of 2, 3, 4, and so forth. However, since these outcomes are not equally likely, the definition for determining the probability of an event with equally likely outcomes cannot be used. As a result, we list all of the outcomes of tossing two dice and then determine which of those outcomes yield sums of 2, 3, 4, and so forth. The sample space, *S*, for this experiment is shown in Figure 11.4(a).

(1,1)	(1,2)	(1,3)	(1,4)	(1,5)	(1,6)
(2,1)	(2,2)	(2,3)	(2,4)	(2,5)	(2,6)
(3,1)	(3,2)	(3,3)	(3,4)	(3,5)	(3,6)
(4,1)	(4,2)	(4,3)	(4,4)	(4,5)	(4,6)
(5,1)	(5,2)	(5,3)	(5,4)	(5,5)	(5,6)
(6,1)	(6,2)	(6,3)	(6,4)	(6,5)	(6,6)

(a)   **(b)**

Figure 11.4

A question that often arises with this experiment is "why do you list both (1,2) and (2,1) when we are only interested in the sum of three?" To better understand this, imagine that the two dice are different colors, red and green. This would mean that 1 dot on the red die and 2 dots on the green die is a *different* outcome than 2 dots on the red die and 1 dot on the green die. Thus both outcomes are listed separately. By looking at the sample space in Figure 11.4(a) and the sums of dots (the numbers at the ends of the arrows) in Figure 11.4(b), the size of the sample space [$n(S) = 36$] and the size of the various subsets representing events can be determined. Using this information, $P(A)$, $P(B)$, and $P(C)$ are shown in Table 11.2.

Table 11.2

EVENT E	$N(E)$	$P(E)$
A	$n(A) = 6$	$P(A) = \frac{6}{36} = \frac{1}{6}$
B	$n(B) = 5$	$P(B) = \frac{5}{36}$
C	$n(C) = 33$	$P(C) = \frac{33}{36} = \frac{11}{12}$

Spotlight on Technology The rolling of two dice and recording the sum of the number of dots on their faces can be simulated using a spreadsheet. Refer to the dynamic spreadsheet, *Roll the Dice*, in the Spreadsheet webmodule. Use the spreadsheet to simulate rolling two dice 200 times. How close are the results of this experiment to the theoretical probabilities in Table 11.2?

www.wiley.com/
college/musser

All of the examples discussed thus far have been experiments consisting of one action. In the case of tossing three coins or rolling two dice, it was still only one action, but performed on more than one object. We now want to consider experiments that consist of doing two or more actions in succession. For example, consider the experiment of tossing one coin three times. Would this experiment have a different sample space than the experiment of tossing three different coins once as in Example 11.4? No. In fact, it is often helpful in listing a sample space for experiments of this type to be aware of this connection. The next example is an illustration of an experiment of two actions done in succession.

Example 11.6   A jar contains four marbles: one red, one green, one yellow, and one white (Figure 11.5). If we draw two marbles from the jar, one after the other, without replacing the first one drawn, what is the probability of each of the following events?

> A: One of the marbles is red.
> B: The first marble is red or yellow.
> C: The marbles are the same color.
> D: The first marble is not white.
> E: Neither marble is blue.

Figure 11.5

Solution The sample space consists of the following outcomes. ("RG," for example, means that the first marble is red and the second marble is green.)

RG	GR	YR	WR
RY	GY	YG	WG
RW	GW	YW	WY

Thus $n(S) = 12$. Since there is exactly one marble of each color and all marbles are physically identical to the touch, we assume that all the outcomes are equally likely. Then

$A = \{$RG, RY, RW, GR, YR, WR$\}$, so $P(A) = \frac{6}{12} = \frac{1}{2}$.

$B = \{$RG, RY, RW, YR, YG, YW$\}$, so $P(B) = \frac{6}{12} = \frac{1}{2}$.

$C = \varnothing$, the empty event. That is, C is impossible, so $P(C) = \frac{0}{12} = 0$.

$D = \{$RG, RY, RW, GR, GY, GW, YR, YG, YW$\}$, so $P(D) = \frac{9}{12} = \frac{3}{4}$.

$E = $ the entire sample space, S. So $P(E) = \frac{12}{12} = 1$.

Notice that event B in Example 11.6 can be represented as the union of two events corresponding to drawing red on the first marble or yellow on the first marble. That is, if we let $L = \{RG, RY, RW\}$ and $M = \{YR, YG, YW\}$, then $B = L \cup M$. Observe that $L \cap M = \varnothing$. If we compute $P(L \cup M)$, $P(L)$, and $P(M)$, we find $P(L \cup M) = P(B) = \frac{1}{2}$, while $P(L) + P(M) = \frac{3}{12} + \frac{3}{12} = \frac{1}{2}$. Hence $P(L \cup M) = P(L) + P(M)$. Thus the probability of B can be found by adding the probabilities of two *disjoint* events whose union is event B, that is, $P(B) = P(L) + P(M)$.

The set of outcomes in the sample space S but not in event D is called the **complement of the event** D, written $\overline{D}$. Because $S = D \cup \overline{D}$ and $D \cap \overline{D} = \varnothing$, we see that $n(D) + n(\overline{D}) = n(S)$ or $n(\overline{D}) = n(S) - n(D)$. Therefore,

$$P(\overline{D}) = \frac{n(\overline{D})}{n(S)} = \frac{n(S) - n(D)}{n(S)} = \frac{n(S)}{n(S)} - \frac{n(D)}{n(S)} = 1 - P(D).$$

Similarly, $P(D) = 1 - P(\overline{D})$. Thus $P(\overline{D})$ in Example 11.6 is the probability that the first marble is white, namely $\frac{3}{12}$ or $\frac{1}{4}$. So $P(D) = 1 - P(\overline{D}) = 1 - \frac{1}{4} = \frac{3}{4}$, as we found directly.

Example 11.7 Figure 11.6 shows a diagram of a sample space S of an experiment with equally likely outcomes. Events A, B, and C are indicated, their outcomes represented by points. Find the probability of each of the following events: $S, \varnothing, A, B, C, A \cup B, A \cap B, A \cup C, \overline{C}$.

Solution In Table 11.3, we tabulate the number of outcomes in each event and their probabilities. For example, $n(A) = 5$ and $n(S) = 15$, so $P(A) = \frac{5}{15} = \frac{1}{3}$.

Problem-Solving Strategy
Draw a Diagram

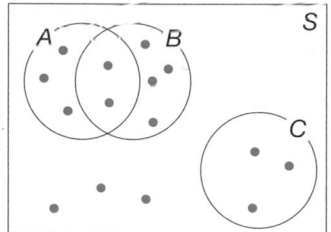

Figure 11.6

Table 11.3

EVENT, E	$n(E)$	$P(E) = \dfrac{n(E)}{n(S)}$
S	15	$\frac{15}{15} = 1$
$\varnothing$	0	$\frac{0}{15} = 0$
A	5	$\frac{5}{15} = \frac{1}{3}$
B	6	$\frac{6}{15} = \frac{2}{5}$
C	3	$\frac{3}{15} = \frac{1}{5}$
$A \cup B$	9	$\frac{9}{15} = \frac{3}{5}$
$A \cap B$	2	$\frac{2}{15}$
$A \cup C$	8	$\frac{8}{15}$
$\overline{C}$	12	$\frac{12}{15} = \frac{4}{5}$

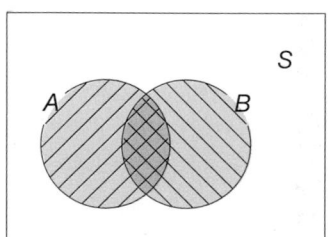

Figure 11.7

In Example 11.7, $P(A \cup B) = \frac{9}{15}$, while $P(A) + P(B) - P(A \cap B) = \frac{5}{15} + \frac{6}{15} - \frac{2}{15} = \frac{9}{15} = P(A \cup B)$. So $P(A \cup B) = P(A) + P(B) - P(A \cap B)$. This result is true for *all* events A and B. In Figure 11.7, observe how the region $A \cap B$ is shaded *twice*, once from A and once from B. Thus to find the number of elements in $A \cup B$, we can calculate $n(A) + n(B)$. *But* we have to subtract $n(A \cap B)$ so that we do not count the elements in $A \cap B$ twice. Hence $n(A \cup B) = n(A) + n(B) - n(A \cap B)$ for sets A and B.

In Example 11.7, events A and C are disjoint, or **mutually exclusive.** That is, they have no outcomes in common. In such cases, $P(A \cup C) = P(A) + P(C)$, since $A \cap C = \varnothing$. Verify this in Example 11.7. Also, observe that $P(C) + P(\overline{C}) = 1$. Occasionally, it is simpler to compute the probability of an event indirectly, using the complement. That is, $P(C) = 1 - P(\overline{C})$.

NCTM Standards 2000
Data Analysis and
Probability
Grades 6–8
All students should understand
and use appropriate terminology
to describe complementary and
mutually exclusive events.

We can summarize our observations about probabilities as follows.

PROPERTY

Properties of Probability

1. For any event A, $0 \leq P(A) \leq 1$.
2. $P(\emptyset) = 0$.
3. $P(S) = 1$, where S is the sample space.
4. For all events A and B, $P(A \cup B) = P(A) + P(B) - P(A \cap B)$.
5. If A denotes the complement of event A, then $P(\overline{A}) = 1 - P(A)$.

Observe in item 4, when $A \cap B = \emptyset$, that is, A and B are mutually exclusive, we have $P(A \cup B) = P(A) + P(B)$. The properties of probability apply to all experiments and sample spaces.

Finally, let's consider the case when the outcomes are *not* equally likely. For example, what if the regions on a spinner are not the same size.

(a)

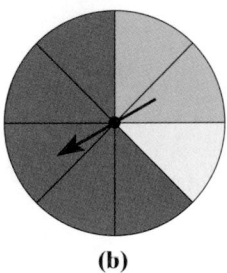

(b)

Figure 11.8

Example 11.8 For the spinner in Figure 11.8(a), what is the probability of pointing to the blue region?

Solution Since the regions are not the same size, it cannot be said that the probability of pointing to the blue region is one out of three. It is clear that the probability of pointing to the blue is greater than half, but how much greater? Because each of the outcomes red, green, and blue are not equally likely, we cannot use the sample space $S = \{R, G, B\}$ to compute the probability. We can, however, determine some type of ratio for the probability. In this case, the spinner can be divided into eight equally shaped and sized regions [see Figure 11.8(b)]. Since five of the eight equally sized regions are blue, we know that the probability of pointing to a blue is the ratio of blue regions to total regions which is $\frac{5}{8}$. ■

Example 11.9 A bag of candy contains 6 red gumballs, 3 green gumballs, and 2 blue gumballs. If one gumball is drawn from the bag, what is the probability that it will be red?

Solution If we try to approach this problem using the sample space $S = \{R, G, B\}$, difficulties arise because there are a different number of each color of gumball. While we could write the sample space in a different way, it is simpler to view this probability as a ratio of gumballs of interest (red) to total gumballs. Since there are 6 red gumballs and a total of 11 gumballs altogether, the probability of getting a red gumball is $\frac{6}{11}$. ■

In summary, probabilities are computed by determining a ratio of the number of objects of interest compared to total number of objects. In some cases this ratio can be determined directly. In other cases, we may list the sample space to ensure that we have accounted for all possible outcomes.

MATHEMATICAL MORSEL

The following true story was reported in a newspaper article. A teacher was giving a standardized true/false achievement test when she noticed that Johnny was busily flipping a coin in the back of the room and then marking his answers. When asked what he was doing he replied, "I didn't have time to study, so instead I'm using a coin. If it comes up heads, I mark true, and if it comes up tails, I mark false." Half an hour later, when the rest of the students were done, the teacher saw Johnny still flipping away. She asked, "Johnny, what's taking you so long?" He replied, "It's like you always tell us. I'm just checking my answers."

Section 11.1 EXERCISE / PROBLEM SET A

EXERCISES

1. According to the weather report, there is a 20% chance of snow in the county tomorrow. Which of the following statements would be appropriate?

   a. Out of the next five days, it will snow one of those days.

   b. Of the 24 hours, snow will fall for 4.8 hours.

   c. Of past days when conditions were similar, one out of five had some snow.

   d. It will snow on 20% of the area of the county.

2. List the elements of the sample space for each of the following experiments.

   a. A quarter is tossed.

   b. A single die is rolled with faces labeled A, B, C, D, E, and F.

   c. A regular tetrahedron die (with four faces labeled 1, 2, 3, 4) is rolled and the number on the bottom face is recorded.

   d. The following "red-blue-yellow" spinner is spun once. (All sectors are equal in size and shape.)

   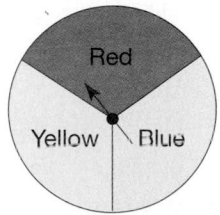

3. An experiment consists of tossing four coins. List each of the following.

   a. The sample space

   b. The event of a head on the first coin

   c. The event of three heads

   d. The event of a head or a tail on the fourth coin

   e. The event of a head on the second coin and a tail on the third coin

4. An experiment consists of tossing a regular dodecahedron die (with 12 congruent faces). List the following.

   a. The sample space

   b. The event of an even number

   c. The event of a number less than 8

   d. The event of a number divisible by 2 and 3

   e. The event of a number greater than 12

5. Identify which of the following events are certain (C), possible (P), or impossible (I).

   a. You throw a 2 on a die.

   b. A student in this class is less than 2 years old.

   c. Next week has only 5 days.

6. One way to find the sample space of an experiment involving two parts is to use the Cartesian product. For example, an experiment consists of tossing a dime and a quarter.

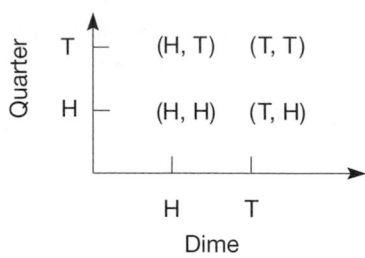

Sample space for dime $D = \{H, T\}$
Sample space for quarter $Q = \{H, T\}$

The sample space of the experiment is

$$D \times Q = \{(H, H), (H, T), (T, H), (T, T)\}.$$

Using this method, construct the sample space of the following experiment.

Toss a coin and roll a tetrahedron die (four faces).

7. A die is rolled 60 times with the following results recorded.

OUTCOME	1	2	3	4	5	6
FREQUENCY	10	9	10	12	8	11

Find the experimental probability of the following events.

a. Getting a 4

b. Getting an odd number

c. Getting a number greater than 3

8. Refer to Example 11.5 which gives the sample space for the experiment of rolling two dice, and give the probabilities of the following events.

a. A 4 on the second die

b. An even number on each die

c. At least 7 dots in total

d. A total of 15 dots

e. A total greater than 1

9. A dropped thumbtack will land point up or point down.

a. Do you think one outcome will happen more often than the other? Which one?

b. The results for tossing a thumbtack 60 times are as follows.

Point up: 42 times
Point down: 18 times

What is the experimental probability that it lands point up? point down?

c. If the thumbtack was tossed 100 times, about how many times would you expect it to land point up? point down?

10. You have a key ring with five keys on it.

a. One of the keys is a car key. What is the probability of picking that one?

b. Two of the keys are for your apartment. What is the probability of selecting an apartment key?

c. What is the probability of selecting either the car key or an apartment key?

d. What is the probability of selecting neither the car key nor an apartment key?

11. Two dice are thrown. If each face is equally likely to turn up, find the following probabilities.

a. The sum is even.

b. The sum is not 10.

c. The sum is a prime.

d. The sum is less than 9.

e. The sum is not less than 9.

12. What is the probability of getting yellow on each of the following spinners?

a.
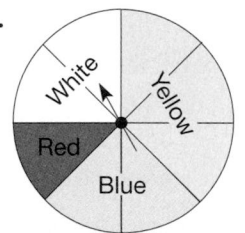
All eight sectors are equally sized and shaped.

b.
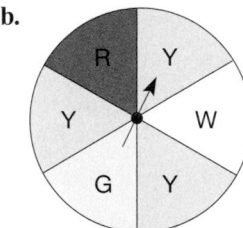
All six sectors are equally sized and shaped.

13. A die is made that has two faces marked with 2s, three faces marked with 3s, and one face marked with a 5. If this die is thrown once, find the following probabilities.

a. Getting a 2

b. Not getting a 2

c. Getting an odd number

d. Not getting an odd number

14. A card is drawn from a standard deck of cards. Find $P(A \cup B)$ in each part.

a. $A = \{getting\ a\ black\ card\}, B = \{getting\ a\ heart\}$

b. $A = \{getting\ a\ diamond\}, \quad B = \{getting\ an\ ace\}$

c. $A = \{getting\ a\ face\ card\}, \quad B = \{getting\ a\ spade\}$

d. $A = \{getting\ a\ face\ card\}, \quad B = \{getting\ a\ 7\}$

15. With the spinner in Example 11.2(c), spin twice and record the color on each spin. For this experiment, consider the sample space and following events.

    A: getting a green on the first spin
    B: getting a yellow on the second spin
    $A \cup B$: getting a green on the first spin or
             a yellow on the second spin

$$A$$

		A	
RR	YR	GR	BR
RY	YY	GY	BY
RG	YG	GG	BG
RB	YB	GB	BB

B labels the second row (RY YY GY BY)

Verify the following:

$$n(S) = 16, n(A) = 4, n(B) = 4$$
$$n(A \cup B) = 7, n(A \cap B) = 1$$
$$P(A) = \frac{4}{16}, P(B) = \frac{4}{16},$$
$$P(A \cup B) = \frac{7}{16}, \text{ and } P(A \cap B) = \frac{1}{16}.$$

Show that $P(A \cup B) = P(A) + P(B) - P(A \cap B)$. Apply this to find $P(A \cup B)$ in the following cases.

a. A: getting a red on first spin
    B: getting same color on both spins

b. A: getting a yellow or blue on first spin
    B: getting a red or green on second spin

16. For the experiment in Problem 15 where a spinner is spun twice, consider the following events:

    A: getting a blue on the first spin
    B: getting a yellow on one spin
    C: getting the same color on both spins

Describe the following events and find their probabilities.

a. $A \cup B$ **b.** $B \cap C$ **c.** $\overline{B}$

17. A student is selected at random. Let A be the event that the selected student is a sophomore and B be the event that the selected student is taking English. Write in words what is meant by each of the following probabilities.

a. $P(A \cup B)$ **b.** $P(A \cap B)$ **c.** $1 - P(A)$

PROBLEMS

18. Two fair six-sided dice are rolled and the sum of the dots on the top faces is recorded.

    a. Complete the table, showing the number of ways each sum can occur.

SUM	2	3	4	5	6	7	8	9	10	11	12
WAYS	1	2	3								

    b. Use the table to find the probability of the following events.

    A: The sum is prime.
    B: The sum is a divisor of 12.
    C: The sum is a power of 2.
    D: The sum is greater than 3.

19. The probability of a "geometric" event involving the concept of measure (length, area, volume) is determined as follows. Let $m(A)$ and $m(S)$ represent the measures of the event A and the sample space S, respectively. Then

$$P(A) = \frac{m(A)}{m(S)}.$$

For example, in the first figure, if the length of S is 12 cm and the length of A is 4 cm, then $P(A) = \frac{4}{12} = \frac{1}{3}$. Similarly, in the second figure, if the area of region B is 10 cm^2 and the area of region S is 60 cm^2, then $P(B) = \frac{10}{60} = \frac{1}{6}$.

A bus travels between Albany and Binghamton, a distance of 100 miles. If the bus has broken down, we want to find the probability that it has broken down within 10 miles of either city.

a. The road from Albany to Binghamton is the sample space. What is $m(S)$?

b. Event A is that part of the road within 10 miles of either city. What is $m(A)$?

c. Find $P(A)$.

20. The dartboard illustrated is made up of circles with radii of 1, 2, 3, and 4 units. A dart hits the target randomly. What is the probability that the dart hits the bull's-eye? (*Hint:* The area of a circle with radius r is πr^2.)

 Section 11.1 EXERCISE / PROBLEM SET B

EXERCISES

1. For visiting a resort area you will receive a special gift.

CATEGORY I	CATEGORY II	CATEGORY III
A. New car	D. 25-inch color TV	G. Meat smoker
B. Food processor	E. AM/FM stereo	H. Toaster oven
C. $2500 cash	F. $1000 cash	I. $25 cash

The probabilities are as follows: A, 1 in 52,000; B, 25,736 in 52,000; C, 1 in 52,000; D, 3 in 52,000; E, 25,736 in 52,000; F, 3 in 52,000; G, 180 in 52,000; H, 180 in 52,000; I, 160 in 52,000.

   a. Which gifts are you most likely to receive?

   b. Which gifts are you least likely to receive?

   c. If 5000 people visit the resort, how many would be expected to receive a new car?

2. List the sample space for each experiment.

   a. Tossing a dime and a penny

   b. Tossing a nickel and rolling a die

   c. Drawing a marble from a bag containing one red and one blue marble and drawing a second marble from a bag containing one green and one white marble

3. A bag contains one each of red, green, blue, yellow, and white marbles. Give the sample space of the following experiments.

   a. One marble is drawn.

   b. One marble is drawn, then replaced, and a second one is then drawn.

   c. One marble is drawn, but not replaced, and a second one is drawn.

4. An experiment consists of tossing a coin and rolling a die. List each of the following.

   a. The sample space

   b. The event of getting a head

   c. The event of getting a 3

   d. The event of getting an even number

   e. The event of getting a head and a number greater than 4

   f. The event of getting a tail or a 5

5. Identify which of the following events are certain (C), possible (P), or impossible (I).

   a. There are at least four Sundays this month.

   b. It will rain today.

   c. You throw a head on a die.

6. Use the Cartesian product to construct the sample space of the following experiment:

   Toss a coin, and draw a marble from a bag containing purple, green, and yellow marbles.

7. A loaded die (one in which outcomes are not equally likely) is tossed 1000 times with the following results.

OUTCOME	1	2	3	4	5	6
NUMBER OF TIMES	125	75	350	250	150	50

Find the experimental probability of the following events.

   a. Getting a 2   **b.** Getting a 5

   c. Getting a 1 or a 5   **d.** Getting an even number

8. Refer to Example 11.4, in which three fair coins are tossed. Assign theoretical probabilities to the following events.

   a. Getting a head on the first coin

   b. Getting a head on the first coin and a tail on the second coin

   c. Getting at least one tail

   d. Getting exactly one tail

9. A snack pack of colored candies contained the following:

COLOR	Brown	Tan	Yellow	Green	Orange
NUMBER	7	3	5	3	4

One candy is selected at random. Find the probability that it is of the following color.

a. Brown   **b.** Tan

c. Yellow   **d.** Green

e. Not brown   **f.** Yellow or orange

10. An American roulette wheel has 38 slots around the rim. Two of them are numbered 0 and 00 and are green; the others are numbered from 1 to 36 and half are red, half are black. As the wheel is spun in one direction, a small ivory ball is rolled along the rim in the opposite direction. The ball has an equally likely chance of falling into any one of the 38 slots, assuming that the wheel is fair. Find the probability of each of the following.

a. The ball lands on 0 or 00.

b. The ball lands on 23.

c. The ball lands on a red number.

d. The ball does not land on 20–36.

e. The ball lands on an even number or a green slot.

11. A card is drawn at random from a deck of 52 playing cards. What is the probability of drawing each of the following?

a. A black card   **b.** A face card

c. Not a face card   **d.** A black face card

e. A black or a face card

f. An ace or a face card

g. Neither an ace nor a face card

h. Not an ace

12. A spinner with three equally sized and shaped sectors is spun once.

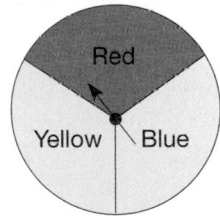

a. What is the probability of spinning red (R)?

b. What is the probability of spinning blue (B)?

c. What is the probability of spinning yellow (Y)?

d. Here the sample space is divided into three different events, R, B, and Y. Find the sum, $P(R) + P(B) + P(Y)$.

e. Repeat the preceding parts with the spinner with eight sectors of equal size and shape. Do you get the same result as in part (d)?

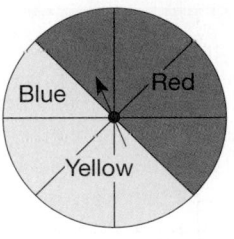

13. One die is thrown. If each face is equally likely to turn up, find the following probabilities.

a. Getting a 6   **b.** Not getting a 6

c. An even number turning up

d. An even number not turning up

e. The number dividing 6

f. The number not dividing 6

14. A bag contains six balls on which are the letters a, a, a, b, b, and c. One ball is drawn at random from the bag. Let A, B, and C be the events that balls a, b, or c are drawn, respectively.

a. What is $P(A)$?   **b.** What is $P(B)$?

c. What is $P(C)$?   **d.** Find $P(A) + P(B) + P(C)$.

e. An unknown number of balls, each lettered c, are added to the bag. It is known that now $P(A) = \frac{1}{4}$ and $P(B) = \frac{1}{6}$. What is $P(C)$?

15. Consider the experiment in Example 11.4 where three coins are tossed. Consider the following events:

    A: The number of heads is 3.
    B: The number of heads is 2.
    C: The second coin lands heads.

Describe the following events and find their probabilities.

a. $A \cup B$ **b.** $\overline{B}$ **c.** $\overline{C}$ **d.** $B \cap C$

16. A bag contains 2 red balls, 3 blue balls, and 1 yellow ball.

a. What is the probability of drawing a red ball?

b. How many red balls must be added to the bag so that the probability of drawing a red ball is $\frac{1}{2}$?

c. How many blue balls must be added to the bag so that the probability of drawing a red ball is $\frac{1}{5}$?

17. What is false about the following statements?

a. Since there are 50 states, the probability of being born in Pennsylvania is $\frac{1}{50}$.

b. The probability that I am taking math is 0.80 and the probability that I am taking English is 0.50, so the probability that I am taking math and/or English is 1.30.

c. The probability that the basketball team wins its next game is $\frac{1}{3}$; the probability that it loses is $\frac{1}{2}$.

d. The probability that I get an A in this course is 1.5.

PROBLEMS

18. A bag contains an unknown number of balls, some red, some blue, and some green. Find the smallest number of balls in the bag if the following probabilities are given. Give the P(green) for each situation.

a. $P(\text{red}) = \frac{1}{6}$, $P(\text{blue}) = \frac{1}{3}$

b. $P(\text{red}) = \frac{3}{5}$, $P(\text{blue}) = \frac{1}{6}$

c. $P(\text{red}) = \frac{1}{5}$, $P(\text{blue}) = \frac{3}{4}$

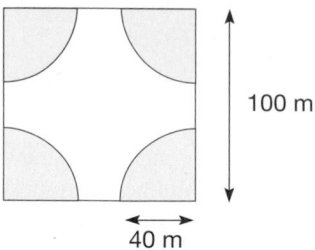

19. A paraglider wants to land in the unshaded region in the square field illustrated, since the shaded regions (four quarter circles) are briar patches. If he lost control and was going to hit the field randomly, what is the probability that he would miss the briar patch?

20. A microscopic worm is eating its way around the inside of a spherical apple of radius 6 cm. What is the probability that the worm is within 1 cm of the surface of the apple? (*Hint*: $V = \frac{4}{3}\pi r^3$, where r is the radius.)

PROBLEMS FOR WRITING/DISCUSSION

1. James says that if there are two children in a family, then there are two girls, two boys, or one of each. So each of the three possibilities must have a probability of 1/3. Do you agree with James? Explain.

2. Melissa was tossing a quarter to try to determine the odds of getting heads after a certain number of tosses. She got five tails in a row! Jennifer said, "You are sure to get heads on the next toss!" Karen said, "No, she's

definitely going to get tails!" Explain the reasoning of each of these students. Do you agree with either one? Explain.

3. Shirley's parents are taking her to New Orleans for a week. At the time of year they are going, the probability of rain on any given day is 40%. Shirley says that means there is a 60% chance it will not rain the whole week she is there. Do you agree? Explain.

11.2 PROBABILITY AND COMPLEX EXPERIMENTS

Two red cubes, one white cube, and one blue cube are placed in a box. One cube is randomly drawn, its color is recorded, and it is returned to the box. A second cube is drawn and its color recorded. What is the probability of drawing a blue and a red cube? (*Hint*: Since order is not specified, this could be a ßR or an Rß.)

Tree Diagrams and Counting Techniques

In some experiments it is inefficient to list all the outcomes in the sample space. Therefore, we develop alternative procedures to compute probabilities.

A **tree diagram** can be used to represent the outcomes of an experiment. The experiment of drawing two marbles, one at a time, from a jar of four marbles without replacement, which was illustrated in Example 11.6, can be conveniently represented by the outcome tree diagram shown in Figure 11.9.

The diagram in Figure 11.9 shows that there are 12 outcomes in the sample space, since there are 12 right-hand endpoints on the tree. Those 12 outcomes are the same

Problem-Solving Strategy
Draw a Diagram

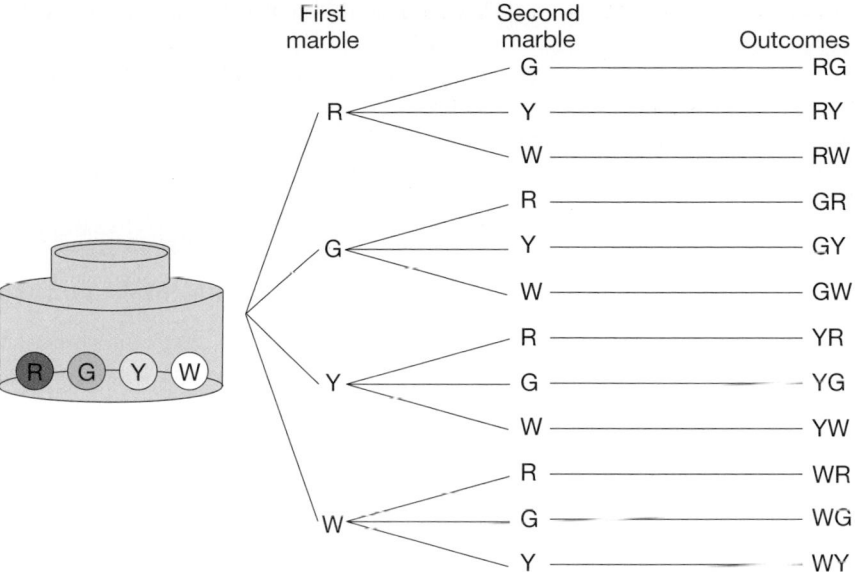

Figure 11.9

as those determined for the sample space of this experiment in Example 11.6. A tree diagram can also be used in the next example.

Example 11.10   Suppose that you can order a new sports car in a choice of five colors, [red, white, green, black, or silver (R, W, G, B, S)] and two types of transmissions, [manual or automatic (M, A)]. How many different types of cars can you order?

Solution Figure 11.10 shows that there are 10 types of cars corresponding to the 10 outcomes.

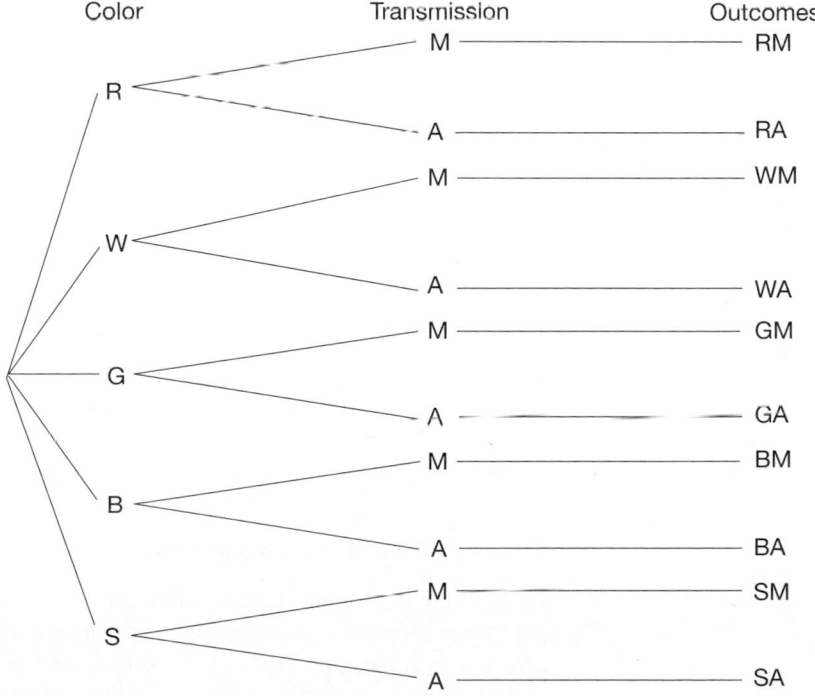

Figure 11.10

There are 10 different paths, or outcomes, for selecting cars in Example 11.10. Rather than count all the outcomes, we can actually compute the number of outcomes by making a simple observation about the tree diagram. Notice that there are five colors (five primary branches) and two transmission types (two secondary branches for each of the original five) or 10 (= 5 · 2) different combinations. This counting procedure suggests the following property.

PROPERTY

Fundamental Counting Property

If an event A can occur in r ways, and for each of these r ways, an event B can occur in s ways, then events A and B can occur, in succession, in $r \cdot s$ ways.

The fundamental counting property can be generalized to more than two events occurring in succession. This is illustrated in the next example.

Example 11.11 Suppose that pizzas can be ordered in 3 sizes (small, medium, large), 2 crust choices (thick or thin), 4 choices of meat toppings (sausage only, pepperoni only, both, or neither), and 2 cheese toppings (regular or double cheese). How many different ways can a pizza be ordered?

Solution Since there are 3 size choices, 2 crust choices, 4 meat choices, and 2 cheese choices, by the fundamental counting property, there are $3 \cdot 2 \cdot 4 \cdot 2 = 48$ different types of pizzas altogether. ∎

Now let's apply the fundamental counting property to compute the probability of an event in a simple experiment.

Example 11.12 Find the probability of getting a sum of 11 when tossing a pair of fair dice.

Solution Since each die has six faces and there are two dice, there are $6 \cdot 6 = 36$ possible outcomes according to the fundamental counting property. There are two ways of tossing an 11, namely (5, 6) and (6, 5). Therefore, the probability of tossing an eleven is $\frac{2}{36}$, or $\frac{1}{18}$. ∎

Example 11.13 A local hamburger outlet offers patrons a choice of four condiments: catsup, mustard, pickles, and onions. If the condiments are added or omitted in a random fashion, what is the probability that you will get one of the following types: catsup and onion, mustard and pickles, or one with everything?

Solution Since we can view each condiment in two ways, namely as being either on or off a hamburger, there are $2^4 = 16$ various possible hamburgers (list them or draw a tree diagram to check this). Since there are three combinations you are interested in, the probability of getting one of the three combinations is $\frac{3}{16}$. ∎

Probability Tree Diagrams

In addition to helping display and count outcomes, tree diagrams can be used to determine probabilities in complex experiments. By weighting the branches of a tree diagram with the appropriate probabilities, we can form a **probability tree diagram,** that in turn, can be used to find probabilities of various events. For example, consider

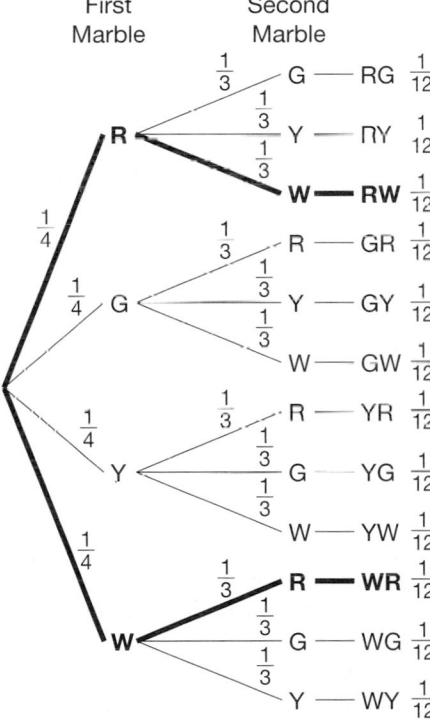

Figure 11.11

the jar containing four marbles—one red, one green, one yellow, and one white—that, was used in Example 11.6 and at the beginning of this section. Suppose a single marble is drawn from the jar. What would the probability tree diagram corresponding to this experiment look like? Since each marble has an equally likely chance of being drawn, the probability of drawing any single marble is $\frac{1}{4}$, as is illustrated on each branch of the probability tree diagram in Figure 11.11. In the next example, two marbles are drawn without replacing the first marble before drawing a second time. This is referred to as **drawing without replacement.** If the marble *had* been replaced, it would be called **drawing with replacement.**

Example 11.14 If two marbles are drawn without replacement from the jar described above, what is the probability of getting a red marble and a white marble?

Solution This problem can be solved by extending the probability tree diagram in Figure 11.11, as shown in Figure 11.12. With only three marbles in the bag after the first marble is drawn, the probability on each branch of the second phase of the experiment is $\frac{1}{3}$. Since there are exactly 12 outcomes for this experiment, the probability of each outcome is represented at the end of each branch as $\frac{1}{12}$. To find the probability of getting a red and a white marble, we note that there are two possible ways of getting that outcome, RW and WR. Thus the probability of getting a red and white marble is

Figure 11.12

$$P(\text{RW}) + P(\text{WR}) = \frac{1}{12} + \frac{1}{12} = \frac{2}{12} = \frac{1}{6}.$$ ■

It is important that some valuable connections be noted in the probability tree diagram shown in Figure 11.12 Consider the probabilities that lead to the outcome of RW, for example. The probability of getting a red on the first draw is $\frac{1}{4}$, the probability of getting a white on the second draw is $\frac{1}{3}$, and the probability of getting a RW as a final outcome is $\frac{1}{12}$. Each of these probabilities was determined based on the number of choices or outcomes. Notice, however, that the probability of the final outcome is equal to the product of the probabilities at the two stages leading to that outcome, namely $\frac{1}{4} \times \frac{1}{3} = \frac{1}{12}$. This observation gives rise to the following property, which is based on the fundamental counting property.

 PROPERTY

Multiplicative Property of Probability

Suppose that an experiment consists of a sequence of simpler experiments. Then the probability of the final outcome is equal to the product of the probabilities of the simpler experiments that make up the sequence.

A second observation can be made about the probability tree diagram in Figure 11.12. The event of getting a red and a white has two possible outcomes $E = \{RW, WR\}$. This set has 2 elements and the sample space has 12 elements, so the probability could be determined by computing the ratio $\frac{2}{12}$. Since the two outcomes of getting a red and white in the event are mutually exclusive, the probability can be determined by adding up the probabilities in the individual outcomes, as was illustrated in the solution to Example 11.14. This method of adding the probabilities gives rise to the additive property of probability.

 PROPERTY

Additive Property of Probability

Suppose that an event E is the union of pairwise mutually exclusive simpler events $E_1, E_2, \ldots, E_n$, where $E_1, E_2, \ldots, E_n$ are from a sample space S. Then

$$P(E) = P(E_1) + P(E_2) + \ldots + P(E_n).$$

The probabilities of the events $E_1, E_2, \ldots, E_n$ can be viewed as those associated with the ends of branches in a probability tree diagram.

Notice that this property is an extension of the property

$$P(A \cup B) = P(A) + P(B) - P(A \cap B)$$

where $A \cap B = \varnothing$, since we required that all the events be pairwise mutually exclusive (i.e., the intersection of all pairs of E's is the empty set.)

The multiplicative and additive properties of probabilities are further illustrated and clarified in the following two examples.

Example 11.15 A jar contains three marbles, two black and one red (Figure 11.13). Two marbles are drawn *with replacement*. What is the probability that both marbles are black? Assume that the marbles are equally likely to be drawn.

Solution 1 Figure 11.14(a) shows $3 \cdot 3 = 9$ equally likely branches in the tree, of which 4 correspond to the event "two black marbles are drawn." Thus the probability of drawing two black marbles with replacement is $\frac{4}{9}$. Instead of comparing the number of successful outcomes (4) with the total number of outcomes (9), we could have simply used the additive property of probability and added the individual probabilities at the ends of the branches in Figure 11.14(b). That is, the probability is $\frac{1}{9} + \frac{1}{9} + \frac{1}{9} + \frac{1}{9} = \frac{4}{9}$. Notice that the end of each branch in Figure 11.14(b) is weighted with a probability of $\frac{1}{9}$, since there are 9 equally likely outcomes. The probability of $\frac{1}{9}$ can also be determined by

Figure 11.13

using the multiplicative property of probability and multiplying the probabilities on each of the branches that lead to the outcomes, $\frac{1}{3} \times \frac{1}{3} = \frac{1}{9}$.

Problem-Solving Strategy
Draw a Diagram

NCTM Standards 2000
Data Analysis and
Probability
Grades 6–8
All students should compute probabilities for simple compound events, using such methods as organized lists, tree diagrams, and area models.

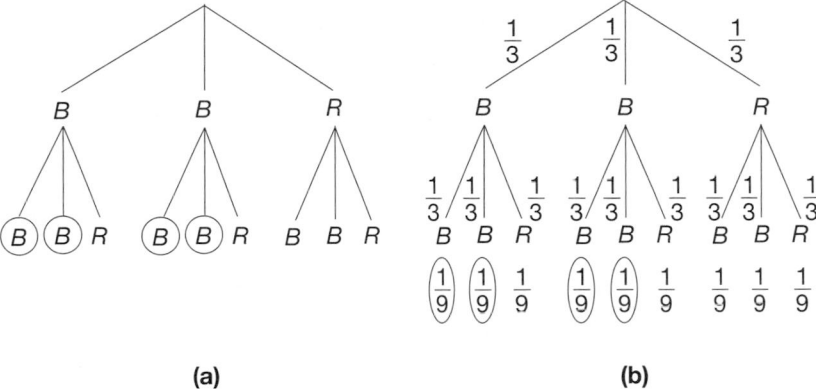

(a)   (b)

Figure 11.14

Solution 2 The solution to this problem can be approached differently by labeling the probability tree diagram in a way that relies on the additive and multiplicative properties of probability. Figure 11.15 illustrates how the number of branches in part (a) can be reduced by collapsing similar branches and then weighting them accordingly, parts (b) and (c).

Problem-Solving Strategy
Draw a Diagram

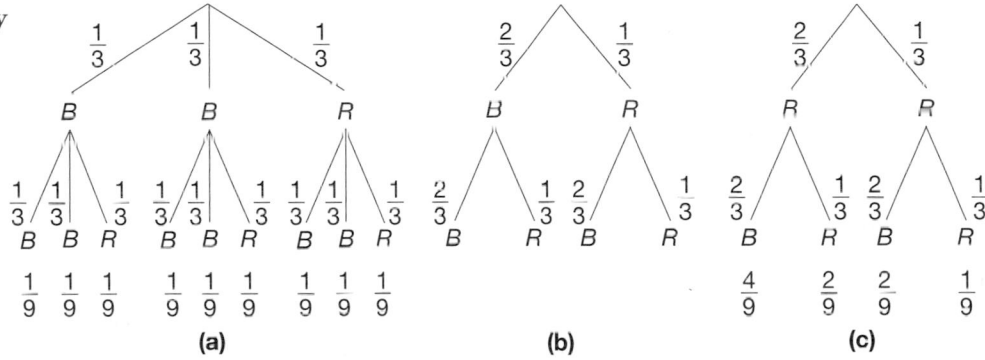

(a)   (b)   (c)

Figure 11.15

Next we must label the ends of the branches by relying on the multiplicative property of probability. Since the probability of drawing the first black marble is $\frac{2}{3}$ and the probability of drawing the second black marble is $\frac{2}{3}$, then the probability of drawing two black marbles in a row is $P(BB) = \frac{2}{3} \times \frac{2}{3} = \frac{4}{9}$, which is consistent with our first solution. The remainder of the diagram in Figure 11.15(c) can be filled out using $P(BR) = \frac{2}{3} \times \frac{1}{3} = \frac{2}{9}$, $P(RB) = \frac{1}{3} \times \frac{2}{3} = \frac{2}{9}$, and $P(RR) = \frac{1}{3} \times \frac{1}{3} = \frac{1}{9}$. ■

While the additive property of probability follows quite naturally from properties of sets, the multiplicative property was based on an observation of patterns in the probability tree diagram in Figure 11.12 and on the fundamental counting property. The next example helps to illustrate why the multiplicative property works.

Example 11.16 Consider a jar with three black marbles and one red marble (Figure 11.16). For the experiment of drawing two marbles with replacement, what is the probability of drawing a black marble and then a red marble in that order?

Figure 11.16

Solution The entries in the 4×4 array in Figure 11.17(a) show all possible outcomes of drawing two marbles with replacement.

		B	B	B	R
	B	BB	BB	BB	BR
First draw	B	BB	BB	BB	BR
	B	BB	BB	BB	BR
	R	RB	RB	RB	RR

All possible draws
Second draw

(a)

First draw B

		B	B	B	R
	B	BB	BB	BB	BR
	B	BB	BB	BB	BR
	B	BB	BB	BB	BR
	R	RB	RB	RB	RR

(b)

First draw B
Second draw R

		B	B	B	R
	B	BB	BB	BB	BR
	B	BB	BB	BB	BR
	B	BB	BB	BB	BR
	R	RB	RB	RB	RR

(c)

Figure 11.17

The outcomes in which B was drawn first, namely those with a B on the left, are surrounded by a rectangle in Figure 11.17(b). Notice that $\frac{3}{4}$ of the pairs are included in the rectangle, since 3 out of 4 marbles are black. In Figure 11.17(c), a dashed rectangle is drawn around those pairs where a B is drawn first and an R is drawn second. Observe that the portion surrounded by the dashed rectangle is $\frac{1}{4}$ of the pairs inside the rectangle, since $\frac{1}{4}$ of the marbles in the jar are red. The procedure used to find the fraction of pairs that are BR in Figure 11.17(c) is analogous to the model we used to find the product of two fractions. Thus the probability of drawing a B then an R with replacement in this experiment is $\frac{3}{4} \times \frac{1}{4} = \frac{3}{16}$, the *products* of the individual probabilities. ■

The next two examples demonstrate the flexibility that probability tree diagrams provide.

Example 11.17 Both spinners shown in Figure 11.18(a) are spun. Find the probability that they stop on the same color.

Solution In order to draw a probability tree diagram, we must first determine the probabilities of stopping on the various colors on each of the spinners. In Section 11.1, the spinners could be divided into equal regions to compute the appropriate probability. In this case, the degree measure can be used to describe the portion of the entire circle that each colored region occupies. On spinner 1, the red region occupies 45° of the total 360° around the center of the circle. Thus, the probability of spinner 1 stopping on a red is $P(R) = \frac{45}{360} = \frac{1}{8}$. Similarly the probabilities of spinner 1 stopping on a yellow, white, or green are $P(Y) = \frac{45 + 60}{360} = \frac{7}{24}$, $P(W) = \frac{120}{360} = \frac{1}{3}$, and $P(G) = \frac{90}{360}$, respectively. For spinner 2 the probabilities are $P(W) = \frac{180}{360} = \frac{1}{2}$, $P(R) = \frac{60}{360} = \frac{1}{6}$, and $P(G) = \frac{120}{360} = \frac{1}{3}$. These probabilities can now be used to label the appropriate branches of the tree diagram, as shown in Figure 11.18(b).

Figure 11.18(a)

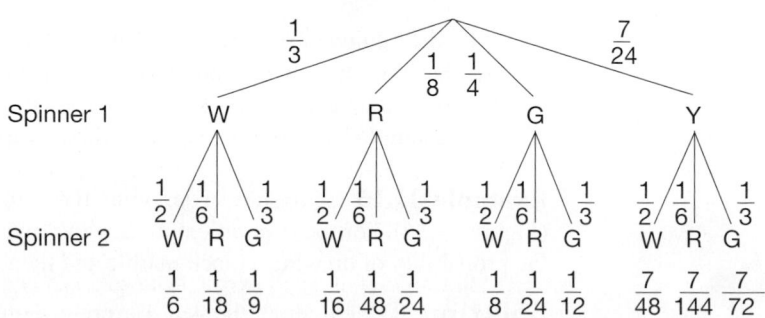

Figure 11.18(b)

The desired event is $\{WW, RR, GG\}$. By the multiplicative property of probability, $P(WW) = \frac{1}{3} \cdot \frac{1}{2} = \frac{1}{6}$, $P(RR) = \frac{1}{8} \cdot \frac{1}{6} = \frac{1}{48}$, and $P(GG) = \frac{1}{4} \cdot \frac{1}{3} = \frac{1}{12}$. By the additive property of probability, $P(\{WW, RR, GG\}) = \frac{1}{6} + \frac{1}{48} + \frac{1}{12} = \frac{13}{48}$. ■

Problem-Solving Strategy
Draw a Diagram

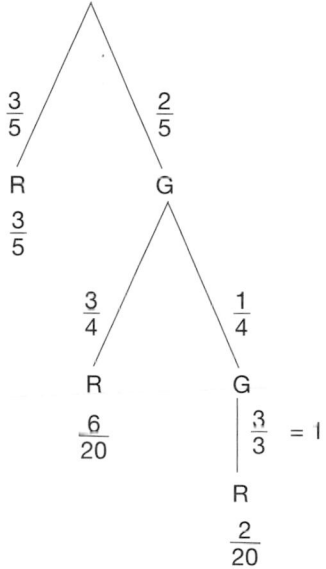

Figure 11.19

Example 11.18   A jar contains three red gumballs and two green gumballs. An experiment consists of drawing gumballs one at a time from the jar, without replacement, until a red one is obtained. Find the probability of the following events.

> A: Only one draw is needed.
> B: Exactly two draws are needed.
> C: Exactly three draws are needed.

Solution   In constructing the probability tree diagram, it is important to remember that this experiment involves drawing until a red gumball appears. As a result, the tree diagram (see Figure 11.19) terminates whenever a red is drawn. Since the gumballs are being drawn without replacement, the number of gumballs in the bag changes, as do the corresponding probabilities, after each gumball is drawn. Using the multiplicative property of probability, the probabilities at the end of each can branch easily be determined. Hence $P(A) = \frac{3}{5}$, $P(B) = \frac{2}{5} \cdot \frac{3}{4} = \frac{6}{20} = \frac{3}{10}$, and $P(C) = \frac{2}{5} \cdot \frac{1}{4} \cdot 1 = \frac{2}{20} = \frac{1}{10}$. ■

In summary, the probability of a complex event can be found as follows:

1. Construct the appropriate probability tree diagram.
2. Assign probabilities to each branch.
3. Multiply the probabilities along individual branches to find the probability of the outcome at the end of each branch.
4. Add the probabilities of the relevant outcomes, depending on the event.

Finally we would like to examine a certain class of experiments whose outcomes can be counted using a more convenient procedure. Such experiments consist of a sequence of smaller identical experiments *each having two outcomes*. Coin-tossing experiments are in this general class since there are only two outcomes (heads/tails) on each toss.

Example 11.19
a. Three coins are tossed. How many outcomes are there?
b. Repeat for 4, 5, and 6 coins.
c. Repeat for n coins, where n is a counting number.

Solution

a. For each coin there are two outcomes. Thus, by the fundamental counting property, there are $2 \times 2 \times 2 = 2^3 = 8$ total outcomes.
b. For 4 coins, by the fundamental counting property, there are $2^4 = 16$ outcomes. For 5 and 6 coins, there are $2^5 = 32$ and $2^6 = 64$ outcomes, respectively.
c. For n coins, there are 2^n outcomes. ■

Counting outcomes in experiments such as coin tosses can be done systematically. Figure 11.20 shows all the outcomes for the experiments in which 1, 2, or 3 coins are tossed.

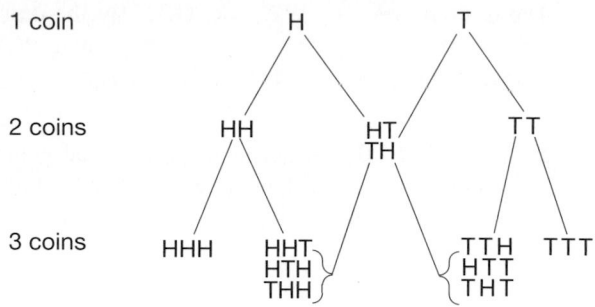

Outcomes in coin experiments

Figure 11.20

From the sample space for the experiment of tossing 1 coin we can determine the outcomes for an experiment of tossing 2 coins (Figure 11.20, second row). The two ways of getting exactly 1 head (middle two entries) are derived from the outcomes for tossing 1 coin. The outcome H for 1 coin yields the outcomes HT for two coins, while the outcome T for one coin yields TH for two coins.

In a similar way, the outcomes for tossing 3 coins (Figure 11.20, third row) are derived from the outcomes for tossing 2 coins. For example, the three ways of getting 2 heads when tossing 3 coins is the *sum* of the number of ways of getting 2 or 1 heads when tossing 2 coins. This can be seen by taking the 1 arrangement for getting 2 heads with 2 coins and making the third coin a tail. Similarly, take the arrangements of getting 1 head with 2 coins, and make the third coin a head. This gives all 3 possibilities.

We can abbreviate this counting procedure, as shown in Figure 11.21.

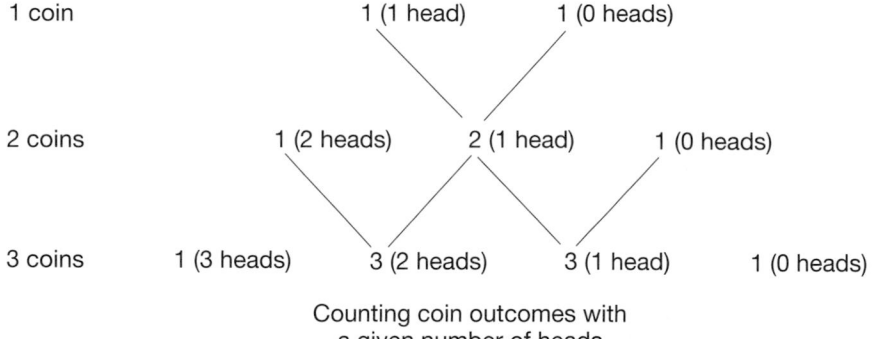

Counting coin outcomes with
a given number of heads

Figure 11.21

Problem-Solving Strategy
Look for a Pattern

Notice that the row of possible arrangements when tossing 3 coins begins with 1. Thereafter each entry is the sum of the two entries immediately above it until the final 1 on the right. This pattern generalizes to any whole number of coins. The number array that we obtain is **Pascal's triangle.** Figure 11.22 shows seven rows of Pascal's triangle.

										Sum
					1					2^0
1 coin					1	1				2^1
2 coins				1	2	1				$4 = 2^2$
3 coins			1	3	3	1				$8 = 2^3$
4 coins		1	4	6	4	1				$16 = 2^4$
5 coins	1	5	10	10	5	1				$32 = 2^5$
6 coins	1	6	15	20	15	6	1			$64 = 2^6$

Figure 11.22

Notice that the sum of the entries in the nth row is 2^n.

Example 11.20   Six fair coins are tossed. Find the probability of getting exactly 3 heads.

Solution   From Example 11.19 there are $2^6 = 64$ outcomes. Furthermore, the 6-coins row of Pascal's triangle (Figure 11.22) may be interpreted as follows:

$$1(6H) \quad 6(5H) \quad 15(4H) \quad 20(3H) \quad 15(2H) \quad 6(1H) \quad 1(0H).$$

Thus there are 20 ways of getting exactly 3 heads, and the probability of 3 heads is $\frac{20}{64} = \frac{5}{16}$.   ■

Notice in Example 11.20 that even though half the coins are heads, the probability is not $\frac{1}{2}$, as one might initially guess.

Example 11.21   Use Pascal's triangle to find the probability of getting at least four heads when tossing seven coins.

Solution   First, by the fundamental counting property, there are 2^7 possible outcomes when tossing 7 coins. Next, construct the row that begins 1, 7, 21, . . . in Pascal's triangle in Figure 11.22.

$$1 \quad 7 \quad 21 \quad 35 \quad 35 \quad 21 \quad 7 \quad 1$$

The first four numbers—1, 7, 21, and 35—represent the number of outcomes for which there are at least four heads. Thus the probability of tossing at least four heads with seven coins is $\dfrac{(1 + 7 + 21 + 35)}{2^7} = \dfrac{64}{128} = \dfrac{1}{2}$.   ■

Pascal's triangle provides a useful way of counting coin arrangements or outcomes in any experiment in which only two equally likely possibilities exist. For example, births (male/female), true/false exams, and target shooting (hit/miss) are sources of such experiments.

MATHEMATICAL MORSEL

The following story of the $500,000 "sure thing" appeared in a national news magazine. A popular wagering device at several race-tracks and jai alai frontons was called Pick Six. To win, one had to pick the winners of six races or games. The jackpot prize would continue to grow until someone won. At one fronton, the pot reached $551,331. Since there were eight possible winners in each of six games, the number of ways that six winners could occur was 8^6, or 262,144. To cover all of these combinations, a group of bettors bought a $2 ticket on every one of the combinations, betting $524,288 in total. Their risk was that someone else would do the same thing or be lucky enough to guess the correct combination, in which case they would have to split the pot. Neither event happened, so the betting group won $988,326.20, for a net pretax profit of $464,038.20. (The jai alai club kept part of the total amount of money bet.)

Section 11.2 EXERCISE / PROBLEM SET A

EXERCISES

1. The simplest tree diagrams have **one stage** (when the experiment involves just one action). For example, consider drawing one ball from a box containing a red, a white, and a blue ball. To draw the tree, follow these steps.

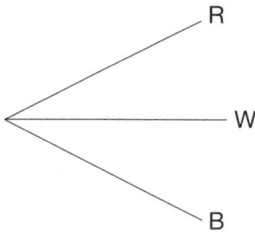

   1. Draw a single dot.
   2. Draw one branch for each outcome.
   3. At the end of the branch, label it by listing the outcome.

   Draw one-stage trees to represent each of the following experiments.

   a. Tossing a dime
   b. Drawing a marble from a bag containing one red, one green, one black, and one white marble
   c. Choosing a TV program from among channels 2, 6, 9, 12, and 13.
   d. Spinning the following spinner, where all central angles are 120°

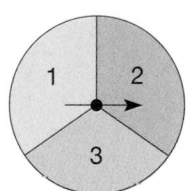

2. In each part, draw **two-stage** trees to represent the following experiments, which involve a sequence of two experiments.

   1. Draw the one-stage tree for the outcomes of the first experiment.
   2. Starting at the end of *each branch* of the tree in step 1, draw the (one-stage) tree for the outcomes of the second experiment.

   a. Tossing a coin twice
   b. Drawing a marble from a box containing one yellow and one green marble, then drawing a marble from a box containing one yellow, one red, and one blue marble
   c. Having two children in the family

3. Trees may have more than two stages. Draw outcome trees to represent the following experiments.

   a. Tossing a coin three times
   b. Having four children in the family (Use *B* for boy and *G* for girl.)

4. In some cases, what happens at the first stage of the tree affects what can happen at the next stage. For example, one ball is drawn from the box containing one red, one white, and one blue ball, but not replaced before the second ball is drawn.

   a. Draw the first stage of the tree.
   b. If the red ball was selected and not replaced, what possible outcomes are possible on the second draw? Starting at *R,* draw a branch to represent these outcomes.
   c. If the white was drawn first, what outcomes are possible on the second draw? Draw these branches.
   d. Do likewise for the case that blue was drawn first.
   e. How many total outcomes are possible?

5. For your vacation, you will travel from your home to New York City, then to London. You may travel to New York City by car, train, bus, or plane, and from New York to London by ship or plane.

   a. Draw a tree diagram to represent possible travel arrangements.
   b. How many different routes are possible?
   c. Apply the fundamental counting property to find the number of possible routes. Does your answer agree with part (b)?

6. Draw a probability tree diagram for drawing a ball from the following containers. An example for the first container is provided.

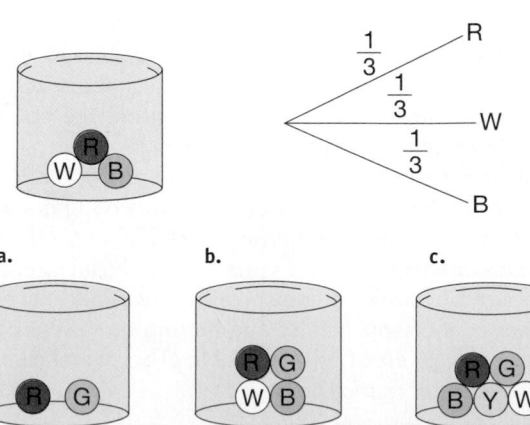

   a.   b.   c.

7. Another white ball is added to the container with one red, one white, and one blue ball. Since there are four balls, we could draw a tree with 4 branches, as illustrated. Each of these branches is equally likely, so we label them with probability $\frac{1}{4}$. However, we could combine the branches, as illustrated. Since two out of the four balls are white, $P(W) = \frac{2}{4} = \frac{1}{2}$, and the branch is so labeled.

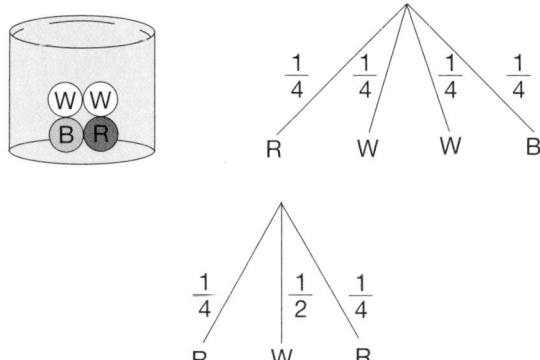

Draw a probability tree representing drawing one ball from the following containers. Combine branches where possible.

8. The branches of a probability tree diagram may or may not represent equally likely outcomes. The given probability tree diagram represents the outcome for each of the following spinners. Write the appropriate probabilities along each branch in each case.

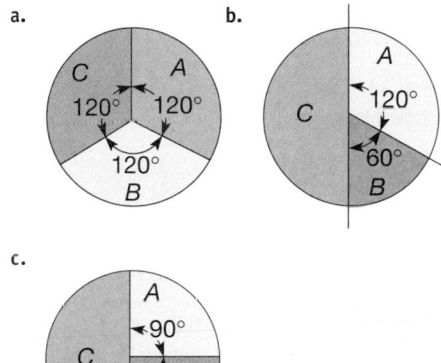

9. The row of Pascal's triangle that starts 1, 4, . . . would be useful in finding probabilities for an experiment of tossing four coins.

  a. Interpret the meaning of each number in the row.

  b. Find the probability of exactly one head and three tails.

  c. Find the probability of at least one tail turning up.

  d. Should you bet in favor of getting exactly two heads or should you bet against it?

PROBLEMS

10. If each of the 10 digits is chosen at random, how many ways can you choose the following numbers?

  a. A two-digit code number, repeated digits permitted

  b. A three-digit identification card number, for which the first digit cannot be a 0

  c. A four-digit bicycle lock number, where no digit can be used twice

  d. A five-digit zip code number, with the first digit not zero

11. a. If eight horses are entered in a race and three finishing places are considered, how many finishing orders are possible?

  b. If the top three horses are Lucky One, Lucky Two, and Lucky Three, in how many possible orders can they finish?

  c. What is the probability that these three horses are the top finishers in the race?

12. Three children are born to a family.

  a. Draw a tree diagram to represent the possible order of boys (*B*) and girls (*G*).

  b. How many of the outcomes involve all girls? two girls, one boy? one girl, two boys? no girls?

  c. How do these results relate to Pascal's triangle?

13. In shooting at a target three times, on each shot you either hit or miss (and we assume these results are equally likely). The 1, 3, 3, 1 row of Pascal's triangle can be used to find the probabilities of hits and misses.

NUMBER OF HITS	3	2	1	0
NUMBER OF WAYS (8 TOTAL)	1	3	3	1
PROBABILITY	$\frac{1}{8}$	$\frac{3}{8}$	$\frac{3}{8}$	$\frac{1}{8}$

a. Use Pascal's triangle to fill in the entries in the following table for shooting 4 times.

NUMBER OF HITS	4	3	2	1	0
NUMBER OF WAYS					
PROBABILITY					

b. Which is more likely, that in three shots you will have three hits or that in four shots you will have three hits and one miss?

14. The Los Angeles Lakers and Portland Trailblazers are going to play a "best two out of three" series. The tree shows the possible outcomes.

a. If the teams are evenly matched, each has a probability of $\frac{1}{2}$ of winning any game. Label each branch of the tree with the appropriate probability.

b. Find the probability that Los Angeles wins the series in two straight games and that Portland wins the series after losing the first game.

c. Find the following probabilities.

   i. Los Angeles wins when three games are played.

  ii. Portland wins the series.

 iii. The series requires three games to decide a winner.

15. Suppose that the Los Angeles Lakers and the Portland Trailblazers are not quite evenly matched in their "best two out of three" series. Let the probability that the Lakers win an individual game with Portland be $\frac{3}{5}$.

a. What is the probability that Portland wins an individual game?

b. Label the branches of the probability tree with the appropriate probability.

c. What is the probability that Portland wins in two straight games?

d. What is the probability that LA wins the series when losing the second game?

e. What is the probability that the series goes for three games?

f. What is the probability that LA wins the series?

16. Team A and team B are playing a "best three out of five" series to determine a champion. Team A is the stronger team with an estimated probability of $\frac{2}{3}$ of winning any game.

a. Team A can win the series by winning three straight games. That path of the tree would look like this:

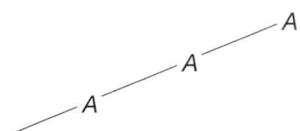

Label the branches with probabilities and find the probability that this occurs.

b. Team A can win the series in four games, losing one game and winning three games. This could occur as $BAAA$, $ABAA$, or $AABA$ (Why not $AAAB$?). Compare the probabilities of the following paths.

  i.

 ii.

What do you observe? What is the probability that team A wins the series in four games?

c. The series could go to five games. Team A could win in this case by winning three games and losing two games (they must win the last game). List the ways in which this could be done. What is the probability of each of these ways? What is the probability of team A winning the series in five games?

d. What is the probability that team A will be the winner of the series? that team B will be the winner?

17. **a.** Complete the tree diagram to show the possible ways of answering a true/false test with three questions.

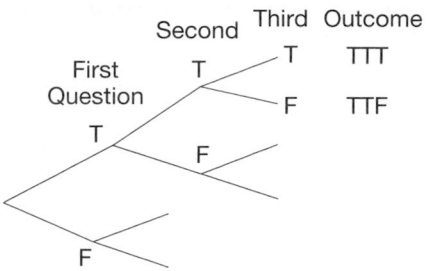

b. How many possible outcomes are there?

c. How many of these outcomes give the correct answers?

d. What is the probability of guessing all the correct answers?

18. Your drawer contains two blue socks, two brown socks, and two black socks. Without looking, you pull out two socks.

a. Draw a probability tree diagram (use E for blue, N for brown, K for black).

b. List the sample space.

c. List the event that you have a matched pair.

d. What is the probability of getting a matched pair?

e. What is the probability of getting a matched blue pair?

19. Your drawer contains two blue socks, two brown socks, and two black socks. What is the minimum number of socks that you would need to pull, at random, from the drawer to be sure that you have a matched pair?

20. A customer calls a pet store seeking a male puppy. An assistant, who is bathing three puppies, is asked whether one is a male. The assistant looks at the one he is toweling and says, "This one is a female." What is the probability that either one of the other two is a male?

21. A box contains four white and six black balls. A second box contains seven white and three black balls. A ball is picked at random from the first box and placed in the second box. A ball is then picked from the second box. What is the probability that it is white?

22. a. How many equilateral triangles of all sizes are in a 6 × 6 × 6 equilateral triangle similar to the one in Problem 17 of Part B in Chapter 1, Section 1.2?

b. How many would be in an 8 × 8 × 8 equilateral triangle?

 Section 11.2 EXERCISE / PROBLEM SET B

EXERCISES

1. Draw one-stage trees to represent each of the following situations.

a. Having one child

b. Choosing to go to Boston, Miami, or Los Angeles for vacation

c. Hitting a free throw or missing

d. Drawing a ball from a bag containing balls labeled A, B, C, D, and E

2. a. Draw a two-stage tree to represent the experiment of tossing one coin and rolling one die.

b. How many possible outcomes are there?

c. In how many ways can the first event (tossing one coin) occur?

d. In how many ways can the second event (rolling one die) occur?

e. According to the fundamental counting property, how many outcomes are possible for this experiment?

3. A coin is tossed. If it lands heads up, a die will be tossed. If it lands tails up, a spinner with equal sections of blue, red, and yellow will be spun. Draw a two-stage tree for the experiment.

4. Outcome tree diagrams may not necessarily be symmetrical. For example, from the box containing one red, one white, and one blue ball, we will draw balls (without replacing) until the red ball is chosen. Draw the outcome tree.

5. Bob has just left town A. There are five roads leading from town A to town B and four roads leading from town B to C. How many possible ways does he have to travel from A to C?

6. The given tree represents the outcomes for each of the following experiments in which one ball is taken from the container. Write the appropriate probabilities along each branch for each case.

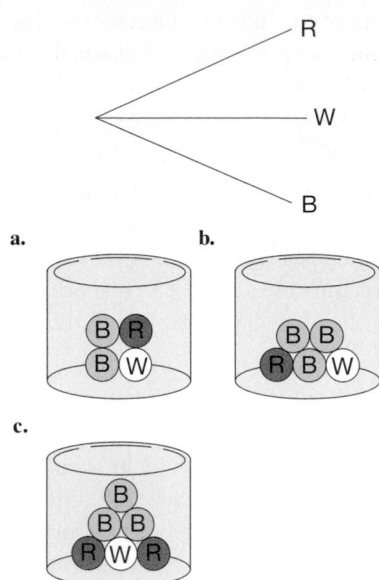

a.

b.

c.

7. A container holds two yellow and three red balls. A ball will be drawn, its color noted, and then replaced. A second ball will be drawn and its color recorded. A tree diagram representing the outcomes is given.

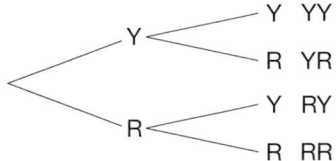

a. On the diagram, indicate the probability of each branch.

b. What is the probability of drawing YY? of drawing RY?

c. What is the probability of drawing at least one yellow?

d. Show a different way of computing part (c), using the complement event.

8. Draw probability tree diagrams for the following experiments.

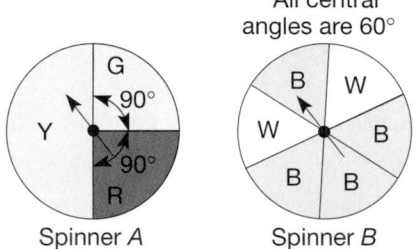

Spinner A   Spinner B

a. Spinner *A* spun once

b. Spinner *B* spun once

c. Spinner *A* spun, then spinner *B* spun [*Hint*: Draw a two-stage tree combining results of parts (a) and (b).]

9. Four coins are tossed.

a. Draw a tree diagram to represent the arrangements of heads (H) and tails (T).

b. How many outcomes involve all heads? three heads, one tail? two heads, two tails? one head, three tails? no heads?

c. How do these results relate to Pascal's triangle?

PROBLEMS

10. A given locality has the telephone prefix of 237.

a. How many seven-digit phone numbers are possible with this prefix?

b. How many of these possibilities have four ending numbers that are all equal?

c. What is the probability of having one of the numbers in part (b)?

d. What is the probability that the last four digits are consecutive (i.e., 1234)?

11. Many radio stations in the United States have call letters that begin with a W or a K and have four letters.

a. How many arrangements of four letters are possible as call letters?

b. What is the probability of having call letters KIDS?

12. A local menu offers choices from eight entrées, three varieties of potatoes, either salad or soup, and five beverages.

a. If you select an entrée with potatoes, salad or soup, and beverage, how many different meals are possible?

b. How many of these meals have soup?

c. What is the probability that a patron has a meal with soup?

d. What is the probability that a patron has a meal with french fries (one of the potato choices) and cola (one of the beverage choices)?

13. A family decides to have five children. Since there are just two outcomes, boy (B) and girl (G), for each birth and since we will assume that each outcome is equally likely (this is not exactly true), Pascal's triangle can be applied.

a. Which row of Pascal's triangle would give the pertinent information?

b. In how many ways can the family have one boy and four girls?

c. In how many ways can the family have three boys and two girls?

d. What is the probability of having three boys? of having at least three boys?

14. The Houston Rockets and San Antonio Spurs will play a "best two out of three" series. Assume that Houston has a probability of $\frac{1}{3}$ of winning any game.

a. Draw a probability tree showing possible outcomes of the series. Label the branches with appropriate probabilities.

b. What is the probability that Houston wins in two straight games? that San Antonio wins in two straight games?

c. What is the probability that the series goes to three games?

d. What is the probability that Houston wins the series after losing the first game?

e. What is the probability that San Antonio wins the series?

15. a. Make a tree diagram to show all the ways that you can choose answers to a multiple-choice test with three questions. The first question has four possible answers, a, b, c, and d; the second has three possible answers, a, b, and c; the third has two possible answers, a and b.

b. How many possible outcomes are there?

c. Apply the fundamental counting property to find the number of possible ways. Does your answer agree with part (b)?

d. If all the answer possibilities are equally likely, what is the probability of guessing the right set of answers?

16. Babe Ruth's lifetime batting average was .343. In three times at bat, what is the probability of the following? (*Hint*: Draw a probability tree diagram.)

a. He gets three hits.   **b.** He gets no hits.

c. He gets at least one hit.

d. He gets exactly one hit.

17. A coin will be thrown until it lands heads up or until the coin has been thrown five times.

a. Draw a probability tree to represent this experiment.

b. What is the probability that the coin is tossed just once? just twice? just three times? just four times?

c. What is the probability of tossing the coin five times without getting a head?

18. You come home on a dark night and find the porchlight burned out. Since you cannot tell which key is which, you randomly try the five keys on your key ring until you find one that opens your apartment

door. Two of the keys on your key ring unlock the door. Find the probability of opening the door on the first or second try.

a. Draw the tree diagram for the experiment.

b. Compute the probability of opening the door with the first or second key.

19. The ski lift at a ski resort takes skiers to the top of the mountain. As the skiers head down the trails, they have a variety of choices. Assume that at each intersection of trails, the skier is equally likely to go left or right. Find the percent (to the nearest whole percent) of the skiers who end up at each lettered location at the bottom of the hill.

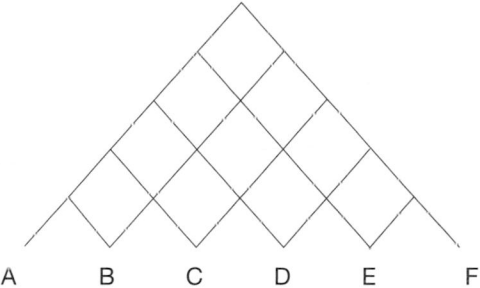

20. A prisoner is given 10 white balls, 10 black balls, and 2 boxes. He is told that his fate depends on drawing a ball from one of the two boxes. If it is white, the prisoner will go free; if it is black, he will remain in prison. Each box has an equally likely chance of being selected, but the prisoner can distribute the balls between the boxes to his advantage. How should he arrange the balls in the boxes to give himself the best chance for freedom?

21. In a television game show, a major prize is hidden behind one of three curtains. A contestant selects a curtain. Then one of the other curtains is opened and the prize is *not* there. The contestant can pick again. Should she switch or stay with her original choice? (To gain a better understanding of this problem, do the Chapter 11 eManipulative activity, *Let's Make a Deal.*)

22. A box contains four white and eight black balls. You pick out a ball with your left hand and don't look at it. Then you pick out a ball with your right hand and don't look at it.

a. What is the probability the ball in your left hand is white?

b. Next, you look at the ball in your right hand and it is black. Now what is the probability that the ball in your left hand is white?

23. Prove or disprove: In any set of four consecutive Fibonacci numbers, the difference of the squares of the middle pair equals the product of the end pair.

PROBLEMS FOR WRITING/DISCUSSION

1. Herman's father was going on an informal business trip, and he wished to minimize his luggage. He brought two pairs of shoes, two shirts, two pairs of trousers, and two sport coats. Assuming he would always wear one of each of these items, Herman says his Dad will have eight different outfits, $2 + 2 + 2 + 2$. Is this correct? If not, how would you help explain this situation?

2. Freda says that the probability of choosing a king from a deck of cards is 4/52 and the probability of choosing a heart is 13/52. So the probability of choosing the king of hearts is 17/52. Before you have a chance to explain to Freda, Mattie jumps in and says, "No, Freda, you don't add, you multiply. So the answer is $52/52^2$." What mistake did Freda make? Is Mattie correct? How would you explain this to your students?

3. Maxwell is looking at a similar problem. He knows how to find the probability of the king of hearts, which is represented by P(king and heart), but he is trying to figure out the probability of drawing a king or a heart at random from a deck of cards. He says, "*Or* means 'plus,' so the answer must be 17/52." Does *or* ever mean "plus"? How would you explain this problem to Maxwell?

11.3 SIMULATION, EXPECTED VALUE, ODDS, AND CONDITIONAL PROBABILITY

 STARTING POINT

For Sterling's weekly lawn-mowing job, his parents have given him two choices for his method of payment.

Choice 1: He receives $10.
Choice 2: His parents place four $1 bills, one $5 bill, and two $10 bills in a bag and Sterling draws two bills from the bag.

In the long run, which is the better deal for Sterling? Justify your answer with mathematical reasoning.

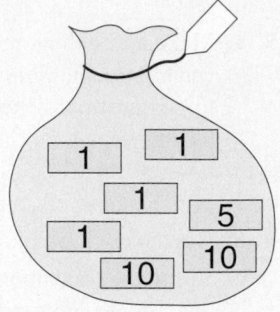

NCTM Standards 2000
Data Analysis and Probability
Grades 6–8
All students should use proportionality and a basic understanding of probability to make and test conjectures about the results of experiments and simulations.

Simulation

In Section 11.1, the difference between theoretical and experimental probability was discussed, and up to this point, the majority of the examples have dealt with theoretical probability. Occasionally, however, an experiment is difficult to analyze theoretically, but the experimental probability can be determined by modeling or simulating the experiment. In these cases, the experimental probability is used to estimate the theoretical probability.

A **simulation** is a representation of an experiment using dice, coins, objects in a bag, or a random-number generator. There is a one-to-one correspondence between outcomes in the original experiment and outcomes in the simulated experiment. The probability that an outcome in the original experiment occurs is estimated to be the experimental probability of its corresponding outcome in the simulated experiment.

Example 11.22   When planning for a family, a husband and wife plan to stop having children after they have either two girls or four children. Since they want to begin saving for their childrens' college educations, they want to predict how many children they should expect to have. If the chances are equally likely of having a girl or a boy, what is the probability that they will have four children?

Solution By assumption, since having a girl or a boy is equally likely, this situation can be simulated using a coin. We will let heads (H) represent a boy and tails (T) represent a girl. In simulating this experiment, we will toss the coin until there are two tails (two girls) or until the coin has been tossed four times (family of four). Below we have simulated the creation of a 40 families by tossing coins. Since the question to be answered is to find the probability of having a family of four, all families of four are in boldface.

HTT	TT	**HHTT**	**HHHH**	**HTHT**	THT	**HTHT**	HTT
HHHT	**HHHH**	**THHH**	**HHHT**	**HTHT**	**HHHH**	**THHH**	**HTHT**
HHTH	**HTHH**	THT	THT	**HTHH**	**HHTH**	THT	THT
HTHT	TT	TT	TT	TT	**HHHT**	TT	TT
THHH	TT	TT	HTT	THT	**HHHT**	TT	**HHTT**

There are 40 families, of which 21 have four children. Thus the probability that the husband and wife have four children is $\frac{21}{40}$, or 52.5%.   ■

This simulation could have been carried out using a spinner divided into two equal parts, drawing two pieces of paper (one marked B and the other G), or using a random-number table. In fact, the next example illustrates how a random-number table can be used to perform simulations.

Example 11.23   A cereal company has put six types of toy cars in its cereal boxes, one car per box. If the cars are distributed uniformly, what is the probability that you will get all six types of cars if you buy 10 boxes?

Problem-Solving Strategy
Do a Simulation

Solution Simulate the experiment by using the whole numbers from 1 through 6 to represent the different cars. Use a table of random digits as the random-number generator (Figure 11.23). (Six numbered slips of paper or chips, drawn at random from a hat, or a six-sided die would also work. In this example we disregard 0, 7, 8, 9, since there are six types of toy cars.) Start anywhere in the table. (We started at the upper left.) Read until 10 numbers from 1 through 6 occur, ignoring 0, 7, 8, and 9. Record the sequence of numbers [Figure 11.23(b)]. Each such sequence of 10 numbers is a simulated outcome. (Simulated outcomes are separated by a vertical bar.) Six of these sequences appear in Figure 11.23(b). Successful outcomes contain 1, 2, 3, 4, 5, and 6 (corresponding to the six cars) and are marked "yes." Based on the simulation, our estimate of the probability is $\frac{2}{6} = 0.\overline{3}$. Using a computer to simulate the experiment yields an estimate of 0.257.

2	2	9	8	5	3	5	1	8	7	⟶	2	2	5	3	5	1	5	4	3	6	yes
7	5	0	4	3	9	6	3	6	4	⟶	3	6	4	6	1	5	3	3	5	6	no
7	7	7	6	1	9	5	9	3	3												
5	6	1	7	2	3	9	6	5	1	⟶	1	2	3	6	5	1	5	6	2	3	no
5	6	2	0	3	2	8	0	5	9	⟶	2	5	3	3	4	6	5	6	6	5	no
3	3	4	8	0	8	6	5	6	6												
9	5	6	7	9	1	3	6	8	3	⟶	6	1	3	6	3	4	4	4	2	5	yes
0	4	4	8	4	2	5	5	9	1	⟶	5	1	1	3	1	2	5	5	1	6	no
8	1	8	7	3	1	8	2	5	5												
1	9	7	6	0	3	2	5	2	3												

(a) Random digits   **(b)** Simulated outcomes

Figure 11.23

■

The previous example used a simulation to find the probability that you would get all six prizes if 10 boxes were purchased. For many collectors, a more useful question would be "How many boxes should I buy in order to get all six prizes?" This question is addressed in the following example.

Example 11.24 A cereal company has put six types of toy cars in its cereal boxes, one car per box. If the cars are distributed uniformly, how many boxes should I buy in order to get all six types of cars?

Solution To simulate this experiment, let the numbers on a die represent each of the six different types of cars. We will roll the die until all six numbers have turned up and then record how many rolls it took to obtain all six numbers. By repeating this 25 times, we will have the data necessary to determine a reasonable estimate of the number of boxes that should be purchased. The numbers below represent five of the 25 trials.

2, 2, 6, 5, 6, 4, 4, 2, 4, 4, 5, 1, 6, 2, 3	→ 15 rolls (boxes)
5, 5, 4, 2, 3, 1, 1, 5, 1, 6	→ 10 rolls (boxes)
2, 5, 5, 4, 4, 5, 6, 3, 2, 2, 6, 3, 4, 4, 2, 1	→ 16 rolls (boxes)
4, 2, 2, 6, 3, 2, 3, 5, 6, 5, 6, 6, 3, 3, 6, 6, 3, 4, 4, 6, 1	→ 21 rolls (boxes)
4, 5, 3, 6, 5, 2, 1	→ 7 rolls (boxes)

After repeating this process 20 more times, we computed the average of the rolls needed to get all six toy cars. Based on this simulation, the average was 15.12 rolls. On average, a collector should buy 15 to 16 boxes of cereal to get all six types of cars. ▰

Spotlight on Technology The simulation for Example 11.24 can also be done using the Chapter 11 eManipulative activity, *Simulation*. Simply click on the numbers 1, 2, 3, 4, 5, and 6. Once these numbers have been placed in the box, press START and let the computer draw numbers from the box until all six numbers have been drawn. Record the number of draws that were required and repeat the process. When a sufficient number of repetitions have been done, compute the average number of draws.

www.wiley.com/college/musser

Another way to phrase the question in the previous example would be to say, "How many boxes would a collector *expect* to have to buy in order to get all six types of toy cars?" This idea of expected outcomes leads us to the next idea.

Expected Value

Probability can be used to determine values such as admission to games (with payoffs) and insurance premiums, using the idea of expected value.

Example 11.25 A cube has three red faces, two green faces, and a blue face. A game consists of rolling the cube twice. You pay $2 to play. If both faces are the same color, you are paid $5 (you win $3). If not, you lose the $2 it costs to play. Will you win money in the long run?

Solution Use a probability tree diagram (Figure 11.24). Let W be the event that you win. Then $W = \{RR, GG, BB\}$, and $P(W) = \frac{1}{2} \cdot \frac{1}{2} + \frac{1}{3} \cdot \frac{1}{3} + \frac{1}{6} \cdot \frac{1}{6} = \frac{7}{18}$. Hence $\frac{7}{18}$ (about 39%) of the time you will win, and $\frac{11}{18}$ (about 61%) of the time you will lose. If you play the game 18 times, you can expect to win 7 times and lose 11 times on average. Hence, your winnings, in dollars, will be $3 \times 7 + (-2) \times 11 = -1$. That is, you can expect to lose $1 if you play the game 18 times. On the average, you will lose $1/18 per game (about 6¢).

Problem-Solving Strategy
Draw a Diagram

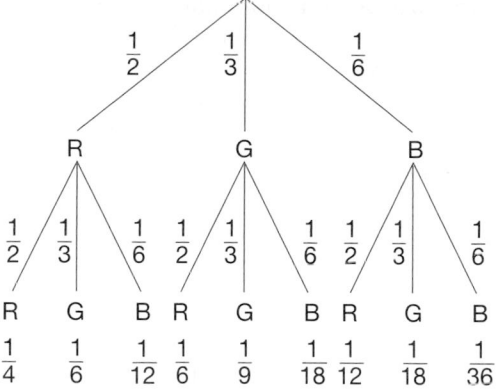

Figure 11.24

In Example 11.25, the amount in dollars that we expect to "win" on each play of the game is $3 \times \frac{7}{18} + (-2) \times \frac{11}{18} = -\frac{1}{18}$, called the expected value. Expected value is defined as follows.

 DEFINITION

Expected Value

Suppose that the outcomes of an experiment are real numbers (values) called $v_1, v_2, \ldots, v_n$, and suppose that the outcomes have probabilities $p_1, p_2, \ldots, p_n$ respectively. The **expected value,** E, of the experiment is the sum

$$E = v_1 \cdot p_1 + v_2 \cdot p_2 + \cdots + v_n \cdot p_n.$$

The expected value of an experiment is the average value of the outcomes over many repetitions. The next example shows how insurance companies use expected values.

Example 11.26 Suppose that an insurance company has broken down yearly automobile claims for drivers from age 16 through 21, as shown in Table 11.4. How much should the company charge as its average premium in order to break even on its costs for claims?

Solution Use the notation from the definition for expected value. Let $n = 6$ (the number of claim categories), and let the values $v_1, v_2, \ldots, v_n$ and the probabilities $p_1, p_2, \ldots, p_n$ be as listed in Table 11.5.

Thus the expected value, $E = 0(0.80) + 2000(0.10) + 4000(0.05) + 6000(0.03) + 8000(0.01) + 10,000(0.01) = 760$. Since the average claim value is $760, the average automobile insurance premium should be set at $760 per year for the insurance company to break even on its claims costs. ■

Odds

The term *odds* is used often in the English language in situations ranging from horse racing to medical research. For example, hepatitis C is a disease of the liver. If a person is a chronic carrier of the virus, the odds of his developing cirrhosis of the liver are 1 : 4. Under certain treatments for hepatitis C, the odds of achieving a substantial decrease in the presence of the virus are 2 : 3. The use of the term *odds* may sound familiar, but what do these odds really mean and how are they related to probability?

Table 11.4

AMOUNT OF CLAIM (NEAREST $2000)	PROBABILITY
0	0.80
$2,000	0.10
4,000	0.05
6,000	0.03
8,000	0.01
10,000	0.01

Table 11.5

V	P
$v_1 = 0$	$p_1 = 0.80$
$v_2 = 2000$	$p_2 = 0.10$
$v_3 = 4000$	$p_3 = 0.05$
$v_4 = 6000$	$p_4 = 0.03$
$v_5 = 8000$	$p_5 = 0.01$
$v_6 = 10,000$	$p_6 = 0.01$

When computing the probability of an event occurring, we examine the ratio of the favorable outcomes compared to the total number of possible outcomes. When people speak about odds in favor of an event, they are comparing the number of favorable outcomes of an event to the number of unfavorable outcomes of the event. This comparison assumes, as we will in this section, that outcomes are equally likely. According to this description, a person who is a chronic carrier of hepatitis C has one chance of developing cirrhosis and four chances of not developing it. Similarly, a person who undergoes a certain treatment has two chances of a substantial benefit and three chances of not having a substantial benefit.

In general, let E be an event in the sample space S and $\overline{E}$ be the event complementary to E. Then odds are defined formally as follows.

DEFINITION

Odds for Events with Equally Likely Outcomes

The **odds in favor** of event E are $n(E):n(\overline{E})$.
The **odds against** event E are $n(\overline{E}):n(E)$.

Example 11.27 If a six-sided die is tossed, what are the odds in favor of the following events?

a. Getting a 4   **b.** Getting a prime
c. Getting a number greater than 0   **d.** Getting a number greater than 6

Solution

a. $1:5$, since there is one 4 and five other numbers
b. $3:3 = 1:1$, since there are three primes (2, 3, and 5) and three nonprimes
c. $6:0$ since all numbers are favorable to this event
d. $0:6$ since no numbers are favorable to this event

Notice that in Example 11.27(c) it is reasonable to allow the second number in the odds ratio to be zero.

Just like the sets E and $\overline{E}$ combine to make the entire sample space, the number of favorable outcomes combines with the number of unfavorable outcomes to yield the total number of possible outcomes. This connection allows a smooth transition between odds and probability.

It is possible to determine the odds in favor of an event E directly from its probability. For example, if $P(E) = \frac{5}{7}$, we would expect that, in the long run, E would occur five out of seven times and not occur two of the seven times. Thus the odds in favor of E would be $5:2$. When determining the odds in favor of E, we compare $n(E)$ and $n(\overline{E})$. Now consider $P(E) = \frac{5}{7}$ and $P(\overline{E}) = \frac{2}{7}$. If we compare these two probabilities in the same order, we have $P(E):P(\overline{E}) = \frac{5}{7}:\frac{2}{7} = \frac{5}{7} \div \frac{2}{7} = \frac{5}{2} = 5:2$, the odds in favor of E. The following discussion justifies the latter method of calculating odds. The odds in favor of E are

$$\frac{n(E)}{n(\overline{E})} = \frac{\dfrac{n(E)}{n(S)}}{\dfrac{n(\overline{E})}{n(S)}} = \frac{P(E)}{P(\overline{E})} = \frac{P(E)}{1 - P(E)}$$

Thus we can find the odds in favor of an event directly from the probability of an event.

THEOREM

The odds in favor of the event E are

$$P(E):1 - P(E) \quad \text{or} \quad P(E):P(\overline{E}).$$

The odds against E are

$$1 - P(E):P(E) \quad \text{or} \quad P(\overline{E}):P(E).$$

Example 11.28   In fact, this result is used to define odds using probabilities in the case of unequally likely outcomes as well as equally likely outcomes.

Find the odds in favor of event E, where E has the following probabilities.

a. $P(E) = \frac{1}{2}$ **b.** $P(E) = \frac{3}{4}$ **c.** $P(E) = \frac{5}{13}$

Solution

a. Odds in favor of $E = \frac{1}{2} : (1 - \frac{1}{2}) = \frac{1}{2} : \frac{1}{2} = 1:1$

b. Odds in favor of $E = \frac{3}{4} : (1 - \frac{3}{4}) = \frac{3}{4} : \frac{1}{4} = 3:1$

c. Odds in favor of $E = \frac{5}{13} : (1 - \frac{5}{13}) = \frac{5}{13} : \frac{8}{13} = 5:8$ ■

Now suppose that you know the odds in favor of an event E. Can the probability of E be found? The answer is "yes!" For example, if the odds in favor of E are $2:3$, this means that the ratio of favorable outcomes to unfavorable outcomes is $2:3$. Thus in a sample space with five elements with two outcomes favorable to E and three unfavorable, $P(E) = \frac{2}{5} = \frac{2}{2 + 3}$. In general, we have the following.

THEOREM

If the odds in favor of E are $a:b$, then

$$P(E) = \frac{a}{a + b}.$$

Example 11.29   Find $P(E)$ given that the odds in favor of (or against) E are as follows.

a. Odds in favor of E are $3:4$.   **b.** Odds in favor of E are $9:2$.
c. Odds against E are $7:3$ **d.** Odds against E are $2:13$.

Solution

a. $P(E) = \dfrac{3}{3 + 4} = \dfrac{3}{7}$ **b.** $P(E) = \dfrac{9}{9 + 2} = \dfrac{9}{11}$

c. $P(E) = \dfrac{3}{7 + 3} = \dfrac{3}{10}$ **d.** $P(E) = \dfrac{13}{2 + 13} = \dfrac{13}{15}$ ■

Conditional Probability

When drawing cards from a standard deck of 52 cards, we know that the probability of drawing an ace is $\frac{4}{52} = \frac{1}{13}$, since there are 4 aces in the deck. If a second draw is made, what is the probability of drawing an ace given that 1 ace has already been drawn? Our sample space is now 51 cards with 3 aces, so the probability is $\frac{3}{51}$. Even though both probabilities deal with drawing an ace, the results are different because the second example has an extra condition that reduces the size of the sample space. When such conditions are added that change the size of the sample space, it is referred to as *conditional* probability.

Example 11.30 When tossing three fair coins, what is the probability of getting two tails given that the first coin came up heads?

Solution When tossing three coins, there are eight outcomes: HHH, HHT, HTH, THH, HTT, THT, TTH, TTT. In this case, however, the condition of the first coin being a head has been added. This changes the possible outcomes to be {HHH, HHT, HTH, HTT}. There are only four possible outcomes in this reduced sample space. The only outcome fitting the description of having two tails in this sample space is HTT. Thus the conditional probability of getting two tails given that the first of the three coins is a head is $\frac{1}{4}$. ▪

Problem-Solving Strategy
Draw a Diagram

(a)

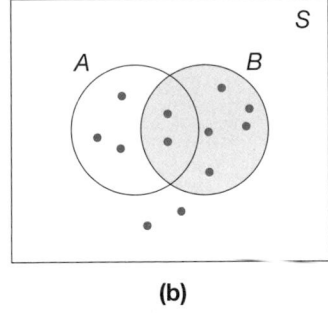

(b)

Figure 11.25

In Example 11.30 the original sample space is reduced to those outcomes having the given condition, namely H on the first coin. Let A be the event that exactly two tails appear among the three coins, and let B be the event the first coin comes up heads. Then $A = \{HTT, THT, TTH\}$ and $B = \{HHH, HHT, HTH, HTT\}$. We see that there is only one way for A to occur given that B occurs, namely HTT. (Note that $A \cap B = \{HTT\}$.) Thus the probability of A given B is $\frac{1}{4}$. The notation $P(A \mid B)$ means "the probability of A given B." So, $P(A \mid B) = \frac{1}{4}$. Notice that $P(A \mid B) = \frac{1}{4} = \frac{1/8}{4/8} = \frac{P(A \cap B)}{P(B)}$. That is $P(A \mid B)$ the relative frequency of event A *within* event B. This suggests the following.

DEFINITION

Conditional Probability

Suppose A and B are events in a sample space S such that $P(B) \neq 0$. The **conditional probability** that event A occurs, given that event B occurs, denoted $P(A \mid B)$, is

$$P(A \mid B) = \frac{P(A \cap B)}{P(B)}.$$

A Venn diagram can be used to illustrate the definition of conditional probability. A sample space S of equally likely outcomes is shown in Figure 11.25(a). The reduced sample space, given that event B occurs, appears in Figure 11.25(b). From Figure 11.25(a) we see that $\frac{P(A \cap B)}{P(B)} = \frac{2/12}{7/12} = \frac{2}{7}$. From Figure 11.25(b) we see that $P(A \mid B) = \frac{2}{7}$. Thus $P(A \mid B) = \frac{P(A \cap B)}{P(B)}$.

The next example illustrates conditional probability in the case of unequally likely outcomes.

Example 11.31 Suppose a 20-sided die has the following numerals on its faces: 1, 1, 2, 2, 2, 3, 3, 4, 5, 6, 7, 8, 9, 10, 11, 12, 13, 14, 15, 16. The die is rolled once and the number on the top face is recorded. Let A be the event the number is prime, and B be the event the number is odd. Find $P(A \mid B)$ and $P(B \mid A)$.

Solution Assuming that the die is balanced, $P(A) = \frac{9}{20}$, since there are 9 ways that a prime can appear. Similarly, $P(B) = \frac{10}{20}$, since there are 10 ways that an odd number can occur. Also, $P(A \cap B) = P(B \cap A) = \frac{6}{20}$, since an odd prime can appear in 6 ways. Thus

$$P(A \mid B) = \frac{P(A \cap B)}{P(B)} = \frac{6/20}{10/20} = \frac{3}{5}$$

and

$$P(B \mid A) = \frac{P(B \cap A)}{P(A)} = \frac{6/20}{9/20} = \frac{2}{3}.$$

These results can be checked by reducing the sample space to reflect the given information, then assigning probabilities to the events as they occur as subsets of the *reduced sample space*. ■

MATHEMATICAL MORSEL

If I drop this needle on those lines, I get a pi?

The French naturalist Buffon devised his famous needle problem from which π may be determined using probability methods. The method is as follows. Draw a number of parallel lines at a distance of d units apart. Then a needle, whose length l is less than d, is dropped *at random* onto the parallel lines. Buffon showed that the probability P that the needle will touch one of the lines is given by $P = 2l/\pi d$. Thus, if this experiment is performed a large number of times, an approximate value of π can be found using the equation $\pi = 2l/Pd$, where here P represents the probability obtained in this experiment.

Section 11.3   EXERCISE / PROBLEM SET A

EXERCISES

Simulation

1. A penny gumball machine contains gumballs in eight different colors. Assume that there are a large number of gumballs equally divided among the eight colors.

   a. Estimate how many pennies you will have to use to get one of each color.

   b. Cut out eight identical pieces of paper and mark them with the digits 1–8. Put the pieces of paper in a container. Without looking, draw one piece and record its number. Replace the piece, mix the pieces up, and draw again. Repeat this process until all digits have appeared. Record how many draws it took. Repeat this experiment a total of 10 times and average the number of draws needed.

2. Use the Chapter 11 eManipulative activity, *Simulation*, to simulate Problem 1 by doing the following.

   1. Click on one each of the numbers 1 through 8.
   2. Press START and watch until all 8 numbers have drawn at least once.
   3. Press PAUSE and record the number of draws.
   4. Clear the draws and repeat. (Perform at least 20 repetitions.)
   5. Average the number of pennies needed.

3. A cloakroom attendant receives five fur coats from five women and gets them mixed up. She returns the coats at random. Follow the following steps to find the probability that at least one woman receives her own coat.

   1. Cut out five pieces of paper, all the same size, and label them A, B, C, D, and E.
   2. Put the pieces in a container and mix them up.
   3. Draw the pieces out, one at a time, without replacing them, and record the order.
   4. Repeat steps 2 and 3 a total of 25 times.
   5. Count the number of times at least one letter is in the appropriate place (A in first place, B in second place, etc.).

   From this simulation, what is the approximate probability that at least one woman receives her own coat?

4. You are going to bake a batch of 100 oatmeal cookies. Because raisins are expensive, you will only put 150 raisins in the batter and mix the batter well. Follow the steps given to find out the probability that a cookie will end up without a raisin.

   1. Draw a 10 × 10 grid as illustrated. Each cell is represented by a two-digit number. The first digit is the horizontal scale and the second digit is the vertical scale. For example, 06 and 73 are shown.

OUTCOME	−2000	0	1000	3000
PROBABILITY	$\frac{1}{4}$	$\frac{1}{6}$	$\frac{1}{4}$	$\frac{1}{3}$

7. A study of attendance at a football game shows the following pattern. What is the expected value of the attendance?

WEATHER	ATTENDANCE	WEATHER PROBABILITY
Extremely cold	30,000	0.06
Cold	40,000	0.44
Moderate	52,000	0.35
Warm	65,000	0.15

2. Given is a portion of a table of random digits. For each two-digit number in the table, place an × in the appropriate cell of your grid.

15	77	01	64	69	69	58	40	81	16
85	40	51	40	10	15	33	94	11	65
47	69	35	90	95	16	17	45	86	29
13	26	87	40	20	40	81	46	08	09
10	55	33	20	47	54	16	86	11	16
60	20	00	84	22	05	06	67	26	77
57	62	94	04	99	65	50	89	18	74
16	70	48	02	00	59	68	53	31	55
74	99	16	92	99	31	31	05	36	48
59	34	71	55	84	91	59	46	44	45
14	85	40	52	68	60	41	94	98	18
42	07	50	15	69	86	97	40	25	88
73	47	16	49	79	69	80	76	16	60
75	16	00	21	11	42	44	84	46	84
49	25	36	12	07	25	90	89	55	25

a. Tally the number of squares that have no raisin indicated. What is the probability of selecting a cookie without a raisin?

b. If your calculator can generate random numbers, generate another set of 150 numbers and repeat this experiment.

5. A young couple is planning their family and would like to have one child of each sex. On average, how many children should they plan for in order to have at least one boy and one girl.

a. Describe a simulation that could be used to answer the above question.

b. Perform at least 30 trials of the simulation and record your results.

c. Repeat parts (a) and (b) using the Chapter 11 eManipulative activity, *Simulation*.

Expected Value

6. From the data given, compute the expected value of the outcome.

8. A player rolls a fair die and receives a number of dollars equal to the number of dots showing on the face of the die.

a. If the game costs $1 to play, how much should the player expect to win for each play?

b. If the game costs $2 to play, how much should the player expect to win per play?

c. What is the most the player should be willing to pay to play the game and not lose money in the long run?

9. A student is considering applying for two scholarships. Scholarship A is worth $1000 and scholarship B is worth $5000. Costs involved in applying are $10 for scholarship A and $25 for scholarship B. The probability of receiving scholarship A is 0.05 and of scholarship B is 0.01.

a. What is the student's expected value for applying for scholarship A?

b. What is the student's expected value for applying for scholarship B?

c. If the student can apply for only one scholarship, which should she apply for?

Odds

10. Which, if either, are more favorable odds, 50:50 or 100:100? Explain.

11. Two dice are thrown.

a. Find the odds in favor of the following events.

   i. Getting a sum of 7

   ii. Getting a sum greater than 3

   iii. Getting a sum that is an even number

b. Find the odds against each of the events in part (a).

12. A die is thrown once.

a. If each face is equally likely to turn up, what is the probability of getting a 5?

b. What are the odds in favor of getting a 5?

c. What are the odds against getting a 5?

13. In each part, you are given the probability of event E. Find the odds in favor of event E and the odds against event E.

a. $\frac{3}{5}$ **b.** $\frac{1}{4}$ **c.** $\frac{5}{6}$

14. In each part, you are given the following odds in favor of event E. Find $P(E)$.

a. $9:1$ **b.** $2:5$ **c.** $12:5$

15. Two fair dice are rolled, and the sum of the dots is recorded. In each part, give an example of an event having the given odds in its favor.

a. $1:1$ **b.** $1:5$ **c.** $1:3$

Conditional Probability

16. The diagram shows a sample space S of equally likely outcomes and events A and B. Find the following probabilities.

a. $P(A)$ **b.** $P(B)$ **c.** $P(A \mid B)$ **d.** $P(B \mid A)$

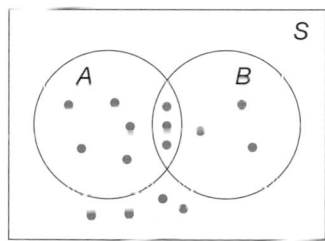

17. The spinner is spun once. (All central angles equal 60°.)

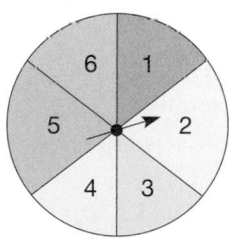

a. What is the probability that it lands on 4?

b. If you are told it has landed on an even number, what is the probability that it landed on 4?

c. If you are told it has landed on an odd number, what is the probability that it landed on 4?

18. A container holds three red balls and five blue balls. One ball will be drawn and discarded. Then a second ball is drawn.

a. What is the probability that the second ball drawn is red if you drew a red ball the first time?

b. What is the probability of drawing a blue ball second if the first ball was red?

c. What is the probability of drawing a blue ball second if the first ball was blue?

19. A six-sided die is tossed. What is the probability that it shows 2 if you know the following?

a. It shows an even number.

b. It shows a number less than 5.

c. It does not show a 6.

d. It shows 1 or 2.

e. It shows an even number less than 4.

f. It shows a number greater than 3.

20. Given is the probability tree diagram for an experiment. The sample space $S = \{a, b, c, d\}$. Also, event $A = \{a, b, c\}$ and event $B = \{b, c, d\}$. Find the following probabilities.

a. $P(A)$ **b.** $P(B)$ **c.** $P(A \cap B)$

d. $P(A \cup B)$ **e.** $P(A \mid B)$ **f.** $P(B \mid A)$

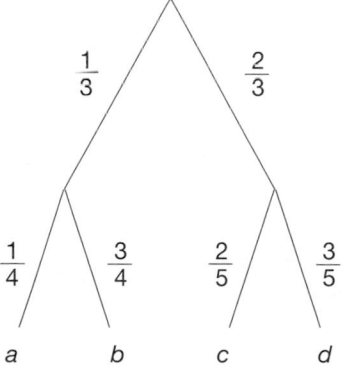

PROBLEMS

21. In the World Series, the team that wins four out of seven games is the winner.

a. Would you agree or disagree with the following statement? The prospects for a long series decrease when the teams are closely matched.

b. If the probability that the American League team wins any game is p, what is the probability that it wins the series in four games?

c. If the probability that the National League team wins any game is q, what is the probability that it wins the series in four games? (NOTE: $q = 1 - p$.)

d. What is the probability that the series ends at four games?

e. Complete the following table for the given odds.

ODDS FAVORING AMERICAN LEAGUE	1:1	2:1	3:1	3:2
p				
q				
P(AMERICAN IN 4 GAMES)				
P(NATIONAL IN 4 GAMES)				
P(4-GAME SERIES)				

  f. What conclusion can you state from this evidence about the statement in part (a)?

22. a. In a five-game World Series, there are four ways the American League could win (*NAAAA*, *ANAAA*, *AANAA*, and *AAANA*). Here, event *A* is an American League win, event *N* a National League victory. If $P(A) = p$ and $P(N) = q$, what is the probability of each sequence? What is the probability of the American League winning the series in five games?

  b. Similarly, there are four ways the National League could win (verify this). What is the probability of the National League winning in five games?

  c. What is the probability the series will end at five games?

23. a. There are ten ways the American League can win a six-game World Series. (There are 10 branches that contain four *A*'s and two *N*'s, where the last one is *A*.) If $P(A) = p$ and $P(N) = q$, what is the probability of the American League winning the World Series in six games? (NOTE: $q = 1 - p$.)

  b. There are also ten ways the National League team can win a six-game series. What is the probability of that event?

  c. What is the probability that the World Series will end at six games?

24. a. There are 20 ways each for the American League team or National League team to win a seven-game World Series. If $P(A) = p$ and $P(N) = q$, what is the probability of the American League winning? (NOTE: $q = 1 - p$.)

  b. What is the probability of the National League winning?

  c. What is the probability of the World Series going all seven games?

25. Summarize the results from Problems 21 to 24. Here

  a. $P(A) = p$ and $P(N) = q$, where $p + q = 1$.

X = NUMBER OF GAMES	4	5	6	7
P(AMERICAN WINS)				
P(NATIONAL WINS)				
P(X GAMES IN SERIES)				

  b. If the odds in favor of the American League are 1:1, complete the following table.

X = NUMBER OF GAMES	4	5	6	7
P(X)				

  c. Find the expected value for the length of the series.

26. A snack company has put five different prizes in its snack boxes, one per box. Assuming that the same number of each toy has been used, how many boxes of snacks should you expect to buy in order to get all five toys?

  a. Describe how to use the Chapter 11 eManipulative activity, *Simulation*, to perform a simulation of this problem.

  b. Perform a simulation of at least 30 trials and record your results.

Section 11.3   EXERCISE / PROBLEM SET B

EXERCISES

Simulation

1. A candy bar company is having a contest. On the inside of each package, N, U, or T is printed in ratios 3:2:1. To determine how many packages you should buy to spell NUT, perform the following simulation.

  1. Using a die, let 1, 2, 3 represent N; let 4, 5 represent U; and let 6 represent T.

  2. Roll the die and record the corresponding letter. Repeat rolling the die until each letter has been obtained.

  3. Repeat step 2 a total of 20 times.

Average the number of packages purchased in each case.

2. Use the Chapter 11 eManipulative activity, *Simulation*, to simulate Problem 1 by doing the following.

  1. Click on one 1, two 2s, and three 3s.

  2. Press START and watch until all three numbers 1, 2, and 3 appear at least once.

  3. Press PAUSE and record the number of draws.

4. Clear the draws and repeat. (Perform at least 20 repetitions.)

5. Average the number of candy bars purchased.

3. A family wants to have five children. To determine the probability that they will have at least four of the same sex, perform the following simulation.

1. Use five coins, where H = girl and T = boy.

2. Toss the five coins and record how they land.

3. Repeat step 2 a total of 30 times.

4. Count the outcomes that have at least four of the same sex.

What is the approximate probability of having at least four of the same sex?

4. A bus company overbooks the 22 seats on its bus to the coast. It regularly sells 25 tickets. Assuming that there is a 0.1 chance of any passenger not showing up, complete the following steps to find the probability that at least one passenger will not have a seat.

1. Let the digit 0 represent not showing up and the digits 1–9 represent showing up. Is $P(0) = 0.1$?

2. Given here is a portion of a random number table. Each row of 25 numbers represents the 25 tickets sold on a given day. In the first row, how many passengers did not show up (how many zeros appear)?

07018	31172	12572	23968	55216
52444	65625	97010	46794	62370
72161	57299	87521	44351	99981
17918	75071	91057	46829	47992
13623	76165	43195	50205	75736
27426	97534	89707	97453	90836
96039	21338	88169	69530	53300
68282	98888	25545	69406	29470
54262	21477	33097	48125	92982
66920	27544	72780	91384	47296
53348	39044	04072	62210	01209
34482	42758	40128	48136	30254
99268	98715	07545	27317	52459
95342	97178	10401	31615	95784
38556	60373	77935	64608	28949
39159	04795	51163	84475	60722
41786	18169	96649	92406	42733
95627	30768	30607	89023	60730
98738	15548	42263	79489	85118
75214	61575	27805	21930	94726
73904	89123	19271	15792	72675
33329	08896	94662	05781	59187
66364	94799	62211	37539	80172
68349	16984	86532	96186	53893
19193	99621	66899	12351	72438

3. Count the number of rows that have two or fewer zeros. They represent days in which someone will not have a seat.

  a. From this simulation, what is the probability that at least one passenger will not have a seat?

  b. If your calculator can generate random numbers, generate another five sets of 25 numbers and repeat the experiment.

5. Explain how to simulate the rolling of die using the random-number table in Problem 4. Simulate 20 rolls of a dice and record your results.

Expected Value

6. From the following data, compute the expected value of the payoff.

PAYOFF	−2	0	2	3
PROBABILITY	0.3	0.1	0.4	0.2

7. A laboratory contains ten electronic microscopes, of which two are defective. Four microscopes are to be tested. All microscopes are equally likely to be chosen. A sample of four microscopes can have zero, one, or two defective ones, with the probabilities given.

NUMBER OF DETECTIVES	0	1	2
PROBADILITY	$\frac{1}{3}$	$\frac{8}{15}$	$\frac{2}{15}$

What is the expected number of defective microscopes in the sample?

8. For visiting a resort, you will receive one gift. The probabilities and manufacturer's suggested retail values of each gift are as follows: gift A, 1 in 52,000 ($9272.00); gift B, 25,736 in 52,000 ($44.95); gift C, 1 in 52,000 ($2500.00); gift D, 3 in 52,000 ($729.95); gift E, 25,736 in 52,000 ($26.99); gift F, 3 in 52,000 ($1000.00); gift G, 180 in 52,000 ($44.99); gift H, 180 in 52,000 ($63.98); gift I, 160 in 52,000 ($25.00). Find the expected value of your gift.

9. According to a publisher's records, 20% of the books published break even, 30% lose $1000, 25% lose $10,000, and 25% earn $20,000. When a book is published, what is the expected income for the book?

Odds

10. Which, if either, are more favorable odds, 60:40 or 120:80? Explain.

11. A card is drawn at random from a standard 52-card deck. Find the following odds.

    a. In favor of drawing a face card (king, queen, or jack)

    b. Against drawing a diamond

    c. In favor of drawing the ace of spades

    d. Against drawing a 2, 3, or 4

12. The spinner is spun once. Find the following odds.

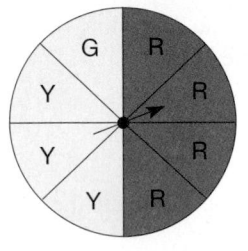

All central angles are 45°

    a. In favor of getting yellow

    b. Against getting green

    c. In favor of getting a primary color (blue, red, or yellow)

    d. Against getting red or green

13. You are given the probability of event E. Find the odds in favor of event E and the odds against event E.

    a. $\frac{1}{8}$ b. $\frac{2}{5}$

14. In each part, you are given the following odds *against* event E. Find $P(E)$ in each case.

    a. $8:1$ b. $5:3$ c. $6:5$

15. Two fair dice are rolled, and the sum of the dots is recorded. In each part, give an example of an event having the given odds in its favor.

    a. $2:1$ b. $4:5$ c. $35:1$

Conditional Probability

16. The diagram shows a sample space S of equally likely outcomes and events A, B, and C. Find the following probabilities.

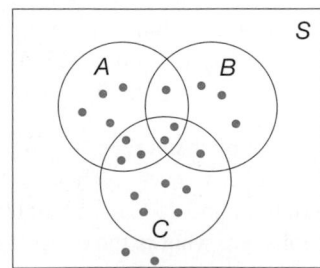

    a. $P(A)$ b. $P(B)$ c. $P(C)$
    d. $P(A \mid B)$ e. $P(B \mid A)$ f. $P(A \mid C)$
    g. $P(C \mid A)$ h. $P(B \mid C)$ i. $P(C \mid B)$

17. A spinner is spun whose central angles are all 45°. What is the probability that it lands on 5 if you know the following?

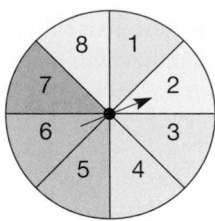

    a. It lands on an odd number.

    b. It lands on a number greater than 3.

    c. It does not land on 7 or 8.

    d. It lands on a factor of 10.

18. One container holds the letters D A D and a second container holds the letters A D D. One letter is chosen randomly from the first container and added to the second container. Then a letter will be chosen from the second container.

    a. What is the probability that the second letter chosen is D if the first letter was A? if the first letter was D?

    b. What is the probability that the second chosen letter is A if the first letter was A? if the first letter was D?

19. Given is a tabulation of academic award winners in a school.

	NUMBER OF STUDENTS RECEIVING AWARDS	NUMBER OF MATH AWARDS
Class 1	15	7
Class 2	16	8
Class 3	14	9
Class 4	20	11
Class 5	19	12
Class 6	21	14
Boys	52	29
Girls	53	32

A student is chosen at random from the award winners. Find the probabilities of the following events.

    a. The student is in class 1.

    b. The student is in class 4, 5, or 6.

    c. The student won a math award.

    d. The student is a girl.

    e. The student is a boy who won a math award.

    f. The student won a math award given that he or she is in class 1.

    g. The student won a math award given that he or she is in class 1, 2, or 3.

h. The student is a girl, given that he or she won a math award.

i. The student won a math award, given that she is a girl.

20. An experiment consists of tossing six coins. Let A be the event that at least three heads appear. Let B be the event that the first coin shows heads. Let C be the event that the first and last coins show heads. Find the following probabilities.

a. $P(A \mid B)$ **b.** $P(B \mid A)$ **c.** $P(A \mid C)$
d. $P(C \mid A)$ **e.** $P(B \mid C)$ **f.** $P(C \mid B)$

PROBLEMS

21. Since you do not like to study for your science test, a 10-question true/false test, you decide to guess on each question. To determine your chances of getting a score of 70% or better, perform the following simulation.

1. Use a coin where H = true and T = false.

2. Toss the coin 10 times, recording the corresponding answers.

3. Repeat step 2 a total of 20 times.

4. Repeat step 2 one more time. This is the answer key of correct answers. Correct each of the 20 "tests."

   a. How many times was the score 70% or better?

   b. What is the probability of a score of 70% or better?

   c. Use Pascal's triangle to compute the probability that you will score 70% or more.

22. How many cards would we expect to draw from a standard deck in order to get two aces? (Do a simulation; use at least 100 trials.)

23. You are among 20 people called for jury duty. If there are to be two cases tried in succession and a jury consists of 12 people, what are your chances of serving on the jury for at least one trial? Assume that all potential jurors have the same chance of being

called for each trial. [Do a simulation; use an icosahedron die (20 faces), 20 playing cards, 20 numbered slips of paper, or better yet, a computer program, and at least 100 trials.]

24. Using a spinner with three equal sectors, do a simulation to solve Problem 21 in Exercise/Problem Set 11.2, Part B.

25. Roll a standard (six-face) die until each of the numbers from 1 through 5 appears. Ignore 6. Count the number of rolls needed. This is one trial. Repeat at least 100 times and average the number of rolls needed in all the trials. Your average should be around 11. Theoretical expected value = 11.42.

26. Describe how to use the Chapter 11 eManipulative activity, *Simulation*, to perform a simulation of Problem 25. Perform a simulation of at least 30 trials using the eManipulative.

27. Eight points are evenly spaced around a circle. How many segments can be formed by joining these points?

28. True or false? The sum of all the numbers in a 3 × 3 additive magic square of whole numbers must be a multiple of 3. If true, prove. If false, give a counterexample. (*Hint:* What can you say about the sums of the three rows?)

PROBLEMS FOR WRITING/DISCUSSION

1. Sanchez is going to the third Cleveland Indians game at the beginning of the season. Julio Franco, who has been up to bat seven times in the two previous games, has gotten a total of three hits. Sanchez says to you, "He got three hits out of seven times at bat, so the odds are 7 : 3 that he won't get a hit in his first at bat of the game." How would you respond?

2. Franco's batting average is .333. He has just had five hits in a row. What are the odds that he gets a hit his next time at bat? Explain.

3. Cookie stated that it is best to do a simulation whenever an experiment is very complex or requires a large number of trials. Do you agree? Explain.

11.4 ADDITIONAL COUNTING TECHNIQUES

Roberto and Darius were having a contest to see who could make the most towers out of combinations of red and green blocks. Each tower must be exactly four blocks high and look different from all of the rest of the four-block towers. How many towers can you make? (Three example towers are shown.)

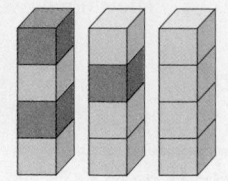

Most of the examples and problems discussed thus far in this chapter have been solved by writing out the sample space or using a tree diagram. Suppose that the sample space is too large and a tree diagram too complex. For example, the question "What is the probability of having four of a kind in a random four-card hand dealt from a standard deck of cards?" has a sample space consisting of all four-card hands. Such a sample space would be unmanageable to list. This section introduces counting techniques that can be used to determine the size of a sample space or the number of elements in an event without having to list them.

The fundamental counting property in Section 11.2 can be used to count the number of ways that several events can occur in succession. It states that if an event A can occur in r ways and an event B can occur in s ways, then the two events can occur in succession in $r \times s$ ways. This property can be generalized to more than two events. For example, suppose that at a restaurant you have your choice of three appetizers, four soups, five main courses, and two desserts. Altogether, you have $3 \times 4 \times 5 \times 2$ or 120 complete meal choices. In this section we will apply the fundamental counting property to develop counting techniques for complicated arrangements of objects.

Permutations

An ordered arrangement of objects is called a **permutation.** For example, for the three letters C, A, and T, there are six different three-letter permutations or "words" that we can make: ACT, ATC, CAT, CTA, TAC, and TCA. If we add a fourth letter to our list, say S, then there are exactly 24 different four-letter permutations, which are listed as follows:

ACST	CAST	SACT	TACS
ACTS	CATS	SATC	TASC
ASCT	CSAT	SCAT	TCAS
ASTC	CSTA	SCTA	TCSA
ATCS	CTAS	STAC	TSAC
ATSC	CTSA	STCA	TSCA

We used a systematic list to write down all the permutations by alphabetizing them in columns. Even so, this procedure is cumbersome and would get out of hand with more and more objects to consider. We need a general principle for counting permutations of several objects.

Let's go back to the case of three letters and imagine a three-letter permutation as a "word" that fills three blanks _ _ _. We can count the number of permutations of the letters A, C, and T by counting the number of choices we have in filling each blank and applying the fundamental counting property. For example, in filling the first blank, we have three choices, since any of the three letters can be used: $\underset{3}{\_}$ _ _. Then, in filling the second blank we have two choices *for each of the first three choices*, since either of the two remaining letters can be used: $\underset{3}{\_}\underset{2}{\_}$ _. Finally, to fill the third blank we have the one remaining letter: $\underset{3}{\_}\underset{2}{\_}\underset{1}{\_}$. Hence, by the fundamental counting property, there are $3 \times 2 \times 1$ or 6 ways to fill all three blanks. This agrees with our list of the six permutations of A, C, and T.

We can apply this same technique to the problem of counting the four-letter permutations of A, C, S, and T. Again, imagine filling four blanks using each of the four letters. We have four choices for the first letter, three for the second, two for the third, and one for the fourth: $\underset{4\ 3\ 2\ 1}{\_\ \_\ \_\ \_}$. Hence, by the fundamental counting property, we have $4 \times 3 \times 2 \times 1$ or 24 permutations, just as we found in our list.

Our observations lead to the following generalization: Suppose that we have n objects from which to form permutations. There are n choices for the first object, $n - 1$ choices for the second object, $n - 2$ for the third, and so on, down to one choice for the last object. Hence, by the fundamental counting property, there are $n \times (n - 1) \times (n - 2) \times \ldots \times 3 \times 2 \times 1$ permutations of the n objects. For every whole number n, $n > 0$, the product $n \times (n - 1) \times (n - 2) \times \ldots \times 3 \times 2 \times 1$ is called **n factorial** and is written using an exclamation point as **$n!$**. (Zero factorial is defined to be 1.)

Example 11.32 Evaluate the following expressions involving factorials.

a. $5!$ **b.** $10!$ **c.** $\dfrac{10!}{7!}$

Solution

a. $5! = 5 \times 4 \times 3 \times 2 \times 1 = 120$

b. $10! = 10 \times 9 \times 8 \times 7 \times 6 \times 5 \times 4 \times 3 \times 2 \times 1 = 3,628,800$

c. $\dfrac{10!}{7!} = \dfrac{10 \times 9 \times 8 \times 7 \times 6 \times 5 \times 4 \times 3 \times 2 \times 1}{7 \times 6 \times 5 \times 4 \times 3 \times 2 \times 1}$

   $= 10 \times 9 \times 8 = 720$

[NOTE: The fraction in part (c) was simplified first to simplify the calculation.] ■

 Spotlight on Technology Many calculators have a factorial key, such as $\boxed{n!}$ or $\boxed{x!}$. Entering a whole number and then pressing this key yields the factorial in the display.

Using factorials, we can count the number of permutations of n distinct objects.

 THEOREM

The number of permutations of n distinct objects, taken all together, is $n!$.

Example 11.33

a. Miss Murphy wants to seat 12 of her students in a row for a class picture. How many different seating arrangements are there?

b. Seven of Miss Murphy's students are girls and 5 are boys. In how many different ways can she seat the 7 girls together on the left, then the 5 boys together on the right?

Solution

a. There are $12! = 479,001,600$ different permutations, or seating arrangements, of the 12 students.

b. There are $7! = 5040$ permutations of the girls and $5! = 120$ permutations of the boys. Hence, by the fundamental counting property, there are $5040 \times 120 = 604,800$ arrangements with the girls seated on the left. ■

We will now consider permutations of a set of objects taken from a larger set. For example, suppose that in a certain lottery game, four different digits are chosen from the digits 0 through 9 to form a four-digit number. How many different numbers can be made? There are 10 choices for the first digit, 9 for the second, 8 for the third, and 7 for the fourth. By the fundamental counting property, then, there are $10 \times 9 \times 8 \times 7$, or 5040, different possible winning numbers. Notice that the number of permutations of 4 digits chosen from 10 digits is $10 \times 9 \times 8 \times 7 = 10!/6! = 10!/(10 - 4)!$.

We can generalize the preceding observation to permutations of r objects from n objects—in the example about 4-digit numbers, $n = 10$ and $r = 4$. Let $_nP_r$ denote the number of permutations of r objects chosen from n objects.

THEOREM

The number of permutations of r objects chosen from n objects, where $0 \leq r \leq n$, is

$$_nP_r = \frac{n!}{(n - r)!}.$$

To justify this result, imagine making a sequence of r of the objects. We have n choices for the first object, $n - 1$ choices for the second object, $n - 2$ choices for the third object, and so on down to $n - r + 1$ choices for the last object. Thus we have

$$_nP_r = n \times (n - 1) \times (n - 2) \times \ldots \times (n - r + 1)$$

$$= \frac{n!}{(n - r)!} \text{ total permutations.}$$

Spotlight on Technology Many calculators have a special key for calculating $_nP_r$. To use this key, press the value of n, then the $\boxed{nPr}$ key, then the value of r, then $\boxed{=}$. The value of $_nP_r$ will be displayed. If such a key is not available, the following key strokes may be used: n $\boxed{x!}$ $\boxed{\div}$ $\boxed{(}$ n $\boxed{-}$ r $\boxed{)}$ $\boxed{x!}$ $\boxed{=}$.

Example 11.34 Using the digits 1, 3, 5, 7, and 9, with no repetitions of digits, how many
a. one-digit numbers can be made?
b. two-digit numbers can be made?
c. three-digit numbers can be made?
d. four-digit numbers can be made?
e. five-digit numbers can be made?

Solution Each number corresponds to a permutation of the digits. In each case, $n = 5$.

a. With $r = 1$, there are $5!/(5 - 1)! = 5$ different one-digit numbers.
b. With $r = 2$, there are $5!/(5 - 2)! = 5!/3! = 20$ different two-digit numbers.
c. With $r = 3$, there are $5!/(5 - 3)! = 60$ different three-digit numbers.
d. With $r = 4$, there are $5!/(5 - 4)! = 120$ different four-digit numbers.
e. With $r = 5$, there are $5!/(5 - 5)! = 5!/0! = 120$ different five-digit numbers. Recall that 0! is defined as 1. ■

Combinations

A collection of objects, *in no particular order*, is called a **combination.** Using the language of sets, we find that a combination is a subset of a given set of objects. For example, suppose that in a group of five students—Barry, Harry, Larry, Mary, and Teri—three students are to be selected to make a team. Each of the possible three-member teams is a combination. How many such combinations are there? We can answer this question by using our knowledge of permutations and the fundamental counting property.

If order did matter in the selection of the three students for this team, permutations would be used and would yield $_5P_3 = 5!/(5 - 3)! = 60$. Since order doesn't matter in this case, permutations would count more teams than there should be, so we need to divide out all of the extra teams. The permutations BHL, BLH, HBL, HLB, LBH, LHB are really just one combination, {B, H, L}. Figure 11.26 shows that for each three-person *combination*, there are six three-person *permutations*. This is consistent with the fact that three objects can be rearranged in $3! = 6$ different ways.

CORRESPONDING COMBINATIONS		ALL POSSIBLE 3-PERSON PERMUTATIONS
{B, H, L}	<—>	BHL, BLH, HBL, HLB, LBH, LHB
{B, H, M}	<—>	BHM, BMH, HBM, HMB, MBH, MHB
{B, H, T}	<—>	BHT, BTH, HBT, HTB, TBH, THB
.		.
.		.
.		.
{L, M, T}	<—>	LMT, LTM, MLT, MTL, TLM, TML
Total number of combinations	=	Total number of permutations divided by 6 ($- 3!$), since there are six arrangements for each combination

Figure 11.26

To compute the number of possible combinations of three students chosen from a group of five, we can compute the number of permutations, $_5P_3 = 5!/(5 - 3)! = 60$, and divide out the repetition, $3! = 6$. This yields

$$_5C_3 = \frac{_5P_3}{3!} = \frac{60}{6} = 10,$$

which could also be written as

$$_5C_3 = \frac{_5P_3}{3!} = \frac{5!}{(5 - 3)!3!} = 10.$$

In general, let $_nC_r$ denote the number of combinations of r objects chosen from a set of n objects. The total number of combinations, $_nC_r$, is equal to the number of permutations, $_nP_r$, divided by $r!$ (the repetition). Thus we have the following result.

● THEOREM

The number of combinations of r objects chosen from n objects, where $0 \le r \le n$, is

$$_nC_r = \frac{n!}{(n - r)! \times r!}.$$

[NOTE: Occasionally, $_nC_r$ is denoted $\binom{n}{r}$ and read "n choose r."]

Spotlight on Technology Many calculators have a key for calculating $_nC_r$. It is used like the $\boxed{nPr}$ key; press the value of n, then $\boxed{nCr}$, then the value of r, followed by $\boxed{=}$. The value of $_nC_r$ will be displayed.

Example 11.35

a. Evaluate $_6C_2$, $_{10}C_4$, $_{10}C_6$, and $_{10}C_{10}$.

b. How many 5-member committees can be chosen from a group of 30 people?

c. How many different 12-person juries can be chosen from a pool of 20 jurors?

Solution

a. $_6C_2 = \dfrac{6!}{(6-2)! \times 2!} = \dfrac{6!}{4! \times 2!} = \dfrac{6 \times 5 \times 4 \times 3 \times 2 \times 1}{(4 \times 3 \times 2 \times 1) \times (2 \times 1)} = 15$

$_{10}C_4 = \dfrac{10!}{(10-4)! \times 4!} = \dfrac{10!}{6! \times 4!} = \dfrac{10 \times 9 \times 8 \times 7 \times 6!}{6! \times (4 \times 3 \times 2 \times 1)} = 210$

$_{10}C_6 = \dfrac{10!}{4! \times 6!} = 210$ from the previous calculations.

$_{10}C_{10} = \dfrac{10!}{0! \times 10!} = 1$

b. The number of committees is $_{30}C_5 = \dfrac{30!}{25! \times 5!} = 142{,}506$.

c. The number of juries is $_{20}C_{12} = \dfrac{20!}{8! \times 12!} = 125{,}970$.   ■

Pascal's Triangle and Combinations

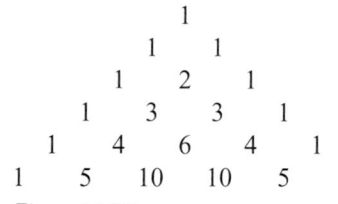

Figure 11.27

Recall Pascal's triangle, the first six rows of which appear in Figure 11.27. It can be shown that the entries are simply values of $_nC_r$. For example, in the row beginning 1, 4, 6 the entries are the values $_4C_0 = 1$, $_4C_1 = 4$, $_4C_2 = 6$, $_4C_3 = 4$, $_4C_4 = 1$. In general, in the row beginning 1, n, the entries are the values of $_nC_r$, where $r = 0, 1, 2, 3, \ldots, n$.

Example 11.36   A fair coin is tossed five times. Find the number of ways that two heads and three tails can appear.

Solution An outcome can be represented as a five-letter sequence of H's and T's representing heads and tails. For example, THHTT represents a successful outcome. To count the successful outcomes, we imagine filling a sequence of five blanks, _ _ _ _ _, with two H's and three T's. If the two H's are placed first, then the three T's will just fill in the remaining spaces. From the five blanks, we will choose two of them to place our H's in. Since the H's are indistinguishable, the order in which they are placed doesn't matter. Therefore, there are $_5C_2 = 10$ ways of placing two H's in five blanks. The three T's go in the remaining three blanks. In the discussions in Section 11.2, it was determined that the number of ways of getting two heads when tossing five coins can be determined by examining the row that begins 1, 5, ... in Pascal's triangle, which can be seen in Figure 11.27.   ■

The next example shows the power of using combinations rather than generating Pascal's triangle.

Example 11.37 On a 30-item true/false test, in how many ways can 27 or more answers be correct?

Solution We can represent an outcome as a 30-letter sequence of C's and I's, for correct and incorrect. To count the number of ways that exactly 27 answers are correct, we count the number of ways that 27 of the 30 positions can have a C in them. There are $_{30}C_{27} = 4060$ such ways. Similarly, there are $_{30}C_{28} = 435$ ways that 28 answers are correct, $_{30}C_{29} = 30$ ways that 29 are correct, and $_{30}C_{30} = 1$ way that all 30 are correct. Thus there are $4060 + 435 + 30 + 1 = 4526$ ways to get 27 or more answers correct. (Using Pascal's triangle to solve this problem would involve generating 30 of its rows—a tedious procedure!) ■

Example 11.38 At Frederico's Pizza they offer 10 different choices of toppings other than cheese. How many different combinations of toppings are available at Frederico's?

Solution The solution to this problem can be viewed in two different ways. One way would be to count how many combinations there are with exactly 0 toppings, 1 topping, 2 toppings, 3 toppings, etc. and add them up. There are $_{10}C_0 = 1$ combinations with 0 toppings, $_{10}C_1 = 10$ combinations with 1 topping, $_{10}C_2 = 45$ combinations with 2 toppings, $_{10}C_3 = 120$ with 3 toppings, etc. Therefore, the total number of topping combinations is $1 + 10 + 45 + 120 + 210 + 252 + 210 + 120 + 45 + 10 + 1 = 1024$, which is the sum of all of the elements of the tenth row of Pascal's triangle.

The second way of looking at this problem is to think of having 10 blanks _ _ _ _ _ _ _ _ _ _, one for each topping. For each blank there are two choices; either put the topping on or leave it off. Thus there are $2 \cdot 2 \cdot 2 \cdot 2 \cdot 2 \cdot 2 \cdot 2 \cdot 2 \cdot 2 \cdot 2 = 2^{10} = 1024$ combinations of toppings. ■

It is interesting to note that the sum of the elements in the row of Pascal's triangle beginning 1, 10, . . . is 2^{10}. Looking back at Figure 11.27, it can be seen that the same pattern holds for the first through fifth rows of Pascal's triangle as well. In general, the sum of all of the elements in the row of Pascal's triangle beginning 1, n, . . . is equal to 2^n.

Probabilities Using Counting Techniques

We will now consider the problem posed at the beginning of the section, "What is the probability of having 4 of a kind in a random 4-card hand dealt from a standard deck of cards?" We know from previous sections that

$$P(4 \text{ of a kind}) = \frac{\text{number of ways to have 4 of a kind}}{\text{number of 4-card hands}}.$$

In determining the number of 4-card hands, it must first be decided whether order matters. Because it only matters which cards you have and *not* the order in which they were dealt, order doesn't matter. There are 52 cards in a standard deck, so the number of 4-card hands is $_{52}C_4 = 270,725$. Since there is only one way to have 4 aces, one way to have 4 kings, one way to have 4 queens, and so forth, the number of ways to have 4 of a kind is 13. Thus,

$$P(4 \text{ of a kind}) = \frac{13}{270,725} = \frac{1}{20,825}.$$

Example 11.39 Hideko and Salina are hoping to be selected from their class of 30 as the president and vice-president of the social committee. If the three-person committee (president, vice-president, and secretary) is selected at random, what is the probability that Hideko and Salina would be president and vice-president of the committee?

Solution If this three-person committee didn't have offices within it, then the order in which the committee was selected wouldn't matter and combinations could be used. Since there are officers on the committee, we will assume that the first person selected is the president, the second person is the vice-president, and the secretary is the last one selected. This makes order important, and thus we will need to use permutations. In general, we want to find

$$P(\text{Pres. \& VP are Salina and Hideko}) = \frac{\text{number of 3-person committees with Salina and Hideko as Pres. and VP}}{\text{total number of 3-person committes}}$$

The total number of possible committees is the number of permutations of 3 objects chosen from 30 objects, or $_{30}P_3 = 30 \cdot 29 \cdot 28 = 24{,}360$.

We now compute the number of committees that have the two friends as president and vice-president. Consider the three slots _ _ _ as the slots of president, vice-president, and secretary, respectively. In order to create the desired type of committee, the first slot would need to be filled by one of the two friends and the second slot by the other. Thus, there are only 2 choices for the first slot and 1 choice for the second slot. The third slot, however, could be filled by any one of the remaining 28 students in the class. The number of committees that would have had Hideko and Salina as the president and vice-president offices is $2 \cdot 1 \cdot 28 = 56$. Thus,

$$P(\text{Pres. \& VP are Salina and Hideko}) = \frac{56}{24{,}360} = \frac{1}{435}. \qquad ■$$

MATHEMATICAL MORSEL

The Rubik's cube, a game that was invented by Erno Rubik in the late 1970s, is a 3-by-3-by-3 cube with colored stickers on the exposed faces of each of the 26 exposed subcubes that make up the 3-by-3-by-3 cube (the middle subcube is omitted to make $26 = 27 - 1$ exposed subcubes). With more than 43 quintillion possible combinations formed by twisting the cube, many strategies require 50 to 100 moves to get the scrambled cube back to its original arrangement. However, Professor Richard Korf from the University of California–Los Angeles claims he has found some significantly better solutions using a computer program on a Sun workstation. Professor Korf's research shows that most scrambled cubes can be solved in less than 18 moves. However, the computer time to find such solutions is as much as several weeks.

Section 11.4 EXERCISE / PROBLEM SET A

EXERCISES

1. Compute each of the following. Look for simplifications first.

   a. $\dfrac{10!}{8!}$ **b.** $\dfrac{12!}{8!\,4!}$ **c.** $_9P_6$ **d.** $_6C_2$

2. Find m and n so that

   a. $\dfrac{9!}{6!} = {}_mP_n$ **b.** $13 = {}_mC_n$

3. Certain automobile license plates consist of a sequence of three letters followed by three digits.

   a. If no repetitions of letters are permitted, how many possible license plates are there?

   b. If no letters and no digits are repeated, how many license plates are possible?

4. A combination lock has 40 numbers on it.

   a. How many different three-number combinations can be made?

   b. How many different combinations are there if the numbers must all be different?

   c. How many different combinations are there if the second number must be different from the first and third?

   d. Why is the name *combination* lock inconsistent with the mathematical meaning of combination?

5. **a.** How many different 5-member teams can be made from a group of 12 people?

   b. How many different 5-card poker hands can be dealt from a standard deck of 52 cards?

6. **a.** Verify that the entries in Pascal's triangle in the 1, 4, 6, 4, 1 row are true values of $_4C_r$ for $r = 0, 1, 2, 3, 4$.

   b. Verify that $_5C_3 = {}_4C_2 + {}_4C_3$.

   c. Show that, in general, $_{n+1}C_r = {}_nC_{r-1} + {}_nC_r$.

   d. Explain how the result in part (c) shows that the entries in the "1, n, . . . " row of Pascal's triangle are the values of $_nC_r$ for $r = 0, 1, 2, \ldots, n$.

7. Ten coins are tossed. Find the probability that the following number of heads appear.

   a. 9   **b.** 7   **c.** 5   **d.** 3   **e.** 1

8. How many different ways can five identical mathematics books and three identical English books be arranged on a shelf? (*Hint*: See Example 11.36.)

9. If a fair coin is tossed eight times, what is the probability of getting exactly three heads?

10. A school dance committee of 4 people is selected at random from a group of 6 ninth graders, 11 eighth graders, and 10 seventh graders.

    a. What is the probability that the committee has all seventh graders?

    b. What is the probability that the committee has no seventh graders?

11. In an effort to promote school spirit, Georgetown High School created ID numbers with just the letters G, H, and S. If each letter is used exactly three times,

    a. how many nine-letter ID numbers can be generated?

    b. what is the probability that a random ID number starts with GHS?

PROBLEMS

12. The license plates in the state of Utah consist of three letters followed by three single-digit numbers.

    a. If Edwardo's initials are EAM, what is the probability that his license plate will have his initials on it (in any order)?

    b. What is the probability that his license plate will have his initials in the correct order?

13. Kofi had forgotten the four-digit combination required to unlock his bike. He could still remember that the digits were 3, 4, 5, and 6 but couldn't remember their order. What is the greatest number of combinations that Kofi will have to try in order to unlock the lock?

14. Find the smallest values of m and n such that

    a. $_mP_n = {}_{10}C_7$.   **b.** $_mC_n = {}_{15}P_2$.

15. In a popular lottery game, five numbers are to be picked randomly from 1 to 36, with no repetitions.

    a. How many ways can these five winning numbers be picked without regard to order?

    b. Answer the same question for picking six numbers.

16. Suppose that there are 10 first-class seats on an airplane. How many ways can the following numbers of first-class passengers be seated?

a. 10   **b.** 9   **c.** 8   **d.** 5

e. r, where $0 \leq r \leq 10$

17. Ten chips, numbered 1 through 10, are in a hat. All of the chips are drawn in succession.

a. In how many different sequences can the chips be drawn?

b. How many of the sequences have chip 5 first?

c. How many of the sequences have an odd-numbered chip first?

d. How many of the sequences have an odd-numbered chip first and an even-numbered chip last?

18. How many five-letter "words" can be formed from the letters P-I-A-N-O if all the letters are different and the following restrictions exist?

a. There are no other restrictions.

b. The first letter is P.

c. The first letter is a consonant.

d. The first letter is a consonant and the last letter is a vowel (a, e, i, o, or u).

19. a. Show that $_{20}C_5 = {_{20}C_{15}}$ without computing $_{20}C_5$ or $_{20}C_{15}$.

b. Show that, in general, $_nC_r = {_nC_{n-r}}$.

c. Given that $_{50}C_7 = 99{,}884{,}400$, find $_{50}C_{43}$.

20. (Refer to the Initial Problem in Chapter 1.) The digits 1 through 9 are to be arranged in the array so that the sum of each side is 17.

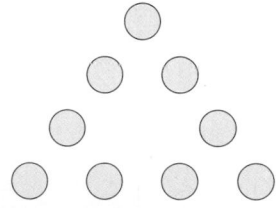

a. How many possible arrangements are there?

b. How many total arrangements are there with 1, 2, and 3 in the corners?

c. Start with 1 at the top, 2 in the lower left corner, and 3 in the lower right corner. Note that the two digits in the 1–2 side must sum to 14. How many two-digit sums of 14 are there using 4, 5, 6, 7, 8, and 9?

d. How many total solutions are there using 1, 2, and 3 as in part (c) and 5 and 9 in the 1–2 side?

e. How many solutions are there for the puzzle, counting all possible arrangements?

The following probability problems involve the use of combinations and permutations.

21. a. Four students are to be chosen at random from a group of 15. How many ways can this be done?

b. If Glenn is one of the students, what is the probability that he is one of the four chosen? (Assume that all students are equally likely to be chosen.)

c. What is the probability that Glenn and Mickey are chosen?

22. Five cards are dealt at random from a standard deck. Find the probability that the hand contains the following cards.

a. 4 aces

b. 3 kings and 2 queens

c. 5 diamonds

d. An ace, king, queen, jack, and ten

23. In a group of 20 people, 3 have been exposed to virus X and 17 have not. Five people are chosen at random and tested for exposure to virus X.

a. In how many ways can the 5 people be chosen?

b. What is the probability that *exactly* one of the people in the group has been exposed to the virus?

c. What is the probability that 1 or 2 people in the group have been exposed to the virus?

 Section 11.4   EXERCISE / PROBLEM SET B

EXERCISES

1. Compute the following:

a. $_{20}P_{15}$ **b.** $\dfrac{23!}{13!\,10!}$

c. $_{10}C_3$ **d.** $\dfrac{(n+1)!}{(n-2)!}$

2. Find m and n so that

a. $\dfrac{16!}{12!\,4!} = {_mC_n}$

b. $23 \cdot 22 \cdot 21 \cdot 20 = {_mP_n}$

3. Which is greater?

    a. $_6P_2$ or $_6C_2$ **b.** $_{12}P_2$ or $_6C_2$

    c. $_{12}C_2$ or $_{12}P_2$ **d.** $_{12}C_9$ or $_{12}P_2$

4. Solve for n.

    a. $_nP_2 = 72$ **b.** $_nC_2 = 66$

5. In how many ways can eight chairs be arranged in a line?

6. If no repetitions are allowed, using the digits 0, 1, 2, 3, 4, 5, 6, 7, 8, 9,

    a. how many two-digit numbers can be formed?

    b. how many of these are odd?

    c. how many of these are even?

    d. how many are divisible by 3?

    e. how many are less than 40?

7. A student must answer 7 out of 10 questions on a test.

    a. How many ways does she have to do this?

    b. How many ways does she have if she must answer the first two?

8. The distance from Lars's home to his school is 11 blocks: 7 blocks to the east and 4 blocks to the north.

How many different paths are there from his house to his school? (NOTE: This is similar to counting the number of arrangements of 7 E's and 4 N's.)

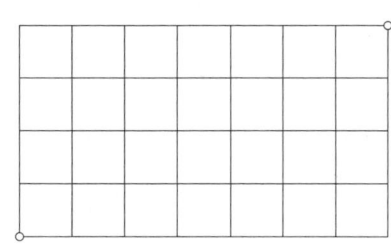

9. Ten children, four boys and six girls, are randomly placed in the bus line. What is the probability that all four boys are standing next to each other?

10. In the high school regional cross-country meet, Chino High, Don Lugo High, and Ontario High fielded six, five, and eight equally skilled runners, respectively. What is the probability that the Chino High team will finish in the top three places?

11. A jar contains three red, five green, and six blue marbles. If all of the marbles are drawn from the bag, what is the probability that the three red marbles are drawn in succession?

PROBLEMS

12. What is the probability of having two aces, two kings, and a queen in a five-card poker hand?

13. Yolanda's Yogurt House offers 3 different kinds of yogurt and 13 different kinds of toppings.

    a. How many different yogurt and topping combinations are possible?

    b. The weekly special is a yogurt with up to 3 toppings for $.99. How many different yogurt and topping combinations are available for the weekly special?

14. Social security numbers are of the form _ _ _ – _ _ – _ _ _ _, where the blanks are filled with the single digit numbers 0–9. If the blanks were filled with letters from the alphabet, instead of numbers, how many more social security numbers would be possible?

15. If a student must take six tests—T1, T2, T3, T4, T5, T6—in how many ways can the student take the tests if

    a. T2 must be taken immediately after T1?

    b. T1 and T2 can't be taken immediately after one another?

16. How many ways can the offices of president, vice-president, treasurer, secretary, parliamentarian, and representative be filled from a class of 30 students?

17. Using the word $MI_1S_1S_2I_2S_3S_4I_3P_1P_2I_4$, where each repeated letter is distinguishable, how many ways can the letters be arranged?

18. In any arrangement (list) of the 26 letters of the English alphabet, which has 21 consonants and 5 vowels, must there be some place where there are at least 3 consonants in a row? 4? 5?

19. If there are 10 chips in a box—4 red, 3 blue, 2 white, and 1 black—and 2 chips are drawn, what is the probability that

    a. the chips are the same color?

    b. exactly 1 is red?

    c. at least 1 is red?

    d. neither is red?

20. In how many ways can the numbers 1, 2, 3, 4, 5, 6, 7 be arranged so that

    a. 1 and 7 are adjacent?

    b. 1 and 7 are not adjacent?

    c. 1 and 7 are exactly three spaces apart?

21. There are 12 books on a shelf: 5 volumes of an encyclopedia, 4 of an almanac, and 3 of a dictionary. How many arrangements are there? How many arrangements are there with each set of titles together?

22. If a team of four players must be made from eight boys and six girls, how many teams can be made if

    a. there are no restrictions?

    b. there must be two boys and two girls?

    c. they must all be boys?

    d. they must all be girls?

PROBLEMS FOR WRITING/DISCUSSION

1. Margaret claims that $\frac{16!}{8!}$ is the same as $\frac{16}{8}$. Explain how you could help her understand the difference.

2. At Julio's subway shop, they offer turkey sandwiches on white or wheat bread with your choice of lettuce, tomatoes, pickles, and onions. Julio claims that his restaurant offers 48 different types of turkey sandwiches. Is he correct? Explain.

3. Wayne claims that permutations should be used to count the number of different committees that could be selected from a group of people. Lowell thinks that combinations should be used. Who is correct? Explain.

END OF CHAPTER MATERIAL

Solution of Initial Problem

At a party, a friend bets you that at least two people in a group of five strangers will have the same astrological sign. Should you take the bet? Why or why not?

Strategy: Do a Simulation

Use a six-sided die and a coin. Make these correspondences.

OUTCOME		SIGN	OUTCOME		SIGN
1H	1	Capricorn	1T	7	Cancer
2H	2	Aquarius	2T	8	Leo
3H	3	Pisces	3T	9	Virgo
4H	4	Aries	4T	10	Libra
5H	5	Taurus	5T	11	Scorpio
6H	6	Gemini	6T	12	Sagittarius

Toss both the die and the coin five times. Record your results as a sequence of numbers from 1 to 12, using the correspondences given in the outcome and sign columns. An example sequence might be 7, 6, 4, 3, 8 (meaning that the die and coin came up 1T, 6H, 4H, 3H, and 2T).

Repeat the experiment 100 times, and determine the percentage of times that two or more matches occur. (A computer program would be an ideal way to do this.) This gives an estimation of the theoretical probability that two or more people in a group of five have the same astrological sign. More repetitions of the experiment should give a more accurate estimation. Your estimate should be around 60%, which means that your friend will win 60% of the time. No, you should not take the bet.

Additional Problems Where the Strategy "Do a Simulation" Is Useful

1. A game is played as follows: One player starts at one vertex of a regular hexagon and tosses a coin. When a head is tossed, the player moves clockwise two vertices. When a tail is tossed, the player moves counterclockwise one vertex. What is the probability that the player goes around the hexagon in fewer than 10 moves?

2. At a restaurant, three couples check their coats using one ticket. What is the probability that one couple gets their coats back if the checker gives them a man's and woman's coat at random?

3. At a bazaar to raise money for the library, parents take a chance to win a prize. They win if they open a book and the hundreds digits of facing pages are the same. What is the probability that they win?

People in Mathematics

Olga Taussky-Todd (1906–1995) Olga Taussky-Todd first met Emmy Noether at the University of Gottingen, where, she recalled, Noether had "a crowd of students." Quite by chance, Taussky-Todd, who was 24 years younger than Noether, went to Bryn Mawr on a graduate scholarship. Noether was there on a Rockefeller fellowship, and Taussky-Todd recalled that "she was almost frightened that I would obtain a position before her." Unlike Noether, Taussky-Todd was fortunate to receive widespread recognition during her lifetime. Her major work was in matrix theory, and she won a Ford prize for her paper "Sums of Squares." In 1966, she was proclaimed "Woman of the Year" by the *Los Angeles Times*, and she lectured at the prestigious Emmy Noether 100th birthday symposium at Bryn Mawr. "I developed rather early a great desire to see the links between the various branches of mathematics. This struck me with great force when I drifted into topological algebra, a subject where one studies mathematical structures from an algebraic and a geometric point of view simultaneously."

Stanislaw Ulam (1909–1984) Stanislaw Ulam helped develop the atomic bomb in Los Alamos, New Mexico, during World War II. After the war, he did further work at Los Alamos and for a time had the dubious distinction of being known as "The Father of the H-Bomb." The title eventually stuck with Edward Teller rather than Ulam. Unlike Teller, he subsequently campaigned in favor of the ban on atmospheric testing of nuclear weapons. In the mathematical world, Ulam is known for his theoretical work in set theory, probability, and topology. The unsolved problem known as "Ulam's conjecture" is discussed in the Chapter 5 Focus On. Ulam wrote an autobiography called *Adventures of a Mathematician* and a book of unsolved mathematics problems. "In learning mathematics, many people—including myself—need examples, practical cases, and not purely formal abstractions and rules, even though mathematics consists of that. We need contact with intuition."

CHAPTER REVIEW

Review the following terms and exercises to determine which require learning or relearning—page numbers are provided for easy reference.

SECTION 11.1: Probability and Simple Experiments

VOCABULARY/NOTATION

Experiment   486
Outcome   486
Sample space   486
Event   486

Equally likely events   488
Probability of an event E, $P(E)$ 488
Impossible event   489
Certain event   490

Theoretical probability   490
Experimental probability   490
Complement of an event D, $\overline{D}$ 493
Mutually exclusive   493

EXERCISES

1. For the experiment "toss a coin and spin a spinner with three equal sectors A, B, and C"

   a. list the sample space, S.

   b. list the event E, "toss a head and spin an A or B."

   c. find $P(E)$.

   d. list $\overline{E}$.

   e. find $P(\overline{E})$.

   f. state the relationship that holds between $P(E)$ and $P(\overline{E})$.

2. Give an example of an event E where

   a. $P(E) = 1$.

   b. $P(E) = 0$.

3. Distinguish between theoretical probability and experimental probability.

4. List two events from the sample space in Exercise 1 that are mutually exclusive.

SECTION 11.2: Probability and Complex Experiments

VOCABULARY/NOTATION

Tree diagram   500
Probability tree diagram   502

Drawing with/without
   replacement   503

Pascal's triangle   508

EXERCISES

1. Draw a tree diagram for the experiment "spin a spinner twice with equal sectors colored red, red, and green."

2. Explain how the fundamental counting property can be used to determine the number of outcomes in the sample space in the experiment in Exercise 1.

3. a. List the first six rows of Pascal's triangle.

   b. Describe an experiment that is represented by the line that begins 1, 5, . . . in Pascal's triangle.

c. Interpret the meaning of a 10 in this row with respect to the experiment.

4. a. Construct the probability tree diagram for the experiment in Exercise 1.

   b. Explain how the multiplication property of probability diagrams is used to determine the probabilities of events for the tree in part (a).

   c. Explain how the addition property of probability diagrams may be used on the tree in part (a).

SECTION 11.3: Simulation, Expected Value, Odds, and Conditional Probability

VOCABULARY/NOTATION

Simulation   516
Expected value   519

Odds in favor of (odds
   against)   520

Conditional probability,
   $P(A \mid B)$ 522

EXERCISES

1. Explain the connection between odds in favor of an event versus odds against an event.

2. Explain the connection between the probability of an event and the odds in favor of an event.

3. What are the odds in favor of getting a sum that is a multiple of 3 when tossing a pair of dice?

4. If $P(E) = 0.57$, what are the odds against E?

5. Describe circumstances under which the computation of conditional probability is required?

6. What is the probability of tossing a multiple of 3 on a pair of dice given that the sum is less than 10?

7. What is the expected value associated with game that pays $1 for a prime number and $2 for a composite number when tossing a pair of dice?

8. a. Describe a situation where a simulation is not only useful, but necessary.

   b. Explain how a table of random digits can be used to simulate tossing a standard six-sided die.

SECTION 11.4: Additional Counting Techniques

VOCABULARY/NOTATION

Permutation   530
n factorial, $n!$ 531

The number of permutations of r
   objects chosen from n objects,
   $_nP_r$ 532

Combination   532
The number of combinations
   of r objects chosen from n
   objects $_nC_r$ 533

EXERCISES

1. True or false?

   a. Since combinations take order into account, there are more combinations than permutations of n objects.

   b. The words *abcd* and *bcad* are the same combination of the letters *a*, *b*, *c*, *d*.

   c. $_{n+1}P_r = {_n}P_{r-1} + {_n}P_r$

   d. The number of combinations of n distinct objects, taken all together, is $n!$.

   e. The entries in Pascal's triangle are the values of $_nC_r$.

2. Out of 12 friends, you want to invite 7 over to watch a football game.

   a. How many ways can this be done?

   b. How many ways can this be done, if two of your friends won't come if a certain other one is there?

   c. If Salvador and Geoff are among those 12 friends, what is the probability that they will be invited?

3. Calculate.

   a. $7!$ **b.** $\dfrac{15!}{9!6!}$ **c.** $_6P_3$ **d.** $_{12}C_4$

4. In how many ways can the questions on a 10-item test be arranged in different orders?

5. From a group of nine men and five women,

   a. How many teams of two men and four women can be formed?

   b. How many ways can this team be seated in a line?

   c. If Damon is one of the men and LaTisha is one of the women, what is the probability that Damon and LaTisha will be on the team?

6. There are five roads between Alpha, Kansas, and Beta, Missouri. Also, there are eight roads between Beta, Missouri, and Omega, Nebraska, and two from Alpha to Omega not through Beta.

   a. How many ways can you get from Alpha to Omega in a round trip, passing through Beta?

   b. How many ways can you get from Alpha to Omega in a round trip, passing through Beta only once?

7. a. Complete $_nC_0 + {_n}C_1 + {_n}C_2 + \ldots + {_n}C_n$ for $n = 3, 4, 5$.

   b. What would the sum be for $n = 6, 10, 20, k$? (Find a formula.)

   c. How is this sum related to Pascal's triangle?

PROBLEMS FOR WRITING/DISCUSSION

1. When throwing two fair dice, the possible sums are from 2 to 12. There are 11 possible sums; thus the probability of tossing a sum of 2 is 1/11. Do you agree? Discuss.

2. An octahedron is a three-dimensional shape with eight sides that are equilateral triangles. This shape is used as a die in some games, such as "Dungeons and Dragons," because all eight sides come up with equal probability. Assuming the sides are numbered 1 through 8, and a person throws two octahedral dice, what are the possible sums? Which sum has the highest probability? Explain.

3. To play the Ohio Lottery, a person has to choose six different numbers from 1 to 50. Once a week, the six winning numbers are selected (without replacement) from a drum that contains 50 balls, each with a number from 1 to 50. When the Ohio Lottery Jackpot reaches $13,000,000, many people purchase $1 tickets to win. If more than one person selects the winning combination, all winners have to split the pot. If no one picks the winning numbers, the $13,000,000 gets added to the Jackpot for the following week. If 2,000,000 tickets are sold, what is the probability that any single ticket would win? What conclusions can you draw about the purchase of a lottery ticket?

4. Irene is playing a board game, and she is only five squares away from Home. To move forward, she tosses a coin; if she gets heads, she moves forward 1 square and if she gets tails, she moves forward 2 squares. It will take her at least three turns (coin tosses) to get to Home. What is the probability that it will take her four turns? Explain. (*Hint:* Make a tree diagram that takes into account *all* the possible ways Irene could get Home.)

5. Explain how you would go about using a simulation with a coin, a die, or a deck of cards to verify your answer to Problem 4. Then do the simulation. About how many trials would it take to conclude reasonably that you had verified, or disproved, your calculations for Problem 4?

6. In the Focus On at the beginning of this chapter, it was stated that you might have had any of 8,388,608 different sets of characteristics when you were conceived. How did the author determine that number? Explain.

7. It was also stated in the Focus On that if you used random guessing on a true/false test with 10 items, your chance at a 70% or more was about 0.17. Explain how the author determined this answer.

8. Insurance companies have mortality tables that tell the likelihood of a person of a particular age, race, and sex living to be 75 years old. Where do these tables come from (how are they created), and why do the insurance companies need them? Do you think the tables are different in different parts of the country? in the world? Why? If the current probability that you will live to be 75 is 72%, will the probability be greater than, less than, or equal to 72% when you are 20 years older? Why?

9. A friend makes a bet with you that if you designate two cards from a deck of cards (say, a 5 and a jack), that at least one of the two cards will always be among the first three cards he pulls at random from the deck (without replacement). (NOTE: The suit is not specified, so there are eight cards that would meet the criteria of the bet.) If he gives you even odds, who has the advantage? (This is a good example to test using a simulation.)

10. When a gambler is playing "craps," he is rolling two dice and looking at their sum. If the sum on his first roll is 7 or 11, he automatically wins; if the sum is 2, 3, or 12, he automatically loses. What are the odds that on his first roll, neither of these things happen? Justify your answer.

CHAPTER TEST

Knowledge

1. True or false?

   a. The experimental probability and theoretical probability of an event are the same.

   b. $P(\overline{A}) = 1 - P(A)$.

   c. The row of Pascal's triangle that begins 1, 10, . . . has 10 numbers in it.

   d. The sum of the numbers in the row of Pascal's triangle that begins 1, 12, . . . is 12^2.

   e. If three dice are tossed, there are 216 outcomes.

   f. If A and B are events of some sample space S, then $P(A \cup B) = P(A) + P(B)$.

   g. $P(A \mid B) = P(A)/P(B)$.

   h. For any event A, $0 < P(A) < 1$.

   i. An ordered arrangement of objects is a combination.

   j. The number of permutations of r objects chosen from n objects, where $0 \leq r < n$, is $\dfrac{n!}{(n - r)!r!}$.

   k. $_nC_r = {_nC_{n-r}}$

2. How are an event and a sample space related?

3. What does "drawing without replacement" mean?

Skill

4. How many outcomes are in the event "Toss two dice and two coins"?

5. Given that $P(A) = \frac{5}{7}$ and $P(B) = \frac{1}{8}$ and $A \cap B = \varnothing$, what is $P(A \cup B)$?

6. Find the probability of tossing a sum that is a prime number when tossing a pair of dice.

7. What is the probability of tossing at least three heads when tossing four coins *given* that at least two heads turn up?

8. Calculate

   a. $_{10}C_3$ b. $_7P_5$ c. $\dfrac{12!}{4!8!}$

9. At Landmark Tech, the ID numbers consist of two letters followed by five numbers with no repeating letters or numbers.

   a. How many different ID numbers are possible?

   b. What is the probability that a randomly selected ID number would have the initials BP on it?

10. A box contains two red, three white, and four blue tickets. Two tickets will be drawn without replacement.

    a. Draw the probability tree diagram for this experiment and label the probability at the end of each branch.

    b. Find P(drawing a red and a blue).

    c. Find P(drawing a red).

    d. Find P(drawing a blue).

    e. Find P(drawing a red or a blue).

11. A bag contains one blue, two green, and three red marbles. A marble is drawn, replaced, and a second marble is drawn.

    a. Draw a probability tree diagram for this experiment with the appropriate labels.

    b. What is the probability of drawing two blues?

    c. What is the probability of drawing at least one blue?

Understanding

12. Given that "If $A \cap B = \emptyset$, then $P(A \cup B) = P(A) + P(B)$," verify that "$P(\overline{A}) = 1 - P(A)$."

13. Explain how tree diagrams and the fundamental counting property are related.

14. Convert the tree diagram of equally likely outcomes into the corresponding probability tree diagram.

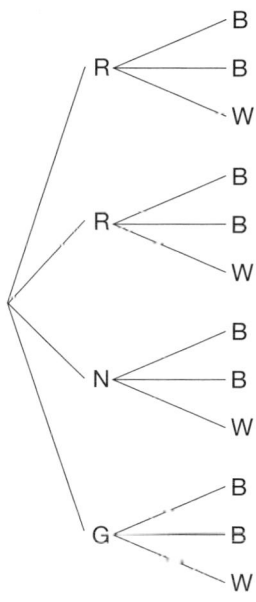

15. Explain how to use a simulation to answer the following question: "A restaurant has four different prizes in their children's meals. What is the probability that you will get all four prizes if you buy seven children's meals?" (Do not do the simulation; just explain how it could be done.)

16. A spinner is numbered $1-6$ in such a way that each number is equally likely. After spinning once, the number is recorded. Describe an event with the odds of $2 : 1$.

17. Hans claims that since a thrown paper cup can land on its bottom, its top, or its side, the probability of it landing on its side is one-third. Merle disagrees. Who is correct? Explain.

18. A bag contains an unknown number of balls, some red, some blue, and some green. On one draw, $P(\text{drawing a red}) = \dfrac{1}{6}$, and $P(\text{drawing a blue}) = \dfrac{3}{8}$.

   a. Find the smallest possible number of balls in the bag.

   b. Find $P(\text{drawing a green})$.

Problem Solving/Application

19. Find the probability of tossing a prime number of heads when tossing ten coins.

20. Show that when tossing a pair of dice, the probability of getting the sum n, where $2 \leq n \leq 12$, is the same as the probability of getting the sum $14 - n$.

21. Suppose that $P(A) = \frac{2}{3}$, $P(B) = \frac{1}{2}$, and $P(A \mid B) = \frac{1}{3}$. What is $P(B \mid A)$?

22. If three letters are chosen from the alphabet and each letter is equally likely to be chosen, what is the probability that all three letters will be the same?

23. If you pay $2 to play a game in which you toss a coin five times and are paid $1 for each time the coin comes up heads, how much would you expect to win each time you played?

References for Reflections from Research

FISCHBEIN, E., & GAZIT, A. (1984). Does the teaching of probability improve probabilistic intuitions? *Educational Studies in Mathematics, 15*(1), 1–24.

JONES, G. A., LANGRALL, C. W., THORNTON, C. A., & MOGILL, A. T. (1999). Students' probabilistic thinking in instruction. *Journal for Research in Mathematics Education, 30*, 487–519.

NUGENT, W. (1990). Tomorrow I am going to turn into a giraffe: Or, is it possible to discuss probability with 5-year-olds? *Mathematics in School, 19*(1), 10–12.

TAYLOR, M., & BIDDULPH, F. (1994). "Context" in probability learning at the primary school level. In A. Jones, A. Begg, B. Bell, F. Biddulph, M. Carr, M. Carr, J. McChesney, E. McKinley, & J. Young-Loveridge (Eds.), *SAME papers 1994* (pp. 96–111). Hamilton, New Zealand: Centre for Science and Mathematics Education Research, University of Waikato.

TRURAN, J. (1995). "But the six doesn't like me"— Reflections on the science and art of teaching probability. In A. Richards (Ed.), *FLAIR—Forging links and integrating resources* (pp. 383–391). Adelaide, Australia: Australian Association of Mathematics Teachers.

NCTM Standards 2000
Geometry
Grades Pre-K–2
All students should recognize, name, build, draw, compare, and sort two- and three-dimensional shapes.

level 1. In our treatment of geometry we will use informal deduction (i.e., the chaining of ideas together to verify general properties of shapes). This is analogous to our observations about properties of number systems in earlier chapters. For example, we will make extensive use of informal deduction in Section 12.2.

Level 3 (Deduction) Reasoning at this level includes the study of geometry as a formal mathematical system. A child who reasons at level 3 understands the notions of mathematical postulates and theorems and can write formal proofs of theorems.

Level 4 (Axiomatics) The study of geometry at level 4 is highly abstract and does not necessarily involve concrete or pictorial models. At this level, the postulates or axioms themselves become the object of intense, rigorous scrutiny. This level of study is not suitable for elementary, middle school, or even most high school students, but it is usually the level of study in geometry courses in college.

Recognizing Geometric Shapes

In the primary grades, children are taught to recognize several types of geometric shapes, such as triangles, squares, rectangles, and circles. Shape-identification items frequently occur on worksheets and on mathematics achievement tests. For example, a child may be asked to "pick out the triangle, the square, the rectangle, and the circle." Children are taught to look for prototype shapes—shapes like those they have seen in their textbook or in physical models.

NCTM Standards 2000
Geometry
Grades 3–5
All students should identify, compare, and analyze attributes of two- and three-dimensional shapes and develop vocabulary to describe the attributes.

Often, however, children have seen only special cases of shapes and do not have a complete idea of the important attributes that a shape must have in order to represent a general type. Referring to the van Hiele theory, we would say that they have recognition ability but not analytic understanding. For example, Figure 12.4 shows a selection of shapes difficult to identify when thinking holistically. Can you see why some children consider shape 1 to be a triangle, shape 2 a square, shape 6 a rectangle, and shape 8 a circle?

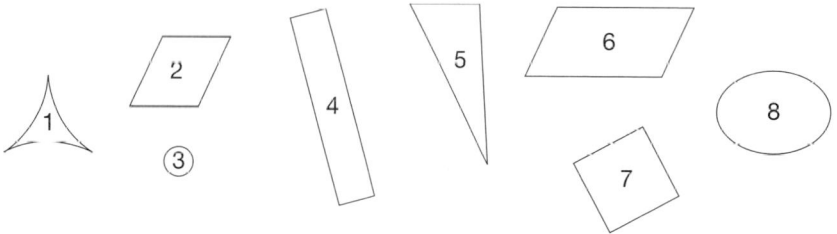

Figure 12.4

Holistic thinking is an important first step in learning about geometric shapes. It lays the groundwork for the analysis of shapes by properties of their components. Students' holistic thinking abilities can be developed by means of visualization activities. For example, finding "hidden" figures can help students visually focus on particular shapes as a whole. Example 12.1 gives an illustration.

Example 12.1   How many different rectangles are formed by the heavy-line segments in this figure?

Solution

Looking for "vertical" rectangles, we find seven.

Looking for "horizontal" rectangles, we find two.

Hence there are nine rectangles altogether. ■

Making new shapes by rearranging other shapes is also a good way for students to develop visualization skills. Tangram puzzles are examples of this kind of activity. Example 12.2 shows a rearrangement activity that provides a "proof" of the Pythagorean theorem, namely, that the sum of the squares on the sides of a right triangle is equal to the square on the hypotenuse.

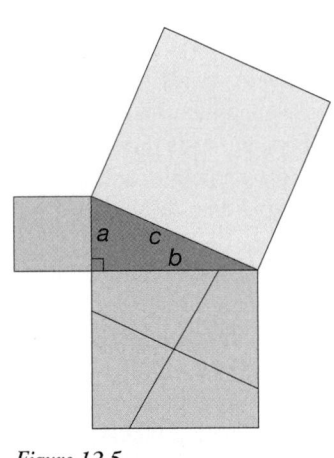

Figure 12.5

Example 12.2 Figure 12.5 shows a right triangle with squares on each of its two sides, labeled a and b, and on its hypotenuse, labeled c. One of the two lines on the square built on side b is constructed parallel to side c and the other is constructed perpendicular to side c. These two lines are placed in the square so that they pass through the center of the square. Trace and cut out the squares on the sides and cut the larger one into four pieces along the solid lines described above. Then rearrange these five pieces to cover the square on the hypotenuse exactly.

Solution

See Figure 12.6 ■

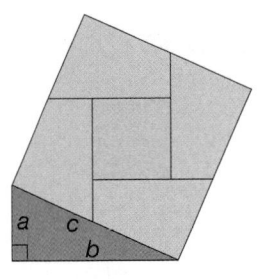

Figure 12.6

The ability to manipulate images is an important visualization skill. Example 12.3 provides an illustration.

Example 12.3 Fold a square piece of paper in half so that the fold is on the dashed line, as shown in Figure 12.7. Then, punch a hole in the folded paper. How will the paper look when unfolded?

Figure 12.7

Solution

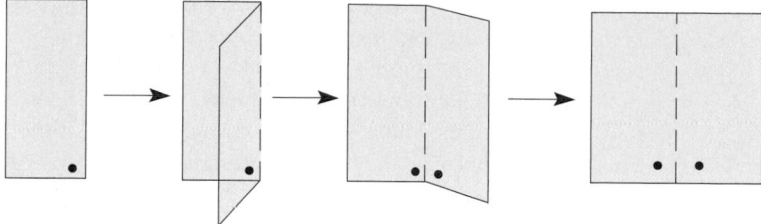

Thus figure (d) is correct. ■

Reflection from Research
Kindergarten children have a great deal of prior knowledge about shapes. Teachers tend to simply elicit and verify this knowledge rather than developing new concepts (Thomas, 1983).

Defining Common Geometric Shapes

Next we study parts of geometric figures using informal methods. We will use activities with dot paper, paper folding, and tracings to reveal characteristics of geometric figures, methods that are currently used when introducing these concepts to children.

The geometric shapes defined in this section are abstractions of physical models from our everyday world. Table 12.1 illustrates many of these shapes.

**NCTM Standards 2000
Geometry
Grades Pre-K – 2**
All students should recognize geometric shapes and structures in the environment and specify their location.

TABLE 12.1

Model		Abstraction
	Top of a window	Line segment
	Vertical flagpole	Right angle (perpendicular segments)
	Yield sign	Triangle (equilateral)
	Open pair of scissors	Angle
	Railroad tracks	Parallel lines
	Floor tile	Square
	Door	Rectangle (that is not a square)
	Railing	Parallelogram
	Diamond	Rhombus
	Kite	Kite
	Water glass silhouette	Trapezoid (isosceles)

Sides and Angles The points of a **square lattice** (i.e., a square array of dots) serve as an effective environment in which to analyze figures such as those in Table 12.1. A geoboard and square dot paper provide concrete representations for such investigations. By joining two points in the shortest possible way, we form a set of points called a (straight) **line segment.** Figure 12.8 shows, on square lattices, several types of figures whose sides are line segments. All the shapes in parts (a) to (c) are **triangles** because they are closed figures composed of exactly three line segments, called **sides.** The shapes in (d) to (h) are **quadrilaterals** because they are closed figures composed of four line segments (sides).

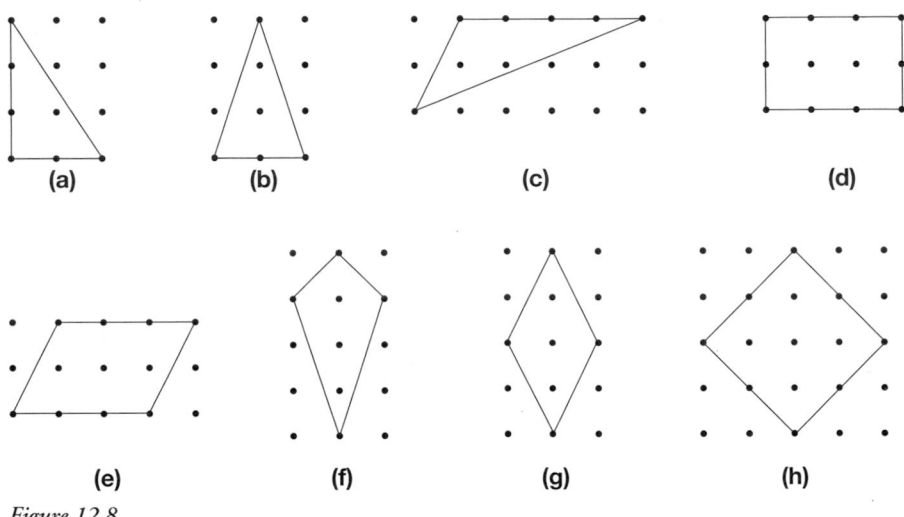

Figure 12.8

Reflection from Research

Angles need to be drawn with varying orientations. Angles are so often represented with one horizontal ray and "opening" to the right that students have been known to refer to 90 degree angles that "open" to the left as left angles (Scally, 1990).

**NCTM Standards 2000
Geometry
Grades Pre-K–2**

All students should describe attributes and parts of two- and three-dimensional shapes.

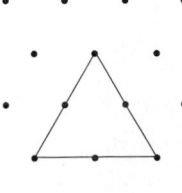

Figure 12.9

Triangles have three angles. An **angle** is the union of two line segments with a common endpoint called a **vertex.** (plural: **vertices**). Quadrilaterals have four angles. (Literally, *triangle* means "three angles" and *quadrilateral* means "four sides." Perhaps *trilateral*, meaning "three sides," would have been a more useful name for a triangle.)

In the remainder of this section, we will describe figures using the concepts of "length," "right angle," and "parallel." We will use these terms informally for now and give precise definitions of them in Section 12.2.

If we consider the triangles in Figure 12.8, we notice several differences among them. For example, the triangle in part (a) has an angle formed by horizontal and vertical sides. Any angle identical to an angle formed by horizontal and vertical line segments is called a **right angle.** In parts (d) and (h) of Figure 12.8, the quadrilaterals each have four right angles. We discuss general procedures for identifying right angles later in this subsection. Two line segments that form a right angle are called **perpendicular.** Triangle (b) has two sides that are the same length. A triangle with two or three sides the same length is called an **isosceles** triangle. A triangle with three sides the same length is called an **equilateral** triangle. An equilateral triangle is shown on *triangular* dot paper in Figure 12.9. Triangle (c) has three sides that are all different lengths. Such triangles are called **scalene** triangles. Thus we can compare and name types of triangles according to their sides.

Figure 12.8 contains a variety of quadrilaterals. For example, the shape in part (h) is a square. A **square** is a quadrilateral with four sides the same length and four right angles. The shape in part (d) is a rectangle. A **rectangle** is a quadrilateral with four right angles. The shape in part (e) is a parallelogram. A **parallelogram** is a quadrilateral with two pairs of parallel sides (point in the same direction). The shape in part (f) is a kite. A **kite** is a quadrilateral with two nonoverlapping pairs of adjacent sides that are the same length. Finally, the shape in part (g) is a rhombus. A **rhombus** is a quadrilateral with four sides the same length. It is also true that shape (h) has four sides the same length and has four right angles.

We will say that two line segments are **congruent line segments** if they have the same length. Any figure whose sides are congruent is called **equilateral.** Two angles are **congruent angles** if they have the same "opening," that is, one angle is an exact copy of the other, except possibly for the lengths of the sides. For example, in a square all four sides are congruent and all four angles are congruent. A figure is said to be **equiangular** if all of its angles are congruent. A square is both equilateral and equiangular.

We notice that rectangle (d) and rhombus (g) in Figure 12.8 also have two pairs of parallel sides. Hence they, too, are parallelograms. Students who are thinking at the analysis level sometimes have difficulty understanding that a figure can represent several types simultaneously. An analogy to membership criteria for clubs can help explain this. For example, shape (h) qualifies for membership in at least five "clubs": the rectangles, parallelograms, kites, rhombuses, and squares.

A quadrilateral with *exactly one pair* of parallel sides is called a **trapezoid** [Figure 12.10(a)]. If the nonparallel sides of a trapezoid are congruent, it is called an **isosceles trapezoid** [Figure 12.10(b)]. Thus a parallelogram is *not* a trapezoid, since it has two pairs of parallel sides.

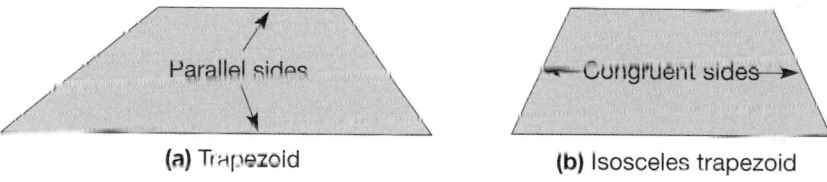

(a) Trapezoid   **(b)** Isosceles trapezoid

Figure 12.10

Section 12.1 EXERCISE / PROBLEM SET A

EXERCISES

1. Answer the following question visually first. Then devise a way to check your answer. If the arrow *A* were continued downward, which arrow would it meet?

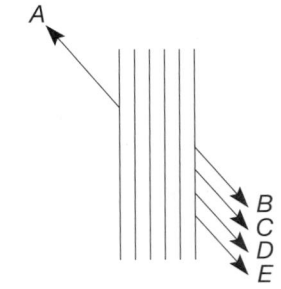

2. Which is longer, *x* or *y*?

a.   b.

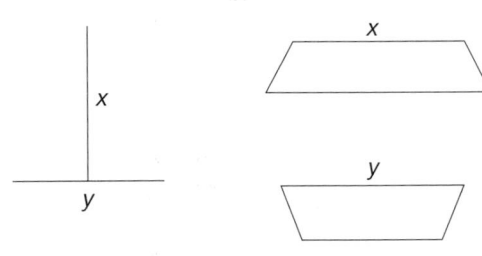

3. How many triangles are in the following design?

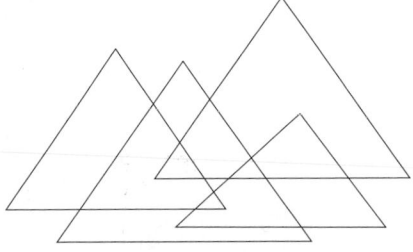

4. How many squares are found in the following figure?

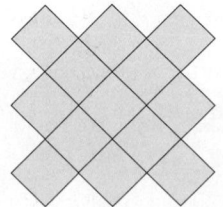

5. Given here are a variety of triangles. Sides with the same length are indicated. Right angles are indicated.

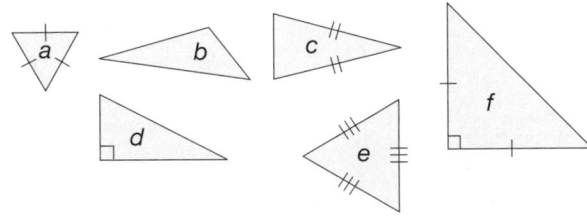

a. Name the triangles that are scalene.
b. Name the triangles that are isosceles.
c. Name the triangles that are equilateral.
d. Name the triangles that contain a right angle.

6. Trace the following figure and cut it into five pieces along the lines indicated. Rearrange the pieces to form a square. You must use all five pieces, have no gaps or overlaps, and not turn the pieces over.

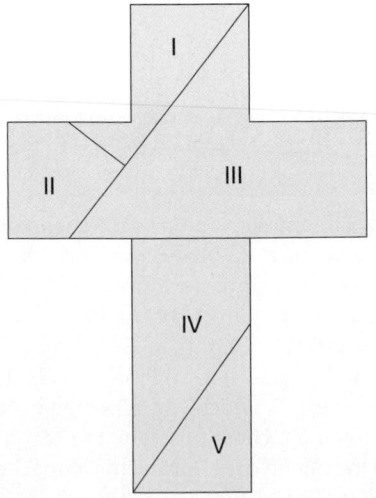

7. Fold a rectangular piece of paper on the dashed line as shown in each of the following figures. Then make cuts in the paper as indicated. Sketch what you think the shape will be when the paper is unfolded. Then unfold your paper to check your picture.

a.

b.

a. **b.**

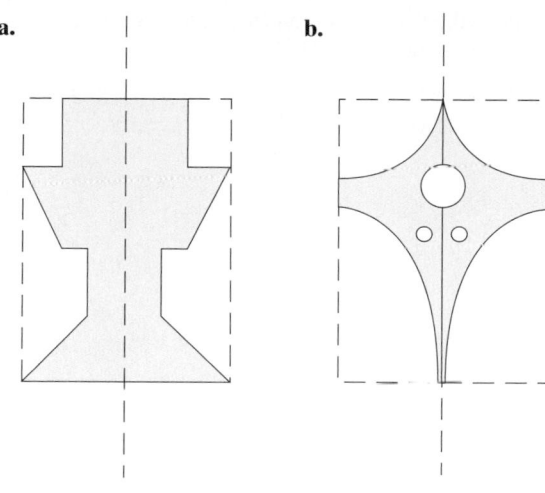

9. Fold a rectangular piece of paper in half vertically (dashed line 1) and then in half again horizontally (dashed line 2). Then make cuts in the paper as indicated. Sketch what you think the shape will be when the paper is unfolded. Unfold your paper to check your picture.

8. Each of the following shapes was obtained by folding a rectangular piece of paper in half vertically (lengthwise) and then making appropriate cuts in the paper. For each figure, draw the folded paper and show the cuts that must be made to make the figure. Try folding and cutting a piece of paper to check your answer.

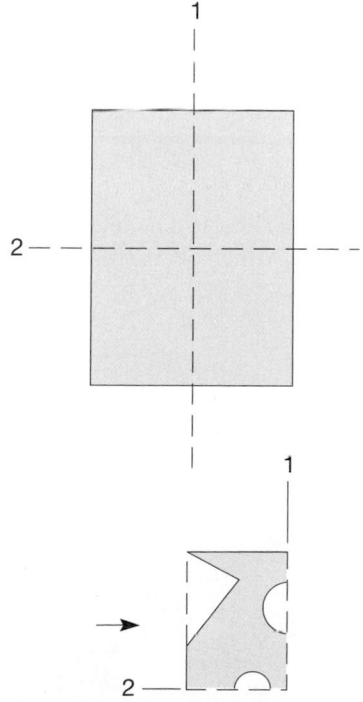

10. Fold the square first on line 1, then on line 2. Next, punch a hole, as indicated.

  a. Draw what you think the resulting shape will be. Unfold to check.

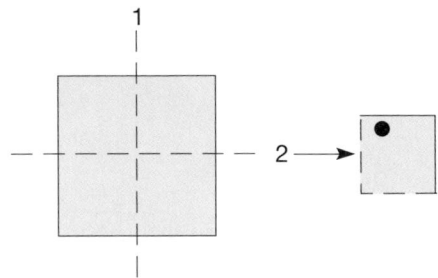

  b. To produce each figure, a square was folded twice, punched once, then unfolded. Find the fold lines and where the hole was punched.

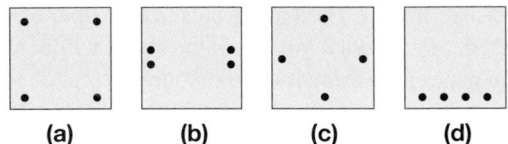

  (a)   (b)   (c)   (d)

11. Find the following shapes in the figure.

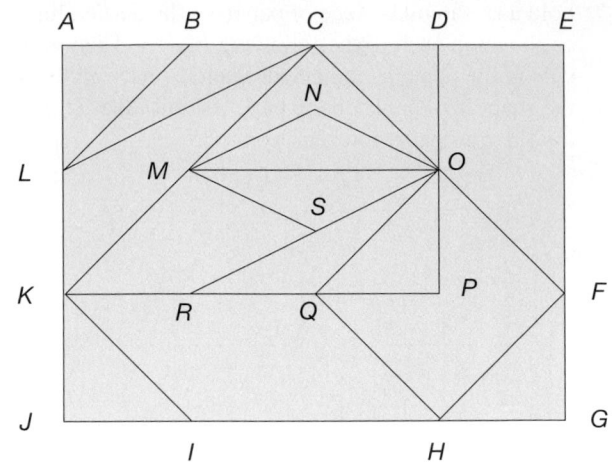

  a. A square

  b. A rectangle that is not a square

  c. A parallelogram that is not a rectangle

  d. An isosceles right triangle

  e. An isosceles triangle with no right angles

  f. A rhombus that is not a square

  g. A kite that is not a rhombus

  h. A scalene triangle with no right angles

  i. A right scalene triangle

  j. A trapezoid that is not isosceles

  k. An isosceles trapezoid

PROBLEMS

12. In the following table, if *A* belongs with *B*, then *X* belongs with *Y*. Which of (i), (ii), or (iii) is the best choice for *Y*?

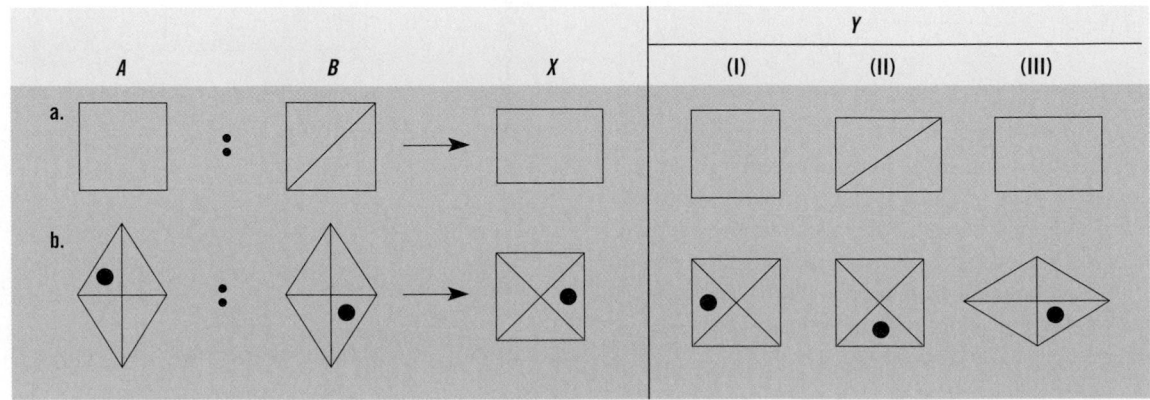

13. A problem that challenged mathematicians for many years concerns the coloring of maps. That is, what is the minimum number of colors necessary to color *any* map? Just recently it was finally proved with the aid of a computer that no map requires more than four colors. Some maps, however, can be colored with fewer than four colors. Determine the smallest number of colors necessary to color each map shown here. (NOTE: Two "countries" that share only one point can be colored the same color; however, if they have more than one point in common, they must be colored differently.)

14. A portion of a triangular lattice is given. Which of the following can be drawn on it?

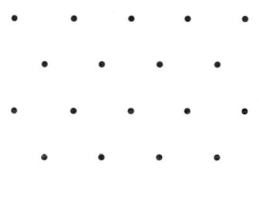

a. Parallel lines
b. Perpendicular lines

15. Which of the following quadrilaterals can be drawn on a triangular lattice?

  a. Rhombus

  b. Parallelogram

  c. Square

  d. Rectangle

16. Given the square lattice shown, draw quadrilaterals having $\overline{AB}$ as a side.

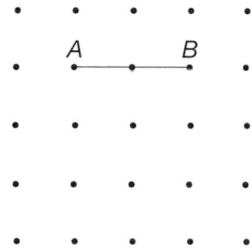

  a. How many parallelograms are possible?

  b. How many rectangles are possible?

  c. How many rhombuses are possible?

  d. How many squares are possible?

17. Trace the following hexagon twice.

  a. Divide one hexagon into three identical parts so that each part is a rhombus.

  b. Divide the other hexagon into six identical kites.

Section 12.1 EXERCISE / PROBLEM SET B

EXERCISES

1. Are the lines labeled *l* and *m* parallel?

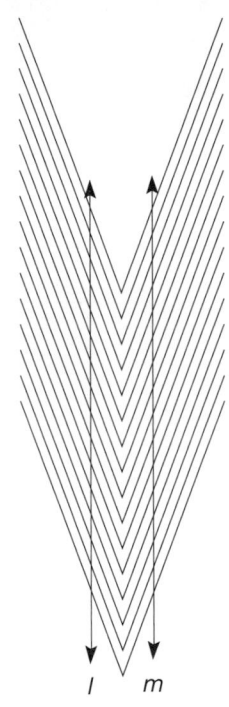

2. Which is longer, *x* or *y*?

a.

b.

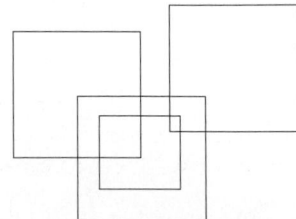

3. How many rectangles are found in the following design?

4. a. How many triangles are in the figure?

   b. How many parallelograms are in the figure?

   c. How many trapezoids are in the figure?

5. Several shapes are pictured here. Sides with the same length are indicated, as are right angles.

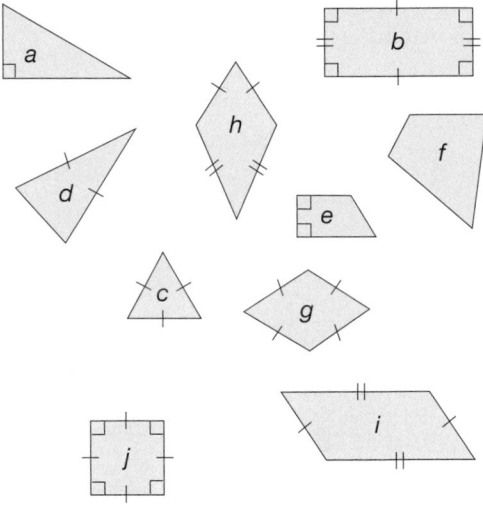

   a. Which figures have a right angle?

   b. Which figures have at least one pair of parallel sides?

   c. Which figures have at least two sides with the same length?

   d. Which figures have all sides the same length?

6. Trace the following figure and cut it into five pieces along the lines indicated. Rearrange the pieces to form a square. You must use all five pieces, have no gaps or overlaps, and not turn the pieces over.

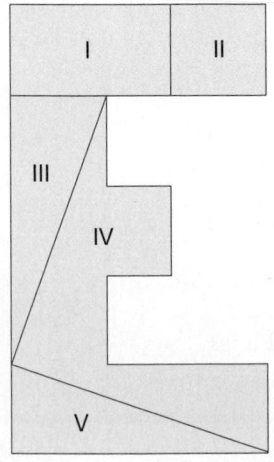

7. Fold a rectangular piece of paper on the dashed line as shown in each of the following figures. Then make cuts in the paper as indicated. Sketch what you think the shape will be when the paper is unfolded. Then unfold your paper to check your picture.

a.

b.

b.

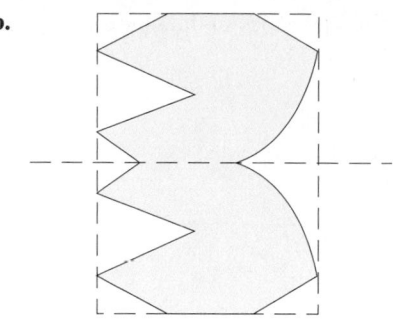

9. Fold a rectangular piece of paper in half vertically (dashed line 1) and then in half again horizontally (dashed line 2). Then make cuts in the paper as indicated. Sketch what you think the shape will be when the paper is unfolded. Unfold your paper to check your picture.

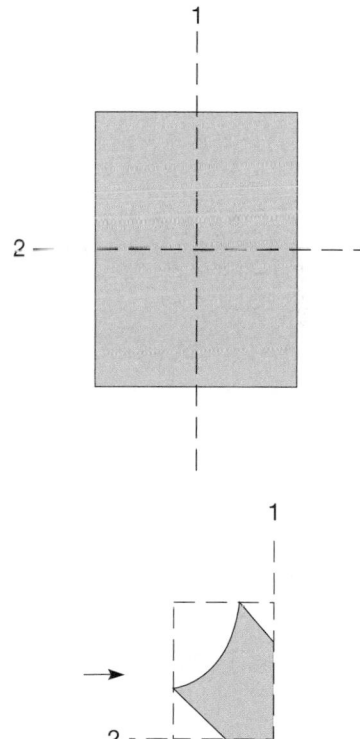

8. Each of the following shapes was obtained by folding a rectangular piece of paper in half horizontally and then making appropriate cuts in the paper. For each figure, draw the folded paper and show the cuts that must be made to make the figure. Try folding and cutting a piece of paper to check your answer.

a.

10. Fold the square first on line 1, then on line 2. Next, punch two holes, as indicated. Draw what you think the resulting shape will be. Unfold to check.

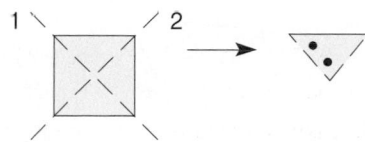

11. Find the following shapes in the figure.

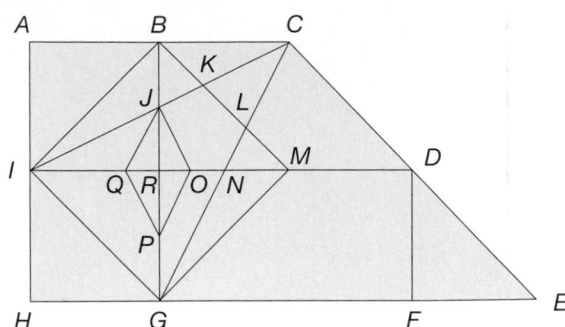

  a. Three squares
  b. A rectangle that is not a square
  c. A parallelogram that is not a rectangle
  d. Seven congruent right isosceles triangles
  e. An isosceles triangle not congruent to those in part (d)
  f. A rhombus that is not a square
  g. A kite that is not a rhombus
  h. A scalene triangle with no right angles
  i. A right scalene triangle
  j. A trapezoid that is not isosceles
  k. An isosceles trapezoid

PROBLEMS

12. In the following table, if A belongs with B, then X belongs with Y. Which of (i), (ii), or (iii) is the best choice for Y?

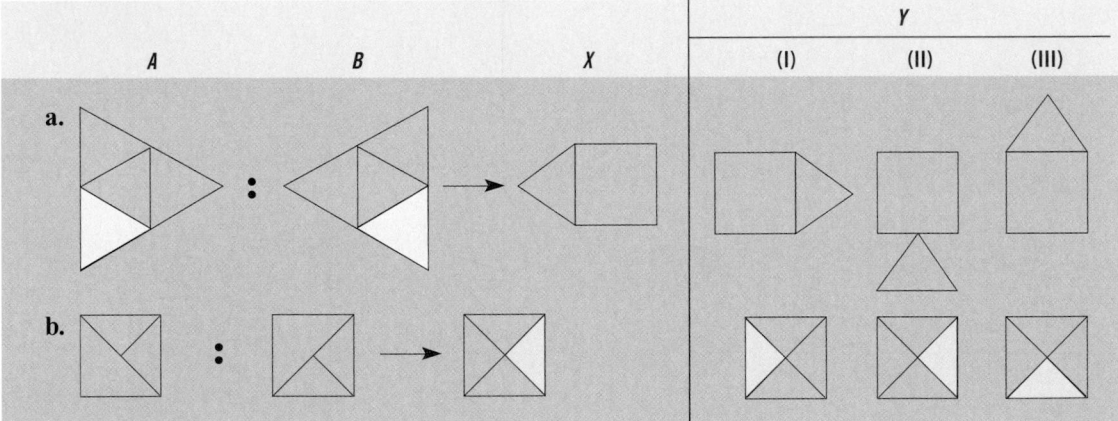

13. Determine the smallest number of colors necessary to color each map. (NOTE: Two "countries" that share only one point can be colored the same color; however, if they have more than one point in common, they must be colored differently.)

  a.

  b.

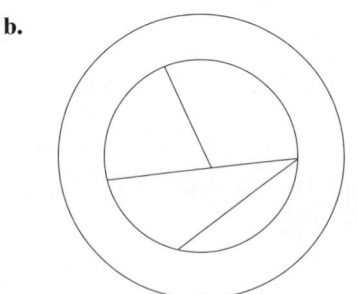

14. A portion of a triangular lattice is shown here. Which of the following triangles can be drawn on it?

  a. Equilateral triangle
  b. Isosceles triangle
  c. Scalene triangle

15. Find the maximal finite number of points of intersection for the following pairs of regular polygons.

  a. A square and a triangle
  b. A triangle and a hexagon
  c. A square and an octagon
  d. An n-gon and an m-gon

16. Trace the hexagon twice.

  a. Divide one hexagon into four identical trapezoids.
  b. Divide the other hexagon into eight identical polygons.

17. a. Make copies of the following large, uncut square. Find ways to cut the squares into each of the following numbers of smaller squares: 7, 8, 9, 10, 11, 12, 13, 14, 15, 16.

If you start with a large square

then you can cut it into 4 smaller squares like this

or into 6 smaller squares like this.

You can cut a square into 10 smaller squares this way

or this way.

  b. Can you find more than one way to cut the squares for some numbers? Which numbers?

  c. For which numbers can you cut the square into equal-sized smaller squares?

PROBLEMS FOR WRITING/DISCUSSION

  1. Whitney says that a square is a kind of rectangle because it has all right angles and its opposite sides are parallel, but Bobby says that's not right because a square has all equal sides and a rectangle has a length and width that have to be different. How would you respond?

  2. Bernie says that any three-sided figure is a triangle, even if the sides are curved. Chandra says the sides have to make angles and the bottom has to be straight. Can you tell what van Hiele level would be indicated by answers such as these? Explain.

  3. Donyall was trying to follow the directions on an activity. It said to put all the rhombus shapes in one pile. Elyse told him to put the squares in there, too, but Donyall said, "No, because the rhombuses have to be slanty." What is your response?

12.2 ANALYZING SHAPES

STARTING POINT

In the figure below, all of the shapes in category I have a common property and all of the shapes in category II do not have that property. Discuss the property you found with another student to see if you came up with the same property. Write a precise mathematical description of that property.

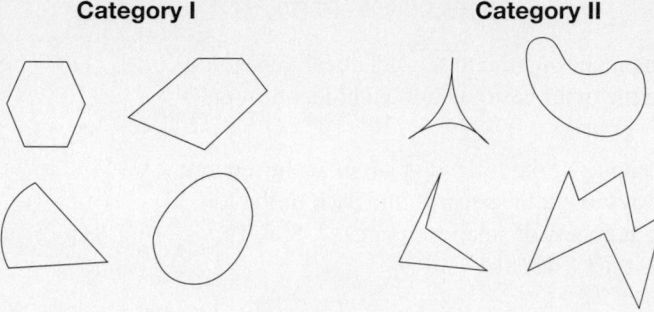

Category I   **Category II**

Symmetry

NCTM Standards 2000
Geometry
Grades 3–5
All students should identify and describe line and rotational symmetry in two- and three-dimensional shapes and designs.

The concept of symmetry can be used in analyzing figures. Two-dimensional figures can have two distinct types of symmetry: reflection symmetry and rotation symmetry. Informally, a figure has **reflection symmetry** if there is a line that the figure can be "folded over" so that one-half of the figure matches the other half perfectly (Figure 12.11).

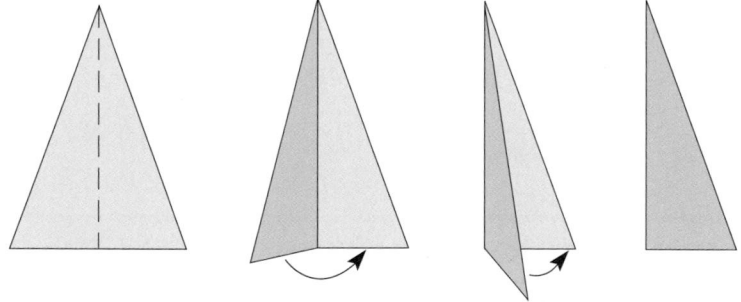

Figure 12.11

NCTM Standards 2000
Geometry
Grades 6–8
All students should examine the congruence, similarity, and line or rotational symmetry of objects using transformations.

The "fold line" just described is called the figure's **line (axis) of symmetry.**

Figure 12.12 shows several figures and their lines of reflection symmetry. The lines of symmetry are dashed. Many properties of figures, such as symmetry, can be demonstrated using tracings and paper folding.

Next, we introduce some convenient notation to help describe geometric shapes and their symmetry properties.

SYMBOL	MEANING
$\overline{AB}$	Line segment with endpoints A and B [Figure 12.13(a)]
$\angle ABC$	Angle with vertex at B and sides $\overline{AB}$ and $\overline{BC}$ [Figure 12.13(b)]
$\triangle ABC$	Triangle with vertices A, B, and C [Figure 12.3(c)]

Example 12.4 uses symmetry to show a property of isosceles triangles.

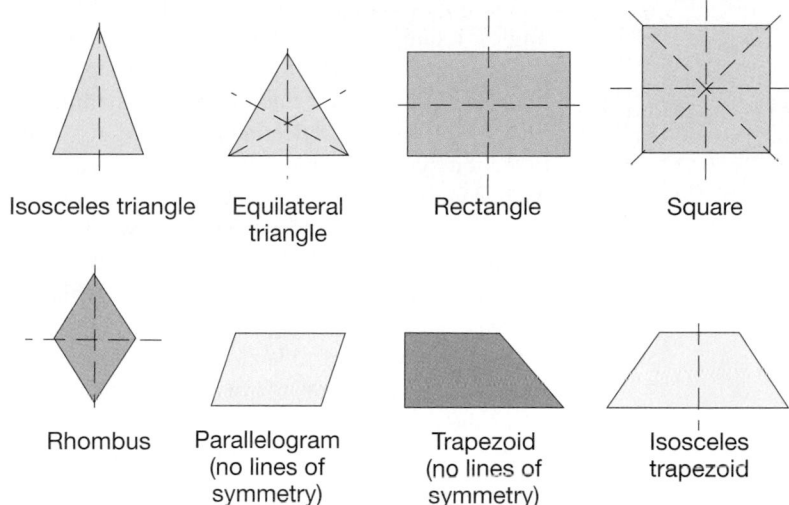

Isosceles triangle   Equilateral triangle   Rectangle   Square

Rhombus   Parallelogram (no lines of symmetry)   Trapezoid (no lines of symmetry)   Isosceles trapezoid

Figure 12.12

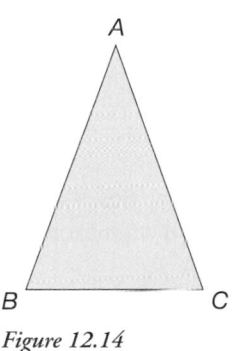

(a)

(b)

(c)

Figure 12.13

Example 12.4 Suppose that $\triangle ABC$ is isosceles with side $\overline{AB}$ congruent to side $\overline{AC}$ (Figure 12.14). Show that $\angle ABC$ is congruent to $\angle ACB$.

Figure 12.14

Solution Fold the triangle so that vertex A remains fixed while vertex B folds onto vertex C. Semitransparent paper works well for this (Figure 12.15).

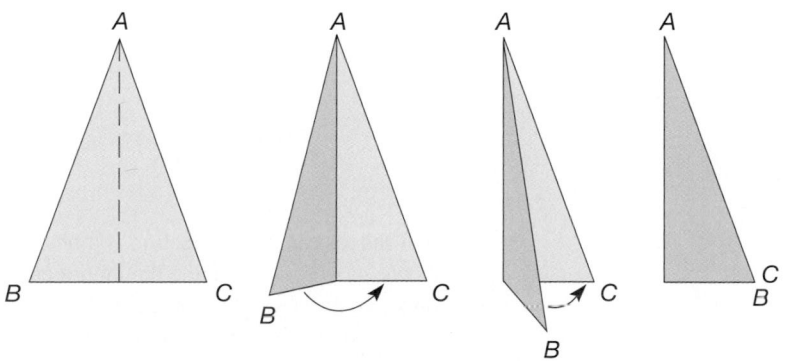

Figure 12.15

NCTM Standard 2001
Geometry
Grades 3–5
All students should make and test conjectures about geometric properties and relationships and develop logical arguments to justify conclusions.

Observe that, after folding, side $\overline{AB}$ coincides with side $\overline{AC}$. Since $\angle ABC$ folds onto and exactly matches $\angle ACB$, they are congruent. ■

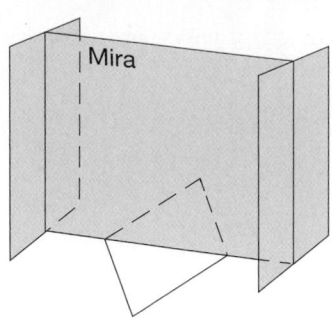

Figure 12.16

Reflection from Research
Rotational symmetry is at least as easy to understand as line symmetry for primary children. Students benefit when the ideas are taught together (Morris, 1987).

In an isosceles triangle, the angles opposite the congruent sides are called **base angles.** Example 12.4 shows that the base angles of an isosceles triangle are congruent. A similar property holds for isosceles trapezoids.

A useful device for finding lines of symmetry is a **Mira®,** a Plexiglas "two-way" mirror. You can see reflections in it and also see through it. Hence, in the case of a reflection symmetry, the reflection image appears to be superimposed on the figure itself. Figure 12.16 shows how to find lines of symmetry in a rhombus using a Mira. The beveled edge must be down and toward you.

The second type of symmetry of figures is rotation symmetry. A figure has **rotation symmetry** if there is a point around which the figure can be rotated, *less than a full turn,* so that the image matches the original figure perfectly. (We will see more precise definitions of reflection and rotation symmetry in Chapter 16.) Figure 12.17 shows an investigation of rotation symmetry for an equilateral triangle. In Figure 12.17 the equilateral triangle is rotated counterclockwise $\frac{1}{3}$ of a turn. It could also be rotated $\frac{2}{3}$ of a turn and, of course, through a full turn to produce a matching image. Every figure can be rotated through a full turn using any point as the center of rotation to produce a matching image. Figures for which only a full turn produces an identical image do *not* have rotation symmetry.

   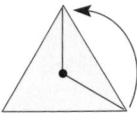

Figure 12.17

Figure 12.18 shows several types of figures and the number of turns up to and including one full turn that makes the image match the figure. See whether you can verify the numbers given. Tracing the figure and rotating your drawing may help you. In Figure 12.18, all figures except the trapezoid have rotation symmetry.

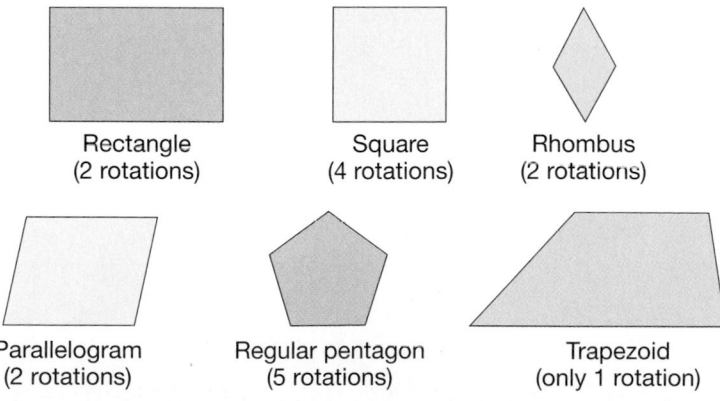

Rectangle (2 rotations) Square (4 rotations) Rhombus (2 rotations)

Parallelogram (2 rotations) Regular pentagon (5 rotations) Trapezoid (only 1 rotation)

Figure 12.18

We see that shapes can have reflection symmetry without rotation symmetry (e.g., Figure 12.12 shows an isosceles triangle that is not equilateral) and rotation symmetry without reflection symmetry (e.g., Figure 12.18 shows a parallelogram that is not a rectangle).

Example 12.5 shows how we can use a rotation to establish a property of parallelograms.

Example 12.5 Show that the opposite sides of a parallelogram are congruent.

Solution Trace the parallelogram and turn the (shaded) tracing one-half turn around its center, the intersection of $\overline{AC}$ and $\overline{BD}$ [Figures 12.19(a), (b), and (c)]. Observe that side $\overline{AB}$ of the tracing coincides with side $\overline{CD}$ and that side $\overline{AD}$ of the tracing coincides with side $\overline{CB}$ [Figure 12.19(d)].

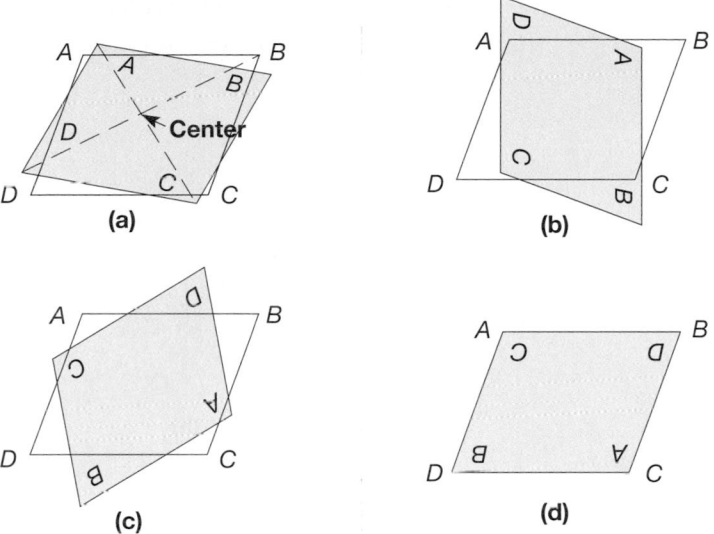

Figure 12.19

Thus both pairs of opposite sides are congruent. ■

Perpendicular and Parallel Line Segments

When folding and tracing figures, it is convenient to have tests to determine when line segments are perpendicular or parallel. To determine whether two line segments l and m are perpendicular, we use the following test (Figure 12.20).

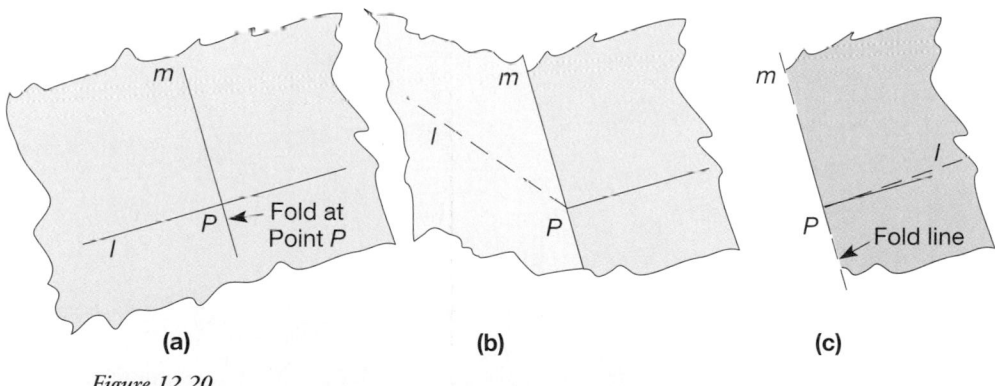

Figure 12.20

Perpendicular Line Segments Test

Let P be the point of intersection of l and m [Figure 12.20(a)]. Fold l at point P so that l folds across P onto itself [Figures 12.20(b) and (c)]. Then l and m are perpendicular if and only if m lies along the fold line [Figure 12.20(c)].

We can also analyze properties of figures using diagonals. A **diagonal** is a line segment formed by connecting nonadjacent vertices (i.e., not on the same side) (Figure 12.21).

Example 12.6 demonstrates a property of the diagonals of a kite.

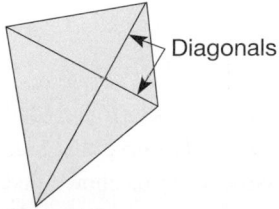

Figure 12.21

Example 12.6   Show that the diagonals of a kite are perpendicular.

Solution   Let $ABCD$ be a kite [Figure 12.22(a)]. Diagonals $\overline{AC}$ and $\overline{DB}$ intersect at point E. Fold $\overline{DE}$ across $\overline{AC}$ onto $\overline{EB}$ [Figures 12.22(b) and (c)]. Notice that diagonal $\overline{AC}$ is on the fold line [Figure 12.22(d)]. Thus the diagonals are perpendicular.

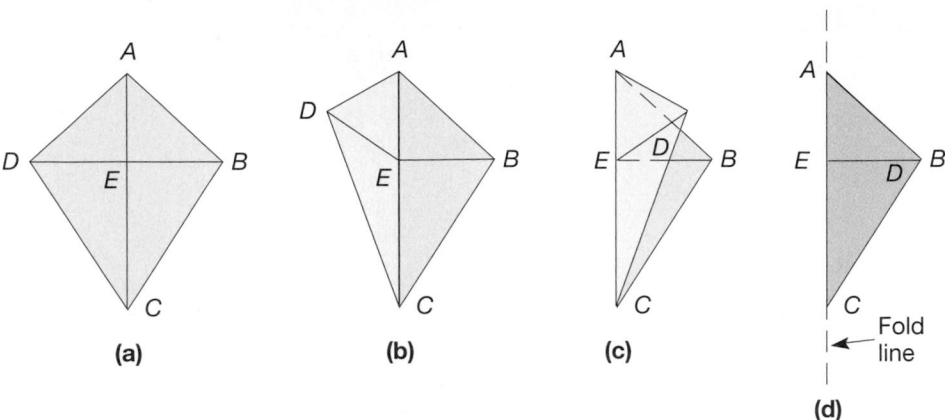

Figure 12.22

To determine whether two lines l and m are parallel, we use the following test (Figure 12.23).

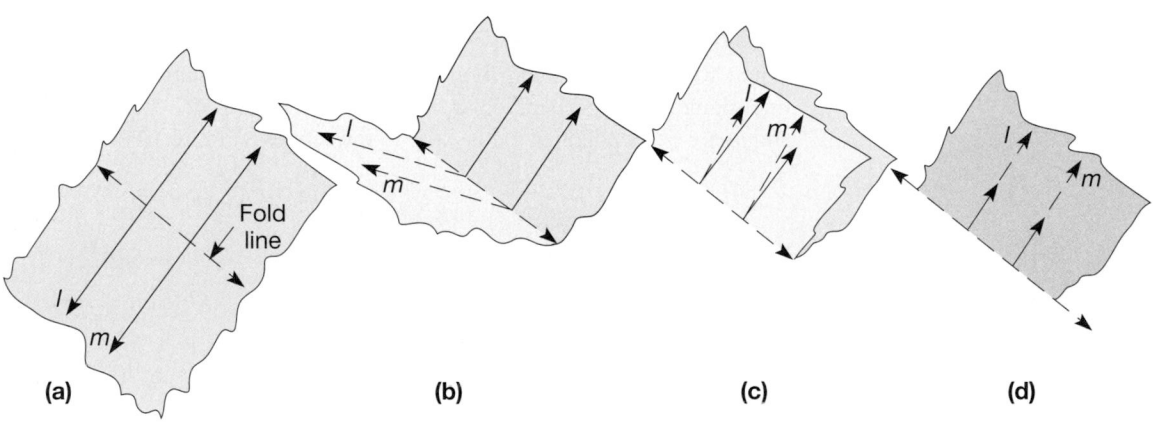

Figure 12.23

Parallel Line Segments Test

Fold so that l folds onto itself [Figures 12.23(a) to (c)]. (Any fold line can be used, as long as l folds onto itself.) Then l and m are parallel if and only if m folds onto itself or an extension of m [Figure 12.23(d)].

Example 12.7 is an application of the test for parallel line segments.

Example 12.7   Show that the opposite sides of a rhombus are parallel.

Solution   Let $ABCD$ be a rhombus [Figure 12.24(a)]. Fold so that side $\overline{AB}$ is folded onto itself [Figure 12.24(b)]. (Extend $\overline{AB}$ and/or $\overline{DC}$, if necessary.) Observe that side $\overline{DC}$ also folds onto itself. Thus $\overline{AB}$ and $\overline{DC}$ are parallel. Similarly, it can be shown that $\overline{AD}$ is parallel to $\overline{BC}$.

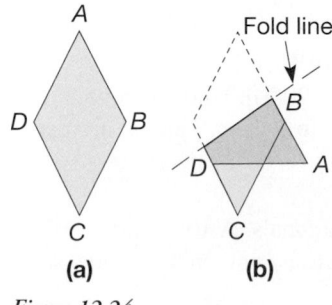

Figure 12.24

Notice that Example 12.7 demonstrates that every rhombus is a parallelogram.

We can tabulate properties of figures and use them to make general comparisons. For example, Table 12.2 gives a list of properties of several types of quadrilaterals. We have demonstrated some of these attributes. Others are in the Exercise/Problem Sets. Deductive verifications of the attributes in Table 12.2 can be made using ideas in Chapter 14, 15, or 16.

Table 12.2 Attributes of Quadrilaterals

ATTRIBUTE	Quadrilateral				
	PARALLELOGRAM	RHOMBUS	RECTANGLE	SQUARE	KITE
All sides congruent		X		X	
All angles congruent			X	X	
Both pairs of opposite sides congruent	X	X	X	X	
Both pairs of opposite sides parallel	X	X	X	X	
Adjacent sides perpendicular			X	X	
Diagonals perpendicular		X		X	X
Has reflection symmetry		X	X	X	X
Has rotation symmetry	X	X	X	X	

Spotlight on Technology To better understand the properties of the various quadrilaterals, it is helpful to be able to see their properties in action. The Geometer's Sketchpad® webmodule activity, *Name That Quadrilateral*, displays seven different quadrilaterals in the shape of a square. However, each quadrilateral is constructed with different properties. Some have right angles, some have congruent sides, and some have parallel sides. By dragging each of the points on each of the quadrilaterals, you can determine the most general name of each quadrilateral. See if you can name all seven of the quadrilaterals.

www.wiley.com/college/musser

Regular Polygons

A **simple closed curve** in the plane is a curve that can be traced with the same starting and stopping points and without crossing or retracing any part of the curve (Figure 12.25). A simple closed "curve" made up of line segments is called a **polygon** (which means "many angles"). A polygon where all sides are congruent and all angles are congruent is called a **regular polygon** or **regular *n*-gon.** Figure 12.26 shows

Figure 12.25

Equilateral triangle
$n = 3$

Square
$n = 4$

Regular pentagon
$n = 5$

Regular hexagon
$n = 6$

Regular heptagon
$n = 7$

Regular octagon
$n = 8$

Figure 12.26

several types of regular *n*-gons. Notice that *n* denotes the number of sides and the number of angles. Since the number of sides in the figure can be any whole number greater than 2, there are infinitely many regular polygons.

The shapes in Figure 12.26 are called **convex,** since each has the following property: A line segment joining any two points inside the figure lies completely inside the figure. Figure 12.27 shows some convex and nonconvex—called **concave**—two-dimensional shapes. It can be seen that all regular *n*-gons are convex.

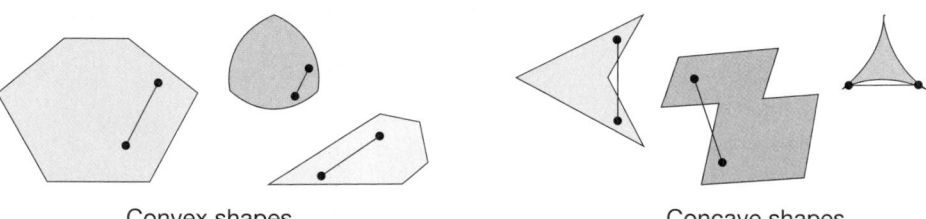

Convex shapes   Concave shapes

Figure 12.27

There are several angles of interest in regular *n*-gons. Figure 12.28 shows three of them: vertex angles, central angles, and exterior angles.

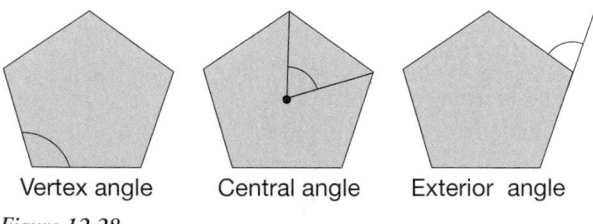

Vertex angle   Central angle   Exterior angle

Figure 12.28

A **vertex angle** (also called an **interior angle**) is formed by two consecutive sides. A **central angle** is formed by the segments connecting consecutive vertices to the center of the regular *n*-gon. An **exterior angle** is formed by one side together with an extension of an adjacent side of the regular *n*-gon, as pictured in Figure 12.28. Notice that the number of vertex angles and the sides of a regular polygon are the same. But there are twice as many exterior angles as interior angles. Vertex angles and exterior angles are formed in all convex shapes whose sides are line segments.

Circles

Figure 12.29

If we consider regular *n*-gons in which *n* is very large, we can obtain figures with many vertices, all of which are the same distance from the center. Figure 12.29 shows a regular 24-gon, for example. A **circle** is the set of *all* points in the plane that are a fixed distance from a given point (called the **center**). The distance from the center to a point on the circle is called the **radius** of the circle. Any segment whose endpoints are the center and a point of the circle is also called a radius. The length of a line segment whose endpoints are on the circle and which contains the center is called a **diameter** of the circle. The line segment itself is also called a diameter. Figure 12.30 shows several circles and their centers.

Figure 12.30

Figure 12.31

A **compass** is a useful device for drawing circles with different radii. Figure 12.31 shows how to draw a circle with a compass. We study techniques for constructing figures with a compass and straightedge in Chapter 14.

If we analyze a circle according to its symmetry properties, we find that it has infinitely many lines of symmetry. Every line through the center of the circle is a line of symmetry (Figure 12.32). Also, a circle has infinitely many rotation symmetries, since every angle whose vertex is the center of the circle is an angle of rotation symmetry (Figure 12.33).

Figure 12.32

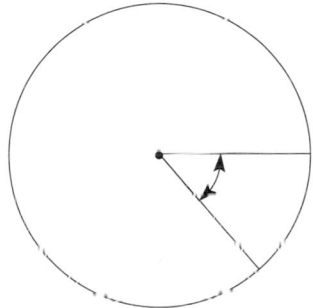

Figure 12.33

Many properties of a circle, including its area, are obtained by comparing the circle to regular *n*-gons with increasingly large values of *n*. We investigate several measurement properties of circles and other curved shapes in Chapter 13.

MATHEMATICAL MORSEL

Road signs come in all different shapes from circles and octagons to triangles and trapezoids. The shape of each sign has a particular use and meaning. For example, circular signs are used at railroad crossings and they represent the most potential danger to a driver. The next level of danger is the need to STOP at intersections, and thus the octagon is the shape used. Diamond- or rhombus-shaped signs are used for caution, while rectangles are used to provide direction and display regulations like the speed limit. The octagon and circle are used exclusively for stop signs and railroad crossings because of the need to be able to identify them at night as well as during the day. Rhombus- or rectangle-shaped signs, however, represent a lower level of danger and thus take on a variety of cautionary or directional meanings.

Section 12.2 EXERCISE / PROBLEM SET A

EXERCISES

1. Three of these figures are identical except for reflecting and/or rotating. Which figure is different from the others? Explain.

a.

b.

c.

d.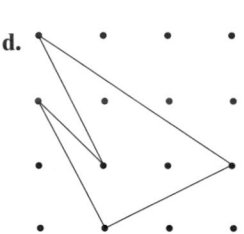

2. Draw the lines of symmetry in the following regular *n*-gons. How many does each have?

a.

b.

c.

d.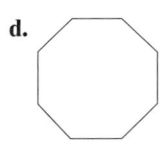

e. This illustrates that a regular *n*-gon has how many lines of symmetry?

3. Given a regular *n*-gon, complete the following statements.

a. If *n* is odd, each line of symmetry goes through a _____ and the _____ of the opposite side.

b. If *n* is even, half of the lines of symmetry connect a _____ to the opposite _____. The other half connect the _____ of one side to the _____ of the opposite side.

4. a. How many lines of symmetry are there for each of the following national flags? Colors are indicated and should be considered. Assume the flags are laying flat.

Argentina   Jamaica

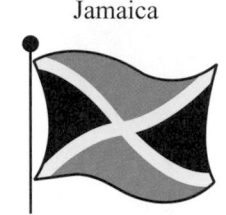

b. Which of the following national flags have rotation symmetry? What are the angles in each case (list measures between 0 and 360°)?

United Kingdom   Japan

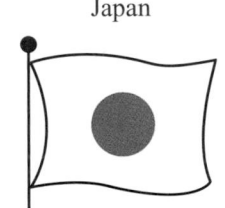

5. For each of the following shapes, determine which of the following descriptions apply.

    S: simple closed curve
    C: convex, simple closed curve
    N: *n*-gon

a.

b.

c.

d.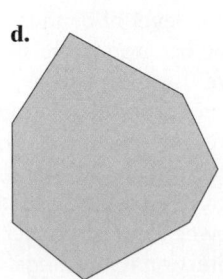

PROBLEMS

6. A **tetromino** is formed by connecting four squares so that connecting squares share a complete edge. Find all the different tetrominos. That is, no two of your tetrominos can be superimposed by reflecting and/or rotating.

A tetromino

Not tetrominos

7. Make two copies of each tetromino shape. Arrange all of those pieces to cover a 5 × 8 rectangle.

8. a. Which of the following pictures of sets best represents the relationship between isosceles triangles and scalene triangles? Label the sets and intersection (if it exists).

i.

ii.   **iii.**

b. Which represents the relationship between isosceles triangles and equilateral triangles?

c. Which represents the relationship between isosceles triangles and right triangles?

d. Which represents the relationship between equilateral triangles and right triangles?

9. Use a tracing to show that the diagonals of a rectangle are congruent.

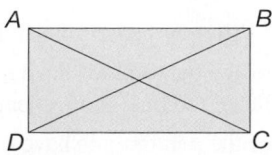

10. Use a tracing to find all the rotation symmetries of a square.

11. Use a tracing to find all the rotation symmetries of an equilateral triangle. (*Hint*: The center is the intersection of the reflection lines.)

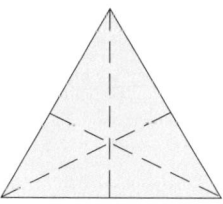

12. Use a tracing to show that the diagonals of a rhombus bisect each other.

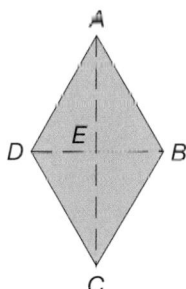

13. a. Use paper folding to show that two of the opposite angles of a kite are congruent. Are the other angles congruent?

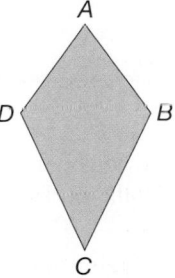

b. What does the result in part (a) tell us about the opposite angles of a rhombus?

Section 12.2 EXERCISE / PROBLEM SET B

EXERCISES

1. Three of these shapes are identical except for reflecting and/or rotating. Which figures is different from the others? Explain.

   a. **b.**

   c. **d.**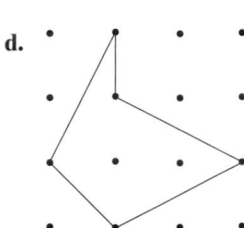

2. Determine the type(s) of symmetry for each figure. Indicate the lines of reflection symmetry and describe the turn symmetries.

   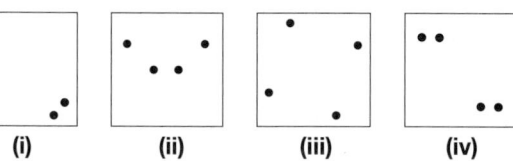

3. Which capital letters of our alphabet have the following symmetry?

   a. Reflection symmetry in vertical line

   b. Reflection symmetry in horizontal line

   c. Rotation symmetry

4. Given here are emblems from national flags. What types of symmetry do they have? Give lines or center and turn angle.

   a. Korea **b.** Burundi

   c. Canada **d.** Taiwan

5. For each of the following shapes, determine which of the following descriptions apply.

   S: simple closed curve
   C: convex, simple closed curve
   N: *n*-gon

   a. **b.**

   c. 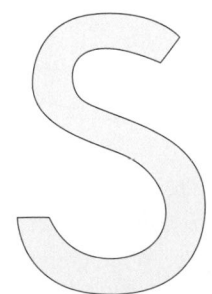 **d.**

PROBLEMS

6. A **pentomino** is made by five connected squares that touch only on a complete side.

   Is a pentomino   Is not a pentomino

   Two pentominos are the same if they can be matched by turning or flipping, as shown.

    and

   Find the 12 different pentomino shapes.

   a. Which of the pentominos have reflection symmetry? Indicate the line(s) of reflection.

   b. Which of the pentominos have rotation symmetry? Indicate the center and angle(s).

7. Look at your set of pentominos. Which of the shapes can be folded into a cubical box without a top?

    a. Find three pentomino shapes that can fit together to form a 3 × 5 rectangle.

    b. Using five of the pentominos, cover a 5 × 5 square.

    c. Using each of the pentomino pieces once, make a 6 × 10 rectangle.

8. a. Which of the following pictures of sets best represents the relationship between rectangles and parallelograms? Label the sets and intersection (if it exists) appropriately.

    i.

    ii.

    iii.
    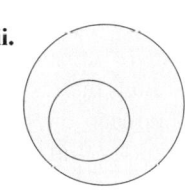

    b. Which represents the relationship between rectangles and rhombuses?

    c. Which represents the relationship between rectangles and squares?

    d. Which represents the relationship between rectangles and isosceles triangles?

9. Use a tracing to show that the diagonals of a parallelogram bisect each other. That is, show that $\overline{AE}$ is congruent to $\overline{CE}$ and that $\overline{DE}$ is congruent to $\overline{BE}$.

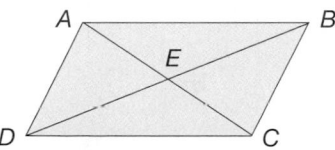

10. Use a tracing to show that a rectangle has rotation symmetry.

11. Use a tracing to show that the opposite sides of a rectangle are congruent.

12. a. Use paper folding to show that an isosceles trapezoid has reflection symmetry.

    b. In a trapezoid, the **bases** are the parallel sides. **Base angles** are a pair of angles that share a base as a common side. What does part (a) show about both pairs of base angles of an isosceles trapezoid?

13. a. Use a tracing to find all the rotation symmetries of the following regular *n*-gons

    i. Regular pentagon

    ii. Regular hexagon

    b. How many rotation symmetries does each regular *n*-gon have?

PROBLEMS FOR WRITING/DISCUSSION

1. Two groups of students were arguing about the lines of symmetry in a regular octagon. One group said the lines of symmetry formed eight congruent triangles. The other group said no, they made eight congruent kites. Could both groups be right? Explain.

2. Gail draws a horizontal line through a parallelogram and says, "If I cut along this line, the two pieces fit on top of each other. So this must be a line of symmetry." Do you agree? Explain.

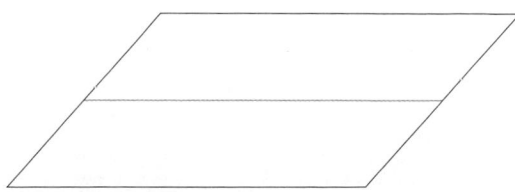

3. Willy says if a plane figure has reflection symmetry, it automatically has rotation symmetry. Is this true? Can you think of a counterexample? Explain.

12.3   PROPERTIES OF GEOMETRIC SHAPES: LINES AND ANGLES

Sketch or describe the following arrangements of three lines. If it is not possible, explain why not.

Arrange three lines to create:

1. Zero points of intersection   **2.** Exactly one point of intersection

3. Exactly two points of intersection   **4.** Exactly three points of intersection

5. Exactly four points of intersection **6.** Zero points of intersection with lines that are not parallel

Points and Lines in a Plane

Imagine that our square lattice is made with more and more points, so that the points are closer and closer together. Imagine also that a point takes up no space. Figure 12.34 gives a conceptual idea of this "ideal" collection of points. Finally, imagine that our lattice extends in every direction in two dimensions, without restriction. This infinitely large flat surface is called a **plane.** We can think of the **points** as locations in the plane. If a line segment $\overline{AB}$ is extended infinitely in two directions as illustrated in Figure 12.35, the resulting figure is called a **line.** Lines are considered to be straight and extend infinitely in each direction [Figure 12.35(a)]. The notation $\overleftrightarrow{AB}$ denotes the line containing points A and B. The intuitive notions of point, line, and plane serve as the basis for the precise definitions that follow.

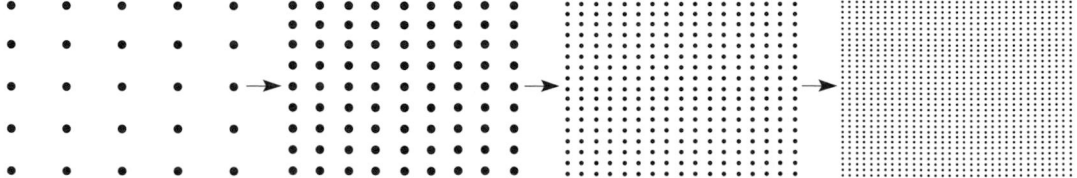

Figure 12.34

Points that lie on the same line are called **collinear points** [C, D, and E are collinear in Figure 12.35(b)]. Two lines *in the plane* are called **parallel lines** if they do not intersect [Figure 12.35(c)] or are the same. Thus a line is parallel to itself.

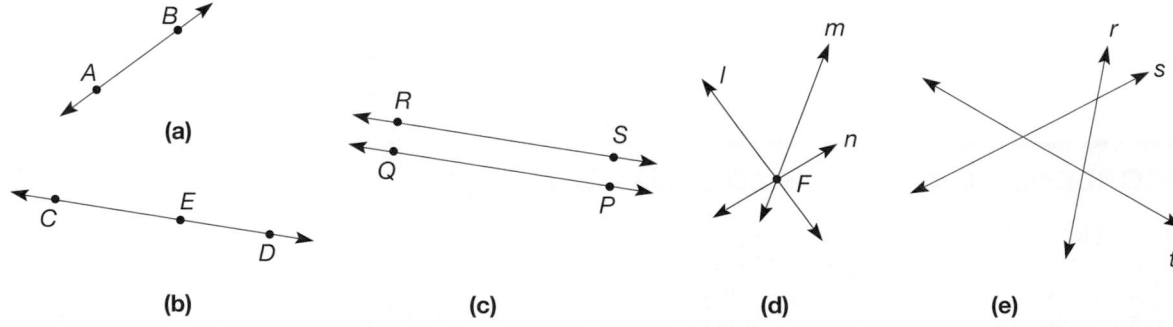

Figure 12.35

Three or more lines that contain the same point are called **concurrent lines.** Lines l, m, and n in Figure 12.35(d) are concurrent, since they all contain point F. Lines r, s, and t in Figure 12.35(e) are not concurrent, since no point in the plane belongs to all three lines.

Because we cannot literally see the plane and its points, the geometric shapes that we will now study are abstractions. However, we can draw pictures and make models to help us imagine shapes, keeping in mind that the shapes exist only in our minds, just as numbers do. We will make certain assumptions about the plane and points in it. They have to do with lines in the plane and the distance between points.

PROPERTY

Points and Lines

1. For each pair of points A, B ($A \neq B$) in the plane, there is a unique line $\overleftrightarrow{AB}$ containing them.

2. Each line can be viewed as a copy of the real number line. The **distance** between two points A and B is the nonnegative difference of the real numbers a and b to which A and B correspond. The distance from A and B is written AB or BA. The numbers a and b are called the **coordinates** of A and B on $\overleftrightarrow{AB}$.

3. If a point P is not on a line l, there is a unique line m, $m \neq l$, such that P is on m and m is parallel to l, We write **$m \parallel l$** to mean m is parallel to l.

Line segment $\overline{AB}$

Ray $\overrightarrow{CD}$

Figure 12.36

We can use our properties of lines to define line segments, rays, and angles. A point P is **between** A and B if the coordinate of P with reference to line $\overleftrightarrow{AB}$ is numerically between the coordinates of A and B. In Figure 12.36, M and P are between A and B. The **line segment,** $\overline{AB}$, consists of all the points between A and B on line $\overleftrightarrow{AB}$ together with points A and B. Points A and B are called the **endpoints** of $\overline{AB}$. The **length** of line segment $\overline{AB}$ is the distance between A and B. The **midpoint**, M, of a line segment $\overline{AB}$ is the point of $\overline{AB}$ that is **equidistant** from A and B, that is, $AM = MB$. The **ray** $\overrightarrow{CD}$ consists of all points of line $\overleftrightarrow{CD}$ on the same side of C as point D, together with the endpoint C (Figure 12.36).

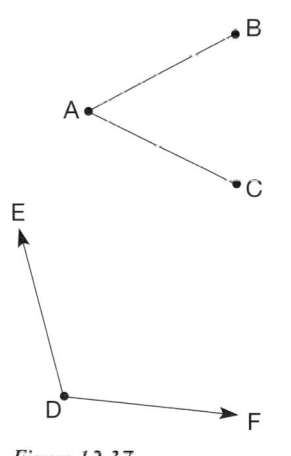

Figure 12.37

Angles

An **angle** is the union of two line segments with a common endpoint *or* the union of two rays with a common endpoint (Figure 12.37). The common endpoint is called the **vertex** of the angle. The line segments or rays comprising the angle are called its **sides.** Angles can be denoted by naming a nonvertex point on one side, then the vertex, followed by a nonvertex point on the other side. For example, Figure 12.37 shows angle BAC and angle EDF. Recall that the symbol $\angle BAC$ is used to denote angle BAC. (We could also call it $\angle CAB$.) We will use line segments and angles in studying various types of shapes in the plane, such as triangles and quadrilaterals.

Reflection from Research
The focus of an angle as a turn is a critical experience for early elementary students. This focus helps students understand what is being measured (the angle) prior to the discussion of unit of measurement (degree) (Wilson & Adams, 1992).

An angle formed by two rays divides the plane into three regions: (1) the angle itself, (2) the **interior** of the angle (i.e., all the points in the plane between the two rays), and (3) the **exterior** of the angle (i.e., all points in the plane not in the angle or its interior). Figure 12.38 illustrates this property. Notice that the interior of the angle is convex, whereas its exterior is concave. (If the two rays form a line, then the angle has no interior.) Two angles that share a vertex, have a side in common, but whose

Figure 12.39

Figure 12.40

Figure 12.38

Figure 12.41

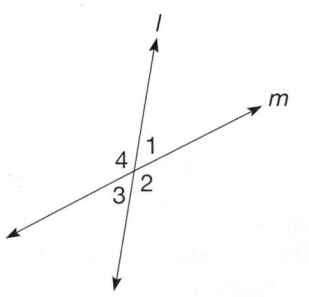

Figure 12.42

interiors do not intersect are called **adjacent angles.** In Figure 12.39, $\angle ABC$ and $\angle CBD$ are adjacent angles.

To measure angles, we use a semicircular device called a **protractor.** We place the center of the protractor at the vertex of the angle to be measured, with one side of the angle passing through the zero-degree (0°) mark (Figure 12.40). The protractor is evenly divided into 180 **degrees,** written 180°. Each degree can be further subdivided into 60 equal minutes, and each minute into 60 equal seconds, or we can use nonnegative real numbers to report degrees (such as 27.428°). The **measure of the angle** is equal to the real number on the protractor that the second side of the angle intersects. For example, the measure of $\angle BAC$ in Figure 12.40 is 120°. The measure of $\angle BAC$ will be denoted **$m(\angle BAC)$**. An angle measuring less than 90° is called an **acute angle,** an angle measuring 90° is called a **right angle,** and an angle measuring greater than 90° but less than 180° is an **obtuse angle.** An angle measuring 180° is called a **straight angle.** An angle whose measure is greater than 180° is called a **reflex angle.** In Figure 12.41, $\angle BAC$ is acute, $\angle BAD$ is a right angle, $\angle BAE$ is obtuse, and $\angle BAF$ is a straight angle.

When two lines intersect, several angles are formed. In Figure 12.42, lines l and m form four angles, $\angle 1$, $\angle 2$, $\angle 3$, and $\angle 4$. We see that

$$m(\angle 1) + m(\angle 2) = 180° \qquad \text{and} \qquad m(\angle 3) + m(\angle 2) = 180°.$$

Hence

$$m(\angle 1) + m(\angle 2) = m(\angle 3) + m(\angle 2),$$

so that

$$m(\angle 1) = m(\angle 3).$$

Similarly, $m(\angle 2) = m(\angle 4)$. Angles 1 and 3 are called a pair of **vertical angles;** they are opposite each other and formed by a pair of intersecting lines. Similarly, angles 2 and 4 are a pair of vertical angles. We have demonstrated that vertical angles have the

Figure 12.43

Figure 12.44

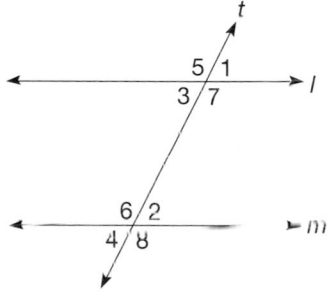

Figure 12.45

same measure. Recall that angles having the same opening, that is, the same measure, are called congruent; similarly, line segments having the same length are called congruent.

Two angles, the sum of whose measures is 180°, are called **supplementary angles.** In Figure 12.42 angles 1 and 2 are supplementary, as are angles 2 and 3. If two lines intersect to form a right angle, the lines are called **perpendicular.** Lines l and m in Figure 12.43 are perpendicular lines. We will write $l \perp m$ to denote that line l is perpendicular to line m. Two angles whose sum is 90° are called **complementary angles.** In Figure 12.43, angles 1 and 2 are complementary, as are angles 3 and 4.

Angles Associated with Parallel Lines

If two lines l and m are intersected by a third line, t, we call line t a **transversal** (Figure 12.44). The three lines in Figure 12.44 form many angles. Angles 1 and 2 are called **corresponding angles,** since they are in the same locations relative to l, m, and t. Angles 3 and 4 are also corresponding angles. Our intuition tells us that if line l is parallel to line m (i.e., they point in the same direction), corresponding angles will have the same measure (Figure 12.45). Look at the various pairs of corresponding angles in Figure 12.45, where $l \parallel m$. Do they appear to have the same measure? Examples such as those in Figure 12.45 suggest the following property.

> ### ● PROPERTY
>
> #### Corresponding Angles
>
> Suppose that lines l and m are intersected by a transversal t. Then $l \parallel m$ if and only if corresponding angles formed by l, m, and t are congruent.

Using the corresponding angles property, we can prove that every rectangle is a parallelogram. This is left for Part A Problem 12 in the Problem Set.

Example 12.8 In Figure 12.46, lines l and m are parallel. Show that $m(\angle 2) = m(\angle 3)$ using the corresponding angles property.

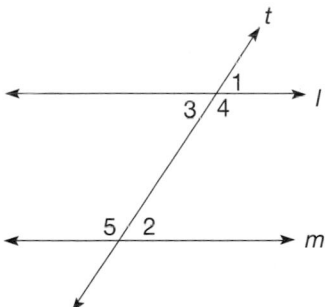

Figure 12.46

Solution Since $l \parallel m$, by the corresponding angles property, $m(\angle 1) = m(\angle 2)$. But also, because $\angle 1$ and $\angle 3$ are vertical angles, we know that $m(\angle 1) = m(\angle 3)$. Hence $m(\angle 2) = m(\angle 3)$. ■

In the configuration in Figure 12.46, the pair $\angle 2$ and $\angle 3$ and the pair $\angle 4$ and $\angle 5$ are called **alternate interior angles,** since they are nonadjacent angles formed by l, m, and t, the union of whose interiors contains the region between l and m. Example 12.8 suggests another property of parallel lines and alternate interior angles.

> ### THEOREM
>
> ### Alternate Interior Angles
>
> Suppose that lines *l* and *m* are intersected by a transversal *t*. Then *l* ∥ *m* if and only if alternate interior angles formed by *l*, *m*, and *t* are congruent.

The complete verification of this result is left for Part A Problem 10 in the Problem Set.

We can use this result to prove a very important property of triangles. Suppose that we have a **triangle, △*ABC.*** (The notation △ *ABC* denotes the triangle that is the union of line segments $\overline{AB}$, $\overline{BC}$, and $\overline{CA}$.) Let line $l = \overleftrightarrow{AC}$ (Figure 12.47). By part three of the properties of points and lines, there is a line *m* parallel to *l* through point *B* in Figure 12.47. Then lines $\overleftrightarrow{AB}$ and $\overleftrightarrow{BC}$ are transversals for the parallel lines *l* and

Problem-Solving Strategy
Draw a Diagram

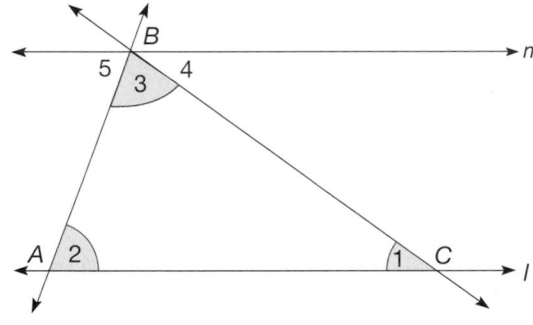

Figure 12.47

m. Hence ∠1 and ∠4 are congruent alternate interior angles. Similarly $m(\angle 2) = m(\angle 5)$. Summarizing, we have the following results:

$$m(\angle 1) = m(\angle 4),$$
$$m(\angle 2) = m(\angle 5),$$
$$m(\angle 3) = m(\angle 3).$$

Notice also that $m(\angle 5) + m(\angle 3) + m(\angle 4) = 180°$, since ∠5, ∠3, and ∠4 form a straight angle. But from the observations above, we see that

$$m(\angle 1) + m(\angle 2) + m(\angle 3) = m(\angle 4) + m(\angle 5) + m(\angle 3) = 180°.$$

This result is summarized next.

> ### THEOREM
>
> ### Angle Sum in a Triangle
>
> The sum of the measures of the three vertex angles in a triangle is 180°.

www.wiley.com/
college/musser

Spotlight on Technology   Even though doing many examples doesn't prove anything, it does help convince a person that a certain property is true. One way to introduce students to the fact that the sum of the angles of a triangle is 180° is to have them construct triangles and measure the angles with a protractor. The tedium of this task limits the number of triangles that can be examined. However, the Geometer's Sketchpad® web-module activity, *Triangle Angle Sum*, allows the student to investigate many more triangles by clicking and dragging the vertices of the triangle. Is it possible to have more than one obtuse angle in a triangle? Why or why not?

As a consequence of this result, a triangle can have at most one right angle or at most one obtuse angle. A triangle that has a right angle is called a **right triangle,** a triangle with an obtuse angle is called an **obtuse triangle,** and a triangle in which *all* angles are acute is called an **acute triangle.** For right triangles, we note that two of the vertex angles must be acute and their sum is 90°. Hence they are complementary. In Figure 12.48, ∠1 and ∠2 are complementary, as are ∠3 and ∠4. Notice in Figure 12.48 that a small symbol " ⌐ " is used to indicate a right angle.

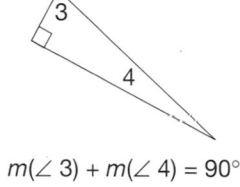

$m(\angle 1) + m(\angle 2) = 90°$ $\qquad$ $m(\angle 3) + m(\angle 4) = 90°$

Figure 12.48

MATHEMATICAL MORSEL

Euler's formula, which relates the number of vertices, edges, and faces of simple polyhedra such as the cube, regular tetrahedron, and so on, is an interesting result about surfaces. Another result about surfaces is due to A. F. Moebius. Start with a rectangular strip ABCD. Twist the strip one-half turn to form the "twisted" strip ABCD. Then tape the two ends AB and CD to form a "twisted loop." Then draw a continuous line down the middle of one side of the loop. What did you find? Next, cut the loop on the line you drew. What did you find? Repeat, drawing a line down the middle of the new loop and cutting one more time. Surprise!

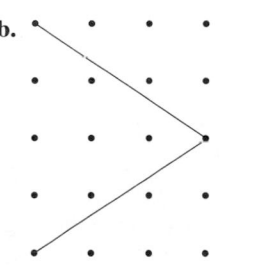

Section 12.3 EXERCISE / PROBLEM SET A

EXERCISES

1. a. How many angles are shown in the following figure?

b. How many are obtuse?

c. How many are acute?

2. Determine which of the following angles represented on a square lattice are right angles. If one isn't, is it acute or obtuse?

3. Consider the square lattice shown here.

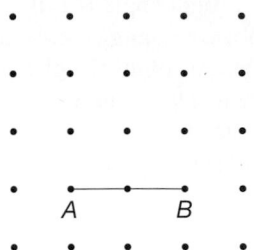

a. How many triangles have $\overline{AB}$ as one side?

b. How many of these are isosceles?

c. How many are right triangles?

d. How many are acute?

e. How many are obtuse?

4. Consider the following sets.

T = all triangles A = acute triangles

S = scalene triangles R = right triangles

I = isosceles triangles O = obtuse triangles

E = equilateral triangles

Draw an example of an element of the following sets, if possible.

a. $S \cap A$ b. $I \cap O$ c. $O \cap E$

5. Find the missing angle measure in the following triangles.

a.   b.

c.   d.

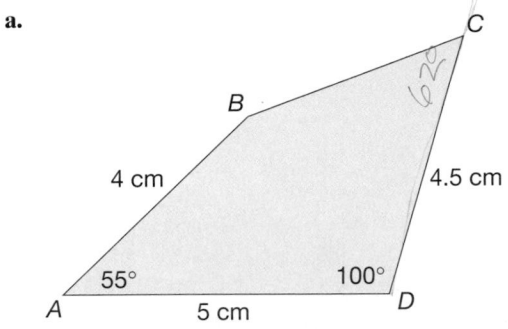

6. Use your ruler and protractor to draw each of the following shapes. Then measure $\angle C$ and diagonal $\overline{AC}$.

a.

b.

PROBLEMS

7. In the figure, $m(\angle BFC) = 55°$, $m(\angle AFD) = 150°$, and $m(\angle BFE) = 120°$. Determine the measures of $\angle AFB$ and $\angle CFD$. (NOTE: Do not measure the angles with your protractor to determine these measures.)

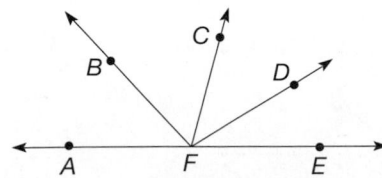

8. In the following figure, the measure of $\angle 1$ is 9° less than half the measure of $\angle 2$. Determine the measures of $\angle 1$ and $\angle 2$.

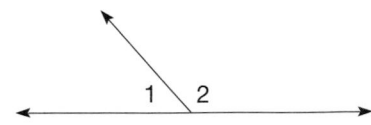

9. Determine the measures of the numbered angles if $m(\angle 1) = 80°$, $m(\angle 4) = 125°$, and l is parallel to m.

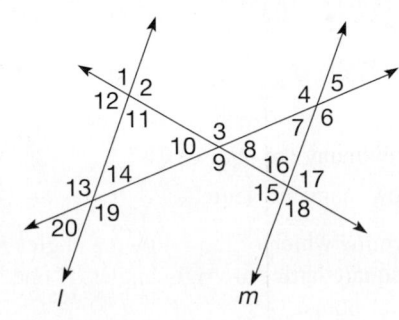

10. The first part of the alternate interior angles theorem was verified in Example 12.8. Verify the second part of the alternate interior angles theorem. In particular, assume that $m(\angle 1) = m(\angle 2)$ and show that $l \parallel m$.

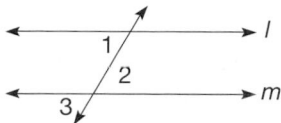

11. Angles 1 and 6 are called **alternate exterior angles.** (Can you see why?) Prove the following statements.

  a. If $m(\angle 1) = m(\angle 6)$, then $l \parallel m$.

  b. If $l \parallel m$, then $m(\angle 1) = m(\angle 6)$.

  c. State the results of parts (a) and (b) as a general property.

12. Using the corresponding angles property, prove that rectangle $ABCD$ is a parallelogram.

13. a. Given a square and a circle, draw an example where they intersect in exactly the number of points given.

    i. No points   **ii.** One point

    iii. Two points   **iv.** Three points

  b. What is the greatest number of possible points of intersection?

14. Use your protractor to measure angles with dots on their vertices in the following semicircle. Make a conjecture based on your findings.

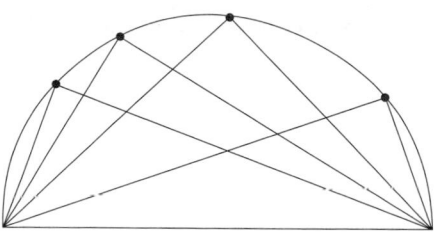

15. Two lines drawn in a plane separate the plane into three different regions if the lines are parallel.

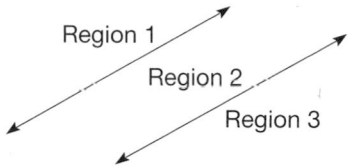

If the lines are intersecting, then they will divide the plane into four regions.

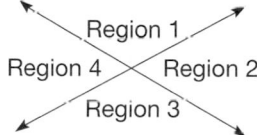

Thus, the greatest number of regions two lines may divide a plane into is four. Determine the greatest number of regions into which a plane can be divided by three lines, four lines, five lines, and ten lines. Generalize to n lines

16. Redo Problem 14 by doing the following construction on the Geometer's Sketchpad®.

  1. Construct a segment $\overline{AB}$.

  2. Construct the midpoint of the segment.

  3. Select the midpoint and point B and construct a circle by center and radius.

  4. Construct a point on the circle and label it point D.

  5. Construct segments to form the angle $\angle ADB$.

  6. Measure $\angle ADB$.

After moving point D around the circle, what conclusions can you draw about the measure of $\angle ADB$? Is this consistent with the results from Problem 14?

Section 12.3 EXERCISE / PROBLEM SET B

EXERCISES

1. How many different line segments are contained in the following portion of a line?

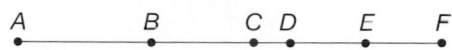

2. Find the angle measure of the following angles drawn on triangular lattices. Use your protractor if necessary.

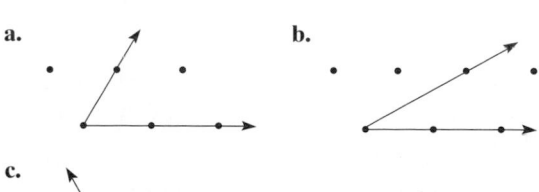

3. Given the square lattice shown, answer the following questions.

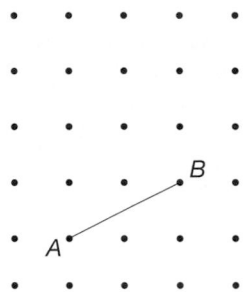

a. How many triangles have $\overline{AB}$ as one side?

b. How many of these are right triangles?

c. How many are acute triangles?

d. How many are obtuse triangles? [*Hint*: Use your answers to part (a) to (c).]

4. Consider the following sets.

T = all triangles A = acute triangles
S = scalene triangles R = right triangles
I = isosceles triangles O = obtuse triangles
E = equilateral triangles

Draw an example of an element of the following sets, if possible.

a. $S \cap R$ b. $T - (A \cup O)$ c. $T - (R \cup S)$

5. Following are the measures of $\angle A$, $\angle B$, and $\angle C$. Can a triangle $\triangle ABC$ be made that has the given angles? Explain.

a. $m(\angle A) = 36$, $m(\angle B) = 78$, $m(\angle C) = 66$

b. $m(\angle A) = 124$, $m(\angle B) = 56$, $m(\angle C) = 20$

c. $m(\angle A) = 90$, $m(\angle B) = 74$, $m(\angle C) = 18$

6. Use your ruler and protractor to draw each of the following shapes. Then measure $\angle C$ and $\overline{AC}$.

a.

b.

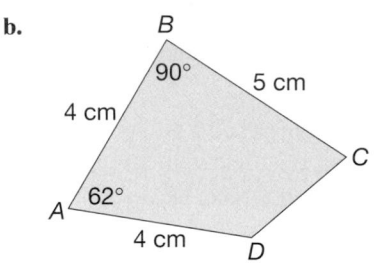

PROBLEMS

7. In the following figure $\overline{AO}$ is perpendicular to $\overline{CO}$. If $m(\angle AOD) = 165°$ and $m(\angle BOD) = 82°$, determine the measures of $\angle AOB$ and $\angle BOC$. (NOTE: Do not measure the angles with your protractor to determine these measures.)

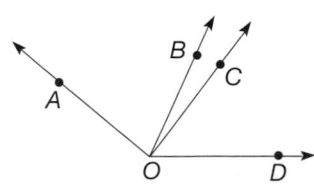

8. The measure of $\angle X$ is 9° more than twice the measure of $\angle Y$. If $\angle X$ and $\angle Y$ are supplementary angles, find the measure of $\angle X$.

9. Find the measures of $\angle 1$, $\angle 2$, $\angle 3$, and $\angle 4$ if some angles formed are related as shown and $l \parallel m \parallel n$.

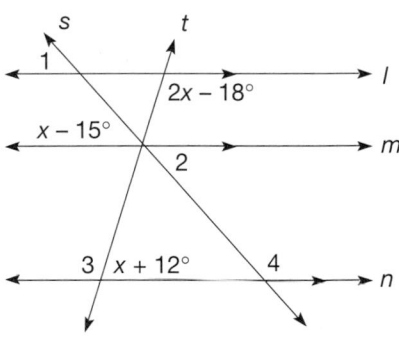

10. In this section we assumed that the corresponding angles property was true. Then we verified the alternate interior angles theorem. Some geometry books assume the alternate interior angles theorem to be true and build results from there. Assume that the only parallel line test we have is the alternate interior angles theorem and show the following to be true.

a. If $l \parallel m$, then corresponding angles have the same measure, namely, $m(\angle 1) = m(\angle 4)$.

b. If $m(\angle 3) = m(\angle 6)$, then $l \parallel m$.

11. Angles 1 and 3 are called **interior angles on the same side of the transversal.**

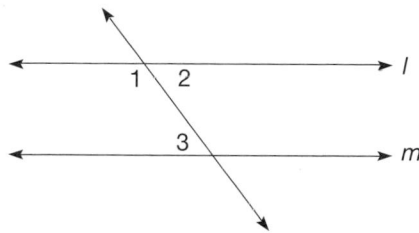

a. If $l \parallel m$, what is true about $m(\angle 1) + m(\angle 3)$?

b. Can you show the converse of the result in part (a): that if your conclusion about $m(\angle 1) + m(\angle 3)$ is satisfied, then $l \parallel m$?

12. In parallelogram $ABCD$, $\angle 1$ and $\angle 2$ are called **consecutive angles,** as are $\angle 2$ and $\angle 3$, $\angle 3$ and $\angle 4$, $\angle 4$ and $\angle 1$. Using the results of Problem 11, what can you conclude about any two consecutive angles of a parallelogram? What can you conclude about two opposite angles (e.g., $\angle 1$ and $\angle 3$)?

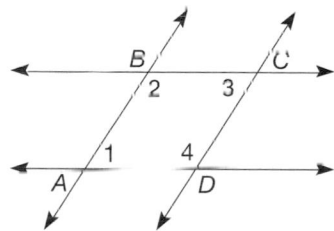

13. a. Given a triangle and a circle, draw an example where they intersect in exactly the number of points given.

   i. No points   **ii.** One point

   iii. Two points   **iv.** Three points

b. What is the greatest number of possible points of intersection?

14. Draw a large copy of $\triangle ABC$ on scratch paper and cut it out.

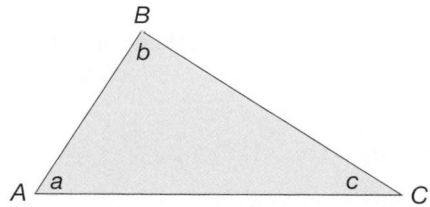

Fold down vertex B so that it lies on $\overline{AC}$ and so that the fold line is parallel to $\overline{AC}$.

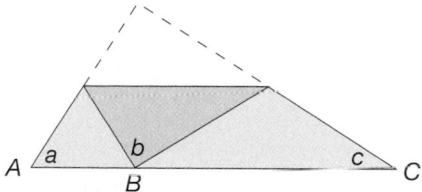

Now fold vertices A and C into point B.

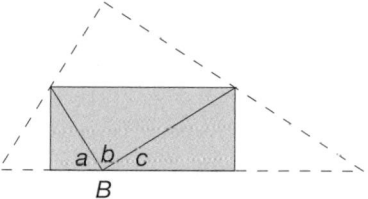

a. What does the resulting figure tell you about the measures of $\angle A$, $\angle B$, and $\angle C$? Explain.

b. What kind of polygon is the folded shape, and what is the length of its base?

c. Try this same procedure with two other types of triangles. Are the results the same?

15. Given three points, there is one line that can be drawn through them if the points are collinear.

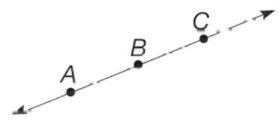

If the three points are noncollinear, there are three lines that can be drawn through pairs of points.

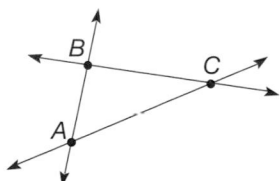

For three points, three is the greatest number of lines that can be drawn through pairs of points. Determine the greatest number of lines that can be drawn for four points, five points, and six points in a plane. Generalize to n points.

16. A famous problem, posed by puzzler Henry Dudenay, presented the following situation. Suppose that houses are located at points A, B, and C. We want to connect each house to water, electricity, and gas located at points W, G, and E, without any of the pipes/wires crossing each other.

A

B

C

W

G

E

a. Try making all of the connections. Can it be done? If so, how?

b. Suppose that the owner of one of the houses, say *B*, is willing to let the pipe for one of his neighbors' connections pass through his house. Then can all of the connections be made? If so, how?

PROBLEMS FOR WRITING/DISCUSSION

1. Barrilee's sister in high school says that the definition of parallel lines in our book is wrong because a line *cannot* be parallel to itself. And the definition of trapezoid is wrong, too; it should be "a quadrilateral with *at least* one pair of parallel sides," not exactly one pair of parallel sides. That's what it says in her book, and she's taking geometry in high school. What is an explanation for these differences?

2. Tisha is trying to determine how many rays are determined by three collinear points, *R*, *S*, and *T*. She thinks there are six: $\overrightarrow{RS}$, $\overrightarrow{ST}$, $\overrightarrow{RT}$, $\overrightarrow{TR}$, $\overrightarrow{TS}$, and $\overrightarrow{SR}$. Do you agree? Explain.

3. Troy says vertical angles have to be straight up and down like vertical lines; they can't be horizontal. Discuss.

12.4   REGULAR POLYGONS AND TESSELLATIONS

STARTING POINT

Two of the known facts about the sums of angles are:

1. The sum of the interior angles of a triangle is 180° degrees.
2. The sum of the angles around a single point is 360° degrees.

Using one or both of these facts, find $a + b + c + d + e$ where *a, b, c, d,* and *e* represent the marked interior angles of the pentagon at the right. Describe at least two methods that you can use for finding this sum.

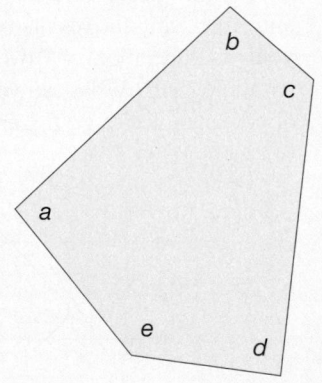

Angle Measures in Regular Polygons

A **regular polygon** (or regular *n*-gon) is both equilateral and equiangular. To find the measure of a central angle in a regular *n*-gon, notice that the sum of the measures of *n* central angles is 360°. Figure 12.49 illustrates this when *n* = 5. Hence the measure of each central angle in a regular *n*-gon is $\dfrac{360°}{n}$.

We can find the measure of the vertex angles in a regular *n*-gon by using the angle sum in a triangle property. Consider a regular pentagon (*n* = 5; Figure 12.50). Let us call the vertex angles $\angle v_1$, $\angle v_2$, $\angle v_3$, $\angle v_4$, and $\angle v_5$. Since all the vertex angles have the same measure, it suffices to find the vertex angle *sum* in the regular pentagon. The measure of each vertex angle, then, is one-fifth of this sum.

To find this sum, subdivide the pentagon into triangles using diagonals $\overline{AC}$ and $\overline{AD}$ (Figure 12.51). For example, *A*, *B*, and *C* are the vertices of a triangle, specifically $\triangle ABC$. Several new angles are formed, namely $\angle a$, $\angle b$, $\angle c$, $\angle d$, $\angle e$, $\angle f$, and $\angle g$. Notice that

$$m(\angle v_1) = m(\angle a) + m(\angle b) + m(\angle c),$$

$$m(\angle v_3) = m(\angle d) + m(\angle e),$$

Figure 12.49

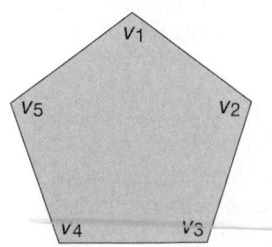

Figure 12.50

Problem-Solving Strategy
Draw a Picture

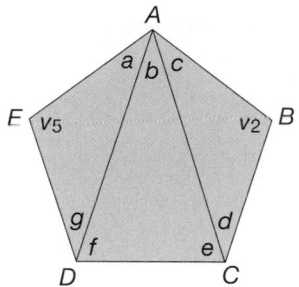

Figure 12.51

and
$$m(\angle v_4) = m(\angle f) + m(\angle g).$$

Within each triangle ($\triangle ABC$, $\triangle ACD$, and $\triangle ADE$), we know that the angle sum is 180°. Hence

$$m(\angle v_1) + m(\angle v_2) + m(\angle v_3) + m(\angle v_4) + m(\angle v_5)$$
$$= m(\angle a) + m(\angle b) + m(\angle c) + m(\angle v_2) + m(\angle d) +$$
$$\quad m(\angle e) + m(\angle f) + m(\angle g) + m(\angle v_5)$$
$$= [m(\angle c) + m(\angle v_2) + m(\angle d)] + [m(\angle b) + m(\angle e) + m(\angle f)] +$$
$$\quad [m(\angle g) + m(\angle v_5) + m(\angle a)]$$
$$= 180° + 180° + 180°,$$

since each bracketed sum is the angle sum in a triangle. Hence the angle sum in a regular pentagon is $3 \times 180° = 540°$. Finally, the measure of each vertex angle in the regular pentagon is $540° \div 5 = 108°$. The technique used here of forming triangles within the polygon can be used to find the sum of the vertex angles in any polygon.

Table 12.3 suggests a way of computing the measure of a vertex angle in a regular n-gon, for $n = 3, 4, 5, 6, 7, 8$. Verify the entries.

Table 12.3

	n	ANGLE SUM IN A REGULAR n-GON	MEASURE OF A VERTEX ANGLE
	3	$1 \cdot 180°$	$180° \div 3 = 60°$
	4	$2 \cdot 180°$	$(2 \times 180°) \div 4 = 90°$
	5	$3 \cdot 180°$	$(3 \times 180°) \div 5 = 108°$
	6	$4 \cdot 180°$	$(4 \times 180°) \div 6 = 120°$
	7	$5 \cdot 180°$	$(5 \times 180°) \div 7 = 128\frac{4}{7}°$
	8	$6 \cdot 180°$	$(6 \times 180°) \div 8 = 135°$

The entries in Table 12.3 suggest a formula for the measure of the vertex angle in a regular n-gon. In particular, we can subdivide any n-gon into $(n - 2)$ triangles. Since each triangle has an angle sum of 180°, the angle sum in a regular n-gon is $(n - 2) \cdot 180°$. Thus each vertex angle will measure $\dfrac{(n - 2) \cdot 180°}{n}$. We can also express this as $\dfrac{180°n - 360°}{n} = 180° - \dfrac{360°}{n}$. Thus any vertex angle is supplementary to any central angle.

To measure the exterior angles in a regular n-gon, notice that the sum of a vertex angle and an exterior angle will be 180°, by the way the exterior angle is formed (Figure 12.52). Therefore, each exterior angle will have measure

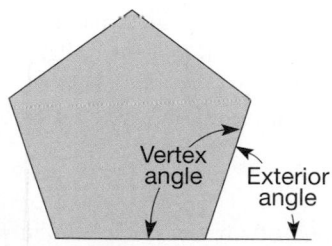

Figure 12.52

$$180° - \left[180° - \frac{360°}{n} \right] = 180° - 180° + \frac{360°}{n} = \frac{360°}{n}.$$ Hence, the measure of any exterior angle is the same as the measure of a central angle!

We can summarize our results about angle measures in regular polygons as follows.

> ### THEOREM
>
> #### Angle Measures in a Regular *n*-gon
>
> | Vertex Angle | Central Angle | Exterior Angle |
> |:---:|:---:|:---:|
> | $\dfrac{(n-2)\cdot 180°}{n}$ | $\dfrac{360°}{n}$ | $\dfrac{360°}{n}$ |

Remember that these results hold only for angles in *regular* polygons—not necessarily in arbitrary polygons. In the problem set, the central angle measure will be used when discussing rotation symmetry of polygons. We will use the vertex angle measure in the next section on tessellations.

Tessellations

A **polygonal region** is a polygon together with its interior. An arrangement of polygonal regions having only sides in common that completely covers the plane is called a **tessellation.** We can form tessellations with arbitrary triangles, as Figure 12.53 shows. Pattern (a) shows a tessellation with a scalene right triangle, pattern (b) shows a tessellation with

Figure 12.53

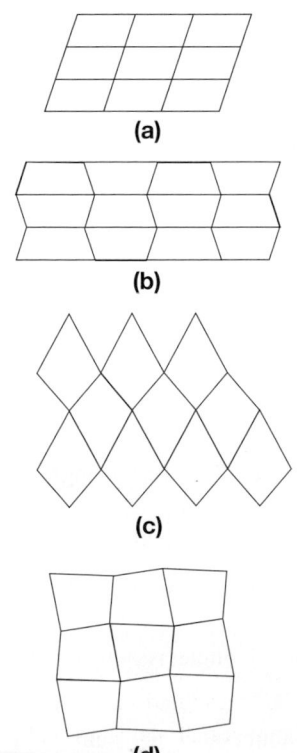

Figure 12.54

an acute isosceles triangle, and pattern (c) shows a tessellation with an obtuse scalene triangle. Note that angles measuring *x, y,* and *z* meet at each vertex to form a straight angle. As suggested by Figure 12.53, every triangle will tessellate the plane.

Every quadrilateral will form a tessellation also. Figure 12.54 shows several tessellations with quadrilaterals. In pattern (a) we see a tessellation with a parallelogram; in pattern (b), a tessellation with a trapezoid; and in pattern (c), a tessellation with a kite. Pattern (d) shows a tessellation with an arbitrary quadrilateral of no special type. We can form a tessellation, starting with *any* quadrilateral, by using the following procedure (Figure 12.55).

1. Trace the quadrilateral [Figure 12.55(a)].
2. Rotate the quadrilateral 180° around the midpoint of any side. Trace the image [Figure 12.55(b)].

3. Continue rotating the image 180° around the midpoint of each of its sides, and trace the new image [Figures 12.55(c) and (d)].

The rotation procedure described here can be applied to any triangle and to any quadrilateral, even nonconvex quadrilaterals.

Several results about triangles and quadrilaterals can be illustrated by tessellations. In Figure 12.53(c) we see that $x + y + z = 180°$, a straight angle. In Figure 12.55(d) we see that $a + b + c + d = 360°$ for the quadrilateral.

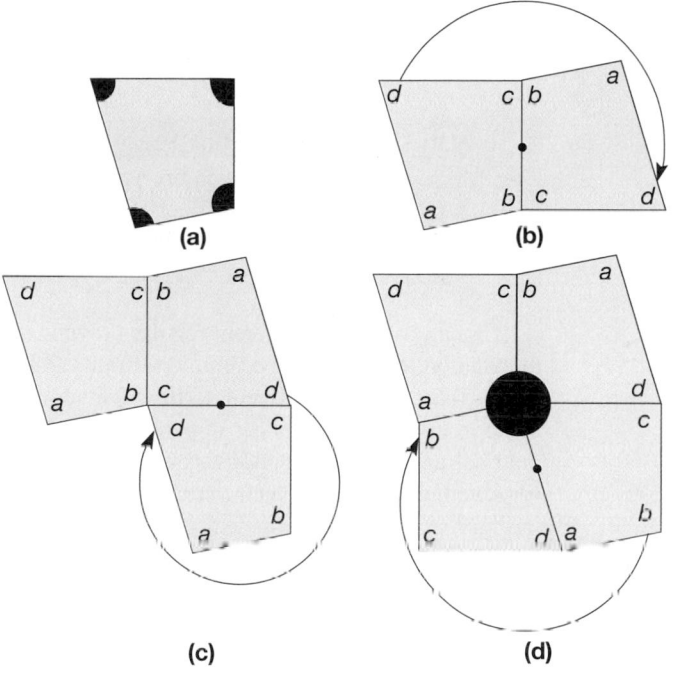

Figure 12.55

Tessellations with Regular Polygons

Figure 12.56 shows some tessellations with equilateral triangles, squares, and regular hexagons. These are examples of tessellations each composed of copies of one regular polygon. Such tessellations are called **regular tessellations.**

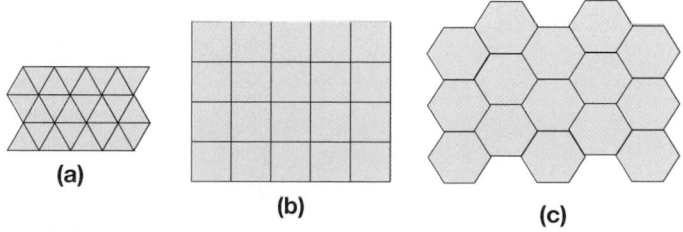

Figure 12.56

Notice that in pattern (a) six equilateral triangles meet at each vertex, in pattern (b) four squares meet at each vertex, and in pattern (c) three hexagons meet at each vertex. We say that the **vertex arrangement** in pattern (a)—that is, the configuration of regular polygons meeting at a vertex—is (3, 3, 3, 3, 3, 3). This sequence of six 3s indicates that six equilateral triangles meet at each vertex. Similarly, the vertex arrangement in pattern (b) is (4, 4, 4, 4), and in pattern (c) it is (6, 6, 6) for three hexagons.

Table 12.4

n	MEASURE OF VERTEX ANGLE IN A REGULAR n-GON
3	60°
4	90°
5	108°
6	120°
7	$128\frac{4}{7}°$
8	135°
9	140°
10	144°
11	$147\frac{3}{11}°$
12	150°

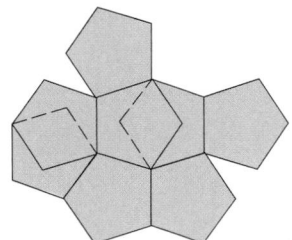

Figure 12.57

Consider the measures of vertex angles in several regular polygons (Table 12.4). For a regular polygon to form a tessellation, its vertex angle measure must be a divisor of 360, since a whole number of copies of the polygon must meet at a vertex to form a 360° angle. Clearly, regular 3-gons (equilateral triangles), 4-gons (squares), and 6-gons (regular hexagons) will work. Their vertex angles measure 60°, 90°, and 120°, respectively, each measure being a divisor of 360°. For a regular pentagon, the vertex angle measures 108°, and since 108 is not a divisor of 360, we know that regular pentagons will not fit together without gaps or overlapping. Figure 12.57 illustrates this fact.

For regular polygons with more than six sides, the vertex angles are larger than 120° (and less than 180°). At least three regular polygons must meet at each vertex, yet the vertex angles in such polygons are too large to make exactly 360° with three or more of them fitting together. Hence we have the following result.

THEOREM

Tessellations Using Only One Type of Regular n-gon

Only regular 3-gons, 4-gons, or 6-gons form tessellations of the plane by themselves.

If we allow several different regular polygons with sides the same length to form a tessellation, many other possibilities result, as Figure 12.58 shows. Notice in Figure 12.58(d) that several different vertex arrangements are possible. Tessellations such as those in Figure 12.58 appear in patterns for floor and wall coverings and other symmetrical designs. Tessellations using two or more regular polygons are called **semiregular tessellations** if their vertex arrangements are identical. Thus, the tessellation in Figure 12.58(d) is *not* a semiregular tessellation, but Figures 12.58 (a), (b), and (c) are. In Chapter 16 we see how the artist M. C. Escher made use of tessellations with polygons to create exotic tessellating patterns.

(4, 8, 8)

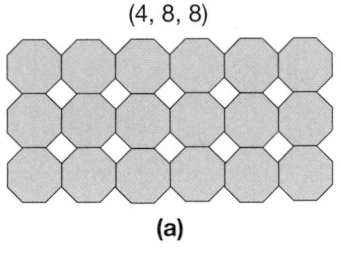

(a)

(3, 6, 3, 6)

(b)

(4, 6, 12)

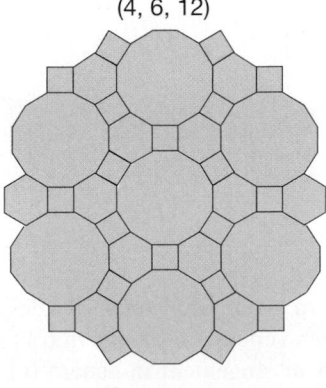

(c)

(3, 3, 3, 3, 3, 3)
(3, 3, 4, 3, 4), (3, 3, 4, 12)

(d)

Figure 12.58

www.wiley.com/
college/musser

Spotlight on Technology The tessellations above can all be constructed on the Chapter 12 eManipulative activity, *Tessellations.* See if you can construct the semiregular tessellation that consists of hexagons, squares, and triangles. In this tessellation, each square is adjacent to two hexagons and two triangles. Remember that the polygons must be arranged in the same way around every point in order to be a semiregular tessellation.

MATHEMATICAL
MORSEL

In 1994 the World Cup Soccer Championships were held in the United States. These games were held in various cities and in a variety of stadiums across the country. Unlike American football, soccer is played almost exclusively on natural grass. This presented a problem for the city of Detroit because its stadium, the Silverdome, is an indoor field with artificial turf. Growing grass in domed stadiums has yet to be done with much success, so the organizers turned to the soil scientists at Michigan State University. They decided to grow the grass outdoors on large pallets and then move these pallets indoors in time for the games. The most interesting fact of this endeavor is the shape of the pallets that they chose—hexagons! Since hexagons are one of the three regular polygons that form a regular tessellation, these pallets would fit together to cover the stadium floor but would be less likely to shift than squares or triangles.

Section 12.4 EXERCISE / PROBLEM SET A

EXERCISES

1. Use your protractor to measure each vertex angle in each of the following polygons. Extend the sides of the polygon, if necessary. Then find the sum of the measures of the vertex angles. What *should* the sum be in each case?

a.

b.

2. Find the missing angle measures in each of the following quadrilaterals.

a.

110°

55°

b.

72°

c.

x x

$x - 30°$ $\frac{1}{2}x + 5°$

3. For the following regular *n*-gons, give the measure of a vertex angle, a central angle, and an exterior angle.

   a. 12-gon   **b.** 16-gon   **c.** 10-gon
   d. 20-gon   **e.** 18-gon   **f.** 36-gon

4. Given are the measures of the vertex angles of regular polygons. What is the measure of the central angle of each one?

   a. 90°   **b.** 176°   **c.** 150°   **d.** $x°$

5. Each vertex angle of a regular polygon measures 165.6°. How many sides does the polygon have?

6. Given are the measures of the exterior angles of regular polygons. How many sides does each one have?

   a. 9°   **b.** 45°   **c.** 10°   **d.** 3°

7. On a square lattice, draw a tessellation with each of the following triangles.

   a.   **b.**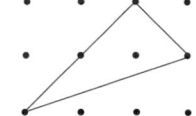

8. Given is a portion of a tessellation based on a scalene triangle. The angles are labeled from the basic tile.

   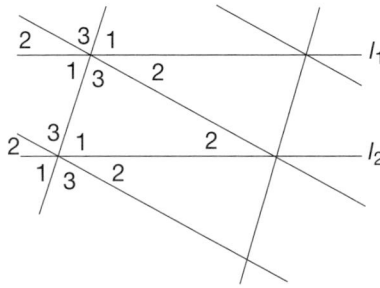

   a. Are lines l_1 and l_2 parallel?
   b. What does the tessellation illustrate about corresponding angles?

   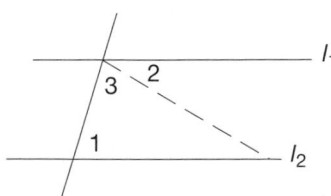

   c. What is illustrated about alternate interior angles?
   d. Angle 1 is an interior angle on the right of the transversal. Angles 2 and 3 together form the other interior angle on the right of the transversal. From the tessellation, what is true about $m(\angle 1) + [m(\angle 2) + m(\angle 3)]$? This result suggests that two lines are parallel if and only if the interior angles on the same side of a transversal are _____ angles.

9. Explain how the shaded portion of the tessellation illustrates the Pythagorean theorem.

10. **a.** Given are portions of the (3, 3, 3, 3, 3, 3), (4, 4, 4, 4), and (6, 6, 6) tessellations. In the first, we have selected a vertex point and then connected the midpoints of the sides of polygons meeting at that vertex. The resulting figure is called the **vertex figure.** Draw the vertex figure for each of the other tessellations.

    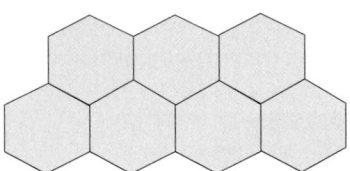

    b. A tessellation is a regular tessellation if it is constructed of regular polygons and has vertex figures that are regular polygons. Which of the preceding tessellations are regular?

11. The **dual** of a tessellation is formed by connecting the centers of polygons that share a common side. The dual tessellation of the equilateral triangle tessellation is shown. Find the dual of the other tessellations.

    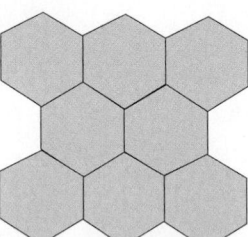

12. Illustrated is a tessellation based on a scalene triangle with sides *a*, *b*, and *c*. The two shaded triangles are similar (have the same shape). For each of the corre-

sponding three sides, find the ratio of the length of one side of the smaller triangle to the length of corresponding side of the larger triangle. What do you observe about corresponding sides of similar triangles?

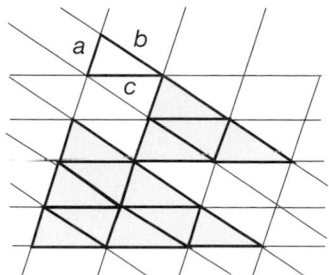

13. A tessellation is a semiregular tessellation if it is made with regular polygons such that each vertex is surrounded by the same arrangement of polygons.

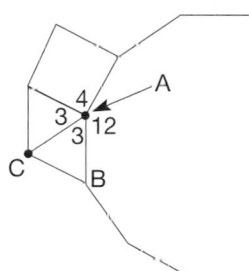

a. One of these arrangements was (3, 3, 4, 12), as shown. Can point B be surrounded by the same arrangement of polygons as point A? What happens to the arrangement at point C?

b. Can the arrangement (3, 3, 4, 12) be extended to form a semiregular tessellation? Explain.

c. Find another arrangement of regular polygons that

fit around a single point but cannot be extended to a semiregular tessellation.

14. It will be shown later in this Exercise/Problem Set that there are only eight semiregular tessellations. They are pictured here. Identify each by giving its vertex arrangement.

a.

b.

c.

d.

e.

f.

g.

h.

PROBLEMS

15. Calculate the measure of each lettered angle. Congruent angles and right angles are indicated.

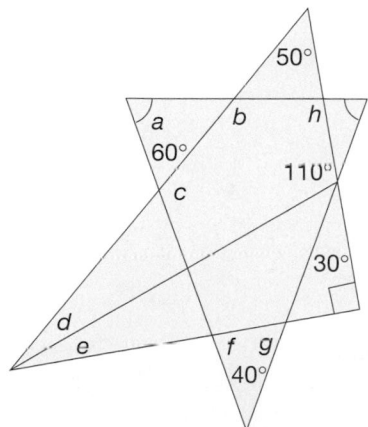

16. Complete the following table. Let V represent the number of vertices, D the number of diagonals from each vertex, and T the total number of diagonals.

POLYGON	V	D	T
Triangle			
Quadrilateral			
Pentagon			
Hexagon			
Heptagon			
Octagon			
.			
.			
.			
n-gon			

17. Suppose that there are 20 people in a meeting room. If every person in the room shakes hands once with every other person in the room, how many handshakes will there be?

18. In the five-pointed star, what is the sum of the angle measures at A, B, C, D, and E? Assume that the pentagon is regular.

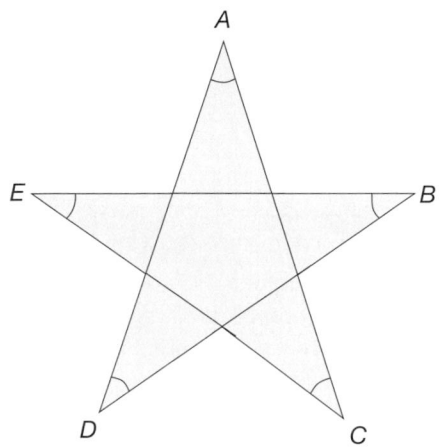

19. A man observed the semiregular floor tiling shown here and concluded after studying it that each angle of a *regular* octagon measures 135°. What was his possible reasoning?

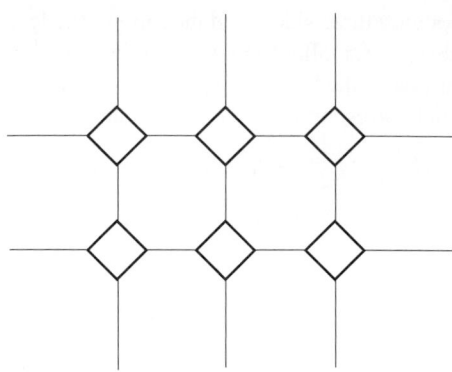

20. Find the maximum number of points of intersection for the following figures. Assume that no two sides coincide exactly.
   a. A triangle and a square
   b. A triangle and a hexagon
   c. A square and a pentagon
   d. An n-gon ($n > 2$) and a p-gon ($p > 2$)

21. Redo Problem 18 by constructing a five-pointed star on the Geometer's Sketchpad®. Measure the angles at the points of the star and add them up by using the Measure and Calculate options in the software. Moving the vertices of the star will change some of the angle measures.
   a. What do you observe about the sum of the measured angles?
   b. Justify your observation from part (a).

 Section 12.4 EXERCISE / PROBLEM SET B

EXERCISES

1. Use your protractor to measure each vertex angle in each polygon shown. Extend the sides of the polygon if necessary. Then find the sum of the measures of the vertex angles. What *should* the sum be in each case?

   a.

   b.

2. Find the missing angle measures in each of the following polygons.

   a.

   b.

   c.

3. Given are the measures of the central angles of regular polygons. How many sides does each one have?

a. 120° **b.** 12° **c.** 15° **d.** 5°

4. Given are the measures of the exterior angles of regular polygons. What is the measure of the vertex angle of each one?

a. 36° **b.** 120° **c.** 2° **d.** $a°$

5. The sum of the measures of the vertex angles of a certain polygon is 2880°. How many sides does the polygon have?

6. Given the following measures of a vertex angle of a regular polygon, determine how many sides it has.

a. 150° **b.** 156° **c.** 174° **d.** 178°

7. On a square lattice, draw a tessellation with each of the following quadrilaterals.

a. **b.**

8. The given scalene triangle is used as the basic tile for the illustrated tessellation.

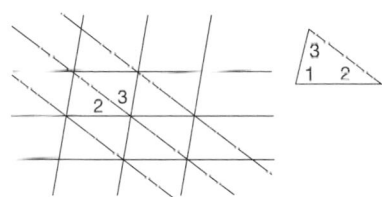

a. Two of the angles have been labeled around the indicated point. Label the other angles (from basic tile).

b. Which geometric results studied in this chapter are illustrated here?

9. One theorem in geometry states the following: The line segment connecting the midpoints of two sides of a triangle is parallel to the third side and half its length. Explain how the figure in the given tessellation suggests this result.

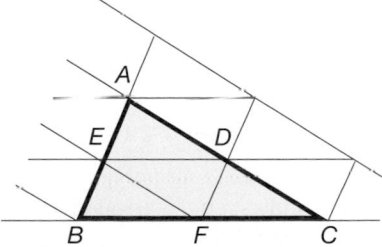

10. Given here are tessellations with equilateral triangles and squares.

a. Draw the vertex figure for each tessellation.

b. Are these tessellations regular tessellations?

11. Complete the following statements.

i. The dual of the regular tessellation with triangles is a regular tessellation with _____.

ii. The dual of the regular tessellation with squares is a regular tessellation with _____.

iii. The dual of the regular tessellation with hexagons is a regular tessellation with _____.

12. A theorem in geometry states the following: Parallel lines intersect proportional segments on all common transversals. In the portion of the tessellation given, lines l_1, l_2, and l_3 are parallel and t_1 and t_2 are transversals. Explain what this geometric result means, and use the portion of the tessellation to illustrate it.

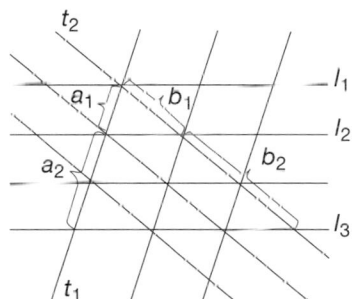

13. Shown are copies of an equilateral triangle, a square, a regular hexagon, a regular octagon, and a regular dodecagon.

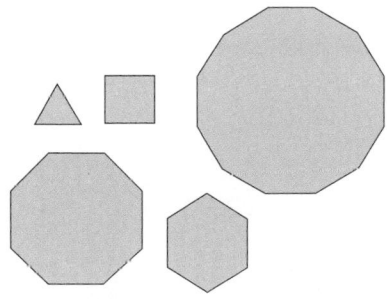

a. Label the measure of one vertex angle for each polygon.

b. Use the Chapter 12 eManipulative activity, *Tessellations*, to find the number of ways you can combine three of these figures (they may be repeated) to surround a point without gaps and overlaps.

c. By sketching, record each way you found.

14. Using the polygons in Exercise 13 and the Chapter 12 eManipulative activity, *Tessellations*, find the ways that you can combine the specified numbers of polygons to surround a point without gaps and over-laps. Record each way you found.

a. Four polygons
b. Five polygons
c. Six polygons
d. Seven polygons

PROBLEMS

15. Calculate the measure of each lettered angle. Con-gruent angles and right angles are indicated.

16. It was shown that a vertex angle of a regular n-gon measures $\dfrac{(n-2)\cdot 180}{n}$ degrees. If there are three regular polygons completely surrounding the vertex of a tessellation, then

$$\frac{(a-2)\cdot 180}{a} + \frac{(b-2)\cdot 180}{b} + \frac{(c-2)\cdot 180}{c} = 360,$$

where the three polygons have a, b, and c sides. Jus-tify each step in the following simplification of the given equation.

$$\frac{a-2}{a} + \frac{b-2}{b} + \frac{c-2}{c} = 2$$

$$1 - \frac{2}{a} + 1 - \frac{2}{b} + 1 - \frac{2}{c} = 2$$

$$1 = \frac{2}{a} + \frac{2}{b} + \frac{2}{c}$$

$$\frac{1}{2} = \frac{1}{a} + \frac{1}{b} + \frac{1}{c}$$

17. Problem 16 gives an equation that whole numbers a, b, and c must satisfy if an a-gon, a b-gon, and a c-gon will completely surround a point.

a. Let $a = 3$. Find all possible whole-number values of b and c that satisfy the equation.

b. Repeat part (a) with $a = 4$.

c. Repeat part (a) with $a = 5$.

d. Repeat part (a) with $a = 6$.

e. This gives all possible arrangements of three poly-gons that will completely surround a point. How many did you find?

18. The following data summarize the possible arrange-ments of three polygons surrounding a vertex point of a tessellation.

3, 7, 42	4, 5, 20	5, 5, 10	6, 6, 6
3, 8, 24	4, 6, 12		
3, 9, 18	4, 8, 8		
3, 10, 15			
3, 12, 12			

The (6, 6, 6) arrangement yields a regular tessella-tion. It has been shown that (3, 12, 12), (4, 6, 12), and (4, 8, 8) can be extended to form a semiregular tessellation. Consider the (5, 5, 10) arrangement.

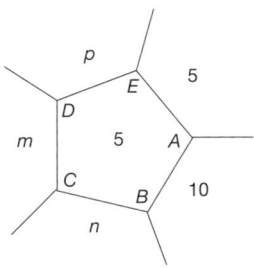

a. Point A is surrounded by (5, 5, 10). If point B is surrounded similarly, what is n?

b. If point C is surrounded similarly, what is m?

c. If point D is surrounded similarly, what is p?

d. What is the arrangement around point E? This shows that (5, 5, 10) cannot be extended to a semiregular tessellation.

e. Show, in general, that this argument illustrates that the rest of the arrangements in the table can-not be extended to semiregular tessellations.

19. In a similar way, when four polygons—an a-gon, b-gon, c-gon, and d-gon—surround a point, it can be shown that the following equation is satisfied.

$$\frac{1}{a} + \frac{1}{b} + \frac{1}{c} + \frac{1}{d} = 1$$

a. Find the four combinations of whole numbers that satisfy this equation.

b. One of these arrangements gives a regular tessellation. Which arrangement is it?

c. The remaining three combinations can each surround a vertex in two different ways. Of those six arrangements, four cannot be extended to a semiregular tessellation. Which are they?

d. The remaining two can be extended to a semiregular tessellation. Which are they?

20. a. When five polygons surround a point, they satisfy the following equation.

$$\frac{1}{a} + \frac{1}{b} + \frac{1}{c} + \frac{1}{d} + \frac{1}{e} = \frac{3}{2}$$

Find the two combinations of whole numbers that satisfy this equation.

b. These solutions yield three different arrangements of polygons that can be extended to semiregular tessellations. Illustrate those patterns.

c. When six polygons surround a point, they satisfy the following equation.

$$\frac{1}{a} + \frac{1}{b} + \frac{1}{c} + \frac{1}{d} + \frac{1}{e} + \frac{1}{f} = 2$$

Find the one combination that satisfies this equation. What type of tessellation is formed by this arrangement?

d. Can more than six regular polygons surround a point? Why or why not?

PROBLEMS FOR WRITING/DISCUSSION

1. Donna says she can tessellate the plane with any kind of triangle, but that's not true for quadrilaterals, because if you have a concave quadrilateral like the one shown, you can't do it. Is she correct? Discuss.

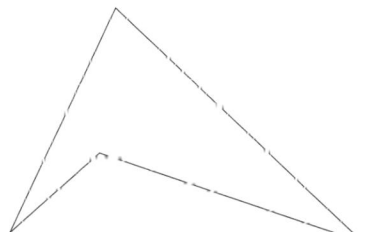

2. Tyrone says if you can tessellate the plane with a regular triangle and a regular quadrilateral, you must be able to tessellate the plane with a regular pentagon. In fact, he has made a rough sketch of the plane tessellated with regular pentagons, and you can see that they seem to fit together. What would be your response?

3. A student who was given a pentagon with four angle measures shown was asked to find the measure of the fifth angle. He said he would use the formula

$$\frac{(n - 2) \cdot 180}{n}$$ to find the missing angle. How's this student thinking? Discuss.

12.5 DESCRIBING THREE-DIMENSIONAL SHAPES

STARTING POINT

The stack of blocks at the right would have the front view and side view as shown. Build two other block stacks that have the same front and side views. Sketch all four views (front, back, two sides) of the two stacks that you have constructed. How do the views for these two stacks compare to each other? How do they compare to the views of the original stack?

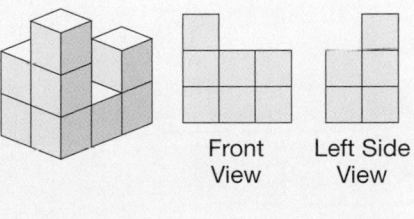

Front View   Left Side View

NCTM Standards 2000
Geometry
Grades Pre-K–2
All students should describe attributes and parts of two-and three-dimensional shapes.

Planes, Skew Lines, and Dihedral Angles

We now consider three-dimensional space and investigate various three-dimensional shapes (i.e., shapes having length, width, *and* height). There are infinitely many planes in three-dimensional space. Figure 12.59 shows several possible relationships among planes in three-dimensional space. The shapes in Figure 12.59 are actually portions of

NCTM Standards 2000
Geometry
Grades 6–8
All students should precisely describe, classify, and understand relationships among types of two- and three-dimensional objects using their defining properties.

Reflection from Research
According to research, spatial ability and problem-solving performance are strongly correlated. This suggests that skill in spatial visualization is a good predictor of mathematical problem solving (Tillotson, 1985).

planes, since planes extend infinitely in two dimensions. Notice in Figures 12.59(b) and (c) that two intersecting planes meet in a line. In three-dimensional space, two planes are either parallel as in Figure 12.59(a) or intersect as in Figure 12.59(b).

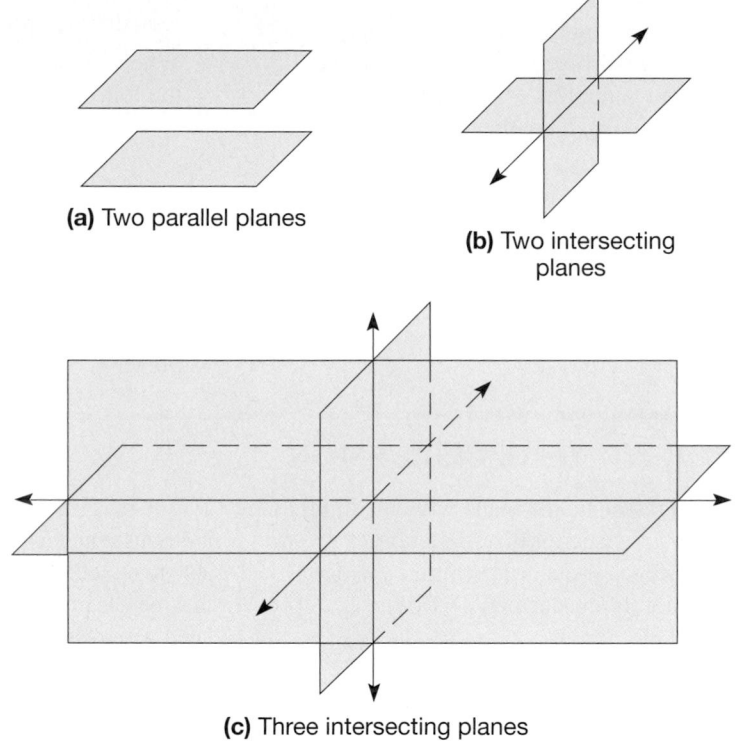

(a) Two parallel planes

(b) Two intersecting planes

(c) Three intersecting planes

Figure 12.59

We can define the angle formed by polygonal regions much as we defined angles in two dimensions. A **dihedral angle** is formed by the union of polygonal regions in space that share an edge. The polygonal regions forming the dihedral angle are called **faces** of the dihedral angle. Figure 12.60 shows several dihedral angles formed by intersecting rectangular regions. (Dihedral angles are also formed when planes intersect, but we will not investigate this situation.)

We can measure dihedral angles by measuring an angle between two lines segments or rays contained in the faces (Figure 12.61). Notice that the line segments forming the sides of the angle in Figure 12.61 are *perpendicular* to the line segment

Figure 12.60

Figure 12.61

Figure 12.62

that is the intersection of the faces of the dihedral angle. Figure 12.62 shows the measurements of several dihedral angles.

From the preceding discussion, we see that planes act in three-dimensional space much as lines do in two-dimensional space. On the other hand, lines in three-dimensional space do not have to intersect if they are not parallel. Such nonintersecting, nonparallel lines are called **skew lines.** Figure 12.63 shows a pair of skew lines, *l* and *m*.

Figure 12.63

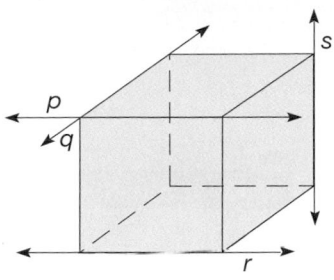

Figure 12.64

Thus in three-dimensional space, there are three possible relationships between two lines: They are parallel, they intersect, or they are skew lines. Figure 12.64 shows these relationships among the edges of a cube. Notice that lines p and r are parallel, lines p and q intersect, and lines q and s are skew lines (as are lines r and s, and lines p and s).

In three-dimensional space a line l is parallel to a plane $\mathscr{P}$ if l and $\mathscr{P}$ do not intersect [Figure 12.65(a)]. A line l is perpendicular to a plane $\mathscr{P}$ if l is perpendicular to every line in $\mathscr{P}$ that l intersects [Figure 12.65(b)].

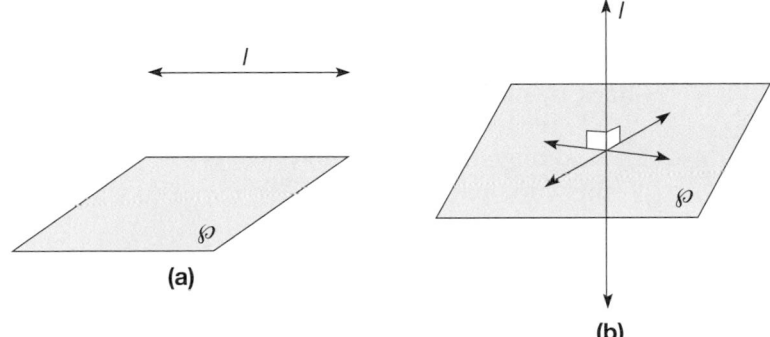

Figure 12.65

Reflection from Research
From grades 3 to 5, students make a move from seeing a three-dimensional cube as an uncoordinated medley of faces to seeing it in terms of layers (Battista & Clements, 1996).

Polyhedra

The cube shown in Figure 12.64 is an example of a general category of three-dimensional shapes called polyhedra. A polyhedron is the three-dimensional analog of a polygon. A **polyhedron** (plural: **polyhedra**) is the union of polygonal regions, any two of which have at most a side in common, such that a connected finite region in space is enclosed without holes. Figure 12.66(a) shows examples of polyhedra, Figure 12.66(b) contains shapes that are not polyhedra. In Figure 12.66(b), shape (i) is not a polyhedron, since it has a hole; shape (ii) is not a polyhedron, since it is curved; and shape (iii) is not a polyhedron, since it does not enclose a finite region in space.

Figure 12.66

Name _____

Date

Student Sheet 4

Painting Cubes

Make your predictions by looking at the picture.
Check by making the package with cubes.

1. Find how many unit cubes are in
   this cube package.

   Number of cubes:

   _____

Suppose that the 6 sides of this package were completely
covered with red paint.

2. How many of the cubes would have 0 faces painted? _____

3. How many of the cubes would have 1 face painted? _____

4. How many of the cubes would have 2 faces painted? _____

5. How many of the cubes would have 3 faces painted? _____

6. How many of the cubes would have 4 faces painted? _____

7. How many of the cubes would have 5 faces painted? _____

8. How many of the cubes would have 6 faces painted? _____

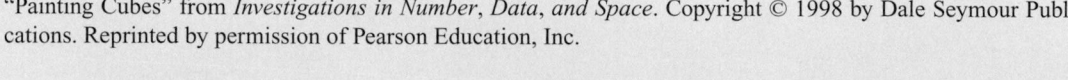

600

A polyhedron is **convex** if every line segment joining two of its points is contained inside the polyhedron or is on one of the polygonal regions. The first two polyhedra in Figure 12.66(a) are convex; the third is not. The polygonal regions of a polyhedron are called **faces,** the line segments common to a pair of faces are called **edges,** and the points of intersection of the edges are called **vertices** [Figure 12.66(c)].

Polyhedra can be classified into several general types. For example, **prisms** are polyhedra with two opposite faces that are identical polygons. These faces are called the **bases.** The vertices of the bases are joined to form **lateral faces** that must be parallelograms. If the lateral faces are rectangles, the prism is called a **right prism,** and the dihedral angle formed by a base and a lateral face is a right angle. Otherwise, the prism is called an **oblique prism.** Figure 12.67 shows a variety of prisms, named according to the types of polygons forming the bases and whether they are right or oblique.

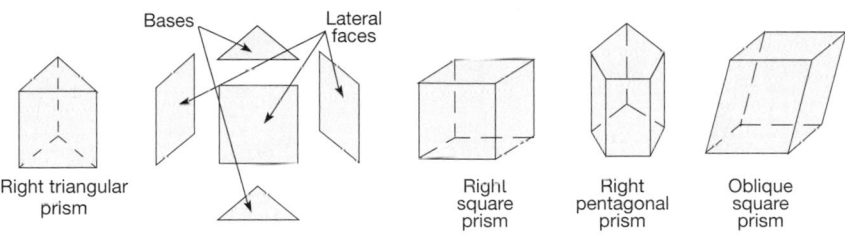

Figure 12.67

Since there are infinitely many types of polygons to use as the bases, there are infinitely many types of prisms.

Pyramids are polyhedra formed by using a polygon for the base and a point not in the plane of the base, called the **apex,** that is connected with line segments to each vertex of the base. Figure 12.68 shows several pyramids, named according to the type of polygon forming the base. Pyramids whose bases are regular polygons fall into two categories. Those whose lateral faces are isosceles triangles are called **right regular pyramids.** Otherwise, they are **oblique regular pyramids.**

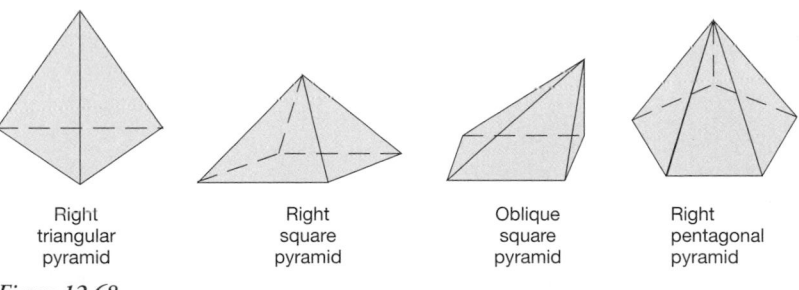

Figure 12.68

Polyhedra with regular polygons for faces have been studied since the time of the ancient Greeks. A **regular polyhedron** is one in which all faces are identical regular polygonal regions and all dihedral angles have the same measure. The ancient Greeks were able to show that there are exactly five regular convex polyhedra, called the

Platonic solids. They are analyzed in Table 12.5, according to number of faces, vertices, and edges, and shown in Figure 12.69. An interesting pattern in Table 12.5 is that $F + V = E + 2$ for all five regular polyhedra. That is, the number of faces plus vertices equals the number of edges plus 2. This result, known as **Euler's formula,** holds for *all* convex polyhedra, not just regular polyhedra. For example, verify Euler's formula for each of the polyhedra in Figures 12.66, 12.67, and 12.68.

Table 12.5

POLYHEDRON	FACES, F	Vertices, V	Edges, E
Tetrahedron	4	4	6
Hexahedron	6	8	12
Octahedron	8	6	12
Dodecahedron	12	20	30
Icosahedron	20	12	30

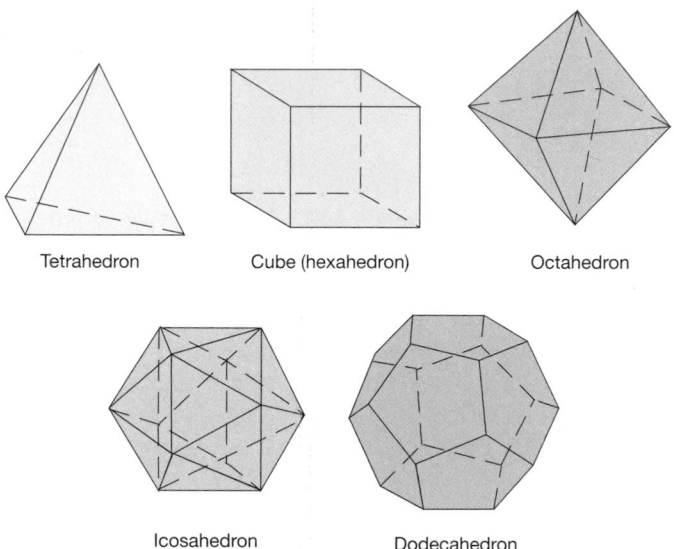

Tetrahedron   Cube (hexahedron)   Octahedron

Icosahedron   Dodecahedron

Figure 12.69

Spotlight on Technology   To gain a better understanding of the Platonic solids and what they actually look like, refer to the Chapter 12 eManipulative activity, *Slicing Solids.* This activity has all five of the regular polyhedra available to look at and manipulate. www.wiley.com/college/musser You can also see what a cross-section of the solid would look like if it were cut by a plane. What types of polygonal cross-sections can you obtain with the cube? Which of them are regular polygons?

If we allow several different regular polygonal regions to serve as the faces, then we can investigate a new family of polyhedra, called semiregular polyhedra. A **semiregular polyhedron** is a polyhedron with several different regular polygonal regions for faces but with the same arrangement of polygons at each vertex. Prisms with square faces and regular polygons for bases are semiregular polyhedra. Figure 12.70 shows several types of semiregular polyhedra.

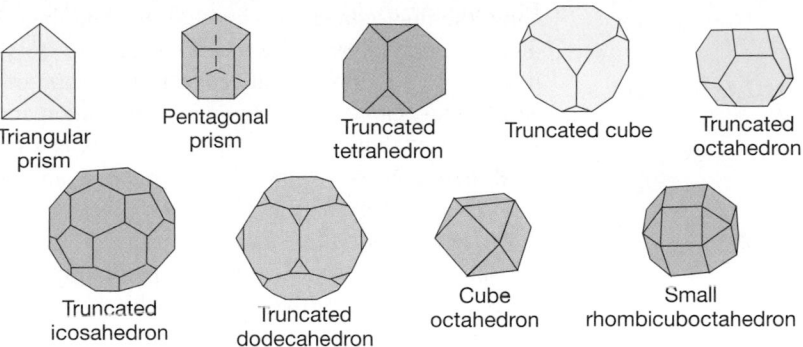

Triangular prism
Pentagonal prism
Truncated tetrahedron
Truncated cube
Truncated octahedron

Truncated icosahedron
Truncated dodecahedron
Cube octahedron
Small rhombicuboctahedron

Figure 12.70

Curved Shapes in Three Dimensions

There are three-dimensional curved shapes analogous to prisms and pyramids, namely cylinders and cones. Consider two identical simple closed curves having the same orientation and contained in parallel planes. The union of the line segments joining corresponding points on the simple closed curves and the interiors of the simple closed curves is called a **cylinder** [Figure 12.71(a)]. Each simple closed curve together with its interior is called a **base of the cylinder.** In a **right circular cylinder,** a line segment $\overline{AB}$ connecting a point A on one circular base to its corresponding point B on the other circular base is perpendicular to the planes of the bases [Figure 12.71(b)]. In an **oblique cylinder,** the bases are parallel, yet line segments connecting corresponding points are not perpendicular to the planes of the bases [Figure 12.71(c)]. In this book we restrict our study to right circular cylinders.

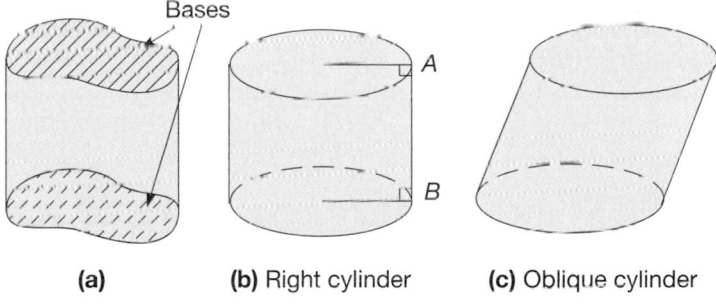

Bases

(a)
(b) Right cylinder
(c) Oblique cylinder

Figure 12.71

A **cone** is the union of the interior of a simple closed curve and all line segments joining points of the curve to a point, called the **apex,** that is not in the plane of the curve. The plane curve together with its interior is called the **base** [Figure 12.72(a)]. We will restrict our attention to circular cones (bases are circles). In a **right circular**

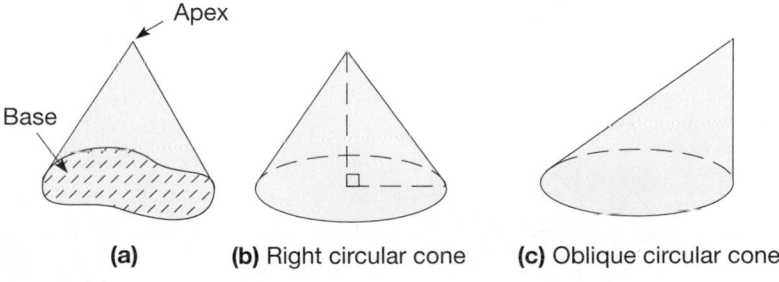

Apex

Base

(a)
(b) Right circular cone
(c) Oblique circular cone

Figure 12.72

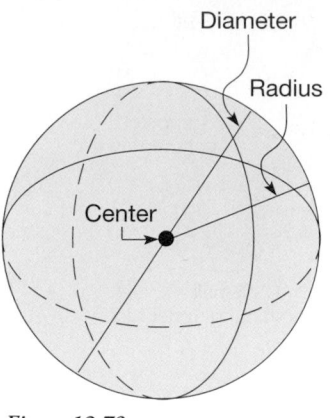

Figure 12.73

cone, the line segment joining the apex and the center of the circular base is perpendicular to the plane of the base [Figure 12.72(b)]. In an **oblique circular cone,** this line segment is not perpendicular to the plane of the base [Figure 12.72(c)]. Cones and cylinders appear frequently in construction and design.

The three-dimensional analog of a circle is a sphere. A **sphere** is defined as the set of all points in three-dimensional space that are the same distance from a fixed point, called the **center** (Figure 12.73). Any line segment joining the center to a point on the sphere is also called a **radius** of the sphere; its *length* is also called *the* radius of the sphere. A segment joining two points of the sphere and containing the center is called a **diameter** of the sphere; its *length* is also called *the* diameter of the sphere. Spherical shapes are important in many areas. Planets, moons, and stars are essentially spherical. Thus measurement aspects of spheres are very important in science. We consider measurement aspects of cones, cylinders, spheres, and other shapes in Chapter 13.

MATHEMATICAL MORSEL

The sphere is one of the most commonly occurring shapes in nature. Hail stones, frog eggs, tomatoes, oranges, soap bubbles, the Earth, and the moon are a very few examples of spherelike shapes. The regular occurrence of the spherical shape is not coincidental. One explanation for the frequency of the sphere's appearance is that for a given surface area, the sphere encloses the greatest volume. In other words, a sphere requires the least amount of natural material to surround a given volume. This may help explain why animals curl up in a ball when it is cold outside.

Section 12.5 EXERCISE/PROBLEM SET A

EXERCISES

1. a. Describe what you see.

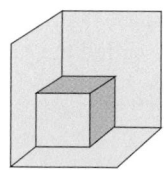

    b. Which is the highest step?

2. How many $1 \times 1 \times 1$ cubes are in the following stack?

3. All faces of the following cube are different.

Which of these cubes could represent a different view of the preceding cube?

a.

b.

c.

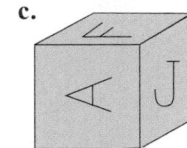

4. Pictured is a stack of cubes. Also given are the top view, the front view, and the right-side view. (Assume that the only hidden cubes are ones that support a pictured cube.)

Top   Front   Right side

Give the three views of each of the following stacks of cubes.

a.   **b.**   **c.**

5. In the figure, the drawing on the left shows a shape. The drawing on the right tells you how many cubes are on each base square. The drawing on the right is called a **base design.**

Front

2	2	3
1	1	1

a. Which is the correct base design for this shape?

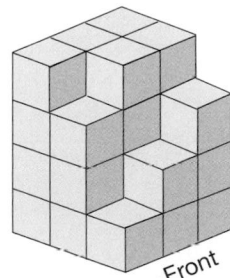

Front

(i)

4	4	4
3	3	3
1	2	4

(ii)

4	4	4
3	4	4
1	2	3

(iii)

4	4	4
3	4	5
1	1	1

b. Make a base design for each shape.

i.

Front

ii.

Front

6. For each of the following prisms, (i) Name the bases of the prism. (ii) Name the lateral faces of the prism. (iii) Name the faces that are hidden from view. (iv) Name the prism by type.

a.

A   B

C

D — — — — — E

F

b.

N   O

M   P

R — — — — — S

Q   T

7. Name the following pyramids according to type.

a. The base is a square.

b. **c.**

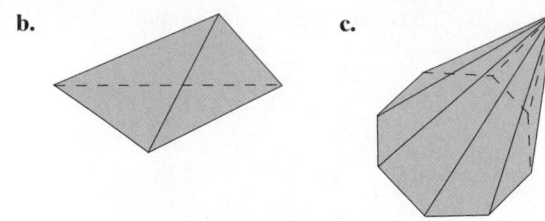

8. Shown are patterns or nets for several three-dimensional figures. Copy and cut each one out. Then fold each one up to form the figure. Name the three-dimensional figure you have made in each case.

a.

b.

c.

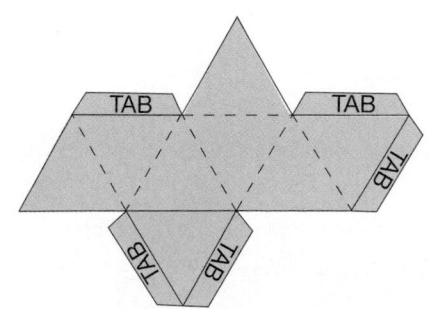

d. Most nets for three-dimensional shapes are not unique. Sketch another net for each shape you made in this exercise. Be sure to include tabs for folding. Try each one to check your answer.

9. Draw a net for each of the following polyhedra. Be sure to include tabs for folding. Cut out and fold your patterns to check your answers.

a.

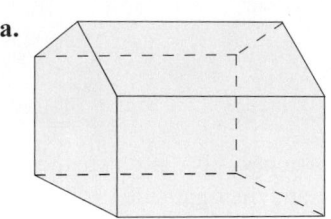

b. A right hexagonal pyramid

10. Which of the following patterns folds into a cube? If one does, what number will be opposite the *X*?

a.

1			
4	X	2	5
3			

b.

1	X	3	
		2	4	5

c.

	3	X	1
5	2	4	

d.

1			
3	5	2	4
			X

e.

1	3	X
		2	4
		5

f.

3	X	
	1	4
	2	5

11. Drawing a prism can be done by following these steps:

Draw the bases.

Connect the vertices.

Dot the hidden edges or leave them out.

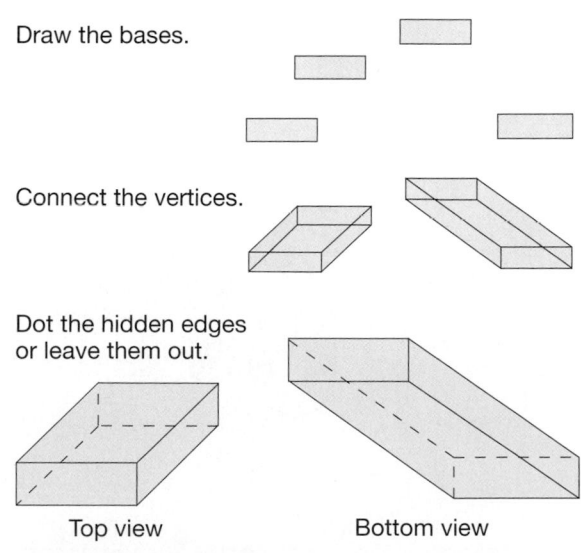

Top view   Bottom view

Draw the following prisms.

a. Square prism

b. Pentagonal prism (bottom view)

12. Given is a prism with bases that are regular pentagons.

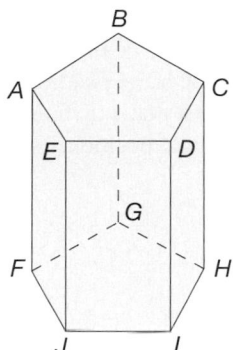

a. Is there a plane in the picture that is parallel to the plane containing points *A*, *B*, *C*, *D*, and *E*? If so, name the points that it contains.

b. Is there a plane in the picture that is parallel to the plane containing points *C*, *D*, *I*, and *H*? If so, name the points that it contains.

c. What is the measure of the dihedral angle between plane *AEJF* and plane *ABGF*?

13. a. Given are samples of prisms. Use these prisms to complete the following table. Let *F* represent the number of faces, *V* the number of vertices, and *E* the number of edges.

BASE	F	V	F + V	E
Triangle				
Quadrilateral				
Pentagon				
Hexagon				
n-gon				

b. Is Euler's formula satisfied for prisms?

14. a. Given are pictures of three-dimensional shapes. Use them to complete the following table. Let *F* represent the number of faces, *V* the number of vertices, and *E* the number of edges.

i.

ii.

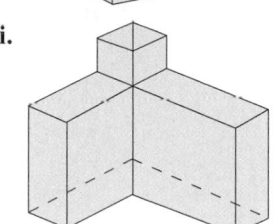

FIGURE	F	V	F + V	E
i.				
ii.				

b. Is Euler's formula satisfied for these figures?

15. The right cylinder is cut by a plane as indicated. Identify the resulting cross-section.

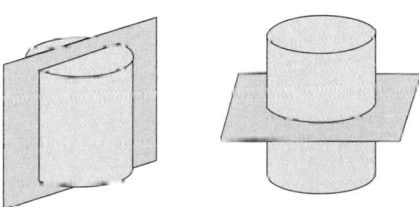

16. When a three-dimensional shape is cut by a plane, the figure that results is a cross-section. Identify the cross-section formed in the following cases. The Chapter 12 eManipulative activity, *Slicing Solids*, may be helpful for parts (a) and (c).

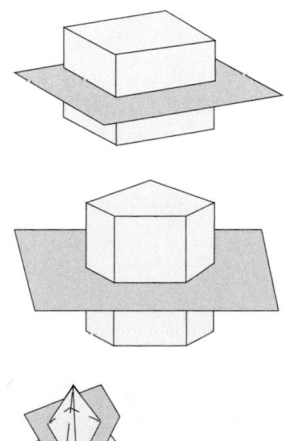

PROBLEMS

17. When folded, the figures on the left become one of the figures on the right. Which one? Make models to check.

a.

(i)

(ii)

(iii)

b.

(iv)

(v)

(vi)

18. If the cube illustrated is cut by a plane midway between opposite faces and the front portion is placed against a mirror, the entire cube appears to be formed. The cutting plane is called a **plane of symmetry,** and the figure is said to have **reflection symmetry.**

a.

How many planes of symmetry of this type are there for a cube?

b.

A plane passing through pairs of opposite edges is also a plane of symmetry, as illustrated. How many planes of symmetry of this type are there in a cube?

c. How many planes of symmetry are there for a cube?

19. The line connecting centers of opposite faces of a cube is an **axis** (plural: **axes**) **of rotational symmetry,** since the cube can be turned about the axis and appears to be in the same position. In fact, the cube can be turned about that axis four times before returning to its original position, as shown.

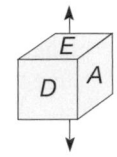

This axis of symmetry is said to have order 4. How many axes of symmetry of order 4 are there in a cube?

20. The line connecting opposite pairs of vertices of a cube is also an axis of symmetry.

a. What is the order of this axis (how many turns are needed to return it to the original arrangement)?

b. How many axes of this order are there in a cube?

21. The line connecting midpoints of opposite edges is an axis of symmetry of a cube.

a. What is the order of this axis?

b. How many axes of this order are there in a cube?

22. What is the shape of a piece of cardboard that is made into a center tube for a paper towel roll?

Section 12.5 EXERCISE / PROBLEM SET B

EXERCISES

1. a. Which dark circle is behind the others in the figure? Look at the figure for one minute before answering.

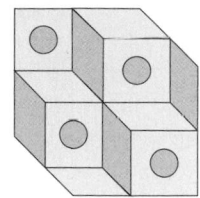

b. Is the small cube attached to the front or the back of the large cube?

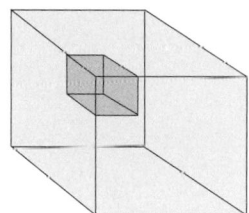

2. How many $1 \times 1 \times 1$ cubes are in the following stack?

3. All the faces of the cube on the left have different figures on them. Which of the three other cubes could represent a different view? Explain.

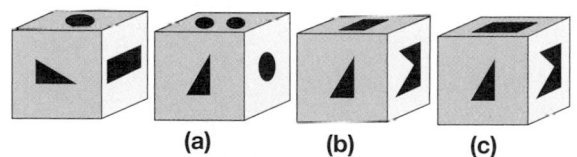

(a) (b) (c)

4. Following is pictured a stack of cubes. (Assume that the only hidden cubes are ones that support a pictured cube; see Exercise 4 in Part A, for example.) Give three views of each of the following stacks of cubes.

a.

b.

5. Following are shown three views of a stack of cubes. Determine the largest possible number of cubes in the stack. What is the smallest number of cubes that could be in the stack? Make a base design for each answer (see Exercise 5 in Part A).

Top:

Front:

Right side:

6. Name the following prisms by type.

a.

b.

c.

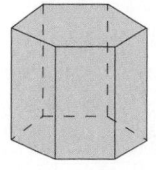

7. Which of the following figures are prisms? Which are pyramids?

a.

b.   c.

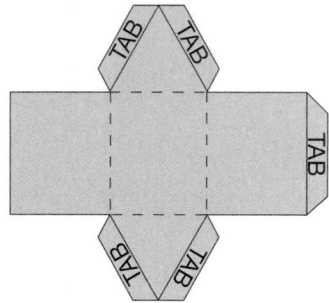

8. Following are patterns or nets for several three-dimensional figures. Copy and cut each one out. Then fold each one up to form the figure. Name the three-dimensional figure you have made in each case.

a.

b.

c.

d. Most nets for three-dimensional shapes are not unique. Sketch another net for each shape you made. Be sure to include tabs for folding. Try each one to check your answer.

9. Draw a net for the following polyhedron. Be sure to include tabs for folding. Cut out and fold your pattern to check your answer.

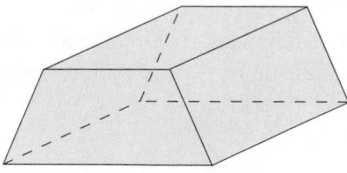

10. Which of the pentominos in Problems 6 and 7 of Set 12.2B will fold up to make a box with no lid? Mark the bottom of the box with an X.

11. Drawing a pyramid can be done by following these steps.

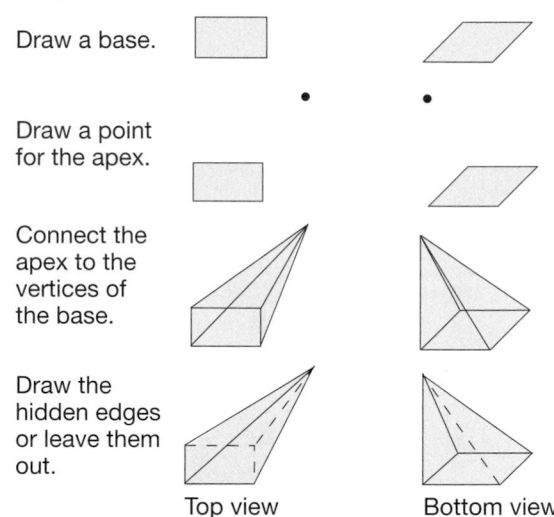

Draw a base.

Draw a point for the apex.

Connect the apex to the vertices of the base.

Draw the hidden edges or leave them out.

Top view   Bottom view

Draw the following pyramids.

a. A triangular pyramid

b. A hexagonal pyramid (bottom view)

12. The dihedral angle, $\angle AED$, of the tetrahedron pictured can be found by the following procedure.

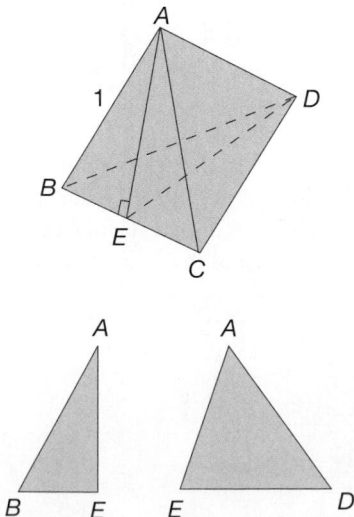

a. The face of the tetrahedron is an equilateral triangle, △*ABC*. As one segment of the dihedral angle, $\overline{AE}$ is perpendicular to $\overline{BC}$. In an equilateral triangle, the perpendicular segment from a vertex to a side cuts the side in half. Find the length of $\overline{BE}$ and $\overline{AE}$, if we assume the edges of the tetrahedron have length 1.

b. Using similar reasoning, find the length of $\overline{DE}$.

c. Label the length of the sides of △*AED*. Use a scale drawing and a protractor to approximate the measure of ∠*AED*.

13. a. Given are samples of pyramids. Use them to complete the following table. Let *F* represent the number of faces, *V* the number of vertices, and *E* the number of edges.

BASE	F	V	F + V	E
Triangle				
Quadrilateral				
Pentagon				
Hexagon				
n-gon				

b. Is Euler's formula satisfied for pyramids?

14. a. Given are pictures of three-dimensional shapes. Use them to complete the following table. Let *F* represent the number of faces, *V* the number of vertices, and *E* the number of edges.

i. **ii.**

FIGURE	F	V	F + V	E
i.				
ii.				

b. Is Euler's formula satisfied for these figures?

15. The following cone is cut by a plane as indicated. Identify the resulting cross-section in each case.

a. **b.** **c.**

16. a. The picture illustrates the intersection between a sphere and a plane. What is true about all such intersections?

b. When the intersecting plane contains the center of the sphere, the cross-section is called a **great circle** of the sphere. How many great circles are there for a sphere?

PROBLEMS

17. Eight small cubes are put together to form one large cube as shown.

Suppose that all six sides of this larger cube are painted, the paint is allowed to dry, and the cube is taken apart.

a. How many of the small cubes will have paint on just one side? on two sides? on three sides? on no sides?

b. Answer the questions from part (a), this time assuming the large cube is formed from 27 small cubes.

c. Answer the questions from part (a), this time assuming the large cube is formed from 64 small cubes.

d. Answer the questions from part (a), but assume the large cube is formed from n^3 small cubes.

18. Use the Chapter 12 eManipulative activity, *Slicing Solids*, to determine which of the following cross-sections are possible when a plane cuts a cube.

    a. A square
    b. A rectangle
    c. An isosceles triangle
    d. An equilateral triangle
    e. A trapezoid
    f. A parallelogram
    g. A pentagon
    h. A regular hexagon

19. Use the Chapter 12 eManipulative activity, *Slicing Solids*, to determine which of the following cross-sections are possible when a plane cuts a octahedron.

    a. A square
    b. A rectangle
    c. An isosceles triangle
    d. An equilateral triangle
    e. A trapezoid
    f. A parallelogram
    g. A pentagon
    h. A regular hexagon

20. How many planes of symmetry do the following figures have? (Models may help.)

    a. A tetrahedron
    b. A square pyramid
    c. A pentagonal prism
    d. A right circular cylinder

21. Find the axes of symmetry for the following figures. Indicate the order of each axis. (Models may help.)

    a. A tetrahedron
    b. A pentagonal prism

22. How many axes of symmetry do the following figures have?

    a. A right square pyramid
    b. A right circular cone
    c. A sphere

23. A regular tetrahedron is attached to a face of a square pyramid with equilateral faces where the faces of the tetrahedron and the pyramid are identical triangles. What is the fewest number of faces possible for the resulting polyhedron? (Use a model—it will suggest a surprising answer. However, a complete mathematical solution is difficult.)

24. Show how to slice a cube with four cuts to make a regular tetrahedron. (*Hint:* Slice a clay cube with a cheese cutter, or draw lines on a paper or plastic cube.)

PROBLEMS FOR WRITING/DISCUSSION

1. Rene says two planes either intersect or they don't. If they don't, then they're parallel. It's the same thing with lines; either they intersect or they're parallel. How would you respond to Rene?

2. Mario says a polygon is a simple closed figure with straight-line sides and a polyhedron is a simple closed figure with polygonal sides. How could you clarify Mario's thinking here?

3. Cheryl says she doesn't know if a right triangular pyramid should have a right triangle base. Can you help her? Explain.

END OF CHAPTER MATERIAL

Solution of Initial Problem

Describe a solid shape that will fill each of the holes in this template as well as pass through each hole.

d

(a)

d

d

(b)

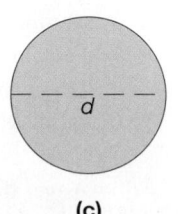

d

(c)

Strategy: Use a Model

A cylinder whose base has diameter d and whose height is d will pass through the square and circle exactly [Figure 12.74(a)]. We will modify a model of this cylinder to get a shape with a triangular cross-section. If we slice the cylinder along the heavy lines in Figure 12.74(b), the resulting model

d

d

(a)

(b)

(c)

Figure 12.74

will pass through the triangular hole exactly. Figure 12.74(c) shows the resulting model that will pass through all three holes exactly.

Additional Problems Where the Strategy "Use a Model" Is Useful

1. Which of the following can be folded into a closed box?

   a.

   b.

   c.

2. If a penny is placed on a table, how many pennies can be placed around it, where each new penny touches the penny in the center and two other pennies?

3. Twenty-five cannonballs are stacked in a 5×5 square rack on the floor. What is the greatest number of cannonballs that can be stacked on these 25 to form a stable pyramid of cannonballs?

People in Mathematics

Cathleen Synge Morawetz (1923–) Cathleen Synge Morawetz said that she liked to construct "engines and levers" as a youngster, but wasn't good in arithmetic. "I used to get bad marks in mental arithmetic." Her father is the Irish mathematician J. L. Synge, and her mother studied mathematics at Trinity College. In college, she gravitated from engineering to mathematics and did her doctoral thesis on the analysis of shock waves. Her professional research has focused on the applications of differential equations. She became the first woman in the United States to head a mathematics institute, the Courant Institute of Mathematical Sciences in New York. "The burden of raising children still falls on the woman, at a time that's very important in her career. I'm about to institute a new plan of life, according to which women would have their children in their late teens and their mothers would bring them up. I don't mean the grandmother would give up her career, but she's already established, so she can afford to take time off to look after the children."

R. L. Moore (1882–1974) A Texan to the core, R. L. Moore was a rugged individualist whose specialty was topology. His methods were highly original, both in research and teaching. As a professor at the University of Texas, he encouraged originality in his students by discouraging them from reading standard expositions and requiring them to work things out for themselves, in true pioneer spirit. His Socratic style became known as the "Moore method." One of his students, Mary Ellen Rudin, describes it this way: "He always looked for people who had not been influenced by other mathematical experiences. His technique was to feed all kinds of problems to us. He gave us lists of mathematical statements. Some were true, some were false, some were very easy to prove or disprove, others very hard. We worked on whatever we jolly well pleased."

CHAPTER REVIEW

Review the following terms and exercises to determine which require learning or relearning—page numbers are provided for easy reference.

SECTION 12.1: Recognizing Geometric Shapes and Definitions

VOCABULARY/NOTATION

Square lattice   554
Line segment   554
Triangle   554
Side   554
Quadrilateral   554
Angle   554
Vertex (vertices)   554
Right angle   554

Perpendicular line segments   554
Isosceles triangle   554
Equilateral triangle   554
Scalene triangle   554
Square   554
Rectangle   554
Parallelogram   554
Kite   555

Rhombus   555
Congruent line segments   555
Equilateral   555
Congruent angles   555
Equiangular   555
Trapezoid   555
Isosceles trapezoid   555

EXERCISES

1. Briefly explain the following four van Hiele levels.

   a. Recognition   **b.** Analysis

   c. Relationships   **d.** Deduction

2. Give examples of how the following shapes are represented in the physical world.

   a. A line segment   **b.** A right angle

   c. A triangle   **d.** An angle

   e. Parallel lines   **f.** A square

   g. A rectangle   **h.** A parallelogram

   i. A rhombus   **j.** A kite

   k. A trapezoid

SECTION 12.2: Analyzing Shapes

VOCABULARY/NOTATION

Reflection symmetry   564
Line of symmetry   564
Axis of symmetry   564
Base angles   566
Mira   566
Rotation symmetry   566
Diagonal   567
Simple closed curve   569

Polygon   569
Regular polygon   569
Regular *n*-gon   569
Convex   570
Concave   570
Vertex angle   570
Interior angle   570

Central angle   570
Exterior angle   570
Circle   570
Center   570
Radius   570
Diameter   570
Compass   571

EXERCISES

1. Describe the lines of symmetry in the following shapes.

   a. An isosceles triangle

   b. An equilateral triangle

   c. A rectangle

   d. A square

   e. A rhombus

   f. A parallelogram

   g. A trapezoid

   h. An isosceles trapezoid

2. Describe the rotation symmetries in the following shapes (not counting one complete rotation as a symmetry).

   a. An isosceles triangle

   b. An equilateral triangle

   c. A rectangle

   d. A square

   e. A rhombus

   f. A parallelogram

   g. A trapezoid

h. An isosceles trapezoid

i. A regular *n*-gon

3. Give paper-folding definitions of

    a. perpendicular lines.   **b.** parallel lines.

4. Distinguish between convex and concave shapes.

5. Sketch a square and label the following.

    a. All vertex angles   **b.** All central angles

    c. All exterior angles

6. Determine the number of types of symmetries of a circle.

    a. Reflection   **b.** Rotation

SECTION 12.3: Properties of Geometric Shapes: Lines and Angles

VOCABULARY/NOTATION

Plane   576
Point, A 576
Line, $\overleftrightarrow{AB}$ 576
Collinear points   576
Parallel lines, $l \parallel m$ 576
Concurrent lines   576
Distance, AB 577
Coordinates   577
Between   577
Line segment, $\overline{AB}$ 577
Endpoints   577
Length   577
Midpoint   577
Equidistant   577

Ray, $\overrightarrow{CD}$ 577
Angle, $\angle ABC$ 577
Vertex of an angle   577
Sides of an angle   577
Interior of an angle   578
Exterior of an angle   578
Adjacent angles   578
Protractor   578
Degrees   578
Measure of an angle, $m(\angle ABC)$ 578
Acute angle   578
Right angle   578
Obtuse angle   578

Straight angle   578
Reflex angle   578
Vertical angles   578
Supplementary angles   579
Perpendicular lines, $l \perp m$ 579
Complementary angles   579
Transversal   579
Corresponding angles   579
Alternate interior angles   579
Triangle, $\triangle ABC$ 580
Right triangle   581
Obtuse triangle   581
Acute triangle   581

EXERCISES

1. Describe physical objects that can be used to motivate abstract definitions of the following.

    a. Point   **b.** Ray

    c. Line   **d.** Plane

    e. Line segment   **f.** Angle

2. Show that any two vertical angles are congruent.

3. Using the result in Exercise 2, show how each of the following statements involving parallel lines infers the other.

    i. Corresponding angles are congruent.

    ii. Alternate interior angles are congruent.

4. Draw and cut out a triangular shape. Tear off the three angular regions and arrange them side to side with their vertices on the same point. How does this motivate the result that the sum of the angles in a triangle is 180°?

SECTION 12.4: Regular Polygons and Tessellations

VOCABULARY/NOTATION

Regular polygon   586
Polygonal region   588

Tessellation   588
Regular tessellation   589

Vertex arrangement   589
Semiregular tessellation   590

EXERCISES

1. How is the measure of a central angle in a regular *n*-gon related to the number of its sides?

2. How is the measure of an exterior angle of a regular *n*-gon related to the measure of a central angle?

3. Use the results in Exercises 1 and 2 to derive the angle measure of a vertex angle in a regular *n*-gon.

4. Which regular *n*-gons tessellate the plane and why?

SECTION 12.5: Describing Three-Dimensional Shapes

VOCABULARY/NOTATION

Dihedral angle   598
Faces of a dihedral angle   598
Skew lines   598
Polyhedron (polyhedra)   599
Convex polyhedron   601
Faces   601
Edges   601
Vertices   601
Prisms   601
Bases   601
Lateral faces   601
Right prism   601

Oblique prism   601
Pyramid   601
Apex of a pyramid   601
Right regular pyramid   601
Oblique regular pyramid   601
Regular polyhedron   601
Platonic solids   602
Euler's formula   602
Semiregular polyhedron   602
Cylinder   603
Base of a cylinder   603

Right circular cylinder   603
Oblique cylinder   603
Cone   603
Apex of a cone   603
Base of a cone   603
Right circular cone   603
Oblique circular cone   604
Sphere   604
Center   604
Radius   604
Diameter   604

EXERCISES

1. Give examples of the following (or portion of the following if the item is infinite) in the physical world.

   a. Parallel planes

   b. Intersecting planes

   c. Three intersecting planes

   d. A dihedral angle

   e. Skew lines

   f. A polyhedron

2. Describe the Platonic solids.

3. State Euler's formula, and illustrate it with one of the Platonic solids.

4. Give examples of how the following are represented in the physical world.

   a. A right cylinder

   b. A right cone

   c. A sphere

PROBLEMS FOR WRITING/DISCUSSION

1. Clifton says that if you have enough sides for your polygon, it will be a circle. How would you respond?

2. Jackie says that if you add up all the exterior angles of a polygon, you get 720°, not 360°. Is she correct? Explain.

3. Rodney says if a triangle can be acute and isosceles at the same time, and another triangle can be equilateral and isosceles at the same time, then every triangle can be described by two of the triangle words. So there must be some triangle that is scalene and isosceles and another that is right and obtuse. What are the limits to Rodney's conjecture? What combinations are possible? Which are not?

4. Naquetta made three categories of quadrilaterals: those whose diagonals are equal, those whose diagonals are perpendicular, and those whose diagonals bisect each other. Were there any quadrilaterals that fit into more than one category? Were there any

quadrilaterals that did not fit into any category? Demonstrate for Naquetta how to correlate the results using a Venn diagram.

5. Marty says the sum of the angles in any plane figure is 180°. He uses a triangle as his example. Heather says "No, the triangle is the exception." The sum of the angles in any plane figure *except the triangle* is 360°. How would you respond?

6. Greg says he is convinced that a regular pentagon can't tessellate the plane, but maybe he could find some weird pentagon that could (if replicated) tessellate the plane. What advice could you give him about the angles of his weird pentagon?

7. Tatiana says that the circle and the sphere have the same definition: a set of points at an equal distance from the center. Do you agree? How could you explain the need for a difference in the two definitions? What would the difference be?

8. It is possible to draw a polygon that has no line of symmetry. Is it possible to find a prism that has no plane of symmetry? Sketch it if you can.

9. The Platonic solids have faces made of regular triangles, regular quadrilaterals, or regular pentagons. Koji asks why you couldn't have a Platonic solid with faces of regular hexagons. How would you respond?

10. Jared wants to know if it is possible to draw a hexagon that has equal sides but not equal angles, or, on the other hand, equal angles but not equal sides. How would you respond?

CHAPTER TEST

Knowledge

1. True or false?

  a. Every isosceles triangle is equilateral.

  b. Every rhombus is a kite.

  c. A circle is convex.

  d. Vertical angles have the same measure.

  e. A triangle has at most one right angle or one obtuse angle.

  f. A regular pentagon has five diagonals.

  g. A cube has 6 faces, 8 vertices, and 12 edges.

  h. There are exactly three different regular tessellations each using congruent regular n-gons, where $n = 3, 4,$ or 6.

  i. A pyramid has a square base.

  j. Skew lines are the same as parallel lines.

  k. A regular hexagon has exactly three reflection symmetries.

  l. The vertex angle of any regular n-gon has the same measure as any exterior angle of the same n-gon.

  m. A circle has infinitely many rotation symmetries.

  n. It is possible to have a right scalene triangle.

2. In the following figure, identify

  a. a pair of corresponding angles.

  b. a pair of alternate interior angles.

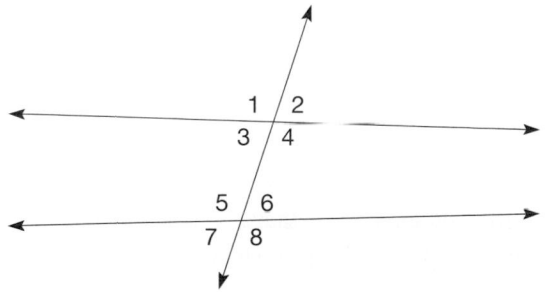

3. Write a precise mathematical definition of a circle.

4. What is the complete name of the following objects?

 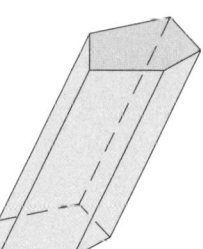

5. Sketch the following. (Please label the sides and angles to emphasize the unique features of the object.)

  a. Obtuse scalene triangle

  b. A trapezoid that is not isosceles

Skill

6. Explain how to use paper folding to show that the diagonals of a rhombus are perpendicular.

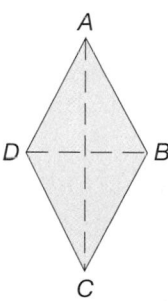

7. Determine the measures of all the dihedral angles of a right prism whose bases are regular octagons.

8. What is the measure of a vertex angle in a regular 10-gon?

9. Determine the number of reflection symmetries a regular 9-gon has. How many rotations less than 360° map a regular 13-gon onto itself?

10. In the following figure, $l \parallel m$. Given the angle measures indicated on the figure, find the measures of the angles identified by a, b, c, d, e, and f.

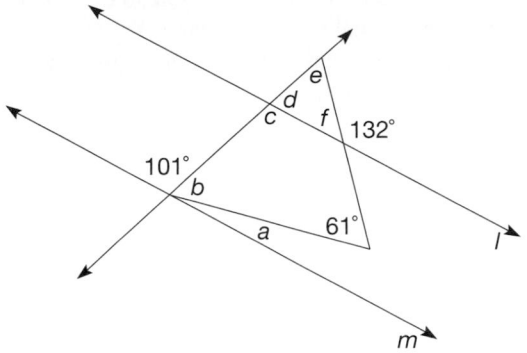

11. Determine the number of faces, vertices, and edges for the hexagonal pyramid shown. Verify Euler's formula for this pyramid.

12. Select a letter of the alphabet that has the following properties. Sketch the lines of symmetry and/or describe the angles of rotation.

   a. Rotational symmetry but not reflexive symmetry

   b. Reflexive but not rotational symmetry

   c. Neither reflexive nor rotational symmetry

Understanding

13. The corresponding angles property states that $m(\angle 1) = m(\angle 2)$ in the figure. Angles $\angle 3$ and $\angle 4$ are called interior angles on the same side of the transversal. Prove that $m(\angle 3) + m(\angle 4) = 180°$.

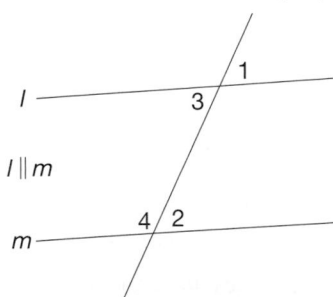

14. Using the result of Problem 13, show that if a parallelogram has one right angle, then the parallelogram must be a rectangle.

15. a. Let one circle represent the set of trapezoids and the other circle represent the set of parallelograms. Which of the following diagrams best represents the relationship between trapezoids and parallelograms?

   b. Let one circle represent the set of kites and the other circle represent the set of rectangles. Which of the following diagrams best represents the relationship between kites and rectangles?

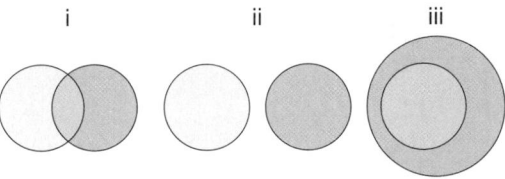

16. The equation for computing the measure of the vertex angle of a regular n-gon can be written as $\dfrac{(n-2)180}{n}$. Explain how it is derived.

17. Given the top view of a stack of blocks where the numbers indicate how high each stack of blocks is, which of the following pictures represents the same stack?

Top view

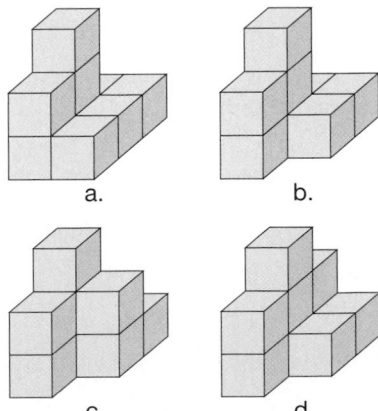

Problem Solving/Application

18. A prism has 96 edges. How many vertices and faces does it have? Explain.

19. Use the figure to show that any convex 7-gon has the sum of its vertex angles equal to 900°.

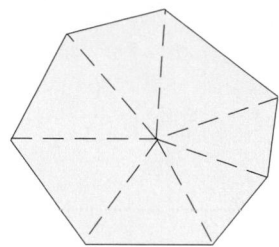

ular octagons will tessellate the plane. Explain why these tessellations work but regular octagons alone will not.

22. In the following seven-pointed star, find the sum of the measures of the angles *A*, *B*, *C*, *D*, *E*, *F*, and *G*.

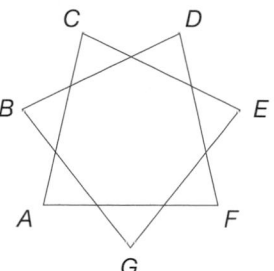

20. Determine whether it is possible to tessellate the plane using only a combination of regular 5-gons and regular 7-gons.

21. We know that squares alone will tessellate the plane. We also know that a combination of squares and reg-

References for Reflections from Research

BATTISTA, M. T., & CLEMENTS, D. H. (1996). Student's understanding of three-dimensional rectangular arrays of cubes. *Journal for Research in Mathematics Education, 27,* 258–292.

FOXMAN, D., & RUDDOCK, G. (1984). Concepts and skills: Line symmetry and angle. *Mathematics in School, 13,* 9–13.

MORRIS, J. P. (1987). Investigating symmetry in the primary grades. In J. M. Hill (Ed.), *Geometry for grades K–6* (pp. 55–60). Reston, VA: National Council for Teachers of Mathematics.

SCALLY, S. (1990). The impact of experience in a Logo learning environment on adolescents' understanding of angle: A van Hiele based clinical assessment. Unpublished doctoral dissertation, Emory University, Atlanta, GA.

THOMAS, B. H. (1983). Kindergarten teachers elicitation and utilization of children's prior knowledge in the teaching of shape concepts. *Dissertation Abstracts International, 43A,* 3506.

TILLOTSON, M. L. (1985). The effect of instruction in spatial visualization on spatial abilities and mathematical problem solving. *Dissertation Abstracts International, 45A,* 2792.

VAN HIELE, P. M. (1984). The child's thought and geometry. In D. Fuys, D. Geddes, & R. Tischler (Eds.), *English translations of selected writings of Dina van Hiele-Geldof and P.M. van Hiele* (pp. 243–252.) Brooklyn, NY: Brooklyn College, School of Education. (ERIC Document Reproduction Service No. 289 697.)

WILSON, P. S., & ADAMS, V. (1992). A dynamic way of teaching angle. *Arithmetic Teacher, 39*(5), 6–13.

CHAPTER 13

FOCUS ON *Archimedes: Mathematical Genius from Antiquity*

Archimedes (287–212 B.C.) is considered to have been the greatest mathematician in antiquity. In fact, he is ranked by many with Sir Isaac Newton and Carl Friedrich Gauss as one of the three greatest mathematicians of all time.

In mathematics, Archimedes discovered and verified formulas for the surface area and volume of a sphere. His method for deriving the volume of a sphere, called the *Archimedean method*, involved a lever principle. He compared a sphere of radius r and a cone of radius $2r$ and height $2r$ to a cylinder also of radius $2r$ and height $2r$, as in the following figure.

Archimedes made many significant contributions to mathematics and physics. He invented a pump for raising water from a river and parabolic "burning mirror," which were used to focus the sun's rays on attacking wooden ships, thereby igniting them. Perhaps the most famous story about him is that of his discovery of the principle of buoyancy; namely, a body immersed in water is buoyed up by a force equal to the weight of the water displaced. Legend has it that he discovered the buoyancy principle while bathing and was so excited that he ran naked into the street shouting "Eureka!"

Using cross-sections, Archimedes deduced that the cone and sphere as solids, placed two units from the fulcrum of the lever, would balance the solid cylinder placed one unit from the fulcrum.

Hence the volume of the cone plus the volume of the sphere equals $\frac{1}{2}$ the volume of the cylinder. But the volume of the cone was known to be $\frac{1}{3}$ the volume of the cylinder, so that the volume of the sphere must be $\frac{1}{6}$ the volume of the cylinder. Thus the volume of the sphere is $\frac{1}{6}(8\pi r^3)$, or $\frac{4}{3}\pi r^3$. The original description of the Archimedean method was thought to be permanently lost until its rediscovery in Constantinople, now Istanbul, in 1906.

Archimedes is credited with anticipating the development of some of the ideas of calculus, nearly 2000 years before its creation by Sir Isaac Newton (1642–1727) and Gottfried Wilhelm Leibniz (1646–1716).

Problem Solving Strategies

1. Guess and Test
2. Use a Variable
3. Draw a Picture
4. Look for a Pattern
5. Make a List
6. Solve a Simpler Problem
7. Draw a Diagram
8. Use Direct Reasoning
9. Use Indirect Reasoning
10. Use Properties of Numbers
11. Solve an Equivalent Problem
12. Work Backward
13. Use Cases
14. Solve an Equation
15. Look for a Formula
16. Do a Simulation
17. Use a Model
18. **Use Dimensional Analysis**

Strategy
Use Dimensional Analysis

The strategy Use Dimensional Analysis is useful in applied problems that involve conversions among measurement units. For example, distance–rate–time problems or problems involving several rates (ratios) are sometimes easier to analyze via dimensional analysis. Additionally, dimensional analysis allows us to check whether we have reported our answer in the correct measurement units.

Initial Problem

David was planning a motorcycle trip across Canada. He drew his route on a map and estimated the length of his route to be 115 centimeters. The scale on his map is 1 centimeter = 39 kilometers. His motorcycle's gasoline consumption averages 75 miles per gallon of gasoline. If gasoline costs $1.25 per gallon, how much should he plan to spend for gasoline? (What additional information does he need?)

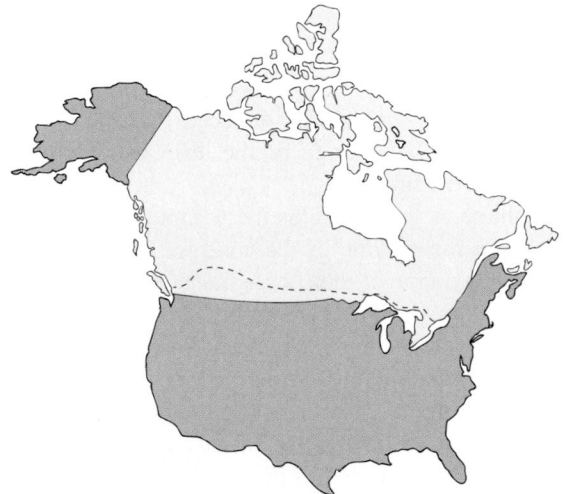

Clues

The Use Dimensional Analysis strategy may be appropriate when

- Units of measure are involved.
- The problem involves physical quantities.
- Conversions are required.

A solution of the Initial Problem appears on page 686.

Figure 13.1

INTRODUCTION

The measurement process allows us to analyze geometric figures using real numbers. For example, suppose that we use a sphere to model the Earth (Figure 13.1). Then we can ask many questions about the sphere, such as "How far is it around the equator? How much surface area does it have? How much space does it take up?" Questions such as these can lead us to the study of the measurement of length, area, and volume of geometric figures, as well as other attributes. In the first section of this chapter we introduce **holistic measurement,** using natural or **nonstandard units** such as "hands" and "paces." We also study two systems of standard units, namely the English system or customary system of units, which we Americans use, and the metric system, or *Système International* (SI), which virtually all other countries use. In the other sections, we study abstract mathematical measurement of geometric shapes, exploring length, area, surface area, and volume.

13.1 MEASUREMENT WITH NONSTANDARD AND STANDARD UNITS

STARTING POINT

When carpet is purchased for a room, a salesman might ask "how many *yards* do you need?" When ordering concrete to pour a sidewalk, the dispatcher will ask "how many *yards* to you need?" Are *yards* in both of these situations the same? Explain.

NCTM Standards 2000
Measurement
Grades Pre-K–2
All students should recognize the attributes of length, volume, weight, area, and time.

Nonstandard Units

The measurement process is defined as follows.

DEFINITION

The Measurement Process

1. Select an object and an attribute of the object to measure, such as its length, area, volume, weight, or temperature.
2. Select an appropriate unit with which to measure the attribute.
3. Determine the number of units needed to measure the attribute. (This may require a measurement device.)

For example, to measure the length of an object, we might see how many times our hand will span the object. Figure 13.2 shows a stick that is four "hand spans" long. "Hands" are still used as a unit to measure the height of horses.

Figure 13.2

Reflection from Research
When learning about measurement, children should use informal, nonstandard units before being introduced to standard units and measuring tools (Van de Walle, 1994).

For measuring longer distances, we might use the length of our feet placed heel to toe or our pace as our unit of measurement. For shorter distances, we might use the width of a finger as our unit (Figure 13.3). Regardless, in every case, we can select

NCTM Standards 2000
Measurement
Grades Pre-K–2
All students should understand how to measure using nonstandard and standard units.

Reflection from Research
A possible teaching sequence for area is to "investigate rectangular covering as a problem in itself, then introduce the area concept" and then use knowledge of covering to measure area (Outhred & Mitchelmore, 2000).

Figure 13.4

Figure 13.5

| A horse that is 16 hands tall | Stepping off a room | A flower that is 5 fingers wide |

1 hand

Figure 13.3

some appropriate unit and determine how many units are needed to span the object. This is an *informal* measurement method of measuring length, since it involves naturally occurring units and is done in a relatively imprecise way.

To measure the area of a region informally, we select a convenient two-dimensional shape as our unit and determine how many such units are needed to cover the region. Figure 13.4 shows how to measure the area of a rectangular rug, using square floor tiles as the unit of measure. By counting the number of squares inside the rectangular border, and estimating the fractional parts of the other squares that are partly inside the border, it appears that the area of the rug is between 15 and 16 square units (certainly, between 12 and 20).

To measure the capacity of water that a vase will hold, we can select a convenient container, such as a water glass, to use as our unit and count how many glassfuls are required to fill the vase (see Figure 13.5). This is an informal method of measuring volume. (Strictly speaking, we are measuring the *capacity* of the vase, namely the amount that it will hold. The volume of the vase would be the amount of material comprising the vase itself.) Other holistic volume measures are found in recipes: a "dash" of hot sauce, a "pinch" of salt, or a "few shakes" of a spice, for example.

Measurement using nonstandard units is adequate for many needs, particularly when accuracy is not essential. However, there are many other circumstances when we need to determine measurements more precisely and communicate them to others. That is, we need standard measurement units as discussed next.

Standard Units

THE ENGLISH SYSTEM The **English system** of units arose from natural, nonstandard units. For example, the foot was literally the length of a human foot and the yard was the distance from the tip of the nose to the end of an outstretched arm (useful in measuring cloth or "yard goods"). The inch was the length of three barley corns, the fathom was the length of a full arm span (for measuring rope), and the acre was the amount of land that a horse could plow in one day (Figure 13.6).

Length The natural English units were standardized so that the foot was defined by a prototype metal bar, and the inch defined as $\frac{1}{12}$ of a foot, the yard the length of 3 feet, and so on for other lengths (Table 13.1). A variety of ratios occur among the English units of length. For example, the ratio of inches to feet is 12:1, of feet to yards is 3:1, of yards to rods is $5\frac{1}{2}$:1, and of furlongs to miles is 8:1. A considerable amount of memorization is needed in learning the English system of measurement.

NCTM Standards 2000
Measurement
Grades 3–5
All students should understand the need for measuring with standard units and become familiar with standard units in their customary and metric systems.

Figure 13.6

TABLE 13.1

UNIT	FRACTION OR MULTIPLE OF 1 FOOT
Inch	$\frac{1}{12}$ ft
Foot	1 ft
Yard	3 ft
Rod	$16\frac{1}{2}$ ft
Furlong	660 ft
Mile	5280 ft

NCTM Standards 2000
Measurement
Grades Pre-K–2
All students should develop common referents for measures to make comparisons and estimates.

NCTM Standards 2000
Measurement
Grades 6–8
All students should understand both metric and customary systems of measurements.

Area Area is measured in the English system using the square foot (written ft²) as the fundamental unit. That is, to measure the area of a region, the number of squares, 1 foot on a side, that are needed to cover the region is determined. This is an application of tessellating the plane with squares (see Chapter 12). Other polygons could, in fact, be used as fundamental units of area. For example, a right triangle, an equilateral triangle, or a regular hexagon could also be used as a fundamental unit of area. For large regions, square yards are used to measure areas, and for very large regions, acres and square miles are used to measure areas. Table 13.2 gives the relationships among various English system units of area. Here again, the ratios between area units are not uniform.

TABLE 13.2

UNIT	MULTIPLE OF 1 SQUARE FOOT
Square inch	1/144 ft²
Square foot	1 ft²
Square yard	9 ft²
Acre	43,560 ft²
Square mile	27,878,400 ft²

Example 13.1 shows how to determine some of the entries in Table 13.2. A more general strategy, called dimensional analysis, appears later in this section.

Example 13.1 Compute the ratios square feet:square yards and square feet:square miles.

Solution Since there are 3 feet in 1 yard and 1 square yard measures 1 yard by 1 yard, we see that there are 9 square feet in 1 square yard [Figure 13.7(a)]. Therefore, the ratio of square feet to square yards is 9:1.

(a)   **(b)**

Figure 13.7

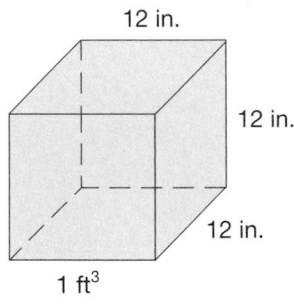

Figure 13.8

Next imagine covering a square, 1 mile on each side, with square tiles, each 1 foot on a side [Figure 13.7(b)]. It would take an array of square with 5280 rows, each row having 5280 tiles. Hence it would take $5280 \times 5280 = 27{,}878{,}400$ square feet to cover 1 square mile. So the ratio of square feet to square miles is 27,878,400:1. ■

Volume In the English system, volume is measured using the cubic foot as the fundamental unit (Figure 13.8). To find the volume of a cubical box that is 3 feet on each side, imagine stacking as many cubic feet inside the box as possible (Figure 13.9). The box could be filled with $3 \times 3 \times 3 = 27$ cubes, each measuring 1 foot on an edge. Each of the smaller cubes has a volume of 1 cubic foot (written ft^3), so that the larger cube has a volume of $27\ \text{ft}^3$. The larger cube is, of course, 1 cubic yard ($1\ \text{yd}^3$). It is common for topsoil and concrete to be sold by the cubic yard, for example. In the English system, we have several cubic units used for measuring volume. Table 13.3 shows some relationships among them. Note the variety of volume ratios in the English system.

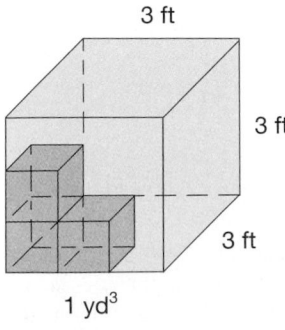

Figure 13.9

TABLE 13.3

UNIT	FRACTION OR MULTIPLE OF A CUBIC FOOT
Cubic inch ($1\ \text{in}^3$)	$1/1728\ \text{ft}^3$
Cubic foot	$1\ \text{ft}^3$
Cubic yard ($1\ \text{yd}^3$)	$27\ \text{ft}^3$

Example 13.2   Verify the ratio of in^3 : ft^3 given in Table 13.3.

Solution Since there are 12 inches in each foot, we could fill a cubic foot with $12 \times 12 \times 12$ smaller cubes, each 1 inch on an edge. Hence there are $12^3 = 1728$ cubic inches in 1 cubic foot. Consequently, each cubic inch is $\frac{1}{1728}$ of a cubic foot.   ■

Figure 13.9 shows cubes, one foot on each side, being stacked *inside* the cubic yard to show that the volume of the box is 27 ft^3. If the larger box were a solid, we would still say that its volume is 27 ft^3. Notice that 27 ft^3 of water can be poured into the open box but no water can be poured *into* a solid cube. To distinguish between these two physical situations, we use the words **capacity** (how much the box will hold) and *volume* (how much material makes up the box). Often, however, the word *volume* is used for capacity. The English system uses the units shown in Table 13.4 to measure capacity for liquids. In addition to these liquid measures of capacity, there are similar dry measures.

TABLE 13.4

UNIT	ABBREVIATION	RELATION TO PRECEDING UNIT
1 teaspoon	tsp	
1 tablespoon	tbsp	3 teaspoons
1 liquid ounce	oz	2 tablespoons
1 cup	c	8 liquid ounces
1 pint	pt	2 cups
1 quart	qt	2 pints
1 gallon	gal	4 quarts
1 barrel	bar	31.5 gallons

Weight In the English system, weight is measured in pounds and ounces. In fact, there are two types of measures of weight—troy ounces and pounds (mainly for precious metals), and avoirdupois ounces and pounds, the latter being more common. We will use the avoirdupois units. The weight of 2000 pounds is 1 English ton. Smaller weights are measured in drams and grains. Table 13.5 summarizes these English system units of weight. Notice how inconsistent the ratios are between consecutive units.

TABLE 13.5   English System Units of Weight (Avoirdupois)

UNIT	RELATION TO PRECEDING UNIT
1 grain	
1 dram	$27\frac{11}{32}$ grains
1 ounce	16 drams
1 pound	16 ounces
1 ton	2000 pounds

Technically, the concepts of weight and mass are different. Informally, mass is the measure of the amount of matter of an object and weight is a measure of the force with which gravity attracts the object. Thus, although your mass is the same on Earth and on the Moon, you weigh more on Earth because the attraction of gravity is greater on Earth. We will not make a distinction between weight and mass. We will use English units of weight and metric units of mass, both of which are used to weigh objects.

212°F	Boiling point of water
98.6°	Body temperature
70°F	Room temperature
32°F	Freezing point of water

Figure 13.10

Temperature Temperature is measured in **degrees Fahrenheit** in the English system. The Fahrenheit temperature scale is named for Gabriel Fahrenheit, a German instrument maker, who invented the mercury thermometer in 1714. The freezing point and boiling point of water are used as reference temperatures. The freezing point is arbitrarily defined to be 32° Fahrenheit, and the boiling point 212° Fahrenheit. This gives an interval of exactly 180° from freezing to boiling (Figure 13.10).

THE METRIC SYSTEM In contrast to the English system of measurement units, the **metric system** of units (or Système International d'Unités) incorporates all of the following features of an ideal system of units.

An Ideal System of Units

1. The fundamental unit can be accurately reproduced without reference to a prototype. (Portability)

2. There are simple (e.g., decimal) ratios among units of the same type. (Convertibility)

3. Different types of units (e.g., those for length, area, and volume) are defined in terms of each other, using simple relationships. (Interrelatedness)

Length In the metric system, the fundamental unit of length is the **meter** (about $39\frac{1}{2}$ inches). The meter was originally defined to be one ten-millionth of the distance from the equator to the North Pole along the Greenwich-through-Paris meridian. A prototype platinum–iridium bar representing a meter was maintained in the International Bureau of Weights and Measures in France. However, as science advanced, this definition was changed so that the meter could be reproduced anywhere in the world. Since 1960, the meter has been defined to be precisely 1,650,763.73 wavelengths of orange-red light in the spectrum of the element krypton 86. Although this definition may seem highly technical, it has the advantage of being reproducible in a laboratory anywhere. That is, no standard meter prototype need be kept. This is a clear advantage over older versions of the English system. We shall see that there are many more.

The metric system is a decimal system of measurement in which multiples and fractions of the fundamental unit correspond to powers of ten. For example, one thousand meters is a **kilometer,** one-tenth of a meter is a **decimeter,** one-hundredth of a meter is a **centimeter,** and one-thousandth of a meter is a **millimeter.** Table 13.6 shows some relationship among metric units of length. Notice the simple ratios among units of length in the metric system. (Compare Table 13.6 to Table 13.1 for

Reflection from Research
Students have difficulty estimating lengths of segments using metric units. In a national assessment only 30% of the thirteen-year-olds successfully estimated segment length to the nearest centimeter (Carpenter, Corbitt, Kepner, Lindquist, & Reys, 1981).

TABLE 13.6

UNIT	SYMBOL	FRACTION OR MULTIPLE OF 1 METER
1 millimeter	1 mm	0.001 m
1 centimeter	1 cm	0.01 m
1 decimeter	1 dm	0.1 m
1 meter	1 m	1 m
1 dekameter	1 dam	10 m
1 hectometer	1 hm	100 m
1 kilometer	1 km	1000 m

the English system, for example.) From Table 13.6 we see that 1 **dekameter** is equivalent to 10 meters, 1 **hectometer** is equivalent to 100 meters, and so on. Also, 1 dekameter is equivalent to 100 decimeters, 1 kilometer is equivalent to 1,000,000 millimeters, and so on. (Check these.)

From the information in Table 13.6, we can make a metric "converter" diagram to simplify changing units of length. Locate consecutive metric abbreviations for units of length starting with the largest prefix on the left (Figure 13.11). To convert from, say, hectometers to centimeters, count spaces from "hm" to "cm" in the diagram, and move the decimal point in the same direction as many spaces as are indicated in the diagram (here, four to the right). For example, 13.23685 hm = 132,368.5 cm. Similarly, 4326.9 mm = 4.3269 m, since we move three spaces to the left in the diagram when going from "mm" to "m." It is good practice to use measurement sense as a check. For example, when converting from mm to hm, we have fewer "hm's" than "mm's," since 1 hm is longer than 1 mm.

Figure 13.11

Figure 13.12 shows *relative* comparisons of lengths in English and metric systems. Lengths that are measured in feet or yards in the English system are commonly measured in meters in the metric system. Lengths measured in inches in the English system are measured in centimeters in the metric system. (By definition, 1 in. is exactly 2.54 cm.) For example, in metric countries, track and field events use meters instead of yards for the lengths of races. Snowfall is measured in centimeters in metric countries, not inches.

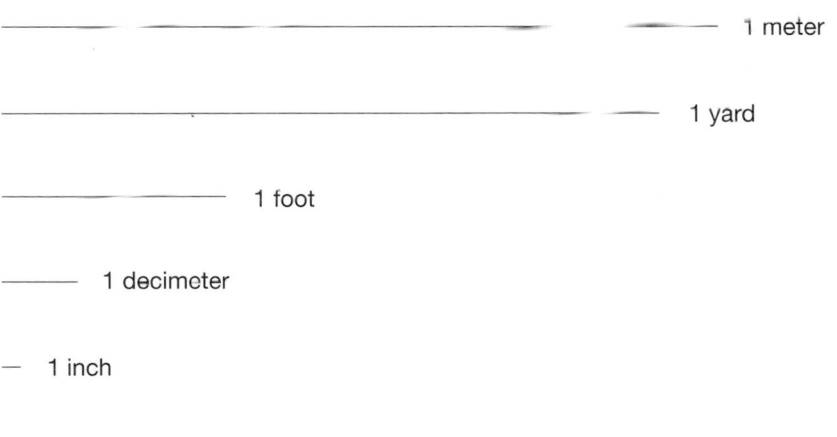

Figure 13.12

From Table 13.6 we see that certain prefixes are used in the metric system to indicate fractions or multiples of the fundamental unit. Table 13.7 gives the meanings of many of the metric prefixes. The three most commonly used prefixes are in italics. We will see that these prefixes are also used with measures of area, volume, and weight. Compare the descriptions of the prefixes in Table 13.7 with their uses in Table 13.6. Notice how the prefixes signify the ratios to the fundamental unit.

TABLE 13.7

PREFIX	MULTIPLE OR FRACTION	
atto-	10^{-18}	
femto-	10^{-15}	
pico-	10^{-12}	Science
nano-	10^{-9}	
micro-	10^{-6}	
milli-	$10^{-3} = \frac{1}{1000}$	
centi-	$10^{-2} = \frac{1}{100}$	
deci-	$10^{-1} = \frac{1}{10}$	Everyday life
deka-	10	
hecto-	$10^2 = 100$	
kilo-	$10^3 = 1000$	
mega-	10^6	
giga-	10^9	
tera-	10^{12}	Science
peta-	10^{15}	
exa-	10^{18}	

Area In the metric system, the fundamental unit of area is the square meter. A square that is 1 meter long on each side has an area of **1 square meter,** written 1 m² (Figure 13.13). Areas measured in square feet or square yards in the English system are measured in square meters in the metric system. For example, carpeting would be measured in square meters.

Smaller areas are measured in square centimeters. A **square centimeter** is the area of a square that is 1 centimeter long on each side. For example, the area of a piece of notebook paper or a photograph would be measured in square centimeters (cm²). Example 13.3 shows the relationship between square centimeters and square meters.

Example 13.3 Determine the number of square centimeters in 1 square meter.

Solution A square with area 1 square meter can be covered with an array of square centimeters. In Figure 13.14 we see part of the array. There are 100 rows, each row

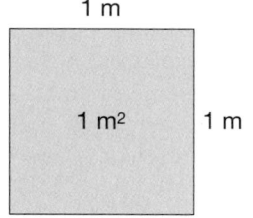

1 m

1 m²   1 m

Figure 13.13

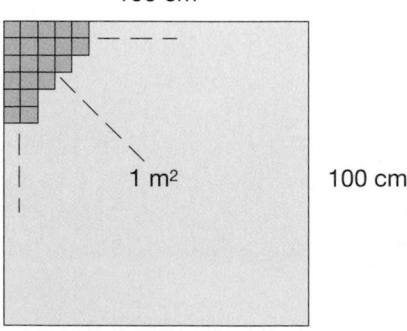

100 cm

1 m²   100 cm

(not to scale)

Figure 13.14

having 100 square centimeters. Hence there are $100 \times 100 = 10\,000$ square centimeters needed to cover the square meter. Thus 1 m² = 10 000 cm². (NOTE: Spaces are used instead of commas to show groupings in large numbers.)   ▪

10 m

1 are
(100 m²)

10 m

Figure 13.15

NCTM Standards 2000
Measurement
Grades 3–5
All students should carry out
simple unit conversions such as
centimeters to meters, within
a system of measurement.

Very small areas, such as on a microscope slide, are measured using square millimeters. A **square millimeter** is the area of a square whose sides are each 1 millimeter long.

In the metric system the area of a square that is 10 m on each side is given the special name **are** (pronounced "air"). Figure 13.15 illustrates this definition. An are is approximately the area of the floor of a large two-car garage and is a convenient unit for measuring the area of building lots. There are 100 m² in 1 are.

An area equivalent to 100 ares is called a **hectare,** written 1 ha. Notice the use of the prefix "hect" (meaning 100). The hectare is useful for measuring areas of farms and ranches. We can show that 1 hectare is 1 square hectometer by converting each to square meters, as follows.

$$1 \text{ ha} = 100 \text{ ares} = 100 \times (100 \text{ m}^2) = 10\,000 \text{ m}^2$$

Also,

$$1 \text{ hm}^2 = (100 \text{ m}) \times (100 \text{ m}) = 10\,000 \text{ m}^2.$$

Thus 1 ha = 1 hm².

Finally, very large areas are measured in the metric system using square kilometers. One **square kilometer** is the area of a square that is 1 kilometer on each side. Areas of cities or states, for example, are reported in square kilometres. Table 13.8 gives the ratios among various units of area in the metric system. See if you can verify the entries in the table.

TABLE 13.8

UNIT	ABBREVIATION	FRACTION OR MULTIPLE OF 1 SQUARE METER
Square millimeter	mm²	0.000001 m²
Square centimeter	cm²	0.0001 m²
Square decimeter	dm²	0.01 m²
Square meter	m²	1 m²
Are (square dekameter)	a (dam²)	100 m²
Hectare (square hectometer)	ha (hm²)	10 000 m²
Square kilometer	km²	1 000 000 m²

From Table 13.8 we see that the metric prefixes for square units should *not* be interpreted in the abbreviated forms as having the same meanings as with linear units. For example, 1 dm² is not one-tenth of 1 m²; rather, 1 dm² is one-hundredth of 1 m². Conversions among units of area can be done if we use the metric converter in Figure 13.16 but move the demical point *twice* the number of spaces that we move between units. This is due to the fact that area involves *two* dimensions. For example, suppose that we wish to convert 3.7 m² to mm². From Figure 13.16, we move three spaces to the right from "m" to "mm," so we will move the decimal point 3 · 2 = 6 (the "2" is due to the *two* dimensions) places to the right. Thus 3.7 m² = 3 700 000 mm². Since 1 m² = (1000 mm)² = 1 000 000 mm², we have 3.7 m² = 3.7 × (1 000 000) mm² = 3 700 000 mm², which is the same result that we obtained using the metric converter.

km　　hm　　dam　　m　　dm　　cm　　mm

Figure 13.16

Figure 13.17

Volume The fundamental unit of volume in the metric system is the liter. A **liter,** abbreviated L, is the volume of a cube that measures 10 cm on each edge (Figure 13.17). We can also say that a liter is 1 **cubic decimeter,** since the cube in Figure 13.17 measures 1 dm on each edge. Notice that the liter is defined with reference to the meter, which is the fundamental unit of length. The liter is slightly larger than a quart. Many soft-drink containers have capacities of 1 or 2 liters.

Imagine filling the liter cube in Figure 13.17 with smaller cubes, 1 centimeter on each edge. Figure 13.18 illustrates this. Each small cube has a volume of 1 **cubic centimeter** (1 cm³). It will take a 10 × 10 array (hence 100) of the centimeter cubes to cover the bottom of the liter cube. Finally, it takes 10 layers, each with 100 centimeter cubes, to fill the liter cube to the top. Thus 1 liter is equivalent to 1000 cm³. Recall that the prefix "milli-" in the metric system means one-thousandth. Thus we see that 1 **milliliter** is equivalent to 1 cubic centimeter, since there are 1000 cm³ in 1 liter. Small volumes in the metric system are measured in milliliters (cubic centimeters). Containers of liquid are frequently labeled in milliliters.

10 cm = 1 dm

10 cm = 1 dm

10 cm = 1 dm

Figure 13.18

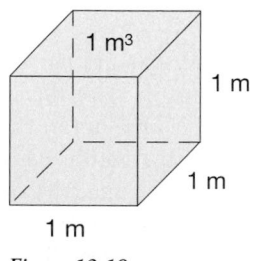

Figure 13.19

Large volumes in the metric system are measured using cubic meters. A **cubic meter** is the volume of a cube that measures 1 meter on each edge (Figure 13.19). Capacities of large containers such as water tanks, reservoirs, or swimming pools are measured using cubic meters. A cubic meter is also called a **kiloliter.** Table 13.9 gives the relationships among commonly used volume units in the metric system.

Table 13.9

UNIT	ABBREVIATION	FRACTION OR MULTIPLE OF 1 LITER
Milliliter (cubic centimeter)	mL (cm³)	0.001 L
Liter (cubic decimeter)	L (dm³)	1 L
Kiloliter (cubic meter)	kL (m³)	1000 L

In the metric system, capacity is usually recorded in liters, milliliters, and so on. We can make conversions among metric volume units using the metric converter (Figure 13.20). To convert among volume units, we count the number of spaces that we move left or right in going from one unit to another. Then we move the decimal point exactly *three* times that number of places, since volume involves three dimensions. For example, in converting 187.68 cm³ to m³, we count two spaces to the left in Figure 13.20 (from cm to m). Then we move the decimal point $2 \cdot 3 = 6$ (the "3" is due to *three* dimensions) places to the left, so that 187.68 cm³ = 0.00018768 m³.

Figure 13.20

Mass In the metric system, a basic unit of mass is the kilogram. One **kilogram** is the mass of 1 liter of water in its densest state. (Water expands and contracts somewhat when heated or cooled.) A kilogram is about 2.2 pounds in the English system. Notice that the kilogram is defined with reference to the liter, which in turn was defined relative to the meter. Figure 13.21 shows a liter container filled with water, hence a mass of 1 kilogram (1 kg). This illustrates the interrelatedness of the metric units meter, liter, and kilogram.

From the information in Table 13.9, we can conclude that 1 milliliter of water weighs $\frac{1}{1000}$ of a kilogram. This weight is called a **gram.** Grams are used for small weights in the metric system, such as ingredients in recipes or nutritional contents of various foods. Many foods are packaged and labeled by grams. About 28 grams are equivalent to 1 ounce in the English system.

We can summarize the information in Table 13.9 with the definitions of the various metric weights in the following way. In the metric system, there are three basic cubes: the cubic centimeter, the cubic decimeter, and the cubic meter (Figure 13.22).

Figure 13.21

1 cm³
= 1 mL of water with mass 1 g

1 dm³
= 1000 cm³
= 1 L of water with mass 1 kg

1 m³
= 1000 dm³
= 1,000,000 cm³
= 1 kL of water with mass 1 tonne

(Drawing not to scale)

Figure 13.22

The cubic centimeter is equivalent in volume to 1 milliliter, and, if water, it weighs 1 gram. Similarly, 1 cubic decimeter of volume is 1 liter and, if water, weighs 1 kilogram. Finally, 1 cubic meter of volume is 1 kiloliter and, if water, weighs 1000 kilograms, called a **metric ton** (tonne). Table 13.10 summarizes these relationships.

Temperature In the metric system, temperature is measured in **degrees Celsius.** The Celsius scale is named after the Swedish astronomer Anders Celsius, who devised it in 1742. This scale was originally called "centigrade." Two reference temperatures are used, the freezing point of water and the boiling point of water. These are defined to be, respectively, zero degrees Celsius (0°C) and 100 degrees Celsius (100°C). A metric thermometer is made by dividing the interval from freezing to boiling into 100 degrees Celsius. Figure 13.23 shows a metric thermometer and some useful metric temperatures.

Table 13.10

CUBE	VOLUME	MASS (WATER)
1 m³	1 kL	1 tonne
1 dm³	1 L	1 kg
1 cm³	1 mL	1 g

Figure 13.23

The relationship between degrees Celsius and degrees Fahrenheit (used in the English system) is derived next.

Example 13.4

a. Derive a conversion formula for degrees Celsius to degrees Fahrenheit.
b. Convert 37°C to degrees Fahrenheit.
c. Convert 68°F to degrees Celsius.

Solution

Figure 13.24

a. Suppose that C represents a Celsius temperature and F the equivalent Fahrenheit temperature. *Since there are 100° Celsius for each 180° Fahrenheit* (Figure 13.24), there is 1° Celsius for each 1.8° Fahrenheit. If C is a temperature above freezing, then the equivalent Fahrenheit temperature, F, is 1.8C degrees Fahrenheit above 32° Fahrenheit, or 1.8C + 32. Thus 1.8C + 32 = F is the desired formula. (This also applies to temperatures at freezing or below, hence to all temperatures.)

b. Using 1.8C + 32 = F, we have 1.8(37) + 32 = 98.6° Fahrenheit, which is normal human body temperature.

c. Using 1.8C + 32 = F and solving C, we find $C = \dfrac{F - 32}{1.8}$. Hence room temperature of 68° Fahrenheit is equivalent to $C = \dfrac{68 - 32}{1.8} = 20°$ Celsius. ■

Water is densest at 4°C. Therefore, the precise definition of the kilogram is the mass of 1 liter of water at 4°C.

From the preceding discussion, we see that the metric system has all of the features of an ideal system of units: portability, convertibility, and interrelatedness. These features make learning the metric system simpler than learning the English system of units. The metric system is the preferred system in science and commerce throughout the world. Moreover, only a handful of countries use a system other than the metric system.

Dimensional Analysis

When working with two (or more) systems of measurement, there are many circumstances requiring conversions among units. The procedure known as dimensional analysis can help simplify the conversion. In **dimensional analysis,** we use unit ratios that are equivalent to 1 and treat these ratios as fractions. For example, suppose that we wish to convert 17 feet to inches. We use the unit ratio 12 in./1 ft (which is 1) to perform the conversion.

$$17\text{ft} = 17\cancel{\text{ft}} \times \frac{12 \text{ in.}}{1 \cancel{\text{ft}}}$$
$$= 17 \times 12 \text{ in.}$$
$$= 204 \text{ in.}$$

Reflection from Research
It is difficult for students to comprehend that it takes more inches than feet to cover the same distance. The inverse relationship that exists because inches are smaller but more of them are required than feet can be confusing (Hart, 1984).

Hence a length of 17 ft is the same as 204 inches. Dimensional analysis is especially useful if several conversions must be made. Example 13.5 provides an illustration.

Example 13.5 A vase holds 4286 grams of water. What is its capacity in liters?

Solution Since 1 mL of water weighs 1 g and 1 L = 1000 mL, we have

$$4286g = 4286g \times \frac{1 \text{ mL}}{1 \text{ g}} \times \frac{1 \text{ L}}{1000 \text{ mL}}$$

$$= \frac{4286}{1000} \text{ L} = 4.286 \text{ L}.$$

Consequently, the capacity of the vase is 4.286 liters. ■

In Example 13.6 we see a more complicated application of dimensional analysis. Notice that treating the ratios as fractions allows us to use multiplication of fractions. Thus we can be sure that our answer has the proper units.

Example 13.6 The area of a rectangular lot is 25,375 ft². What is the area of the lot in acres? Use the fact that 640 acres = 1 square mile.

Solution We wish to convert from square feet to acres. Since 1 mile = 5280 ft, we can convert from square feet to square miles. That is, 1 mile² = 5280 ft × 5280 ft = 27,878,400 ft². Hence

$$25,375 \text{ ft}^2 = 25,375 \text{ ft}^2 \times \frac{1 \text{ mile}^2}{27,878,400 \text{ ft}^2} \times \frac{640 \text{ acres}}{1 \text{ mile}^2}$$

$$= \frac{25,375 \times 640}{27,878,400} \text{ acres} = 0.58 \text{ acre (to two places).} ■$$

Example 13.7 shows how to make conversions between English and metric system units. We do not advocate memorizing such conversion ratios, since rough approximations serve in most circumstances. However, there are occasions when accuracy is needed. In fact, the English system units are now legally defined *in terms* of metric system units. Recall that the basic conversion ratio for lengths is 1 inch : 2.54 centimeters, exactly.

Example 13.7 A pole vaulter vaulted 19 ft $4\frac{1}{2}$ in. Find the height in meters.

Solution Since 1 meter is a little longer than 1 yard and the vault is about 6 yards, we estimate the vault to be 6 meters. Actually,

$$19 \text{ ft } 4\frac{1}{2} \text{ in.} = 232.5 \text{ in.}$$

$$= 232.5 \text{ in.} \times \frac{2.54 \text{ cm}}{1 \text{ in.}} \times \frac{1 \text{ m}}{100 \text{ cm}}$$

$$= \frac{232.5 \times 2.54}{100} \text{ m} = 5.9055 \text{ m.} ■$$

Our final example illustrates how we can make conversions involving different types of units, here distance and time.

Example 13.8 Suppose that a bullet train is traveling 200 mph. How many feet per second is it traveling?

Solution

$$200\frac{\text{mi}}{\text{hr}} \cdot \frac{5280 \text{ ft}}{1 \text{ mi}} \cdot \frac{1 \text{ hr}}{3600 \text{ sec}} = 293\frac{1}{3} \text{ ft/sec.} ■$$

Problem-Solving Strategy
Use Dimensional Analysis

NCTM Standards 2000
Measurement
Grades Pre-K–2
All students should compare and order objects by attributes of length, volume, weight, area, and time.

Problem-Solving Strategy
Use Dimensional Analysis

Problem-Solving Strategy
Use Dimensional Analysis

Problem-Solving Strategy
Use Dimensional Analysis

MATHEMATICAL MORSEL

In 1958, fraternity pledges at M.I.T. (where "Math Is Truth") were ordered to measure the length of Harvard Bridge—not in feet or meters, but in "Smoots," one Smoot being the height of their 5-foot 7-inch classmate, Oliver Smoot. Handling him like a ruler, the pledges found the bridge to be precisely 364.4 Smoots long. Thus began a tradition: The bridge has been faithfully. "re-Smooted" each year since, and its new sidewalk is permanently scored in 10-Smoot intervals. Oliver Smoot went on to become an executive with a trade group in Washington, D.C.

 Section 13.1 EXERCISE / PROBLEM SET A

EXERCISES

1. In your elementary classroom, you find the following objects. For each object, list attributes that could be measured and how you could measure them.

   a. A student's chair **b.** A wastebasket

   c. A bulletin board **d.** An aquarium

2. Calculate the following.

   a. How many inches in a mile?

   b. How many yards in a mile?

   c. How many square yards in 43,560 square feet?

   d. How many cubic inches in a cubic yard?

   e. How many ounces in 500 pounds?

   f. How may cups in a quart?

   g. How many cups in a gallon?

   h. How many tablespoons in a cup?

3. Convert the following (to the nearest degree).

   a. Moderate oven (350°F) to degrees Celsius

   b. A spring day (60°F) to degrees Celsius

   c. 20°C to degrees Fahrenheit

   d. Ice-skating weather (0°F) to degrees Celsius

   e. −5°C to degrees Fahrenheit

4. The metric prefixes are also used with measurement of time. If "second" is the fundamental unit of time, what multiple or fraction of a second are the following measurements?

   a. Megasecond **b.** Millisecond

   c. Microsecond **d.** Kilosecond

   e. Centisecond **f.** Picosecond

5. Using the meanings of the metric prefixes, how do the following units compare to a meter? If it exists, give an equivalent name.

   a. "Kilomegameter" **b.** "Hectodekameter"

   c. "Millimillimicrometer" **d.** "Megananometer"

6. Use the metric converter to complete the following statements.

   | km | hm | dam | m | dm | cm | mm |

   a. 1 dm = _____ mm **b.** 7.5 cm = _____ mm

   c. 31 m = _____ cm **d.** 3.06 m = _____ mm

   e. 0.76 hm = _____ m **f.** 0.93 cm = _____ m

   g. 230 mm = _____ dm **h.** 3.5 m = _____ hm

   i. 125 dm = _____ hm **j.** 764 m = _____ km

7. Use the metric converter to complete the following statements.

   a. $1 \text{ cm}^2 = $ _____ mm^2

   b. $610 \text{ dam}^2 = $ _____ hm^2

   c. $564 \text{ m}^2 = $ _____ km^2

   d. $821 \text{ dm}^2 = $ _____ m^2

   e. $0.382 \text{km}^2 = $ _____ m^2

   f. $9.5 \text{ dm}^2 = $ _____ cm^2

   g. $6\ 540\ 000 \text{ m}^2 = $ _____ km^2

   h. $9610 \text{ mm}^2 = $ _____ m^2

8. Use the metric converter to answer the following questions.

   a. One cubic meter contains how many cubic decimeters?

b. Based on your answer in part (a), how do we move the decimal point for each step to the right on the metric converter?

c. How should we move the decimal point for each step left?

9. Using a metric converter if necessary, convert the following measurements of mass.

    a. 95 mg = _____ cg

    b. 7 kg = _____ g

    c. 940 mg = _____ g

10. Convert the following measures of capacity.

    a. 5 L = _____ cL

    b. 53 L = _____ daL

    c. 4.6 L = _____ mL

11. Choose the most realistic measures of the following objects.

    a. The length of a small paper clip: 28 mm, 28 cm, or 28 m?

    b. The height of a 12-year-old boy: 48 mm, 148 cm, or 48 m?

    c. The length of a shoe: 27 mm, 27 cm, or 27 m?

12. Choose the most realistic measures of the volume of the following objects.

    a. A juice container: 90 mL, 900 cL, or 900 L?

    b. A tablespoon: 15 mL, 15 cL, or 15 L?

    c. A pop bottle: 473 mL, 473 cL, or 473 L?

13. Choose the most realistic measures of the mass of the following objects.

    a. A 6-year-old boy: 23 mg, 23 g, or 23 kg?

    b. A pencil: 10 mg, 10 g, or 10 kg?

    c. An eyelash: 305 mg, 305 g, 305 kg?

14. Choose the best estimate for the following temperatures.

    a. The water temperature for swimming: 22°C, 39°C, or 80°C?

    b. A glass of lemonade: 10°C, 5°C, or 40°C?

15. A container holds water at its densest state. Give the missing numbers or missing units in the following table.

	VOLUME	CAPACITY	MASS
a.	? cm^3	34 mL	34 g
b.	? dm^3	? l	18 kg
c.	23 cm^3	23 ?	23 g
d.	750 dm^3	750 L	750 ?
e.	19^7 ?	19 L	19 ?
f.	72 cm^3	72 ?	72 ?

16. By using dimensional analysis, make the following conversions.

    a. 3.6 lb to oz

    b. 55 mi/hr to ft/min

    c. 35 mi/hr to in./sec

    d. $575 per day to dollars per minute

17. Prior to conversion to a decimal monetary system, the United Kingdom used the following coins.

    1 pound = 20 shillings   1 penny = 2 half-pennies

    1 shilling = 12 pence   1 penny = 4 farthings

    (Pence is the plural of penny.)

    a. How many pence were there in a pound?

    b. How many half-pennies in a pound?

    c. How many farthings were equal to a shilling?

18. One inch is defined to be exactly 2.54 cm. Using this ratio, convert the following measurements.

    a. 6-inch snowfall to cm

    b. 100-yard football field to m

    c. 440-yard race to m

    d. 1 km racetrack to mi

PROBLEMS

19. A gallon of water weighs about 8.3 pounds. A cubic foot of water weighs about 62 pounds. How many gallons of water (to one decimal place) would fill a cubic foot container?

20. An adult male weighing about 70 kg has a red blood cell count of about 5.4×10^6 cells per microliter of blood and a blood volume of approximately 5 liters.

Determine the approximate number of red blood cells in the body of an adult male.

21. The density of a substance is the ratio of its mass to its volume:

$$\text{Density} = \frac{\text{mass}}{\text{volume}}.$$

Density is usually expressed in terms of grams per cubic centimeter (g/cm^3). For example, the density of copper is 8.94 g/cm^3.

a. Express the density of copper in kg/dm^3.

b. A chunk of oak firewood weighs about 2.85 kg and has a volume of 4100 cm^3. Determine the density of oak in g/cm^3, rounding to the nearest thousandth.

c. A piece of iron weighs 45 ounces and has a volume of 10 in^3. Determine the density of iron in g/cm^3, rounding to the nearest tenth.

22. The features of portability, convertibility, and interrelatedness were described as features of an ideal measurement system. Through an example, explain why the English system has none of these features.

23. Light travels 186,282 miles per second.

a. Based on a 365-day year, how far in miles will light travel in one year? This unit of *distance* is called a **light-year.**

b. If a star in Andromeda is 76 light-years away from Earth, how many miles will light from the star travel on its way to Earth?

c. The planet Jupiter is approximately 480,000,000 miles from the sun. How long does it take for light to travel from the sun to Jupiter?

24. A train moving 50 miles per hour meets and passes a train moving 50 miles per hour in the opposite direction. A passenger in the first train sees the second train pass in 5 seconds. How long is the second train?

25. a. If 1 inch of rainfall fell over 1 acre of ground, how many cubic inches of water would that be? How many cubic feet?

b. If 1 cubic foot of water weighs approximately 62 pounds, what is the weight of a uniform coating of 1 inch of rain over 1 acre of ground?

c. The weight of 1 gallon of water is about 8.3 pounds. A rainfall of 1 inch over 1 acre of ground means about how many gallons of water?

26. A ruler has marks placed at every unit. For example, an 8-unit ruler has a length of 8 and has seven marks on it to designate the unit lengths.

This ruler provides three direct ways to measure a length of 6; from the left end to the 6 mark, from the 1 mark to the 7 mark, and from the 2 to the 8.

a. Show how all lengths from 1 through 8 can be measured using only the marks at 1, 4, and 6.

b. Using a blank ruler 9 units in length, what is the fewest number of marks necessary to be able to measure lengths from 1 to 10 units? How would marks be placed on the ruler?

c. Repeat for a ruler 10 units in length.

27. A father and his son working together can cut 48 ft^3 of firewood per hour.

a. If they work an 8-hour day and are able to sell all the wood they cut at $100 per cord, how much money can they earn? A cord is defined as 4 feet × 4 feet × 8 feet.

b. If they split the money evenly, at what hourly rate should the father pay his son?

c. If the delivery truck can hold 100 cubic feet, how many trips would it take to deliver all the wood cut in a day?

d. If they sell their wood for $85 per truckload, what price are they getting per cord?

28. A hiker can average 2 km per hour uphill and 6 km per hour downhill. What will be his average speed for the entire trip if he spends no time at the summit?

29. There are about 1 billion people in China. If they lined up four to a row and marched past you at the rate of 25 rows per minute, how long would it take the parade to pass you?

30. A restaurant chain has sold over 80 billion hamburgers. A hamburger is about one-half inch thick. If the moon is 240 thousand miles away, what percent of the distance to the moon is the height of a stack of 80 billion hamburgers?

 Section 13.1 EXERCISE / PROBLEM SET B

EXERCISES

1. Many attributes of the human body are measured in the normal activities of life. Name some of these attributes that would be measured by the following people.

a. A dressmaker **b.** A shoe salesperson

c. A doctor **d.** An athletic coach

2. Calculate the following.

   a. How many yards in a furlong?

   b. How many rods in a mile?

   c. How many acres in a square mile?

   d. How many cubic feet in a cubic rod?

   e. How many drams in a ton?

   f. How many cups in half-pint?

   g. How many quarts in a barrel?

   h. How many teaspoons in a cup?

3. Convert the following (to the nearest degree).

   a. World's highest temperature recorded (136°F) at Azizia, Tripolitania, in northern Africa on September 13, 1922, to degrees Celsius

   b. 90°C to degrees Fahrenheit

   c. −30°C to degrees Fahrenheit

   d. World's record low temperature (−126.9°F) at the Antarctic station Vostok on August 24, 1960, to degrees Celsius

   e. −18°C to degrees Fahrenheit

4. Indentify the following amounts.

   a. "Decidollar"

   b. "Centidollar"

   c. "Dekadollar"

   d. "Kilodollar"

5. A state lottery contest is called "Megabucks." What does this imply about the prize?

6. Use the metric converter to complete the following.

   km   hm   dam   m   dm   cm   mm

   a. 1200 cm = _____ m

   b. 35 690 mm = _____ km

   c. 260 km = _____ cm

   d. 786 mm = _____ m

   e. 384 mm = _____ cm

   f. 12 m = _____ km

   g. 13 450 m = _____ cm

   h. 1900 cm = _____ km

   i. 46 780 000 mm = _____ m

   j. 89 000 cm = _____ hm

7. Use the metric converter to convert metric measurements of area.

   a. Each square meter is equivalent to how many square centimeters?

   b. To move from m^2 to cm^2, how many decimal places do we need to move?

   c. For each step *right*, how do we move the decimal point?

   d. For each step *left*, how do move the decimal point?

   e. What are more common names for dam^2 and hm^2?

8. Convert the following measures.

   a. 2 m^3 = _____ cm^3

   b. 5m^3 = _____ mm^3

   c. 16 dm^3 = _____ cm^3

   d. 620 cm^3 = _____ dm^3

   e. 56 000 cm^3 = _____ m^3

   f. 1 200 000 mm^3 = _____ cm^3

9. Using a metric converter, if necessary, convert the following measurements of mass.

   a. 475 cg = _____ mg   b. 57 dg = _____ hg

   c. 32 g = _____ mg

10. Convert the following measures of capacity.

    a. 350 mL = _____ dL   b. 56 cL = _____ L

    c. 520 L = _____ kL

11. Choose the most realistic measures of the following objects.

    a. The height of a building: 205 cm, 205 m, or 205 km?

    b. The height of a giant redwood tree: 72 cm, 72 m, or 72 km?

    c. The distance between two cities: 512 cm, 512 m, or 512 km?

12. Choose the most realistic measures of the volume of the following objects.

    a. A bucket: 10 mL, 10 L, or 10 kL?

    b. A coffee cup: 2 mL, 20 mL, or 200 mL?

    c. A bath tub: 5 L, 20 L, or 200 L?

13. Choose the most realistic measures of the mass of the following objects.

    a. A tennis ball: 25 mg, 25 g, or 25 kg?

    b. An envelope: 7 mg, 7 g, or 7 kg?

    c. A car: 715 mg, 1715 g, 1715 kg?

14. Choose the best estimate for the following temperatures.

a. A good day to go skiing: $-5°C$, $15°C$, or $35°C$?

b. Treat yourself for a fever: $29°C$, $39°C$, or $99°C$?

15. a. A rectangular prism that measures 24 inches by 18 inches by 9 inches is filled with water. How much does the water weigh? (1 gallon equals 231 cubic inches and weighs 8.3 pounds.)

b. A similar container measuring 64 cm by 48 cm by 12 cm is filled with water. What is the weight of the water in grams?

c. Which of the preceding questions involved less work in finding the answer?

16. Change the following measurements to the given units.

a. 40 kg/m to g/cm

b. 65 kg/L to g/cm^3

c. 72 lb/ft^3 to ton/yd^3

d. 144 ft/sec to mi/hr

17. In performing a dimensional analysis problem, a student does the following:

$$22 \text{ ft} = 22 \text{ ft} \times \frac{1 \text{ ft}}{12 \text{ in.}} = \frac{22}{12} \text{ in.} = 1.83 \text{ in.}$$

a. What has the student done wrong?

b. How would you explain to the student a way of checking that units are correct?

18. The speed of sound is 1100 ft/sec at sea level.

a. Express the speed of sound in mi/hr.

b. Change the speed of sound to mi/year. Let 365 days = 1 year.

PROBLEMS

19. A teacher and her students established the following system of measurements for the Land of Names.

1 jack = 24 jills
1 james = 8 jacks
1 jennifer = 60 jameses
1 jessica = 12 jennifers

Complete the following table

	jill	jack	james	jennifer	jessica
1 jack =	24	1			
1 james =		8	1		
1 jennifer =			60	1	
1 jessica =				12	1

20. The **horsepower** is a nonmetric unit of power used in mechanics. It is equal to 746 watts. How many watts of power does a 350-horsepower engine generate?

21. A midwestern farmer has about 210 acres planted in wheat. Express this cultivated area to the nearest hectare.

22. The speed limit on some U.S. highways is 55 mph. If metric highway speed limit signs are posted, what will they read? Use 1 inch = 2.54 cm, the official link between the English and metric system.

23. Glaciers on coastal Greenland are relatively fast moving and have been observed to flow at a rate of 20 m per day.

a. How long does it take at this rate for a glacier to move 1 kilometer?

b. Use dimensional analysis to express the speed of the glacier in feet/hour to the nearest tenth of a foot.

24. Energy is sold by the **joule,** but in common practice, bills for electrical energy are expressed in terms of a kilowatt-hour (kWh), which is 3,600,000 joules.

a. If a household uses 1744 kWh in a month, how many joules are used?

b. The first 300 kWh are charged at a rate of 4.237 cents per kWh. Energy above 300 kWh is charged at a rate of 5.241 cents per kWh. What is the monthly charge for 1744 kWh?

25. What temperature is numerically the same in degrees Celsius and degrees Fahrenheit?

26. The *Pioneer 10* spacecraft passed the planet Jupiter on December 12, 1973, and exited the solar system on June 14, 1983. The craft traveled from Mars to Jupiter, a distance of approximately 1 billion kilometers, in one year and nine months.

a. Calculate the approximate speed of the craft in kilometers per second.

b. Assuming a constant speed, approximately how many kilometers did *Pioneer 10* travel between the time it passed Jupiter and the time it left the solar system?

27. An astronomical unit used to measure distance is a **parsec,** which is approximately 1.92×10^{13} miles. A parsec is equivalent to how many light-years?

28. A car travels 20 km per hour between two cities. How fast must the car travel on the return trip to average 40 km per hour for the round trip?

29. The production of plastic fiber involves several steps. Each roll measures 400 feet and weighs 100 pounds.

a. The plastic formulation process takes 15 hr per 0.75 ton. Find the ratio of hr/roll.

b. The cold sheeting process produces 120 ft/min. How many hours does each roll take?

c. If the maximum production is 130 tons, how many rolls can be produced?

30. Noah's ark was 300 cubits long, 50 cubits wide, and 30 cubits high. Use a rectangular prism with no top as an approximation to the shape of the ark. What is the surface area of the ark in square meters? What is the capacity of the ark in cubic meters? (A cubit equals 21 inches, and 1 inch = 2.54 cm.)

PROBLEMS FOR WRITING/DISCUSSION

1. Jhoti is looking at the ratio of feet to yards. Since there are 3 feet in 1 yard, she says there must be 3 square feet in 1 square yard. Do you agree? Explain, using a sketch.

2. Monique says she wants to know the length and width of a square plot of land that measures 14 acres in size. If an area is 43,560 ft^2, should she take the square root of 43,560 to find each side of a one acre square, and then multiply by 14? How would you help?

3. Scotty just moved into a new house and the landscaper ordered 1 cubic yard of topsoil for his 15' by 24' garden. If the topsoil is spread evenly, about how thick will it be: a light dusting, about 1", or about 1'? Discuss.

13.2 LENGTH AND AREA

With a partner or in a group, discuss the following questions.

1. What is area?
2. Why are squares used to measure area?
3. What are some other possible units that could be used to measure area?

Write your conclusions for each question.

Length

In Section 13.1 we discussed measurement from a scientific point of view. That is, the measurements we used would be obtained by means of measuring instruments, such as rulers, tape measures, balance scales, thermometers, and so on. In this section we consider measurement from an abstract point of view, in which no physical measuring devices would be required. In fact, none would be accurate enough to suit us! We begin with length and area.

From Chapter 12 we know that every line can be viewed as a copy of the real number line (Figure 13.25). Suppose that P and Q are points on a line such that P corresponds to the real number p, and Q corresponds to the real number q. Recall that the numbers p and q are called coordinates of points P and Q, respectively. The **distance** from P to Q, written PQ, is the real number obtained as the nonnegative difference of p and q.

Reflection from Research
Some students have difficulty using a ruler. They often begin measuring at a point other than zero (such as 1) (Post, 1992).

Figure 13.25

Reflection from Research
Students who make connections between geometric forms and numerical ideas in length problems have more powerful and flexible solution strategies for solving spatial problems. The lack of connection appears to limit growth in number sense, geometric knowledge, and problem-solving ability (Clements, Battista, Sarama, Saminathan, & McMillen, 1997).

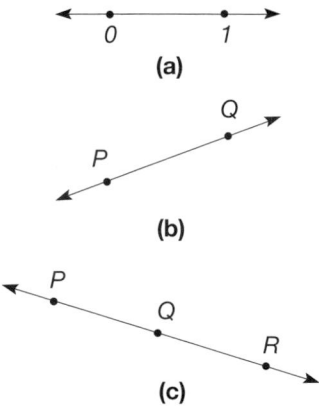

Figure 13.26

Example 13.9   Suppose that P, Q, and R are points on a line such that P corresponds to -4.628, Q corresponds to 18.75, and R corresponds to 27.5941. Find PQ, QR, and PR.

Solution   In this situation, $p = -4.628$, $q = 18.75$, and $r = 27.5941$. Hence

$$PQ = 18.75 - (-4.628) = 23.378,$$
$$QR = 27.5941 - (18.75) = 8.8441,$$
$$PR = 27.5941 - (-4.628) = 32.2221.$$

Note that here, since Q is between P and R, we have $PQ + QR = PR$.   ■

From Example 13.9 and similar examples we can observe several properties of distance.

PROPERTIES

Distance on a Line

1. The distance from 0 to 1 on the number line is 1 and is called the **unit distance** [Figure 13.26(a)].
2. For all points P and Q, $PQ = QP$ [Figure 13.26(b)].
3. If P, Q, and R are points on a line and Q is between P and R, then $PQ + QR = PR$ [Figure 13.26(c)].

Property 1 establishes a unit of distance on a line. All distances are thus expressed in terms of this unit. For instance, in Example 13.9, the distance PQ is 23.378 units. Property 1 follows from our definition of distance, since $1 - 0 = 1$.

Property 2 states that the distance from point P to point Q is equal to the distance from Q to P. Property 2 also follows from our definition of distance, since in calculating PQ and QP we use the *unique* nonnegative difference of p and q.

In property 3, point Q is between P and R if and only if its coordinate q is numerically between p and r, the coordinates P and R, respectively. Property 3 states that distances between *consecutive* points on a line segment can be added to determine the total length of the segment.

To verify property 3, suppose that Q is between P and R, and P, Q, and R have coordinates p, q, and r, respectively. Suppose also that $p < q < r$. Then $PQ = q - p$, $PR = r - p$, and $QR = r - q$. Hence

$$PQ + QR = (q - p) + (r - q)$$
$$= q + (-p) + r + (-q) = r - p = PR.$$

Thus $PQ + QR = PR$. The case that $r < q < p$ is similar.

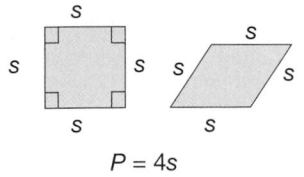

$P = 4s$

Figure 13.27

PERIMETER   The **perimeter** of a polygon is the sum of the lengths of its sides. *Peri* means "around" and *meter* represents "measure"; hence *perimeter* literally means "the measure around." Perimeter formulas can be developed for some common quadrilaterals. A square and a rhombus both have four sides of equal length. If one side is of length s, then the perimeter of each of them can be represented by $4s$ (Figure 13.27).

In rectangles and parallelograms, pairs of opposite sides are congruent. This property will be verified formally in Chapter 14. Thus, if the lengths of their sides are a and b, then the perimeter of a rectangle or a parallelogram is $2a + 2b$. A similar formula can be used to find the perimeter of a kite (Figure 13.28).

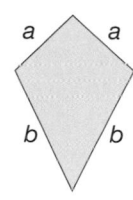

$P = 2a + 2b$

Figure 13.28

Perimeters of Common Quadrilaterals

FIGURE	PERIMETER
Square with sides of length s	$4s$
Rhombus with sides of length s	$4s$
Rectangle with sides of lengths a and b	$2a + 2b$
Parallelogram with sides of lengths a and b	$2a + 2b$
Kite with sides of lengths a and b	$2a + 2b$

Example 13.10 Find the perimeters of the following (Figure 13.29).
a. A triangle whose sides have length 5 cm, 7 cm, and 9 cm
b. A square with sides of length of 8 ft
c. A rectangle with one side of length 9 mm and another side of length 5 mm
d. A rhombus one of whose sides has length 7 in.
e. A parallelogram with sides of length 7.3 cm and 9.4 cm
f. A kite whose shorter sides are $2\frac{2}{3}$ yd and whose longer sides are $6\frac{1}{5}$ yd
g. A trapezoid whose bases have lengths 13.5 ft and 7.9 ft and whose other sides have lengths 4.7 ft and 8.3 ft

Solution

a. $P = 5 \text{ cm} + 7 \text{ cm} + 9 \text{ cm} = 21 \text{ cm}$
b. $P = 4 \times 8 \text{ ft} = 32 \text{ ft}$
c. $P = 2(9 \text{ mm}) + 2(5 \text{ mm}) = 28 \text{ mm}$
d. $P = 4 \times 7 \text{ in.} = 28 \text{ in.}$
e. $P = 2(7.3 \text{ cm}) + 2(9.4 \text{ cm}) = 33.4 \text{ cm}$
f. $P = 2(2\frac{2}{3} \text{ yd}) + 2(6\frac{1}{5} \text{ yd}) = 5\frac{1}{3} \text{ yd} + 12\frac{2}{5} \text{ yd} = 17\frac{11}{15} \text{ yd}$
g. $P = 13.5 \text{ ft} + 7.9 \text{ ft} + 4.7 \text{ ft} + 8.3 \text{ ft} = 34.4 \text{ ft}$

Figure 13.29

CIRCUMFERENCE The "perimeter" of a circle, namely the length of the circle, is given the special name **circumference** (Figure 13.30). In every circle, the ratio of the circumference C to the diameter d, namely C/d, is a constant called π (the Greek letter "**pi**"). We can approximate π by measuring the circumferences and diameters of several cylindrical cans, then averaging the ratios of circumference to diameter. For example, the can shown in Figure 13.31 measures $C = 19.8$ cm and $d = 6.2$ cm. Thus in this case our approximation of π is the ratio $\dfrac{19.8 \text{ cm}}{6.2 \text{ cm}} = 3.2$ (to one decimal

Figure 13.30

6.2

19.8

Figure 13.31

place). Actually, $\pi = 3.14159 \ldots$ and is an irrational number. In every circle, the following relationships hold.

Distances in a Circle

Let r, d, and C be the radius, diameter, and circumference of a circle, respectively. Then $d = 2r$ and $C = \pi d = 2\pi r$.

Area

RECTANGLES To determine the area of a two-dimensional figure, we imagine the interior of the figure completely filled with square regions called **square units** [Figure 13.32(a)]. To find the area of a rectangle whose sides have whole-number lengths, as in Figure 13.32(b), we determine the number of unit squares needed to fill the rectangle. In Figure 13.32(b), the rectangle is composed of $4 \times 3 = 12$ square units. This procedure can be extended to rectangles whose dimensions are decimals, as illustrated next.

Reflection from Research
Both primary and upper-grade students have difficulty distinguishing between area and perimeter (Wilson & Rowland, 1993).

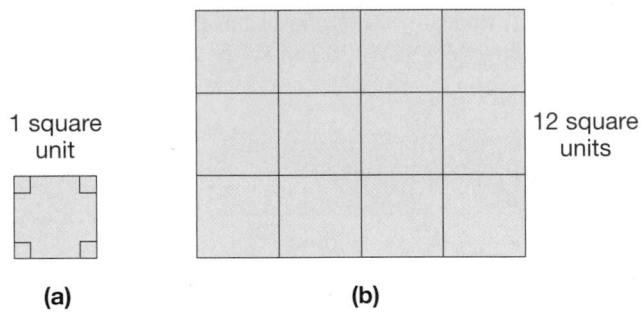

1 square
unit

12 square
units

(a)   (b)

Figure 13.32

Example 13.11 Suppose that a rectangle has length 4.2 units and width 2.5 units. Find the area of the rectangle in square units (Figure 13.33).

Reflection from Research
The construction and coordination of units is a fundamental component of children's construction of area (Reynolds & Wheatley, 1996).

4   0.2

2

0.5

Each large square
has area 1.

Each rectangle
has area 0.1.

Each small square
has area $0.1 \times 0.1 = 0.01$.

Figure 13.33

Solution In Figure 13.33 notice that there are $4 \times 2 = 8$ large squares, plus the equivalent of 2 more large squares made up of 20 horizontal rectangular strips. Also, there are 4 vertical strips plus 10 small squares (i.e., the equivalent of 5 strips altogether). Hence the area is $8 + 2 + 0.5 = 10.5$. Notice that the 8 large squares were found by multiplying 4 times 2. Similarly, the product $4.2 \times 2.5 = 10.5$ is the area of the entire rectangular region. ■

NCTM Standards 2000
Measurement
Grades 3–5
All students should develop, understand, and use formulas to find the area of rectangles and related triangles and parallelograms.

As Example 13.11 suggests, the area of a rectangle is found by multiplying the lengths (real numbers) of two perpendicular sides. Of course, the area would be reported in square units.

NCTM Standards 2000
Measurement
Grades 6–8
All students should develop and use formulas to determine the circumference of circles and the area of triangles, parallelograms, trapezoids, and circles, and develop strategies to find the area of more complex shapes.

Reflection from Research
Seeing the connection between the lengths of the sides and the area of a rectangle may seem natural to adults, but is not obvious to children (Outhred & Mitchelmore, 2000).

 DEFINITION

Area of a Rectangle

The area A of a rectangle with perpendicular sides of lengths a and b is

$$A = ab.$$

The formula for the area of a square is an immediate consequence of the area of a rectangle formula, since every square is a rectangle.

 THEOREM

Area of a Square

The area A of a square whose sides have length s is

$$A = s^2.$$

Probably the reason that we read s^2 as "s squared" is that it gives the area of a square with side length s.

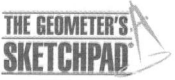
www.wiley.com/college/musser

Spotlight on Technology Now that both perimeters and areas of rectangles have been presented, an interesting question that arises is whether or not the area and perimeter are related. This question can be investigated using the Geometer's Sketchpad® webmodule activity, *Rectangle Area*. Use the activity to determine if all rectangles with a perimeter of 20 centimeters have the same area. If they do not have the same area, what type of rectangle appears to yield the largest area?

TRIANGLES The formula for the area of a triangle also can be determined from the area of a rectangle. Consider first a right triangle $\triangle ABC$ [Figure 13.34(a)]. Construct rectangle $ABDC$ where $\triangle DCB$ is a copy of $\triangle ABC$ [Figure 13.34(b)]. The area of rectangle $ABDC$ is bh, and the area of $\triangle ABC$ is one-half the area of the rectangle. Hence the area of $\triangle ABC = \frac{1}{2} bh$.

(a)

(b)

Figure 13.34

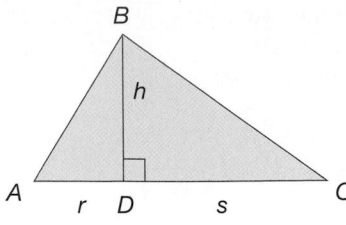

Figure 13.35

More generally, suppose that we have an arbitrary triangle, $\triangle ABC$ (Figure 13.35). In our figure, $\overline{BD} \perp \overline{AC}$. Consider the right triangles $\triangle ADB$ and $\triangle CDB$. The area of $\triangle ADB$ is $\frac{1}{2} rh$, where $r = AD$. Similarly, the area of $\triangle CDB = \frac{1}{2} sh$, where $s = DC$. Hence

$$\begin{aligned}
\text{area of } \triangle ABC &= \frac{1}{2} rh + \frac{1}{2} sh \\
&= \frac{1}{2} (r + s) h \\
&= \frac{1}{2} bh \qquad \text{where } b = r + s, \text{ the length of } \overline{AC}.
\end{aligned}$$

We have verified the following formula.

THEOREM

Area of a Triangle

The area A of a triangle with base of length b and corresponding height h is

$$A = \tfrac{1}{2} bh.$$

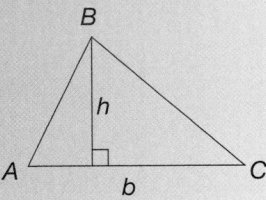

When calculating the area of a triangle, any side may serve as a **base.** The perpendicular distance from the opposite vertex to the line containing the base is the **height** corresponding to this base. Hence each triangle has *three* bases and *three* corresponding heights. In the case of an obtuse triangle, the line segment used to find the height may lie outside the triangle as in $\triangle ABC$ in Figure 13.36.

In this case, the area of $\triangle ABC$ is $\frac{1}{2}h(x + b) - \frac{1}{2}hx = \frac{1}{2}bh$, the same as in the preceding theorem.

Figure 13.36

www.wiley.com/
college/musser

Spotlight on Technology According to the equation for the area of a triangle, two different looking triangles could have the same area as long as the base, b, and height, h, are the same. The two triangles, $\triangle ABC$ and $\triangle ABD$, at the right have the same area because of the base of length 3 and height of length 3. This idea can be tested by constructing triangles on the Chapter 13 eManipulative activity, *Geoboard.* On the eManipulative, construct three or more triangles with a base of 4 and a height of 5. Are the areas the same? What about the perimeters?

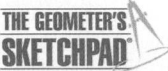

www.wiley.com/
college/musser

Spotlight on Technology Because the area of a triangle is dependant only on the length of the base and length of the height, two very differently shaped triangles will have the same area as long as the base and height of the two triangles are the same. This property is demonstrated in the Geometer's Sketchpad® webmodule activity, *Same Base, Same Height, Same Area.* Use the activity to find an example of an acute, obtuse, and right triangle that all have the same area. How do the areas and perimeters appear to be related?

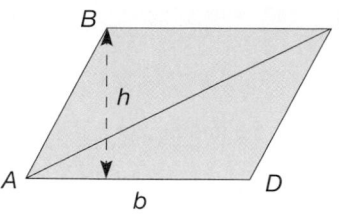

Figure 13.37

PARALLELOGRAMS We can determine the area of a parallelogram by drawing in a diagonal to form two triangles with the same height (Figure 13.37). Notice that in $\triangle ACD$, if we use AD as a base, then h, the distance between lines $\overleftrightarrow{AD}$ and $\overleftrightarrow{BC}$, is the **height** corresponding to $\overline{AD}$. Similarly, in $\triangle ABC$, if we use BC as a base, then h is also the corresponding height. Observe also that $BC = AD = b$, since opposite sides of the parallelogram $ABCD$ have the same length. Hence

$$\text{area of } ABCD = \text{area of } \triangle ABC + \text{area of } \triangle ACD$$
$$= \frac{1}{2}bh + \frac{1}{2}bh$$
$$= bh.$$

THEOREM

Area of a Parallelogram

The area A of a parallelogram with base b and height h is

$$A = bh.$$

Spotlight on Technology A common question that arises when studying the area of rectangles and parallelograms is whether two parallelograms with the same perimeter would also have the same area. This question can be investigated in the Geometer's Sketchpad® webmodule activity, *Parallelogram Areas*. Use this activity to discuss the question, "Does a larger perimeter always yield a larger area?"

www.wiley.com/college/musser

TRAPEZOIDS The area of a trapezoid can also be derived from the area of a triangle. Suppose that we have a trapezoid $PQRS$ whose bases have lengths a and b and whose **height** is h, the distance between the parallel bases (Figure 13.38).

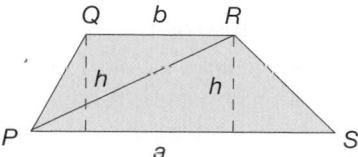

Figure 13.38

The diagonal $\overline{PR}$ divides the trapezoid into two triangles with the same height, h, since $QR \parallel PS$. Hence the area of the trapezoid is the sum of the areas of the two triangles, or $\frac{1}{2}ah + \frac{1}{2}bh = \frac{1}{2}(a + b)h$.

> ### THEOREM
>
> #### Area of a Trapezoid
>
> The area A of a trapezoid with parallel sides of lengths a and b and height h is
>
> $$A = \frac{1}{2}(a + b)\,h.$$
>
>

CIRCLES Our final area formula will be for a circle. Imagine a circle of radius r inscribed in a regular polygon. Figure 13.39 shows an example using a regular octagon with O the center of the inscribed circle.

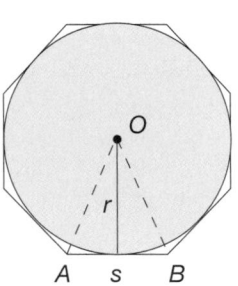

Figure 13.39

Let s be the length of each side of the regular octagon. Then the area of $\triangle ABO$ is $\frac{1}{2}sr$. Since there are eight such triangles within the octagon, the area of the entire octagon is $8(\frac{1}{2}\,sr.) = \frac{1}{2}r \times 8s$. Notice that $8s$ is the perimeter of the octagon. In fact, the area of every circumscribed regular polygon is $\frac{1}{2}r \times P$, where P is the perimeter of the polygon. As the number of sides in the circumscribed regular polygon increases, the closer P is to the circumference of the circle, C, and the closer the polygon's area is to that of the circle. Thus we expect the area of the circle to be $\frac{1}{2}r \times C = \frac{1}{2}r \times (2\pi r) = \pi r^2$. This is, indeed, the area of a circle with radius r.

> ### THEOREM
>
> #### Area of a Circle
>
> The area A of a circle with radius r is
>
> $$A = \pi r^2.$$
>
>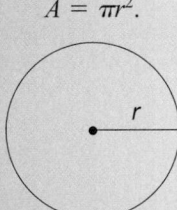

A rigorous verification of this formula cannot be done without calculus-level mathematics. However, areas of irregular two-dimensional regions can be approximated by covering the region with a grid.

The Pythagorean Theorem

The Pythagorean theorem, perhaps the most spectacular result in geometry, relates the lengths of the sides in a right triangle; the longest side is called the **hypotenuse** and the other two sides are called **legs**. Figure 13.40 shows a special instance of the Pythagorean theorem in an arrangement involving isosceles right triangles. Notice that the area of the large square, c^2, is equal to the area of four of the shaded triangles, which, in turn, is equal to the sum of the areas of the two smaller squares, $a^2 + b^2$. Therefore, $a^2 + b^2 = c^2$. In the particular case shown, $a = b$. This result generalizes to all right triangles. In words, it says "the area of the square on the hypotenuse is equal to the sum of the areas of the squares on the two sides."

Figure 13.40

THEOREM

The Pythagorean Theorem

In a right triangle, if the legs have lengths a and b and the hypotenuse has length c, then

$$a^2 + b^2 = c^2.$$

To prove the Pythagorean theorem, we construct a square figure consisting of four right triangles surrounding a smaller square [Figure 13.41(a)]. First, the sequence of

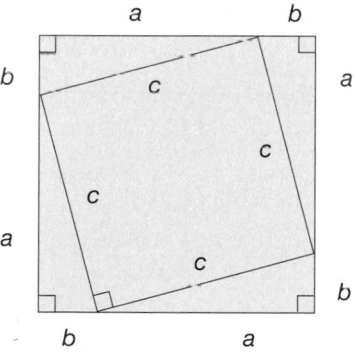

Figure 13.41(a)

pictures in Figure 13.41(b) shows a visual "proof." Since the amount of space occupied by the four triangles is constant, the areas of the square region(s) must be. Thus $c^2 = a^2 + b^2$.

Problem-Solving Strategy
Use a Model

Figure 13.41(b)

Spotlight on Technology Sometimes a visual proof, such as this geometric proof of the Pythagorean theorem, is clearer if you can actually move the physical objects yourself. Such geometric manipulation is possible on the Chapter 13 eManipulative activity, *Phythagorean Theorem*. How many different ways are there to arrange the squares and triangles?

www.wiley.com/
college/musser

Spotlight on Technology A geometric demonstration of the Pythagorean theorem can be more powerfully made when the actual regions dynamically move from a^2 and b^2 to fill c^2. Such a demonstration can be seen in the Geometer's Sketchpad® web-module activity, *Dynamic Pythagorean Theorem*. After using this activity, discuss how the proof illustrated in Figure 13.41(b) is similar to and yet different from the demonstration in *Dynamic Pythagorean Theorem*.

www.wiley.com/
college/musser

Next we give an algebraic justification. Observe that the legs of the four right triangles combine to form a large square. The area of the large square is $(a + b)^2$ by the area of a square formula. On the other hand, the area of each triangle is $\frac{1}{2}ab$ and the area of the smaller square (verify that is a square) is c^2. Thus the area of the large square is also $4(\frac{1}{2}ab) + c^2 = 2ab + c^2$. Thus $(a + b)^2 = 2ab + c^2$. But

Problem-Solving Strategy
Use a Variable

$$\begin{aligned}
(a + b)^2 &= (a + b)(a + b) \\
&= (a + b) \cdot a + (a + b) \cdot b \\
&= a^2 + ba + ab + b^2 \\
&= a^2 + ab + ab + b^2 \\
&= a^2 + 2ab + b^2.
\end{aligned}$$

Combining these results, we find that

$$a^2 + 2ab + b^2 = 2ab + c^2, \qquad \text{so that}$$
$$a^2 + b^2 = c^2.$$

This proves the Pythagorean theorem. The Pythagorean theorem enables us to find lengths in the plane. Example 13.12 illustrates this.

Example 13.12 Suppose that we have points in the plane arranged in a square lattice. Find the length of $\overline{PQ}$ (Figure 13.42).

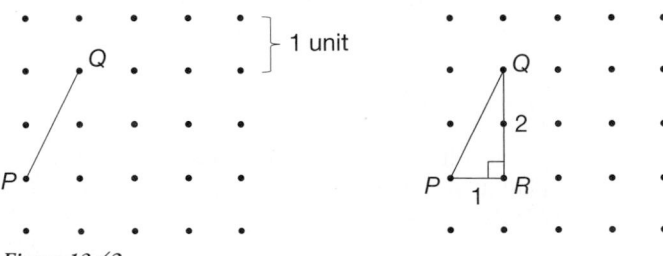

Figure 13.42

Solution Draw the right traingle $\triangle PRQ$ with right angle $\angle R$. Then $PR = 1$ and $QR = 2$. We use the Pythagorean theorem to find PQ, namely, $PQ^2 = 1^2 + 2^2 = 5$, or $PQ = \sqrt{5}$. ■

Example 13.13 shows how the Pythagorean theorem can be used to construct a line segment whose length is the square root of a whole number.

Example 13.13 Construct a length of $\sqrt{13}$ in the plane.

Solution Observe that $13 = 2^2 + 3^2$. Thus, in a right triangle whose legs have lengths 2 and 3, the hypotenuse will have length $\sqrt{13}$, by the Pythagorean theorem (Figure 13.43). Hence the construction of such a right triangle will yield a segment of length $\sqrt{13}$. ■

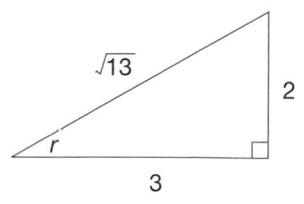

Figure 13.43

A final observation that we can make about distance in the plane is called the triangle inequality.

THEOREM

Triangle Inequality

If P, Q, and R are points in the plane, then $PQ + QR \geq PR$.

www.wiley.com/
college/musser

Spotlight on Technology This theorem can be investigated further by using the Geometer's Sketchpad® webmodule activity, *Triangle Inequality*. Use this activity to answer the question, "When is the equation $PQ + QR = PR$ true?"

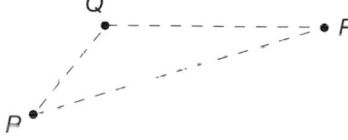

Figure 13.44

The triangle inequality states that the distance from P to Q plus the distance from Q to R is always greater than or equal to the distance from P to R (see Figure 13.44). That is, the sum of the lengths of two sides of a triangle is always greater than the length of the third side. (We will have $PQ + QR = PR$ if and only if P, Q, and R are collinear with Q between P and R.)

MATHEMATICAL MORSEL

The United States remains an island in a metric world. At present, the only nonmetric country in the world other than the United States is Burma. Actually, our units of measure are defined in terms of the metric units. For example, in 1959 1 inch was defined to be exactly 2.54 centimeters. Even though many industries in the United States, including the automobile and pharmaceutical industries, already use metric tools and measures, the change to everyday use of the metric system has been very gradual. In 1988, President Reagan signed a bill that required all government agencies to be metric by 1992. However, as can easily be seen, we are not a completely metric country yet.

Section 13.2 EXERCISE / PROBLEM SET A

EXERCISES

1. Points P, Q, R, and S are located on line l, as illustrated next.

The corresponding real numbers are $p = -3.78$, $q = -1.35$, $r = 0.56$, and $s = 2.87$. Find each of the following lengths.

  a. PR **b.** RQ **c.** PS **d.** QS

2. Let points P and Q be points on a line l with corresponding real numbers p and q, respectively.

  a. If $p < q$, find the distance between points P and Q.

  b. If $p < q$, then find $\frac{1}{2}PQ$.

  c. Add the value in part (b) to p and simplify. This gives the real number corresponding to the midpoint of segment $\overline{PQ}$.

  d. Repeat parts (a) to (c) if $q < p$, except add the value in part (b) to q. Do you get the same result?

  e. Use the formula you found in part (c) to find the real number corresponding to the midpoint if $p = -2.5$ and $q = 13.9$.

3. Find the real number corresponding to the midpoints of the segments whose endpoints correspond to the following real numbers.

  a. $p = 3.7$, $q = 15.9$

  b. $p = -0.3$, $q = 6.2$

4. Let points P and Q be points on a line with corresponding real numbers p and q, respectively.

  a. Let $p < q$ and find the distance between points P and Q.

  b. Find $m = p + \frac{1}{3}PQ$ and simplify your result.

  c. Find $n = p + \frac{2}{3}PQ$ and simplify.

  d. Use your results from parts (b) and (c) to find the real numbers corresponding to the points that divide $\overline{PQ}$ into three segments of the same length if $p = -3.6$ and $q = 15.9$.

5. Given below is the real number corresponding to the midpoint M of segment PQ. Also given is the real number corresponding to one of the endpoints. Find the real number corresponding to the other endpoint.

  a. $m = 12.1$, $p = 6.5$ **b.** $m = -2.5$, $q = 3.5$

6. Find the area of each figure illustrated on a square lattice. Use the unit square shown as the fundamental unit of area.

  a.

  b.

  c.

  d. Verify your results from parts (a), (b), and (c) by using the Chapter 13 eManipulative activity, *Geoboard*. Which region has the largest area? By how much?

7. Any figure that tessellates a plane could be used as a unit measuring area. For example, here you are given a triangular, a hexagonal, and a parallelogram

unit of area. Using each of the given units, find the area of the large figure.

a. **b.** **c.**

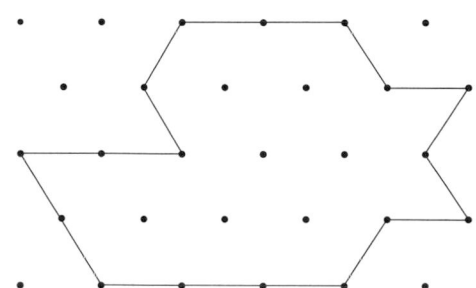

8. Information is given about the illustrated rectangle. Find the information indicated. P = perimeter, A = area.

a. $P = 45.6$, $b = 15.2$. Find a and A.

b. $P = 37.6$, $a = 6.8$. Find b and A.

c. $a = 14.1$, $A = 501.96$. Find b and P.

9. After measuring the room she wants to carpet (illustrated here), Sally proceeds to compute how much carpet is needed as shown in the following calculation.

$$
\begin{array}{lll}
10 \text{ ft} \times 8 \text{ ft} & = 80 & \text{ft}^2 \\
9 \text{ in.} \times 6 \text{ in.} = 54 \text{ in.}^2 & = \underline{0.375} & \text{ft}^2 \\
& \overline{80.375 \text{ ft}^2}
\end{array}
$$

If Sally buys 81 square feet of carpet, will she have enough? If not, what part of the room will not be carpeted?

10. Find the perimeter and area of each parallelogram

a.   **b.**

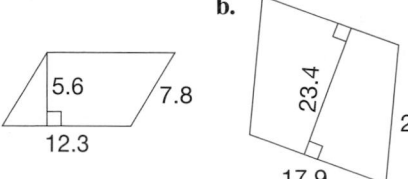

11. Find the perimeter and area of each triangle.

a.   **b.**

 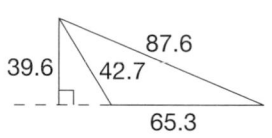

12. Find the circumference and area of each circle.

a.   **b.**

 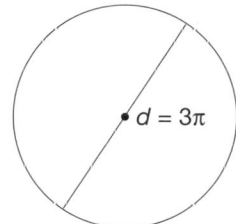

13. Hero's formula can be used to find the area of a triangle if the lengths of the three sides are known. According to this formula, the area of a triangle is $\sqrt{s(s - a)(s - b)(s - c)}$, where a, b, and c are the lengths of the three sides and $s = (a + b + c)/2$. Use Hero's formula to find the area of the triangle whose sides are given (round to one decimal place).

a. 5 cm, 12 cm, 13 cm   **b.** 4 m, 5 m, 6 m

14. A trapezoid is sometimes defined as a quadrilateral with at *least* one pair of parallel sides. This definition allows parallelograms to be considered trapezoids. A parallelogram is shown.

a. Using the area of a parallelogram formula, find the area of the given parallelogram.

b. Using the area of a trapezoid formula, find the area of the given parallelogram.

c. Do both formulas yield the same results?

15. Following are two rhombuses that have the same perimeter. Using the fact that diagonals of a rhombus are perpendicular and bisect each other, find the area of each rhombus.

a. **b.**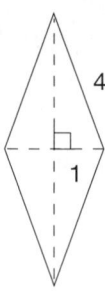

16. a. Triangle *ABC* is shown here on a square lattice. What is its area?

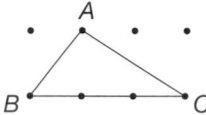

b. Each dimension of the triangle is doubled in the second triangle shown. What is the area of △*DEF*?

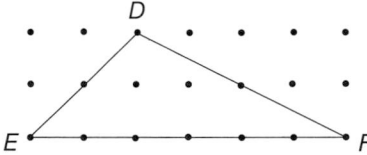

c. The ratio of the lengths of the sides of △*ABC* to the lengths of sides of △*DEF* is 1:2. What is the ratio of their areas?

17. Apply the Pythagorean theorem to find the following lengths represented on a square lattice.

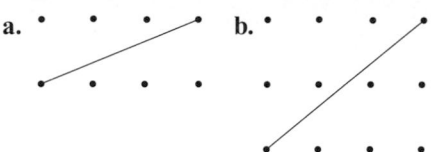

18. Find the length of the side not given.

PROBLEMS

19. A ladder is leaning against a building. If the ladder reaches 20 feet high on the building and the base of the ladder is 15 feet from the bottom of the building, how long is the ladder?

20. A small pasture is to be fenced off with 96 meters of new fencing along an existing fence, using the existing fence as one side of a rectangular enclosure. What whole-number dimensions yield the largest area that can be enclosed by the new fencing?

21. George is building a large model airplane in his workshop. If the door to his workshop is 3 feet wide and $6\frac{1}{2}$ feet high and the airplane has a wingspan of 7.1 feet, will George be able to get his airplane out of the workshop?

22. The proof of the Pythagorean theorem that was presented in this section depended on a figure containing squares and right triangles. Another famous proof of the Pythagorean theorem also uses squares and right triangles. It is attributed to a Hindu mathematician, Bhaskara (1114–1185), and it is said that he simply wrote the word *Behold* above the figure, believing that the proof was evident from the drawing. Use algebra and the areas of the right triangles and squares in the figure to verify the the Pythagorean theorem.

Behold!

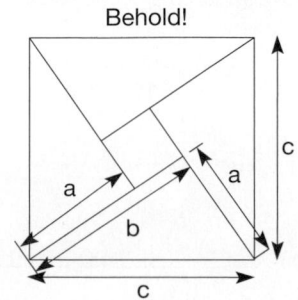

23. Shown is a rectangular prism with length l, width w, and height h.

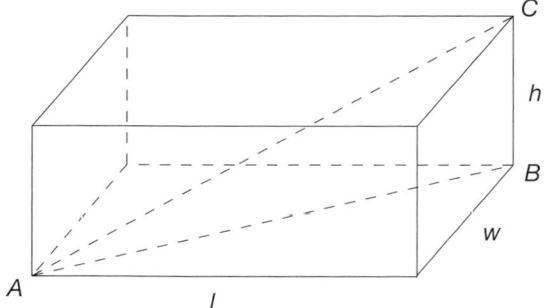

a. Find the length of the diagonal from A to B.

b. Using the result of part (a), find the length of the diagonal from A to C.

c. Use the result of part (b) to find the length of the longest diagonal of a rectangular box 40 cm by 60 cm by 20 cm.

24. Jason has an old trunk that is 16 inches wide, 30 inches long, and 12 inches high. Which of the following objects would he be able to store in his trunk?

a. A telescope measuring 40 inches

b. A baseball bat measuring 34 inches

c. A tennis racket measuring 32 inches

25. The following result, known as **Pick's theorem,** gives a method of finding the area of a polygon on a square lattice, such as on square dot paper or a geoboard. Let b be the number of lattice points on the polygon (i.e., on the "boundary"), and let i be the number of lattice points inside the polygon. Then the area of the polygon is $(b/2 + i - 1)$ square units. For example, for the following polygon $b = 12$ and $i = 8$. Hence the area of the polygon is $\frac{12}{2} + 8 - 1 = 13$ square units.

a. Verify, without using Pick's theorem, that the area of the following polygon is 13 square units.

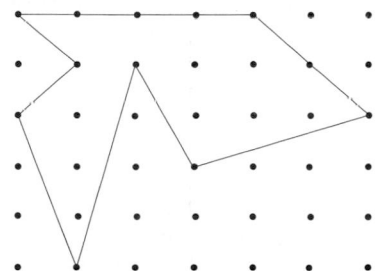

b. Find the area of each of the following polygons using Pick's theorem.

i.

ii.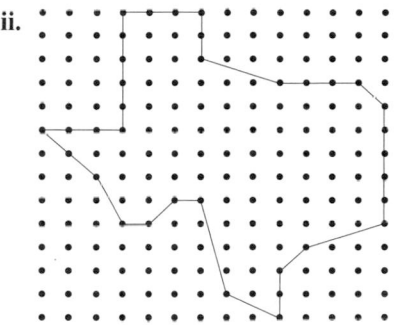

26. A rectangle whose length is 3 cm more than its width has an area of 40 square centimeters. Find the length and width.

27. Use the Chapter 13 eManipulative activity, *Geoboard*, to determine whether or not an equilateral triangle can be constructed on the portion of a square lattice shown here. Show why or why not.

28. Given are the lengths of the sides of a triangle. Indicate whether the triangle is a right triangle. If it is not a right triangle, indicate whether it is an acute triangle or an obtuse triangle.

a. 70, 54, 90   **b.** 63, 16, 65

c. 24, 48, 52   **d.** 27, 36, 45

e. 48, 46, 50   **f.** 9, 40, 46

29. Find the area of the quadrilateral given. Give the answer to one decimal place. (*Hint:* Apply Hero's formula from Exercise 13.)

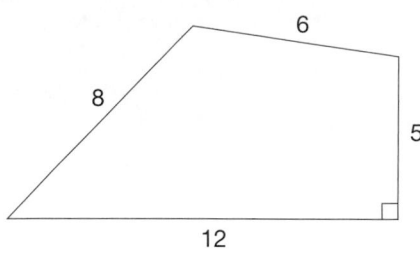

30. The Greek mathematician Eratosthenes, who lived about 255 B.C., was the first person known to have calculated the circumference of the Earth. At Syene, it was possible to see the sun's reflection in a deep well on a certain day of the year. At the same time on the same day, the sun cast a shadow of 7.5° in Alexandria, some 500 miles to the north.

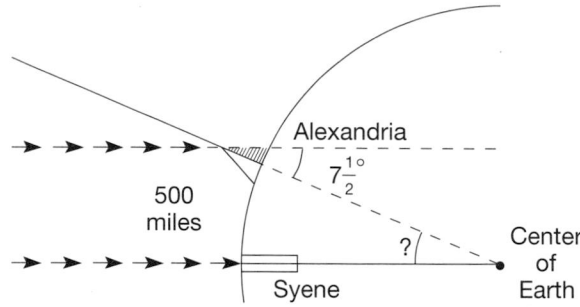

a. What is the measure of the indicated angle at the center of the Earth? By what property?

b. Using this angle, find the circumference of the Earth.

c. With today's precision instruments, the Earth's equatorial circumference has been calculated at 24,901.55 miles. How close was Eratosthenes in miles?

31. Square plugs are often used to check the diameter of a hole. What must the length of the side of the square be to test a hole with diameter 3.16 cm? Round *down* to the nearest 0.01 cm.

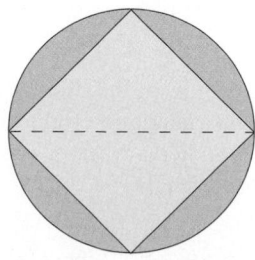

32. Segment $\overline{AB}$, which is 1 unit long, is tangent to the inner circle at A and touches the outer circle at B. What is the area of the region between the two circles? (*Hint:* The radius of the inner circle that has endpoint A is also perpendicular to $\overline{AB}$.)

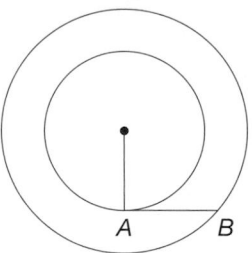

33. Find the area of the shaded region where the petals are formed by constructing semicircles. For each semicircle, the center is the midpoint of a side.

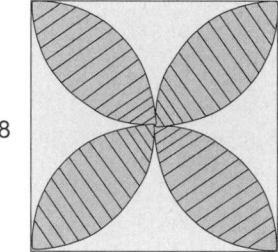

34. A farmer has a square field that measures 100 m on a side. He has a choice of using one large circular irrigation system or four smaller ones, as illustrated.

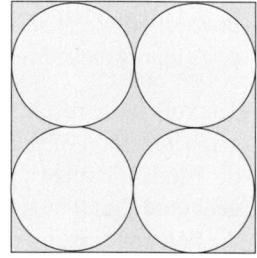

a. What percent of the field will the larger system irrigate?

b. What percent of the field will the smaller system irrigate?

c. Which system will irrigate more land?

d. What generalization does your solution suggest?

35. The following figure shows five concentric circles. If the width of each of the rings formed is the same, how do the areas of the two shaded regions compare?

36. If the price per square centimeter is the same, which is the better buy—a circular pie with a 10-centimeter diameter or a square pie 9 centimeters on each side?

37. Which, if either, of the following two triangles has the larger area?

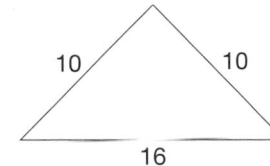

38. Suppose that every week the average American eats one-fourth of a pizza. The average pizza has a diameter of 14 inches and costs $8. There are about 250,000,000 Americans, and there are 640 acres in a square mile.

a. About how many acres of pizza do Americans eat every week?

b. What is the cost per acre of pizza in America?

Section 13.2   EXERCISE / PROBLEM SET B

EXERCISES

1. Given are points on line l and their corresponding real numbers. Find the distances specified.

$$A = -\frac{9}{2} \quad B = \sqrt{3} \quad C = \frac{1}{4} \quad D = 2\sqrt{3} \quad E = 2\pi$$

a. AB **b.** DB

c. AD (to two decimal places)

d. CE (to two decimal places)

2. Let points P and Q be points on a line l with corresponding real numbers $p = -6$ and $q = 12$.

a. Find the distance between points P and Q.

b. Find $\frac{1}{2}PQ$.

c. Add the value in part (b) to p. This gives the real number corresponding to the midpoint, M, of segment PQ. What is that real number?

d. Verify that this point is the midpoint M, by finding PM and QM.

3. Find the real number corresponding to the midpoints of the segments whose endpoints correspond to the following real numbers.

a. $p = -16.3, q = -5.5$

b. $p = 2.3, q = -7.1$

4. Let points P and Q be points on a line l with corresponding real numbers $p = 3$ and $q = 27$.

a. Find the distance between points P and Q.

b. Let M be the point with real number $m = p + \frac{1}{3}PQ$ and N be the point corresponding to $n = p + \frac{2}{3}PQ$. Find m and n.

c. Points M and N divide segment $\overline{PQ}$ into how many equal pieces?

d. Explain how you could divide $\overline{PQ}$ into four segments of equal length.

5. Given is the real number corresponding to the midpoint M of segment PQ. Also given is the real number corresponding to one of the endpoints.

Find the real number corresponding to the other endpoint.

a. $m = -5.8, p = -1.4$

b. $m = -13.2, q = -37.5$

6. For parts (a), (b), and (c), find the area of the figure illustrated on the square lattice. Use the unit square shown as the fundamental unit of area.

a.

b.

c.

 d. Verify your results from parts (a), (b), and (c) by using the Chapter 13 eManipulative activity, *Geoboard*. Which region has the largest area? by how much?

7. Using the triangular unit shown as the fundamental area unit, find the area of the following figures.

a.

b.

c.

8. Find the perimeter and area of each rectangle.

a.

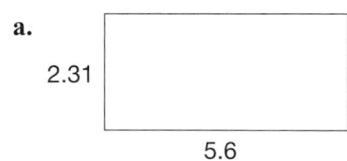

2.31

5.6

b.

37.9

37.9

9. How many pieces of square floor tile, 1 foot on a side, would you have to buy to tile a floor that is 11 feet 6 inches by 8 feet?

10. Shown are two pairs of parallelograms. In each case, the pairs are drawn with sides of the same length.

i.

ii.

a. For each pair of parallelograms shown, use the Chapter 13 eManipulative activity, *Geoboard*, to determine the lengths of the sides and the area of the parallelograms.

b. Based on what you found in part (a), how would you respond to the statement "The area of a parallelogram is the product of the lengths of its sides"?

11. a. Find the area of an equilateral triangle whose sides have a length of 6 units.

b. If an equilateral triangle has sides of length a, apply Hero's formula to derive a formula for the area of an equilateral triangle.

12. Information is given about a circle in the following table. Fill in the missing entries of the table. r = radius, d = diameter, C = circumference, A = area. Use a calculator and give answers to two decimal places.

	r	d	C	A
a.				231.04π
b.		26.8		
c.	$\sqrt{15}$			
d.		18π		

13. Use Hero's formula to find the area of the triangle whose sides are given (round to one decimal place).

  a. 4 km, 5 km, 8 km   **b.** 8 m, 15 m, 17 m

14. A trapezoid is pictured here.

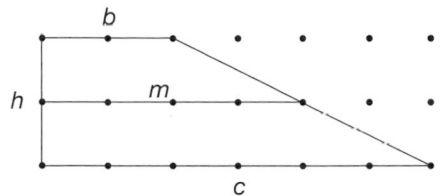

  a. Part of the area formula for a trapezoid is $\frac{1}{2}(b+c)$, the average of the two parallel sides. Find $\frac{1}{2}(b+c)$ for this trapezoid.

  b. The segment pictured with length m is called the **midsegment** of the trapezoid because it connects midpoints of the nonparallel sides. Find m.

  c. How do the results of parts (a) and (b) compare?

15. Find the area of each rhombus.

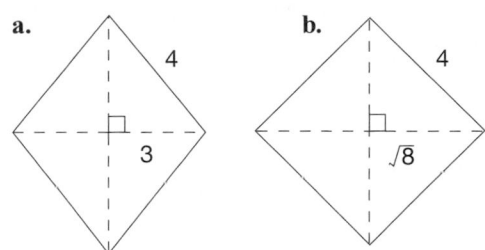

16. a. A trapezoid is illustrated on a square lattice. What is its area?

  b. If all dimensions of the trapezoid are tripled, what is the area of the resulting trapezoid?

  c. If the ratio of lengths of sides of two trapezoids is 1 : 3, what is the ratio of the areas of the trapezoids?

17. Represent the following lengths on a square lattice.

  a. $\sqrt{5}$ **b.** $\sqrt{17}$ **c.** $\sqrt{18}$ **d.** $\sqrt{29}$

18. Find the length of the side not given.

  a.   **b.**

PROBLEMS

19. a. In building roofs, it is common for each 12 feet of horizontal distance to rise 5 feet in vertical distance. Why might this be more common than a roof that rises 6 feet for each 12 feet? (Consider distance measured along the roof.)

  b. Find the area of the roof on the pictured building.

  c. How many sheets of 4 feet × 3 feet plywood would be needed to cover the roof?

  d. Into what dimensions would you cut the plywood?

20. There is an empty lot on a corner that is 80 m long and 30 m wide. When coming home from school, Gail cuts across the lot diagonally. How much distance (to the nearest meter) does she save?

21. A room is 8 meters long, 5 meters wide, and 3 meters high. Find the following lengths.

  a. Diagonal of the floor

  b. Diagonal of a side wall

  c. Diagonal of an end wall

  d. Diagonal from one corner of the floor to the opposite corner of the ceiling.

22. Consecutive terms in a Fibonacci sequence can be used to generate Pythagorean triples, whole numbers that could represent the lengths of the three sides in a right triangle. The process works as follows:

1. Chose any four consecutive terms of any Fibonacci sequence.
2. Let a be the product of the first and last of these four terms.
3. Let b be twice the product of the middle two terms.
4. Then a and b are the legs of a right triangle. To find the length of the hypotenuse, use $c = \sqrt{a^2 + b^2}$.

Use the Fibonacci sequence 1, 1, 2, 3, 5, 8, 13, 21, . . . to answer the following questions.

a. Using the terms 2, 3, 5, and 8, find values of a, b, and c.

b. Using the terms 5, 8, 13, and 21, find values of a, b, and c.

c. Using the terms starting with 13, find values of a, b, and c.

d. Write out more terms of the sequence. Is c one of the terms in this sequence in each of parts (a), (b), and (c)? Verify that a, b, and c in parts (a), (b), and (c) satisfy $a^2 + b^2 = c^2$.

23. A regular hexagon can be divided into six equilateral triangles.

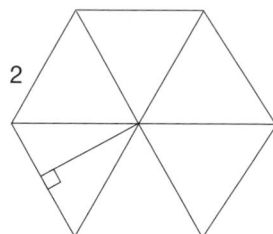

a. The altitude of an equilateral triangle bisects the base. If each side has length 2, find the length of the altitude.

b. What is the area of one triangle?

c. What is the area of the regular hexagon?

24. An artist is drawing a scale model of the design plan for a new park. If she is using a scale of 1 inch = 12 feet, and the area of the park is 36,000 square feet, what area of the paper will the scale model cover?

25. There are only two rectangles whose sides are whole numbers and whose area and perimeter are the same numbers. What are they?

26. A baseball diamond is a square 90 feet on a side. To pick off a player stealing second base, how far must the catcher throw the ball?

27. A man has a garden 10 meters square to fence. How many fence posts are needed if each post is 1 meter from the adjacent posts?

28. Given are lengths of three segments. Will these segments form a triangle? If so, is it a right, an acute, or an obtuse triangle?

a. 48, 14, 56
b. 54, 12, 37
c. 21, 22, 23
d. 15, 8, 16
e. 61, 11, 60
f. 84, 13, 100

29. The diagram here was used by President James Garfield to prove the Pythagorean theorem.

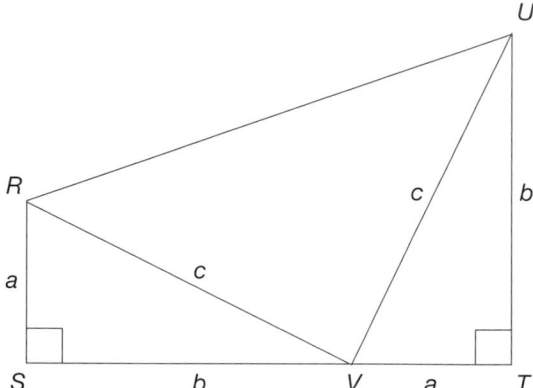

a. Explain why quadrilateral $RSTU$ is a trapezoid.

b. What is the area of $RSTU$?

c. Show that $\triangle RVU$ is a right triangle.

d. Find the areas of the three triangles.

e. Prove the Pythagorean theorem using parts (a)–(d).

30 a. Imagine the largest square plug that fits into a circular hole. How well does the plug fit? That is, what percentage of the circular hole does the square plug occupy?

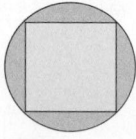

b. Now imagine the largest circular plug that fits into a square hole. How well does this plug fit? That is, what percentage of the square hole does the circular plug occupy?

c. Which of the two plugs described in parts (a) and (b) fits the hole better?

31. Find *x*.

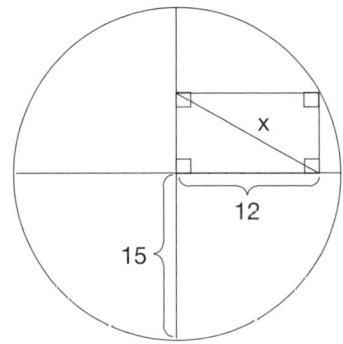

32. A spider and a fly are in a room that has length 8 m, width 4 m, and height 4 m. The spider is on one end wall 1 cm from the floor midway from the two side walls. The fly is caught in the spider's web on the other end wall 1 cm from the ceiling and also midway from the two side walls. What is the shortest distance the spider can walk to enjoy his meal? (*Hint*: Draw a two-dimensional picture.)

33. a. Trace the square, cut along the solid lines, and rearrange the four pieces into a rectangle (that is not a square). Find the areas of the square and the rectangle. Is your result surprising?

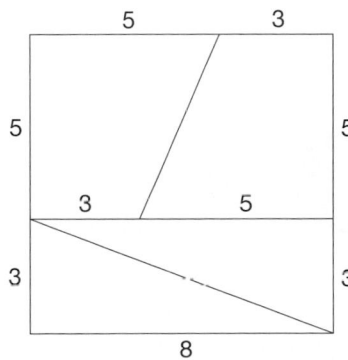

b. Change the dimensions 3, 5, 8 in the square in part (a) to 5, 8, 13, respectively. Now what is the area of the square? the rectangle? In connection with part (a), are these results even more surprising? Try again with 8, 13, 21, and so on.

34. Find the area of the shaded region.

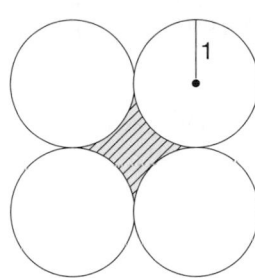

35. A **hexafoil** is inscribed in a circle of radius 1. Find its area. (The petals are formed by swinging a compass of radius 1 with the center at the endpoints of the petals.)

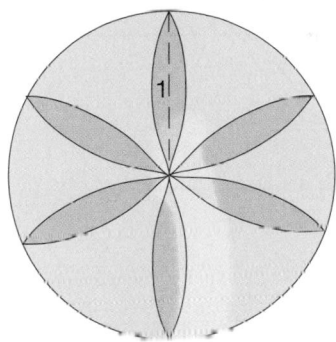

36. The circles in the figure have radii 6, 4, 4, and 2. Which is larger—the shaded area inside the big circle or the shaded area outside the big circle?

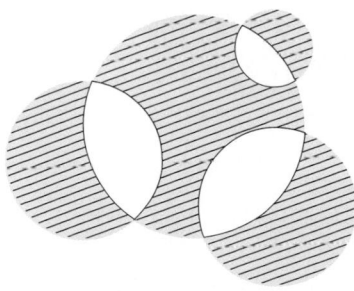

37. There are about 5 billion people on Earth. Suppose that they all lined up and held hands, each person taking about 2 yards of space.

a. How long a line would the people form?

b. The circumference of the Earth is about 25,000 miles at the equator. How many times would the line of people wrap around the Earth?

38. a. In the dart board shown, the radius of circle
A is 1, of circle B is 2, and of circle C is 3.
Hitting A is worth 20 points; region B,
10 points; and region C, 5 points. Is this
a fair dart board? Discuss.

b. What point structure would make it a fair board if
region A is worth 30 points?

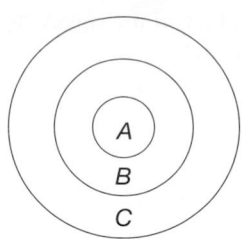

PROBLEMS FOR WRITING/DISCUSSION

1. Larry says the area of a parallelogram can be found
by multiplying length times width. So the area of the
parallelogram below must be $20 \times 16 = 320$ in².
Do you agree? If not, what could you do to give
Larry an intuitive feeling about its area? Is it
possible to find the exact area in this case?
Discuss.

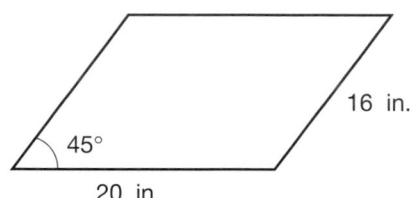

45°

16 in.

20 in.

2. Dana says that the area of a square becomes larger as
the perimeter of a square increase, so that must be true
for a rectangle as well. Do you agree with Dana?
If not, show some figures that explore this idea.
Explain.

3. Billie wants a way to remember the difference between
the formulas for circumference and area in a circle.
He says, "In the formula $2\pi r$ there is just one r because circumference is one-dimensional, and in the
formula πr^2 there are two r's because area is two-
dimensional." Is Billie onto something? Does this
work with any other figures?

13.3   SURFACE AREA

STARTING POINT

At Bobbi's Baby Bargains, they make and sell baby blocks in sets of 24 blocks.
Bobbi has asked you to design a box to package these blocks that will require the
least amount of cardboard. What is your recommendation? Provide a justification
as to why your design is the most efficient.

Problem-Solving Strategy
Use a Model

The **surface area** of a three-dimensional figure is, literally, the total area of its exterior surfaces. For three-dimensional figures having bases, the **lateral surface area** is
the surface area minus the areas of the bases. For polyhedra such as prisms and pyramids, the surface area is the sum of the areas of the polygonal faces.

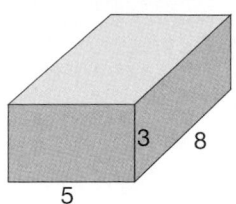

Figure 13.45

Prisms

Example 13.14 shows how to find the surface area of a right rectangular prism.

Example 13.14   Find the surface area of a box in the shape of a right prism whose bases are rectangles with side lengths 5 and 8, and whose height is 3 (Figure 13.45).

Solution We can "disassemble" this box into six rectangles (Figure 13.46). If we consider the 5 × 8 faces to be the bases, the lateral surface area of this box is

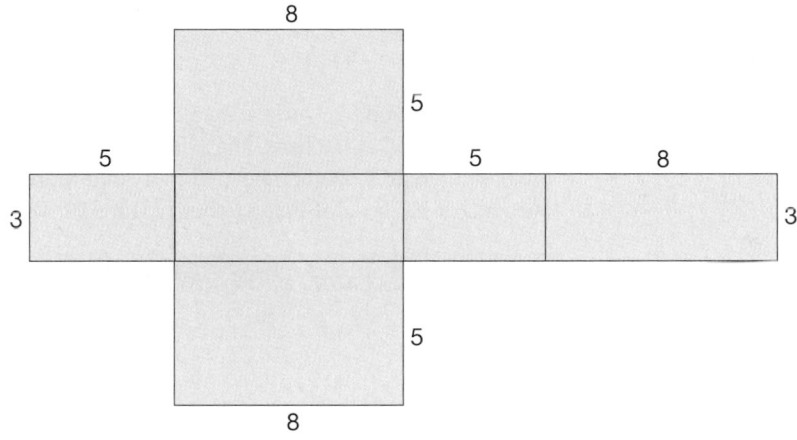

Figure 13.46

$2[(3 \times 5) + (3 \times 8)] = 78$ square units. Since each base has area $5 \times 8 = 40$ square units, the surface area is $78 + 80 = 158$ square units.   ■

Observe that the lateral surface area in Example 13.14 also can be viewed as $3 \times (5 + 8 + 5 + 8)$, or 3 times the perimeter of the base. In general, let h be the height of a prism, P the perimeter of its base, and A the area of each base. Then, according to Example 13.14, the surface area of the prism is $2A + Ph$.

⬤ THEOREM

Surface Area of a Right Prism

The surface area S of a right prism with height h whose bases each have area A and perimeter P is

$$S = 2A + Ph.$$

Cylinders

The surface area of a right circular cylinder can be approximated using a sequence of right regular prisms with increasingly many faces (Figure 13.47).

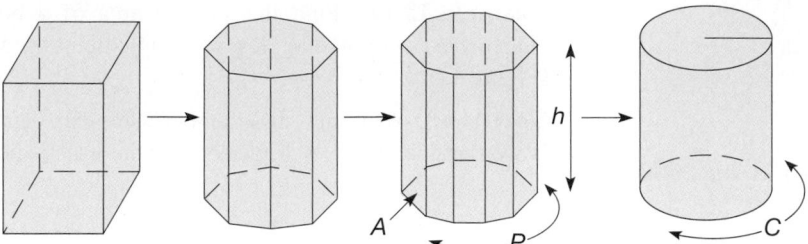

Figure 13.47

For each prism, the surface area is $2A + Ph$, where A and P are the area and perimeter, respectively, of the base, and h is the height of the prism. As the number of sides of the base increases, the perimeter P more and more closely approximates the circumference, C, of the base of the cylinder (Figure 13.47). Thus we have the following result.

 THEOREM

Surface Area of a Right Circular Cylinder

The surface area S of a right circular cylinder whose base has area A, radius r, and circumference C, and whose height is h is

$$S = 2A + Ch$$
$$= 2(\pi r^2) + (2\pi r)h = 2\pi r(r + h).$$

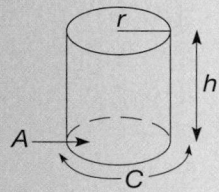

NCTM Standards 2000
Measurement
Grades 6–8
All students should use two-dimensional representations of three-dimensional objects to visualize and solve problems such as those involving surface area and volume.

We can verify the formula for the surface area of a right circular cylinder by "slicing" the cylinder open and "unrolling" it to form a rectangle plus the two circular bases (Figure 13.48). The area of each circular base is πr^2. The area of the rectangle is $2\pi rh$, since the length of the rectangle is the circumference of the cylinder. Thus the total surface area is $2\pi r^2 + 2\pi rh$.

Figure 13.48

NOTE: Rather than attempt to memorize this formula, it is easier to imagine the cylinder sliced open to form a rectangle and two circles and then use area formulas for rectangles and circles, as we have just done.

Pyramids

The surface area of a pyramid is obtained by summing the areas of the triangular faces and the base. Example 13.15 illustrates this for a square pyramid.

Example 13.15 Find the surface area of a right square pyramid whose base measures 20 units on each side and whose faces are isosceles triangles with edges of length 26 units [Figure 13.49(a)].

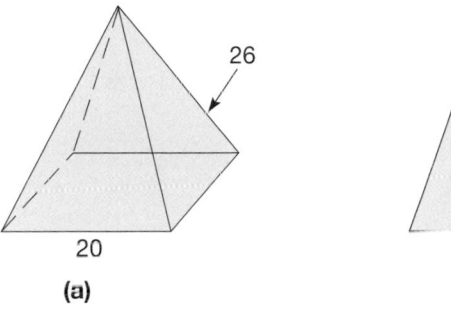

(a)   (b)

Figure 13.49

Solution The area of the square base is $20^2 = 400$ square units. Each face is an isosceles triangle whose height, l, we must determine [Figure 13.49(b)]. By the Pythagorean theorem, $l^2 + 10^2 = 26^2 = 676$, so $l^2 = 576$. Hence $l = \sqrt{576} = 24$. Thus the area of each face is $\frac{1}{2} (20 \cdot 24) = 240$ square units. Finally, the surface area of the prism is the area of the base plus the areas of the triangular faces, or $400 + 4(240) = 1360$ square units. ■

The height, l, as in Figure 13.49(b), of each triangular face of a right regular pyramid is called the **slant height** of the pyramid. In general, the surface area of a right regular pyramid is determined by the slant height and the base. Recall that a right regular pyramid has a regular n-gon as its base.

The sum of the areas of the triangular faces of a right regular pyramid is $\frac{1}{2}Pl$. This follows from the fact that each face has height l and base of length P/n, where n is the number of sides in the base. So each face has area $\frac{1}{2}(P/n)l$. Since there are n of these faces, the sum of the areas is $n[\frac{1}{2}(P/n)l] = \frac{1}{2}Pl$. Thus we have the following result.

THEOREM

Surface Area of a Right Regular Pyramid

The surface area S of a right regular pyramid whose base has area A and perimeter P, and whose slant height is l is

$$S = A + \tfrac{1}{2}Pl.$$

Cones

The surface area of a right circular cone can be obtained by considering a sequence of right regular pyramids with increasing numbers of sides in the bases (Figure 13.50).

Figure 13.50

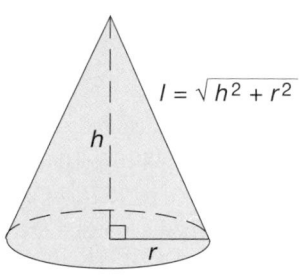

Figure 13.51

The surface area of each right pyramid is $A + \frac{1}{2}Pl$, where A is the area of the base of the pyramid, P is the perimeter of the base, and l is the slant height. As the number of sides in the bases of the pyramids increases, the perimeters of the bases approach the circumference of the base of the cone (Figure 13.50). For the right circular cone, the **slant height** is the distance from the apex of the cone to the base of the cone measured along the surface of the cone (Figure 13.51). If the height of the cone is h and the radius of the base is r, then the slant height, l, is $\sqrt{h^2 + r^2}$. The lateral surface area of the cone is one-half the product of the circumference of the base ($2\pi r$) and the slant height. This is analogous to the sum of the areas of the triangular faces of the pyramids. Combining the area of the base and the lateral surface area, we obtain the formula for the surface area of a right circular cone.

> ### ◆ THEOREM
>
> #### Surface Area of a Right Circular Cone
>
> The surface area S of a right circular cone whose base has area A and circumference C, and whose slant height is l is
>
> $$S = A + \frac{1}{2}Cl.$$
>
> If the radius of the base is r and the height of the cone is h, then
>
> $$S = \pi r^2 + \frac{1}{2}(2\pi r)l = \pi r^2 + \pi r \sqrt{h^2 + r^2}.$$
>
>

The lateral surface area of a cone is the surface area minus the area of the base. Thus the formula for the lateral surface area of a cone is $\pi r \sqrt{h^2 + r^2}$.

Spheres

Archimedes made a fascinating observation regarding the surface area and volume of a sphere. Namely, the surface area (volume) of a sphere is two-thirds the surface area (volume) of the smallest cylinder containing the sphere. (Archimedes was so proud of this observation that he had it inscribed on his tombstone.) The formula for the surface area of a sphere is derived next and the formula for the volume will be derived in the next section.

Figure 13.52 shows a sphere of radius r contained in a cylinder whose base has radius r and whose height is $2r$. The surface area of the cylinder is $2\pi r^2 + 2\pi r(2r) = 6\pi r^2$. Thus, from Archimedes' observation, the formula for the surface area of a sphere of radius r is $\frac{2}{3}(6\pi r^2) = 4\pi r^2$.

Figure 13.52

THEOREM

Surface Area of a Sphere

The surface area S of a sphere of radius r is

$$S = 4\pi r^2.$$

A **great circle** of a sphere is a circle on the sphere whose radius is equal to the radius of the sphere. It is interesting that the surface area of a sphere, $4\pi r^2$, is exactly *four* times the area of a great circle of the sphere, πr^2. A great circle is the intersection of the sphere with a plane through the center of the sphere (Figure 13.53).

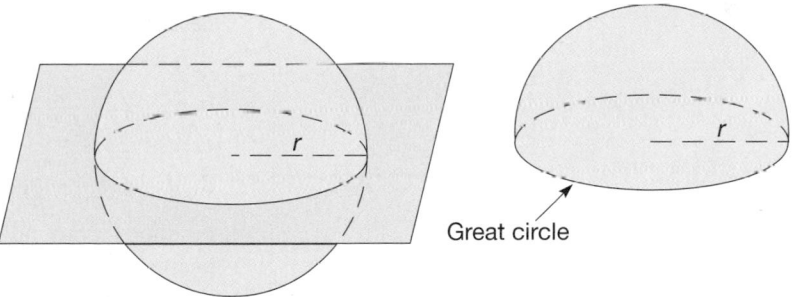

Great circle

Figure 13.53

If the Earth were a perfect sphere, the equator and the circles formed by the meridians would be great circles. There are infinitely many great circles of a sphere (Figure 13.54).

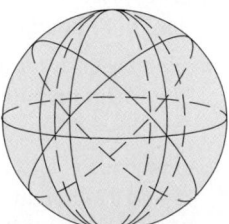

Figure 13.54

MATHEMATICAL MORSEL

Rubik's cube was one of the most popular toys in the 1980s. It was developed by a Hungarian design professor, Erno Rubic, to help his students better understand three-dimensional solids. Each face of the cube is made up of nine squares. The nine squares on each of the six faces are the same color *in their initial position,* six colors in all. The cube can be twisted in such a way as to move the smaller square faces around to other faces. In fact, with as few as four twists of an original cube, the faces can be so completely scrambled that most people cannot rearrange the cube back to where the faces all the same color. This should not be surprising, since there are over 43 quintillion (!) different arrangements of the cube.

Let's see... That's eight .. or was that my ninth move?

 Section 13.3 EXERCISE / PROBLEM SET A

EXERCISES

1. Find the surface area of the following prisms and cylinders.

a.

(rectangular prism: 10, 15, 10)

b.

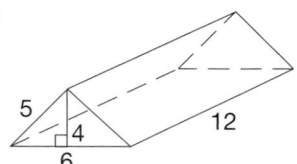

(triangular prism: 5, 4, 6, 12)

c.

(cylinder: 10, 10)

d.

(cylinder: 17.9, 3.1)

2. Find the surface area of the following square pyramids and cones.

a.

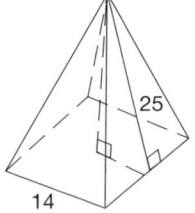

(pyramid: 13, 10, 10)

b.

(pyramid: 25, 14)

c.

(cone: 5, 13)

d.

(cone: 2, 1.5)

3. Find the surface area of the following spheres (to the nearest whole square unit).

  a. $r = 6$

  b. $r = 2.3$

  c. $d = 24$

  d. $d = 6.7$

4. Find the surface area of the following cans to the nearest square centimeter.

  a. Coffee can $r = 7.6$ cm, $h = 16.3$ cm

  b. Soup can $r = 3.3$ cm, $h = 10$ cm

5. Find the surface area of each right prism with the given features.

  a. The bases are equilateral triangles with sides of length 8; height = 10.

  b. The bases are trapezoids with bases of lengths 7 and 9 perpendicular to one side of length 6; height = 12.

  c. The base is a right triangle with legs of length 5 and 12; height = 20.

6. Refer to the following figure.

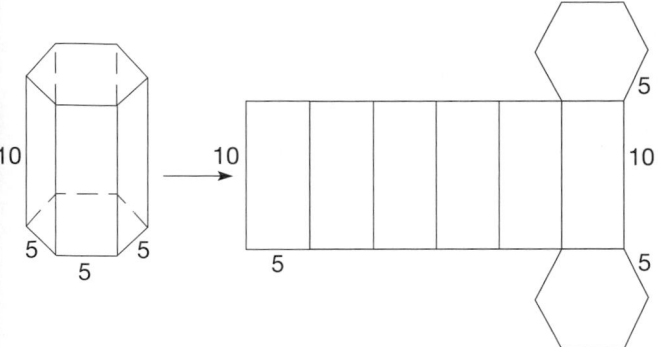

a. Find the area of each hexagonal base.
b. Find the total surface area of the prism.

7. Find the surface area.

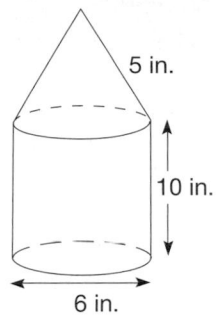

8. Which has the larger surface area—a right circular cone with diameter of base 1 and height $\frac{1}{2}$ or a right circular cylinder with diameter of base 1 and height 1?

PROBLEMS

9. A room measures 4 meters by 7 meters and the ceiling is 3 meters high. A liter of paint covers 20 square meters. How many liters of paint will it take to paint all but the floor of the room?

10. A scale model of a new engineering building is being built for display. A scale of 5 cm = 3 m is being used. It took 27,900 square centimeters of cardboard to construct the exposed surfaces of the model. What will be the area of the exposed surfaces of the building in square meters?

11. Suppose that you have 36 unit cubes like the one shown. Those cubes could be arranged to form right rectangular prisms of various sizes.

a. Sketch an arrangement of the cubes in the shape of a right rectangular prism that has a surface area of exactly 96 square units.

b. Sketch an arrangement of the cubes in the shape of a right rectangular prism that has a surface area of exactly 80 square units.

c. What arrangement of the cubes gives a right rectangular prism with the smallest possible surface area? What is this minimum surface area?

d. What arrangement of the cubes gives a right rectangular prism with the largest possible surface area? What is this maximum surface area?

12. A new jumbo-sized cereal box is to be produced. Each dimension of the regular-sized box will be doubled. How will the amount of cardboard required to make the new box compare to the amount of cardboard required to make the old box?

13. a. Assuming that the Earth is a sphere with an equatorial diameter of 12,760 kilometers, what is the radius of the earth?

b. What is the surface area of the Earth?

c. If the land area is 135,781,867 square kilometers, what percent of the Earth's surface is land?

14. Suppose that the radius of a sphere is reduced by half. What happens to the surface area of the sphere?

15. A square 6 centimeters on a side is rolled up to form the lateral surface of a right circular cylinder. What is the surface area of the cylinder, including the top and the bottom?

16. Given a sphere with diameter 10, find the surface area of the smallest cylinder containing the sphere.

Section 13.3 EXERCISE / PROBLEM SET B

EXERCISES

1. Find the surface area of each prism and cylinder.

   a.

   b.

   c. **d.**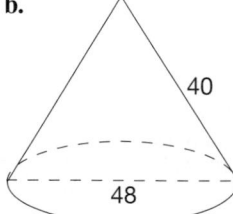

2. Find the surface area of each cone and rectangular pyramid (to the nearest whole square unit).

   a. **b.**

   c. **d.**

3. **a.** Find the surface area of a sphere with radius 3 cm in terms of π.

   b. Find the surface area of a sphere with diameter 24.7 cm.

   c. Find the diameter, to the nearest centimeter, of a sphere with surface area 215.8 cm².

4. Find the surface area of the following cans to the nearest square centimeter.

   a. Juice can $r = 5.3$ cm, $h = 17.7$ cm

   b. Shortening can $r = 6.5$ cm, $h = 14.7$ cm

5. Find the surface area of each right pyramid with the given features.

   a. The base is a regular hexagon with sides of length 12; height = 14.

   b. The base is a 10-by-18 rectangle; height = 12.

6. A right prism has a base in the shape of a regular hexagon with a 12-cm side and height to a side of $6\sqrt{3}$ cm as shown. If the sides of the prism are all squares, determine the total surface area of the prism.

   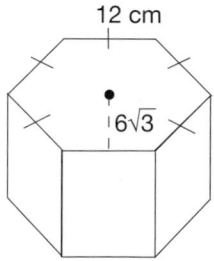

7. Find the surface area. Round your answers to the nearest square inch.

8. Which has the larger surface area—a cube with edge length 1 or a sphere with diameter 1?

PROBLEMS

9. The top of a rectangular box has an area of 96 square inches. Its side has area 72 square inches, and its end has area 48 square inches. What are the dimensions of the box?

10. A right circular cylinder has a surface area of 112π. If the height of the cylinder is 10, find the diameter of the base.

11. Thirty unit cubes are stacked in square layers to form a tower. The bottom layer measures 4 cubes × 4 cubes, the next layer 3 cubes × 3 cubes, the next layer 2 cubes × 2 cubes, and the top layer a single cube.

  a. Determine the total surface area of the tower of cubes.

  b. Suppose that the number of cubes and the height of the tower were increased so that the bottom layer of cubes measured 8 cubes × 8 cubes. What would be the total surface area of this tower?

  c. What would be the total surface area of the tower if the bottom layer measured 20 cubes × 20 cubes?

12. a. If the ratio of the sides of two squares is $2:5$, what is the ratio of their areas?

  b. If the ratio of the edges of two cubes is $2:5$, what is the ratio of their surface areas?

  c. If all the dimensions of a rectangular box are doubled, what happens to its surface area?

13. A tank for storing natural gas is in the shape of a right circular cylinder. The tank is approximately 380 feet high and 250 feet in diameter. The sides and top of the cylinder must be coated with a special primer. How many square feet of surface must be painted?

14. A paper cup has the shape shown in the following drawing (called a **frustum** of a right circular cone).

If the cup is sliced open and flattened, the sides of the cup have the shape shown next.

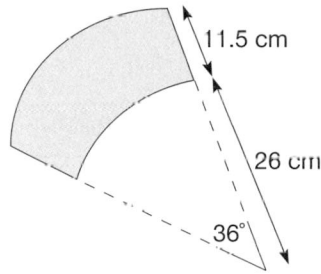

Use the dimensions given to calculate the number of square meters of paper used in the construction of 10,000 of these cups.

15. Let a sphere with surface area 64π be given.

  a. Find the surface area of the smallest cube containing the sphere.

  b. Find the surface area of the largest cube contained in the sphere.

16. A barber pole consists of a cylinder of radius 10 cm on which one red, one white, and one blue helix, each of equal width, are painted. The cylinder is 1 meter high. If each stripe makes a constant angle of 60° with the vertical axis of the cylinder, how much surface area is covered by the red stripe?

PROBLEMS FOR WRITING/DISCUSSION

1. In making a (two-dimensional) net of a cylinder, Jalen was confused. He thought that since the bases were circles, the part that is the side of a cylinder must be round at the end. How could that part turn out to be a rectangle? How would you help Jalen visualize what the net should be?

2. Ella wants to draw her own map of the world and then paste it onto a globe. She asks you if you know how to cover the globe with paper. How would you go about it?

3. Mark wants to make a tall skinny cone and a short fat cone (without their bases). He wants to know if he can make both of them from two circular pieces of paper having the same size or if one piece would have to be larger than the other. Can he? Defend your answer by using paper models.

13.4 VOLUME

STARTING POINT The box has a volume of 12 cubic feet. If all three dimensions were doubled, how much would that affect the volume of the new box? Would the volume be doubled, tripled, ...?

A college student who was 4 ft, 6 in. tall and weighed 80 pounds wanted to play professional basketball. He read about some magic pills that would double his height to a dominant 9 ft tall. If his proportions were similar, what would he expect to weigh at his new height? How agile do you think that he would be?

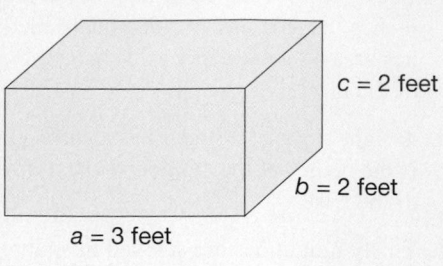

$c = 2$ feet
$b = 2$ feet
$a = 3$ feet

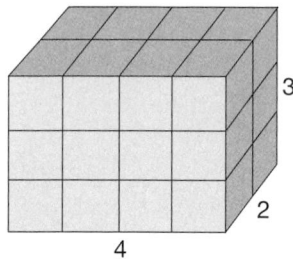

Figure 13.55

Reflection from Research

When considering volumes of three-dimensional objects made of cubes, students tend only to count those cubes that form the outer shell of the solid and ignore the inside cubes (Wilson & Rowland, 1993).

0   1

Figure 13.56

Reflection from Research

Learning how to visualize how many cubes are contained in a rectangular box can be complex for students. "Having students make predictions (of box contents) on the basis of pictures of boxes and (box) patterns, along with changing presentation formats" may be critical in helping students see these objects more abstractly (Battista, 1999).

The **volume** of a three-dimensional figure is a measure of the amount of space that it occupies.

Prisms

To determine the volume of a three-dimensional figure, we imagine the figure filled with unit cubes. A rectangular prism whose sides measure 2, 3, and 4 units, respectively, can be filled with $2 \cdot 3 \cdot 4 = 24$ unit cubes (Figure 13.55). The volume of a cube that is 1 unit on each edge is 1 **cubic unit.** Hence the volume of the rectangular prism in Figure 13.55 is 24 cubic units.

As with units of area, we can subdivide 1 cubic unit into smaller cubes to determine volumes of rectangular prisms with dimensions that are terminating decimals. For example, we can subdivide our unit of length into 10 parts and make a tiny cube whose sides are $\frac{1}{10}$ of a unit on each side (Figure 13.56). It would take $10 \cdot 10 \cdot 10 = 1000$ of these tiny cubes to fill our unit cube. Hence the volume of our tiny cube is 0.001 cubic unit. This subdivision procedure can be used to motivate the following volume formula, which holds for any right rectangular prism whose sides have real number lengths.

● DEFINITION

Volume of a Right Rectangular Prism

The volume V of a right rectangular prism whose dimensions are positive real numbers a, b, and c is

$$V = abc.$$

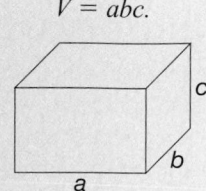

c
b
a

From the formula for the volume of a right rectangular prism, we can immediately determine the volume of a cube, since every cube is a special right rectangular prism with all edges the same length. Volume is reported in cubic units.

THEOREM

Volume of a Cube

The volume V of a cube whose edges have length s is

$$V = s^3.$$

A useful interpretation of the volume of a right rectangular prism formula is that the volume is the product of the area of a base and the corresponding height. For example, the area of one base is $a \cdot b$ and the corresponding height is c. We could choose any face to serve as a base and measure the height perpendicularly from that base. Imagine a right prism as a deck of very thin cards that is transformed into an oblique prism (Figure 13.57). It is reasonable to assume that the oblique prism has

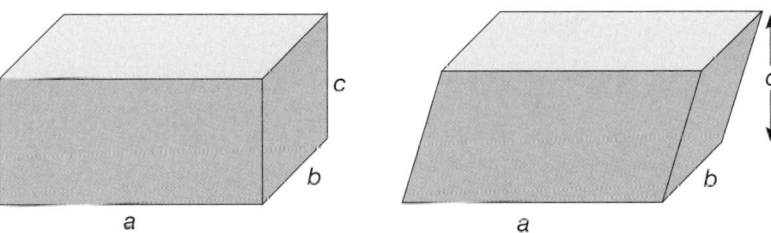

Figure 13.57

the same volume as the original prism (thinking again of a deck of cards). Thus we can obtain the volume of the oblique prism by calculating the product of the area of a base and its corresponding height. The height is c, the distance between the planes containing its bases. This general result holds for all prisms.

THEOREM

Volume of a Prism

The volume V of a prism whose base has area A and whose height is h is

$$V = Ah.$$

4.1 Filling a Cylinder

The *volume* of a container is the number of unit cubes it will hold. In the last investigation, you saw that you could find the volume of a prism-shaped box by figuring out how many unit cubes will fit in a single layer at the bottom of the box and then multiplying by the total number of layers needed to fill the box. In this problem, you will develop a method for determining how many cubes will fit inside a cylinder.

Problem 4.1

Make a cylinder by taping together the ends of a sheet of paper. Use the same size paper you used to make the prism shapes in Problem 3.3.

A. Set the cylinder on its base on a sheet of centimeter grid paper. Trace the cylinder's base. Look at the centimeter squares inside your tracing. How many cubes would fit in one layer at the bottom of the cylinder? Consider whole cubes and parts of cubes.

B. How many layers of cubes would it take to fill the cylinder?

Trace the base.   How many cubes would fit in one layer?   How many layers would it take to fill the cylinder?

C. What is the volume of the cylinder?

■ Problem 4.1 Follow-Up

1. How can you use the dimensions of the cylinder to help you estimate its volume more accurately? Explain.

2. How does the volume of the cylinder compare to the volumes of the prisms you made in Problem 3.3?

Example 13.16 gives an application of the volume of a prism formula.

Example 13.16   Find the volume of a right triangular prism whose height is 4 and whose base is a right triangle with legs of lengths 5 and 12 (Figure 13.58).

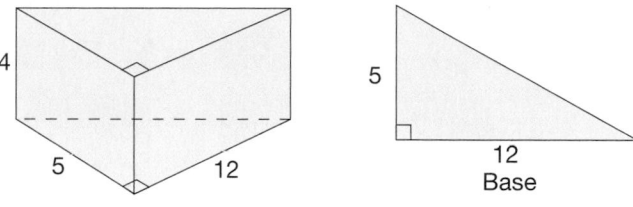

Figure 13.58

Solution   The base is a right triangle whose area is $(5 \times 12)/2 = 30$ square units. Hence $A = 30$ and $h = 4$, so the volume of the prism is $30 \times 4 = 120$ cubic units.   ■

Cylinders

The volume of a cylinder can be approximated using prisms with increasing numbers of sides in their bases (Figure 13.59) The volume of each prism is the product of the area of its base and its height. Hence we would expect the same to be true about a cylinder. This suggests the following volume formula (which can be proved using calculus).

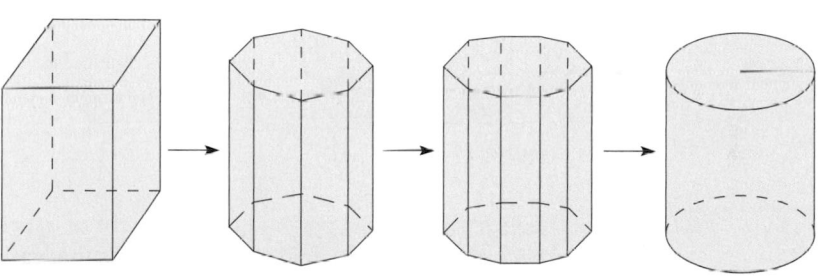

Figure 13.59

THEOREM

Volume of a Cylinder

The volume V of a cylinder whose base has area A and whose height is h is

$$V = Ah.$$

If the base of the cylinder is a circle of radius r, then $V = \pi r^2 h$.

Note that the volume of an arbitrary cylinder, such as those in Figure 13.60, is simply the product of the area of its base and its height.

Figure 13.60

Pyramids

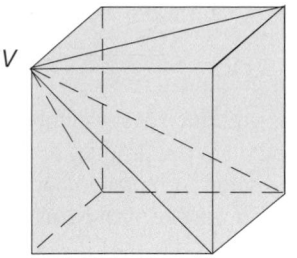

Figure 13.61

To determine the volume of a square pyramid, we start with a cube and consider the four diagonals from a particular vertex to the other vertices (Figure 13.61). Taking the diagonals three at a time, we can identify three pyramids inside the cube (Figure 13.62). The pyramids are identical in size and shape and intersect only in faces or

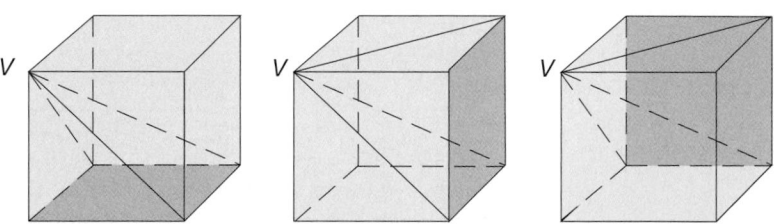

Figure 13.62

edges, so that each pyramid fills one-third of the cube. (Three copies of the pattern in Figure 13.63 can be folded into pyramids that can be arranged to form a cube). Thus the volume of each pyramid is one-third of the volume of the cube. This result holds in general for pyramids with any base.

Figure 13.63

THEOREM

Volume of a Pyramid

The volume V of a pyramid whose base has area A and whose height is h is

$$V = \frac{1}{3} Ah.$$

Cones

We can determine the volume of a cone in a similar manner by considering a sequence of pyramids with increasing numbers of sides in the bases (Figure 13.64). Since the volume of each pyramid is one-third of the volume of the smallest prism containing it, we would expect the volume of a cone to be one-third of the volume of the smallest cylinder containing it. This is, in fact, the case. That is, the volume of a cone is one-third of the product of the area of its base and its height. This property holds for right and oblique cones.

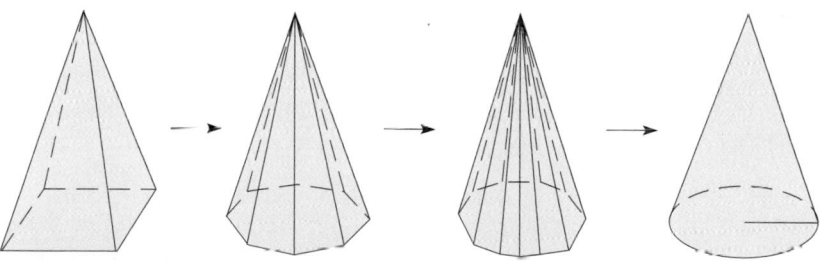

Figure 13.64

THEOREM

Volume of a Cone

The volume V of a cone whose base has area A and whose height is h is

$$V = \frac{1}{3} Ah.$$

For a cone with a circular base of radius r, the volume of the cone is $\frac{1}{3}\pi r^2 h$.

Figure 13.65

Spheres

In Section 13.3 it was stated that Archimedes observed that the volume of a sphere is two-thirds the volume of the smallest cylinder containing the sphere. Figure 13.65 shows this situation. The volume of the cylinder is

$$V = (\pi r^2)2r = 2\pi r^3.$$

Hence the volume of the sphere is $\frac{2}{3}(2\pi r^3)$, or $\frac{4}{3}\pi r^3$. Thus we have derived a formula for the volume of a sphere.

THEOREM

Volume of a Sphere

The volume V of a sphere with radius r is $V = \dfrac{4}{3}\pi r^3$.

As an aid to recall and distinguish between the formulas for the surface area and volume of a sphere, observe that the r in $4\pi r^2$ is *squared*, an area unit, whereas the r in $\frac{4}{3}\pi r^3$ is *cubed*, a volume unit.

Table 13.11 summarizes the volume and surface area formulas for right prisms, right circular cylinders, right regular pyramids, right circular cones, and spheres. The indicated dimensions are the area of the base, A; the height, h; the perimeter or circumference of the base, P or C; and the slant height, l. By observing similarities, one can minimize the amount of memorization.

TABLE 13.11

GEOMETRIC SHAPE	SURFACE AREA	VOLUME
Right prism	$S = 2A + Ph$	$V = Ah$
Right circular cylinder	$S = 2A + Ch$	$V = Ah$
Right regular pyramid	$S = A + \frac{1}{2}Pl$	$V = \frac{1}{3}Ah$
Right circular cone	$S = A + \frac{1}{2}Cl$	$V = \frac{1}{3}Ah$
Sphere	$S = 4\pi r^2$	$V = \frac{4}{3}\pi r^3$

Cavalieri's Principle

The remainder of this section presents a more formal derivation of the volume and surface area of a sphere. First, to find the volume of a sphere, we use Cavalieri's principle, which compares solids were cross-sections have equal areas.

Cavalieri's Principle

Suppose that two three-dimensional solids are contained between two parallel planes such that every plane parallel to the two given planes cuts cross-sections of the solids with equal areas. Then the volumes of the solids are equal.

Figure 13.66 shows an illustration of Cavalieri's principle applied to cylinders. Notice that a plane cuts each cylinder, forming circular cross-sections of area πr^2. Hence, by Cavalieri's principle, the cylinders have equal volume.

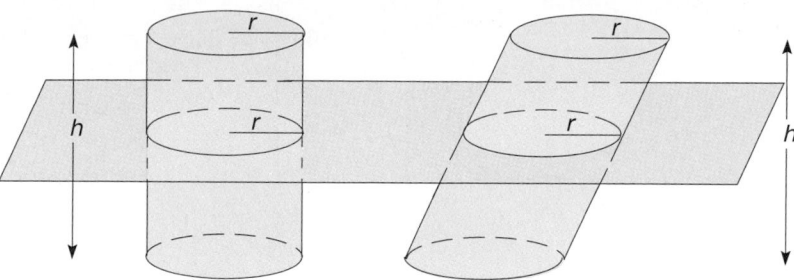

Figure 13.66

We can also apply Cavelieri's principle to the prisms in Figure 13.57. Cavalieri's principle explains why the volume of a prism or cylinder depends only on the base and height.

To determine the volume of a sphere, consider the solid shape obtained by starting with a cylinder of radius r and height $2r$, and removing two cones. We will call the resulting shape S (Figure 13.67).

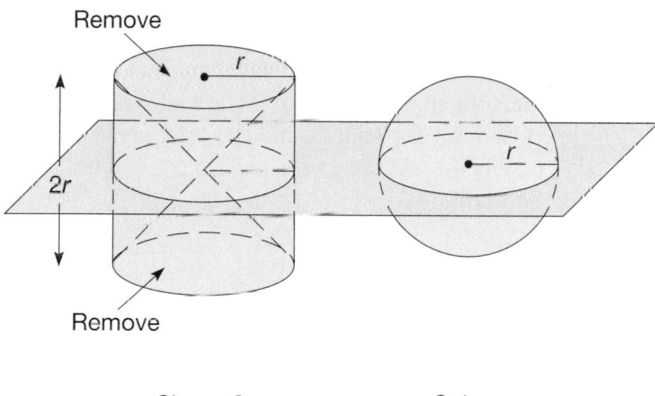

Figure 13.67

Imagine cutting shape S and the sphere with a plane that is a units above the center of the sphere. Figure 13.68 shows front and top views.

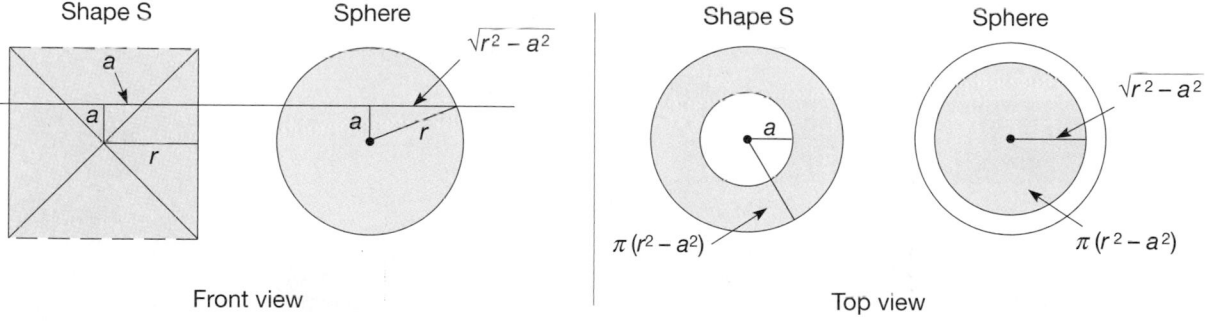

Figure 13.68

Using the top view, we show next that each cross-sectional area is $\pi(r^2 - a^2)$. First, for shape S, the cross-section is a "washer" shape with outside radius r and inside radius a. Therefore, its area is $\pi r^2 - \pi a^2 = \pi(r^2 - a^2)$. Second, for the sphere, the cross-section is a circle of radius $\sqrt{r^2 - a^2}$. (Refer to the right triangle in the front view and apply the Pythagorean theorem.) Hence, the cross-sectional area of the sphere is $\pi(\sqrt{r^2 - a^2})^2$, or $\pi(r^2 - a^2)$ also. Thus the plane cuts equal areas, so that by Cavalieri's principle, the sphere and shape S have the *same* volume. The volume of shape S is the volume of the cylinder minus the volume of two cones that were removed. Therefore,

$$\text{volume of shape } S = \pi r^2 \cdot (2r) - 2\left(\frac{1}{3}\pi r^2 \cdot r\right)$$

$$= 2\pi r^3 - \frac{2\pi}{3}r^3$$

$$= \frac{6\pi r^3}{3} - \frac{2\pi r^3}{3}$$

$$= \frac{4}{3}\pi r^3.$$

Figure 13.69

Since the sphere and shape S have the same volume, the volume of the sphere is $\frac{4}{3}\pi r^3$.

To determine the surface area of a sphere, we imagine the sphere comprised of many "pyramids" of base area A and height r, the radius of the sphere. In Figure 13.69, the "pyramid" has a base of area A and volume V. The ratio $\frac{A}{V}$ is

$$\frac{A}{V} = \frac{A}{\frac{1}{3}Ar} = \frac{3}{r}.$$

If we fill the sphere with a large number of such "pyramids," of arbitrarily small base area A, the ratio of $\frac{A}{V}$ should also give the ratio of the surface area of the sphere to the volume of the sphere. (The total volume of the "pyramids" is approximately the volume of the sphere, and the total area of the bases of the "pyramids" is approximately the surface area of the sphere.) Hence, for the sphere we expect

$$\frac{A}{V} = \frac{3}{r},$$

so

$$A = \frac{3}{r} \cdot V$$

$$= \frac{3}{r} \cdot \frac{4}{3}\pi r^3$$

$$= 4\pi r^2.$$

This is, in fact, the surface area of the sphere. Again, we would need calculus to verify the result rigorously.

Notice that the formulas obtained from Cavalieri's principle were the same as those obtained from Archimedes' observation.

MATHEMATICAL MORSEL

On the TV quiz show *Who Wants to Be a Millionaire?*, contestants are asked more and more difficult questions and receive more money for each correct answer. They continue until they either answer a question incorrectly or have earned a million dollars. After answering the $32,000 question correctly, contestant David Honea moved on to the $64,000 question. The question was "Which of the five Great Lakes is the second largest in area after Lake Superior?" David answered Lake Huron, but the show said that the correct answer was Lake Michigan. After being encouraged by other contestants, he challenged the answer a short time later. When the show producers investigated the question, they found that Lake Michigan has the second largest volume but, as David indicated, Lake Huron has the second largest area. He was invited back to the show and eventually won $125,000.

Section 13.4 EXERCISE / PROBLEM SET A

EXERCISES

1. Find the volume of each prism and cylinder.

a.

b.

c.

d.

c.

d.

3. Find the volume of each can.

   a. Coffee can $r = 7.6$ cm, $h = 16.3$ cm

   b. Soup can $r = 3.3$ cm, $h = 10$ cm

4. Find the volume of the following spheres (to the nearest whole cubic unit).

   a. A sphere with $r = 6$

   b. A sphere with $d = 24$

2. Find the volume of each square pyramid and cone.

a.

b.

PROBLEMS

5. Following are shown base designs for stacks of unit cubes (see the Problem Sets in Section 12.1). For each one, determine the volume and total surface area (including the bottom) of the stack described.

a.

3	4	2
1	1	3

b.

1	4
2	

c.

3	3	3
1	2	3
1	2	3

6. Find the volume of each of the following solid figures, rounding to the nearest cubic inch.

a.

b.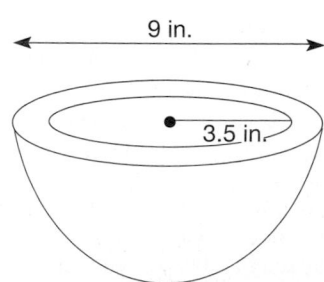

7. A standard tennis ball can is a cylinder that holds three tennis balls.

   a. Which is greater, the circumference of the can or its height?

   b. If the radius of a tennis ball is 3.5 cm, what percent of the can is occupied by air, not including the air inside the balls?

8. Find the volume of each right prism with the given features.

   a. The bases are equilateral triangles with sides of length 8; height = 10.

   b. The bases are trapezoids with bases of lengths 7 and 9 perpendicular to one side of length 6; height = 12.

   c. The base is a right triangle with legs of length 5 and 12; height = 20.

9. A cylindrical aquarium has a circular base with diameter 2 feet and height 3 feet. How much water does the aquarium hold, in cubic feet?

10. The Great Wall of China is about 1500 miles long. The cross-section of the wall is a trapezoid 25 feet high, 25 feet wide at the bottom, and 15 feet wide at the top. How many cubic yards of material make up the wall?

11. The Pyramid Arena in Memphis, Tennessee, has a square base that measures approximately 548 feet on a side. The arena is 321 feet high.

    a. Calculate its volume.

    b. Calculate its lateral surface area.

12. a. A pipe 8 inches in diameter and 100 yards long is filled with water. Find the volume of the water in the pipe, in cubic yards.

    b. A pipe 8 centimeters in diameter and 100 meters long is filled with water. Find the volume of the water in the pipe, in cubic meters.

    c. Which is the easier computation, part (a) or part (b), or are they equivalent?

13. A scale model of a new engineering building is being built for display, using a scale of 5 cm = 3 m. The volume of the scale model is 396,000 cubic centimeters. What will be the volume of the finished structure in cubic meters?

14. Two designs for an oil storage tank are being considered: spherical and cylindrical. The two tanks would have the same capacity and would each have an inside diameter of 60 feet.

    a. What would be the height of the cylindrical tank?

    b. If 1 cubic foot holds 7.5 gallons of oil, what is the capacity of each tank in gallons?

    c. Which of the two designs has the smallest surface area and would thus require less material in its construction?

15. A sculpture made of iron has the shape of a right square prism topped by a sphere. The metal in each part of the sculpture is 2 mm thick. If the dimensions are as shown and the density of iron is 7.87 g/cm³, calculate the approximate weight of the sculpture in kilograms.

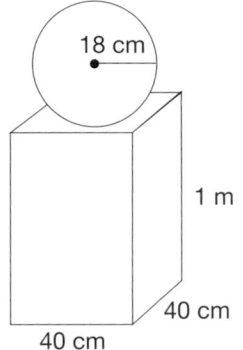

16. The volume of an object with an irregular shape can be determined by measuring the volume of water it displaces.

    a. A rock placed in an aquarium measuring $2\frac{1}{2}$ feet long by 1 foot wide causes the water level to rise $\frac{1}{4}$ inch. What is the volume of the rock?

    b. With the rock in place, the water level in the aquarium is $\frac{1}{2}$ inch from the top. The owner wants to add to the aquarium 200 solid marbles, each with a diameter of 1.5 cm. Will the addition of these marbles cause the water in the aquarium to overflow?

17. Suppose that all the dimensions of a square prism are doubled.

    a. How would the volume change?

    b. How would the surface area change?

18. a. How does the volume of a circular cylinder change if its radius is doubled?

    b. How does the volume of a circular cylinder change if its height is doubled?

19. In designing a pool, it could be filled with three pipes each 9 centimeters in diameter, two pipes each 12 centimeters in diameter, or one pipe 16 centimeters in diameter. Which design will fill the pool the fastest?

20. a. Find the volume of a cube with edges of length 2 meters.

b. Find the length of the edges of a cube with volume twice that of the cube in part (a).

21. A do-it-yourselfer wants to dig some holes for fence posts. He has the option of renting posthole diggers with diameter 6 inches or 8 inches. The amount of dirt removed by the larger posthole digger is what percent greater than the amount removed by the smaller?

22. A water tank is in the shape of an inverted circular cone with diameter 10 feet and height 15 feet. Another conical tank is to be built with height 15 feet but with one-half the capacity of the larger tank. Find the diameter of the smaller tank.

23. The following sphere, right circular cylinder, and right circular cone have the same volume. Find the height of the cylinder and the slant height of the cone.

  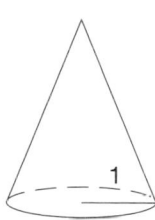

24. Lumber is measured in board feet. A **board foot** is the volume of a square piece of wood measuring 1 foot long, 1 foot wide, and 1 inch thick. A surfaced "two by four" actually measures $1\frac{1}{2}$ inches thick by $3\frac{1}{2}$ inches wide, a "two by six" measures $1\frac{1}{2}$ by $5\frac{1}{2}$, and so on ($\frac{1}{4}$ inch is planed off each rough surface). Plywood is sold in exact dimensions and is differentiated by thickness (e.g., $\frac{1}{2}$ inch, $\frac{5}{8}$ inch, etc.). Find the number of board feet in the following pieces of lumber.

a. A 6-foot long two by four

b. A 10-foot two by eight

c. A 4 foot-by-8 foot sheet of $\frac{3}{4}$-inch plywood

d. A 4 foot-by-6 foot sheet of $\frac{5}{8}$-inch plywood

25. Suppose that you have 10 separate unit cubes. Then the total volume is 10 cubic units and the total surface area is 60 square units. If you arrange the cubes as shown, the volume is still 10 cubic units, but now the surface area is only 36 square units (convince yourself this is true by counting faces). For each of the following problems, assume that all the cubes are stacked to form a single shape sharing complete faces (no loose cubes allowed).

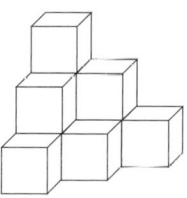

a. How can you arrange 10 cubes to get a surface area of 34 square units? Draw a sketch.

b. What is the greatest possible surface area you can get with 10 cubes? Sketch the arrangement.

c. How can you arrange the 10 cubes to get the least possible surface area? What is this area?

d. Answer the questions in parts (b) and (c) for 27 and 64 cubes.

e. What arrangement has the greatest surface area for a given number of cubes?

f. What arrangement seems to have the least surface area for a given number of cubes? (Consider cases with n^3 cubes for whole numbers n.)

g. Biologists have found that an animal's surface area is an important factor in its regulation of body temperature. Why do you think desert animals such as snakes are long and thin? Why do furry animals curl up in a ball to hibernate?

 Section 13.4   EXERCISE / PROBLEM SET B

EXERCISES

1. Find the volume of each prism and cylinder.

a.

b.

c.

d.

2. Find the volume of each pyramid and cone.

a. **b.**

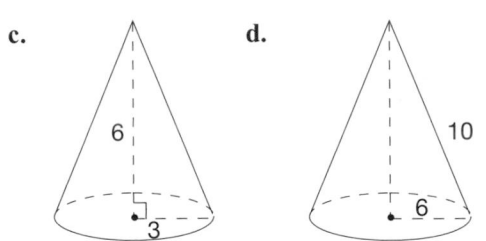

c. **d.**

3. Find the volume of each can.

a. Juice can $r = 5.3$ cm, $h = 17.7$ cm

b. Shortening can $r = 6.5$ cm, $h = 14.7$ cm

4. Find the volume of the following spheres (to the nearest whole cubic unit).

a. A sphere with $r = 2.3$.

b. A sphere with $d = 6.7$.

5. Following are base designs for stacks of unit cubes (see the Problem Sets in Section 12.5). For each one, determine the volume and surface area (including the bottom) of the stack described.

a.

1	2	4	3

b.

2	3
1	5

c.

1	4	5	6
2	3		

6. a. How many square meters of tile are needed to tile the sides and bottom of the swimming pool illustrated?

b. How much water does the pool hold?

PROBLEMS

7. a. Find the volume, to the nearest cubic centimeter, of a soft-drink can with a diameter of 5.6 centimeters and a height of 12 centimeters.

b. If the can is filled with water, find the weight of the water in grams.

8. Given are three cardboard boxes.

a. Find the volume of each box.

b. Find the surface area of each box.

c. Do boxes with the same volume always have the same surface area?

d. Which box used the least amount of cardboard?

9. The first three steps of a 10-step staircase are shown.

a. Find the amount of concrete needed to make the exposed portion of the 10-step staircase.

b. Find the amount of carpet needed to cover the fronts, tops, and sides of the concrete steps.

15 cm

80 cm

20 cm

10. The Pyramid of Cheops has a square base 240 yards on a side. Its height is 160 yards.

a. What is its volume?

b. What is the surface area of the four exterior sides?

11. A vegetable garden measures 20 feet by 30 feet. The grower wants to cover the entire garden with a layer of mushroom compost 2 inches thick. She plans to haul the compost in a truck that will hold a maximum of 1 cubic yard. How many trips must she make with the truck to haul enough compost for the garden?

12. A soft-drink cup is in the shape of a right circular cone with capacity 250 milliliters. The radius of the circular base is 5 centimeters. How deep is the cup?

13. A 4-inch-thick concrete slab is being poured for a circular patio 10 feet in diameter. Concrete costs $50 per cubic yard. Find the cost of the concrete, to the nearest cent.

14. The circumference of a beach ball is 73 inches. How many cubic inches of air does the ball hold? Round your answer to the nearest cubic inch.

15. a. You want to make the smallest possible cubical box to hold a sphere. If the radius of the sphere is r, what percent of the volume of the box will be air (to the nearest percent)?

b. For a child's toy, you want to design a cube that fits inside a sphere such that the vertices of the cube just touch the sphere. If the radius of the sphere is r, what percent of the volume of the sphere is occupied by the cube?

16. An aquarium measures 25 inches long by 14 inches wide by 12 inches high. How much does the water filling the aquarium weigh? (One cubic foot of water weighs 62.4 pounds.)

17. a. How does the volume of a sphere change if its radius is doubled?

b. How does the surface area of a sphere change if its radius is doubled?

18. a. If the ratio of the sides of two squares is $2:5$, what is the ratio of their areas?

b. If the ratio of the edges of two cubes is $2:5$, what is the ratio of their volumes?

c. If all the dimensions of a rectangular box are doubled, what happens to its volume?

19. It is estimated that the average diameter of peeled logs coming into your sawmill is 16 inches.

a. What is the thickness of the largest square timber that can be cut from the average log?

b. If the rest of the log is made into mulch, what percent of the original log is the square timber?

20. The areas of the faces of a right rectangular prism are 24, 32, and 48 square centimeters. What is the volume of the prism?

21. While rummaging in his great aunt's attic, Bernard found a small figurine that he believed to be made out of silver. To test his guess, he looked up the density of silver in his chemistry book and found that it was 10.5 g/cm^3. He found that the figure weighed 149 g. To determine its volume, he dropped it into a cylindrical glass of water. If the diameter of the glass was 6 cm and the figurine was pure silver, by how much should the water level in the glass rise?

22. A baseball is composed of a spherical piece of cork with a 2-centimeter radius, which is then wrapped by string until a sphere with a diameter of 12 centimeters is obtained. If an arbitrary point is selected in the ball, what is the probability that the point is in the string?

23. An irrigation pump can pump 250 liters of water per minute. How many hours should the system work to water a rectangular field 75 m by 135 m to a depth of 3 cm?

24. If a tube of caulking lays a 40-foot cylindrical bead $\frac{1}{4}$ inch in diameter, how long will a $\frac{1}{8}$-inch bead be?

25. A rectangular piece of paper can be rolled into a cylinder in two different directions. If there is no overlapping, which cylinder has the greater volume, the one with the long side of the rectangle as its height, or the one with the short side of the rectangle as its height, or will the volumes be the same?

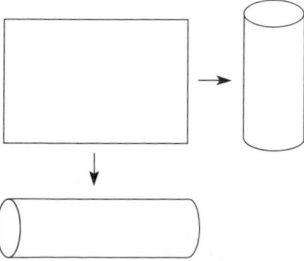

PROBLEMS FOR WRITING/DISCUSSION

1. Nedra was trying to find the volume of a square pyramid, and she needed to find the height. The problem was that there seemed to be too many heights. She didn't know whether to use *h*, *l*, or *e*. Are they related? Discuss.

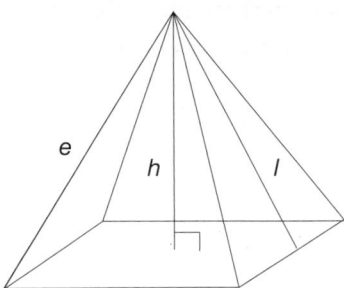

2. Hester Ann wants to build a big box in the shape of a cube to keep her blocks in. The blocks are all little cubes 3″ on a side, and she has 56 blocks. She needs to know what the inside dimensions of the box should be to make sure all the blocks will fit, yet have the big box be as small as possible. How would you help her figure out the problem? Would there be any space left over in the box for extra blocks later on?

3. Douglas is a future entrepreneur. He's been thinking about the fact that if he has a product to sell, and he wants to use the smallest package possible for his product, he could fit the largest volume inside a spherical package. He's wondering why other manufacturers haven't realized this. Why aren't more products sold in the shape of a sphere? Are there any products you can think of that do come in a spherical, or near spherical, shape?

END OF CHAPTER MATERIAL

Solution of Initial Problem

David was planning a motorcycle trip across Canada. He drew his route on a map and estimated the length of his route to be 115 centimeters. The scale on his map is 1 centimeter = 39 kilometers. His motorcycle's gasoline consumption averages 75 miles per gallon of gasoline. If gasoline costs $1.25 per gallon, how much should he plan to spend for gasoline? (What additional information does he need?)

Strategy: Use Dimensional Analysis

David set up the following ratios.

$$1 \text{ cm}/39 \text{ km (map scale)}$$
$$75 \text{ miles}/1 \text{ gallon (gasoline consumption)}$$

The length of his trip, then, is about

$$115 \text{ cm} \times \frac{39 \text{ km}}{1 \text{ cm}} = 115 \times 39 \text{ km} = 4485 \text{ km}.$$

If he knew how many kilometers are in 1 mile, he could convert the length of his trip to miles. (This is the additional information that he needs.) David looked this ratio up in an almanac and found 1 mile = 1.61 km (to two places). Thus the length of his trip is

$$4485 \text{ km} \times \frac{1 \text{ mile}}{1.61 \text{ km}} = \frac{4485}{1.61} \text{ miles}$$
$$= 2785.7 \quad \text{miles (to one decimal place).}$$

Hence David computed his gasoline expenses as follows.

$$2785.7 \text{ miles} \times \frac{1 \text{ gallon}}{75 \text{ miles}} \times \frac{1.25 \text{ dollars}}{\text{gallon}} =$$
$$\frac{2785.7 \times 1.25}{75} \text{ dollars} = \$46.43$$

To use the strategy Use Dimensional Analysis, set up the ratios of units (such as km/cm) so that when the units are simplified (or canceled) as fractions, the resulting unit is the one that was sought.

Notice how the various units cancel to produce the end result in dollars. Summarizing, David converted distance (the length of his trip) to dollars (gasoline expense) via the product of ratios.

$$115 \text{ cm} \times \frac{39 \text{ km}}{1 \text{ cm}} \times \frac{1 \text{ mile}}{1.61 \text{ km}} \times \frac{1 \text{ gallon}}{75 \text{ miles}} \times \frac{1.25 \text{ dollars}}{1 \text{ gallon}}$$
$$= \$46.43$$

Additional Problems Where the Strategy "Use Dimensional Analysis" Is Useful

1. Bamboo can grow as much as 35.4 inches per day. If the bamboo continues to grow at this rate, about how many meters tall, to the nearest tenth of a meter, would it be at the end of a week? (Use 1 in. = 2.54 cm.)

2. A foreign car's gas tank holds 50 L of gasoline. What will it cost to fill the tank if regular gas is selling for $1.09 a gallon? (1 L = 1.057 qt.)

3. We see lightning before we hear thunder because light travels faster than sound. If sound travels at about 1000 km/hr through air at sea level at 15°C and light travels at 186,282 mi/sec, how many times faster is the speed of light than the speed of sound?

People in Mathematics

Leonhard Euler (1707–1783)
Leonhard Euler was one of the most prolific of all mathematicians. He published 530 books and papers during his lifetime and left much unpublished work at the time of his death. From 1771 on, he was totally blind, yet his mathematical discoveries continued. He would work mentally, then dictate to assistants, sometimes using a large chalkboard on which to write the formulas for them. His writings are a model of clear exposition, and much of our modern mathematical notation has been influenced by his style. For instance, the modern use of the symbol π is due to Euler. In geometry, he is best known for the Euler line of a triangle and the formula $V - E + F = 2$, which relates the number of vertices, edges, and faces of any simple closed polyhedron.

Maria Agnesi (1718–1799)
Maria Agnesi was famous for the highly regarded *Instituzioni Analitiche*, a 1020-page, two-volume presentation of algebra, analytic geometry, and calculus. Published in 1748, it brought order and clarity to the mathematics invented by Descartes, Newton, Leibniz, and others in the seventeenth century. Agnesi was the eldest of 21 children in a wealthy Italian family. She was a gifted child, with an extraordinary talent for languages. Her parents encouraged her to excel, and she received the best schooling available. Agnesi began work on *Instituzioni Analitiche* at age 20 and finished it 10 years later, supervising its printing on presses installed in her home. After its publication, she was appointed honorary professor at the University of Bologna. But instead, Agnesi decided to dedicate her life to charity and religious devotion, and she spent the last 45 years of her life caring for the sick, aged, and indigent.

CHAPTER REVIEW

Review the following terms and exercises to determine which require learning or relearning—page numbers are provided for easy reference.

SECTION 13.1: Measurement with Nonstandard and Standard Units
VOCABULARY/NOTATION

Holistic measurement   623
Nonstandard units: "hand," "pace,"
   "dash," "pinch," etc.   624
Standard units   624
English system of units for
Length: inch (in.)   625
   foot (ft)   625
   yard (yd)   625
   mile (mi)   625
Area: square inch (in^2)   625
   square foot (ft^2)   625
   square yard (yd^2)   625
   acre   625
   square mile (mi^2)   625

Volume: cubic inch (in^3)   626
   cubic foot (ft^3)   626
   cubic yard (yd^3)   626
Capacity: teaspoon (tsp)   627
   tablespoon (tbsp)   627
   liquid ounce (oz)   627
   cup (c)   627
   pint (pt)   627

   quart (qt)   627
   gallon (gal)   627
   barrel (bar)   627
Weight: ounce (oz)   627
   pound (lb)   627
   ton (t)   627
Temperature: degrees Fahrenheit
   (°F)   628

Metric system of units for
Length: meter (m)   628
           decimeter (dm)   628
           centimeter (cm)   628
           millimeter (mm)   628
           dekameter (dam)   628
           hectometer (hm)   628
           kilometer (km)   628
Area: square meter (m²)   630
           square centimeter (cm²)
               630

square millimeter (mm²)
    631
are (a)   631
hectare (ha)   631
square kilometer (km²)
    631
Volume: liter (L)   632
           cubic decimeter (dm³)   632
           cubic centimeter (cm³)
               632

milliliter (mL)   632
cubic meter (m³)   632
kiloliter (kL)   632
Mass: kilogram (kg)   633
           gram (g)   633
           metric ton (T)   633
Temperature: degrees Celsius (°C)
               633
Dimensional analysis   634

EXERCISES

1. List the three steps in the measurement process.

2. What is meant by an informal measurement system?

3. Names three units of measurement used to measure the following in the English system.

   a. Length   b. Area
   c. Volume   d. Capacity
   e. Weight

4. List the three attributes of an ideal system of units.

5. Name three units of measurement used to measure the following in the metric system.

   a. Length   b. Area
   c. Volume   d. Capacity
   e. Mass

6. Name five common prefixes in the metric system.

7. Convert 54°C to °F.

8. A speed of 70 miles per hour is equivalent to how many kilometers per hour (use 1 in. = 2.54 cm)?

SECTION 13.2: Length and Area

VOCABULARY / NOTATION

Distance from point P to point Q,
    PQ,   641
Unit distance   642
Perimeter   642
Circumference   643

pi (π)   643
Area   644
Square unit   644
Base of a triangle   646
Height of a triangle   646

Height of a parallelogram   647
Height of a trapezoid   647
Hypotenuse of a right triangle
    648
Legs of a right triangle   648

EXERCISES

1. Find perimeters of the following.

   a. A rectangle with side lengths 5 and 7
   b. A parallelogram with side lengths 11 and 14
   c. A rhombus whose sides have length 3.5
   d. A kite with side lengths 3 and 6.4
   e. A square whose sides have length 6
   f. A circle whose radius is 5

2. Find areas of the following.

   a. A right triangle whose legs have length 4.1 and 5.3
   b. A circle whose diameter is 10
   c. A parallelogram with sides of length 8 and 10, and height 6 to the shorter side

   d. A square whose sides have length 3.5
   e. A trapezoid whose bases have length 7 and 11 and whose height is 4.5
   f. A rhombus whose sides have length 9 and whose height to one side is 6

3. State the Pythagorean theorem in the following ways.

   a. Geometrically in terms of squares
   b. Algebraically in terms of squares

4. What does the triangle inequality have to say about a triangle two of whose sides are 7 and 9?

SECTION 13.3: Surface Area
VOCABULARY / NOTATION

Surface area   662   Slant height   665   Great circle   667
Lateral surface area   662

EXERCISES

1. Sketch a right rectangular prism, label lengths of its sides 4, 5, and 6, and find its surface area.

2. Find the surface area of a right cylinder whose base has radius 3 and whose height is 7.

3. Find the surface area of a right square pyramid whose base has side lengths of 6 and whose height (not slant height) is 4.

4. Find the surface area of a right circular cone whose base has radius 5 and whose height is 12.

5. Find the surface area of a sphere whose diameter is 12.

SECTION 13.4: Volume
VOCABULARY / NOTATION

Volume   672   Cubic unit   672

EXERCISES

1. Sketch a right rectangular prism, label lengths of its sides 4, 5, and 6, and find its volume.

2. Find the volume of a right cylinder whose base has radius 3 and whose height is 7.

3. Find the volume of a right square pyramid whose base has side lengths of 6 and whose height (not slant height) is 4.

4. Find the volume of a right circular cone whose base has radius 5 and whose height is 12.

5. Find the volume of a sphere whose diameter is 12.

PROBLEMS FOR WRITING/DISCUSSION

1. When Carol was finding the area of a rectangle that had a length of 13 cm and a width of 12 cm, she got an answer of 156 cm^2, so she squared 156 and got an answer of 24 336 sq cm. Did she do something wrong? Discuss.

2. Amy said that if a centimeter is 0.01 of a meter, then 1 cm^2 must be 0.001 of a square meter and 1 cm^3 must be 0.0001 of a cubic meter. Is she correct? Discuss. What visual means can you use to demonstrate?

3. Tyrone says that he can take any parallelogram and make one straight line cut in it and, by rearranging the two pieces, turn it into a rectangle. It's also possible to turn the parallelogram into a kite or an isosceles trapezoid with just one cut. So he wants to know if there is a way to turn any parallelogram into a square with one cut. How would you explore this with Tyrone?

4. Consuella likes turning figures into parallelograms. She says if she takes two congruent triangles, she can arrange them to form a parallelogram. She can do it with two congruent trapezoids, too. She wants to know if there are any other figures she can turn into parallelograms. How should you respond?

5. Dan says the formula for the area of a trapezoid works for squares, too. He wants to know if it works for any other quadrilaterals. Discuss.

6. Diana says she knows the formula for the area of a triangle is $\frac{1}{2}bh$. Would it make a difference which side you take for the base? For example, in the next picture, if she knows AD is 5.5, could she use 10 for the base? Is there some way to determine the length of CE? Explain.

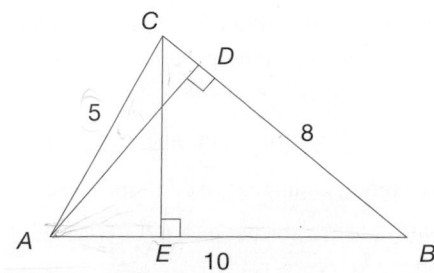

7. Marcy brought in a can of tomato soup for the hunger drive at your school. Before she handed it to you, she asked you to point out where the lateral surface area was, where the total surface area was, and where the volume was. How can you help her distinguish among these three concepts?

8. Diana and Marcy were discussing the results in Problem 6. Diana says that since a triangle can be viewed as having three different heights, so can a cone. Is she correct? Discuss.

9. Alberto asked how to find the height of an oblique cylinder. How would you help him decide?

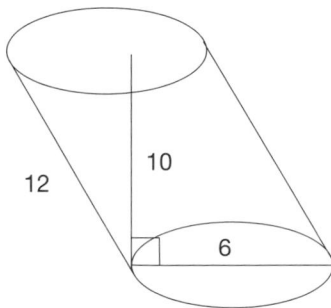

10. Temperatures can vary widely in the American Midwest in the spring. One day in Indianapolis the temperature changed from 41°F to 82°F in 6 hours when a weather front passed through. Jeffrey says, "That means it's now twice as warm as it was this morning!" Is Jeffrey correct? Discuss. (*Hint*: What would Jeffrey say if he applied the appropriate metric measurement to the same temperatures?)

CHAPTER TEST

Knowledge

1. True or false?

a. The prefix *milli* means "one thousand times."

b. The English system has all the properties of an ideal measurement system.

c. The formula for the volume of a circular cylinder is $V = \pi r^2 h$, where r is the radius of the base and h is the height.

d. The formula for the surface area of a sphere is $A = \frac{4}{3}\pi r^2$.

e. If, in a right triangle, the length of the hypotenuse is a and the lengths of the other two sides are b and c, then $a^2 + b^2 = c^2$.

f. The formula for converting degrees Celsius into degrees Fahrenheit is $F = \frac{9}{5}C + 32$.

g. One milliliter of water in its densest state has a mass of 1 kilogram.

h. The surface area of a right square pyramid whose base has sides of length s and whose triangular faces have height h is $2hs + s^2$.

2. The mass of 1 cm³ of water is _____ gram(s).

3. What geometric shape is used to measure

a. area?

b. volume?

Skill

4. If 1 inch is exactly 2.54 cm, how many kilometers are in a mile?

5. Seven cubic hectometers are equal to how many cubic decimeters?

6. What is the area of a circle whose circumference is 2?

7. What is the volume of a prism whose base is a rectangle with dimensions 7.2 cm by 3.4 cm and whose height is 5.9 cm?

8. Find the volume of a pyramid whose base is a pentagon with perimeter 17 cm and area 13 cm² and whose height is 12 cm.

9. If all three dimensions of a box are tripled, the volume of the new box is _____ times bigger than the volume of the original box.

10. Find the perimeter of the following figure and leave the result in exact form.

11. Perform each of the following conversions

    a. 1 yd   = _____ in.

    b. 1 gallon   = _____ pints

    c. 8 yd^3 = _____ ft^3

    d. 543 mm^2 = _____ cm^2

    e. 543 cm^3 = _____ m^3

    f. 15 mm   = _____ m

    g. 225 cm^3 = _____ mL

    h. 3.78 g   = _____ mg

Understanding

12. Show how one can use the formula for the area of a rectangle to derive the area of a parallelogram.

13. Explain why the interrelatedness attribute of an ideal system of measurement is useful in the metric system.

14. Describe one aspect of the metric system that should make it much easier to learn than the English system.

15. List the following from smallest to largest.

    i. The perimeter of a square with 6-cm sides.

    ii. The perimeter of a rectangle with one side 7 cm and the other side 6 cm.

    iii. The perimeter of a triangle with one side 6 cm and one side 6 cm, and the length of the third side not given.

16. Choose the most realistic measure for the following objects.

    a. The weight of a cinder block
      10 kg   100 kg   100 g

    b. The height of a two-story building
      60 cm   6 m   0.6 km

    c. The volume of a can of soda
      500 mL   50 L   50 mL

17. Given the area of a rectangle is bh and the area of a parallelogram is bh, explain why the area of the triangle with base b and height h, indicated in the following figure, can be found by using the equation $A = \frac{1}{2} b \cdot h$.

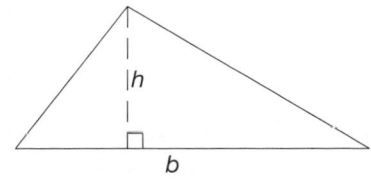

18. If a cylinder and a cone have congruent bases and congruent volumes, are the height of the cone and the height of the cylinder related? If so, how? If not, why not?

Problem Solving/Application

19. The cube shown has edges of length s.

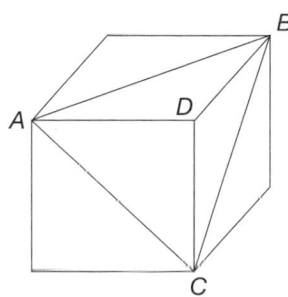

    a. Find the area of $\triangle ABC$.

    b. Find the volume of pyramid $ABCD$.

20. Sound travels 1100 feet per second in air. Assume that the Earth is a sphere of diameter 7921 miles. How many hours would it take for a plane to fly around the equator at the speed of sound and at an altitude of 6 miles?

21. Find the surface area and volume of the following solids:

    a. Four faces are rectangles; the other two are trapezoids with two right angles.

    b. Right circular cylinder

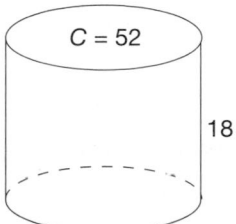

22. Find the area of the shaded region in the following figure. Note that the quadrilateral is a square and the arc is a portion of a circle with radius 2 ft and center on the lower left vertex of the square.

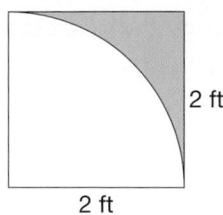

2 ft

2 ft

23. A sketch of the Surenkov home is shown in the following figure, with the recent sidewalk addition shaded. Using the measurements indicated on the figure and the fact that the sidewalk is 4 inches thick with right angles at all corners, determine how many yards of concrete it took to create the new sidewalk.

24. An airplane flying around the equator travels 24,936 miles in an entire orbit and the circumference of the Earth of the equator is 24,901 miles.

a. What is the altitude of the airplane in miles (*exactly*)?

b. *Approximately* what was the plane's altitude in feet (within 100 ft)?

References for Reflections from Research

BATTISTA, M. T. (1999). Fifth graders' enumeration of cubes in 3D arrays: Conceptual progress in an inquiry-based classroom. *Journal for Research in Mathematics Education, 30,* 417–448.

BOURGEOIS, R. D. (1986). Third graders' ability to associate foldout shapes with polyhedra. *Journal for Research in Mathematics Education, 13,* 222–230.

CARPENTER, T. P., CORBITT, M. K., KEPNER, H. S., JR., LINDQUIST, M. M., & REYS, R. E. (1981). *Results from the second mathematics assessment of the National Assessment of Educational Progress.* Reston, VA: National Council of Teachers of Mathematics.

CLEMENTS, D. H., BATTISTA, M. T., SARAMA, J., SWAMINATHAN, S., & McMILLEN, S. (1997). Students' development of length concepts in a logo-based unit on geometric paths. *Journal for Research in Mathematics Education, 28,* 70–95.

HART, K. M. (1984). Which comes first—length, area, or volume? *Arithmetic Teachers, 31*(1), 16–18, 26–27.

OUTHRED, L. N., & MITCHELMORE, M. C. (2000). Young children's intuitive understanding of rectangular area measurement. *Journal for Research in Mathematics Education, 31,* 144–167.

POST, T. R. (1992). *Teaching mathematics in grades K–8: Research based methods* (2nd ed.). Boston: Allyn and Bacon.

REYNOLDS, A., & WHEATLEY, G. H. (1996). Elementary students' construction and coordination of units in an area setting. *Journal for Research in Mathematics Education, 27,* 564–581.

VAN DE WALLE, J. A. (1994). *Elementary school mathematics: Teaching developmentally* (2nd ed.). White Plains, NY: Longman.

WILSON, P. S., & ROWLAND, R. (1993). Teaching measurement. In R. J. Jensen (Ed.), *Research ideas for the classroom: Early childhood mathematics* (pp. 171–194). New York: Macmillan.

CHAPTER 14

Geometry Using Triangle Congruence and Similarity

FOCUS ON Euclid: Father of Geometry

Euclid of Alexandria (circa 300 B.C.) has been called the "father of geometry." Euclid authored many works, but he is most famous for *The Elements*, which consisted of thirteen books, five of which are concerned with plane geometry, three with solid geometry, and the rest with geometric explanations of mathematics now studied in algebra.

After Plato (circa 400 B.C.) developed the method of forming a proof, and Aristotle (circa 350 B.C.) distinguished between axioms and postulates, Euclid organized geometry into a single logical system. Although many of the results of Euclidean geometry were known, Euclid's unique contribution was the use of definitions, postulates, and axioms with statements to be proved, called propositions or theorems. The first such proposition was "Describe an equilateral triangle on a given finite straight line," which showed how to construct an equilateral triangle with a given side length using only a compass and straightedge. Other famous theorems included in *The Elements* are the Pythagorean theorem, for which Euclid has his own original proof (see the figure to the right), the Pons Asinorum theorem (the angles at the base of an isosceles triangle are congruent), and the proof of the infinitude of primes.

Modern geometers have revised Euclid's work to ensure more rigor. For example, Euclid defined a point as "that which has no parts," a line as "length without breadth," and a plane as "that which has only length and breadth."

Euclid

In modern geometry, these terms are left as undefined because it is impossible to state precise definitions for all terms. Also, some of Euclid's theorems are now taken as postulates because the "proofs" that he offered had logical shortcomings. Nevertheless, most of the theorems and much of the development contained in a typical high school geometry course today are taken from Euclid's *Elements*.

Euclid founded the first school of mathematics in Alexandria, Greece. As one story goes, a student who had learned the first theorem asked Euclid, "But what shall I get by learning these things?" Euclid called his slave and said, "Give him three pence, since he must make gain out of what he learns." As another story goes, a king asked Euclid if there were not an easier way to learn geometry than by studying *The Elements*. Euclid replied by saying, "There is no royal road to geometry."

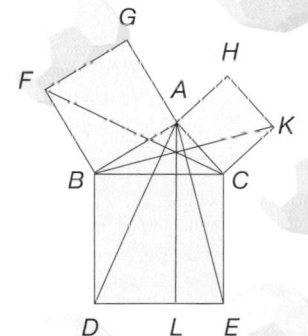

Problem Solving Strategies

1. Guess and Test
2. Use a Variable
3. Draw a Picture
4. Look for a Pattern
5. Make a List
6. Solve a Simpler Problem
7. Draw a Diagram
8. Use Direct Reasoning
9. Use Indirect Reasoning
10. Use Properties of Numbers
11. Solve an Equivalent Problem
12. Work Backward
13. Use Cases
14. Solve an Equation
15. Look for a Formula
16. Do a Simulation
17. Use a Model
18. Use Dimensional Analysis
19. **Identify Subgoals**

Strategy
Identify Subgoals

Many complex problems can be broken down into *subgoals*—that is, intermediate results that lead to a final solution. Instead of seeking a solution to the entire problem directly, we can often obtain information that we can piece together to solve the problem. One way to employ the Identify Subgoals strategy is to think of other information that you wish the problem statement contained. For example, saying, "If I only knew such and such, I could solve it," suggests a subgoal, namely, the missing information.

Initial Problem

An eastbound bicycle enters a tunnel at the same time that a westbound bicycle enters the other end of the tunnel. The eastbound bicycle travels at 10 kilometers per hour, the westbound bicycle at 8 kilometers per hour. A fly is flying back and forth between the two bicycles at 15 kilometers per hour, leaving the eastbound bicycle as it enters the tunnel. The tunnel is 9 kilometers long. How far has the fly traveled in the tunnel when the bicycles meet?

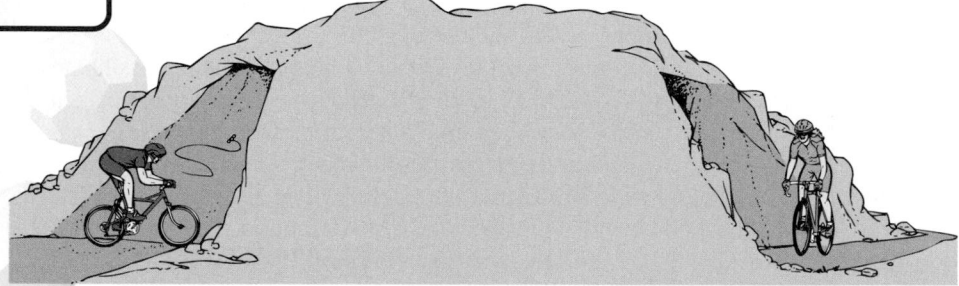

Clues

The Identify Subgoals strategy may be appropriate when

- A problem can be broken down into a series of simpler problems.
- The statement of the problem is very long and complex.
- You can say, "If I only knew . . . , then I could solve the problem."
- There is a simple, intermediate step that would be useful.

A solution of the Initial Problem appears on page 749.

INTRODUCTION

NCTM Standards 2000
Geometry
Grades 3–5
All students should explore
congruence and similarity.

In Chapters 12 and 13 we studied a variety of two- and three-dimensional shapes and their properties. In this chapter we study congruence and similarity of triangles and applications of these ideas. Applications of congruence will include the construction of two-dimensional geometric shapes using specific instruments or tools. The classical construction instruments are an unmarked straightedge, a compass, and a writing implement, such as a pencil. From the time of Plato, the ancient Greeks studied geometric constructions. Applications of similarity will include indirect measurement and several other constructions.

14.1   CONGRUENCE OF TRIANGLES

STARTING POINT

For the two triangles below, Corey said that triangle A was *congruent* to triangle B. Whitney claimed that triangle A was *equal* to triangle B. Who is correct, and what is the difference between equality and congruence?

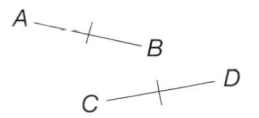

In an informal way, we say that two geometric figures are congruent if they can be superimposed so as to coincide. We will make this idea precise for specific figures.

Recall that if two line segments $\overline{AB}$ and $\overline{CD}$ have the same length, we say that they are **congruent line segments.** Similarly, if two angles $\angle PQR$ and $\angle STU$ have the same measure, we call them **congruent angles.** We indicate congruent segments and angles using marks as shown in Figure 14.1. Suppose that we have two triangles, $\triangle ABC$ and $\triangle DEF$, and suppose that we pair up the vertices, $A \leftrightarrow D$, $B \leftrightarrow E$, $C \leftrightarrow F$ (Figure 14.2). This notation means that vertex A in $\triangle ABC$ is paired with vertex D in $\triangle DEF$, vertex B is paired with vertex E, and vertex C is paired with vertex F. Then we say that we have formed a **correspondence** between $\triangle ABC$ and $\triangle DEF$. Side $\overline{AB}$ in $\triangle ABC$ corresponds to side $\overline{DE}$, side $\overline{BC}$ corresponds to side $\overline{EF}$, and side $\overline{AC}$ corresponds to side $\overline{DF}$. Similarly, $\angle ABC$, $\angle BAC$, and $\angle ACB$ correspond to $\angle DEF$, $\angle EDF$, and $\angle DFE$, respectively. We are especially interested in correspondences between triangles such that all corresponding sides and angles are congruent. If such a correspondence exists, the triangles are called congruent triangles (Figure 14.3).

Figure 14.1

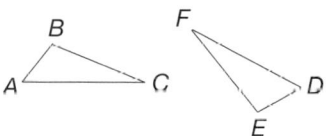

Figure 14.2

DEFINITION

Congruent Triangles

Suppose that $\triangle ABC$ and $\triangle DEF$ are such that under the correspondence $A \leftrightarrow D$, $B \leftrightarrow E$, $C \leftrightarrow F$ all corresponding sides are congruent and all corresponding vertex angles are congruent. Then $\triangle ABC$ is **congruent** to $\triangle DEF$, and we write $\triangle ABC \cong \triangle DEF$.

Figure 14.3

Date   Time

Congruent Figures

Math Message

Carefully examine the figures in Examples a–f.

The following pairs of figures are **congruent** to each other.

The following pairs of figures are *not* congruent to each other.

a.

b.

c.

d.

e.

f.

1. Write a definition of "congruent polygons." Then compare your definition to the definition on page 166 in your *Student Reference Book*.

_____

| Line segments are **congruent** if they have the same length. | Angles are **congruent** if they have the same degree measure. |

2. Draw wavy lines to connect each pair of congruent line segments below. Use a ruler to measure line segments if needed to help you.

3. Draw wavy lines to connect each pair of congruent angles below. Use a protractor to measure angles if needed to help you.

184   Use with Lesson 5.6.

Reflection from Research

The dominant strategy in young children for verifying congruence is edge matching (Beilin, 1982).

If two triangles are congruent, they have the same size and shape. However, they may be positioned differently in a plane or in space. Note that the symbol "$\cong$" stands for "is congruent to." Every triangle is congruent to itself under the correspondence that pairs each vertex with itself. To demonstrate that two triangles are congruent, we need to give the explicit correspondence between vertices and verify that corresponding sides and angles are congruent. Example 14.1 gives an illustration.

Example 14.1   Show that the diagonal $\overline{BD}$ of rectangle $ABCD$ on the square lattice in Figure 14.4 divides the rectangle into two congruent triangles $\triangle ABD$ and $\triangle CDB$.

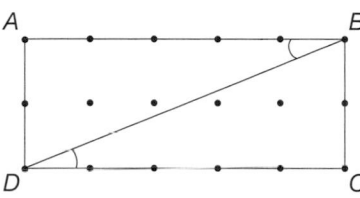

Figure 14.4

Solution We observe that $AB = CD = 5$, $AD = CB = 2$, and $BD = DB$. Since $\overline{AB} \parallel \overline{DC}$, we have that $m(\angle ABD) = m(\angle CDB)$ by the alternate interior angle theorem. Similarly, since $\overline{AD} \parallel \overline{BC}$, we have $m(\angle BDA) = m(\angle DBC)$. Also, $m(\angle A) = m(\angle C) = 90°$, since $ABCD$ is a rectangle. Consequently, under the correspondence $A \leftrightarrow C$, $B \leftrightarrow D$, $D \leftrightarrow B$, all corresponding sides and corresponding angles are congruent. Thus $\triangle ABD \cong \triangle CDB$.   ■

Example 14.1 shows that it is important to choose the correspondence between vertices in triangles *carefully*. For example, if we use the correspondence $A \leftrightarrow C$, $B \leftrightarrow B$, $D \leftrightarrow D$, it is *not* true that corresponding sides are congruent. For example, side $\overline{AB}$ corresponds to side CB, yet $\overline{AB} \ncong \overline{CB}$. Corresponding angles are not congruent under this correspondence either, since $\angle ABD$ is not congruent to $\angle CBD$.

We can apply simpler conditions to verify the congruence of two triangles. Suppose that instead of having the three side lengths and three angle measures specified for a triangle, we are given only two of the side lengths and the measure of the angle formed by the two sides. Figure 14.5 shows an example.

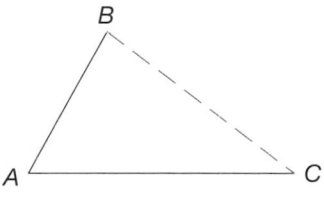

Figure 14.5

We can complete the triangle ($\triangle ABC$) in only one way, namely by connecting vertex B to vertex C. That is, the two given sides and the included angle determine a unique triangle. This observation is the basis of the side–angle–side congruence property.

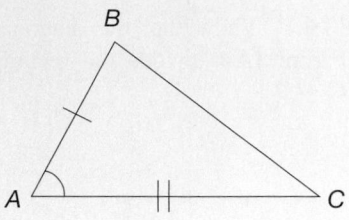

PROPERTY

Side–Angle–Side (SAS) Congruence

If two sides and the included angle of a triangle are congruent, respectively, to two sides and the included angle of another triangle, then the triangles are congruent. Here, $\triangle ABC \cong \triangle DEF$.

The SAS congruence property tells us that it is sufficient to verify that two sides and an included angle of one triangle are congruent, respectively, to their corresponding parts of another triangle, to establish that the triangles are congruent. Example 14.2 gives an illustration.

Example 14.2   In Figure 14.6, $\overline{AB} \cong \overline{AC}$ and $\angle BAP \cong \angle CAP$. Show that $\triangle BAP \cong \triangle CAP$.

Solution   Consider the correspondence $B \leftrightarrow C$, $A \leftrightarrow A$, $P \leftrightarrow P$. We have (i) $\overline{AP} \cong \overline{AP}$, (ii) $\angle BAP \cong \angle CAP$, and (iii) $\overline{AB} \cong \overline{AC}$. Hence, by (i), (ii), (iii), and the SAS congruence property, $\triangle BAP \cong \triangle CAP$.   ▪

From the result of Example 14.2, we can conclude that $\angle ABP \cong \angle ACP$ in Figure 14.6, since these angles correspond in the congruent triangles. Thus the base angles of an isosceles triangle are congruent. In Section 14.3 Part A Problem 17, we investigate the converse result, namely, that if two angles of a triangle are congruent, the triangle is isosceles.

A second congruence property for triangles involves two angles and their common side. Suppose that we are given two angles, the sum of whose measures is less than 180°. Also suppose that they share a common side. Figure 14.7 shows an example. The extensions of the noncommon sides of the angles intersect in a unique point C. That is, a unique triangle, $\triangle ABC$, is formed. This observation can be generalized as the angle–side–angle congruence property.

Figure 14.6

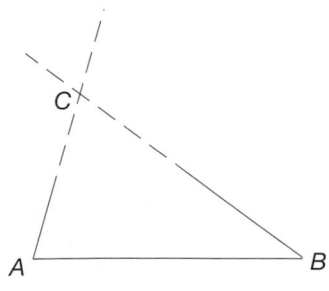

Figure 14.7

PROPERTY

Angle–Side–Angle (ASA) Congruence

If two angles and the included side of a triangle are congruent, respectively, to two angles and the included side of another triangle, then the two triangles are congruent. Here, $\triangle ABC \cong \triangle DEF$.

NOTE: Although we are assuming ASA congruence as a property, it actually can be shown to be a theorem that follows from the SAS congruence property.

Example 14.3 illustrates an application of the ASA congruence property.

Example 14.3   Show that the diagonal in Figure 14.8 divides a parallelogram into two congruent triangles.

NCTM Standards 2000
Geometry
Grades 6–8
All students should create and critique inductive and deductive arguments concerning geometric ideas and relationships, such as congruence, similarity, and the Pythagorean relationship.

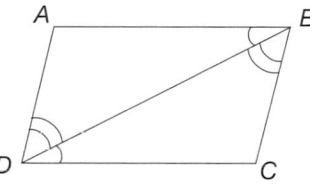

Figure 14.8

NCTM Standards 2000
Reasoning and Proof
Instructional programs should enable all students to recognize reasoning and proof as essential and powerful parts of mathematics.

Solution   Line $\overleftrightarrow{DB}$ is a transversal for lines $\overleftrightarrow{AB}$ and $\overleftrightarrow{DC}$. Since $\overleftrightarrow{AB} \parallel \overleftrightarrow{DC}$, we know (i) $\angle ABD \cong \angle CDB$ by the alternate interior angle property. Similarly, $\angle ADB$ and $\angle CBD$ are alternate interior angles formed by the transversal $\overleftrightarrow{BD}$ and parallel lines $\overleftrightarrow{AD}$ and $\overleftrightarrow{BC}$. Hence (ii) $\angle ADB \cong \angle CBD$. Certainly, (iii) $\overline{BD} \cong \overline{DB}$. Thus by (i), (ii), (iii), and the ASA congruence property, we have established that $\triangle ABD \cong \triangle CDB$.   ■

Since $\triangle ABD \cong \triangle CDB$, the six corresponding parts of the two triangles are congruent. Thus we have the following theorem.

THEOREM

Opposite Sides and Angles of a Parallelogram

Opposite sides of a parallelogram are congruent.
Opposite angles of a parallelogram are congruent.

The complete verifications of these results about parallelograms are left for Part A Problem 5 in the Problem Set.

The third and final congruence property for triangles that we will consider involves just the three sides. Suppose that we have three lengths x, y, and z units long, where the sum of any two lengths exceeds the third, with which we wish to form triangles as the lengths of the sides. If we lay out the longest side, we can pivot the shorter sides from the endpoints. Figure 14.9 illustrates this process. Notice that in pivoting the shorter sides [Figure 14.9(c)], we are drawing parts of two circles of radii x and y units, respectively. The two circles intersect at point C above $\overline{AB}$ and form the unique triangle $\triangle ABC$. [NOTE: We could also have extended our circles below $\overline{AB}$ so that they would intersect in another point, say D (Figure 14.10).]

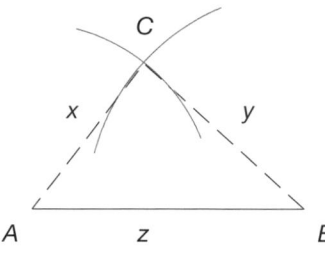

Lay off the longest side.

(a)

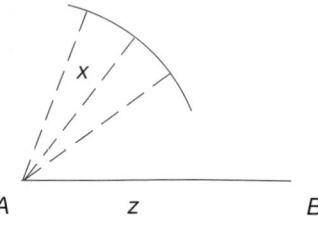

Pivot a shorter side from one endpoint.

(b)

Pivot the third side from the other end.

(c)

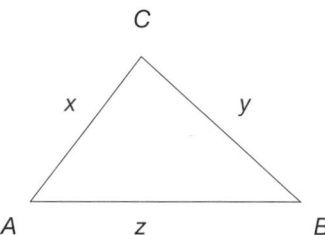

The two shorter sides can meet in only one point, *C*, above $\overline{AB}$.

(d)

Figure 14.9

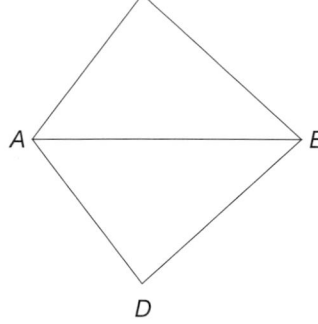

Figure 14.10

Once points *A* and *B* have been located and the position of point *C* has been found (above $\overline{AB}$ here) *only one* such triangle, $\triangle ABC$, can be formed. This observation is the basis of the side–side–side congruence property. (NOTE: This property can also be proved from the SAS congruence property.)

⬡ PROPERTY

Side–Side–Side (SSS) Congruence

If three sides of a triangle are congruent, respectively, to three sides of another triangle, then the two triangles are congruent. Here, $\triangle ABC \cong \triangle DEF$.

By the SSS congruence property it is sufficient to verify that corresponding sides in two triangles are congruent in order to establish that the triangles are congruent. Example 14.4 gives an application of the SSS congruence property.

Spotlight on Technology If you were given two sides and an angle and asked to construct a triangle with the angle between the two sides, would you always end up with the same shape of triangle no matter how you rearranged the pieces? According to the SAS congruence property, you would always get the same shape triangle. What if you were asked to construct a triangle with two sides and an angle, but the angle was *not between* the two sides? Would you always get the same shape triangle no matter how you rearranged the two sides and angle? You can investigate this question for yourself on the Chapter 14 eManipulative activity, *Congruence*. Try the SSA option and test your hypothesis.

www.wiley.com/
college/musser

Example 14.4   Suppose that $ABCD$ is a kite with $\overline{AB} \cong \overline{AD}$ and $\overline{BC} \cong \overline{DC}$. Show that the diagonal $\overline{AC}$ divides the kite into two congruent triangles (Figure 14.11).

Problem-Solving Strategy
Draw a Picture

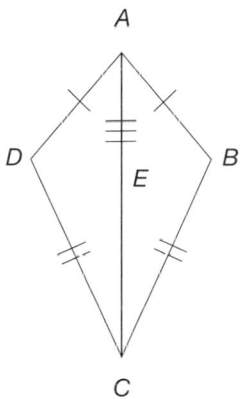

Figure 14.11

Solution We know (i) $\overline{AB} \cong \overline{AD}$ and (ii) $\overline{BC} \cong \overline{DC}$. Also, (iii) $\overline{AC} \cong \overline{AC}$. Using the correspondence $A \leftrightarrow A$, $B \leftrightarrow D$, and $C \leftrightarrow C$, we have that all three pairs of corresponding sides of $\triangle ABC$ and $\triangle ADC$ are congruent. Thus $\triangle ABC \cong \triangle ADC$ by (i), (ii), (iii), and the SSS congruence property. ■

From the result of Example 14.4, we can make several observations about kites. In particular, $\angle BAC \cong \angle DAC$, since they are corresponding angles in the congruent triangles (Figure 14.11). That is, $\overleftrightarrow{AC}$ divides $\angle DAB$ into two congruent angles, and we say that line $\overleftrightarrow{AC}$ is the **angle bisector** of $\angle DAB$. Notice that $\overleftrightarrow{AC}$ is the angle bisector of $\angle BCD$ as well, since $\angle BCA \cong \angle DCA$. We also observe that $\angle ADC \cong \angle ABC$, since they are corresponding angles in the congruent triangles, namely $\triangle ADC$ and $\triangle ABC$. Thus two of the opposite angles in a kite are congruent.

We might wonder whether there are "angle–angle–angle," "angle–angle–side," or "side–side–angle" congruence properties. In the Problem Set, we will see that only one of these properties is a congruence property.

MATHEMATICAL MORSEL

In his *Elements*, Euclid showed that in four cases—SAS, ASA, AAS, and SSS—if three corresponding parts of two triangles are congruent, all six parts are congruent in pairs. Interestingly, it is possible to have *five* (of the six) parts of one triangle congruent to *five parts* of a second triangle *without* the two triangles being congruent (i.e., the sixth parts are not congruent). Although it seems impossible, there are infinitely many such pairs of "5-con" triangles, as they have been named by a mathematics teacher. These 5-con triangles have three angles and two sides congruent. However, the congruent sides are not corresponding sides. Two such triangles are pictured.

Section 14.1 EXERCISE / PROBLEM SET A

EXERCISES

1. Given that $\triangle RST \cong \triangle JLK$, complete the following statements.

   a. $\triangle TRS \cong \triangle$_____

   b. $\triangle TSR \cong \triangle$_____

   c. $\triangle SRT \cong \triangle$_____

   d. $\triangle JKL \cong \triangle$_____

2. In the given pairs of triangles, congruent sides and angles are marked. Write an appropriate congruence statement about the triangles:

   a.

   b.

   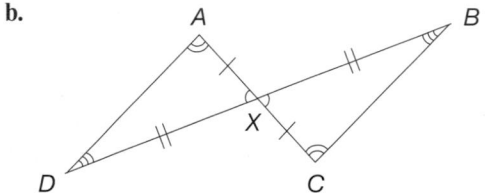

3. You are given $\triangle RST$ and $\triangle XYZ$ with $\angle S \cong \angle Y$.

   a. To show $\triangle RST \cong \triangle XYZ$ by the SAS congruence property, what more would you need to know?

   b. To show $\triangle RST \cong \triangle XYZ$ by the ASA congruence property, what more would you need to know? Give two different answers.

4. Could the SAS, ASA, or SSS congruence property be used to show that the following pairs of triangles are congruent? If not, why not?

   a.

   b.

   c.

   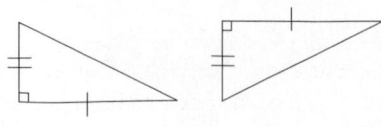

5. Are the following pairs of triangles congruent? Justify your answer.

   a.

   b.

   c.

   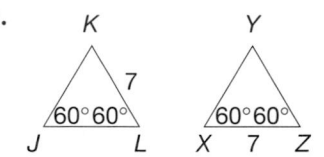

6. $\triangle ABC$ and $\triangle WXY$ are shown.

   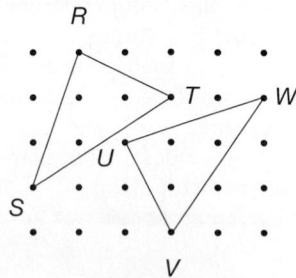

   a. To apply the SAS congruence property to prove $\triangle ABC \cong \triangle WXY$, you could show that $\overline{AB} \cong$?, that $\angle B \cong$?, and that $\overline{BC} \cong$?.

   b. Name two other sets of corresponding information that would allow you to apply the SAS congruence property.

7. Verify that the following triangles are congruent. Give the justification of your answer.

8. a. Identify the pairs of corresponding parts of
△*ABC* and △*DEF* that are congruent.

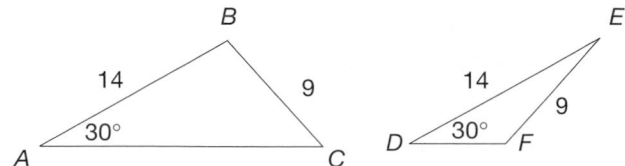

b. Does △*ABC* appear to be congruent to △*DEF*?

c. Can triangles be shown to be congruent by an SSA property? Explain your answer.

9. Verify that two congruent corresponding parts are not sufficient to guarantee that two triangles are congruent by drawing the following figures.

a. Draw △*ABC* and △*XYZ* with *AB* = 5 cm, *XY* = 5 cm, *AC* = 4 cm, *XZ* = 4 cm, but $m(\angle A) = 70°$, $m(\angle X) = 40°$. How do sides $\overline{BC}$ and $\overline{YZ}$ compare?

b. Draw △*ABC* and △*XYZ* with *AB* = 8 cm, *XY* = 8 cm, *AC* = 6 cm, *XZ* = 6 cm, but *BC* = 10 cm and *YZ* = 8 cm. How do ∠*A* and ∠*X* compare?

10. The parts of a *right* triangle are given special names, as indicated. Given are pairs of congruent triangles and the corresponding congruent parts. Identify which congruence property of general triangles applies.

a. Leg–leg

b. Leg–acute angle

c. Hypotenuse–acute angle

PROBLEMS

11. Two hikers, Ken and Betty, are standing on the edge of a river at point *A*, directly across from tree *T*. They mark off a certain distance to point *B*, where Betty remains. Ken travels that same distance to point *C*. Then he turns and walks directly away from the river to point *D*, where he can see Betty lined up with the tree.

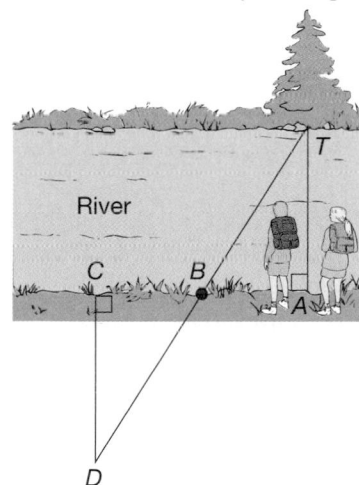

a. Identify the corresponding pairs of sides and angles that are congruent.

b. Is △*ABT* ≅ △*CBD*? Why or why not?

c. How can they use the information they have to find the width of the river?

12. If possible, draw two noncongruent triangles that satisfy the following conditions. If not possible, explain why not.

a. Three pairs of corresponding parts are congruent.

b. Four pairs of corresponding parts are congruent.

c. Five pairs of corresponding parts are congruent.

d. Six pairs of corresponding parts are congruent.

13. Two quadrilaterals are given in which three sides and the two included angles of one are congruent, respectively, to three sides and the two included angles of the other. A proof that the two quadrilaterals are congruent verifies the SASAS congruence property for quadrilaterals.

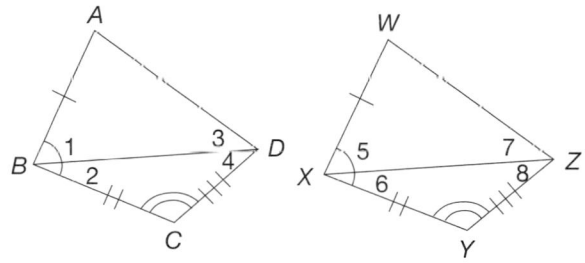

a. Draw diagonals $\overline{BD}$ and $\overline{XZ}$. Which of the triangles formed are congruent? What is the reason?

b. Show that ∠1 ≅ ∠5.

c. Show that △*ABD* ≅ △*WXZ*. What additional corresponding parts of the quadrilateral are therefore congruent?

d. Show that ∠*ADC* ≅ ∠*WZY*.

e. Have all the corresponding parts of quadrilaterals *ABCD* and *WXYZ* been shown to be congruent?

14. Justify the following statement: If $\angle D$ and $\angle E$ are supplementary and congruent, they are right angles.

15. Given parallelogram $ABCD$, prove the following properties using congruent triangles.

a. $\overline{AB} \cong \overline{CD}$, $\overline{BC} \cong \overline{DA}$ (opposite sides are congruent).

b. $\angle A \cong \angle C$, $\angle B \cong \angle D$ (opposite angles are congruent).

Section 14.1 EXERCISE / PROBLEM SET B

EXERCISES

1. The congruence $\triangle ABC \cong \triangle EFG$ can be rewritten as $\triangle ACB \cong \triangle EGF$. Rewrite this congruence in four other ways.

2. Each of the following triangles is congruent to $\triangle ABC$. Identify the correspondence and complete this statement: $\triangle ABC \cong \triangle$ _____.

a.

b.

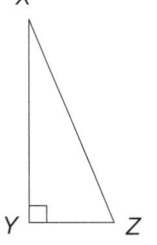

3. You are given $\triangle ABC$ and $\triangle GHI$ with $\overline{AB} \cong \overline{GH}$.

a. To show $\triangle ABC \cong \triangle GHI$ by the SSS congruence property, what more would you need to know?

b. To show $\triangle ABC \cong \triangle GHI$ by the SAS congruence property, what more would you need to know? Give two different answers.

c. To show $\triangle ABC \cong \triangle GHI$ by the ASA congruence property, what more would you need to know?

4. Identify the congruence property—SSS, SAS, or ASA—that could be used to show that the following pairs of triangles are congruent.

a.

b.

c.

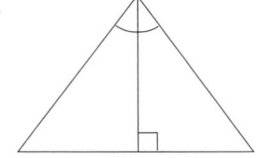

5. Are the following triangles congruent? Justify your answer.

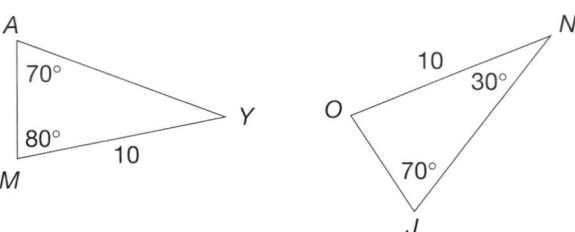

6. $\triangle LMN$ and $\triangle PQR$ are shown.

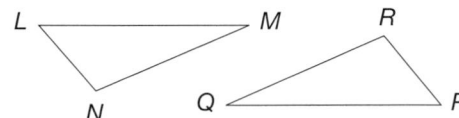

a. To use the ASA congruence property to prove $\triangle LMN \cong \triangle PQR$, could you show that $\angle L \cong ?$, that $\overline{LM} \cong ?$, and that $\angle M \cong ?$

b. Name two other sets of corresponding information that would allow you to apply the ASA congruence property.

7. Verify that the following triangles are congruent.

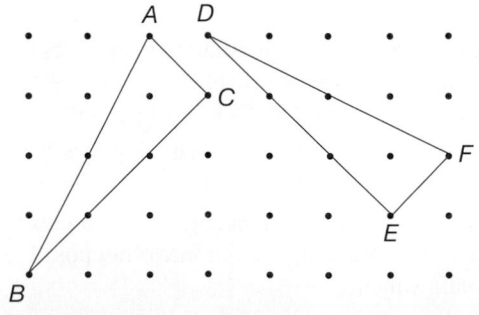

8. a. Identify the pairs of corresponding parts of △PQR and △STU that are congruent.

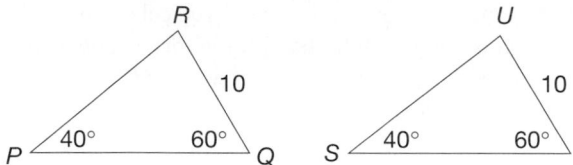

b. Does △PQR appear to be congruent to △STU?

c. Show that the triangles are congruent by ASA.

9. a. Identify the pairs of corresponding parts of △ABC and △XYZ that are congruent.

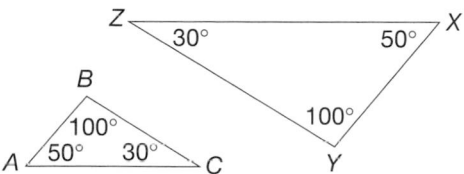

b. Does △ABC appear to be congruent to △XYZ?

c. Do you think triangles can be shown to be congruent by an AAA property? Explain your answer.

10. Shown are two right triangles.

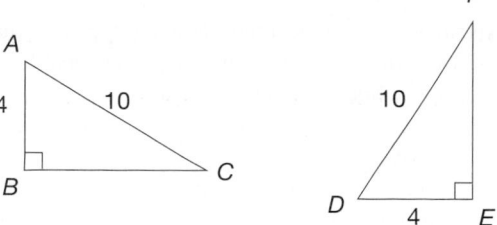

a. Identify the pairs of corresponding congruent parts.

b. Is there an SSA congruence property for general triangles that shows △ABC ≅ △DEF?

c. By applying the Pythagorean theorem, what other pair of corresponding parts are congruent?

d. Can we say that △ABC ≅ △DEF? Why? [NOTE: This demonstrates the hypotenuse–leg (HL) congruence property for right triangles.]

PROBLEMS

11. A saw blade is made by cutting six right triangles out of a regular hexagon as shown. If $\overline{XY}$ is cut the same at each tooth, why are the sharp points of the blade all congruent angles?

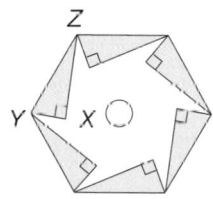

12. Draw two noncongruent triangles that satisfy the following conditions.

a. Three pairs of parts are congruent.

b. Four pairs of parts are congruent.

c. Five pairs of parts are congruent.

13. Two quadrilaterals are congruent if any three angles and the included sides of one are congruent, respectively, to three angles and the included sides of the other (ASASA for congruent quadrilaterals). Use the following figures to prove this statement.

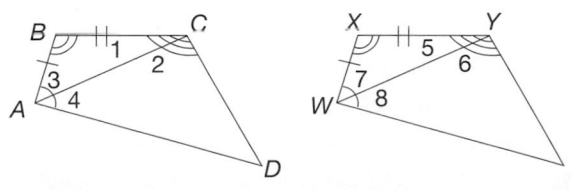

14. Justify the hypotenuse–leg congruence property for right triangles. In particular, right triangles △ABC and △XYZ are given with right angles at B and Y. Legs $\overline{AB}$ and $\overline{XY}$ are congruent and have length a. Hypotenuses $\overline{AC}$ and $\overline{XZ}$ are congruent with length c. Verify that △ABC ≅ △XYZ.

15. a. Draw two noncongruent quadrilaterals that satisfy the following description: a quadrilateral with four sides of length 5 units.

b. Draw two noncongruent quadrilaterals that satisfy the following description: a quadrilateral with two opposite sides of length 4 units and the other two sides of length 3 units.

c. The SSS congruence property was sufficient to show that two triangles were congruent. Is a similar pattern (SSSS) sufficient to show that two quadrilaterals are congruent? Justify your answer.

PROBLEMS FOR WRITING/DISCUSSION

1. Courtney was wondering how many types of quadrilaterals could be divided into two congruent triangles by drawing one diagonal. She knew a kite would work, but she was wondering about the others, particularly the parallelogram. What do you think? What other quadrilaterals can be split into two congruent triangles by one diagonal? Can you prove the two triangles are congruent?

2. Paul was looking at the following picture. He could see two triangles, $\triangle ABD$ and $\triangle ABC$, that seemed to have a number of parts that were congruent. Shouldn't the triangles be congruent by SAS? Discuss.

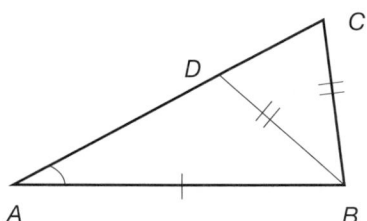

3. Allison says that if a triangle is isosceles, you can say it is congruent to itself. So in this example, you could say $\triangle ABC$ is congruent to $\triangle CAB$. Do you agree? Discuss.

14.2 SIMILARITY OF TRIANGLES

STARTING POINT

Write a description of what is meant by "this object is *similar* to that object." Use your description to determine whether the following pairs of objects are similar.

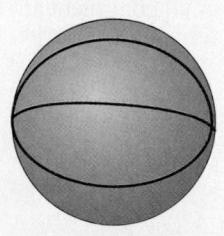

1. a volleyball and a basketball
2. a father and his son
3. two squares
4. you and your picture
5. a small soda cup and a medium soda cup from a fast-food restaurant
6. a piece a paper with writing on it and a clean piece of paper

Discuss how the English definition of *similar* and your understanding of the mathematical definition of *similar* compare.

Triangle Similarity

Informally, two geometric figures that have the same shape, but not *necessarily* the same size, are called similar. In the case of triangles we have the following definition.

Reflection from Research

Because the term *similar* is used in both mathematical and nonmathematical situations, students often have difficulty with its mathematical definition. For instance, in everyday life triangles are similar because they all have three sides; however, they may not be similar in a mathematical sense (Chazan, 1988).

DEFINITION

Similar Triangles

Suppose that $\triangle ABC$ and $\triangle DEF$ are such that under the correspondence $A \leftrightarrow D$, $B \leftrightarrow E$, $C \leftrightarrow F$, all corresponding sides are proportional and all corresponding vertex angles are congruent. Then $\triangle ABC$ is **similar** to $\triangle DEF$, and we write $\triangle ABC \sim \triangle DEF$.

Saying that corresponding sides in $\triangle ABC$ and $\triangle DEF$ are proportional means that the ratios of corresponding sides are all equal. That is, if $\triangle ABC \sim \triangle DEF$, then $\frac{AB}{DE} = \frac{BC}{EF} = \frac{AC}{DF}$.

Example 14.5 Suppose that $\triangle ABC \sim \triangle DEF$ with $AB = 5$, $BC = 8$, $AC = 11$, and $DF = 3$ (Figure 14.12). Find DE and EF.

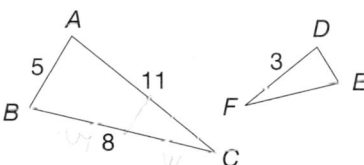

Figure 14.12

NCTM Standards 2000
Measurement
Grades 6–8

All students should solve problems involving scale factors, using ratio and proportion.

Solution Since the triangles are similar under the correspondence $A \leftrightarrow D$, $B \leftrightarrow E$, $C \leftrightarrow F$, we know that $\frac{AB}{DE} = \frac{AC}{DF}$. Hence

$$\frac{5}{DE} = \frac{11}{3},$$

so that

$$DE = \frac{15}{11} = 1\frac{4}{11}.$$

Similarly, $\frac{BC}{EF} = \frac{AC}{DF}$, so that

$$\frac{8}{EF} = \frac{11}{3}.$$

Therefore,

$$EF = \frac{24}{11} = 2\frac{2}{11}.$$

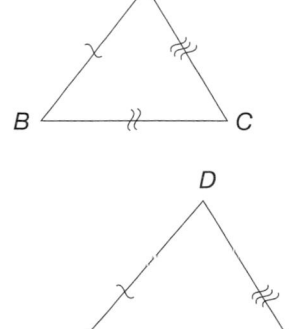

Figure 14.13

Suppose that $\triangle ABC \sim \triangle DEF$ (Figure 14.13). From the proportions, $\frac{AB}{DE} = \frac{BC}{EF} = \frac{AC}{DF}$, we see that there are several other proportions that we can form. For example, the proportion $\frac{AB}{BC} = \frac{DE}{EF}$ tells us that the ratio of the lengths of two sides of $\triangle ABC$, say $\frac{AB}{BC}$, is equal to the corresponding ratio from $\triangle DEF$, namely $\frac{DE}{EF}$.

There are similarity properties for triangles analogous to the SAS, ASA, and SSS congruence properties for triangles. For example, suppose that $\triangle ABC$ and $\triangle DEF$ correspond, so that $\dfrac{AB}{DE} = \dfrac{AC}{DF}$ and $\angle BAC \cong \angle EDF$; that is, two pairs of corresponding sides are proportional, and their included angles are congruent (Figure 14.14). Then $\triangle ABC \sim \triangle DEF$. Thus we have an SAS similarity property for triangles,

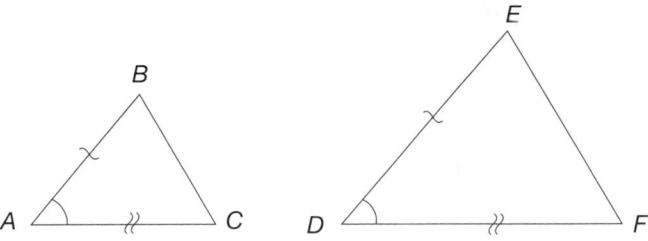

Figure 14.14

just as we have an SAS congruence property. We summarize the triangle similarity properties as follows.

PROPERTIES

Similarity Properties of Triangles

Two triangles, $\triangle ABC$ and $\triangle DEF$, are similar if and only if at least one of the following three statements is true.

1. Two pairs of corresponding sides are proportional and their included angles are congruent (SAS similarity).

2. Two pairs of corresponding angles are congruent (AA similarity).

3. All three pairs of corresponding sides are proportional (SSS similarity).

Notice that AA similarity is equivalent to AAA similarity, since the measure of the third angle is known once the measures of two angles are known.

Indirect Measurement

Example 14.6 illustrates an application of the AA similarity property in *indirect mea-surement* [as opposed to direct measurement where a ruler (protractor) is placed on the segment (angle) to be measured].

Example 14.6   A student who is 1.5 meters tall wishes to determine the height of a tree on the school grounds. The tree casts a shadow 37.5 m long at the same time that the student casts a shadow that is 2.5 m long (Figure 14.15). Assume that the tree and student are on level ground. How tall is the tree?

Problem-Solving Strategy
Draw a Picture

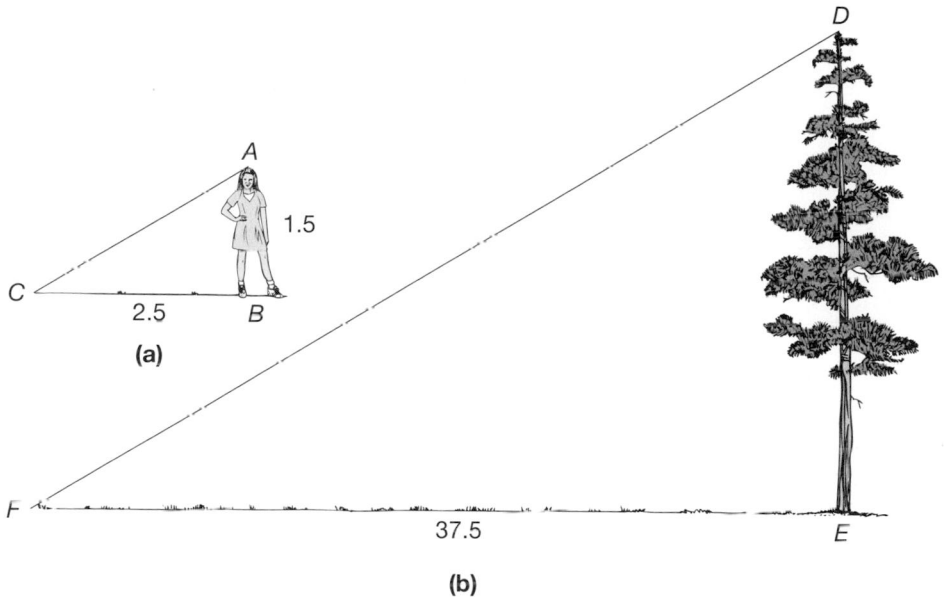

(a)

(b)

Figure 14.15

Solution Let $\triangle ABC$ be a triangle formed by the line segment joining the top of the student's head and the ground, $\overline{AB}$, and the student's shadow, $\overline{BC}$. Notice that $\overline{AC}$ can be considered part of a light ray from the sun. Similarly, $\triangle DEF$ is formed by $\overline{DE}$, a line segment from the top of the tree to the ground, and the tree's shadow, $\overline{EF}$. Assume that the light ray containing $\overline{DF}$ is parallel to the ray containing $\overline{AC}$, so that $\angle ACB \cong \angle DFE$. (Use the corresponding angles property to verify this.) Then we have the pair of right triangles, $\triangle ABC$ and $\triangle DEF$.

We wish to find the distance DE. Using the AA similarity property, we see that $\triangle ABC \sim \triangle DEF$. Hence $\dfrac{DE}{AB} = \dfrac{EF}{BC}$, so that $\dfrac{DE}{1.5} = \dfrac{37.5}{2.5}$, and

$$DE = \frac{1.5 \times 37.5}{2.5} = 22.5$$

Thus the tree is 22.5 meters tall.   ■

www.wiley.com/
college/musser

Spotlight on Technology Since the above problem assumes that the shadows of the girl and tree are measured at the same time of day, we know that their heights and shadows are proportional. Any other tree's height and shadow would be proportional to the girl's at the same time of day. By moving the point X on the Geometer's Sketchpad® web-module activity, *Tree Height*, we can see the proportional heights of any other tree whose shadow was measured at that same time of day. In addition to being able to find the height of a tree that casts a 37.5-foot shadow, how can the proportional height measurement be used to find the height of a tree that casts a 28-meter shadow?

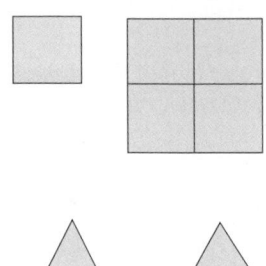

Fractals and Self-Similarity

In Section 9.3 we studied various types of functions and their graphs. These functions and others are used to model physical phenomena to solve problems. However, in many instances, such as the shapes of waves and prices in the stock market, behavior does not conform to "nice" functions. In 1982, Benoit Mandelbrot's book *The Fractal Geometry of Nature* popularized a form of geometry that attempts to study chaotic behaviors. The following discussion provides an introduction to the notion of self-similarity, which is part of this modern field of study.

Squares and equilateral triangles are simple examples of reptiles, namely tiles that when arranged in the proper way produced new tiles of the same shape. (Figure 14.16). Observe that as new shapes are constructed, they are similar to each of the previous shapes. Some trees also exhibit this idea. Figure 14.17 displays a part of a tree that begins with two branches and then grows two similar ones at the end of each new branch.

Figure 14.16

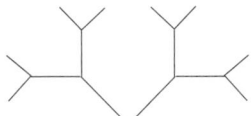

Figure 14.17

A more intricate pattern is shown in Figure 14.18. This construction begins with an equilateral triangle. Next, equilateral triangles are constructed on the middle thirds of the original triangle. The curve formed by repeating this process *indefinitely* is known as the **Koch curve.** Notice how each small triangle formed is similar to the preceding triangle. The Koch curve is said to be **self-similar,** since the curve looks the same when magnified. In addition to being self-similar, the Koch curve has a finite area but an *infinite* perimeter!

  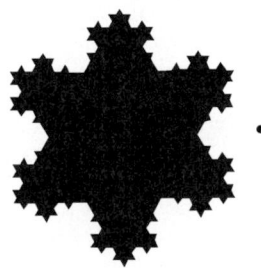

Figure 14.18

Another well-known self-similar shape is called the **Sierpinski triangle** or **Sierpinski gasket.** This shape results from starting with an equilateral triangle and removing successively smaller ones from the centers of the newly formed triangles (Figure 14.19).

Figure 14.19

Shapes that occur in nature and exhibit self-similarity somewhat are broccoli, acorns, and breaking waves. Fractal geometry and chaos theory are examples of two of the new fields of mathematics that have been popularized in the past 30 large part due to the availability of high-speed computers.

MATHEMATICAL MORSEL

The Pythagorean theorem can be stated in words as follows: In a right triangle, the area of the square on the hypotenuse is equal to the sum of the areas of the squares on the two sides. Interestingly, this theorem also holds for shapes other than squares. For example, the area of the semicircle on the hypotenuse is equal to the sum of the areas of the semicircles on the two sides. The semicircles can be replaced by any regular polygons and the same relationship still holds. Even more surprising, this "Pythagorean" relationship holds for the areas of any three shapes constructed on the three sides of a right triangle, as long as the figures are similar.

Section 14.2 EXERCISE / PROBLEM SET A

EXERCISES

1. Which of the following pairs of triangles are similar? If they are similar, explain why.

a.

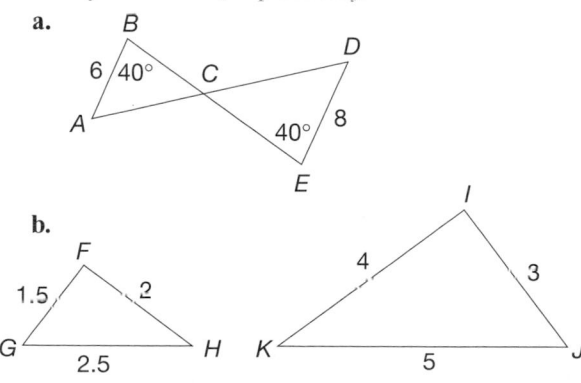

b.

2. Given are pairs of similar triangles with some dimensions specified. Find the measures of the other sides.

a.

b.

c.

d.

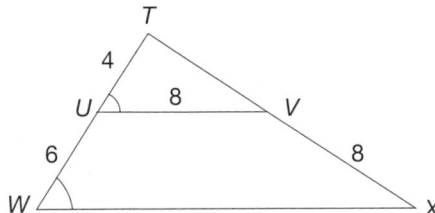

3. Using the measurements given, find the distance PQ across the river. (NOTE: Point O is on $\overline{MQ}$, $PO = 10$ m, and P, O, N are collinear.)

4. True or false? Justify your reasoning.

  a. If two triangles are similar, they are congruent.

  b. If two triangles are congruent, they are similar.

  c. All equilateral triangles are congruent.

  d. All equilateral triangles are similar.

PROBLEMS

5. Suppose that parallel lines l_1, l_2, and l_3 are intersected by parallel transversals m and n.

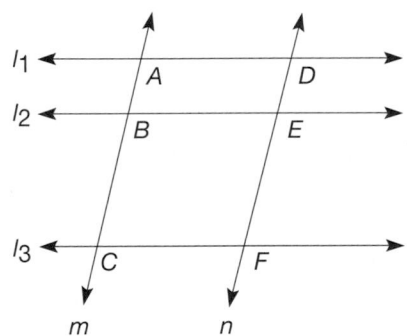

  a. Justify that quadrilaterals $ABED$ and $BCFE$ are parallelograms.

  b. Justify that $AB = DE$ and $BC = EF$.

  c. Complete the proportion $\dfrac{AB}{BC} = \dfrac{?}{?}$.

  d. Have parallel lines l_1, l_2, and l_3 intercepted proportional segments on transversals m and n?

6. Suppose that parallel lines l_1, l_2, and l_3 are intersected by transversals m and n, which intersect at a point P. Let a, b, c, x, y, and z represent the lengths of the segments shown.

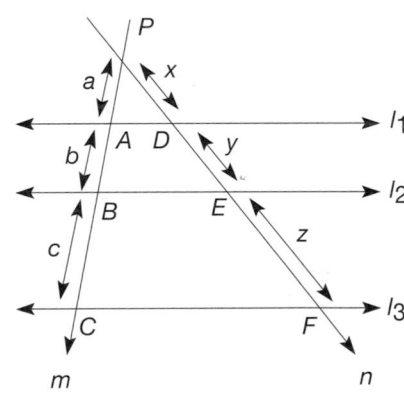

  a. Verify that $\triangle PAD \sim \triangle PBE \sim \triangle PCF$.

  b. Show that $ay = bx$.

  c. Show that $ay + az = bx + cx$.

  d. Show that $az = cx$.

  e. Combine parts (b) and (d) to show that $\dfrac{b}{c} = \dfrac{y}{z}$.

  f. Have parallel lines l_1, l_2, and l_3 intercepted proportional segments on transversals m and n?

7. The conclusions of Problems 5 and 6 can be summarized: Parallel lines intercept proportional segments on all transversals. Apply this result to complete the following proportions when $l_1 \parallel l_2 \parallel l_3 \parallel l_4$.

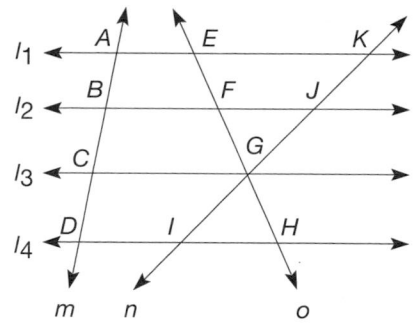

a. $\dfrac{AB}{BC} = \underline{\quad\quad} = \underline{\quad\quad}$

b. $\dfrac{FG}{GH} = \underline{\quad\quad} = \underline{\quad\quad}$

c. $\dfrac{IJ}{JK} = \underline{\quad\quad} = \underline{\quad\quad}$

8. At a particular time, a tree casts a shadow 29 m long on horizontal ground. At the same time, a vertical pole 3 m high casts a shadow 4 m long. Calculate the height of the tree to the nearest meter.

9. Another method of determining the height of an object uses a mirror placed on level ground. The person stands at an appropriate distance from the mirror so that he or she sees the top of the object when looking in the mirror.

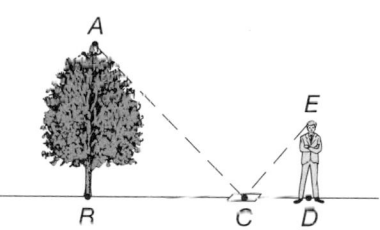

a. Name two similar triangles in the diagram. Why are they similar?

b. Find the height of the tree if a person 1.5 meters tall sees the top of the tree when the mirror is 18 meters from the base of the tree and the person is standing 1 meter from the mirror.

10. a. A person 6 feet tall is in search of a tree 100 feet tall. If the person's shadow is 9 feet, what is the length of the shadow of the tree?

b. The person in part (a) walks 60 feet from the base of a tree and finds that the shadows of his head and the tree coincide. How tall is the tree?

11. Suppose that a film is being shown in class when a student sitting 5 feet in front of the projector puts his hand between the projector and the screen as shown here.

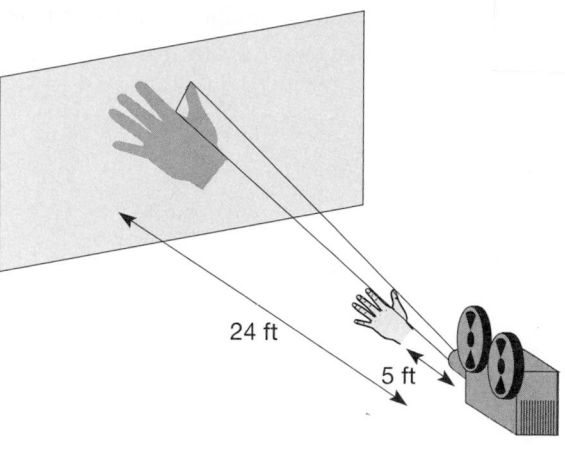

24 ft

5 ft

a. If the projector is 24 feet from the screen and the student's thumb is 2 inches long, how long does his thumb appear to be on the screen?

b. If the student were 10 feet in front of the projector, how would that change the image of the thumb on the screen?

12. Suppose that a tree growing on level ground must be cut down and the approximate height of the tree needs to be calculated to determine where it should fall. To calculate that height, you can use a right isosceles triangle cut from cardboard or wood. You must sight along the hypotenuse of the right triangle and walk forward or backward as necessary until the top of the tree is exactly in line with the hypotenuse. Also, the bottom side of the triangle must be in a horizontal line with the place where you are going to cut. The point at which you now stand is where the top of the tree will fall.

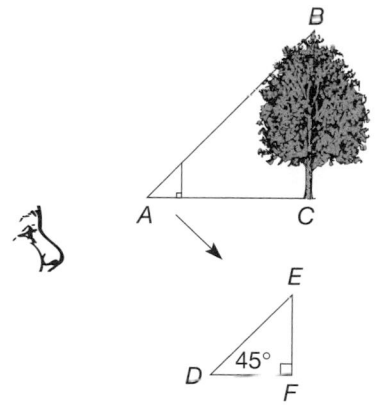

Use similar triangles to explain why this method works.

13. Some hikers wanted to measure the distance across a canyon. They sighted two boulders A and B on the opposite side. Measuring between C and D (points across from A and B), they found $AB = 60$ m.

Find the distance across the canyon, BD, using the distances in the diagram. Assume that $\overleftrightarrow{AB} \parallel \overleftrightarrow{CD}$.

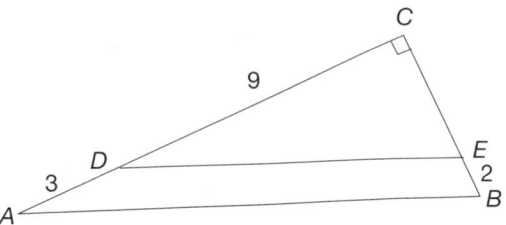

14. Two right triangles are similar, and the lengths of the sides of one triangle are twice the lengths of the corresponding sides of the other. Compare the areas of the triangles.

15. Explain how the figure shown can be used to find $\sqrt{a}$ for any given length a. (*Hint*: Prove that $x^2 = a$.)

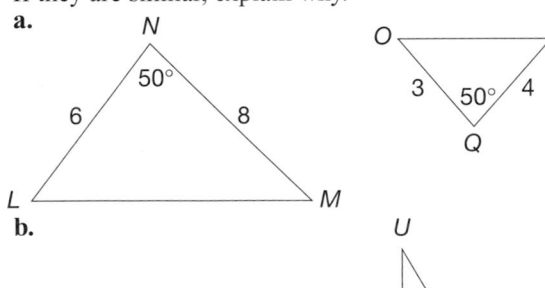

16. Given $\triangle ABC$, where $\overline{DE} \parallel \overline{AB}$, find AB.

17. Prove the Pythagorean theorem using the following diagram and similar triangles.

18. Assume that the original triangle in the construction of the Koch curve has sides of length 1.

   a. What is the perimeter of the initial curve (the triangle)?

   b. What is the perimeter of the second curve?

   c. What is the perimeter of the third curve?

   d. What is the perimeter of the nth curve?

19. Assume that the original triangle in the construction of the Koch curve has area 9.

   a. What is the area of the second curve?

   b. What is the area of the third curve?

   c. What is the area of the fourth curve?

   d. What is the area of the nth curve?

Section 14.2   EXERCISE / PROBLEM SET B

EXERCISES

1. Which of the following pairs of triangles are similar? If they are similar, explain why.

   a.

   b.

   a.

   b.

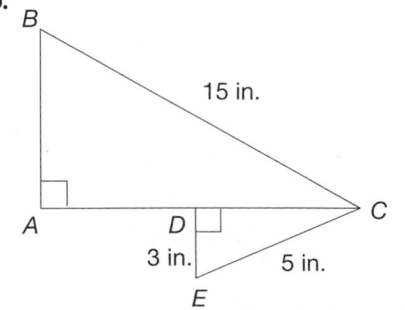

2. The following pairs are similar triangles with some dimensions specified. Find the measures of the other sides.

c.

d.

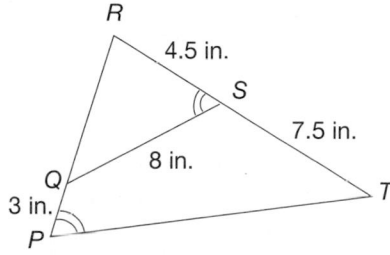

3. Given △*ABC* as shown, where $\overline{DE} \parallel \overline{AB}$, find *AD*.

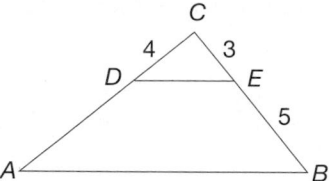

4. True of false? Justify your reasoning.

   a. All isosceles triangles are congruent.

   b. All isosceles triangles are similar.

   c. All isosceles right triangles are congruent.

   d. All isosceles right triangles are similar.

PROBLEMS

5. Lines *k*, *l*, *m*, and *n* are parallel. Find *a*, *b*, *c*, and *d*.

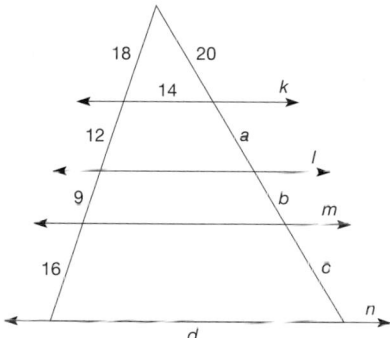

6. a. Is $n \parallel \overleftrightarrow{AB}$? Explain.

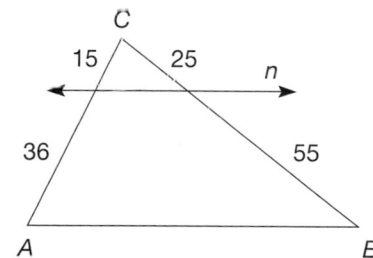

   b. Is $m \parallel \overleftrightarrow{CD}$? Explain.

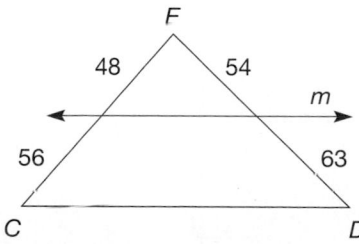

7. Compute the ratios requested for the following pairs of figures.

   a. Find the ratios of base : base, height : height, and area : area for this pair of similar triangles.

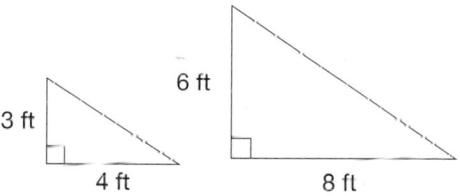

   b. Find the ratios of base : base, height : height, and area : area for this pair of similar triangles.

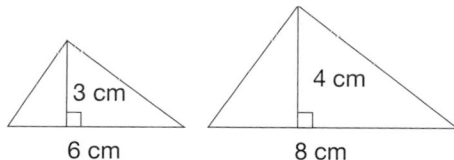

   c. Find the ratios of length : length, width : width, and area : area for this pair of similar rectangles.

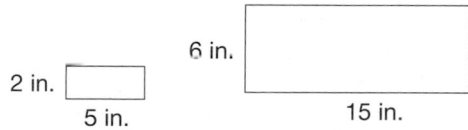

   d. Do you see a pattern in the relationship between the ratios of the dimensions and the ratios of the areas? Test your conjecture by drawing several other pairs of similar geometric figures.

8. Is $\triangle ADC \sim \triangle CDE$? Explain.

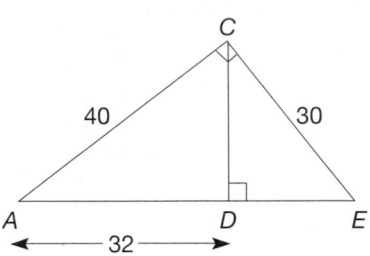

9. *PQRS* is a trapezoid.

a. Why is $\triangle PQT \sim \triangle RST$?

b. Find a and b.

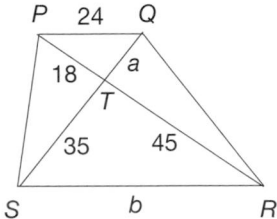

10. Tom and Carol are playing a shadow game. Tom is 6 feet tall and Carol is 5 feet tall. If Carol stands at the "shadow top" of Tom's head, their two combined shadows total 15 feet. How long is each shadow?

11. A boy and his friend wish to calculate the height of a flagpole. One boy holds a yardstick vertically at a point 40 feet from the base of the flagpole, as shown. The other boy backs away from the pole to a point where he sights the top of the pole over the top of the yardstick. If his position is 1 foot 9 inches from the yardstick and his eye level is 2 feet above the ground, find the height of the flagpole.

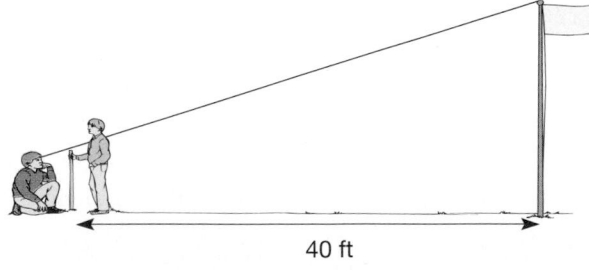

40 ft

12. A new department store opens on a hot summer day. Kathy's job is to stand outside the main entrance and hand out a special supplement to incoming customers. The building is 30 feet tall and casts a shadow 8 feet wide in front of the store. If Kathy is 5 ft 6 in. tall, how far away from the building can she stand and still be in the shade?

30 ft

8 ft

13. Some scouts want to measure the distance *AB* across a gorge. They estimated the distance *AC* to be 70 feet and *AD* to be 50 feet. How could they find the distance *AB*? Assume that *C*, *B*, and *E* are collinear, as are *D*, *B*, and *F*. Also assume that $\angle CAD$ and $\angle FBE$ are right angles.

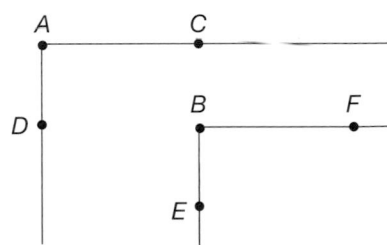

14. Prove: Two isosceles triangles, $\triangle ABC$ and $\triangle XYZ$, are similar if their nonbase angles, $\angle B$ and $\angle Y$, are congruent.

15. The Pythagorean theorem is often interpreted in terms of areas of squares, as shown in the following figure.

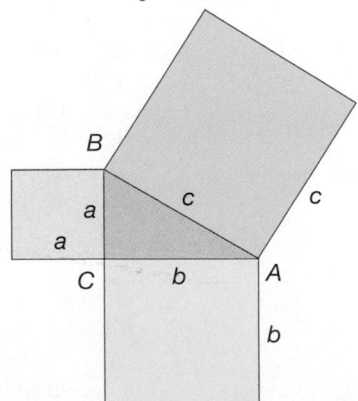

The equation $a^2 + b^2 = c^2$ means that the sum of the areas of the squares drawn on the legs of the right triangle equals the area of the square drawn on the hypotenuse. In fact, the theorem can be generalized to mean that if similar figures are drawn on each side of the right triangle, the sum of the areas of the two smaller figures equals the area of the larger figure. Verify that this is the case for each figure that follows.

a.

b.

c.

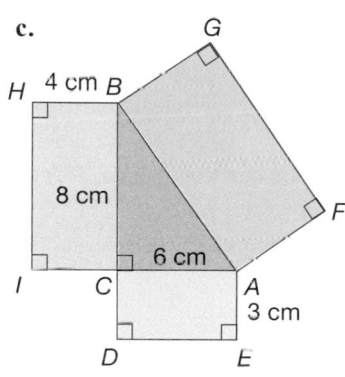

d. (NOTE: Parallel sides are marked by arrowheads.)

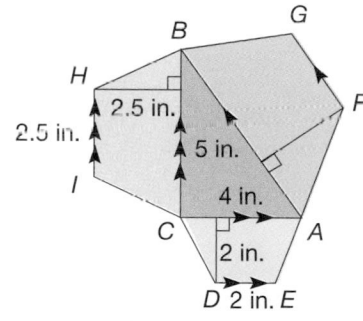

16. Given $\overline{AB} \parallel \overline{CD}$, $BE = 1$, $CD = 5$, $CE = 3$, and $AD = 7$, find $AB, AE,$ and DE.

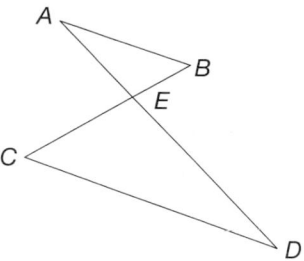

17. Prove that triangles are similar if their sides are respectively parallel to each other.

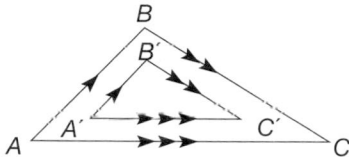

18. Assume that the original Sierpinski triangle has perimeter 3 (refer to Figure 14.19).

    a. What is the perimeter of the black portion of the second curve?

    b. What is the perimeter of the black portion of the third curve?

    c. What is the perimeter of the black portion of the fourth curve?

    d. What is the perimeter of the black portion of the nth curve?

19. Assume that the original Sierpinski triangle has area 1 (refer to Figure 14.19).

    a. What is the area of the black portion of the second curve?

    b. What is the area of the black portion of the third curve?

    c. What is the area of the black portion of the fourth curve?

    d. What is the area of the black portion of the nth curve

PROBLEMS FOR WRITING/DISCUSSION

1. Barbara wanted to get a few of her vacation photos enlarged. The originals are 4″ by 6″, and she wants them enlarged to 5″ by 8″. She wants to know whether these two rectangles are similar and, if not, whether the photos will be distorted in some way. How would you respond?

2. Kim says if you draw the diagonals in an isosceles trapezoid, four triangles are formed: Two of the triangles are congruent to each other and the other two are similar to each other. Do you agree with Kim? Discuss.

3. Marvin wants to find the height of a building using the sun, his height, and similar triangles. He goes out during his lunch break at noon on a sunny day but complains that this method doesn't seem to work. What might be his problem?

14.3 BASIC EUCLIDEAN CONSTRUCTIONS

Identify all of the properties of the diagonals of a parallelogram and a rhombus. Are there any properties that a rhombus has that a parallelogram does not? If so, what are they? Are there any properties that a parallelogram has that a rhombus does not? If so, what are they?

Parallelogram   **Rhombus**

In this section we study many of the classical compass and straightedge constructions. The following properties will be applied to constructions with a compass and straightedge.

Compass and Straightedge Properties

1. For every positive number r and for every point C, we can construct a circle of radius r and center C. A connected portion of a circle is called an **arc** [Figure 14.20(a)].

2. Every pair of points P and Q can be connected by our straightedge to construct the line $\overleftrightarrow{PQ}$, the ray $\overrightarrow{PQ}$, and the segment $\overline{PQ}$ [Figure 14.20(b)].

3. A line l can be constructed if and only if we have located two points that are on l [Figure 14.20(c)]. Points are located only by the intersection of lines, rays, segments, or arcs [Figure 14.20(d)].

CONSTRUCTION 1   Copy a line segment.

Given line segment $\overline{AB}$ [Figure 14.21(a)], line l, and point P [Figure 14.21(b)], locate point Q on l so that $\overline{PQ} \cong \overline{AB}$ [Figure 14.21(d)].

Figure 14.20

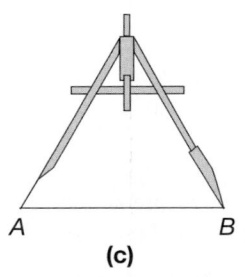

Figure 14.21

Procedure (Figure 14.21)

1. Open the compass to length AB [Figure 14.21(c)].

2. With the point of the compass at P, mark off an arc of radius AB that intersects line l. Let Q be the point of intersection of the arc and line l [Figure 14.21(d)]. Then $\overline{PQ} \cong \overline{AB}$.

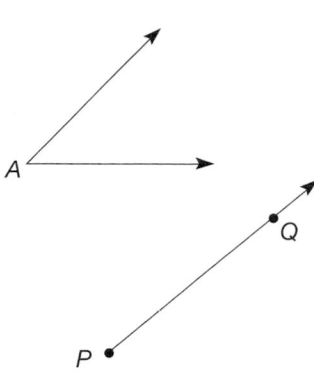

Figure 14.22

Justification (Figure 14.21): On line $\overleftrightarrow{AB}$, the distance AB is a positive real number, say r. By the compass and straightedge property 1, we can construct an arc of a circle of radius r with center at P. The intersection of the arc of the circle and line l is the desired point Q. ■

CONSTRUCTION 2   Copy an angle.

Given an angle $\angle A$ and a ray $\overrightarrow{PQ}$, locate point S so that $\angle SPQ \cong \angle A$ (Figure 14.22).

Procedure (Figure 14.23)

1. With the point of the compass at A, construct an arc that intersects each side of $\angle A$. Call the intersection points B and C [Figure 14.23(a)].

2. With the compass open to the radius AB, place the point at P and construct an arc of radius AB that intersects ray $\overrightarrow{PQ}$. Call the point of intersection point R [Figure 14.23(b)].

3. Place the point of the compass at C and open the compass to radius CB. Then, with the *same* compass opening, put the point of the compass at R and construct an arc of radius CB intersecting the first arc. Call the point of intersection of the two arcs point S [Figure 14.23(b)].

4. Construct ray $\overrightarrow{PS}$. Then $\angle BAC \cong \angle SPR$ (Figure 14.24).

Figure 14.23

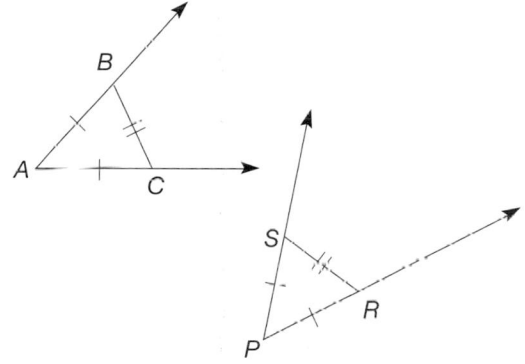

Figure 14.24

Justification (Figure 14.24): Construct the line segments $\overline{BC}$ and $\overline{SR}$, and consider $\triangle BAC$ and $\triangle SPR$. From the construction procedure, we know $\overline{AB} \cong \overline{AC} \cong \overline{PS} \cong \overline{PR}$ and $\overline{BC} \cong \overline{SR}$. Consider the correspondence $A \leftrightarrow P$, $B \leftrightarrow S$, $C \leftrightarrow R$. Then $\triangle BAC \cong \triangle SPR$ by the SSS congruence property. Consequently, $\angle BAC \cong \angle SPR$, as desired. ■

CONSTRUCTION 3   Construct the perpendicular bisector of a line segment.

Given a line segment $\overline{AB}$, construct line l so that $l \perp \overline{AB}$ and l intersects $\overline{AB}$ at the midpoint of $\overline{AB}$ (Figure 14.25).

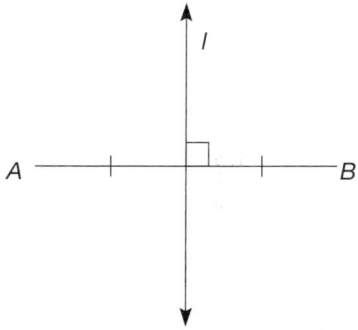

Figure 14.25

Procedure (Figure 14.26)

1. Place the compass point at A and open the compass to a radius r such that $r > \frac{1}{2}AB$; that is, r is more than one-half the distance AB. Construct arcs of radius r on each side of $\overline{AB}$ [Figure 14.26(a)].

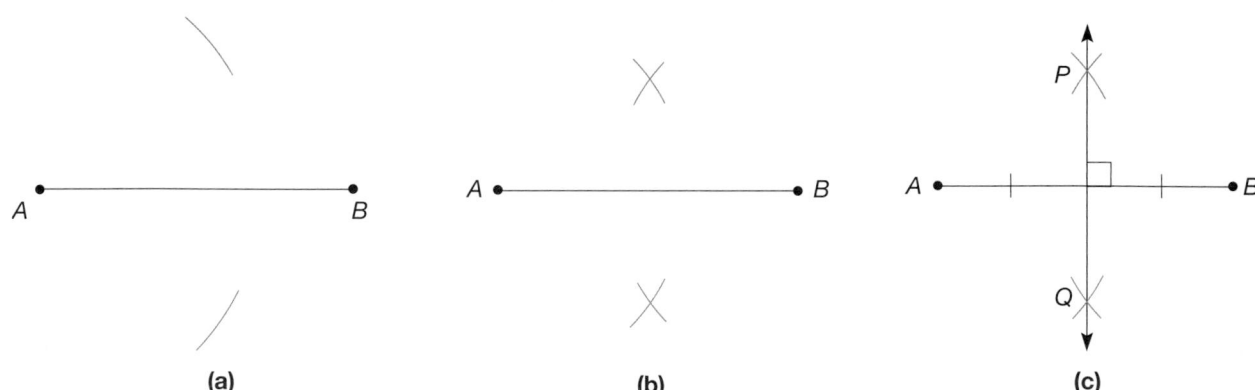

(a)   **(b)**   **(c)**

Figure 14.26

2. With the same compass opening, r, place the point of the compass at B and swing arcs of radius r on each side of $\overline{AB}$ [Figure 14.26(b)].

3. Let P be the intersection of the arcs on one side of $\overline{AB}$, and let Q be the intersection of the arcs on the other side of $\overline{AB}$. Construct line $\overleftrightarrow{PQ}$. Then line $\overleftrightarrow{PQ}$ is the perpendicular bisector of line segment $\overline{AB}$ [Figure 14.26(c)].

Justification (Figure 14.27): We will give the major steps. Construct segments $\overline{PA}$, $\overline{PB}$, $\overline{QA}$, and $\overline{QB}$. Let R be the intersection of $\overline{PQ}$ and $\overline{AB}$. By the construction procedure, $PA = PB = QA = QB$ [Figure 14.27(a)]. Also, $\overline{PQ} \cong \overline{PQ}$. Hence $\triangle APQ \cong \triangle BPQ$ by the SSS congruence property. Thus $\angle APQ \cong \angle BPQ$ [Figure 14.27(b)]. Consider $\triangle APR$ and $\triangle BPR$. They are congruent by the SAS congruence condition. Consequently, $AR = BR$, so $\overline{PQ}$ bisects $\overline{AB}$. We know that $\angle PRA$ and $\angle PRB$ are supplementary, so that all that remains is to show $\angle PRA \cong \angle PRB$. But this follows from the fact that $\triangle APR \cong \triangle BPR$. Therefore, $\overline{PQ} \perp \overline{AB}$.

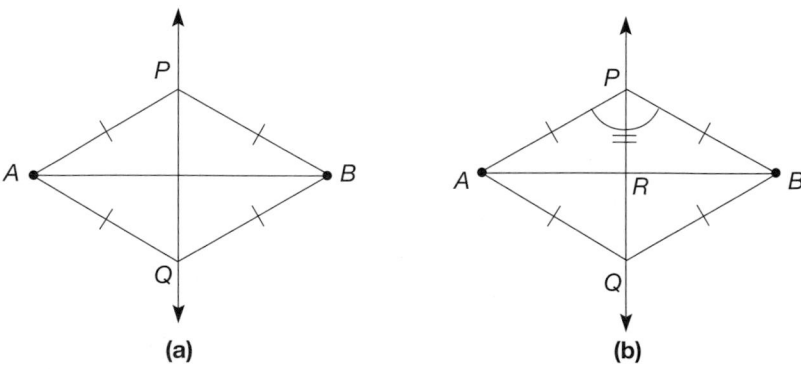

(a)   **(b)**

Figure 14.27

CONSTRUCTION 4 Bisect an angle.

Given an angle $\angle ABC$ [Figure 14.28(a)], construct a line $\overleftrightarrow{BR}$ such that $\angle ABR \cong$ $\angle CBR$; that is, $\overleftrightarrow{BR}$ is the angle bisector of $\angle ABC$ [Figure 14.28(b)].

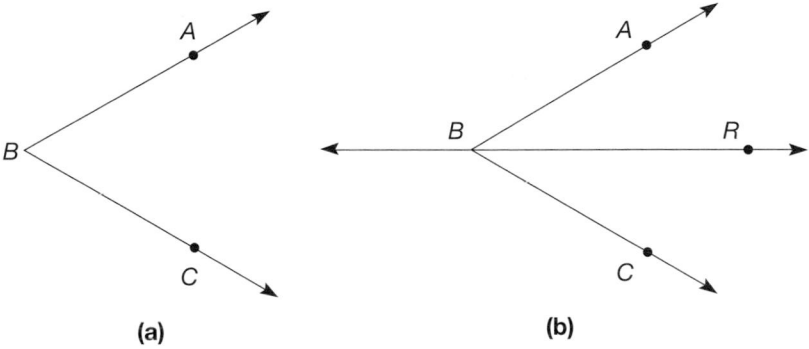

(a) **(b)**

Figure 14.28

Procedure (Figure 14.29)

1. Put the compass point at B and construct an arc that intersects sides $\overrightarrow{BA}$ and $\overrightarrow{BC}$. Label the points of intersection P and Q, respectively [Figure 14.29(a)].

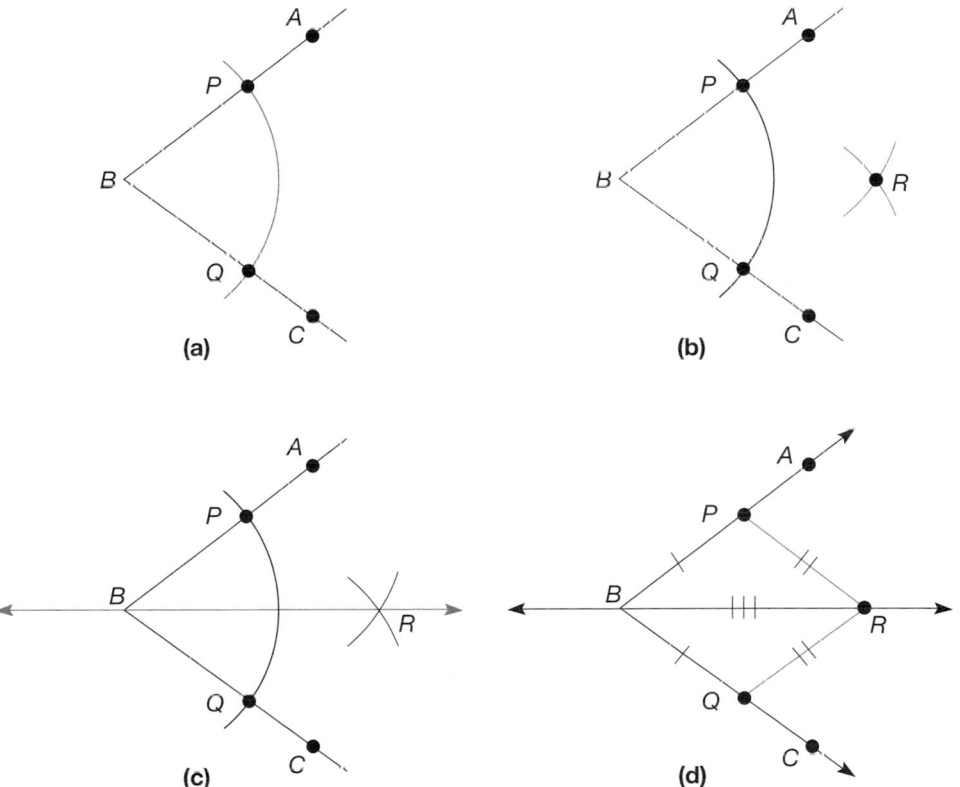

Figure 14.29

2. Put the compass point at P and then at Q, and construct intersecting arcs of the *same* radius. Label the intersection of the arcs R [Figure 14.29(b)].
3. Construct line $\overleftrightarrow{BR}$, the angle bisector of $\angle ABC$ [Figure 14.29(c)].

Figure 14.30

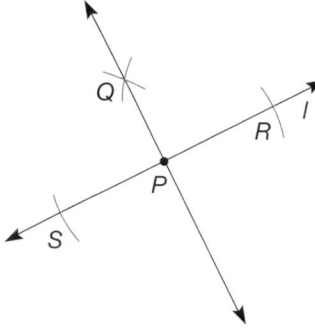

Figure 14.31

Justification [Figure 14.29(d)]: By step 1, $\overline{PB} \cong \overline{QB}$, and by step 2, $\overline{RQ} \cong \overline{RP}$. Certainly $\overline{BR} \cong \overline{BR}$. Thus $\triangle PBR \cong \triangle QBR$ by the SSS congruence property, so that $\angle PBR \cong \angle QBR$, as desired. ■

CONSTRUCTION 5 Construct a line perpendicular to a given line through a specified point on the line.

Given point P on l, construct $\overleftrightarrow{QP}$ such that $\overleftrightarrow{QP} \perp l$ (Figure 14.30).

Procedure (Figure 14.31)

1. Place the point of the compass at P and construct arcs of a circle that intersect line l at points S and R.
2. Bisect the straight angle $\angle SPR$ using construction 4. Let point Q be the intersection of the arcs constructed in step 2 of construction 4.
3. The angle bisector, $\overleftrightarrow{QP}$, is perpendicular to line l.

Justification (Figure 14.31): We know that $\angle SPR$ is a straight angle, since points S, P, and R are all on l. Hence $m(\angle SPR) = 180°$, so angle bisector $\overleftrightarrow{QP}$ divides $\angle SPR$ into two congruent angles, each measuring 90°. Thus $m(\angle QPR) = 90°$. ■

CONSTRUCTION 6 Construct a line perpendicular to a given line through a specified point not on the line.

Given a line l and a point P, not on l [Figure 14.32(a)], construct a line $\overleftrightarrow{QP}$ such that $\overleftrightarrow{QP} \perp l$ [Figure 14.32(b)].

(a)   **(b)**

Figure 14.32

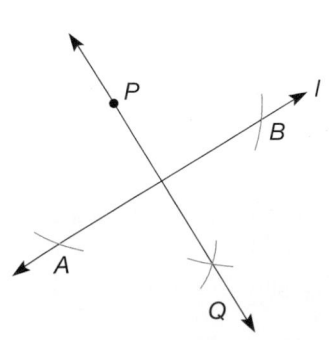

Figure 14.33

Procedure (Figure 14.33)

1. Place the point of the compass at P and construct an arc that intersects line l in two points. Label the points of intersection A and B.
2. With the *same* compass opening as in step 1, place the point of the compass at A, and then at B, to construct intersecting arcs on the side of l that does not contain P. Label the point of intersection of the arcs point Q.
3. Construct line $\overleftrightarrow{PQ}$. Then $\overleftrightarrow{PQ}$ contains P and is perpendicular to l.

Justification (Figure 14.34): Let R be the intersection of $\overline{PQ}$ and $\overline{AB}$. Then the justification is exactly the same as for construction 3; that is, $\overline{PQ}$ is the perpendicular

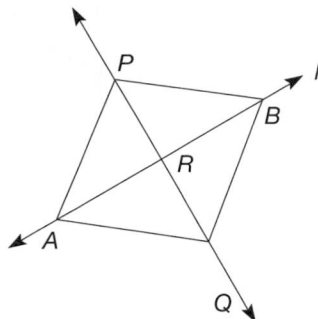

Figure 14.34

bisector of $\overline{AB}$, so that $\overleftrightarrow{PQ} \perp l$. (NOTE: The compass openings in step 2 can be different from those in step 1, as long as the arcs intersect *and AQ = BQ*.) ■

CONSTRUCTION 7 Construct a line parallel to a given line through a specified point not on the line.

Given a line l and a point P, not on l [Figure 14.35(a)], construct a line m such that $m \parallel l$ and P is on m [Figure 14.35(b)].

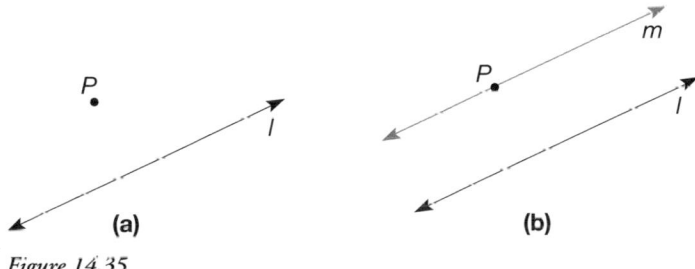

Figure 14.35

Procedure (Figure 14.36)

Reflection from Research

Because many computer drawing programs enable the user to move geometric figures after they have been drawn, the sequence in which steps of a construction are done becomes important. Constructing a point on a line may not be the same as constructing a line through a point. If a line is drawn through a point and then the line is moved, the point may not move with the line; the point would need to be constructed on the line to ensure the movement (Finzer & Bennett, 1995).

1. Let Q be any point on l and construct line $\overleftrightarrow{PQ}$.
2. Let R be another point on l [Figure 14.36(a)].

Copy $\angle PQR$ using construction 2 so that the vertex is at P, one side is on line $\overleftrightarrow{QP}$, and the other is on line m [Figure 14.36(b)]. Then $m \parallel l$.

Justification [Figure 14.36(b)]: By construction 2, the pair of alternate interior angles at P and Q are congruent. Hence, by the alternate interior angles theorem, $m \parallel l$.

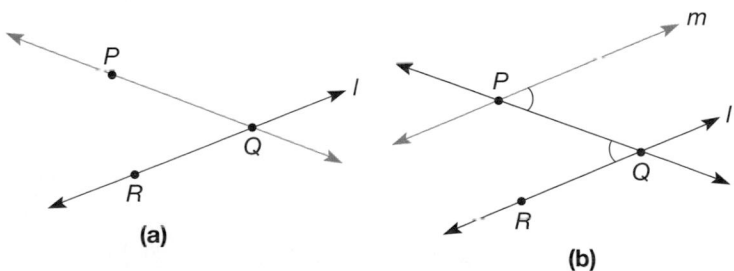

Figure 14.36

MATHEMATICAL MORSEL

There are three famous problems of antiquity to be done using only a compass and straightedge.

1. Given a circle, construct a square of equal area.
2. Trisect any given angle; that is, construct an angle exactly one-third the measure of the given angle.
3. Construct a cube that has twice the volume of a given cube.

The ancients failed to solve these problems, not because their solutions were too difficult, but because the problems have *no* solutions! That is, mathematicians were able to prove that all three of these constructions were impossible using *only* a compass and straightedge.

 Section 14.3 EXERCISE / PROBLEM SET A

EXERCISES

1. Given are an angle and a ray. Copy the angle such that the ray is one side of the copied angle.

2. Construct the perpendicular bisector for each of the following segments.

a.   **b.**

3. Construct the angle bisector for each of the following angles.

a.   **b.**

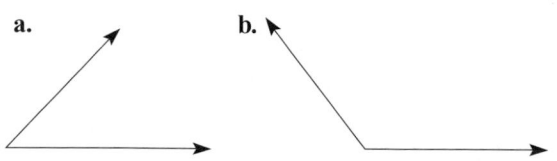

4. Construct a line perpendicular to the given line through point *P*.

a.   *P*

      • *P*

b.

5. Construct a line through point *P* parallel to the given line.

a.   **b.**

     • *P*   • *P*

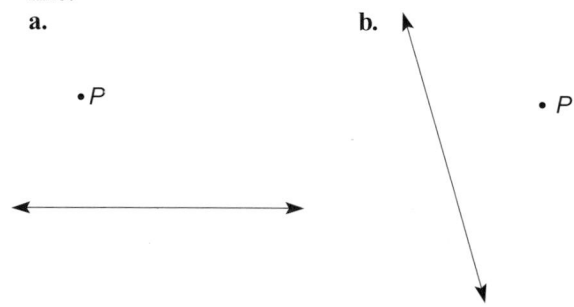

6. Using only a compass and straightedge, construct angles with the following measures.

a. 45°   **b.** 60°   **c.** 30°

7. Use your compass and straightedge and a unit segment to construct the figures described.

a. Construct a right triangle with legs 3 units and 4 units in length. How long *should* the hypotenuse of your right triangle be? Use your compass to mark off units along the hypotenuse to check your answer.

b. Construct a right triangle with legs 5 units and 12 units in length. How long *should* the hypotenuse of your right triangle be? Use your compass to mark off units along the hypotenuse to check your answer.

c. Construct a right triangle with a leg 8 units and hypotenuse 17 units in length. How long *should* the other leg be? Use your compass to mark off units along the leg to check your answer.

8. Use △ABC to perform the following construction.

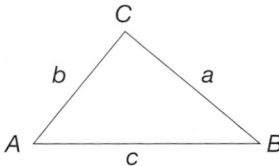

a. Use your compass and straightedge to construct △PQR such that PQ = 3c, PR = 3b, and QR = 3a.

b. How do the measures of ∠A, ∠B, and ∠C compare to the measures of ∠P, ∠Q, and ∠R? (Use your protractor to check.)

c. What can you conclude about the relationship between △ABC and △PQR? Justify your answer.

d. Which of the three similarity properties of triangles does this construction verify?

9. A **median** of a triangle is a segment joining a vertex and the midpoint of the opposite side. Construct the three medians of the given triangle. What do you notice about how the three medians intersect?

10. Draw a figure similar to the one shown.

a. Construct the line perpendicular to line *l* through point *P*. Call this line *m*.

b. Construct a line through point *P* that is perpendicular to line *m*. Call this line *k*.

c. What is the relationship between line *k* and line *l*? Explain why.

11. Use △ABC to perform the following construction: Use your compass and straightedge to construct △PQR such that ∠P ≅ ∠A and ∠Q ≅ ∠B.

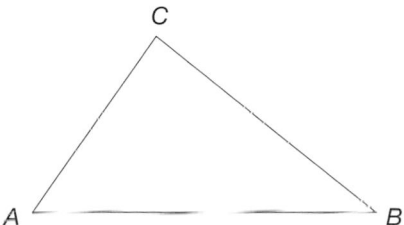

a. What is the ratio of the lengths of corresponding sides of the triangles? That is, find $\frac{PQ}{AB}, \frac{PR}{AC}$, and $\frac{QR}{BC}$. (Use your ruler here.) How do the ratios compare?

b. What can you conclude about the relationship between △ABC and △PQR? Justify your answer.

c. Which of the three similarity properties of triangles does this construction verify?

PROBLEMS

12. Both the medians and the angle bisectors of a triangle contain the vertices of the triangle. Under what circumstances will a median and an angle bisector coincide?

13. Use the Geometer's Sketchpad® to construct a triangle, △ABC, with all three angle bisectors and all three medians. By moving the vertices A, B, and/or C, determine what type(s) of triangles have exactly one median that coincides with an angle bisector.

14. Both the perpendicular bisectors and medians of a triangle pass through the midpoints of the sides of the triangles. Under what circumstances will a perpendicular bisector and median coincide?

15. Use the Geometer's Sketchpad® to construct a triangle, △ABC, with all three perpendicular bisectors and all three medians. By moving the vertices A, B, and/or C, determine what type(s) of triangles have exactly one median that coincides with a perpendicular bisector.

16. Complete the justification of construction 3, that is, that $\overleftrightarrow{PQ}$ is the perpendicular bisector of $\overline{AB}$.

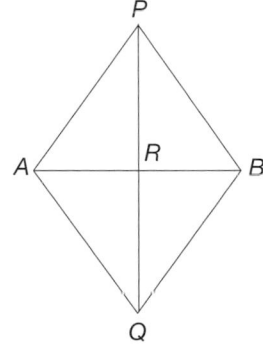

a. To show that △APQ ≅ △BPQ by the SSS congruence property, identify the three pairs of corresponding congruent sides.

b. To show that △APR ≅ △BPR by the SAS congruence property, identify the three pairs of corresponding congruent parts.

c. Explain why $\overline{PQ} \perp \overline{AB}$.

d. Explain why $\overline{PQ}$ bisects $\overline{AB}$.

17. Show the following result: If two angles of a triangle are congruent, the triangle is isosceles. (*Hint*: Bisect the third angle and apply AAS.)

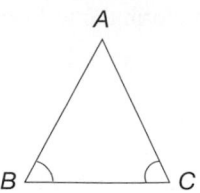

Section 14.3   EXERCISE / PROBLEM SET B

EXERCISES

1. Construct the perpendicular bisector of $\overline{PQ}$ using a compass and straightedge.

2. Construct the bisector of $\angle R$ using a compass and straightedge.

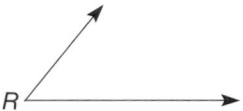

3. Construct the line perpendicular to l through P using a compass and straightedge.

4. Construct the line perpendicular to l through P using a compass and straightedge.

5. Draw an angle like the one shown, but with longer sides. Construct the following lines using a compass and straightedge.

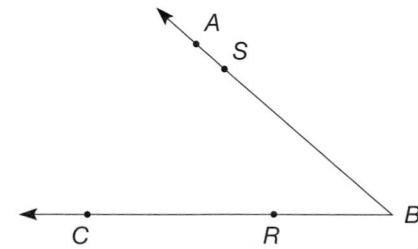

a. The line perpendicular to $\overline{AB}$ at point S

b. The line perpendicular to $\overline{BC}$ through point S

c. The line parallel to $\overline{AB}$ through point R

d. The line parallel to $\overline{BC}$ through point A

6. Given are two acute angles with measures a and b. Using a compass and straightedge, construct the following.

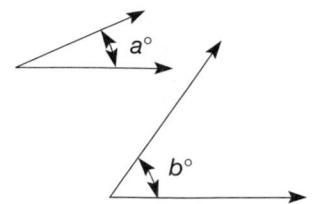

a. An angle with measure $a + b$

b. An angle with measure $2a$

c. An angle with measure $b - a$

d. An angle with measure $(a + b)/2$

7. Given are $\overline{AB}$, $\angle C$, and $\angle D$. Using construction techniques with a compass and straightedge, construct the following.

a. A triangle with angles congruent to $\angle C$ and $\angle D$ and the included side congruent to $\overline{AB}$

b. An isosceles triangle with two sides of length AB and the included angle congruent to $\angle D$

8. a. Given is a construction procedure for copying a triangle. Follow it to copy $\triangle RST$.

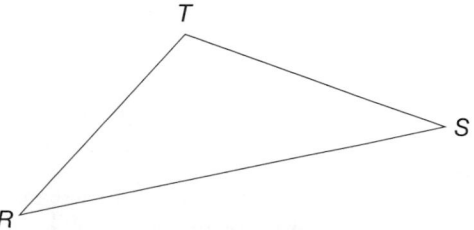

1. Draw a ray and copy segment $\overline{RS}$ of the triangle. Call the copy $\overline{DE}$.

2. Draw an arc with center D and radius RT.

3. Draw an arc with center E and radius ST. This arc should intersect the arc drawn in step 2. Call the intersection point F.

4. With a straightedge, connect points D and F and points E and F.

b. Write a justification of the construction procedure.

9. An **altitude** of a triangle is a segment from one vertex perpendicular to the line containing the opposite side. Construct the three altitudes of the given triangle. What do you notice about how the three altitudes intersect?

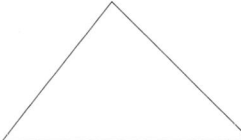

10. A method sometimes employed by drafters to bisect a line segment $\overline{AB}$ follows. Explain why this method works.

Angles of 45° are drawn at points A and B, and the point of intersection of their sides is labeled C. A perpendicular is drawn from point C to $\overline{AB}$. Point D bisects $\overline{AB}$.

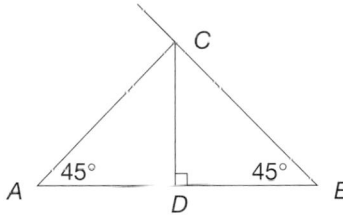

11. Use $\triangle ABC$ and your compass and straightedge to perform the following construction: Construct $\triangle PQR$ where $PQ = 2c$, $PR = 2b$, and $\angle P \cong \angle A$.

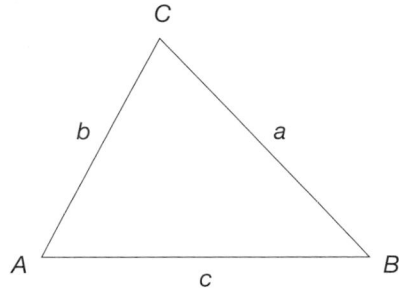

a. How does the length of $\overline{RQ}$ compare to the length of $\overline{CB}$? (Use your compass to check your answer.) How do the measures of $\angle B$ and $\angle C$ compare to the measures of $\angle Q$ and $\angle R$? (Use your compass or a protractor to compare the angles.)

b. What can you conclude about the relationship between $\triangle ABC$ and $\triangle PQR$? Justify your answer.

c. Which of the three similarity properties of triangles does this construction verify?

PROBLEMS

12. Both the perpendicular bisectors and altitudes of a triangle are perpendicular to the line containing the sides. Under what circumstances will a perpendicular bisector and altitude coincide?

13. Use the Geometer's Sketchpad® to construct a triangle, $\triangle ABC$, with all three perpendicular bisectors and all three altitudes. By moving the vertices A, B, and/or C, determine what type(s) of triangles have exactly one altitude that coincides with a perpendicular bisector.

14. Using AB as unit length, construct segments of the given length with a compass and straightedge.

a. $\sqrt{10}$ **b.** $\sqrt{6}$ **c.** $\sqrt{12}$ **d.** $\sqrt{15}$

15. A rectangle similar to rectangle $ABCD$ can be constructed as follows.

1. Draw diagonal $\overline{AC}$ in rectangle $ABCD$. Extend the diagonal through point C if you want a rectangle larger than $ABCD$.

2. Pick any point on $\overleftrightarrow{AC}$ and call it P.

3. Construct perpendiculars from point P to $\overleftrightarrow{AB}$ and to $\overleftrightarrow{AD}$.

4. Label the points of intersection Q and R. $ABCD \sim AQPR$. Explain why this is true.

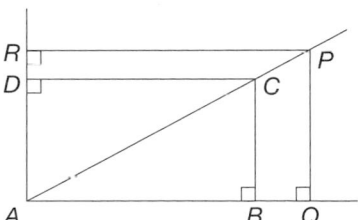

16. Prove the following result: If a point is equidistant from the endpoints of a segment, it is on the perpendicular bisector of the segment. (*Hint*: Connect C with the midpoint D of segment $\overline{AB}$ and show that $\overline{CD}$ is perpendicular to $\overline{AB}$.)

17. Two neighbors at points A and B will share the cost of extending electric service from a road to their houses. A line will be laid that is equidistant from their two houses. How can they determine where the line should run?

PROBLEMS FOR WRITING/DISCUSSION

1. Tammy is constructing a perpendicular bisector of a segment. She wonders if it would make any difference if, after she draws the arcs from one end of the segment, she changes the compass before she draws the arcs from the other end. The line still looks perpendicular. How would you respond?

2. Glen is trying to construct the altitude from one of the acute angles in an obtuse triangle, but he can't get it to stay inside the triangle. He asks you, "Isn't the altitude supposed to be inside the triangle?" What do you say?

3. Gwennette is looking at an isosceles triangle. She says, "I thought in an isosceles triangle, the altitude,

the median, and the angle bisector were all supposed to be the same line segment. Mine are all different." How should you respond?

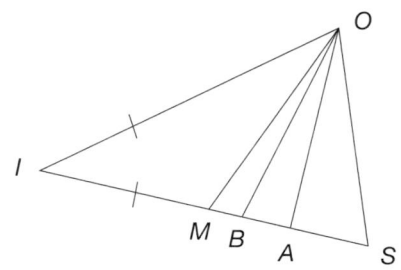

14.4   ADDITIONAL EUCLIDEAN CONSTRUCTIONS

STARTING POINT

The three neighboring cities of Logan, Mendon, and Clarkston decided to combine resources to build an airport. Each city, however, wanted an assurance that their residents would not have to drive any farther than the residents from any other city to get to the new airport. Based on the map of the cities shown here, sketch your proposed location of the new airport. Explain how you located it and why it satisfies each city's criterion.

Mendon
○

Logan   Clarkston
○   ○

Constructing Circumscribed and Inscribed Circles

We can perform several interesting constructions that involve triangles and circles. In particular, every triangle can have a circle circumscribed around it, and every triangle can have a circle inscribed within it (Figure 14.37). The **circumscribed circle** contains the vertices of the triangle as points on the circle. The **inscribed circle** touches each side of the triangle at exactly one point.

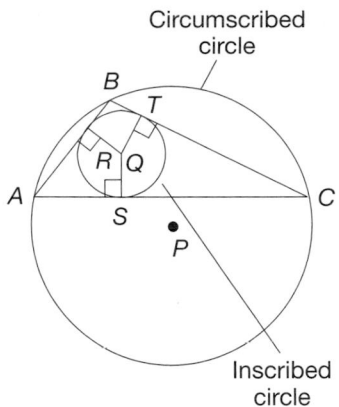

Figure 14.37

In Figure 14.37, line $\overleftrightarrow{AB}$ is said to be **tangent** to the inscribed circle, since the line and circle intersect at exactly one point, and all other points of the circle lie entirely on one side of the line. Similarly, lines $\overleftrightarrow{BC}$ and $\overleftrightarrow{AC}$ are tangent to the inscribed circle.

In Figure 14.37, point P is the center of the circumscribed circle, so $PA = PB = PC$. Thus P is equidistant from the vertices of $\triangle ABC$. Point P is called the **circumcenter** of $\triangle ABC$. Point Q is the center of the inscribed circle and is called the **incenter** of $\triangle ABC$. The inscribed circle intersects each of the three sides of $\triangle ABC$ at R, S, and T. Notice that $QR = QS = QT$, since each length is the radius of the inscribed circle. To construct the circumscribed and inscribed circles for a triangle, we need to construct the circumcenter and the incenter of the triangle. Example 14.7 provides the basis for constructing the circumcenter.

Example 14.7   Suppose that $\overline{AB}$ is a line segment with perpendicular bisector l. Show that point P is on l if and only if P is equidistant from A and B; that is, $AP = BP$ (Figure 14.38).

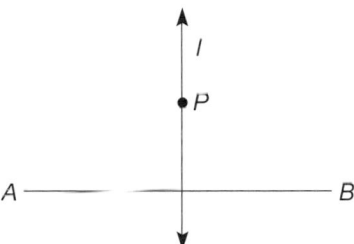

Figure 14.38

Solution   Suppose that P is on l, the perpendicular bisector of $\overline{AB}$. Let M be the midpoint of $\overline{AB}$ (Figure 14.39). Then $\triangle PMA \cong \triangle PMB$ by the SAS congruence property (verify this). Hence $PA = PB$, so P is equidistant from A and B. This shows that the

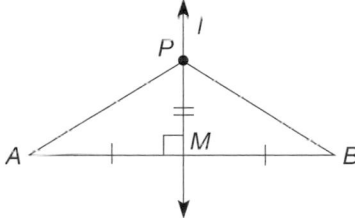

Figure 14.39

points on the perpendicular bisector of $\overline{AB}$ are equidistant from A and B. To complete the argument, we would have to show that if a point is equidistant from A and B, then it must be on l. This is left for Part B Problem 11 in the Problem Set.   ■

Example 14.7 shows that the circumcenter of a triangle must be a point on each of the perpendicular bisectors of the sides. Thus to find the circumcenter of a triangle, we find the perpendicular bisectors of the sides of the triangle. (Actually, any two of the perpendicular bisectors will suffice.)

CONSTRUCTION 8   Construct the circumscribed circle of a triangle.

Procedure (Figure 14.40): Given $\triangle ABC$, construct point P that is equidistant from A, B, and C.

    1. Using construction 3, construct line l, the perpendicular bisector of side $\overline{AC}$ [Figure 14.40(a)].

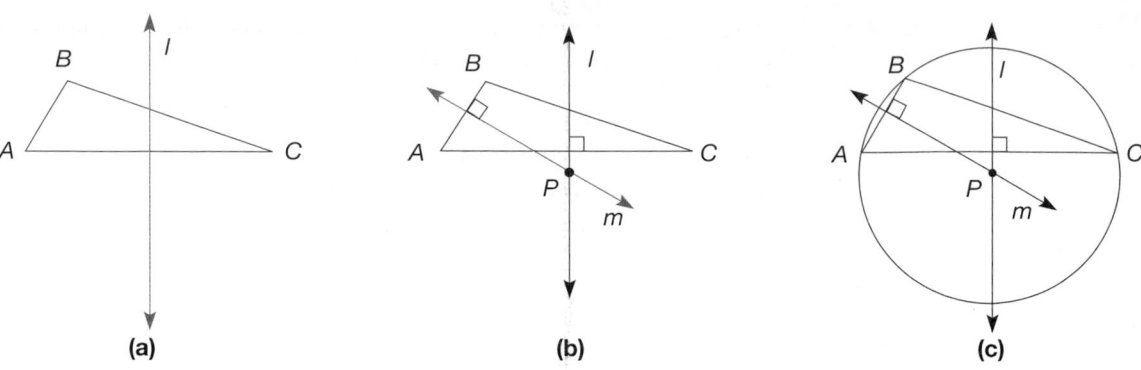

Figure 14.40

2. Similarly, construct line *m*, the perpendicular bisector of side $\overline{AB}$. The intersection of lines *l* and *m* is point *P*, the circumcenter of $\triangle ABC$ [Figure 14.40(b)]. The circle with center *P* and radius *PA* is the circumscribed circle of $\triangle ABC$ [Figure 14.40(c)].

Justification (Figure 14.40): Since *P* is on line *l*, *P* is equidistant from *A* and *C*, by Example 14.7. Hence $PA = PC$. Also, *P* is on line *m*, so *P* is equidistant from *A* and *B*. Thus $PA = PB$. Combining results, we have $PA = PB = PC$. Thus the circle whose center is *P* and whose radius is *PA* will contain points *A*, *B*, and *C*. ■

Spotlight on Technology The location of the circumcenter of a triangle varies depending on the type and shape of the triangle. Constructing enough triangles and circumcircles by hand to identify any type of pattern would be a tedious task. The use of dynamic geometric software can aid in this process. Use the Geometer's Sketchpad® webmodule activity, *Circumcircle*, to investigate the location of the circumcenter for a variety of triangles. Based on your observations, describe where the circumcenter lies in acute, obtuse, and right triangles.

www.wiley.com/
college/musser

To find the incenter of a triangle, we need to define what is meant by the distance from a point *P* to a line *l* [Figure 14.41(a)]. Suppose that $\overleftrightarrow{PQ}$ is the line through

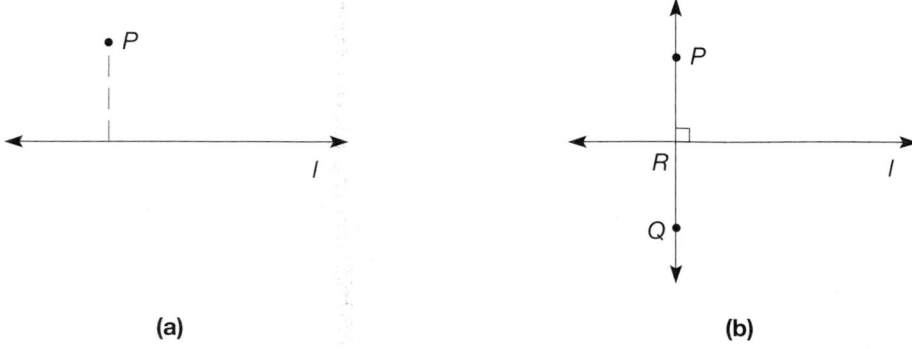

Figure 14.41

P that is perpendicular to *l* (construction 6). Let *R* be the intersection of line $\overleftrightarrow{PQ}$ and line *l* [Figure 14.41(b)]. Then we define the **distance from *P* to *l*** to be the distance *PR*. That is, we measure the distance from a point to a line by measuring along a line that is *perpendicular* to the given line, here *l*, through the given point, here *P*. Point *R* is the point on line *l* closest to point *P*.

To find the incenter of a triangle, we must locate a point that is equidistant from the sides of the triangle. Construction 9 shows us how to do this.

CONSTRUCTION 9   Construct the inscribed circle of a triangle.

Procedure (Figure 14.42):

1. Using construction 4, construct line *l*, the bisector of ∠*CAB* [Figure 14.42(a)].

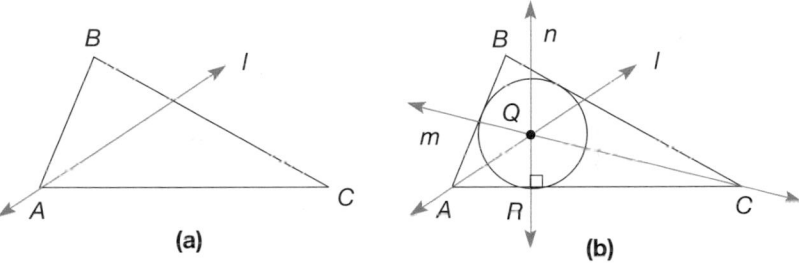

Figure 14.42

2. Similarly, construct line *m*, the bisector of ∠*BCA*. Let *Q* be the point of intersection of lines *l* and *m*. Then *Q* is the incenter of △*ABC* [Figure 14.42(b)]. To construct the inscribed circle, first construct the line *n* containing *Q* such that *n* is perpendicular to $\overline{AC}$. Let *R* be the intersection of line *n* and $\overline{AC}$. Then construct the circle, center at *Q*, whose radius is *QR*. This is the inscribed circle of △*ABC* [Figure 14.42(b)].

Justification: The justification for this construction is developed in the problem set. ■

Two other centers are commonly associated with triangles, the orthocenter and the centroid. The **orthocenter** is the intersection of the altitudes, and the **centroid** is the intersection of the medians of a triangle. The centroid has the property that it is the center of mass of a triangular region. That is, if a triangular shape is cut out of some material of uniform density, the triangle will balance at the centroid (Figure 14.43).

Figure 14.43

Constructing Regular Polygons

There are infinitely many values of *n* for which a regular *n*-gon can be constructed with compass and straightedge, *but* not for every *n*. In this subsection we will see how to construct several infinite families of regular *n*-gons. We will also learn a condition on the prime factorization of *n* that determines which regular *n*-gons can be constructed.

CONSTRUCTION 10   Construct and equilateral triangle.

Procedure [Figure 14.44(a)]:

1. Choose points *A* and *B* arbitrarily.
2. Place the compass point at *A* and open the compass to the distance *AB*.
3. With the compass point at *A*, construct arc 1 of radius *AB*. Do the same thing with the compass point at *B* to construct arc 2. Label the intersection of the arcs point *C*. Then △*ABC* is equilateral.

Reflection from Research
Individual steps in a construction should be placed on separate transparencies. Overlaying these transparencies in the appropriate sequence helps students follow the sequence and allows teachers to refer back to any step at any time (Sobel & Maletsky, 1988).

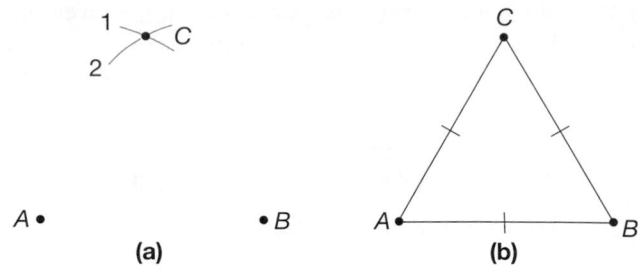

(a) **(b)**

Figure 14.44

Justification [Figure 14.44(b)]: From steps 2 and 3, we find that $AB = AC = BC$. Hence $\triangle ABC$ is equilateral. ■

We can use the construction of an equilateral triangle as the basis for constructing an infinite family of regular n-gons. For example, suppose that we find the circumscribed circle of an equilateral triangle [Figure 14.45(a)]. Let P be the circumcenter.

(a) **(b)**

Figure 14.45

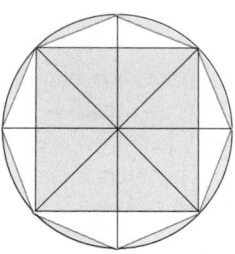

Figure 14.46

Bisect the central angles, $\angle V_1 P V_2$, $\angle V_2 P V_3$, and $\angle V_3 P V_1$, to locate points V_4, V_5, and V_6 on the circle [Figure 14.45(b)]. These six points are the vertices of a regular 6-gon (hexagon). Next bisect the central angles in the regular 6-gon, inscribed in a circle, to construct a regular 12-gon, then a 24-gon, and so on. Theoretically, then, we can construct an infinite family of regular n-gons, namely the family for $n = 3, 6, 12, 24, 48, \ldots, 3 \cdot 2^k, \ldots$, where k is any whole number.

Because we know how to construct right angles, we can construct a square. Then if a square is inscribed in a circle, we can bisect the central angles to locate the vertices of a regular 8-gon, then a 16-gon, and so on (Figure 14.46). Thus we could theoretically construct a regular n-gon for $n = 2^k$, where k is any whole number greater than 1.

In general, once we have constructed a regular n-gon, we can construct an infinite family of regular polygons, namely those with $n \cdot 2^k$ sides, where k is any whole number. In the Problem Set, we will investigate this family with $n = 5$. We will show that it is possible to construct a regular pentagon, and hence to construct regular n-gons for $n = 5, 10, 20, 40, 80, \ldots, 5 \cdot 2^k, \ldots$, where k is a whole number.

A remarkable result about the construction of regular n-gons tells us precisely the values of n for which a regular n-gon can be constructed. To understand the result, we need a certain type of prime number, called a Fermat prime. A **Fermat prime** is a prime number of the form $F_k = 2^{(2^k)} + 1$, where k is a whole number.

For the first few whole-number values of k, we obtain the following results.

$$F_0 = 2^{(2^0)} + 1 = 2^1 + 1 = 3, \text{ a prime;}$$
$$F_1 = 2^{(2^1)} + 1 = 2^2 + 1 = 5, \text{ a prime;}$$
$$F_2 = 2^{(2^2)} + 1 = 2^4 + 1 = 17, \text{ a prime;}$$

$$F_3 = 2^{(2^3)} + 1 = 2^8 + 1 = 257, \text{ a prime;}$$
$$F_4 = 2^{(2^4)} + 1 = 2^{16} + 1 = 65,537, \text{ a prime;}$$
$$F_5 = 2^{(2^5)} + 1 = 2^{32} + 1 = (641) \cdot (6,700,417), \textit{ not a prime.}$$

Thus there are at least five Fermat primes, namely 3, 5, 17, 257, and 65,537, but not every number of the form $2^{(2^k)} + 1$ is a prime. [Also, not every prime is of the form $2^{(2^k)} + 1$. For example, 7 is a prime, but not a Fermat prime.] A result, due to the famous mathematician Gauss, gives the conditions that n must satisfy in order for a regular n-gon to be constructible.

THEOREM

Gauss's Theorem for Constructible Regular n-gons

A regular n-gon can be constructed with straightedge and compass if and only if the only odd prime factors of n are distinct Fermat primes.

Gauss's theorem tells us that for constructible regular n-gons, the only odd primes that can occur in the factorization of n are Fermat primes with no Fermat prime factor repeated. The prime 2 can occur to any whole-number power. At this time, no Fermat primes larger than 65,537, F_4, are known, nor is it known whether any others *exist*. (As of 1999, it is known that F_5 through F_{23}, as well as over 100 other Fermat numbers, are composite.) Example 14.8 illustrates several applications of Gauss's theorem.

Example 14.8 For which of the following values of n can a regular n-gon be constructed?

a. 40   **b.** 45   **c.** 60   **d.** 64   **e.** 21

Solution

a. $n = 40 = 2^3 \cdot 5$. Since the only odd prime factor of 40 is 5, a Fermat prime, a regular 40-gon can be constructed.

b. $n = 45 = 3^2 \cdot 5$. Since the (Fermat) prime 3 occurs more than once in the factorization of n, the odd prime factors are not *distinct* Fermat primes. Hence a regular 45-gon cannot be constructed.

c. $n = 60 = 2^2 \cdot 3 \cdot 5$. The odd prime factors of n are the distinct Fermat primes 3 and 5. Therefore, a regular 60-gon can be constructed.

d. $n = 64 = 2^6$. There are no odd factors to consider. Hence a regular 64-gon can be constructed.

e. $n = 21 = 3 \cdot 7$. Since 7 is not a Fermat prime, a regular 21-gon cannot be constructed. ■

The proof of Gauss's theorem is very difficult. The theorem is a remarkable result in the history of mathematics and helped make Gauss one of the most respected mathematicians of all time.

Constructing Segment Lengths

The use of similar triangles allows us to construct products and quotients of real-number lengths. Example 14.9 gives the construction for the product of two real numbers.

Example 14.9 Suppose that a and b are positive real numbers representing the lengths of line segments (Figure 14.47) and we have a segment of length 1. Show how to construct a line segment whose length is $a \cdot b$.

Figure 14.47

Solution Let $\overline{PQ}$ be a line segment of length a [Figure 14.48(a)]. Let R be any point not on line $\overleftrightarrow{PQ}$ such that $PR = 1$ [Figure 14.48(b)]. Let S be a point on ray $\overrightarrow{PR}$ such that $PS = b$ [Figure 14.48(b)]. Construct segment $\overline{QR}$, and construct a line l through point S such that $l \parallel \overleftrightarrow{QR}$ [Figure 14.48(c)]. Let T be the intersection of lines l

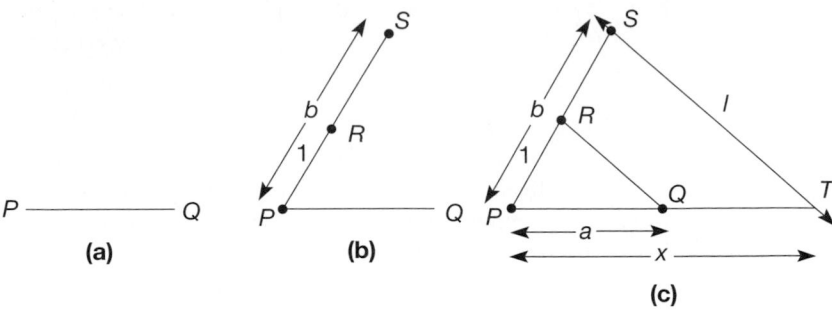

Figure 14.48

and $\overleftrightarrow{PQ}$. Then $\angle PQR \cong \angle PTS$ by the corresponding angles property. Since $\angle RPQ \cong \angle SPT$, we know that $\triangle PRQ \sim \triangle PST$ by the AA similarity property. Let $x = PT$. Then, using similar triangles,

$$\frac{a}{1} = \frac{x}{b},$$

so that $a \cdot b = x$. Thus we have constructed the product of the real numbers a and b. ■

Other construction procedures with real-number lengths appear in the Problem Set.

MATHEMATICAL MORSEL

In writing his book on geometry, called *The Elements,* Euclid produced a new proof of the Pythagorean theorem. In 1907, when Elisha Loomis was preparing the manuscript for the book *The Pythagorean Proposition* (which eventually had over 370 *different* proofs of the Pythagorean theorem), he noted that there were two or three American textbooks on geometry in which Euclid's proof does not appear. He mused that the authors must have been seeking to show their originality or independence. However, he said, "The leaving out of Euclid's proof is like the play of *Hamlet* with Hamlet left out."

Section 14.4 EXERCISE / PROBLEM SET A

EXERCISES

1. Copy the given triangle and construct the circle circumscribed about the triangle.

2. Use the Geometer's Sketchpad® to construct a triangle and a circle circumscribed about the triangle. Submit a printout of the construction.

3. Copy the given triangle and construct the circle inscribed inside the triangle.

4. Use the Geometer's Sketchpad® to construct a triangle and a circle inscribed in the triangle. Submit a printout of the construction.

5. Construct an equilateral triangle with sides congruent to the given segment.

_____

6. Use the Geometer's Sketchpad® to construct an equilateral triangle. Submit a printout of the construction and describe the similarities between the compass and straightedge construction in Problem 5 and the construction done on the computer.

7. Using only a compass and straightedge, construct angles with the following measures.

 a. 15°   **b.** 75°   **c.** 105°

8. Construct a triangle with angles of 30°, 60°, and 90°. With your ruler, measure the lengths in centimeters of the hypotenuse and the shortest leg. Next, construct two more triangles of different sizes but with angles of 30°, 60°, and 90°. Again measure the lengths of the hypotenuse and the shortest leg. What is the relationship between the length of the hypotenuse and the length of the shorter leg in a 30°−60°−90° triangle?

9. a. Follow steps 1 to 6 to inscribe a particular regular *n*-gon in a circle.

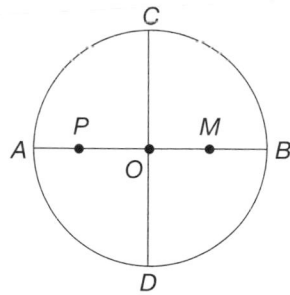

 1. Draw a circle with center *O*.

 2. In this circle, draw a diameter $\overline{AB}$.

 3. Construct another diameter, $\overline{CD}$, that is perpendicular to $\overline{AB}$.

 4. Bisect $\overline{OB}$. Let *M* be its midpoint.

 5. Using *M* as the center and $\overline{CM}$ as the radius, draw an arc intersecting $\overline{AO}$. Call the intersection point *P*.

 6. Mark off arcs of radius *CP* around the circle and connect consecutive points.

 b. What regular *n*-gon have you constructed?

10. a. If you bisected the central angles of the regular *n*-gon constructed in the preceding problem and connected the consecutive points along the circle, what regular *n*-gon would be constructed?

 b. Repeating the bisecting process to this new regular *n*-gon, what regular *n*-gon would be constructed?

 c. List two other regular polygons of this family that can be constructed.

11. Which of the following regular *n*-gons can be constructed with compass and straightedge?

 a. 120-gon   **b.** 85-gon   **c.** 36-gon

 d. 80-gon   **e.** 63-gon   **f.** 75-gon

 g. 105-gon   **h.** 255-gon   **i.** 340-gon

12. The following construction procedure can be used to divide a segment into any given number of congruent segments. Draw a segment and follow the steps listed.

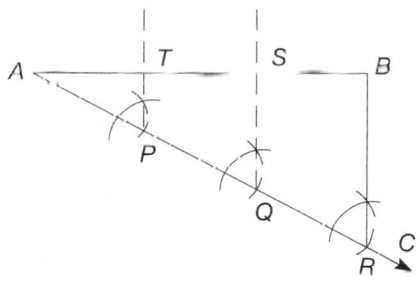

 1. Construct any ray $\overrightarrow{AC}$ not collinear with $\overline{AB}$.

 2. With any arbitrary compass setting, mark off three congruent segments on $\overrightarrow{AC}$ (here, $\overline{AP}$, $\overline{PQ}$, and $\overline{QR}$).

 3. Construct $\overline{BR}$.

 4. Construct lines parallel to $\overline{BR}$ through *P* and *Q*.

 Into how many congruent pieces has $\overline{AB}$ been divided? (NOTE: To divide $\overline{AB}$ into *k* congruent segments, where *k* is a whole number, mark off *k* congruent segments on $\overrightarrow{AC}$ in step 2.)

13. We can simplify the procedure described in the preceding exercise by constructing only $\overline{SQ}$ parallel to $\overline{BR}$. Then use the compass opening as $\overline{SB}$ and mark off congruent segments along $\overline{AB}$. Use this technique to divide $\overline{AB}$ into six congruent pieces.

$A \;\rule{4cm}{0.4pt}\; B$

PROBLEMS

14. a. Draw an acute triangle and find its circumcenter.

    b. Repeat part (a) with a different acute triangle.

    c. What do you notice about the location of the circumcenter of an acute triangle?

15. a. Construct an obtuse triangle and find its circumcenter.

    b. Repeat part (a) with a different obtuse triangle.

    c. What do you notice about the location of the circumcenter of an obtuse triangle?

16. An interesting result attributed to Napoleon Bonaparte can be observed in the following construction.

    1. Draw any triangle $\triangle PQR$.

    2. Using a compass and straightedge, construct an equilateral triangle on each side of $\triangle PQR$.

    3. Use your compass and straightedge to locate the centroid of each equilateral triangle: C_1, C_2, C_3.

    4. Connect C_1, C_2, and C_3 to form a triangle.

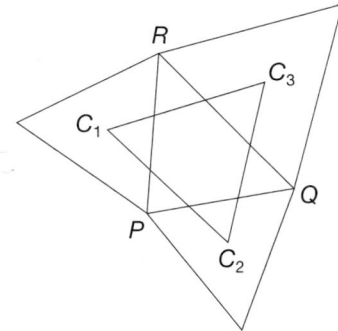

    a. Draw a triangle and perform the steps 1–4. What kind of triangle is $\triangle C_1C_2C_3$? Use your ruler and protractor to check.

    b. Repeat the construction for two different types of triangles $\triangle PQR$. What kind of triangle is $\triangle C_1C_2C_3$?

    c. Can you summarize your observations?

17. In this section a construction was given to find the product of any two lengths. Use that construction to find the length $1/a$ for any given length a. The case $a > 1$ is shown in the following figure.

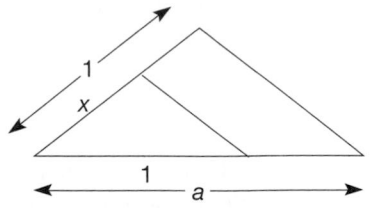

18. a. If $\dfrac{a}{x} = \dfrac{x}{b}$ then x is called the **mean proportional** or **geometric mean** between a and b. One method of constructing the geometric mean is pictured. Assuming $a \geq b$, mark off AC of length a, and find point B such that BC has length b, where B is between A and C. Then mark off BD of length a, and draw two large arcs with centers A and D and radius a. If the arcs intersect at E, then $x = EB$. Following this method, construct the geometric mean between 1 and 2 where the length 1 is given. What length have you constructed?

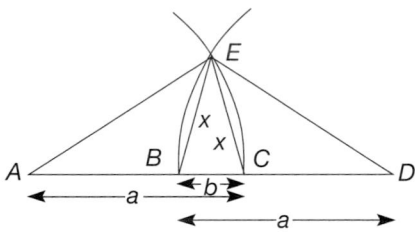

    b. Prove that the x in the diagram is, in fact, the geometric mean between the a and b given.

19. A woman wants to divide a short strip of plastic into five congruent pieces but has no ruler available. If she has a pencil and a sheet of lined paper, how can she use them to mark off five congruent segments?

Section 14.4 EXERCISE / PROBLEM SET B

EXERCISES

1. Copy the given triangle and use a compass and straightedge to find the following.

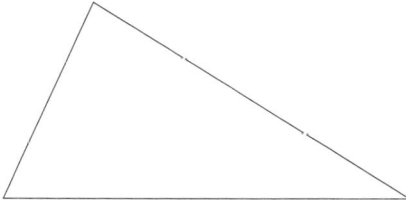

   a. The circumcenter of the triangle

   b. The incenter of the triangle

2. The three medians of a triangle are concurrent at a point called the centroid. This point is the center of gravity or balance point of a triangle. Construct the three medians of the following triangles and complete the statement in part (a).

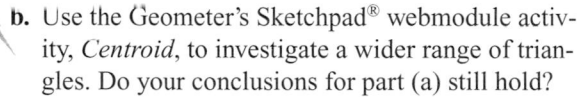

   a. The centroid always lies _____ the triangle.

   b. Use the Geometer's Sketchpad® webmodule activity, *Centroid*, to investigate a wider range of triangles. Do your conclusions for part (a) still hold?

3. The lines containing the altitudes of a triangle meet at a single point, called the orthocenter. The position of the orthocenter is determined by the measures of the angles. Construct the three altitudes for each of the following triangles. Then complete the statements in parts (a)–(c).

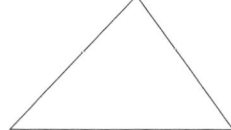

   a. The orthocenter of an acute triangle lies _____ the triangle.

   b. The orthocenter of a right triangle is the _____.

   c. The orthocenter of an obtuse triangle lies _____ the triangle.

   d. Use the Geometer's Sketchpad® webmodule activity, *Orthocenter*, to investigate a wide range of acute, obtuse, and right triangles. Do your conclusions for parts (a), (b), and (c) still hold?

4. Explain how to construct angles with the following measures.

   a. 135°   **b.** 75°   **c.** 72°   **d.** 108°

5. a. Construct a circle using any compass setting. Without changing the compass setting, mark off arcs of the radius around the circle (each mark serving as center for next arc). Join consecutive marks to form a polygon. Is the polygon a regular polygon? If so, which one?

   b. Prove your assertion in part (a).

6. Follow the given steps to construct a regular decagon. (A justification of this construction follows in Problem 13 of Exercise/Problem Set 14.5B.)

   a. Taking AB as a unit length, construct a segment $\overline{CD}$ of length $\sqrt{5}$. (*Hint:* Apply the Pythagorean theorem.)

   b. Using $\overline{AB}$ and $\overline{CD}$, construct a segment $\overline{EF}$ of length $\sqrt{5} - 1$.

   c. Bisect segment $\overline{EF}$ forming segment $\overline{EG}$. What is the length of $\overline{EG}$?

   d. Construct a circle with radius AB.

   e. With a compass open a distance EG, make marks around the circle. Connecting adjacent points will yield a decagon.

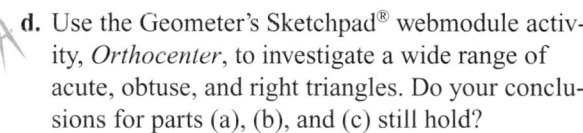

7. It has been shown that a regular n-gon can be constructed using a Mira if and only if n is of the form $2^r \cdot 3^s \cdot p_1 \ldots p_k$, where the $p_1, \ldots, p_k$ are primes of the form $2^u 3^v + 1$. Find the first 10 regular n-gons that can be constructed using a Mira.

8. List all regular polygons with fewer than 100 sides that can be constructed with compass and straightedge. (*Hint*: Apply Gauss's theorem.)

9. A golden rectangle, as described in Chapter 7, can be constructed using a compass and straightedge as follows.

    1. Construct any square $ABCD$.

    2. Bisect side $\overline{AB}$ and call the midpoint M.

    3. Set the radius of your compass as MC. Using point M as the center of your arc, make an are that intersects $\overleftrightarrow{AB}$ at P.

    4. Construct $\overline{PQ} \parallel \overline{AD}$ and $\overline{DQ} \parallel \overline{AB}$.

    5. Now $APQD$ is a golden rectangle.

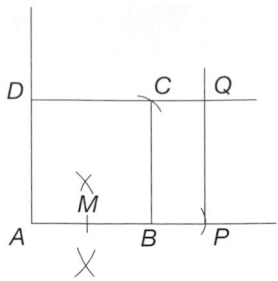

Construct a golden rectangle starting with a square that has sides of some length you chose. Using a ruler, measure the length and width of your rectangle in centimeters. Calculate the ratio of length : width for your rectangle. How does your ratio compare to the golden ratio?

10. a. Use the procedure in Exercise 13 of Part A to divide $\overline{AB}$ into four congruent pieces.

$A \underline{\hspace{5cm}} B$

    b. Find another procedure that can be used to divide $\overline{AB}$ into four congruent parts (using construction techniques from Section 14.3).

11. Complete the Solution for Example 14.7.

PROBLEMS

12. a. Construct a right triangle and find its circumcenter.

    b. Repeat part (a) with a different right triangle.

    c. What do you notice about the location of the circumcenter of a right triangle?

13. By constructing a variety of acute, right, and obtuse triangles and finding their incenters, determine whether the incenter is always inside the triangle.

14. An interesting result called Aubel's theorem can be observed in the following construction.

    1. Draw any quadrilateral $ABCD$.

    2. Using a compass and straightedge, construct a square on each side of quadrilateral $ABCD$.

    3. Locate the midpoint of each square: M_1, M_2, M_3, M_4. Connect the midpoints of opposite squares with line segments.

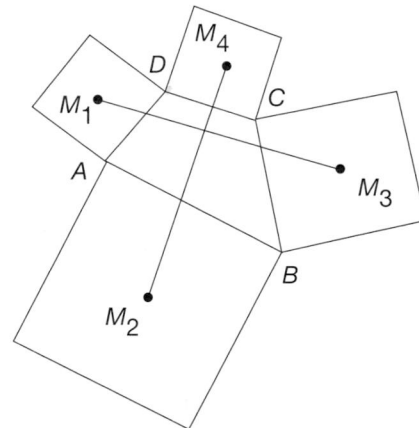

a. Draw a convex quadrilateral and perform the preceding steps. Use your ruler to measure the lengths of segments $\overline{M_1 M_3}$ and $\overline{M_2 M_4}$. Use your protractor to measure the angles formed where $\overline{M_1 M_3}$ and $\overline{M_2 M_4}$ intersect.

b. Repeat the construction for two more quadrilaterals. Let one quadrilateral be concave, in which case the squares will overlap. Measure the segments and angles described in part (a).

c. What conclusion can you draw?

15. By Gauss's theorem we know that it is not possible to construct a regular heptagon (7-gon) using only straightedge and compass. It is possible, however, to make an angle measuring $\frac{180°}{7}$, or approximately 25.7°, with toothpicks using a technique attributed to C. Johnson, *Mathematical Gazette*, No. 407, 1975. Seven congruent toothpicks can be arranged as shown in the following figure, where points A, B, C, and D are collinear. When the toothpicks are arranged in this way, the angle at A will measure $\frac{180°}{7}$.

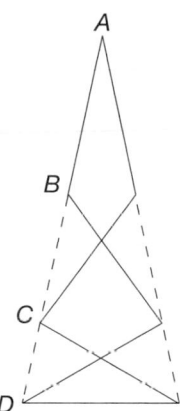

a. Arrange seven toothpicks as shown and then use your protractor to measure the angle at A.

b. What is the measure of the central angle of a regular heptagon?

c. If you can construct an angle of $\frac{180°}{7}$, how can you construct a regular heptagon?

16. To locate the incenter of a triangle, we need to locate a point that is equidistant from the sides of the triangle. Suppose that point A is equidistant from $\overrightarrow{YX}$ and $\overrightarrow{YZ}$. Show that $\overrightarrow{YA}$ is the angle bisector of $\angle XYZ$.

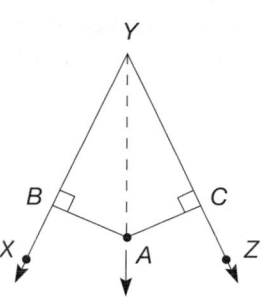

17. If line l is the bisector of $\angle BAC$ and point Q is on l, verify that Q is equidistant from the sides $\overleftrightarrow{AB}$ and $\overleftrightarrow{AC}$ of $\angle BAC$ by completing the following.

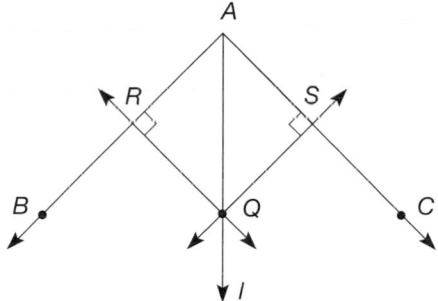

a. Let line $\overleftrightarrow{QR}$ be perpendicular to $\overleftrightarrow{AB}$, where R is on $\overleftrightarrow{AB}$. What is the distance from Q to $\overleftrightarrow{AB}$?

b. Let line $\overleftrightarrow{QS}$ be perpendicular to $\overleftrightarrow{AC}$, where S is on $\overleftrightarrow{AC}$. What is the distance from Q to $\overleftrightarrow{AC}$?

c. Is $\triangle ARQ \cong \triangle ASQ$? Justify your answer.

d. Explain why Q is therefore equidistant from $\overleftrightarrow{AB}$ and $\overleftrightarrow{AC}$.

e. Use these results to justify construction 9, the procedure for constructing the incenter of a triangle.

PROBLEMS FOR WRITING/DISCUSSION

1. Roseanne was trying to find the circumcenter of a triangle. She constructed the perpendicular bisectors of two of the sides, but she was wondering if she needed to construct all three. How should you respond?

2. Craig said he had a new way to construct a regular hexagon. He said a regular hexagon is just six equilateral triangles stuck together, so he could just construct one equilateral triangle, and then construct matching triangles on two of its sides, and just keep going that way until he had six of them. Will Craig end up with a regular hexagon? How can you be sure?

3. Joan wanted to construct a segment that would be $\sqrt{5}$ inches long, but she didn't know how. Roberto said, "You can make it the diagonal of a certain rectangle." Joan tells you she doesn't understand that. Is Roberto correct? Discuss.

14.5 GEOMETRIC PROBLEM SOLVING USING TRIANGLE CONGRUENCE AND SIMILARITY

The two parallelograms below have congruent corresponding sides, but the parallelograms themselves are not congruent. The two triangles below have congruent corresponding sides and, by the SSS triangle congruence, the triangles are congruent. These two ideas are related to some principles of fence building.

When building a gate for a fence, a crosspiece (*A*), like the one shown, is added to ensure a stronger more stable gate that won't sag. Why does the diagonal (*A*) add so much strength that the 2 parallel pieces (*B* and *C*) couldn't provide? How is this strengthening crosspiece related to the SSS triangle congruence?

Problem-Solving Strategy
Draw a Picture

In this section we apply triangle congruence and similarity properties to prove properties of geometric shapes. Many of these results were observed informally in Chapter 12. Our first result is an application of the SAS congruence property that establishes a property of the diagonals of a rectangle.

Example 14.10 Show that the diagonals of a rectangle are congruent.

Solution Suppose that $ABCD$ is a rectangle [Figure 14.49(a)]. Then $ABCD$ is a parallelogram (from Chapter 12). By a theorem in Section 14.1, the opposite sides of $ABCD$ are congruent [Figure 14.49(b)]. In particular, $\overline{AB} \cong \overline{DC}$. Consider $\triangle ABC$ and $\triangle DCB$; $\angle ABC \cong \angle DCB$, since they are both right angles. Also, $\overline{CB} \cong \overline{BC}$. Hence, $\triangle ABC \cong \triangle DCB$ by the SAS congruence property. Consequently, $\overline{AC} \cong \overline{BD}$, as desired.

 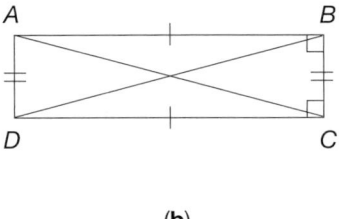

Figure 14.49

The next result is a form of a converse of the theorem in Example 14.10.

Example 14.11 In parallelogram $ABCD$, if the diagonals are congruent, it is a rectangle.

Solution Suppose that $ABCD$ is a parallelogram with $\overline{AC} \cong \overline{BD}$ [Figure 14.50(a)]. Since $ABCD$ is a parallelogram, $\overline{AD} \cong \overline{BC}$. Therefore, since $\overline{DC} \cong \overline{DC}$, $\triangle ADC \cong \triangle BCD$ by SSS [Figure 14.50(b)]. By corresponding parts, $\angle ADC \cong \angle BCD$. But

Figure 14.50

∠*ADC* and ∠*BCD* are also supplementary because $\overline{AD} \parallel \overline{BC}$. Consequently, m ∠*ADC* = m ∠*BCD* − 90° and *ABCD* is a rectangle. ■

Next we verify that every rhombus is a parallelogram using the ASA congruence property and the alternate interior angles theorem.

Example 14.12 Show that every rhombus is a parallelogram [Figure 14.51(a)].

Problem-Solving Strategy
Draw a Picture

Solution Let *ABCD* be a rhombus. Thus $\overline{AB} \cong \overline{BC} \cong \overline{CD} \cong \overline{DA}$. Construct diagonal $\overline{BD}$ and consider △*ABD* and △*CDB* [Figure 14.51(b)]. Since $\overline{BD} \cong \overline{DB}$, it follows that △*ABD* ≅ △*CDB* by the SSS congruence property. Hence ∠*ABD* ≅ ∠*CDB*, since they are corresponding angles in the congruent triangles. By the alternate interior angles theorem, $\overline{AB} \parallel \overline{DC}$. Also ∠*ADB* ≅ ∠*CBD*, so that $\overline{AD} \parallel \overline{BC}$. Therefore, *ABCD* is a parallelogram, since the opposite sides are parallel.

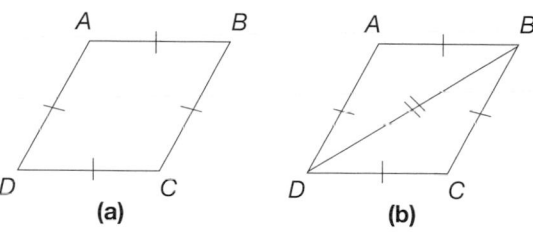

Figure 14.51 ■

Next we prove a result about quadrilaterals that is applied in the Epilogue, following Chapter 16.

Example 14.13 If two sides of a quadrilateral are parallel and congruent, then the quadrilateral is a parallelogram.

Solution Let *ABCD* be a quadrilateral with $\overline{AD} \parallel \overline{BC}$ and $\overline{AD} \cong \overline{BC}$ [Figure 14.52(a)]. Draw in diagonal $\overline{AC}$ [Figure 14.52(b)]. Since $\overline{AD} \parallel \overline{BC}$, $\overline{AC}$ is a transversal and ∠*DAC* ≅ ∠*BCA* [Figure 14.52(c)]. Thus △*DAC* ≅ △*BCA* by SAS, since $\overline{AC}$ is common to both triangles. By corresponding parts, ∠*ACD* ≅ ∠*CAB*. Therefore, $\overline{AB} \parallel \overline{DC}$, since ∠*ACD* and ∠*CAB* are congruent alternate interior angles. Finally, *ABCD* is a parallelogram, since $\overline{AD} \parallel \overline{BC}$ and $\overline{AB} \parallel \overline{DC}$.

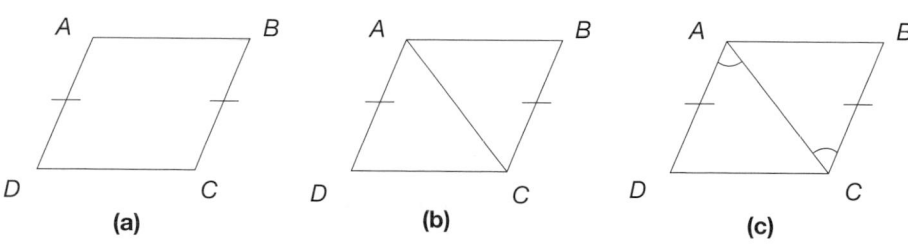

Figure 14.52 ■

Using several geometric constructions and the SSS congruence property, we can prove an important result about right triangles, namely the converse of the Pythagorean theorem.

Example 14.14 Suppose that the lengths of the sides of △*ABC* are *a*, *b*, and *c* with $a^2 + b^2 = c^2$ (Figure 14.53). Show that △*ABC* is a right triangle.

Solution Construct a segment $\overline{DE}$ of length *b* using construction 1 [Figure 14.54(a)]. Next, using construction 5, construct line $\overleftrightarrow{EF}$ such that $\overleftrightarrow{EF} \perp \overline{DE}$ at point *E* [Figure 14.54(b)]. Next, locate point *G* on line $\overleftrightarrow{EF}$ so that *EG* = *a*, using construction 1

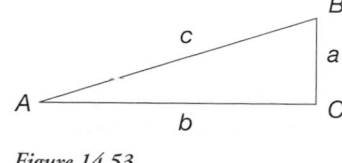

Figure 14.53

[Figure 14.54(c)]. Then $\triangle DEG$ is a right triangle. By the Pythagorean theorem, $DG^2 = DE^2 + EG^2 = a^2 + b^2$. Hence $DG^2 = c^2$, since $a^2 + b^2 = c^2$ by assumption. Thus $DG = c$ [Figure 14.54(d)]. But then $\triangle ACB \cong \triangle DEG$ by the SSS congruence property. Therefore, $\angle ACB \cong \angle DEG$, a right angle, so that $\triangle ACB$ is a right triangle.

Problem-Solving Strategy
Draw a Picture

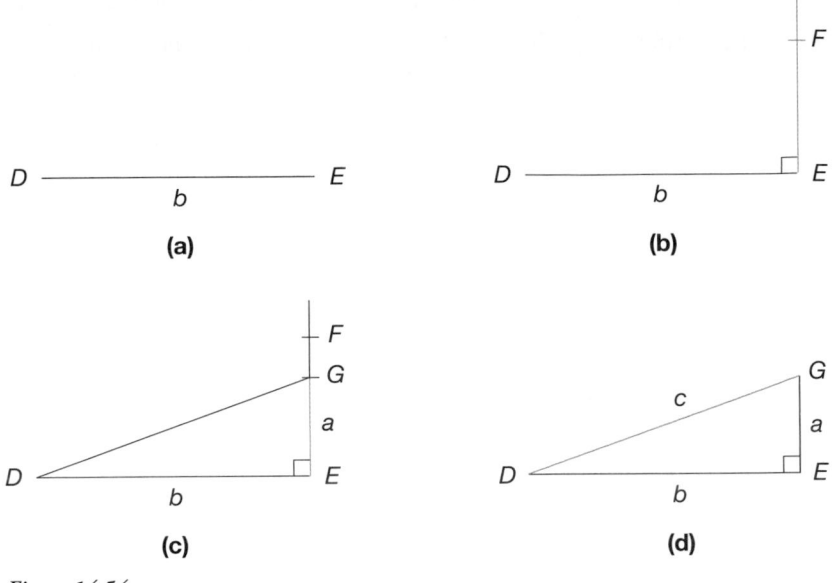

(a)

(b)

(c)

(d)

Figure 14.54   ■

THEOREM

Converse of the Pythagorean Theorem

A triangle having sides of lengths a, b, and c, where $a^2 + b^2 = c^2$, is a right triangle.

The converse of the Pythagorean theorem has an interesting application. When carpenters erect the walls of a house, usually they need to make the walls perpendicular to each other. A common way to do this is to use a 12-foot string loop with knots at 1-foot intervals (Figure 14.55). If this loop is stretched into a $3-4-5$ triangle, the angle between the "3" and "4" sides must be a right angle by the converse of the Pythagorean theorem, since $3^2 + 4^2 = 5^2$.

The next example presents an interesting result about the midpoints of the sides of a triangle using the SAS similarity property, the SSS similarity property, and the SAS congruence property.

Figure 14.55

Example 14.15   Given $\triangle ABC$, where P, Q, R are the midpoints of the sides $\overline{AB}$, $\overline{BC}$, and $\overline{AC}$, respectively [Figure 14.56(a)], show that $\triangle APR$, $\triangle PBQ$, $\triangle RQC$, and $\triangle QRP$ are all congruent and that each triangle is similar to $\triangle ABC$.

Solution   Consider $\triangle ABC$ and $\triangle PBQ$ [Figure 14.56(b)]. We will first show that these triangles are similar using the SAS similarity property. Since P and Q are the midpoints of their respective sides, we know that $PB = \frac{1}{2}AB$ and that $BQ = \frac{1}{2}BC$. Certainly, $\angle ABC \cong \angle PBQ$, so that $\triangle ABC \sim \triangle PBQ$ by the SAS similarity property. Using a similar argument, we can show that $\triangle APR \sim \triangle ABC$ [Figure 14.56(c)] and that $\triangle RQC \sim \triangle ABC$ [Figure 14.56(d)]. Also, $\triangle QRP \sim \triangle ABC$ by the SSS similarity property (verify). Since $AP = PB$, $\triangle APR \cong \triangle PBQ$ by the ASA congruence property (verify). In similar fashion, we have $\triangle PBQ \cong \triangle RQC$. Combining our results, we can $\triangle RQC \cong \triangle QRP$ using the SSS congruence property. Thus we have that all ɪᴜᴄ smaller triangles are congruent.

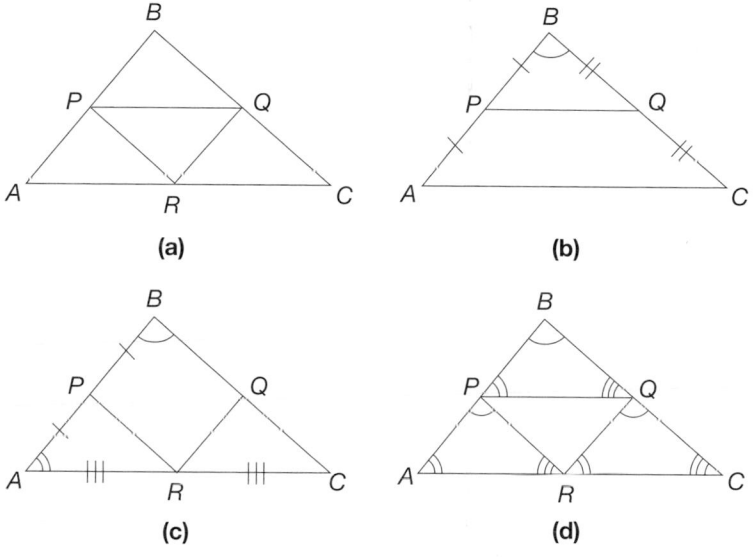

(a) (b)

(c) (d)

Figure 14.56

The next result is related to Example 14.15.

Example 14.16   Refer to Figure 14.57(a). Suppose that $\triangle ABC$ is a triangle and points P and Q are on $\overline{AB}$ and $\overline{BC}$, respectively, such that $\dfrac{BP}{BA} = \dfrac{BQ}{BC}$; that is, P and Q divide $\overline{BA}$ and $\overline{BC}$ proportionally. Show that $\overline{PQ} \parallel \overline{AC}$ and $\dfrac{PQ}{AC} = \dfrac{BP}{BA}$.

Solution   Consider $\triangle BPQ$ [Figure 14.57(b)]. Since $\dfrac{BP}{BA} = \dfrac{BQ}{BC}$ and $\angle PBQ \cong \angle ABC$, we have that $\triangle ABC \sim \triangle PBQ$ by the SAS similarity property. Hence $\angle BPQ \cong \angle BAC$, since they are corresponding angles in the similar triangles [Figure 14.57(c)].

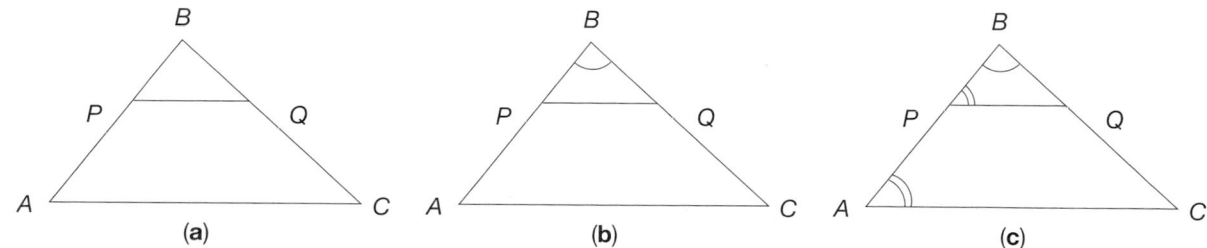

(a) (b) (c)

Figure 14.57

Thus $\overline{PQ} \parallel \overline{AC}$. Also, $\dfrac{PQ}{AC} = \dfrac{BP}{BA}$, since corresponding sides are proportional in the similar triangles (verify this).

From Example 14.16 we see that a line segment that divides two sides of a triangle proportionally is parallel to the third side and proportional to it in the same ratio.

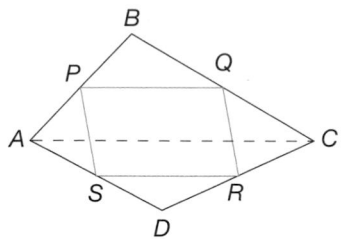

Figure 14.58

In particular, if points P and Q in Example 14.16 were midpoints of the sides, then $\overline{PQ} \parallel \overline{AC}$ and $PQ = \frac{1}{2}AC$. The segment, such as $\overline{PQ}$, that joins the midpoints of two sides of a triangle is called a **midsegment** of the triangle.

Using the result of Example 14.16 regarding the midsegment of a triangle, we can deduce a surprising result about quadrilaterals. Suppose that $ABCD$ is any quadrilateral in the plane (Figure 14.58). Let P, Q, R, and S be the midpoints of the sides. We call $PQRS$ the **midquad** of $ABCD$, since it is a quadrilateral that is formed by joining midpoints of the sides of $ABCD$. By Example 14.16, $\overline{PQ} \parallel \overline{AC}$ and $\overline{SR} \parallel \overline{AC}$. Thus $\overline{PQ} \parallel \overline{SR}$. Similarly, $\overline{PS} \parallel \overline{QR}$. Therefore, $PQRS$ is a parallelogram.

⚽ THEOREM

Midquad Theorem

The midquad of any quadrilateral is a parallelogram.

NCTM Standards 2000
Reasoning and Proof
Instructional programs should enable all students to make and investigate mathematical conjectures.

The preceding proof shows that $PQRS$ is a parallelogram. But could it be a square? a rectangle? a rhombus? Part A Problem 10 in the Problem Set contains some problems that will lead you to decide precisely under what conditions these special quadrilaterals are possible.

THE GEOMETER'S SKETCHPAD
www.wiley.com/
college/musser

Spotlight on Technology In addition to the midquad of any quadrilateral being a parallelogram, there is an interesting property that relates the area of the midquad to the area of the original quadrilateral. Use the Geometer's Sketchpad® webmodule activity, *Midquad*, to investigate this relationship. What relationship do you observe?

MATHEMATICAL MORSEL

Although the name of the Greek mathematician Pythagoras (circa 500 B.C.) is associated with the famous Pythagorean theorem, there is no doubt that this result was known prior to the time of Pythagoras. In fact, the discovery of a Babylonian method for finding the diagonal of a square, given the length of the side of the square, suggests that the theorem was known more than 1000 years before Pythagoras. Interestingly, it has been asserted that Pythagoras' greatest achievement was that he was the first European who insisted that postulates must be set down first when developing geometry, a contribution to mathematics often attributed to Euclid.

Section 14.5 EXERCISE / PROBLEM SET A

PROBLEMS

1. Answer the questions to prove the following property: If a line bisects the vertex angle of an isosceles triangle, it is the perpendicular bisector of the base.

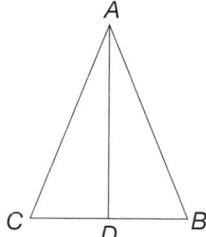

a. You are given that $\triangle ABC$ is isosceles with base $\overline{BC}$ and that $\overline{AD}$ bisects $\angle CAB$. What pairs of angles or segments are congruent because of the given information?

b. What other pair of corresponding angles of $\triangle ABD$ and $\triangle ACD$ are congruent? Why?

c. What congruence property can be used to prove $\triangle ABD \cong \triangle ACD$?

d. Why is $\angle ADC \cong \angle ADB$ and $\overline{DC} \cong \overline{DB}$?

e. Why is $\overline{AD} \perp \overline{BC}$?

f. Why is $\overline{AD}$ the perpendicular bisector of $\overline{BC}$?

2. Given rhombus $ABCD$ with diagonals meeting at point E, prove that the diagonals of a rhombus are perpendicular to each other. (*Hint*: Show that $\triangle ABE \cong \triangle CBE$.)

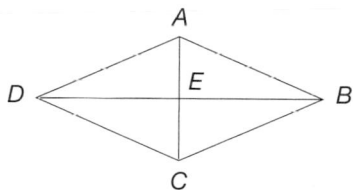

3. Quadrilateral $STUV$ is a rhombus and $\angle S$ is a right angle. Show that $STUV$ is a square.

4. Prove that the diagonals of a parallelogram bisect each other.

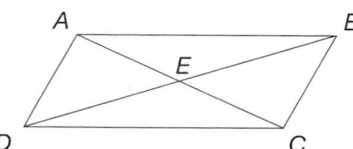

5. Construct a parallelogram with adjacent sides and one diagonal congruent to the given segments.

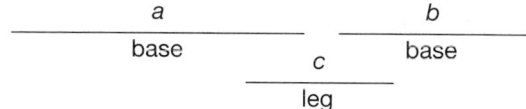

6. Quadrilateral $STUV$ is a rhombus and diagonals $\overline{SU}$ and $\overline{TV}$ are congruent. Show that $STUV$ is a square.

7. Construct a rhombus with sides and one diagonal congruent to the given segment.

_____ a _____

8. Construct an isosceles trapezoid with bases and legs congruent to the given segments.

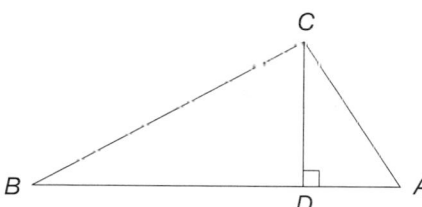

9. If $\overline{CD} \perp \overline{AB}$ in $\triangle ABC$ and AC is the geometric mean of AD and AB, prove that $\triangle ABC$ is a right triangle. (*Hint*: Show that $\triangle ADC \sim \triangle ACB$.)

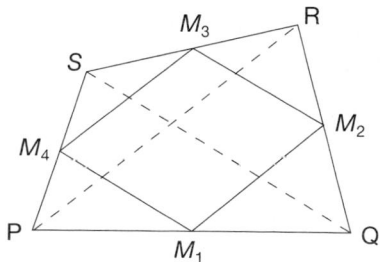

10. The midquad theorem in this section states that the midquad of any quadrilateral $PQRS$ is a parallelogram.

a. Use the fact that each side of the midquad is parallel to and one-half the length of a diagonal of the quadrilateral to determine under what conditions the midquad $M_1M_2M_3M_4$ will be a rectangle.

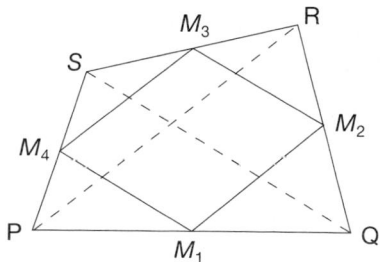

b. Under what conditions will the midquad $M_1M_2M_3M_4$ be a rhombus?

c. Under what conditions will the midquad $M_1M_2M_3M_4$ be a square?

11. Complete the following argument, which uses similarity to prove the Pythagorean theorem. Let △ABC have ∠C as a right angle. Let $\overline{CD}$ be perpendicular to $\overline{AB}$.

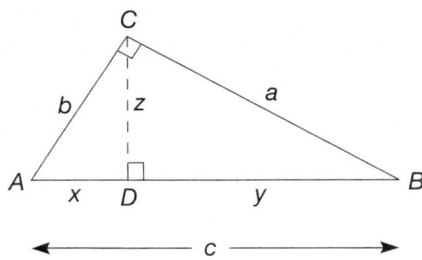

a. Then △ADC ~ △ACB. Why?

b. Also, △BDC ~ △BCA. Why? Thus $\dfrac{b}{x} = \dfrac{x+y}{b}$, or $b^2 = x^2 + xy$. Also $\dfrac{a}{y} = \dfrac{x+y}{a}$, or $a^2 = xy + y^2$.

c. Show that $a^2 + b^2 = c^2$.

12. a. Show that the diagonals of kite ABCD are perpendicular. (*Hint*: Show that △AEB ≅ △AED.)

b. Find a formula for the area of a kite in terms of the lengths of its diagonals.

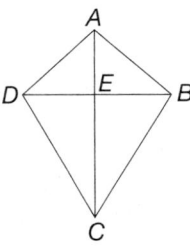

13. Show that the SSS congruence property follows from the SAS congruence property. (*Hint*: Referring to the following figure, assume the SAS congruence property and suppose that the respective sides of △ABC and △A′B′C′ are congruent as marked. Assume that ∠A is acute and then construct △ABD as illustrated so that ∠BAD ≅ ∠B′A′C′ and AD = A′C′. Without using the SSS congruence property, show △BAD ≅ △B′A′C′, △BAD ≅ △BAC, etc.)

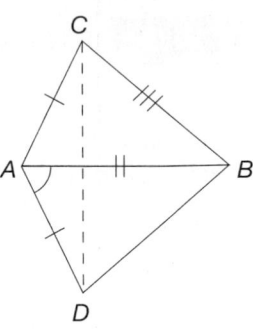

14. Show that the AA similarity property follows from the SAS similarity property. Referring to the following figure, suppose that ∠A ≅ ∠A′ and ∠B ≅ ∠B′. Show that △ABC ~ △A′B′C′ without using the AA similarity property. (*Hint*: If $\dfrac{AC}{AB} = \dfrac{A'C'}{A'B'}$, then △ABC ~ △A′B′C′ by the SAS similarity property. If $\dfrac{AC}{AB} \neq \dfrac{A'C'}{A'B'}$, a D′ can be found on $\overline{A'C'}$ such that $\dfrac{AC}{AB} = \dfrac{A'D'}{A'B'}$. Use the SAS similarity property to reach a contradiction.)

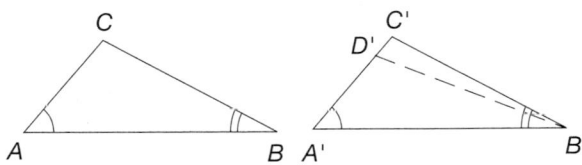

15. Euclid's proof of the Pythagorean theorem is as follows. Refer to the figure and justify each part.

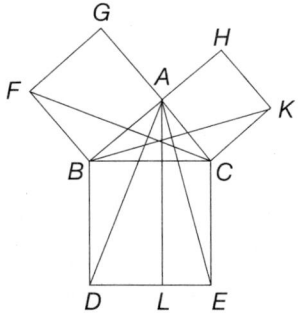

a. Show that △ABD ≅ △FBC and △ACE ≅ △KCB.

b. Show that the area of △ABD plus the area of △ACE is one-half the area of square BCED.

c. Show that the area of △FBC is one-half the area of square ABFG, and that the area of △KCB is one-half the area of square ACKH.

d. Show that the area of square ABFG plus the area of square ACKH is the area of square BCED.

e. How does this prove the Pythagorean theorem?

Section 14.5 EXERCISE / PROBLEM SET B

PROBLEMS

1. Answer the following questions to prove that the diagonals of a rhombus bisect the vertex angles of the rhombus.

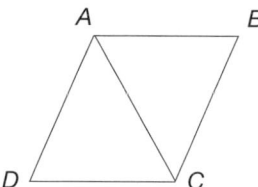

a. Given the rhombus $ABCD$ and diagonal $\overline{AC}$, what pairs of corresponding sides of $\triangle ABC$ and $\triangle ADC$ are congruent?

b. What other pair of corresponding sides are congruent? Why?

c. What congruence property can be used to show that $\triangle ABC \cong \triangle ADC$?

d. Why is $\angle BAC \cong \angle DAC$ and $\angle BCA \cong \angle DCA$?

e. Why does $\overline{AC}$ bisect $\angle DAB$ and $\angle DCB$?

2. Another justification that the diagonal of a rhombus bisects the vertex angles follows from the following questions.

a. Since a rhombus is a parallelogram, $AB \parallel \overline{CD}$ and $\overline{AD} \parallel \overline{BC}$. What pairs of angles are thereby congruent?

b. $\angle 1 \cong \angle 2$ and $\angle 3 \cong \angle 4$. Why?

c. Can we say $\angle 1 \cong \angle 4$ and $\angle 2 \cong \angle 3$? Why?

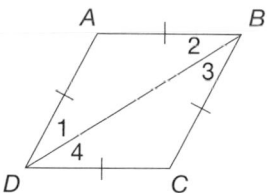

3. Given that $\triangle PQR$ is an equilateral triangle, show that it is also equiangular.

4. Prove: If a trapezoid is isosceles, its opposite angles are supplementary.

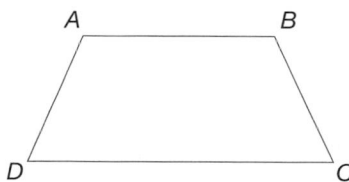

5. A rhombus is sometimes defined as a parallelogram with two adjacent congruent sides. If parallelogram

$DEFG$ has congruent sides $\overline{DE}$ and $\overline{EF}$, verify that it has four congruent sides (thus satisfying our definition of a rhombus).

6. Prove that every rectangle is a parallelogram.

7. Quadrilateral $HIJK$ is a rectangle, and adjacent sides $\overline{HI}$ and $\overline{IJ}$ are congruent. Prove that $HIJK$ is a square.

8. Construct a rectangle with a side and a diagonal congruent to the given segments.

side	diagonal

9. Construct a square with diagonals congruent to the given segment.

d

10. a. Prove: If diagonals of a quadrilateral are perpendicular bisectors of each other, the quadrilateral is a rhombus.

b. Construct a rhombus with diagonals congruent to the two segments given.

a
b

11. Prove: Two isosceles triangles, $\triangle DEF$ and $\triangle RST$, are similar if a base angle of one is congruent to a base angle of the other. (Let $\angle D$ and $\angle R$ be the congruent base angles and $\angle E$ and $\angle S$ be the nonbase angles.)

12. In $\triangle ABC$, $\overline{CD} \perp \overline{AB}$ and CD is the geometric mean of AD and DB. Prove that $\triangle ABC$ is a right triangle.

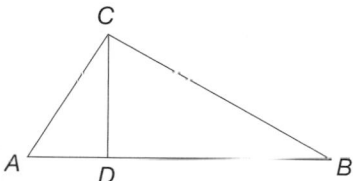

13. Refer to the next figure. To inscribe a regular decagon in a circle of radius 1, it must be possible to construct the length x.

a. What are $m(\angle BAC)$, $m(\angle ABC)$, and $m(\angle ACB)$?

b. An arc of length x is constructed with center B, meeting $\overline{AC}$ at point D. What are $m(\angle BCD)$ and $m(\angle CBD)$?

c. What is $m(\angle ABD)$? What special kind of triangle is $\triangle ABD$?

d. What are the lengths of $\overline{AD}$ and $\overline{DC}$?

e. Consider the following triangles copied from the preceding drawing. Label angle and side measures that are known. Are these triangles similar?

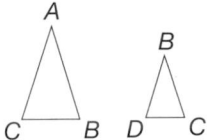

f. Complete the proportions: $\dfrac{AC}{?} = \dfrac{BC}{?}$ or
$\dfrac{1}{?} = \dfrac{x}{?}$.

g. Solve this proportion for x. [*Hint*: You may need to recall the quadratic formula. To solve the equation $ax^2 + bx + c = 0$, use $x = (-b \pm \sqrt{b^2 - 4ac})/2a$.]

h. Can we construct a segment of length x?

14. Show that the ASA congruence property follows from the SAS congruence property. (*Hint*: Referring to the following figure, if $AC = A'C'$, then $\triangle ABC \cong \triangle A'B'C'$ by the SAS congruence property. If not, find a D' on $\overline{A'C'}$ such that $AC = A'D'$, show that $\triangle ABC \cong \triangle A'B'D'$, and use the SAS congruence property to reach a contradiction.)

15. Show that the SSS similarity property follows from the SAS similarity property. (*Hint*: Referring to the figure, assume the SAS similarity property and suppose that the sides in $\triangle ABC$ and $\triangle A'B'C'$ are proportional, as marked. Assume that $\angle A$ is acute and construct $\triangle ABD$ as illustrated so that $\angle BAD \cong \angle B'A'C$, and $\dfrac{AD}{AB} = \dfrac{A'C'}{A'B'}$. Show that $\triangle BAD \sim \triangle B'A'C'$ and $\triangle BAD \cong \triangle BAC$; use the SAS congruence property.)

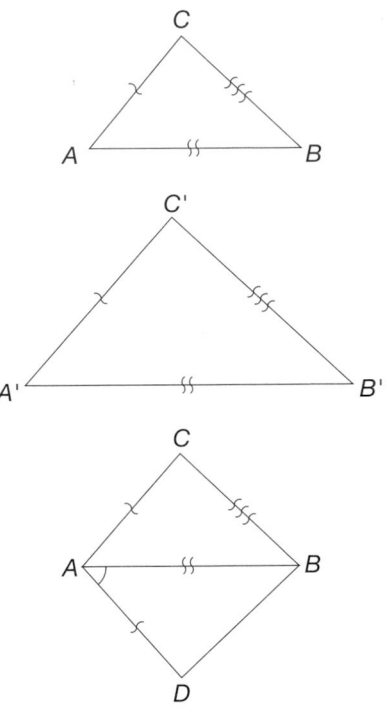

PROBLEMS FOR WRITING/DISCUSSION

1. Willard says, "Why do I have to prove that a rhombus is a parallelogram? Isn't it obvious from looking at it?" What is your response?

2. Caesar says, "I know a rhombus is a parallelogram because having two pairs of parallel sides is one of the properties of a rhombus." Does this constitute a proof? You may want to refer back to what you know about van Hiele levels.

3. Victoria wants to prove that the angle bisector of the angle opposite the base in an isosceles triangle is the same as the median, but she doesn't know where to begin. Can she assume that $PI = IC$? They look equal. Can she assume that $\angle PIK$ and $\angle KIC$ are right angles? How would you explain?

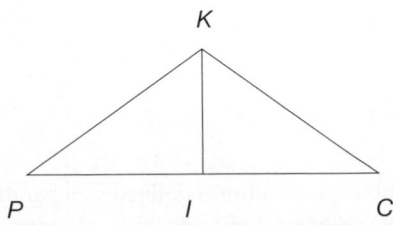

END OF CHAPTER MATERIAL

Solution of Initial Problem

An eastbound bicycle enters a tunnel at the same time that a westbound bicycle enters the other end of the tunnel. The eastbound bicycle travels at 10 kilometers per hour, the westbound bicycle at 8 kilometers per hour. A fly is flying back and forth between the two bicycles at 15 kilometers per hour, leaving the eastbound bicycle as it enters the tunnel. The tunnel is 9 kilometers long. How far has the fly traveled in the tunnel when the bicycles meet?

Strategy: Identify Subgoals

We know the rate at which the fly is flying (15 km/h). If we can determine the time that the fly is traveling, we can determine the distance the fly travels, since distance = rate × time. Therefore, our subgoal is to find the time that the fly travels. But this is the length of time that it takes the two bicycles to meet.

Let t be the time in hours that it takes for the bicycles to meet. The eastbound bicycle travels $10 \cdot t$ kilometers and the westbound bicycle travels $8 \cdot t$ kilometers. This yields

$$10t + 8t = 9,$$

so that

$$18t = 9,$$

or

$$t = \frac{1}{2}.$$

Therefore, the time that it takes for the bicycles to meet is $\frac{1}{2}$ hour. (This reaches our subgoal.) Consequently, the fly travels for $\frac{1}{2}$ hour, so that the fly travels $15 \times \frac{1}{2} = 7\frac{1}{2}$ km.

Additional Problems Where the Strategy "Identify Subgoals" Is Useful

1. Find the smallest square that has a factor of 360.
2. The areas of the sides of a rectangular box are 24 cm², 32 cm², and 48 cm². What is the volume of the box?
3. Thirty-two percent of n is 128. Find n mentally.

People in Mathematics

Hypatia (370?–415) Hypatia is the first woman mathematician to be mentioned in the history of mathematics. She was the daughter of the mathematician Theon of Alexandria, who is chiefly known for his editions of Euclid's *Elements*. At the university in Alexandria, she was a famous lecturer in philosophy and mathematics, but we do not know if she had an official teaching position. It is said that she followed the practice of philosophers of her time, dressing in a tattered cloak and holding public discussions in the center of the city. Hypatia became a victim of the prejudice of her time. Christians in Alexandria were hostile toward the university and the pagan Greek culture it represented. There were periodic outbreaks of violence, and during one of these incidents Hypatia was killed by a mob of Christian fanatics.

Benoit Mandelbrot (1924–   ) Benoit Mandelbrot once said, "Clouds are not spheres, mountains are not cones, coastlines are not circles, and bark is not smooth, nor does lightning travel in a straight line." This is how he describes the inspiration for fractal geometry, a new field of mathematics that finds order in chaotic, irregular shapes and processes. Mandelbrot was largely responsible for developing the mathematics of fractal geometry while at IBM's Watson Research Center. Before Mandelbrot, other mathematicians had considered the requisite mathematics, but they described it as "pathological," giving rise to "mathematical monstrosities." "The question I raised in 1967 is, 'How long is the coast of Britain?' and the correct answer is 'It all depends.' It depends on the size of the instrument used to measure length. As the measurement becomes increasingly refined, the measured length will increase. Thus the coastline is of infinite length in some sense."

CHAPTER REVIEW

Review the following terms and exercises to determine which require learning or relearning—page numbers are provided for easy reference.

SECTION 14.1: Congruence of Triangles

VOCABULARY/NOTATION

Congruent line segments, $\overline{AB} \cong \overline{DE}$
695

Congruent angles, $\angle ABC \cong \angle DEF$
695

Correspondence between $\triangle ABC$ and
$\triangle DEF$, $A \leftrightarrow D$, $B \leftrightarrow E$, $C \leftrightarrow F$
695

Congruent triangles, $\triangle ABC \cong \triangle DEF$
695

Angle bisector   701

EXERCISES

1. State the definition of congruent triangles.

2. State the following congruence properties.

   a. SAS   **b.** ASA   **c.** SSS

3. Decide whether $\triangle ABC \cong \triangle DEF$ under the following conditions. Which of the properties in Exercise 2 justify the congruences? If the triangles are not congruent, sketch a figure to show why not.

   a. $\overline{AB} \cong \overline{DE}$, $\overline{BC} \cong \overline{EF}$, $\overline{CA} \cong \overline{FD}$

   b. $\overline{AB} \cong \overline{DE}$, $\angle C \cong \angle F$, $\overline{BC} \cong \overline{EF}$

   c. $\angle A \cong \angle D$, $\angle B \cong \angle E$, $\overline{AB} \cong \overline{DE}$

   d. $\angle B \cong \angle E$, $\overline{BC} \cong \overline{EF}$, $\overline{AB} \cong \overline{DE}$

SECTION 14.2: Similarity of Triangles

VOCABULARY / NOTATION

Similar triangles, $\triangle ABC \sim \triangle DEF$
707

Indirect measurement   709

Fractals   710

Koch curve   710

Self-similar   710

Sierpinski triangle or gasket   710

EXERCISES

1. State the definition of similar triangles.

2. State the following similarity properties.

   a. SAS   **b.** AA   **c.** SSS

3. Decide whether $\triangle ABC \sim \triangle DEF$ under the following conditions. Which of the properties in Exercise 2 justify the similarity? If the triangles are not similar, sketch a figure to show why not.

   a. $\dfrac{AB}{DE} = \dfrac{BC}{EF}$, $\angle A \cong \angle D$ **b.** $\dfrac{AB}{DE} = \dfrac{BC}{FC} = \dfrac{AC}{EF}$

   c. $\angle B \cong \angle E$, $\angle C \cong \angle F$

4. Describe three ways to calculate the height of a tree using similarity.

SECTION 14.3: Basic Euclidean Constructions

VOCABULARY / NOTATION

Arc   718

EXERCISES

1. Draw a line segment and copy it.

2. Draw an angle and copy it.

3. Draw a line segment and construct its perpendicular bisector.

4. Draw an angle and bisect it.

5. Draw a line and mark point P on it. Construct a line through P perpendicular to the line.

6. Draw a line and a point P not on the line. Construct a line through P perpendicular to the line.

7. Draw a line and a point P not on the line. Construct a line through P parallel to the line.

SECTION 14.4: Additional Euclidean Constructions

VOCABULARY / NOTATION

Circumscribed circle   728
Inscribed circle   728
Tangent line to a circle   729

Circumcenter   729
Incenter   729
Distance from a point to a line   730

Orthocenter   731
Centroid   731
Fermat prime   732

EXERCISES

1. List the steps required to construct the circumscribed circle of a triangle.

2. List the steps required to construct the inscribed circle of a triangle.

3. Draw a line segment and construct an equilateral triangle having the line segment as one of its sides.

4. Describe how to construct the following regular *n*-gons.
   a. A square
   b. A hexagon
   c. An octagon

5. Draw a line segment $\overline{AB}$ and construct a second line segment whose length is $AB\sqrt{3}$.

SECTION 14.5: Geometric Problem Solving Using Triangle Congruence and Similarity

VOCABULARY / NOTATION

Midsegment of a triangle   744   Midquad   744

EXERCISES

1. State and prove the converse of the Pythagorean theorem.

2. Show how the midsegment theorem is used to prove the midquad theorem.

PROBLEMS FOR WRITING/DISCUSSION

1. Ricardo says these two triangles must be congruent by AAS. Do you agree? Why or why not?

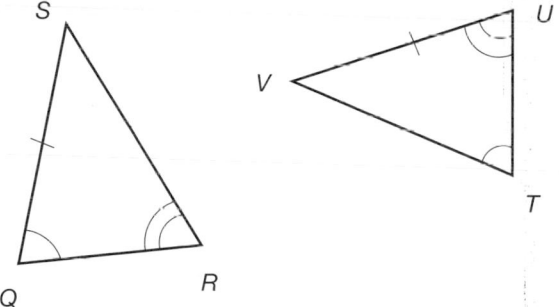

2. All cubes are similar to each other; thus all rectangular prisms are similar to each other. True or false? Explain.

3. If one cube has a side of 3 m and another cube has a side of 5 m, what is the ratio of their heights? of their front faces? of their volumes? Explain.

4. Is the circumcenter always inside the triangle? Is the orthocenter always inside the triangle? How about the incenter? the centroid? Discuss, using examples.

5. When constructing triangles with three line segments of different lengths, Latisha says you have to draw the longest side first. Marlena says it doesn't matter; you can even start with the shortest side. Latisha says, "Then the triangles won't match." Which student is correct? Discuss.

6. Angelo says the diagonal of a rectangle bisects its angles. Juan says not always. What do you say? How would you respond to these students? Could you prove the diagonal was an angle bisector?

7. If you knew two figures were rectangles, how many parts of one would have to be congruent to the corresponding parts of the other for you to be sure the two rectangles were congruent? If two figures were parallelograms, what is the minimum number of parts of one that would have to match the other for you to be sure they were congruent? Discuss.

8. Dwight was trying to find x in the following diagram. He knew that the two triangles were similar, so he made the following proportion: $\dfrac{6}{10} = \dfrac{8}{x}$. The answer didn't look quite right in the picture, but he knew that diagrams aren't always drawn to scale. Is Dwight correct? Discuss.

9. When Rachel compares the shape of a horse to the shape of an elephant, she notices that the legs of the elephant are much fatter than the legs of the horse. She asks you if the elephant has fatter legs than the horse because it is fatter generally. Or is it because the elephant has more weight to carry? How would you respond? (Suppose the back of the horse is about 5 feet high and the back of the elephant is about 8 feet high. If you assumed their body shapes were roughly similar, what would be the ratio of their volumes? What would be the ratio of their masses?)

10. Darrell is wondering how to find the volume of this truncated cone. He thinks that it would help if he

drew in the part of the cone that was cut off. Can similar triangles be useful here? Discuss.

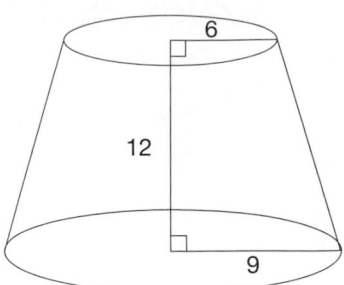

CHAPTER TEST

Knowledge

1. True or false?

   a. Two triangles are congruent if two sides and the included angle of one triangle are congruent, respectively, to two sides and the included angle of the other triangle.

   b. Two triangles are similar if two sides of one triangle are proportional to two sides of the other triangle.

   c. The opposite sides of a parallelogram are congruent.

   d. The diagonals of a kite are perpendicular.

   e. Every rhombus is a kite.

   f. The diagonals of a parallelogram bisect each other.

   g. The circumcenter of a triangle is the intersection of the altitudes.

   h. The incenter of a triangle is equidistant from the vertices.

2. Which of the following are congruence properties for triangles?

   SAS, ASA, SSA, SSS, AAA

Skill

3. For which of the following values of n can a regular n-gon be constructed with a compass and straightedge?

   a. 36   b. 85

   c. 144   d. 4369

4. Construct a regular 12-gon with a compass and straightedge.

5. Construct the circumcenter and incenter for the same equilateral triangle. What conclusion can you draw?

6. Determine which of the following pairs of triangles are congruent. Justify your conclusion.

   a.

   b.
   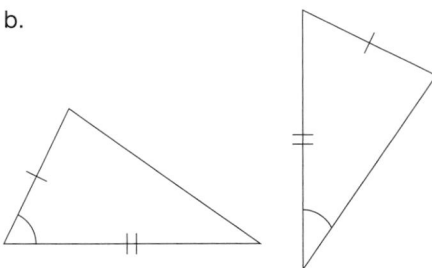

7. In the following figure, $AC = 20$, $CE = 5$, $DE = 3$, and $BE = 9$. Determine if $\triangle ABE \sim \triangle CDE$. Justify your answer.

   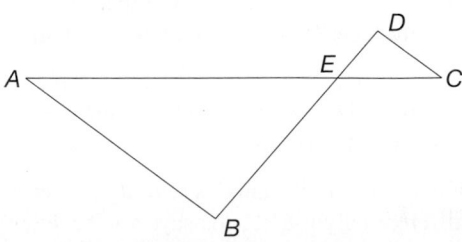

8. Construct the line parallel to line l through point P using a compass and straightedge.

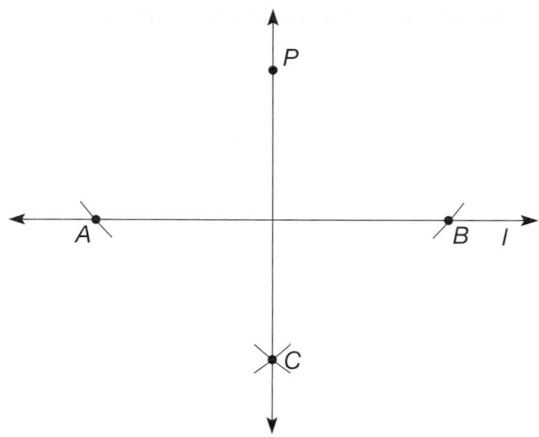

Understanding

9. Given segment $\overline{AB}$ as the unit segment, construct a segment $\overline{AC}$ where the length of $\overline{AC}$ is $\sqrt{5}$. Then construct a square with area 5.

$$\overline{}$$
$A \qquad\quad B$

10. Prove or disprove: If $\triangle ABC \cong \triangle CBA$, then $\triangle ABC$ is isosceles.

11. Prove or disprove: If $\triangle ABC \cong \triangle BCA$, then $\triangle ABC$ is equilateral.

12. If possible, construct two noncongruent triangles that have corresponding sides of length 1.5 inches and corresponding angles with measure 75°. If this is not possible, explain why not.

13. Explain how similar triangles can be used to determine the height of a tree.

14. Explain, in detail, what it means for two triangles to be congruent by the SAS congruence property.

15. In the following figure, line *l* and point *P* are given. The rest of the marks on the figure indicate the construction of a line through *P* that is perpendicular to *l*. The following steps describe the construction.

   a. Draw an arc with center *P* to intersect *l* in two places. Label these points of intersection *A* and *B*.

   b. Draw an arc with center *A* on the side of *l* that is opposite of *P*.

   c. Keeping the same measure on the compass as in part (b), draw an arc with center *B* to intersect the arc drawn in part (b), Label this point of intersection *C*.

   d. Draw line $\overline{PC}$. This is the desired perpendicular.

Explain why this series of steps yields the desired result of "a line through *P* that is perpendicular to *l*."

16. **a.** State the mathematical definition of *similar*.

   b. Determine whether the following statements are true or false according to the definition.

   i. Notebook paper (8.5 in. by 11 in.) is similar to an index card (3 in. by 5 in.).

   ii. A right triangle is similar to an equilateral triangle.

   iii. A circle of radius 1 inch is similar to a circle of radius 5 meters.

Problem Solving Application

17. Given: trapezoid *ABCD*.

   a. Prove: If $\angle A \cong \angle B$, then $\overline{AD} \cong \overline{BC}$.

   b. Prove: If $\overline{AD} \cong \overline{BC}$, then $\angle A \cong \angle B$.

18. **a.** According to Gauss's theorem, a regular 9-gon cannot be constructed with a compass and straightedge. Why?

   b. What is the measure of a central angle in a regular 9-gon?

   c. Suppose that one wanted to trisect a 60° angle (i.e., divide it into three congruent angles) with a compass and straightedge. What angle would be constructed?

d. What conclusion can you draw from parts (a), (b), and (c) regarding the possibility of trisecting a 60° angle?

19. In $\triangle ABC$, segment $\overline{PQ} \parallel \overline{BC}$ and $\angle AQP$ is a right angle.

a. Find the length of $\overline{PQ}$.

b. Find the area of $\triangle ABC$.

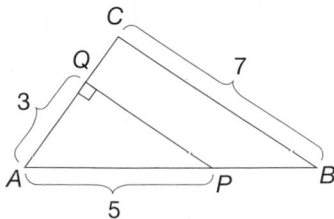

20. On her early morning walk, Jinhee noticed that when she walked under a streetlight, her shadow would get longer the farther she was away from the light. She decided to use her shadow to find out how tall the light was. When she was 12 feet from the base of the light, her shadow was 4 feet long. She is 5 feet 6 inches tall. How tall is the light?

References for Reflections from Research

BEILIN, H. (1982). *Strategies and structures in understanding geometry.* (ERIC Document Reproduction Service No. ED 255 808.)

CHAZAN, D. (1988). *Similarity, exploring the understanding of a geometric concept.* (ERIC Document Reproduction Service No. 295 822.)

FINZER, W. F., & BENNETT, D. S. (1995). From drawing to construction with *The Geometer's Sketchpad. Mathematics Teacher, 88,* 428–431.

SOBEL, M. A., & MALETSKY, E. M. (1988). *Teaching mathematics: A source book of aids, activities, and strategies* (2nd ed.). Upper Saddle River, NJ: Prentice Hall.

FOCUS ON René Descartes and Coordinate Geometry

The subjects of algebra and geometry had evolved on parallel tracks until René Descartes (1596–1650) developed a method of joining them. This important contribution made possible the development of the calculus. Because of this contribution, Descartes has been called the "father of modern mathematics." The coordinate system used in analytic geometry is called the Cartesian coordinate system in his honor.

Descartes's analytic geometry was designed to study the mathematical attributes of lines and curves by representing them via equations. These equations were obtained by picturing the curves in the plane. Each point, P, in the plane was labeled using pairs of numbers, or "coordinates," determined by two perpendicular reference lines (Figure 1).

A second convenient way of representing curves in the plane is through the use of polar coordinates, where every point, P, of the plane can be located using a reference angle, θ, whose vertex is called the origin, and a distance, r, from the origin (Figure 2).

What is impressive about the coordinate approach, either Cartesian or polar, is that geometric problems can be represented using algebraic equations. Then algebra can be applied to these equations without regard to their geometric representations. Finally, the result of the algebra can be reinterpreted to produce a solution to the original geometric problem.

René Descartes

Cartesian coordinates

Figure 1

Polar coordinates

Figure 2

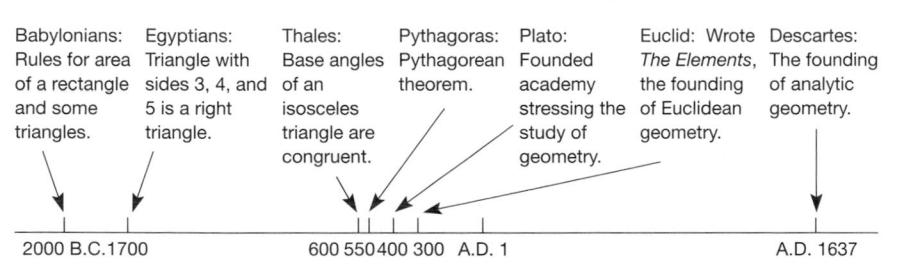

Brief Timeline for Geometry

Babylonians: Rules for area of a rectangle and some triangles.

Egyptians: Triangle with sides 3, 4, and 5 is a right triangle.

Thales: Base angles of an isosceles triangle are congruent.

Pythagoras: Pythagorean theorem.

Plato: Founded academy stressing the study of geometry.

Euclid: Wrote *The Elements*, the founding of Euclidean geometry.

Descartes: The founding of analytic geometry.

2000 B.C. 1700   600 550 400 300   A.D. 1   A.D. 1637

Problem Solving Strategies

1. Guess and Test
2. Use a Variable
3. Draw a Picture
4. Look for a Pattern
5. Make a List
6. Solve a Simpler Problem
7. Draw a Diagram
8. Use Direct Reasoning
9. Use Indirect Reasoning
10. Use Properties of Numbers
11. Solve an Equivalent Problem
12. Work Backward
13. Use Cases
14. Solve an Equation
15. Look for a Formula
16. Do a Simulation
17. Use a Model
18. Use Dimensional Analysis
19. Identify Subgoals
20. Use Coordinates

Strategy
Use Coordinates

In many two-dimensional geometry problems, we can use a "grid" of squares overlaid on the plane, called a coordinate system, to gain additional information. This numerical information can then be used to solve problems about two-dimensional figures. Coordinate systems also can be used in three-dimensional space and on curved surfaces such as a sphere (e.g., the Earth).

Initial Problem

A surveyor plotted a triangular building lot, drew the following diagram, and recorded the following data. What is the area of the lot, in square feet? (NOTE: East 207′ means 207 feet east of stake S.)

STAKE	POSITION RELATIVE TO S
U	East 207′, North 35′
T	East 40′, North 185′

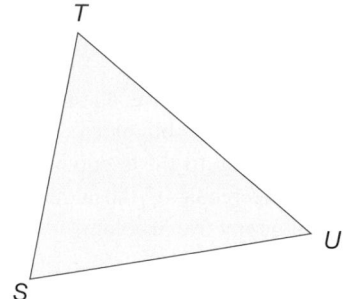

Clues

The Use Coordinates strategy may be appropriate when

- A problem can be represented using two variables.
- A geometry problem cannot easily be solved by using traditional Euclidean methods.
- A problem involves finding representations of lines or conic sections.
- A problem involves slope, parallel lines, perpendicular lines, and so on.
- The location of a geometric shape with respect to other shapes is important.
- A problem involves maps.

A solution of the Initial Problem appears on page 792.

INTRODUCTION

Reflection from Research
An understanding of coordinate graphing develops over an extended period of time (Demana & Waits, 1988).

In this chapter we study geometry using the coordinate plane. Using a coordinate system on the plane, which was introduced in Section 9.3, we are able to derive many elegant geometrical results about lines, polygons, circles, and so on. In Section 15.1 we introduce the basic ideas needed to study geometry in the coordinate plane. Then in Section 15.2 we prove properties of geometric shapes using these concepts. Finally, Section 15.3 contains many interesting problems that can be solved using coordinate geometry.

15.1   DISTANCE AND SLOPE IN THE COORDINATE PLANE

STARTING POINT

The points $A = (0, 0)$, $B = (2, 3)$, and $C = (5, -1)$ are plotted on the axes at the right. Locate a fourth point D such that A, B, C, and D are the vertices of a parallelogram. Justify your selection. Are there other points that will work? If so, how many?

Figure 15.1

Distance

The use of coordinates as developed in Section 9.3 allows us to analyze many properties of geometric figures. For example, we can find distances between points in the plane using coordinates. Consider points $P(x_1, y_1)$ and $Q(x_2, y_2)$ (Figure 15.1). We can use point $R(x_2, y_1)$ to form a right triangle, $\triangle PQR$. Notice that the length of the horizontal segment $\overline{PR}$ is $x_2 - x_1$ and that the length of the vertical segment $\overline{QR}$ is $y_2 - y_1$. We wish to find the length of $\overline{PQ}$. By the Pythagorean theorem,

$$PQ^2 = PR^2 + QR^2,$$

so

$$PQ = \sqrt{PR^2 + QR^2}.$$

But

$$PR^2 = (x_2 - x_1)^2 \text{ and } QR^2 = (y_2 - y_1)^2.$$

Hence $PQ = \sqrt{(x_2 - x_1)^2 + (y_2 - y_1)^2}$. This yields the following distance formula.

NCTM Standards 2000
Geometry Grades 3–5
All students should find the distance between points along horizontal and vertical lines of a coordinate system.

THEOREM

Coordinate Distance Formula

If P is the point (x_1, y_1) and Q is the point (x_2, y_2), the distance from P to Q is

$$PQ = \sqrt{(x_2 - x_1)^2 + (y_2 - y_1)^2}.$$

$Q(x_2, y_2)$

$P(x_1, y_1)$

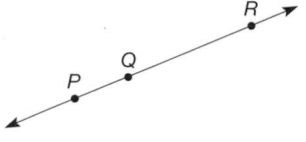

Figure 15.2

We have verified the coordinate distance formula in the case that $x_2 \geq x_1$ and $y_2 \geq y_1$. However, this formula holds for *all* pairs of points in the plane. For example, if $x_1 \geq x_2$, we would use $(x_1 - x_2)^2$ in the formula. But $(x_1 - x_2)^2 = (x_2 - x_1)^2$, so that the formula will yield the same result.

We can use the coordinate distance formula to determine whether three points are collinear. Recall that points P, Q, and R are collinear with Q between P and R if and only if $PQ + QR = PR$; that is, the distance from P to R is the sum of the distances from P to Q and Q to R (Figure 15.2).

Example 15.1 Use the coordinate distance formula to show that the points $P = (-5, -4)$, $Q = (-2, -2)$, and $R = (4, 2)$ are collinear.

Solution

$$PQ = \sqrt{[(-5) - (-2)]^2 + [(-4) - (-2)]^2} = \sqrt{9 + 4} = \sqrt{13}$$

$$QR = \sqrt{[(-2) - 4]^2 + [(-2) - 2]^2} = \sqrt{36 + 16} = 2\sqrt{13}$$

$$PR = \sqrt{[(-5) - 4]^2 + [(-4) - 2]^2} = \sqrt{81 + 36} = 3\sqrt{13}$$

Thus $PQ + QR = \sqrt{13} + 2\sqrt{13} = 3\sqrt{13} = PR$, so P, Q, and R are collinear. ■

Spotlight on Technology Example 15.1 can also be investigated by using the Chapter 15 eManipulative activity, *Coordinate Geoboard*. If a band is stretched between two points and perimeter is selected, the distance between the two points will be displayed. By moving the cursor around on the screen, locate the points P, Q, and R on the geoboard. Stretch a band PQ, measure its length by clicking on PERIMETER, and record the displayed value. Repeat for segments QR and PR. According to the displayed distances, are P, Q, and R collinear? What is the difference between the length of PQ computed above and the length displayed on the eManipulative?

www.wiley.com/college/musser

Example 15.1 is a special case of the following theorem.

THEOREM

Collinearity Test

Points $P(x_1, y_1)$, $Q(x_2, y_2)$, and $R(x_3, y_3)$ are collinear with Q between P and R if and only if $PQ + QR = PR$, or, equivalently,

$$\sqrt{(x_2 - x_1)^2 + (y_2 - y_1)^2} + \sqrt{(x_3 - x_2)^2 + (y_3 - y_2)^2}$$
$$= \sqrt{(x_3 - x_1)^2 + (y_3 - y_1)^2}.$$

Next we determine the midpoint of a line segment (Figure 15.3).

Figure 15.3

Consider $P(x_1, y_1)$ and $Q(x_2, y_2)$. Let M be the intersection of the vertical line through $\left(\dfrac{x_1 + x_2}{2}, y_1\right)$ and the horizontal line through $\left(x_2, \dfrac{y_1 + y_2}{2}\right)$ [Figure 15.3(a)]. Notice that $\left(\dfrac{x_1 + x_2}{2}, y_1\right)$ and $\left(x_2, \dfrac{y_1 + y_2}{2}\right)$ are midpoints of $\overline{PR}$ and $\overline{QR}$, respectively. Hence $M = \left(\dfrac{x_1 + x_2}{2}, \dfrac{y_1 + y_2}{2}\right)$. We can verify that M is the midpoint of segment $\overline{PQ}$ by showing that $PM = MQ$ and that P, M, and Q are collinear [Figure 15.3(b)]. This is left for Part A Problem 19 in the Problem Set.

NCTM Standards 2000
Reasoning and Proof
Instructional programs should enable all students to develop and evaluate mathematical arguments and proofs.

THEOREM

Midpoint Formula

If P is the point (x_1, y_1) and Q is the point (x_2, y_2), the midpoint, M, of $\overline{PQ}$ is the point

$$\left(\frac{x_1 + x_2}{2}, \frac{y_1 + y_2}{2}\right).$$

In words, the coordinates of the midpoint of a segment are the averages of the x-coordinates and y-coordinates of the endpoints, respectively.

Example 15.2   Find the coordinates of the midpoints of the three sides of $\triangle ABC$, where $A = (-6, 0)$, $B = (0, 8)$, $C = (10, 0)$ [Figure 15.4(a)].

Solution

$$\text{midpoint of } \overline{AB} = \left(\frac{-6 + 0}{2}, \frac{0 + 8}{2}\right) = (-3, 4)$$

$$\text{midpoint of } \overline{BC} = \left(\frac{0 + 10}{2}, \frac{8 + 0}{2}\right) = (5, 4)$$

$$\text{midpoint of } \overline{AC} = \left(\frac{-6 + 10}{2}, \frac{0 + 0}{2}\right) = (2, 0) \text{ [Figure 15.4(b)]}$$

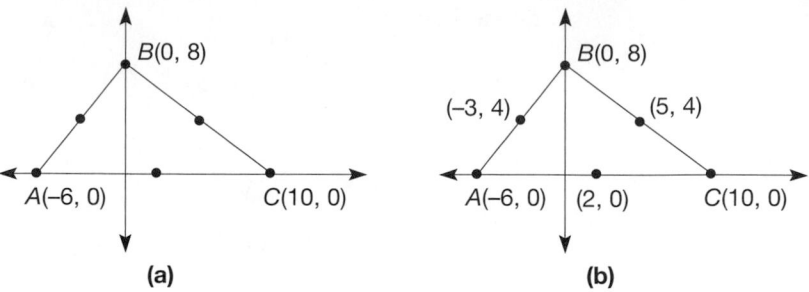

Figure 15.4

Slope

The slope of a line is a measure of its inclination from the horizontal.

DEFINITION

Slope of a Line

Suppose that P is the point (x_1, y_1) and Q is the point (x_2, y_2).

The **slope of line** $\overleftrightarrow{PQ}$ is the ratio $\dfrac{y_2 - y_1}{x_2 - x_1}$, provided $x_1 \neq x_2$. If $x_1 = x_2$, that is,

$\overleftrightarrow{PQ}$ is vertical, then the slope of $\overleftrightarrow{PQ}$ is undefined.

Note that $\dfrac{y_2 - y_1}{x_2 - x_1} = \dfrac{y_1 - y_2}{x_1 - x_2}$, so that it does not matter which endpoint we use first in computing the slope of a line. However, we must be consistent in the numerator and denominator; that is, we subtract the coordinates of Q from the coordinates of P, or vice versa. The slope of a line is often defined informally as "rise over the run." The **slope of a line segment** is the slope of the line containing it.

Example 15.3   Find the slope of these lines: (a) line l containing $P(-8, -6)$ and $Q(10, 5)$, (b) line m containing $R(2, 1)$ and $S(20, 12)$, and (c) line n containing $T(-3, 11)$ and $U(4, 11)$ (Figure 15.5).

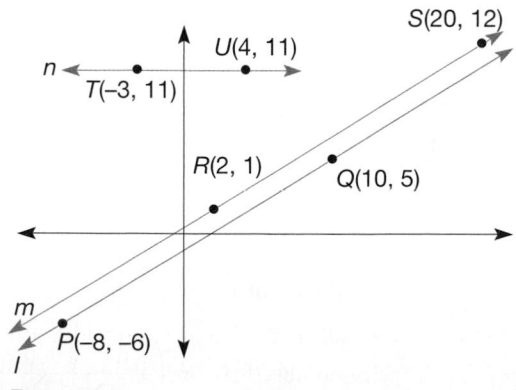

Figure 15.5

Solution

a. Using the coordinates of P and Q, the slope of $l = \dfrac{5 - (-6)}{10 - (-8)} = \dfrac{11}{18}$.

b. Using the coordinates of R and S, the slope of $m = \dfrac{12 - 1}{20 - 2} = \dfrac{11}{18}$. Hence lines l and m have equal slopes.

c. Using points T and U, the slope of line $n = \dfrac{11 - 11}{4 - (-3)} = 0$. Note that line n is horizontal. ■

Spotlight on Technology Gaining a sense of how the numerical values of the slope are related to the visual appearance of a line can be difficult. The Geometer's Sketchpad® webmodule activity, www.wiley.com/ college/musser *Slope*, can aid in this process. By moving the line you can see the slope change dynamically. After using the webmodule activity, describe what a line with slope 5, -7 or $\dfrac{1}{3}$ would look like.

Figure 15.6 shows examples of lines with various slopes. A horizontal line, such as line n in Example 15.3, has slope 0. As the slope increases, the line "rises" to the right. A line that rises steeply from left to right has a large positive slope. A vertical line has no slope. On the other hand, a line that declines steeply from left to right has a *small* negative slope. For example, in Figure 15.6, the line with slope -8 is steeper than the line with slope -1. A line with a negative slope near zero, such as the line in Figure 15.6 having slope $-\frac{1}{8}$, declines gradually from left to right.

Using slopes, we can determine whether several points are collinear. For example, if points P, Q, and R are collinear, then the slope of segment $\overline{PQ}$ is equal to the slope of segment $\overline{PR}$ (Figure 15.7). That is, if P, Q, and R are collinear, then $\dfrac{y_2 - y_1}{x_2 - x_1} = \dfrac{y_3 - y_1}{x_3 - x_1}$ provided that the slopes exist. If P, Q, and R are collinear and lie on a vertical line, then segments $\overline{PQ}$ and $\overline{PR}$ have no slope.

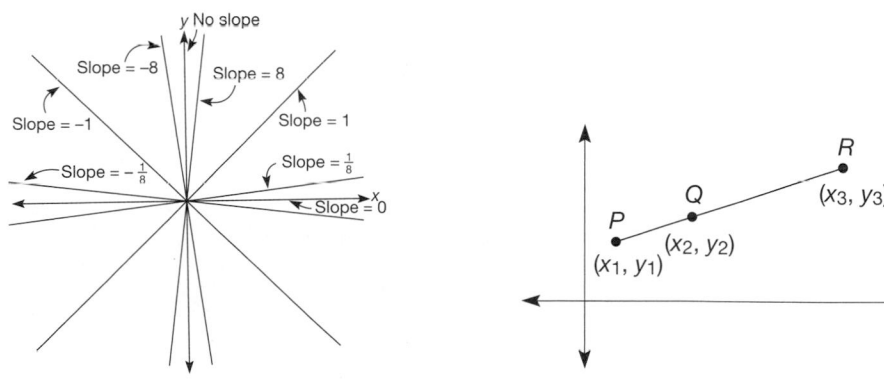

Figure 15.6

Figure 15.7

On the other hand, suppose that P, Q, and R are such that the slope of segment $\overline{PQ}$ is equal to the slope of segment $\overline{QR}$. It can be shown that the points P, Q, and R are collinear.

Mr. O

We use the plastic figure **Mr. O** to help us make coordinate maps. The O in Mr. O stands for "origin." The origin is another name for the point (0, 0) on a coordinate graph. Mr. O helps us keep track of directions when we make a map.

The imaginary line running from left to right through Mr. O is called the *x*-axis or the left-right axis. Mr. O's right hand is shown with a circle. It points to the positive part of the *x*-axis. The line running from back to front through Mr. O is called the *y*-axis or the front-back axis. The positive *y*-axis is always in front of Mr. O. His front is the side with the buttons. In this picture Mr. O's back is to us.

One way to describe the location of an object relative to Mr. O is to use directions (left or right, front or back) and distances. For example, Shannon placed her Mr. O in the center of her class and said that the center of the teacher's desk was 200 centimeters to the left and 150 centimeters behind Mr. O.

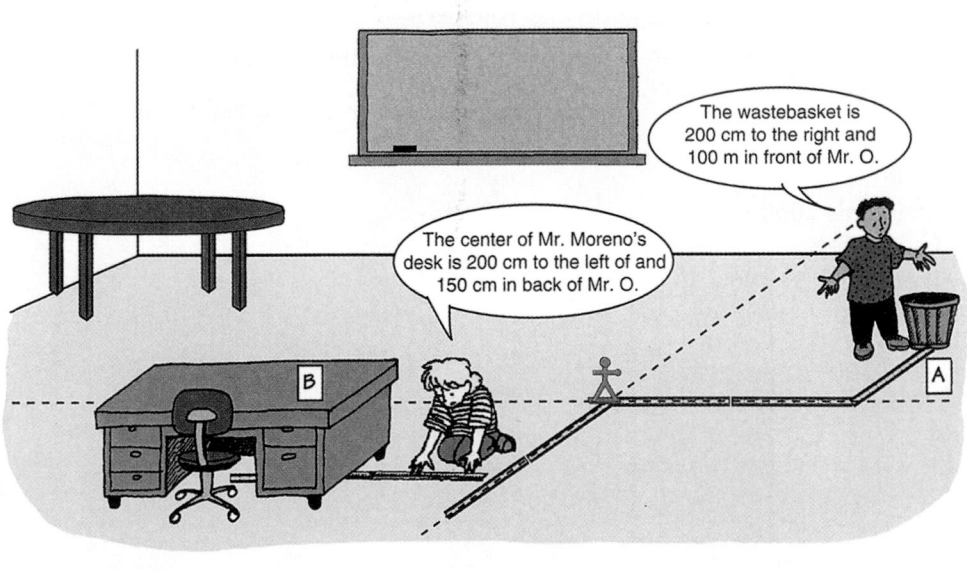

Mr. O   Unit 10 • Lesson 4   335

From *Math Trailblazers,* Grade 5 Student Guide p. 395, by the *TIMS PROJECT.* Copyright © 1997 by Kendall/Hunt Publishing Company. Reprinted with permission.

THEOREM

Slope and Collinearity

Points P, Q, and R are collinear if and only if

1. the slopes of $\overline{PQ}$ and $\overline{QR}$ are equal, or
2. the slopes of $\overline{PQ}$ and $\overline{QR}$ are undefined (i.e., P, Q, and R are on the same vertical line).

In Figure 15.5 it appears that lines l and m, which have the same slope, are parallel. We can determine whether two lines are parallel by computing their slopes.

THEOREM

Slopes of Parallel Lines

Two lines in the coordinate plane are parallel if and only if

1. their slopes are equal, or
2. their slopes are undefined.

In Example 15.3, lines l and m each have slope $\frac{11}{18}$ and thus are parallel by the slopes of parallel lines theorem. The verification of the Slopes of Parallel Lines Theorem is left for Part B Problem 20 in the Problem Set.

Just as we are able to determine whether lines are parallel using their slopes, we can also identify perpendicular lines by means of their slopes. For example, consider line l in Figure 15.8(a). Since l contains $(0, 0)$ and (x_1, y_1), the slope of l is $\frac{y_1 - 0}{x_1 - 0} = \frac{y_1}{x_1}$. If line l is rotated $90°$ clockwise around $(0, 0)$ to l', then l is perpendicular to l' [Figure 15.8(b)]. Also, point $(y_1, -x_1)$ is on l'. So the slope of l' is $\frac{-x_1 - 0}{y_1 - 0} = \frac{-x_1}{y_1}$. Therefore, the product of the slopes of the perpendicular lines l and l' is $\frac{y_1}{x_1} \times \frac{-x_1}{y_1} = -1$ Conversely, to show that *if* the product of the slopes of two lines

**NCTM Standards 2000
Geometry Grades 6–8**
All students should use coordinate geometry to examine special geometric shapes such as regular polygons or those with pairs of parallel or perpendicular sides.

**NCTM Standards 2000
Geometry Grades 6–8**
All students should use coordinate geometry to represent and examine the properties of geometric shapes.

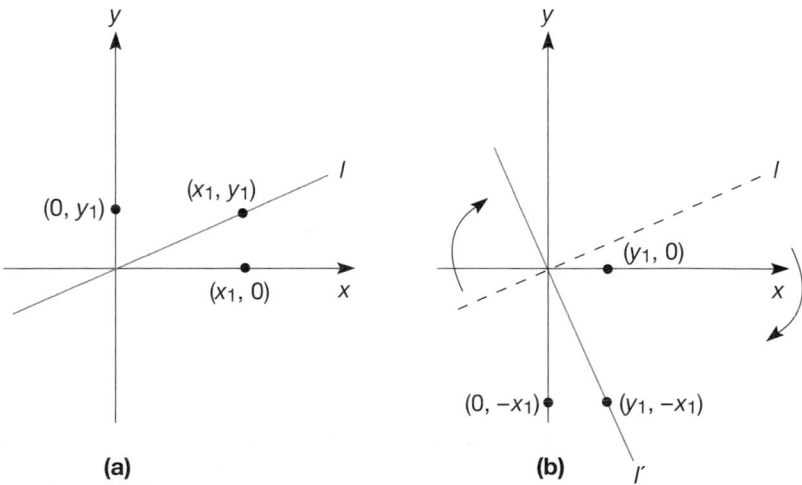

(a) **(b)**

Figure 15.8

is −1, *then* the lines are perpendicular, we can use a similar argument. This is left for Part B Problem 18 in the Problem Set. In summary, we have the following result.

THEOREM

Slopes of Perpendicular Lines

Two lines in the coordinate plane are perpendicular if and only if

1. the product of their slopes is −1, or
2. one line is horizontal and the other is vertical.

www.wiley.com/ college/musser

Spotlight on Technology Being able to see many examples of perpendicular lines where the product of their slopes is equal to −1 does not prove this theorem, but it does clearly support its truth. Generating many such examples is easily done on the Geometer's Sketchpad® webmodule activity, *Perpendicular Lines*. If a line has a slope of 0.2, what is the slope of its perpendicular? Use the webmodule activity to verify your conclusion.

Example 15.4 shows how slopes can be used to analyze the diagonals of a rhombus.

Example 15.4   Show that the diagonals of *PQRS* in Figure 15.9 form right angles at their intersection.

Solution

The slope of diagonal $\overline{PR}$ is $\dfrac{2}{-2} = -1$, and the slope of diagonal $\overline{QS}$ is $\dfrac{4}{4} = 1$.

Since the product of their slopes is −1, the diagonals form right angles at *T* by the slopes of perpendicular lines theorem. Each side of *PQRS* has length $\sqrt{10}$. Thus it is a rhombus. In fact, the result in Example 15.4 holds for *any* rhombus. This result is presented as a problem in Section 15.3. ■

Figure 15.9

www.wiley.com/ college/musser

Spotlight on Technology The problem in Example 15.4 can be investigated using the Chapter 15 eManipulative activity, *Coordinate Geoboard*. Construct a rhombus *PQRS* and the diagonals of *PQRS* with two separate rubber bands. By selecting each diagonal separately, the slope can be determined. Verify that the diagonals of a rhombus are, in fact, perpendicular.

MATHEMATICAL MORSEL

Descartes was creative in many fields: philosophy, physics, cosmology, chemistry, physiology, and psychology. But he is best known for his contributions to mathematics. He was a frail child of a noble family. As one story goes, due to his frailty, Descartes had a habit of lying in bed, thinking for extended periods. One day, while watching a fly crawling on the ceiling, he set about trying to describe the path of the fly in mathematical language. Thus was born analytic geometry—the study of mathematical attributes of lines and curves.

Section 15.1 EXERCISE / PROBLEM SET A

EXERCISES

1. Find the distance between the following pairs of points.

   a. $(0, 0)$, $(3, -2)$

   b. $(-4, 2)$, $(-2, 3)$

2. Use the distance formula to determine whether points P, Q, and R are collinear.

   a. $P(-1, 4)$, $Q(-2, 3)$, and $R(-4, 1)$

   b. $P(-2, 1)$, $Q(3, 4)$, and $R(12, 10)$

3. The endpoints of a segment are given. Find the coordinates of the midpoint of the segment.

   a. $(0, 2)$ and $(-3, 2)$

   b. $(-5, -1)$ and $(3, 5)$

   c. $(-2, 3)$ and $(-3, 6)$

   d. $(3, -5)$ and $(3, -7)$

4. Find the slopes of the lines containing the following pairs of points.

   a. $(3, 2)$ and $(5, 3)$

   b. $(-2, 1)$ and $(-5, -3)$

5. Use the ratio $\dfrac{y_2 - y_1}{x_2 - x_1}$ and the ratio $\dfrac{y_1 - y_2}{x_1 - x_2}$ to compute the slopes of the lines containing the following points. Do both ratios give the same result?

   a. $(-4, 5)$ and $(6, -3)$

   b. $(-2, -3)$ and $(3, 2)$

6. Use slopes to determine whether $\overline{AB} \parallel \overline{PQ}$.

   a. $A(-1, 0)$, $B(4, 5)$, $P(3, 9)$, $Q(-2, 4)$

   b. $A(0, 4)$, $B(6, 8)$, $P(-4, -6)$, $Q(2, -2)$

7. Use slopes to determine whether the points $A(3, -2)$, $B(1, 2)$, and $C(-3, 10)$ are collinear.

8. Determine whether the quadrilaterals with the given vertices are parallelograms.

   a. $(1, 4)$, $(4, 4)$, $(5, 1)$, and $(2, 1)$

   b. $(1, -1)$, $(6, -1)$, $(6, -4)$, and $(1, -4)$

   c. $(1, -2)$, $(4, 2)$, $(6, 2)$, and $(3, -2)$

   d. $(-10, 5)$, $(-5, 10)$, $(10, -5)$, and $(5, -10)$

9. In each part, use the the Chapter 15 eManipulative activity, *Coordinate Geoboard*, to determine whether any of the line segments joining the given points are perpendicular.

   a. $(2, 2)$, $(2, 4)$, and $(5, 4)$

   b. $(-3, 4)$, $(0, -1)$, and $(5, 2)$

   c. $(-5, -4)$, $(3, 2)$, and $(5, 2)$

   d. $(-2, -2)$, $(1, 4)$, and $(5, -4)$

10. Consider the following quadrilateral.

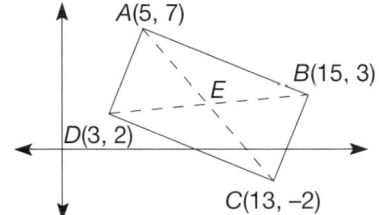

   a. Verify that $ABCD$ is a rectangle.

   b. What do you observe about the lengths BD and AC?

   c. What do you observe about $\overline{AE}$ and $\overline{CE}$ about $\overline{BE}$ and $\overline{DE}$?

   d. Are $\overline{AC}$ and $\overline{BD}$ perpendicular? Explain.

   e. Summarize the properties you have observed about rectangle $ABCD$.

11. Using *only* the array of points and points $A(2, 4)$ and $R(4, 4)$ as the endpoints of one side of a quadrilateral, answer the following questions.

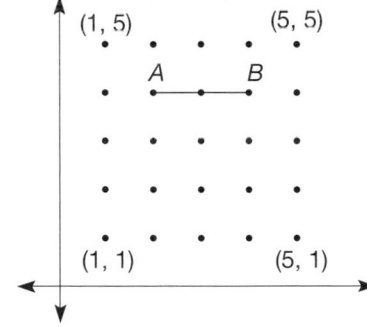

   a. Use coordinates to list all possible parallelograms that can be constructed on the above array.

   b. Use coordinates to list all possible rectangles.

   c. Use coordinates to list all possible rhombi.

   d. Use coordinates to list all possible squares.

12. Give the slope of a line perpendicular to $\overleftrightarrow{AB}$.

   a. $A(1, 6)$, $B(2, 5)$

   b. $A(0, 4)$, $B(-6, -5)$

   c. $A(4, 2)$, $B(-5, 2)$

   d. $A(-1, 5)$, $B(-1, 3)$

13. On the Chapter 15 eManipulative activity, *Coordinate Geoboard*, construct triangles that have vertices with the given coordinates. Describe the triangles as scalene, isosceles, equilateral, acute, right, or obtuse. Explain.

   a. $(0, 0), (0, -4), (4, -4)$

   b. $(-3, 1), (1, 3), (5, -4)$

   c. $(-3, -1), (1, 2), (5, -1)$

   d. $(-4, -2), (-1, 3), (4, -2)$

14. Given are the coordinates of the vertices of a triangle. Use the coordinate distance formula to determine whether the triangle is a right triangle.

   a. $A(-2, 5), B(0, -1), C(12, 3)$

   b. $D(2, 3), E(-2, -3), F(-6, 1)$

   c. $G(-3, -2), H(5, -2), I(1, 2)$

15. Draw the quadrilateral *ABCD* whose vertices are $A(3, 0), B(6, 6), C(6, 9)$, and $D(0, 6)$. Divide each of the coordinates by 3 and graph the new quadrilateral $A'B'C'D'$. For example, A' has coordinates $(1, 0)$. How do the lengths of corresponding sides compare?

PROBLEMS

16. A pole is supported by two sets of guy wires fastened to the ground 15 meters from the pole. The shorter set of wires has slope $\pm\frac{4}{3}$. The wires in the longer set are each 50 meters long.

50 m

Slope $\frac{4}{3}$

← 15 m →

   a. How high above the ground is the shorter set of wires attached?

   b. What is the length of the shorter set of wires?

   c. How tall is the pole to the nearest centimeter?

   d. What is the slope of the longer set of wires to two decimal places?

17. A freeway ramp connects a highway to an overpass 10 meters above the ground. The ramp, which starts 150 meters from the overpass, is 150.33 meters long and 9 meters wide. What is the **percent grade** (rise/run expressed as a percent) of the ramp to three decimal places?

18. Let P, Q, R, and S be any points on line l as shown. By drawing horizontal and vertical segments, draw right triangles $\triangle PQO$ and $\triangle RST$. Follow the given steps to verify that the slope of line l is independent of the pairs of points selected.

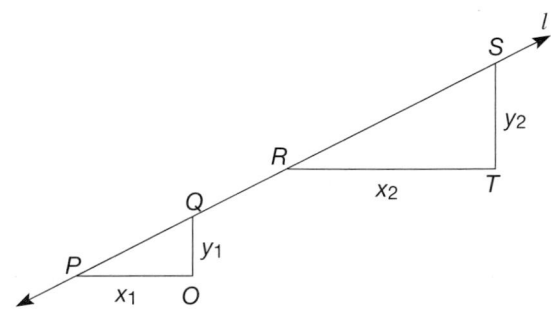

   a. Show that $\triangle PQO \sim \triangle RST$.

   b. Show that $\dfrac{y_1}{x_1} = \dfrac{y_2}{x_2}$.

   c. Is the slope of $\overline{PQ}$ equal to the slope of $\overline{RS}$? Explain.

19. In the development of the midpoint formula, points P and Q have coordinates (x_1, y_1) and (x_2, y_2), respectively, and M is the point $\left(\dfrac{x_1 + x_2}{2}, \dfrac{y_1 + y_2}{2}\right)$. Use the coordinate distance formula to verify that $P, M,$ and Q are collinear and that $PM = MQ$.

20. Verify the Slopes of Parallel Lines Theorem.

21. Cartesian coordinates may be generalized to three-dimensional space. A point in space is determined by giving its location relative to three axes as shown. Point P with coordinates (x_1, y_1, z_1) is plotted by going x_1 along the x-axis, y_1 along the y-direction, and z_1 in the z-direction. Plot the following points in three-dimensional space.

a. $(2, 1, 3)$ **b.** $(-2, 1, 0)$ **c.** $(3, -1, -2)$

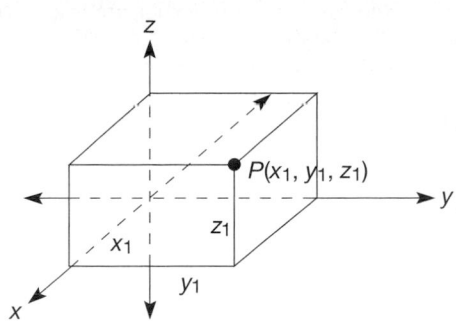

Section 15.1   EXERCISE / PROBLEM SET B

EXERCISES

1. Find the distance between the following pairs of points.

a. $(2, 3), (-1, -5)$

b. $(-3, 5), (-3, -2)$

2. Use the distance formula to determine whether points P, Q, and R are collinear.

a. $P(-2, -3)$, $Q(2, -1)$, and $R(10, 3)$

b. $P(2, 7)$, $Q(-2, -7)$, and $R(3, 10.5)$

3. The point M is the midpoint of $\overline{AB}$. Given the coordinates of the following points, find the coordinates of the third point.

a. $A(-3, -1)$, $M(-1, 3)$

b. $B(-5, 3)$, $M(-7, 3)$

c. $A(1, -3)$, $M(4, 1)$

d. $M(0, 0)$, $B(-2, 5)$

4. Find the slope of each line containing the following pairs of points.

a. $(-1, 2)$ and $(6, -3)$

b. $(6, 5)$ and $(6, -2)$

5. Given are the slopes of several lines. Indicate whether each line is horizontal, vertical, rises to the right, or rises to the left.

a. $\frac{3}{4}$ **b.** no slope

c. 0 **d.** $-\frac{5}{6}$

6. Determine which pairs of segments are parallel.

a. The segment from $(3, 5)$ to $(8, 3)$ and the segment from $(0, 8)$ to $(8, 5)$.

b. The segment from $(-4, 5)$ to $(4, 2)$ and the segment from $(-3, -2)$ to $(5, -5)$.

c.

d.

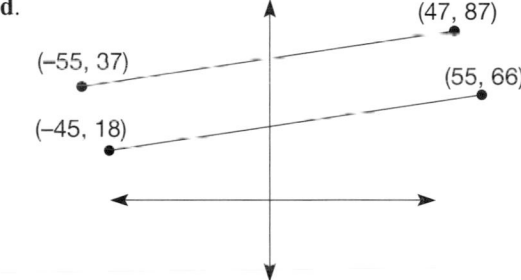

7. Use slopes to determine if the points $A(0, 7)$, $B(2, 11)$, and $C(-2, 1)$ are collinear.

8. Determine which of the quadrilaterals, with the given vertices, is a rectangle.

a. $(0, 0)$, $(12, 12)$, $(16, 8)$, and $(4, -4)$

b. $(-3, 8)$, $(0, 12)$, $(12, 3)$, and $(9, -1)$

c. $(-10, -5)$, $(-6, 15)$, $(14, 11)$, and $(10, -9)$

9. In each part, use the Chapter 15 eManipulative activity, *Coordinate Geoboard*, to determine which, if any, of the triangles with the given vertices is a right triangle.

a. $(-5, -4)$, $(-1, 4)$, and $(1, 2)$

b. $(4, -4)$, $(0, 2)$, and $(-3, 0)$

c. $(2, -3)$, $(4, 4)$, and $(-1, -2)$

10. Which of the following properties are true of the given kites? Explain.

a. The diagonals are congruent.

b. The diagonals are perpendicular to each other.

c. The diagonals bisect each other.

d. The kite has two right angles.

i.

ii.

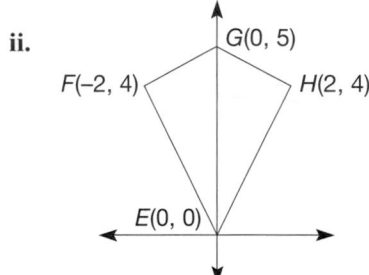

11. Using only the 5 × 5 array of points, how many segments can be drawn making a right angle at an endpoint of the given segment?

a.

b.

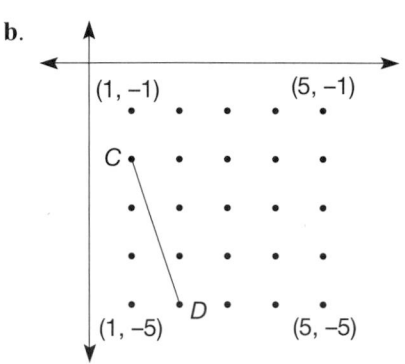

12. Use slopes to show that $\overline{AB} \perp \overline{PQ}$.

a. $A(0, 4)$, $B(-6, 3)$, $P(-2, -2)$, $Q(-3, 4)$

b. $A(-2, -1)$, $B(2, 3)$, $P(4, 1)$, $Q(0, 5)$

13. What general type of quadrilateral is $ABCD$, where $A = (0, 0)$, $B = (-4, 3)$, $C = (-1, 7)$, and $D = (6, 8)$? Describe it as completely as you can.

14. Find the distance between the following pairs of points.

a. $(1, 4)$ and $(-2, -3)$ **b.** $(-5, 2)$ and $(1, -4)$

PROBLEMS

15. Three of the vertices of a parallelogram have coordinates $P(2, 3)$, $Q(5, 7)$, and $R(10, -5)$.

a. Find the coordinates of the fourth vertex of the parallelogram. (*Hint*: There is more than one answer.)

b. Determine the area of each parallelogram.

16. a. Draw quadrilateral $ABCD$ where $A(4, -2)$, $B(4, 2)$, $C(-2, 2)$, and $D(-2, -2)$.

b. Multiply each coordinate by 3 and graph quadrilateral $A'B'C'D'$. For example, A' has coordinates $(12, -6)$.

c. How do the perimeters of $ABCD$ and $A'B'C'D'$ compare?

d. How do the areas of $ABCD$ and $A'B'C'D'$ compare?

e. Repeat parts (b) to (d), but divide each coordinate by 2.

17. The percent grade of a highway is the amount that the highway rises (or falls) in a given horizontal distance. For example, a highway with a 4% grade rises 0.04 mile for every 1 mile of horizontal distance.

a. How many feet does a highway with a 6% grade rise in 2.5 miles?

b. How many feet would a highway with a 6% grade rise in 90 miles if the grade remained constant?

c. How is percent grade related to slope?

18. Prove the following statement: If the product of the slopes of *l* and *m* is -1, lines *l* and *m* are perpendicular. (*Hint*: Show that $\triangle OPQ$ is a right triangle.)

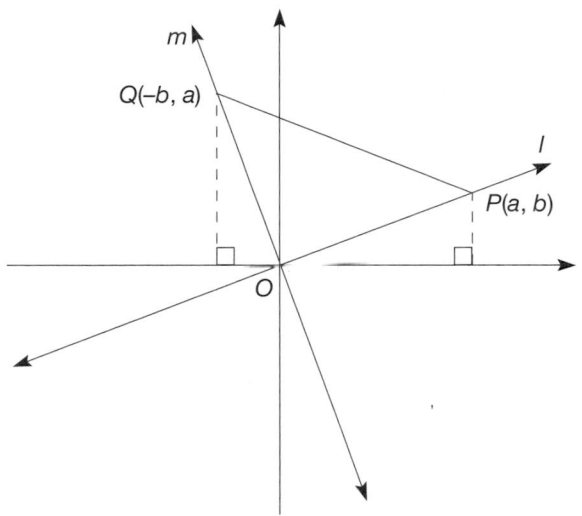

19. Locations on the Earth's surface are measured by two sets of circles. **Parallels of latitude** are circles at constant distances from the equator used to identify locations north or south, called **latitude**. The latitude of the North Pole, for example, is 90°N, that of the equator is 0°, and that of the South Pole is 90°S. Great circles through the North and South poles, called **meridians**, are used to identify locations east or west, called **longitude**. The half of the great circle through the poles and Greenwich, England, is called the **prime meridian**. Points on the prime meridian have longitude 0°E. Points east of Greenwich and less than halfway around the world from it have longitudes between 0 and 180°E. Points west of Greenwich and less than halfway around the world from it have longitudes between 0 and 180°W. Here are the latitudes and longitudes of several cities, to the nearest degree.

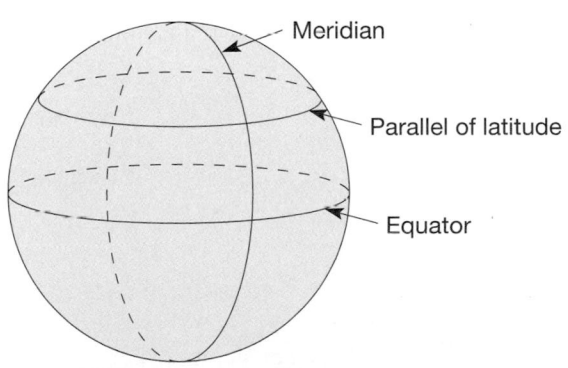

CITY	LATITUDE	LONGITUDE
London	52°N	0°E
New York	41°N	74°W
Moscow	56°N	38°E
Nome, Alaska	64°N	165°W
Beijing	40°N	116°E
Rio de Janeiro	23°S	43°W
Sydney	34°S	151°E

a. Which cities are above the equator? Which are below?

b. Which city is farthest from the equator?

c. Are there points in the United States, excluding Alaska and Hawaii, with east longitudes? Explain.

d. What is the latitude of all points south of the equator and the same distance from the equator as London?

e. What is the longitude of a point exactly halfway around the world (north of the equator) from New York?

f. What are the latitude and longitude of a point diametrically opposite Sydney? That is, the point in question and Sydney are the endpoints of a diameter of the Earth.

20. The coordinate distance formula can also be generalized to three-dimensional space. Let *P* have coordinates (a, b, c) and *Q* have coordinates (x, y, z). The faces of the prism are parallel to the coordinate planes.

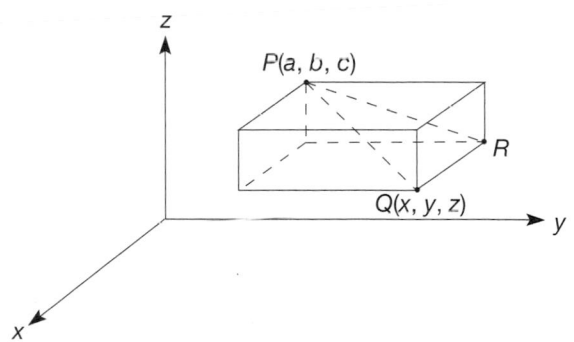

a. What are the coordinates of point *R*?

b. What is the distance *PR*? (*Hint*: Pythagorean theorem.)

c. What is the distance *QR*?

d. What is the distance *PQ*? (*Hint*: Pythagorean theorem.)

PROBLEMS FOR WRITING/DISCUSSION

1. Janiece was trying to find the distance between $(3, 7)$ and $(9, 6)$ in the coordinate plane. She knew the formula was $D = \sqrt{(9 - 3)^2 + (6 - 7)^2}$. So she took the square roots and got $(9 - 3) + (6 - 7) = 5$. Did Janiece get the right answer? Will her method always work? Discuss.

2. Edmund was working on the same problem, but the numbers under the radical looked different: $D = \sqrt{(9 - 3)^2 + (7 - 6)^2}$. Shirdena told him he couldn't subtract the numbers that way; he had to subtract the coordinates in the same order. So he had to put $6 - 7$, not $7 - 6$. Who is correct? What explanation would you give to them?

3. Shirdena was trying to find the slope of the segment whose endpoints were $(-2, 7)$ and $(-5, -8)$. She knew she had to subtract both numbers the same way, so she wrote $\dfrac{7 - (-8)}{-2 - (-5)}$. She got $\dfrac{15}{3}$, which she said equals 5. Edmund put $\dfrac{-8 - 7}{-5 - (-2)}$. He got $\dfrac{-15}{-3}$, which he said equals -5. Is it acceptable for them to get two different answers for this problem or is there something wrong here? Discuss.

15.2 EQUATIONS AND COORDINATES

STARTING POINT

In the graph at the right, line l contains the point $P = (-1, 4)$ and has a slope of $m = -\dfrac{2}{3}$. Identify three other points on line l and justify how you know each lies on the line.

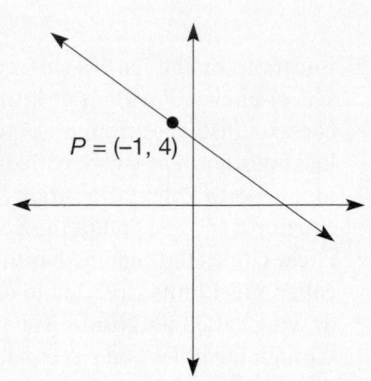

$P = (-1, 4)$

Equations of Lines

We can determine equations that are satisfied by the points on a particular line. For example, consider the line l containing points $(-4, 2)$ and $(2, 5)$ (Figure 15.10). Suppose that (x, y) is an arbitrary point on line l. We wish to find an equation in x and y that is satisfied by the coordinates of the point (x, y). We will use the slope of l to do this. Using the points $(-4, 2)$ and $(2, 5)$, the slope of l is $\dfrac{5 - 2}{2 - (-4)} = \dfrac{1}{2}$. Using the points $(-4, 2)$ and (x, y), the slope of l is $\dfrac{y - 2}{x - (-4)} = \dfrac{y - 2}{x + 4}$. Since the slope of l is $\dfrac{1}{2}$ and $\dfrac{y - 2}{x + 4}$, we have

$$\frac{y - 2}{x + 4} = \frac{1}{2}.$$

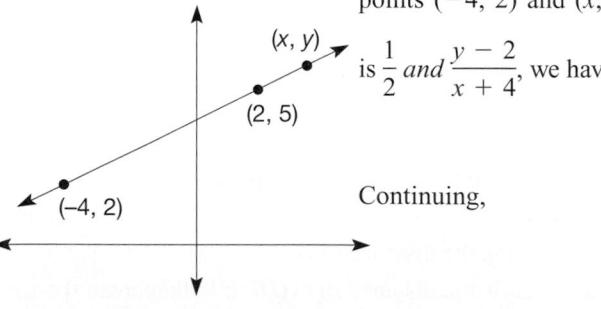

(x, y)

$(2, 5)$

$(-4, 2)$

Figure 15.10

Continuing,

$$y - 2 = \frac{1}{2}(x + 4),$$

$$y - 2 = \frac{1}{2}x + 2,$$

or finally,

$$y = \frac{1}{2}x + 4.$$

That is, we have shown that every point (x, y) on line l satisfies the equation $y = \frac{1}{2}x + 4$. [NOTE: We could also have used the points $(2, 5)$ and (x, y), and solved $\dfrac{y - 5}{x - 2} = \dfrac{1}{2}$ to obtain $y = \frac{1}{2}x + 4$.]

In our equation for line l, the "x" term is multiplied by the slope of l, namely $\frac{1}{2}$. Also, the constant term, 4, is the y-coordinate of the point at which l intersects the y-axis.

We can show that every line in the plane that is not vertical has an equation of the form $y = mx + b$, where m is the slope of the line and b, called the **y-intercept**, is the y-coordinate of the point at which the line intersects the y-axis (Figure 15.11).

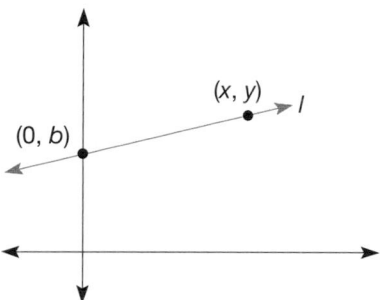

Figure 15.11

Generalizing from the preceding argument, suppose that l is a line containing the point $(0, b)$ such that the slope of l is m and that (x, y) is an arbitrary point on l (Figure 15.11). Then, since the slope of l is m, we have

$$\frac{y - b}{x - 0} = m,$$

so that

$$y - b = mx,$$
$$y = mx + b.$$

Thus every point (x, y) on l satisfies the equation $y = mx + b$.

It is also true that if (x, y) is a point on the plane such that $y = mx + b$, then (x, y) is on line l. Thus the equation $y = mx + b$ describes all points (x, y) that are on line l.

If a line l is vertical and hence has no slope, it must intersect the horizontal axis at a point, say $(a, 0)$. Then all of the points on l will satisfy the equation $x = a$ (Figure 15.12). That is, the x-coordinate of each point on l is a, and the y-coordinate is an arbitrary real number.

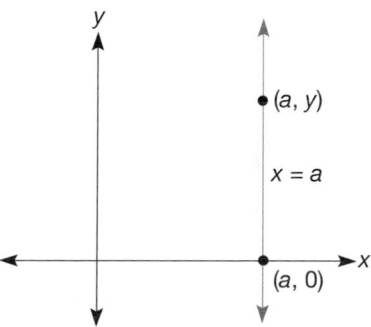

Figure 15.12

We can summarize our results about equations of lines in the coordinate plane as follows:

> ### THEOREM
>
> #### Slope-Intercept Equation of a Line
>
> Every line in the plane has an equation of the form (1) $y = mx + b$ where m is the slope of the line and b is the y-intercept, or (2) $x = a$ if the slope of the line is undefined (i.e., the line is vertical).

The equation $y = mx + b$ is called the **slope-intercept equation of a line**, since m is the slope and b is the y-intercept of the line.

Example 15.5   Find the equations for the lines l_1, l_2, l_3, and l_4 satisfying the following conditions (Figure 15.13).

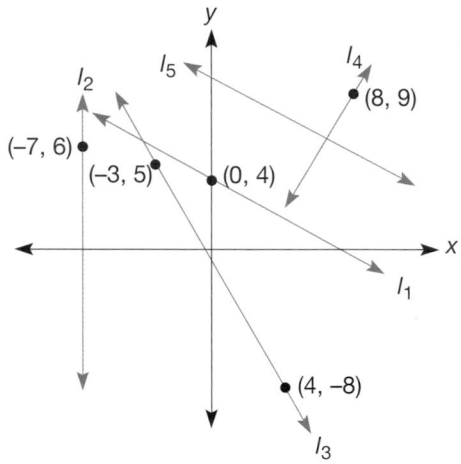

Figure 15.13

a. l_1 has slope $\dfrac{-3}{5}$ and y-intercept 4.

b. l_2 is a vertical line containing the point $(-7, 6)$.

c. l_3 contains the points $(-3, 5)$ and $(4, -8)$.

d. l_4 contains the point $(8, 9)$ and is perpendicular to the line l_5, whose equation is
$$y = \frac{-4}{7}x + 10.$$

Solution

a. By the equation of a line formula (1) in the Slope-Intercept Equation of a Line Theorem, the slope-intercept equation of l_1 is $y = \dfrac{-3}{5}x + 4$, since the slope of l_1 is $\dfrac{-3}{5}$ and the y-intercept is 4.

b. The line l_2 is a vertical line containing the point $(-7, 6)$, so that l_2 also contains the point $(-7, 0)$. Therefore, the equation of l_2 is $x = -7$.

c. The slope of l_3 is $\dfrac{5 - (-8)}{-3 - 4} = \dfrac{13}{-7} = \dfrac{-13}{7}$, so l_3 has an equation of the form
$y = \dfrac{-13}{7}x + b$. We can find b by using the fact that the point $(-3, 5)$ is on l_3. We substitute -3 and 5 for x and y, respectively, in the equation of l_3, as follows:

$$5 = \frac{-13}{7}(-3) + b,$$

$$5 = \frac{39}{7} + b,$$

so

$$5 - \frac{39}{7} = b,$$

$$\frac{-4}{7} = b.$$

Therefore, the equation of l_3 is

$$y = \frac{-13}{7}x - \frac{4}{7}.$$

We could also have used the fact that $(4, -8)$ is on l_3 to find b.

d. Since l_4 is perpendicular to the line $y = \frac{-4}{7}x + 10$, we know that the slope of l_4 is $\frac{7}{4}$, by the Slopes of Perpendicular Lines Theorem. Hence l_4 has an equation of the form $y = \frac{7}{4}x + b$. Since the point $(8, 9)$ is on l_4, we can substitute 8 for x and 9 for y in the equation $y = \frac{7}{4}x + b$. Thus we have

$$9 = \frac{7}{4} \cdot 8 + b,$$

$$9 = 14 + b,$$

$$-5 = b.$$

Consequently, the equation of l_4 is

$$y = \frac{7}{4}x - 5.$$ ■

In Example 15.5(d) the coordinates of a point, $(8, 9)$, and the slope of the line, $\frac{7}{4}$, were known. Even though we did not know *both* the slope and the y-intercept, we were able to find the equation of the line. Generalizing, suppose that (x_1, y_1) is a point on a line l having slope m. If (x, y) is any other point on l, then

$$\frac{y - y_1}{x - x_1} = m \qquad \text{or} \qquad y - y_1 = m(x - x_1).$$

This is summarized next.

THEOREM

Point-Slope Equation of a Line

If a line contains the point (x_1, y_1) and has slope m, then the point-slope equation of the line is

$$y - y_1 = m(x - x_1).$$

Simultaneous Equations

Consider the equations $y = 4x + 2$ and $y = -3x + 5$. The first line has slope 4, and the second line has slope -3, so that the lines must intersect (Figure 15.14). We can find the point P where the two lines intersect by using the fact that P lies on *both*

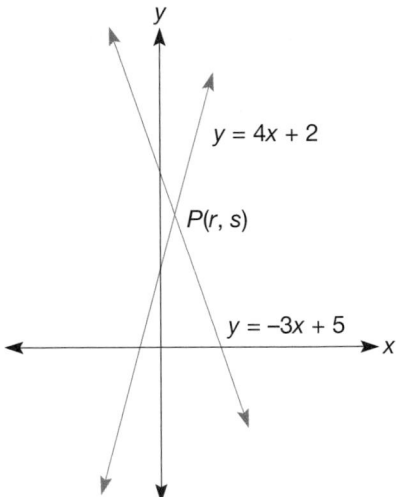

Figure 15.14

lines. That is, the coordinates of P must satisfy both equations. Hence if r and s are the coordinates of P, we must have $s = 4r + 2$ and $s = -3r + 5$, so that

$$4r + 2 = -3r + 5.$$

Therefore,

$$7r = 3 \qquad \text{or} \qquad r = \frac{3}{7}.$$

Thus the x-coordinate of P is $\frac{3}{7}$. Using the first of the two equations, we find

$$s = 4\left(\frac{3}{7}\right) + 2,$$

or

$$s = \frac{26}{7}.$$

Consequently, $P = (\frac{3}{7}, \frac{26}{7})$ is the point of intersection of the two lines. (We could have used either equation to find s, since r and s must satisfy both equations.) We say that the point $P = (\frac{3}{7}, \frac{26}{7})$ is a **simultaneous solution** of the equations, since it satisfies both of them. The equations whose simultaneous solution we seek are called **simultaneous equations** or a system of equations.

The algebraic process of solving simultaneous equations has an interesting geometric interpretation. When we solve a pair of simultaneous equations such as

$$(1)\ ax + by = c$$

and

$$(2)\ dx + ey = f,$$

where a, b, c, d, e, and f represent constant coefficients and x and y are variables, we are finding the point of intersection of two lines in the coordinate plane. Note that x

and y appear to the first power only. In the case that $b \neq 0$ in equation (1), and $e \neq 0$ in equation (2), we can rewrite these equations as follows. (Verify this.)

$$(1)' \quad y = -\frac{a}{b}x + \frac{c}{b}$$

and

$$(2)' \quad y = -\frac{d}{e}x + \frac{f}{e}.$$

We recognize these equations of *lines* in the plane. Suppose that line l has equation $(1)'$ as its equation and line m has equation $(2)'$ as its equation. Then there are three possible geometric relationships between lines l and m.

a. $l = m$ [Figure 15.15(a)].
b. $l \parallel m$ and $l \neq m$ [Figure 15.15(b)].
c. l intersects m in exactly one point (x, y) [Figure 15.15(c)].

If $l = m$ as in case (a), then *all* the points (x, y) that satisfy the equation of l will also satisfy the equation of m. Thus, for this case, equations (1) and (2) will have infinitely many simultaneous solutions. For case (b), in which the lines l and m are different parallel lines, there will be no points in common for the two lines. Hence equations (1) and (2) will have no simultaneous solutions in this case. Finally, for case (c), in which the lines intersect in a unique point $P = (x, y)$, we will have only one simultaneous solution to the equations (1) and (2), namely, the x- and y-coordinates of point P.

Now let us consider this situation starting with the equations of the lines. If they have infinitely many solutions, the lines that they represent are coincident. If they have no solutions, their lines are different parallel lines. Finally, if they have a unique solution, their lines intersect at only one point. We can find conditions on the numbers a, b, c, d, e, and f in equations (1) and (2) in order to determine how many simultaneous solutions there are for the equations. This is left for Part A Problem 24 in the Problem Set.

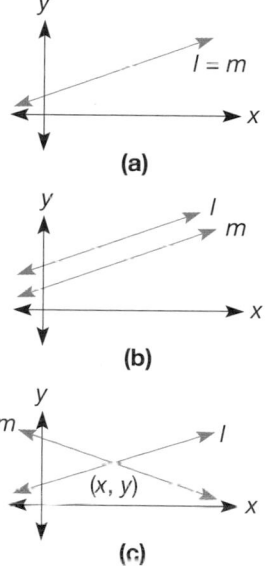

Figure 15.15

(a)

(b)

(x, y)

(c)

⬢ THEOREM

Solutions of Simultaneous Equations

Let a, b, c, d, e, and f be real-number constants and x and y be variables. Then the equations

$$ax + by = c$$

and

$$dx + ey = f$$

have zero, one, or infinitely many solutions if and only if the lines they represent are parallel, intersect in exactly one point, or are coincident, respectively.

The following example illustrates the preceding geometric interpretation of simultaneous equations.

Example 15.6 Graph the following pairs of equations, and find their simultaneous solutions.

a. $x + y = 7$
$-28 = -4x - 4y$

b. $2x + y = 5$
$-12 + 3y = -6x$

c. $x + y = 7$
$2x + y = 5$

Solution

a. We can rewrite the equations as follows:

$$(1)\, x + y = 7$$

and

$$(2)\, 4x + 4y = 28$$

or, multiplying both sides of the second equation by $\frac{1}{4}$,

$$(1)'\, x + y = 7$$

and

$$(2)'\, x + y = 7.$$

Hence the equations represent the *same* line, namely the line $y = -x + 7$ [Figure 15.16(a)]. Every point on this line is a simultaneous solution of the pair of equations.

b. Rewrite the equations in slope-intercept form.

$$y = -2x + 5$$
$$y = -2x + 4$$

Here the equations represent lines with the same slope (i.e., parallel lines) but different y-intercepts. Therefore the equations have no simultaneous solution [Figure 15.16(b)].

c. Rewrite the equations in slope-intercept form.

$$y = -x + 7$$
$$y = -2x + 5$$

Here the equations represent lines with different slopes, namely -1 and -2. The lines are intersecting lines [Figure 15.16(c)], so the equations will have a unique simultaneous solution. Equating the expressions for y, we obtain

$$-x + 7 = -2x + 5$$
$$x + 7 = 5$$
$$x = -2.$$

Substituting -2 for x in the first equation, we have $y = -(-2) + 7 = 9$. Thus the point $(-2, 9)$ is the only simultaneous solution of the two equations. [Check to see that $(-2, 9)$ is a simultaneous solution.] ■

Equations of Circles

Circles also have equations that can be determined using the distance formula. Recall that a circle is the set of points that are a fixed distance (i.e., the radius) from the center of the circle (Figure 15.17). Let the point $C = (a, b)$ be the center of the circle

(a)

(b)

(c)

Figure 15.16

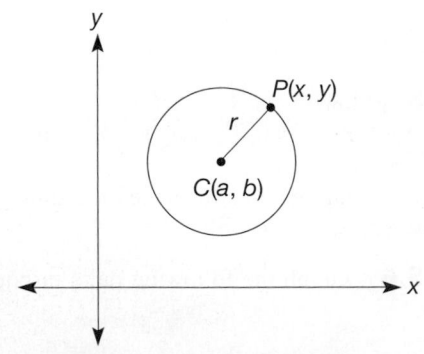

Figure 15.17

and r be the radius. Suppose that the point $P = (x, y)$ is on the circle. Then, by the definition of the circle, $PC = r$, so that $PC^2 = r^2$. But by the distance formula,

$$PC^2 = (x - a)^2 + (y - b)^2.$$

Therefore, $(x - a)^2 + (y - b)^2 = r^2$ is the equation of the circle.

 THEOREM

Equation of a Circle

The circle with center (a, b) and radius r has the equation

$$(x - a)^2 + (y - b)^2 = r^2.$$

Example 15.7   Find the equation of the circle whose center is $(-5, 6)$ and whose radius is 3.

Solution

In the equation of a circle formula, $(a, b) = (-5, 6)$ and $r = 3$. Consequently, the equation of the circle (shown in Figure 15.18) is

$$[x - (-5)]^2 + (y - 6)^2 = 3^2 \qquad \text{or} \qquad (x + 5)^2 + (y - 6)^2 = 9.$$

Figure 15.18

MATHEMATICAL MORSEL

Many words in mathematics have their origins in Hindu and Arabic words. The earliest Arabic arithmetic is that of al-Khowarizmi (circa A.D. 800). In referring to his book on Hindu numerals, a Latin translation begins "Spoken has Algoritmi." Thus we obtain the word *algorithm,* which is a procedure for calculating. The mathematics book *Hisab-al-jabr-w'almugabalsh,* also written by al-Khowarizmi, became known as "al-jabr," our modern-day "algebra."

EXERCISES

1. Show that point P lies on the line with the given equation.

   a. $y = 7x - 2$; $P(1, 5)$

   b. $y = -\frac{2}{3}x + 5$; $P(-6, 9)$

   c. $-2x = 6y + 3$; $P(7.5, -3)$

   d. $3y = 4x + 2$; $P(4, 6)$

2. Write each equation in the form $y = mx + b$. Identify the slope and y-intercept.

   a. $2y = 6x + 12$ **b.** $4y - 3x = 0$

   c. $8y - 2 = 0$ **d.** $3x - 4y = 12$

3. Write the equation of the line, given its slope m and y-intercept b.

   a. $m = 3, b = 7$ **b.** $m = -1, b = -3$

   c. $m = \frac{2}{3}, b = 5$ **d.** $m = -3, b = -\frac{1}{4}$

4. Write the equation in (i) point-slope form and (ii) slope-intercept form for $\overleftrightarrow{AB}$.

   a. $A(6, 3), B(0, 2)$ **b.** $A(-4, 8), B(3, -6)$

5. Point P has coordinates $(-2, 3)$.

   a. Give the coordinates of three other points on a horizontal line containing P.

   b. Give the coordinates of two other points on a vertical line containing P.

6. Write the equation of each line that satisfies the following.

   a. Vertical through $(1, 3)$

   b. Vertical through $(-5, -2)$

   c. Horizontal through $(-3, 6)$

   d. Horizontal through $(3, -3)$

7. Write the equation of a line that passes through the given point and is parallel to the line whose equation is given.

   a. $(5, -1)$; $y = 2x - 3$ **b.** $(1, -2)$; $y = -x - 2$

   c. $(2, -5)$; $3x + 5y = 1$ **d.** $(-1, 0)$; $3x + 2y = 6$

8. Graph the line described by each equation.

   a. $y = 2x - 1$ **b.** $y = -3x + 2$

   c. $y = \frac{1}{2}x + 1$ **d.** $x = -2$

   e. $y = 3$ **f.** $2x = -6y$

9. **a.** Graph the following lines on the same coordinate system.

      i. $y = 2x + 3$ **ii.** $y = -3x + 3$

      iii. $y = \frac{1}{2}x + 3$

   b. What is the relationship between these lines?

   c. Describe the lines of the form $y = cx + d$, where d is a fixed real number and c can be any real number.

10. The vertices of a triangle have coordinates $(0, 0)$, $(1, 5)$, and $(-4, 3)$. Find the equations of the lines containing the sides of the triangle.

11. Find the equation of the line containing the median $\overline{AD}$ of $\triangle ABC$ with vertices $A(3, 7)$, $B(1, 4)$, and $C(11, 2)$.

12. Find the equation of the line containing altitude $\overline{PT}$ of triangles PRS with vertices $P(3, 5)$, $R(-1, 1)$, and $S(7, -3)$.

13. One method of solving simultaneous linear equations is the **graphical method**. The two lines are graphed and, if they intersect, the coordinates of the intersection point are determined. Graph the following pairs of lines to determine their simultaneous solutions, if any exist.

    a. $y = 2x + 1$ $y = \frac{1}{2}x + 4$

    b. $x + 2y = 4$ $x + 2y = -2$

    c. $-2x + 3y = 9$ $x + y = -2$

    d. $-2x + 3y = 9$ $4x - 6y = -18$

14. One algebraic method for solving a system of equations is the **substitution method**. Solve the pair of equations

    $$2x + y = 3$$
    $$x - 2y = 5$$

    using the following steps:

    1. Express y in terms of x in the first equation.
    2. Since the y-value of the point of intersection satisfies both equations, we can substitute this new name for y in place of y in the second equation. Do this.
    3. The resulting equation has only the variable x. Solve for x.
    4. By substituting the x-value into either original equation, the value of y is found. Solve for y.

    Solve using the substitution method.

    a. $y = -2x + 3$ **b.** $2x - y = 6$

        $y = 3x - 5$ $5x - y = 5$

15. Another algebraic method of solving systems of equations, the **elimination method**, involves elimi-

nating one variable by adding or subtracting equivalent expressions. Consider the system

$$2x + y = 7$$
$$3x - y = 3.$$

1. Add the left-hand sides of the equations and the right-hand sides. Since the original terms were equal, the resulting sums are also equal. Notice that the variable y is eliminated.

2. Solve the equation you obtained in step 1.

3. Substitute this value of the variable into one of the original equations to find the value of the other variable.

Sometimes another operation is necessary before adding the equations of a system in order to eliminate one variable.

a. What equation results when adding the given equations? Is one variable eliminated?

$$2x - 3y = 6$$
$$4x + 5y = 1$$

b. Now multiply the first equation by -2. Is one variable eliminated when the two equations are added?

c. What is the solution of the system of equations?

16. Solve the following systems of equations, using any method.

a. $y = 6x + 2$
$\quad y = 3x - 7$

b. $2x + y = -8$
$\quad x - y = -4$

c. $3x - y = 4$
$\quad 6x + 3y = -12$

d. $3x + 5y = 9$
$\quad 4x - 8y = 17$

17. Identify whether the following systems have a unique solution, no solution, or infinitely many solutions.

a. $y = 2x + 5$
$\quad y = 2x - 3$

b. $3x - 2 = y$
$\quad 3x - y = 2$

c. $y = -x + 3$
$\quad y = 2x - 1$

d. $2x - 3y = 5$
$\quad 3x - 2y = 5$

e. $4x - y = 6$
$\quad 8x - 2y = 6$

f. $3x - y = 5$
$\quad -6x + 2y = -10$

18. Show that point P lies on the circle with the given equation.

a. $P(3, 4)$; $x^2 + y^2 = 25$

b. $P(-3, 5)$; $x^2 + y^2 = 34$

19. Identify the center and radius of each circle whose equation is given.

a. $(x - 3)^2 + (y - 2)^2 = 25$

b. $(x + 1)^2 + (y - 3)^2 = 49$

20. **a.** Write the equation of a circle with center $C(-2, 3)$ and radius of length 2.

b. Write the equation of the circle with center $C(3, -4)$ that passes through $P(2, -6)$.

c. Write the equation of the circle that has center $C(-3, -5)$ and passes through the origin.

d. Write the equation of the circle for which $A(-2, -1)$ and $B(6, -3)$ are the endpoints of a diameter.

21. Find the equation of the circumscribed circle for the triangle whose vertices are $A(-1, 2)$, $B(-1, 8)$, and $C(-5, 4)$.

22. **a.** Use the graphical method to predict solutions to the simultaneous equations

$$x^2 + y^2 = 1$$
$$y = \frac{x}{2} + 1.$$

How many solutions do you expect?

b. Use the substitution method to solve the simultaneous equations.

PROBLEMS

23. A catering company will cater a reception for $4.50 per person plus fixed costs of $200.

a. Complete the following chart.

NUMBER OF PEOPLE	30	50	75	100	n
TOTAL COST, y					

b. Write a linear equation representing the relationship between number of people (x) and total costs (y).

c. What is the slope of this line? What does it represent?

d. What is the y-intercept of this line? What does it represent?

24. For the system of equations

$$ax + by = c$$
$$dx + ey = f,$$

find the conditions on $a, b, c, d, e,$ and f, where b and e are nonzero, such that the equations have

a. infinitely many solutions.

b. no solution.

c. a unique solution.

25. Another coordinate system in the plane, called **polar coordinates**, identifies a point with an angle θ and a real number r. For example, $(3, 60°)$ gives the coordinates of point P shown. The positive x-axis serves as the initial side of the angle. Angles may be measured positively (counterclockwise) or negatively (clockwise). Plot the following points, and indicate which quadrant they are in or which axis they are on.

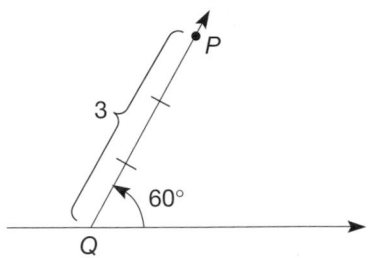

a. $(5, 45°)$ **b.** $(3, 125°)$ **c.** $(1, -170°)$

d. $(2, 240°)$ **e.** $(1.5, 300°)$ **f.** $(4, -270°)$

26. Rectangle $ABCD$ is given. Point P is a point within the rectangle such that the distance from P to A is 3 units, from P to B is 4 units, and from P to C is 5 units. How far is P from D?

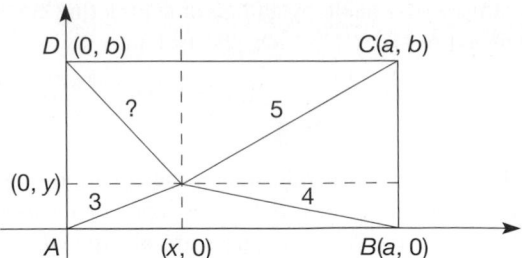

27. The junior class is planning a dance. The band will cost \$400, and advertising costs will be \$100. Food will be supplied at \$2 per person.

   a. How many people must attend the dance in order for the class to break even if tickets are sold at \$7 each?

   b. How many people must attend the dance in order for the class to break even if tickets are sold at \$6 each?

   c. How many people must attend the dance if the class wants to earn a \$400 profit and sells tickets for \$6 each?

Section 15.2 EXERCISE / PROBLEM SET B

EXERCISES

1. For each of the following equations, find three points whose coordinates satisfy the equation.

   a. $x - y = 4$ **b.** $2x - 3y = 6$

   c. $x = 3$ **d.** $x + 4y = 0$

2. Identify the slope and the y-intercept for each line.

   a. $y = -3x + 2$ **b.** $y = \frac{3}{2}x - 5$

   c. $2y = 5x - 6$ **d.** $2x - 7y = 8$

3. Write the equation of each line, given its slope m and y-intercept b.

   a. $m = -2, b = 5$ **b.** $m = \frac{7}{3}, b = -2$

4. Write the equation in (i) point-slope form and (ii) slope-intercept form for $\overleftrightarrow{AB}$.

   a. $A(-5, 2), B(-3, 1)$ **b.** $A(4, 7), B(10, 7)$

5. a. Graph the following lines on the same coordinate system.

     i. $y = 2x$ **ii.** $y = 2x + 3$

     iii. $y = 2x - 5$

   b. What is the relationship among these lines?

   c. Describe the lines of the form $y = cx + d$, where c is a fixed real number and d can be any real number.

6. Find the equation of the lines described.

   a. Slope -3 and y-intercept -5

   b. Vertical line through $(-2, 3)$

   c. Contains $(6, -1)$ and $(3, 2)$

7. Write the equation of the line that passes through the given point and is perpendicular to the line whose equation is given.

   a. $(-2, 5); y = -2x + 1$

   b. $(6, 0); y = \frac{2}{3}x - 1$

   c. $(1, -3); 2x + 4y = 6$

   d. $(-5, -4); 3x - 2y = 8$

8. Graph the line described by each equation.

   a. $y = 2x + 5$ **b.** $y = \frac{1}{3}x - 2$

   c. $y = 3$ **d.** $x = -4$

9. a. Graph the following lines on the same coordinate system.

     i. $x + y = 3$ **ii.** $x + y = -4$ **iii.** $x + y = 9$

   b. What is the relationship among these lines?

   c. Describe the lines of the form $x + y = c$, where c is any constant.

10. Find the equation of the perpendicular bisector of the segment whose endpoints are $(-3, -1)$ and $(6, 2)$.

11. Find the equations of the diagonals of the rectangle $PQRS$ with vertices $P(-2, -1)$, $Q(-2, 4)$, $R(8, 4)$, and $S(8, -1)$.

12. Find the equation of the perpendicular bisector of side $\overline{AB}$ of $\triangle ABC$, where $A = (0, 0)$, $B = (2, 5)$, and $C = (10, 5)$.

13. Solve the following simultaneous equations using the graphical method. (See Exercise 13, Part 15.2A).

   a. $y = x$ $y = -x + 4$

   b. $y = 2x$ $y = \frac{1}{2}x + 6$

   c. $x + y = 5$ $y = -x - 5$

   d. $3y = 5x + 1$ $-10x + 6y = 2$

14. Use the substitution method to find the solution of the following systems of linear equations, if a solution exists. If no solution exists, explain. (See Exercise 14, Part 15.2A).

   a. $y = 2x - 4$ $y = -5x + 17$

   b. $4x + y = 8$ $5x + 3y = 3$

   c. $x - 2y = 1$ $x = 2y + 3$

   d. $x - y = 5$ $2x - 4y = 7$

15. Use the elimination method to solve the following systems of equations. (See Exercise 15, Part 15.2A.)

   a. $5x + 3y = 17$ b. $4x - 4y = -3$
      $2x - 3y = -10$ $7x + 2y = 6$

16. Solve the following systems of equations, using any method.

   a. $y = 3x - 15$ $y = -2x + 10$

   b. $x + y = 5$ $2x + y = 6$

   c. $2x - 5y = 1$ $x - 2y - 1$

17. Determine whether the following systems have a unique solution, no solution, or infinitely many solutions.

   a. $2x - 3y = 6$ $4x - 6y = -7$

   b. $3x = 2y$ $4x - y = 2$

   c. $3y = 2x - 6$ $4x - 6y = 12$

18. Show that point P lies on the circle with the given equation.

   a. $P(-3, 7)$; $(x + 1)^2 + (y - 2)^2 = 29$

   b. $P(\sqrt{5}, -3)$; $x^2 + (y + 5)^2 = 9$

19. Identify the center and radius of each circle identified by the following equations.

   a. $(x - 2)^2 + (y + 5)^2 = 64$

   b. $(x + 3)^2 + (y - 4)^2 = 20$

20. Write the equation for each circle described as follows.

   a. Center $(-1, -2)$ and radius $\sqrt{5}$

   b. Center $(2, -4)$ and passing through $(-2, 1)$

   c. Endpoints of a diameter at $(-1, 6)$ and $(3, 2)$

21. Find the equation of the circumscribed circle for the triangle whose vertices are $J(4, 5)$, $K(8, -3)$, and $L(-4, 3)$.

22. a. Use the graphical method to predict solutions to the simultaneous equations

$$x^2 + y^2 = 1$$
$$x^2 + (y - 3)^2 = 1.$$

   How many solutions do you expect?

   b. Use the substitution method to solve the simultaneous equations.

PROBLEMS

23. A cab company charges a fixed fee of $0.60 plus $0.50 per mile.

   a. Find the cost of traveling 10 miles; of traveling 25 miles.

   b. Write an expression for the cost, y, of a trip of x miles.

24. a. A manufacturer can produce items at a cost of $0.65 per item with an operational overhead of $350. Let y represent the total production costs and x represent the number of items produced. Write an equation representing costs.

   b. The manufacturer sells the items for $1 per item.

   Let y represent the revenue and x represent the number of items sold. Write an equation representing revenue.

   c. How many items does the manufacturer need to sell to break even?

25. a. Sketch the graph of the equation $xy = 1$. Choose a variety of values for x. For example, use $x = -10$, -5, -1, -0.5, -0.1, 0.1, 0.5, 1, 5, 10, and other values. The graph is called a **hyperbola**.

   b. Why can't x or $y = 0$?

   c. What happens to the graph when x is near 0? Be sure to include cases when $x > 0$ and when $x < 0$.

26. a. Sketch the graph of the equation $y = x^2$. Choose a variety of values for x. For example, use $x = -5$, $-2, -1, 0, 1, 2, 5$, and other values. The graph is called a **parabola**.

  b. Sketch a graph of the equation $y = -x^2$. How is its graph related to the graph in part (a)?

27. a. Sketch the graph of the equation $\dfrac{x^2}{4} + \dfrac{y^2}{9} = 1$.

(*Hint*: Choose values of x between -2 and 2, and note that each value of x produces two values of y.) The graph is called an **ellipse**.

  b. Sketch the graph of the equation $\dfrac{x^2}{9} + \dfrac{y^2}{4} = 1$.

  Choose values of x between -3 and 3. How is the graph related to the graph in part (a)?

PROBLEMS FOR WRITING/DISCUSSION

1. Jimmie was trying to figure out the equation of the line containing the points $(3, 7)$ and $(-5, 9)$. He thought the slope was $-\frac{1}{4}$, so he could put that number in place of the m in the slope-intercept form of a linear equation, $y = mx + b$. But he was very worried about which of the two points to use to substitute for the x and y in the equation. Should he use $(3, 7)$ or $(-5, 9)$? Discuss.

2. Sondra was working on solving simultaneous linear equations. She had the equations $y = 4x - 5$ and $3x + 2y = 7$, and after substituting the value of y from the first equation into the second she got the answer $x = \dfrac{17}{11}$. Is she finished? In your explanation, include a picture of the two lines and indicate what an "answer" means in this problem.

3. Hakim was trying to solve a problem about circles that asked whether $(-5, 4)$ was on the circle $(x + 5)^2 + (y - 4)^2 = 9$. He suddenly realized that $(-5, 4)$ was the center of the circle. Therefore, he said, "Yes, $(-5, 4)$ is on the circle." Do you agree? What explanation would you give Hakim?

15.3   GEOMETRIC PROBLEM SOLVING USING COORDINATES

STARTING POINT

The figure at the right is a rhombus. The diagonals of a rhombus have a variety of properties. Select one of these properties and use the coordinates provided to justify that property.

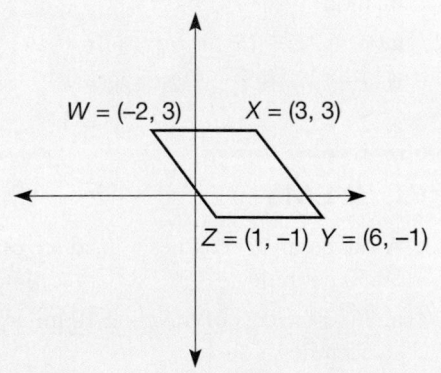

$W = (-2, 3)$ $X = (3, 3)$

$Z = (1, -1)$ $Y = (6, -1)$

We can use coordinates to solve a variety of geometric problems. The following property of triangles provides an example.

Example 15.8   Suppose that two medians of a triangle are congruent [Figure 15.19(a)]. Show that the triangle is isosceles. (Recall that a median is a line segment joining a vertex to the midpoint of the opposite side.)

Problem-Solving Strategy
Draw a Picture

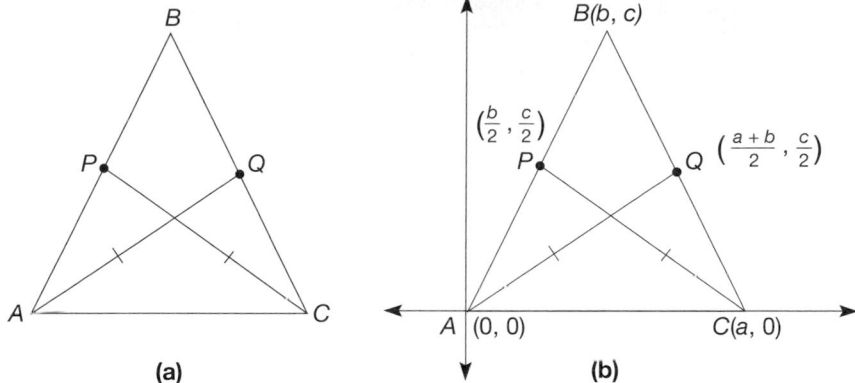

(a) **(b)**

Figure 15.19

Solution

Choose a coordinate system so that $A = (0, 0)$, $C = (a, 0)$, and $B = (b, c)$ [Figure 15.19(b)]. Let P and Q be the midpoints of sides $\overline{AB}$ and $\overline{BC}$, respectively. Then $P = \left(\dfrac{b}{2}, \dfrac{c}{2}\right)$ and $Q = \left(\dfrac{a + b}{2}, \dfrac{c}{2}\right)$. We wish to show that $AB = BC$; that is, that $\sqrt{b^2 + c^2} = \sqrt{(b - a)^2 + c^2}$. Squaring both sides, we must show $b^2 + c^2 = b^2 - 2ab + a^2 + c^2$ or, simplifying, that $2ab = a^2$. We know that $AQ = CP$, so that

$$\left(\frac{a + b}{2}\right)^2 + \left(\frac{c}{2}\right)^2 = \left(\frac{b}{2} - a\right)^2 + \left(\frac{c}{2}\right)^2$$
$$= \left(\frac{b - 2a}{2}\right)^2 + \left(\frac{c}{2}\right)^2.$$

Expanding, we have

$$\frac{a^2 + 2ab + b^2}{4} + \frac{c^2}{4} = \frac{b^2 - 4ab + 4a^2}{4} + \frac{c^2}{4}$$
$$a^2 + 2ab + b^2 + c^2 = 4a^2 - 4ab + b^2 + c^2$$
$$6ab = 3a^2,$$

so that

$$2ab = a^2,$$

as desired. Thus $\overline{AB} \cong \overline{BC}$, so that $\triangle ABC$ is isosceles.   ■

We can use coordinates to verify an interesting result about the three medians of any triangle.

 THEOREM

Centroid of a Triangle

The medians of $\triangle PQR$ are concurrent at a point G that divides each median in a ratio of $2:1$.

The point G is called the **centroid** of $\triangle PQR$.

Proof Choose a coordinate system having $P(0, 0)$, $R(c, 0)$, and $Q(a, b)$ (Figure 15.20).

Problem-Solving Strategy
Draw a Picture

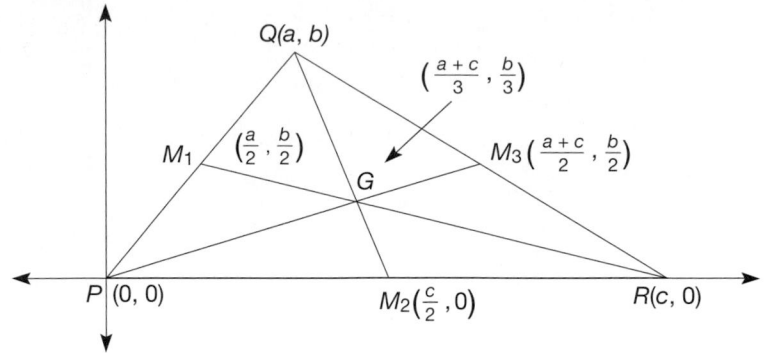

Figure 15.20

Let M_1, M_2, and M_3 be the midpoints of sides $\overline{PQ}$, $\overline{PR}$, and $\overline{QR}$.

Then $M_1 = \left(\dfrac{a}{2}, \dfrac{b}{2}\right)$, $M_2 = \left(\dfrac{c}{2}, 0\right)$, and $M_3 = \left(\dfrac{a+c}{2}, \dfrac{b}{2}\right)$. Consider the point $G = \left(\dfrac{a+c}{3}, \dfrac{b}{3}\right)$. Using slopes, we will show that P, G, and M_3 are collinear.

$$\text{slope of } \overline{PG} = \frac{\dfrac{b}{3} - 0}{\dfrac{a+c}{3} - 0} = \frac{b}{a+c}$$

$$\text{slope of } \overline{PM_3} = \frac{\dfrac{b}{2} - 0}{\dfrac{a+c}{2} - 0} = \frac{b}{a+c}$$

Therefore, P, G, and M_3 are collinear.

In a similar way, we can show that Q, G, and M_2 are collinear, as are R, G, and M_1. This is left for Part B Problem 12 in the Problem Set. Hence point G is on all three medians, so that the medians intersect at G.

Finally, we will show that G divides the median $\overline{PM_3}$ in a ratio of $2:1$. The similar verification for the other two medians is left for Part B Problem 13 in the Problem Set.

$$PG = \sqrt{\left(\frac{a+c}{3}\right)^2 + \left(\frac{b}{3}\right)^2}$$

$$= \frac{\sqrt{(a+c)^2 + b^2}}{3}$$

$$GM_3 = \sqrt{\left(\frac{a+c}{2} - \frac{a+c}{3}\right)^2 + \left(\frac{b}{2} - \frac{b}{3}\right)^2}$$

$$= \sqrt{\left(\frac{a+c}{6}\right)^2 + \left(\frac{b}{6}\right)^2}$$

$$= \frac{\sqrt{(a+c)^2 + b^2}}{6}$$

$$= \frac{1}{2} PG$$

Thus the ratio $PG : GM_3 = 2:1$. ■

The next result shows how equations of lines can be used to verify properties of triangles.

> ### THEOREM
>
> #### Orthocenter of a Triangle
>
> The altitudes of $\triangle PQR$ are concurrent at a point O called the **orthocenter** of the triangle.

Proof Consider $\triangle PQR$ with altitudes l, m, and n from P, Q, and R, respectively [Figure 15.21(a)]. Choose a coordinate system having $P(0, 0)$, $Q(a, b)$, and $R(c, 0)$ [Figure 15.21(b)]. Since $l \perp \overleftrightarrow{QR}$, the slope of l is $\dfrac{c - a}{b}$. (Verify.)

Problem-Solving Strategy
Draw a Picture

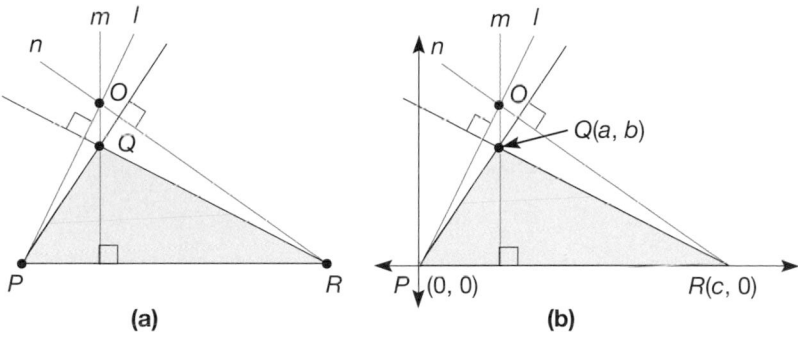

(a)   **(b)**

Figure 15.21

Hence, the equation of l is $y = \dfrac{c - a}{b} x$, since l contains $(0, 0)$. The equation of m is $x = a$, since m is a vertical line through $Q(a, b)$. Thus l and m intersect at point $O = \left(a, \dfrac{(c - a)a}{b} \right)$. (Verify.) To find the equation of n, we first find its slope. Since $n \perp \overleftrightarrow{PQ}$, the slope of n is $\dfrac{-a}{b}$. (Verify.) Hence the equation of n is of the form $y = -\dfrac{a}{b} x + d$ for some d. Using the fact that $R = (c, 0)$ is on n, we have

Problem-Solving Strategy
Solve an Equation

$$0 = \frac{-a}{b} c + d, \qquad \text{so} \qquad d = \frac{ac}{b}.$$

Thus the equation of n is $y = \dfrac{-a}{b} x + \dfrac{ac}{b}$. To show that l, m, and n meet at one point, all we need to show is that point $O = \left(a, \dfrac{(c - a)a}{b} \right)$ is on line n. Substituting a for x in the equation of n, we obtain

$$
\begin{aligned}
y &= \frac{-a}{b} a + \frac{ac}{b} \\
&= \frac{ac}{b} - \frac{aa}{b} \\
&= \frac{(c - a)a}{b},
\end{aligned}
$$

the y-coordinate of O! Hence the three altitudes—l, m, and n—intersect at point O. ■

The next example illustrates a geometric construction in the coordinate plane using equations of lines and circles.

Example 15.9   Find the equation of the circumscribed circle for the triangle whose vertices are $O = (0, 0)$, $P = (2, 4)$, and $Q = (6, 0)$ (Figure 15.22).

Problem-Solving Strategy
Draw a Picture

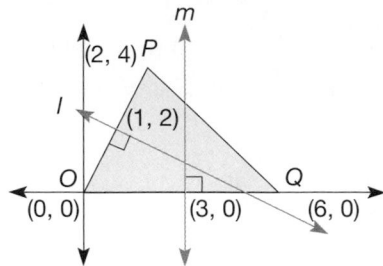

Figure 15.22

Solution

The circumscribed circle for a triangle contains all three vertices (see Chapter 14). First, we find the equations of lines l and m, the perpendicular bisectors of $\overline{OP}$ and $\overline{OQ}$. The intersection of lines l and m is the circumcenter of $\triangle OPQ$. To find the equation of line l, we need its slope. The slope of $\overline{OP}$ is $\dfrac{4 - 0}{2 - 0} = 2$, so that the slope of l is $-\frac{1}{2}$ by the slopes of perpendicular lines theorem. Hence the equation of line l is $y = -\frac{1}{2}x + b$, for some b. The midpoint of $\overline{OP}$ is $(1, 2)$, by the midpoint formula, so the point $(1, 2)$ satisfies the equation of line l. Thus $2 = (-\frac{1}{2})(1) + b$, so $b = \frac{5}{2}$. Therefore, the equation of line l is $y = -\frac{1}{2}x + \frac{5}{2}$.

Line m is vertical and contains $(3, 0)$, the midpoint of $\overline{OQ}$. Hence the equation of line m is $x = 3$. To find the circumcenter of $\triangle OPQ$, then, we need to find the point (x, y) satisfying the following simultaneous equations:

Problem-Solving Strategy
Solve an Equation

$$y = -\frac{1}{2}x + \frac{5}{2} \quad \text{and} \quad x = 3.$$

Using $x = 3$, we have

$$y = -\frac{1}{2}(3) + \frac{5}{2}, \quad \text{or} \quad y = 1.$$

Thus the point $C = (3, 1)$ is the circumcenter of $\triangle OPQ$.

To find the radius of the circumscribed circle, we use the distance formula. Since $(0, 0)$ is on the circle (we can use any vertex), the radius is $\sqrt{(3 - 0)^2 + (1 - 0)^2} = \sqrt{10}$. Thus, by the equation of a circle formula, the equation of the circumscribed circle is

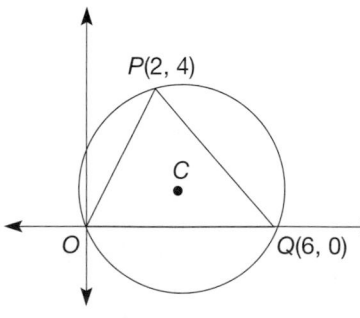

Figure 15.23

$$(x - 3)^2 + (y - 1)^2 = 10.$$

As a check, verify that all the vertices of the triangle—namely $(0, 0)$, $(6, 0)$, and $(2, 4)$—satisfy this equation. Hence all are on the circle. Figure 15.23 shows the circumscribed circle. ■

In this chapter we have restricted our attention to equations of circles and lines. However, using coordinates, it is possible to write equations for other sets of points in the plane and thus to investigate many other geometric problems, such as properties of curves other than lines and circles.

MATHEMATICAL MORSEL

Any three noncollinear points are contained on a circle. However, a remarkable result concerning nine points in a triangle, known as the nine-point circle theorem, states that all the following nine points lie on a single circle determined by △*PQR*.

    A, B, C: the midpoints of the sides
    D, E, F: the "feet" of the altitudes
    G, H, I: the midpoints of the segments joining the vertices (*P, Q, R*) to the orthocenter, *O*

This circle is called the "Feuerbach circle" after a German mathematician, Karl Feuerbach, who proved several results about it.

Section 15.3 EXERCISE / PROBLEM SET A

EXERCISES

1. The coordinates of three vertices of a parallelogram are given. Find the coordinates of the fourth vertex. (There are three correct answers for each part.)

    a. $(0, 0), (0, 5), (3, 0)$

    b. $(-2, -2), (2, 3), (5, 3)$

2. The coordinates of three vertices of a square are given. Find the coordinates of the fourth vertex.

    a. $(-2, -1), (3, -1), (3, 4)$

    b. $(-3, 0), (0, -2), (2, 1)$

3. When using coordinate methods to verify results about polygons, it is often important how you choose the axes of the coordinate system. For example, it is often advantageous to put one vertex at the origin. Label the missing coordinates in the following diagrams.

    a. Square *ABCD*

    b. Rectangle *EFGH*

4. Right triangle *QRS* is placed in a coordinate system as shown.

    a. If $QR = 6$ and $QS = 4$, find the coordinates of the vertices of △*QRS*.

    b. If $QR = a$ and $QS = b$, find the coordinates of the vertices of △*QRS*.

5. Given is isosceles triangle *XYZ* with $XY = YZ, XZ = 8$, and the altitude from *Y* having length 5. Find the coordinates of the vertices in each of the coordinate systems described.

a. X is at the origin, $\overleftrightarrow{XZ}$ is the x-axis, and Y is in the first quadrant.

b. $\overleftrightarrow{XZ}$ is the x-axis, the y-axis is a line of symmetry, and the y-coordinate of Y is positive.

6. Given $R(5, -2)$, $S(3, 0)$, $T(-4, -1)$, and $U(-2, -3)$, show that $RSTU$ is a parallelogram.

7. Given the coordinates of $A(4, 1)$, $B(0, 7)$, $C(3, 9)$, and $D(7, 3)$, show that $ABCD$ is a rectangle.

8. Given is $\triangle ABC$ with $A(-3, 6)$, $B(5, 8)$, and $C(3, 2)$.

a. Let M be the midpoint of $\overline{AC}$. What are its coordinates?

b. Let N be the midpoint of $\overline{BC}$. What are its coordinates?

c. Find the slope of $\overline{MN}$ and the slope of $\overline{AB}$. What do you observe?

d. Find the lengths of $\overline{MN}$ and $\overline{AB}$. What do you observe?

PROBLEMS

9. Use coordinates to prove that the diagonals of a rectangle are congruent.

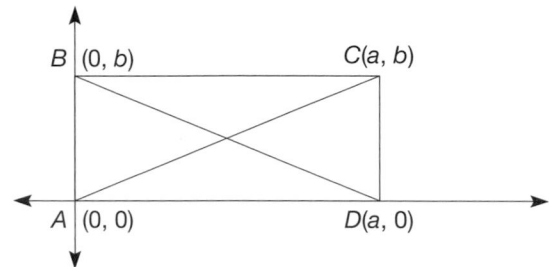

10. Given is $\triangle ABC$ with vertices $A(0, 0)$, $B(24, 0)$, and $C(18, 12)$.

a. Find the equation of the line containing the median from vertex A.

b. Find the equation of the line containing the median from vertex B.

c. Find the equation of the line containing the median from vertex C.

d. Find the intersection of the lines in parts (a) and (b). Does this point lie on the line in part (c)?

e. What result about the medians is illustrated?

11. Given $P(a, b)$, $Q(a + c, b + c)$, $R(a + d, b - d)$, and $S(a + c + d, b + c - d)$, determine whether the diagonals of $PQRS$ are congruent.

12. Given in the following figure is $\triangle ABC$ with vertices $A(0, 0)$, $B(a, b)$, and $C(c, 0)$. If $\triangle ABC$ is an isosceles triangle with $AB = BC$, show the following results.

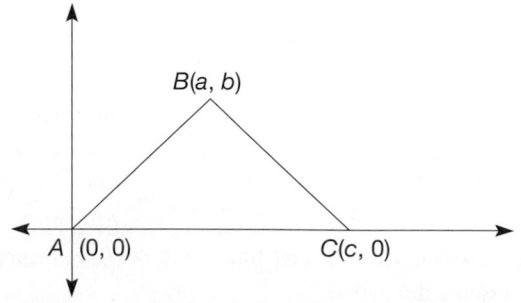

a. $c = 2a$.

b. The median from B is perpendicular to $\overline{AC}$.

13. Given is $\triangle RST$ with vertices $R(0, 0)$, $S(8, 6)$, and $T(11, 0)$.

a. Find the equation of the line containing the altitude from vertex R.

b. Find the equation of the line containing the altitude from vertex S.

c. Find the equation of the line containing the altitude from vertex T.

d. Find the intersection point of the lines in parts (a) and (b). Does this point lie on the line in part (c)? What point is this?

14. Use coordinates to show that the diagonals of a parallelogram bisect each other.

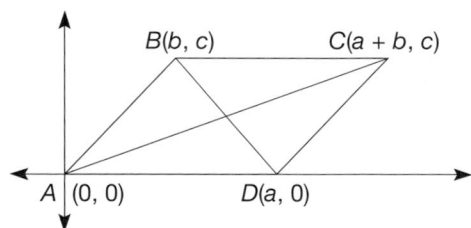

15. In the proof in this section concerning the orthocenter of a triangle, verify the following statements.

a. The slope of l is $\dfrac{c - a}{b}$.

b. The lines l and m intersect at the point $\left(a, \dfrac{(c - a)a}{b} \right)$.

c. The slope of n is $-\dfrac{a}{b}$.

16. Can an equilateral triangle with a horizontal side be formed on a square lattice? If so, show one. If not, explain why not.

17. The other day, I was taking care of two girls whose parents are mathematicians. The girls are both whizzes at math. When I asked their ages, one girl replied, "The sum of our ages is 18." The other stated, "The difference of our ages is 4." What are the girls' ages?

18. Seven cycle riders and nineteen cycle wheels go past. How many bicycles and how many tricycles passed by the house?

19. Mike and Joan invest $11,000 together. If Mike triples his money and Joan doubles hers, they will have $29,000. How much did each invest?

20. Marge went to a bookstore and paid $16.25 for a used math book, using only quarters and dimes. How many quarters and dimes did she have if she spent all of her 110 coins?

21. **a.** How many paths of length 7 are there from *A* to *C*? (*Hint*: At each vertex, write the number of ways to get there directly from *A*. Look for a pattern.)

b. How many of these paths go through *B*? (*Hint*: Apply the fundamental counting property.)

c. What is the probability that the path will go through *B*?

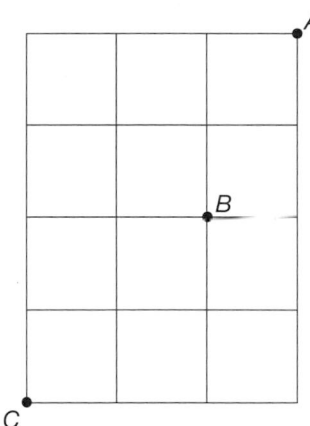

EXERCISES

1. The coordinates of three vertices of a rectangle are given. Find the coordinates of the fourth vertex.

   a. $(4, 2), (4, 5), (-1, 2)$

   b. $(-2, 1), (0, -1), (3, 2)$

2. Two vertices of a figure are $(-4, 0)$ and $(2, 0)$.

   a. Name the coordinates of the third vertex above the *x*-axis if the figure is an equilateral triangle. (*Hint*: One of the coordinates is irrational.)

   b. Name the coordinates of the other two vertices above the *x*-axis if the figure is a square.

3. Parallelogram *IJKL* is placed in a coordinate system such that *I* is at the origin and $\overline{IJ}$ is along the *x*-axis. The coordinates of *I*, *J*, and *L* are shown. Give the coordinates of point *K* in terms of *a*, *b*, and *c*.

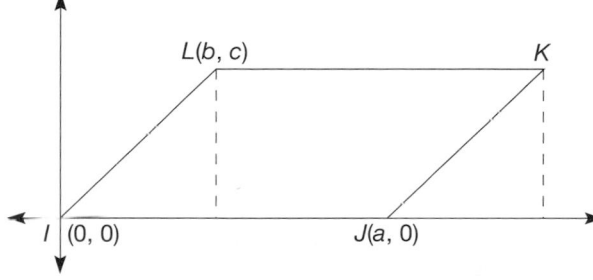

4. Rhombus *MNOP* is placed in a coordinate system such that *M* is at the origin and $\overline{MN}$ is along the *x*-axis. The coordinates for points *M*, *N*, and *P* are given.

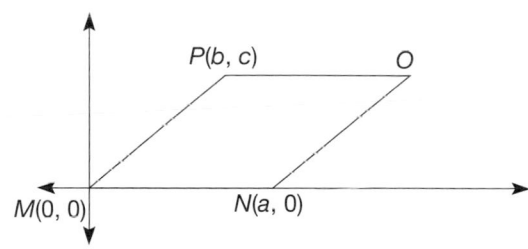

   a. Find the coordinates of point *O* in terms of *a*, *b*, and *c*.

   b. What special relationship exists among *a*, *b*, and *c* because *MNOP* is a rhombus?

5. The coordinate axes may be established in different ways. Suppose that rectangle *ABCD* is a rectangle with $AB = 10$ and $AD = 8$. Find the coordinates of the vertices in each of the coordinate systems described.

   a. $\overleftrightarrow{AB}$ is the *x*-axis, and the *y*-axis is a line of symmetry.

b. The x-axis is a horizontal line of symmetry (let $\overleftrightarrow{AB}$ also be horizontal), and the y-axis is a vertical line of symmetry.

6. Given the points $A(-4, -1)$, $B(1, -1)$, $C(4, 3)$, and $D(-1, 3)$, show that $ABCD$ is a rhombus.

7. Given the points $A(-3, -2)$, $B(1, -3)$, $C(2, 1)$, and $D(-2, 2)$, show that $ABCD$ is a square.

8. Determine whether the diagonals of $EFGH$ bisect each other, where $E(-1, -7)$, $F(-3, -5)$, $G(-2, 2)$, and $H(0, 0)$.

PROBLEMS

9. Use coordinates to show that the midpoint of the hypotenuse of a right triangle is equidistant from all three vertices.

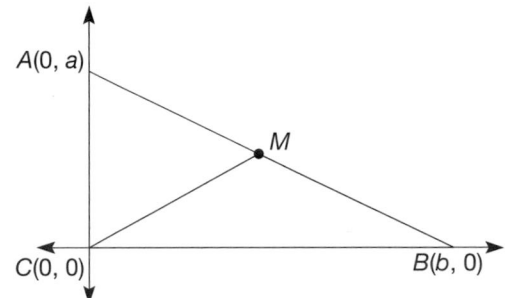

10. In Problem 10, Part 15.3A, let M be the centroid of the triangle (i.e., the point where the three medians are concurrent).

a. Find the length of the median from A, the length AM, and the ratio of AM to the length of the median from A.

b. Find the length of the median from B, the length BM, and the ratio of BM to the length of the median from B.

c. Find the length of the median from C, the length CM, and the ratio of CM to the length of the median from C.

d. Describe the location of the centroid.

11. Use coordinates to verify that the diagonals of a rhombus are perpendicular. (*Hint:* $a^2 = b^2 + c^2$.)

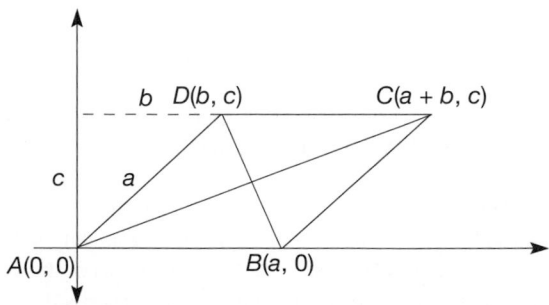

12. In the proof in this section concerning the centroid of a triangle, verify the following statements.

a. Points Q, G, and M_2 are collinear.

b. Points R, G, and M_1 are collinear.

13. In the proof in this section concerning the centroid of a triangle, verify the following statements.

a. The point G divides the median QM_2 in a ratio $2:1$.

b. The point G divides the median RM_1 in a ratio $2:1$.

14. Given is an equilateral triangle on a coordinate system.

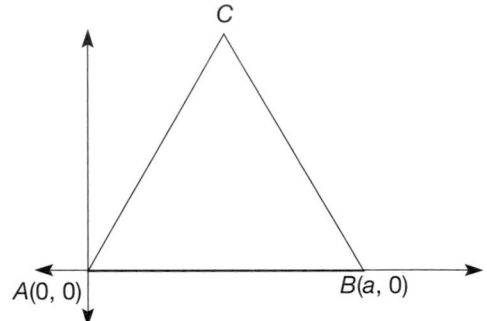

a. Find the coordinates of point C.

b. Find the perpendicular bisector of $\overline{AB}$, the median from point C, and the altitude from point C. Do these share points?

c. Do the perpendicular bisector of $\overline{BC}$, the median, and the altitude from point A share points?

d. Do the perpendicular bisector of $\overline{AC}$, the median, and the altitude from point B share points?

e. What general conclusion about equilateral triangles have you shown?

15. a. Given that $ABCD$ is an arbitrary quadrilateral, and points M and N are the midpoints of the diagonals $\overline{AC}$ and $\overline{BD}$, respectively, show that

$$AB^2 + BC^2 + CD^2 + DA^2$$
$$= BD^2 + AC^2 + 4(MN)^2.$$

b. What does the result in part (a) imply about a parallelogram?

16. Arrange the numbers 1, 2, 3, 4, 5, 6, 8, 9, 10, 11, 12, 13 around the cube shown so that the sum of the four edges that determine a face is always 28 and the sum of the three edges that lead into any vertex is 21.

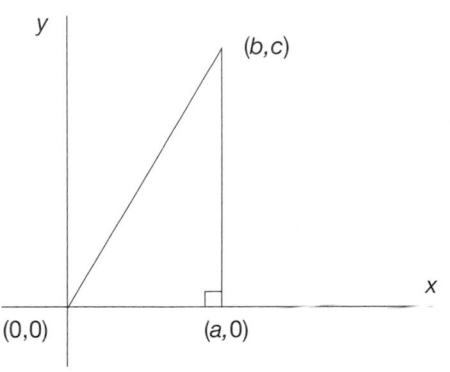

17. A quiz had some 3-point and some 4-point questions. A perfect score was 100 points. Find out how many questions were of each type if there were a total of 31 questions on the quiz.

18. A laboratory produces an alloy of gold, silver, and copper having a weight of 44 grams. If the gold weighs 3 grams more than the silver and the silver weighs 2 grams less than the copper, how much of each element is in the alloy?

19. The sum of two numbers is 148 and their difference is 16. What are the two numbers?

20. Six years ago, in a state park, the deer outnumbered the foxes by 80. Since then, the number of deer has doubled and the number of foxes has increased by 20. If there is now a total of 240 deer and foxes in the park, how many foxes were there six years ago?

21. My son gave me a set of table mats he bought in Mexico. They were rectangular and made of straw circles joined together in this way: All the circles on the edges of each mat were white and the inner circles black. I noted that there were 20 white circles and 15 black circles. Is it possible to make such a rectangular mat where the number of black circles is the same as the number of white circles?

PROBLEMS FOR WRITING/DISCUSSION

1. Jolene needed to do a coordinate proof involving a right triangle, but she couldn't decide how to place it on the axes. Can she do it like this? Can you think of a better placement for the triangle? How do you determine what is a "better" way? Would there be a way to rename the point (b, c) in her diagram in light of other facts given in the diagram? Explain.

2. Herbert wants to find the equation of the perpendicular bisector of the hypotenuse of the right triangle

shown. He knows the midpoint of the hypotenuse is $\left(\dfrac{a}{2}, \dfrac{b}{2}\right)$, so he uses that point and $(0, 0)$ to get the equation $y = \left(\dfrac{b}{a}\right) x$. The line goes through the midpoint and hence is the perpendicular bisector of the hypotenuse. Is he correct? Discuss.

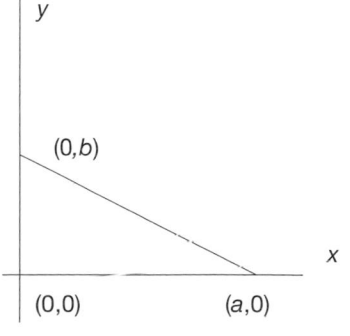

3. Shelley was placing a rhombus on coordinate axes as shown. She wanted to name the vertices using the

fewest number of letters. Suppose the (0, 0) and (*a, b*) are correct. Is she assuming too much to think that the other two vertices could be labeled (0, 2*b*) and (−*a, b*)? What would Shelley have to explain in order to justify her labeling?

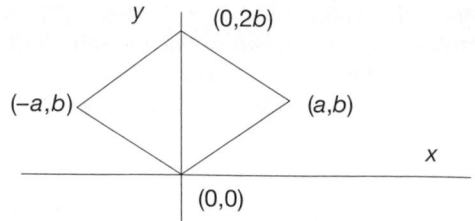

END OF CHAPTER MATERIAL

Solution of Initial Problem

A surveyor plotted a triangular building lot, drew the following diagram, and recorded the following data. What is the area of the lot, in square feet?

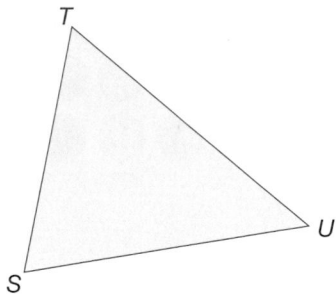

STAKE	POSITION RELATIVE TO *S*
U	East 207′, North 35′
T	East 40′, North 185′

Strategy: Use Coordinates

First, place the triangle on a coordinate system and then surround it with a rectangle (Figure 15.24). Each triangle, *A*, *B*, and *C*, is a right triangle. We can compute the area of each triangle, then subtract their total areas from the area of the rectangle:

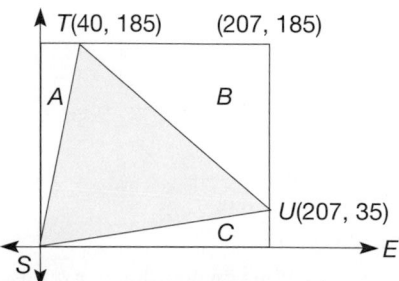

Figure 15.24

$$\text{Area of triangle } A = \frac{40 \times 185}{2} = 3700 \text{ ft}^2$$

$$\text{Area of triangle } B = \frac{167 \times 150}{2} = 12{,}525 \text{ ft}^2$$

$$\text{Area of triangle } C = \frac{207 \times 35}{2} = 3622.5 \text{ ft}^2$$

$$\text{Area of rectangle} = 207 \times 185 = 38{,}295 \text{ ft}^2$$

Hence the area of a surveyed triangle = 38,295 ft² − (3700 + 12,525 + 3622.5) ft² = 18,447.5 ft².

Additional Problems Where the Strategy "Use Coordinates" Is Useful

1. Prove that the diagonals of a kite are perpendicular. [*Hint*: Consider the kite with coordinates (0, 0), (*a, b*), (−*a, b*), and (0, *c*), where *c* > *b*.]

2. An explorer leaves base camp and travels 4 km north, 3 km west, and 2 km south. How far is he from the base camp?

3. Prove that $\overline{BC}$ is parallel to $\overline{DE}$, where *D* and *E* are the centers of the squares (Figure 15.25). (*Hint*: Use slopes.)

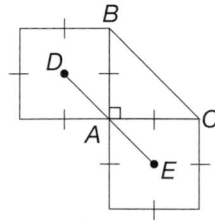

Figure 15.25

People in Mathematics

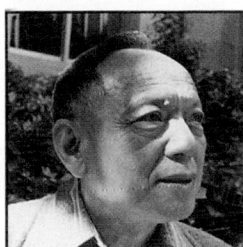

Shiing-Shen Chern (1911-) Shiing-Shen Chern is noted for his pioneering work in differential geometry, a branch of mathematics that has been used to extend Einstein's theory of general relativity. Born and educated in China, Chern did advanced study in Germany and France during the 1930s. He returned to China to organize a mathematics institute in Shanghai. The largest part of his working life has been spent in the United States, at the Institute of Advanced Study, the University of Chicago, and the University of California at Berkeley. In 1982, the National Science Foundation created a center for advanced mathematical study at Berkeley, and Chern was chosen to become its first director. Its official name is the Mathematical Sciences Research Institute; the acronym MSRI is commonly pronounced "misery" by the researchers at the institute, perhaps in recognition of the frustrations they have experienced when attacking difficult problems.

H. S. M. Coxeter (1907-) H. S. M. Coxeter is known for his research and expositions of geometry. He is the author of 11 books, including *Introduction to Geometry, Projective Geometry, Non-Euclidean Geometry, The Fifty-Nine Icosahedra*, and *Mathematical Recreations and Essays*. He contends that Russia, Germany, and Austria are the countries that do the best job of teaching geometry in the schools, because they still regard it as a subject worth studying. "In English-speaking countries, there was a long tradition of dull teaching of geometry. People thought that the only thing to do in geometry was to build a system of axioms and see how you would go from there. So children got bogged down in this formal stuff and didn't get a lively feel for the subject. That did a lot of harm."

CHAPTER REVIEW

Review the following terms and exercises to determine which require learning or relearning—page numbers are provided for easy reference.

SECTION 15.1: Distance and Slope in the Coordinate Plane

VOCABULARY/NOTATION

Slope of a line   760   Slope of a line segment   760

EXERCISES

The points $P(3, 4)$, $Q(5, -2)$, $R(6, 8)$, $S(10, -4)$, and $T(7, 3)$ are used in the following.

1. Find the distance PQ.

2. Find the midpoint M of $\overline{PQ}$.

3. Determine whether P, Q, and M are collinear.

4. Find the slopes of $\overline{PM}$ and $\overline{MQ}$. What does your answer prove?

5. Determine whether $\overleftrightarrow{PQ} \parallel \overleftrightarrow{RS}$.

6. Determine whether $\overline{TM} \perp \overline{PQ}$.

SECTION 15.2: Equations and Coordinates

VOCABULARY/NOTATION

y-intercept   771   Simultaneous solutions   774   Simultaneous equations   774
Slope-intercept equation of a line
    772

EXERCISES

The points $P(4, -7)$, $Q(0, 3)$, $R(3, 2)$, $S(5, -1)$, and $T(-2, 5)$ are used in the following.

1. Write the slope-intercept form of $\overleftrightarrow{PQ}$.

2. Write the point-slope form of $\overleftrightarrow{RS}$.

3. Describe the three types of outcomes possible when solving two linear equations simultaneously.

4. Write the equation of the circle with center at T and diameter 10.

SECTION 15.3: Geometric Problem Solving Using Coordinates

VOCABULARY/NOTATION

Centroid   783   Orthocenter   785

EXERCISES

The points $P(0, 0)$, $Q(0, 5)$, and $R(12, 0)$ are used in the following.

1. Find the centroid of $\triangle PQR$.

2. Find the orthocenter of $\triangle PQR$.

3. Find the center of the circumscribed circle of $\triangle PQR$.

PROBLEMS FOR WRITING/DISCUSSION

1. Mickey said he had a new way to find the midpoint of a segment. He compared it to finding a midpoint on a number line. On a number line, if you want the midpoint between 4 and 9, say, you can take the difference (5), take half of it (2.5), and add that number to the smaller number (4 + 2.5)—and that will give you the midpoint (6.5). So in the coordinate plane, if you want the midpoint between (3, 7) and (11, 4), you can subtract the x's and y's (8 and 3), take half of each (4 and 1.5), and add them onto the first number (3 + 4 and 7 + 1.5)—and that will give you the midpoint (7, 8.5). Does any of this make sense? Explain how you could help Mickey.

2. Joel was thinking about horizontal and vertical lines. He said "zero slope" and "no slope" sound like the same thing to him, since zero means nothing. Explain how you could help Joel understand the difference.

3. Lewis says he knows that the slopes of two lines that are perpendicular have slopes whose product is -1; for example, 2/3 and $-3/2$. He asks, "What happens if the product of the slopes is $+1$, like 2/3 and 3/2? Does that mean anything special?" How would you respond?

4. Kimberly says she knows that the slopes of two parallel lines are equal. But what if they are opposites, like 4 and -4? Does that mean anything special? What would you say to Kimberly?

5. Bruce says, "In the plane, the horizontal axis is x and the vertical axis is y, so why is $x = 5$ a vertical line and $y = 3$ a horizontal line? Shouldn't it be the other way around?" How would you explain this to Bruce?

6. When Marla was sketching the graph of a linear equation, $y = -2x + 5$, without graph paper, she found that her line seemed to bend, as shown in the figure. What went wrong?

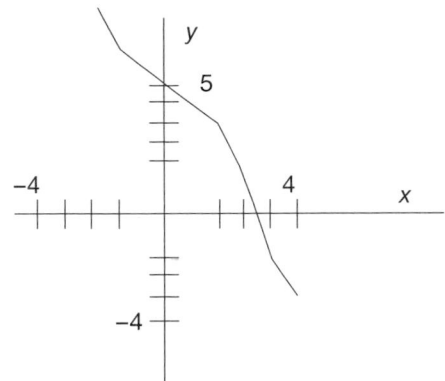

7. This is a riddle. An explorer left his base camp and walked due south for 4 miles. He then traveled due west for 2 miles, then due north for 4 miles. This brought him back to his base camp, where he saw a bear getting into his food supplies. What color was the bear? What does this riddle tell us about a coordinate system on a curved surface?

8. Warren said sometimes he could tell whether two lines were parallel just from looking at their equations. For example, if the two equations were $2x + 5y = 7$ and $4x + 10y = 15$, he would know immediately that the lines were parallel. How could he tell? How could you change the 15 to make the lines coincident instead of parallel?

9. What are two ways to determine whether the following points are the vertices of a right triangle? Show both methods and include a sketch and an explanation: $(-1, 3)$, $(1, 6)$, and $(4, 4)$.

10. Holly wants to prove that the figure formed by connecting the midpoints of the four sides of any quadrilateral is a parallelogram. She has drawn the accompanying quadrilateral, which does not have any of the special properties that would make it a trapezoid, kite, or any other special quadrilateral. Can she use any fewer letters than she has to name the vertices? Explain how she would go about proving this theorem.

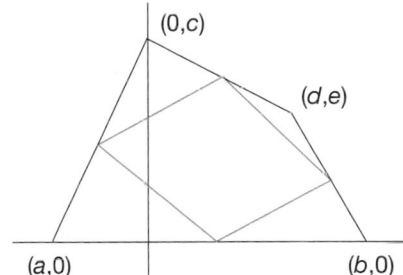

CHAPTER TEST

Knowledge

1. True or false?

   a. A point $(a, 0)$ is on the x-axis.

   b. The quadrants are labeled I–IV clockwise beginning with the upper left quadrant.

   c. The midpoint of the segment with endpoints $(a, 0)$ and $(b, 0)$ is $((a + b)/2, 0)$.

   d. The y-intercept of a line is always positive.

   e. A pair of simultaneous equations of the form $ax + by = c$ may have *exactly* 0, 1, or 2 simultaneous solutions.

   f. The orthocenter of a triangle is the intersection of the altitudes.

   g. The equation $x^2 + y^2 = r^2$ represents a circle whose center is the origin and whose radius is $\sqrt{r^2}$.

   h. If two lines are perpendicular and neither line is vertical, the slope of each line is the multiplicative inverse of the slope of the other.

2. Name and write the equations for two different forms of linear equations.

Skill

3. Find the length, midpoint, and slope of the line segment with endpoints $(1, 2)$ and $(5, 7)$.

4. Find the equations of the following lines.

   a. The vertical line containing $(-1, 7)$

   b. The horizontal line containing $(-1, 7)$

   c. The line containing $(-1, 7)$ with slope 3

   d. The line containing $(-1, 7)$ and perpendicular to the line $2x + 3y = 5$

5. Find the equation of the circle with center $(-3, 4)$ and radius 5.

6. Without finding the solutions, determine whether the following pairs of equations have zero, one, or infinitely many simultaneous solutions.

    a. $3x + 4y = 5$
       $6x + 8y = 11$

    b. $3x - 2y = -9$
        $x + y = -1$

    c. $x - y = -1$
       $y - x = 1$

    d. $x + 5 = 0$
       $2x + 7y = 10$

7. Write the equation $3x - 4y = 8$ in slope-intercept form.

8. Find the equation of the perpendicular bisector of the segment described in Exercise 3.

Understanding

9. Determine how many simultaneous solutions the equations $x^2 + y^2 = r^2$ and $ax + by = c$ *may* have. Explain.

10. Explain why the following four equations could not contain the four sides of a rectangle, but *do* contain the four sides of a parallelogram.

$$2x - 4y = 7$$

$$2x - 4y = 13$$

$$3x + 5y = 8$$

$$3x + 5y = -2$$

11. Find 3 points on the circle described in Exercise 5.

12. Explain how the Pythagorean theorem is related to the distance formula.

13. Plot the points $L(2, 2)$, $M(5, 1)$, $N(6, 4)$, and $O(3, 5)$ on a set of axes and determine exactly what type of quadrilateral $LMNO$ is. Justify your conclusion.

14. If the midpoint of a segment is $(3, 5)$ and one endpoint is $(-1, 7)$, what are the coordinates of the other endpoint?

15. If line l has a slope of 2 and contains the point $(-1, -2)$, what are three other points that lie on l?

16. Let $A = (2, 3)$, $B = (3, 6)$, and $C = (6, 5)$.

    a. Sketch $\triangle ABC$ on a set of axes.

    b. Determine if $\triangle ABC$ is equilateral, isosceles, or scalene. Explain your reasoning.

    c. Determine if $\triangle ABC$ is acute, obtuse, or right. Explain your reasoning.

Problem Solving Application

17. Give the most complete description of the figure $ABCD$, where A, B, C, and D are the midpoints of the square determined by the points $(0, 0)$, $(a, 0)$, (a, a), and $(0, a)$, and where a is positive. Prove your assertion.

18. For the triangle pictured, prove the following relationships.

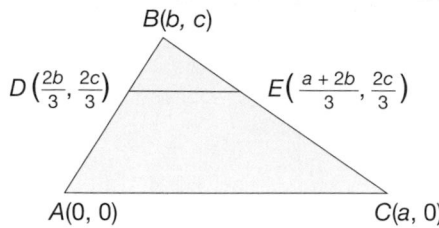

    a. $\overline{DE} \parallel \overline{AC}$

    b. $DE = \frac{1}{3}AC$

State the new theorem that you have proved.

19. The quadrilateral $LMNO$ in the following figure is a parallelogram.

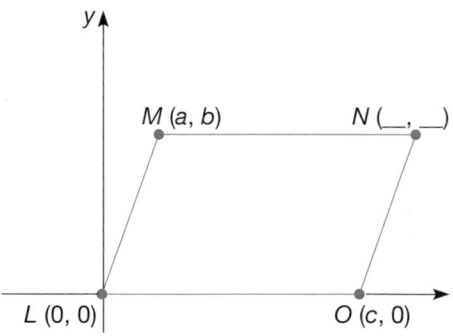

    a. Find the coordinates of vertex N based on the coordinates of the other vertices already listed in the figure.

    b. Using the given information and the results of part (a), show that the diagonals of a parallelogram bisect each other.

References for Reflections from Research

DEMANA, E., & WAITS, B. (1988). Pitfalls in graphical computation, or why a single graph isn't enough. *The College Mathematics Journal, 19*, 177–183

FOCUS ON *The Geometric Art of M. C. Escher*

aurits Escher was born in the Netherlands in 1898. Although his school experience was largely a negative one, he looked forward with enthusiasm to his two hours of art each week. His father urged him into architecture to take advantage of his artistic ability. However, that endeavor did not last long. It became apparent that Escher's talent lay more in the area of decorative arts than in architecture, so Escher began the formal study of art when he was in his twenties. His work includes sketches, woodcuts, mezzotints, lithographs, and watercolors.

Escher's links with mathematics and mathematical form are apparent. The following works illustrate various themes related to mathematics.

Approaches to Infinity

Circle Limit III illustrates one of three Circle Limit designs based on a hyperbolic tessellation. Notice how the fish seem to swim to infinity. This work gave rise to a paper by H. S. M. Coxeter entitled "The Non-Euclidean Symmetry of Escher's Picture *Circle Limit III*."

Circle Limit III

Symmetries

Shells and Starfish, which was developed from a pattern of stars and diamond shapes on a square grid, possesses several rotation symmetries.

Metamorphosis

Escher is perhaps most famous for his ever-changing pictures. *Fish* shows arched fish evolving, appearing, and disappearing across the drawing. Methods that lead to constructions such as these are discussed in this chapter.

Shells and Starfish

M. C. Escher in his studio in 1967.

Fish

Problem Solving Strategies

1. Guess and Test
2. Use a Variable
3. Draw a Picture
4. Look for a Pattern
5. Make a List
6. Solve a Simpler Problem
7. Draw a Diagram
8. Use Direct Reasoning
9. Use Indirect Reasoning
10. Use Properties of Numbers
11. Solve an Equivalent Problem
12. Work Backward
13. Use Cases
14. Solve an Equation
15. Look for a Formula
16. Do a Simulation
17. Use a Model
18. Use Dimensional Analysis
19. Identify Subgoals
20. Use Coordinates
21. **Use Symmetry**

Strategy
Use Symmetry

Several types of geometric and numerical symmetry can occur in mathematical problems. Geometric symmetry involves a correspondence between points that preserves shape and size. For example, the actions of sliding, turning, and flipping lead to types of symmetry. Numerical symmetry occurs, for example, when numerical values can be interchanged and yet the results are equivalent. As an illustration, suppose that 5 coins are tossed. Knowing that 3 heads and 2 tails can occur in 10 ways, we can determine the number of ways that 2 heads and 3 tails can occur. We simply replace each "head" by "tail," and vice versa, using the fact that each arrangement of n heads and m tails ($n + m = 5$) corresponds to exactly one arrangement of m heads and n tails. Hence there are also 10 ways that 2 heads and 3 tails can occur.

Initial Problem

Houses A and B are to be connected to a television cable line l, at a transformer point P. Where should P be located so that the sum of the distances, $AP + PB$, is as small as possible?

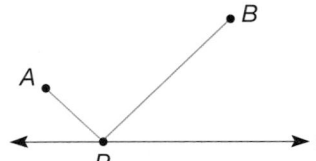

Clues

The Use Symmetry strategy may be appropriate when

- Geometry problems involve transformations.
- Interchanging values does not change the representation of the problem.
- Symmetry limits the number of cases that need to be considered.
- Pictures or algebraic expressions are symmetric.

A solution of the Initial Problem appears on page 847.

INTRODUCTION

NCTM Standards 2000
Geometry
Grades Pre-K–2
All students should recognize and
apply slides, flips, and turns.

In Chapter 12 we observed informally that many geometric figures have symmetry properties, such as rotation or reflection symmetry. In this chapter we give a precise description of symmetry in the plane in terms of functions or mappings between points. Mappings of points in the plane will be called transformations. Using transformations, we give precise meanings to the ideas of congruence of figures and similarity of figures. Finally, by studying congruence and similarity via transformations, we can derive many important geometric properties that can be used to solve geometry problems.

16.1   TRANSFORMATIONS

Each of the following pairs of triangles are congruent, which means they are the same shape and size. Since they are congruent, one triangle in each pair could be moved to lie exactly on top of the other. Trace $\triangle ABC$ and cut out your tracing. Lay your tracing on $\triangle ABC$ and move it to $\triangle A'B'C'$. Describe the movement in terms of a slide, flip, or turn. Repeat for $\triangle DEF$.

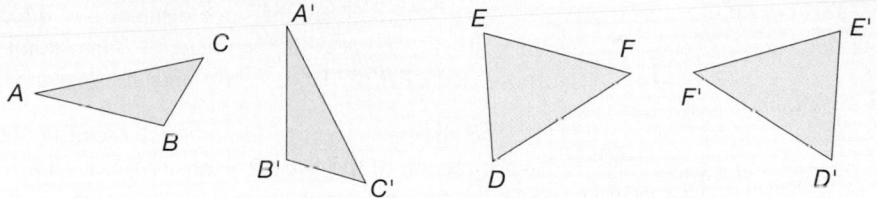

Reflection from Research
Learning about transformations
in a computer-based environment
significantly increases students'
two-dimensional visualization
(Dixon, 1995).

Isometries

In Chapter 12 we investigated symmetry properties of geometric figures by means of motions that make a figure coincide with itself. For example, the kite in Figure 16.1 has reflection symmetry, since there is a line, $\overleftrightarrow{BD}$, over which the kite can be folded to make the two halves match.

Notice that when we fold the kite over $\overleftrightarrow{BD}$, we are actually forming a one-to-one correspondence between the points of the kite. For example, points A and C correspond to each other, points along segments $\overline{AB}$ and $\overline{CB}$ correspond, and points along segments $\overline{AD}$ and $\overline{CD}$ correspond. In this chapter we will investigate correspondences between points of the plane. A **transformation** is a one-to-one correspondence between points in the plane such that each point P is associated with a unique point P', called the **image** of P.

Transformations that preserve the size and shape of geometric figures are called **isometries** (*iso* means "same" and *metry* means "measure") or **rigid motions.** In the remainder of this subsection, we'll study the various types of isometries.

TRANSLATIONS Consider the following transformation that acts like a "slide."

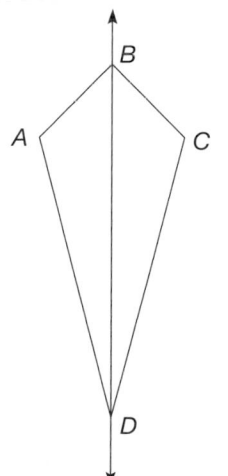

Figure 16.1

Example 16.1 Describe a transformation that will move △*ABC* of Figure 16.2 to coincide with △*A′B′C′*.

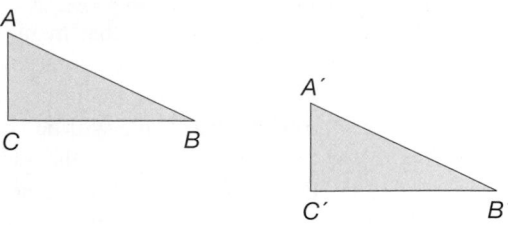

Figure 16.2

Solution Slide the triangle so that *A* moves to *A′* (Figure 16.3).

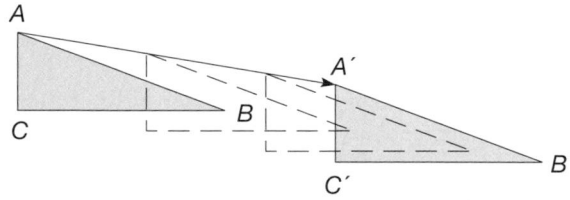

Figure 16.3

Since *B′* and *C′* are the same distance and direction from *B* and *C*, respectively, as *A′* is from *A*, point *B′* is the image of *B* and point *C′* is the image of *C*. Thus △*ABC* moves to △*A′B′C′*. Trace △*ABC* and slide it using the arrow from *A* to *A′*. ■

The sliding motion of Example 16.1 can be described by specifying the distance and direction of the slide. The arrow from *A* to *A′* in Figure 16.3 conveys this information. A transformation that "slides" each point in the plane in the same direction and for the same distance is called a translation. For the transformations considered in this section, we will assume that we can obtain the image of a polygon by connecting the images of the vertices of the original polygon, as we did in Example 16.1.

To give a precise definition to a translation or "sliding" transformation, we need the concept of directed line segment. Informally, a line segment $\overline{AB}$ can be directed in two ways: (1) pointing from *A* to *B* or (2) pointing from *B* to *A* (Figure 16.4). We denote the **directed line segment** from *A* to *B* as $\overrightarrow{AB}$. Two directed line segments are called **equivalent** if they are parallel, have the same length, and point in the same direction.

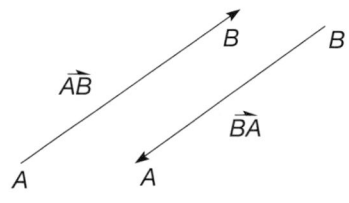

Figure 16.4

Reflection from Research
Translations are the easiest transformations for students to visualize when compared to reflections and rotations (Schultz & Austin, 1983).

DEFINITION

Translation

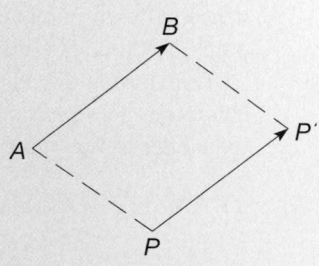

Suppose that *A* and *B* are points in the plane. The **translation** associated with directed line segment $\overrightarrow{AB}$, denoted $\boldsymbol{T_{AB}}$, is the transformation that maps each point *P* to the point *P′* such that $\overrightarrow{PP′}$ is equivalent to $\overrightarrow{AB}$.

Directed segment $\overrightarrow{PP'}$ is equivalent to $\overrightarrow{AB}$ so that $\overrightarrow{PP'} \parallel \overrightarrow{AB}$ and $PP' = AB$. Thus quadrilateral $PP'BA$ is a parallelogram, since it has a pair of opposite sides that are parallel and congruent. We can imagine that P is "slid" by the translation T_{AB} in the direction from A to B for a distance equal to AB.

Spotlight on Technology Translations can be better understood by using the Chapter 16 eManipulative activity, *Translation Transformations*. Select several different blocks and group them together to create a nonsymmetrical object. The translation of your object will automatically be constructed. After moving the object and manipulating the directed line segment, answer the following question: "Does the direction or length of the directed line segment affect the size of the image?" Repeat similar investigations in *Rotation Transformations* and *Reflection Transformations* as you study those transformations over the the next few pages.

ROTATIONS An isometry that corresponds to turning the plane around a fixed point is described next.

Example 16.2 Describe a transformation that will move $\triangle ABC$ of Figure 16.5 to coincide with $\triangle A'B'C'$.

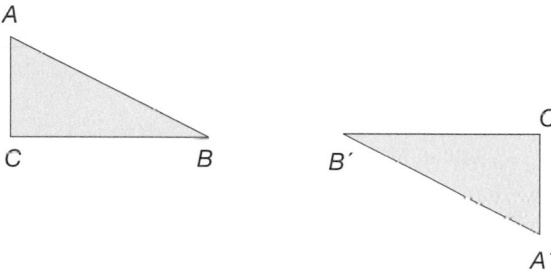

Figure 16.5

Reflection from Research
The dynamic presentation of rotations is more appropriate than the static presentation for young children. Students were more successful performing rotations after being taught about them using motion than not using motion (Moyer, 1978).

Solution We can turn $\triangle ABC$ $180°$ around point P, the midpoint of segment $\overline{BB'}$, to coincide with $\triangle A'B'C'$ (Figure 16.6).

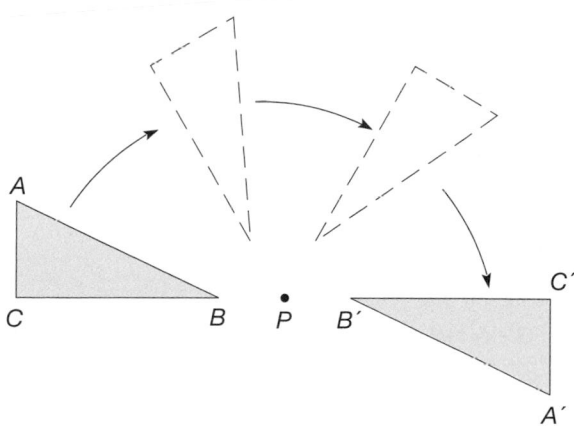

Figure 16.6

Trace $\triangle ABC$, and turn your tracing around point P to verify this. ■

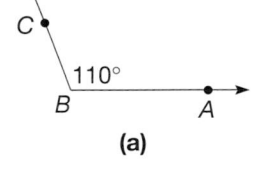

Figure 16.7

A transformation that corresponds to a turning motion as in Example 16.2 is called a rotation. To define a rotation, we need the concept of directed angle. Angle ∠*ABC* is said to be a **directed angle** if it satisfies the following properties:

1. If $m(\angle ABC) = 0$, then the measure of the directed angle is 0°.
2. If ∠*ABC* is a straight angle, then the measure of the directed angle is 180°.
3. See Figure 16.7.
   a. Let ray $\overrightarrow{BA}$ be turned around point *B* through the smallest possible angle so that the image of ray $\overrightarrow{BA}$ coincides with ray $\overrightarrow{BC}$.
   b. If the direction of the turn is *counterclockwise*, the **measure of the directed angle** is the *positive* number $m(\angle ABC)$. If the direction is *clockwise*, the measure is the *negative number* $-m(\angle ABC)$. We denote the directed angle ∠*ABC* by ∡*ABC*.

For directed angle ∡*ABC*, ray $\overrightarrow{BA}$ is called the **initial side** and ray $\overrightarrow{BC}$ is called the **terminal side.** In directed angle ∡*ABC*, the initial side is given by the ray whose vertex is the vertex of the angle, here *B*, and that contains the point listed first in the name of the angle, here *A*. For example, in directed angle ∡*CBA* the initial side is $\overrightarrow{BC}$. Notice that the measure of directed angle ∡*CBA* is the *opposite* of the measure of directed angle ∡*ABC*, since the initial side of directed angle ∡*CBA* is ray $\overrightarrow{BC}$, while the initial side of directed angle ∡*ABC* is $\overrightarrow{BA}$. Example 16.3 gives several examples of directed angles.

Example 16.3 Find the measure of each of the directed angles ∡*ABC* in Figure 16.8.

Solution

a. The measure of directed angle ∡*ABC* is 110°, since initial side $\overrightarrow{BA}$ can be turned counterclockwise through 110° around point *B* to coincide with terminal side $\overrightarrow{BC}$.
b. The measure of directed angle ∡*ABC* is −75°, since initial side $\overrightarrow{BA}$ can be turned clockwise through 75° to coincide with terminal side $\overrightarrow{BC}$.
c. The measure of directed angle ∡*ABC* is 180°, since ∠*ABC* is a straight angle.
d. The measure of directed angle ∡*ABC* is 0°, since $m(\angle ABC) = 0°$. ■

We can now define a rotation. In Section 16.2 we prove that rotations are isometries.

(a)

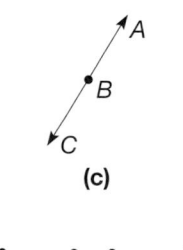

(b)

(c)

(d)

Figure 16.8

DEFINITION

Rotation

The **rotation** with center *O* and angle with measure *a*, denoted $\boldsymbol{R}_{O,a}$, is the transformation that maps each point *P* other than *O* to the point *P'* such that

1. the measure of directed angle ∡*POP'* is *a*, and
2. $OP' = OP$.

Point *O* is mapped to itself by $R_{O,a}$.

NOTE: If a is positive, $R_{O,a}$ is counterclockwise, and if a is negative, $R_{O,a}$ is clockwise. Intuitively, point P is "turned" by $R_{O,a}$ around the center, O, through a directed angle of measure a to point P'.

REFLECTIONS Another isometry corresponds to flipping the plane over a fixed line.

Example 16.4   Describe a transformation that will move $\triangle ABC$ of Figure 16.9 to coincide with $\triangle A'B'C'$.

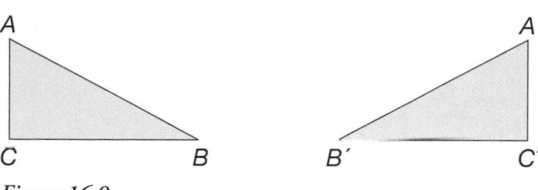

Figure 16.9

Solution Flip $\triangle ABC$ over the perpendicular bisector of segment $\overline{AA'}$ (Figure 16.10).

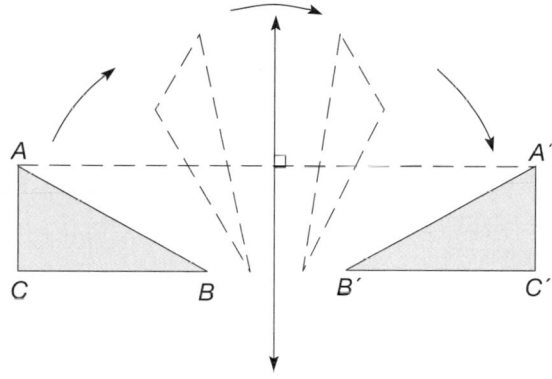

Figure 16.10

Then point A moves to point A', point B to B', and C to C'. Hence $\triangle ABC$ moves to $\triangle A'B'C'$. Trace Figure 16.9, and fold your tracing to verify this.   ■

A transformation that "flips" the plane over a fixed line is called a reflection.

DEFINITION

Reflection

Suppose that l is a line in the plane. The **reflection** in line l, denoted M_l, is the transformation that maps points as follows:

1. Each point P not on line l is mapped to the point P' such that l is the perpendicular bisector of segment $\overline{PP'}$.
2. Each point Q on line l is mapped to itself.

LESSON 4

HANDS ON

Slides, Flips, and Turns

▶ **Explore**

A plane figure can be moved in different ways.

a → b
slide

a | b
flip

a → b
turn

Quick Review

Tell if each figure is congruent to the figure at the right. Write *yes* or *no*.

1. ▢ 2. ▢
3. ▢ 4. ▢
5. ▢

VOCABULARY
slide   flip   turn

MATERIALS
pattern blocks, triangle dot paper

Activity

Use pattern blocks to slide, flip, and turn figures.

• Choose a pattern block. Show different ways to move the block.

STEP 1
Trace the block on triangle dot paper.

STEP 3
Flip the block and trace it. Label the drawing "flip."   **flip**

STEP 2
Slide the block and trace it. Label the drawing "slide."   **slide**

STEP 4
Turn the block and trace it. Label the drawing "turn."   **turn**

• Choose a different pattern block. Repeat the steps above.

Talk About It

• Look at your drawings. Does a slide ever look like a flip? Does a flip ever look like a turn?

• **REASONING** Does the size or shape of the block change when you slide, flip, or turn it? Explain.

338

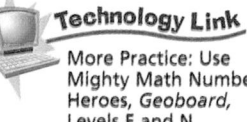

Technology Link
More Practice: Use Mighty Math Number Heroes, Geoboard, Levels F and N.

"Slides, Flips, and Turns" from HARCOURT MATH, Grade 3, copyright © 2002 by Harcourt, Inc., reprinted by permission of the publisher.

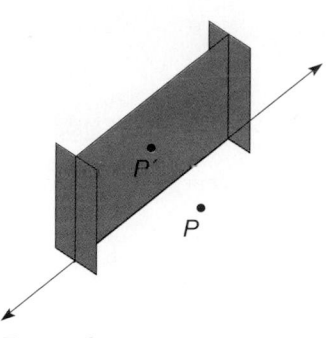

One can envision the effect of the reflection in line *l* by imagining a mirror in line *l* perpendicular to the plane. Then points on either side of *l* are mapped to the other side of *l*, and points on *l* remain fixed. A Mira can be used to find reflection images easily (Figure 16.11). We prove that reflections are isometries in the next section.

Figure 16.11

GLIDE REFLECTIONS Next we define a transformation that is a combination of a translation and a reflection, called a glide reflection.

Example 16.5   Is there a translation that will move $\triangle ABC$ of Figure 16.12 to coincide with $\triangle A'B'C'$? What about a rotation? a reflection?

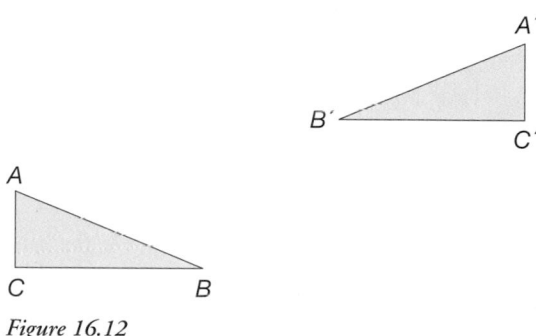

Figure 16.12

Solution No single transformation that we have studied thus far will suffice. Use tracings to convince yourself. However, with a combination of a translation and a reflection, we can move $\triangle ABC$ to $\triangle A'B'C'$ (Figure 16.13).

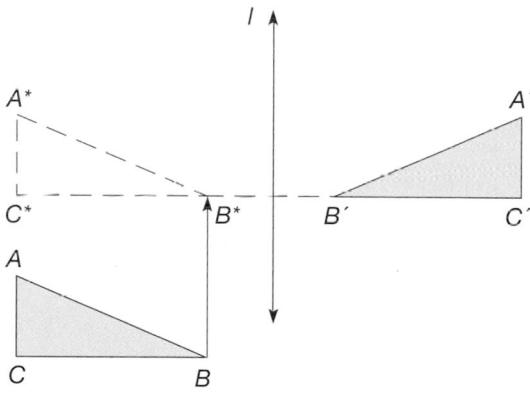

Figure 16.13

First, apply the translation T_{BB*} to move $\triangle ABC$ to $\triangle A*B*C*$, a triangle that can be reflected onto $\triangle A'B'C'$. Then reflect $\triangle A*B*C*$ in line *l* onto $\triangle A'B'C'$. Notice that directed line segment $\overrightarrow{BB*}$ is parallel to the reflection line *l*.   ■

A transformation formed by combining a translation and a reflection over a line parallel to the directed line segment of the translation, as in Example 16.5, is called a glide reflection.

DEFINITION

Glide Reflection

Suppose that A and B are different points in the plane and that line l is parallel to directed line segment $\overrightarrow{AB}$. The combination of the translation T_{AB} followed by the reflection M_l is called the **glide reflection** determined by $\overrightarrow{AB}$ and **glide axis** l. That is, P is first mapped to P^* by T_{AB}. Then P^* is mapped to P' by M_l. The combination of T_{AB} followed by M_l maps P to P'.

It can be shown that as long as $l \parallel \overrightarrow{AB}$, the glide reflection image can be found by translating first, then reflecting, or vice versa. Example 16.6 shows the effect of a glide reflection on a triangle.

Example 16.6 In Figure 16.14(a), find the image of $\triangle PQR$ under the glide reflection T_{AB} followed by M_l.

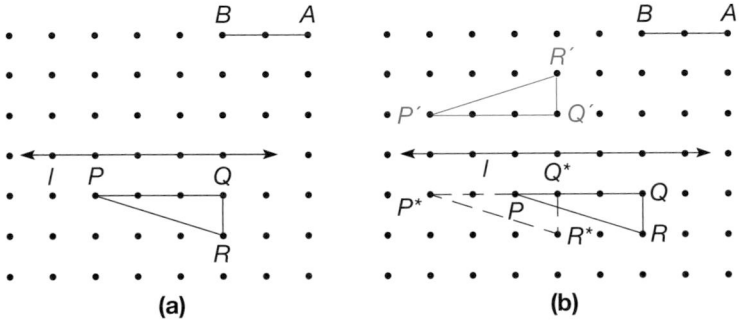

Figure 16.14

Solution We observe that the translation T_{AB} maps each point two units to the left [Figure 16.14(b)]. That is, T_{AB} maps $\triangle PQR$ to $\triangle P^*Q^*R^*$. The reflection M_l reflects $\triangle P^*Q^*R^*$ across line l to $\triangle P'Q'R'$. Equivalently, we can reflect $\triangle PQR$ across line l, then slide its image to the left. In each case, the image of $\triangle PQR$ is $\triangle P'Q'R'$. Since glide reflections are combinations of two isometries, a translation and a reflection, they, too, are isometries. ■

In Example 16.6 observe that $\triangle PQR$ was translated, then reflected across line l to $\triangle P'Q'R'$. Thus the "orientation" of $\triangle P'Q'R'$ is opposite that of $\triangle PQR$. In Figure 16.15, $\triangle PQR$ is said to have **clockwise orientation,** since tracing the triangle from P to Q to R is a clockwise tracing. Similarly, $\triangle P'Q'R'$ in Figure 16.15 has **counterclockwise orientation,** since a tracing from P' to Q' to R' is counterclockwise.

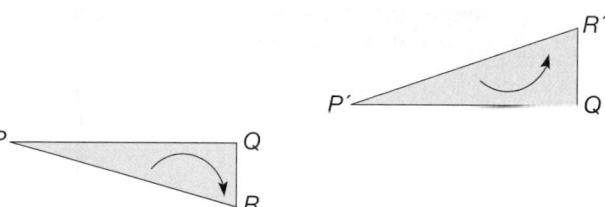

Figure 16.15

From the examples in this section, we can observe that translations and rotations preserve orientation, whereas reflections and glide reflections reverse orientation.

In elementary school, translations, rotations, reflections, and glide reflections are frequently called "slides," "turns," "flips," and "slide flips," respectively. Next, we will see how to apply these transformations to analyze symmetry patterns in the plane.

NCTM Standards 2000
Geometry
Grades Pre-K–2
All students should recognize and create shapes that have symmetry.

Symmetry

Consider a tessellation of the plane with parallelograms (Figure 16.16).

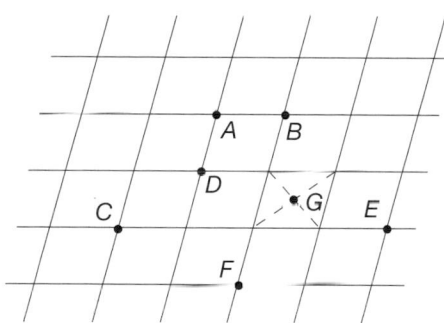

Figure 16.16

Reflection from Research
Car hubcaps or toys such as the Spirograph can be used to help students investigate rotational symmetry (Flores, 1992).

We can identify several translations that map the tessellation onto itself. For example, the translations T_{AB}, T_{CD}, and T_{EF} all map the tessellation onto itself. To see that T_{AB} maps the tessellation onto itself, make a tracing of the tessellation, place the tracing on top of the tessellation, and move the tracing according to the translation T_{AB}. The tracing will match up with the original tessellation. (Remember that the tessellation fills the plane.) A figure has **translation symmetry** if there is a translation that maps the figure onto itself. Every tessellation of the plane with parallelograms like the one in Figure 16.16 has translation symmetry.

For the tessellation in Figure 16.16, there are several rotations, through less than 360°, that map the tessellation onto itself. For example, the rotations $R_{A,180}$ and $R_{G,180}$ map the tessellation onto itself. Note that G is the intersection of the diagonals of a parallelogram. (Use your tracing paper to see that these rotations map the tessellation onto itself.) A figure has **rotation symmetry** if there is a rotation through an angle greater than 0° and less than 360° that maps the figure onto itself.

In Figure 16.17, a tessellation with isosceles triangles and trapezoids is pictured. Again, imagine that the tessellation fills the plane. In Figure 16.17, reflection M_l maps the tessellation onto itself, as does M_m. A figure has **reflection symmetry** if there is a reflection that maps the figure onto itself. The tessellation in Figure 16.17 has translation symmetry and reflection symmetry, but not rotation symmetry.

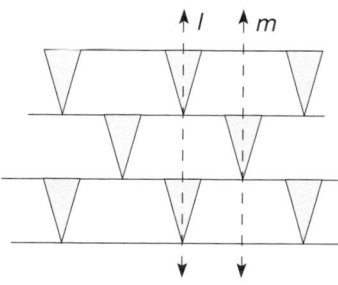

Figure 16.17

Figure 16.18 illustrates part of a tessellation of the plane that has translation, rotation, and reflection symmetry.

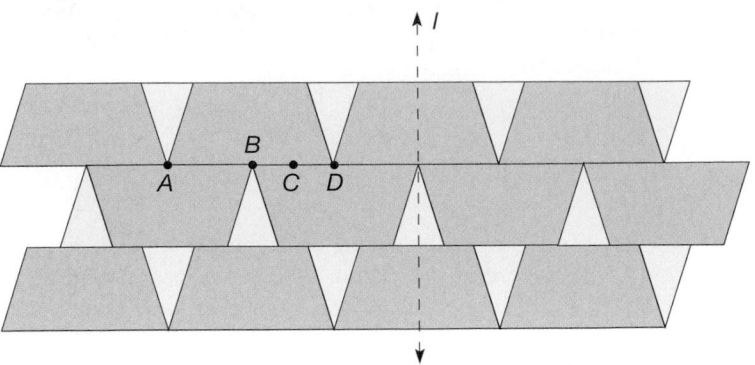

Figure 16.18

For example, $R_{C,180}$ is a rotation that maps the tessellation onto itself, where point C is the midpoint of segment $\overline{BD}$. (You can use a tracing of the tessellation to check this.) The translation T_{AD} can be used to show that the tessellation has translation symmetry, while the reflection M_l can be used to show reflection symmetry. This tessellation also has glide reflection symmetry. For example, consider the glide reflection formed by T_{AB} followed by M_{AB}. This glide reflection maps the tessellation onto itself. A figure has **glide reflection symmetry** if there is a glide reflection that maps the figure onto itself. (Notice that, in this case, neither the translation T_{AB}, nor the reflection M_{AB} alone, maps the tessellation to itself.)

Symmetrical figures appear in nature, art, and design. Interestingly, all symmetrical patterns in the plane can be analyzed using translations, rotations, reflections, and glide reflections.

Making Escher-Type Patterns

The artist M. C. Escher used tessellations and transformations to make intriguing patterns that fill the plane. Figure 16.19 shows how to produce such a pattern. Side $\overline{AB}$ of the square $ABDC$ [Figure 16.19(a)] is altered to form the outline of a cat's head [Figure 16.19(b)]. Then the curved side from A' to B' is translated so that A' is mapped to C' and B' is mapped to D'. Thus the curve connecting C' to D' is the same size and shape as the curve connecting A' to B'. All other points remain fixed. The resulting shape will tessellate the plane [Figure 16.19(c)]. Using translations, tessellations of the plane with parallelograms can be altered to make Escher-type patterns.

NCTM Standards 2000
Geometry
Grades 6–8
All students should recognize and apply geometric ideas and relationships in areas outside the mathematics classroom, such as art, science, and everyday life.

(a)

(b)   **(c)**

Figure 16.19

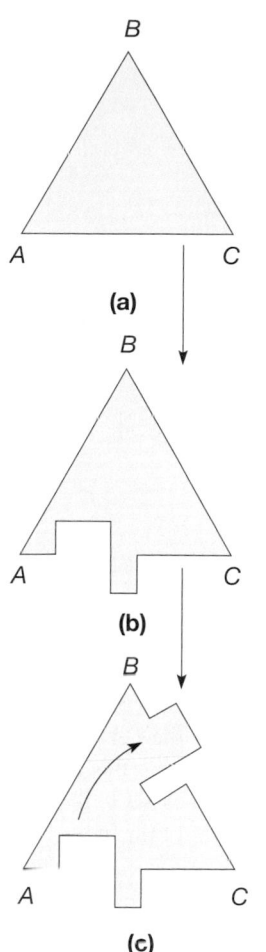

(a)

(b)

(c)

Figure 16.20

Rotations can also be used to make Escher-type drawings. Figure 16.20 shows a triangle that has been altered by rotation to produce an Escher-type pattern. Side $\overline{AC}$ of $\triangle ABC$ [Figure 16.20(a)] is altered arbitrarily, provided that points A and C are not moved [Figure 16.20(b)]. Then, using point C as the center of a rotation, altered side $\overline{AC}$ is rotated so that A is rotated to B [Figure 16.20(c)]. The result is an alteration of side $\overline{BC}$. The shape in Figure 16.20(c) will tessellate the plane as shown in Figure 16.20(d). Other techniques for making Escher-type patterns appear in the Exercise/Problem Sets. Many Escher-type patterns are tessellations of the plane having a variety of types of symmetry. For example, the tessellation in Figure 16.19(c) has translation and reflection symmetry, while the tessellation in Figure 16.20(d) has translation and rotation symmetry.

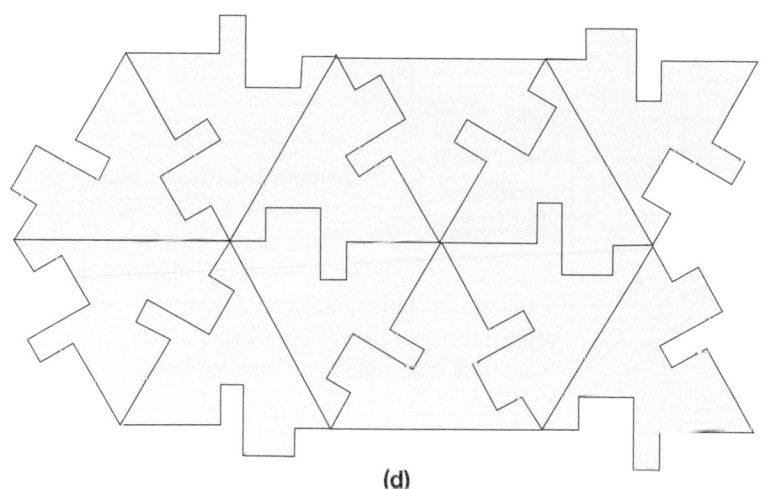

(d)

Similitudes

Thus far we have investigated transformations that preserve size and shape, namely isometries. Next we investigate transformations that preserve shape but not necessarily size.

SIZE TRANSFORMATIONS First we consider transformations that can change size.

Example 16.7 In Figure 16.21, find the image of $\triangle ABC$ under each of the following transformations.

a. Each point P is mapped to the point P' on the ray $\overrightarrow{OP}$ such that $OP' = 2 \cdot OP$. That is, OP' is twice the distance OP.

b. Each point P is mapped to the point P'' on the ray $\overrightarrow{OP}$ such that $OP'' = \frac{1}{2} \cdot OP$.

Solution

a. To locate A', imagine ray $\overrightarrow{OA}$ [Figure 16.22(a)]. Then A' is the point on $\overrightarrow{OA}$ so that $OA' = 2 \cdot OA$. Locate B' and C' similarly. The image of $\triangle ABC$ is $\triangle A'B'C'$.

b. To locate A'', imagine ray $\overrightarrow{OA}$ [Figure 16.22(b)]. Locate A'' on $\overrightarrow{OA}$ so that $OA'' = \frac{1}{2} OA$. Locate B'' and C'' similarly. The image of $\triangle ABC$ is $\triangle A''B''C''$.

Figure 16.21

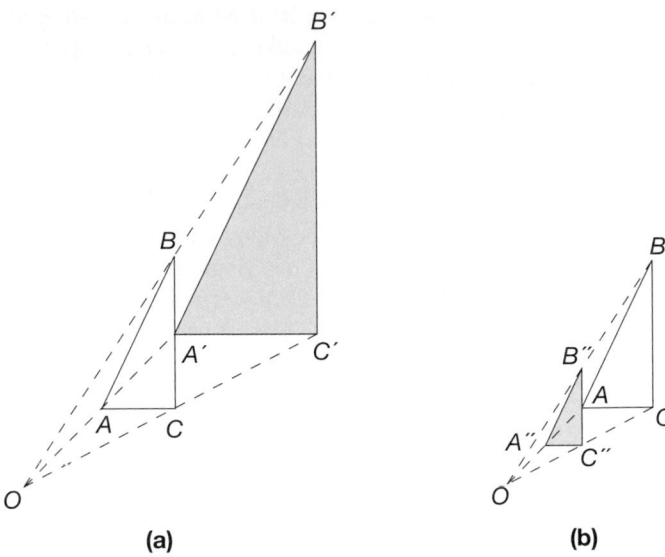

(a)   **(b)**

Figure 16.22   ■

Spotlight on Technology Being able to visualize how the location of the point O affects the image in a size transformation is sometimes difficult to do. The Geometer's Sketchpad® webmodule activity, *Size Transformation*, allows you to dynamically move the center of the size transformation and see the effects on the resulting image. After using this activity, answer the question, "Does moving the center of a size transformation closer to the original figure make the image smaller, larger, or have no effect on the size of the image?"

Transformations such as those in Example 16.7 that uniformly stretch or shrink geometric shapes are called size transformations.

DEFINITION

Size Transformations

The **size transformation** $S_{O,k}$, with **center** O and **scale factor** k (where k is a positive real number), is the transformation that maps each point P to the point P' such that P' is on ray $\overrightarrow{OP}$, and $OP' = k \cdot OP$ where

a. if $k > 1$,
    then P is between O and P', or

b. if $k < 1$,
    then P' is between O and P.

(NOTE: Size transformations are also called **magnifications, dilations,** and **dilitations.**)

Notice that points O, P, and P' are collinear. If $k > 1$, a size transformation enlarges shapes and if $k < 1$, a size transformation shrinks shapes. If $k = 1$, then

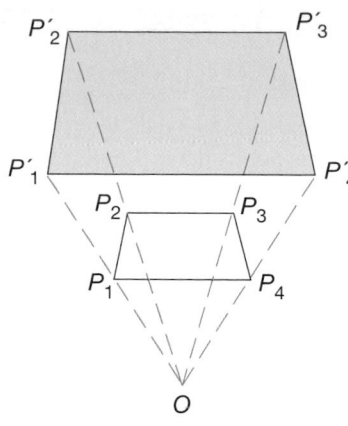

Figure 16.23

$P' = P$ (i.e., each point is mapped to itself). Figure 16.23 illustrates the effect of a size transformation on a quadrilateral, with $k > 1$. A size transformation maps a polygon $\mathcal{P}$ to a polygon $\mathcal{P}'$ having the same shape, as illustrated in Figure 16.23. Also, we can show that a size transformation maps a triangle to a similar triangle.

SIMILITUDES Next we consider the combination of a size transformation followed by an isometry. Figure 16.24 illustrates this is a special case.

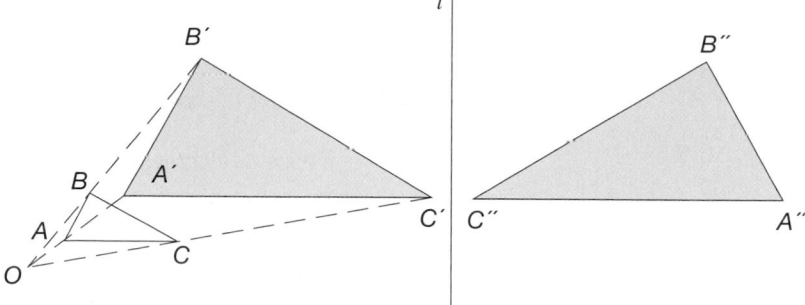

Figure 16.24

The size transformation $S_{O,k}$ maps $\triangle ABC$ to $\triangle A'B'C'$. By properties of size transformations, corresponding angles of $\triangle A'B'C'$ and $\triangle ABC$ are congruent, and corresponding sides of the two triangles are proportional. Thus $\triangle A'B'C' \sim \triangle ABC$. The reflection, M_l, maps $\triangle A'B'C'$ to $\triangle A''B''C''$. Since M_l is an isometry, we know that $\triangle A'B'C' \cong \triangle A''B''C''$. Therefore, corresponding angles of $\triangle A'B'C'$ and $\triangle A''B''C''$ are congruent, as are corresponding sides. Combining our results, we see that corresponding angles of $\triangle ABC$ and $\triangle A''B''C''$ are congruent and that corresponding sides are proportional. Hence $S_{O,k}$ followed by M_l maps $\triangle ABC$ to a triangle similar to it, namely $\triangle A''B''C''$.

Generalizing the foregoing discussion, it can be shown that given similar triangles $\triangle ABC$ and $\triangle A''B''C''$, there exists a combination of a size transformation followed by an isometry that maps $\triangle ABC$ to $\triangle A''B''C''$.

⬡ DEFINITION

Similitude

A **similitude** is a combination of a size transformation followed by an isometry.

In Figure 16.24 we also could have first flipped $\triangle ABC$ across l and then magnified it to $\triangle A''B''C''$. In general, it can be shown that any similitude also can be expressed as the combination of an isometry followed by a size transformation.

MATHEMATICAL MORSEL

Two symmetrical patterns are considered to be equivalent if they have exactly the same types of symmetry. As recently as 1891, it was finally proved that there are only 17 inequivalent symmetry patterns in the plane. However, the Moors, who lived in Spain from the eighth to the fifteenth centuries, were aware of all 17 types of symmetry patterns. Examples of the patterns, such as the one shown here, were used to decorate the Alhambra, a Moorish fortress in Granada.

EXERCISES

1. In each part, draw the image of the quadrilateral under the translation T_{AB}. It may be helpful to use the Chapter 13 eManipulative activity, *Geoboard*, to determine the images.

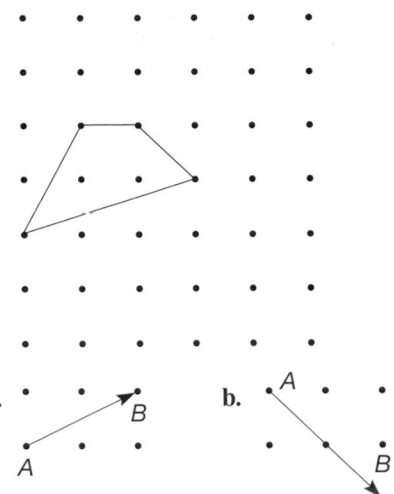

2. Draw $\overline{PQ}$ and $\overline{AB}$. With tracing paper on top, trace segment $\overline{PQ}$ and point A. Slide the tracing paper (without turning) so that the traced point A moves to point B. Make impressions of points P and Q by pushing your pencil tip down. Label these impressions P' and Q'. Draw segment $\overline{P'Q'}$, the translation image of segment $\overline{PQ}$.

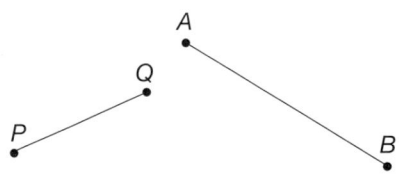

3. Use the following graph to answer the questions in parts (a), (b), and (c).

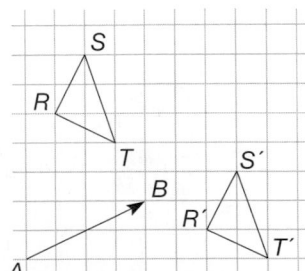

   a. On graph paper, draw three other directed line segments that describe T_{AB}. (*Hint:* The directed line segments must have the same length and direction.)

   b. Draw three directed line segments that describe a translation that moves points down 3 units and right 4 units.

   c. Draw two directed line segments that describe the translation that maps $\triangle RST$ to $\triangle R'S'T'$.

4. According to the definition of a translation, the quadrilateral $PP'BA$ is a parallelogram where P' is the image of P under T_{AB}. Use this to construct the image, P', with a compass and straightedge. (*Hint:* Construct the line parallel to $\overline{AB}$ through P.)

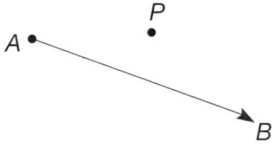

5. Find the measure of each of the following directed angles $\measuredangle ABC$.

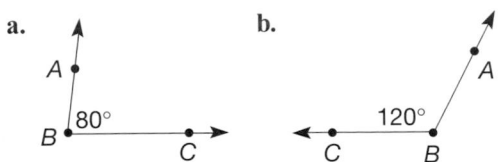

6. A protractor and tracing paper may be used to find rotation images. For example, find the image of point A under a rotation of $-50°$ about center O by following these four steps.

   1. Draw ray $\overrightarrow{OA}$.
   2. With ray $\overrightarrow{OA}$ as the initial side, use your protractor to draw a directed angle $\measuredangle AOB$ of $-50°$.
   3. Place tracing paper on top and trace point A.
   4. Keep point O fixed and turn the tracing paper until point A is on ray $\overrightarrow{OB}$. Make an imprint with your pencil for A'.

7. Using a protractor and tracing paper, find the rotation image of point A about point O for the following directed angles.

   a. $75°$ b. $-90°$ c. $-130°$ d. $180°$

8. Find the rotation image of $\overline{AB}$ about point O for each of the following directed angles.

   a. $-90°$

   b. $90°$

   c. $180°$

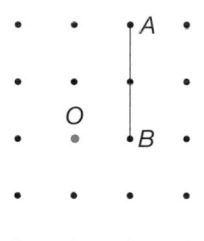

9. Give the coordinates of P', the point that is the image of P under $R_{O,90°}$. (*Hint:* Think of rotating $\triangle OPQ$.)

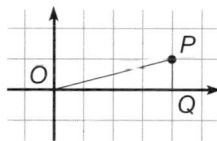

10. Give the coordinates of the images of the following points under $R_{O,90°}$.

   a. $(2, 3)$ **b.** $(-1, 3)$ **c.** $(-1, -4)$

   d. $(-4, -2)$ **e.** $(2, -4)$ **f.** (x, y)

11. Give the coordinates of the images of the following points under $R_{O,180°}$.

   a. $(3, -1)$ **b.** $(-6, -3)$

   c. $(-4, 2)$ **d.** (x, y)

12. The rotation image of a point or figure may be found using a compass and straightedge. The procedure is similar to that with a protractor except that the directed angle is constructed rather than measured with a protractor. Also recall that $OA = OA'$. Construct the rotation image of A about point O for the following directed angles.

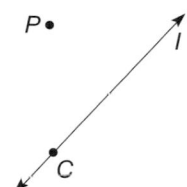

   a. $-90°$ **b.** $45°$ **c.** $180°$

13. The reflection image of point P can be found using tracing paper as follows.

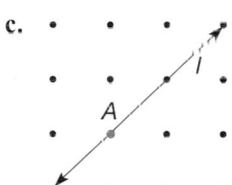

   1. Choose a point C on line l.
   2. Trace line l and points P and C on your tracing paper.
   3. Flip your tracing paper over, matching line l and point C.
   4. Make an impression for P'.

   Using this procedure, find P'.

14. Find the reflection of point A in each of the given lines.

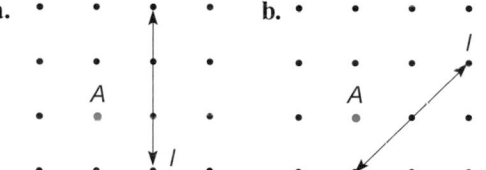

15. **a.** Let M_x be the reflection in the x-axis. Graph the triangle with vertices $A(1, 2)$, $B(3, 5)$, and $C(6, 1)$ and its image under the reflection M_x.

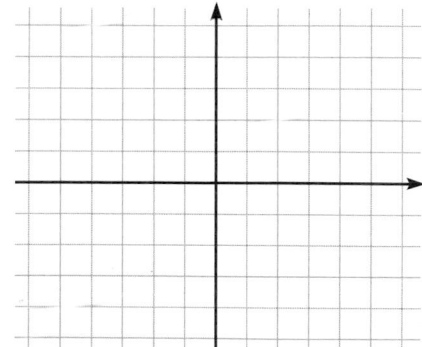

   b. What are the coordinates of the images of points A, B, and C under the reflection M_x?

   c. If point P has coordinates (a, b), what are the coordinates of its image under M_x?

16. The reflection image of point A in line l can be constructed with a compass and straightedge. Recall that line l is the perpendicular bisector of $\overline{AA'}$. If point P is the intersection of $\overline{AA'}$ and l, then $\overline{AA'} \perp l$ and $AP = PA'$. Using a compass and straightedge, find A'.

17. **a.** Graph $\triangle ABC$ with $A(-2, 1)$, $B(0, 3)$, and $C(3, 2)$ and its image under this glide reflection: T_{PQ} followed by M_x.

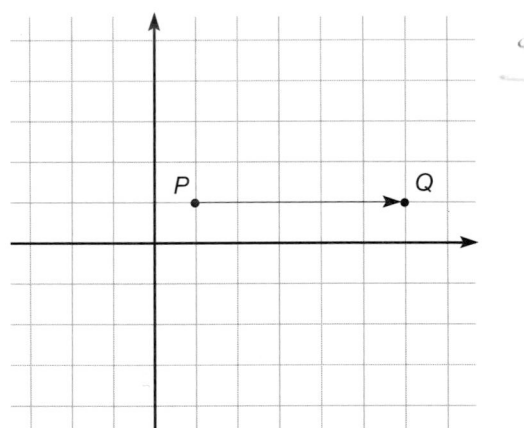

   b. What are the coordinates of the images of points A, B, and C under this glide reflection: T_{PQ} followed by M_x?

   c. If point R has coordinates (a, b), what are the coordinates of its image under this glide reflection: T_{PQ} followed by M_x?

18. Using a compass and straightedge, construct the glide reflection image of $\overline{AB}$ under the glide reflection: T_{XY} followed by M_l.

19. Which of the following triangles have the same orientation as the given triangle? Explain.

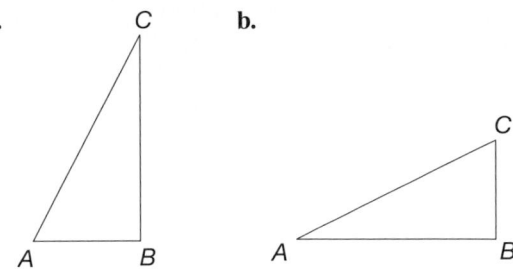

20. Use dot paper, a ruler, possibly a protractor, and the Chapter 13 eManipulative activity, *Geoboard*, if necessary, to draw the image of quadrilateral $ABCD$ under the transformation specified in each part.

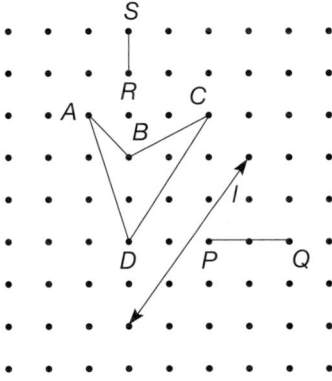

   a. T_{RS} **b.** $R_{B,90°}$ **c.** M_l
   d. M_l followed by T_{PQ}

21. Identify the types of symmetry present in the following patterns. Assume that they are infinite patterns.

a.

b.

c.

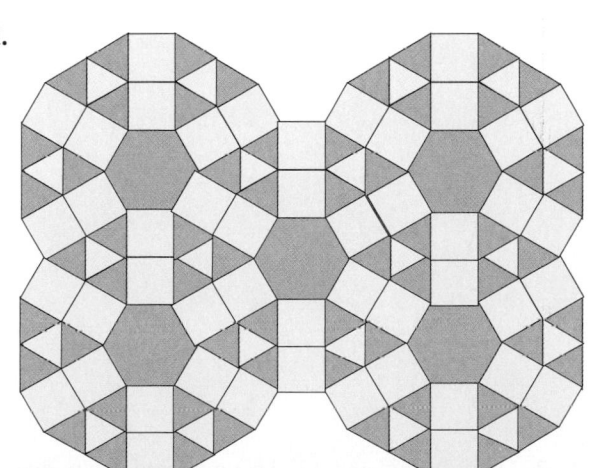

d.

22. Trace a translation of the curve to the opposite side of the parallelogram. Verify that the resulting shape will tessellate the plane.

a.

b.

c.

d.

23. On the square lattice portions here, find $S_{O,2}(P)$.

a. ·   ·   ·   ·

·   ·   ·   ·

O P
·   ·   ·   ·

·   ·   ·   ·

b. ·   ·   ·   ·   ·
        O

·   ·   ·   ·   ·
                P
·   ·   ·   ·   ·

·   ·   ·   ·   ·

c. O
·   ·   ·   ·   ·   ·
        P
·   ·   ·   ·   ·   ·

·   ·   ·   ·   ·   ·

·   ·   ·   ·   ·   ·

24. Use tracing paper and a ruler to draw the image of each figure under the given size transformation.

a. $S_{P,3}$

b. $S_{P,2/3}$

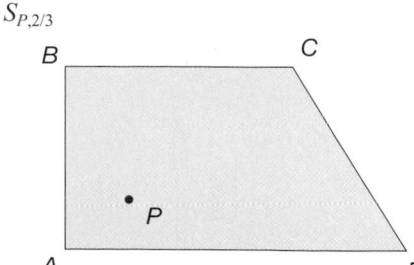

PROBLEMS

25. Give an example of a transformation of each of the following types that maps A to A'.

  a. Translation

  b. Rotation

  c. Reflection

  d. Glide reflection

26. Give an example, if possible, of a transformation of each of the following types that maps $\overline{AB}$ to $\overline{A'B'}$.

  a. Translation

  b. Rotation

  c. Reflection

  d. Glide reflection

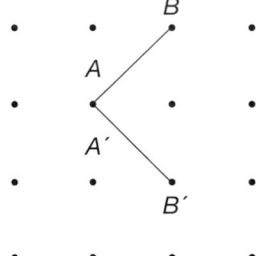

27. For each given transformation, plot $\triangle ABC$, with $A(2, 3)$, $B(-1, 4)$, and $C(-2, 1)$, and its image. Decide whether the transformation is a translation, rotation, reflection, glide reflection, or none of these. The notation $F(x, y)$ denotes the image of the point (x, y) under transformation F.

  a. $F(x, y) = (y, x)$

  b. $F(x, y) = (y, -x)$

  c. $F(x, y) = (x + 2, y - 3)$

28. Using the Chapter 16 eManipulative activity, *Isometries*, perform a translation of any combination of pattern blocks that you would like. By manipulating the directed line segment, answer the following question: When constructing translations, does it matter where you draw the directed line segment?

Section 16.1   EXERCISE / PROBLEM SET B

EXERCISES

1. In each part, draw the image of the quadrilateral under the translation T_{AB}. It may be helpful to use the Chapter 13 eManipulative activity, *Geoboard*, to determine the images.

  a.

  b.

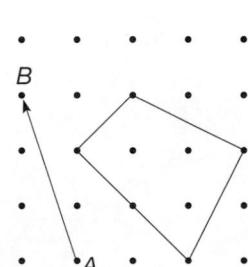

2. Draw $\triangle EFG$ and $\overline{XY}$. Using tracing paper, draw the image of $\triangle EFG$ under translation T_{XY}.

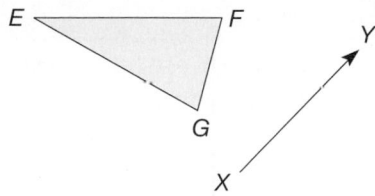

3. a. Find the coordinates of the images of the vertices of quadrilateral $ABCD$ under T_{OX}.

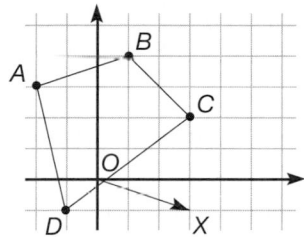

b. Given a point (x, y), what are the coordinates of its image under T_{OX}?

4. Using a compass and straightedge, construct the image of $\triangle ABC$ under the translation that maps R to S.

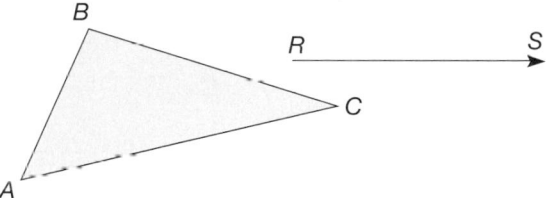

5. Find the measure of each of the following directed angles $\angle ABC$.

a.

b.

6. Given $\overline{AB}$ and point O, use a protractor and tracing paper to find the image of $\overrightarrow{AB}$ under $R_{O,a}$ for each of the following values of a.

a. $60°$ **b.** $-90°$ **c.** $180°$

7. Use a protractor and ruler to find the $90°$ clockwise rotation of $\triangle ABC$ about point O.

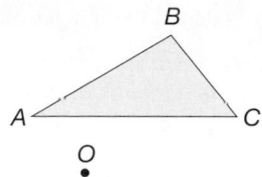

8. Find the $90°$ clockwise rotation about the point O for each of the following quadrilaterals. It may be helpful to use the Chapter 13 eManipulative activity, *Geoboard*, to determine the images.

a.

b.

c.

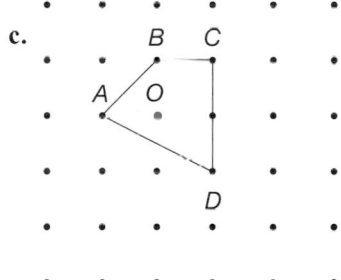

9. Draw the image of $\triangle ABC$ under $R_{O,-90°}$. What are the coordinates of A', B', and C'?

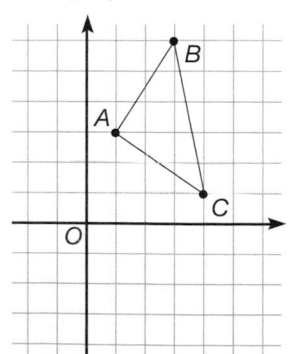

10. Give the coordinates of the images of the following points under $R_{O,-90°}$.

   a. $(1, 5)$ **b.** $(-1, 3)$ **c.** $(-2, -4)$

   d. $(-3, -1)$ **e.** $(5, -2)$ **f.** (x, y)

11. We could express the results of $R_{O,90°}$ applied to $(4, 2)$ in the following way:

$$(4, 2) \xrightarrow{R_{o,90°}} (-2, 4)$$

   Complete the following statements.

   a. $(x, y) \xrightarrow{R_{o,90°}} (?, ?)$

   b. $(x, y) \xrightarrow{R_{o,-90°}} (?, ?)$

   c. $(x, y) \xrightarrow{R_{o,180°}} (?, ?)$

12. Using a compass and straightedge, construct the 90° clockwise rotation of $\triangle ABC$ about point O.

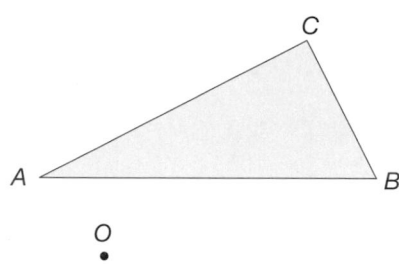

13. Using tracing paper, find the image of $\overline{AB}$ under M_l for the following segments.

   a.

   b.

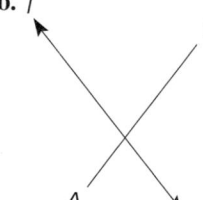

14. Find the reflection images of point P, segment $\overline{RS}$, and $\triangle ABC$ in line l.

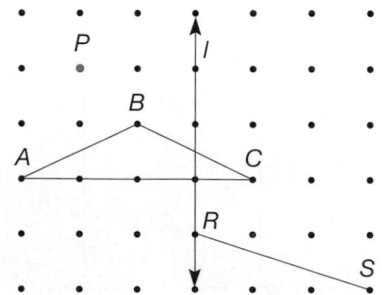

15. **a.** Graph $\triangle ABC$ with $A(2, 1)$, $B(3, -5)$, and $C(6, 3)$ and its image under M_y, the reflection in the y-axis.

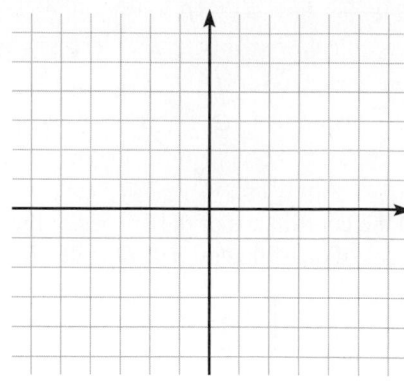

   b. What are the coordinates of the points A, B, and C under M_y?

   c. If point P has coordinates (a, b), what are the coordinates of its image under M_y?

16. Using a compass and straightedge, construct the reflection of the following figures in line l.

   a.

   b.

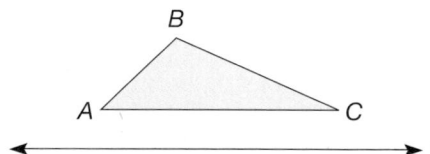

17. **a.** Graph $\triangle ABC$, with $A(1, 1)$, $B(3, 1)$, and $C(4, 6)$, and its image under this glide reflection: T_{XY} followed by M_l where l is the line $y = x$

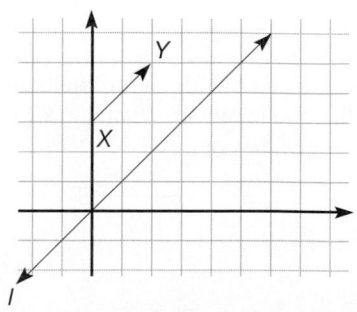

   b. What are the coordinates of the images of A, B, and C?

c. If the point P has coordinates (x, y), what are the coordinates of its image under this glide reflection: T_{XY} followed by M_l?

18. Using a compass and straightedge, construct the glide reflection image of $\overline{AB}$ under the glide reflection: T_{YX} followed by M_l.

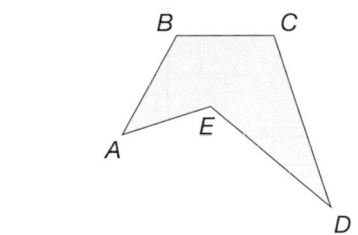

19. Which of the following polygons has the same orientation as the given polygon? Explain.

a.

b.

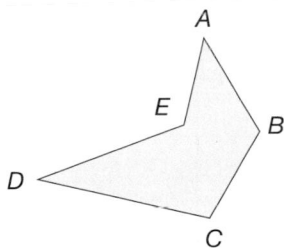

c.

20. Use dot paper, a ruler, possibly a protractor, and the Chapter 13 eManipulative activity, *Coordinate Geoboard*, if necessary, to draw the image of quadrilateral $ABCD$ under the transformation specified in each part.

a. T_{PQ} **b.** $R_{Q,180°}$ **c.** M_l

d. M_l followed by T_{SR}

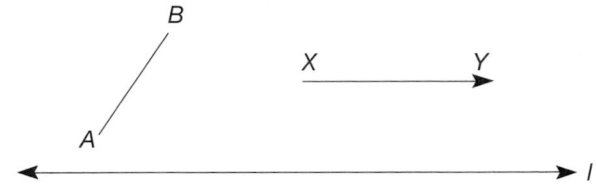

21. Identify the types of symmetry present in the following patterns. Assume that they are infinite patterns.

a. *Summer Stars*

b. *Seesaw*

c. *Road to California*

d. *Log Cabin*

22. Trace the translation of the curves to the opposite sides to create a shape that tessellates. Use the grid to show that the shape will tessellate the plane.

a.

b.

23. Find the image of $\overline{AB}$ under each of the transformations shown.

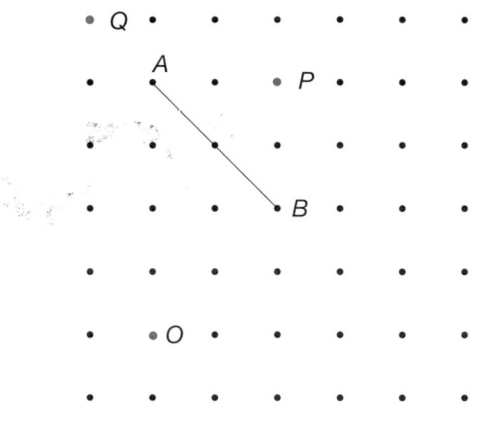

a. $S_{O,1/2}$ **b.** $S_{P,3/2}$ **c.** $S_{Q,2}$

24. Use tracing paper and a ruler to draw the image of each figure under the given size transformation.

a. $S_{P,1/2}$

b. $S_{P,3}$

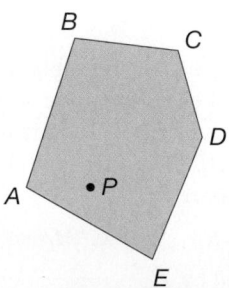

PROBLEMS

25. Describe a transformation of each of the following types (if possible) that maps $\overline{AB}$ to $\overline{A'B'}$.

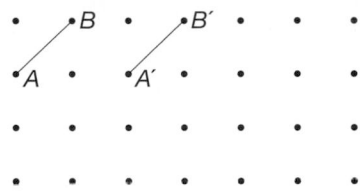

   a. Translation   **b.** Rotation

   c. Reflection   **d.** Glide reflection

26. Describe a transformation of each of the following types (if possible) that maps $\overline{AB}$ to $\overline{A'B'}$.

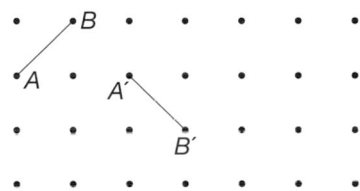

   a. Translation   **b.** Rotation

   c. Reflection   **d.** Glide reflection

27. For each given transformation, plot $\triangle ABC$—with $A(2, 3)$, $B(-1, 4)$, and $C(-2, 1)$—and its image. Decide whether the transformation is a translation, rotation, reflection, glide reflection, or none of

these. The notation $F(x, y)$ denotes the image of the point (x, y) under transformation F. The Chapter 15 eManipulative activity, *Coordinate Geoboard*, may help in the process.

   a. $F(x, y) = (2x, -y)$

   b. $F(x, y) = (-x + 4, -y + 2)$

   c. $F(x, y) = (-x, y + 2)$

28. a. Draw the image of the circle C_1 under $S_{O,2}$.

     b. Draw the image of the circle C_2 under $S_{P,1/2}$.

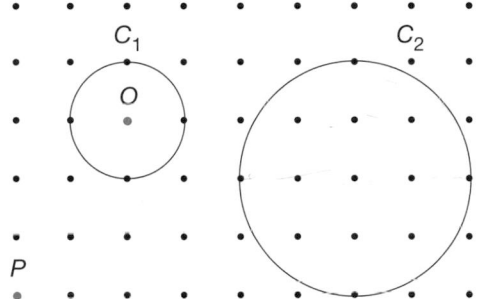

29. Using the Chapter 16 eManipulative activity, *Isometries,* perform a rotation of any combination of pattern blocks that you would like. Move the center of rotation and describe how the image moves. Does the location of the center affect the size or shape of the image? Explain.

PROBLEMS FOR WRITING/DISCUSSION

1. Marjorie needed to turn a figure 180° clockwise about a fixed point. She asks, "If I turned it counterclockwise 180° instead, would the image be different?" In your explanation, include an example about a turn of 90° clockwise and its equivalent.

2. Kwan Lee says if you have to slide a figure 4 squares down and 4 squares to the right, you have to count

that as two separate slides. Maureen says, "No, you can do it all at once: it's sort of like going southeast on a map." Do you agree? Discuss.

3. Owen says a 180° degree turn is the same thing as flipping a figure over a line. Is this ever true? Discuss.

16.2 CONGRUENCE AND SIMILARITY USING TRANSFORMATIONS

STARTING POINT

Trace the figure at the right and sketch the location of the image of $\triangle XYZ$ after being reflected around line *l*. Label this image $\triangle X'Y'Z'$. Now sketch the image of $\triangle X'Y'Z'$ after being reflected around line *m*. Label this final triangle $\triangle X''Y''Z''$. Describe a single isometry that would map $\triangle XYZ$ directly to $\triangle X''Y''Z''$.

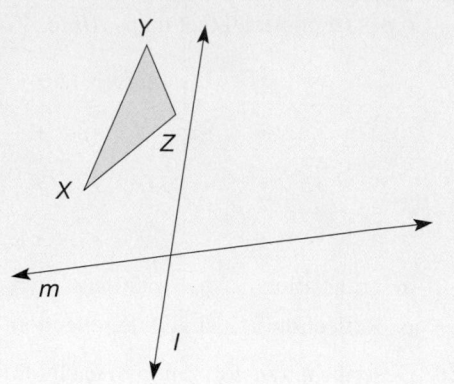

Congruence

In this section we study special properties of translations, rotations, reflections, and glide reflections. We apply some results on triangle congruence from Section 14.1 to verify some of these properties.

We will use the notation in Table 16.1 to denote images of points under transformations (Figure 16.25).

Table 16.1

TRANSFORMATION	IMAGE OF POINT P
Translation, T_{AB}	$T_{AB}(P)$ [Figure 16.25(a)]
Rotation, $R_{O,a}$	$R_{O,a}(P)$ [Figure 16.25(b)]
Reflection, M_l	$M_l(P)$ [Figure 16.25(c)]
Glide reflection T_{AB} followed by M_l	$M_l(T_{AB}(P))$ [Figure 16.25(d)]

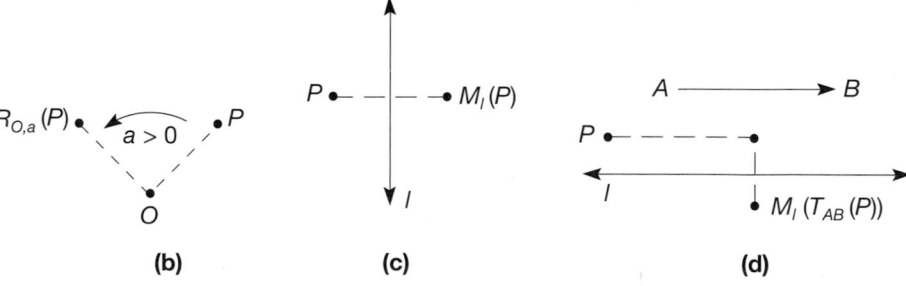

(a)   (b)   (c)   (d)

Figure 16.25

For example, $T_{AB}(P)$ is read "T sub AB of P" or "the image of point P under the translation T_{AB}" [Figure 16.25(a)]. Similarly, $R_{O,a}(P)$ is read "R sub O, a of P" and denotes the image of point P under the rotation $R_{O,a}$ [Figure 16.25(b)]. The reflection image of point P in line l is denoted by $M_l(P)$ and read "M sub l of P" [Figure 16.25(c)]. Finally, the glide reflection image of point P, $M_l(T_{AB}(P))$, is read "M sub l of T sub AB of P" [Figure 16.25(d)]. Note that in the notation for the glide reflection, the transformation T_{AB} is applied first.

Next, we will investigate properties of the transformations listed in Table 16.1. In particular, we first will determine whether they preserve distance; that is, whether the distance between two points is the same as the distance between their images.

Suppose that we have a translation T_{AB} and that we consider the effect of T_{AB} on a line segment $\overline{PQ}$ (Figure 16.26). Let $P' = T_{AB}(P)$ and $Q' = T_{AB}(Q)$. According to the definition of a translation, $\overline{PP'} \parallel \overline{AB}$ and $PP' = AB$. Similarly, $\overline{QQ'} \parallel \overline{AB}$ and $QQ' = AB$. Combining our results, we see that $\overline{PP'} \parallel \overline{QQ'}$ and $PP' = QQ'$.

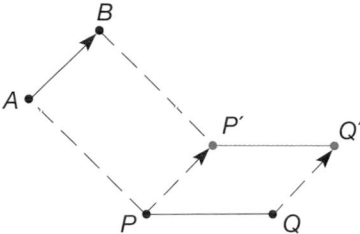

Figure 16.26

Thus $PP'Q'Q$ is a parallelogram, since opposite sides, $\overline{PP'}$ and $\overline{QQ'}$, are parallel and congruent. Consequently, $PQ = P'Q'$. We have verified that translations preserve distance; that is, that the distance $P'Q'$ is equal to the distance PQ. (Also, since $PQ \parallel P'Q'$, we can deduce that a translation maps a line to a line parallel to the original line.)

Next, we show that rotations also preserve distance. Suppose that $R_{O,a}$ is a rotation with center O and angle with measure a. Consider the effect of $R_{O,a}$ on a line segment $\overline{PQ}$ (Figure 16.27). We wish to show that $PQ - P'Q'$. To do this, we will

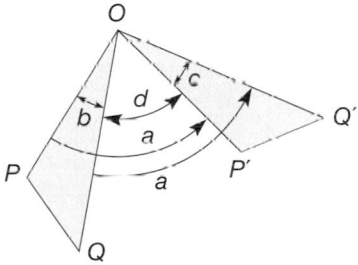

Figure 16.27

establish that $\triangle POQ \cong \triangle P'OQ'$ using the SAS congruence property. Since $OP = OP'$ and $OQ = OQ'$ by the definition of rotation $R_{O,a}$, all that remains is to show that $\angle POQ \cong \angle P'OQ'$. Let $b = m(\angle POQ)$, $c = m(\angle P'OQ')$, and $d = m(\angle QOP')$ (Figure 16.27). Here we are assuming that P rotates counterclockwise to P' and Q to Q'. (If it does not, a similar argument can be developed.) Then we have

$$b + d = a = d + c \qquad \text{so that} \qquad b + d = d + c.$$

Hence $b = c$. so that $m(\angle POQ) = m(\angle P'OQ')$. Thus $\triangle POQ \cong \triangle P'OQ'$, by the SAS congruence property. Consequently, we have that $\overline{PQ} \cong \overline{P'Q'}$, since they are corresponding sides in the congruent triangles. This shows that rotations preserve distance. Unlike translations, a rotation, in general, does not map a line to a line parallel to the original line. In fact, only rotations through multiples of 180° do.

Using triangle congruence, we can show that reflections also preserve distance. There are four cases to consider: (1) P and Q are on l; (2) only one of P or Q is on l; (3) P and Q are on the same side of l; and (4) P and Q are on opposite sides of l.

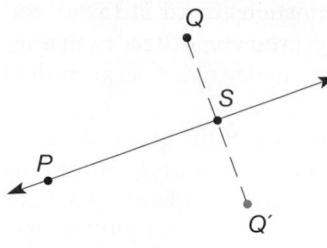

Figure 16.28

CASE 1: P and Q are fixed by M_l; that is, $M_l(P) = P' = P$, and $M_l(Q) = Q' = Q$, so that $P'Q' = PQ$.

CASE 2: Suppose that P is on line l and Q is not on l (Figure 16.28). Let $Q' = M_l(Q)$ and let S be the intersection of segment $\overline{QQ'}$ and line l. Then $QS = Q'S$ and $\angle QSP$ is a right angle, by the definition of $M_l(Q)$. Hence $\triangle QSP \cong \triangle Q'SP$ by the SAS congruence condition. Consequently, $QP = Q'P'$ as desired.

Cases 3 and 4 are somewhat more complicated and are left for Part A Problem 24 and Part B Problem 24, respectively, in the Problem Set.

In the case of a glide reflection, since both the translation and the reflection comprising the glide reflection preserve distance, the glide reflection must also preserve distance.

In the first section, a transformation that preserved size and shape was called an isometry. More formally, an **isometry** is a transformation that preserves distance (*iso* = "equal," *metry* = "measure"). We have just shown that translations, rotations, reflections, and glide reflections are isometries. It can also be shown that isometries map lines to lines; that is, the image of a line l under an isometry is another line l'. Figure 16.29 illustrates this result for a translation, rotation, and reflection.

Figure 16.29

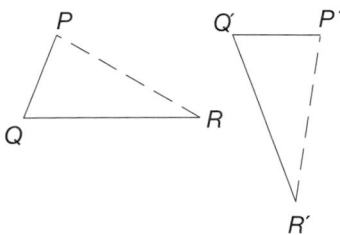

Figure 16.30

We can show that every isometry also preserves angle measure; that is, an isometry maps an angle to an angle that is congruent to the original angle (Figure 16.30). Consider $\angle PQR$ and its image, $\angle P'Q'R'$, under an isometry. Form $\triangle PQR$ and its image $\triangle P'Q'R'$ (Figure 16.30). We know that $PQ = P'Q'$, $QR = Q'R'$, and $PR = P'R'$. Thus $\triangle PQR \cong \triangle P'Q'R'$ by the SSS congruence property, so that $\angle PQR \cong \angle P'Q'R'$.

Because isometries preserve distance, we know that isometries map triangles to congruent triangles. Also, using the corresponding angles property, it can be shown that isometries preserve parallelism. That is, isometries map parallel lines to parallel lines. A verification of this is left for Part B Problem 20 in the Problem Set. We can summarize properties of isometries as follows.

 THEOREM

Properties of Isometries

1. Isometries map lines to lines, segments to segments, rays to rays, angles to angles, and polygons to polygons.
2. Isometries preserve angle measure.
3. Isometries map triangles to congruent triangles.
4. Isometries preserve parallelism.

We can analyze congruent triangles by means of isometries. Suppose, for example, that $\triangle ABC$ and $\triangle A'B'C'$ are congruent, they have the same orientation, and the three pairs of corresponding sides are parallel, as in Figure 16.31. Since the corresponding sides are parallel and congruent, it can be shown that the translation $T_{AA'}$ maps $\triangle ABC$ to $\triangle A'B'C'$.

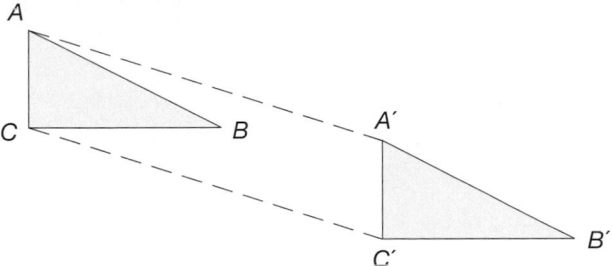

Figure 16.31

If $\triangle ABC$ and $\triangle A'B'C'$ are congruent, they have the same orientation, and if $\overline{AB} \not\parallel \overline{A'B'}$, there is a rotation that maps $\triangle ABC$ to $\triangle A'B'C'$ (Figure 16.32).

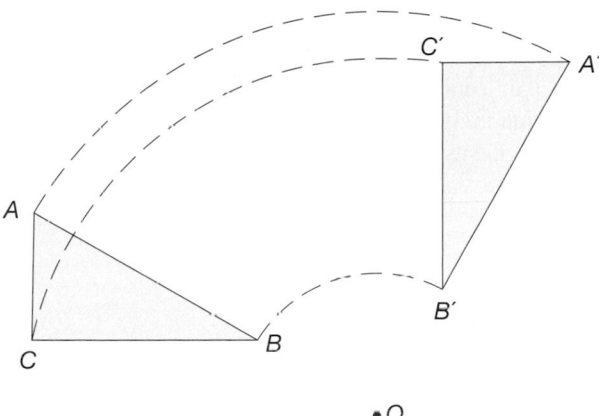

Figure 16.32

Example 16.8 In Figure 16.33, $\triangle ABC \cong \triangle A'B'C'$. Find a rotation that maps $\triangle ABC$ to $\triangle A'B'C'$.

Solution To find the center, O, of the rotation, we use the fact that O is equidistant from points A and A'. Hence O is on the perpendicular bisector, l, of segment $\overline{AA'}$ (Figure 16.34).

But O is also equidistant from B and B', so O is on m, the perpendicular bisector of $\overline{BB'}$. Hence $\{O\} = l \cap m$. The angle of the rotation is $\angle AOA'$ (Figure 16.35).

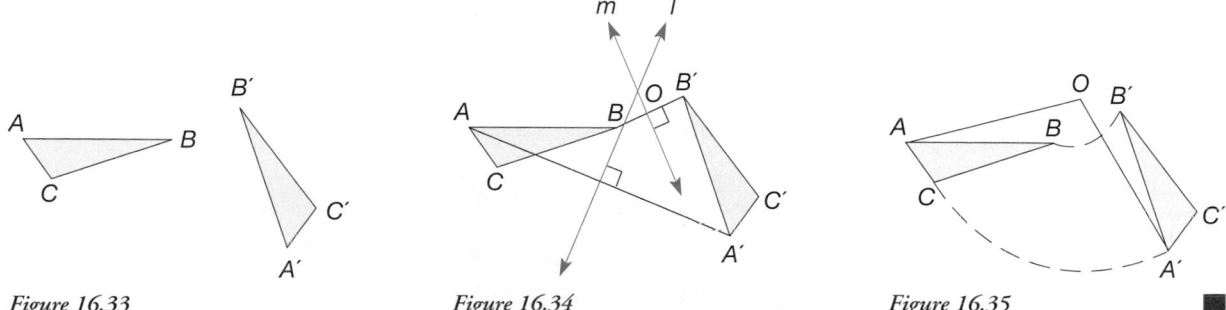

Figure 16.33 *Figure 16.34* *Figure 16.35* ■

Thus, if two congruent triangles have the same orientation, and a translation will not map one to the other, there is a rotation that will.

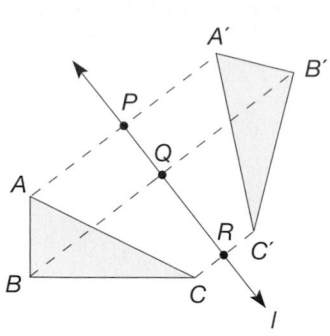

Figure 16.36

Next, suppose that $\triangle ABC$ and $\triangle A'B'C'$ are congruent and have opposite orientation. Further assume that there is a line l that is the perpendicular bisector of $\overline{AA'}$, $\overline{BB'}$, and $\overline{CC'}$ (Figure 16.36). Then, by the definition of a reflection, M_l maps $\triangle ABC$ to $\triangle A'B'C'$. If there is no reflection mapping $\triangle ABC$ to $\triangle A'B'C'$, then a glide reflection maps $\triangle ABC$ to $\triangle A'B'C'$. The next example shows how to find the glide axis of a glide reflection.

Example 16.9 In Figure 16.37, $\triangle ABC \cong \triangle A'B'C'$. Find a glide reflection that maps $\triangle ABC$ to $\triangle A'B'C'$.

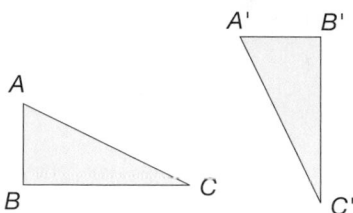

Figure 16.37

Solution Since $\triangle ABC$ and $\triangle A'B'C'$ have opposite orientation, we know that either a reflection or glide reflection is needed. Since $\triangle A'B'C'$ does not appear to be a reflection image of $\triangle ABC$, we will find a glide reflection. Find the midpoints P, Q, and R of segments $\overline{AA'}$, $\overline{BB'}$, and $\overline{CC'}$, respectively (Figure 16.38).

Figure 16.38

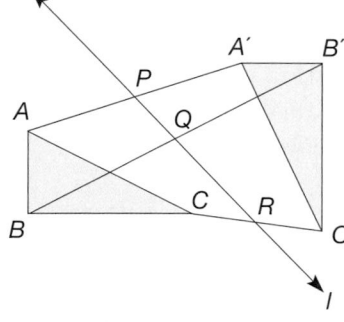

Figure 16.39

Then P, Q, and R are collinear and the line $\overleftrightarrow{PQ}$ is the glide axis of the glide reflection (Figure 16.39). (This result follows from Hjelmslev's theorem, which is too technical for us to prove here.) We reflect $\triangle ABC$ across line $\overleftrightarrow{PQ}$ to obtain $\triangle A*B*C*$. Then $\triangle A*B*C*$ is mapped to $\triangle A'B'C'$ by $T_{A*A'}$. Thus we see the effect of the glide reflection, M_{PQ} followed by $T_{A*A'}$, which maps $\triangle ABC$ to $\triangle A'B'C'$. ■

Thus, if two congruent triangles $\triangle ABC$ and $\triangle A'B'C'$ have opposite orientation, there exists either a reflection or a glide reflection that maps one to the other. We can summarize our results about triangle congruence and isometries as follows.

> ### THEOREM
>
> **Triangle Congruence and Isometries**
>
> $\triangle ABC \cong \triangle A'B'C'$ if and only if there is an isometry that maps $\triangle ABC$ to $\triangle A'B'C'$. If the triangles have the same orientation, the isometry is either a translation or a rotation. If the triangles have opposite orientation, the isometry is either a reflection or a glide reflection.

NCTM Standards 2000
Geometry
Grades 6–8
All students should examine the congruence, similarity, and line or rotational symmetry of objects using transformations.

Based on the foregoing discussion, it can be shown that there are only four types of isometries in the plane: translations, rotations, reflections, and glide reflections.

Isometries allow us to define congruence between general types of shapes (i.e., collections of points) in the plane.

● DEFINITION

Congruent Shapes

Two shapes, $\mathscr{S}$ and $\mathscr{S}'$, in the plane are **congruent** if and only if there is an isometry that maps $\mathscr{S}$ onto $\mathscr{S}'$.

Figure 16.40 shows several pairs of congruent shapes. Can you identify the type of isometry, in each case, that maps shape $\mathscr{S}$ to shape $\mathscr{S}'$? In parts (a), (b), (c), and (d), respectively, of Figure 16.40, a translation, rotation, reflection, and glide reflection will map shape $\mathscr{S}$ to shape $\mathscr{S}'$.

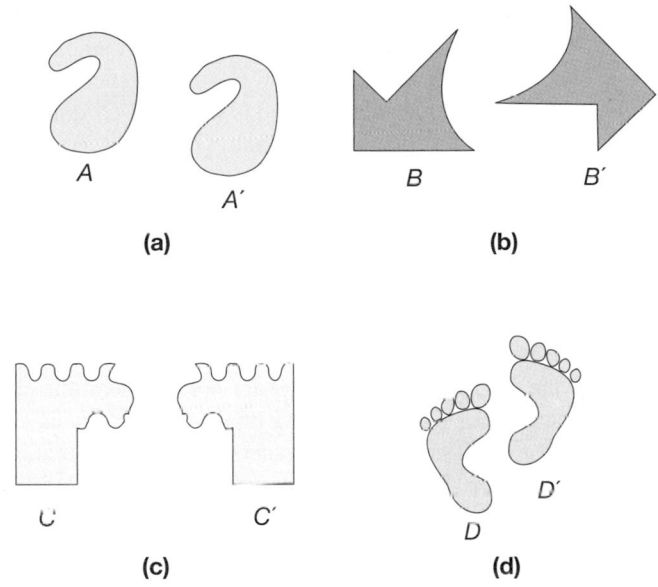

Figure 16.40

We can determine when two polygons are congruent by means of properties of their sides and angles. Suppose that there is a one-to-one correspondence between polygons $\mathscr{P}$ and $\mathscr{P}'$ such that all corresponding sides are congruent, as are all corresponding angles. We can show that $\mathscr{P}$ is congruent to $\mathscr{P}'$. To demonstrate this, consider the polygons in Figure 16.41(a). Suppose that the vertices correspond as indicated and that all pairs of corresponding sides and angles are congruent. Choose three vertices in $\mathscr{P}$—say A, B, and C—and their corresponding vertices A', B', and

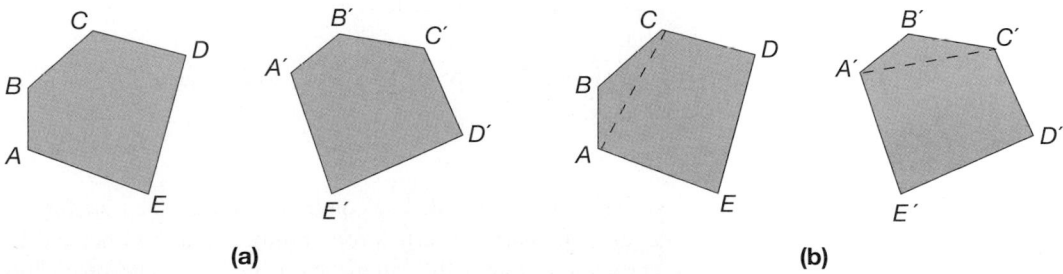

Figure 16.41

C' in $\mathcal{P}'$ [Figure 16.41(b)]. By the side–angle–side congruence condition, $\triangle ABC \cong \triangle A'B'C'$. Thus there is an isometry T that maps $\triangle ABC$ to $\triangle A'B'C'$. But then T preserves $\angle BCD$ and distance CD. Since $\mathcal{P}$ and $\mathcal{P}'$ have the same orientation, T must map segment $\overline{CD}$ to segment $\overline{C'D'}$. Similarly, T maps segment $\overline{DE}$ to segment $\overline{D'E'}$ and segment $\overline{EA}$ to segment $\overline{E'A'}$. From this we see that T maps polygon $\mathcal{P}$ to polygon $\mathcal{P}'$ so that the polygons are congruent.

THEOREM

Congruent Polygons

Suppose that there is a one-to-one correspondence between polygons $\mathcal{P}$ and $\mathcal{P}'$ such that all pairs of corresponding sides and angles are congruent. Then $\mathcal{P} \cong \mathcal{P}'$.

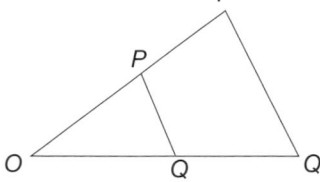

Figure 16.42

Similarity

Next we study properties of size transformations and similitudes. Isometries preserve distance, whereas size transformations, hence similitudes, preserve *ratios* of distances. To see this, consider $\overline{PQ}$ and its image $\overline{P'Q'}$ under the size transformation $S_{O,k}$, where $k > 1$ and where O, P, and Q are not collinear (Figure 16.42). By definition,

$$OP' = k \cdot OP, \quad \text{so} \quad \frac{OP'}{OP} = k, \quad \text{and} \quad OQ' = k \cdot OQ, \quad \text{so} \quad \frac{OQ'}{OQ} = k. \quad \text{Thus} \quad \frac{OP'}{OP} =$$

$\dfrac{OQ'}{OQ}$. Since $\angle POQ = \angle P'OQ'$ and $\dfrac{OP'}{OP} = \dfrac{OQ'}{OQ}$, we can conclude that

$\triangle POQ \sim \triangle P'OQ'$ by SAS similarity. By corresponding parts, $\dfrac{P'Q'}{PQ} = k$. In the case when O, P, and Q are not collinear, the size transformation $S_{O,k}$ takes every segment $\overline{PQ}$ to a segment k times as long. This is also true in the case when O, P, and Q are collinear. Thus, in general, size transformations preserve ratios of distances.

Since size transformations preserve ratios of distances, the image of any triangle is similar to the original triangle by SSS similarity. Thus size transformations also preserve angle measure. A proof of this result and others in the following theorem are left for the problem set.

THEOREM

Properties of Size Transformations

1. The size transformation $S_{O,k}$ maps a line segment $\overline{PQ}$ to a parallel line segment $\overline{P'Q'}$. In general, size transformations map lines to parallel lines and rays to parallel rays.
2. Size transformations preserve ratios of distances.
3. Size transformations preserve angle measure.
4. Size transformations preserve parallelism.
5. Size transformations preserve orientation.

Recall that a similitude is a combination of a size transformation and an isometry. Thus the following properties of similitudes can be obtained by reasoning from the properties of size transformations and isometries. The verification of these properties is left for the problem set.

THEOREM

Properties of Similitudes

1. Similitudes map lines to lines, segments to segments, rays to rays, angles to angles, and polygons to polygons.
2. Similitudes preserve ratios of distances.
3. Similitudes preserve angle measure.
4. Similitudes map triangles to similar triangles.
5. Similitudes preserve parallelism.

The next theorem and following example display the connection between the general notion of similarity and similar triangles.

THEOREM

Triangle Similarity and Similitudes

$\triangle ABC \sim \triangle A'B'C'$ if and only if there is a similitude that maps $\triangle ABC$ to $\triangle A'B'C'$.

Example 16.10   Suppose $\triangle ABC$ and $\triangle A'B'C'$ in Figure 16.43 are similar under the correspondence $A \leftrightarrow A'$, $B \leftrightarrow B'$, and $C \leftrightarrow C'$. Suppose also that $AC = 4$, $BC = 9$, $AB = 12$, and $A'C' = 7$.

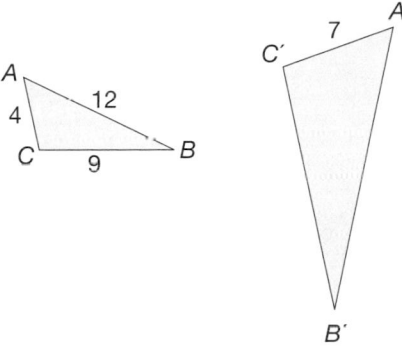

Figure 16.43

a. Find $B'C'$ and $A'B'$.
b. Find a similitude that maps $\triangle ABC$ to $\triangle A'B'C'$.

Solution

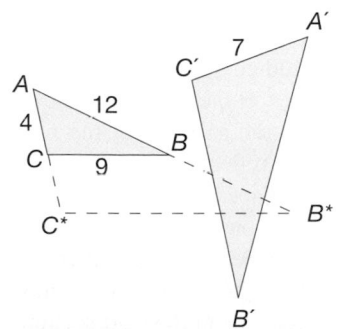

Figure 16.44

a. Since corresponding sides are proportional, we must have $\dfrac{B'C'}{BC} = \dfrac{A'C'}{AC}$, or $\dfrac{B'C'}{9} = \dfrac{7}{4}$. Solving for $B'C'$, we find $B'C' = \dfrac{63}{4} = 15\dfrac{3}{4}$. Similarly, $\dfrac{A'C'}{AC} = \dfrac{A'B'}{AB}$, so that $\dfrac{A'B'}{12} = \dfrac{7}{4}$, from which we find $A'B' = 21$.

b. Consider the size transformation $S_{A,7/4}$. Figure 16.44 shows the effect of $S_{A,7/4}$ on $\triangle ABC$. Note that B^* and C^* are the images of B and C, respectively, under this size transformation. Calculate that $AC^* = 7$, $AB^* = 21$, and $B^*C^* = 15\frac{3}{4}$. Hence $\triangle AB^*C^* \cong \triangle A'B'C'$ by the SSS congruence property. (In fact, any size transformation with scale factor $\frac{7}{4}$ will map $\triangle ABC$ to a triangle congruent to $\triangle A'B'C'$. For convenience, we chose point A as the center of the size transformation. However, we could have chosen any point as the center.)

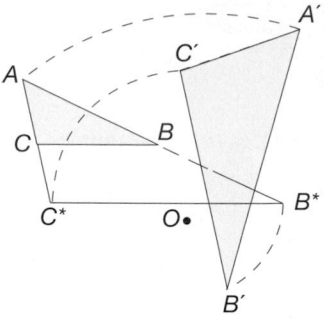

Figure 16.45

Observe that $\triangle AB^*C^*$ and $\triangle A'B'C'$ have the same orientation. However, $\triangle A'B'C'$ is not a translation image of $\triangle AB^*C^*$. Therefore, there is a rotation that maps $\triangle AB^*C^*$ to $\triangle A'B'C'$. Thus $S_{A,7/4}$ followed by a rotation is a similitude that maps $\triangle ABC$ to $\triangle A'B'C'$ (Figure 16.45).   ■

We can define similarity of shapes in the plane via similitudes.

DEFINITION

Similar Shapes

Two shapes, $\mathcal{S}$ and $\mathcal{S}'$, in the plane are **similar** if and only if there is a similitude that maps $\mathcal{S}$ to $\mathcal{S}'$.

Using the triangle similarity and similitudes theorem, we can show that two polygons are similar if there is a one-to-one correspondence between them such that all pairs of corresponding sides are proportional and all pairs of corresponding angles are congruent (Figure 16.46).

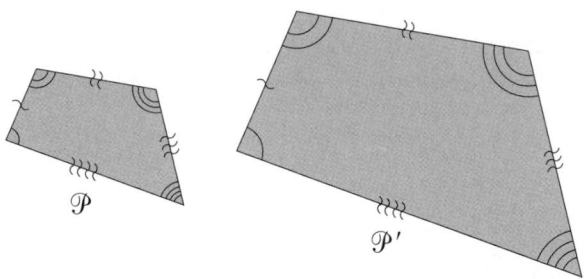

Figure 16.46

THEOREM

Similar Polygons

Suppose that there is a one-to-one correspondence between polygons $\mathcal{P}$ and $\mathcal{P}'$ such that all pairs of corresponding sides are proportional and all pairs of corresponding angles are congruent. Then $\mathcal{P} \sim \mathcal{P}'$.

From the definition of similar shapes, we see that all congruent shapes are similar, since we can use the size transformation with scale factor 1 to serve as the similitude in mapping one congruent shape to the other. Hence all transformations that we have studied in this chapter—namely, isometries (translations, rotations, reflections, glide reflections), size transformations, and combinations of these transformations—are similitudes. Thus all the transformations that we have studied preserve shapes of figures. Finally, since there are only four types of isometries in the plane, it follows that every similitude is a combination of a size transformation and one of the four types of isometries: a translation, rotation, reflection, or glide reflection.

The approach to congruence and similarity of geometric shapes via isometries and similitudes is called **transformation geometry.** Transformation geometry provides additional problem-solving techniques in geometry that effectively complement approaches using triangle congruence and similarity and approaches using coordinates. We explore the use of transformations to solve geometry problems in the next section.

MATHEMATICAL MORSEL

When Memphis, Tennessee, officials wanted an eye-catching new sports arena, they decided to take a page from the book on their sister city, Memphis, Egypt. A $52 million stainless-steel clad pyramid, two-thirds the size of the world's largest pyramid, the Great Pyramid of Cheops, was the result. The square pyramid is 321 feet, or 32 stories, high and its base covers 300,000 square feet, or about six football fields. In addition to housing sporting events and circuses, the pyramid houses a museum of American music.

 Section 16.2 EXERCISE / PROBLEM SET A

EXERCISES

1. a. What are the coordinates of points A and B?

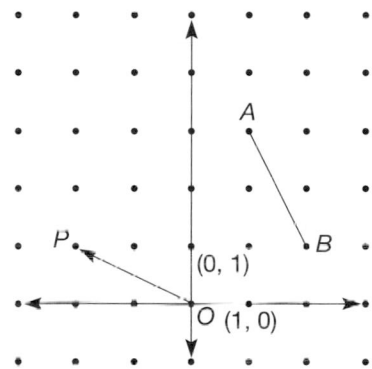

b. What are the coordinates of A' and B', where $A' = T_{OP}(A)$ and $B' = T_{OP}(B)$?

c. Use the distance formula to verify that this translation has preserved distances (i.e., show that $AB = A'B'$).

2. Consider $P(p, q)$, T_{OP}, $X(x, y)$, and $Y(x + p, y + q)$.

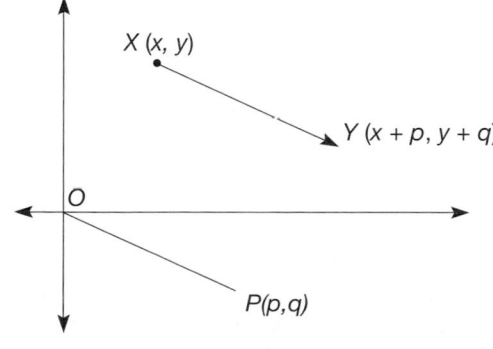

a. Are the directed line segments $\overrightarrow{OP}$ and $\overrightarrow{XY}$ parallel?

b. Do $\overrightarrow{OP}$ and $\overrightarrow{XY}$ have the same length? Explain.

c. Is $Y = T_{OP}(X)$?

3. Consider $X(x, y)$ and $Y(-y, x)$.

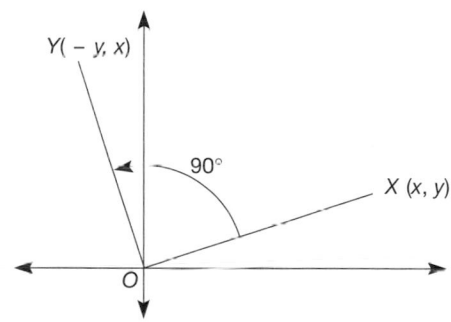

a. Verify that $m(\angle XOY) = 90°$.

b. Verify that $OX = OY$.

c. Is $Y = R_{O,90°}(X)$? Why or why not?

4. Given that $R_{O,90°}(x, y) = (-y, x)$, find the coordinates of A' and B', where $A' = R_{O,90°}(A)$, $B' = R_{O,90°}(B)$, and A and B have coordinates $(5, 2)$ and $(3, -4)$, respectively. Verify that $R_{O,90°}$ preserves the distance AB.

5. a. What are the coordinates of points A and B?

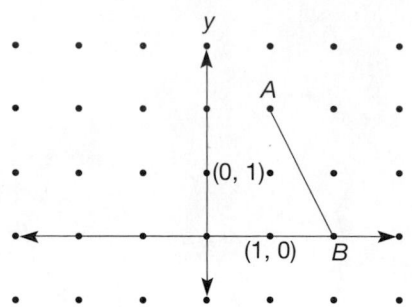

b. What are the coordinates of A' and B' for $A' = M_y(A)$, $B' = M_y(B)$, where M_y is the reflection in the y-axis?

c. Use the distance formula to verify that this reflection has preserved the distance AB (i.e., show that $AB = A'B'$).

6. Let A be a point in the plane with coordinates (a, b).

a. What are the coordinates of $A' = M_x(A)$, where M_x is the reflection in the x-axis?

b. If A and B have coordinates (a, b) and (c, d), respectively, verify that M_x preserves distances.

7. Consider $X(x, y)$ and $Y(y, x)$.

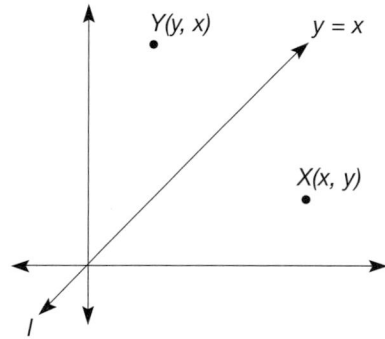

a. Verify that the midpoint of $\overline{XY}$ lies on line l whose equation is $y = x$.

b. Verify that $\overline{XY} \perp l$.

c. Is $Y = M_l(X)$? Why or why not?

8. a. What are the coordinates of points A and B?

b. What are the coordinates of A' and B' where $A' = M_x(T_{PQ}(A))$ and $B' = M_x(T_{PQ}(B))$?

c. Use the distance formula to verify that this glide reflection has preserved the distance AB (i.e., show that $AB = A'B'$).

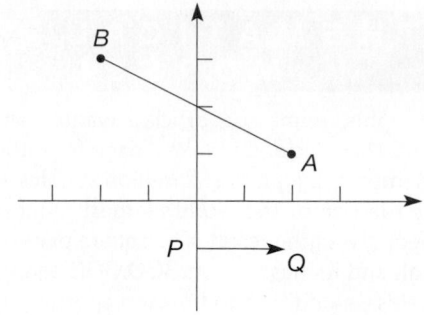

9. Determine the type of isometry that maps the shape on the left onto the shape on the right.

a.

b.

c.

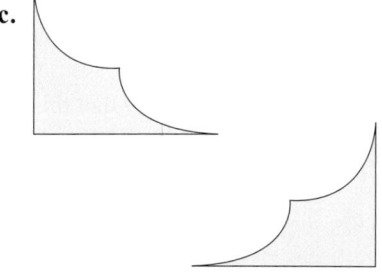

10. Find a translation, rotation, reflection, or glide reflection that maps $ABCD$ onto $A'B'C'D'$ in each case.

a.

b.

c.

d.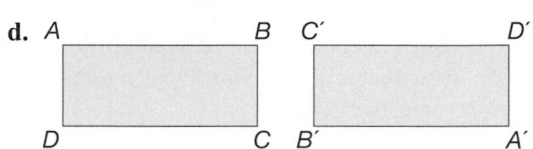

13. Is there a size transformation that maps $\triangle RST$ to $\triangle R'S'T'$? If so, find its center and scale factor. If not, explain why not.

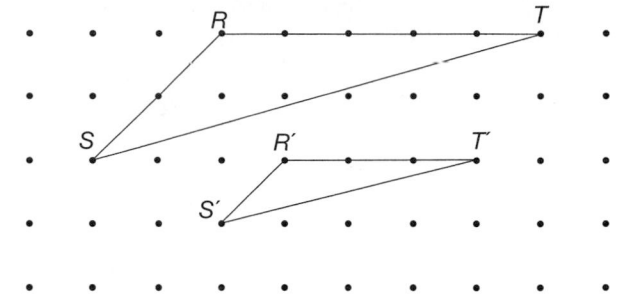

11. a. Find the image of $\triangle ABC$ under the transformation $S_{P,2}$.

b. Find the lengths of $\overline{AB}$ and $\overline{A'B'}$. What is the ratio $A'B'/AB$?

c. Find the lengths of $\overline{BC}$ and $\overline{B'C'}$. What is the ratio $B'C'/BC$?

d. Find the lengths of $\overline{AC}$ and $\overline{A'C'}$. What is the ratio $A'C'/AC$?

e. In addition to their lengths, what other relationship exists between a segment and its image?

14. For each part, find a similitude that maps $\triangle ABC$ to $\triangle A'B'C'$. Describe each similitude as completely as you can.

a.

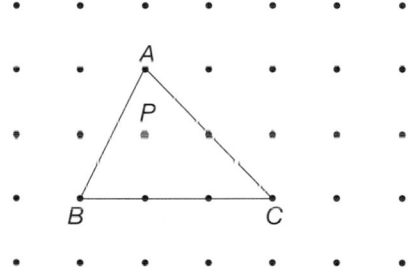

12. a. Find the image of $\angle ABC$ under $S_{P,2}$.

b. How do the measures of $\angle ABC$ and $\angle A'B'C'$ compare?

b.

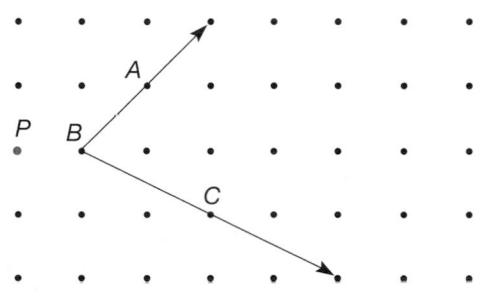

PROBLEMS

15. Let A, X, and B be points on line l with X between A and B and let A', X', and B' be the images of A, X, and B, respectively, under a translation T_{PQ}.

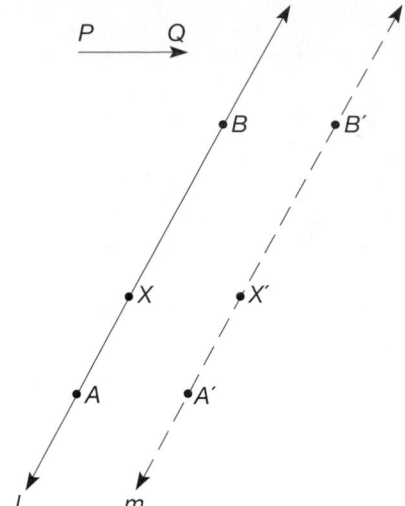

a. Show that $BB'X'X$ and $BB'A'A$ are both parallelograms.

b. Combine conclusions from part (a) and the uniqueness of line m through B' such that $l \parallel m$ to verify that A', X', and B' are collinear. This verifies that the translation image of a line is a set of collinear points. [NOTE: To show that $m = T_{PQ}(l)$ goes beyond the scope of this book.]

16. Suppose there is a translation that maps P to P', Q to Q', and R to R'. Verify that translations preserve angle measure; that is, show that $\angle PQR \cong \angle P'Q'R'$. (*Hint:* Consider $\triangle PQR$ and $\triangle P'Q'R'$.)

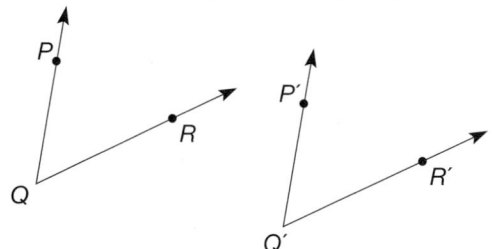

17. Given are parallel lines p and q. Suppose that a rotation maps p to p' and q to q'. Verify that $p' \parallel q'$ (i.e., that rotations preserve parallelism).

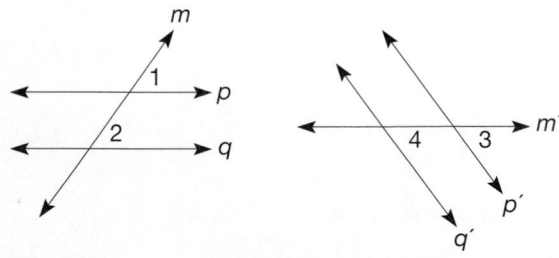

18. Suppose there is a reflection that maps A to A', B to B', and C to C'. Verify that reflections preserve collinearity; that is, if A, B, and C are collinear, show that A', B', and C' are collinear.

19. Verify that reflections preserve parallelism; that is, if $p \parallel q$, show that $p' \parallel q'$. (*Hint:* Draw a reflection line and the images p', q', and m'.)

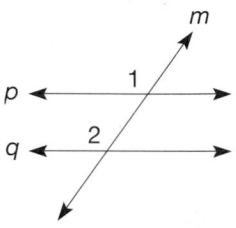

20. Given is $\triangle ABC$. An isometry is applied yielding images A', B', and C' of points A, B, and C, respectively. Verify that isometries map triangles to congruent triangles (i.e., show that $\triangle ABC \cong \triangle A'B'C'$).

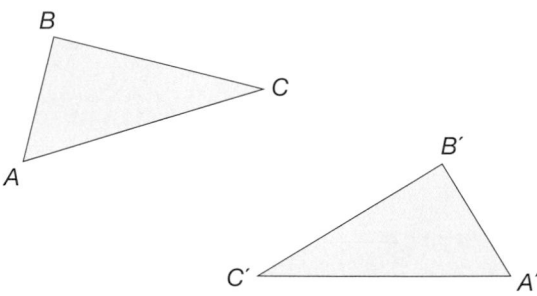

21. Let P and Q be any two points.

a. How many translations are possible that map P to Q? Describe them.

b. How many rotations are possible that map P to Q? Describe them.

22. a. Find the center of the magnification that maps P to P' and Q to Q'.

b. Is the scale factor less than 1 or greater than 1?

c. Repeat parts (a) and (b) for the following points.

•*P*

•*P'*

•*Q'*

•*Q*

23. The size transformation $S_{P,k}$ maps Q to Q'. If P is on line l, describe how you would construct $S_{P,k}(R)$.

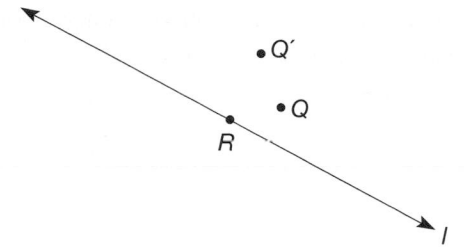

24. Suppose that P and Q are on the same side of line l, $P' = M_l(P)$, and $Q' = M_l(Q)$. Show that $P'Q' = PQ$.

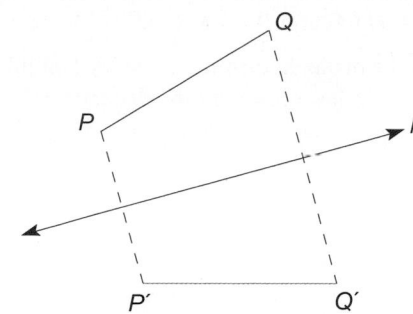

25. Use the Chapter 16 eManipulative activity, *Compositions,* to create a reflection about two parallel lines. Describe how the original object and the image appear to be related. Is there a single transformation that would map the original object to its image? If yes, what is it?

Section 16.2   EXERCISE / PROBLEM SET B

EXERCISES

1. a. What are the coordinates of points A and B?

  b. Point P has coordinates $(4, 5)$. Let $A' = T_{OP}(A)$ and $B' = T_{OP}(B)$. What are the coordinates of A' and B'?

  c. Verify that T_{OP} has preserved the length of $\overline{AB}$.

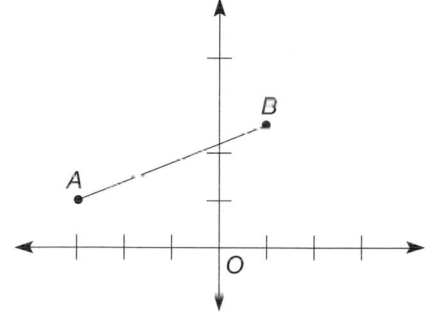

2. Given that $T_{OP}(x, y) = (x + p, y + q)$ and that points A and B have coordinates (a, b) and (c, d), respectively, answer the following.

  a. Find AB.

  b. What are the coordinates of A' and B' where $A' = T_{OP}(A)$ and $B' = T_{OP}(B)$?

  c. Find $A'B'$.

  d. Does this general translation preserve distances?

3. Consider $\triangle ABC$ pictured on the graph. The rotation $R_{O,-90°}$ takes a point with coordinates (x, y) to a point with coordinates $(y, -x)$.

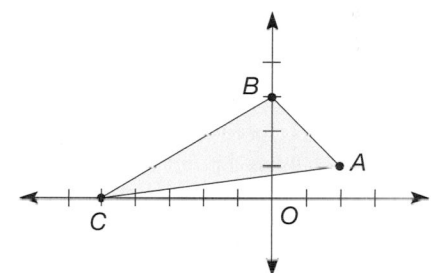

  a. Find the coordinates of A', B', and C' where $A' = R_{O,-90°}(A)$, $B' = R_{O,-90°}(B)$, and $C' = R_{O,-90°}(C)$.

  b. Is $\triangle ABC \cong \triangle A'B'C'$? Verify your answer.

  c. Is $\angle ABC \cong \angle A'B'C'$? Verify.

4. Given that $R_{O,180°}(x, y) = (-x, -y)$, find the coordinates of A' and B' where $A' = R_{O,180°}(A)$ and $B' = R_{O,180°}(B)$ and A and B have coordinates $(-2, 3)$ and $(-3, -1)$, respectively. Verify that $R_{O,180°}$ preserves the distance AB.

5. a. What are the coordinates of points A and B?

b. What are the coordinates of A' and B' where $A' = M_x(A)$ and $B' = M_x(B)$?

c. Use the distance formula to verify that this reflection has preserved the distance AB (i.e., show that $AB = A'B'$).

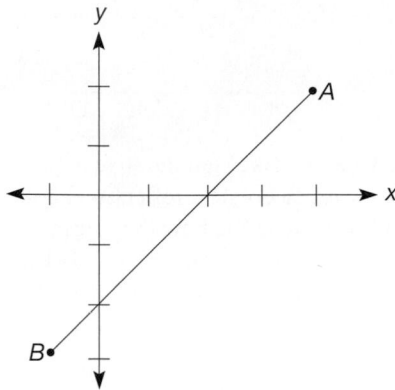

6. Let A be a point in the plane with coordinates (a, b).

a. What are the coordinates of $A' = M_y(A)$?

b. If points A and B have coordinates (a, b) and (c, d), respectively, verify that M_y preserves the distance AB.

7. Consider $\triangle ABC$ pictured on the following graph. The reflection M_l takes a point with coordinates (x, y) to a point with coordinates (y, x).

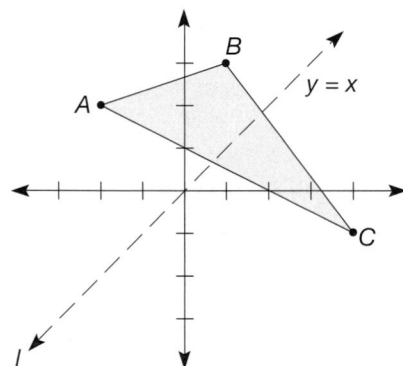

a. Find the coordinates of A', B', and C', where $A' = M_l(A)$, $B' = M_l(B)$, and $C' = M_l(C)$.

b. Is $\triangle ABC \cong \triangle A'B'C'$? Verify.

c. Is $\angle ABC \cong \angle A'B'C'$? Verify.

8. a. What are the coordinates of points A and B?

b. For $P(p, 0)$, what are the coordinates of A' and B', where $A = M_x(T_{OP}(A))$ and $B' = M_x(T_{OP}(B))$?

c. Verify that $M_x(T_{OP})$ preserves the distance AB.

9. Determine the type of isometry that maps the shape on the left onto the shape on the right.

a.

b.

c.

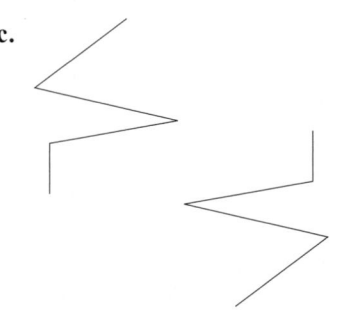

10. Find a translation, rotation, reflection, or glide reflection that maps $\triangle ABC$ to $\triangle A'B'C'$ in each case.

a.

b.

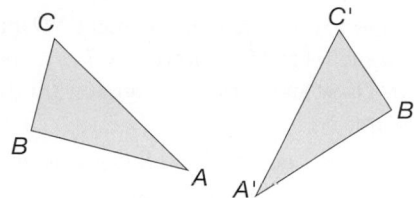

11. a. Find the image of $\overline{AB}$ under the transformation $S_{P,3}$.
   b. Verify that $PA' = 3PA$.
   c. Verify that $PB' = 3PB$.
   d. Find the length of $\overline{AB}$ and $\overline{A'B'}$. How do these lengths compare?

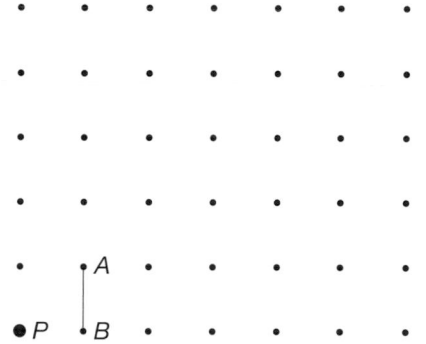

12. a. Find the center P and a scale factor k such that the transformation $S_{P,k}$ maps the small figure to the large figure.
   b. If $S_{P,h}$ maps the large figure onto the small figure, find the scale factor h.
   c. How are k and h related?

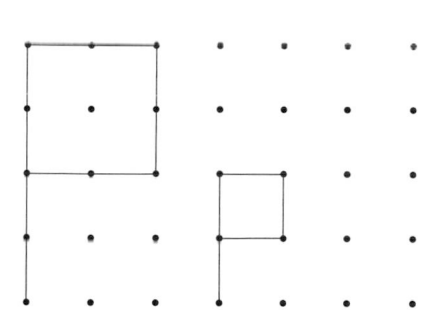

13. a. Describe an isometry followed by a size transformation that maps circle A_1 to circle A_2.
   b. Are all circles similar? Explain why or why not.

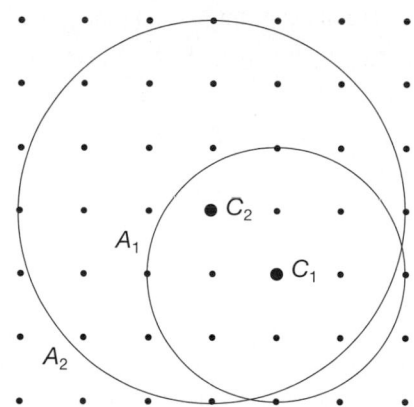

14. In each part, find a similitude that maps $\triangle ABC$ to $\triangle A'B'C'$. Describe each similitude as completely as possible.

a.

b.

c.

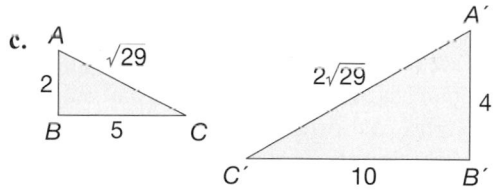

PROBLEMS

15. Suppose there exists a translation that maps line p to p' and line q to q'. Verify that translations preserve parallelism; that is, if $p \parallel q$, show that $p' \parallel q'$.

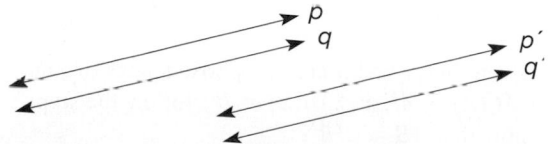

16. Let $R_{O,a}$ be a rotation that maps A to A', B to B', and C to C'. Verify that rotations preserve collinearity; that is, if points A, B, and C are also collinear, show that points A', B', and C' are also collinear. (*Hint:* Show $A'B' + B'C' = A'C'$.)

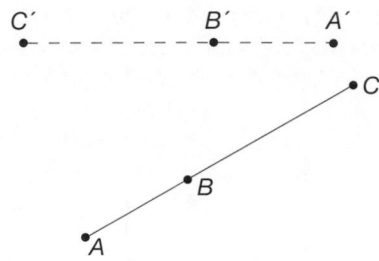

17. Let $R_{O,a}$ be a rotation that maps A to A', B to B', and C to C'. Verify that rotations preserve angle measure; that is, show that $\angle BAC \cong \angle B'A'C'$. (*Hint:* Consider $\triangle ABC$ and $\triangle A'B'C'$.)

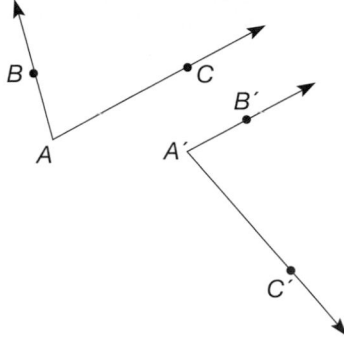

18. Let line l be chosen such that $B' = M_l(B)$. Let P be a point on l and Q be the point where $\overrightarrow{BB'}$ intersects l. Show that $\angle BPQ \cong \angle B'PQ$.

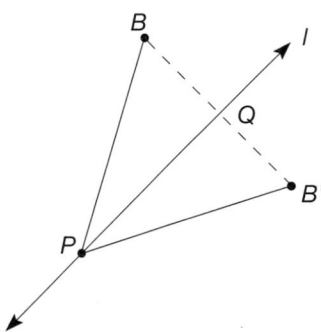

19. Given are two points A and B. A right triangle is drawn that has $\overline{AB}$ as its hypotenuse and point C at the vertex of the right angle. Line l is the perpendicular bisector of $\overline{AC}$.

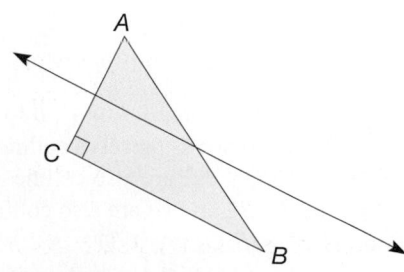

a. Verify that $l \parallel \overline{CB}$.

b. Verify that M_l followed by T_{CB} maps A to B.

c. Find another directed line segment $\overrightarrow{NO}$ and line m such that M_m followed by T_{NO} maps A to B. (*Hint:* Draw another right triangle with $\overline{AB}$ as its hypotenuse.)

d. At what point do line l and line m intersect? Will this be true for other glide axes?

20. Given are parallel lines p and q. Line p' is the image of line p under a certain isometry, and line q' is the image of line q under the same isometry. Verify that the isometry preserves parallelism (i.e., show that $p' \parallel q'$). (*Hint:* Use corresponding angles.)

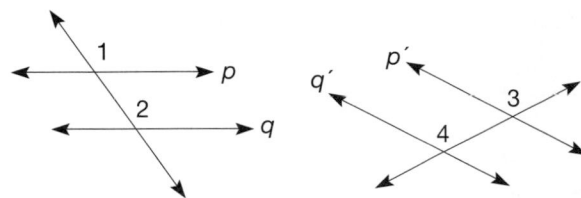

21. Let P and Q be any two points.

a. How many reflections map P to Q? Describe them.

b. How many glide reflections map P to Q? Describe them.

22. Construct the image of quadrilateral $ABCD$ under $S_{P,k}$, where $k = PA'/PA$. Describe your procedure.

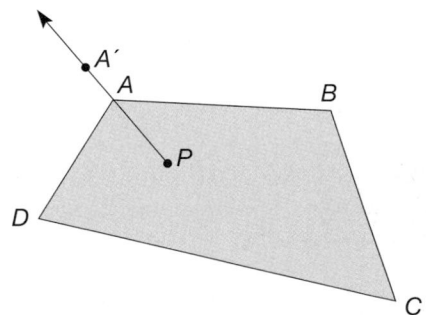

23. Given a size transformation that maps P to P' and Q to Q', describe how to construct the image of R under the same size transformation.

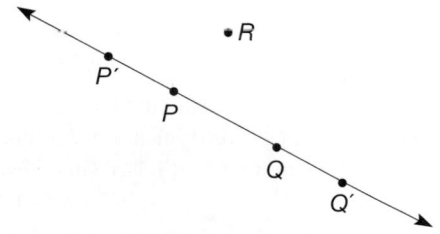

24. Given that A and B are on opposite sides of line l, $M_l(A) = A'$, and $M_l(B) = B'$, follow the steps to show that $AB = A'B'$.

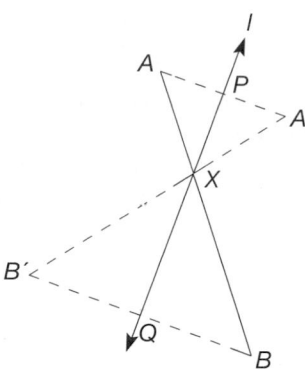

3. Let $a = m(\angle AXP)$ and $b = m(\angle A'XB)$. Use the fact that A, X, and B are collinear to show that $m(\angle AXP) + m(\angle PXA') + m(\angle A'XB) = a + a + b = 180°$. Determine the value for $m(\angle A'X'B')$ and justify your answer. Can we conclude that A', X', and B' are collinear?

4. Since X is on line l, we can conclude that $AX = A'X'$. Similarly, $BX = B'X'$. What is the reason for these conclusions?

5. Use what has been shown to verify $AB = A'B'$ and justify.

1. Let P be the intersection of l and $\overline{AA'}$ and Q be the intersection of l and $\overline{BB'}$. Let X be the point where $\overline{AB}$ intersects line l. Let $X' = M_l(X)$. Where is X'?

2. Next, we wish to show that A', X', and B' are collinear. Give reasons why the following angles are congruent (one reason for each congruent symbol): $\angle BXQ \cong \angle AXP \cong \angle A'X'P \cong \angle B'X'Q$.

25. Use the Chapter 16 eManipulative activity, *Compositions*, to create a reflection about two intersecting lines. Describe how the original object and the image appear to be related. Is there a single transformation that would map the original object to its image? If yes, what is it?

PROBLEMS FOR WRITING/DISCUSSION

1. Monica asks you this question about isometries and parallel lines: "If a figure has parallel sides, will they still be parallel after the transformation? And what about the corresponding parts of a figure and its image? Will they be parallel?" Discuss.

2. Thomas wants to know: "In a size transformation, would the corresponding line segments of a figure and its image be parallel?" How would you answer?

What would you say if Thomas asked this question about a similitude?

3. Kristie wants to know: "If there are two congruent shapes anywhere on my paper, will I always be able to find an isometry that maps one onto the other, even if one is the flip image of the other, like two mittens where the right-hand one is horizontal and the left-hand one is vertical?" Discuss.

16.3   GEOMETRIC PROBLEM SOLVING USING TRANSFORMATIONS

STARTING POINT

You and your friends are playing pool on the pool table as shown when you are confronted with three collinear balls. One of the rules of the game is that you cannot hit the eight-ball first. Also, you are penalized if you don't hit the other ball with the cue ball. Describe a path that the cue ball (the white one) can take so that it will miss the eight-ball (the black one) but hit the other ball. Find another such path.

The use of transformations provides an alternative approach to geometry and gives us additional problem-solving techniques. Our first example is a transformational proof of a familiar property of isosceles triangles.

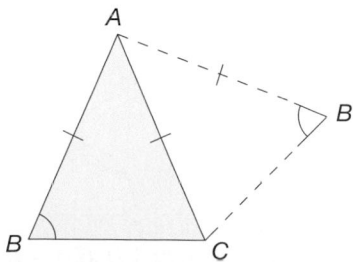

Figure 16.47

Example 16.11   Use isometries to show that the base angles of an isosceles triangle are congruent.

Solution Let $\triangle ABC$ be isosceles with $\overline{AB} \cong \overline{AC}$ (Figure 16.47). Reflect $\triangle ABC$ in $\overleftrightarrow{AC}$, forming $\triangle AB'C$. As a result, we know that $\angle ABC \cong \angle AB'C$ and $\angle BAC \cong \angle B'AC$, since reflections preserve angle measure. Next, consider the rotation with center A and directed angle $\angle B'AC$. Since $\angle B'AC \cong \angle BAC$, and since $\overline{AB} \cong \overline{AC} \cong \overline{AB'}$, we know

Reflection from Research
Students' development of understanding of concepts in transformation geometry is consistent with the van Hiele theory (Soon, 1989).

that this rotation maps $\triangle AB'C$ to $\triangle ACB$. Hence $\angle AB'C \cong \angle ACB$. Combining this with our proceding observation that $\angle AB'C \cong \angle ABC$, we have that $\angle ABC \cong \angle ACB$. ■

A particular type of rotation, called a half-turn, is especially useful in verifying properties of polygons. A **half-turn,** H_O, is a rotation through $180°$ with any point, O, as the center. Figure 16.48, shows a half-turn image of $\triangle ABC$, with point O as the center. In Figure 16.48, $\overline{AB}$ is rotated by H_O to $\overline{A'B'}$, where it appears that $\overline{A'B'} \parallel \overline{AB}$. Next we verify that the half-turn image of a line is indeed parallel to the original line.

Figure 16.48

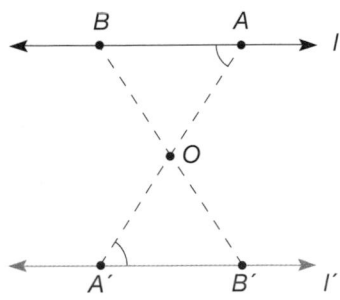

Figure 16.49

In Figure 16.49, let l be a line and let O be the center of a half-turn. Notice that in this case O is not on l. Since H_O is an isometry, it maps l to a line l'. Let A and B be points on l. Then A' and B', the images of A and B under the half-turn H_O, are on l'. Also, and most important, A, O, and A' are collinear, so that line $\overleftrightarrow{AA'}$ is a transversal for lines l and l' containing point O. Since H_O is an isometry, $\angle BAO \cong \angle B'A'O$. Thus, by the alternate interior angles theorem, $l \parallel l'$. In summary, we have shown that a half-turn, H_O, maps a line l to a line l' such that $l' \parallel l$. Figure 16.50 shows the two possible cases; namely, O is on l [Figure 16.50(a)] or O is not on l [Figure 16.50(b)]. If O is on l, the result follows immediately, since every line is parallel to itself.

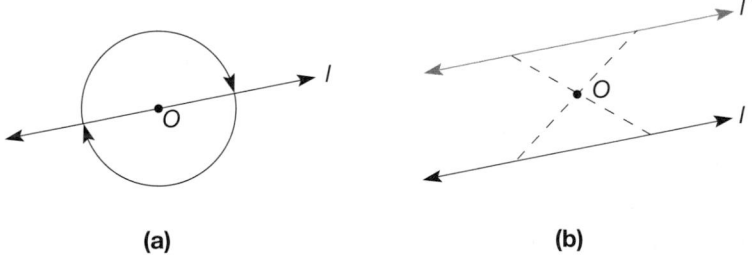

(a)   **(b)**

Figure 16.50

Example 16.12 illustrates the use of half-turns to verify a property of quadrilaterals.

Example 16.12 Show that if the diagonals of a quadrilateral bisect each other, the quadrilateral is a parallelogram.

Solution Suppose that $ABCD$ is a quadrilateral with diagonals $\overline{AC}$ and $\overline{BD}$ intersecting at point O, the midpoint of each diagonal (Figure 16.51).

Problem-Solving Strategy
Draw a Picture

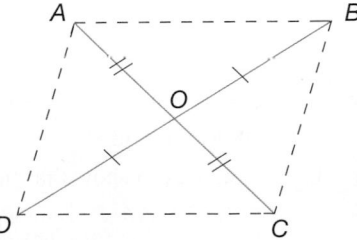

Figure 16.51

Consider the half-turn H_O. Then $H_O(A) = C$, $H_O(B) = D$, $H_O(C) = A$, and $H_O(D) = B$ (verify). Thus H_O maps side $\overline{AB}$ of quadrilateral $ABCD$ to side $\overline{CD}$ so that $\overline{AB} \parallel \overline{CD}$.

Also, H_O maps $\overline{AD}$ to $\overline{CB}$ so that $\overline{AD} \parallel \overline{CB}$. Hence quadrilateral $ABCD$ is a parallelogram, since both pairs of its opposite sides are parallel. (NOTE: Since H_O is an isometry, this also shows that opposite sides of a parallelogram are congruent.) ■

Transformations can also be used to solve certain applied problems. Consider the following pool table problem.

Example 16.13 Cue ball A is to hit cushion l, then strike object ball B (Figure 16.52). Assuming that there is no "spin" on the cue ball, show how to find the desired point P on cushion l at which to aim the cue ball.

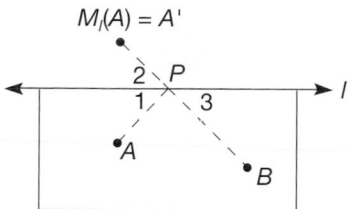

Figure 16.52

Solution Reflect the cue ball, A, in line l. That is, find $M_l(A) = A'$ (Figure 16.52). Let P be the point at which the line $\overline{A'B}$ intersects cushion l. Then $\angle 1 \cong \angle 2$, since an angle is congruent to its reflection image, and $\angle 2 \cong \angle 3$, because they are vertical angles. Since the angle of incidence is congruent to the angle of reflection, we have that the cue ball should be aimed at point P. ■

Examples of pool shot paths caroming, or "banking," off several cushions appear in the Exercise/Problem Set. Our next example concerns a minimal distance problem involving a translation.

Example 16.14 Towns A and B are on opposite sides of a river (Figure 16.53). The towns are to be connected with a bridge, $\overline{CD}$, perpendicular to the river, so that the distance $AC + CD + DB$ is as small as possible. Where should the bridge be located?

Solution No matter where the bridge is located, distance CD, the width of the river, will be a constant in the sum $AC + CD + DB$ [Figure 16.54(a)]. Hence we wish to minimize the sum $AC + DB$. Let S be a translation in a direction from B toward the river and perpendicular to it, for a distance equal to the width of the river, d. Let $B' = S(B)$. Then the segment $\overline{AB'}$ is the shortest path from A to B'. Let point C be the intersection of $\overline{AB'}$ and line m, one side of the river [Figure 16.54(b)].

Figure 16.53

Problem-Solving Strategy
Look for a Pattern

(a)

(b)

Figure 16.54

Let point D be the point opposite C on the other side of the river, where $\overline{CD} \perp m$. That is, $\overline{CD} \parallel \overline{B'B}$ and $\overline{CD} = \overline{B'B}$. Hence quadrilateral $BB'CD$ is a parallelogram, since the opposite sides $\overline{CD}$ and $\overline{B'B}$ are congruent and parallel. Thus the sum $AC + CD + DB$ is as small as possible. ■

MATHEMATICAL MORSEL

The following sequence of diagrams suggests a transformational proof of the Pythagorean theorem.

Section 16.3   EXERCISE / PROBLEM SET A

EXERCISES

1. Figure *ABCD* is a kite. Point *E* is the intersection of the diagonals. Which of the following transformations can be used to show that $\triangle ABC \cong \triangle ADC$ using the transformation definition of congruence? Explain.

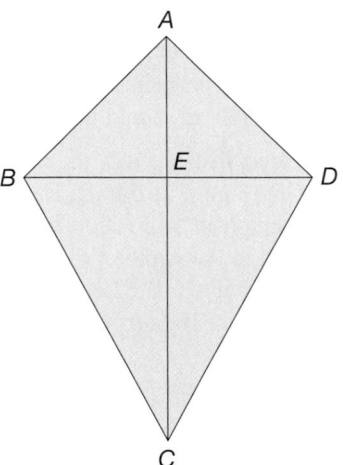

  a. H_E **b.** T_{BE} **c.** $R_{E,90°}$ **d.** M_{AC}

2. *ABCD* is a rectangle. Points *E*, *F*, *G*, *H* are the midpoints of the sides. Find all the reflections and rotations that map *ABCD* onto itself.

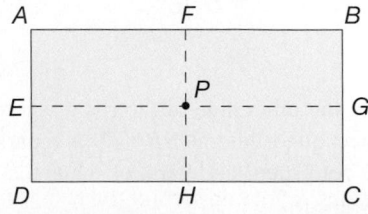

3. *ABCDEF* is a regular hexagon with center *O*.

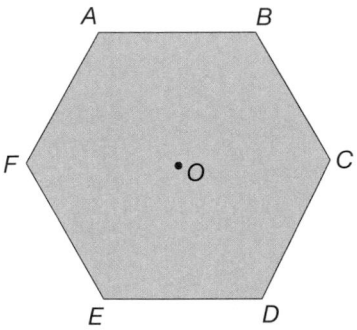

  a. List three reflections and three rotations that map the hexagon onto itself.

  b. How many isometries are there that map the hexagon onto itself?

4. *ABCD* is an isosceles trapezoid. Are there two isometries that map *ABCD* onto itself? Explain.

5. On the lattice shown. *ABCD* is a parallelogram.

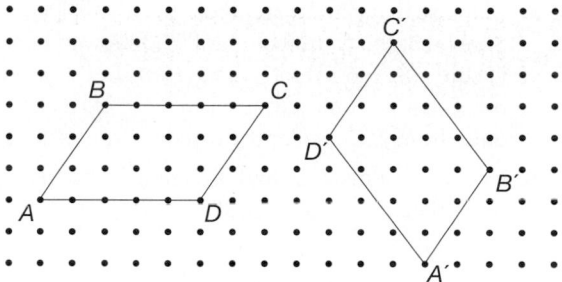

a. Find the image of point *P* under the following sequence of half-turns: H_A, then H_B, then H_C, then H_D. That is, find $H_D(H_C(H_B(H_A(P))))$.

b. Find $H_D(H_C(H_B(H_A(Q))))$.

c. Write a conjecture based on your observations.

6. Find a combination of isometries that map *ABCD* to *A'B'C'D'*, or explain why this is impossible.

7. a. Show how the combination of $R_{B,90°}$ followed by $S_{O,1/2}$ will map $\triangle ABC$ onto $\triangle A'B'C'$.

b. Is $\triangle ABC \sim \triangle A'B'C'$? Explain.

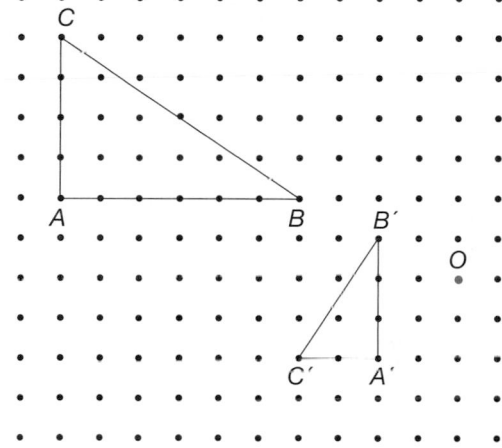

PROBLEMS

8. *ABCD* is a parallelogram. Show that the diagonal $\overline{AC}$ divides *ABCD* into two congruent triangles using the transformation definition of congruence. (*Hint:* Use a half-turn.)

9. Use the results of Problem 8 to show that the following statements are true.

a. Opposite angles of a parallelogram are congruent.

b. Opposite sides of a parallelogram are congruent.

10. Suppose that point *B* is equidistant from points *A* and *C*. Show that *B* is on the perpendicular bisector of $\overline{AC}$. (*Hint:* Let *P* be a point on $\overline{AC}$ so that $\overline{BP}$ is the bisector of $\angle ABC$. Then use M_{BP}.)

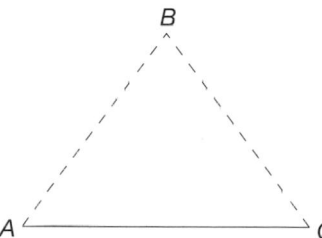

11. Let *ABCD* be a kite with *AB = AD* and *BC = DC*. Explain how Problem 10 shows that the following statements are true.

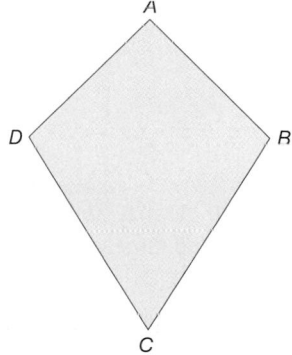

a. The diagonals of a kite are perpendicular.

b. A kite has reflection symmetry.

12. a. Suppose that r and s are lines such that $r \parallel s$. Show that the combination of M_r followed by M_s is equivalent to a translation. [*Hint:* Let A be any point that is x units from r. Let $A' = M_r(A)$ be y units from s. Consider the distance from A to A'.]

b. How are the distance and direction of the translation related to lines r and s?

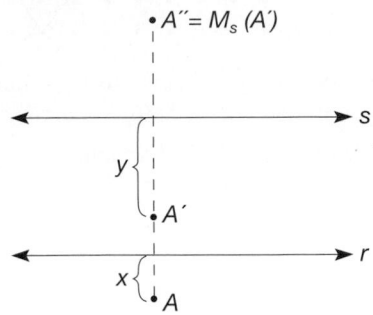

13. On the billiard table, ball A is to carom off two of the rails (sides) and strike ball B.

a. Draw the path for a successful shot.

b. Using a reflection and congruent triangles, give an argument justifying your drawing in part (a).

14. $ABCD$ is a square with side length a, while $EFGH$ is a square with side length b. Describe a similarity transformation that will map $ABCD$ to $EFGH$.

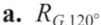

Section 16.1 EXERCISE / PROBLEM SET B

EXERCISES

1. Triangle ABC is equilateral. Point G is the circumcenter (also the incenter). Which of the following transformations will map $\triangle ABC$ onto itself?

a. $R_{G,120°}$ **b.** $R_{G,60°}$ **c.** M_{AF} **d.** $S_{C,1}$

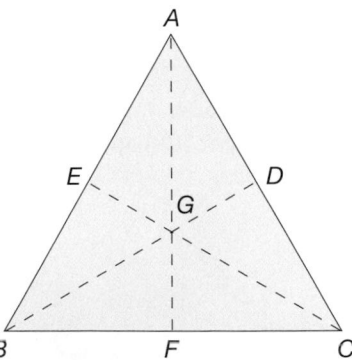

2. For equilateral triangle ABC in Exercise 1, list three different rotations and three different reflections that map $\triangle ABC$ onto itself.

3. $ABCDE$ is a regular pentagon with center O. Points F, G, H, I, J are the midpoints of the sides. List all the reflections and all the rotations that map the pentagon onto itself.

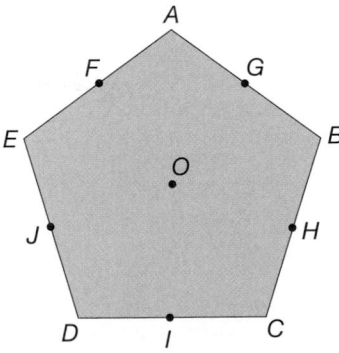

4. $ABCD$ is a parallelogram. List all the isometries that map $ABCD$ onto itself.

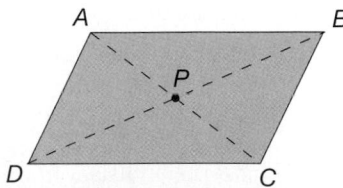

5. a. Using the triangle ABC, find the image of point P under the following sequence of half-turns:
$$H_C(H_B(H_A(H_C(H_B(H_A(P))))))$$

b. Apply the same sequence to point Q.

c. Write a conjecture based on your observations.

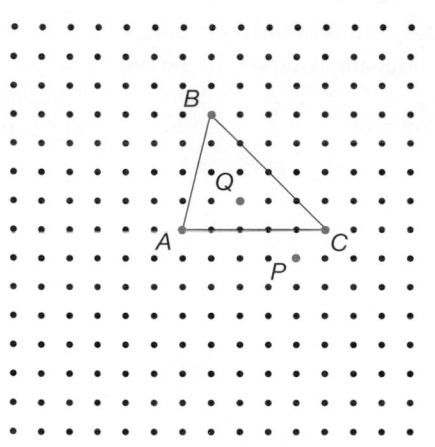

6. Find a combination of isometries that will map $\triangle ABC$ to $\triangle A'B'C'$, or explain why this is impossible.

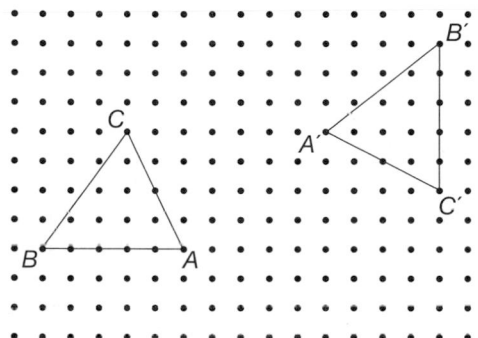

7. Show how the combination of M_r, followed by $S_{O,1/2}$ will map $\triangle ABC$ onto $\triangle A'B'C'$.

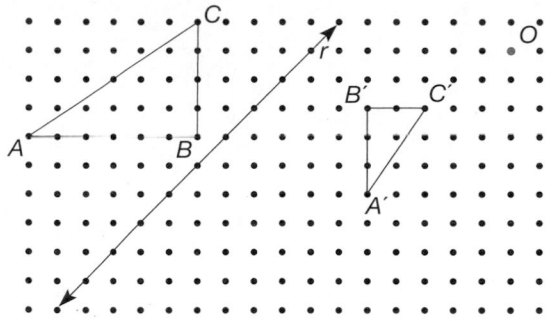

PROBLEMS

8. Points P, Q, and R are the midpoints of the sides of $\triangle ABC$.

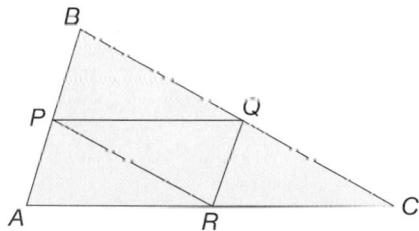

a. Show $S_{A,2}(\triangle APR) = \triangle ABC$, $S_{B,2}(\triangle PBQ) = \triangle ABC$, and $S_{C,2}(\triangle QCR) = \triangle BCA$.

b. How does part (a) show that $PBQR$ is a parallelogram?

9. Suppose that $ABCD$ is a parallelogram. Show that the diagonals $\overline{AC}$ and $\overline{BD}$ bisect each other.

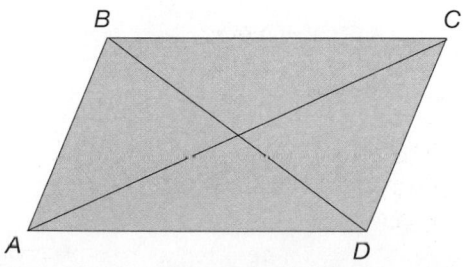

[*Hint:* Let P be the midpoint of $\overline{AC}$ and show that $H_p(B) = D$.]

10. Suppose that point B is on the perpendicular bisector l of $\overline{AC}$. Use M_l to show that $AB = BC$ (i.e., that B is equidistant from A and C).

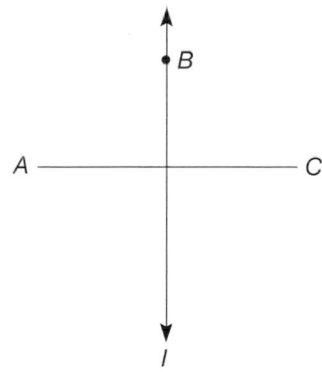

11. Suppose that lines r and s intersect at point P.

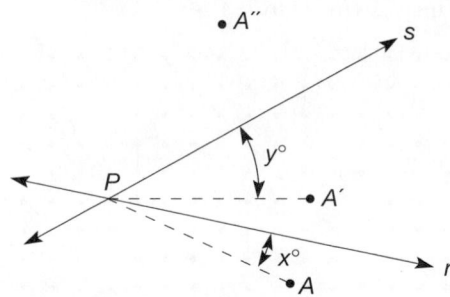

a. Show that M_r followed by M_s is equivalent to a rotation.

b. How are the center and angle of the rotation related to lines r and s?
[*Hint:* Let $A' = M_r(A)$ and suppose that the angle formed by $\overrightarrow{PA}$ and r measures x. Let $A'' = M_s(A')$ and suppose that the angle formed by $\overrightarrow{PA}$ and s measures y.]

12. On the billiard table, ball A is to carom off three rails, then strike ball B.

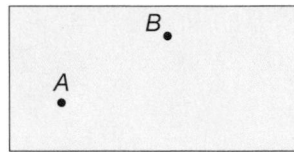

a. Draw the path for a successful shot.

b. Using three reflections, give an argument justifying your drawing in part (a).

13. Suppose that $ABCD$ is a rhombus. Use reflections M_{AC} and M_{BD} to show that $ABCD$ is a parallelogram.

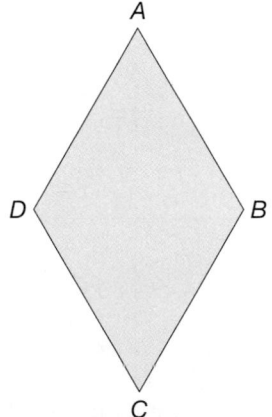

14. Euclid's proof of the Pythagorean theorem involves the following diagram. In the proof, Euclid states that $\triangle ABD \cong \triangle FBC$ and that $\triangle ACE \cong \triangle KCB$. Find two rotations that demonstrate these congruences.

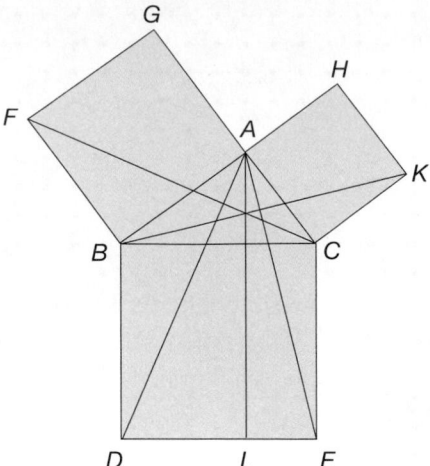

15. A **Reuleaux triangle** is a curved three-sided shape (see the figure). Each curved side is a part of a circle whose radius is the length of the side of the equilateral triangle. Find the area of a Reuleaux triangle if the length of the side of the triangle is 1.

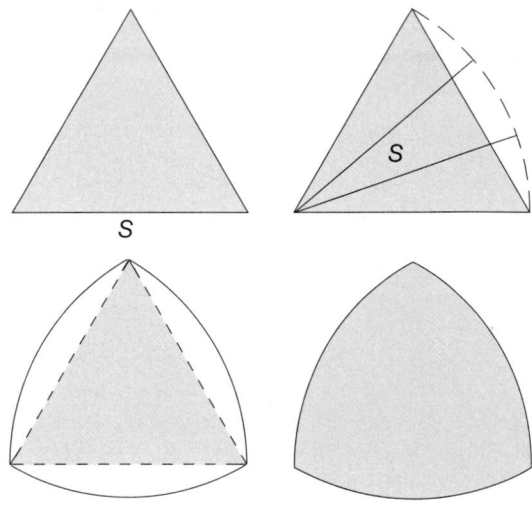

PROBLEMS FOR WRITING/DISCUSSION

1. Jaime drew this picture of one hole at a miniature golf course. He says he can hit the ball from point A and have it follow the path he showed and end up in the hole at point B. How accurate is his thinking on this problem? Discuss.

2. Annie has reflected an isosceles triangle over its nonequal side. She says the triangle together with its image seems to have the shape of a rhombus. Is she correct? Explain.

3. Lee says a parallelogram has a line of symmetry in between two of the parallel sides. What properties of reflection could you use to explain that this is not a line of symmetry?

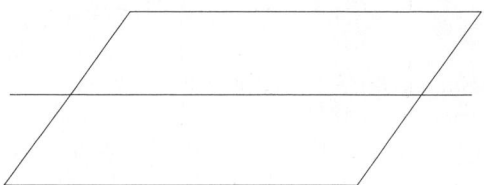

END OF CHAPTER MATERIAL

Solution of Initial Problem

Houses A and B are to be connected to a television cable line l, at a transformer point P. Where should P be located so that the sum $AP + PB$ is as small as possible?

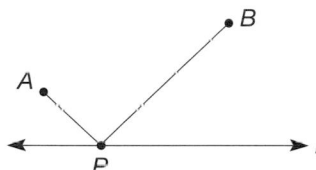

Strategy: Use Symmetry

Reflect point B across line l to point B'. Then $\triangle BPB'$ is isosceles, and line l is a line of reflection symmetry for $\triangle BPB'$. Hence $BP = B'P$, so the problem is equivalent to locating P so that the sum $AP + PB'$ is as small as possible. By the triangle inequality, we must have A, P, and B' collinear.

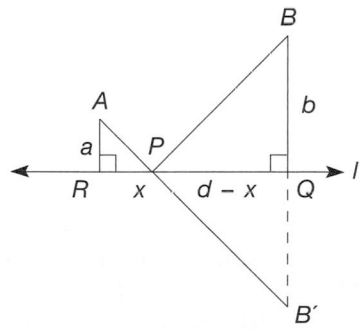

Let point Q be the intersection of $\overline{BB'}$ and l. Let R be the point on l such that $AR \perp l$. Since points A, P, and B' are collinear and $\triangle BPB'$ is isosceles, we have $\angle APR \cong \angle B'PQ \cong \angle BPQ$. But then, $\triangle APR \sim \triangle BPQ$ by the AA similarity property. Thus

corresponding sides are proportional in these triangles. Let $RP = x$ and $RQ = d$, so that $PQ = d - x$. Then, by similar triangles,

$$\frac{x}{d-x} = \frac{a}{b},$$

so that

$$bx = ad - ax$$
$$ax + bx = ad$$
$$x(a + b) = ad$$
$$x = \frac{ad}{a+b},$$

Hence, locate point P along $\overline{RQ}$ so that $RP = \frac{ad}{a+b}$.

Additional Problems Where the Strategy "Use Symmetry" Is Useful

1. The 4×4 quilt of squares shown here has reflective symmetry.

Explain how to find all such quilts having reflective symmetry that are made up of 12 light squares and 4 dark squares.

2. Find all three-digit numbers that can serve as house numbers when the numbers are installed upside-down or right-side-up. Assume that the 1 and 8 are read the same both ways.

3. The 4th number in the 41st row of Pascal's triangle is 9880. What is the 38th number of the 41st row?

People in Mathematics

Edward G. Begle (1914–1978)
Edward G. Begle could be called the father of the "New Math." Influenced by the success of *Sputnik* in 1957, the U.S. government, through its National Science Foundation, embarked on a systematic revision of the K–12 curriculum in the late 1950s. Although Begle was well on his way to becoming a first-rate research mathematician, he was asked to lead this effort, called the School Mathematics Study Group (SMSG), due to his unique talent for administration. He moved to Stanford, where he coordinated the SMSG for many years. In addition to this project, he initiated the National Longitudinal Study of Mathematical Abilities (NLSMA), which set a standard for subsequent such studies. Begle, whose respect for mathematics education grew as he worked with SMSG, stated that "Mathematics education is more complicated than you expected even though you expected it to be more complicated than you expected."

Jaime Escalante (1930–)
Jaime Escalante began teaching at Garfield High in East Los Angeles as a seasoned mathematics teacher, having taught for 11 years in Bolivia. But he was not prepared for this run-down inner-city school, where gang violence abounded and neither parents nor students were interested in education. After the discouraging first day on the job, he vowed, "First I'm going to teach them responsibility, and I'm going to teach them respect, and then I'm going to quit." He succeeded but stayed on to build, year after year, a team of mathematics students with the Advanced Placement calculus exam as their Olympic competition. He built their self-confidence and trained, coached, and prodded them as a coach might train athletes. Students would go to the Advanced Placement exam wearing their school jackets, yelling "Defense, Defense!" Today, Garfield High is, Escalante says, "one of the best schools. I feel great when I see our kids going to the best colleges now." "My skills are really to motivate these kids, to make them learn, to give them 'ganas'—the desire to do something—to make them believe they can learn." The movie *Stand and Deliver* was about Escalante's successes as a teacher at Garfield.

CHAPTER REVIEW

Review the following terms and exercises to determine which require learning or relearning—page numbers are provided for easy reference.

SECTION 16.1: Transformations

VOCABULARY/NOTATION

Transformation, T 799
Image of a point, P' 799
Isometry   799
Rigid motion   799
Directed line segment, $\overrightarrow{AB}$ 800
Equivalent directed line segments   800
Translation, T_{AB} 800
Directed angle, $\angle ABC$ 802
Measure of a directed angle   802
Initial side   802

Terminal side   802
Rotation with center O and angle with measure a, $R_{O,a}$ 803
Reflection in line l, M_l (or M_{AB} if $l = \overleftrightarrow{AB}$)   803
Glide reflection determined by directed line segment $\overrightarrow{AB}$ and glide axis l (or T_{AB} followed by M_{AB})   806
Clockwise orientation   806
Counterclockwise orientation   806

Translation symmetry   807
Rotation symmetry   807
Reflection symmetry   807
Glide reflection symmetry   808
Escher-type patterns   808
Size transformation $S_{O,k}$ with center O and scale factor k 810
Magnification   810
Dilation   810
Dilitation   810
Similitude   811

EXERCISES

1. Draw directed line segment $\overrightarrow{AB}$ and P anywhere. Show how to find the image of P determined by T_{AB}.

2. Draw a directed angle of measure a and vertex O and P anywhere. Show how to find the image of P determined by $R_{O,a}$.

3. Draw a line l, Q on l, and P anywhere. Show how to find the images of Q and P determined by M_l.

4. Draw a line l, a directed line segment $\overrightarrow{AB}$ parallel to l, and P anywhere. Show how to find the image of P determined by the glide reflection l and $\overrightarrow{AB}$.

5. Sketch a pattern that has translation symmetry. What must be true about such patterns?

6. Sketch a pattern that has a rotation symmetry of less than $180°$.

7. Sketch a pattern that has reflection symmetry.

8. Sketch a pattern that has glide reflection symmetry. What must be true about such patterns?

9. Draw $\triangle ABC$ and point O anywhere. Show how to find the image of $\triangle ABC$ determined by $S_{O,2}$.

10. Using the idea of a similitude, show that any two equilateral triangles are similar.

SECTION 16.2: Congruence and Similarity Using Transformations
VOCABULARY / NOTATION

Image of a point P under a translation, $T_{AB}(P)$ 822
Image of a point P under a rotation, $R_{O,a}(P)$ 822
Image of a point P under a reflection, $M_l(P)$ 822

Image of a point P under a glide reflection: T_{AB} followed by M_l, $M_l(T_{AB}(P))$ 822
Isometry   824
Congruent shapes $\mathscr{S} \cong \mathscr{S}'$ 827
Congruent polygons, $\mathscr{P} \cong \mathscr{P}'$ 827

Similar shapes, $\mathscr{S} \sim \mathscr{S}'$ 830
Similar polygons, $\mathscr{P} \sim \mathscr{P}'$ 830
Transformation geometry   830

EXERCISES

1. Name the four types of isometries.

2. Given that an isometry maps line segments to line segments and preserves angle measure, show that the isometry maps any triangle to a congruent triangle.

3. Given that an isometry maps lines to lines and preserves angle measure, show that the isometry maps parallel lines to parallel lines.

4. Describe how isometries are used to prove that two triangles are congruent.

5. Given that size transformations map line segments to line segments and preserve angle measure, show that size transformations map any triangle to a similar triangle.

6. Explain why size transformations preserve parallelism.

7. Describe how similarity is used to prove that two triangles are similar.

SECTION 16.3: Geometric Problem Solving Using Transformations
VOCABULARY / NOTATION

Half-turn with center O, H_O 840

EXERCISE

1. Given a triangle and any point O, find the half-turn image of the triangle determined by the point O.

PROBLEMS FOR WRITING/DISCUSSION

1. If you saw a figure, and its image after a translation, explain how you would go about reconstructing the direction and distance of the slide.

2. If you saw a figure, and its image after a reflection, explain how you would go about reconstructing the flip line.

3. If you saw a figure, and its image after a rotation, explain how you would go about reconstructing its center and the degree and direction of the turn.

4. If you saw a figure, and its image after a glide reflection, explain how you would go about reconstructing its glide axis.

5. If you saw a figure, and its image after a size transformation, explain how you would go about reconstructing the center of the transformation and the scale factor.

6. Chungsim has taken an L-shaped figure and reflected it over a line, *p*. She then took the image and reflected that over a second line, *q*. The two lines meet in a 40° angle at point *F*. Chungsim asks you, "Did I have to do two motions? Could I have done it with just one flip?" How would you respond? Be specific.

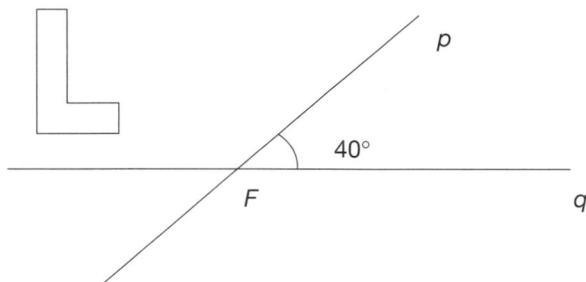

7. Mackie says any slide can be replaced by one flip if a figure is symmetric, two flips if it isn't. Is he correct? Explain. What are the restrictions on the flip lines?

8. Penny says any turn can be replaced by two flips. If you asked her to elaborate, what specifics would you expect her to include?

9. Emir says a glide reflection could not be replaced by flips. Do you agree? Explain.

10. Chris says he can move any figure in the plane onto its congruent image using only flips, no matter how difficult the task may seem. What is the most challenging problem you can think of to give him? Include your solution, of course.

CHAPTER TEST
Knowledge

1. True or false?

   a. A translation maps a line *l* to a line parallel to *l*.

   b. If the direction of a turn is clockwise, the measure of the directed angle associated with the turn is positive.

   c. A reflection reverses orientation.

   d. A regular tessellation of square tiles has translation, rotation, reflection, and glide reflection symmetry.

   e. An isometry preserves distance and angle measure.

   f. An isometry preserves orientation.

   g. A size transformation preserves angle measure and ratios of length.

   h. A similarity transformation is a size transformation followed by an isometry.

2. List the properties that are preserved by isometries but not size transformations.

3. Which of the transformations leaves exactly one point fixed when performed on the entire plane?

4. Which of the following transformations map the segment $\overline{AB}$ to $\overline{A'B'}$ in such a way that $\overline{AB} \parallel \overline{A'B'}$? (There may be more than one correct answer.)

   a. Translation   b. Rotation

   c. Reflection   d. Glide reflection

   e. Size transformation

5. Which of the following transformations map the segment $\overline{AB}$ to $\overline{A'B'}$ in such a way that $\overline{AA'} \parallel \overline{BB'}$? (There may be more than one correct answer.)

   a. Translation   b. Rotation

   c. Reflection   d. Glide reflection

   e. Size transformation

6. Each of the following notations describes a specific transformation. Identify the general type of transformation corresponding to each notational description.

a. $S_{M,3}(Q)$ **b.** $R_{N,b}(Q)$ **c.** $M_n(Q)$

d. $M_n(T_{xy}(Q))$ **e.** $T_{xy}(Q)$

Skill

7. For each of the following, trace the figure onto a piece of paper and perform the indicated transformation on the quadrilateral.

a. Reflect about line m.

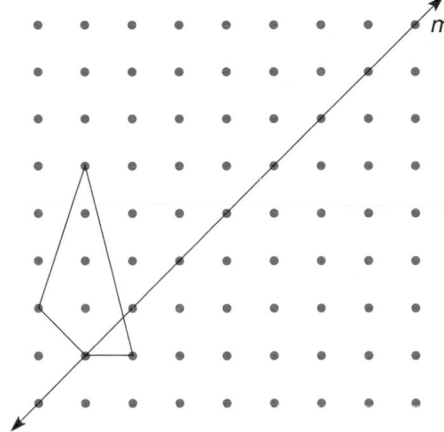

b. Rotate $90°$ about point O.

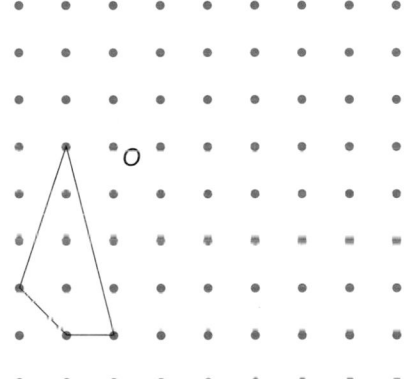

c. Translate parallel to the directed line segment $\overrightarrow{MN}$.

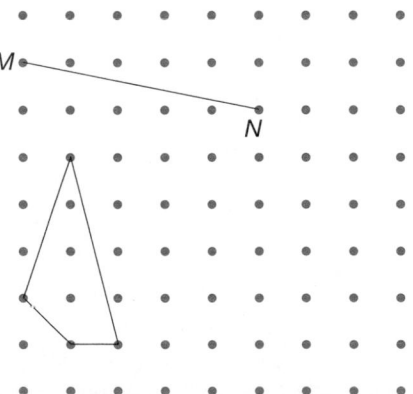

8. Find the following points on the square lattice.

  a. $T_{AB}(P)$

  b. $R_{C,90°}(P)$

  c. $M_{OC}(P)$

  d. $T_{PB}(M_{OC}(P))$

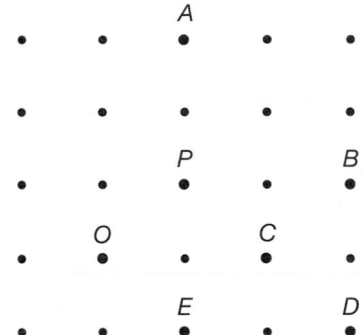

9. Trace the following grid and triangle on a piece of paper and find $S_{O,3}(\triangle ABC)$.

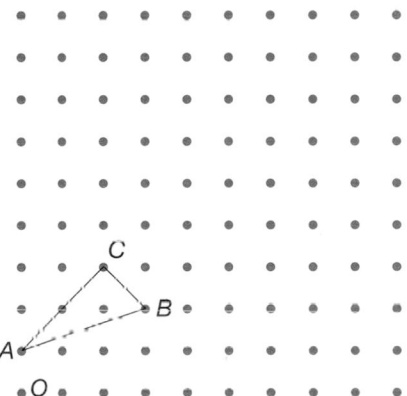

10. Determine which of the following types of symmetry apply to the tessellation shown here: translation, rotation, reflection, glide reflection (assume that the tessellation fills the plane).

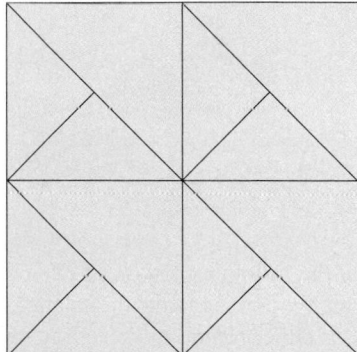

11. Describe the following isometries as they relate to the triangles shown.

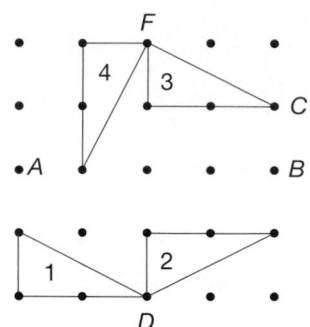

a. The reflection that maps 3 to 2

b. The rotation that maps 3 to 4

c. The translation that maps 3 to 1

Understanding

12. Explain how to prove that the square $ABCD$ is similar to the square $EFGH$

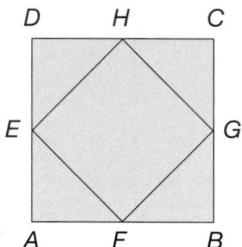

13. Explain why performing two glide reflections, one after the other, yields either a translation or a rotation.

14. Given that l, m, and n are perpendicular bisectors of sides $\overline{AB}$, $\overline{BC}$, and $\overline{AC}$, respectively, find the image of B after applying successively M_l followed by M_n, followed by M_m.

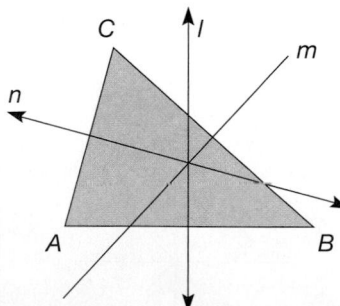

15. In each of the following cases $\triangle XYZ \cong \triangle X'Y'Z'$. Identify the type of isometry that maps $\triangle XYZ$ to $\triangle X'Y'Z'$ as either rotation, translation, reflection, glide reflection, or none.

a.

b.

c.

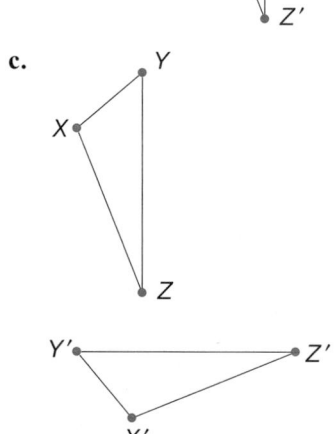

16. Trace the following figure onto a piece of paper. Sketch the approximate location of the image of $\triangle XYZ$ under the rotation $R_{O,60°}$.

17. Let $M = (-1, 5)$ and $N = (3, -1)$. Give the coordinates of the images of the points $A = (1, 1)$, $B = (-2, -4)$, and $C = (x, y)$ under the transformation T_{MN}.

Problem Solving Application

18. Find AB, AC, and CE for the figure shown.

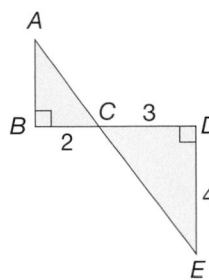

19. Given isosceles $\triangle ABC$, where M is the midpoint of $\overline{AB}$, prove that $\overleftrightarrow{CM}$ is a symmetry line for $\triangle ABC$.

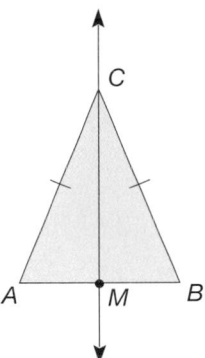

20. In the following figure, $\triangle ABC \cong \triangle A'B'C'$. Completely describe a transformation that maps $\triangle ABC$ to $\triangle A'B'C'$ (i.e., if the transformation is a reflection, then construct the line of reflection; if the transformation is a translation, then construct the directed line segment, etc.).

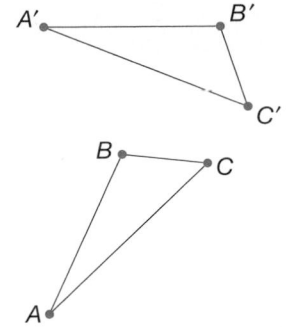

21. In the following figure, is $\triangle ABC$ the image of $\triangle XYZ$ under a size transformation? Justify your conclusion.

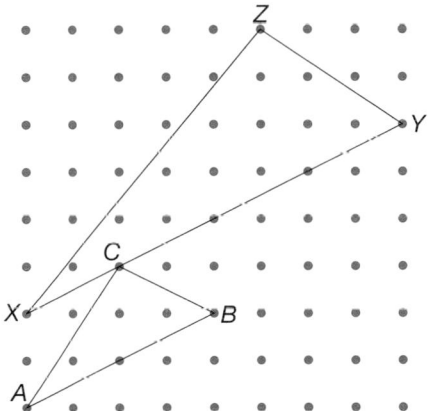

References for Reflections from Research

DIXON, J. K. (1995). English language proficiency and spatial visualization in middle school students' construction of the concepts of reflections and rotation using *The Geometer's Sketchpad*. Unpublished doctoral dissertation, University of Florida.

FLORES, A. (1992). Mathematical connections with a Spirograph. *Mathematics Teacher, 85,* 129–137.

MOYER, J. C. (1978). The relationship between the mathematical structure of Euclidean transformations and the spontaneously developed cognitive structures of young children. *Journal for Research in Mathematics Education, 9,* 83–92.

SCHULTZ, K. A., & AUSTIN, J. D. (1983). Directional effects in transformation tasks. *Journal for Research in Mathematics Education, 14,* 95–101.

SOON, Y. P. (1989). An investigation of van Hiele levels of learning transformation geometry of secondary school students in Singapore. (Doctoral dissertation, Florida State University, Tallahassee, 1989). *Dissertation Abstract International, 50*(3), 619A.

An Eclectic Approach to Geometry

INTRODUCTION

NCTM Standards 2000
Reasoning and Proof
Instructional programs should enable all students to select and use various types of reasoning and methods of proof.

Three approaches to geometry were presented in Chapters 14–16:

1. The traditional Euclidean approach using congruence and similarity
2. The coordinate approach
3. The transformation approach

A fourth common approach is the vector approach. The value of multiple approaches to problem solving is that a theorem may be proved using *any* of several methods, one of which may lead to an *easy* proof. Facility using these various approaches gives one "mathematical power" when making proofs in geometry. This section gives a proof of the midsegment theorem using each of the three approaches. The problem set contains problems where you may choose the approach that you feel will lead to an easy solution.

The Midsegment Theorem

In Section 14.5 it was shown that the midsegment of a triangle is parallel and equal to one-half the length of the third side. Following are three different proofs, the first using congruence, the second using coordinates, and the third using transformations.

Congruence Proof Let $\overline{PQ}$ be a midsegment of $\triangle ABC$ as shown in Figure E.1(a). Extend $\overline{PQ}$ through Q to R so that $PQ = QR$, and draw $\overline{CR}$ [Figure E.1(b)].

Figure E.1

By SAS, $\triangle PBQ \cong \triangle RCQ$, since $\angle PQB$ and $\angle RQC$ are vertical angles. Consequently, $\angle PBQ \cong \angle RCQ$ by corresponding parts. Viewing these parts as a pair of congruent alternate interior angles, we have $\overline{AP} \parallel \overline{CR}$. Again, by corresponding parts, $\overline{PB} \cong \overline{CR}$. Also, since $\overline{AP} \cong \overline{PB}$, we have $\overline{AP} \cong \overline{CR}$ [Figure E.1(c)]. Thus, by Example 14.13, $APRC$ is a parallelogram, since $\overline{AP} \parallel \overline{CR}$ and $\overline{AP} \cong \overline{CR}$. It follows that $\overline{PQ} \parallel \overline{AC}$ and $PQ = \frac{1}{2}AC$. ∎

Coordinate Proof Let $\overline{PQ}$ be a midsegment of $\triangle ABC$ with coordinates as shown in Figure E.2. By the midpoint formula, the coordinates of P are $(\frac{a}{2}, \frac{b}{2})$ and of Q are $(\frac{a+c}{2}, \frac{b}{2})$. Since P and Q have the same y-coordinate, namely $\frac{b}{2}$, $\overline{PQ}$ is horizontal; hence it is parallel to the x-axis and thus to $\overline{AC}$. Also, $PQ = \frac{a+c}{2} - \frac{a}{2} = \frac{c}{2}$ and $AC = c$. Thus $PQ = \frac{1}{2}AC$.

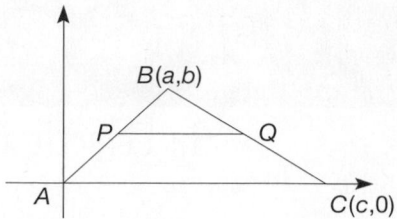

Figure E.2

Transformation Proof Let $\overline{PQ}$ be a midsegment of $\triangle ABC$ as shown in Figure E.3. Consider the size transformation $S_{B,2}$. Under $S_{B,2}$, the image of P is A and the image of Q is C. Thus, according to the properties of size transformations, $\overline{PQ} \parallel \overline{AC}$ and $PQ = \frac{1}{2}AC$, since the scale factor is 2.

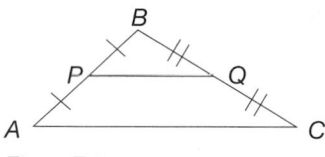

Figure E.3

If the coordinate and transformation proofs seem to be much easier, it is because much work went into developing concepts *before* we applied them in these proofs. For example, we applied the midpoint formula in the coordinate proof and properties of size transformations in the transformation proof.

The following Problem Set will provide practice in proving geometric relationships using the three approaches. Your choice of approach is a personal one. You may find one approach to be preferable (easier?) to a friend's. You will find that comparing the various proofs and discussing the merits of the various approaches is worthwhile.

E   EXERCISE / PROBLEM SET A

1. Prove: Consecutive angles of a parallelogram $ABCD$ are supplementary. (Use congruence geometry.)

2. The sides of $DEFG$ have midpoints M, N, O, and P, as shown. Verify that $MNOP$ is a parallelogram.

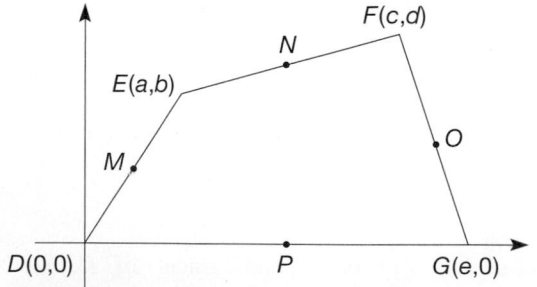

3. Suppose that $\triangle ABC$ is isosceles with $AB = AC$. Let P be the point on $\overline{BC}$ so that $\overline{AP}$ bisects $\angle BAC$. Use the transformation M_{AP} to show that $\angle ABC \cong \angle ACB$.

4. In quadrilateral $ABCD$, both pairs of opposite sides are congruent. Prove that $ABCD$ is a parallelogram. (*Hint:* Draw diagonal $\overline{BD}$.) (Do two proofs, one congruence and one coordinate.)

5. Prove: In an isosceles triangle, the medians to the congruent sides are congruent. (Do two proofs, one congruence and one coordinate.)

Prove Problems 6–8 using any approach.

6. A rectangle is sometimes defined as a parallelogram with at least one right angle. If parallelogram $PQRS$ has a right angle at P, verify that $PQRS$ has four right angles.

7. Prove: The diagonals of a square are perpendicular.

8. In quadrilateral $PQRS$, both pairs of opposite angles are congruent. Prove that $PQRS$ is a parallelogram.

E EXERCISE / PROBLEM SET B

1. If a pair of opposite sides of *ABCD* are parallel and congruent, then it is a parallelogram. (*Hint:* Let $\overline{AB} \parallel \overline{DC}$, $\overline{AB} \cong \overline{DC}$ and draw $\overline{BD}$.) (Use congruence geometry.)

2. Given is trapezoid *ABCD* with $AB \parallel CD$. *M* is the midpoint of $\overline{AD}$ and *N* is the midpoint of $\overline{BC}$. Show that $MN = \frac{1}{2}(AB + DC)$ and $\overline{MN} \parallel \overline{AB}$. (Use coordinates.)

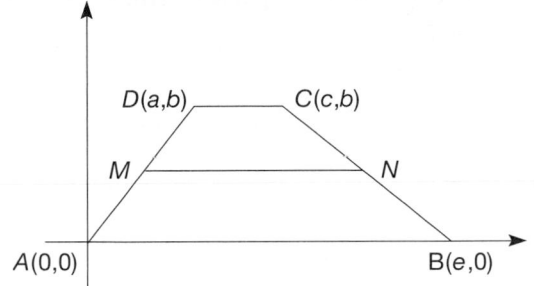

3. Suppose that *ABCD* is a parallelogram and *P* is the intersection of the diagonals.

   a. Show that $H_P(A) = C$ and $H_P(B) = D$.

   b. How does part (a) show that a parallelogram has rotation symmetry?

4. In *ABCD*, the diagonals bisect each other at *E*. Prove that *ABCD* is a parallelogram. (Use coordinates.)

5. Verify that the diagonals of a rhombus are perpendicular. (Do two proofs, one congruence and one coordinate.)

Prove Problems 6–8 using any approach.

6. Given parallelogram *LMNO* with perpendicular diagonals $\overline{LN}$ and $\overline{MO}$ intersecting at *P*, prove that *LMNO* is a rhombus.

7. Show that the diagonals of an isosceles trapezoid are congruent.

8. Quadrilateral *HIJK* is a rectangle where *HJ* and *IK* intersect at *L* and are perpendicular. Prove that *HIJK* is a square.

ELEMENTARY LOGIC

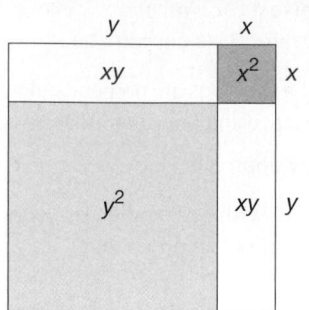

Figure T1.1

Logic allows us to determine the validity of arguments, in and out of mathematics. The validity of an argument depends on its logical form, not on the particular meaning of the terms it contains. For example, the argument, "All X's are Y's; all Y's are Z's; therefore all X's are Z's" is valid no matter what X, Y, and Z are. In this topic section we will study how logic can be used to represent arguments symbolically and to analyze arguments using tables and diagrams.

Statements

Often, ideas in mathematics can be made clearer through the use of variables and diagrams. For example, the equation $2m + 2n = 2(m + n)$, where the variables m and n are whole numbers, can be used to show that the sum of any two arbitrary even numbers, $2m$ and $2n$ here, is the even number $2(m + n)$. Figure T1.1 shows that $(x + y)^2 = x^2 + 2xy + y^2$, where each term in the expanded product is the area of the rectangular region so designated.

In a similar fashion, symbols and diagrams can be used to clarify logic. Statements are the building blocks on which logic is built. A **statement** is a declarative sentence that is true or false but not both. Examples of statements include the following:

1. Alaska is geographically the largest state of the United States. (True)
2. Texas is the largest state of the United States in population. (False)
3. $2 + 3 = 5$. (True)
4. $3 < 0$. (False)

The following are not statements.

1. Oregon is the best state. (Subjective)
2. Help! (An exclamation)
3. Where were you? (A question)
4. The rain in Spain. (Not a sentence)
5. This sentence is false. (Neither true nor false!)

Statements are usually represented symbolically by lowercase letters (e.g., p, q, r, and s).

New statements can be created from existing statements in several ways. For example, if p represents the statement "The sun is shining," then the **negation** of p, written $\sim p$ and read "not p," is the statement "The sun is not shining." When a statement is true, its negation is false and when a statement is false, its negation is true; that is, a statement and its negation have opposite truth values. This relationship between a statement and its negation is summarized using a **truth table:**

p	$\sim p$
T	F
F	T

This table shows that when the statement p is T, then $\sim p$ is F and when p is F, $\sim p$ is T.

Logical Connectives

Two or more statements can be joined, or connected, to form **compound statements.** The four commonly used **logical connectives** "and," "or," "if–then," and "if and only if" are studied next.

AND If p is the statement "It is raining" and q is the statement "The sun is shining," then the **conjunction** of p and q is the statement "It is raining and the sun is shining" or, symbolically, "$p \wedge q$." The conjunction of two statements p and q is true exactly when both p and q are true. This relationship is displayed in the next truth table.

p	q	$p \wedge q$
T	T	T
T	F	F
F	T	F
F	F	F

Notice that the two statements p and q each have two possible truth values, T and F. Hence there are four possible combinations of T and F to consider.

OR The **disjunction** of statements p and q is the statement "p or q," symbolically, "$p \vee q$." In practice, there are two common uses of "or": the exclusive "or" and the inclusive "or." The statement "I will go or I will not go" is an example of the use of the **exclusive "or,"** since either "I will go" is true or "I will not go" is true, but both cannot be true at the same time. The **inclusive "or"** (called "and/or" in everyday language) allows for the situation in which both parts are true. For example, the statement "It will rain or the sun will shine" uses the inclusive "or"; it is true if (1) it rains, (2) the sun shines, or (3) it rains and the sun shines. That is, the inclusive "or" in $p \vee q$ allows for both p and q to be true. In mathematics, we agree to use the inclusive "or," whose truth values are summarized in the next truth table.

p	q	$p \vee q$
T	T	T
T	F	T
F	T	T
F	F	F

Example T1.1 Determine whether the following statements are true or false, where p represents "Rain is wet" and q represents "Black is white."
a. $\sim p$ **b.** $p \wedge q$ **c.** $(\sim p) \vee q$
d. $p \wedge (\sim q)$ **e.** $\sim (p \wedge q)$ **f.** $\sim [p \vee (\sim q)]$

Solution

a. p is T, so $\sim p$ is F.
b. p is T and q is F, so $p \wedge q$ is F.
c. $\sim p$ is F and q is F, so $(\sim p) \vee q$ is F.
d. p is T and $\sim q$ is T, so $p \wedge (\sim q)$ is T.
e. p is T and q is F, so $p \wedge q$ is F and $\sim (p \wedge q)$ is T.
f. p is T and $\sim q$ is T, so $p \vee (\sim q)$ is T and $\sim [p \vee (\sim q)]$ is F. ■

IF–THEN One of the most important compound statements is the implication. The statement "If p, then q," denoted by "$p \rightarrow q$," is called an **implication** or **conditional** statement; p is called the **hypothesis,** and q is called the **conclusion.** To determine the truth table for $p \rightarrow q$, consider the following conditional promise given to a math class: "If you average at least 90% on all tests, then you will earn an A." Let p represent "Your average is at least 90% on all tests" and q represent "You earn an A." Then there are four possibilities:

AVERAGE AT LEAST 90%	EARN AN A	PROMISE KEPT
Yes	Yes	Yes
Yes	No	No
No	Yes	Yes
No	No	Yes

Notice that the only way the promise can be broken is in line 2. In lines 3 and 4, the promise is not broken, since an average of at least 90% was not attained. (In these cases, a student may still earn an A—it does not affect the promise either way.) This example suggests the following truth table for the conditional.

p	q	$p \to q$
T	T	T
T	F	F
F	T	T
F	F	T

One can observe that the truth values for $p \wedge q$ and $q \wedge p$ are always the same. Also, the truth tables for $p \vee q$ and $q \vee p$ are identical. However, it is not the case that the truth tables of $p \to q$ and $q \to p$ are identical. Consider this example: Let p be "You live in New York City" and q be "You live in New York State." Then $p \to q$ is true, whereas $q \to p$ is not true, since you may live in Albany, for example. The conditional $q \to p$ is called the converse of $p \to q$. As the example shows, a conditional may be true, whereas its converse may be false. On the other hand, a conditional and its converse may both be true. Two other variants of a conditional occur in mathematics, the contrapositive and the inverse.

> Given conditional: $p \to q$
> The **converse** of $p \to q$ is $q \to p$.
> The **inverse** of $p \to q$ is $(\sim p) \to (\sim q)$.
> The **contrapositive** of $p \to q$ is $(\sim q) \to (\sim p)$.

The following truth table displays the various truth values for these four conditionals.

p	q	$\sim p$	$\sim q$	CONDITIONAL $p \to q$	CONTRAPOSITIVE $\sim q \to \sim p$	CONVERSE $q \to p$	CONVERSE $\sim p \to \sim q$
T	T	F	F	T	T	T	T
T	F	F	T	F	F	T	T
F	T	T	F	T	T	F	F
F	F	T	T	T	T	T	T

Notice that the columns of truth values under the conditional $p \to q$ and its contrapositive are the same. When this is the case, we say that the two statements are logically equivalent. In general, two statements are **logically equivalent** when they have the same truth tables. Similarly, the converse of $p \to q$ and the inverse of $p \to q$ have the same truth table; hence, they, too, are logically equivalent. In mathematics, replacing a conditional with a logically equivalent conditional often facilitates the solution of a problem.

Example T1.2 Prove that if x^2 is odd, then x is odd.

Solution Rather than trying to prove that the given conditional is true, consider its logically equivalent contrapositive: If x is not odd (i.e., x is even), then x^2 is not odd (i.e., x^2 is even). Even numbers are of the form $2m$, where m is a whole number. Thus the square of $2m$, $(2m)^2 = 4m^2 = 2(2m^2)$, is also an even number since it is of the form $2n$, where $n = 2m^2$. Thus if x is even, then x^2 is even. Therefore, the contrapositive of this conditional, our original problem, is also true. ■

IF AND ONLY IF The connective "p if and only if q," called a **biconditional** and written $p \leftrightarrow q$, is the conjunction of $p \rightarrow q$ and its converse $q \rightarrow p$. That is, $p \leftrightarrow q$ is logically equivalent to $(p \rightarrow q) \wedge (q \rightarrow p)$. The truth table of $p \leftrightarrow q$ follows.

p	q	$p \rightarrow q$	$q \rightarrow p$	$(p \rightarrow q) \wedge (q \rightarrow p)$	$p \leftrightarrow q$
T	T	T	T	T	T
T	F	F	T	F	F
F	T	T	F	F	F
F	F	T	T	T	T

Notice that the biconditional $p \leftrightarrow q$ is true when p and q have the same truth values and false otherwise.

Often in mathematics the words *necessary* and *sufficient* are used to describe conditionals and biconditionals. For example, the statement "Water is necessary for the formation of ice" means "If there is ice, then there is water." Similarly, the statement "A rectangle with two adjacent sides the same length is a sufficient condition to determine a square" means "If a rectangle has two adjacent sides the same length, then it is a square." Symbolically we have the following:

$p \rightarrow q$ means q **is necessary for p**
$p \rightarrow q$ means p **is sufficient for q**
$p \leftrightarrow q$ means p **is necessary and sufficient for q**

Arguments

Deductive or **direct reasoning** is a process of reaching a conclusion from one (or more) statements, called the hypothesis (or hypotheses). This somewhat informal definition can be rephrased using the language and symbolism in the preceding section. An **argument** is a set of statements in which one of the statements is called the conclusion and the rest comprise the hypothesis. A **valid argument** is an argument in which the conclusion must be true whenever the hypothesis is true. In the case of a valid argument, we say that the conclusion *follows from* the hypothesis. For example, consider the following argument: "If it is snowing, then it is cold. It is snowing. Therefore, it is cold." In this argument, when the two statements in the hypothesis—namely "If it is snowing, then it is cold" and "It is snowing"—are both true, then one can conclude that "It is cold." That is, this argument is valid since the conclusion follows from the hypothesis.

An argument is said to be an **invalid argument** if its conclusion can be false when its hypothesis is true. An example of an invalid argument is the following: "If it is raining, then the streets are wet. The streets are wet. Therefore, it is raining." For convenience, we will represent this argument symbolically as $[(p \rightarrow q) \wedge q] \rightarrow p$. This is an invalid argument, since the streets could be wet from a variety of causes (e.g., a street cleaner, an open fire hydrant, etc.) without having had any rain. In this example, $p \rightarrow q$ is true and q may be true, while p is false. The next truth table also shows that this argument is invalid, since it is possible to have the hypothesis $[(p \rightarrow q) \wedge q]$ true with the conclusion p false.

p	q	$p \rightarrow q$	$(p \rightarrow q) \wedge q$
T	T	T	T
T	F	F	F
F	T	T	**T**
F	F	T	F

The argument with hypothesis $[(p \rightarrow q) \wedge \sim p]$ and conclusion $\sim q$ is another example of a common invalid argument form, since when p is F and q is T, $[(p \rightarrow q) \wedge \sim p]$ is T and $\sim q$ is F.

Three important valid argument forms, used repeatedly in logic, are discussed next.

MODUS PONENS: $[(p \rightarrow q) \wedge p] \rightarrow q$ In words **modus ponens,** which is also called the **law of detachment,** says that whenever a conditional statement and its hypothesis are true, the conclusion is also true. That is, the conclusion can be "detached" from the conditional. An example of the use of this law follows.

> If a number ends in zero, then it is a multiple of 10.
> Forty is a number that ends in zero.
> Therefore, 40 is a multiple of 10.

(NOTE: Strictly speaking, the sentence "a number ends in zero" is an "open" sentence, since no particular number is specified; hence the sentence is neither true nor false as given. The sentence "Forty is a number that ends in zero" is a true statement. Since the use of open sentences is prevalent throughout mathematics, we will permit such "open" sentences in conditional statements without pursuing an in-depth study of such sentences.)

The following truth table verifies that the law of detachment is a valid argument form.

p	q	$p \rightarrow q$	$(p \rightarrow q) \wedge p$
T	**T**	T	**T**
T	F	F	F
F	T	T	F
F	F	T	F

Notice that in line 1 in the preceding truth table, when the hypothesis $(p \rightarrow q) \wedge p$ is true, the conclusion, q, is also true. This law of detachment is used in everyday language and thought.

Diagrams can also be used to determine the validity of arguments. Consider the following argument.

> All mathematicians are logical.
> Pólya is a mathematician.
> Therefore, Pólya is logical.

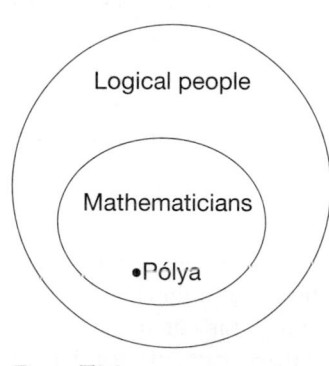

Figure T1.2

This argument can be pictured using an **Euler diagram** (Figure T1.2). The "mathematician" circle within the "logical people" circle represents the statement "All mathematicians are logical." The point labeled "Pólya" in the "mathematician" circle represents "Pólya is a mathematician." Since the "Pólya" point is within the "logical people" circle, we conclude that "Pólya is logical."

The second common valid argument form follows.

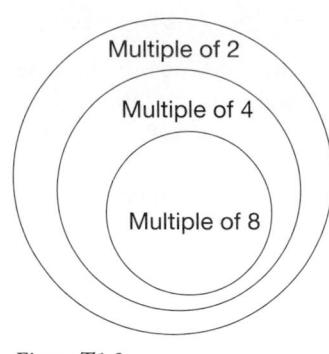

Figure T1.3

HYPOTHETICAL SYLLOGISM: $[(p \rightarrow q) \wedge (q \rightarrow r)] \rightarrow (p \rightarrow r)$ The following argument is an application of this law:

> If a number is a multiple of 8, then it is a multiple of 4.
> If a number is a multiple of 4, then it is a multiple of 2.
> Therefore, if a number is a multiple of 8, it is a multiple of 2.

Hypothetical syllogism, also called the **chain rule,** can be verified using an Euler diagram (Figure T1.3). The circle within the "multiples of 4" circle represents the "multiples of 8" circle. Then the "multiples of 4" circle is within the "multiples of 2" circle. Thus, from the diagram, it must follow that "If a number is a multiple of 8, then it is a multiple of 2," since all the multiples of 8 are within the "multiples of 2" circle.

The following truth table also proves the validity of hypothetical syllogism.

p	q	r	$p \rightarrow q$	$q \rightarrow r$	$p \rightarrow r$	$(p \rightarrow q) \wedge (q \rightarrow r)$
T	T	T	T	T	T	T
T	T	F	T	F	F	F
T	F	T	F	T	T	F
T	F	F	F	T	F	F
F	T	T	T	T	T	T
F	T	F	T	F	T	F
F	F	T	T	T	T	T
F	F	F	T	T	T	T

Observe that in rows 1, 5, 7, and 8 the hypothesis $(p \rightarrow q) \wedge (q \rightarrow r)$ is true. In both of these cases, the conclusion, $p \rightarrow r$, is also true; thus the argument is valid.

The final valid argument we study here is used often in mathematical reasoning.

MODUS TOLLENS: $[(p \rightarrow q) \wedge \sim q] \rightarrow \sim p$ Consider the following argument:

> If a number is a power of 3, then it ends in a 9, 7, 1, or 3.
> The number 3124 does not end in a 9, 7, 1, or 3.
> Therefore, 3124 is not a power of 3.

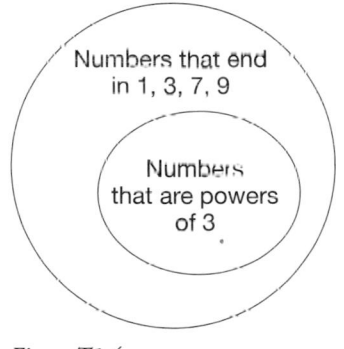

Figure T1.4

This argument is an application of **modus tollens.** Figure T1.4 illustrates this argument. All points outside the larger circle represent numbers not ending in 1, 3, 7, or 9. Clearly, any point outside the larger circle must be outside the smaller circle. Thus, since 3124 is outside the "powers of 3" circle, it is not a power of 3. In words, modus tollens says that whenever a conditional is true and its conclusion is false, the hypothesis is also false.

The next truth table provides a verification of the validity of this argument form.

p	q	$p \rightarrow q$	$(p \rightarrow q) \wedge \sim q$	$\sim p$
T	T	T	F	F
T	F	F	F	F
F	T	T	F	T
F	F	T	T	T

Notice that row 4 is the only instance when the hypothesis $(p \rightarrow q) \wedge \sim q$ is true. In this case, the conclusion of $[(p \rightarrow q) \wedge (\sim q)] \rightarrow \sim p$, namely $\sim p$, is also true. Hence the argument is valid. Notice how the validity of modus tollens also can be shown using modus ponens with a contrapositive:

$$[(p \rightarrow q) \wedge \sim q] \leftrightarrow [(\sim q \rightarrow \sim p) \wedge \sim q] \text{ and } [(\sim q \rightarrow \sim p) \wedge \sim q] \rightarrow \sim p.$$

All three of these valid argument forms are used repeatedly when reasoning, especially in mathematics. The first two should seem quite natural, since we are schooled in them informally from the time we are young children. For example, a parent might say to a child: "If you are a good child, then you will receive presents." Needless to say, every little child who wants presents learns to be good. This, of course, is an application of the law of detachment.

Similarly, consider the following statements:

If you are a good child, then you will get a new bicycle.
If you get a new bicycle, then you will have fun.

The conclusion children arrive at is "If I am good, then I will have fun," an application of the law of syllogism.

The three argument forms we have been studying can also be applied to statements that are modified by "quantifiers," that is, words such as *all*, *some*, *every*, or their equivalents. Here, again, Euler diagrams can be used to determine the validity or invalidity of various arguments. Consider the following argument:

All logicians are mathematicians.
Some philosophers are not mathematicians.
Therefore, some philosophers are not logicians.

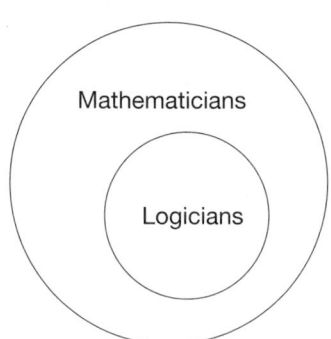

Figure T1.5

The first line of this argument is represented by the Euler diagram in Figure T1.5. However, since the second line guarantees that there are "some" philosophers outside the "mathematician" circle, a dot is used to represent at least one philosopher who is *not* a mathematician (Figure T1.6). Observe that, due to the dot, there is always a philosopher who is not a logician; hence the argument is valid. (Note that the word *some* means "at least one.")

Next consider the argument:

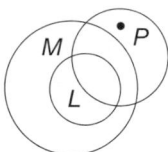

Figure T1.6

All rock stars have green hair.
No presidents of banks are rock stars.
Therefore, no presidents of banks have green hair.

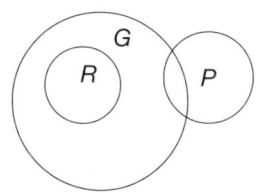

Figure T1.7

An Euler diagram that represents this argument is shown in Figure T1.7, where G represents all people with green hair, R represents all rock stars, and P represents all bank presidents. Note that Figure T1.7 allows for presidents of banks to have green hair, since the circles G and P may have an element in common. Thus the argument, as stated, is invalid since the hypothesis can be true while the conclusion is false. The validity or invalidity of the arguments given in the Exercise/Problem Set can be determined in this way using Euler diagrams. Be sure to consider *all* possible relationships among the sets before drawing any conclusions.

 T1   EXERCISE / PROBLEM SET A

EXERCISES

1. Determine which of the following are statements.

   a. What's your name?

   b. The rain in Spain falls mainly in the plain.

   c. Happy New Year!

   d. Five is an odd number.

2. Write the following in symbolic form using $p, q, r,$ $\sim, \wedge, \vee, \rightarrow, \leftrightarrow,$ where $p, q,$ and r represent the following statements:

p: The sun is shining.
q: It is raining.
r: The grass is green.

a. If it is raining, then the sun is not shining.

b. It is raining and the grass is green.

c. The grass is green if and only if it is raining and the sun is shining.

d. Either the sun is shining or it is raining.

3. If p is T, q is F, and r is T, find the truth values for the following:

a. $p \wedge \sim q$

b. $\sim(p \vee q)$

c. $(\sim p) \rightarrow r$

d. $(\sim p \wedge r) \leftrightarrow q$

e. $(\sim q \wedge p) \vee r$

f. $p \vee (q \leftrightarrow r)$

g. $(r \wedge \sim p) \vee (r \wedge \sim q)$

h. $(p \wedge q) \rightarrow (q \vee \sim r)$

4. Write the converse, inverse, and contrapositive for each of the following statements.

a. If I teach third grade, then I am an elementary school teacher.

b. If a number has a factor of 4, then it has a factor of 2.

5. Construct one truth table that contains truth values for all of the following statements and determine which are logically equivalent.

a. $(\sim p) \vee (\sim q)$

b. $(\sim p) \vee q$

c. $(\sim p) \wedge (\sim q)$

d. $p \rightarrow q$

e. $\sim(p \wedge q)$

f. $\sim(p \vee q)$

PROBLEMS

6. Determine the validity of the following arguments.

a. All professors are handsome.
Some professors are tall.
Therefore, some handsome people are tall.

b. If I can't go to the movie, then I'll go to the park.
I can go to the movie.
Therefore, I will not go to the park.

c. If you score at least 90%, then you'll earn an A.
If you earn an A, then your parents will be proud.
You have proud parents.
Therefore, you scored at least 90%.

d. Some arps are bomps.
All bomps are cirts.
Therefore, some arps are cirts.

e. All equilateral triangles are equiangular.
All equiangular triangles are isosceles.
Therefore, all isosceles triangles are equilateral.

f. If you work hard, then you will succeed.
You do not work hard.
Therefore, you will not succeed.

g. Some girls are teachers.
All teachers are college graduates.
Therefore, all girls are college graduates.

h. If it doesn't rain, then the street won't be wet.
The street is wet.
Therefore, it rained.

7. Determine a valid conclusion that follows from each of the following statements and explain your reasoning.

a. If you study hard, then you will be popular.
You will study hard.

b. If Scott is quick, then he is a basketball star.
Scott is not a basketball star.

c. All friends are respectful.
All respectful people are trustworthy.

d. Every square is a rectangle.
Some parallelograms are rhombuses.
Every rectangle is a parallelogram.

8. Which of the laws (modus ponens, hypothetical syllogism, or modus tollens) is being used in each of the following arguments?

a. If Joe is a professor, then he is learned. If you are learned, then you went to college. Joe is a professor, so he went to college.

b. All women are smart. Helen of Troy was a woman. So Helen of Troy was smart.

c. If you have children, then you are an adult. Bob is not an adult, so he has no children.

d. If today is Tuesday, then tomorrow is Wednesday. Tomorrow is Saturday, so today is not Tuesday.

e. If I am broke, I will ride the bus. When I ride the bus, I am always late. I'm broke, so I am going to be late.

9. Decide the truth value of each of the following.

a. Alexander Hamilton was once president of the United States.

b. The world is flat.

c. If dogs are cats, then the sky is blue.

d. If Tuesday follows Monday, then the sun is hot.

e. If Christmas day is December 25, then Texas is the largest state in the United States.

10. Draw an Euler diagram to represent the following argument and decide whether it is valid.

> All timid creatures (T) are bunnies (B).
> All timid creatures are furry (F).

Some cows (C) are furry.
Therefore, all cows are timid creatures.

 T1 EXERCISE / PROBLEM SET B

EXERCISES

1. Let r, s, and t be the following statements:

> r: Roses are red.
> s: The sky is blue.
> t: Turtles are green.

Translate the following statements into English.

a. $r \wedge s$ **b.** $r \wedge (s \vee t)$

c. $s \rightarrow (r \wedge t)$ **d.** $(\sim t \wedge t) \rightarrow \sim r$

2. Fill in the headings of the following table using p, q, $\wedge$, $\vee$, $\sim$, and $\rightarrow$.

p	q				
T	T	T	F	T	T
T	F	F	T	F	T
F	T	T	T	F	F
F	F	T	T	F	T

3. Suppose that $p \rightarrow q$ is known to be false. Give the truth values for the following:

a. $p \vee q$ **b.** $p \wedge q$ **c.** $q \rightarrow p$ **d.** $\sim q \rightarrow p$

4. Prove that the conditional $p \rightarrow q$ is logically equivalent to $\sim p \vee q$.

5. State the hypothesis (or hypotheses) and conclusion for each of the following arguments.

a. All football players are introverts. Tony is a football player, so Tony is an introvert.

b. Bob is taller than Jim, and Jim is taller than Sue. So Bob is taller than Sue.

c. All penguins are elegant swimmers. No elegant swimmers fly, so penguins don't fly.

6. Use a truth table to determine which of the following are always true.

a. $(p \rightarrow q) \rightarrow (q \rightarrow p)$ **b.** $\sim p \rightarrow p$

c. $[p \wedge (p \rightarrow q)] \rightarrow q$ **d.** $(p \vee q) \rightarrow (p \wedge q)$

e. $(p \wedge q) \rightarrow p$

7. Using each pair of statements, determine whether (i) p is necessary for q; (ii) p is sufficient for q; (iii) p is necessary and sufficient for q.

a. p: Bob has some water.
q: Bob has some ice, composed of water.

b. p: It is snowing.
q: It is cold.

c. p: It is December.
q: 31 days from today it is January.

PROBLEMS

8. If possible, determine the truth value of each statement. Assume that a and b are true, p and q are false, and x and y have unknown truth values. If a value can't be determined, write "unknown."

a. $p \rightarrow (a \vee b)$ **b.** $b \rightarrow (p \vee a)$

c. $x \rightarrow p$ **d.** $a \vee p$

e. $b \wedge q$ **f.** $b \rightarrow x$

g. $a \wedge (b \vee x)$ **h.** $(y \vee x) \rightarrow a$

i. $(y \wedge b) \rightarrow p$ **j.** $(a \vee x) \rightarrow (b \wedge q)$

k. $x \rightarrow a$ **l.** $x \vee p$

m. $\sim x \rightarrow x$ **n.** $x \vee (\sim x)$

o. $\sim [y \wedge (\sim y)]$

9. Rewrite each argument in symbolic form, then check the validity of the argument.

a. If today is Wednesday (w), then yesterday was Tuesday (t). Yesterday was Tuesday, so today is Wednesday.

b. The plane is late (l) if it snows (s). It is not snowing. Therefore, the plane is not late.

c. If I do not study (s), then I will eat (e). I will not eat if I am worried (w). Hence, if I am worried, I will study.

d. Meg is married (m) and Sarah is single (s). If Bob has a job (j), then Meg is married. Hence Bob has a job.

10. Use the following Euler diagram to determine which of the following statements are true. (Assume that there is at least one person in every region within the circles.)

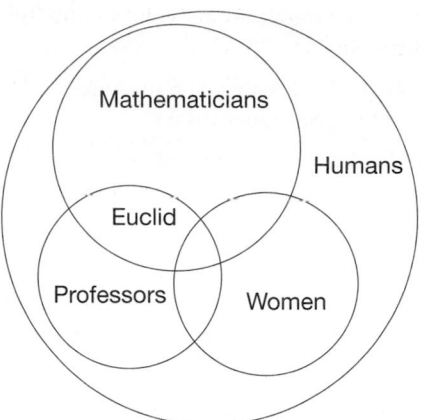

a. All women are mathematicians.

b. Euclid was a woman.

c. All mathematicians are men.

d. All professors are humans.

e. Some professors are mathematicians.

f. Euclid was a mathematician and human.

TOPIC REVIEW

VOCABULARY/NOTATION

Statement, p 858
Negation, $\sim p$ 858
Truth table   858
Compound statements   859
Logical connectives   859
Conjunction (and), $p \wedge q$ 859
Disjunction (or), $p \vee q$ 859
Exclusive "or"   859
Inclusive "or"   859
Implication/conditional
  (if . . . then), $p \rightarrow q$ 859

Hypothesis   859
Conclusion   859
Converse   860
Inverse   860
Contrapositive   860
Logically equivalent statements
  860
Biconditional (if and only if),
  $p \leftrightarrow q$ 861
Is necessary for   861
Is sufficient for   861

Is necessary and sufficient for   861
Deductive/direct reasoning   861
Argument   861
Valid argument   861
Invalid argument   862
Modus ponens (law of
  detachment)   862
Euler diagram   862
Hypothetical syllogism (chain
  rule)   863
Modus tollens   863

ELEMENTARY LOGIC TEST

Knowledge

1. True or false?

a. The disjunction of p and q is true whenever p is true and q is false.

b. If $p \rightarrow q$ is true, then $\sim p \rightarrow \sim q$ is true.

c. In the implication $q \rightarrow p$, the hypothesis is p.

d. $[(p \rightarrow q) \wedge (q \rightarrow r)] \rightarrow (p \rightarrow r)$ is the modus tollens.

e. "I am older than 20 or younger than 30" is an example of an exclusive "or."

f. A statement is a sentence that is true or false, but not both.

g. The converse of $p \rightarrow q$ is $\sim p \rightarrow \sim q$.

h. $p \rightarrow q$ means p is necessary for q.

Skill

2. Find the converse, inverse, and contrapositive of each.

a. $p \rightarrow \sim q$

b. $\sim p \rightarrow q$

c. $\sim q \rightarrow \sim p$

3. Decide the truth value of each statement.

a. $4 + 7 = 11$ and $1 + 5 = 6$.

b. $2 + 5 = 7 \leftrightarrow 4 + 2 = 8$.

c. $3 \cdot 5 = 12$ or $2 \cdot 6 = 11$.

d. If $2 + 3 = 5$, then $1 + 2 = 4$.

e. If $3 + 4 = 6$, then $8 \cdot 4 = 31$.

f. If 7 is even, then 8 is even.

4. Use Euler diagrams to check the validity of each argument.

   a. Some men are teachers. Sam Jones is a teacher. Therefore, Sam Jones is a man.

   b. Gold is heavy. Nothing but gold will satisfy Amy. Hence nothing that is light will satisfy Amy.

   c. No cats are dogs. All poodles are dogs. So some poodles are not cats.

   d. Some cows eat hay. All horses eat hay. Only cows and horses eat hay. Frank eats hay, so Frank is a horse.

   e. All chimpanzees are monkeys. All monkeys are animals. Some animals have two legs. So some chimpanzees have two legs.

5. Complete the following truth table.

p	q	$p \wedge q$	$p \vee q$	$p \rightarrow q$	$\sim p$	$\sim q$	$q \leftarrow p$	$\sim q \rightarrow \sim p$
T				T				
		T	F					
F			F					T
		T	F					

Understanding

6. Using an Euler diagram, display an invalid argument. Explain.

7. Is it ever the case that the conjunction, disjunction, and implication of two statements are all true at the same time? all false? If so, what are the truth values of each statement? If not, explain why not.

Problem Solving/Application

8. In a certain land, every resident either always lies or always tells the truth. You happen to run into two residents, Bob and Sam. Bob says, "If I am a truth teller, then Sam is a truth teller." Is Bob a truth teller? What about Sam?

9. The binary connective $\updownarrow$ is defined by the following truth table:

p	q	$p \updownarrow q$
T	T	F
T	F	T
F	T	T
F	F	T

Compose a statement using only the connective $\updownarrow$ that is logically equivalent to

   a. $\sim p$

   b. $p \wedge q$

   c. $p \vee q$

CLOCK ARITHMETIC: A MATHEMATICAL SYSTEM

The mathematical systems that we studied in Chapters 1 through 8 consisted of the infinite sets of whole numbers, fractions, and integers, together with their usual operations and properties. However, there are also mathematical systems involving finite sets.

Clock Arithmetic

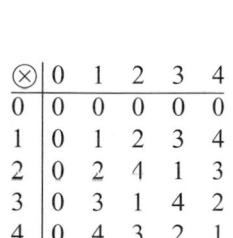

Figure T2.1

The hours of a 12-clock are represented by the finite set $\{1, 2, 3, 4, 5, 6, 7, 8, 9, 10, 11, 12\}$. The problem "If it is 7 o'clock, what time will it be in 8 hours?" can be represented as the addition problem $7 \oplus 8$ (we use a circle around the "plus" sign here to distinguish this clock addition from the usual addition). Since 8 hours after 7 o'clock is 3 o'clock, we write $7 \oplus 8 = 3$. Notice that $7 \oplus 8$ can also be found simply by adding 7 and 8, then subtracting 12, the clock number, from the sum, 15. Instead of continuing to study 12-clock arithmetic, we will simplify our discussion about clock arithmetic by considering the 5-clock next (Figure T2.1).

In the 5-clock, the sum of two numbers is found by adding the two numbers as whole numbers, except that when this sum is greater than 5, 5 is subtracted. Thus, in the 5-clock, $1 \oplus 2 = 3$, $3 \oplus 4 = 2$ (i.e., $3 + 4 - 5$), and $3 \oplus 3 = 1$. Since $1 \oplus 5 = 1$, $2 \oplus 5 = 2$, $3 \oplus 5 = 3$, $4 \oplus 5 = 4$, and $5 \oplus 5 = 5$, the clock number 5 acts like the additive identity. For this reason, it is common to replace the clock number with a zero. Henceforth, 0 will be used to designate the clock number. Addition in the 5-clock is summarized in the table in Figure T2.2.

$\oplus$	0	1	2	3	4
0	0	1	2	3	4
1	1	2	3	4	0
2	2	3	4	0	1
3	3	4	0	1	2
4	4	0	1	2	3

Figure T2.2

It can be shown that 5-clock **addition** is a commutative, associative, and closed binary operation. Also, 0 is the additive identity, since $a \oplus 0 = a$ for all numbers a in the 5-clock. Finally, every 5-clock number has an opposite or additive inverse: $1 \oplus 4 = 0$ (the identity), so 4 and 1 are opposites of each other; $2 \oplus 3 = 0$, so 2 and 3 are opposites of each other; and $0 \oplus 0 = 0$, so 0 is its own opposite.

Subtraction in the 5-clock can be defined in three equivalent ways. First, similar to the take-away approach for whole numbers, a number can be subtracted by counting backward. For example, $2 \ominus 4 = 3$ on the 5-clock, since counting backward 4 from 2 yields 1, 0, 4, 3. One can also use the missing-addend approach, namely $2 \ominus 4 = x$ if and only if $2 = 4 \oplus x$. Since $4 \oplus 3 = 2$, it follows that $x = 3$. Finally, $2 \ominus 4$ can be found by the adding-the-opposite method; that is, $2 \ominus 4 = 2 \oplus 1 = 3$, since 1 is the opposite of 4.

Example T2.1 Calculate in the indicated clock arithmetic.
a. $6 \oplus 8$ (12-clock) **b.** $4 \oplus 4$ (5-clock) **c.** $7 \oplus 4$ (9-clock)
d. $8 \ominus 2$ (12-clock) **e.** $1 \ominus 4$ (5-clock) **f.** $2 \ominus 5$ (7-clock)

Solution

a. In the 12-clock, $6 \oplus 8 = 6 + 8 - 12 = 2$.
b. In the 5-clock, $4 \oplus 4 = 4 + 4 - 5 = 3$.
c. In the 9-clock, $7 \oplus 4 = 7 + 4 - 9 = 2$.
d. In the 12-clock, $8 \ominus 2 = 6$ since $8 = 2 \oplus 6$.
e. In the 5-clock, $1 \ominus 4 = 1 + 1 = 2$ by adding the opposite.
f. In the 7-clock, $2 \ominus 5 = 2 + 2 = 4$.

$\otimes$	0	1	2	3	4
0	0	0	0	0	0
1	0	1	2	3	4
2	0	2	4	1	3
3	0	3	1	4	2
4	0	4	3	2	1

Figure T2.3

Multiplication in clock arithmetic is viewed as repeated addition. In the 5-clock, $3 \otimes 4 = 4 \oplus 4 \oplus 4 = 2$. The 5-clock multiplication table is shown in Figure T2.3.

As with addition, there is a shortcut for finding products. For example, to find $3 \otimes 4$ in the 5-clock, first multiply 3 and 4 as whole numbers. This result, 12, exceeds 5, the number of the clock. In the 5-clock, imagine counting 12 starting with 1, namely, 1, 2, 3, 4, 5, 1, 2, 3, 4, 5, 1, 2. Here you must go around the circle twice ($2 \times 5 = 10$) plus two more clock numbers. Thus $3 \otimes 4 = 2$. Also, notice that 2 is the remainder when 12 is divided by 5. In general, to multiply in any clock, first take the whole-number product of the two clock numbers. If this product exceeds the clock number, divide by the clock number—the remainder will be the clock product. Thus $7 \otimes 9$ in the 12-clock is 3, since 63 leaves a remainder of 3 when divided by 12.

As with clock addition, clock multiplication is a commutative and associative closed binary operation. Also, $1 \otimes n = n \otimes 1 = n$, for all n, so 1 is the multiplicative identity. Since $1 \otimes 1 = 1$, $2 \otimes 3 = 1$, and $4 \otimes 4 = 1$, every nonzero element of the 5-clock has a reciprocal or multiplicative inverse. Notice that $0 \otimes n = 0$ for all n, since 0 is the additive identity (zero); this is consistent with all of our previous number systems, namely zero times any clock number is zero.

Division in the 5-clock can be viewed using either of the following two equivalent approaches: (1) missing factor or (2) multiplying by the reciprocal of the divisor. For example, using (1), $2 \oplus 3 = n$ if and only if $2 = 3 \otimes n$. Since $3 \otimes 4 = 2$, it follows that $n = 4$. Alternatively, using (2), $2 \oplus 3 = 2 \otimes 2 = 4$, since 2 is the reciprocal of 3 in the 5-clock.

Although every nonzero number in the 5-clock has a reciprocal, this property does not hold in every clock. For example, consider the multiplication table for the 6-clock (Figure T2.4). Notice that the number 1 does not appear in the "2" row. This means that there is no number n in the 6-clock such that $2 \otimes n = 1$. Also consider 2 in the 12-clock and the various multiples of 2. Observe that they are always even; hence 1 is never a multiple of 2. Thus 2 has no reciprocal in the 12-clock. This lack of reciprocals applies to every n-clock, where n is a composite number. For example, in the 9-clock, the number 3 (as well as 6) does not have a reciprocal. Thus, in composite number clocks, some divisions are impossible.

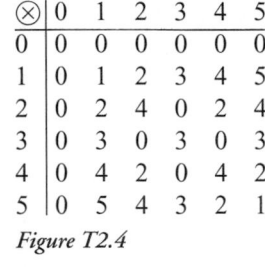

$\otimes$	0	1	2	3	4	5
0	0	0	0	0	0	0
1	0	1	2	3	4	5
2	0	2	4	0	2	4
3	0	3	0	3	0	3
4	0	4	2	0	4	2
5	0	5	4	3	2	1

Figure T2.4

Example T2.2 Calculate in the indicated clock arithmetic (if possible).
a. $5 \otimes 7$ (12-clock) **b.** $4 \otimes 2$ (5-clock)
c. $6 \otimes 5$ (8-clock) **d.** $1 \oplus 3$ (5-clock)
e. $2 \oplus 5$ (7-clock) **f.** $2 \oplus 6$ (12-clock)

Solution

a. $5 \otimes 7 = 11$ in the 12-clock, since $5 \times 7 = 35$ and 35 divided by 12 has a remainder of 11.
b. $4 \otimes 2 = 3$ in the 5-clock, since $4 \times 2 = 8$ and 8 divided by 5 has a remainder of 3.
c. $6 \otimes 5 = 6$ in the 8-clock, since 30 divided by 8 has a remainder of 6.
d. $1 \oplus 3 = 1 \otimes 2 = 2$ in the 5-clock, since 2 is the reciprocal of 3.
e. $2 \oplus 5 = 2 \otimes 3 = 6$ in the 7-clock, since 3 is the reciprocal of 5.
f. $2 \oplus 6$ in the 12-clock is not possible, because 6 has no reciprocal. ■

Other aspects of various clock arithmetics that can be studied, such as ordering, fractions, and equations, are covered in the Exercise/Problem Set.

Congruence Modulo m

Clock arithmetics are examples of finite mathematical systems. Interestingly, some of the ideas found in clock arithmetics can be extended to the (infinite) set of integers. In clock arithmetic, the clock number is the additive identity (or the zero). Thus a natural association of the integers with the 5-clock, say, can be obtained by wrapping the integer number line around the 5-clock, where 0 corresponds to 5 on the 5-clock, 1 with 1 on the clock, -1 with 4 on the clock, and so on (Figure T2.5).

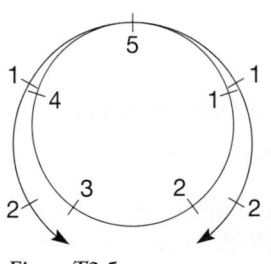

Figure T2.5

In this way, there are infinitely many integers associated with each clock number. For example, in the 5-clock in Figure T2.5, the set of integers associated with 1 is $\{\ldots, -14, -9, -4, 1, 6, 11, \ldots\}$. It is interesting to note that the difference of any two of the integers in this set is a multiple of 5. In general, this fact is expressed symbolically as follows:

DEFINITION

Congruence Mod m

Let a, b, and m be integers, $m \geq 2$. Then $a \equiv b \bmod m$ if and only if $m \mid (a - b)$.

In this definition, we need to use an extended definition of divides to the system of integers. We say that $a \mid b$, for integers $a \ (\neq 0)$ and b, if there is an integer x such that $ax = b$. The expression $a \equiv b \bmod m$ is read *a is congruent to b mod m*. The term "mod m" is an abbreviation for "modulo m."

Example T2.3   Using the definition, determine which are true. Justify your conclusion.

a. $13 \equiv 7 \bmod 2$ **b.** $5 \equiv 11 \bmod 6$
c. $-5 \equiv 14 \bmod 6$ **d.** $-7 \equiv -22 \bmod 5$

Solution

a. $13 \equiv 7 \bmod 2$ is true, since $13 - 7 = 6$ and $2 \mid 6$.
b. $5 \equiv 11 \bmod 6$ is true, since $5 - 11 = -6$ and $6 \mid -6$.
c. $-5 \equiv 14 \bmod 6$ is false, since $-5 - 14 = -19$ and $6 \nmid -19$.
d. $-7 \equiv -22 \bmod 5$ is true, since $-7 - (-22) = 15$ and $5 \mid 15$. ■

If the "mod m" is omitted from the congruence relation $a \equiv b \bmod m$, the resulting expression, $a \equiv b$, looks much like the equation $a = b$. In fact, congruences and equations have many similarities, as can be seen in the following seven results. (For simplicity, we will omit the "mod m" henceforth unless a particular m needs to be specified. As before, $m \geq 2$.)

1. $a \equiv a$ for all clock numbers a.
   This is true for any m, since $a - a = 0$ and $m \mid 0$.
2. If $a \equiv b$, then $b \equiv a$.
   This is true since if $m \mid (a - b)$, then $m \mid -(a - b)$ or $m \mid (b - a)$.
3. If $a \equiv b$ and $b \equiv c$, then $a \equiv c$.
   The justification of this is left for the Problem Set, Part A, 10.
4. If $a \equiv b$, then $a + c \equiv b + c$.
   If $m \mid (a - b)$, then $m \mid (a - b + c - c)$, or $m \mid [(a + c) - (b + c)]$; that is, $a + c \equiv b + c$.
5. If $a \equiv b$, then $ac \equiv bc$.
   The justification of this is left for the Problem Set, Part B, 12.
6. If $a \equiv b$ and $c \equiv d$, then $ac \equiv bd$.
   Results 5 and 3 can be used to justify this as follows: If $a \equiv b$, then $ac \equiv bc$ by result 5. Also, if $c \equiv d$, then $bc \equiv bd$ by result 5. Since $ac \equiv bc$ and $bc \equiv bd$, we have $ac \equiv bd$ by result 3.
7. If $a \equiv b$ and n is a whole number, then $a^n \equiv b^n$.
   This can be justified by using result 6 repeatedly. For example, since $a \equiv b$ and $a \equiv b$ (using $a \equiv b$ and $c \equiv d$ in result 6), we have $aa \equiv bb$ or $a^2 \equiv b^2$. Continuing, we obtain $a^3 \equiv b^3$, $a^4 \equiv b^4$, and so on.

Congruence mod m can be used to solve a variety of problems. We close this section with one such problem.

Example T2.4 What are the last two digits of 3^{30}?

Solution The number 3^{30} is a large number, and its standard form will not fit on calculator displays. However, suppose that we could find a smaller number, say n, that did fit on a calculator display so that n and 3^{30} have the same last two digits. If n and 3^{30} have the same last two digits, then $3^{30} - n$ has zeros in its last two digits, and vice versa. Thus we have that $100 \mid (3^{30} - n)$, or $3^{30} \equiv n \bmod 100$. We now proceed to find such an n. Since 3^{30} can be written as $(3^6)^5$, let's first consider $3^6 = 729$. Because the last two digits of 729 are 29, we can write $3^6 \equiv 29 \bmod 100$. Then, from result 7, $(3^6)^5 \equiv 29^5 \bmod 100$. Since $29^5 = 20,511,149$ and $20,511,149 \equiv 49 \bmod 100$, by result 3 we can conclude that $(3^6)^5 \equiv 49 \bmod 100$. Thus, 3^{30} ends in 49. ■

  T2 EXERCISE / PROBLEM SET A

EXERCISES

1. Calculate in the clock arithmetics indicated.

   a. $8 \oplus 11$ (12-clock) **b.** $1 \ominus 5$ (7-clock)

   c. $3 \otimes 4$ (6-clock) **d.** $3 \oslash 2$ (5-clock)

   e. $7 \oplus 6$ (10-clock) **f.** $5 \ominus 7$ (9-clock)

   g. $4 \otimes 7$ (11-clock) **h.** $2 \oslash 9$ (13-clock)

2. Find the opposite and reciprocal (if it exists) for each of the following.

   a. 3 (7-clock) **b.** 5 (12-clock)

   c. 7 (8-clock) **d.** 4 (8-clock)

3. In clock arithmetics, a^n means $a \times a \times \ldots \times a$ (n factors of a). Calculate in the clocks indicated.

   a. 7^3 (8-clock) **b.** 4^5 (5-clock)

   c. 2^6 (7-clock) **d.** 9^4 (12-clock)

4. Determine whether these congruences are true or are false.

   a. $14 \equiv 3 \bmod 3$ **b.** $-3 \equiv 7 \bmod 4$

   c. $43 \equiv -13 \bmod 14$ **d.** $7 \equiv -13 \bmod 2$

   e. $23 \equiv -19 \bmod 7$ **f.** $-11 \equiv -7 \bmod 8$

5. Explain how to use the 5-clock addition table to find $1 \ominus 4$ in the 5-clock.

6. Using the 5-clock table, explain why 5-clock addition is commutative.

7. In the 5-clock, $\frac{1}{3}$ is defined to be $1 \oslash 3$, which equals $1 \otimes 2 = 2$. Using this definition of a clock fraction, calculate $\frac{1}{3} \oplus \frac{1}{2}$. Then add $\frac{1}{3}$ and $\frac{1}{2}$ as you would fractions, except do it in 5-clock arithmetic. Are your answers the same in both cases? Try adding, subtracting, multiplying, and dividing $\frac{3}{4}$ and $\frac{2}{3}$ in 5-clock in this way.

PROBLEMS

8. Suppose that "less than" is defined in the 5-clock as follows: $a < b$ if and only if $a \oplus c = b$ for some nonzero number c. Then $1 < 3$ since $1 \oplus 2 = 3$. However, $3 < 1$ also since $3 \oplus 3 = 1$. Thus, although this definition is consistent with our usual definition, it produces a result very different from what happens in the system of whole numbers. For each of the following, find an example that is inconsistent with what one would expect to find for whole numbers.

   a. If $a < b$, then $a \oplus c < b \oplus c$.

   b. If $a < b$ and $c \neq 0$, then $a \otimes c < b \otimes c$.

9. Find all possible replacements for x to make the following true.

   a. $3 \otimes x = 2$ in the 7-clock

   b. $2 \otimes x = 0$ in the 12-clock

   c. $5 \otimes x = 0$ in the 10-clock

   d. $4 \otimes x = 5$ in the 8-clock

10. Prove: If $a + c \equiv b + c$, then $a \equiv b$.

11. Prove: If $a \equiv b$ and $b \equiv c$, then $a \equiv c$.

12. Find the last two digits of 3^{48} and 3^{49}.

13. Find the last three digits of 4^{101}.

T2 EXERCISE / PROBLEM SET B

EXERCISES

1. Calculate in the clock arithmetics indicated.

   a. $3 \otimes (4 \oplus 5)$ and $(3 \otimes 4) \oplus (3 \otimes 5)$ in the 7-clock

   b. $2 \otimes (3 \oplus 6)$ and $(2 \otimes 3) \oplus (2 \otimes 6)$ in the 12-clock

   c. $5 \otimes (7 \ominus 3)$ and $(5 \otimes 7) \ominus (5 \otimes 3)$ in the 9-clock

   d. $4 \otimes (3 \ominus 5)$ and $(4 \otimes 3) \ominus (4 \otimes 5)$ in the 6-clock

   e. What do parts (a) to (d) suggest?

2. Calculate as indicated [i.e., in $2^4 \otimes 3^4$, calculate 2^4, then 3^4, then multiply your results, and in $(2 \otimes 3)^4$, calculate $2 \otimes 3$, then find the fourth power of your product].

   a. $3^2 \otimes 5^2$ and $(3 \otimes 5)^2$ in the 7-clock

   b. $2^3 \otimes 3^3$ and $(2 \otimes 3)^3$ in the 6-clock

   c. $5^4 \otimes 6^4$ and $(5 \otimes 6)^4$ in the 10-clock

   d. What do parts (a) to (c) suggest?

3. Make a 7-clock multiplication table and use it to find the reciprocals of 1, 2, 3, 4, 5, and 6.

4. Find the following in the 6-clock.

   a. -2 **b.** -5

   c. $(-2) \otimes (-5)$ **d.** $2 \otimes 5$

   e. -3 **f.** -4

   g. $(-3) \otimes (-4)$ **h.** $3 \otimes 4$

   What general result similar to one in the integers is suggested by parts (c), (d), (g), and (h)?

5. In each part, describe all integers n, where $-20 \leq n \leq 20$, which make these congruences true.

   a. $n \equiv 3 \bmod 5$ **b.** $4 \equiv n \bmod 7$

   c. $12 \equiv 4 \bmod n$ **d.** $7 \equiv 7 \bmod n$

6. Show, by using an example in the 12-clock, that the product of two nonzero numbers may be zero.

7. List all of the numbers that do not have reciprocals in the clock given.

   a. 8-clock **b.** 10-clock **c.** 12-clock

   d. Based on your findings, predict the numbers in the 36-clock that don't have reciprocals. Check your prediction.

PROBLEMS

8. Find reciprocals of the following:

   a. 7 in the 8-clock **b.** 4 in the 5-clock

   c. 11 in the 12-clock **d.** 9 in the 10-clock

   e. What general idea is suggested by parts (a) to (d)?

9. State a definition of "square root" for clock arithmetic that is consistent with our usual definition. Then find all square roots of the following if they exist.

   a. 4 in the 5-clock **b.** 1 in the 8-clock

   c. 3 in the 6-clock **d.** 7 in the 12-clock

   e. What do you notice that is different or similar about square roots in clock arithmetics?

10. The system of rational numbers was divided into the three disjoint sets: (i) negatives, (ii) zero, and (iii) positives. The set of positives was closed under both addition and multiplication. Show that it is impossible to find two disjoint nonempty sets to serve as positives and negatives in the 5-clock. (*Hint:* Let 1 be positive and another number be

negative, say $-1 = 4$. Then show that if the set of positive 5-clock numbers is closed under addition, this situation is impossible. Observe that this holds in all clock arithmetics.)

11. Explain why multiplication is closed in any clock.

12. Prove: If $a \equiv b$, then $ac \equiv bc$.

13. Prove or disprove: If $ac \equiv bc \bmod 6$ and $c \not\equiv 0 \bmod 6$, then $a \equiv b \bmod 6$.

14. Suppose that you want to know the remainder when 3^{100} is divided by 7. If r is the remainder and q is the quotient, then $3^{100} = 7q + r$ or $3^{100} - r = 7q$. Thus $7 \mid (3^{100} - r)$ or $3^{100} \equiv r \bmod 7$. (Recall that for the remainder r, we have $0 \leq r < 7$.) Now $3^5 = 243 \equiv 5 \bmod 7$. So $(3^5)^2 \equiv 5^2 \bmod 7$ or $3^{10} \equiv 25 \equiv 4 \bmod 7$. Thus $3^{100} = (3^{10})^{10} \equiv 4^{10} \bmod 7$. But $4^{10} = 16^5 \equiv 2^5 \equiv 4 \bmod 7$. Thus the remainder is 4. Find the remainder when 7^{101} is divided by 8. (*Hint:* $7^{101} = 7^{100} \cdot 7$.)

TOPIC REVIEW

VOCABULARY/NOTATION

Clock arithmetic   869
  Addition, $a \oplus b$ 869
  Subtraction, $a \ominus b$ 869

Multiplication, $a \otimes b$ 869
Division, $a \oslash b$ 870

Congruence modulo, m,
  $a \equiv b \bmod m$ 870

CLOCK ARITHMETIC TEST

Knowledge

1. True or false?

   a. The 12-clock is comprised of the numbers 0, 1, 2, 3, 4, 5, 6, 7, 8, 9, 10, 11, 12.

   b. Addition in the 5-clock is associative.

   c. The number 1 is the additive identity in the 7-clock.

   d. The number 4 is its own multiplicative inverse in the 5-clock.

   e. Every clock has an additive inverse for each of its elements.

   f. Every number is congruent to itself mod m.

   g. If $a \equiv b \bmod 7$, then either $a - b = 7$ or $b - a = 7$.

   h. If $a \equiv b$ and $c \equiv b$, then $a \equiv c$.

Skill

2. Calculate.

   a. $5 \oplus 9$ in the 11-clock

   b. $8 \otimes 8$ in the 9-clock

   c. $3 \ominus 7$ in the 10-clock

   d. $4 \oslash 9$ in the 13-clock

   e. 2^4 in the 5-clock

   f. $(2 \ominus 5)^3 \otimes 6$ in the 7-clock

3. Show how to do the following calculations easily mentally by applying the commutative, associative, identity, inverse, or distributive properties.

   a. $3 \oplus (9 \oplus 7)$ in the 10-clock

   b. $(8 \otimes 3) \otimes 4$ in the 11-clock

   c. $(5 \otimes 4) \oplus (5 \otimes 11)$ in the 15-clock

   d. $(6 \otimes 3) \oplus (3 \otimes 4) \oplus (3 \otimes 3)$ in the 13-clock

4. Find the opposite and the reciprocal (if they exist) of the following numbers in the indicated clocks. Explain.

   a. 4 in the 7-clock   **b.** 4 in the 8-clock

   c. 0 in the 5-clock   **d.** 5 in the 12-clock

5. In each part, describe the set of all numbers n that make the congruence true.

   a. $n \equiv 4 \bmod 9$ where $-15 \le n \le 15$

   b. $15 \equiv 3 \bmod n$ where $1 < n < 20$

   c. $8 \equiv n \bmod 7$

Understanding

6. Using a clock as a model, explain why 4 does not have a reciprocal in the 12-clock.

7. Explain (a) why 0 cannot be used for m and (b) why 1 is not used for m in the definition of $a \equiv b \bmod m$.

8. Explain why $a \equiv a \bmod m$.

Problem Solving/Application

9. If January 1 of a non-leap year falls on a Monday, show how congruence mod 7 can be used to determine the day of the week for January 1 of the next year.

INTRODUCTION TO GRAPH THEORY

Introduction

Visualizing geometric objects has been discussed in various sections throughout the text. In this topic, we discuss a type of visual model that can be used to represent relationships between objects or paths between locations. These visual models can be used to solve problems involving paths of snowplows and garbage trucks or the routes of a traveling salesman.

During the 1700s in the Prussian city of Königsberg (it is now called Kaliningrad, Russia), there were seven bridges in the center of the city over the Pregel River. These bridges went from the sides of the river onto islands in the river (see Figure T3.1). When citizens of Königsberg would take their Sunday walks, they would often try to walk across each bridge once and only once. When the townspeople were unable to find such a path, they took this problem to the mathematician Leonhard Euler. He not only solved this problem but was able to describe a general solution to any problem of this type.

Figure T3.1   Seven Bridges of Königsberg

Vertex-Edge Graphs (Networks)

The first element of solving this problem is to devise an alternate representation of the situation. When one identifies each landmass as a point and draws a line connecting the points to represent each bridge, the diagram in Figure T3.2 results. Each point in the graph is called a **vertex** and each line is called an **edge.** Thus, this type of representation is called a **vertex-edge graph** or **network.** In Figure T3.2, the vertices and edges represent land and bridges respectively. However, they can represent a wide variety of objects in other vertex-edge graphs. Since a vertex-edge graph is not a "picture" of a situation, but simply a representation of paths or relationships among a finite number of objects, the edges can be drawn either straight or curved. The study of the properties and uses of vertex-edge graphs is a branch of mathematics called **graph theory.** In Chapter 9, we talked about graphs as a way to represent functions. In Chapter 10, graphs were used to organize and represent data. In this topic, we use graphs as yet another type of representation. Although the word *graph* has various meanings, the term *graph* will be used to refer to a vertex-edge graph throughout the rest of this topic.

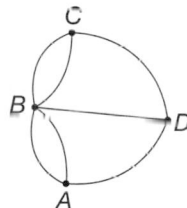

Figure T3.2

Problem-Solving Strategy
Draw a Diagram

NCTM Standards 2000
Geometry
Grades 6–8
All students should use visual tools such as networks to represent and solve problems.

Example T3.1 Consider the map of the interstate highways in the states of Idaho, Oregon, and Washington, as shown in Figure T3.3.

Figure T3.3

a. Sketch a graph representing the interstate highway connections between the cities Bellingham, Eugene, Olympia, Portland, Seattle, Spokane, and Twin Falls, using I-5, I-84, and I-90.

b. Sketch a graph representing the interstate highway connections between the cities Olympia, Pendleton, Portland, Pullman, Salem, and Spokane using I-5, I-84, and I-90.

Solution

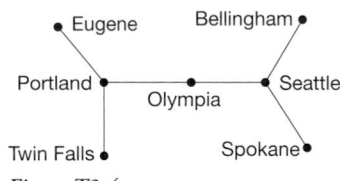

Figure T3.4

a. The cities of Bellingham, Seattle, Olympia, Portland, and Eugene lie along I-5 in that order. From Seattle you can take I-90 to Spokane, and from Portland you can take I-84 to Twin Falls. There are no other connections using the designated highways. This information yields the vertex-edge graph in Figure T3.4.

b. In constructing a graph of this type, it is helpful to first identify the vertices that will be used and then identify whether or not an edge or edges need to be constructed between the vertices. The cities will function as vertices, and the edges will be drawn between a pair of vertices if there is an interstate highway that connects one with another. Let's examine the resulting graph (Figure T3.5) and discuss some of its properties. Although there are roads that connect Pullman to the other cities, there are no interstate highways leading to or from Pullman. Thus, there are no edges drawn from the vertex representing Pullman. Notice that there is an edge between Olympia and Spokane because there are interstate highways that connect those two cities. Even though a person would have to drive through Seattle to get from Olympia to Spokane, Seattle is not shown as a vertex along the edges between these two cities because it is not under consideration for the current graph. ■

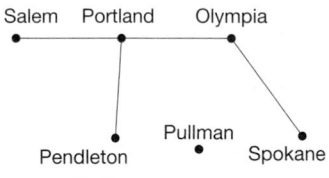

Figure T3.5

In a vertex-edge graph, a **path** is a curve traced by following a sequence of edges in the graph where no edge is retraced. For example, in the graph in Figure T3.4, there is a path from Eugene to Spokane that passes through the cities (vertices) of Portland, Olympia, and Seattle. A graph is said to be **connected** if there is a path between every pair of vertices in the graph. The graph in Figure T3.4 is connected because there is a path from any city to any other city in the graph. The graph in Figure T3.5, however, is not connected because there is no path from Pullman to any of the other cities.

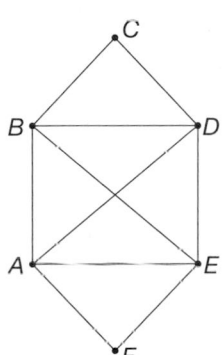

Figure T3.6

Traversable Graphs, Euler Paths, and Circuits

For the seven bridges of Königsberg problem, we are seeking a path that uses all of the bridges (edges) once and only once. This task can be thought of as using a pencil to trace the entire graph in Figure T3.2 without lifting the pencil or redrawing any edge. If this can be done, the graph is said to be **traversable** and the path traced out is called an **Euler path.** If the path begins and ends at the same vertex, it is called an **Euler circuit.** The name, Euler, was given to this type of path because of Leonhard Euler's work with traversable graphs.

The graph in Figure T3.6 has a path that is described by the numbering of edges: 1-2-3-4-5-6-7-8-9. This path could also be described by listing the vertices in the order that they are traversed, namely, A-F-E-B-A-E-D-C-B-F. Notice that because the path uses all of the edges, it is an Euler path. However, since this path begins at vertex A and ends at vertex F, it is not an Euler circuit. The graph in Figure T3.7 contains an Euler circuit that is described by the following list of vertices: B-C-D-E-B-D-A-F-E-A-B (check this). Since the first and last vertex in the list are the same and the path is Euler, it is an Euler circuit. There are many other Euler circuits that start and end at vertex B. In fact, Euler circuits can be constructed to start and end at any of the other vertices in the graph. A discussion of the attributes of a graph that determine whether or not an Euler path or circuit exists follows.

In the case of the seven bridges, Euler noticed that each time a bridge (edge) led *to* a landmass (vertex), there needed to be another bridge (edge) going *from* that landmass (vertex) in order to continue on the path. This led Euler to conclude that a vertex with an even number of edges emanating from it was critical to the solution of the problem. The number of edges that emanate from a vertex is called the **degree of a vertex.** A vertex with an odd number of edges emanating from it is said to have an **odd degree,** while a vertex with an even number of edges emanating from it has an **even degree.**

Example T3.2 Determine the degree of the vertices in each of the graphs in Figures T3.6 and T3.7.

Solution

Table T3.1

GRAPH	VERTEX AND ITS DEGREE					
	A	B	C	D	E	F
Figure T3.6	3	4	2	2	4	3
Figure T3.7	4	4	2	4	4	2

Figure T3.8

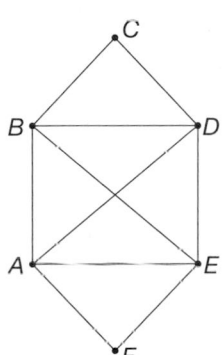

Figure T3.7

To gain a better understanding of when Euler paths or circuits can be constructed, we will examine the paths through certain vertices and their corresponding degrees. Euler noted that every vertex in a path must have an even degree except for beginning and ending vertices. This can be seen in the paths in the graphs of Figure T3.6 and Figure T3.7. Each time the path passes through a vertex, two edges are used: one edge to enter the vertex and one edge to exit the vertex. A closer look at the path through vertex E of Figure T3.6 illustrates this (see Figure T3.8). The first time vertex E is traversed, the blue edges are used: one to enter and one to exit. The second time vertex E is traversed, the orange edges are used: one to enter and one to exit.

We will now examine the beginning and ending vertices, A and F, of the Euler path A-F-E-B-A-E-D-C-B-F in Figure T3.6. From Table T3.1, we can see that both of these vertices have an odd degree, namely 3. The beginning vertex, A, uses one of the odd number of edges (green) to start the path, leaving an even number of unused edges emanating from A. When the path later passes through vertex A, the remaining two blue

(a)

(b)

Figure T3.9

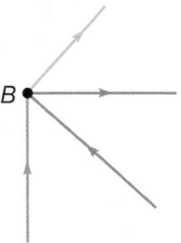

Figure T3.10

edges are used [see Figure T3.9(a)]. On the other hand, the ending vertex, F, uses the two blue edges when the path passes through it, leaving one red edge emanating from it. This red edge is the last edge traversed in the path [see Figure T3.9(b)].

Finally, we now examine the beginning and ending vertex, B, of the Euler circuit in Figure T3.7. After using the green edge beginning at B (Figure T3.10), an odd number of edges that emanate from vertex B remain to be used. When the path passes through vertex B, the two blue edges are used: one to enter and one to exit. This leaves one last red edge to be used. After all of the other edges in the graph have been used, this red edge is traversed to complete the circuit. Any of the other vertices in this graph could also be used as the beginning and ending vertices of an Euler circuit. The vertices with a degree of 4 could be traversed in a similar way to vertex B. Vertices with a degree of 2 (C or F) could be beginning and ending vertices, with one edge being the first edge in the circuit and the other edge being the last edge in the circuit.

In the graph representing the seven bridges of Königsberg in Figure T3.2, it can be seen that three of the four vertices have a degree of 3 and the fourth vertex has a degree of 5. Thus, according to Euler, there is no way to walk across each of the bridges once and only once because in the vertex-edge graph that represents the bridges, there are *no even vertices*. Euler generalized these observations in the following theorem.

Notice that this theorem is stated only in terms of graphs that are connected. Since graphs that are not connected may or may not be traversable, this theorem and our discussion of it is limited to connected graphs only.

◆ THEOREM

Euler's Traversable Graph Theorem

Connected vertex edge graphs are traversable if and only if

1. every vertex in the graph has an even degree. In this case, the beginning and ending vertex of the Euler path is the same, making the path an Euler circuit. This beginning and ending vertex could be any vertex in the graph.
2. there are exactly two vertices with an odd degree, which must be the beginning and ending vertices of the Euler path.

This theorem can now be applied to the following arrangement of twelve bridges.

Example T3.3 Consider the arrangement of rivers, islands, and bridges in Figure T3.11.

Figure T3.11

a. Construct a vertex-edge graph representing the bridges and landmasses.
b. Determine if the graph is traversable (i.e., is it possible to walk across each bridge once and only once?). Explain why or why not.
c. Describe any Euler path, or circuit, if possible.

Solution

a. The landmasses from Figure T3.11 are labeled A, B, C, D, E, and F in Figure T3.12(a) and drawn as vertices in Figure T3.12(b). The edges in Figure T3.12(b) are the bridges.

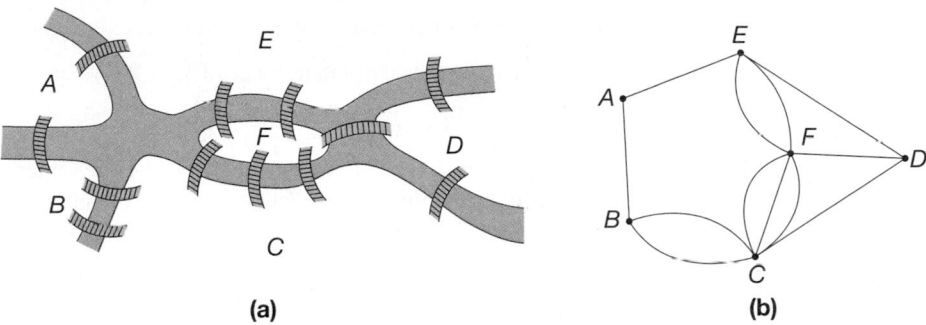

(a)   (b)

Figure T3.12

b. The degrees of the vertices in the vertex-edge graph of Figure T3.12(b) are A-2, B-3, C-6, D-3, E-4, and F-6. Since there are exactly two vertices with an odd degree, the graph is traversable, an Euler path exists, and the beginning and ending vertices must be B and D, in either order. The odd vertices also indicate that no Euler circuit exists.

c. Two of the many different Euler paths are shown in the vertex-edge diagrams in Figure T3.13, with the edges being numbered in the order that they are to be traversed.

Figure T3.13

(a)

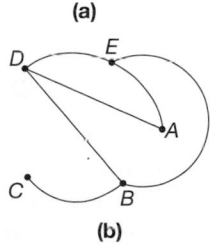

(b)

Figure T3.14

As was mentioned earlier, vertex-edge graphs can be used for a variety of different problems, and constructing such graphs can be a challenge. The important aspect of the graphs is the relationships that are represented. For example, two vertices are said to be **adjacent** if there is an edge joining them. Two graphs are considered to be **equivalent** if they have the same number of vertices connected to each other in the same way, even if the edges look different. How the edge *looks* is not as significant as the *existence* of the edge. The graphs in Figures T3.14(a) and T3.14(b) are equivalent even though they appear to be quite different.

Table T3.2

VERTEX	DEGREE GRAPH (a)	GRAPH (b)
A	2	2
B	3	3
C	1	1
D	3	3
E	3	3

Figure T3.15

Figure T3.16

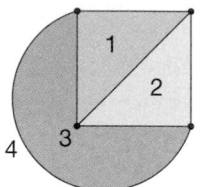

Figure T3.17

The corresponding vertices in each graph have the same degree (see Table T3.2). Also, each graph has the following pairs of adjacent vertices: A and E, A and D, D and E, D and B, B and C.

In the graph of Figure T3.14(a), the edges BE and AD appear to intersect. However, since there is no dot at the intersection, there is no vertex there. This is similar to the way two roads may appear to cross each other on a highway map without there being a way to drive from one road to the other because there is an overpass, but no interchange. The graph in Figure T3.14(b) is equivalent to the one in Figure T3.14(a), but it is drawn so that the edges AD and BE don't intersect.

Example T3.4 Construct a graph having four vertices with edges connecting each pair of vertices so that the edges do not intersect.

Solution The graph in Figure T3.15 shows one such graph. ■

Planar Graphs

Graphs that can be constructed so that edges intersect only at the vertices are called **planar graphs.** To further understand planar graphs, consider the graph in Figure T3.16. It is equivalent to the graph in Figure T3.15 because each vertex in each graph is adjacent to all three of the other vertices in the graph. This means that each vertex has a degree of 3. The main difference between the two graphs is that two of the edges intersect in the graph in Figure T3.16. Is this graph planar? Yes. A planar graph is a graph that *can be* drawn so that edges only intersect at the vertices. Since the graph in Figure T3.16 *can be* drawn like the graph in Figure T3.15, then it is planar. Are all graphs planar graphs? In other words, can all graphs be drawn so that edges intersect only at points representing vertices? The answer to this question is "no," but the justification is beyond the scope of this book. An example of a non-planar graph is a graph with 5 vertices and with edges drawn between each pair of vertices (10 edges in all). This graph cannot be drawn without some edges intersecting at places other than vertices. Try sketching this graph to be planar and you will quickly see that it is non-planar.

Just like other graphs that have been discussed, planar graphs have vertices and edges. However, the edges of these graphs also determine regions. For example, the planar graph in Figure T3.15 determines four regions (see Figure T3.17). The area outside of the graph is considered to be a region. An interesting relationship between the number of vertices, edges, and regions in a planar graph is illustrated in the following example.

Example T3.5 Determine the number of regions (R), vertices (V), and edges (E) for each of the graphs in Figure T3.18.

Solution

Table T3.3

GRAPH	R	V	E
(a)	5	4	7
(b)	6	8	12
(c)	8	8	14
(d)	3	6	7

■

(a)   (b)

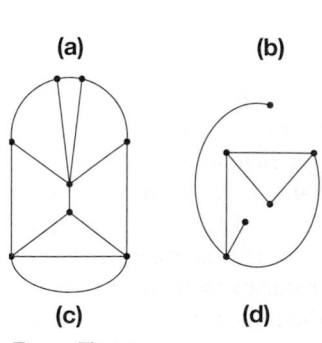

(c)   (d)

Figure T3.18

An examination of Table T3.3 reveals that the number of regions plus the number of vertices is two more than the number of edges in each case (check this). Before we conclude that this relationship holds for all graphs, we must first look to see if there are other properties that these four examples have in common. It can be seen that all four of these graphs are both planar and connected. Thus, we state this relationship between the number of regions, vertices, and edges in terms of connected, planar graphs.

(a)

(b)

(c)

Figure T3.19

(a)

(b)

(c)

Figure T3.20

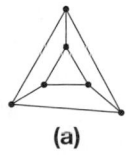

(a)

Figure T3.21(a)

THEOREM

Euler's Formula Theorem

In any connected, planar, vertex-edge graph, the following relationship holds for the number of regions (R), vertices (V), and edges (E).

$$R + V = E + 2$$

We have two ways to determine if Euler's formula holds for a graph. First, we can simply find the number of regions, vertices, and edges and check to see if the formula holds. Second, we can apply the theorem which states that if a graph is connected and planar, then the formula holds. What can be said if Euler's formula does not hold? In this case, we know that the graph cannot be both connected and planar (for in this case the theorem says that the formula must hold).

Example T3.6 Determine whether Euler's formula holds for each of the graphs in Figure T3.19. If the formula does not hold, discuss what conclusions can be drawn about the graph.

Solution

a. The number of vertices is seven and the number of edges is eight. There are two enclosed regions and one outside. Thus, there are three regions. Hence,

$$R + V = 7 + 3 = 8 + 2 = E + 2$$

So Euler's formula holds.

b. For this graph, $R = 5$, $V = 7$, and $E = 9$, and $R + V \neq E + 2$. Since Euler's formula does not hold, we know that either the graph is not planar or it is not connected. It can be seen that the graph is planar, so we will check to see if it is connected. To be connected, it must be possible to find a path from any vertex to any other vertex. There are no paths from the top four vertices to the bottom three vertices, so the graph is not connected.

c. We can see that this graph is both connected and planar, so we can apply the theorem and say that Euler's formula must hold. ■

The connection between Euler's formula for polyhedra, which was studied in Section 12.5, and Euler's formula for vertex-edge graphs is more than just a coincidence. If the faces of a polyhedron are viewed as the regions of a graph, each polyhedron can be represented as a planar vertex-edge graph. For example, the graph in Figure T3.18(b) is a representation of a cube. There are 8 vertices and 12 edges, like a cube, and each region is bounded by 4 edges due to the fact that each face on a cube is a quadrilateral. This relationship can further be visualized by imagining the view of a cube from the top. If the top of the cube were pushed down and the bottom of the cube spread out as a result, the resulting shape would look like Figure T3.18(b). Notice that the outside region represents the bottom of the cube. The vertex-edge graph that represents a polyhedron is referred to as the **net** of the polyhedron.

Example T3.7 Construct the net for each of the polyhedra in Figure T3.20.

Solution

a. Similar to the net of the cube in Figure T3.18(b), the net of this prism is viewed as if the top triangular base were pushed down to fit inside of the bottom triangular base. The bottom triangular base corresponds to the region outside of the net [see Figure T3.21(a)].

(b)

(c)

Figure T3.21

b. Once again, this net is constructed by imagining the apex of the pyramid being pushed down into the plane containing the base [Figure T3.21(b)].

c. The dodecahedron is by far the most complicated of these examples in which to find the net. First we determine the number of vertices (20), edges (30), and faces (12). In the polyhedron, each vertex has 3 edges coming from it. Similarly, every vertex in the net has a degree of 3 [see Figure T3.21(c)]. Finally, every region in the net is bounded by 5 edges, due to the fact that every face on the polyhedron is a pentagon. ■

Now that the properties of vertex-edge graphs have been established, along with how they are constructed, we will examine how they can be used to solve a variety of problems.

Example T3.8 The Pioneer Historical Museum is arranged with displays adjacent to each doorway. To prevent congestion at the doorways, the tour guide wants to see if she can design a tour that passes through each door once and only once. Is it possible to design such a tour for the floor plan in Figure T3.22? If so, sketch the path. If not, explain why not.

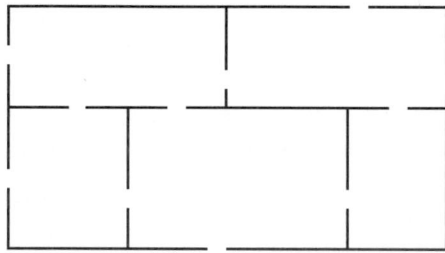

Figure T3.22 Pioneer Historical Museum Floor Plan

Solution The problem can be solved by constructing a vertex-edge graph and determining if it is traversable and hence has an Euler path. It is quite natural to have the rooms be the vertices of the graph and the edges be the paths between the rooms through the doorways. The less obvious part of the construction is to have one vertex represent the outside of the museum, as shown in Figure T3.23(a).

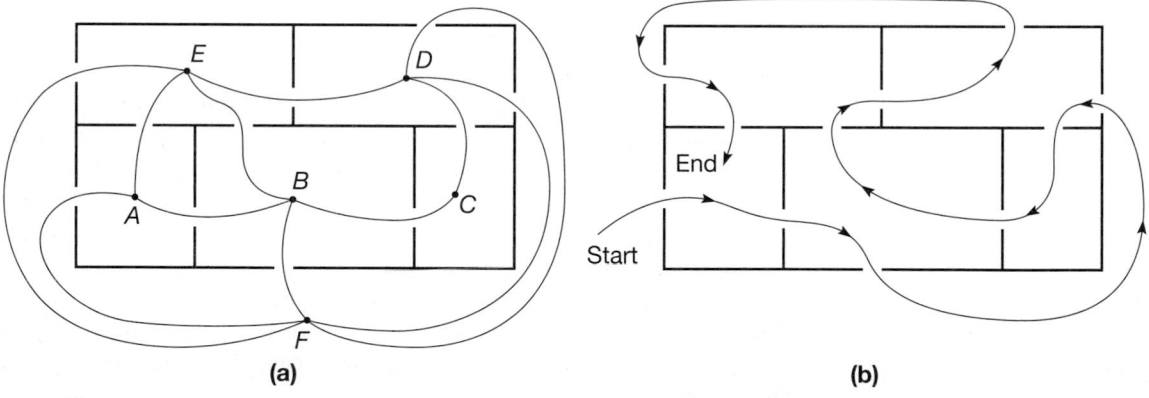

(a)

(b)

Figure T3.23

The degrees of the vertices are A-3, B-4, C-2, D-4, E-4, and F-5. Since there are exactly two vertices of odd degree, by Euler's theorem for traversable graphs, there is an Euler path beginning at F and ending at A. The path corresponding to F-A-B-F-D-C-B-E-D-F-E-A is shown in Figure T3.23(b). ■

Hamiltonian Paths and Circuits

As we have seen, Euler paths traverse each *edge* once and only once. Another type of problem involving vertex-edge graphs would be to find a path that passes through each *vertex* once and only once. If such a path exists, it is called a **Hamiltonian path.** A Hamiltonian path that begins and ends with the same vertex is a **Hamiltonian circuit.** When finding a Hamiltonian path or circuit it is *not* necessary to traverse each edge.

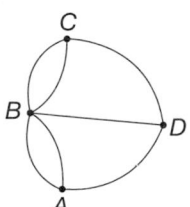

Figure T3.24

Example T3.9 Although it is not possible to walk across each of the seven bridges of Königsberg once and only once, is it possible to visit each landmass in the center of Königsberg once and only once?

Solution Visiting each landmass is the same as finding a Hamiltonian path or circuit in the graph representing the seven bridges of Königsberg. This graph is shown again in Figure T3.24, with the vertices (landmasses) labeled. The path, A-B-C-D, traverses each vertex once and only once. The path A-B-C-D-A begins and ends on the same vertex (landmass) thus creating a Hamiltonian circuit. Thus, we see that it is possible to have a graph that contains a Hamiltonian circuit, but not an Euler circuit. ■

In general, if a vertex-edge graph has n vertices where $n > 2$, and each vertex has a degree of at least $\frac{n}{2}$, then the graph has a Hamiltonian circuit. In Example T3.9 there were 4 vertices and each vertex had a degree of 3 or more so a Hamiltonian circuit existed.

The following example illustrates why a problem that involves a Hamiltonian circuit is often referred to as a **traveling salesman problem.**

Example T3.10 Siope is the sales representative for a paper products company. The vertex-edge graph in Figure T3.25 represents his sales territory of northern Utah and southern Idaho, where the vertices are the cities he needs to visit and the edges represent the major roads that connect those cities. To be as efficient as possible, he would like to do as little backtracking as possible. Find a path that visits each city once and only once and begins and ends in Siope's hometown of Brigham City. If this is not possible, find a route that involves the least amount of backtracking.

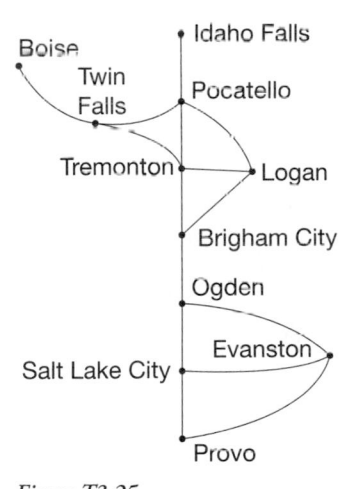

Figure T3.25

Solution Euler paths are known to exist if there are no odd vertices or exactly two odd vertices. When searching for Hamiltonian paths, there is no clear-cut criterion to know if one exists. In this graph, we can see that a path to Boise must go through Twin Falls in both directions. The same is true for Idaho Falls and Pocatello. Similarly, a path must pass through Brigham City and Ogden in both directions to get from the north to the south end of the territory. Thus, there is no Hamiltonian path in this vertex-edge graph. Since four cities—Twin Falls, Pocatello, Brigham City, and Ogden—must be traversed twice, if a route can be found that passes through these cities at most twice, and all other cities only once, then it is a minimal path. A possible route that minimizes the amount of backtracking is described below, where each city is represented by the first two letters of the city name.

Br–Lo–Po–Id–Po–Tw–Bo–Tw–Tr–Br–Og–Ev–Pr–Sa–Og–Br

In this route, the duplicated cities are Pocatello, Twin Falls, Brigham City, and Ogden. ■

T3 EXERCISE / PROBLEM SET A

EXERCISES

1. For each of the following graphs, determine the degree of each of the vertices.

a.

b.

c.

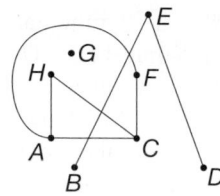

2. For each of the following graphs:

(i) List the vertices that are adjacent to vertex A.

(ii) List all pairs of adjacent vertices.

If there are two or more edges for a pair of vertices, indicate that as part of your answer.

a.

b.

c.

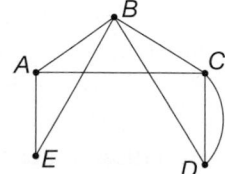

3. Refer to Figure T3.3 and sketch a graph representing the interstate highway connections between the following cities.

a. Boise, Grants Pass, Idaho Falls, Olympia, Pendleton, and Portland.

b. Boise, Eugene, Portland, Spokane, and Twin Falls.

c. Bellingham, Olympia, Pendleton, Portland, Salem, and Spokane.

4. Which of the following graphs are connected. Justify your conclusion.

a.

b.

c.

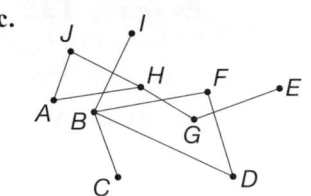

5. Determine which of the following graphs are equivalent.

(i)

(ii)

(iii)

(iv)

(v)

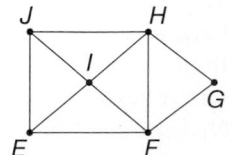

6. Determine which of the following graphs contain an Euler path, Euler circuit, or neither. Justify your conclusions. For each graph where a path or circuit exists, describe that path or circuit by sketching the graph and numbering the edges.

a.

b.

c.

d.

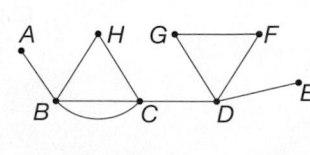

7. For each graph in Exercise 6, describe a Hamiltonian path or circuit where one exists.

8. Each of the following graphs is planar. Redraw each of the following graphs so that the edges intersect only at the vertices.

   a.   **b.** 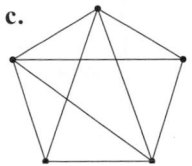 **c.**

9. For each of the following graphs, determine whether or not Euler's formula holds. Explain your reasoning.

   a.   **b.**

c.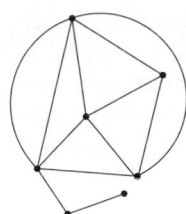

10. Draw the net for each of the following polyhedra.

   a.   **b.**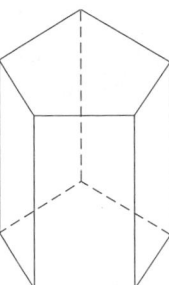

PROBLEMS

11. For each of the graphs in Exercises 1 and 2:
    a. Determine the number of odd vertices and number of even vertices.
    b. What pattern, if any, do you notice about the number of odd vertices in each of these graphs. (*Hint:* Do you ever have one odd vertex or three or five odd vertices?)

12. Construct a connected, planar graph with 5 vertices and 11 edges. How many regions does your graph have? Construct a different connected, planar graph with 5 vertices and 11 edges. How many regions does the second graph have? Is it possible to construct a different graph with 5 vertices, 11 edges, and a different number of regions?

13. The graph below is not traversable. Add exactly one edge to make the graph traversable and describe the Euler path.

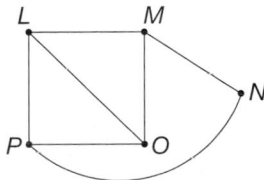

14. The graph below contains many Euler circuits. Describe five different circuits with at least two different starting points.

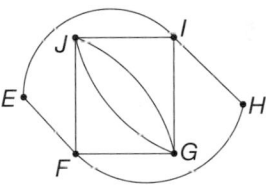

15. There are six small towns in Benton County, all connected by dirt roads, as shown below. The county has finally agreed to pave the roads so that a person can get from any city in the county to any other city in the county along a paved road. Using the distances in miles indicated on the graph below, find the shortest total length of road that would need to be paved to meet this goal. Describe the roads that would be paved to accomplish this shortest total distance.

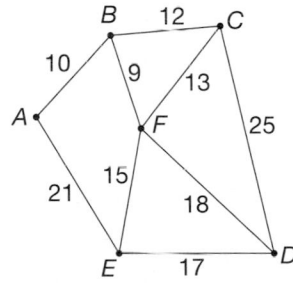

16. Consider the bridge arrangement below and assume that the rivers continue on to the left and right.

If possible, construct a path that crosses each bridge once and only once and that starts and ends at the same location. If such a path is not possible, construct a path that starts and ends at different locations. If neither type of path is possible, explain why not.

17. McKye has the responsibility of servicing the automated teller machines (ATMs) in a certain part of the city (see map below) where there is an ATM at

every intersection or street end (indicated by the white squares on the map below). To make the best use of travel time, she wants to pass by each ATM only once. Describe a path, if possible, that meets this goal.

T3 EXERCISE / PROBLEM SET B

EXERCISES

1. For each of the following graphs, determine the degree of each of the vertices.

a.

b.

c.

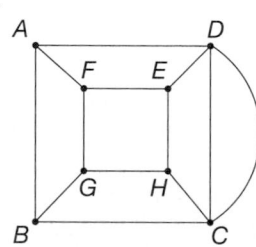

2. For each of the graphs in Exercise 1:

   a. List the vertices that are adjacent to vertex A, adjacent to vertex B, and adjacent to vertex C. If there are two or more edges for a pair of vertices, indicate that as part of your answer.

   b. Describe any observed connections between the number of vertices adjacent to A, B, and C and the degrees of vertices A, B, and C.

3. The Big-Little Airline of Texas (BLAT) offers flights between the following cities (in both directions): Amarillo–Oklahoma City, Austin–Dallas,

Austin–San Antonio, Dallas–Oklahoma City, Dallas–Shreveport, Dallas–Houston, Dallas–San Antonio, El Paso–San Antonio, and Houston–San Antonio. Construct a graph representing the BLAT connections between all of these cities.

4. Which of the following graphs are connected? Justify your conclusion.

   a.

   b.

   c.

   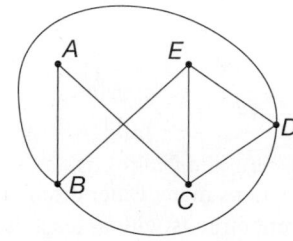

5. Determine which of the following graphs are equivalent.

(i)

(ii)

(iii)

(iv)

(v)

6. If the vertices in a connected graph have the following degrees:

   (i) Is it traversable? Justify your answer.

   (ii) Does it have an Euler path or an Euler circuit? Justify your answer.

   a. 2, 2, 3, 4, 1, 6, 4

   b. 5, 4, 4, 6, 2, 3, 4, 7, 2, 2, 1

   c. 4, 2, 2, 4, 2, 6

   d. 4, 6, 6, 3, 1, 2, 4, 4

7. For each of the graphs in Exercise 4, describe a Hamiltonian path or circuit where one exists.

8. Each of the following graphs is planar. Redraw each of them so that the edges intersect only at the vertices.

   a.

   b.

   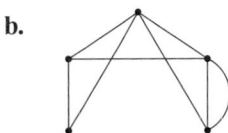

9. In a connected planar graph with 8 regions and 13 edges, how many vertices are there?

10. Each graph below is the net for a polyhedron. Describe the corresponding polyhedron.

   a.   **b.**

   c.

   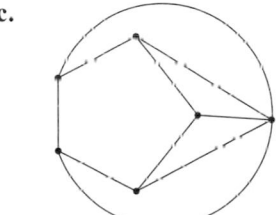

PROBLEMS

11. The graph below is not traversable. What is the minimum number of edges that would need to be added in order to construct an Euler circuit? Describe those edges and the Euler circuit in the new graph.

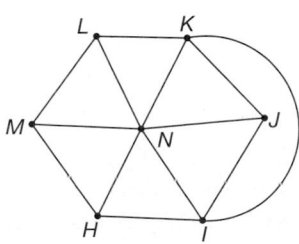

12. Draw two different pictures for each of the following graphs.

   a. Vertices: A, B, C, D, E
Adjacent vertices: A and B, A and C, A and E, C and B, B and D, B and E, and C and D.

   b. Vertices: K, R, U, Z, T
Adjacent vertices: K is adjacent to R and U; R is adjacent to K, Z, and T; U is adjacent to K and Z; Z is adjacent to R, U, and T; T is adjacent to R and Z.

13. Redo Exercise 3 from Part A, but in this case, assume that there is a new interstate highway between Pendleton and Spokane.

14. Answer the following for each of the graphs in Exercises 1 and 4.

   a. What is the sum of all of the degrees of all of the vertices?

   b. What is the total number of edges in each graph?

   c. Describe the relationship, if any, between the results of parts (a) and (b).

15. Consider the museum floor plan below. Devise a tour that passes through each door once and only once.

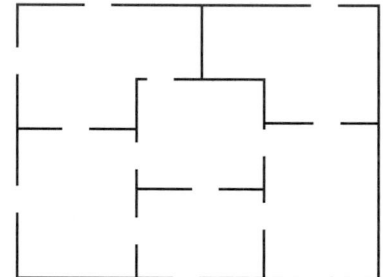

16. Answer the following for each of the graphs in Exercise 1.

   a. Determine the minimum number of edges that could be added to the graph to make all of the vertices have an even degree.

   b. List all of the new edges for each graph.

   c. If a graph had six odd vertices and three even vertices, what would be the minimum number of edges that would need to be added to make all of the vertices have an even degree?

17. Police officer Davis has been given the responsibility of patrolling Park Meadows. In order to be more efficient, he would like to be able to drive down each street once and only once every three hours. If possible, describe a path that he could use for the neighborhood. Is there more than one path for the neighborhood? If so, describe at least one additional path.

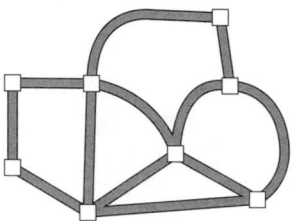

Park Meadows

TOPIC REVIEW

VOCABULARY/NOTATION

Vertex 875	Traversable 877	Equivalent 879
Edge 875	Euler path 877	Planar graphs 880
Vertex-edge graph 875	Euler circuit 877	Net 882
Network 875	Degree of a vertex 877	Hamiltonian path 883
Graph theory 875	Odd degree 877	Hamiltonian circuit 883
Path 876	Even degree 877	Traveling salesman problem 883
Connected 876	Adjacent 879	

GRAPH THEORY TEST

Knowledge

1. True or false?

   a. Every graph that has a Euler circuit also has a Hamiltonian circuit.

   b. If a graph is connected, then Euler's formula holds.

   c. If a graph is traversable, then it has at most two vertices with an odd degree.

   d. An Euler circuit is just another name for an Euler path.

   e. If one graph has all straight edges and another graph has some curved edges, then these two graphs cannot be equivalent.

Skill

Refer to the two graphs below for Problems 2–6

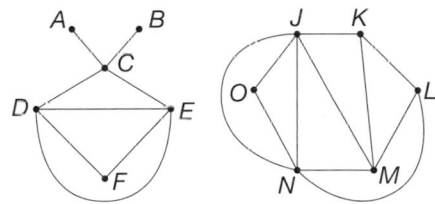

2. List all pairs of adjacent vertices in both graphs.

3. List the degree of each vertex in each graph.

4. Describe an Euler path or circuit in each graph. If such a path or circuit does not exist, explain why not.

5. Verify Euler's formula for each graph.

6. For each graph, describe a Hamiltonian path or circuit where one exists.

Understanding

7. The following graph contains at least one Euler path. Why?

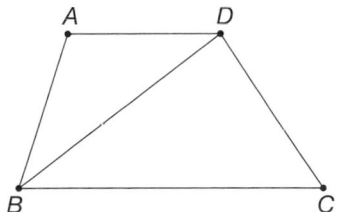

   a. How many Euler paths originate from point A?

   b. How many Euler paths originate from point B?

   c. How many Euler paths originate from point C?

   d. How many Euler paths originate from point D?

8. Draw a different graph for each of the following descriptions.

   a. A planar graph

   b. A connected graph

   c. A nonconnected graph

   d. A graph that contains an Euler path

   e. A graph that contains an Euler circuit

   f. A graph that does not contain a Hamiltonian path or circuit

Problem Solving/Application

9. Reno drives a snowplow in the winter and wants to do the job as quickly as possible by having to do no backtracking. Describe a path in the neighborhood below that meets Reno's goals. If it is not possible, explain why not. (NOTE: Two roads crossing without a white square indicates an overpass.)

Exercise/Problem Sets — Part A, Chapter Reviews, Chapter Tests, and Topics Section

Section 1.1A

1. 8

2. 36 ft × 78 ft

3. 88

4. $9 = 4 + 5$. If n is odd, then both $n - 1$ and $n + 1$ are even and $n = \dfrac{n - 1}{2} + \dfrac{n + 1}{2}$.

5. $6 \div 6 + 6 + 6 = 13$

6.

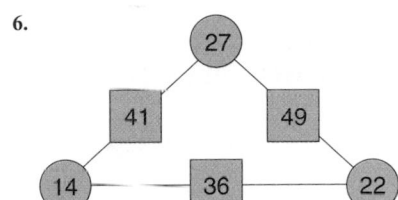

7.

8. No; $0 + 1 + 2 + 3 + 4 + 5 + 6 + 7 + 8 + 9 = 45$, which is too large.

9. For example, beginning at corner: 8, 2, 6, 7, 3, 4, 9, 5, 1

10. Row 1: 9, 3, 4; row 2: 8, 2, 5; row 3: 7, 6, 1

11. 52

12. Bill

13. a. 1839   **b.** 47

14. For example, row 1: 3, 5; row 2: 7, 1, 8, 2; row 3: 4, 6

15. U = 9, S = 3, R = 8, A = 2, P = 1, E = 0, C = 7

16. 3

17. Top pair: 8, 5; second pair from the top: 4, 1; third pair from the top: 6, 3; bottom pair: 2, 7. There are other correct answers.

18. $\dfrac{4(n + 10) + 200}{4} - n = (n + 10) + 50 - n$
$= n + 60 - n = 60$

19. For example, $98 - 7 + 6 + 5 - 4 + 3 - 2 + 1 = 100$, and $9 - 8 + 76 - 5 + 4 + 3 + 21 = 100$.

20. 1 and 12, 9 and 10

Section 1.2A

1. a. 9, 16, 25   **b.** 9   **c.** 13
   d. 23 $[1 + 3 + 5 + \cdots + (2n - 1) = n^2]$

2. a. 32   **b.** $\dfrac{1}{27}$ **c.** 21   **d.** 1287

3. a.

D	D	D
D	D	
	□	

   b.

○		
		→

4. a. $5556^2 - 4445^2 = 11,111,111$
   b. $55555556^2 - 44444445^2 = 1,111,111,111,111,111.$

5.

60	6	10
30	6	5
2	1	2

6. a.

TRIANGLE NUMBER	NUMBER OF DOTS IN SHAPE
1	1
2	3
3	6
4	10
5	15
6	21

   b.

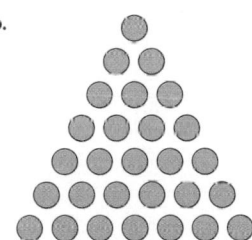

   c. 55 dots   **d.** Yes, the 13th number.
   e. No, the 16th number has 136 and the 17th number has 153.
   f. $\dfrac{n(n + 1)}{2}$ **g.** $\dfrac{100(101)}{2} = 5050$

7. a. $3 + 6 = 9$ **b.** $10 + 15 = 25$
   c. $45 + 55 = 100$, $190 + 210 = 400$, $(n - 1)$st + nth
   d. 36 is the 8th triangular number and is the 6th square number.
   e. Some possible answers: $4 - 1 = 3$, $49 - 4 = 45$, $64 - 49 = 15$, $64 - 36 = 28$, $64 - 9 = 55$, $169 - 64 = 105$.

8. $10,737,418.23 if paid the second way

9. For n triangles, perimeter $= n + 2$

10. a. In the 4, 6, 12, 14, . . . column
   b. In the 2, 8, 10, 16, . . . column
   c. In the 3, 7, 11, 15, . . . column
   d. In the 5, 13, . . . column

11. $100^3 = 1,000,000$

12. 34, 55, 89, 144, 233, 377; 144 · 233 = 33,552

13. 987

14. a. Sums are 1, 1, 2, 3, 5, 8, 13. Each sum is a Fibonacci number.
   b. Next three sums: 21, 34, 55

15. a. Sum is 20.
   b. Sum of numbers inside the circle is always twice the number directly below the circle.

16. a.

Step 5

Step 6

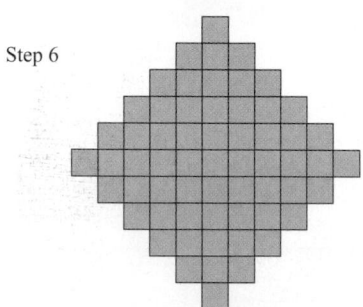

b.

STEP	NUMBER OF SQUARES
1	1
2	5
3	13
4	25
5	41
6	61

   c. 85   **d.** 10th, 181; 20th, 761; 50th, 4901

17. 23

18. a. 18   **b.** 66

CHAPTER REVIEW

Section 1.1

1. Try Guess and Test

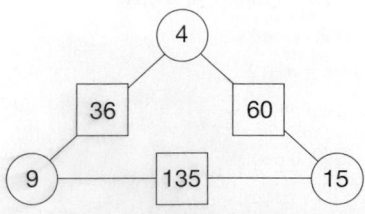

2. Use a Variable or Guess and Test

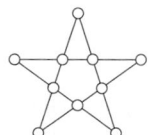

3. Draw a Picture—289 tiles

Section 1.2

1. Look for a Pattern
   1234321 × (1 + 2 + 3 + 4 + 3 + 2 + 1) = 4444²

2. Solve a Simpler Problem
   a. 9   **b.** 1296

3. Make a List
   a. 3: 1, 3, 9   **b.** 4: 1, 3, 9, 27   **c.** 364 grams

Chapter 1 Test

1. Understand the problem; devise a plan; carry out the plan; look back

2. Guess and Test; Use a Variable; Look for a Pattern; Make a List; Solve a Simpler Problem; Draw a Picture

3. $5 allowance.

4. Answers may vary.

5. Amanda had 31 hard-boiled eggs to sell.

6. Exercises are routine applications of known procedures, whereas problems require the solver to take an original mental step.

7. Any of the 6 clues under Guess and Test.

8. Any of the 8 clues under Use a Variable.

9. 4 × 4: 1, 2, 3, 4; 3, 4, 1, 2; 4, 3, 2, 1; 2, 1, 4, 3. The 2 × 2 is impossible. 3 × 3: 1, 3, 2; 3, 2, 1; 2, 1, 3.

10. 6

11. 30

12. Head and tail are 4 inches long and the body is 22 inches long.

13. 256

14.

15.

X	X	X	X	X	X
X	X	X			
X	X	X		X	
X	X	X			X

16. 2 nickels & 10 dimes; 5 nickels, 6 dimes, & 1 quarter; 8 nickels, 2 dimes, & 2 quarters.

17. Let $x, x + 1$, and $x + 2$ be any three consecutive numbers. Their sum is $(x) + (x + 1) + (x + 2) = 3x + 3 = 3(x + 1)$.

18. 4 different triangles. 2, 6, 6; 3, 5, 6; 4, 5, 5; 4, 4, 6

19. Baseball is 0.5 pounds, football is 0.75 pounds, soccer ball is 0.85 pounds.

Section 2.1A

1. a. {6, 7, 8}   **b.** {2, 4, 6, 8, 10, 12, 14}
   c. {2, 4, 6, . . . , 150}   **d.** {9, 10, 11, . . .}
   e. {1, 3, . . . , 99}   **f.** { }

2. a. T   **b.** F   **c.** T   **d.** F
   e. T   **f.** T   **g.** F   **h.** T
   i. F   **j.** T

3. ∅, {a}, {b}, {c}, {a, b}, {a, c}, {b, c}, {a, b, c}

4. ∅, {△}, {○}

5.

6. a.

b.

c.

7. a.

b.

c.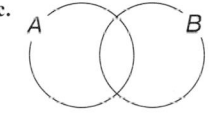

8. a. $\{b, c\}$ **b.** $\{b, c, e\}$ **c.** $\{a\}$

9. a. Women *or* Americans who have won Nobel Prizes
  b. Nobel Prize winners who are American women
  c. American winners of the Nobel Prize in chemistry

10. a. $\{0, 1, 2, 3, 4, 5, 6, 8, 10\}$ **b.** $\{0, 2, 4, 6, 8, 10\}$
  c. $\{0, 2, 4\}$ **d.** $\{0, 4, 8\}$
  e. $\{2, 6, 10\}$ **f.** $\{1, 2, 3, 5, 6, 10\}$

11. a. {January, June, July, August}
  b. {January}
  c. $\varnothing$
  d. {January, June, July}
  e. {March, April, May, September, October, November}
  f. {January}

12. a. Yes; compare Figures 2.4 and 2.5.
  b. Not necessarily; if $x \in X - Y$, then $x \in X \cup Y$, but $x \notin X \cap Y$.

13. a.

b.

c.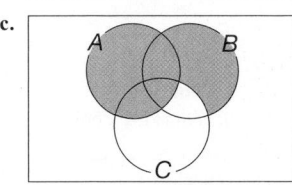

14. a. $(B \cap C) - A$ **b.** $C - (A \cup B)$
  c. $[A \cup (B \cap C)] - (A \cap B \cap C)$. Note: There are many other correct answers.

15. a. Yes
  b. $\{3, 6, 9, 12, 15, 18, 21, 24, \ldots\}$
  c. $\{6, 12, 18, 24, \ldots\}$
  d. $A \cup B = A, A \cap B = B$

16. a. Region inside circle or triangle
  b. Region inside both circle and rectangle
  c. Region inside rectangle combined with region inside both circle and triangle
  d. Region inside any of the three figures
  e. Small corner of rectangle that is also inside triangle and circle
  f. Same as part (e)

17. a. $\overline{A \cup B} = \overline{A} \cap \overline{B} = \{6\}$. Yes, the sets are the same.
  b. $\overline{A \cup B}$ and $\overline{A} \cap \overline{B}$ are both represented by

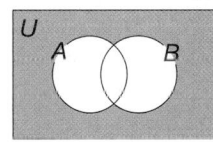

  Yes, the diagrams are the same.

18. a. $\{(a, b), (a, c)\}$
  b. $\{(5, a), (5, b), (5, c)\}$
  c. $\{(a, 1), (a, 2), (a, 3), (b, 1), (b, 2), (b, 3)\}$
  d. $\{(2, 1), (2, 4), (3, 1), (3, 4)\}$
  e. $\{(a, 5), (b, 5), (c, 5)\}$
  f. $\{(1, a), (2, b), (3, a), (1, b), (2, b), (3, b)\}$

19. a. 8   **b.** 12

20. a. 2   **b.** 4   **c.** Not possible
  d. 25   **e.** 0   **f.** Not possible

21. a. $A = \{a\}, B = \{2, 4, 6\}$
  b. $A = B = \{a, b\}$

22. a. T   **b.** F   **c.** F   **d.** F   **e.** F

23. a. 2   **b.** 99   **c.** 201
  d. infinite set   **e.** infinite set

24. a. Three elements; eight elements
  b. y elements; $x + y$ elements

25. 24

26. a. 1   **b.** 2   **c.** 4   **d.** 8   **e.** 32
  f. $2 \cdot 2 \cdot 2 \cdots 2$ (2 appears n times)

27. a. Possible   **b.** Not possible

28. a. When $D \subseteq E$ **b.** When $E \subseteq D$ **c.** When $E = D$

29. The Cartesian product of the set of skirts with the set of blouses will determine how many outfits can be formed—56 in this case.

30. 31 matches

31. Yes. Use lines perpendicular to the base.

32. Yes

33. a. 7   **b.** 19   **c.** 49

34. Twenty-five were butchers, bakers, *and* candlestick makers.

Section 2.2A

1. 314-781-9804, identification: 13905, identification; 6, cardinal; 7814, identification; 28, ordinal; $10, cardinal; 20, ordinal

2. a. Attribute common to all sets that match the set $\{a, b, c, d, e, f, g\}$
   b. Attribute common to all sets that match $\{a\}$
   c. Impossible
   d. How many elements are in the empty set?

3. Put in one-to-one correspondence with the set $\{1, 2, 3, 4, 5, 6\}$.

4. 8; 5

5. 9 is greater than 4; counting chant: 4 comes before 9; whole-number line; 4 is to the left of 9; set method: a set of 4 elements can be matched to a proper subset of a set with 9 elements.

6. If $A = \{a, b, c, d, e\}$, then $n(A) = 5$. If $B \subset A$, then $n(B) = 0, 1, 2, 3$, or 4, since if B is a proper subset of A, A must contain at least one element that is not in B. So the numbers smaller than 5 are 0, 1, 2, 3, and 4.

7. a. |||||||||

   b. ∩∩|||

   c. 𝟫𝟫𝟫𝟫∩∩∩∩|||

   d. 𝟫𝟫∩∩∩|

8. a. LXXVI   **b.** XLIX
   c. CXCII   **d.** MDCCXLI

9. a.

   b.

   c.

   d.

10. a.

   b.

   c.

d.

11. a. 12   **b.** 4270   **c.** 3614   **d.** 1991
   e. 976   **f.** 3245   **g.** 42   **h.** 404
   i. 3010   **j.** 14   **k.** 52   **l.** 333

12. a.

   b. CXXXI

   c.

13. a. Egyptian
   b. Mayan
   c. No. For example, to represent 10 requires two symbols in the Mayan system, but only one in either the Egyptian or Babylonian systems.

14. a. (i) 42, (ii) 625, (iii) 3533, (iv) 89,801
   b. (i) $\pi\epsilon$, (ii) $\psi,\mu\delta$, (iii) $\beta\rho\upsilon\gamma$, (iv) $\kappa\alpha\phi\lambda\delta$
   c. No.

15. IV and VI, IX and XI, and so on; the Egyptian system was not positional, so there should not be a problem with reversals.

16. a. (i) 30, (ii) 24, (iii) 47, (iv) 57
   b. Add the digits of the addends (or substrahend and minuend).

17. MCMXCIX. It was introduced in the fall of 1998.

18. 18 pages

19. $1993 \times (1 + 2 + 3 + 4 + \cdots + 1994)$

20. Do a three-coin version first. For five coins, start by comparing two coins. If they balance, use a three-coin test on the remaining coins. If they do not balance, add in one of the good coins and use a three-coin test.

Section 2.3A

1. a. $7(10) + 0(1)$
   b. $3(100) + 0(10) + 0(1)$
   c. $7(100) + 4(10) + 6(1)$
   d. $9(100) + 8(10) + 4(1)$
   e. $6(10^7) + 6(10^3) + 6(10)$
   f. $8(10^5) + 4(10^4) + 1(1)$

2. a. 1207   **b.** 500,300   **c.** 8,070,605
   d. 2,000,033,040   **e.** 60,900,000

3. a. Two billion
   b. Eighty-seven trillion
   c. Fifty-two trillion six hundred seventy-two billion four hundred five million one hundred twenty-three thousand one hundred thirty-nine
   d. Ninety-eight quadrillion

4. Any three of the following digits: 0, 1, 2, 3, 4, 5, 6, 7, 8, 9; grouping by tens; place value; additive; multiplicative

5. a. For example, loop all columns having three *x*'s. Then, group these loops in sets of three. Finally, draw one loop around three of these groups.
   b. 1121_{three}

6. 3223_{four}

7. 1, 2, 1, 3

8. a.

b.

c.

9. a.

b.

c.

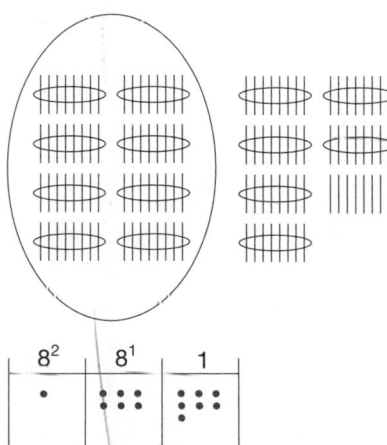

10. a. 222_{five}

   b. 333_{five}; 32143_{five}

11. a. $15_{\text{seven}} = 1(7) + 5(1)$

   b. $123_{\text{seven}} = 1(7^2) + 2(7) + 3(1)$

   c. $5046_{\text{seven}} = 5(7^3) + 0(7^2) + 4(7) + 6(1)$

12. a. In base five, 1, 2, 3, 4, 10, 11, 12, 13, 14, 20, 21, 22, 23, 24, 30, 31, 32, 33, 34, 40, 41, 42, 43, 44, 100

   b. In base two, 1, 10, 11, 100, 101, 110, 111, 1000, 1001, 1010, 1011, 1100, 1101, 1110, 1111, 10000

   c. In base three, 1, 2, 10, 11, 12, 20, 21, 22, 100, 101, 102, 110, 111, 112, 120, 121, 122, 200, 201, 202, 210, 211, 212, 220, 221, 222, 1000

   d. 255, 300, 301, 302 (in base six)

   e. 310_{four}

   f. 1000_{nine}

13. a. 613_{eight} **b.** 23230_{four} **c.** 110110_{two}

14. a. 194   **b.** 328   **c.** 723   **d.** 129

   e. 1451   **f.** 20,590

15. a. 202_{six}; 62_{twelve}

   b. 332_{six}; $T8_{\text{twelve}}$

   c. 550_{six}; 156_{twelve}

   d. 15142_{six}; $14E2_{\text{twelve}}$

16. a. 7_{nine} **b.** 60_{nine} **c.** 255_{nine}

17. 23

18. Improper digit symbols for the given bases—can't have an 8 in base eight or a 4 in base three

19. a. Seven   **b.** Forty-seven

   c. Twelve   **d.** $x > 5, x = 3y - 5$

20. a. It must be 0, 2, 4, 6, or 8.

   b. It must be 0 or 2.

   c. It must be a 0.

   d. It may be any digit in base 5.

21. 1024 pages

22. 57

23. a. If final answer is *abcdef*, then the first two digits (*ab*) give the month of birth, the second two (*cd*) give the date of birth, and the last two (*ef*) give the year of birth.

   b. If birthday is *ab/cd/ef*, then the result will be $100,000a + 10,000b + 1,000c + 100d + 10e + f$. For example, begin by calculating $4(10a + b) + 13$.

Section 2.4A

1. a. $\{(a, a), (a, b), (b, c), (c, b)\}$

   b. $\{(1, x), (2, y), (3, y), (4, z)\}$

   c. $\{(a, b), (b, a), (a, c), (c, a), (b, c), (c, b)\}$

2. a.

b.

c.

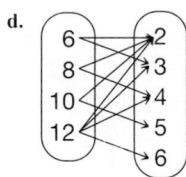

Broncos → San Francisco
Vikings → St. Louis
49ers → Oakland
Cowboys → Dallas
Rams → Denver
→ Minnesota

d.

6, 8, 10, 12 → 2, 3, 4, 5, 6

3. a. R, T   **b.** S   **c.** T
  d. R, S, T, equivalence relation

4. a. Each person is contained in a subset having all people with the same surname.
  b. The partition has 10 subsets. The numbers in each subset have the same tens digit.
  c. All residents in the United States are in disjoint subsets where residents of the same state are together.

5. a. Transitive only
  b. All three, therefore an equivalence relation
  c. Reflexive and transitive only
  d. All three, thus an equivalence relation

6. a. Not a function, since b is paired with two different numbers
  b. Function
  c. Function
  d. Not a function, since 3 is paired with two different numbers

7. a. (0, 0), (2, 10), (4, 116). Range: {0, 10, 116}
  b. (1, 3), (2, 4), (9, 11). Range: {3, 4, 11}
  c. $(1, 2), \left(2, \dfrac{9}{4}\right), \left(3, \dfrac{64}{27}\right)$. Range: $\left\{1, \dfrac{9}{4}, \dfrac{64}{27}\right\}$

8. a. Yes   **b.** Yes
  c. No, since the number 1 is paired with two different numbers.
  d. Yes
  e. No, since the letter b is paired with both b and c (and the letter d is paired with both e and f).

9. a. 100   **b.** 81   **c.** 3   **d.** 2

10. a. Function
  b. Function
  c. Not a function, since some college graduates have more than one degree
  d. Function

11. a. {(0, 0), (1, 0), (4, 60)}, $\begin{matrix} 0 \to 0 \\ 1 \to 0 \\ 4 \to 60 \end{matrix}$

x	f(x)
0	0
1	0
4	60

  b. $f(x) = \sqrt{x}$ for $x \in \{1, 4, 9\}$, $\begin{matrix} 1 \to 1 \\ 4 \to 2 \\ 9 \to 3 \end{matrix}$

x	f(x)
1	1
4	2
9	3

  c. $f(x) = 2x$ for $x \in \{1, 2, 10\}$, {(1, 2), (2, 4), (10, 20)}

x	f(x)
1	2
2	4
10	20

  d. $f(x) = 11x$ for $x \in \{5, 6, 7\}$,
  {(5, 55), (6, 66), (7, 77)}, $\begin{matrix} 5 \to 55 \\ 6 \to 66 \\ 7 \to 77 \end{matrix}$

12. a. 29, 18, 17   **b.** 7, 10, 4   **c.** $\dfrac{7}{9}, \dfrac{6}{9}, \dfrac{5}{6}$ **d.** 5, 3, 4

13. a. Arithmetic, 5, 1002
  b. Geometric, 2, 14×2^{199}
  c. Arithmetic, 10, 1994
  d. Neither

14. 228

15. a. 0.44   **b.** 0.56   **c.** 0.67   **d.** 4.61

16. Fraction equality is an equivalence relation. The equivalence class containing $\frac{1}{2}$ is $\{\frac{1}{2}, \frac{2}{4}, \frac{3}{6}, \frac{4}{8}, \frac{5}{10}, \dots\}$.

17. a. 32; 212; 122; -40 **b.** 0; 100; 40; -40
  c. Yes; -40

18. 3677

19. a. $C(x) = 85 + 35x$
  b. $C(18) = 715$. The total amount spent by a member after 18 months is $715.
  c. After 27 months

20. a. $r = \dfrac{1}{2}$ **b.** 2400, 1200, 600, 300, 150, 75

21. a.

n	T(n)
1	4
2	12
3	20
4	28
5	36
6	44
7	52
8	60

  b. Arithmetic sequence with $a = 4$ and $d = 8$
  c. $T(n) = 4 + (n - 1)8$ or $T(n) = 8n - 4$
  d. $T(20) = 156$; $T(150) = 1196$
  e. Domain: {1, 2, 3, 4, ...}
  Range: {4, 12, 20, 28, ...}

22. a.

n	$T(n)$
1	3
2	9
3	18
4	30
5	45
6	63
7	81
8	108

b. Neither

c. $T(n) = \dfrac{3n(n+1)}{2}$

d. $T(15) = 360.$ $T(100) = 15{,}150$

e. Domain: $\{1, 2, 3, 4, \ldots\}$
Range: $\{3, 9, 18, 30, \ldots\}$

23. a.

n = NUMBER OF YEARS	ANNUAL INTEREST EARNED	VALUE OF ACCOUNT
0	0	100
1	5	105
2	5	110
3	5	115
4	5	120
5	5	125
6	5	130
7	5	135
8	5	140
9	5	145
10	5	150

b. Arithmetic sequence with $a = 100$ and $d = 5$.
$A(n) = 100 + 5n$

24. a.

n = NUMBER OF YEARS	ANNUAL INTEREST EARNED	VALUE OF ACCOUNT
0	0	100
1	5	105
2	5.25	110.25
3	5.51	115.76
4	5.79	121.55
5	6.08	127.63
6	6.38	134.01
7	6.70	140.71
8	7.04	147.75
9	7.39	155.13
10	7.76	162.89

b. Geometric sequence with $a = 100$ and $r = 1.05$.
$A(n) = 100(1.05)^n$

c. $12.89

25. $h(1) = 48$, $h(2) = 64$, $h(3) = 48$; 4 seconds

26. Convert the number to base two. Since the largest possible telephone number, 999–9999, is between $2^{23} = 8388608$ and $2^{24} = 16777216$, the base two numeral will have at most 24 digits. Ask, in order, whether each digit is 1. This process takes 24 questions. Then convert back to base ten.

PROBLEMS WHERE THE STRATEGY "DRAW A DIAGRAM" IS USEFUL

1. Draw a tree diagram. There are $3 \cdot 2 \cdot 2 = 12$ combinations.

2. Draw a diagram tracing out the taxi's path: 5 blocks north and 2 blocks east.

3. Draw a diagram showing the four cities: 15,000 arrive at Canton.

CHAPTER REVIEW
Section 2.1

1. Verbal description, listing, set-builder notation

2. a. T **b.** T **c.** T **d.** T **e.** T **f.** T
g. F **h.** F **i.** F **j.** F **k.** T **l.** F

3. $\{1, 2, 3, 4, 5, 6, 7\}$

4. An infinite set can be matched with a proper subset of itself.

5. 7

Section 2.2

1. No—it should be house *numeral*.

2. a. How much money is in your bank account?
b. Which place did you finish in the relay race?
c. What is your telephone number?

3. a. T **b.** T **c.** F **d.** T **e.** T **f.** T
g. F **h.** F

4. a. 111 **b.** 114 **c.** 168

5. a. ∩ ∩ ∩ | | | | | | | **b.** XXXVII

c.

6. IV ≠ VI shows that the Roman system is positional. However, this system does not have place value. Every place value system is positional.

Section 2.3

1. a. Digits tell how many of each place value is required.
b. Grouping by ten establishes the place values.
c. Place values allow for large numbers with few numerals.
d. Digits are *multiplied* by the place values and then all resulting values are *added*.

2. The names of 11 and 12 are unique; the names of 13–19 read the ones digits first, then say "teen." The numerals 21–29 are read from left to right, where twenty means 2 tens and the second digit is the number of ones.

3. a. F **b.** T **c.** F **d.** T

4. It gives you insight into base 10.

Section 2.4

1. a. Yes. **b.** Neither symmetric nor transitive
c. Not transitive

2. a. $\{(1, 10), (2, 9), (3, 8), (4, 7), (5, 6), (6, 5), (7, 4), (8, 3), (9, 2), (10, 1)\}$, symmetric
b. $\{(12, 8), (11, 7), (10, 6), (9, 5), (8, 4), (7, 3), (6, 2), (5, 1)\}$
c. $\{(1, 12), (12, 1), (2, 6), (6, 2), (3, 4), (4, 3)\}$, symmetric
d. $\{(12, 6), (10, 5), (8, 4), (6, 3), (4, 2), (2, 1)\}$

3. a. (i) 1, 7, 13, 19, 25; (ii) 2, 8, 32, 128, 512   **b.** (i) 6; (ii) 4

4. a. T   **b.** F   **c.** F   **d.** F

5. a. Dawn→Jones, Jose→Ortiz, Amad→Rasheed

b.

FIRST NAME	SURNAME
Dawn	Jones
Jose	Ortiz
Amad	Rasheed

   c. (Dawn, Jones), (Jose, Oritz), (Amad, Rasheed)

6.

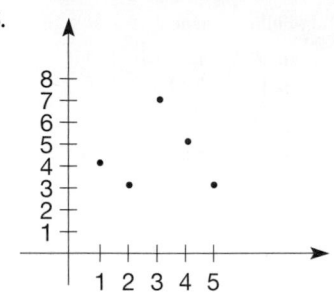

Range = {3, 4, 5, 7}

7. For example, the area of a circle with radius r is πr^2, the circumference of a circle with radius r is $2\pi r$, and the volume of a cube having side length s is s^3.

Chapter 2 Test

1. a. F   **b.** T   **c.** T   **d.** T   **e.** F   **f.** F
   g. T   **h.** F   **i.** F   **j.** F   **k.** F   **l.** T

2. 19

3. The intersection is an empty set.

4. Arrow Diagrams, Tables, Machines, Ordered Pairs, Graphs, Formulas, Geometric Transformations (any 6 is sufficient)

5. a. {a, b, c, d, e}   **b.** { } or ∅   **c.** {b, c}
   d. {$(a, e), (a, f), (a, g), (b, e), (b, f), (b, g), (c, e), (c, f), (c, g)$}
   e. {d}   **f.** {e}

6. a. 32   **b.** 944   **c.** 381   **d.** 96   **e.** 21   **f.** 142

7. a. $7 \times 100 + 5 \times 10 + 9$ **b.** $7 \times 1000 + 2$
   c. $1 \times 2^6 + 1 \times 2^3 + 1$

8.

9.

Babylonian:

Roman: CLVII

Egyptian: ꝲꝲꝲꝲꝲꝲꝲꝵꝵꝵꝵꝵꝵꝵ

Mayan:

10. 4034_{five}

11. $[A - (B \cup C)] \cup (B \cap C)$ There are other correct answers.

12. a. {$(a, c), (b, c), (c, a), (c, d), (d, a), (d, e), (e, b)$}
   b. {$(a, a), (a, b), (b, a), (c, e), (d, d), (e, c), (e, e)$}, symmetric
   c. {$(1, 2), (2, 1), (-2, 3), (-1, -1), (-3, -2), (-2, -3), (3, -2)$}, symmetric

13. IV ≠ VI; thus position is important, but there is no place value as in 31 ≠ 13, where the first 3 means "3 tens" and the second three means "3 ones."

14. a. True for all A and B
   b. True for all A and B
   c. True whenever $A = B$
   d. True whenever $A = B$ or where A or B is empty

15. $(b, a), (b, c), (d, a), (d, c)$

16. 2, 6, 10, 14, . . . is an arithmetic sequence, and 2, 6, 18, 54, . . . is geometric.

17. Zero, based on groups of 20, 18 · 20, etc.

18.

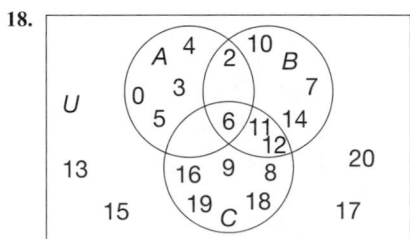

19. No. There are 26 letters and 40 numbers.

20. Yes; No, 3 has no image; No, two arrows from 2.

21.

3^3	3^2	3^1	3^0

22. a. {$(1, 1), (2, 2), (3, 3), (4, 4)$}   **b.** None
   c. {$(1, 1), (2, 2), (3, 3), (4, 4), (1, 4), (4, 1), (3, 2), (2, 3)$}
   d. Same as part (c)

23. 97

24. $a = 6, b = 8$

25. 3

26. a. $241   **b.** $C(n) = 4(n - 1)^2 + 3(2n - 1)$

27. $187, 3 + (n - 1) \cdot 4$

28. a.

1 → 2
2 → 4
3 → 8
4 → 16
5 → 32
6 → 64

b.

n	2^n
1	2
2	4
3	8
4	16
5	32
6	64

c.

d. $f(n) = 2^n$

29. $f(x) = 0.75(220 - x)$

Section 3.1A

1. a.

b.

2. Only (a) and (b)

3. a. Closed **b.** Closed
  c. Not closed, $1 + 2 = 3$
  d. Not closed, $1 + 2 = 3$
  e. Closed **f.** Closed
  g. Not closed, $1 + 1 = 2$
  h. Not closed, $1 + 1 = 2$
  i. Closed
  j. Not closed, $1 + 16 = 17$

4. a. Closure **b.** Commutativity
  c. Associativity **d.** Identity
  e. Commutativity
  f. Associativity and commutativity

5. Associative property and commutative property for whole-number addition

6. a. $7 - 2 = 5$, set model, take-away
  b. $7 - 3 = 4$, measurement model, missing addend
  c. $6 - 4 = 2$, set model, comparison approach

7. a. $140; (94 + 6) + (27 + 13)$
  b. $121; (5 + 25) + (13 + 47) + 31$

8. a. $8 - 3$ is 8 "take away" 3, or 5; $8 - 3 = c$ if and only if $8 = 3 + c$, or $c = 5$.

b.

c.

d.

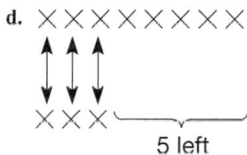

9. a. Yes **b.** Yes **c.** No
  d. Yes **e.** No **f.** No

10. a. No; that is, $3 - 5$ is not a whole number.
  b. No; that is, $3 - 5 \neq 5 - 3$.
  c. No; that is, $(6 - 3) - 1 \neq 6 - (3 - 1)$.
  d. No, $5 - 0 = 5$ but $0 - 5 \neq 5$.

11. a. Take-away model, since \$120 has been removed from the original amount of \$200:
$$200 - 120 = r$$

  b. Comparison approach, since two different sets of tomato plants are being compared:
$$24 - 18 = x$$

  c. Missing-addend model, since we need to know what additional amount will make savings equal \$1795
$$1240 + x = 1795$$

12. a.

+	0	1	2	3	4
0	0	1	2	3	4
1	1	2	3	4	10
2	2	3	4	10	11
3	3	4	10	11	12
4	4	10	11	12	13

b. (i) 4_{five}, (ii) 3_{five}, (iii) 3_{five}, (iv) 3_{five}

13. a. $4_{\text{five}} + 3_{\text{five}} = 12_{\text{five}}, 12_{\text{five}} - 4_{\text{five}} = 3_{\text{five}}, 12_{\text{five}} - 3_{\text{five}} = 4_{\text{five}}$
  b. $1_{\text{five}} + 4_{\text{five}} = 10_{\text{five}}, 10_{\text{five}} - 1_{\text{five}} = 4_{\text{five}}, 10_{\text{five}} - 4_{\text{five}} = 1_{\text{five}}$
  c. $2_{\text{five}} + 4_{\text{five}} = 11_{\text{five}}, 4_{\text{five}} + 2_{\text{five}} = 11_{\text{five}}, 11_{\text{five}} - 2_{\text{five}} = 4_{\text{five}}$

14. The rest of the counting numbers

15. $123 - 45 - 67 + 89 = 100$

16.

25	11	12	22
14	20	19	17
18	16	15	21
13	23	24	10

17. Sums of numbers on all six sides are the same as are sums on the "half-diagonals," lines from center to edge.

18. a. (i) 363, **(ii)** 4884, **(iii)** 55
  b. 69, 78, 79, or 89

19. 4, 8, 12, 16, 20

20. One arrangement has these sides: 1, 5, 9, 2; 2, 4, 8, 3; 1, 6, 7, 3.

Section 3.2A

1. Partitive. The 28 students are the groups, and the 60 cupcakes are broken into 28 groups to find out how many are in each group.

2. The problem should include the idea of 91 objects being broken into 7 equal groups. Answers may vary.

3. a. 2×4 **b.** 4×2 **c.** 3×7

4. a.

  b.

  0 6 12 18 24

  c.
  × × × × × ×
  × × × × × ×
  × × × × × ×
  × × × × × ×

5. a. No   **b.** Yes   **c.** No   **d.** Yes   **e.** Yes
  f. Yes   **g.** Yes   **h.** Yes   **i.** Yes   **j.** Yes

6. a. Commutative   **b.** Commutative
  c. Distributive over addition   **d.** Identity
  e. Distributive over subtraction   **f.** Associative
  g. Multiplication by 0   **h.** Distributive over addition

7. a. $4 \cdot 60 + 4 \cdot 37$ **b.** $21 \cdot 6 + 35 \cdot 6$
  c. $3 \cdot 29 + 3 \cdot 30 + 3 \cdot 6$ **d.** $5x - 5 \cdot 2y$
  e. $37 \cdot 60 - 37 \cdot 22$ **f.** $a \cdot 7 - ab + az$

8. a. $(6 \times 100) - (6 \times 1) = 594$
  b. $(5 \times 50) - (5 \times 1) = 245$
  c. $(7 \times 20) - (7 \times 1) = 133$
  d. $(6 \times 50) - (6 \times 3) = 282$

9. a. $45(11) = 45(10 + 1)$ **b.** $39(102) = 39(100 + 2)$
  c. $23(21) = 23(20 + 1)$ **d.** $97(101) = 97(100 + 1)$

10. a. Cartesian product, since the set of possibilities is {small, medium, large} × {cola, diet cola, lemon-lime, root beer, orange}:
$$x = 3 \cdot 5$$
  b. Rectangular array approach, since students form a moving array of 72 rows and 4 columns:
$$n = 72 \cdot 4$$
  c. Repeated addition, since the bill could be found by adding $70¢ + 70¢ + 70¢ + \cdots + 70¢$, where the sum has 25 terms:
$$c = 25 \cdot 70$$

11. a. $5(23 \times 4) = 23(5 \times 4) = 23 \times 20 = 460$
  b. $12 \times 25 = 3(4 \times 25) = 300$

12. a. $48 = 8 \times 6$ **b.** $51 = 3 \cdot x$ **c.** $x = 5 \cdot 13$
  d. $24 = 12 \cdot x$ **e.** $x = 27 \cdot 3$ **f.** $a = b \cdot x$

13. a. 0   **b.** 2   **c.** 12   **d.** 8   **e.** 32   **f.** 13

14. a. (In base five)

×	0	1	2	3	4
0	0	0	0	0	0
1	0	1	2	3	4
2	0	2	4	11	13
3	0	3	11	14	22
4	0	4	13	22	31

  b. (i) $3_{\text{five}} \times 2_{\text{five}} = 11_{\text{five}}, 11_{\text{five}} \div 3_{\text{five}} = 2_{\text{five}}, 11_{\text{five}} \div 2_{\text{five}} = 3_{\text{five}}$
     (ii) $3_{\text{five}} \times 4_{\text{five}} = 22_{\text{five}}, 4_{\text{five}} \times 3_{\text{five}} = 22_{\text{five}}, 22_{\text{five}} \div 4_{\text{five}} = 3_{\text{five}}$
     (iii) $2_{\text{five}} \times 4_{\text{five}} = 13_{\text{five}}, 4_{\text{five}} \times 2_{\text{five}} = 13_{\text{five}}, 13_{\text{five}} \div 4_{\text{five}} = 2_{\text{five}}$

15. a. $3 \div 2 \neq$ whole number   **b.** $4 \div 2 \neq 2 \div 4$
  c. $(12 \div 3) \div 2 \neq 12 \div (3 \div 2)$ **d.** $5 \div 1 = 5$, but $1 \div 5 \neq 5$
  e. $12 \div (4 + 2) \neq 12 \div 4 + 12 \div 2$

16. $3.84

17. Approximately $2.48.

18. $90,000

19. Push 1; multiplicative identity

20. Yes

21. a. Row 1: 4, 3, 8; row 2: 9, 5, 1; row 3: 2, 7, 6
  b. Row 1: $2^4, 2^3, 2^8$; row 2: $2^9, 2^5, 2^1$; row 3: $2^2, 2^7, 2^6$

22. $31 + 33 + 35 + 37 + 39 + 41 = 216$;
$43 + 45 + 47 + 49 + 51 + 53 + 55 = 343$;
$57 + 59 + 61 + 63 + 65 + 67 + 69 + 71 = 512$

23. 9, 5, 4, 6, 3, 2, 1, 7, 8

24. $\dfrac{2(n + 10) + 100}{2} - n = 60$

25. 1st place: Pounce, Michelle
2nd place: Hippy, Kevin
2nd place: Hoppy, Jason
3rd place: Bounce, Wendy

26. 3 cups of tea, 2 cakes, and 7 people

27. 3^{29}

28. Put three on each pan. If they balance, the lighter one of the other two will be found in the next weighing. If three of the coins are lighter, then weigh one of these three against another of these three. If they balance, the third coin is the lighter one. If they do not balance, choose the lighter one.

29. Yes, providing $c \neq 0$.

Section 3.3A

1. a. 19   **b.** 16

2. $2 < 10, 8 < 10, 10 > 2, 10 > 8$

3. Yes

4. a. Yes   **b.** No. $2 \neq 3$ and $3 \neq 2$, but $2 = 2$.

5. a. 3^4 **b.** $2^4 \cdot 3^2$ **c.** $6^3 \cdot 7^2$
   d. $x^2 y^4$ **e.** $a^2 b^2$ or $(ab)^2$ **f.** $5^3 6^3$ or $(5 \cdot 6)^3$

6. a. $3 \cdot x \cdot x \cdot y \cdot y \cdot y \cdot y \cdot y \cdot z$
   b. $7 \cdot 5 \cdot 5 \cdot 5$
   c. $7 \cdot 5 \cdot 7 \cdot 5 \cdot 7 \cdot 5$

7. a. 5^7 **b.** 3^{10} **c.** 10^7
   d. 2^8 **e.** 5^4 **f.** 6^7

8. $3^2 \cdot 3^4$ is an abbreviated form of $(3 \cdot 3)(3 \cdot 3 \cdot 3 \cdot 3)$, so there is a total of 6 factors of 3, which can be written as 3^6. The student's answer means a product of six 9s.

9. In general, $(a + b)^n \neq a^n + b^n$. For example, $(1 + 2)^2 = 3^2 = 9$, but $1^2 + 2^2 = 1 + 4 = 5$.

10. a. 1,679,616   **b.** 50,625   **c.** 1875

11. a. $x = 6$ **b.** $x = 5$ **c.** x can be any whole number.

12. a. $6^{10} = (2 \cdot 3)^{10} = 2^{10} \cdot 3^{10} < 3^{10} \cdot 3^{10} = 3^{20}$
   b. $9^9 = (3^2)^9 = 3^{18} < 3^{20}$
   c. $12^{10} = (4 \cdot 3)^{10} = 4^{10} \cdot 3^{10} > 3^{10} \cdot 3^{10} = 3^{20}$

13. a. 200¢ or $2.00   **b.** 6400¢ or $64.00
   c. Price $= 25 \cdot 2^n$ cents

14. When $a = n(A)$ and $b = n(B)$, $a < b$ means A can be matched to a proper subset of B. Also, $b < c$ when $c = n(C)$ means the B can be matched to a proper subset of C. In that matching, the proper subset of B that matches A is matched to a proper subset of a proper subset of C. Thus, since A can be matched to a proper subset of C, $a < c$.

15. a. $17 + 18 + 19 + \cdots + 25 = 4^3 + 5^3$;
     $26 + 27 + 28 + \cdots + 36 = 5^3 + 6^3$
   b. $9^3 + 10^3 = 82 + 83 + \cdots + 100$
   c. $12^3 + 13^3 = 145 + \cdots + 169$
   d. $n^3 + (n + 1)^3 = (n^2 + 1) + (n^2 + 2) + \cdots + (n + 1)^2$

16. $4(2^4) = 64$

17. a. The only one-digit squares are 1, 4, and 9. The only combination of these that is a perfect square is 49.
   b. 169, 361
   c. 1600, 1936, 2500, 3600, 4900, 6400, 8100, 9025
   d. 1225, 1444, 4225, 4900
   e. 1681
   f. 1444, 4900, 9409

18. The second one

19. a. If $a < b$, then $a + n = b$ for some nonzero n.
     Then $(a + c) + n = b + c$, or $a + c < b + c$.
   b. If $a < b$, then $a - c < b - c$ for all c, where $c \leq a, c \leq b$.
     Proof: If $a < b$, then $a + n = b$ for some nonzero n.
     Hence $(a - c) + n = b - c$, or $a - c < b - c$.

PROBLEMS WHERE THE STRATEGY "USE DIRECT REASONING" IS USEFUL

1. Since the first and last digits are the same, their sum is even. Since the sum of the three digits is odd, the middle digit must be odd.

2. Michael, Clyde, Jose, Andre, Ralph

3. The following triples represent the amount in the 8-, 3-, and 5-liter jugs, respectively, after various pourings: (8, 0, 0), (5, 3, 0), (5, 0, 3), (2, 3, 3), (2, 1, 5), (7, 1, 0), (7, 0, 1), (4, 3, 1), (4, 0, 4).

CHAPTER REVIEW

Section 3.1

1. a. $5 + 4 = n(\{a, b, c, d, e\}) + n(\{f, g, h, i\}) = n(\{a, b, c, d, e\} \cup \{f, g, h, i\}) = 9$
   b.

2. a. Associative   **b.** Identity   **c.** Commutative
   d. Closure

3. a. $5 + 6 = 5 + (5 + 1) = (5 + 5) + 1 = 10 + 1 = 11$; associativity for addition, doubles, adding ten
   b. $7 + 9 = (6 + 1) + 9 = 6 + (1 + 9) = 6 + 10 = 16$; associativity, combinations to ten, adding ten

4. a. $7 - 3 = n(\{a, b, c, d, e, f, g\} - \{e, f, g\}) = n(\{a, b, c, d\}) = 4$.
   b. $7 - 3 = n$ if and only if $7 = 3 + n$. Thus, $n = 4$.

5. To find $7 - 2$, find 7 in the "2" column. The answer is in the row containing 7, namely 5.

6. None

Section 3.2

1. a. 15 altogether:

   b. 15 altogether:

c.

d.

2. a. Identity   **b.** Commutative   **c.** Associative   **d.** Closure

3. a. $7 \times 27 + 7 \times 13 = 7(27 + 13) = 7(40) = 280$
   b. $8 \times 17 - 8 \times 7 = 8(17 - 7) = 8(10) = 80$

4. a. $6 \times 7 = 6(6 + 1) = 6 \times 6 + 6 \times 1 = 36 + 6 = 42$; distributivity
   b. $9 \times 7 = (10 - 1)7 = 10 \times 7 - 7 = 70 - 7 = 63$; distributivity

5. a. $17 \div 3 = 5$ remainder 2:

   b. $17 \div 3 = 5$ remainder 2:

6. To find $63 \div 7$, look for 63 in the "7" column. The answer is the row containing 63, namely 9.

7. a. $7 \div 0 = n$ if and only if $7 = 0 \times n$. Since $0 \times n = 0$ for all n, there is no answer for $7 \div 0$.
   b. $0 \div 7 = n$ if and only if $0 = 7 \times n$. Therefore, $n = 0$.
   c. $0 \div 0 = n$ if and only if $0 = 0 \times n$. Since any number will work for n, there is no unique answer for $0 \div 0$.

8. $39 \div 7 : 39 = 7 \times 5 + 4$ where 5 is the quotient and 4 is the remainder

9. None

10. This diagram shows how subtraction, multiplication, and division are all connected to addition.

Section 3.3

1. $a < b \ (b > a)$ if there is nonzero whole number n such that $a + n = b$.

2. a. $a + c < b + c$ **b.** $a \times c < b \times c$

3. $5^4 = 5 \times 5 \times 5 \times 5$

4. a. $7^{3 \times 4} = 7^{12}$ **b.** $(3 \times 7)^5 = 21^5$ **c.** $5^{(7-3)} = 5^4$
d. $4^{12+13} = 4^{25}$

5. Use a pattern: $5^3 = 125, 5^2 = 25, 5^1 = 5, 5^0 = 1$, since we divided by 5 each time.

Chapter 3 Test

1. a. F   **b.** T   **c.** T   **d.** F   **e.** F
f. F   **g.** F   **h.** T   **i.** F   **j.** T

2.

	ADD	SUBTRACT	MULTIPLY	DIVIDE
Closure	T	F	T	F
Commutative	T	F	T	F
Associative	T	F	T	F
Identity	T	F	T	F

3. a. Commutative for multiplication (CM)
b. IM   **c.** AA   **d.** AM   **e.** D   **f.** CA

4. a. $30 + 10 + 9 + 2$ **b.** $40 + 80 + 7 + 7$
c. $(5 \cdot 2)73$ **d.** $10 \times 33 + 2 \times 33$

5. 64 R1

6. a. 3^{19} **b.** 5^{24} **c.** 7^{15} **d.** 2^2 **e.** 14^{15} **f.** 36^{12}

7. a. $13(97 + 3)$; distributivity
b. $(194 + 6) + 86$; associativity and commutativity
c. $23(7 + 3)$; commutativity and distributivity
d. $(25 \cdot 8)123$; commutativity and associativity

8. a. partitive   **b.** measurement   **c.** measurement

9. a. Since there are two sets, comparison can be used with either missing-addend, $137 + x = 163$, or take-away, $163 - 137 = 26$.
b. missing-addend, $973 + x = 1500$
c. take-away, $\$5 - \$1.43 = \$3.57$

10. A

11. a. $(7^3)^4 = (7 \cdot 7 \cdot 7)^4 = (7 \cdot 7 \cdot 7)(7 \cdot 7 \cdot 7)(7 \cdot 7 \cdot 7)(7 \cdot 7 \cdot 7) = 7^{12}$
b. $(7^3)^4 = 7^3 \cdot 7^3 \cdot 7^3 \cdot 7^3 = 7^{3+3+3+3} = 7^{12}$

12. $3 \div 0 = n$ if and only if $n \cdot 0 = 3$. But $n \cdot 0 = 0$

13. $a^m \cdot b^m = \underbrace{a \cdot a \cdots a}_{m} \cdot \underbrace{b \cdot b \cdots b}_{m} =$
$\underbrace{ab \cdot ab \cdots ab}_{m} = (a \cdot b)^m$

14. $(2 \cdot 3)^2 = 36$ but $2 \cdot 3^2 = 2 \cdot 9 = 18$

15. $\{2, 3, 4, 5, \ldots\}$

16. One number is even and one number is odd.

17. a.

Three added together 4 times is 12.

b.

Four rows of three make 12 squares.

18.

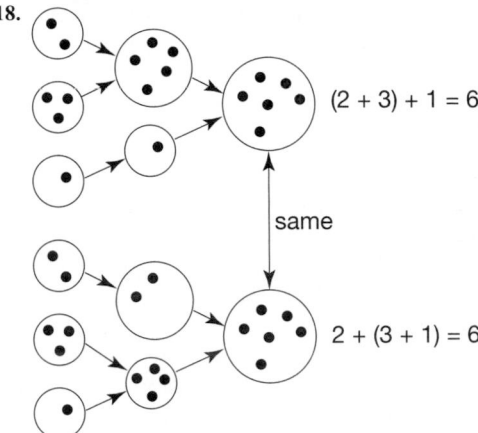

$(2 + 3) + 1 = 6$

same

$2 + (3 + 1) = 6$

19. a.

How many more need to be added to the set of 5 to make it a set of 8?

b.

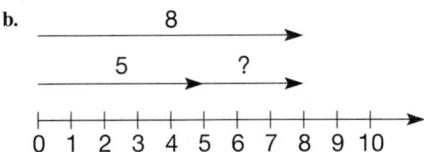

20.

$4 \begin{array}{|c|} \hline 3 \\ \hline \end{array} = 3 \begin{array}{|c|} \hline 4 \\ \hline \end{array}$

21. $64 = 8^2 = 4^3$

22. $2 \cdot 2 = 2 + 2$ and $0 \cdot 0 = 0 + 0$

Section 4.1A

1. a. 105   **b.** 4700   **c.** 1300   **d.** 120

2. a. $43 - 17 = 46 - 20 = 26$
b. $62 - 39 = 63 - 40 = 23$
c. $132 - 96 = 136 - 100 = 36$
d. $250 - 167 = 283 - 200 = 83$

3. a. 579   **b.** 903   **c.** 215   **d.** 333

4. a. $198 + 387 = 200 + 385 = 585$
  b. $84 \times 5 = 42 \times 10 = 420$
  c. $99 \times 53 = 5300 - 53 = 5247$
  d. $4125 \div 25 = 4125 \times \frac{4}{100} = 165$

5. a. 290,000,000,000   **b.** 14,700,000,000
  c. 91,000,000,000   **d.** 84×10^{14}
  e. 140×10^{15} **f.** 102×10^{15}

6. a. (i) 4000 to 6000, (ii) 4000, (iii) 4900, (iv) about 5000
  b. (i) 1000 to 5000, (ii) 1000, (iii) 2400, (iv) about 2700
  c. (i) 7000 to 9000, (ii) 7000, (iii) 8100, (iv) about 8400

7. a. 600 to 1200   **b.** 20,000 to 60,000   **c.** 3200 to 4000

8. a. $63 \times 97 \approx 63 \times 100 = 6300$
  b. $51 \times 212 \approx 50 \times 200 = 10,000$
  c. $3112 \div 62 \approx 3000 \div 60 = 50$
  d. $103 \times 87 \approx 100 \times 87 = 8700$
  e. $62 \times 58 \approx 60 \times 60 = 3600$
  f. $4254 \div 68 \approx 4200 \div 70 = 60$

9. a. 370   **b.** 700   **c.** 1130   **d.** 460   **e.** 3000

10. a. $4 \times 350 = 1400$ **b.** 60^3 **c.** 500^4
  d. $5 \times 800 = 4000$

11. a. $32 + 20 = 52, 52 + 9 = 61, 61 + 50 = 111, 111 + 6 = 117$
  b. $54 + 20 = 74, 74 + 8 = 82, 82 + 60 = 142, 142 + 7 = 149$
  c. $19 + 60 = 79, 79 + 6 = 85, 85 + 40 = 125, 125 + 9 = 134$
  d. $62 + 80 = 142, 142 + 4 = 146, 146 + 20 = 166, 166 + 7 = 173, 173 + 80 = 253, 253 + 1 = 254$

12. Underestimate so that fewer than the designated amount of pollutants will be discharged.

13. There are many acceptable estimates. One reasonable one is listed for each part.
  a. 42 and 56   **b.** 12 and 20   **c.** 1 and 4

14. a. $52 - 35: 52 - 30 = 22, 22 - 5 = 17$
  b. $173 - 96: 173 - 90 = 83, 83 - 6 = 77$
  c. $241 - 159: 241 - 100 = 141, 141 - 50 = 91, 91 - 9 = 82$
  d. $83 - 55: 83 - 50 = 33, 33 - 5 = 28$

15. a. $84 \div 14 = 42 \div 7 = 6$
  b. $234 \div 26 = 117 \div 13 = 9$
  c. $120 \div 15 = 240 \div 30 = 8$
  d. $168 \div 14 = 84 \div 7 = 12$

16. a. $16 \times 21 = 8 \times 42 = 4 \times 84 = 2 \times 168 = 336$
  b. $4 \times 72 = 2 \times 144 = 288$
  c. $8 \times 123 = 4 \times 246 = 2 \times 492 = 984$
  d. $16 \times 211 = 8 \times 422 = 4 \times 844 = 2 \times 1688 = 3376$

17. a. 4   **b.** 13

18. a. $17 \times 817 \times 100 = 1,388,900$
  b. $10 \times 98 \times 673 = 659,540$
  c. $50 \times 4 \times 674 \times 899 = 119,837,200$
  d. $8 \times 125 \times 783 \times 79 = 61,857,000$

19. a. 4^5 **b.** 3^7 **c.** 4^7 **d.** 3^6

20. a. 12, 7   **b.** 31, 16   **c.** 6, 111   **d.** 119, 828

21. $10^2 + 100^2 = 10,100; 588^2 + 2353^2 = 5,882,353$

22. Yes, yes, no

23. a. Yes   **b.** Yes   **c.** Yes

24. Yes, yes, yes

25. a. 1357×90 **b.** 6666×66
  c. $78 \times 93 \times 456$ **d.** $123 \times 45 \times 67$

26. To find a range for $742 - 281$, find $700 - 200 = 500$ and $700 - 300 = 400$. The answer is between 400 and 500.

27. 177,777,768,888,889

28. 5643, 6237

29. a. 4225, 5625, 9025
  b. $(10a + 5)^2 = 100a^2 + 100a + 25 = 100a(a + 1) + 25$

30. Yes

31. The first factor probably ends in 9 rather than 8.

32. a. $54 \times 46 = 50^2 - 4^2 = 2484$
  b. $81 \times 79 = 80^2 - 1 = 6399$
  c. $122 \times 118 = 120^2 - 2^2 = 14,396$
  d. $1210 \times 1190 = 1200^2 - 10^2 = 1,439,900$

33. True, Express the product as $(898,000 + 423) \times (112,000 + 303)$. Use distributivity twice, then add.

34. $(439 \times 6852) \times 1000 + 268 \times 6852 = 3,009,864,336$

35. a. $76 \times (54 + 97)$ **b.** $(4 \times 13)^2$
  c. $13 + (59^2 \times 47)$ **d.** $(79 - 43) \div 2 + 17^2$

36. a. $57 \times 53 - 3021$
  b. $(10a + b)(10a + 10 - b) = 100a^2 + 100a + 10b - b^2 = 100a(a + 1) + b(10 - b)$.
  c. Problem 32 is the special case when $b = 5$.

37. (i) Identify the digit in the place to which you are rounding. (ii) If the digit in the place to its right is a 5, 6, 7, 8, or 9, add one to the digit to which you are rounding. Otherwise, leave the digit as it is. (iii) Put zeros in all the places to the right of the digit to which you are rounding.

38. $3 \cdot 5 \cdot 7 \cdot 9 \cdot 11 \cdot 13 \cdot 15 \cdot 17 = 34,459,425$

39. Pour as much as possible from two of the 3-liter pails into the 5-liter pail; one liter will be left in the 3-liter pail.

Section 4.2A

1. a.

  b.

2. Expanded form; commutative and associative properties of addition; distributive property of multiplication over addition; single-digit addition facts; place value.

3. a. 986   **b.** 747   **c.** 2822

4. a. 1229   **b.** 13,434

5. a. 751   **b.** 1332

6. a. Simple; requires more writing
   b. Simple; requires more space; requires drawing lattice

7. a. 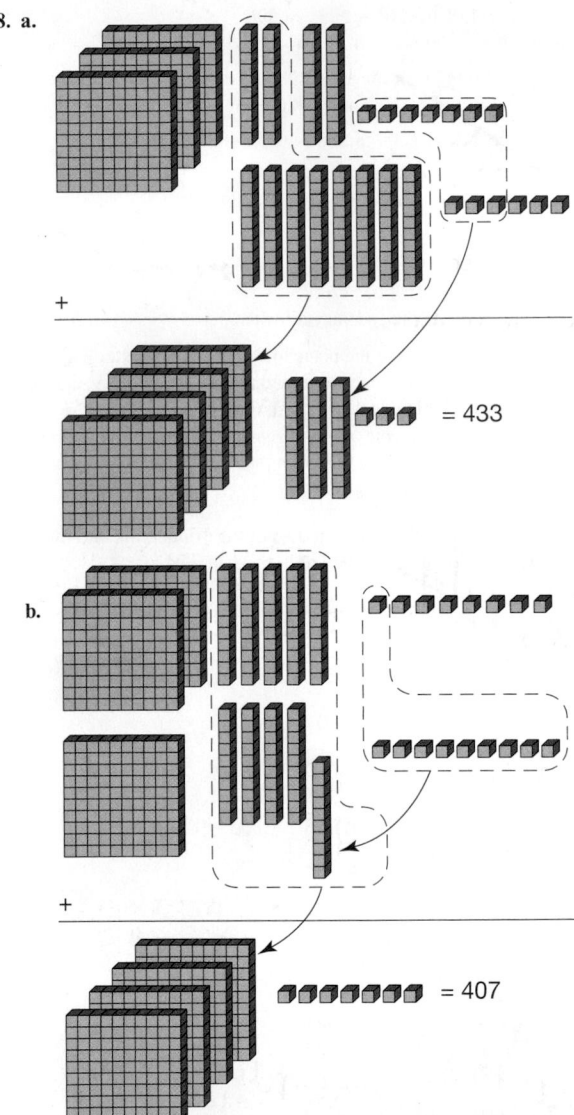   **b.** ... //

   c. /////

8. a.

9. 8, 12, 13, 12

10. (b), (a), (c)

11. a. 477   **b.** 776   **c.** 1818

12. a. 358; 47,365; 1,814,736
   b. Complement of $B = 999 - B$, so
    $A + (999 - B) =$

$A + 1000 - B - 1 = 1000 + (A - B) - 1$;
so to get $A - B$ cross off the 1 in the 1000s place and add 1 to
$A + (999 - B)$.

13. Left-hand sum; compare sum of each column, from left to right.

14. The sum is 5074 both ways!

15.

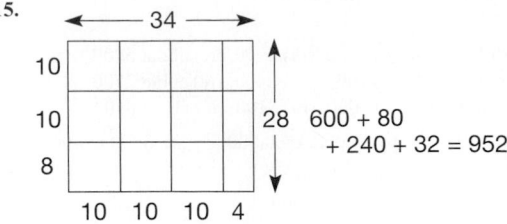

$600 + 80$
$+ 240 + 32 = 952$

16. Expanded form; distributivity; expanded form; associativity for $\times$; place value; place value; addition

17. a. 1426   **b.** 765

18. a. 3525   **b.** 153,244   **c.** 684,288

19. a. 56   **b.** 42   **c.** 60

20. Subtract 6 seven times to reach 0.

21. a. 9, R = 2   **b.** 11, R = 1   **c.** 12, R = 3

22. Bringing down the 3 is modeled by exchanging the 7 leftover flats for 70 longs, making a total of 73 longs.

23. Larry is not carrying properly; Curly carries the wrong digit; Moe forgets to carry.

24. One answer is $359 + 127 = 486$.

25. a. For example, $863 + 742 = 1605$
   b. For example, $347 + 268 = 615$

26. $1 + 2 + 34 + 56 + 7 = 100$; also,
   $1 + 23 + 4 + 5 + 67 = 100$

27. a. $990 + 077 + 000 + 033 + 011$
   b. (i) $990 + 007 + 000 + 003 + 111$;
     (ii) $990 + 070 + 000 + 030 + 111$;
     (iii) $000 + 700 + 000 + 300 + 111$

28. a. Equal   **b.** Differ by 2   **c.** Yes
   d. Difference of products is 10 times the vertical 10s-place difference.

29. a.

X	X	X	X	X
X	X	X	X	X
X	X	X	X	X
X	X	X	X	X

   b. $1 + 2 + 3 + 4 = \frac{1}{2}(4 \times 5)$
   c. $\frac{1}{2}(50 \times 51) = 1275$; $\frac{1}{2}(75 \times 76) = 2850$

30. $888 + 777 + 444 = 2190$; $888 + 666 + 555 = 2109$

31. Bob: 184; Jennifer: 120; Suzie: 206; Tom: 2081

32.

$$
\begin{array}{r}
5314 \times 79 \\
\hline
28 \\
736 \\
2109 \\
3527 \\
45 \\
\hline
419806
\end{array}
$$

33. All eventually arrive at 6174, then these digits are repeated.

Section 4.3A

1. a.

b.

c.

d.

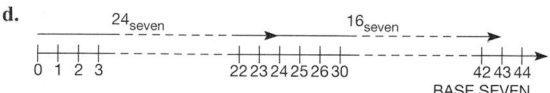

2. a. 114_{six} **b.** 654_{seven} **c.** 10012_{four}

3. a. 3_{four} **b.** 100_{four} **c.** 331_{four} **d.** 12013_{four}

4. a. 154_{nine} **b.** $1TT_{twelve}$

5. a. 1201_{five} **b.** 1575_{eight}

6. a. 4_{six} **h.** 456_{seven} **c.** 2322_{four}

7. a. 13_{four} **b.** 31_{four} **c.** 103_{four}

8. $10201_{three} - 2122_{three} = 10201_{three} + 100_{three} - 10000_{three} + 1_{three} = 1002_{three}$; the sums, in columns, of a number and its complement must be all twos.

9. a. 122_{four} **b.** 234_{five} **c.** 132_{four}

10. a. 11_{six} **b.** 54_{seven} **c.** 132_{four}

11. a. 3_{four} **b.** 5_{six} **c.** 4_{eight}

12.

Thought One

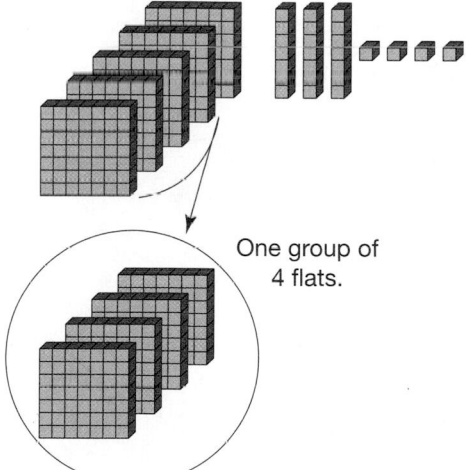

One group of
4 flats.

Thought Two

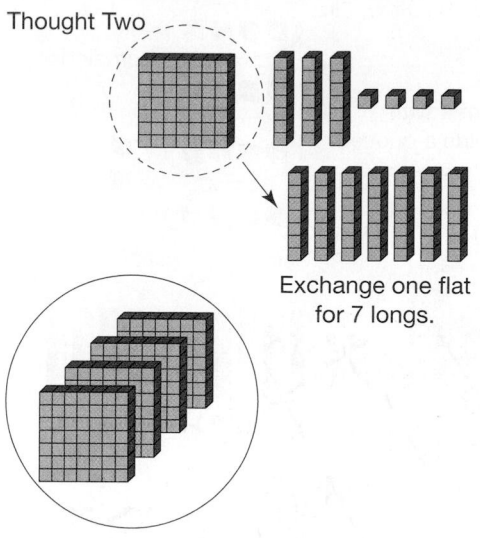

Exchange one flat
for 7 longs.

Thought Three

Two groups of 4 longs.

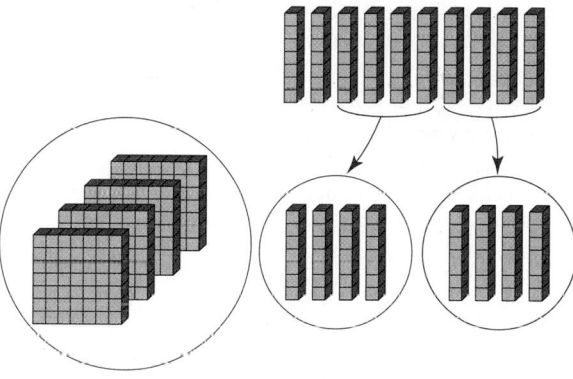

Thought Four

Exchange two longs
for 14 ones.

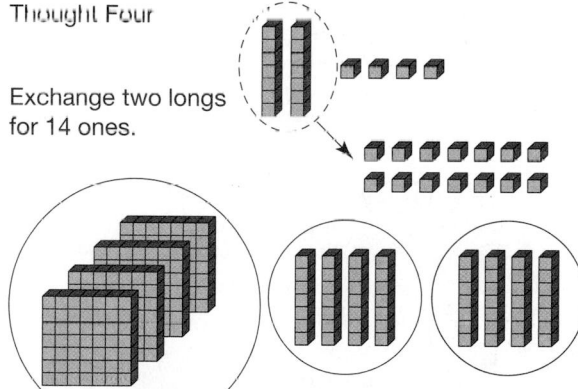

Thought Five

Four groups of 4 with
2 left over yields a quotient
of 124_{seven}
remainder 2_{seven}.

Remainder

13. Six

14. Steve has $2, Tricia has $23, Bill has $40, Jane has $50.

15. 39,037,066,084

16. 125

PROBLEMS WHERE THE STRATEGY "USE INDIRECT REASONING" IS USEFUL

1. Assume that x can be even. Then $x^2 + 2x + 1$ is odd. Therefore, x cannot be even.

2. Suppose that n is odd. Then n^4 is odd; therefore, n cannot be odd.

3. Assume that both x and y are odd. Then $x = 2m + 1$ and $y = 2n + 1$ for whole numbers m and n. Thus $x^2 = 4m^2 + 4m + 1$ and $y^2 = 4n^2 + 4n + 1$, or $x^2 + y^2 = 4(m^2 + n^2 + m + n) + 2$, which has a factor of 2 but not 4. Therefore, it cannot be a square, since it only has one factor of 2.

CHAPTER REVIEW

Section 4.1

1. a. $97 + 78 = 97 + (3 + 75) = (97 + 3) + 75 = 100 + 75 = 175$; associativity

 b. $267 \div 3 = (270 - 3) \div 3 = (270 \div 3) - (3 \div 3) = 90 - 1 = 89$; right distributivitity of division over subtraction

 c. $(16 \times 7) \times 25 = 25 \times (16 \times 7) = (25 \times 16) \times 7 = 400 \times 7 = 2800$; commutativity, associativity, compatible numbers

 d. $16 \times 9 - 6 \times 9 = (16 - 6) \times 9 = 10 \times 9 = 90$; distributivity

 e. $92 \times 15 = 92(10 + 5) = 920 + 460 = 1380$; distributivity

 f. $17 \times 99 = 17(100 - 1) = 1700 - 17 = 1683$; distributivity

 g. $720 \div 5 = 1440 \div 10 = 144$; compensaton

 h. $81 - 39 = 82 - 40 = 42$; compensation

2. a. $400 < 157 + 371 < 600$ **b.** 720,000 **c.** 1400

 d. $25 \times 56 = 5600 \div 4 = 1400$

3. a. 47,900 **b.** 4750 **c.** 570

4. a. Not necessary **b.** $7 \times (5 - 2) + 3$

 c. $15 + 48 \div (3 \times 4)$

5. a. 11 **b.** 6 **c.** 10 **d.** 8 **e.** 10 **f.** 19

Section 4.2

1. 982 in all parts

2. 172 in all parts

3. 3096 in all parts

4. 9 R 10 in all parts

Section 4.3

1. 1111_{six} in all parts

2. 136_{seven} in all parts

3. 1332_{four} in all parts

4. 2_{five} R 31_{five} in all parts

Chapter 4 Test

1. a. F **b.** F **c.** F **d.** F

2. a. One possibility is

$$\begin{array}{r} 376 \\ + 594 \\ \hline 10 \\ 160 \\ 800 \\ \hline 970 \end{array}$$

 b. One possibility is

$$\begin{array}{r} 56 \\ \times \quad 73 \\ \hline 18 \\ 150 \\ 420 \\ 3500 \\ \hline 4088 \end{array}$$

3. a.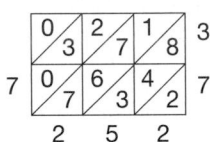

 b.

4. a. $54 + 93 + 16 + 47 = 54 + 16 + 93 + 47 = 70 + 140 = 210$

 b. $9225 - 2000 = 7225$

 c. $3497 - 1362 = 2135$

 d. $25 \times 52 = \frac{100}{4} \times 52 = 100 \times \frac{52}{4} = 1300$

5. 234 R 8

6. a. (i) 2500, (ii) 2500 to 2900, (iii) 2660, (iv) 2600

 b. (i) 350,000, (ii) 350,000 to 480,000, (iii) 420,000, (iv) 420,000

7. $32 \times 21 = (30 + 2)(20 + 1)$
$= (30 + 2)20 + (30 + 2)1$
$= 30 \cdot 20 + 2 \cdot 20 + 30 \cdot 1 + 2 \cdot 1$
$= 600 + 40 + 30 + 2 = 672$

8. Since we are finding 321×20, not simply 321×2

9. Commutativity and associativity

10.

11. Answers may vary

$$
\begin{array}{r}
168 \ \text{R } 37 \\
8 \\
\hline
60 \\
100 \\
43\overline{)7261} \\
-4300 \\
\hline
2961 \\
-2580 \\
\hline
381 \\
-\ 344 \\
\hline
37
\end{array}
$$

12. Thought One

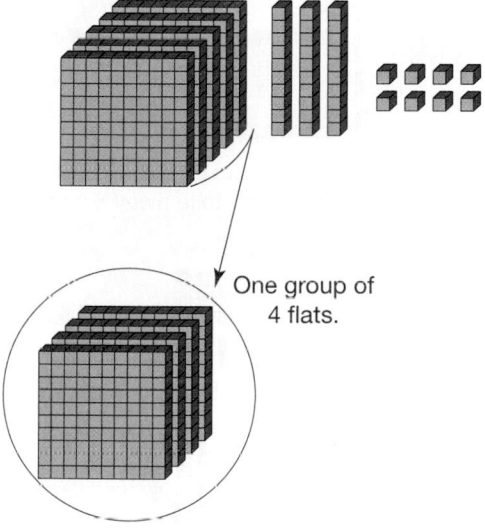

One group of
4 flats.

Thought Two

Exchange one flat
for 10 longs.

Thought Three

Three groups of 4 longs.

Thought Four

Exchange one long
for 10 ones.

Remainder

Thought Five

Four groups
of 4 units.

Quotient 134, Remainder: 2

13.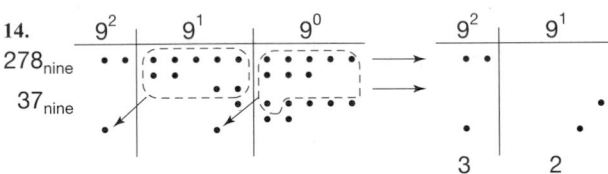

Note enough units to take away three units

Exchange a long for four units.

Take away one long
Take away three units

Leaves 13₍four₎

14.

	9^2	9^1	9^0		9^2	9^1
278_{nine}	• •			→	• •	
37_{nine}				→		
					3	2

15. a.

Exchange 10 units for 1 long.

Exchange 10 longs for 1 flat.

Yields 403

b.

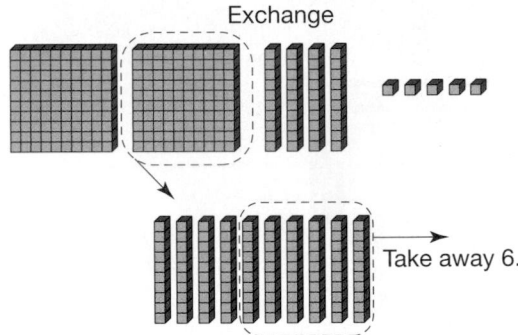

Exchange

Can't take away 8 units from 3 so exchange 1 long for 10 units. Now take away 8 units.

Exchange

Take away 6.

Can't take away 6 longs from 4 so exchange 1flat for 10 longs. Now take away 6 longs to leave 185.

c.

Thought One

One group of 5 flats.

Thought Two

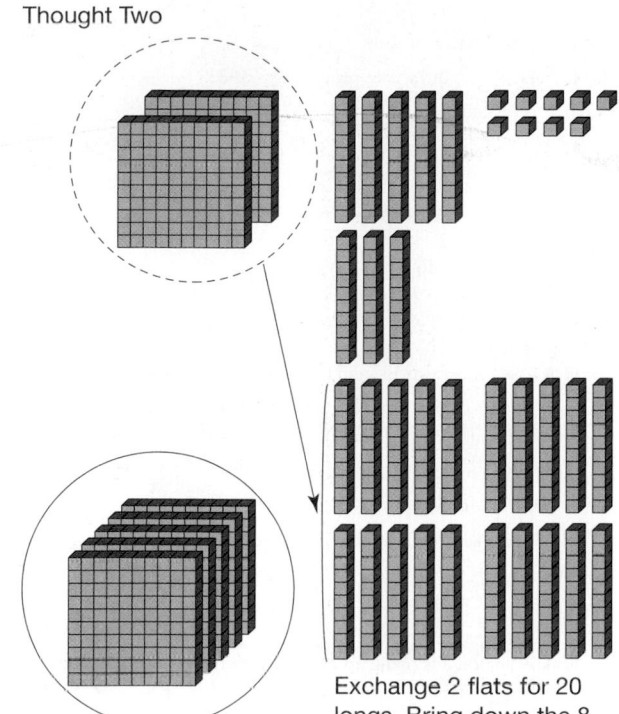

Exchange 2 flats for 20 longs. Bring down the 8.

Thought Three

Five groups of 5 longs.

Exchange 3 longs for 30 units. Bring down the 9.

Thought Four

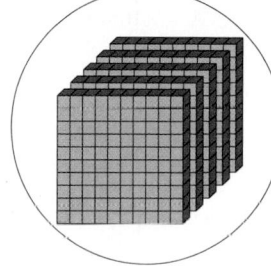

Seven groups of 5 units with 4 remaining yields a quotient of 157 and remainder of 4.

16.

Intermediate	Standard
492	2
× 37	6 1
14	492
630	× 37
2800	3444
60	14760
2700	18204
12000	
18204	

In both cases the ones (7) in the number 37 is multiplied by each of the ones, tens, and hundreds of 492. Similarly the tens (3) of 37 is multiplied by each of the ones, tens, and hundreds of 492.

17. The advantage of the standard algorithm is that it is short. The disadvantage is that because of its brevity, it loses some meaning. The advantage of the lattice is that all of the multiplication is done first and then all of the addition, which eliminates some confusion. The disadvantage is its length.

18. The subtract-from-the base algorithm appears to be more natural for young students. The only disadvantage is its lack of use because of the tradition of the standard algorithm.

19.

200	30	$\begin{array}{r} 200 \\ 140 \\ 30 \\ + 21 \\ \hline 391 \end{array}$
140	21	

20. H = 2, E = 5, S = 6

21. $a = 7, b = 5, c = 9$; 62,015

22. A = 5, B = 6; A = 4, B = 7; A = 3, B = 8; A = 2, B = 9. The roles of A and B can be reversed. In all cases C = 1, D = 2.

Section 5.1A

1. 2, 3, 5, 7, 11, 13, 17, 19, 23, 29, 31, 37, 41, 43, 47, 53, 59, 61, 67, 71, 73, 79, 83, 89, 97

2. a. $2^2 \times 3^2$ **b.** 2×3^3 **c.** $2 \times 3 \times 17$ **d.** $2^3 \times 5^3$

3. a. $2^3 \times 3^3$ **b.** $2^2 \times 3 \times 5 \times 7^2$ **c.** $3 \times 5^2 \times 11$
d. $2 \times 3^2 \times 7 \times 11^2 \times 13$

4. a. T, • • •
    • • •
    • • •
  b. F, There is no whole number x such that $12x = 6$.
  c. T, • • • • • • •
    • • • • • • •
    • • • • • • •
  d. F, There is no whole number x such that $6x = 3$.
  e. T, • • • •
    • • • •
    • • • •
    • • • •
  f. F, There is no whole number x such that $0x = 5$.
  g. T, •
    •
    •
    •
    •
    •
    •
    •
    •
  h. T, • • •
    • • •
    • • •
    • • •
    • • •
    • • •
    • • •
    • • •
    • • •
    • • •
    • • •
    • • •

5. a. F; $3 \nmid 40$ **b.** F; $3 \nmid 2000$
  c. T; $4 \mid 00$ **d.** T; $4 \mid 32,304$ and $3 \mid 32,304$

6. 1, 3, and 7

7. a. $8 \mid 152$, since $8 \times 19 = 152$ **b.** $x = 15,394$ by long division
  c. Yes. $15,394 \times 8 = 123,152$

8. a. 4 only **b.** 3, 4

9. a. T, 3 is a factor of 9
  b. T, 3 and 11 are different prime factors of 33

10. a. F. $4 \nmid 5$ and $4 \nmid 3$, but $4 \mid (5 + 3)$ **b.** T

11. a. $2 \mid 12$ **b.** $3 \mid 123$ **c.** $2 \mid 1234$ **d.** $5 \mid 12,345$

12. (a) and (c)

13. a. $2^2 \times 3^2$ **b.** 1, 2, 3, 4, 6, 9, 12, 18, 36
  c. $4 = 2^2, 6 = 2 \times 3, 9 = 3^2, 12 = 2^2 \times 3,$
    $18 = 2 \times 3^2, 36 = 2^2 \times 3^2$
  d. The divisors of 36 have the same prime factors as 36, and they appear at most as many times as they appear in the prime factorization of 36.
  e. It has at most two 13s and five 29s and has no other prime factors.

14. For 5, $5 \mid 10(a \cdot 10 + b)$ or $5 \mid (a \cdot 10^2 + b \cdot 10)$; therefore, if $5 \mid c$, then $5 \mid (a \cdot 10^2 + b \cdot 10 + c)$. Similar for 10.

15. (a), (b), (d), and (e)

16. a. Yes **b.** No **c.** Composite numbers greater than 4

17. 333,333,331 has a factor of 17.

18. $p(0) = 17, p(1) = 19, p(2) = 23, p(3) = 29$:
$p(16) = 16^2 + 16 + 17 = 16(17) + 17$ is not prime.

19. a. They are all primes.
  b. The diagonal is made up of the numbers from the formula $n^2 + n + 41$.

20. The numbers with an even number of ones have 11 as a factor. Also, numbers that have a multiple-of-three number of ones (e.g., 111) have 3 as a factor. That leaves the numbers with 5, 7, 11, 13, and 17 ones to factor.

21. Only $7(= 5 + 2)$. For the rest, since one of the two primes would have to be even, 2 is the only candidate, but the other summand would then be a multiple of 5.

22. a. 5, 13, 17, 29, 37, 41, 53, 61, 73, 89, and 97.
  b. $5 = 1 + 4, 13 = 9 + 4, 17 = 1 + 16, 29 = 4 + 25, 37 = 1 + 36, 41 = 16 + 25, 53 = 4 + 49, 61 = 25 + 36, 73 = 9 + 64, 89 = 25 + 64, 97 = 16 + 81$

23. There are no other pairs, since every even number besides 2 is composite.

24. 3 and 5, 17 and 19, 41 and 43, 59 and 61, 71 and 73, 101 and 103, 107 and 109, 137 and 139, 149 and 151, 179 and 181, 191 and 193, 197 and 199

25. a. Many correct answers are possible.
  b. Let n be an odd whole number greater than 6. Take prime p (not 2) less then n. $n - p$ is an even number that is a sum of primes a and b. Then $n = a + b + p$.

26. Yes

27. 34,227 and 36,070

28. a. 6, Each has a factor of 2 and 3.
  b. 3, The only common factor is 3.

29. 2520

30. $2^2 \times 3 \times 5 = 60$

31. 3. Proof: $n + (n + 1) + (n + 2) = 3n + 3 = 3(n + 1)$

32. Use a variable; the numbers $a, b, a + b, a + 2b, 2a + 3b, 3a + 5b, 5a + 8b, 8a + 13b, 13a + 21b, 21a + 34b$ have a sum of $55a + 88b$, which is $11(5a + 8b)$, or 11 times the seventh number.

33. a. Use distributivity.
  b. $1001! + 2, 1001! + 3, \ldots, 1001! + 1001$

34. $\$3.52 - \$2.91 = \$.61 = 61¢$ is not a multiple of 3.

35. 504. Since the number is a multiple of 7, 8, and 9, the only three-digit multiple is $7 \cdot 8 \cdot 9$.

36. 61

37. $abcabc = abc(1001) = abc(7 \cdot 11 \cdot 13)$, 7 and 11

38. a. Apply the test for divisibility by 11 to any four-digit palindrome.
   b. A similar proof applies to every palindrome with an even number of digits.

39. 151 and 251

40. 7 | 2443 (349 times), 7 | 443,002 (63,286 times).
   If $7 \mid (1000a + b)$, then show $7 \mid (1000b + a)$. $7 \mid (1000a + b)$ means $7n = 1000a + b$.
   Since 7 | 1001, $7 \mid [(1001a + 1001b) - (1000a + b)]$, or $7 \mid (a + 1000b)$.

41. $289 = 17^2$ is the first non-prime.

42. $11 \mid [a(1001) + b(99) + c(11) - a + b - c + d]$ if and only if $11 \mid (-a + b - c + d)$. Therefore, we only need to check the $-a + b - c + d$ part.

43. $11 \times 101,010,101 = 1,111,111,111$
   $13 \times 8,547,008,547 = 111,111,111,111$
   $17 \times 65,359,477,124,183 = 1,111,111,111,111,111$

44. a. $n = 10$ **b.** $n = 15$ **c.** $n = 10$

45. $n = 16$; $p(17) = 323 = 17 \cdot 19$, composite, $p(18) = 359$, prime

Section 5.2A

1. a. 6   **b.** 12   **c.** 60

2. a. $2 \cdot 2 \cdot 3 \cdot 3$
   b. $1, 2, 3, 4 = 2 \cdot 2, 6 = 2 \cdot 3, 9 = 3 \cdot 3, 12 = 2 \cdot 2 \cdot 3, 18 = 2 \cdot 3 \cdot 3, 36 = 2 \cdot 2 \cdot 3 \cdot 3$
   c. Every prime factor of a divisor of 36 is a prime factor of 36.
   d. It contains only factors of 7^4 or 17^2.

3. Multiples, generally; exceptions are 0 (a multiple of 18 but not a divisor) and 18 (both a multiple and divisor).

4. a. 2   **b.** 6   **c.** 6

5. a. 6   **b.** 121   **c.** 3   **d.** 2

6. a. 6   **b.** 1   **c.** 5   **d.** 14   **e.** 13   **f.** 29

7. a. 24   **b.** 20   **c.** 63   **d.** 30   **e.** 40   **f.** 72

8. a. $2^3 \cdot 3^2 \cdot 5 \cdot 7$ **b.** $2^2 \cdot 3^2 \cdot 5 \cdot 7 \cdot 11$
   c. $2^4 \cdot 3 \cdot 5 \cdot 7$

9. a. 6   **b.** 13   **c.** 8   **d.** 37

10. a. All except 6, 12, 18, 20, 24   **b.** 12, 18, 20, 24
   c. 6

11. (a)

12. a. amicable   **b.** not amicable
   c. amicable   **d.** 18,416

13. a. $a = 2 \times 3^3$ **b.** $a = 2^2 \times 7^3 \times 11^2$

14. a. 1   **b.** $2^1 = 2$ **c.** $2^2 = 4$
   d. $2^1 \times 3^1 = 6$ **e.** $2^4 = 16$ **f.** $2^2 \times 3 = 12$
   g. $2^6 = 64$ **h.** $2^3 \times 3 = 24$

15. a. 2, 3, 5, 7, 11, 13; primes
   b. 4, 9, 25, 49, 121, 169; primes squared
   c. 6, 10, 14, 15, 21, 22; the product of two primes, or 8, 27, 125 or any prime to the third power
   d. $2^4, 3^4, 5^4, 7^4, 11^4, 13^4$; a prime to the fourth power

16. 6, 28, 496, 8128

17. 1, 5, 7, 11, 13, 17, 19, 23

18. 1, 4, 9, 16, 25, . . . ; all lockers numbered with a perfect square number

19. 16 candy bars

20. Chickens, \$2; ducks, \$4; and geese, \$5

21. None, since each has only one factor of 5

22. 773

23. a. 11, 101, 1111   **b.** 1111

24. 41, 7, 11, 73, 67, 17, 13

25. 31

26. $343 = 7 \cdot 49$. Let $a + b = 7$. Then $7 \mid (10a + 10b)$. But 7 | 91, so 7 | 91a. Then $7 \mid (10a + 10b + 91a)$ or $7 \mid (100a + 10b + a)$.

27. GCF(54, 27) = 27, LCM(54, 27) = LCM(54, 18) = LCM(18, 27) = 54

PROBLEMS WHERE THE STRATEGY "USE PROPERTIES OF NUMBERS" IS USEFUL

1. Mary is 71 unless each generation married and had children very young.

2. Four folding machines and three stamp machines, since the LCM of 45 and 60 is 180

3. Let p and q be any two primes. Then p^6q^{12} will have $7 \cdot 13 = 91$ factors.

CHAPTER REVIEW

Section 5.1

1. $17 \times 13 \times 11 \times 7$

2. 90, 91, 92, 93, 94, 95, 96, 98, 99, 100

3. a. F   **b.** F   **c.** T   **d.** F   **e.** T   **f.** T
   g. T   **h.** T

4. All are factors.

5. Check to see whether the last two digits are 00, 25, 50, or 75.

Section 5.2

1. 24

2. 36

3. 27

4. 432

5. Multiply each prime by 2.

6. $81 \times 135 = \text{GCF}(81, 135) \times \text{LCM}(81, 135)$

Chapter 5 Test

1. a. F   **b.** T   **c.** T   **d.** F   **e.** T   **f.** T
   g. T   **h.** F   **i.** F   **j.** T

2. a. Three can be divided into 6 evenly.
   b. Six divided by 3 is 2.
   c. The statement 3 divides 6 is true. (Answers may vary)

3. a. $2^3 \cdot 5 \cdot 3$ **b.** $2^4 \cdot 5^2 \cdot 3^3$
   c. $3^2 \cdot 7 \cdot 13$

4. a. 2, 4, 8, 11   **b.** 2, 3, 5, 6, 10
   c. 2, 3, 4, 5, 6, 8, 9, 10

5. a. 24   **b.** 16   **c.** 27

6. a. $2^3 \cdot 3$; $2^4 \cdot 3^2 \cdot 5$ **b.** 7; $2 \cdot 3 \cdot 5 \cdot 7^2$
   c. $2^3 \cdot 3^4 \cdot 5^3$; $2^7 \cdot 3^5 \cdot 5^7$ **d.** 41; 128,207
   e. 1; 6300

7.
$$\begin{array}{r} 6\ \text{R}\ 123 \\ 1025\overline{)6273} \end{array}$$
$$\begin{array}{r} 8\ \text{R}\ 41 \\ 123\overline{)1025} \end{array}$$
$$\begin{array}{r} 3\ \text{R}\ 0 \\ 41\overline{)123} \end{array}$$
$$\text{GCF}(1025, 6273) = 41$$

8. LCM(18, 24) = 72

9. All the crossed-out numbers greater than 1 are composite.

10. No, because if two numbers are equal, they must have the same prime factorization.

11. $x + (x + 1) + (x + 2) + (x + 3) = 4x + 6 = 2(2x + 3)$

12. a. $4 \mid 36$ and $6 \mid 36$ but $24 \nmid 36$.
   b. If $2 \mid m$ and $9 \mid m$ then $18 \mid m$.

13. LCM$(a, b) = (a \cdot b)/\text{GCD}(a, b) = 270/3 = 90$.

14.
```
 • •      • • •
 • •      • • •
 • •      • •
 • •
 4 | 8    3 ∤ 8
```

15. $n = m$ because they have the same prime factorization; Fundamental Theorem of Arithmetic

16. $2^3 \cdot 3^2 \cdot 5 \cdot 7 = 2520$

17. If two other prime numbers differ by 3, one is odd and one is even. The even one must have a factor of 2.

18. a. $2^3 \cdot 5$ **b.** $2^3 \cdot 3^3 \cdot 5$

19. 24, 25, 26, 27, 28; or 32, 33, 34, 35, 36

20. 1, 4, 9, 16; They are perfect squares.

21. $n = 11$

22. $a = 15, b = 180$; and $a = 45, b = 60$

23. 36

Section 6.1A

1. a.

   b.

   c.

2. a.
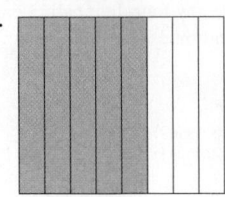

d.

3. Yes. The parts have equal areas.

4. a. $\frac{1}{10}$ **b.** $\frac{1}{4}$ **c.** $\frac{1}{3}$ **d.** $\frac{1}{3}$

5.
 =

6. (a), (b), and (d)

7. a. Not equal   **b.** Not equal   **c.** Equal   **d.** Equal

8. a. $\frac{3}{4}$ **b.** $\frac{7}{8}$ **c.** $\frac{9}{13}$ **d.** $\frac{11}{5}$

9. a. $5\frac{15}{32}$ **b.** $2\frac{185}{216}$

10. a. (i) $\frac{11}{17} < \frac{12}{17} < \frac{13}{17}$ (ii) $\frac{1}{7} < \frac{1}{6} < \frac{1}{5}$
   b. Increasing numerators, decreasing denominators

11. a. $\frac{17}{23} < \frac{51}{68}$; $\frac{68}{91}$ **b.** $\frac{50}{687} < \frac{43}{567}$; $\frac{93}{1254}$
   c. $\frac{597}{2511} < \frac{214}{897}$; $\frac{811}{3408}$ **d.** $\frac{93}{2811} < \frac{3}{87}$; $\frac{96}{2898}$

12. a. $\frac{51}{92}, \frac{55}{100}$ **b.** $\frac{1}{4}, \frac{25}{100}$ **c.** $\frac{110}{141}, \frac{78}{100}$

13. a. The fractions are decreasing.
   b. The fraction may be more than 1.

14. Texas had the higher rate.

15. a.   **b.**

   c.   **d.**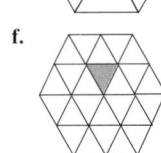

   e.

   f.

16. Yes, since $\dfrac{288 \cdots 86}{588 \cdots 83} = \dfrac{26 \cdot 11 \cdots 1}{53 \cdot 11 \cdots 1} = \dfrac{26}{53}$.

17. $\frac{1}{8}$

18. a. False   **b.** False   **c.** True   **d.** True

19. Both $12 \div 2$ and $18 \div 3$ are the GCF(12, 18)
   a. 24   **b.** 26

20. Only (c) is correct.

21. 15

22. 562,389

23. 41

24. 2200

25. 15

26. a. 50, 500, etc.   **b.** 25, 250, etc.   **c.** 4, 40, 400, etc.
   d. 75, 750, etc.

27. There are infinitely many such fractions. Two are $\frac{15}{28}$ and $\frac{31}{56}$.

Section 6.2A

1. a.

$$\frac{2}{5} \qquad \frac{1}{3} \qquad \frac{11}{15}$$

b.

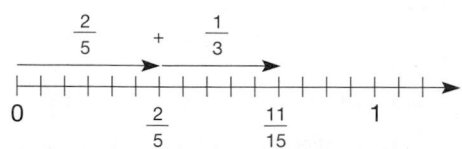

$$\frac{2}{5} \quad + \quad \frac{1}{3}$$

2. a.

b.

c.

3. a. 3/4   **b.** 3/4   **c.** 16/21   **d.** 167/144
e. 460/663   **f.** 277/242   **g.** 617/1000
h. 99/100   **i.** 15,059/100,000

4. a. $\frac{23}{6}$ **b.** $\frac{23}{8}$ **c.** $\frac{26}{5}$ **d.** $\frac{64}{9}$

5. a.

b.

c.

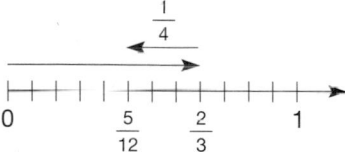

6. a. 4/11   **b.** 13/63   **c.** 1/20   **d.** 23/54
e. 154/663   **f.** 11/1000

7. a. $3\frac{11}{12}; 1\frac{5}{12}$ **b.** $13\frac{8}{21}; 2\frac{1}{21}$ **c.** $38\frac{1}{12}; 6\frac{1}{4}$

8. a. $1\frac{1}{9}$ **b.** $2\frac{5}{6}$ **c.** $10\frac{1}{5}$

9. a. $8\frac{3}{7} - 3 = 5\frac{3}{7}$ **b.** $9\frac{4}{8} - 3 = 6\frac{1}{2}$ **c.** $11\frac{5}{7} - 7 = 4\frac{5}{7}$
d. $8\frac{2}{6} - 4 = 4\frac{1}{3}$

10. a. (i) 13 to 15, (ii) 14   **b.** (i) 13 to 15, (ii) $14\frac{1}{2}$
c. (i) 15 to 18, (ii) 16

11. a. $10 + 3\frac{1}{2} = 13\frac{1}{2}$ **b.** $9\frac{1}{2} + 5\frac{1}{2} = 15$
c. $7 + 5 + 2\frac{1}{2} = 14\frac{1}{2}$

12. 15

13. a. $\frac{3}{7} + \frac{2}{7} = \frac{5}{7}$ **b.** $\frac{1}{3} + \frac{1}{6} = \frac{1}{2}$

14. a. 29/20 or $1\frac{9}{20}$ **b.** 13/45

15. a. $\frac{59}{56} = 1\frac{3}{56}$ **b.** $\frac{1}{35}$

16. $\frac{5}{12}$

17. Let t = years of lifetime, t = 72 years

18. $\frac{7}{12}$

19. $\frac{13}{30}$

20. $\frac{1}{36}$

21. When borrowing 1, he does not think of it as $\frac{5}{5}$. Have him use blocks (i.e., base five pieces could be used with long = 1).

22. a. 1   **b.** 1   **c.** Yes; only perfect numbers

23. Yes. $\dfrac{1 + 3 + 5 + 7 + 9}{11 + 13 + 15 + 17 + 19}$,

$\dfrac{1 + 3 + 5 + 7 + 9 + 11}{13 + 15 + 17 + 19 + 21 + 23}$. In general, the numerator is $1 + 3 + \cdots + (2n - 1) = n^2$ and the denominator is $[1 + 3 + \cdots + (2m - 1)] - [1 + 3 + \cdots + (2n - 1)]$, where $m = 2n$. This difference is $m^2 - n^2 = 4n^2 - n^2 = 3n^2$. Thus the fraction is always $n^2/3n^2 = \frac{1}{3}$.

24. $1 - \dfrac{1}{2^{100}} = \dfrac{2^{100} - 1}{2^{100}}$

25. a. $\frac{3}{6}$ **b.** 18   **c.** 56   **d.** $\frac{18}{56}$
e. No, $\frac{3}{10} \oplus \frac{1}{2} = \frac{4}{12} = \frac{1}{3} \neq \frac{9}{26} = \frac{6}{20} \oplus \frac{3}{6}$

26. The sum is 1.

27. a. $\frac{1}{5} = \frac{1}{6} + \frac{1}{30}$ **b.** $\frac{1}{7} = \frac{1}{8} + \frac{1}{56}$ **c.** $\frac{1}{17} = \frac{1}{18} + \frac{1}{306}$

28. 28 matches

29. 1299 0s are necessary. 597 9s are necessary.

Section 6.3A

1. a.

b.

c.

2. a. $\frac{3}{5} \times \frac{3}{4} = \frac{9}{20}$ **b.** $\frac{4}{7} \times \frac{1}{6} = \frac{4}{42}$

3. a. $\frac{21}{11}$ **b.** $\frac{1}{3}$ **c.** $\frac{9}{121}$ **d.** $\frac{1}{108}$

4. a. $<$ **b.** $\frac{4}{3} > \frac{2}{3}$ **c.** Order is reversed

5. a. 5   **b.** $\frac{4}{3}$ **c.** $\frac{33}{39}$ or $\frac{11}{13}$

6. a. $\frac{5}{4}$ **b.** 1   **c.** $\frac{13}{7}$ **d.** $\frac{1}{2}$

7. a. $\frac{3}{14}$ **b.** $\frac{1}{5}$ **c.** $\frac{2}{5}$ **d.** $\frac{15}{26}$ **e.** $\frac{6}{49}$
   f. $\frac{40}{189}$ **g.** $\frac{49}{50}$ **h.** $\frac{5}{8}$ **i.** $\frac{5}{18}$ **j.** $\frac{17}{24}$

8. a. $11\frac{5}{9}$ **b.** $\frac{341}{32} = 10\frac{21}{32}$ **c.** 9   **d.** $\frac{250}{63} = 3\frac{61}{63}$
   e. $\frac{15}{4} = 3\frac{3}{4}$ **f.** 6

9. a. $21 \times \frac{3}{7} = 9$ **b.** $35 \times \frac{3}{7} = 15$ **c.** $1\frac{1}{9}$
   d. $3 \times 54 + \frac{5}{9} \times 54 = 162 + 30 = 192$

10. a.

$4 \div \frac{1}{3} = 12.$

b.

$2\frac{1}{2} \div \frac{1}{4} = 10.$

c.

$3 \div \frac{3}{4} = 4.$

11. a. $30 \times 5 = 150$ **b.** $56 \div 8 = 7$
   c. $72 \div 9 = 8$ **d.** $31 \times 6 = 186$

12. a. $12 \times 12 = 144$ **b.** $5^3 = 125$

13. a. 127/144   **b.** 61/96

14. a. $\frac{98}{117}$ **b.** $\frac{4}{9}$

15. a. Associativity for fraction addition
   b. Distributivity for multiplication over addition
   c. Associativity for fraction multiplication

16. a. $\frac{15}{31}$ **b.** $\frac{56}{67}$ **c.** $\frac{231}{102}$ or $\frac{77}{34}$

17. a. No   **b.** No

18. a. 14/15   **b.** 14/5 or $2\frac{4}{5}$

19. 32 loads

20. Approximately 14,483,000 barrels per day

21. 432

22. a. $12\frac{4}{5}$ gallons, or nearly 13 gallons
   b. About $5\frac{1}{2}$ gallons more

23. 60

24. 8:00

25. a. $2\frac{1}{2}$ cups   **b.** $\frac{5}{8}$ cup   **c.** $\frac{25}{12}$ or $2\frac{2}{12}$ or cups

26. Gale, 9 games; Ruth, 5 games; Sandy, 10 games

27. a. $54,150   **b.** After 8 years

28. 1

29. a. $\dfrac{11}{16 \times 5}$ **b.** Yes
   c. $4\frac{11}{8} \div 2 = 2\frac{11}{16}$; $10\frac{9}{16} \div 2 = 5\frac{9}{32}$

30. Sam: $\frac{18}{12} = 1\frac{1}{2}$, addition (getting common denominator);
   Sandy: $\frac{20}{9} = 2\frac{2}{9}$, division (using reciprocal).

31. 60

32. 21 years old

PROBLEMS WHERE THE STRATEGY "SOLVE AN EQUIVALENT PROBLEM" IS USEFUL

1. Solve by finding how many numbers are in $\{7, 14, 21, \ldots, 392\}$ or in $\{1, 2, 3, \ldots, 56\}$.

2. Rewrite 2^{30} as 8^{10} and 3^{20} as 9^{10}. Since $8 < 9$, we have $8^{10} < 9^{10}$.

3. First find eight such fractions between 0 and 1, namely $\frac{1}{9}, \frac{2}{9}, \frac{3}{9}, \ldots, \frac{8}{9}$. Then divide each of these fractions by 3: $\frac{1}{27}, \frac{2}{27}, \frac{3}{27}, \ldots, \frac{8}{27}$.

CHAPTER REVIEW
Section 6.1

1. Because $4 > 2$

2.

3. The numerator of the improper fraction is greater than the denominator. A mixed number is the sum of a whole number and a proper fraction.

4. a. $\dfrac{8}{19} < \dfrac{24}{56}$ **b.** Equal

5. $\dfrac{24}{56} = \dfrac{3}{7}, \dfrac{8}{19}, \dfrac{12}{28} = \dfrac{15}{35} = \dfrac{3}{7}$

6. $\dfrac{2}{5} < \dfrac{2 + 5}{5 + 12} < \dfrac{5}{12}$

Section 6.2

1. a.

$\longleftarrow \frac{7}{12} \longrightarrow$

$\frac{1}{8} \nearrow$

2. a. $1\frac{14}{45}$ **b.** $\frac{16}{75}$

3. a. Commutative   **b.** Identity   **c.** Associative
   d. Closure

4. None

5. a. $5\frac{2}{8} + \frac{1}{8} + 3\frac{7}{8} = 9\frac{1}{4}$. Compensation, associativity
   b. $31\frac{1}{8} - 5 = 26\frac{1}{8}$. Equal additions
   c. $1\frac{3}{5}$. Commutativity, associativity

6. a. 12 to 14   **b.** $17 + 24\frac{1}{2} = 41\frac{1}{2}$ **c.** 23

Section 6.3

1.

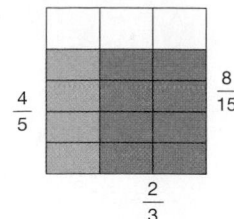

$\dfrac{4}{5}$ $\dfrac{8}{15}$ $\dfrac{2}{3}$

2. a. $\frac{4}{15}$ **b.** $\frac{3}{2}$

3. a. Inverse   **b.** Associative   **c.** Identity
   d. Closure   **e.** Associative

4. $\dfrac{a}{b}\left(\dfrac{c}{d}+\dfrac{e}{f}\right)=\dfrac{a}{b}\times\dfrac{c}{d}+\dfrac{a}{b}\times\dfrac{e}{f}$;

$\dfrac{3}{17}\times\dfrac{4}{9}+\dfrac{14}{17}\times\dfrac{4}{19}=\left(\dfrac{3}{17}+\dfrac{14}{17}\right)\times\dfrac{4}{9}=\dfrac{4}{9}$

5. $\dfrac{12}{25}\div\dfrac{1}{5}=\dfrac{12}{25}\div\dfrac{5}{25}=\dfrac{12}{5}$

$\dfrac{12}{25}\div\dfrac{1}{5}=\dfrac{12}{25}\times\dfrac{5}{5}=\dfrac{12}{5}$

6. None

7. a. $(\frac{2}{3}\div 9)\times 5=6\times 5=30$. Commutativity and associativity

   b. $(25\times 2)+(25\times\frac{2}{5})=50+10=60$. Distributivity

8. a. 35 to 48   **b.** $3\frac{1}{2}\times 4=14$

Chapter 6 Test

1. a. T   **b.** F   **c.** F   **d.** T   **e.** T   **f.** F
   g. T   **h.** F

2. Number: relative amount represented
Numeral: representing a part-to-whole relationship

3. Closure for division of nonzero elements or multiplicative inverse of nonzero elements

4. a. $\frac{2}{3}$ **b.** $\frac{17}{18}$ **c.** $\frac{2}{3}$ **d.** $\frac{41}{189}$

5. a. $\frac{38}{11}$ **b.** $5\frac{11}{16}$ **c.** $\frac{37}{7}$ **d.** $11\frac{2}{11}$

6. a. $\frac{3}{4}$ **b.** $\frac{7}{3}$ **c.** $\frac{16}{92}$

7. a. $\frac{31}{36}$ **b.** $\frac{11}{75}$ **c.** $\frac{3}{4}$ **d.** $\frac{64}{49}$

8. a. $\frac{5}{2}\cdot(\frac{3}{4}\cdot\frac{2}{5})=(\frac{5}{2}\cdot\frac{2}{5})\cdot\frac{3}{4}=\frac{3}{4}$

   b. $\frac{4}{7}\cdot\frac{3}{5}+\frac{4}{7}\cdot\frac{3}{5}=(\frac{4}{7}+\frac{4}{7})\frac{3}{5}=\frac{48}{35}\cdot\frac{3}{5}=\frac{144}{175}$

   c. $(\frac{13}{17}+\frac{5}{11})+\frac{4}{17}=(\frac{13}{17}+\frac{4}{17})+\frac{5}{11}=1\frac{5}{11}$

   d. $\frac{3}{8}\cdot\frac{5}{7}-\frac{4}{9}\cdot\frac{3}{8}=\frac{3}{8}(\frac{5}{7}-\frac{4}{9})=\frac{3}{8}\cdot\frac{17}{63}=\frac{51}{504}=\frac{17}{168}$

9. a. $35\frac{4}{5}\div 9\frac{2}{7}\approx 36\div 9=4$

   b. $3\frac{5}{8}\times 14\frac{2}{3}\approx 4\times 15=60$

   c. $3\frac{4}{9}+13\frac{1}{5}+\frac{3}{13}=(3+13)+(\frac{4}{9}+\frac{1}{5}+\frac{3}{13})$

     $\approx 16+1=17$
     Answers may vary.

10. The fraction $\frac{6}{12}$ represents 6 of 12 equivalent parts (or 6 eggs), whereas $\frac{12}{24}$ represents 12 of 24 equivalent parts (or 12 halves of eggs). NOTE: This works best when the eggs are hard-boiled.

11. $\dfrac{a}{b}<\dfrac{c}{d}$ if and only if $\dfrac{ad}{bd}<\dfrac{bc}{bd}$ if and only if $ad<bc$

12. NOTE: For simplicity we will express our fractions using a common denominator.

$\dfrac{a}{c}\left(\dfrac{b}{c}-\dfrac{d}{c}\right)=\dfrac{a}{c}\left(\dfrac{b-d}{c}\right)=\dfrac{a(b-d)}{c^2}=\dfrac{ab-ab}{c^2}$

$=\dfrac{ab}{c^2}-\dfrac{ad}{c^2}=\dfrac{a}{c}\cdot\dfrac{b}{c}-\dfrac{a}{c}\cdot\dfrac{d}{c}.$

13.

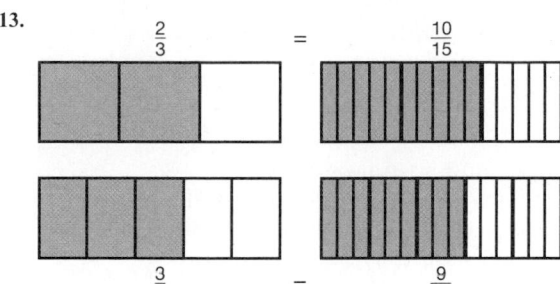

$\dfrac{2}{3}$ = $\dfrac{10}{15}$

$\dfrac{3}{5}$ = $\dfrac{9}{15}$

14.

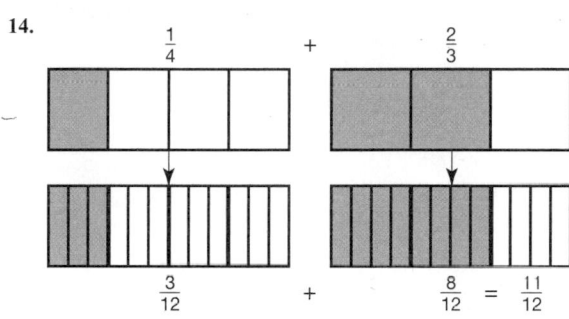

$\dfrac{1}{4}$ + $\dfrac{2}{3}$

$\dfrac{3}{12}$ + $\dfrac{8}{12}$ = $\dfrac{11}{12}$

15.

$\dfrac{3}{4}$

$\dfrac{3}{5}$ = $\dfrac{9}{20}$

16. a. Problem should include 2 groups of size $\frac{3}{4}$. How much all together?

   b. Problem should include 2 wholes being broken into groups of size $\frac{1}{3}$. How may groups?

   c. Problem should include $\frac{2}{5}$ of a whole being broken into 3 groups. How big is each group?

17. a.

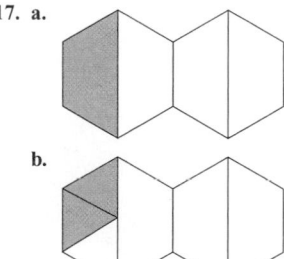

   b.

18. $\dfrac{n}{n+1}<\dfrac{n+1}{n+2}$ if and only if $n(n+2)<(n+1)^2$.
However, since $n^2+2n<n^2+2n+1$, the latter inequality is always true when $n\geq 0$.

19. 90

20. $240,000

21. $\frac{2}{5} = \frac{56}{140} < \frac{57}{140}, \frac{58}{140}, \frac{59}{140} < \frac{60}{140} = \frac{3}{7}$

22. $4 \div \frac{2}{3} = 6$

Section 7.1A

1. a. 75.603   **b.** 0.063   **c.** 306.042

2. a. (i) 4(1/10) + 5(1/100); (ii) 45/100
   b. (i) 3 + 1(1/10) + 8(1/100) + 3(1/1000); (ii) 3183/1000
   c. 2(10) + 4 + 2(1/10) + 5(1/10,000); (ii) 242,005/10,000

3. a. 746,000   **b.** 0.746   **c.** 746,000,000

4. a. Thirteen thousandths
   b. Sixty-eight thousand four hundred eighty five and five hundred thirty-two thousandths
   c. Eighty-two ten thousandths
   d. Eight hundred fifty-nine and eighty thousand five hundred nine millionths

5. (b), (c), (d), and (e)

6. a. R   **b.** T, 3 places   **c.** R   **d.** T, 4 places
Explanation: Highest power of 2 and/or 5

7. a. 0.085, 0.58, 0.85
   b. 780.9999, 781.345, 781.354
   c. 4.09, 4.099, 4.9, 4.99
   d. 8.0019929, 8.010019, 8.01002
   e. 0.5, 0.5005, 0.505, 0.55

8. a. $\frac{5}{9} < \frac{19}{34}$ **b.** $\frac{18}{25} < \frac{38}{52}$

9. There should be no "and." The word "and" is reserved for indicating the location of the decimal point.

10. a. $18.47 - 10 = 8.47$; equal additions
   b. $1.3 \times 70 = 91$; commutativity and distributivity
   c. $7 + 5.8 = 12.8$; commutativity and associativity
   d. $17 \times 2 = 34$; associativity and commutativity
   e. 0.05124; powers of ten
   f. 39.07, left to right
   g. $72 + 4 = 76$; distributivity
   h. 15,000; powers of ten

11. a. 5.9×10^1 **b.** 4.326×10^3 **c.** 9.7×10^4
   d. 1.0×10^6 **e.** 6.402×10^7 **f.** 7.1×10^{10}

12. a. 6,750,000   **b.** 0.00019514
   c. 296 followed by 26 zeros   **d.** 29,600

13. a. 4.16×10^{16} m   **b.** 3.5×10^9 m

14. a. $\frac{1}{4} \times 44 = 11$ **b.** $\frac{3}{4} \times 80 = 60$
   c. $35 \times \frac{2}{5} = 14$ **d.** $\frac{1}{5} \times 65 = 13$
   e. $65 \times \frac{4}{5} = 52$ **f.** $380 \times \frac{1}{20} = 19$

15. a. 16 to 19; $5 + 6 + 7 = 18$
   b. 420 to 560; $75 \times 6 = 450$
   c. 10   **d.** 40

16. a. $48 \div 3 = 16$ **b.** $\frac{1}{4} \times 88 = 22$
   c. $125 \times \frac{1}{5} = 25$ **d.** $56,000 \times \frac{1}{4} = 14,000$
   e. $15,000 \div 750 = 20$ **f.** $\frac{3}{5} \times 500 = 300$

17. a. 97.3   **b.** 350   **c.** 350   **d.** 0.018
   e. 0.0183   **f.** 0.5   **g.** 0.50

18. One possible answer:

26.2	20.96	47.16
52.4	31.44	10.48
15.72	41.92	36.68

19. At least 90 cents per hour

Section 7.2A

1. a. (i) 47,771, (ii) 485.84   **b.** Same as in part (a)

2. a. (i) 0.17782, (ii) 4.7   **b.** Same as in part (a)

3. a. 2562.274   **b.** 37.6   **c.** 5844.237   **d.** 6908.3

4. None

5. a. 0.72   **b.** 3.41   **c.** 36.9

6. a. 3.658×10^6 **b.** 5.893×10^9

7. a. 5.2×10^2 **b.** 8.1×10^3

8. a. 1.0066×10^{15} **b.** 1.28×10^{14}

9. a. 1.286×10^9, 3.5×10^7 **b.** About 36.7 times greater

10. a. $0.\overline{7}$ **b.** $0.4\overline{712}$ **c.** $0.\overline{18}$ **d.** $0.35\overline{0}$
   e. $0.\overline{14}$ **f.** $0.45\overline{31596}$

11. a. 0.317417417417   **b.** 0.317474747474
   c. 0.317444444444

12. a. $\frac{16}{99}$ **b.** $\frac{43}{111}$ **c.** $\frac{359}{495}$

13. Approximately 1600 light-years

14. Nonterminating; denominator is not divisible by only 2 or 5 after simplification.

15. a. $\frac{1}{8}$ **b.** $\frac{1}{16}$ **c.** $1/5^8$ **d.** $1/2^{17}$

16. a. $\frac{3}{9} = \frac{1}{3}$ **b.** $\frac{5}{9}$ **c.** $\frac{7}{9}$ **d.** $2\frac{8}{9}$ **e.** 6

17. a. $\frac{3}{99} = \frac{1}{33}$ **b.** $\frac{5}{99}$ **c.** $\frac{7}{99}$ **d.** $\frac{37}{99}$ **e.** $\frac{64}{99}$
   f. $5\frac{97}{99}$

18. a. $\frac{3}{999} = \frac{1}{333}$ **b.** $\frac{5}{999}$ **c.** $\frac{7}{999}$ **d.** $\frac{19}{999}$ **e.** $\frac{827}{999}$
   f. $3\frac{217}{999}$

19. a. (i) $\frac{23}{99}$, (ii) $\frac{10}{999}$, (iii) $\frac{769}{999}$, (iv) $\frac{9}{9} = 1$, (v) $\frac{57}{99} = \frac{19}{33}$,
   (vi) $\frac{1827}{9999} = \frac{203}{1111}$

20. a. $1/99999 = 0.\overline{00001}$
   b. $x/99999$ where $1 \le x \le 99998$, where digits in x are not all the same

21. a. 2   **b.** 6   **c.** 0   **d.** 7

22. Disregarding the first two digits to the right of the decimal point in the decimal expansion of $\frac{1}{71}$, they are the same.

23. $0.94376 \approx 364 \div 365 \times 363 \div 365$ and so on

24. $7.93

25. $31,250

26. $8.91

27. 32

28. $83.33

29. 20.32 cm by 25.4 cm

30. Approximately $100

31. 2.4-liter 4-cylinder is 0.6 liter per cylinder.
3.5-liter V-6 is 0.583 liter per cylinder.
4.9-liter V-8 is 0.61 liter per cylinder.
6.8 liter V-10 is 0.68 liter per cylinder.

32. 14 moves

Section 7.3A

1. a. 5:6　　**b.** $\frac{5}{11}$　　**c.** Cannot be determined　　**d.** 15

2. Each is an ordered pair of numbers. For example,
  (a) Measures efficiency of an engine
  (b) Measures pay per time
  (c) Currency conversion rate
  (d) Currency conversion rate

3. a. $\frac{1}{4}$　　**b.** $\frac{2}{5}$　　**c.** $\frac{5}{1}$ or 5

4. a. No　　**b.** Yes

5. 3.8, yes

6. a. 20　　**b.** 18　　**c.** 8　　**d.** 30

7. a. 0.64　　**b.** 8.4　　**c.** 0.93　　**d.** 1.71　　**e.** 2.17
  f. 0.11

8. a. $24:2 = 48:4 = 96:8 = 192:16$
  b. $13.50:1 = 27:2 = 81:6$
  c. $300:12 = 100:4 = 200:8$
  d. $20:15 = 4:3 = 16:12$
  e. $32:8 = 16:4 = 48:12$

9. $\dfrac{36¢}{42¢} = \dfrac{18\ oz}{21\ oz}, \dfrac{18\ oz}{36¢} = \dfrac{21\ oz}{42¢}, \dfrac{42¢}{36¢} = \dfrac{21\ oz}{18\ oz}$

10. 62.5 mph

11. a. 17 cents for 15 ounces
  b. 29 ounces for 13 cents
  c. 73 ounces for 96 cents

12. 40 ounces

13. $16\frac{1}{2}$ days

14. 15

15. 1024 ounces

16. About $30\frac{2}{3}$ years

17. 4.8 pounds

18. 24,530 miles

19. About 1613 feet

20. About 29″

21. a. 30　　**b.** $942.86　　**c.** $1650

22. a. 2.48 AU　　**b.** 93,000,000 miles or 9.3×10^7 miles
  c. 2.31×10^8 miles

23. a. Approximately 416,666,667
  b. Approximately 6,944,444
  c. Approximately 115,741
  d. About 12 noon
  e. About 22.5 seconds before midnight
  f. Less than $\frac{1}{10}$ of a second before midnight (0.0864 second before midnight)

24. 120 miles away

25. 1, 2, 4, 8, 16, 32, 2816 cents

26. Eric: .333　　Morgan: .333

27. 81 dimes

28. $17.50

29. 119¢ (50, 25, 10, 10, 10, 10, 1, 1, 1, 1); 219¢ if a silver dollar is used.

30. Yes; the first player always wins by going to a number with ones digit one.

31. Start both timers at the same time. Start cooking the object when the 7-minute timer runs out—there will be 4 minutes left on the 11-minute timer. When the 11-minute timer runs out, turn it over to complete the 15 minutes.

32. $\frac{8}{7} \times 11 = 12\frac{4}{7}$ seconds

Section 7.4A

1. 1/2, 0.5; 7/20, 35%; 0.25, 25%; 0.125, 12.5%; 1/80, 1.25%; 5/4, 1.25; 3/4, 75%

2. a. (i) 5, (ii) 6.87, (iii) 0.458, (iv) 3290
  b. (i) 12, (ii) 0.93, (iii) 600, (iv) 3.128
  c. (i) 13.5, (ii) 7560, (iii) 1.08, (iv) 0.0099

3. a. 252　　**b.** 144　　**c.** 231　　**d.** 195　　**e.** 40　　**f.** 80

4. a. 56　　**b.** 76　　**c.** 68　　**d.** 37.5　　**e.** 150　　**f.** $133\frac{1}{3}$

5. a. 32　　**b.** 37　　**c.** 183　　**d.** 70　　**e.** 122　　**f.** 270

6. a. $40\% \times 70 = 28$　　**b.** $60\% \times 30 = 18$
  c. $125\% \times 60 = \frac{5}{4} \times 60 = 75$　　**d.** $50\% \times 200 = 100$
  e. $20\% \times 70 = 14$　　**f.** $10\% \times 300 = 30$
  g. $1\% \times 60 = 0.6$　　**h.** $400\% \times 180 = 4 \times 180 = 720$

7. a. 56%
  (i)

  How many squares are equal to 42?

  75

  (ii) $\dfrac{42}{75} = \dfrac{x}{100}$　　(iii) $42 = x \cdot 75$

  b. 163.88
  (i)
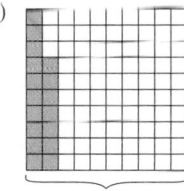

  964

  (ii) $\dfrac{17}{100} = \dfrac{x}{964}$　　(iii) $0.17 \cdot 964 = x$

  c. $423\dfrac{9}{27}$
  (i)

  156.6

  (ii) $\dfrac{156.6}{x} = \dfrac{37}{100}$　　(iii) $0.37 \cdot x = 156.6$

d. approximately 71%

(i)

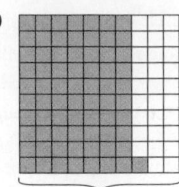

How many squares are equal to $8\frac{3}{4}$?

$12\frac{1}{3}$

(ii) $\dfrac{8\frac{3}{4}}{12\frac{1}{3}} = \dfrac{x}{100}$ (iii) $8\frac{3}{4} = x \cdot 12\frac{1}{3}$

e. $5\frac{13}{27}$

(i)

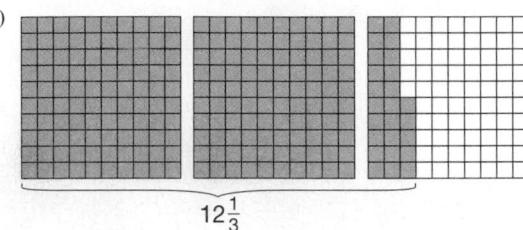

$12\frac{1}{3}$

(ii) $\dfrac{225}{100} = \dfrac{12\frac{1}{3}}{x}$ (iii) $2.25 \cdot x = 12\frac{1}{3}$

8. a. 33.6   **b.** 2.7   **c.** 82.4   **d.** 48.7%
   e. 55.5%   **f.** 123.5   **g.** 33.3%   **h.** 213.3
   i. 0.5   **j.** 0.1

9. a. 56.7   **b.** 115.5   **c.** 375.6   **d.** 350
   e. 2850   **f.** 15,680   **g.** 4400   **h.** 22
   i. 0.6   **j.** 70   **k.** 650

10. a. $1.65   **b.** $2.25   **c.** $5.25   **d.** $3.60

11. 8.5%

12. 1946 students

13. a. $5120.76   **b.** About $53.05 more

14. $(100)(1.0004839)^{15} = 100.73$, about 73 cents

15. 5.7%; 94.3%

16. a. About 5.72×10^{10} **b.** 55.3%

17. a. 72.5 quadrillion BTU
   b. Nuclear, 10.6%; crude oil, 17.2%; natural gas, 30.1%;
   renewables 9.9%; coal, 32.1%. Percentages don't add up to
   100% due to rounding.

18. The discount is 13% or the sales price should be $97.75.

19. $5000

20. a. 250   **b.** 480   **c.** 15

21. $4875

22. a. About 16.3%   **b.** About 34.8%
   c. 3.64×10^{14} square meters
   d. 0.44% or about $\frac{11}{25}$ of 1%

23. No; 3 grams is 4% of 75 grams, but 7 grams is 15% of 46.6 grams,
giving different U.S. RDA of protein.

24. 31.68 inches

25. The result is the same

26. 32%

27. 119 to 136

28. If the competition had x outputs, then $x + 0.4x = 6$, or $1.4x = 6$.
There is no whole number for x, therefore, the competition couldn't
have had x outputs.

29. $10\% + 5\% = 15\%$ off, whereas 10% off, then 5% off is equivalent
to finding $90\% \times 95\% = 85.5\%$, or 14.5% off. Conclusion: Add
the percents.

30. An increase of about 4.9%

31. The player who is faced with 3 petals loses. Reasoning backward,
so is the one faced with 6, since whatever she takes, the opponent
can force her to 3. The same for 9. Thus the first player will lose.
The key to this game is to leave the opponent on a multiple 3.

32. Let P be the price. Option (i) is $P \times 80\% \times 106\%$, whereas (ii) is
$P \times 106\% \times 80\%$. By commutativity, they are equal.

33. $14,751.06

34. $59,000

35. $9052.13

36. $\dfrac{4.7}{172.8} \approx 2.72\%$

37. $50,000. If you make a table, you can see that you will keep more
of your money up to $50,000, namely 50% of $50,000, or $25,000.
However, at $51,000 you keep only 49% of $51,000, or $24,990,
and it goes down from there until you keep $0 at $100,000!
Observe that there is symmetry around $50,000.

38. $9.25

39. 35 or 64

40. 34, 36, 44, 54, 76, 146

41. Pilot should fly when there is no wind.

PROBLEMS WHERE THE STRATEGY "WORK BACKWARD" IS USEFUL

1. Working backward, we have $87 - 59 + 18 = 46$. So they must
have gone 46 floors the first time.

2. If she ended up with 473 cards, she brought $473 - 9 + 2 - 4 - 2$
$+ 7 - 5 + 3 = 465$.

3. Working backward, $\{[(13 \cdot 4 + 6)3 \div 2] - 9\} \div 6 = 13$ is the
original number.

CHAPTER REVIEW

Section 7.1

1. $3 \times 10 + 7 + 1 \times (1/10) + 4 \times (1/100) + 9 \times (1/1000)$

2. Two and three thousand seven hundred ninety-eight
ten thousandths

3. (a) and (c)

4. a. Shade 24 small squares and 3 strips of ten squares.
Thus, $0.24 < 0.3$.
   b. 0.24 is to the left of 0.3.   **c.** $\frac{24}{100} < \frac{30}{100} (= \frac{3}{10})$
   d. Since $2 < 3$, $0.24 < 0.3$.

5. a. 24.6. Use commutativity and associativity to find $0.25 \times 8 = 2$.
   b. 9.6. Use commutativity and distributivity to find $2.4(1.3 + 2.7)$.
   c. 18.72. Use compensation to find $15.72 + 3.00$.
   d. 7.53. Use equal additions to find $27.53 - 20.00$.

6. a. Between 48 and 108   **b.** 14
   c. $8.5 - 2.4 = 6.1$ **d.** $400 \div 50 = 8$

Section 7.2

1. a. 21.009   **b.** 36.489   **c.** 153.55   **d.** 36.9

2. a. $0.\overline{384615}$ **b.** $0.3\overline{96}$ **c.** $\frac{1}{2}$

3. a. $3\frac{674}{999}$ **b.** $\frac{23{,}891}{990}$

Section 7.3

1. A ratio is an ordered pair, and a proportion is a statement saying that two ratios are equal.

2. a. No, since $\frac{7}{13} \neq \frac{3}{5}$.   **b.** Yes, since $12 \times 25 = 15 \times 20$.

3. $\frac{a}{b} = \frac{c}{d}$ if and only if (i) $ad = bc$ or (ii) $\frac{a}{b}$ and $\frac{c}{d}$ are equivalent to the same fraction.

4. a. $\frac{58}{24} < \frac{47}{16}$, so 58¢ for 24 oz is the better buy.

b. $\frac{3.45}{7} > \frac{5.11}{11}$, so \$5.11 for 11 pounds is the better buy.

5. $4\frac{1}{3}$ cups.

Section 7.4

1. a. $56\% = 0.56 = \frac{56}{100}(= \frac{14}{25})$
b. $0.48 = 48\% = \frac{48}{100}(= \frac{12}{25})$
c. $\frac{1}{8} = 0.125 = 12.5\%$

2. a. $48 \times \frac{1}{4} = 12$ **b.** $\frac{1}{3} \times 72 = 24$
c. $\frac{3}{4} \times 72 = 54$ **d.** $\frac{1}{5} \times 55 = 11$

3. a. $25\% \times 80 = 20$ **b.** $50\% \times 200 = 100$
c. $33\frac{1}{3}\% \times 60 = 20$ **d.** $66\frac{2}{3}\% \times 300 - 200$

4. a. \$16,000   **b.** 59%

Chapter 7 Test

1. a. F   **b.** T   **c.** T   **d.** F   **e.** F   **f.** T
g. T   **h.** T

2. a. $3 \cdot 10^1 + 2 \cdot 1 + 1 \cdot \left(\frac{1}{10^1}\right) + 9\left(\frac{1}{10^2}\right) + 8\left(\frac{1}{10^3}\right)$

b. $3 \cdot \left(\frac{1}{10^4}\right) + 4 \cdot \left(\frac{1}{10^5}\right) + 2 \cdot \left(\frac{1}{10^6}\right)$

3. Hundred

4. a. The ratio of red to green is $9:14$, or the ratio of green to red is $14:9$.
b. $9:23$ or $14:23$

5. a. 17.519   **b.** 6.339   **c.** 83.293   **d.** 500

6. a. $\frac{103}{1000} < \frac{400}{1000}$ and $0.1 < 0.4$; therefore, $0.103 < 0.4$
b. $\frac{997}{10{,}000} < \frac{1000}{10{,}000}$ and $0.09 < 0.10$; therefore, $0.0997 < 0.1$

7. a. $0.\overline{285714}$ **b.** 0.625   **c.** 0.14583 **d.** $0.\overline{4}$

8. a. Terminating   **b.** Nonterminating   **c.** Terminating

9. a. $\frac{4}{11}$ **b.** $\frac{11}{30}$ **c.** $\frac{909}{2500}$

10. a. $0.52, \frac{52}{100}$ **b.** $125\%, \frac{125}{100}$ **c.** $0.68, 68\%$

11. 18

12. a. $53 \times 0.48 \approx 52 \times 0.5 = 52 \div 2 = 26$
b. $1469.2 \div 26.57 = 14.692 \div 0.2657 \approx 16 \div 0.25 = 16 \div \frac{1}{4} = 16 \times 4 = 64$
c. $33 \div 0.76 \approx 33 \div 0.75 = 33 \times \frac{4}{3} - 44$
d. $442.78 \times 18.7 \approx 450 \times 20 = 9000$

13. $3\%, \frac{2}{7}, 0.3, \frac{1}{3}$

14. 123,456,789 has prime factors other than 2 or 5.

15. 37 $\boxed{\div}$ 100 $\boxed{\times}$ 58 is 37% of 58.

16. a. Bernard got 80% of the questions correct on his math test. If he got 48 correct, how many questions were on the test?
b. Of his 140 times at bat for the season, Jose got a hit 35 times. What percent of the time did he get a hit? (Answers may vary.)

17. If we convert 1.3 and 0.2 to fractions before adding, the denominator of the sum is 10 and thus the sum has one digit to the right of the decimal. $\left(\frac{13}{10} + \frac{2}{10} = \frac{15}{10} = 1.5\right)$. When multiplying, the denominators are multiplied, giving a denominator of 10^2 (two digits to the right of the decimal) in the product $\left(\frac{13}{10} \times \frac{2}{10} = \frac{26}{10^2} = 0.26\right)$.

18. 7

19. \$2520

20. 522

21. 9.6 inches

22. 5.37501, 5.37502, 5.37503 (Answers may vary.)

23. 28

24. If the competition has 4 new styles, then 6 new styles is 50% more. If the competition has 5 new styles, then 6 new styles is 20% more. In other words, 6 styles is 40% more than 4.28 styles and 0.28 of a style makes no sense.

25. \$870

Section 8.1A

1. All are integers
a. Positive   **b.** Negative   **c.** Neither

2. a. *RRRRB*   **b.** *BRRRRRRB*
c.   **d.**

3. a. *BBB*   **b.** *RRRRR*

c. *BR*

4. a. -3 **b.** 4   **c.** 0   **d.** 168   **e.** -56 **f.** 1235

5. a. *I*   **b.** $\{\ldots, -4, -3, -2, -1, 1, 2, 3, 4, \ldots\}$ **c.** $\varnothing$

6. \$64

7. a.

or *BBBBBRRR = BB*; 2.

b.

or *RRR RR* = -5.

8. a. $-14 + 6 = [-8 + (-6)] + 6 = -8 + (-6 + 6) = -8 + 0 = -8$

b. $17 + (-3) = (14 + 3) + (-3) = 14 + (3 + (-3)) = 14 + 0 = 14$

9. a. Commutative property of addition
b. Additive inverse property

10. a. 635 **b.** -17

11. a.

b. $BBBB \; BBBBB$ = 9

$RRRRR$

12. a. -4 **b.** 12 **c.** 1 **d.** 1

13. a. 26 **b.** -5 **c.** 370 **d.** -128

14. a. -5 **b.** 12 **c.** -78 **d.** 1 **e.** 9 **f.** 8

15. a. T **b.** F **c.** F **d.** T

16. a. Five minus two
b. Negative six or opposite of six (both equivalent)
c. Opposite of three
d. Opposite of negative five, for example
e. Ten minus the opposite of negative two, for example
f. Opposite of p or additive inverse of p

17. a. 5 **b.** 17 **c.** 2 **d.** -2 **e.** -2 **f.** 2

18. Top: 5; second: $-1, 6$; third: $-2, 1$

19. a. Yes; $-3 - 7$ is an integer **b.** No; $3 - 2 \neq 2 - 3$
c. No; $5 - (4 - 1) \neq (5 - 4) - 1$ **d.** No; $5 - 0 \neq 0 - 5$

20. If $a - b = c$, then $a + (-b) = c$. Then $a + (-b) + b = c + b$, or $a = b + c$.

21. a. (i) When a and b have the same sign or when one or both are 0, (ii) when a and b have opposite signs, (iii) never, (iv) all integers will work.
b. Only condition (iv)

22. First row: $7, -14, 1$; second row: $-8, -2, 4$; third row: $-5, 10, -11$

23. a. (i) $9 - 4$, (ii) $4 - 9$, (iii) $4 - 4$,
(iv) $9 - [(4 - 4) - 4]$, (v) $(9 - 4) - 4$,
(vi) $[(9 - 4) - 4] - 4$
b. All integers
c. Any integer that is multiple of 4
d. If $GCF(a, b) = 1$, then all integers; otherwise, just multiples of GCF

24. Second: $2, -24$; third: $4, -2, -22$; bottom: -7

25. As long as we have integers, this algorithm is correct. Justification: $72 - 38 = (70 + 2) - (30 + 8) = (70 - 30) + (2 - 8) = 40 + (-6) = 34$.

26.

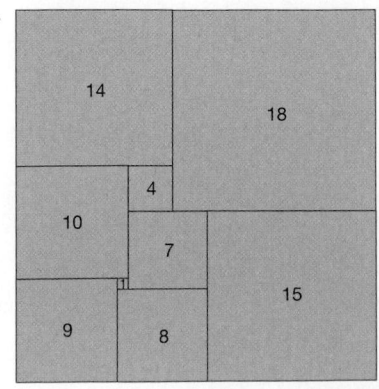

Section 8.2A

1. a. $2 + 2 + 2 + 2 = 8$ or $4 \times 2 = 8$
b. $(-3) + (-3) + (-3) = -9$ or $3 \times (-3) = -9$
c. $(-1) + (-1) + (-1) + (-1) + (-1) + (-1) = -6$ or $6 \times (-1) = -6$

2. a. (i) $6 \times (-1) = -6, 6 \times (-2) = -12, 6 \times (-3) = -18$;
(ii) $9 \times (-1) = -9, 9 \times (-2) = -18, 9 \times (-3) = -27$
b. Positive times negative equals negative.

3. a. -30 **b.** 32 **c.** -15 **d.** 39

4. a. $RR \; RR \; RR = -6$

b. $BBBBBBBBBBBB = 12$

$RRRRRRRRRRRR$

5. Distributivity of multiplication over addition; additive inverse; multiplication by 0

6. a. 16 **b.** -27 **c.** 16 **d.** 25 **e.** -243
f. 64

7. Positive: (c), (d); negative: (e)

8. Adding the opposite approach to subtraction; distributivity of multiplication over addition; $(-a)b = -(ab)$; adding opposite approach; distributivity of multiplication over subtraction.

9. a. -6 **b.** 5 **c.** -15 **d.** 0 **e.** 4 **f.** 36

10. a. -2592 **b.** 1938 **c.** $97,920$ **d.** -47
e. -156 **f.** 1489

11. Yes

12. a. $\frac{1}{100}$ **b.** $\frac{1}{64}$ **c.** $\frac{1}{64}$ **d.** $\frac{1}{125}$

13. a. $\frac{1}{4^2} \cdot 4^6 = 4^4$ **b.** $4^{-2+6} = 4^4$ **c.** $\frac{1}{5^4} \cdot \frac{1}{5^2} = \frac{1}{5^6}$

14. a. $\frac{1/3^2}{3^5} = \frac{1}{3^7}$ **b.** $3^{-2-5} = 3^{-7} = \frac{1}{3^7}$ **c.** $6^{10}, 6^{10}$ **d.** Yes

15. a. $3^3 = 27$ **b.** 6 **c.** $3^8 = 6561$

16. a. 0.000037 **b.** 0.0000000245

17. a. 4×10^{-4} **b.** 1.6×10^{-6} **c.** 4.95×10^{-10}
d. 8.071×10^{-20}

18. a. 7.22×10^{-25} **b.** 8.28×10^{-26}
c. 2.5×10^{-10} **d.** 4×10^{-37}
e. 8×10^{14} **f.** 2.05×10^{-7}

19. a. -3 is left of 2. **b.** -6 is left of -2.
c. -12 is the left of -3.

20. a. $-5, -2, 0, 2, 5$ **b.** $-8, -6, -5, 3, 12$
c. $-11, -8, -5, -3, -2$
d. $-108, -72, -36, 23, 45$

21. a. $<$ **b.** $>$

22. $43,200, -240, -180, 12, -5, 3$

23. a. -10 and -8 **b.** -8 **c.** No

24. a. ? $-$
b. (i) ? $+$ (ii) $+ \; -$ (iii) $+ \; -$
$- \; ?$ $- \; +$ $- \; +$

25. a. (i) When x is negative, (ii) when x is nonnegative (zero or positive), (iii) never, (iv) all integers
b. Only (iv)

26. This is correct, by $a(-1) = -a$.

27. Put the amounts on a number line, where positive numbers represent assets and negative numbers represent liabilities. Clearly, $-10 < -5$.

28. First row: $-2, -9, 12$; second row: $-36, 6, -1$; third row: $3, -4, -18$

29. $x < y$ means $y = x + p$ for some $p > 0$, $y^2 = (x + p)^2 = x^2 + 2xp + p^2$. Since $x > 0$ and $p > 0$, $2xp + p^2 > 0$. Therefore, $x^2 < y^2$.

30. 1.99×10^{-23} grams per atom of carbon

31. a. 1.11×10^{-2}
  b. About 2.33×10^8 seconds, or 7.37 years

32. 100 sheep, 0 cows, and 0 rabbits or 1 lamb, 19 cows, and 80 rabbits

33. True. Every whole number can be expressed in the form $3n, 3n + 1$, or $3n + 2$. If these three forms are squared, the squares will be of the form $3m$ or $3m + 1$.

34. 30 cents

35. Assume $ab = 0$ and $b \neq 0$. Then $ab = 0 \cdot b$. Since $ac = bc$ and $c \neq 0$ implies that $a = b$, we can cancel the b's in $ab = 0 \cdot b$. Hence $a = 0$.

PROBLEMS WHERE THE STRATEGY "USE CASES" IS USEFUL

1. Case 1: odd + even + odd = even.
Case 2: even + odd + even = odd.
Since only Case 1 has an even sum, two of the numbers must be odd.

2. $m^2 - n^2$ is positive when $m^2 > n^2$.
Case 1: $m > 0, n > 0$. Here m must be greater than n.
Case 2: $m > 0, n < 0$. Here $m > -n$.
Case 3: $m < 0, n > 0$. Here $-m > n$.
Case 4: $m < 0, n < 0$. Here $m < n$.

3. Case 1: If $n = 5m$, then $n^2 = 25m^2$ and hence is a multiple of 5.
Case 2: If $n = 5m + 1$, then $n^2 = 25m^2 + 10m + 1$, which is one more than a multiple of 5.
Case 3: If $n = 5m + 2$, then $n^2 = 25m^2 + 20m + 4$, which is 4 more than (hence one less than) a multiple of 5.
Case 4: If $n = 5m + 3$, then $n^2 = 25m^2 + 30m + 9$, which is one less than a multiple of 5.
Case 5: If $n = 5m + 4$, then $n^2 = 25m^2 + 40m + 16$, which is one more than a multiple of 5.

CHAPTER REVIEW

Section 8.1

1. a. Use black chips for positive integers and red chips for negative integers.
  b. Arrows representing positive integers point to the right, and arrows representing negative integers points to the left.

2. a. $BBBBBBBRRRR = BBB$
  b.

$$0\ 1\ 2\ 3\ 4\ 5\ 6\ 7$$

3. a. Identity **b.** Inverse **c.** Commutativity
  d. Associativity **e.** Closure

4. a.

$BBBBB\ \boxed{RR}$ $3 - (-2) = 5$

  b. $3 - (-2) = 3 + 2 = 5$
  c. $3 - (-2) = n$ if and only if $3 = (-2) + n$; therefore, $n = 5$.

5. (a) only

Section 8.2

1. a. $(-2) + (-2) + (-2) + (-2) + (-2) = -10$
  b. $(-5)2 = -10, (-5)1 = -5, (-5)0 = 0, (-5)(-1) = 5, (-5)(-2) = 10$

2. a. Commutativity **b.** Associativity **c.** Closure
  d. Identity **e.** Cancellation

3. Let $a = 3$ and $b = 4$.

4. $n = 0$; zero divisors

5. $a \div b = c$ if and only if $a = bc$.

6. None

7. a. Positive—even number of negative numbers
  b. Negative—odd number of negative numbers
  c. 0—zero is a factor

8. $7^3 = 7 \times 7 \times 7, 7^2 = 7 \times 7, 7^1 = 7, 7^0 = 1, 7^{-1} = \frac{1}{7}$, etc.

9. a. 7.9×10^{-5} **b.** 0.0003 **c.** 4.58127×10^2
  d. 23,900,000

10. a. -21 is to the left of 17 **b.** $-21 + 4 = -17$

11. a. $>$: Property of less than and multiplication by a negative
  b. $<$: Transitivity
  c. $<$: Property of less than and multiplication by a positive
  d. $<$: Property of less than and addition

Chapter 8 Test

1. a. T **b.** F **c.** F **d.** T **e.** F **f.** F
  g. F **h.** T

2. $a^{-n} = \dfrac{1}{a^n}$

3. (b) and (c)

4. Take-away, missing-addend, add-the-opposite

5. a. -6 **b.** 42 **c.** 48 **d.** -8 **e.** -30
  f. 3 **g.** -52 **h.** -12

6. a. $3(-4 + 2) = 3(-2) = -6, 3(-4) + 3(2) = -12 + 6 = -6$
  b. $-3[-5 + (-2)] = -3(-7) = 21, (-3)(-5) + (-3)(-2) = 15 + 6 = 21$

7. a. 8.2×10^{12} **b.** 6×10^{-6}

8. $n = -4$

9. a. Associativity **b.** Associativity and commutativity
  c. Distributivity **d.** Commutativity and distributivity

10. a. i. $BBBBBBBBBBBBB\!R\!\!R\!\!R\!\!R\!\!R = 13$
    ii. $8 - (-5) = 8 + 5 = 13$
    iii. $8 - (-5) = c$ if and only if $8 = c + (-5); c = 13$.
  b. i. $RR \rightarrow BBBBB\!R\!\!R\!\!R\!\!R\!\!R\!\!R = 5$
    ii. $(-2) - (-7) = -2 + 7 = 5$
    iii. $(-2) - (-7) = c$ if and only if $-2 = c + (-7); c = 5$.

11. a. Negative **b.** Negative **c.** Positive **d.** Positive

12. a.

b.

c.

13. (i) take-away

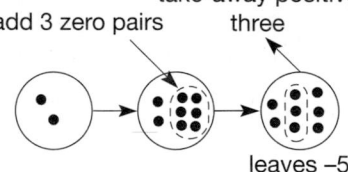

add 3 zero pairs — take-away positive three

leaves –5

(ii) missing-addend
What needs to be
added to a set of
3 to get −2?

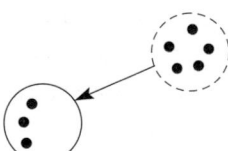

14. a. $3 \times 4 = 12$
$2 \times 4 = 8$
$1 \times 4 = 4$
$0 \times 4 = 0$
$-1 \times 4 = -4$
$-2 \times 4 = -8$

b. $-2 \times 4 = -8$
$-2 \times 3 = -6$
$-2 \times 2 = -4$
$-2 \times 1 = -2$
$-2 \times 0 = 0$
$-2 \times -1 = 2$
$-2 \times -2 = 4$
$-2 \times -3 = 6$
$-2 \times -4 = 8$

15. No; let $a = 2$, $b = 3$, $c = 4$, then $a(b \cdot c) = 24$, but $a \cdot b \times a \cdot c = 48$.

16. a. $30, -30$ **b.** $120, 60$ **c.** $-900, -3600$
d. $-1, -2$

17.

9	−12	3
−6	0	6
−3	12	−9

18.

−256	2	−64
8	32	128
−16	512	−4

19. $a - b = b - a$ is the same as $a - b = -(a - b)$. The only number that is equal to its opposite is 0, so $a - b = 0$ which means $a = b$.

20. a. 20   **b.** 18   **c.** 6

Section 9.1A

1. a. $\frac{-2}{3}$ where $-2, 3$ are integers
   b. $\frac{-31}{6}$ where $-31, 6$ are integers
   c. $\frac{10}{1}$ where $10, 1$ are integers

2. $\frac{-3}{1}, \frac{3}{-1}, -\frac{3}{1}, -\frac{-3}{-1}$

3. (a) and (b)

4. a. $\frac{-5}{7}$ **b.** $\frac{-3}{5}$ **c.** $\frac{2}{5}$ **d.** $\frac{-4}{5}$

5. a. $\frac{-1}{9}$ **b.** $\frac{-4}{3}$ **c.** $\frac{1}{4}$ **d.** $\frac{-1}{8}$

6. a. $2\frac{5}{8}$ **b.** $1\frac{3}{5}$

7. a. 2   **b.** $-\frac{5}{3}$

8. a. $\frac{2}{3}$ **b.** 2   **c.** $\frac{5}{7}$ **d.** $\frac{-31}{36}$

9. a. $\frac{14}{27}$ **b.** $\frac{-35}{18}$ **c.** $\frac{5}{18}$ **d.** $\frac{1}{4}$

10. a. $\frac{-11}{17}$ **b.** $\frac{-3}{14}$ **c.** $\frac{31}{21}$ **d.** $\frac{2}{7}$

11. a. $\frac{4}{3}$ **b.** $\frac{-1}{6}$ **c.** $\frac{-9}{20}$ **d.** $\frac{-7}{5}$

12. a. $\frac{24}{143}$ **b.** $1\frac{123}{245}$

13. a. $\frac{-9}{11} < \frac{-3}{11}$ **b.** $\frac{-1}{3} < \frac{2}{5}$ **c.** $\frac{-9}{10} < \frac{-5}{6}$ **d.** $\frac{-9}{8} < \frac{-10}{9}$

14. a. $\frac{-152}{201} < \frac{-231}{356}$ **b.** $\frac{-500}{345} < \frac{-761}{532}$

15. a. I, N, Q   **b.** Q   **c.** W, F, I, N, Q   **d.** I, Q
   e. W, F, I, Q

16. a. Associative—addition
   b. Commutative—multiplication
   c. Distributive—multiplication over addition
   d. Property of less than and addition

17. a. $x < \dfrac{-4}{3}$ **b.** $x < \dfrac{-1}{12}$

18. a. $x < \dfrac{3}{2}$ **b.** $x < \dfrac{-3}{4}$

19. a. $x > \dfrac{5}{4}$ **b.** $x > -\dfrac{3}{2}$

20. a. $-90{,}687$ **b.** -77

21. a. $\frac{-164}{837}$ **b.** $\frac{-19}{528}$

22. a. $\frac{-43}{88} < \frac{-37}{76}, \frac{-80}{164} = \frac{-20}{41}$ **b.** $\frac{-59}{97} < \frac{-68}{113}, \frac{-127}{210}$

23. There are many correct answers.
   a. For example, $\frac{-2}{3}, \frac{-5}{7}$, and $\frac{-3}{5}$
   b. For example, $\frac{-6}{7}, \frac{-11}{13}$, and $\frac{-13}{15}$

24. $a/b = an/bn$ if and only if $a(bn) = b(an)$. The last equation is true due to associativity and commutativity of integer multiplication.

25. a. $\frac{a}{b} \cdot \frac{c}{d} = \frac{ac}{bd}$ (definition of multiplication), ac and bd are integers (closure of integer multiplication); therefore, $\frac{ac}{bd}$ is a rational number. Similar types of arguments hold for parts (b) to (e).

26. a. $a/b = c/d + e/f$
   b. If $a/b - c/d = e/f$, then $a/b + (-c/d) = e/f$. Add c/d to both sides. Then $a/b = c/d + e/f$. Also, if $a/b = c/d + e/f$, add $-c/d$ to both sides. Then $a/b + (-c/d) = e/f$ or $a/b - c/d = e/f$.
   c. If $a/b - c/d = e/f$, then $a/b = c/d + e/f$. Adding $-c/d$ to both sides will yield $a/b + (-c/d) = e/f$. Hence, $a/b - c/d = a/b + (-c/d)$.

27. $\frac{a}{b}\left(\frac{c}{d} + \frac{e}{f}\right) = \frac{a}{b}\left(\frac{cf + de}{df}\right) = \frac{a\,(cf + de)}{bdf} =$

$\frac{acf + ade}{bdf} = \frac{acf}{bdf} + \frac{ade}{bdf} = \frac{ac}{bd} + \frac{ae}{bf} =$

$\frac{a}{b} \cdot \frac{c}{d} + \frac{a}{b} \cdot \frac{e}{f}$, using addition and multiplication of rational numbers and distributivity of integers

28. If $a/b < c/d$, then $a/b + p/q = c/d$ for some positive p/q. Therefore, $a/b + p/q + e/f = c/d + e/f$, or $a/b + e/f + p/q = c/d + e/f$ for positive p/q. Thus $a/b + e/f < c/d + e/f$.

29. $\left(-\frac{a}{b}\right) + \left[-\left(-\frac{a}{b}\right)\right] = \left(-\frac{a}{b}\right) + \frac{a}{b}$. Therefore, by additive cancellation, $-\left(-\frac{a}{b}\right) = \frac{a}{b}$.

30. Start both timers. When the 5-minute timer expires, start it again. When the 8-minute timer expires, start it again; the 5-minute timer will have 2 minutes left on it. When the 5-minute timer expires, start measuring, since the 8-minute timer will have 6 minutes left.

Section 9.2A

1. a. Irrational   **b.** Rational   **c.** Irrational
   d. Rational   **e.** Irrational   **f.** Irrational
   g. Rational   **h.** Rational

2. No; if it did, π would be a rational number. This is an approximation to π.

3. $0.56, 0.565565556\ldots, 0.565566555666\ldots, 0.5\overline{6}, 0.5\overline{66}, 0.56656665\ldots, 0.5\overline{66}$

4. There are many correct answers. One is $0.37414243\ldots$

5. For example, $\sqrt{10}, \sqrt{11}, \sqrt{12}, 3.060060006\ldots$

6. a. Distributive of multiplication over addition
   b. Yes; 8π
   c. No

7. a. $2 \times 3 = 6$ **b.** $2 \times 5 = 10$ **c.** $3 \times 4 = 12$
   d. $3 \times 5 = 15$ **e.** $\sqrt{a} \times \sqrt{b} = \sqrt{a \times b}$

8. a. 19   **b.** 27

9. a. 10   **b.** 22

10. a. $\sqrt{2}$ **b.** $\sqrt{3}$

11. a. $\sqrt{34}$ **b.** $\sqrt{20} = 2\sqrt{5}$ **c.** 6

12. a. 2.65   **b.** 3.95   **c.** 0.19

13. The numbers decrease in size, 1.

14. a. $0.3 < 0.5477225$ **b.** $0.5 < 0.7071067$
   Square root is larger than number.

15. a. 5   **b.** 2   **c.** 243   **d.** 81   **e.** 8   **f.** $\frac{1}{125}$

16. a. -3 **b.** Not real   **c.** 2

17. a. 25   **b.** 3.804 (rounded)
   c. 7,547,104.282 (rounded)
   d. 9,018,968.484 (rounded)

18. a. $\frac{22}{7}$ **b.** $\sqrt[3]{37}$

19. a. -8 **b.** 5   **c.** $\frac{-5}{9}$ **d.** $3\sqrt{2}$

20. a. 9   **b.** 5   **c.** 5   **d.** $\frac{9}{8}$ **e.** $\frac{-7}{6}$ **f.** 2π

21. a. $x > \frac{-11}{3}$ **b.** $x \le 4$ **c.** $x > \frac{9}{5}$ **d.** $x \le \frac{22}{27}$

22. Let $\sqrt{3} = a/b$. Then $3 = a^2/b^2$ or $a^2 = 3b^2$. Count prime factors.

23. When you get to the step $a^2 = 9 \cdot b^2$, this can be written as $a^2 = 3^2 \cdot b^2$. Thus both sides have an even number of prime factors and no contradiction arises.

24. Assume not. Then $(a/b)^3 = 2$ for some rational a/b.

25. a. By closure of real-number multiplication, $5\sqrt{3}$ is a real number, and thus a rational or an irrational number. Assume that it is rational, say m. $\sqrt{3} = m/5$. Since $m/5$ is rational and $\sqrt{3}$ is irrational, we have a contradiction. Therefore, $5\sqrt{3}$ must be irrational.
   b. Argue as in part (a); replace 5 with any nonzero rational and $\sqrt{3}$ with my irrational.

26. a. $1 + \sqrt{3} = a/b$ so $\sqrt{3} = (a - b)/b$, which is a rational number, and this is a contradiction because $\sqrt{3}$ is an irrational number.
   b. Argue as in part (a); assume that the number is rational and solve for $\sqrt{3}$.

27. a. Apply 25(b).
   b. Apply 26(b).
   c. Apply 26(b).

28. $\sqrt{a} + \sqrt{b} \ne \sqrt{a + b}$ except when $a = 0$ or $b = 0$. There is no consistent analogy between multiplication and addition.

29. $\sqrt{a} \cdot \sqrt{b} = \sqrt{ab}$ is true for all a and b, where $a \ge 0$ and $b \ge 0$.

30. $\{(3n, 4n, 5n) \mid$ is a nonzero whole number$\}$ is an infinite set of Pythagorean triples.

31. For example, if $u = 2, v = 1$, then $a = 4, b = 3, c = 5$. If $u = 3, v = 2$, then $a = 12, b = 5, c = 13$.

32. $3, 4, 5; 1, 2, 3; 2, 3, 4; -1, 0, 1$

33. Yes; 1 or -1

34. Cut from the longer wire a piece that is $\frac{1}{3}$ the sum of the lengths of the original pieces.

35. Mr. Milne

36. 20 and 64

Section 9.3A

1. a.

b.

c.   **d.**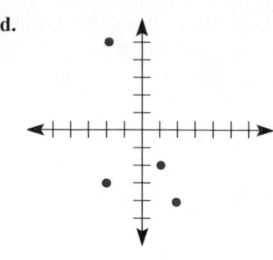

2. a. III and IV   **b.** IV   **c.** III

3.

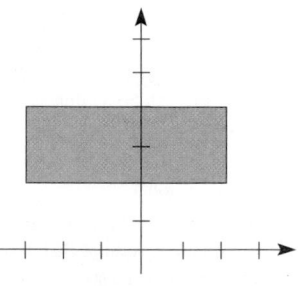

4. a. Domain $= \{x \mid -2 \le x \le 3\}$
Range $= \{y \mid -1 \le y \le 3\}$
   b. Not a function
   c. Not a function
   d. Domain is the set of all real numbers. Range is the set of all positive real numbers.

5. a. (i) 3, (ii) -4, (iii) 0
   b. Domain $= \{x \mid -3 \le x \le 6\}$
Range $= \{y \mid -4 \le y \le 3\}$
   c. 0, 2, 5

6. a. $d(4) = 2.4$, $d(5.5) \approx 2.81$
   b. Approximately 2.16 miles
   c. Domain is the set of all nonnegative real numbers.
Range is the set of all nonnegative real numbers up to the farthest number of miles one can see.

7. a.

x	f(x)
−2	−1
−1	1
0	3
1	5
2	7

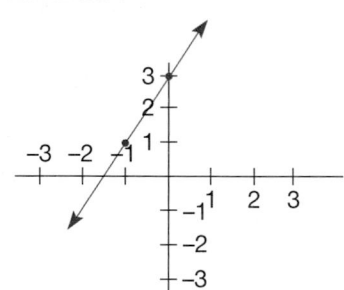

b.

x	m(x)
−2	50
−1	45
0	40
1	35
2	30

c.

x	g(x)
−2	−18.9
−1	−11.7
0	−4.5
1	2.7
2	9.9

8. a.

x	h(x)
−2	0
−1	−0.5
0	0
1	1.5
2	4

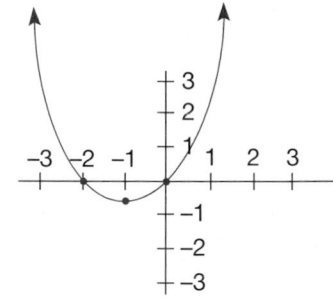

b.

x	r(x)
−2	$\frac{1}{9}$
−1	$\frac{1}{3}$
0	1
1	3
2	9

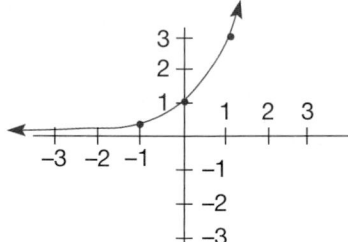

c.

x	s(x)
−2	10
−1	3
0	2
1	1
2	−6

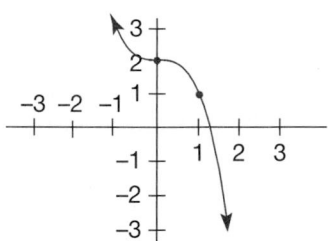

9. a. (i) 2, (ii) 7, (iii) -5, (iv) 0
   b.

10. a. (i)

(ii)

(iii)

(iv)

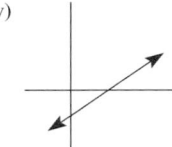

b. The larger the coefficient of x, the greater the slope or steeper the slant.

c. It changes the slant from lower left to upper right to a slant from upper left to lower right.

(i)

(ii)

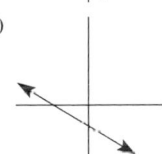

11. a. The line gets closer to being vertical.
 b. The line is horizontal.
 c. The line slants from upper left to lower right.

12. a. (i)

(ii)

(iii)

(iv)

(v)

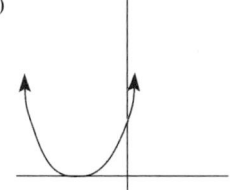

b. (ii) shifts the graph of (i) two units up, (iii) shifts the graph of (i) two units down, (iv) shifts the graph of (i) two units to the right, (v) shifts the graph of (i) two units to the left.

c. The graph of $f(x) = x^2 + 4$ should be the same as the graph in (i) except it is shifted up 4 units. The graph of $f(x) = (x - 3)^2$ should be the same as the graph in (i) except it is shifted 3 units to the right.

13. a. Changing b has the effect of moving the parabola to the left or right.
 b. Changing c has the effect of moving the parabola up or down.

14. a. (i)

(ii)

(iii)

(iv)

b. When the base is greater than 1, the larger the base, the steeper the rise of its graph from left to right, especially in the first quadrant. When the base is between 0 and 1, the closer to zero, the steeper the fall of its graph from left to right, especially in the second quadrant.

c.

$f(x) = 10^x$

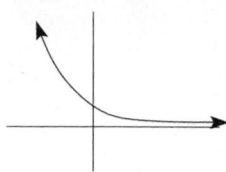

$f(x) = (0.95)^x$

15. a. The right part comes closer to the *y*-axis and the left part gets closer to the *x*-axis.
b. It is a horizontal line.
c. The graph is decreasing from left to right instead of increasing.

16. a. (i) 34¢, (ii) $1.49, (iii) $2.87, (iv) $3.10
b. Domain is 0 oz through 16 oz.
Range = {34¢, 57¢, 80¢, $1.03, $1.26, $1.49, $1.72, $1.95, $2.18, $2.41, $2.64, $2.87, $3.10}
c.

Cost in cents

Ounces
Graph for first class
mail up to 6 oz

d. 20 × 34 cents = $6.80 for 20 pieces or $\frac{3}{4}$ × 20 = 15 oz is $3.10.

17. a.

b.

c.

d.

18. a. Exponential　　**b.** Quadratic　　**c.** Cubic

19. a. The length of the shadow varies as time passes. Exponential.
b. $L(5) = 150$, $L(8) = 1100$, $L(2.5) = 50$
c. 4.5, 6
d. It is too dark to cast a shadow.

20. a.

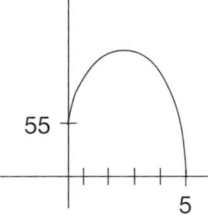

55

5

b. Approximately 0.55 second and 3.8 seconds
c. In approximately 5.1 seconds
d. Approximately 131 feet

21. a.

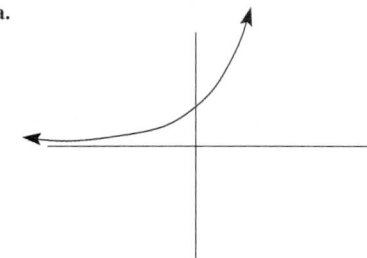

b. 5.86 billion
c. Approximately 34.5 years
d. Approximately 41 years

22. (a)

23. 130 drops 160 off on the top floor and returns. 210 takes the elevator to the top while 130 stays behind. 160 returns and comes up to the top with 130.

PROBLEMS WHERE THE STRATEGY "SOLVE AN EQUATION" IS USEFUL

1. $27,000

2. 840

3. 4

CHAPTER REVIEW
Section 9.1

1. Every fraction and every integer is a rational number and the operations on fractions and integers are the same as the corresponding operations on rational numbers.

2. The a and b in $\frac{a}{b}$ are nonzero integers for rationals but are whole numbers for fractions.

3. The restriction that denominators are positive must be stated when dealing with rational numbers.

4. The number $-\frac{3}{4}$ is the additive inverse of $\frac{3}{4}$, and $\frac{-3}{4}$ is read "negative three over four"; however, they are equal.

5. a. T　　**b.** T　　**c.** F　　**d.** T　　**e.** T　　**f.** T
　　g. T　　**h.** F　　**i.** F　　**j.** T　　**k.** T　　**l.** T

6. a. Commutativity for addition
　　b. Associativity for multiplication
　　c. Multiplicative identity
　　d. Distributivity
　　e. Associativity for addition
　　f. Multiplicative inverse
　　g. Closure for addition
　　h. Additive inverse
　　i. Additive indentity
　　j. Closure for multiplication
　　k. Commutativity for multiplication
　　l. Additive cancellation

7. a. No, since $\frac{-5}{11}$ is to the left of $\frac{-3}{7}$.
　　b. $\frac{-33}{77} < \frac{-35}{77}$ is false.
　　c. $\frac{-3}{7} = \frac{-5}{11} + \frac{2}{77}$
　　d. $-33 < -35$ is false.

8. a. $\frac{-2}{3} < \frac{7}{5}$; transitivity
　　b. $<$; property of less than and multiplication by a positive
　　c. $\frac{5}{8}$; property of less than and addition
　　d. $<$; property of less than and multiplication by a negative
　　e. Between; density property

Section 9.2

1. Every rational number is a real number, and operations on rational numbers as real numbers are the same as rational-number operations.

2. Rational numbers can be expressed in the form $\frac{a}{b}$, where a and b are integers, $b \neq 0$, irrational numbers cannot. Also rational numbers have repeating decimal representations, whereas irrational numbers do not.

3. None

4. Completeness. Real numbers fill the entire number line, whereas the rational-number line has "holes" where the irrationals are.

5. a. T　　**b.** T　　**c.** T　　**d.** F　　**e.** T　　**f.** F
　　g. T　　**h.** F

6. i. $a^m a^n = a^{m+n}$　　ii. $a^m b^m = (ab)^m$
　　iii. $(a^m)^n = a^{mn}$　　iv. $a^m \div a^n = a^{m-n}$

7. $x = -\frac{13}{3}$ in all four cases.

8. a. $\frac{3}{7}$　　**b.** $x < \frac{29}{22}$

Section 9.3

1. a. Cubic

b. Exponential

c. Quadratic

d. Linear

2.

3.

Chapter 9 Test

1. a. F **b.** T **c.** F **d.** F **e.** T **f.** F
 g. T **h.** F

2. a. i, ii, iii **b.** i, ii, iii **c.** i, iii **d.** i, iii **e.** i, ii, iii

3. a. $\frac{-23}{21}$ **b.** $\frac{-6}{55}$ **c.** $\frac{-1}{28}$

4. a. Commutativity and associativity
 b. Commutativity, distributivity, and identity for multiplication

5. a. $\left\{x \mid x > \frac{-12}{7}\right\}$ **b.** $\frac{177}{98}$

6. a. 729 **b.** 128 **c.** $\frac{1}{243}$

7. a.   **b.**

 c.

8. $14.1\%, \dfrac{7}{5}, \underline{1.41411411\ldots}, 1.\overline{41}, \sqrt{2}, 1.41\overline{42}$

9. a. 16 **b.** $6\sqrt{3}$ **c.** $7\sqrt{5}$ **d.** -1

10. $\dfrac{-3}{7} = \dfrac{-3}{7} \cdot \dfrac{-1}{-1} = \dfrac{(-3)(-1)}{7(-1)} = \dfrac{3}{-7}$

11. No. For example, $\frac{1}{-2} < \frac{-1}{3}$; however, $3 > 2$.

12. $\dfrac{1}{5^{-7}} = \dfrac{1}{(1/5^7)} = 5^7$

13.

$$2x + 3 = 9$$

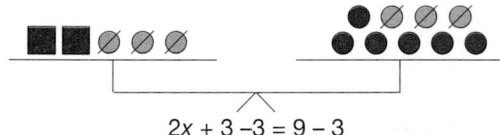

$$2x + 3 - 3 = 9 - 3$$

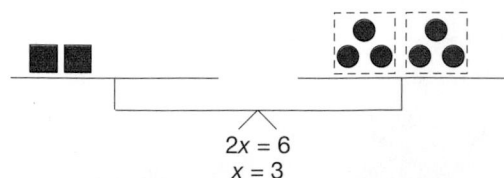

$$2x = 6$$
$$x = 3$$

14. Since $\sqrt{17}$ is irrational, it has a nonrepeating, nonterminating decimal representation. But $4.123105\overline{62}$ is repeating, so it is rational. Thus, the two numbers cannot be equal.

15. a. Exponential **b.** Quadratic **c.** Cubic

16. Suppose $\sqrt{8} = \dfrac{a}{b}$, where $\dfrac{a}{b}$ is a rational number. Then $8b^2 = a^2$. But this is impossible, since $8b^2 = 2^3 b^2$ has an odd number of prime factors, whereas a^2 has an even number.

17. 105

18. Only when $x = 0$ or when $a = b$

19. $t = 3$

20. $0.45455455545555\ldots, 0.45616116111\ldots, 0.46363663666\ldots$ (Answers may vary.)

21. Any a and b where both a and b are not zero.

22. $F(C) = 1.8C + 32$

Section 10.1A

1. a. 58, 63, 65, 67, 69, 70, 72, 72, 72, 74, 74, 76, 76, 76, 76, 78, 78, 80, 80, 80, 82, 85, 85, 86, 88, 92, 92, 93, 95, 98
 b. 58, 98 **c.** 76
 d.

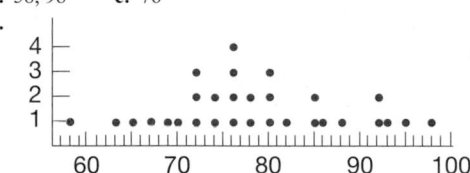

 e.

51–60	1
61–70	5
71–80	14
81–90	5
91–100	5

 f.

 g. 71–80
 h.

 i. For increment 5, 73 to 78 and 78 to 83 both have 6. For increment 8, 74 to 82 has 11. For increment 5, the 12 in 73–83 is close to the 11 in 74 to 82 for increment 8.

2.

15.	8 9
16.	1 3 4
17.	0 5
18.	1 2 5 5 5
19.	2 4
20.	2 3 6 9 9
21.	1 4 8
22.	0 0 1

3. a.

b.

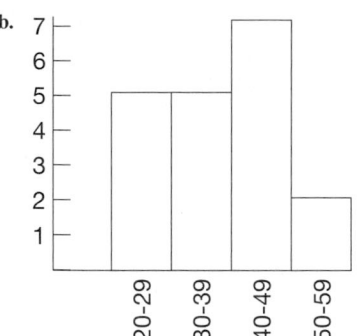

4. a.

CLASS 2		CLASS 1
	5	7 8 9
8 7 6	6	0 2
9 7 7 5	7	2 5 6 6 9
7 7 5 5 4 3 2	8	0 0 1 6 6 6 7
5 2 2 2 0 0	9	3 3 3

b. Class 2

5. a. $15,000,000   **b.** $5,000,000   **c.** $85,000,000

6. a.

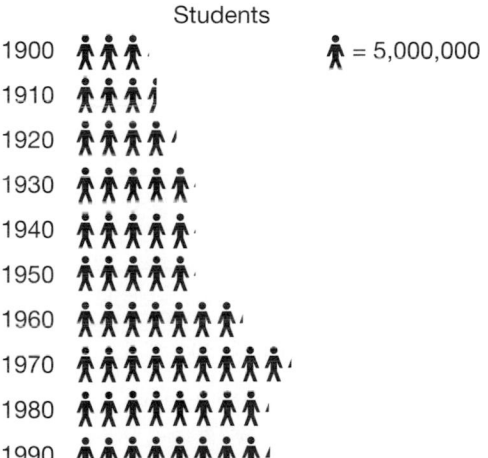

Students

1900
1910
1920
1930
1940
1950
1960
1970
1980
1990

= 5,000,000

Each stick figure represents 5,000,000 students

b. 1900s, 1910s, 1920s, 1950s, 1960s

c. Bar or line graph

7. a. Portland

b. 4 months; 0 month

c. December (6.0 inches); July (0.5 inch)

d. August (4.0 inches); January (2.7 inches)

e. New York City (40.3 inches) (Portland's total = 37.6 inches)

8. a.

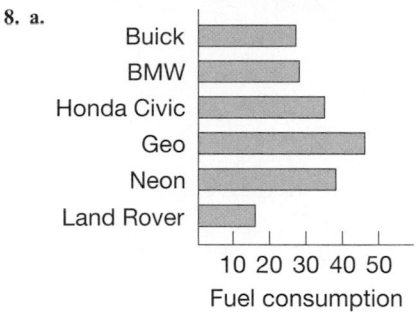

b. Land Rover; Geo

c. Geo; Land Rover

d. Buick, $3822.22; BMW, $3685.71; Honda Civic, $2948.57; Geo, $2243.48; Neon, $2715.79; Land Rover, $6450

e. A histogram could not be used because the categories on the horizontal axis are not numbers that can be broken into different intervals.

9. a.

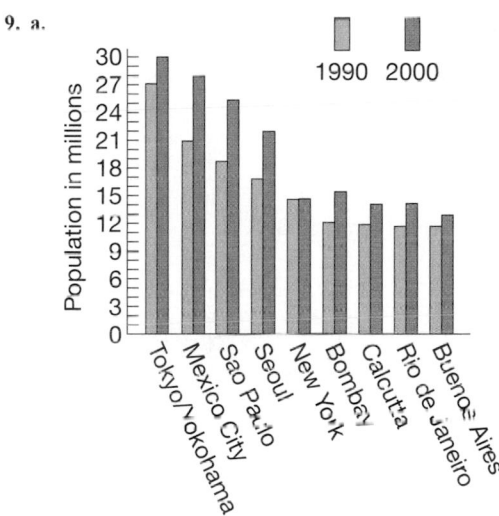

World's Largest Urban Areas
(*Source: World Almanac*)

b. Sao Paulo   **c.** New York

10. a.

b.

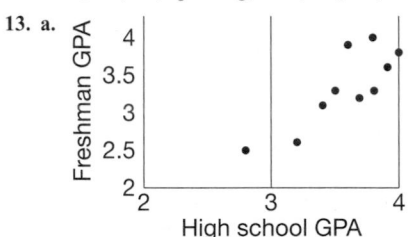

c. The first; the second

11. a. Taxes   **b.** 20.3%   **c.** 64°   **d.** Natural resources
   e. Social assistance, transportation, health and rehabilitation, and natural resources
   f. 23°, 26°

12. Grants to local governments, $1,269,000,000; salaries and fringe benefits, $1,161,000,000; grants to organizations and individuals, $873,000,000; operating, $621,000,000; other, $576,000,000

13. a.

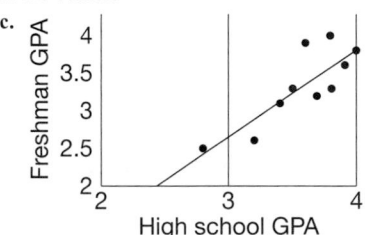

b. No outliers
c.

d. No outliers, so no change

14. a.

b. No outliers
c.

d. No outliers, so no change

15. a. and **b.**

c. They should look similar.

16. a. and **b.**

c. They should look similar.

17. a. 80 or 81   **b.** 85 to 87

18. a. Double bar graph or pictograph for comparing two sets of data.
b.

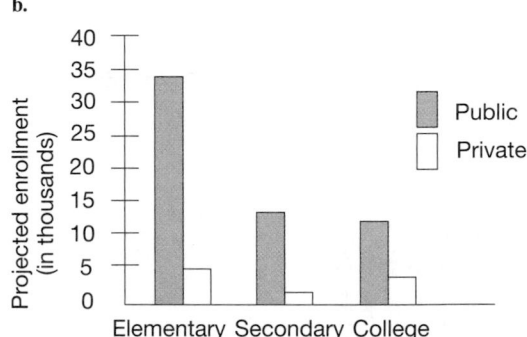

19. a. Circle graph—compare parts of a whole
b.

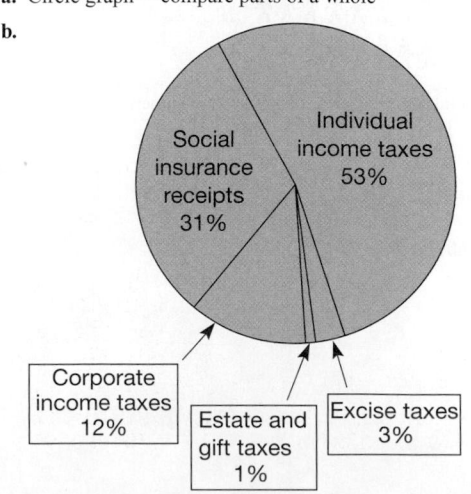

20. a. Double line graph or bar graph to show trends

b.

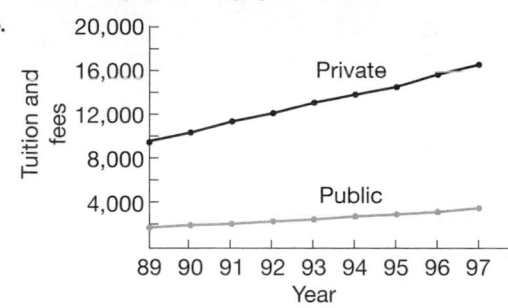

c. Private—graph is generally steeper

21. a. Bar graph or line graph to show a trend.

b.

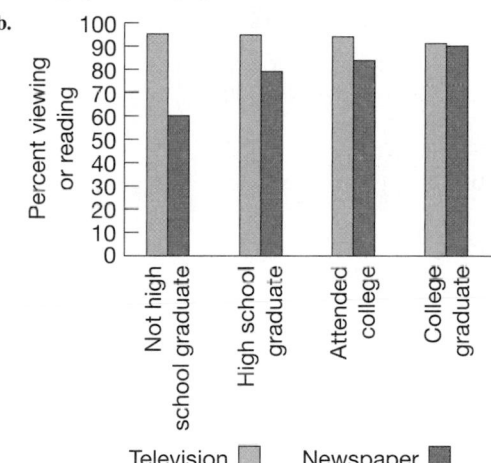

22. a. Multiple bar graph.

b.

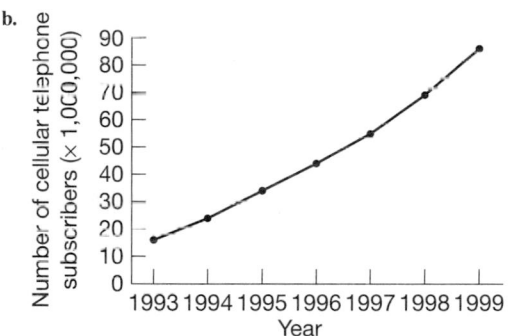

23. a. Multiple bar graph or line graph to show a trend

b.

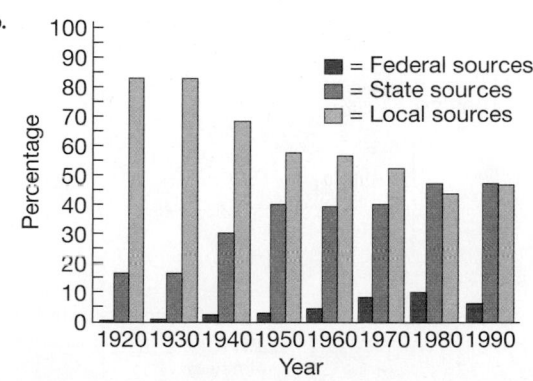

c. Federal funds increased steadily until sometime during the 1980s, then decreased. State funds increased steadily. Local funds decreased steadily until the 1980s and provide less than half of school funds.

24. a–b.

c. 6

25.

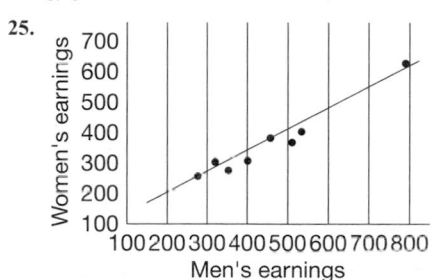

The median weekly salary for a woman is $400.

26. a. True　**b.** True

c. Suppose that $a^2 + b^2 + c^2 = d^2 + e^2 + f^2$. Show that $(10a + d)^2 + (10b + e)^2 + (10c + f)^2$ equals $(10d + a)^2 + (10e + b)^2 + (10f + c)^2$.

27. 4624, 6084, 6400, 8464

Section 10.2A

1. a. $9.8\overline{3}$; **9.5**; 9　　**b.** $14.1\overline{6}$; 13.5; no mode
c. $0.48\overline{3}$; 1.9; no mode　**d.** $-4.\overline{2}$; 0; 0

2. a. $3.\overline{3}$; 3.5; 5　　**b.** 6; 6; no mode
c. $11.5\overline{4}$; 12; 10　**d.** $-10/7$; 0; 5

3. No student is average overall. On the math test, Doug is closest to the mean; on the reading test, Rob is closest.

4. 584 students

5. a. {1}　**b.** {1, 7, 7}

6.

7. a.

b. Class 2; all five statistics are higher than their counterparts for Class 1.

8. a. 0; 0

   b. $6.\overline{6}$; 2.58 (to two places)

   c. 371.61; 19.28 (to two places)

9. a. 2; $\sqrt{2}$ **b.** 18; $3\sqrt{2}$ **c.** 50; $5\sqrt{2}$

   d. 72; $6\sqrt{2}$. If the variance is v and the standard deviation is s, and if all data are multiplied by r, the new variance is $r^2 v$ and the new standard deviation is $\sqrt{r^2} \cdot s$.

   e. Their standard deviations are all the same and all three sets of data are arithmetic sequences with a difference of 5.

10. 35; 30; 30; 275; 16.58 (to two places)

11. $-0.55, -1.76, 0.36, 1.71, -0.32, -0.1, 0.66$

12.

A trend toward greater growth west of the Mississippi

13. a.

```
7 | 14 55
6 | 60
5 | 04 11 12 12 21 21 34 36 48 63 73 86
4 | 07 11 14 26 28 42 52 57 65 75 75 93
```

   b. Aaron's and Ruth's totals are both mild outliers.

14. a. Fiftieth percentile

   b.

z-SCORE	PERCENTILE
1	84 or 85
2	98
−1	15 or 16
−2	2

15. 87th percentile

16. 23.8 or 24

17. Approximately 38.3

18. 293

19. 76.81 to two places

20. 1456

21. Test 1: her z-score (0.65) is slightly higher than on test 2 (0.63).

22. Mode, since this represents the most frequently sold size

23. a. The distribution with the smaller variance

   b. The distribution with the larger mean

24. a. 1.14 (to two places)

   b. 1.99 (to two places)

   c. 97.5%

25. Impossible to qualify

26. a. 1, 6, 12, 8, 0

   b. $4 \times 4 \times 4$; 8, 24, 24, 8, 0; $5 \times 5 \times 5$; 27, 54, 36, 8, 0

   c. $n \times n \times n$: $(n-2)^3, 6(n-2)^2, 12(n-2), 8, 0$

Section 10.3A

1. a.

   b. It makes the downward trend more apparent.

2. a.

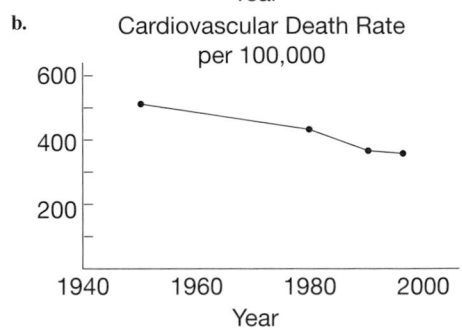

Cardiovascular Death Rate per 100,000

   b.

Cardiovascular Death Rate per 100,000

3.

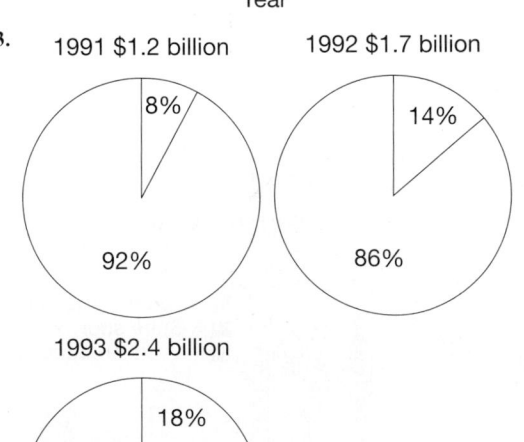

1991 $1.2 billion

1992 $1.7 billion

1993 $2.4 billion

It gives the impression that every graph represents the same amount of money.

4.

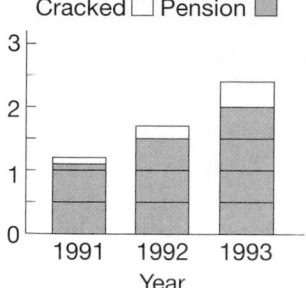

Cracked Nest Eggs
Cracked ☐ Pension ▨

5. a. Yes   **b.** Different vertical scale   **c.** i.   **d.** ii.

6.

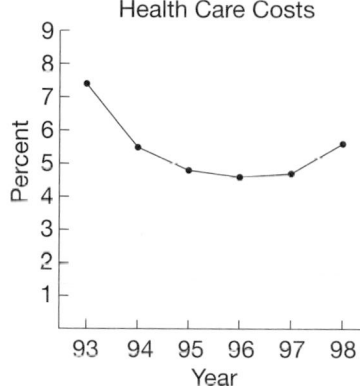

Year-to-Year Increases in Health Care Costs

7.

New Car Sales

8.

1998

9. a.

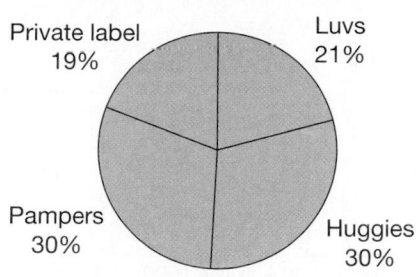

52 weeks ending June 13, 1992

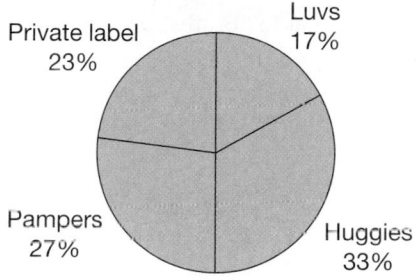

52 weeks ending December 11, 1993

  b. New ones represent relative amounts more accurately.
  c. No

10. Cropped vertical axis, horizontal instead of vertical bars, reverse the order of the categories.

11. a. (ii), (iii), and (iv).
  b. In (i), the volume represented on the right is actually 8 times as large.

12. Population = set of lightbulbs manufactured.
Sample = package of 8 chosen.

13. Population = set of full-time students enrolled at the university.
Sample = set of 100 students chosen to be interviewed.

14. a. $\sqrt{2}$ or about 1.4 in. Because the graphs are two-dimensional, their revenues vary as the square of their radii and $1^2 : \sqrt{2}^2 = 1:2 = 5,000,000:10,000,000$.
  b. $\sqrt[3]{2}$ or about 1.3 in. Because the graphs are three-dimensional, their revenues vary as the cube of their radii and $1^3 : \sqrt[3]{2}^3 = 1:2 = 5,000,000:10,000,000$.

15.

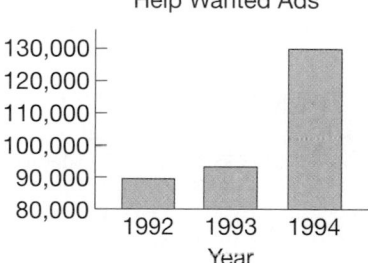

Help Wanted Ads

16.

Federal Tax Burden per Capita

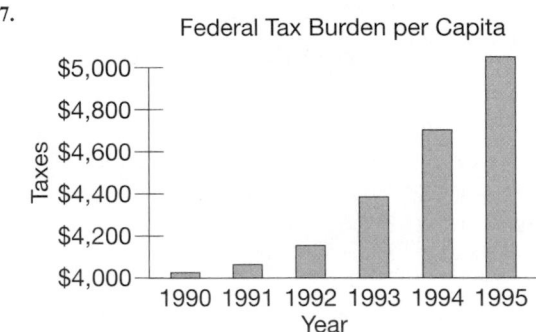

17.

Federal Tax Burden per Capita

18.

Agricultural Prices

19. Population = the set of fish in the lake. Sample = the 500 fish that are caught and are examined for tags. Bias results from the fact that some of the tagged fish may be caught or die before the sample is taken and the fish might not re-distribute throughout the lake.

20. Population = set of all doctors. Sample = the set of 20 doctors chosen. Bias results from the fact that they will commission studies until they get the result they want.

PROBLEMS WHERE THE STRATEGY "LOOK FOR A FORMULA" IS USEFUL

1. The first allowance yields $7 + 21 + 35 + \cdots + 7(2 \cdot 30 - 1)$, which equals $7(1 + 3 + 5 + \cdots + 59)$. Since $1 + 3 + 5 + \cdots + (2n - 1) = n^2$ and 59 is $2 \cdot 30 - 1$, the total is $7 \cdot 30^2 = \$63$. The other way, the total is $30 \cdot 2 = \$60$. He should choose the first way.

2. Let x be its original height. Its height after several days would be given by $x\left(\dfrac{3}{2}\right)\left(\dfrac{4}{3}\right)\left(\dfrac{5}{4}\right) \cdots$. One can see that the product of these fractions leads to this formula: $x\left(\dfrac{3}{2}\right)\left(\dfrac{4}{3}\right)\left(\dfrac{5}{4}\right) \cdots \left(\dfrac{n+1}{n}\right) = \dfrac{n+1}{2}$.

Therefore, since $\dfrac{n+1}{2} > 100$ when $n + 1 > 200$, or when $n > 199$, it would take 199 days.

3. Pairing the first ray on the right with the remaining rays would produce 99 angles. Pairing the second ray on the right with the remaining ones would produce 98 angles. Continuing in this way, we obtain $99 + 98 + 97 + \cdots + 1$ such angles. But this sum is $(100 \cdot 99)/2$ or 4950. Thus 4950 different angles are formed.

CHAPTER REVIEW
Section 10.1

1.

CLASS 1		CLASS 2
	1	7
3 3	2	5 9
9 7	3	9
1	4	0 0 0 0 9
	5	1 2 2
	6	
9 8 6 4 4 2	7	
2 1 0	8	0 5 9
6 4 4 4 0	9	2 5 7 7 9

2.

3.

4.

5.

6.

Sporting Good Sales vs. Rain

The point (18, 340) is an outlier.
Fifteen inches of rain should correspond to $245,000 in sales.
For sales of $260,000, the rain should be around 13.5 inches.

Section 10.2

1. Mode = 14, median = 9, mean = 8.4

2.

1 3   9   14

3. Range = 13, variance = 23.42, standard deviation = 4.84

4. $2: -1.27$; $5: -0.68$; $14: 1.11$

5. It represents a data point's number of standard deviations away
from the mean in which above the mean is positive and below the
mean is negative.

6. 68%

7. 95%

8. 2 is the 10th or 11th percentile.
5 is the 25th percentile.
14 is the 86th or 87th percentile.

Section 10.3

1.

2. a.

b.

3.

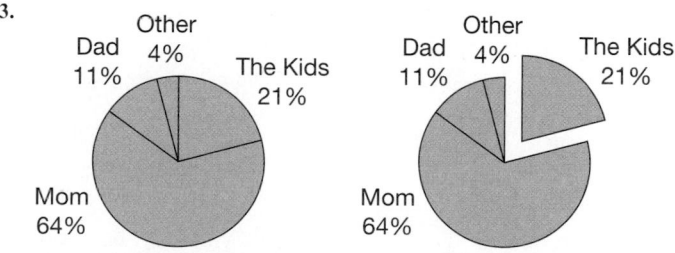

Who makes the kids' lunch?   Who makes the kids' lunch?

4. Because the size of the people in the "marry" category is larger, it gives the section a much more dominant appearance over the small person representing the "live alone" category. Answers may vary.

5. Population: all voters in town. Sample: adult passersby near high school. Bias: Since the most in-line skaters are high school–aged students, people near the high school are more likely to have a polarized opinion about the issue.

6. Local dentists may be more likely to use a local product than dentists across the country.

Chapter 10 Test

1. **a.** F   **b.** F   **c.** F   **d.** F   **e.** T   **f.** T
   g. F   **h.** T   **i.** F   **j.** F   **k.** F

2. Measures of central tendency: mean, median, mode
   Measures of dispersion: variance, standard deviation

3. Bar and line graphs are good for comparisons and trends and circle graphs are not.

   Circle graphs are good for relative amounts, not for trends.

4. 108°

5. Mean is 6; median is 6; mode is 3; range is 7.

6. 11, 14, 20, 23

7. 5.55

8. The lineman is in the 98th percentile and the receiver is in the 8th percentile.

9.

10.

11. **a.**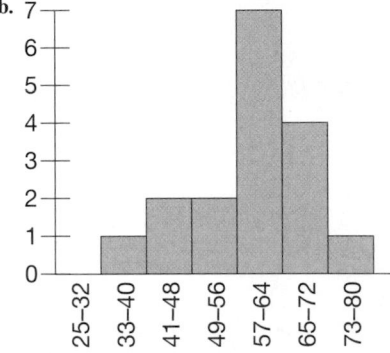

   b.

12. Population: families with school-aged children in school system
    Sample: families of 200 students with home addresses

13. 0, 6, 6, 7, 8, 9. There are many other possibilities.

14. 3, 3 (Actually, any *single* nonzero number is a correct answer.)

15. The professor may look at both of them to determine how to assign grades depending on the distribution. The histogram in part (a) would indicate 4 A grades and 7 B grades while the histogram in part (b) would indicate 1 A grade and 4 B grades. The histogram in part (b) also gives a better sense of how dispersed the scores are. Answers may vary.

16. To indicate an increase (or decrease) in the data being measured, sometimes the size of the picture in the pictograph is incorrectly increased instead of the number of pictures being increased. Answers may vary.

17. The data set {4, 5, 6} has a mean of 5 and a standard deviation of $\sqrt{\frac{2}{3}}$, while the data set {0, 5, 10} has a mean of 5 and a standard deviation of $5\sqrt{\frac{2}{3}}$.

    Answers may vary.

18. Line graphs can be deceptive by cropping either the vertical or horizontal axis. They are also distorted by making the graph excessively narrow or wide. Answers may vary.

19. A line graph could be good to display this data because it shows the trend over time

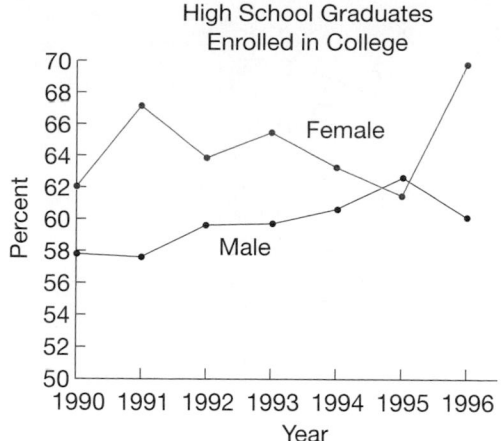

High School Graduates Enrolled in College

or a bar graph could be good to display the year to year comparisons.

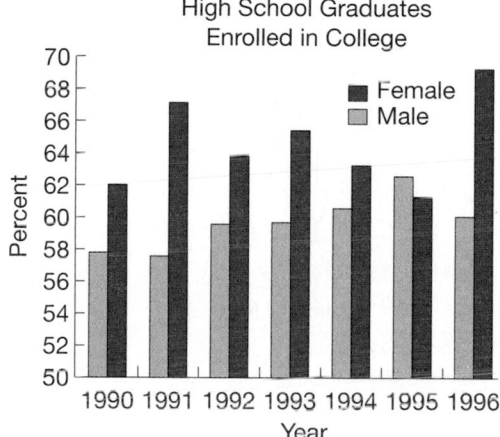

High School Graduates Enrolled in College

20.

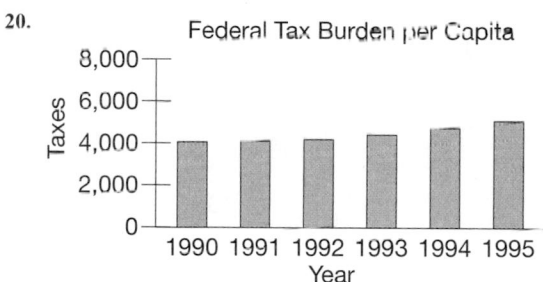

Federal Tax Burden per Capita

21. 15

22. 23

23. Science, since its z-score is the highest

24. Customers are more likely to prefer the lemon-lime so that they will be on television and to please the people making the commercial.

25. Because the picture of the men's lacrosse player is larger, it gives the upper graphs a more dominant effect. Also the width of the bars representing the men's champions is greater, so the bar for the 4 championships for Syracuse looks more than 2 times as large as the bar for the 2 championships for Temple. Answers may vary.

Section 11.1A

1. (c)

2. a. {H, T}   **b.** {A, B, C, D, E, F}   **c.** {1, 2, 3, 4}
   d. {red, yellow, blue}

3. a. {HHHH, HHHT, HHTH, HTHH, THHH, HHTT, HTHT, THHT, HTTH, THTH, TTHH, HTTT, THTT, TTHT, TTTH, TTTT}
   b. {HHHH, HHHT, HHTH, HTHH, HHTT, HTHT, HTTH, HTTT}
   c. {HHHT, HHTH, HTHH, THHH}
   d. Same as part (a)
   e. {HHTH, HHTT, THTH, THTT}

4. a. {1, 2, 3, 4, 5, 6, 7, 8, 9, 10, 11, 12}   **b.** {2, 4, 6, 8, 10, 12}
   c. {1, 2, 3, 4, 5, 6, 7}   **d.** {6, 12}   **e.** ∅

5. a. P   **b.** I   **c.** I

6. {(H, 1), (H, 2), (H, 3), (H, 4), (T, 1), (T, 2), (T, 3), (T, 4)}

7. a. $\frac{12}{60} = \frac{1}{5}$ **b.** $\frac{28}{60} = \frac{7}{15}$ **c.** $\frac{31}{60}$

8. a. $\frac{1}{6}$ **b.** $\frac{9}{36} = \frac{1}{4}$ **c.** $\frac{21}{36} = \frac{7}{12}$ **d.** 0   **e.** 1

9. a. Point up is generally more likely
   b. $\frac{42}{60} = \frac{7}{10}; \frac{18}{60} = \frac{3}{10}$ **c.** 70; 30

10. a. $\frac{1}{5}$ **b.** $\frac{2}{5}$ **c.** $\frac{3}{5}$ **d.** $\frac{2}{5}$

11. a. $\frac{1}{2}$ **b.** $\frac{11}{12}$ **c.** $\frac{5}{12}$ **d.** $\frac{13}{18}$ **e.** $\frac{5}{18}$

12. a. $\frac{3}{8}$ **b.** $\frac{1}{2}$(or $\frac{3}{6}$)

13. a. $\frac{1}{3}$ **b.** $\frac{2}{3}$ **c.** $\frac{2}{3}$ **d.** $\frac{1}{3}$

14. a. $\frac{3}{4}$ **b.** $\frac{4}{13}$ **c.** $\frac{11}{26}$ **d.** $\frac{4}{13}$

15. a. $\frac{7}{16}$ **b.** $\frac{12}{16} = \frac{3}{4}$

16. a. Getting a blue on the first spin or a yellow on one spin; $\frac{10}{16} = \frac{5}{8}$
   b. Getting a yellow on both spins: $\frac{1}{16}$
   c. Not getting a yellow on either spin: $\frac{9}{16}$

17. a. Probability that the student is a sophomore or is taking English
   b. Probability that the student is a sophomore taking English
   c. Probability that the student is not a sophomore

18. a. 4, 5, 6, 5, 4, 3, 2, 1   **b.** $\frac{5}{12}, \frac{1}{3}, \frac{1}{4}, \frac{11}{12}$

19. a. 100   **b.** 20   **c.** $\frac{20}{100} = \frac{1}{5}$

20. $\frac{1}{16}$

Section 11.2A

1. a.

b.

c.

d.

2. a.

b.

c.

3. a.

b.

4. a–d.

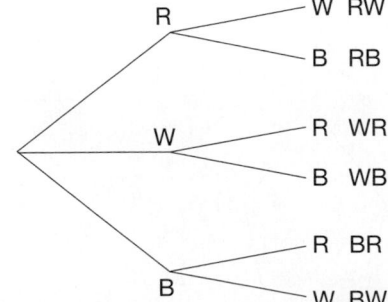

e. 6 outcomes

5. a.

b. 8   **c.** $4 \cdot 2 = 8$, yes

6. a.   **b.**

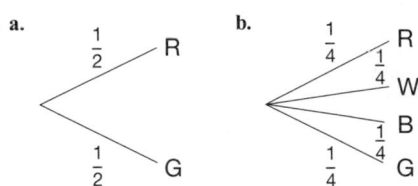

c.

7. a. $R: \frac{2}{5}, W: \frac{3}{5}$ **b.** $B: \frac{1}{3}, G: \frac{2}{3}$

8. a. $A: \frac{1}{3}, B: \frac{1}{3}, C: \frac{1}{3}$ **b.** $A: \frac{1}{3}, B: \frac{1}{6}, C: \frac{1}{2}$
c. $A: \frac{1}{4}, B: \frac{1}{4}, C: \frac{1}{2}$

9. a. Number of ways of getting 0 heads (1), 1 head (4), 2 heads (6), 3 heads (4), or 4 heads (1)
b. $\frac{4}{16} = \frac{1}{4}$ **c.** $\frac{15}{16}$ **d.** Against

10. a. $10 \times 10 = 100$
b. $9 \times 10 \times 10 = 900$
c. $10 \times 9 \times 8 \times 7 = 5040$
d. $9 \times 10 \times 10 \times 10 \times 10 = 90,000$

11. a. $8 \cdot 7 \cdot 6 = 336$ **b.** $3 \cdot 2 \cdot 1 = 6$ **c.** $\frac{6}{336} = \frac{1}{56}$

12. a.

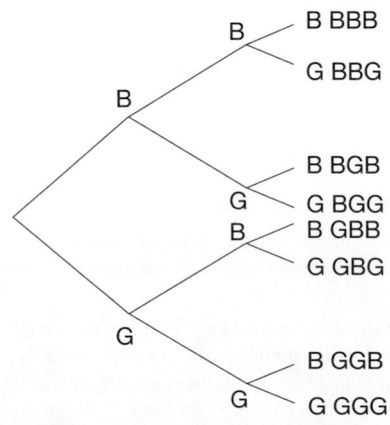

b. 1; 3; 3; 1
c. They are the 1, 3, 3, 1, row

13. a. $1, 4, 6, 4, 1; \frac{1}{16}, \frac{1}{4}, \frac{3}{8}, \frac{1}{4}, \frac{1}{16}$ **b.** 3 hits and 1 miss

14. a. Each branch has probability of $\frac{1}{2}$

  b. $\frac{1}{2} \times \frac{1}{2} = \frac{1}{4}$ (top branch), $\frac{1}{2} \times \frac{1}{2} \times \frac{1}{2} = \frac{1}{8}$ (*LPP*)

  c. (i) $\frac{1}{8} + \frac{1}{8} = \frac{1}{4}$ (*PLL* and *LPL*), (ii) $\frac{1}{8} + \frac{1}{8} + \frac{1}{4} = \frac{1}{2}$ (*LPP*, *PLP*, and *PP*), (iii) $\frac{1}{8} + \frac{1}{8} + \frac{1}{8} + \frac{1}{8} = \frac{1}{2}$ (*LPL*, *LPP*, *PLL*, and *PLP*)

15. a. $\frac{2}{5}$ **b.** $L = \frac{3}{5}, P = \frac{2}{5}$ **c.** $\frac{4}{25}$ **d.** $\frac{18}{125}$
  e. $\frac{12}{25}$ **f.** $\frac{81}{125}$

16. a. $\dfrac{2}{3}$ for each branch; $\dfrac{8}{27}$

  b. Both paths have probability $\left(\dfrac{2}{3}\right)^3\left(\dfrac{1}{3}\right) = \dfrac{8}{81}$;
  $$\frac{8}{81} + \frac{8}{81} + \frac{8}{81} = \frac{8}{27}$$

  c. *BBAAA, BABAA, BAABA, ABBAA, ABABA, AABBA*;
  $$\left(\frac{2}{3}\right)^3\left(\frac{1}{3}\right)^2 = \frac{8}{243}; \frac{16}{81}$$

  d. $\dfrac{8}{27} + \dfrac{8}{27} + \dfrac{16}{81} = \dfrac{64}{81}; \dfrac{17}{81}$

17. a.

  b. 8   **c.** 1   **d.** $\frac{1}{8}$

18. a.

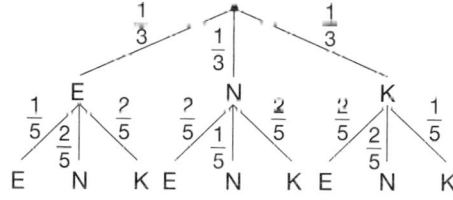

  b. $\{(E, E), (E, N), (E, K), (N, E), (N, N), (N, K), (K, E), (K, N), (K, K)\}$

  c. $\{(E, E), (N, N), (K, K)\}$

  d. $\frac{1}{5}$ **e.** $\frac{1}{15}$

19. 4 socks

20. $\frac{6}{7}$. This is the probability of having at least one male among three puppies given that one is a female.

21. $\frac{37}{55}$

22. (a) 78 (b) 170

Section 11.3A

1. (a) Answers will vary. **(b)** Answers will vary, but theoretically it should take about 22 attempts.

2. Average should be near 22.

3. Answers will vary; theoretical value is $0.6\overline{3}$.

4. a. $\frac{22}{100} = \frac{11}{50}$ **b.** Answers will vary.

5. a. On a standard die, let a boy be an even number and a girl be an odd number. Toss a die until you get one of each and count the number of tosses.
  b. 3
  c. Let a boy be 0 and a girl be 1. "Draw" until you get one of each. Count the number of draws.

6. 750

7. 47,350 people

8. a. \$2.50   **b.** \$1.50   **c.** \$3.50

9. a. \$40.00   **b.** \$25   **c.** Scholarship *A*

10. They each equal 1:1, so are equivalent.

11. a. (i) 6:30 or 1:5, (ii) 33:3 or 11:1, (iii) 18:18 or 1:1
  b. (i) 5:1, (ii) 1:11, (iii) 1:1

12. a. $\frac{1}{6}$ **b.** 1:5   **c.** 5:1

13. a. 3:2, 2:3   **b.** 1:3, 3:1   **c.** 5:1, 1:5

14. a. $\frac{9}{10}$ **b.** $\frac{2}{7}$ **c.** $\frac{12}{17}$

15. For example, the sum is
  a. even.   **b.** 7.   **c.** 5 or 6.

16. a. $\frac{8}{15}$ **b.** $\frac{6}{15} = \frac{2}{5}$ **c.** $\frac{1}{2}$ **d.** $\frac{3}{8}$

17. a. $\frac{1}{6}$ **b.** $\frac{1}{3}$ **c.** 0

18. a. $\frac{2}{7}$ **b.** $\frac{5}{7}$ **c.** $\frac{4}{7}$

19. a. $\frac{1}{3}$ **b.** $\frac{1}{4}$ **c.** $\frac{1}{5}$ **d.** $\frac{1}{2}$ **e.** 1   **f.** 0

20. a. $\frac{3}{5}$ **b.** $\frac{11}{12}$ **c.** $\frac{31}{60}$ **d.** 1   **e.** $\frac{31}{55}$ **f.** $\frac{31}{36}$

21. a. Disagree to be correct.
  b. p^4 **c.** q^4 **d.** $p^4 + q^4$
  e. For $1:1 - \frac{1}{2}, \frac{1}{2}, \frac{1}{16}, \frac{1}{16}, \frac{1}{8} = 0.13$;
  for $2:1 - \frac{2}{3}, \frac{1}{3}, \frac{16}{81}, \frac{1}{81}, \frac{17}{81} = 0.21$;
  for $3:1 - \frac{3}{4}, \frac{1}{4}, \frac{81}{256}, \frac{1}{256}, \frac{82}{256} = 0.32$;
  for $3:2 - \frac{3}{5}, \frac{2}{5}, \frac{81}{625}, \frac{16}{625}, \frac{97}{625} = 0.15$.
  f. The prospect for series longer than 4 games is greater when teams are evenly matched.

22. a. $p^4q; 4p^4q$ **b.** $4pq^4$ **c.** $4p^4q + 4pq^4$

23. a. $10p^4q^2$ **b.** $10p^2q^4$ **c.** $10p^4q^2 + 10p^2q^4$

24. a. $20p^4q^3$ **b.** $20p^3q^4$ **c.** $20p^4q^3 + 20p^3q^4$

25. a. For $X = 4, p^4, q^4, p^4 + q^4$; for $X = 5, 4p^4q, 4pq^4, 4p^4q + 4pq^4$; for $X = 6, 10p^4q^2, 10p^2q^4, 10p^4q^2 + 10p^2q^4$; for $X = 7, 20p^4q^3, 20p^3q^4, 20p^4q^3 + 20p^3q^4$
  b. 0.125, 0.25, 0.3125, 0.3125
  c. 5.8 games

26. Select numbers 1–5. Have the computer draw until all 5 numbers appear. Record the number of draws needed. This is one trial. Repeat at least 100 times and average the number of rolls needed in all the trials. Your average should be around 11. Theoretical expected value = 11.42.

Section 11.4A

1. a. 90   **b.** 495   **c.** 60,480   **d.** 15

2. a. $m = 9, n = 3$ **b.** $m = 13, n = 1$

3. a. 15,600,000   **b.** 11,232,000

4. a. 64,000   **b.** 59,280   **c.** 60,840
  d. The order of the numbers is important

5. a. $_{12}C_5 = 792$ **b.** $_{52}C_5 = 2,598,960$

6. a. $_4C_0 = \dfrac{4!}{(4-0)!0!} = 1$; $_4C_1 = \dfrac{4!}{(4-1)!1!} = 4$, and so on

b. $_5C_3 = \dfrac{5!}{3!\,2!} = 10$, $_4C_2 = \dfrac{4!}{2!\,2!} = 6$.

$_4C_3 = \dfrac{4!}{3!\,1!} = 4$, and $10 = 6 + 4$

c. $_nC_{r-1} + {}_nC_r = \dfrac{n!}{(r-1)!(n-r+1)!} + \dfrac{n!}{r!(n-r)!}$

$= \dfrac{n!\,r}{r!(n-r+1)!} + \dfrac{n!(n-r+1)}{r!(n-r+1)!}$

$= \dfrac{(n+1)!}{r!(n+1-r)!} = {}_{n+1}C_r$

d. Each "inside" entry is equal to the sum of the nearest two entries above it.

7. a. $\dfrac{_{10}C_9}{2^{10}}$ **b.** $\dfrac{_{10}C_7}{2^{10}}$ **c.** $\dfrac{_{10}C_5}{2^{10}}$ **d.** $\dfrac{_{10}C_3}{2^{10}}$ **e.** $\dfrac{_{10}C_1}{2^{10}}$

8. $_8C_5 = 56$

9. $\dfrac{_8C_3}{2^8} = \dfrac{7}{32}$

10. a. $\dfrac{_{10}C_4}{_{27}C_4} = \dfrac{7}{585}$ **b.** $\dfrac{_{17}C_4}{_{27}C_4} = \dfrac{238}{1755}$

11. a. 1680 **b.** $\dfrac{3}{56}$

12. a. $\dfrac{6}{26^3}$ **b.** $\dfrac{1}{26^3}$

13. $4! = 24$

14. a. $m = n = 5$ **b.** $m = 10, n = 4$

15. a. 376,992 **b.** 1,947,792

16. a. 10! **b.** 10! **c.** $_{10}C_8 \cdot 8!$ **d.** $_{10}C_5 \cdot 5!$
e. $_{10}C_r \cdot r!$

17. a. 10! **b.** 9! **c.** $5 \cdot 9!$ **d.** $25 \cdot 8!$

18. a. 5! **b.** 4! **c.** $2 \cdot 4!$ **d.** $2 \cdot 3 \cdot 3!$

19. a. $\dfrac{20!}{15!\,5!} = \dfrac{20!}{5!\,15!}$ **b.** $\dfrac{n!}{(n-r)!\,r!} = \dfrac{n!}{r!(n-r)!}$
c. 99,884,400

20. a. 9! **b.** 6! **c.** 2 **d.** 8 **e.** 96

21. a. $_{15}C_4 = 1365$ **b.** $\dfrac{364}{1365}$ **c.** $\dfrac{78}{1365}$

22. a. $\dfrac{48}{_{52}C_5}$ **b.** $\dfrac{24}{_{52}C_5}$ **c.** $\dfrac{_{13}C_5}{_{52}C_5}$ **d.** $\dfrac{4^5}{_{52}C_5}$

23. a. $_{20}C_5$ **b.** $\dfrac{3 \cdot {}_{17}C_4}{_{20}C_5} = 0.46$

c. $\dfrac{_3C_1 \cdot {}_{17}C_4 + {}_3C_2 \cdot {}_{17}C_3}{_{20}C_5} = 0.59$

PROBLEMS WHERE THE STRATEGY "DO A SIMULATION" IS USEFUL

1. Sketch a hexagon, flip coins, and play the game several times to determine the experimental probability of winning.

2. Toss a die twice. If a 1 or a 2 turns up on the die, the man received his coat. Toss it again. If a 1 or 2 turns up, the woman received her coat. Repeat several times. Another simulation could be done using pieces of paper labeled 1 through 6.

3. Using your textbook, perform several trials of this situation to determine the experimental probability.

CHAPTER REVIEW

Section 11.1

1. a. $S = \{(H, A), (H, B), (H, C), (T, A), (T, B), (T, C)\}$
b. $E = \{(H, A), (H, B)\}$
c. $P(E) = \dfrac{2}{6} = \dfrac{1}{3}$
d. $\overline{E} = \{(H, C), (T, A), (T, B), (T, C)\}$
e. $P(\overline{E}) = \dfrac{4}{6} = \dfrac{2}{3}$
f. $P(E) + P(\overline{E}) = 1$

2. a. E = toss a sum less than 13 on a pair of standard dice
b. E = toss a sum of 13 on a pair of standard dice.

3. Theoretical probability is the probability that should occur under perfect conditions. Experimental probability is the probability that occurs when an experiment is performed.

4. For example, E and $\overline{E}$ as listed in Exercise 1 are mutually exclusive, since $E \cap \overline{E} = \varnothing$.

Section 11.2

1.

```
        R
    R   R
        G
        R
    R   R
        G
        R
    G   R
        G
```

2. There are 3 equally likely outcomes for each of the two spins. Thus there are $3 \times 3 = 9$ outcomes.

3. a.

```
              1
            1   1
          1   2   1
        1   3   3   1
      1   4   6   4   1
    1   5   10   10   5   1
```

b. Toss 5 coins.
c. The number of ways to obtain 3 heads and 2 tails when tossing 5 coins

4. a.

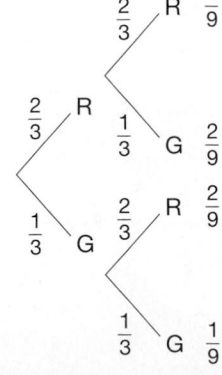

b. The probabilities along successive branches are multiplied to obtain the $\frac{4}{9}, \frac{2}{9}, \frac{2}{9}$, and $\frac{1}{9}$.

c. To find, for example, the probability of spinning RG or GR, you find $\frac{2}{9} + \frac{2}{9} = \frac{4}{9}$.

Section 11.3

1. If $a:b$ are the odds in favor of an event, then $b:a$ are the odds against the event.

2. If $P(E) = \dfrac{a}{b}$, then the odds in favor of E are $a:(b - a)$.

3. 12:24 or 1:2

4. 43:57

5. When a special condition is imposed on the sample space

6. $\frac{11}{30}$

7. $1\frac{7}{12}$, or about $1.58

8. a. Testing to see how many times one must shoot an arrow to hit an apple on your professor's head
b. Use the digits 1, 2, 3, 4, 5, 6 to represent the faces of the dice, disregarding 0, 7, 8, 9.

Section 11.4

1. a. F   **b.** T   **c.** F   **d.** F   **e.** T

2. a. $_{12}C_7 = 792$ **b.** $_9C_6 + {}_{11}C_7 = 414$ **c.** $\dfrac{_{10}C_5}{_{12}C_7} = \dfrac{252}{792}$

3. a. 5040   **b.** 5005   **c.** 120   **d.** 495

4. $_{10}P_{10} = 10! = 3,628,800$

5. a. $_9C_2 \cdot {}_5C_4 = 36 \cdot 5 = 180$
b. Any team of 6 players can be seated in $_6P_6 = 6! = 720$ ways in a line.
c. $\dfrac{_8C_1 \cdot {}_4C_3}{_9C_2 \cdot {}_5C_4} = \dfrac{32}{180} = \dfrac{8}{45}$

6. a. $5 \cdot 8 = 40$ **b.** $5 \cdot 8 \cdot 2 = 80$

7. a. 8 for $n = 3$, 16 for $n = 4$, 32 for $n = 5$
b. 64, 1024, $2^{20} = 1,048,576$, 2^n
c. It is the sum of the entries in row n.

Chapter 11 Test

1. a. F   **b.** T   **c.** F   **d.** F   **e.** T   **f.** F
g. F   **h.** F   **i.** F   **j.** F   **k.** T

2. The event is a subset of the sample space.

3. When drawing from a container, an object is drawn and not replaced before drawing a second object.

4. 144

5. $\frac{47}{56}$

6. $\frac{5}{12}$

7. $\frac{5}{11}$

8. a. 120   **b.** 2520   **c.** 495

9. a. 19,656,000   **b.** $\frac{1}{650}$

10. a.

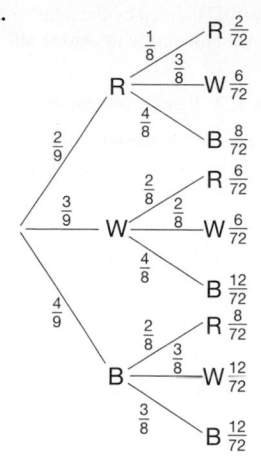

b. $\frac{2}{9}$ **c.** $\frac{30}{72}$ **d.** $\frac{52}{72}$ **e.** $\frac{11}{12}$

11. a.

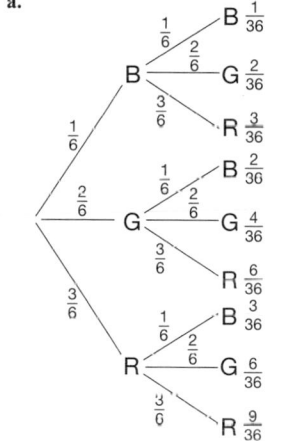

b. $\frac{1}{36}$ **c.** $\frac{11}{36}$

12. $1 = P(A \cup \overline{A}) = P(A) + P(\overline{A})$; therefore, $P(\overline{A}) = 1 - P(A)$

13. Both can be used to find the total number of outcomes in an event.

14.

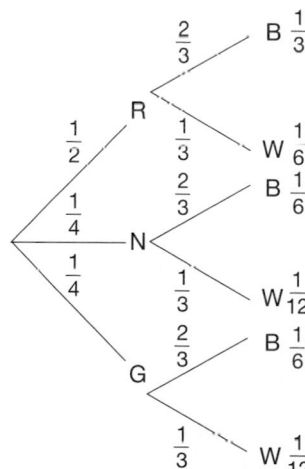

15. In a bag place 4 pieces of paper numbered 1–4. Draw from the bag 7 times (with replacement), keeping track of which numbers are drawn. At the end of the 7 draws, if all 4 numbers have been drawn, record a "yes" for the trial. Repeat this process at least 20 times, recording "yes" or "no" at the end of each trial. After all of the trials, compute the number of "yeses" divided by the number of trials. This will be the experimental probability of getting all 4 prizes in 7 tries.

16. The odds of getting the numbers 1, 2, 3, or 4. Answers may vary.

17. Merle is correct because in order to have a one-third probability in this situation, each outcome would have to be equally likely, and that is not the case.

18. a. 24   **b.** $\frac{11}{24}$

19. $\frac{537}{1024}$

20.

SUMS n	2	3	4	5	6	7	8	9	10	11	12
WAYS	1	2	3	4	5	6	5	4	3	2	1
$14 - n$	12	11	10	9	8	7	6	5	4	3	2

Note the symmetry in this table.

21. $\frac{1}{4}$

22. $\dfrac{26}{26^3} = \dfrac{1}{26^2}$

23. $.50

Section 12.1A

1. Arrow D

2. Same length in both cases

3. 12 triangles

4. 18

5. a. b, d **b.** a, c, e, f **c.** a, e **d.** d, f

6.

7. a.

b.

8. a.   **b.**

9.

10. a.

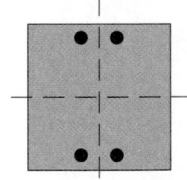

b. Several possibilities exist for each part.

11. a. FHQO
b. ADPK, and so on
c. KQHI, and so on
d. ABL, FGH, OPQ
e. MNO, MOS, COM
f. MNOS
g. COSM, CONM
h. CLK, and so on
i. CAL, ROP
j. DEFO, MORK, KQHJ, and so on
k. BCKL

12. a. (ii), draw a diagonal   **b.** (i), rotate $\frac{1}{2}$ turn

13. a. 3   **b.** 2

14. Both types of lines

15. All but (c)

16. a. 12   **b.** 4   **c.** 1   **d.** 1

17. a.   **b.**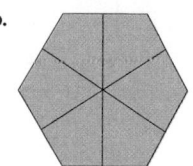

Section 12.2A

1. (d)

2. a. 5 lines   **b.** 6 lines   **c.** 7 lines   **d.** 8 lines
e. n lines

3. a. Vertex, midpoint
b. Vertex, vertex, midpoint, midpoint

4. a. 2   **b.** 180°

5. a. S, N **b.** S **c.** None   **d.** C, S, N

6.

7.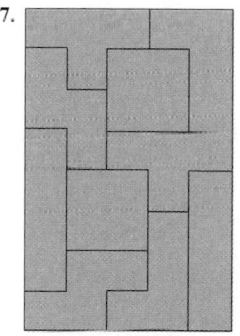

8. a. (i)
b. (iii), equilateral triangles inside isosceles
c. (ii), intersection is "isosceles right triangles"
d. (i), equilateral triangles have 60° angles

9. Flip the tracing over so that point A of the tracing is matched with point D and point B of the tracing is matched with point C. Then diagonal $\overline{AC}$ of the tracing will coincide with diagonal $\overline{DB}$.

10. Rotate $\frac{1}{4}, \frac{1}{2}, \frac{3}{4}$, and 1 full turn around the center.

11. Rotate $\frac{1}{3}, \frac{2}{3}$, and 1 full turn around the center.

12. Fold one diagonal along itself so that opposite vertices coincide. Then the other diagonal lies along the fold line.

13. a. Fold on diagonal $\overline{AC}$. Then $\angle ADC$ coincides with $\angle ABC$. $\angle A$ is not necessarily congruent to $\angle C$.
b. *Both* pairs of opposite angles are congruent, since a rhombus is a kite in two ways.

Section 12.3A

1. a. 10   **b.** 4   **c.** 6

2. a. Right   **b.** Acute

3. a. 20   **b.** 6   **c.** 10   **d.** 2   **e.** 8

4. a.   **b.**
c. Not possible

5. a. 30°   **b.** 20°   **c.** 60°   **d.** Not possible

6. a. $m(\angle C) = 62°$, $\overline{AC} = 6.3$ cm
b. $m(\angle C) = 110°$, $\overline{AC} = 3.8$ cm

7. $m(\angle AFB) = 60°$, $m(\angle CFD) = 35°$

8. $m(\angle 1) = 54°$, $m(\angle 2) = 126°$

9.
$m(\angle 1) = 80°$	$m(\angle 11) = 80°$
$m(\angle 2) = 100°$	$m(\angle 12) = 100°$
$m(\angle 3) = 135°$	$m(\angle 13) = 125°$
$m(\angle 4) = 125°$	$m(\angle 14) = 55°$
$m(\angle 5) = 55°$	$m(\angle 15) = 100°$
$m(\angle 6) = 125°$	$m(\angle 16) = 80°$
$m(\angle 7) = 55°$	$m(\angle 17) = 100°$
$m(\angle 8) = 45°$	$m(\angle 18) = 80°$
$m(\angle 9) = 135°$	$m(\angle 19) = 125°$
$m(\angle 10) = 45°$	$m(\angle 20) = 55°$

10. $m(\angle 1) = m(\angle 2)$, given; $m(\angle 2) = m(\angle 3)$, vertical angles have the same measure; $m(\angle 1) = m(\angle 3)$; $l \parallel m$, corresponding angles property

11. a. $m(\angle 1) = m(\angle 6)$, given; $m(\angle 1) = m(\angle 3)$, vertical angles have the same measure; $m(\angle 3) = m(\angle 6)$; $l \parallel m$, corresponding angles property
b. $l \parallel m$, given; $m(\angle 1) = m(\angle 4)$, corresponding angles property; $m(\angle 4) = m(\angle 6)$, vertical angles have the same measure; $m(\angle 1) = m(\angle 6)$
c. Two lines are parallel if and only if at least one pair of alternate exterior angles formed have the same measure.

12. Since $\angle DAB$ is a right angle, $\overleftrightarrow{DA} \perp \overleftrightarrow{AB}$ and $\angle 1$ is a right angle also. However, since both are right angles, $\angle 1 \cong \angle ADC$ and $\overleftrightarrow{AB} \parallel \overleftrightarrow{DC}$ by the corresponding angles property. Similarly, show $\overline{AD} \parallel \overline{BC}$.

13. a. (i)   (ii)

(iii)   (iv)

b. 8 points

14. All measure 90°. Any angle drawn from endpoints of a diameter of a circle and with its vertex on the circle will measure 90°.

15. 3 lines → 7 regions, 4 lines → 11 regions, 5 lines → 16 regions, 10 lines → 56 regions,

n lines → $\dfrac{n(n + 1)}{2}$ + 1 regions

16. All measure 90°. Yes.

Section 12.4A

1. a. 540° **b.** 1080°

2. a. 105° **b.** 108° **c.** 110°, 60°, 80°, 110°

3. a. 150°, 30°, 30° **b.** 157.5°, 22.5°, 22.5°
  c. 144°, 36°, 36° **d.** 162°, 18°, 18°
  e. 160°, 20°, 20° **f.** 170°, 10°, 10°

4. a. 90° **b.** 4° **c.** 30° **d.** $(180 - x)°$

5. 25 sides

6. a. 40 **b.** 8 **c.** 36 **d.** 120

7. a.   **b.**

These patterns can be continued.

8. a. Yes **b.** Have equal measure
  c. Have same measure **d.** Equals 180°, supplementary

9. The triangle surrounded by the shaded regions is a right triangle. The two small squares include a total of four triangles—the same area covered by the larger square. Thus, if two short sides of the triangle are a and b, and the hypotenuse is c, we have $a^2 + b^2 = c^2$.

10. a. Square vertex figure, triangular vertex figure

b. All

11.

12. All ratios equal $\dfrac{2}{3}\left(\dfrac{2a}{3a} = \dfrac{2}{3}\right)$. They are proportional.

13. a. Yes; point C will have all triangles if pattern is continued.
  b. (3, 3, 4, 12), (3, 3, 6, 6), (3, 4, 4, 6), (3, 4, 3, 12)

14. a. (4, 8, 8) **b.** (4, 6, 12) **c.** (3, 3, 3, 3, 6)
  d. (3, 3, 4, 3, 4) **e.** (3, 4, 6, 4) **f.** (3, 3, 3, 4, 4)
  g. (3, 12, 12) **h.** (3, 6, 3, 6)

15. $a = 70°, b = 130°, c = 120°, d = 20°, e = 20°, f = 80°, g = 60°,$
  $h = 100°$

16. 3, 0, 0; 4, 1, 2; 5, 2, 5; 6, 3, 9; 7, 4, 14; 8, 5, 20; $n, n - 3$; $\dfrac{n(n - 3)}{2}$

17. 190

18. 180°

19. Each small tile is a square with vertex angles of 90°. Each large tile is a nonregular octagon. Each pair of octagon vertex angles meeting a vertex of the square must add up to 360° − 90° = 270°. So each angle measures 135°. Thus all the angles in this octagon measure 135°. The measures of all vertex angles in a regular octagon are equal so they must also be 135°.

20. a. 6 points **b.** 6 points **c.** 8 points
  d. If $n \le p$, then $2n$ points; otherwise $2p$ points

21. a. 180°
  b. The sum of the pentagon's interior angles is 540°. The sum of their vertical angles is thus 540°. The sum of the base angles of the triangles on the pentagon is 5 · 360° − (540° + 540°) = 720°. The sum of the angles in question is 5 · 180° − 720° = 180°.

Section 12.5A

1. a. A cube in a corner or a cube outside on the outside corner of a cube
  b. One of the corners

2. 14

3. (c)

4. a.

Top	Front	Right Side

b.

Top	Front	Right Side

c.

Top	Front	Right Side

5. a. (ii)

i. 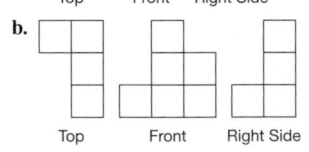 ii.

3	2	4	2
3	2	4	2

6. a. (i) *ABC, DEF*, (ii) *ACFD, BCFE, ABED*, (iii) *DEF, ABED*,
  (iv) triangular prism
  b. (i) *MPTQ, NOSR*, (ii) *MNOP, OSTP, MNRQ, RSTQ*,
  (iii) *MNRQ, NOSR, RSTQ*,
  (iv) right trapezoidal prism

7. a. Square pyramid **b.** Triangular pyramid
  c. Octagonal pyramid

8. a. Right square pyramid **b.** Right hexagonal prism
  c. Regular octahedron

d.

9. a.

b.

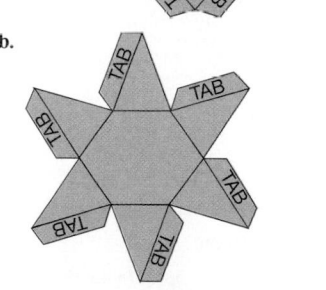

10. a. Yes; 5 **b.** Yes; 4 **c.** No **d.** Yes; 1
 e. No **f.** Yes; 2

11. a.   **b.**

12. a. Yes; F, G, H, I, J **b.** No **c.** 108°

13. a. Triangle: 5, 6, 11, 9; quadrilateral: 6, 8, 14, 12; pentagon: 7, 10, 17, 15; hexagon: 8, 12, 20, 18; n-gon: $n + 2, 2n, 3n + 2, 3n$
 b. Yes

14. a. (i) 7, 10, 17, 15 (ii) 12, 17, 29, 27
 b. Yes

15. a. Rectangle **b.** Circle

16. a. Rectangle **b.** Pentagon **c.** Kite

17. a. (iii) **b.** (v)

18. a. 3 **b.** 6 **c.** 9

19. 3

20. a. Order 3 **b.** 4

21. a. Order 2 **b.** 6

22. A parallelogram

PROBLEMS WHERE THE STRATEGY "USE A MODEL" IS USEFUL

1. Trace, cut out, and fold these shapes as a check. Only (b) forms a closed box.

2. Try this arrangement with pennies. Six can be placed around one.

3. Try this with several tennis balls. The maximum number that can be stacked into a pyramid is $25 + 16 + 9 + 4 + 1 = 55$.

CHAPTER REVIEW

Section 12.1

1. **a.** *Recognition*: A person can recognize a geometric shape but does not know any of its attributes.
 b. *Analysis*: A person can analyze a geometric shape for its various attributes.
 c. *Relationships*: A person can see relationships among geometric shapes. For example, a square is a rectangle, a rectangle is a parallelogram, etc.
 d. *Deduction*: A person can deduce relationships. For example, a person can prove that a quadrilateral with four right angles must have opposite sides parallel. Hence, a rectangle is a parallelogram.

2. **a.** Pencil **b.** Corner
 c. Yield sign **d.** Intersecting roads
 e. Railroad tracks **f.** Tiles
 g. Window **h.** Stair railing
 i. Diamond **j.** Kite
 k. Silhouette of a water glass

Section 12.2

1. **a.** Perpendicular bisector of the base
 b. Perpendicular bisector of each side
 c. Perpendicular bisector of each side
 d. Perpendicular bisector of each side and angle bisector of each angle
 e. Angle bisector
 f. None
 g. None
 h. Perpendicular bisector of the bases

2. **a.** None
 b. 120° and 240° around its center
 c. 180° around its center

d. 90°, 180°, and 270° around its center

e. 180° around its center

f. None

g. None

h. None

i. $\dfrac{360°}{n}, \dfrac{720°}{n}, \ldots, \dfrac{(n-1)360°}{n}$

3. a. If one line is the fold line, all perpendicular lines must fold onto themselves.

b. If one line folds onto itself, so must any parallel line (other than the fold line).

4. A geometric shape is convex if any line segment is in the interior of the shape whenever its endpoints are in the interior of the shape.

5. a. **b.**

c.

6. (a) and (b) are both infinite.

Section 12.3

1. a. A dot **b.** An arrow

c. A stiff piece of wire **d.** A taut sheet

e. A pencil

f. Blades of an open pair of scissors

2.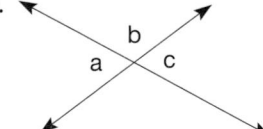

$a + b = 180° = c + b$; therefore $a = c$.

3.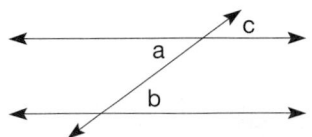

(i) → (ii): Given: $c = b$. Show: $a = b$. First, $a = c$, since they are vertical angles. From $a = c$ and $c = b$, we have $a = b$.

(ii) → (i): Given: $a = b$. Show: $b = c$. First, $a = c$, since they are vertical angles. From $a = c$ and $a = b$, we have $b = c$.

4.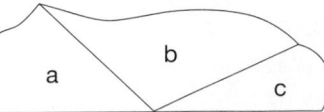

$a + b + c = 180°$. Thus the sum of the angle measures in a triangle is 180°.

Section 12.4

1. $\dfrac{360°}{n}$

2. Equal

3. $180° - \dfrac{360°}{n}$

4. Regular 3-gon, 4-gon, and 6-gon, since the measure of their vertex angles divided evenly into 360°.

Section 12.5

1. a. Two floors in a building

b. An intersecting wall and floor

c. Two intersecting walls and their ceiling

d. The angle at which two walls intersect

e. Telephone pole and telephone wire attached to a crossbar

f. A cube

2. The five polyhedron all of whose faces are congruent regular polygons.

3. $F + V = E + 2$. For a cube, $F = 6$, $V = 8$, and $E = 12$. Thus, $6 + 8 = 12 + 2$.

4. a. Can **b.** Ice cream cone **c.** Ball

Chapter 12 Test

1. a. F **b.** T **c.** T **d.** T **e.** T **f.** T **g.** T

h. T **i.** F **j.** F **k.** F **l.** F **m.** T **n.** T

2. a. 1, 5 or 3, 7 or 2, 6 or 4, 8. **b.** 3, 6, or 4, 5

3. The set of all points a fixed distance from a given point.

4. a. Right circular cylinder

b. Oblique pentagonal prism

5. a. $\angle ABC$ is obtuse

b. $\overline{AB} \parallel \overline{CD}, \overline{AC} \not\parallel \overline{BD}, \overline{AC} \not\cong \overline{BD}$

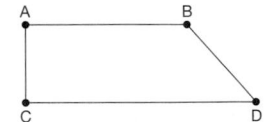

6. Fold so that point A folds onto point C. Observe that $\overline{BD}$ lies along the fold line. Thus $\overline{AC} \perp \overline{BD}$.

7. 90° and 135°

8. 144°

9. 9; 12 (not including a 0° or 360° rotation)

10. $a = 13°, b = 66°, c = 101°, d = 79°, e = 53°, f = 48°$

11. $F = 7, V = 7, E = 12$;
Euler's formula: $7 + 7 = 12 + 2$

12. a. N; 180° rotation **b.** A **c.** F

13. $m(\angle 3) + m(\angle 4) = 180°$.
Proof: $180° = m(\angle 2) + m(\angle 4) = m(\angle 3) + m(\angle 4)$
since $m(\angle 1) = m(\angle 2)$ and $m(\angle 1) = m(\angle 3)$.

14. By 13, any two consecutive interior angles are supplementary. Thus if one angle measures 90°, they all must.

15. a. (ii) **b.** (i)

16. By drawing diagonals from one vertex of an n-sided polygon, $(n - 2)$ triangles are created. The angles of all of the triangles make up all of the interior angles of the original polygon. Since the sum of the angles of a triangle is 180, the sum of the interior angles of the n-gon is $(n - 2)180$. Since all of the angles in the n-gon are congruent, the measure of each angle is $\dfrac{(n - 2)180}{n}$.

17. (b)

18. 64 vertices, 34 faces

19. Since there are 7 triangles, the sum of all the angle measures is $7 \cdot 180° = 1260°$. If the measures of the central angles are subtracted, the result, $1260° - 360° = 900°$, yields the sum of the measures of all the vertex angles.

20. The measures of the vertex angles of regular 5-gons and regular 7-gons are $108°$ and $128\frac{4}{7}°$, respectively, and there is no combination of them that will total $360°$. Thus it is impossible to tessellate the plane using only regular 5-gons and regular 7-gons.

21. Four squares meet at a point with angles that add up to $4 \cdot 90° = 360°$. Two octagons and a square meet at a point with angles that add up to $2 \cdot 135° + 90° = 360°$. However, the angles of two octagons are only $270°$, while the angles of 3 octagons meeting at a point add up to $405°$, neither of which is exactly $360°$.

22. $540°$

Section 13.1A

1. a. Height, width (with ruler); weight (scale); how much weight it will hold (by experiment)
 b. Diameter, height (with ruler); volume (pouring water into it); weight (scale)
 c. Height, length (with ruler); surface area (cover with sheets of paper); weight (scale)
 d. Height, length, width (with ruler); volume (pour water into it); surface area (cover it); weight (scale)

2. a. 63,360 inches **b.** 1760 yards **c.** 4840
 d. 46,656 **e.** 8000 **f.** 4
 g. 16 **h.** 16

3. a. 177 °C **b.** 16 °C **c.** 68 °F **d.** −18 °C **e.** 23 °F

4. a. 10^6 **b.** 10^{-3} **c.** 10^{-6} **d.** 10^3 **e.** 10^{-2}
 f. 10^{-12}

5. a. 10^9; gigameter **b.** 10^3; kilometer
 c. 10^{-12}; picometer **d.** 10^{-3}; millimeter

6. a. 100 **b.** 75 **c.** 3100 **d.** 3060
 e. 76 **f.** 0.0093 **g.** 2.3 **h.** 0.035
 i. 0.125 **j.** 0.764

7. a. 100 **b.** 6.1 **c.** 0.000564 **d.** 8.21
 e. 382,000 **f.** 950 **g.** 6.54 **h.** 0.00961

8. a. 1000 dm^3 **b.** 3 places right **c.** 3 places left

9. a. 9.5 **b.** 7000 **c.** 0.94

10. a. 500 **b.** 5.3 **c.** 4600

11. a. 28 mm **b.** 148 cm **c.** 27 cm

12. a. 900 mL **b.** 15 mL **c.** 473 mL

13. a. 23 kg **b.** 10 g **c.** 305 mg

14. a. 22°C **b.** 5°C

15. a. 34 **b.** 18, 18 **c.** mL **d.** kg **e.** dm^3, kg
 f. mL, g

16. a. 57.6 oz **b.** 4840 ft/min **c.** 616 in./sec
 d. \$0.40/min

17. a. 240 **b.** 480 **c.** 48

18. a. 15.24 cm **b.** 91.44 m **c.** 402.336 m
 d. 0.621 mi

19. 7.5 gallons

20. 2.7×10^{13} cells

21. a. 8.94 kg/dm^3
 b. 0.695 g/cm^3
 c. 7.8 g/cm^3

22. The length of a foot is based on a prototype and is not exactly reproducible. Converting linear measure, for example, uses ratios: 12 inches:1 foot; 3 feet:1 yard; 1760 yards:1 mile; so measures are not easily convertible. Volumes of in^3, quarts, and pounds are not related directly.

23. a. Approximately 5,874,600,000,000 miles
 b. Approximately 446,470,000,000,000 miles
 c. Approximately 43 minutes

24. $\dfrac{100 \text{ mi}}{\text{hr}} \times \dfrac{5280 \text{ ft}}{1 \text{ mi}} \times \dfrac{1 \text{ hr}}{3600 \text{ sec}} = 146\frac{2}{3}$ ft/sec.
 Therefore, the length of the second is
 $5 \text{ sec} \times 146\frac{2}{3} \text{ ft/sec} = 733\frac{1}{3}$ ft.

25. a. 6,272,640 cubic inches, 3630 cubic feet
 b. 225,060 pounds
 c. 27,116 gallons

26. a. 1, 4, 6 are measured directly. 2 is 4 to 6, 3 is 1 to 4, 5 is 1 to 6, and 7 is 1 to 8.
 b. 4. There are several ways. One is 1, 4, 6, 7.
 c. 4. There are several ways. One is 1, 4, 6, 8.

27. a. \$300 **b.** \$18.75/hr
 c. 4 **d.** \$108.80

28. 3 km/hour

29. About 19 years

30. About 263%

Section 13.2A

1. a. 4.34 **b.** 1.91 **c.** 6.65 **d.** 4.22

2. a. $q - p$ **b.** $\dfrac{q - p}{2}$ **c.** $p + \dfrac{q - p}{2} = \dfrac{p + q}{2}$
 d. Yes **e.** $\dfrac{-2.5 + 13.9}{2} = 5.7$

3. a. 9.8 **b.** 2.95

4. a. $q - p$ **b.** $\dfrac{2p + q}{3}$ **c.** $\dfrac{p + 2q}{3}$
 d. $m = 2.9, n = 9.4$

5. a. 17.7 **b.** −8.5

6. a. 5.5 square units **b.** 9 square units **c.** 12 square units
 d. c, 3 square units

7. a. 29 **b.** $4\frac{5}{6}$ **c.** $14\frac{1}{2}$

8. a. $a = 7.6, A = 115.52$ **b.** $b = 12, A = 81.6$
 c. $b = 35.6, P = 99.4$

9. No

10 ft   9 in.

8 ft

6 in.

Shaded area would be carpeted. Unshaded would not.

10. a. 40.2; 68.88   **b.** 90; 418.86

11. a. 49.1; 111.87   **b.** 195.6; 1292.94

12. a. $9.6\pi \approx 30.16$; $(4.8)^2\pi \approx 72.38$
b. $3\pi^2 \approx 29.61$; $(3\pi/2)^2\pi \approx 69.76$

13. a. 30 cm^2 **b.** 9.9 m^2

14. a. $b \cdot h$ **b.** $\frac{1}{2}(b + b) \cdot h = \frac{1}{2}(2b) \cdot h = b \cdot h$ **c.** Yes

15. a. $8\sqrt{3}$ **b.** $2\sqrt{15}$

16. a. $\frac{3}{2}$ **b.** 6   **c.** 1:4

17. a. $\sqrt{10}$ **b.** $\sqrt{13}$

18. a. 15   **b.** 104

19. 25 feet

20. 24 by 48

21. Yes

22. Area of large square = sum of areas of smaller pieces:
$$c^2 = 4(\tfrac{1}{2}ab) + (b - a)^2$$
$$c^2 = 2ab + b^2 - 2ab + a^2$$
$$c^2 = a^2 + b^2$$

23. a. $\sqrt{l^2 + w^2}$ **b.** $\sqrt{l^2 + w^2 + h^2}$ **c.** $\sqrt{5600} \approx 74.8$ cm

24. (b) and (c).

25. a. Subdivide. Areas are indicated. Total area = 13.

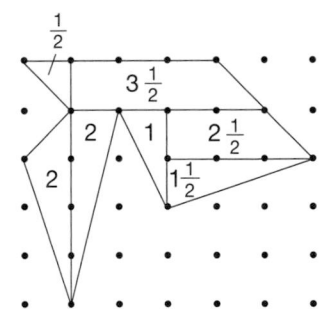

b. (i) $\frac{14}{2} + 0 - 1 = 6$ (ii) $\frac{35}{2} + 68 - 1 = 84\frac{1}{2}$

26. 8 cm by 5 cm

27. No. Try all cases.

28. a. Obtuse   **b.** Right   **c.** Acute   **d.** Right
e. Acute   **f.** Obtuse

29. 46.7 square units

30. a. 7.5°; when lines are parallel, alternate interior angles have the same measure.
b. $\dfrac{500}{7.5} = \dfrac{x}{360}$, $x = 24,000$ miles
c. He was off by 901.55 miles.

31. 2.23 cm

32. Area of region = π

33. $32\pi - 64$

34. a. $\pi/4$ or 78.5%   **b.** $\pi/4$ or 78.5%
c. They both irrigate the same amount.
d. It doesn't pay to use more sprinklers with a smaller radius. Check this in the $n \times n$ case.

35. They are the same.

36. Same

37. Equal

38. a. 1534 acres   **b.** $325,982.58 per acre

Section 13.3A

1. a. 800   **b.** 216   **c.** 150π **d.** 130.2π

2. a. 360   **b.** 896   **c.** 300π **d.** 6π

3. a. 452   **b.** 66   **c.** 1810   **d.** 141

4. a. 1141 cm^2 **b.** 276 cm^2

5. a. SA $= 2 \times \frac{1}{2} \times 8 \times 4\sqrt{3} + 3 \times 8 \times 10 = 32\sqrt{3} + 240$
b. SA $= 96 + 12(22 + 2\sqrt{10})$
c. SA $= 60 + 30 \times 20 = 660$

6. a. $B = 6 \times \frac{1}{2} \times \frac{5}{2}\sqrt{3} \times 5 = \frac{75}{2}\sqrt{3}$
b. $A = 2(\frac{75}{2}\sqrt{3}) + 6 \times 5 \times 10 = 75\sqrt{3} + 300$

7. 264 in^2

8. Cylinder

9. 5

10. 10,044 m^2

11. a. A $6 \times 6 \times 1$ prism of cubes
b. A $9 \times 2 \times 2$ prism of cubes
c. A $3 \times 4 \times 3$ prism of cubes. Surface area is 66 square units.
d. A $36 \times 1 \times 1$ prism of cubes. Surface area is 146 square units.

12. The new box will require 4 times as much cardboard as the old box.

13. a. 6380 km   **b.** 5.12×10^8 km^2 **c.** 26.5%

14. Surface area is $\frac{1}{4}$ of the original.

15. SA $= 36 + 2\pi\left(\dfrac{3}{\pi}\right)^2 = 36 + \dfrac{18}{\pi}$

16. 150π

Section 13.4A

1. a. 1500   **b.** 144   **c.** 250π **d.** 172.019π

2. a. 400   **b.** 1568   **c.** 240π **d.** 1.5π

3. a. 2958 cm^3 **b.** 342 cm^3

4. a. 905   **b.** 7238

5. a. Volume = 14; surface area = 46
b. Volume = 7; surface area = 30
c. Volume = 21; surface area = 54

6. a. 545 in^3 **b.** 101 in^3

7. a. Circumference $(2\pi r)$ is greater than height $(6r)$.
b. $33\frac{1}{3}$% (one-third) of the can

8. a. $V = \frac{1}{2} \times 8 \times 4\sqrt{3} \times 10 = 160\sqrt{3}$
b. $V = 48 \times 12 = 576$
c. $V = \frac{1}{2} \times 5 \times 12 \times 20 = 600$

9. About 9.42 (exactly 3π)

10. 1.47×10^8 yd³

11. a. Approximately 32,100,000 ft³   **b.** Approximately 463,000 ft²

12. a. $V \approx 3.88$ yd³   **b.** $V \approx 0.5$ m³
 c. The computation in (b) is easier.

13. 85,536 m³

14. a. $h = 40$ feet   **b.** Approximately 848,000 gallons
 c. The sphere has the smaller surface area.

15. 36.3 kg

16. a. 90 in³   **b.** No

17. a. 8 times   **b.** 4 times

18. a. 4 times   **b.** 2 times

19. 12-cm pipes

20. a. 8 m³   **b.** $\sqrt[3]{16} = 2\sqrt[3]{2}$

21. $100 \times \dfrac{64 - 36}{36}\% \approx 78\%$

22. $\dfrac{10}{\sqrt{2}} \approx 7.07$ ft

23. Height $= \frac{4}{3}$, slant height $= \sqrt{17}$

24. a. 2.625   **b.** 9.375   **c.** 24   **d.** 15

25. a.

 b. 42. Make a $1 \times 1 \times 10$ stack.
 c. 30. A $2 \times 2 \times 2$ stack with 2 on the top.
 d. 110 and 54; 258 and 96
 e. A $1 \times 1 \times n$ stack for n cubes
 f. The most cubical arrangement
 g. Maximal surface area is coolest; minimal surface is warmest.

ADDITIONAL PROBLEMS WHERE THE STRATEGY "USE DIMENSIONAL ANALYSIS" IS USEFUL

1. 6.3 m

2. $14.40

3. Light is 1,079,270 times faster than sound.

CHAPTER REVIEW

Section 13.1

1. (i) Select an attribute to be measured. (ii) Select a unit. (iii) Determine the number of units in the object to be measured.

2. Units are based on some convenient unit rather than a scientifically based unit.

3. a. Inch, foot, yard
 b. Square inch, square foot, acre
 c. Cubic inch, cubic foot, cubic yard
 d. Teaspoon, cup, pint
 e. Ounce, pound, ton

4. (i) Portability, (ii) convertibility, (ii) interrelatedness

5. a. Meter, kilometer, centimeter
 b. Square meter, square kilometer, square centimeter
 c. Cubic meter, cubic kilometer, cubic centimeter

 d. Liter, kiloliter, milliliter
 e. Gram, kilogram, milligram

6. Kilo-, centi-, milli-, hecto-, deci-

7. 129.2°F

8. 112.65 kph

Section 13.2

1. a. 24   **b.** 50   **c.** 14   **d.** 18.8   **e.** 24   **f.** 10π

2. a. 10.865 square units   **b.** 25π square units
 c. 48 square units   **d.** 12.25 square units
 e. 40.5 square units   **f.** 54 square units

3. a. The sum of the areas of the squares on the sides of a right triangle equals the area of the square on the hypotenuse.
 b. If the sides of a triangle have lengths a and b and the hypotenuse has length c, then $a^2 + b^2 = c^2$.

4. The length of the third side is less than $7 + 9 = 16$.

Section 13.3

1.

SA = 148 square units

2. 60π square units

3. 96 square units

4. 90π square units

5. 144π square units

Section 13.4

1.

V = 120 cubic units

2. 63π cubic units

3. 48 cubic units

4. 100π cubic units

5. 288π cubic units

Chapter 13 Test

1. a. F   **b.** F   **c.** T   **d.** F   **e.** F   **f.** T   **g.** F   **h.** T

2. 1 gram

3. a. squares   **b.** cubes

4. $1 \text{ mile} \cdot \dfrac{5280 \text{ feet}}{1 \text{ mile}} \cdot \dfrac{12 \text{ inches}}{1 \text{ foot}} \cdot \dfrac{2.54 \text{ cm}}{1 \text{ inch}} \cdot \dfrac{1 \text{ km}}{100,000 \text{ cm}} = 1.609$ km

5. 7,000,000,000 dm³; from hm³ to dm³ is a move right of three steps on the metric converter, and each step involves moving the decimal point three places.

6. Area is $1/\pi$ or approximately 0.318 cubic unit.

7. Volume $= (7.2)(3.4)(5.9)$ cm$^3 = 144.432$ cm^3

8. Volume $= \dfrac{(13)(12)}{3} = 52$ cm^3

9. 27 times bigger

10. $6 + 3\sqrt{5} + \sqrt{13}$

11. **a.** 36　　**b.** 8　　**c.** 216　　**d.** 5.43
　　e. 0.000543　　**f.** 0.015　　**g.** 225　　**h.** 3780

12. Cutting off one piece with a cut perpendicular between two bases and reassembling gives us a rectangle. The two sides of the rectangle correspond to the base and height of the parallelogram and thus the formula follows.

13. It aids in comparing and converting measurements of volume, capacity, and mass; for example, 1 cm^3 of volume equals 1 mL and, if water, weighs 1 g.

14. The convertibility of the metric system makes it easier to learn because the prefixes have the same meaning for all measurements, and converting between measurements involves factors of 10 and thus just movement of the decimal point.

15. iii < i < ii

16. **a.** 10 kg　　**b.** 6 m　　**c.** 500 mL

17. Place an identical copy of the triangle next to the original as shown. The new figure has a side $A'C'$ at the top that is congruent to AC at the bottom. In the figure $A'B'$ on the right is congruent to AB on the left. Thus the new figure is a parallelogram which has an area of bh. Since the original triangle is exactly half of the parallelogram, the area of the triangle is $\frac{1}{2}bh$.

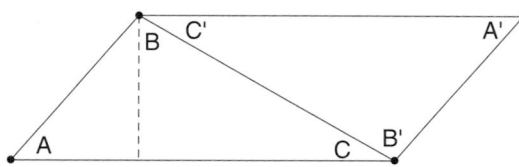

18. The height of the cone is 3 times larger.

19. **a.** Area $= \sqrt{3}s^2/2$ square units; $\triangle ABC$ is an equilateral triangle with sides of length $s\sqrt{2}$ and height $\sqrt{6}s/2$.
　　b. Use $\triangle ADC$ as a base. Its area is $s^2/2$ and the height BD from this base is s, so the volume equals $s^3/6$.

20. The circumference flown is 7933π miles;

$$7933\pi \text{ miles} \cdot \frac{5280 \text{ feet}}{1 \text{ mile}} \cdot \frac{1 \text{ second}}{1100 \text{ feet}} \cdot \frac{1 \text{ hour}}{3600 \text{ seconds}} \approx 33 \text{ hours.}$$

21. **a.** Surface area $= 300$ square units; volume $= 300$ cubic units.
　　b. Surface area $= 936 + 1352/\pi$
　　≈ 1366 square units; volume $= 12{,}168/\pi$
　　≈ 3873 cubic units

22. $4 - \pi$

23. $\frac{365}{81} \approx 4.5$ yd^3

24. **a.** $\dfrac{35}{2\pi}$ miles　　**b.** Between 29,311 and 29,512 feet

Section 14.1A

1. **a.** *KJL*　　**b.** *KLJ*　　**c.** *LJK*　　**d.** *RTS*

2. **a.** $\triangle ABC \cong \triangle EFD$ or equivalent statement
　　b. $\triangle AXD \cong \triangle CXB$ or equivalent statement

3. **a.** $\overline{RS} \cong \overline{XY}, \overline{ST} \cong \overline{YZ}$
　　b. $\overline{ST} \cong \overline{YZ}, \angle T \cong \angle Z$ or $\overline{RS} \cong \overline{XY}, \angle R \cong \angle X$

4. **a.** Yes　　**b.** No, congruent angles are not included angles.
　　c. Yes

5. **a.** Yes; $m(\angle C) = 70°, m(\angle A) = 40°, m(\angle E) = m(\angle F) = 70°$, so $\triangle ABC \cong \triangle DEF$ by SAS or ASA.
　　b. No; $m(\angle T) = 50°, VU = 4, m(\angle V) = 50°$, but there is no correspondence of the sides.
　　c. Yes, $m(\angle K) = 60°, XZ = 7$, so $\triangle JKL \cong \triangle YZX$ by ASA.

6. **a.** $\overline{WX}; \angle X; \overline{XY}$
　　b. $\overline{BC} \cong \overline{XY}, \angle C \cong \angle Y, \overline{CA} \cong \overline{YW}; \overline{CA} \cong \overline{YW}, \angle A \cong \angle W, \overline{AB} \cong \overline{WX}$

7. Use SSS.

8. **a.** $\angle A \cong \angle D, \overline{AB} \cong \overline{DE}, \overline{BC} \cong \overline{EF}$　　**b.** No
　　c. No; this example is a counterexample.

9. **a.**

$BC > YZ$

　　b.

$m(\angle A) = 90° > m(\angle X)$

10. **a.** SAS　　**b.** ASA　　**c.** ASA

11. **a.** $\overline{AB} \cong \overline{CB}$ (they measured it off), $\angle TAB$ and $\angle DCB$ are both right angles (directly across and directly away from), $\angle TBA \cong \angle DBC$ (vertical angles).
　　b. Yes; ASA
　　c. $\overline{DC} \cong \overline{TA}$, so they can measure $\overline{DC}$ and that equals the width of the river.

12. **a.** For example, have 3 pairs of angles congruent.
　　b. Not possible. Consider possible cases: (1) 3 sides, 1 angle, apply SSS; (2) 2 sides, 2 angles (third angle would also have to be), apply ASA; (3) 1 side, 3 angles, apply ASA.
　　c. Not possible, $\cong$ by either SSS or ASA.
　　d. Not possible, $\cong$ by definition.

13. **a.** $\triangle BCD \cong \triangle XYZ$, by SAS congruence property
　　b. $\angle ABC \cong \angle WXY$ (given), $\angle 2 \cong \angle 6$ [corresponding parts of congruent triangles in part (a)], thus $m(\angle ABC) - m(\angle 2) = m(\angle WXY) - m(\angle 6)$ or $m(\angle 1) = m(\angle 5)$, so $\angle 1 \cong \angle 5$.
　　c. $\overline{AB} \cong \overline{WX}$ (given), $\angle 1 \cong \angle 5$ [part (b)], $\overline{BD} \cong \overline{XZ}$ [corresponding parts of congruent triangles in part (a)], so $\triangle ABD \cong \triangle WXZ$ by SAS congruence property; $\angle A \cong \angle W, \overline{AD} \cong \overline{WZ}$.
　　d. $\angle 3 \cong \angle 7$ [corresponding parts of congruent triangles in part (c)], $\angle A \cong \angle 8$ [corresponding parts of congruent triangles in part (a)], so $m(\angle 3) + m(\angle 4) = m(\angle 7) + m(\angle 8)$ and $m(\angle ADC) = m(\angle WZY)$, so $\angle ADC \cong \angle WZY$.
　　e. Yes, and the quadrilaterals are thus congruent.

14. $m(\angle D) + m(\angle E) = 180°$ (supplementary),
$m(\angle D) = m(\angle E)$ (congruent),
$m(\angle D) + m(\angle D) = 180°$ (substitution),
$2m(\angle D) = 180°$, so $m(\angle D) = 90°$ and $m(\angle E) = 90°$.

15. a. Show $\triangle ABD \cong \triangle CDB$ as in Example 14.3.
   b. $\angle A \cong \angle C$ follow because they deal with corresponding parts.
      Show $\triangle ACD \cong \triangle CAB$ similarly, show $\angle B \cong \angle D$.

Section 14.2A

1. a. $\triangle ABC \sim \triangle DEC$, by AA similarity
   b. $\triangle FGH \sim \triangle IJK$, by SSS similarity

2. a. $EF = 10$, $DF = 14$
   b. $RS = 6$, $RT = 6\sqrt{10}$, $LN = \sqrt{10}$
   c. $EI = 10$, $HI = 3\sqrt{3}$, $FI = 5\sqrt{3}$
   d. $TV = \frac{16}{3}$, $WX = 20$

3. 25 meters

4. a. F; triangle may have sides with different lengths
   b. T; by AA
   c. F; see part (a)
   d. T; by AA

5. a. $\overline{AB} \parallel \overline{DE}$ and $\overline{AD} \parallel \overline{BE}$ from given information, and
      therefore $ABED$ is a parallelogram by definition. Similarly,
      $\overline{BC} \parallel \overline{EF}$, $\overline{BE} \parallel \overline{CF}$, and $BCFE$ is a parallelogram
   b. Opposite sides of a parallelogram are congruent.
   c. DE/EF
   d. Yes

6. a. $\angle P \cong \angle P \cong \angle P$, $\angle PAD \cong \angle PBE \cong \angle PCF$ (corresponding
      angles property) so that $\triangle PAD \sim \triangle PBE \sim \triangle PCF$ by AA simi-
      larity property
   b. $a/(a + b) = x/(x + y)$, so $a(x + y) = x(a + b)$, $ax + ay = xa +$
      xb, or $ay = bx$
   c. $a/(a + b + c) = x/(x + y + z)$, so $a(x + y + z) = x(a + b + c)$,
      $ax + ay + az = ax + bx + cx$, or $ay + az = bx + cx$
   d. Combining parts (b) and (c) yields
      $bx + az = bx + cx$ or $az = cx$.
   e. $bx/cx = ay/az$ or $b/c = y/z$
   f. Yes

7. a. $EF/FG = KJ/JG$ **b.** $BC/CD = JG/GI$
   c. $DB/BA = HF/FE$

8. 22 meters

9. a. $\triangle ABC \sim \triangle EDC$, by AA similarity. We assume that both the
      tree and the person are perpendicular to the ground, and the an-
      gle of incidence, $\angle ECD$, is congruent to the angle of reflection,
      $\angle ACB$.
   b. 27 meters

10. a. 150 feet   **b.** 46 feet

11. a. 9.6 inches
   b. Image would be half as long (i.e., the image of his thumb would
      be 4.8 inches long).

12. $\triangle ABC \sim \triangle DEF$, so $\triangle ABC$ is also a right isosceles triangle. There-
    fore, the height $\overline{BC}$ is the same length as the leg $\overline{AC}$.

13. $\dfrac{40}{30} = \dfrac{40 + BD}{60}$, so $BD = 40$.

14. The area of the larger triangle will be four times the area of the
    smaller triangle.

15. $\triangle ADC \sim \triangle CDB$; therefore, $\dfrac{a}{x} = \dfrac{x}{1}$, or $a = x^2$

16. $\dfrac{9}{3} = \dfrac{CE}{2}$, so $CE = 6$. Thus $8^2 + 12^2 = AB^2$, so $AB = \sqrt{208}$
    $= 4\sqrt{13}$.

17. The three triangles are similar by AA similarity. Therefore, $\dfrac{a}{x} = \dfrac{c}{a}$,
    or (i) $a^2 = cx$ and $\dfrac{b}{c - x} = \dfrac{c}{b}$, or (ii) $b^2 = c^2 - cx$. Substituting a^2
    for cx in (ii) we have $b^2 = c^2 - a^2$, or $a^2 + b^2 = c^2$.

18. a. 3   **b.** 4   **c.** $5\frac{1}{3}$

   d. $3\left[1 + \dfrac{1}{3} + 4\left(\dfrac{1}{3^2}\right) + \cdots + 4^{n-2}\left(\dfrac{1}{3^{n-1}}\right)\right]$, $n > 1$.

19. a. 12   **b.** $13\frac{1}{3}$ **c.** $13\frac{25}{27}$

   d. $3\left[3 + 1 + 4\left(\dfrac{1}{3^2}\right) + \cdots + 4^{n-2}\left(\dfrac{1}{3^{2n-4}}\right)\right]$, $n > 1$.

Section 14.3A

1. Follow the steps of construction 2.

2. Follow the steps of construction 3.

3. Follow the steps of construction 4.

4. Follow the steps of constructions 5 and 6.

5. Follow the steps of construction 7.

6. a. Construct a pair of perpendicular segments, then bisect a
      90° angle.
   b. Construct equilateral triangle.
   c. Bisect angle in part (b).

7.

8. b. $\angle A \cong \angle P$, $\angle B \cong \angle Q$, $\angle C \cong \angle R$
   c. $\triangle ABC \sim \triangle PQR$, since angles are congruent and all sides are
      proportional
   d. SSS similarity

9. They meet in a single point.

10. c. $k \parallel l$ since corresponding angles are congruent (right angles).

11. a. Ratios are the same: $PQ/AB = PR/AC = QR/BC$.
   b. $\triangle ABC \sim \triangle PQR$, since angles are congruent and sides are pro-
      portional.
   c. AA similarity

12. They do in an equilateral triangle. In every isosceles triangle
    the median to the base and the angle bisector of the vertex angle
    coincide.

13. An isosceles triangle that is not equilateral

14. They do in an equilateral triangle. In every isosceles triangle the
    perpendicular bisector of the base and median to the base coincide.

15. An isosceles triangle that is not equilateral

16. a. $\overline{PA} \cong \overline{PB}$, $\overline{QA} \cong \overline{QB}$ (by construction), $\overline{PQ} \cong \overline{PQ}$.
   b. $\overline{PA} \cong \overline{PB}$, $\angle APR \cong \angle BPR$ [corresponding angles of congruent
      triangles in part (a)], $\overline{PR} \cong \overline{PR}$.

c. ∠*PRA* and ∠*PRB* are supplementary by definition since *A*, *R*, and *B* are collinear, ∠*PRA* ≅ ∠*PRB* since they are corresponding angles of congruent triangles in part (b). Since these angles are supplementary and congruent, they are right angles.

d. $\overline{AR}$ ≅ $\overline{BR}$ since they are corresponding sides of congruent triangles in part (b). Hence, by definition, $\overline{PQ}$ bisects $\overline{AB}$.

17. Bisect ∠*A* and call the intersection of the angle bisector with $\overline{BC}$ point *D*. Then ∠*B* ≅ ∠*C* (given), ∠*BAD* ≅ ∠*CAD* (angle bisector), and $\overline{AD}$ ≅ $\overline{AD}$. Therefore, △*BAD* ≅ △*CAD* and corresponding sides $\overline{AB}$ and $\overline{AC}$ are congruent. By definition △*ABC* is isosceles.

Section 14.4A

1. Follow the steps of construction 8.

2. Printouts will vary depending on the shape of the triangle.

3. Follow the steps of construction 9.

4. Printouts will vary depending on the shape of the triangle.

5. Follow the steps of construction 10.

6. Answers will vary.

7. a. Construct equilateral triangle, bisect one angle, and bisect one of the bisected angles.
b. Add 15° and 60° angles.   **c.** Add 15° angle to a right angle.

8. The hypotenuse is twice as long as the shortest leg.

9. b. Regular pentagon

10. a. Regular pentagon   **b.** Regular 20-gon
c. 40, 80, any of the form $5 \cdot 2^k$

11. (a), (b), (d), (h), and (i).

12. The resulting segments $\overline{AT}$, $\overline{TS}$, and $\overline{SB}$ are congruent, thus dividing $\overline{AB}$ into three congruent segments.

13.

14. c. It lies inside the triangle.

15. c. It is outside the triangle.

16. △$C_1C_2C_3$ is always an equilateral triangle (Napoleon's theorem).

17. Case 1: *a* > 1.

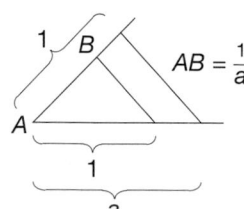

$AB = \dfrac{1}{a}$

Case 2: *a* < 1.

$AB = \dfrac{1}{a}$

Case 3: If *a* = 1, then $\dfrac{1}{a}$ = 1.

18. a. √2
b. △*AEC* and △*EBC* are both isosceles triangles sharing base angle ∠*ECB* and are therefore similar by AA similarity property. Corresponding sides are thus proportional. so *AE/EB* = *EC/BC* or *a/x* = *x/b*.

19. Lay the piece diagonally across the ruled paper so that the edge of the piece acts as a transversal. If the piece crosses six parallel lines, portions of the strip between them will be congruent.

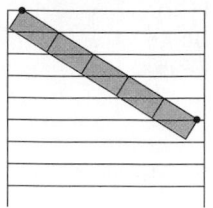

Section 14.5A

1. a. $\overline{AC}$ ≅ $\overline{AB}$, ∠*CAD* ≅ ∠*BAD*
b. ∠*C* ≅ ∠*B*, opposite congruent sides
c. ASA
d. Corresponding parts of congruent triangles are congruent.
e. ∠*ADC* and ∠*ADB* are right angles, since they are congruent and supplementary.
f. $\overline{AD}$ ⊥ $\overline{BC}$ and $\overline{AD}$ bisects $\overline{BC}$ (divides it into 2 congruent pieces).

2. $\overline{AB}$ ≅ $\overline{CB}$ (rhombus), ∠*ABE* ≅ ∠*CBE* (△*ABD* ≅ △*CBD*, so vertex angle bisected by diagonal), $\overline{BE}$ ≅ $\overline{BE}$ (common side), △*ABE* ≅ △*CBE* (SAS), so ∠*AEB* ≅ ∠*CEB* (corresponding parts). Thus $\overline{AC}$ is perpendicular to $\overline{BD}$, since ∠*AEB* and ∠*CEB* are congruent and supplementary.

3. Since *STUV* is a rhombus, it has 4 congruent sides. We need to show that it has 4 right angles. Since a rhombus is a parallelogram, opposite angles ∠*S* and ∠*U* are congruent (right angles) and adjacent angles are supplementary; ∠*V* and ∠*T* are thus right angles.

4. Since $\overline{AB}$ ∥ $\overline{CD}$, we have ∠*EBA* ≅ ∠*EDC* and ∠*EAB* ≅ ∠*ECD*. Also, $\overline{AB}$ ≅ $\overline{CD}$. Therefore, △*EAB* ≅ △*ECD* (ASA congruence property). By corresponding parts, $\overline{AE}$ ≅ $\overline{CE}$ and $\overline{BE}$ ≅ $\overline{DE}$.

5. Using the SSS congruence property, construct △*ABC*, where *AB* = *a*, *BC* = *b*, and *AC* = *d*. Using $\overline{AC}$ as one side, similarly construct △*CDA*, where *CD* = *a* and *DA* = *b*. *ABCD* will be the desired parallelogram.

6. $\overline{SV}$ ≅ $\overline{TU}$ (all sides are congruent), $\overline{ST}$ ≅ $\overline{TS}$, and $\overline{TV}$ ≅ $\overline{SU}$ (diagonals congruent), so △*STV* ≅ △*TSU* (SSS congruence property). Thus supplementary angles ∠*TSV* and ∠*STU* (adjacent angles of parallelogram are supplementary) are also congruent (corresponding parts of congruent triangles). Therefore, ∠*TSV* and ∠*STU* are both right angles. Similarly, ∠*SVU* and ∠*TUV* are right angles.

7. Construct an equilateral △*ABC*. Using $\overline{AC}$ as one side, construct equilateral △*CDA*. *ABCD* is the desired rhombus.

8. Construct $\overline{AB}$, the length of the longer base. Construct a segment whose length is *a* − *b* and bisect this segment. Mark off an arc centered at *A* with length (*a* − *b*)/2, intersecting $\overline{AB}$ at *R*, and an arc centered at *B* with the same length, intersecting $\overline{AB}$ at *S*. At *R* and *S* construct segments perpendicular to $\overline{AB}$. With compass set at length *c*, mark off an arc centered at *B*, intersecting perpendicular from *S* at point *C*. Similarly, draw an arc from *A*, intersecting the perpendicular from *R* at point *D*. *ABCD* is the desired isosceles trapezoid.

9. $AD/AC = AC/AB$ (AC is geometric mean) and $\angle A \cong \angle A$, so $\triangle ADC \cong \triangle ACB$ (SAS similarity property). Therefore, $\angle ADC \cong \angle ACB$ and since $\angle ADC$ is a right angle, so is $\angle ACB$. Thus $\triangle ABC$ is a right triangle.

10. **a.** $M_1M_2M_3M_4$ will be a rectangle when the diagonals $\overline{PR}$ and $\overline{QS}$ are perpendicular.
    b. $M_1M_2M_3M_4$ will be a rhombus when the diagonals $\overline{PR}$ and $\overline{QS}$ are congruent.
    c. $M_1M_2M_3M_4$ will be a square when the diagonals $\overline{PR}$ and $\overline{QS}$ are both perpendicular and congruent.

11. **a.** AA similarity property
    b. AA similarity property
    c. $a^2 + b^2 = x^2 + xy + xy + y^2 = x^2 + 2xy + y^2 = (x + y)^2 = c^2$.

12. **a.** By SSS, $\triangle ABC \cong \triangle ADC$. Hence $\angle BAC \cong \angle DAC$, so $\triangle AEB \cong \triangle AED$ by SAS. Thus, $\angle BEA$ and $\angle DEA$ are congruent supplementary angles, so each is a right angle.
    b. Area $= (AE \times BD)/2 + (CE \times BD)/2 = (AC \times BD)/2$.

13. $\triangle BAD \cong \triangle B'A'C'$ by SAS. Therefore, $BD = B'C' = BC$. Since $\triangle ACD$ and $\triangle BDC$ are both isosceles, their base angles are congruent. By addition, $\angle ACB \cong \angle ADB$. Thus $\triangle BAD \cong \triangle BAC$ by SAS. Therefore, $\triangle B'A'C' \cong \triangle BAC$, since they are both congruent to $\triangle BAD$.

14. $\triangle ABC \sim \triangle A'B'D'$. Thus $\angle ABC \cong \angle A'B'D'$. Also $m\angle A'B'D' < m\angle A'B'C'$, so $m\angle ABC < m\angle A'B'C'$. But $\angle ABC \cong \angle A'B'C'$ was given. Thus we have a contradiction. A similar contradiction is reached if $m\angle A'B'D' > m\angle A'B'C'$.

15. **a.** $\triangle ABD \cong \triangle FBC$ and $\triangle ACE \cong \triangle KCB$ by SAS.
    b. The triangles have congruent bases and the sum of their heights is BE. The sum of their areas is $1/2$ the area of the square.
    c. This verification uses the same method as in part (b).
    d. Combine parts (a), (b), and (c).
    e. The sum of the area of the squares on the legs of a right $\triangle ABC$ is equal to the area of the square on the hypotenuse. This is the geometric statement of the Pythagorean theorem.

ADDITIONAL PROBLEMS WHERE THE STRATEGY "IDENTIFY SUBGOALS" IS USEFUL

1. Factoring 360 into its prime factorization, we have $360 = 2^3 \cdot 3^2 \cdot 5$. To find the smallest square having $2^3 \cdot 3^2 \cdot 5$ as a factor, we need to find the smallest number with the same prime factors but with *even* exponents. Thus $2^4 \cdot 3^2 \cdot 5^2 = 3600$ is the smallest such number.

2. Subgoal: Find the lengths of the sides. Volume is 192 cm^3.

3. If 32% of n is 128, then 16% of n is 64, or 8% of n is 32, or 1% of n is 4. Therefore, $n = 400$.

CHAPTER REVIEW
Section 14.1

1. $\triangle ABC \cong \triangle DEF$ if and only if $\overline{AB} \cong \overline{DE}$, $\overline{BC} \cong \overline{EF}$, $\overline{AC} \cong \overline{DF}$, $\angle A \cong \angle D$, $\angle B \cong \angle E$, $\angle C \cong \angle F$.

2. **a.** If two sides and the included angle of one triangle are congruent, respectively, to two sides and the included angle of another triangle, the triangles are congruent.
   b. If two angles and the included side of one triangle are congruent, respectively, to two angles and the included side of another triangle, the triangles are congruent.
   c. If three sides of one triangle are congruent, respectively, to three sides of another triangle, the triangles are congruent.

3. **a.** SSS   **b.** Not necessarily congruent

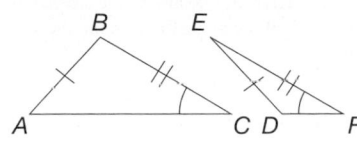

   c. ASA   **d.** SAS

Section 14.2

1. $\triangle ABC \sim \triangle DEF$ if and only if $\angle A \cong \angle D$, $\angle B \cong \angle E$, $\angle C \cong \angle F$, $\dfrac{AB}{DE} = \dfrac{BC}{EF} = \dfrac{AC}{DF}$.

2. **a.** If two sides of one triangle are proportional, respectively, to two sides of another triangle and their included angles are congruent, the triangles are similar.
   b. If two angles of one triangle are congruent, respectively, to two angles of another triangle, the triangles are similar.
   c. If three sides of one triangle are proportional, respectively, to three sides of another triangle, the triangles are similar.

3. **a.** Not necessarily similar.

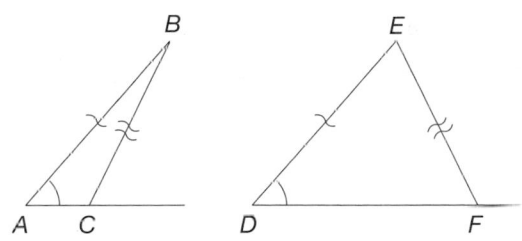

   b. SSS   **c.** AA

4.

| Shadow and stick | Reflection in a mirror | Direct Sighting |

Section 14.3

1. See Figure 14.21.
2. See Figure 14.23.
3. See Figure 14.26.
4. See Figure 14.29.
5. See Figure 14.31.
6. See Figure 14.33.
7. See Figure 14.36.

Section 14.4

1. Construct the perpendicular bisectors of two of the sides. Use the distance from their intersection to any vertex as a radius to draw the circle.

2. Construct the angle bisectors of two angles. Then construct a perpendicular from their intersection to any of the sides. Use the distance from the intersection of the angle bisectors to the selected side as the radius of the circle.

3. See Figure 14.44.

4. **a.** Construct a pair of perpendicular lines. Mark off a pair of congruent segments having endpoints at the point of intersection. Then construct two lines perpendicular at the other ends of the segments. A square should be apparent.

   b. Draw a circle. Using the radius, mark off six points around the circle, putting the compass point at the next pencil point. Connect the six resulting points consecutively on the circle to form a hexagon.

   c. Construct a square, its circumscribed circle, and the perpendicular bisectors of two adjacent sides of the square extended to intersect the circle. Connect the eight consecutive points on the circle to form an octagon.

5.

Section 14.5

1. See Example 14.14.

2. See the discussion preceding Figure 14.58.

Chapter 14 Test

1. **a.** T **b.** F **c.** T **d.** T **e.** T **f.** T
   g. F **h.** F

2. SAS, ASA, SSS

3. (b) and (d)

4. Construct an equilateral triangle and circumscribe a circle about it. Then bisect the central angles twice.

5. The circumcenter and incenter for an equilateral triangle are the same point.

6. **a.** Yes. The triangle on the left is isosceles so the base angles are 75° and the triangle on the right has a third angle of 75°. Thus, the triangles are congruent by ASA.

   b. No. In the triangle on the right, the congruent angle isn't between the congruent sides.

7. Since $\dfrac{BE}{ED} = \dfrac{9}{3} = \dfrac{AE}{EC} = \dfrac{15}{5}$ and $\angle AEB \cong \angle DEC$, the triangles are similar by SAS.

8.

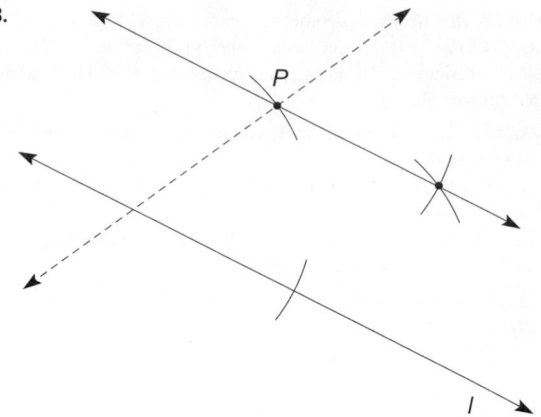

9. Construct a right triangle with sides of length 1 and 2. The hypotenuse will have length $\sqrt{5}$. Construct a square with sides of length $\sqrt{5}$.

10. From $\triangle ABC \cong \triangle CBA$, we have $\angle A \cong \angle C$. Sides opposite congruent angles are congruent and thus $\triangle ABC$ is isosceles.

11. From $\triangle ABC \cong \triangle BCA$, we have $\angle A \cong \angle B$ and $\angle B \cong \angle C$. Thus $\angle A \cong \angle B \cong \angle C$ and $\triangle ABC$ is equilateral.

12.

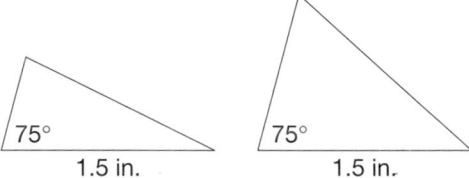

13. Measure the height of a person (h_p) and the length of the person's shadow (s_p) and the length of the shadow of the tree (s_t). Set up the proportion $\dfrac{h_p}{s_p} = \dfrac{h_t}{s_t}$ and solve for h_t, which is the height of the tree.

14. It means that if two sides and the included angle of one triangle are congruent, respectively, to two sides and the included angle of another triangle, then all sides and angles of one triangle are congruent to the corresponding parts of the other triangle.

15. Since $\overline{PA} \cong \overline{PB}$ and $\overline{AC} \cong \overline{BC}$, $PACB$ is a kite that has perpendicular diagonals. Thus, $\overleftrightarrow{PC} \perp \overleftrightarrow{AB}$.

16. **a.** Two objects are similar if all pairs of corresponding angles are congruent and all pairs of corresponding sides are proportional (i.e., the objects are the same shape).

   b. (i) F   (ii) F   (iii) T

17. **a.** Let P and Q be points on $\overline{AB}$ such that $\overline{DP} \perp \overline{AB}$ and $\overline{CQ} \perp \overline{AB}$. Since parallel lines are always equidistant, $\overline{DP} \cong \overline{CQ}$. Also $\angle APD \cong \angle BQC$, since they are both right angles and $\angle A \cong \angle B$ (given). Thus $\angle ADP \cong \angle BCQ$. Hence $\triangle APD \cong \triangle BQC$ by the ASA congruence property and $\overline{AD} \cong \overline{BC}$.

   b. As in part (a), draw $\overline{DP}$ and $\overline{CQ}$. Then show that $\overline{AP} \cong \overline{BQ}$ by the Pythagorean theorem. Thus $\triangle APD \cong \triangle BQC$ by the SSS congruence property and $\angle A \cong \angle B$.

18. **a.** Because the prime factorization of 9 includes two 3s.
    b. 40°   **c.** 20°   **d.** It is impossible.

19. **a.** 4   **b.** $\frac{147}{8}$

20. 22 feet tall

Section 15.1A

1. a. $\sqrt{13}$ **b.** $\sqrt{5}$

2. a. $\sqrt{2} + 2\sqrt{2} = 3\sqrt{2}$; yes
   b. $\sqrt{34} + \sqrt{117} \neq \sqrt{277}$; no

3. a. $\left(\dfrac{-3}{2}, 2\right)$ **b.** $(-1, 2)$ **c.** $\left(\dfrac{-5}{2}, \dfrac{9}{2}\right)$ **d.** $(3, -6)$

4. a. $\frac{1}{2}$ **b.** $\frac{4}{3}$

5. a. $\dfrac{-3-5}{6-(-4)} = \dfrac{-8}{10} = \dfrac{-4}{5}$ and $\dfrac{5-(-3)}{-4-6} = \dfrac{8}{-10} = \dfrac{-4}{5}$; yes
   b. $\dfrac{2-(-3)}{3-(-2)} = \dfrac{-3-2}{-2-3} = 1$; yes

6. a. Slopes of $\overline{AB}$ and $\overline{PQ}$ equal 1; parallel
   b. Slopes equal $\frac{2}{3}$; parallel

7. Yes

8. a. Top and bottom are both horizontal, $\dfrac{4-1}{1-2} = -3$, $\dfrac{4-1}{4-5} = -3$; parallelogram

   b. Top, bottom are both horizontal, sides are vertical; parallelogram
   c. Top, bottom are horizontal, $\dfrac{2-(-2)}{4-1} = \dfrac{4}{3}$, $\dfrac{2-(-2)}{6-3} = \dfrac{4}{3}$; parallelogram

   d. $\dfrac{10-(-5)}{-5-10} = \dfrac{15}{-15} = -1$, $\dfrac{5-(-10)}{-10-5} = \dfrac{15}{-15} = -1$, parallel;
   $\dfrac{10-5}{-5-(-10)} = 1$; $\dfrac{-5-(-10)}{10-5} = \dfrac{5}{5} = 1$, parallelogram

9. a. Yes   **b.** Yes   **c.** No   **d.** No

10. a. $\overline{AD}$ and $\overline{BC}$ have slope $\frac{5}{2}$, $\overline{AB}$ and $\overline{CD}$ have slope $-\frac{2}{5}$, so $\overline{AB} \perp \overline{AD}$, $\overline{AB} \perp \overline{BC}$, $\overline{BC} \perp \overline{CD}$, and $\overline{AD} \mid \overline{CD}$.
   b. $AC = \sqrt{(5-13)^2 + [7-(-2)]^2} = \sqrt{145}$;
   $BD = \sqrt{(15-3)^2 + (3-2)^2} = \sqrt{145}$, so $AC = BD$.
   c. All are equal.
   d. No, the slope of $\overline{AC} = -\frac{9}{8}$, the slope of $\overline{BD} = \frac{1}{12}$.
   e. Diagonals are congruent and bisect each other but are not necessarily perpendicular

11. A and B with the following pairs:
   a. (1, 5), (3, 5); (2, 5), (4, 5); (3, 5), (5, 5); (1, 3), (3, 3); (2, 3), (4, 3); (3, 3), (5, 3); (1, 2), (3, 2); (2, 2), (4, 2); (3, 2), (5, 2); (1, 1), (3, 1); (2, 1), (4, 1); (3, 1), (5, 1)
   b. (2, 5), (4, 5); (2, 3), (4, 3); (2, 2), (4, 2); (2, 1), (4, 1)
   c. (2, 2), (4, 2)   **d.** (2, 2), (4, 2)

12. a. 1   **b.** $\dfrac{-2}{3}$ **c.** No slope   **d.** 0

13. a. Isosceles right   **b.** Scalene obtuse
   c. Obtuse isosceles   **d.** Scalene acute

14. a. $AB = \sqrt{40}$, $BC = \sqrt{160}$, $AC = \sqrt{200}$. Since $AC^2 = AB^2 + BC^2$, $\triangle ABC$ is a right triangle.
   b. $DE = \sqrt{52}$, $EF = \sqrt{32}$, $DF = \sqrt{68}$. Since $DF^2 \neq DE^2 + EF^2$, $\triangle DEF$ is not a right triangle.
   c. $GH = 8$, $HI = \sqrt{32} = GI$. Since $GH^2 = HI^2 + GI^2$, $\triangle GHI$ is a right triangle.

15. Sides of $A'B'C'D'$ are $\frac{1}{3}$ the length of the corresponding sides of $ABCD$.

16. a. 20 m   **b.** 25 m   **c.** 4770 cm   **d.** ±3.18

17. 6.667 %

18. a. Since $\overline{PO} \parallel \overline{RT}$ (both horizontal), $\angle QPO \cong \angle SRT$. Also $\angle O \cong \angle T$ (both right angles). Thus $\triangle PQO \sim \triangle RST$ by AA similarity.
   b. $\overline{OP}$ and $\overline{TR}$ are corresponding sides, as are $\overline{OQ}$ and $\overline{TS}$; since the triangles are similar, corresponding sides are proportional. Interchange means of proportion.
   c. y_1/x_1 is the slope of $\overline{PQ}$ and y_2/x_2 is the slope of $\overline{RS}$. By part (b) they are equal.

19. $PM + MQ = \sqrt{\left(\dfrac{x_2 - x_1}{2}\right)^2 + \left(\dfrac{y_2 - y_1}{2}\right)^2} +$

$\qquad\qquad \sqrt{\left(\dfrac{x_2 - x_1}{2}\right)^2 + \left(\dfrac{y_2 - y_1}{2}\right)^2}$

$\qquad = 2\sqrt{\dfrac{(x_2 - x_1)^2 + (y_2 - y_1)^2}{4}}$

$\qquad = \sqrt{(x_2 - x_1)^2 + (y_2 - y_1)^2}$ and

$PQ = \sqrt{(x_2 - x_1)^2 + (y_2 - y_1)^2}$; since $PM + MQ = PQ$, P, M, and Q are collinear. Also,

$PM^2 = \left(\dfrac{x_1 + x_2}{2} - x_1\right)^2 + \left(\dfrac{y_1 + y_2}{2} - y_1\right)^2$

$\qquad = \left(\dfrac{x_1 + x_2}{2} - \dfrac{2x_1}{2}\right)^2 + \left(\dfrac{y_1 + y_2}{2} - \dfrac{2y_1}{2}\right)^2$

$\qquad = \left(\dfrac{x_2 - x_1}{2}\right)^2 + \left(\dfrac{y_2 - y_1}{2}\right)^2$

$MQ^2 = \left(x_2 - \dfrac{x_1 + x_2}{2}\right)^2 + \left(y_2 - \dfrac{y_1 + y_2}{2}\right)^2$

$\qquad = \left(\dfrac{x_2 - x_1}{2}\right)^2 + \left(\dfrac{y_2 - y_1}{2}\right)^2 = PM^2$

Hence $PM = MQ$.

20. a.

   b.

   c.

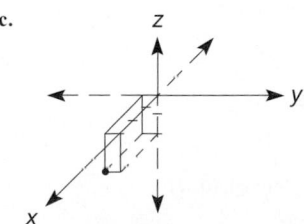

Section 15.2A

1. **a.** $5 = 7(1) - 2 = 5$
   b. $9 = -\frac{2}{3}(-6) + 5 = 4 + 5 = 9$
   c. $-2(7.5) = 6(-3) + 3, -15 = -18 + 3 = -15$
   d. $3(6) = 4(4) + 2, 18 = 16 + 2 = 18$

2. **a.** $y = 3x + 6; 3; 6$
   b. $y = \frac{3}{4}x; \frac{3}{4}; 0$
   c. $y = \frac{1}{4}; 0; \frac{1}{4}$
   d. $y = \frac{3}{4}x - 3; \frac{3}{4}; -3$

3. **a.** $y = 3x + 7$
   b. $y = -x - 3$
   c. $y = \frac{2}{3}x + 5$
   d. $y = -3x - \frac{1}{4}$

4. **a.** $y - 3 = \frac{1}{6}(x - 6)$ and $y = \frac{1}{6}x + 2$
   b. $y - 8 = -2(x + 4)$ or $y + 6 = -2(x - 3)$ and $y = -2x$

5. **a.** Any point of form $(x, 3)$ for any x
   b. Any point of form $(-2, y)$ for any y

6. **a.** $x = 1$ **b.** $x = -5$ **c.** $y = 6$ **d.** $y = -3$

7. **a.** $y = 2x - 11$ **b.** $y = -x - 1$
   c. $y = -\frac{3}{5}x - \frac{19}{5}$ **d.** $y = -\frac{3}{2}x - \frac{3}{2}$

8. **a.**   **b.**

   c.   **d.**

   e.   **f.**

9. **a.**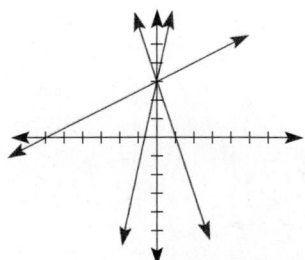
   b. They all pass through $(0, 3)$.
   c. A family of lines passing through $(0, d)$.

10. $y = 5x, y = -\frac{3}{4}x, y = \frac{2}{5}x + \frac{23}{5}$

11. Point D is $(6, 3)$; equation of median is $y = -\frac{4}{3}x + 11$

12. $y = 2x - 1$

13. **a.** $(2, 5)$ **b.** No solution   **c.** $(-3, 1)$
    d. Infinitely many solutions of the form $(x, \frac{2}{3}x + 3)$.

14. **a.** $x = \frac{8}{5}, y = -\frac{1}{5}$ **b.** $x = -\frac{1}{3}, y = -\frac{20}{3}$

15. **a.** $6x + 2y = 7$; no   **b.** Yes   **c.** $x = \frac{3}{2}, y = -1$

16. **a.** $(-3, -16)$ **b.** $(-4, 0)$ **c.** $(0, -4)$ **d.** $\left(\frac{157}{44}, -\frac{15}{44}\right)$

17. **a.** No solution   **b.** Infinitely many
    c. Unique solution   **d.** Unique solution
    e. No solution   **f.** Infinitely many

18. **a.** $3^2 + 4^2 = 9 + 16 = 25$
    b. $(-3)^2 + 5^2 = 9 + 25 = 34$

19. **a.** $(3, 2); r = 5$ **b.** $(-1, 3); r = 7$

20. **a.** $(x + 2)^2 + (y - 3)^2 = 4$
    b. $(x - 3)^2 + (y + 4)^2 = 5$
    c. $(x + 3)^2 + (y + 5)^2 = 34$
    d. $(x - 2)^2 + (y + 2)^2 = 17$

21. $(x + 2)^2 + (y - 5)^2 = 10$

22. **a.** 2 **b.** $(0, 1)$ and $\left(-\frac{4}{5}, \frac{3}{5}\right)$

23. **a.** $\$335, \$425, \$537.50, \$650, \$4.50n + 200$
    b. $y = 4.5x + 200$ **c.** 4.5; cost per person
    d. 200; the fixed costs

24. **a.** $ae = bd$ and $ce = bf$ **b.** $ae = bd$ and $ce \neq bf$
    c. $ae \neq bd$

25. **a.** I   **b.** II   **c.** III   **d.** III   **e.** IV   **f.** y-axis

26. $AP: x^2 + y^2 = 9$ ①
    $BP: (a - x)^2 + y^2 = 16$ ②
    $CP: (a - x^2) + (b - y)^2 = 25$ ③
    $DP:$ Want to find $x^2 + (b - y)^2 = DP^2$
    ③ − ② $(b - y)^2 - y^2 = 9$
    $+$ ① $x^2 + y^2 = 9$
    $\overline{\qquad\qquad\qquad\qquad\qquad\qquad}$
    $(b - y)^2 + x^2 = 18$, so $DP = \sqrt{18}$

27. **a.** 100 people   **b.** 125 people   **c.** 225 people

Section 15.3A

1. **a.** $(3, 5), (-3, 5),$ or $(3, -5)$
   b. $(1, -2), (-5, -2),$ or $(9, 8)$

2. **a.** $(-2, 4)$ **b.** $(-1, 3)$

3. **a.** $C(a, a), D(0, a)$ **b.** $G(a, b)$

4. **a.** $Q(0, 0), R(6, 0), S(0, 4)$ **b.** $Q(0, 0), R(a, 0), S(0, b)$

5. **a.** $(0, 0), (8, 0), (4, 5)$ **b.** $(-4, 0), (4, 0), (0, 5)$

6. Slope of $\overline{RS} = \dfrac{-2 - 0}{5 - 3} = -1$;
   slope of $\overline{TU} = \dfrac{-1 + 3}{-4 + 2} = -1; \overline{RS} \parallel \overline{TU}$;
   slope of $\overline{ST} = \dfrac{0 + 1}{3 + 4} = \dfrac{1}{7}$;
   slope of $\overline{RU} = \dfrac{-2 + 3}{5 + 2} = \dfrac{1}{7}; \overline{ST} \parallel \overline{RU}$. Since both pairs of opposite sides are parallel, $RSTU$ is a parallelogram.

7. Slope of $\overline{AB} = -\frac{3}{2}$ and slope of $\overline{CD} = -\frac{3}{2}$, so $\overline{AB} \parallel \overline{CD}$.
   Slope of $\overline{BC} = \frac{2}{3}$ and slope of $\overline{AD} = \frac{2}{3}$, so $\overline{BC} \parallel \overline{AD}$. Since

$(-\frac{3}{2})(\frac{2}{3}) = -1, \overline{AB} \perp \overline{BC}$. Thus $ABCD$ is a parallelogram (opposite sides parallel) with a right angle, and thus a rectangle.

8. a. $(0, 4)$ **b.** $(4, 5)$
  c. Both equal 1/4, $\overline{MN} \parallel \overline{AB}$
  d. $MN = \sqrt{17}, AB = \sqrt{68} = 2\sqrt{17}$,
  $MN = (1/2)\,AB$

9. $AC = \sqrt{a^2 + b^2}; BD = \sqrt{(0 - a)^2 + (b - 0)^2} = \sqrt{a^2 + b^2}$

10. a. $y = \frac{2}{7}x$ **b.** $y = -\frac{2}{5}x + \frac{48}{5}$
  c. $y = 2x - 24$ **d.** $(14, 4)$; yes
  e. The medians are concurrent (meet at a single point).

11. Yes

12. a. If $AB = BC$, then $\sqrt{a^2 + b^2} = \sqrt{(a - c)^2 + b^2}$ or $a^2 = (a - c)^2$, $a^2 = a^2 - 2ac + c^2, c^2 = 2ac$, and then $c = 2a$.
  b. The midpoint of $\overline{AC}$ has coordinates $(a, 0)$, and thus the median from B is vertical and thereby perpendicular to horizontal $\overline{AC}$

13. a. $y = \frac{1}{2}x$ **b.** $x = 8$ **c.** $y = -\frac{4}{3}x + \frac{44}{3}$
  d. $(8, 4)$, yes, orthocenter

14. The midpoint of $\overline{AC}$ is $\left(\dfrac{a + b}{2}, \dfrac{c}{2}\right)$. The midpoint of $\overline{BD}$ is $\left(\dfrac{b + a}{2}, \dfrac{c}{2}\right)$. The diagonals meet at the midpoint of each, thus bisecting each other.

15. a. The slope of $\overline{QR}$ is $\dfrac{b}{a - c}$, so the slope of l (perpendicular to $\overline{QR}$) is $-\left(\dfrac{a - c}{b}\right)$ or $\dfrac{c - a}{b}$.
  b. Since the point has an x-coordinate of a, it is on line m. Substituting into $y = \dfrac{c - a}{b}x$ yields $\dfrac{(c - a)a}{b} = \left(\dfrac{c - a}{b}\right)a$, which is satisfied, so the point lies on line l also.
  c. The slope of $\overline{PQ}$ is $\dfrac{b}{a}$, so the slope of n (perpendicular to $\overline{PQ}$) is $\dfrac{-a}{b}$.

16. Impossible. The length of the horizontal side is $2a$. The height is b, a whole number. Also, $\sqrt{a^2 + b^2} = 2a$, so $a^2 + b^2 = 4a^2, b^2 = 3a^2$, $\dfrac{b}{a} = \sqrt{3}$, which is irrational.

17. 7 and 11

18. 5 tricycles and 2 bicycles

19. Mike, $7000; Joan, $4000

20. 75 dimes and 35 quarters

21. a. 35   **b.** 18   **c.** $\frac{18}{35}$

ADDITIONAL PROBLEMS WHERE THE STRATEGY "USE COORDINATES" IS USEFUL

1. One of the diagonals of the kite is on the y-axis and the other is parallel to the x-axis. Thus they are perpendicular.

2. On a coordinate map, starting at $(0, 0)$, where north is up, he goes to $(0, 4)$, then to $(-3, 4)$, then to $(-3, 2)$. Thus his distance from base camp is $\sqrt{3^2 + 2^2} = \sqrt{13}$ km.

3. Place the figure on a coordinate system with A at the origin, $B = (0, 2m)$, and $C = (2m, 0)$. Then $E = (m, -m)$ and $D = (-m, m)$. The slope of $\overline{BC} = -1$, as does the slope of $\overline{DE}$. Thus they are parallel.

CHAPTER REVIEW

Section 15.1

1. $\sqrt{40} = 2\sqrt{10}$

2. $(4, 1)$

3. Yes

4. P, Q, and M are collinear.

5. Yes

6. No

Section 15.2

1. $y = -\frac{5}{2}x + 3$

2. $y - 2 = (-\frac{3}{2})(x - 3)$

3. There are one, none, or infinitely many solutions.

4. $(x + 2)^2 + (y - 5)^2 = 25$

Section 15.3

1. $(4, \frac{5}{3})$

2. $(0, 0)$

3. $(6, 2\frac{1}{2})$

Chapter 15 Test

1. a. T   **b.** F   **c.** T   **d.** F   **e.** F   **f.** T
  g. T   **h.** F

2. Slope-intercept: $y = mx + b$
  Point-slope: $(y - y_0) = m(x - x_0)$

3. Length is $\sqrt{41}$; midpoint is $(3, 4.5)$; slope is $\frac{5}{4}$.

4. a. $x = -1$ **b.** $y = 7$ **c.** $y = 3x + 10$ **d.** $2y - 3x = 17$

5. $(x + 3)^2 + (y - 4)^2 = 5^2$, or $x^2 + 6x + y^2 - 8y = 0$

6. a. 0   **b.** 1   **c.** Infinitely many   **d.** 1

7. $y = \frac{3}{4}x - 2$

8. $(y - 4\frac{1}{2}) = -\frac{4}{5}(x - 3)$

9. 0, 1, or 2, since a circle and a line may meet in 0, 1, or 2 points

10. The first pair of lines is parallel, the last pair is parallel, but no two of the lines are perpendicular.

11. $(-3, -1), (-3, 9), (-8, 4), (2, 4)$, any values of x and y that satisfy the equation.

12. As seen in the following figure

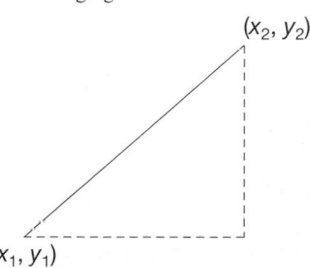

a right triangle can be constructed between the pair of points and the legs of the triangle have lengths $|x_2 - x_1|$ and $|y_2 - y_1|$. Using the Pythagorean theorem, we can find the length of the hypotenuse as $\sqrt{(x_2 - x_1)^2 + (y_2 - y_1)^2}$, which is the distance formula.

13. All sides have length $\sqrt{10}$. The slope of $\overline{LM}$ is $-\frac{1}{3}$ and the slope of $\overline{MN}$ is 3, so $\angle LMN$ is a right angle. Thus, $LMNO$ is a square.

14. $(7, 3)$

15. Any point on the line $y = 2x$ [e.g., $(0, 0), (1, 2), (2, 4)$]

16. a.

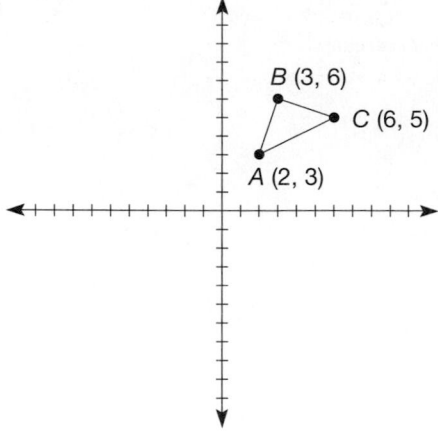

b. Isosceles triangle:
$AB = \sqrt{10}, BC = \sqrt{10}, AC = \sqrt{20}$

c. Right triangle: $AB^2 + BC^2 = AC^2$

17. $ABCD$ is a square, since it is a parallelogram whose diagonals are perpendicular and congruent (verify).

18. a. The slopes of $\overline{DE}$ and $\overline{AC}$ are both zero.

b. $DE = \dfrac{a + 2b}{3} - \dfrac{2b}{3} = \dfrac{a}{3}$. Therefore, $DE = \dfrac{1}{3}AC$. In $\triangle ABC$, if $DB = \dfrac{1}{3}AB$ and $EB = \dfrac{1}{3}CB$, then $DE = \dfrac{1}{3}AC$ and $\overline{DE} \parallel \overline{AC}$.

19. a. $N = (a + c, b)$

b. The midpoint of $\overline{LN}$ is $\left(\dfrac{a + c}{2}, \dfrac{b}{2}\right)$ and the midpoint of $\overline{MO}$ is $\left(\dfrac{a + c}{2}, \dfrac{b}{2}\right)$. Since the midpoints coincide, the diagonals bisect each other.

Section 16.1A

1. a. **b.**

2.

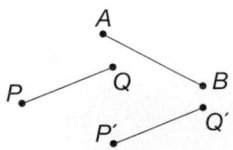

3. a. Any directed line segment that goes right 4, up 2
b. **c.** Down 4, right 5

4. Construct a line through P parallel to $\overleftrightarrow{AB}$. Then with a compass, mark off $\overline{PP'}$ having the length of $\overline{AB}$.
NOTE: P' should be to the right and above B.

5. a. $-80°$ **b.** $120°$

6.

7. a. **b.**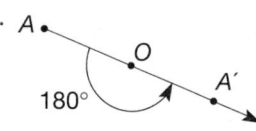

c. **d.**

8. a. **b.**

c.

9. $(-1, 4)$

10. a. $(-3, 2)$ **b.** $(-3, -1)$ **c.** $(4, -1)$
d. $(2, -4)$ **e.** $(4, 2)$ **f.** $(-y, x)$

11. a. $(-3, 1)$ **b.** $(6, 3)$ **c.** $(4, -2)$ **d.** $(-x, -y)$

12. a. **b.**

c.

13.

14. a. **b.**

c.

15. a.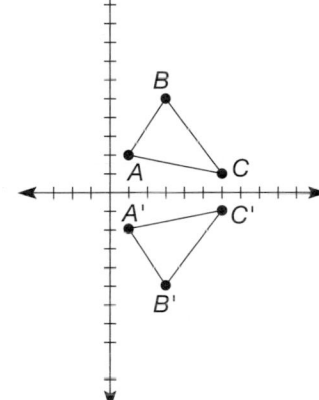

b. $(1, -2), (3, -5), (6, -1)$ **c.** $(a, -b)$

16. Construct a line through A perpendicular to l (to point P on l), extend beyond l, and mark off A' such that $PA' = AP$.

17. a.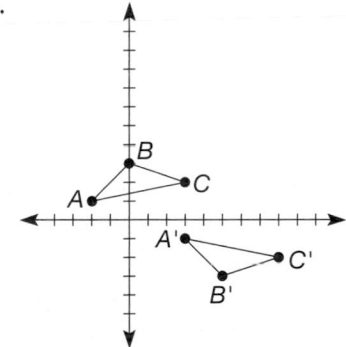

b. $(3, -1), (5, -3), (8, -2)$ **c.** $(a + 5, -b)$

18. Construct lines, through A and B, parallel to $\overleftrightarrow{XY}$ and mark off the translation. Then construct perpendiculars to l through A' and B' to find the reflection of the translated image.

19. a. Same; A to B to C is counterclockwise in each case.
b. Opposite **c.** Opposite

20. a.

b.

c.

d.

21. a. Translation, rotation, reflection, glide reflection
b. Translation, rotation, reflection, glide reflection
c. Translation, rotation, reflection, glide reflection
d. Translation, rotation, reflection, glide reflection

22. a. **b.**

c. **d.**

23. a.

b.

c.

24. a.

b.

25. a. $R_{0,-90}$ is one possibility.

b. M_l

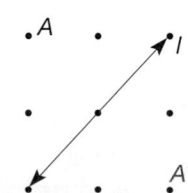

c. T_{XY} followed by M_l is one possibility.

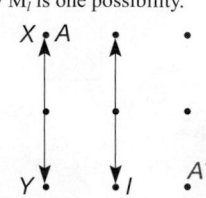

26. a. Not possible

b. 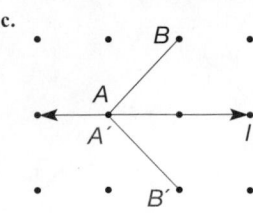 **c.**

d. Not possible

27. a. Reflection

b. Rotation

c. Translation

28. No.

Section 16.2A

1. a. $(1, 3); (2, 1)$ **b.** $(-1, 4); (0, 2)$

c. $AB = \sqrt{(1 - 2)^2 + (3 - 1)^2} = \sqrt{5}$;
$A'B' = \sqrt{(-1 - 0)^2 + (4 - 2)^2} = \sqrt{5}$

2. a. Yes, both have slope $\dfrac{q}{p}$.

b. Yes, both have length $\sqrt{p^2 + q^2}$.

c. Yes, by definition.

3. a. $\overline{OX} \perp \overline{OY}$ since (slope of $\overline{OX}$) (slope of $\overline{OY}$) $=$ $\left(\dfrac{y}{x}\right) \cdot \left(\dfrac{x}{-y}\right) = -1$.

b. $OX = \sqrt{x^2 + y^2}$, $OY = \sqrt{(-y)^2 + x^2} = \sqrt{y^2 + x^2}$

c. Yes, by definition.

4. $A' = (-2, 5)$, $B' = (4, 3)$; $AB = \sqrt{2^2 + 6^2} = 2\sqrt{10}$ and $A'B' = \sqrt{(-6)^2 + 2^2} = 2\sqrt{10}$, so $AB = A'B'$.

5. a. $(1, 2)$ and $(2, 0)$ **b.** $(-1, 2)$ and $(-2, 0)$

c. $AB = \sqrt{(1 - 2)^2 + (2 - 0)^2} = \sqrt{5}$

d. $A'B' = \sqrt{(-1 + 2)^2 + (2 - 0)^2} = \sqrt{5}$

6. a. $(a, -b)$

b. $AB = \sqrt{(a - c)^2 + (b - d)^2}$;
$A' = (a, -b)$, $B' = (c, -d)$, and
$A'B' = \sqrt{(a - c)^2 + (-b + d)^2}$
$= \sqrt{(a - c)^2 + (b - d)^2}$

7. a. The midpoint of $\overline{XY} = \left(\dfrac{x + y}{2}, \dfrac{y + x}{2}\right)$. Since its x- and y-coordinates are equal, it lies on line l.

b. The slope of $\overline{XY} = \dfrac{x - y}{y - x} = -1$, and the slope of line l is 1. Since $(-1)(1) = -1$, $\overline{XY} \perp l$.

c. Yes, line l is the perpendicular bisector of $\overline{XY}$.

8. a. $(2, 1); (-2, 3)$ **b.** $(4, -1); (0, -3)$

c. $AB = \sqrt{(2 + 2)^2 + (1 - 3)^2} = 2\sqrt{5}$;
$A'B' = \sqrt{(4 - 0)^2 + (-1 + 3)^2} = 2\sqrt{5}$

9. a. Rotation

b. Translation

c. Glide reflection

10. a. Translation   **b.** Reflection
   c. Glide reflection   **d.** Rotation

11. a.

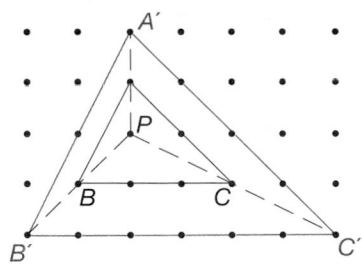

   b. $\sqrt{5}, 2\sqrt{5}; 2; 2$ **c.** 3, 6; 2
   d. $2\sqrt{2}, 4\sqrt{2}; 2; 2$ **e.** They are parallel.

12. a.

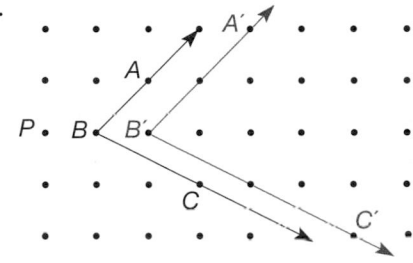

   b. They are equal.

13. No; the lines $\overleftrightarrow{SS'}$, $\overleftrightarrow{RR'}$ and $\overleftrightarrow{TT'}$ do not meet at a common point. (If it were a size transformation, they would meet at the center.) Also $RS/R'S' = 2$ but $RS/R'T' = \frac{5}{3} \neq 2$, so the ratios of sides are not equal.

14. a. A size transformation of scale factor $\frac{3}{2}$ followed by a rotation.

   b. A size transformation of scale factor $\frac{1}{3}$ followed by a reflection or glide reflection.

15. a. Since $\overrightarrow{PQ}$, $\overrightarrow{BB'}$, $\overrightarrow{XX'}$, and $\overrightarrow{AA'}$ are equivalent directed line segments by the definition of T_{PQ}, $\overline{PQ} \parallel \overline{BB'} \parallel \overline{XX'} \parallel \overline{AA'}$ and $\overline{PQ} \cong \overline{BR'} \cong \overline{XX'} \cong \overline{AA'}$. In each case, one pair of opposite sides is congruent and parallel, so $BB'X'X$ and $BB'A'A$ are both parallelograms.

   b. $\overleftrightarrow{B'X'} \parallel \overleftrightarrow{BA}$ and $\overleftrightarrow{B'A'} \parallel \overleftrightarrow{BA}$, since they contain opposite sides of parallelograms. However, since through B' there can only be one line parallel to $\overleftrightarrow{BA}$ $\overleftrightarrow{B'X'}$ and $\overleftrightarrow{B'A'}$ must be the same line. Therefore, A', X', and B' are collinear.

16. Since translations preserve distances, $PQ = P'Q'$, $QR = Q'R'$, and $RP = R'P'$. Thus $\triangle PQR \cong \triangle P'Q'R'$, Therefore, $\angle PQR \cong \angle P'Q'R'$, since they are corresponding parts of congruent triangles.

17. $p \parallel q$ implies that $\angle 1 \cong \angle 2$. Since rotations preserve angle measures, $\angle 1 \cong \angle 3$ and $\angle 2 \cong \angle 4$. Thus $\angle 3 \cong \angle 4$ and $p' \parallel q'$ by the corresponding angles property.

18. Since reflections preserve distances, $AB = A'B'$, $BC = B'C'$, and $AC = A'C'$. Since A, B, and C are collinear, $AB + BC = AC$. Therefore, $A'B' + B'C' = AB + BC = AC = A'C'$ and A', B', and C' are collinear.

19. $q \parallel p$ implies that $\angle 1 \cong \angle 2$. Since reflections preserve angle measures, $\angle 1 \cong \angle 1'$ and $\angle 2 \cong \angle 2'$, where $\angle 1'$ and $\angle 2'$ are the images, respectively, of $\angle 1$ and $\angle 2$. Thus $\angle 2' \cong \angle 1'$ and $p' \parallel q'$ by the corresponding angles property.

20. Since isometries map segments to segments and preserve distances, $\overline{AB} \cong \overline{A'B'}$, $\overline{BC} \cong \overline{B'C'}$, and $\overline{CA} \cong \overline{C'A'}$. Thus, by the SSS congruence property, $\triangle ABC \cong \triangle A'B'C'$.

21. a. One, just T_{PQ}

   b. Infinitely many; the center C may be any point on the perpendicular bisector of $\overline{PQ}$, and $\angle PCQ$ is the rotation angle.

22. a. The point where $\overleftrightarrow{PP'}$ and $\overleftrightarrow{QQ'}$ intersect

   b. Greater than 1

   c. Where $\overleftrightarrow{PP'}$ and $\overleftrightarrow{QQ'}$ intersect, less than 1

23. Construct line through Q' parallel to $\overleftrightarrow{QR}$. The intersection of that line and l is R'.

24. Let point R be the intersection of line l and segment $\overline{PP'}$ and let S be the intersection of l and $\overline{QQ'}$. Then $\triangle QRS \cong \triangle Q'RS$ as in case 2. Hence $RQ = RQ'$ and $\angle QRS \cong \angle Q'RS$. Thus $\triangle PRQ \cong \triangle P'RQ'$. We can see this by subtracting $m(\angle QRS)$ from $90°$, which is the measure of $\angle PRS$), and subtracting $m(\angle Q'RS$ from $90°$, which is the measure of $\angle P'RS$. Thus $\underline{\triangle PRQ} \cong \underline{\triangle P'RQ'}$ by the SAS congruence property. Consequently, $\overline{PQ} \cong \overline{P'Q'}$, since these sides correspond in $\triangle PRQ$ and $\triangle P'RQ'$. Thus $PQ = P'Q'$, as desired.

25. Yes, a translation

Section 16.3A

1. (d), since $A \to A, B \to D, C \to D, D \to B$

2. $M_{EG}, M_{FH}, H_P, R_{P,360°}$

3. a. For example, $M_{AD}, M_{BE}, M_{CF}, R_{O,60°}, R_{O,120°}$, and $R_{O,180°}$

   b. 11 (6 reflections and 5 rotations)

4. Yes. Let E and F be the midpoints of sides $\overline{AB}$ and CD. Then M_{EF} and $R_{A,360°}$ will work.

5. a. $H_D(H_C(H_B(H_A(P)))) = P$

   b. $H_D(H_C(H_B(H_A(Q)))) = Q$

   c. This combination of four half-turns around the vertices of a parallelogram maps each point to itself.

6. Impossible. Even though corresponding sides have the same length, corresponding diagonals do not. Yet isometries preserve distance.

7. b. Yes; $R_{B,90°}$ followed of $S_{O,1/2}$ is a similarity transformation.

8. Let M be the midpoint of $\overline{AC}$. Hence $H_M(A) = C, H_M(C) = A$. We know that $H_M(B)$ is on $\overleftrightarrow{CD}$, since $H_M(\overleftrightarrow{AB}) \parallel \overleftrightarrow{AB}$ and C is on $H_M(\overleftrightarrow{AB})$. Similarly, $H_M(B)$ is on $\overleftrightarrow{AD}$, so that $H_M(B)$ is on $\overleftrightarrow{CD} \cap \overleftrightarrow{AD}$. That is, $H_M(B) = D$. Hence $(\triangle ABC) = \triangle CDA$ so that $\triangle ABC \cong \triangle CDA$.

9. a. $H_M(\angle ADC) = \angle CBA$, so that $\angle ADC \cong \angle CBA$ Similarly, $\angle BAD \cong \angle DCB$.

   b. $H_M(\overline{AB}) = (\overline{DC})$, so $\overline{AB} \cong \overline{DC}$, and so on.

10. Let $l = \overleftrightarrow{BP}$. Then $M_l(A)$ is on $\overleftrightarrow{BC}$, but since $AB = BC$, we must have $M_l(A) = C$. Thus $M_l(\triangle ABP) = \triangle CBP$, so $\triangle ABP \cong \triangle CBP$. Hence $\angle BPA \cong \angle BPC$, but since these angles are supplementary, each is a right angle. Since $AP = CP$, $\overleftrightarrow{BP}$ is the perpendicular bisector of $\overline{AC}$.

11. a. From Problem 10, points A and C are on the perpendicular bisector of $\overline{BD}$, so $\overline{AC} \perp \overline{BD}$.

   b. Since $\overleftrightarrow{AC}$ is the perpendicular bisector of $\overline{BD}, M_{AC}(B) = D$, $M_{AC}(D) = B, M_{AC}(A) = A$, and $M_{AC}(C) = C$. Hence $M_{AC}(ABCD) = ADCB$, so the kite has reflection symmetry.

12. a. $AA' = 2x$ and $A'A'' = 2y$, so that $AA'' = 2(x + y)$. Also, A, A', and A'' are collinear since $\overline{AA'} \perp r, r, \parallel s$ and $\overline{A'A''} \perp s$. Hence, M_r, followed by M_s is equivalent to the translation $T_{AA''}$. Since A was arbitrary, M_r followed by M_s is $T_{AA''}$ since orientation is preserved.

   b. The direction of the translation is perpendicular to r and s, from r toward s, and the distance is twice the distance between r and s.

13. a. (Any two intersecting rails can be used.)

Let $B' = M_l(B)$, and $B'' = M_m(B')$.

Let $P = \overleftrightarrow{AB''} \cap m$. Shoot ball A toward point P.

b. Let $Q = \overline{PB'} \cap l$. Then use an argument as in Example 16.14.

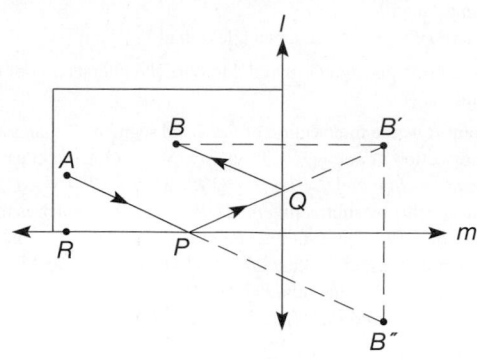

14. Consider $S_{A,bla}$. This size transformation will map $ABCD$ to a square $A'B'C'D'$ congruent to $EFGH$. Then from Section 16.2, we know that there is an isometry J that maps $A'B'C'D'$ to $EFGH$. Hence the combination of $S_{A,bla}$ and J is the desired similarity transformation.

ADDITIONAL PROBLEMS WHERE THE STRATEGY "USE SYMMETRY" IS USEFUL

1. Place any two squares on a 4×4 square grid. Reflect those two squares across a diagonal and across a vertical line through the center as shown. If two more squares are produced in either of these cases, that pattern will have reflective symmetry with four dark squares.

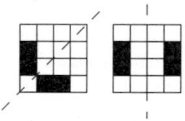

2. There are three digits that read the same upside down: 0, 1, and 8. Since house numbers do not begin with zero, there are $2 \cdot 3 \cdot 3 = 18$ different such house numbers.

3. Pascal's triangle has reflective symmetry along a vertical line through its middle. In the 41st row, the 1st and 41st numbers are equal, as are the 2nd and 40th, the 3rd and 39th, and 4th and 38th. Thus the 38th number is 9880.

CHAPTER REVIEW

Section 16.1

1.

2.

3.

4.

5. They must be infinite in one direction.

6.

7.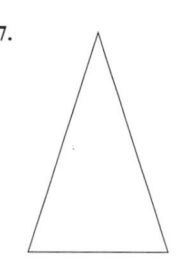

8. They must be infinite in one direction.

9.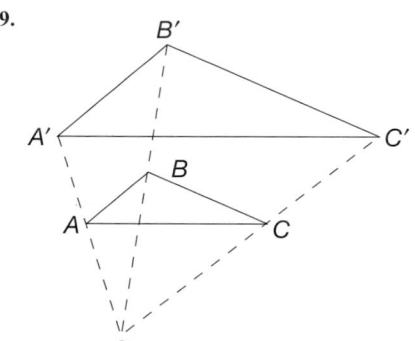

10. Apply a size transformation to get the triangles congruent, then use an isometry to map one to the other.

Section 16.2

1. Translations, rotations, reflections, and glide reflections

2. The image of a triangle will be a triangle with sides and angles congruent to the original triangle, hence congruent to it.

3. The corresponding alternate interior angles formed by the transversals will be congruent, hence the image of parallel lines will be parallel.

4. One triangle is mapped to the other using a combination of a translation, rotation, or reflection.

5. A triangle will map to a triangle with corresponding angles congruent. Thus, the triangles are similar by AA.

6. Similitudes preserve angle measure. Congruent alternate interior angles formed by a translation will map to congruent alternate interior angles.

7. Using a size transformation, the triangles can be made to be congruent. Then an isometry can be used to map one triangle to the other. The combination of the size transformation and the isometry is a similarity that takes one triangle to the other.

Section 16.3

1.

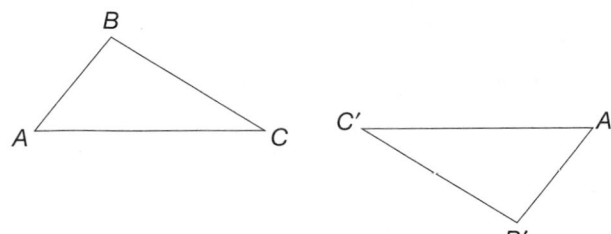

Chapter 16 Test

1. **a.** T   **b.** F   **c.** T   **d.** T   **e.** T   **f.** F
   g. T   **h.** T

2. Distance

3. Rotation

4. (a) and (e)

5. (a) and (c)

6. **a.** Size transformation   **b.** Rotation   **c.** Reflection
   d. Glide reflection   **e.** Translation

7. **a.**

   b.

   c.

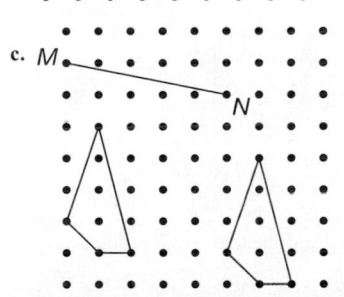

8. **a.** D **b.** E **c.** E **d.** D

9.

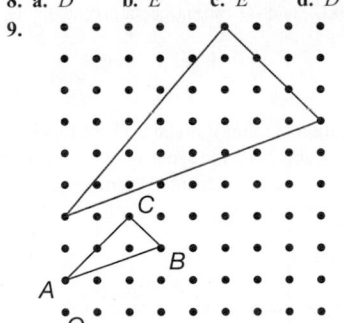

10. Translation, reflection, and glide reflection

11. **a.** M_{AB} **b.** $R_{F,-90°}$ **c.** T_{CD}

12. Let P be the intersection of $\overline{EG}$ and $\overline{FH}$. Then $R_{P,45°}$
    $(S_{P,\sqrt{2}}(EFGH)) = ABCD$; thus $ABCD$ is similar to $EFGH$.

13. The result of two glide reflections is an isometry that preserves orientation. Therefore, the isometry must be a translation or a rotation.

14. B

15. **a.** Reflection   **b.** Translation   **c.** Rotation

16.

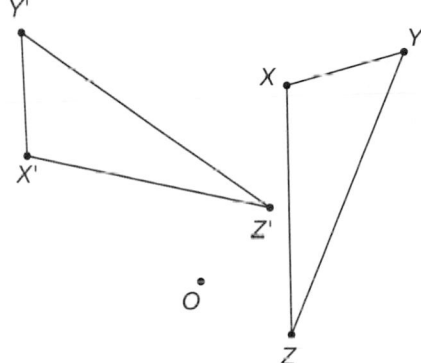

17. $A' = (5, -5)$
    $B' = (2, -10)$
    $C' = (x + 4, y - 6)$

18. $AB = \frac{8}{3}$; $AC = \frac{10}{3}$; $CE = 5$

19. $\triangle AMC \cong \triangle BMC$ by SSS. Therefore, $\angle AMC \cong \angle BMC$, or
    $m(\angle AMC) \cong m(\angle BMC) = 90°$.
    Since $M_{CM}(A) = B$ and $M_{CM}(C) = C$, we have $M_{CM}(\triangle ABC) - \triangle BAC$.
    This means that $\overleftrightarrow{CM}$ is a symmetry line for $\triangle ABC$.

20.

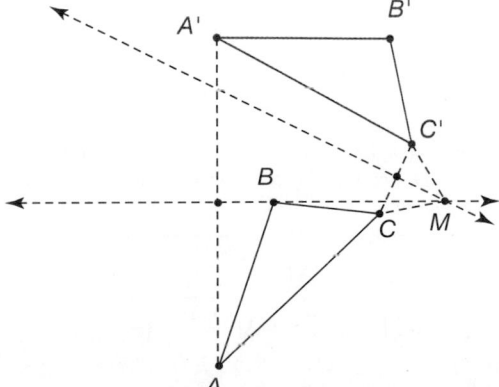

The transformation is a rotation with the center labeled M and $\angle CMC'$ is the angle of rotation.

21. No, because the lines $\overleftrightarrow{XA}$, $\overleftrightarrow{ZC}$, and $\overleftrightarrow{BY}$ are not concurrent.

Section E-A

1. $\overline{AB} \parallel \overline{DC}$ by definition of a parallelogram; $\angle A$ and $\angle D$ are supplementary, since they are interior angles on the same side of a transversal. Since $\overline{AD} \parallel \overline{BC}$, $\angle A$ and $\angle B$ are supplementary. Similarly, $\angle C$ is supplementary to $\angle B$ and $\angle D$.

2. Slope of $\overline{MN}$ = slope of $\overline{OP} = \dfrac{d}{c}$, so $\overline{MN} \parallel \overline{OP}$.

Slope of $\overline{MN}$ = slope of $\overline{ON} = \dfrac{b}{a-e}$, so $\overline{MP} \parallel \overline{ON}$.

Therefore $MNOP$ is a parallelogram.

3. Let $l = \overleftrightarrow{AP}$. Then $M_l(B)$ is on $\overrightarrow{AC}$, since $\angle BAP \cong \angle CAP$. Because $AB = AC$, however, we must have $M_l(B) = C$. Thus $M_l(C) = B$, so that $M_l(\triangle ABP) = \triangle ACP$ Hence $\angle ABP \cong \angle ACP$.

4. *Congruence proof*: $AB = CD$, $AD = CB$, and $BD = DB$. Therefore $\triangle ABD \cong \triangle CDB$ by SSS. By corresponding parts, $\angle ADB \cong \angle CBD$, so $\overline{AD} \parallel \overline{CB}$. Since $\overline{AD}$ and $\overline{CB}$ are parallel and congruent, $ABCD$ is a parallelogram.
Coordinate proof: If A, B, and D have coordinates $(0, 0)$, (a, b), and $(c, 0)$, respectively, then C must have coordinates $(a + c, b)$, since both pairs of opposite sides are congruent.

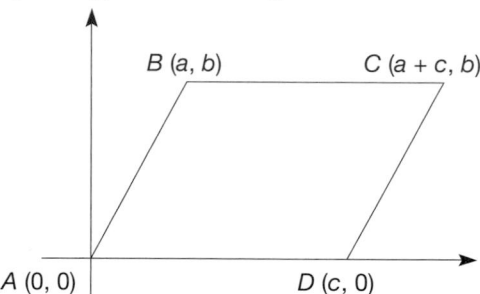

Using slopes, we have $\overline{AB} \parallel \overline{DC}$ and $\overline{AD} \parallel \overline{BC}$.

5. Consider the following isosceles triangle with the appropriate coordinates.

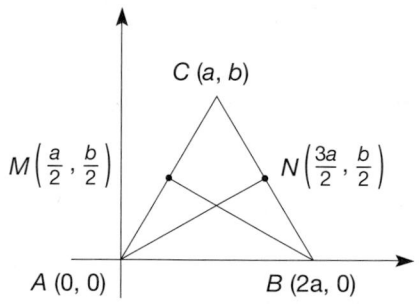

Congruence proof: $AM = BN$, $\angle A \cong \angle B$, and $AB = BA$. Thus $\triangle ABN \cong \triangle BAM$ by SAS. By corresponding parts, $AN = BM$.
Coordinate proof:

$$AN = \sqrt{\left(2a - \frac{a}{2}\right)^2 + \left(-\frac{b}{2}\right)^2} = \sqrt{\left(\frac{3a}{2}\right)^2 + \left(\frac{b}{2}\right)^2};$$

$$BM = \sqrt{\left(a + \frac{a}{2}\right)^2 + \left(-\frac{b}{2}\right)^2} = \sqrt{\left(\frac{3a}{2}\right)^2 + \left(\frac{b}{2}\right)^2}.$$

6. Because $\overline{PQ} \parallel \overline{SR}$ and $\overline{PS} \parallel \overline{QR}$ and interior angles on the same side of the transversal are supplementary, $\angle Q$ and $\angle S$ must also be right angles since they are supplementary to $\angle P$. Further, since opposite angles of a parallelogram are congruent, $\angle R$ must also be a right angle.

7. Slope of $\overline{AC} = \dfrac{a - 0}{a - 0} = 1$;

slope of $\overline{BD} = \dfrac{a - 0}{0 - a} = -1$;

since $1(-1) = -1$, $\overline{AC} \perp \overline{BD}$.

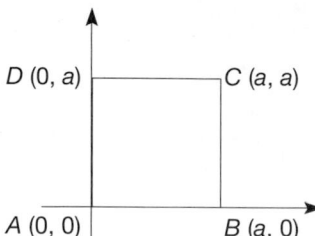

8. $m(\angle P) = m(\angle R)$ and $m(\angle Q) = m(\angle S)$ (opposite angles are congruent); $m(\angle P) + m(\angle Q) + m(\angle R) + m(\angle S) = 360°$ (vertex angles of quadrilateral total $360°$); $m(\angle P) + m(\angle Q) + m(\angle P) + m(\angle Q) = 360°$, so $m(\angle P) + m(\angle Q) = 180°$; thus $\angle P$ and $\angle Q$ are supplementary and $\overline{PS} \parallel \overline{QR}$ (interior angles on same side of transversal are supplementary). Similarly, $m(\angle P) + m(\angle S) + m(\angle P) + m(\angle S) = 360°$, $m(\angle P) + m(\angle S) = 180°$, P and S are supplementary, and $\overline{PQ} \parallel \overline{SR}$. Since both pairs of opposite sides are parallel, $PQRS$ is a parallelogram.

Section T1A

1. (b) and (d)

2. **a.** $q \rightarrow \sim p$ **b.** $q \wedge r$ **c.** $r \leftrightarrow (q \wedge q)$
   d. $p \vee q$

3. **a.** T   **b.** F   **c.** T   **d.** T   **e.** T   **f.** T
  g. T   **h.** T

4. **a.** If I am an elementary school teacher, then I teach third grade. If I do not teach third grade, then I am not an elementary school teacher. If I am not an elementary school teacher, then I do not teach third grade.
   b. If a number has a factor of 2, then it has a factor of 4. If a number does not have a factor of 4, then it does not have a factor of 2. If a number does not have a factor of 2, then it does not have a factor of 4.

5.

p	q	$\sim p$	$\sim q$	$(\sim p)$ $\vee$ $(\sim q)$	$(\sim p)$ $\vee$ q	$(\sim p)$ $\wedge$ $(\sim q)$	$p \rightarrow q$	$\sim(p \wedge q)$	$\sim(p \vee q)$
T	T	F	F	F	T	F	T	F	F
T	F	F	T	T	F	F	F	T	F
F	T	T	F	T	T	F	T	T	F
F	F	T	T	T	T	T	T	T	T

$(\sim p) \vee (\sim q)$ is logically equivalent to $\sim(p \wedge q)$.

$(\sim p) \vee q$ is logically equivalent to $p \rightarrow q$.

$(\sim p) \wedge (\sim q)$ is logically equivalent to $\sim(p \vee q)$.

6. a. Valid **b.** Invalid **c.** Invalid **d.** Valid
e. Invalid **f.** Invalid **g.** Invalid **h.** Valid

7. a. You will be popular. **b.** Scott is not quick.
c. All friends are trustworthy.
d. Every square is a parallelogram.

8. a. Hypothetical syllogism
b. Modus ponens
c. Modus tollens
d. Modus tollens
e. Hypothetical syllogism

9. a. F **b.** F **c.** T **d.** T **e.** F

10. Invalid

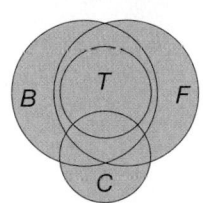

ELEMENTARY LOGIC TEST

1. a. T **b.** F **c.** F **d.** F **e.** F
f. T **g.** F **h.** F

2. a. $\sim q \to p, \sim p \to q, q \to \sim p$
b. $q \to \sim p, p \to \sim q, \sim q \to p$
c. $\sim p \to \sim q, q \to p, p \to q$

3. a. T **b.** F **c.** F **d.** F **e.** T **f.** T

4. a. Invalid **b.** Valid **c.** Valid
d. Invalid **e.** Invalid

5.

p	q	$p \wedge q$	$p \vee q$	$p \to q$	$\sim p$	$\sim q$	$\sim q \leftrightarrow p$	$\sim q \to \sim p$
T	T	T	T	T	F	F	F	T
F	T	F	T	T	T	F	T	T
F	F	F	F	T	T	T	F	T
T	F	F	T	F	F	T	T	F

6. For example: Some B's are A's. All C's are B's. Therefore, all C's are A's.

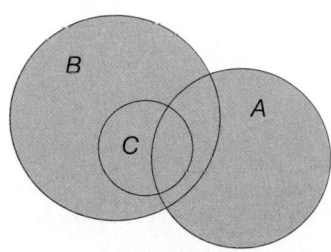

7. All are true when both the hypothesis and conclusion are true. The only time an implication is false, the disjunction is true. Therefore, they are not all false at the same time.

8. Both Bob and Sam are truth tellers.

9. a. $p \updownarrow p$ **b.** $(p \updownarrow q) \updownarrow (p \updownarrow q)$
c. $(p \updownarrow p) \updownarrow (q \updownarrow q)$

Section T2A

1. a. 7 **b.** 3 **c.** 0 **d.** 4 **e.** 3 **f.** 7
g. 6 **h.** 6

2. a. 4, 5 **b.** 7, 5 **c.** 1, 7 **d.** 4, does not exist

3. a. 7 **b.** 4 **c.** 1 **d.** 9

4. a. F **b.** F **c.** T **d.** T **e.** T **f.** F

5. $1 - 4 = n$ if and only if $1 = 4 + n$. Look for a "1" in the "4" row; the number heading the column that the "1" is in represents n, namely 2.

6. The table is symmetric across the upper left/lower right diagonal.

7. $\frac{1}{3} \oplus \frac{1}{2} = 2 \oplus 3 = 5, \frac{1}{3} \oplus \frac{1}{2} = \frac{2}{1} \oplus \frac{3}{1} = 5$ (NOTE: Normally $\frac{1}{3} = \frac{2}{6}$, but $6 = 1$ in the 5-clock.) Yes. For example, $\frac{3}{4} \oplus \frac{2}{3} = 2 \oplus 4 = 1$. On the other hand, $\frac{3}{4} \oplus \frac{2}{3} = \frac{17}{12}$, and $\frac{17}{12} = \frac{2}{2} = 1$ in 5-clock arithmetic.

8. a. If $1 < 2$, then $1 + 3 < 2 + 3$. But $4 \not< 0$ in the whole numbers.
b. If $2 < 3$ and $2 \neq 0$, then $2 \cdot 2 < 2 \cdot 3$. But $4 \not< 1$ in the whole numbers.

9. a. $\{3\}$ **b.** $\{0, 6\}$ **c.** $\{0, 2, 4, 6, 8\}$ **d.** $\{\ \}$

10. If $a + c \equiv b + c$, then $a + c + (-c) \equiv b + c + (-c)$, or $a \equiv b$.

11. If $a \equiv b$ and $b \equiv c$, then $m \mid (a - b)$ and $m \mid (b - c)$. Therefore, $m \mid [(a - b) + (b - c)]$ or $m \mid (a - c)$. Thus $a \equiv c$.

12. 61, 83

13. 504

CLOCK ARITHMETIC TEST

1. a. F **b.** T **c.** F **d.** T **e.** F
f. T **g.** F **h.** T

2. a. 3 **b.** 1 **c.** 6 **d.** 12 **e.** 1 **f.** 6

3. a. $3 \oplus (9 \ominus 7) = 10 \oplus 9 = 9$
b. $(8 \otimes 3) \otimes 4 = 8 \otimes 1 = 8$
c. $(5 \otimes 4) \oplus (5 \otimes 11) = 5 \otimes 0 = 0$
d. $(6 \otimes 3) \oplus (3 \otimes 4) \oplus (3 \otimes 3) = 3 \otimes 0 = 0$

4. a. 3, 2
b. 4; the reciprocal doesn't exist since all multiples of 4 are either 4 or 8 in the 8-clock.
c. 0; the reciprocal doesn't exist since all multiples of 0 are 0 in the 5-clock.
d. 7, 5

5. a. $\{-14, -5, 4, 13\}$ **b.** $\{2, 3, 4, 6, 12\}$
c. $\{7k + 1; k \text{ is any integer}\}$

6. All multiples of 4 land on 4, 8, or 12, never on 1.

7. a. 0 cannot be a divisor.
b. 1 divides everything, thus all numbers would be congruent.

8. Because m divides $a - a$.

9. There are 365 days in a nonleap year and $365 \equiv 1 \bmod 7$. Thus January 1 will fall one day later, or on a Tuesday.

Section T3A

1. a. L = 2, M = 3, N = 2, O = 1
b. U = 2, V = 4, W = 2, X = 2, Y = 3, Z = 1
c. A = 3, B = 1, C = 3, D = 1, E = 2, F = 2, G = 0, H = 2

2. a. (i) B, B, C, C, F; (ii) AB(2), AC(2), AE, BC, CD, CE
b. (i) B, H, G; (ii) AB, AG, AH, BC, CH, CD, DH, DE, EF, EG, FG
c. (i) B, E, C; (ii) AB, AE, AC, BC, BD, BE, CD(2)

3. a.

b.

c.

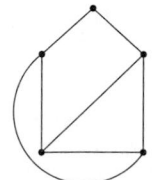

4. a. Not connected because, for example, there is no path from H to I.
   b. Connected since there is a path between any two points.
   c. Not connected because, for example, there is no path between I and H.

5. (i), (iii), and (v) are equivalent; (ii) and (iv) are equivalent.

6. a. JHGFHIEFIJE (path)
   b. Not possible because there are 4 odd vertices.
   c. SVUTSXWZYWVUZYTS (circuit)
   d. ABCHBCDFGDE (path)

7. a. JHGFIEJ (path)
   b. LMQNPO (path)
   c. SVUTYZWXS (circuit)
   d. none

8. a.

   b.

c.

9. a. No. The graph is not connected.
   b. Yes. The graph is connected and planar.
   c. Yes. The graph is connected and planar.

10. a.

   b.

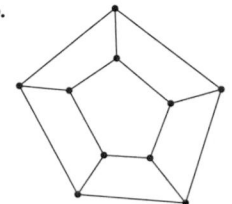

11. a. 1a: 2 odd and 2 even; 1b: 2 odd and 5 even; 1c: 4 odd and 4 even; 2a: 4 odd and 1 even; 2b: 6 odd and 2 even; 2c: 2 odd and 3 even
   b. There is an even number of odd vertices.

12.

Eight regions

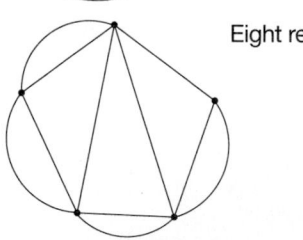

Eight regions

Every connected planar graph with 5 vertices and 11 edges must have 8 regions because it must satisfy Euler's formula.

13. Connect any pair of vertices with an odd degree like LP. An Euler path with new LP in place is OMNPLOPLM.

14. Many possibilities. IEFGJFHI, IEFJGFHI, FHIJGIEF, FHIGHIEF, HIJGIEFH are five circuits.

15. Paved roads BF, BA, BC, FE, ED yield a total distance of 10 + 9 + 12 + 15 + 17 = 63 miles.

16. Yes. There are exactly two vertices with an odd degree.

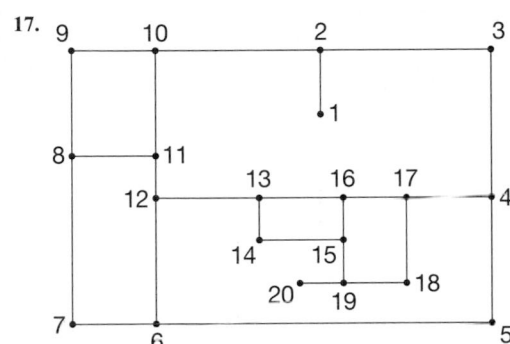

17.

GRAPH THEORY TEST

1. a. F   **b.** F   **c.** T   **d.** F   **e.** F

2. (i) AC, BC, CD, CE, DE(2), DF, EF
   (ii) JK, JM, JN(2), JO, KL, KM, LM, LN, MN, NO

3. (i) A-1, B-1, C-4, D-4, E-4, F-2,
   (ii) J-5, K-3, L-3, M-4, N-5, O-2

4. (i) ACDEFDECB
   (ii) Not possible, 4 odd vertices

5. (i) R = 4, V = 6, E = 8, 4 + 6 = 8 + 2
   (ii) R = 7, V = 6, E = 1, 7 + 6 = 11 + 2

6. (i) No path can go through C exactly once.
   (ii) OJNMLK is a Hamiltonian path and JONMLKJ is a Hamiltonian circuit.

7. Degrees: A-2, B-3, C-3, D-4. Since the graph has exactly two vertices of odd degree, there is an Euler path.
   a. 0
   b. 6 BADCBD, BADBCD, BDABCD, BDCBAD, BCDABD, BCDBAD
   c. Same paths as b done backwards
   d. 0

8. Answer will vary
   a, b, and **e.**

   c.

   d.

   f.

9.

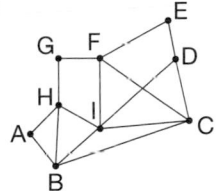

One path is IFGHABHIBCFEDICD

PHOTOGRAPH CREDITS

Chapter 1
Page 1: ©AP/Wide World Photos. Page 31 (left & right): The Granger Collection, New York.

Chapter 2
Page 37: Courtesy Andreas Fuls, Technical University of Berlin, Institute of Geodesy and GIS. Page 86 (left): Courtesy of the Bryn Mawr College Library. Page 86 (right): Courtesy of Professor G. L. Alexanderson.

Chapter 3
Page 93: J-L Charmet/Science Photo Library/Photo Researchers. Page 132 (left): The Bettmann Archive, New York. Page 132 (right): Courtesy of George M. Bergman, University of California, Berkeley.

Chapter 4
Page 137, fig. 1: Will & Demi McIntyre/Photo Researchers. Page 137, fig. 2: E.R. Degginger/Photo Researchers. Page 137, figs. 3 & 4: National Museum of American History ©2002 Smithsonian Institution. Page 137, figs. 5 & 6: NMPFT/Science & Society Picture Library. Page 137, fig. 7: Corbis Images. Page 137, fig. 8: Blair Seitz/Photo Researchers. Page 137, fig. 9: Courtesy of Texas Instruments Incorporated. Page 137, fig. 10: Photo courtesy of Apple Computer, Inc. Page 145: Courtesy of Texas Instruments Incorporated. Page 177 (left): ACME/UPI/The Bettmann Archive, New York. Page 177 (right): Courtesy of Dartmouth College Library, Hanover, New Hampshire.

Chapter 5
Page 183: Granger Collection, New York. Page 210 (left): Reproduced by permission of the Syndics of Cambridge University Library. Page 210 (right): Courtesy of Constance Reid.

Chapter 6
Page 225: The Art Archive/British Museum. Page 271 (left): Courtesy of Evelyn Granville. Page 271 (right): Courtesy of Professor G. L. Alexanderson.

Chapter 7
Page 277: Eberhard Otto/FPG International.

Chapter 8
Page 317: The Needham Research Institute, Cambridge, England. Page 330 (left): George M. Bergman, University of California, Berkeley. Page 330 (right): The Mittag-Leffler Institute, Djursholm, Sweden. Page 348 (left): Courtesy of Sylvia Wiegand. Page 348 (right): Courtesy Kadon Enterprises, Inc.

Chapter 9
Page 353: Newberry Library/SUPERSTOCK. Page 407 (left): Courtesy of Paul Cohen. Page 407 (right): Courtesy of Leon Harkleroad.

Chapter 10
Page 477 (left): UPI/Corbis-Bettmann. Page 477 (right): Laura Wulf/Harvard University News Office.

Chapter 11
Page 483: Granger Collection, New York. Page 523 (left): Photo by Joe Munroe/Ohio Historical Society/Courtesy Caltech Archives. Page 523 (right): UPI/Corbis-Bettmann.

Chapter 12
Page 547 (top & bottom): Courtesy of Dr. Pierre van Hiele. Page 613 (left): Courtesy of Cathleen Singe Morawetz. Photo by James Hamilton. Page 613 (right): The Center for American History, The University of Texas at Austin.

Chapter 13
Page 621: The Granger Collection, New York. Page 687 (left): Corbis-Bettmann. Page 687 (right): Culver Pictures, Inc.

Chapter 14
Page 693: The Granger Collection, New York. Page 749 (left): Corbis-Bettmann. Page 749 (right): Courtesy of International Business Machines Corporation. Unauthorized use not permitted.

Chapter 15
Page 755: Sheila Terry/Science Photo Library/Photo Researchers. Page 793 (left): Courtesy of George Bergman. Page 793 (right): Courtesy of H.S.M. Coxeter, University of Toronto, Canada.

Chapter 16
Page 797 (left): Photo by Ralph A. Raimi. Page 797 (top, right): ©1999 Cordon Art B.V.-Baarn-Holland. All rights reserved. Page 797 (center, right): M.C. Escher, Shells and Starfish ©Cordon Art B.V.-Baarn-Holland. All rights reserved. Page 797 (bottom, right): M.C. Escher, Design Drawing for Intarsia Wood Panel with Fish. ©Cordon Art B.V.-Baarn-Holland. All rights reserved. Page 848 (left): News and Publications Service, Stanford University, Stanford, California. Page 848 (right): FASE Corporate (Foundation for Advancements in Science & Education).

P1

A

Abacists, 93
Abacus:
  Chinese, 93, 137
  chip, 62, 153–55
  Japanese, 93, 137
  Roman, 93
  sand tray, 93
  soroban, 137
  suan-pan, 137
Absolute value, of an
      integer, 329
Abundant number, 207
Acre, 625–26
Acute angle, 581, 703
Acute triangle, 581
Addends, 96
  missing:
    for fractions, 234–35
    for integers, 319–24
    for whole numbers, 103
Adding the complement,
      subtraction by, 165
Adding the opposite:
  integers, 326
  rationals, 361
Addition:
  addend, 96
  additive cancellation property,
      108, 323, 361
  additive inverse property:
    for integers, 323
    for rational numbers, 360
    for real numbers, 376
  algorithms, 153–55
  associative property:
    for fractions, 233
    for integers, 323
    for rational numbers, 360
    for real numbers, 376
    for whole numbers, 99
  binary operation, 96
  closure property:
    for fractions, 233
    for integers, 323
    for rational numbers, 360
    for real numbers, 376
    for whole numbers, 97
  commutative property:
    for fractions, 233
    for integers, 323
    for rational numbers, 360
    for real numbers, 376
    for whole numbers, 97
  compensation, 140
  decimals, 275
  estimation, for fractions, 236,
      250–51
  fractions, 230–34
    with common denominators,
      231

  with unlike denominators,
      231
  identity property:
    for fractions, 233
    for integers, 323
    for rationals, 360
    for real numbers, 376
    for whole numbers, 99
  integers, 319
  order, 123–25
  order of operations, 145
  property with less than, 124
  rational numbers, 357–61
  real numbers, 376
  regrouping, 100
  repeated, 109
  scratch, 164
  set model, 95, 320
  sum, 96
  summands, 96
  of ten, 100
  thinking strategies for learning
      addition facts, 100–1
  of two negatives, 321
  of two positives, 321
  using a chip abacus, 153–55
  using place value pieces,
      153–54
  on the whole number line, 96
  whole numbers, 97–102
  of zero, 321
Addition approach:
  to ordering integers, 340–42
  to ordering rational numbers,
      366
Additive cancellation property:
  for integers, 323
  for rational numbers, 347
  for whole numbers, 108
Additive compensation, 140
Additive identity property:
  fractions, 233
  integers, 323
  rational numbers, 360
  real numbers, 376
  whole numbers, 99
Additive inverse property:
  integers, 323
  rational numbers, 360
  real numbers, 376
Additive magic square, 14, 196
Additive property, of probability,
      504
Additive system, 54
Adjacent
  angles, 578
  vertices, 876
Aesthetics, golden ratio, 263
Agnesi, Maria, 687
Ahmes Papyrus, 215
Algebra, 375–89
  solving equations, 379

  solving inequalities, 384–85
Algebraic logic, 145–46
Algorists, 93
Algorithms, 153–63
  adding the complement, 165
  addition of whole numbers, 96,
      97–99, 153–55
  cashier's, 168
  defined, 153
  decimal operations, 274
  division of whole numbers,
      115–18, 159–63
  duplication, 169
  equal-additions, 168
  Euclidean, 201
  German low-stress, 167
  intermediate for whole number:
    addition, 154, 172
    division, 161–62
    multiplication, 159, 173
  lattice for addition, 155
  lattice for multiplication, 159
  multiplication of whole
      numbers, 109–15,
      158–63
  Russian peasant, 169
  scaffold method for division,
      161, 174
  scratch addition, 164
  standard for whole-number:
    addition, 153
    long division, 173–74
    multiplication, 158
    subtraction, 155
  subtract-from-the-base, 156
  subtraction of whole numbers,
      102–3
Al-Khowarizimi, 93, 777
Alternate exterior angles, 583
Alternate interior angles, 580
Alternate interior angles theorem,
      580
Altitude of a triangle, 727
Amicable pairs, 207
Analysis, 549
Analytical thinking, 533
Analytic geometry, 755
Ancient Egyptian numbers, 54
"And" connective, 859
Angle(s), 42, 554, 577–81
  acute, 578
  adjacent, 578
  alternate exterior, 583
  alternate interior, 580
  angle-angle-similarity property
      (AAA), 708
  angle-side-angle (ASA)
      congruence, 698–700
  associated with parallel lines,
      579–81
  base, 575
  bisector, 701, 721–22

  central, 570
  complementary, 579
  congruent, 695
  consecutive, 585
  copying, 719
  corresponding, 579
  degree, 578
  dihedral, 598
  directed, 802
  exterior, 570, 578
  included, 697
  initial side, 802
  interior, 570, 578
  interior angles on the same side
      as the transversal, 585
  measure of, 578
  measures of a regular n-gon,
      588
  measuring with a protractor, 578
  minutes, 578
  obtuse, 578
  in a pie chart, 447–48
  reflex, 578
  right, 555
  of rotation, 801
  seconds, 578
  side-angle-side (SAS)
      congruence, 697–98
  similarity, 708
  sides, 554, 577
  straight, 578
  sum in a triangle property, 580
  supplementary, 579
  terminal side, 784
  vertex, 570, 577
  vertical, 578
Angle-side-angle (ASA)
      congruence, 698–700
Angle sum in a triangle, 580
Apex, 601
  cone, 603
  pyramid, 601
Apple computer, 137
Apple Macintosh, 137
Arabic, 294
Arc, 718
Archimedean method, 621
Archimedes, 621, 667
Are (square dekameter), 631
Area, 630–31, 644–48
  acre, 625
  circles, 648
  English system of units, 625–26
  formulas, See inside back cover
  Hero's formula, 653
  lateral surface, 662
  metric system, 630–31
  parallelograms, 647
  Pick's theorem, 655
  rectangles, 644–45
  regular polygons, 731–33
  square, 645

Area *(Continued)*
  surface, 662–67
  trapezoids, 647
  triangles, 645–46
Arguments, 861–64
  invalid, 861
  valid, 861
Aristotle, 353, 693
Arithmetica (Diophantus), 317
Arithmetic average, 438
Arithmetic, Fundamental Theorem
  of, 186
Arithmetic logic, 145
Arithmetic sequence, 73
Arithmogon, 12
Array model, 110
Arrow diagrams, 71
  functions as, 76
Ars Magna (Cardano), 317
ASA congruence, 698–700
ASASA for congruent
  quadrilaterals, 698–700
Associative property:
  fraction addition, 233
  fraction multiplication, 245
  integer addition, 323
  integer multiplication, 334
  rational-number addition, 376
  rational-number multiplication,
    376
  real-number addition, 362
  real-number multiplication, 362
  whole-number addition, 100
  whole-number multiplication,
    111–13
Astronomical unit (AU), 293
Atto-, 612
Average:
  arithmetic, 458
  mean, 438–39
  median, 438
  mode, 437
Avoirdupois units, 627
Axiomatics, 551
Axis:
  glide, 806
  manipulation and scaling,
    458–60
  of reflective symmetry, 564–65
  of rotational symmetry, 566
  x- and *y*-, 391

B

Babbage, Charles, 137
Babylonian numeration system,
  55–56
  placeholder, 55
  place value, 55
Bach, J. S, 389
Back-to-back stem and leaf plot,
  416
Balancing method, 380
Bar graphs, 417–20
  misleading, 458–60
Barrel, 627
Base, 61, 125, 601

angles, 566, 575
cone, 603
cylinder, 603
design, 605
exponent, 125
five, 171–74
of a numeration system, 61
parallelogram, 647
power, 125
prism, 663
pyramid, 601
ten pieces, 62
triangle, 647
Base angles, 565–66, 575
  of an isosceles trapezoid, 575
  of an isosceles triangle, 565–66
Base design, 605
Base eight, 66–67
Base five operations, 171–74
  addition, 171–72
  division, 173–74
  multiplication, 173
  subtraction, 172–73
Bases of a trapezoid, 575
Base ten pieces, 62
Base twelve, 66–67
Base two, 66–67
Begle, Edward G., 848
Bell-shaped curve, 447–48
Bertrand conjecture, 196
Betrothed numbers, 209
Between, 577
Bhaskara, 251
Bias surveys, common sources
  of, 469
Biconditional, 861
Bidder, George Parker, 174
Billion, 63
Binary operation, 96
"Birthday problem," 483
Bisect, 701
Bisector:
  angle, 701, 721–22
  perpendicular, 719–20
Black and red chip model for
    integers, 319–25
Blackwell, David, 312
Board foot, 683
Borrowing, 155
Box and whisker plots, 439–43
  extreme outlier, 453
  interquartile range (IQR), 440
  lower quartile, 439
  mild outlier, 453
  outlier, 424, 440, 453
  upper quartile, 439
Brahmagupta, 215, 317
Braille numerals, 60
Buckyballs, iv
Buffon's needle problem, 523
Bundles-of-sticks model, 61

C

Calculatorists, 93
Calculators, 145–47
  adding fractions, 232

algebraic logic, 145–46
arithmetic logic, 145
change-of-sign key, 327
CLEAR key, 141
constant functions, 146
cross-multiplication with
    fractions, 221, 223
decimal, 276
DEL key, 145
division with remainders, 163
exponent keys, 146–47
fraction, 232
GCF, 200
graphics, 394
integers, 327
irrational numbers, 376
logic, 145
long division, 163
memory functions, 147
M+ key, 147
M− key, 147
MR key, 147
multiplication of large
    numbers, 147
*n*th root, 377
ON key, 145
order of operations, 145
parentheses, 146
percent, 297–98, 302
rational exponents, 378
rational numbers, 362
real exponents, 379
RCL key, 147
scientific notation, 147, 282
simplifying fractions, 222–23
square root, 191, 375–76
standard deviation, 444–45
statistics, 439
STO key, 147
SUM key, 147
TI-34 II, 145
Calendar math, 390
Canterbury Puzzles,
    The (Dudeney), 193
Capacity, 624, 627
Cardano, 317
Cardinal number, 51
Carrying, 153
Carry out the plan, 4
Cartesian coordinate system,
    391–92
  coordinates, 391
  origin, 391
  quadrants, 392
  x-axis, 391
  x-coordinate, 391
  y-coordinate, 391
Cartesian product approach, to
    multiplication, 110
Cartesian product of sets, 44
Cashier's, 168
Cavalieri's principle, 678–80
Cayley, Arthur, 342
Celsius:
  conversion to Fahrenheit, 634
  degrees, 633
Celsius, Anders, 633

Center:
  centroid, 783
  circle, 570
  circumcenter, 729
  incenter, 729
  orthocenter, 731, 785
  of rotation, 802
  sphere, 604
Centi-, 630
Centigrade, 633
Centimeter, 628
  cubic, 632
  square, 630
Central angle, 570
Central tendency, measuring,
    437–43
  arithmetic average, 438
  box and whisker plots, 439–43
  mean, 438
  median, 438
  mode, 437
  percentiles, 443
Centroid of a triangle, 783
Certain event, 490
Cevian, 311
Change-of-sign key, 327
Characteristic, 339
Charts and graphs, 417–25
  bar graphs, 417–20
  circle graphs/pie charts, 421–22
  line graphs, 420–21
  pictographs, 422
  pictorial embellishments,
    422–23
  scatterplots, 423–25
Chern, Shiing-Shen, 793
Chinese abacus, 137
Chinese numeration system, 60
Chips, 137
Chip abacus, 62, 153–55
Circle graphs, 447–48
  and misleading statistics,
    464–65
Circle Limit III, 779
Circles, 570–71
  area of, 648
  center, 570
  circumference, 643
  circumscribed, 728–31
  and compass, 571
  concentric, 656
  distances in, 644
  diameter of, 570
  equation, 776–77
  graph, 421–22
  inscribed, 728–31
  radius of, 570
Circuit, Euler, 877
Circumcenter, 729
Circumference, 643
Circumscribed circles, 728–30
  circumcenter, 729
  defined, 728
Classification of isometries,
    799–808
Clinton, William (Bill) Jefferson,
    468

Clock arithmetic 869–74
  congruence modulo *m*, 870–72
Clockwise orientation, 806
Closed curve (simple), 569
Closure property:
  fraction addition, 233
  fraction multiplication, 245
  integer addition, 323
  integer multiplication, 334
  rational-number addition, 360
  rational-number
    multiplication, 363
  real-number addition, 376
  real-number multiplication, 376
  whole-number addition, 97
  whole-number
    multiplication, 111
Clues, 8
Cluster, 416
Cluster estimation, 148
COBOL, 281
Codomain, 75
Coefficients, 380
Cohen, Paul, 407
Coin tossing, 507–9
Cole, Frank Nelson, 192
Collinearity, and slope, 763
Collinearity test, 758
Collinear points, 576
Combinations, 532–35
Combinations to, 100
Commission, 309
Common denominators, 231, 235,
  247, 361
Common difference of a
  sequence, 73
Common factor, 198–201
Common fraction, use of term, 215
Common multiple, 201–3
Common-positive-denominator
  approach, to ordering
  rational numbers, 366
Common ratio of a sequence, 74
Commutative property:
  fraction addition, 233
  fraction multiplication, 245
  integer addition, 323
  integer multiplication, 334
  rational-number addition, 360
  rational-number
    multiplication, 363
  real-number addition, 376
  real-number multiplication, 376
  whole-number addition, 97
  whole-number
    multiplication, 111
Comparison approach, to
  subtraction, 103
Compass, 571
  straightedge constructions and,
    718–28
  straightedge properties and, 718
Compatible numbers, 140
  decimals, 268
  rounding to, 144
  whole numbers, 140, 144
Compensation, 140

Complement:
  of an event, 493
  of a set, 42
Complementary angles, 579
Completeness, 377
Complex fractions, 250
Composite numbers, 185–87
Compound:
  inequality, 128
  interest, 303
  statements, 859
Compounded quarterly,
  use of term, 303
Computational estimation,
  141–47, 236, 250–51,
  268–70, 298–99
  decimals, 268–70
    using fractional equivalents,
    297–98
  fractions, 236, 250–51
  front-end estimation, 141–43
    with adjustment, 142–43
  one-column, 142
  range, 141–42
  rounding, 143–44
  two-column, 142
  whole-number operations,
    141–47
Computer language
  COBOL, 281
Concave shapes, 570
Concentric circles, 656
Conclusion, 859
Concurrent lines, 576
Conditional:
  equations, 79
  probability, 521–23
    and Venn diagram, 523
  statement, 859
Cones, 603, 666
  apex, 603
  base, 603
  height, 677
  lateral surface area, 666
  oblique circular, 604
  right circular, 603–4
  slant height, 666
  surface area, 666
  volume, 667
Congruence modulo *m*, 870–72
Congruence of triangles,
  695–701
  alternate exterior angles, 583
  alternate interior angles, 580
  angle-side-angle (ASA)
    congruence, 698
  base angles, 575
  correspondence, 695
  geometric problem solving
    using, 740–44
  modulo *m*, 870–72
  opposite sides and angles of a
    parallelogram, 699
  polygons, 828
  shapes, 827
  side-angle-side (SAS)
    congruence, 697–98

side-side-side (SSS)
  congruence, 700–1
  using transformations, 828
Congruent:
  angles, 695
  line segments, 555, 695
  polygons, 828
  shapes, 827
  triangles, 695
  vertical angles, 578
Conjecture:
  Goldbach's, 183, 193
  odd perfect number, 183
  twin prime, 183, 193
  Ulam's, 183
Conjunction, 859
Connected graph, 876
Consecutive angles, 585
Constant key on a calculator, 146
Constructions:
  bisect an angle, 721–22
  bisect a segment, 719–20
  circumscribed circle, 728–31
  compass and straightedge
    properties, 718
  construct a line parallel to
    a given line through
    a specified point not on a
    line, 723
  construct a line perpendicular
    to a given line through a
    specified point on a line,
    722
  construct a line perpendicular
    to a given line through a
    specified point not on a
    line, 722–23
  construct an equilateral
    triangle, 731–33
  construct the circumscribed
    circle of a triangle,
    729–31
  construct the inscribed circle
    of a triangle, 731
  construct the perpendicular
    bisector of a line segment,
    719–20
  copy a line segment, 718–19
  copy an angle, 719
  inscribed circle, 728–31
  regular polygons, 731–33
  segment lengths, 733–34
Contrapositive, 860
Converse, 860
  of the Pythagorean theorem,
    742
Conversions:
  between bases, 66–67
  from Celsius to Fahrenheit, 634
  from Fahrenheit to Celsius, 634
  among percents, fractions, and
    decimals, 297–98
  units of length, 628
Convertibility, 628
Convex polygon, 570
Convex polyhedron, 601
Convex shapes, 570

Coordinate distance formula, 757
Coordinates, 391, 577
  Cartesian, 391
  distance, 757–59
    collinearity test, 758
    coordinate distance
      formula, 757
    midpoint formula, 759
  and equations, 770–79
    equations of circles, 776–77
    equations of lines, 770–73
    point-slope equation of
      a line, 773
    simultaneous equations,
      774–76
    slope-intercept equation of
      a line, 772
    solutions of simultaneous
      equations, 775
    y-intercept, 771
  geometric problem solving
    using, 782–87
    centroid of a triangle, 783
    orthocenter of a triangle, 785
  geometry using, 755–56
  slope(s), 760–64
    and collinearity, 763
    of a line, 760–61
    of a line segment, 760
    of parallel lines, 763–64
    of perpendicular lines, 764
Correlation, 424
Correspondence:
  between triangles, 695
  one-to-one, 40
Corresponding:
  angles, 579
  angle property, 579
  parts of congruent triangles, 695
  sides, 695
Counterclockwise orientation, 806
Counting:
  chant, 52
  factors, 197–98
  fundamental property of, 502
  numbers, 16, 39
  techniques, and
    probabilities, 530
Counting methods:
  combinations, 532–35
  permutations, 530–32
  n factorial, 531
Counting on, 100
Cover Up strategy, 380
Coxeter, H. S. M., 793
Cropping, 461–62
Cross-multiplication, 220
  fraction equality, 220–21
  of fraction inequality, 223
  of rational-number
    inequality, 367
Cross-products, 220
Cross-section, 678–79
Cryptarithm, 7
Cube, 602–3
  truncated, 603
  volume of, 673

Cubic centimeter (milliliter), 632
Cubic decimeter (liter), 632
Cubic foot, 626
Cubic functions, graphs of, 396
Cubic inch, 626
Cubic meter, 632
Cubic units, 626
Cubic yard, 626
Cup, 627
Curriculum and Evaluation
    Standards for School
    Mathematics, 3
Curve:
    normal, 447–48
    simple closed, 569
Cylinders, 603, 664–65
    base, 603
    circular, 603
    height, 664–65
    lateral surface area, 664–65
    oblique, 603
    right circular, 603
    surface area of, 664–65
    volume of, 675–76

D

Data:
    box and whisker plots,
        439–43
    cluster, 416
    gap, 416
    mean, 438
    median, 438
    mode, 437
    standard deviation, 444
    z-score, 446–51
Debugging, 271
Deceptive pictorial embellishments,
    466–67
Deci-, 630
Decimals, 263–86
    addition, 275
    algorithms for operations with,
        274–78
    compatible numbers, 140, 144
    decimal point, 265
    defined, 265
    dividing by powers of, 10, 269
    division, 275–78
    estimation, 268–70
    expanded form, 265
    fraction equivalents, 297–98
    fractions with terminating
        decimal representations,
        266
    hundreds square, 265
    infinite, 374
    magic square, 196
    mental math, 268–70
    model for, 265–66
    multiplication, 275
    multiplying by powers of,
        10, 269
    nonrepeating, 374
    notation, 271
    number line, 265–66

operations with, 274–81
ordering, 267
percents to, 297
reading, 265
repeating:
    classifying, 278–81
    defined, 279
    nonterminating, 280
    period, 279
repetend, 279
subtraction, 275
terminating, 266
Decimal notation, 271
Decimeter, 628
Deduction, 551
Deductive reasoning:
    biconditional, 861
    chain rule, 863
    conclusion, 859
    conditional statement, 859
    contrapositive, 860
    converse, 860
    Euler diagram, 862
    hypotheses, 859
    invalid argument, 861
    inverse, 860
    law of detachment, 862
    logically equivalent
        statements, 860
    valid argument, 861
Deficient number, 207
Degree:
    even, 877
    odd, 877
    of a vertex, 877
Degrees, 578
    angle measure, 578
    Celsius, 633
    Fahrenheit, 628
    minutes, 578
    seconds, 578
Deka-, 630
Dekameter, 628
Deming, W. Edwards, 415
Deming Award, 415
DeMorgan's laws, 47, 49
Denominator, 218
    common, 231–32, 235, 247–48
    least common (LCD), 232
    unlike, 231, 235, 248–49
Density, 621
Density property
    fractions, 225
    rational numbers, 367
    real numbers, 377
Descartes, Rene, 44, 755, 764
Detachment, law of, 862
Deviation, standard, 443–46
Devise a plan, 4
Diagonal, 567–68
Diagram:
    Euler, 862
    tree, 111, 500–9
    Venn, 40
Diameter:
    circle, 570
    sphere, 604

Dienes blocks, 62
Difference:
    common, in a sequence, 73
    order of operations, 145
    sets, 42
    whole numbers, 103
Difference Engine, 137
Digits, 62
Dihedral angle, 598
    faces of, 598
Dimensional analysis, 622, 635
Diophantus, 317
Directed angle, 802
    initial side, 802
    measure of, 802
    terminal side, 802
Directed line segment, 800
Direct reasoning, 868
Disjoint sets, 40
Disjunction, 859
Dispersion, measuring, 443–46
    range, 443
    standard deviation, 443–44
    variance, 443–44
    z-score, 446
Distance(s), 642
    in a circle, 644
    between two points, 577
    coordinates, 757–59
        collinearity test, 758
        coordinate distance
            formula, 757
        midpoint formula, 759
    formula, 757
    from a point to a line, 730
    preserving mappings, 824
    unit, 642
Distributions, 447–51
    defined, 447
    normal, 448
    of physical measurements, 448
    relative frequency, 447
Distributive property
    multiplication:
        over addition of fractions, 246
        over addition of integers, 335
        over addition of rational
            numbers, 363
        over addition of real numbers,
            376
        over addition of whole
            numbers, 113
        over subtraction of whole
            numbers, 114
Dividend, 116
Dividing by powers of 10, 269
Divine proportion, 263
Divisibility, test for, 187–91
Divisible by, 187
Division:
    algorithm for whole numbers,
        117
    in base five, 173–74
    compensation, 149
    decimals, 275–78
    dividend, 116
    divisor, 116, 117, 187

estimation, 161
fractions, 246–50
    with common denominators,
        247–48
    with unlike denominators,
        248–49
integers, 337–38
    defined, 337
measurement, 115
missing factor, 116
order of operations, 145
partitive, 115
property of zero, 116
quotient, 116–17
rational numbers, 364–65
real numbers, 376
remainder, 117
repeated subtraction, 117–18
scaffold method, 161, 174
standard algorithm, 162
whole numbers, 115–18,
    159–63
Divisor, 116–17, 187
Do a Simulation strategy, 484, 517
Dodecahedron, 602
Domain, 75
Dot plots, 415
Doubles, 100
Dram, 627
Draw a Diagram strategy, 38,
    117–18, 124–25, 380,
    493, 501, 505, 507–8,
    519, 522, 580
Drawing with replacement, 503
Drawing without replacement, 503
Draw a Picture strategy, 10–12, 99,
    111–12, 225–26, 380–85,
    587, 701, 709, 740–42,
    783–86, 840
Dual tessellation, 592
Dudeney, Henry, 193
Duplication algorithm, 169

E

Earned run average, 295
Edge, 875
Edges, polyhedron, 601
Egyptian numeration system, 54
    as additive system, 54
Einstein, Albert, 406–7
Elementary logic, 858–68
    "and" connective, 859
    arguments, 861–64
    biconditional, 861
    compound statements, 859
    conclusion, 859
    conditional statement, 859
    conjunction, 859
    connectives, 859–61
    contrapositive, 860
    converse, 860
    direct reasoning, 861
    disjunction, 859
    equivalent statements, 860
    Euler diagram, 862–64
    Exclusive "or," 859

hypothesis, 859
hypothetical syllogism, 863
"if and only if" connective, 861
"if-then" connective, 859 61
implication, 859
Inclusive "or," 865
invalid argument, 861
inverse, 860
law of detachment, 862
logical connectives, 859
logically equivalent statements, 860
modus ponens, 862
modus tollens, 863–64
"necessary," use of term, 861
negation, 858
"or" connective, 859
statements, 858
"sufficient," use of term, 861
truth table, 858
valid argument, 861
Elements of a set, 39
Elements, The (Euclid), 353, 693, 701, 734
Elimination method, of solving simultaneous equations, 778–79
Elliott wave theory, 398
Ellipse, 782
Ellipsis, 16
eManipulatives:
    Balance Beam Algebra, 383
    Base Blocks: Addition, 154
    Base Blocks: Subtraction, 158
    Chips Minus, 325
    Chips Plus, 320
    Congruence, 701
    Counterfeit Coin, 22
    Adding Fractions, 232
    Comparing Fractions, 224
    Dividing Fractions, 249
    Equivalent Fractions, 219
    Function Grapher, 394
    Geoboard, 646, 758, 764
    Histogram, 417
    Multibase Blocks, 65
    Number Line, 97
    Percent Gauge, 301
    Pythagorean Theorem, 650
    Scatterplots, 425
    Sieve of Eratosthenes, 186
    Simulation, 518
    Slicing Solids, 602
    Tessellations, 591
    Tower of Hanoi, 23
    Translation transformation, 801
    Venn Diagrams, 42
Empty set, 39
Endpoints, 577
English system of units, 624–28
    area, 625–26
    cubic units, 626–27
    cup, 627

degree Fahrenheit, 628
foot, 625
gallon, 627
inch, 625
length, 624 25
linear units, 625
mile, 625
ounce, avoirdupois, 627
ounce, liquid, 627
pint, 627
pound, 627
quart, 627
square units, 625–26
temperature, 628
volume, 626–27
weight, 627
yard, 625
ENIAC, 137
Equal-additions algorithm, 168
Equal additions method, 140
Equal:
    fractions, 220–21
    ratios, 287
    sets, 39
Equally likely outcomes:
    odds, 519–21
    probability, 488
Equation approach, to solving percent problems, 301–4
Equation(s):
    and coordinates, 770–77
    circles, 776–77
    defined, 379
    lines, 770–73
        point-slope equation of a line, 773
    percent, 301–4
    simultaneous, 774–76
        elimination method, 778–79
        graphical method, 778
        solutions of, 775–76
        substitution method, 778
    slope-intercept equation of a line, 772
    solution set, 379
    solving, 379
    systems, 774
Equiangular, 555
Equidistant, 577
Equilateral, 555
Equilateral triangle, 554
Equivalence relation, 72
Equivalent:
    directed line segments, 800
    graphs, 879
    sets, 39
    statements, 860
Eratosthenes, 656
    sieve of, 185
Erdos, Paul, 257
Escalante, Jaime, 848
Escher, M. C., 590, 797, 808
Escher-type patterns, 808–9
Estimation:
    cluster, 148
    compatible number, 144

computational, 141–48, 236, 250–51, 298–99
decimals, 268–70
fractions, 236, 250–51, 298–99
front-end, 141–43
    with adjustment, 142–43
one-column front-end, 142
percents, using fractional equivalents, 298–99
range, 141–42
round-a-five-up, 143
round down, 143
rounding, 143–44
round to compatible numbers, 144
round to the nearest even, 144
round up, 143
two-column front-end, 142
Euclid, 353, 693, 701, 734
Euclidean algorithm, 201
Euclidean constructions, 718–28
Eudoxus, 353
Euler, Leonhard, 186, 687
Euler:
    circuit, 877
    diagram, 862–64
    path, 877
Euler's:
    formula, 602
    Formula Theorem, 881
    Transversable Graph Theorem, 878
Even:
    degree, 877
    numbers, 16
Event(s), 486
    certain, 490
    complement of, 493
    disjoint, 493
    experimental, 490–91
    impossible, 489–90
    mutually exclusive, 493
Exa-, 630
Exchanging:
    addition, 154
    subtraction, 156
Exercise, 3
Expanded notation (expanded form), 62
    decimal, 265
    whole number, 62
Expected value, 519
Experimental probability, 490–91
Experiments, 486
Exploding a circle graph sector, 465
Exponent, 66, 123–28
    base of, 123
    on a calculator, 379
    integer, 338
    keys, 146–47
    negative, 338
    power, 16, 125
    properties, 126–27, 379
    rational, 377–79
    real, 379

in scientific notation, 339
unit fraction, 378
whole numbers, 125–28
zero as an, 128
Exponential:
    functions, graphs of, 394–95
    growth, 74
Exterior angle, 570, 578
Extreme outliers, 453
Extremes, 288

F

Faces, polyhedron, 601
Factorial, 183, 531
Factor tree, 186
Factorization, prime, 185, 197–201, 202
Factors, 110, 186
    common, 198
    counting, 197–98
    greatest common, 198–201
    missing, for whole numbers, 116
    number of, 197–98
    proper, 207
Facts:
    addition, 100–1
    multiplication, 114–15
Fahrenheit, degrees, 628
    converting to Celsius, 634
Fahrenheit, Gabriel, 628
Fathom, 624
Femto-, 630
Fermat, Pierre de, 183, 192–93
Fermat prime, 732–33
Fermat's Last Theorem, 183
Fermi problems, 179
Feuerbach, Karl, 787
Feuerbach circle, 787
Fibonacci sequence, 16, 29, 197, 390
Finger multiplication, 165–66
Finite sets, 45
Fish, 797
5-clock, 869–74
5-con triangles, 701
Flannery, Sarah, 342
Flat, in place value pieces, 63
Flip, 803
Foot, 625
    cubic, 626
    square, 626
Formula, midpoint, 759
Formulas, functions as, 77
Four-fact families, 103
Fractal Geometry of Nature, The (Mandelbrot), 710
Fractals and self-similarity, 710–11
Fraction(s), 215 61, 355 56
    addition, 230–34
    additive identity property for, 233
    associative property for addition, 233
    associative property for multiplication, 245

Fraction(s) *(Continued)*
closure property for
addition, 233
closure property for
multiplication, 245
common denominators, 231
commutative property for
addition, 233
commutative property for
multiplication, 245
comparing, 223
complex, 250
computational estimation,
236, 250–51
concept of, 217–18
converting to decimals and
percents, 297–98
cross-multiplication for
equality, 220
cross-multiplication for
inequality, 223
cross-products, 220
decimals, 268, 297–98
defined, 218
denominator, 218
density property of, 225
distributive property of
multiplication over
addition, 246
division, 246–50
Egyptian, 215
in elementary mathematics,
217–18
equality, 219, 297–98
equivalent, 286–87
estimation, 236, 250–51
greater than, 223
identity for addition, 233
identity for multiplication, 245
improper fractions, 222
inequality, 223
invert and multiply, 248
least common denominator
(LCD), 232
less than, 223
lowest terms, 221
mental math, 236, 250–51
method of ordering decimals,
222–25
mixed numbers, 222
multiplication, 241–46
multiplicative identity
property, 245
multiplicative inverse, 245
number line, 223
as numerals and numbers, 219
numerator, 218
ordering, 222–25
origin of term, 215
percents to, 297
product, 242
properties of addition, 233
properties of multiplication,
245
ratios, 287
reciprocal of, 245
reducing, 220

with repeating nonterminating
decimal representations,
280
set of, 218
simplest forms of, 221
simplified fractions, 219–20
strips, 219
subtraction, 234–35, 362
with terminating decimal
representations, 266
unitary, 238
unlike denominators, 231
Frangere, 215
Franklin, Benjamin, 104
Frequency:
of a number, 416
relative, 447
Front-end estimation, 141–43
with adjustment, 142–43
one-column, 142
range, 141–42
two-column, 142
Frustum, 671
Fuller, Buckminster, iv
Function(s), 72–77
arithmetic sequence, 73
as arrow diagrams, 76
Cartesian coordinate system,
391–92
codomain, 75
common difference of a
sequence, 73
common ratio of a sequence, 73
cubic, 396
domain, 75
exponential functions, 394–95
exponential growth, 74
as formulas, 77
function notation, 75
geometric sequence, 74
as geometric transformations,
77
as graphs, 76, 391–98
greatest integer, 400
initial term, 73
linear, 392–93
as machines, 76
memory, 147
notation, 75
quadratic, 393–94
range, 75
representations of, 75–77
as sets of ordered pairs, 76
as a spreadsheet, 76
step functions, 397
as tables, 76
vertical line test, 390
Fundamental counting property,
502
Fundamental Theorem of
Arithmetic, 186
Furlong, 625

G

Gallon, 627
Gap, 416

Gardner, Martin, 348
Gasket, Sierpinski, 710
Gauss, Carl Friedrich, 25, 28,
31, 621
Gauss's theorem for
constructible regular
n-gons, 733
GCF (greatest common factor),
198–9
Geometer's Sketchpad activities:
Circumcircle, 730
Dynamic Pythagorean
Theorem, 650
Midquad, 744
Name That Quadrilateral,
569
Parallelogram Areas, 647
Perpendicular Lines, 764
Rectangle Area, 645
Same Base, Same Height,
Same Area, 646
Size Transformation, 810
Slope, 761
Tree Height, 709
Triangle Angle Sum, 580
Triangle Inequality, 651
Geometric constructions,
718–28
Geometric fallacy, golden
ratio, 263
Geometric mean, 736
Geometric sequence, 71
Geometric series, 240
Geometric shapes, 547–619
analyzing, 564–71
angles, 42, 554, 577–81
alternative interior, 579–80
angle sum in a triangle, 580
associated with parallel
lines, 579–81
base, 566, 575
central, 570
complementary, 579
consecutive, 585
corresponding, 579
exterior, 570, 578
interior, 570, 578
interior angles on the
same side of the
transversal, 585
supplementary, 579
vertex, 570
base angles, 575
central angle, 570
circles, 570–71
common, defining, 553–55
concave shapes, 570
cone, 603
congruent line segments, 555
convex shapes, 570
cylinder, 603
diagonal, 567–68
diameter, sphere, 604
equiangular, 555
equilateral, 555
equilateral triangle, 555
exterior angle, 570, 578

interior angle, 570, 578
isosceles trapezoid, 555,
565–66
isosceles triangle, 554, 565–66
kite, 555
line segment, 554
oblique circular cone, 603
oblique cylinder, 603
parallel line segments, 567–69
parallelogram, 554
perpendicular, 554, 579
perpendicular line segments,
567–69
points and lines in a plane,
576–77
polygon, 569–70
properties of, 576–81
quadrilaterals, 554
attributes of, 569
radius, sphere, 604
recognizing, 551–52
rectangle, 554
regular polygons, 569–70
angular measures in, 586–88
tessellations in, 588–91
rhombus, 555
right angle, 554
right circular cone, 603
right circular cylinder, 603
scalene triangle, 554
sides, 554, 577
simple closed curve, 569
sphere, 604
square, 554
square lattice, 554
symmetry, 564–67
base angles, 566
line of, 564
Mira, 566
reflection, 564, 608
rotation, 566, 608
three-dimensional curved
shapes, 603–4
three-dimensional shapes,
597–604
dihedral angle, 598
planes, 597–98
polyhedra, 599–603
skew lines, 598
trapezoid, 555
triangles, 554
acute, 581
obtuse, 581
right, 581
van Hiele theory of
development in geometry,
549–51
analysis (level 1), 549–50
axiomatics (level 4), 551
deduction (level 3), 551
recognition (level 0), 549
relationships (level 2),
550–51
vertex, 554, 577
vertex angle, 578
Geometric transformations,
functions as, 77

Geometry:
  brief timeline for, 755
  congruence of triangle,
      695–701
    angle-side-angle (ASA)
      congruence, 698
    congruent angles, 695
    congruent line segments, 695
    correspondence, 695
    geometric problem solving
      using, 740–44
    opposite sides and angles of
      a parallelogram, 699
    side-angle-side (SAS)
      congruence, 697–98
    side-side-side (SSS)
      congruence, 700–1
  eclectic approach to, 855–57
  Euclidean constructions,
      718–28
    circumscribed and inscribed
      circles, 728–31
    compass and straightedge
      properties, 718–23
    regular polygons, 731–33
    segment lengths, 733–34
  midsegment theorem,
      855–57
  similarity of triangles,
      706–17
    fractals and self-similarity,
      710–11
    geometric problem solving
      using, 740–44
    indirect measurement, 709
    Koch curve, 710
    Sierpinski triangle
      (Sierpinski gasket), 710
    similarity properties, 708
  transformations, 797–853
    defined, 799
    directed line segment, 800
    equivalent directed line
      segments, 800
    image, 799
    isometries, 799–807
    rigid motions, 799
  using coordinates, 755–96
    distance and slope in the
      coordinate plane, 757–64
    equations and coordinates,
      770–77
    geometric problem solving
      using, 782–87
    See also Coordinates
  van Hiele theory of
      development in, 549–51
  See also Geometric shapes
Germain, Sophie, 24, 31
German low stress algorithm, 167
Giga-, 630
Gleason, Andrew, 477
Glide axis, 806
Glide reflections, 805–7
  symmetry, 808
Goldbach's conjecture, 183, 193
Golden ratio, 263

Golden rectangle, 263
Grade, percent, 766
Grain, 627
Gram, 633
Granville, Evelyn Boyd, 257
Graphical method, of solving
      simultaneous equations,
      778
Graphs, 417–25
  bar, 417–20
  box-and-whisker, 439–43
  circle, 421–22
  connected, 876
  of cubic functions, 396
  equivalent, 879
  of exponential functions,
      394–95
  of functions, 390–406
  functions as, 76
  histogram, 417
  horizontal axis, 391–92
  as linear functions, 392–93
  line, 420–21
  misleading, 457–67
  pairs of equations, 765–68
  pictographs, 422
  pictorial embellishments,
      422–23
  pie charts, 447–48
  planar, 880
  of quadratic functions, 393–94
  scatterplots, 423–25
  of step functions, 397
  stem and leaf plots, 416–17
  vertical axis, 391–92
  vertical line test, 390
  See also Misleading
      graphs/statistics
Graph theory, 875
Great circle of a sphere, 688
Greater than, 124
  for fractions, 223
  general set formation of, 52
  See also Less than
Greater than or equal to, 124
  for fractions, 223
Greatest common factor (GCF),
      198–99
  calculator, 201
  Euclidean algorithm, 201
  and LCM, 201–3
  prime factorization method,
      197–201
  set intersection method, 202
Greatest integer function, 400
Great Mental Calculators, The
      (Smith), 148
Great Pyramid of Cheops, 586
Great Wall of China, 682
Greek musical scale, 296
Grid approach, to solving percent
      problems, 299–300
Grouping:
  by tens, 62
  tally numeration system, 53–54
Guess and Test strategy, 5–8,
      379–80

clues, 8
inferential guess and test, 6
random guess and test, 6
solving equations, 379
systematic guess and test, 6

H

Half-turn, 823
Halmos, Paul, 132
Halving and doubling method, 145
Hamann, Arthur, 196
Hamiltonian:
  Circuit, 883
  Path, 883
Hands, 623
Hardy, George, 211
Harmonic triangle, 240
HDL, 292
Hectare (square hectometer), 631
Hecto-, 630
Hectometer, 628
Height:
  cone, 677
  cylinder, 664–65
  parallelogram, 647
  prism, 663
  pyramid, 677
  slant, 665
  trapezoid, 647
  triangles, 646
Heptagon, regular, 589
Hero's formula, 653
Hershiser, Orel, 295
Hexafoil, 661
Hexagon:
  tessellation, 589–90
Hexahedron, 602
Hilbert, David, 86
Hindu-Arabic numeration
      system, 61–67
  base, 61
  base ten pieces, 62, 64
  bundles of sticks, 61
  chip abacus, 62
  digits, 61
  expanded notation (expanded
      form), 62, 65
  exponents, 65
  grouping by tens, 61
  and nondecimal numeration
      systems, 64
  numerals, naming, 63
  place value, 62
Hippasus, 353
Histograms, 417
Holistic measurement, 623
Holistic thinking, and geometric
      shapes, 551
Hoppe, Oscar, 193
Hopper, Grace Brewster Murray,
      177, 271
Horizontal axis, 391
Horsepower, 640
How to Solve It (Polya), 1
Hundreds square, 265
Hundredths, 265

Hypatia, 749
Hyperbola, 781
Hypotenuse, 648
Hypothesis, 859
Hypothetical syllogism, 863

I

Icosahedron, 602
Ideal system of units, 628
Identification numbers, 51
Identify Subgoals strategy, 694
Identity elements (zero),
      See Identity properties
Identity for addition, 100
Identity for multiplication, 112
Identity property:
  fraction addition, 233
  fraction multiplication, 245
  integer addition, 323
  integer multiplication, 334
  rational-number addition, 360
  rational-number
      multiplication, 363
  real-number addition, 376
  real-number multiplication, 376
  whole-number addition, 99
  whole-number
      multiplication, 112
"If and only if" statement, 861
"If-then" statement, 859–61
Image, 799
Implication, 859
Impossible event, 489–90
Improper fractions, 222
Incenter of a triangle, 729
Inch, 625
  cubic, 626
  square, 66
Index of a radical, 377
Indirect measurement, and
      similarity of triangles, 709
Indirect reasoning, 138, 206,
      373–74
Inductive reasoning, 16
Inequalities, 379
  solving, 384–85
Inferential guess and test, 6–8
Infinite decimals, 374
Infinite geometric series, 240
Infinite of primes, 205
Infinite sets, 45
Informal measurement
      methods, 623
Initial side of a directed angle, 802
Initial term, 73
Inscribed circles, 728–31
  defined, 728
  incenter, 729
  tangent, 729
Inscribed polygon, 732
Integer(s), 317–51, 345–46
  absolute value of, 329
  adding the opposite, 325–26
  addition, 319–24
  additive cancellation, 323
  additive identity, 323

Integer(s) *(Continued)*
  additive inverse property, 323
  associative property for
    addition, 323
  associative property for
    multiplication, 334
  black and red chip model,
    319–25
  on a calculator, 327
  closure property for
    addition, 323
  closure property for
    multiplication, 334
  commutative property for
    addition, 323
  commutative property for
    multiplication, 334
  defined, 319
  distributivity of multiplication
    over addition of integers,
    335
  division, 337–38
  exponents, 338–40
  identity property for
    addition, 323
  identity property for
    multiplication, 334
  inequality, 340–41
  less than, 340
  measurement model, 320
  missing addend, 326–27
  multiplication, 332–36
  multiplicative cancellation, 336
  multiplicative identity, 334
  multiplying by opposites,
    335–36
  multiplying opposites, 341–42
  negative, 319
  negative integer exponent,
    338–40
  number line, 319–20
  opposite, 320
  ordering, 340–42
  positive, 319
  product, 332–33
  positive integers, 319
  properties of addition, 323
  properties of multiplication, 334
  properties of ordering, 341
  set model, 320
  subtraction, 324–27
  take-away, 324–25
  zero divisors, 336
Intercept, *y*-, 771
Interest, compound, 303
Interior angle, 570, 578
Interior angles on the same side
  of the transversal, 585
Intermediate algorithm:
  addition of whole numbers,
    154, 172
  division of whole numbers, 162
  multiplication of whole
    numbers, 159
Interquartile range (IQR), 440
Interrelatedness, 628
Intersection of sets, 41–2

Invalid argument, 861
Inverse, 860
  additive for, 23, 310
  additive for rational numbers,
    360
  additive for real numbers, 376
  multiplicative for fractions, 245
  multiplicative for rational
    numbers, 363
  multiplicative for real numbers,
    376
Invert the divisor and multiply,
    364–65
Ionian numeration system, 58
IQR (interquartile range), 440
Irrational numbers, 353, 374
  operations with, 389
  square root, 375–76
Is an element of, 39
Is divisible by, 186
Is greater than, 52
Is greater than or equal to, 52
Is less than, 52, 123
Is less than or equal to, 52
Is not an element of, 39
Isometries, 799–807, 826–27
  clockwise orientation, 806
  congruence of shapes, 827
  counterclockwise orientation,
    806
  directed angle, 802
  directed line segment, 800
  equivalent directed line
    segments, 800
  glide reflections, 805–7
  image, 799
  initial side, 802
  measure of the directed
    angle, 802
  properties of, 824
  reflections, 803–5
  rigid motions, 799
  rotations, 801–3
  terminal side, 802
  translations, 799–801
  triangle congruence, 826
Isosceles trapezoid, 555
Isosceles triangle, 554

J

Japanese abacus, 93, 137
Jefferson, Thomas, 425
Joule, 640

K

Kemeny, John, 177
al-Khowarizimi, 93, 777
Kilo-, 630
Kilogram, 633
Kiloliter (cubic meter), 632
Kilometer, 628
Kilowatt hour, 623
Kite, 554–55
Koch curve, 27, 710
Koch snowflake, 27

Konigsberg bridge problem, 875
Korf, Richard, 536
Kovalevskaya, Sonya, 312
Kurtz, Thomas, 177

L

"Ladder" of numbers, 368
Landon, Alfred, 469
Lateral faces, 601
  prism, 601
  pyramid, 601
Latitude, 769
Lattice method:
  for addition, 155
  for multiplication, 159
Lattice rod, 137
Lattice, square, 554
Law of detachment, 862
LCM (least common multiple),
    201–3
Leaf, stem and leaf plot, 416–17
Least common denominator
    (LCD), 232
Least common multiple (LCM),
    201–3
  build-up method, 202–3
  prime factorization method, 202
  set intersection method, 202
LeBlanc, Antoine, See Germain,
    Sophie
Leffler, Ann Charlotte, 312
Legs of a right triangle, 648
Lehmer, D. H., 196
Left-to-right methods, 140–41
Leibniz, Gottfried Wilhelm, 137,
    621
Leibniz's reckoning machine, 137
Length, 577, 641–44
  Circumference, 643–44
  distance, 641
  of a line segment, 577
  metric system, 628–29
  perimeter, 642–43
Less than, 52, 124
  addition, 124, 341
  fractions, 223
  integers, 340
  multiplication by a negative,
    341
  multiplication by a positive, 341
  ordering, and whole-number
    operations, 123–25
  real numbers, 376
  transitive property, 123–24
  whole numbers, 124–25
Less than or equal to, 123–24
  for fractions, 223
Levels, van Hiele, 549–51
Light-year, 638
Lilavat (Bhaskara), 251
Line(s), 576–77
  concurrent, 576
  equation, 770–73
  graph, 420–21
  number, 25, 52–53, 223, 320
  parallel, 579–81

  parallel to a plane, 598–99
  plot, 415
  point-slope equation of, 773
  of reflection, 803–5
  segment, 554, 577
  skew, 598
  slope-intercept of, 772
  of symmetry, 564
  tangent, 729
Linear functions:
  algebraic form, 393
  graphs of, 392–93
Linear units of measure:
  English, 624–28
  metric, 628–34
  nonstandard, 623–24
Line graphs, 420–21
  and cropping, 461–62
Line plots, 415
Line segment(s), 554, 577
  congruent, 555, 695
  directed, 800
  endpoints, 577
  equivalent directed, 800
  length of, 577
  midpoint, 577
  parallel, 567–69
  perpendicular, 567–69
  slopes of, 760–61
Liquid ounce, 627
Liter, 632
Literary Digest poll, 469
Logarithms, 137
Logic, 858–68
  algebraic, 145–46
  "and" connective, 859
  arguments, 861–64
  arithmetic, 145
  biconditional, 861
  compound statements, 859
  conclusion, 859
  conditional statement, 859
  conjunction, 859
  connectives, 859–61
  contrapositive, 860
  converse, 860
  direct reasoning, 861
  disjunction, 859
  equivalent statements, 860
  Euler diagram, 862–64
  Exclusive "or," 859
  hypothesis, 859
  hypothetical syllogism, 863
  "if and only if" connective, 861
  "if-then" connective, 859–61
  implication, 859
  Inclusive "or," 865
  invalid argument, 861
  inverse, 860
  law of detachment, 862
  logical connectives, 859
  logically equivalent statements,
    860
  modus ponens, 862
  modus tollens, 863–64
  "necessary," use of term, 861
  negation, 858

"or" connective, 859
statements, 858
"sufficient," use of term, 861
truth table, 858
valid argument, 861
Logical connectives, 859–61
Logically equivalent statements, 860
Loomis, Elisha, 734
Long division, 159–63
Long, in place value pieces, 62
Longitude, 769
Look back, 4
Look for a Formula strategy, 414
Look for a Pattern strategy, 15–19, 127, 197–98, 280, 324–25, 333, 338, 508–9, 840
Lower quartile, 439
Lowest terms, fractions, 221

M

Macintosh computer, 137
Machines, functions as, 76
Magic square, additive, 14, 196
Make a List strategy, 19–21
Mandarin, 294
Mandelbrot, Benoit, 710, 749
Mantissa, 339
Mapping, See Transformations
Mass, metric system, 633
Matching set, 40
Mayan numeration system, 56–57
Maya people, 37
Mean, 438–39
    arithmetic, 438
    geometric, 736
    proportional, 736
Means, 288
Measurement, 621–89
    area, 644–48
        circle, 648
        indirect, 709
        informal, 623–24
        parallelogram, 647
        process, 623
        rectangle, 644 45
        square, 645
        trapezoid, 647
        triangle, 645–46
    Cavalieri's principle, 678–80
    dimensional analysis, 634–35
    English system, 624–28
        area, 625–26
        length, 624–25
        temperature, 628
        volume, 626–27
        weight, 627
    holistic, 623
    length, 641–44
        circumference, 643–44
        distance, 641
        perimeter, 642–43
    metric system, 628–34, 651
        are, 631
        area, 630–31
        centimeter, 628

cubic centimeter, 632
cubic decimeter, 632
cubic meter, 632
decimeter, 628
degrees Celsius, 633
dekameter, 629
gram, 633
hectare (square hectometer), 631
hectometer, 629
kilogram, 633
kiloliter (cubic meter), 632
kilometer, 628
length, 628–29
liter, 632
mass, 633
metric ton, 633
milliliter, 632
square centimeter, 630–31
square kilometer, 631
square meter, 630 31
square millimeter, 631
temperature, 633–34
volume, 632–33
nonstandard units, 623–24
Pythagorean theorem, 387, 648–51, 693, 711, 842
standard units, 624–34
surface area, 662–67
    cones, 666
    cylinders, 664–65
    defined, 662
    lateral, 662
    prisms, 663
    of a right circular cone, 666
    of a right circular cylinder, 664
    of a right prism, 663
    of a right regular pyramid, 665
    slant height, 665
    spheres, 667
volume, 672–78
    cones, 677
    cylinders, 675–76
    prisms, 672–75
    pyramids, 676–77
    spheres, 678
Measurement division, 115
Measurement model, 320–21
Measure(s):
    angle, 578
    central tendency, 437–43
    dispersion, 443–46
Median, 437–38
Mega-, 630
Members of a set, 39
Memory function, 147
Memory key, 147
Mental math, 139–41
    additive compensation, 140
    compatible numbers, 140
    compensation, 140
    decimals, 268–70
    division compensation, 149
    equal additions, 140
    fractions, 236, 250–51

halving and doubling, 149
left-to-right-methods, 140–41
multiplication, 140
multiplicative compensation, 140
multiplying by special factors, 141
multiplying powers of 10, 141
percents, 298–99
powers of 10, 141
properties, 140
scaling up/down, 290
special factors, 141
thinking strategies for addition, 100–1
thinking strategies for multiplication, 114
Meridian, 769
    prime, 769
Mersenne number, 196
Meter:
    cubic, 632
    square, 630
Metric converter, 628
Metric prefixes, 630
Metric system, 628–34
    are, 631
    area, 630–31
    capacity, 632
    centimeter, 628
    cubic centimeter, 632
    cubic decimeter, 632
    cubic meter, 632
    cubic units, 632–33
    decimeter, 628
    degrees Celsius, 633
    dekameter, 629
    gram, 633
    hectare (square hectometer), 631
    hectometer, 629
    kilogram, 633
    kiloliter (cubic meter), 632
    kilometer, 628
    length, 628–29
    liter, 632
    linear units, 623–26
    mass, 633
    meter, 628
    metric ton, 633
    milliliter, 632
    millimeter, 628
    prefixes, 630
    square centimeter, 630–31
    square kilometer, 631
    square meter, 630–31
    square millimeter, 631
    square units, 630–31
    temperature, 633–34
    tonne, 633
    volume, 632–33
Metric ton, 633
Micro-, 630
Midpoint, 577
Midpoint formula, 759
Midquad theorem, 744
Midsegment:

trapezoid, 659
triangle, 744
Midsegment theorem, 855–857
Mild outliers, 453
Mile, 625
    square, 626
Milli-, 630
Milliliter, 632
Millimeter, 628
Million, 63
Minuend, 103
Minus, 103
Minute, 578
Mira, 566
Misleading graphs/statistics, 457–67
Missing-addend approach, to subtraction, 103
Missing factor, 116
Missing-factor approach to division, 116
Mixed numbers, 222
Mnemonic for pi, 385
Mode, 437
Models:
    black and red chips, 319–25
    bundles of sticks, 61
    chip abacus, 62,153–55
    decimal squares, 265–66
    for fractions, 219
    fraction strips, 219
    measurement, 96, 102–3, 109–10
    number lines, See Number line
    place value pieces, 61,153 63
    set, 95, 102–3, 109–10
Modulo, 870–72
Modus ponens, 862
Modus tollens, 863–64
Moebius, A. F., 581
Moebius strip, 581
Moore, R. L., 613
Morawetz, Cathleen Synge, 613
Multibase pieces, 61
Multiple, 187
    common, 201
    least common, 201–3
Multiple-bar graphs, 417
Multiplication:
    algorithms, 158–63
    array model, 110
    associative property:
        for fractions, 245
        for integers, 334
        for rationals, 363
        for reals, 376
        for whole numbers, 111
    base five, 173
    Cartesian product approach, 110
    closure property
        for fractions, 245
        for integers, 334
        for rationals, 363
        for reals, 376
        for whole numbers, 111
    commutative property
        for fractions, 245

Multiplication *(Continued)*
for integers, 334
for rationals, 363
for reals, 376
for whole numbers, 111
decimals, 277
distributive property over addition, 113, 363
distributive property over subtraction, 114
duplication algorithm, 169
facts for whole numbers, 114
finger, 165–66
fraction of a fraction, 242
of fractions, 241–46
fraction times a whole number, 241–42
German low-stress algorithm, 167
identity property:
for fractions, 245
for integers, 334
for rational numbers, 363
for real numbers, 376
for whole numbers, 112
integers, 332–36
lattice method, 159
mental, 139–40
order of operations, 145
of a positive and a negative, 334
by powers of 10, 141, 269–70
properties of, 111–13, 245, 334, 363
property of zero, 113
rational numbers, 362–64
real numbers, 376
rectangular array, 110
repeated addition, 110
Russian peasant method, 169
thinking strategies, 114–15
tree diagram approach, 111
of two negatives, 334
of two positives, 334
whole numbers, 109–15
Cartesian product approach, 110–11
rectangular array approach, 110
repeated-addition approach, 109–10
tree diagram approach, 111
of zero, 336
Multiplicative cancellation property:
integers, 336
whole numbers, 121
Multiplicative compensation, 140
Multiplicative identity:
fractions, 245
integers, 334
rational numbers, 363
real numbers, 376
whole numbers, 114
Multiplicative inverse:
fractions, 245
rational numbers, 363
real numbers, 376

Multiplicative numeration system, 55
Multiplicative property of: probability, 504
Multiplying by opposites, 335
Multiplying/dividing by powers of 10, 141, 269
Multiplying by special factors, 141
Multiplying powers of 10, 141
Musical scales, 296
Mutually exclusive events, 493

N

Naming numbers, 63
Nano-, 630
Napier, John, 137, 271
Napier's bones, 137
Napier's "decimal point" notation, 271
National Council of Teachers of Mathematics, 3
National Longitudinal Study of Mathematical Abilities (NLSMA), 848
Natural numbers, 39
Negation, 858
Negative integer exponent, 338–40
Negative integers, 319
Negative rational numbers, 359
Negative real numbers, 375
Negative slope, 761
Net of a polyhedron, 881–82
Network, 875
Newton, Isaac, 12, 621
n-factorial, 531
n-gon, regular, 569
Nine-point circle theorem, 787
NLSMA, 848
Noah's ark, 641
Noether, Emmy, 86
Nondecimal numeration systems, 64–65
Nonstandard units, 623–24
Normal curve, 447–48
Normal distribution, 448–51
Notation:
decimal, 265, 271
expanded, 62, 65
function, 75
Napier's "decimal point," 271
scientific, 147, 339
set-builder, 39
*n*th percentile, 443
*n*th root, 377–78
on a calculator, 378
Null set, 39
Number of elements in a finite set, 52
Number-line approach, to ordering rational numbers, 366
Number(s):
abundant, 207
amicable, 207
base, 61
betrothed, 209
cardinal, 52

compatible, 140
composite, 185
counting, 16
defined, 52
decimal, 263–86
deficient, 207
Egyptian, 54
of elements in a set, 52
even, 16
of factors, 197–98
identification, 48
integers, 317–51, 345–46
irrational, 353, 374
line, 25, 52–53, 223, 320
mixed, 222
naming, 63
natural, 39
negative, 319
odd, 16
ordering, See Ordering
ordinal, 52
palindrome, 106
pentagonal, 28
perfect, 207
positive, 319
powers of, 16, 125
prime, 185
rational, 355–72
reading, 63
real, 355, 373–90
rectangular, 28, 74
relatively prime, 207
Smith, 210
square, 16
theory, 183–214
triangular, 25
whole, 39, 51–53, 93–132, 137–81
Number line:
fraction, 223
integer, 319–20
rational, 359
real, 375
whole, 52–53
Number theory, 183–214
composite numbers, 185
counting factors, 197–98
greatest common factor, 198–99
prime factorization method, 199
set intersection method, 199
least common multiple (LCM), 202
build-up method, 202–3
prime factorization method, 202
set intersection method, 202
prime numbers, 185
prime factorization, 186
Sieve of Eratosthenes, 185
tests for divisibility, 187–91
twin primes, 193
Numerals, 52
Braille, 60
defined, 52
Numeration system, 53–61

compatible, 140
additive, 54
Babylonian, 55–56
base, 61
Braille, 60
Chinese, 60
converting between bases, 65–66
decimal, 61
digit, 61
Egyptian, 54, 57
expanded form, 63
expanded notation, 63
grouping, 53
Hindu-Arabic, 61–68
Ionian, 58
Mayan, 56–57
multiplicative, 55
nondecimal, 64–67
placeholder, 55
place-value, 55
positional, 55
Roman, 54–55, 57
subtractive, 54
tally, 53–54, 57
zero, 56
Numerator, 218

O

Oblique:
circular cone, 604
cylinder, 603
prism, 601
regular pyramids, 601
Obtuse angle, 578
Obtuse triangle, 581
Octagon, regular, 569
Octahedron, 602
Odd:
degree, 877
numbers, 16
Odd perfect number conjecture, 183
Odds, 519–21
One-column front-end estimation, 142
One-stage tree diagrams, 510
One-to-one correspondence, 40
Operations:
in base five, 171–74
binary, 96
with irrational numbers, 389
order of, 141
with sets, 40–45
See also Addition; Subtraction; Multiplication; Division
Opposite of an integer, 32
Opposite of the opposite for rational numbers, 361
Opposite sides and angles of a parallelogram, 699
Opposites, multiplying by, 335–36
"Or" connective, 859
exclusive, 859
inclusive, 859
Ordered pairs, 44
functions as, 76

Ordering:
  decimals, 267
  fractions, 222–25
  integers, 340–42
    addition approach, 340
    number-line approach, 240
    property of less than and
      addition, 341
    property of less than and
      multiplication by a
      negative, 341
    property of less than and
      multiplication by a
      positive, 341
  rational numbers, 365–67
  real numbers, 377
  whole numbers, 52–53,123–25
Order of operations, 145
Order properties, See Less than
Ordinal numbers, 51
Organizing/picturing information,
  415–27
  central tendency, measuring,
    437–43
  charts and graphs, 417–25
  dispersion, measuring, 443–46
  distributions, 447–51
  histograms, 417
  line plots, 415
  misleading graphs/statistics,
    457–67
  stem and leaf plots, 416–17
  See also Charts and graphs
Orientation:
  clockwise, 806
  counterclockwise, 806
Origin, 391
Orthocenter, 731
  of a triangle, 785
Ounce:
  avoirdupois, 627
  liquid, 627
Outcome, 486
  equally likely, 488
Outliers, 424, 440, 453
  extreme, 453
  mild, 453

P

Pairs of equations, graphing,
  774–76
Palindrome, 106
Pan balance, 21
Papyrus, Ahmes, 215
Parabola, 782
Parallel lines, 576
  segments, 567–69
  slopes of, 763–64
Parallelograms, 554–55
  area, 647
  base, 647
  height, 647
  opposite sides and angles of,
    699
Parallels of latitude, 769
Parentheses, 146

Parsec, 640
Parthenon at Athens, 263
Partition of a set, 72
Partitive division, 115
Part-to-part comparison, 287
Part-to-whole comparison, 287
Pascal, Blaise, 137, 483
Pascal's adding machine, 137
Pascal's triangle, 16, 263, 508–9
  and combinations, 532–35
Path, 876
Pentagonal numbers, 28
Pentomino, 574
Percent, 297–304
  calculator, 145–47
  converting, 297–98
  decimals to, 297
  discount, 302
  equation approach, 301–4
  estimation using fractional
    equivalents, 298–99
  fraction equivalents, 297
  grade, 766
  grid approach, 299–300
  mark-down/up, 309
  mental math, 298–99
  origin of term, 297
  proportion approach, 300–1
  solving problems, 299–304
  symbol for, 297
Percentiles, 443
Perfect number, 207
Perimeter(s), 642–43
  circle, 643
  kite, 642
  parallelogram, 643
  polygon, 643
  rectangle, 643
  rhombus, 643
  square, 643
Period of a repeating decimal, 279
Permutations, 530–32
  n factorial, 531
Perpendicular, 554, 579
  bisector, 721–22
  line segments, 567–68
Perpendicular lines:
  slopes of, 764
Peta-, 630
Peter, Rozsa, 407
Pi, 371, 643
  area of a circle, 648
  circumference of a circle, 643
  mnemonic for, 385
Pick's theorem, 655
Pico-, 630
Pictographs, 422
Pictorial embellishments, 422–23
  deceptive, 466–67
Pie charts, 447–48
Pint, 627
Placeholder, 55
Place value, 55, 62, 65
Planar graph, 880
Plane, 576
  of symmetry, 608
Plato, 693

Platonic solids, 602–3
Point(s), 576–77
  between, 577
  collinear, 576
  distance between two, 577
  end-, 577
  mid-, 577
Points and lines in a plane, 576–77
Point-slope equation of a line,
  773
Polar coordinates, 780
Polya, George, 1–3, 128
  four-step process, 1, 4
Polygonal region, 588
Polygon(s), 569–70
  angle, 570
  central angle, 570
  concave, 570
  congruent, 828
  convex, 570
  constructible regular, Gauss's
    theorem for, 733
  diagonal, 567–68
  equiangular, 555
  equilateral, 555
  exterior angle, 570
  inscribed, 732
  interior angle, 570
  perimeter, 643
  regular, 569–70
  side, 569
  similar, 830
  tessellations in, 590
  vertices, 601
Polyhedra, 599–603
  apex, 601
  bases, 601
  convex polyhedron, 601
  defined, 599
  edges, 601
  Euler's formula, 602
  faces, 601
  lateral faces, 601
  oblique prism, 601
  oblique regular pyramids, 601
  Platonic solids, 602–3
  prisms, 601
  pyramids, 601
  regular polyhedron, 601–2
  right prism, 601
  right regular pyramids, 601
  semiregular polyhedron, 602
  vertices, 601
Pons Asinorum theorem, 693
Population, 468
Portability, 628
Positional numeration system,
  55, 57
Positive integers, 319
Positive rational number, 359
Positive real number, 375
Positive slope, 760
Pound, 627
Powell, J. H., 469
Power, 125
Powers, See Exponents
Powers of 10,

multiplying/dividing decimals
  by, 269
Precious Mirror of the Four
  Elements (Chu), 317
Prefixes, metric, 630
Prime:
  factorization, 185, 197–201
  factor test, 191
  Fermat, 732–33
  infinitude of, 205
  meridian, 769
  Mersenne, 192 ,196
  numbers, 185–87
  relatively, 207
  triples, 196
Prime factorization:
  greatest common factor (GCF),
    198–201
  least common multiple (LCM),
    201–2
Primitive Pythagorean triple, 387
Principles and Standards for
  School Mathematics, ix
Principal square root, 375
Prisms, 618, 663
  base, 601
  height, 663
  lateral face, 601
  oblique, 601
  rectangular, 672
  right, 601, 672
  surface area of right, 663
  triangular, 601
  volume, 663
Probability, 483 545
  additive property of, 504
  "birthday problem," 483
  of a certain event, 490
  coin tossing, 507–9
  combinations, 532–35
    and Pascal's triangle,
      534 35
  complement of an event, 493
  conditional, 521–23
  counting techniques, 530
  definition of, 488
  disjoint events, 493
  drawing with/without
    replacement, 503
  equally likely outcomes, 488
  event,486
  expected value, 518–19
  experimental, 490–91
  experiments, 486
  fundamental counting property,
    502
  geometric, 497
  of an impossible event,
    489–90
  multiplicative property of, 504
  mutually exclusive events, 493
  odds, 519–21
  outcome, 486
  Pascal's triangle, 508–9
  permutations, 530–32
  probability tree diagrams,
    502–9

Probability *(Continued)*
  properties of, 494
  sample space, 486
  and simple experiments,
    485–88
    computing probabilities in,
      488–94
  simulation, 484,516–18
  theoretical, 490
  tree diagrams, 500–9
    one-stage, 510
    two-stage, 510
Problem, 3
Problem of the points, 483
Problem solving, 1–34
  four-step process for, 1–5
    carry out plan, 4
    devise of plan, 4
    look back, 4
    understand the problem, 4
  successful problem solvers,
    suggestions from, 23–24
Problem-solving strategies, 5–23
  Do a Simulation strategy,
    484, 517
  Draw a Diagram strategy, 38,
    117–18, 124–25, 380,
    493, 501, 505, 507–8,
    519, 522, 580
  Draw a Picture strategy,
    10–12, 99, 111–12,
    225–26, 380–85, 587,
    701, 709, 740–42,
    783–85, 786, 840
  Guess and Test strategy, 5–7
  Identify Subgoals strategy, 694
  Look for a Formula strategy,
    414
  Look for a Pattern strategy,
    15–19, 127, 197–98, 280,
    324–25, 333, 338, 508–9,
    840
  Make a List strategy, 19–21
  Solve an Equation strategy,
    354, 785, 786
  Solve an Equivalent Problem
    strategy, 216
  Solve a Simpler Problem
    strategy, 21
  Use Cases strategy, 318
  Use Coordinates strategy, 756
  Use Dimensional Analysis
    strategy, 621, 635
  Use Direct Reasoning strategy,
    94, 868
  Use Indirect Reasoning
    strategy, 138, 206,
    373–74
  Use a Model strategy, 548,
    649, 662
  Use Properties of Numbers
    strategy, 184
  Use Symmetry strategy, 798
  Use a Variable strategy, 8–10,
    354, 650
  Work Backward strategy, 264,
    366

Product, 110
  of fractions, 242
  of integers, 332–33
  order of operations, 145
  of rational numbers, 362–63
  of whole numbers, 110
Proper factors, 207
Proper subset, 40
Properties:
  additive of probability, 504
  compass and straightedge, 718
  density of fractions, 225
  distance on a line, 577
  distributive, 113–14, 246, 335,
    363, 376
  exponents, 125–28, 379
  fraction addition, 233
  fraction multiplication, 245
  fundamental counting, 502
  inequalities, See Properties of
    less than and
  integer addition, 323
  integer multiplication, 334
  of isometries, 807
  of multiplication, 113, 245–46
  multiplication by zero, 113
  multiplicative of probability,
    504
  ordering integers, 341
  ordering rational numbers, 367
  ordering real numbers, 377
  of points and lines, 577
  rational-number addition, 360
  rational-number exponents,
    377–79
  rational-number multiplication,
    363
  real-number operations, 376
  reflexive, 71
  of similitudes, 829
  of size transformations,828
  symmetric, 71–72
  transitive, 72
  whole-number addition,
    95–100
  whole-number exponents,
    125–28
  whole-number multiplication,
    111–14
Properties of less than and
  addition:
    for fractions, 223
    for integers, 340
    for rational numbers, 367
    for real numbers, 377
    for whole numbers,124
  multiplication:
    by a negative for integers,
      341
    by a negative for rational
      numbers, 367
    by a negative for real
      numbers, 377
    by a positive for integers,
      341
    by a positive for rational
      numbers, 367

  by a positive for real
    numbers, 377
Proportion, 288–91
  defined, 277
  divine, 263
  extremes, 288
  means, 288
  rates, 288
  scaling up/scaling down, 290
Proportion approach, to solving
  percent problems, 300–1
Proportional mean, 736
Protractor, 578
Purser, Michael, 342
Pyramid, 601
  apex, 601
  base, 601
  Cheops, 831
  Giza, 237
  height, 677
  lateral face, 601
  Memphis, 831
  oblique regular, 601
  right regular, 601
  slant height, 665
  surface area, 677
  volume, 677
Pythagoras, 280, 353, 744
Pythagorean Proposition,
  The (Loomis), 734
Pythagorean theorem, 387,
  648–51, 693, 711, 842
  converse of, 742
Pythagorean triple, 372

Q

Quadrants, 392
Quadratic formula, 730–31
Quadratic functions, graphs of,
  393–94
Quadrilaterals, 553–55
  ASASA for congruent,
    698–700
  attributes of, 569
  isosceles trapezoid, 555
  kite, 554–55
  midquad theorem, 744
  parallelogram, 554–55
  rectangle, 554
  rhombus, 555
  square, 554
  tessellations, 590
  trapezoid, 555
Quadrillion, 63
Quart, 627
Quartile, 439
  lower, 439
  upper, 439
Quotient, 116–17

R

Radical, 377
  index of, 377
Radicand, 377
Radioactive decay, 395

Radius:
  circle, 570
  sphere, 604
Ramanujan, Srinivasa, 14, 211
Random guess and test, 6
Random number generator, 517
Range, 443
  data, 443
  estimation, 141–42
  functions, 75
Rate, 288
Ratio, 286–88
  defined, 286
  equality, 287
  extremes, 287
  golden, 263
  means, 287
  part-to-part, 287
  part-to-whole, 287
  rates, 288
  scaling up/down, 290
  whole-to-part, 287
  See also Proportion
Rational numbers, 355–72
  adding the opposite, 361
  addition, 357–61
  additive cancellation for, 361
  additive inverse property for
    addition, 360
  associative property for
    addition, 360
  associative property for
    multiplication, 363
  on a calculator, 362
  closure property for addition,
    360
  closure property for
    multiplication, 363
  commutative property for
    addition, 360
  commutative property for
    multiplication, 363
  cross-multiplication of
    inequality, 367
  defined, 356
  density, 621
  distributive property of
    multiplication over
    addition, 363
  division, 364–65
  equality, 356–57
  examples of, 356
  exponents, 377–79
  as extension of fractions and
    integers, 355–57
  identity property for addition,
    360
  identity property for
    multiplication, 363
  inequality, 379
  inverse for addition, 360
  inverse for multiplication, 363
  lowest terms, 357
  multiplication of, 362–64
  multiplicative inverse, 363
  negative, 359
  number line, 359

opposite of the opposite, 361
ordering, 365–67
positive, 359
properties of addition, 360
properties of multiplication, 363
properties of ordering, 367
reciprocal, 363
simplest form, 357
subtraction, 361–62
Ray, 577
Reading numbers, 63
Real number(s), 355, 373–90
  addition, 376
  algebra, 379–85
  coefficients, 380
  conditional equations, 379–80
  defined, 374
  division, 376
  equation, 379
  exponents, 378
  inequalities, 379
    solving, 384–85
  irrational numbers, 374
  multiplication, 376
  number line, 375
  operations, 376
  ordering, 377
  principal square root, 375
  properties of operations, 376
  properties of ordering, 377
  rational exponents, 377–79
  solution, 379–85
  square root, 376
  subtraction, 376
  variables, 379
Reasoning:
  direct, 94, 861
  indirect, 138, 206, 373–74
  inductive, 16
Reciprocal, 363
Recognition, 549
Rectangle, 554
  area, 644–45
  perimeter, 642–43
  squared, 330
Rectangular:
  array, 110
  numbers, 28, 74
  prism, 672
Reducing fractions, 220
Rees, Mina, 477
Reflection, 803–5
Reflection symmetry, 564, 566,
  608, 807
Reflex angle, 578
Reflexive property, 71
Region, 880
Regression line, 424
Regrouping, 100
Regular polygon (regular n-gon),
  586–88
  angular measures in, 586–88
  area of, 731–33
  central angle, 570
  constructible, 731–33
  exterior angle, 570, 578
  Fermat prime, 732–33

tessellations in, 588–91
  vertex angle, 570
Regular polyhedron, 601–2
Regular tessellations, 590
Reid, Constance Bowman, 211
Relations, 71–72
  arrow diagrams, 71
  defined, 71
  equivalence, 72
  partition, 72
  reflective, 71
  symmetric, 71–72
  transitive, 72
Relationships, 550
Relative complement of sets, 42
Relative frequency, 447
Relatively prime numbers, 207
Remainder, 117
Repeated addition, 109–10
Repeated subtraction, 117–18
Repeating decimals, 279
  calculator, 271, 279
  classifying, 278–81
  defined, 279
  fractions with repeating,
    nonterminating decimal
    representations, 266
  period, 279
Repetend, 279
Replacement:
  drawing with, 503
  drawing without, 503
Reuleaux triangle, 846
"Reversals" stage, 57
Rhind Papyrus, 215
Rhombus, 555
Riese, Adam, 271
Right angle, 555
Right circular cone, 603–4
  surface area of, 666
  volume, 677
Right circular cylinder, 603
  surface area of, 664
  volume, 675–76
Right distributivity of division
  over addition, 140
Right prism, 601
  surface area of, 663
  volume, 672–75
Right regular pyramids, 601
  surface area of, 665
  volume, 676
Right triangle, 581
  hypotenuse, 648–49
  legs, 648
Rigid motions, 799
Robinson, Julia Bowman,
  132, 211
Rod, 625
Roman numeral system, 93
Roman numeration system, 54–55
  as multiplicative system, 55
  as positional system, 55
  subtractive principle, 54
Roosevelt, Franklin, 469
Root:
  on a calculator, 376

nth, 377–78
  square, 191, 376
Rotation:
  angle of, 801–3
  center, 801–3
Rotation symmetry, 566, 807
Rounding, 143–44
  to compatible numbers, 144
  decimals, 269–70
  down, 143
  a five up technique, 143
  fractions, 236
  to the nearest even, 143
  truncate, 143
  up, 143
  whole numbers, 143–44
Rubik, Erno, 536, 668
Rubik's cube, 536,668
Run, 760
Russian Peasant algorithm, 169

S

Samples and bias, 468–69
  bias, defined, 468
  bias surveys, common
    sources of, 469
  population, 468
  sample, defined, 468
Sample space, 486
SAS congruence property, 697–98
SAS similarity property, 708
Scaffold method for division,
  161, 174
Scalene triangle, 554
Scaling:
  and axis manipulation, 458–60
  up/scaling down, 290
Scatterplots, 423–25
  correlation, 424
  outliers, 424, 440, 453
  regression line, 424
School Mathematics Study Group
  (SMSG), 848
Scientific notation, 147, 339
  characteristics, 339
  mantissa, 339
Scratch addition, 164
Second, 578
Segment(s):
  bisector, 721–22
  constructing line, 733–34
  congruent line, 555, 695
  copying, 718–19
  directed line, 800
  endpoints, 577
  equivalent directed line, 800
  length of, 641–42
  line, 555, 695
  midpoint, 719, 759
  parallel line, 567–69
  perpendicular line, 567–69
Segment lengths, constructing,
  733–34
Self-similarity, 710–11
Semiregular polyhedron, 602
Semiregular tessellations, 590

Sequence, 16
  arithmetic, 73, 89
  common difference, 73
  common ratio, 74
  Fibonacci, 29, 197, 390
  geometric, 73, 89
  initial term, 73
  terms, 16
Set-builder notation, 39
Set intersection method, 197–98
  greatest common factor (GCF),
    199
  least common multiple (LCM),
    202
Set(s), 39–51
  Cartesian product of, 44
  complement of, 42
  counting numbers, 39
  DeMorgan's laws, 47, 49
  difference of, 42
  disjoint, 40
  elements of, 39
  empty, 39
  equal, 39
  equivalent, 40
  finite, 45
  infinite, 45
  inherent rules regarding, 40
  intersection of, 41–42
  matching, 40
  members of, 39
  null, 39
  one-to-one correspondence, 34
  operations on, 40–44
  ordered pair, 44
  proper subset, 40
  relative complement, 42
  set-builder notation, 39
  subset, 40
  union of, 41
  universal, 40
  universe, 40
  Venn diagrams, 40
  whole numbers, 39
Shape identification, geometric
  shapes, 551–53
Shape(s):
  congruent, 827
  similar, 830
Shells and Starfish, 797
Shi-Ku, Chu, 317
Side, 554, 577
  included, 698
Side-angle-side (SAS) congruence
  property, 697–98
Side-angle-side (SAS) similarity
  property, 708
Side-side-side (SSS) congruence
  property, 700–1
Side-side-side (SSS) similarity
  property, 708
Sierpinski gasket (triangle), 610
Sierpinski triangle (gasket), 610
Sieve of Eratosthenes, 185, 192,
  195
Similarity of triangles, 706–17
  See also Triangles

Similar polygons, 830
Similar shapes, 830
Similitudes, 811
  properties of, 829
  similarity of shapes, 830
  transformation geometry, 830
  triangle similarity, 829
Simple closed curve, 569
Simplest form:
  fractions, 221
  rational numbers, 357
Simplifying fractions, 219–20
Simplifying rational numbers, 357
Simulation, 516–18
Simultaneous equations, 774–76
  methods of solving:
    elimination method, 778–79
    graphical method, 778
    substitution method, 778
Simultaneous solution, 775
Size transformation, 809–11
Skew lines, 598
Slant height, 666
  cones, 666
  pyramids, 665
Slide flip, 803
Slide rule, 137
Slope-intercept equation of a line, 772
Slope(s), 760
  and collinearity, 758
  of a line, 760
  of a line segment, 760
  negative, 761
  of parallel lines, 763–64
  of perpendicular lines, 764
  positive, 760
  rise, 760
  run, 760
  undefined, 760
  vertical line, 760
Smith, Steven B., 148
Smith number, 210
Smoot, Oliver, 636
SMSG, 848
Solution, 379
  equations, 379–85
  inequalities, 384–85
  simultaneous, 775
Solution set, 379
Solve an Equation strategy, 354, 785, 786
Solve an Equivalent Problem strategy, 216
Solve a Simpler Problem strategy, 21–22
Solving equations, 379–84
  balancing method, 380
  Cover Up strategy, 380
  Draw a Picture strategy, 380–82, 587
  Guess and Test strategy, 379–80
  simultaneous:
    elimination, 778–79
    graphically, 778
    substitution, 778
  to inequalities, 384–85

transposing, 384
Work Backward strategy, 380
Solving inequalities, 384–85
Soroban, 137
Special factors, multiplying by, 141
Spheres, 604, 662, 667
  center of, 604
  diameter of, 604
  great circle of, 667
  radius of, 604
  surface area of, 667
  volume of, 678
Spotlights in Technology:
  eManipulatives:
    Balance Beam
      Algebra, 383
    Base Blocks: Addition, 154
    Base Blocks: Subtraction, 158
    Chips Minus, 325
    Chips Plus, 320
    Congruence, 701
    Counterfeit Coin, 22
    Adding Fractions, 232
    Comparing Fractions, 224
    Dividing Fractions, 249
    Equivalent Fractions, 219
    Function Grapher, 394
    Geoboard, 646, 758, 764
    Histogram, 417
    Multibase Blocks, 65
    Number Line, 97
    Percent Gauge, 301
    Pythagorean Theorem, 650
    Scatterplots, 425
    Sieve of Eratosthenes, 186
    Simulation, 518
    Slicing Solids, 602
    Tessellations, 591
    Tower of Hanoi, 23
    Translation
      Transformations, 801
    Venn Diagrams, 42
  Geometer's Sketchpad:
    Circumcircle, 730
    Dynamic Pythagorean
      Theorem, 650
    Midquad, 744
    Name That Quadrilateral, 569
    Parallelogram Areas, 647
    Perpendicular Lines, 764
    Rectangle Area, 645
    Same Base, Same Height, Same Area, 646
    Size Transformation, 810
    Slope, 761
    Tree Height, 709
    Triangle Angle Sum, 580
    Triangle Inequality, 651
  Spreadsheets:
    Base Converter, 67
    Circle Graph Budget, 422
    Coin Toss, 491
    Consecutive Integer Sum, 9
    Cubic, 396
    Euclidean, 201

Function Machines and
  Tables, 76
Roll the Dice, 492
Scaffold Division, 161
Standard Deviation, 445
Sum of the Odds, 15
Spreadsheet, 76
Spreadsheet activities:
  Base Converter, 67
  Circle Graph Budget, 422
  Coin Toss, 491
  Consecutive Integer Sum, 9
  Cubic, 396
  Euclidean, 201
  Function Machines and
    Tables, 76
  Roll the Dice, 492
  Scaffold Division, 161
  Standard Deviation, 445
  Sum of the Odds, 15
Square, 554
  area of, 645
  centimeter, 630
  dekameter (are), 631
  foot, 626
  hectometer, 631
  inch, 626
  kilometer, 631
  lattice, 554
  magic, 14, 196
  meter, 630
  mile, 626
  millimeter, 631
  numbers, 16
  perimeter of, 642–43
  root, 191, 376
  tessellation, 588
  units, 625, 631
  units, English, 626
  units, metric, 630–31
  yard, 626
Square root, 191, 375–76
  on a calculator, 376
  irrational numbers, 375–76
  principal, 375
Squared rectangle, 330
Squared square, 330
SSS congruence property, 700–1
SSS similarity property, 708
Standard algorithms:
  addition, 153
  division, 159–61
  multiplication, 158
  subtraction, 155
Standard deviation, 443–46
  defined, 444
  unbiased, 456
Standard units:
  English system, 624–28
  metric system, 628–34
Statements, 864
Statistics, 413–82
  bar graphs, 417–20
  box and whisker plots, 439–43
  on a calculator, 439
  central tendency, measuring, 437–43

charts and graphs, 417–25
circle graphs, 447–48, 464–65
cluster, 416
deceptive pictorial
  embellishments, 466–67
dispersion, 443–46
distributions, 447–51
frequency, 416
gap, 416
histogram, 417
interquartile range (IQR), 440
line graphs, 420–21
lower quartile, 439
mean, 438
measures of central tendency, 437–43
median, 438
mode, 437
misleading graphs and, 457–67
normal curve, 448
normal distribution, 448–51
organizing/picture and
  information, 415–27
percentile, 443
pie chart, 447–48
range, 443
relative frequency, 447
samples and bias, 468–69
scaling, and axis manipulation, 458–60
standard deviation, 444
stem and leaf plot, 416–17
three-dimensional effects, 462–64
unbiased standard deviation, 456
z-score, 446–51
Stem and leaf plots, 416–17
  back to back, 416
Step functions, 397
Stevin, Simon, 271
Stiller, Lewis, 555
Straight angle, 578
Straightedge, 718–28
Straight line, See Line(s)
Strategy clues, 8
Strategy, defined, 4
  See also Problem-solving
    strategies
Subgoals, 694
Subset, 40
  number of elements in, 52
  proper, 40
Substitution method, 778
Subtract-from-the-base algorithm, 156
Subtraction:
  adding the complement, 161
  algorithms, 155–58
  in base five, 172–73
  cashier's algorithm, 168
  comparison approach, 103
  decimals, 275
  difference, 103
  equal additions algorithm, 168
  estimation, 236
  fractions, 234–35

integers, 324–27
  adding the opposite
    approach, 326–27
  missing-addend approach,
    326–27
  take-away approach, 324–25
  minuend, 103
  order of operations, 145
  rational numbers, 361–62
  real numbers, 376
  regrouping, 100
  standard algorithm, 155
  subtrahend, 103
  whole numbers, 103
    comparison approach, 103
    four-fact families, 103
    missing-addend approach,
      103
Subtractive principle, roman
  numeration system, 54–55
Subtrahend, 103
Sum, 96
  of fractions, 230–31
  of integers, 320–21
  order of operations, 145
  of rationals, 358
  of reals, 376
  vertex angles in a regular
    n-gon, 577
  vertex angles in a triangle,
    580
  of whole numbers, 96
Summands, 96
Supplementary angles, 579
Surface area, 662–68
  lateral, 662
  right circular cone, 666
  right circular cylinder, 664
  right prism, 663
  right regular pyramid, 665
  spheres, 667
Syllogism, hypothetical, 863–64
Symbols, See inside back cover
Symmetric property, 71
Symmetry, 564–67, 807–8
  axis of reflective, 564–65
  base angles, 566
  glide reflection, 808
  line of, 564
  plane of, 608
  Mira, 566
  reflection, 564, 608, 807
  rotation, 566, 807
  translation, 807–8
Synge, J. L., 613
Systematic guess and test, 6
Systeme International (SI),
  623, 628
System of equations, See
  Simultaneous equations

T

Table(s):
  functions as, 76
  truth, 858
Tablespoon, 627

Take-away approach, 102, 324–25
  integers, 324–25
  whole numbers, 103
Tally numeration system, 53–54,
  57
  grouping, 53
Tangent, 729
Tangram puzzles, 552
Taussky-Todd, Olga, 541
Taylor, Richard, 183
Tchebyshev, 190
Teaspoon, 627
Teller, Edward, 541
Temperature:
  Celsius (metric), 633
  Fahrenheit (English), 628
Tempered musical scale, 389
"Ten Commandments for Teachers"
  (Polya), 1
Tera-, 630
Terminal side of a directed angle,
  802
Terminating decimals, 266
Terms, 16
  initial, 73
  of a sequence, 16
Tessellations, 588–91
  dual, 592
  Escher-like, 808–9
  with hexagons, 589
  regular, 589
  with regular n-gons, 590
  semiregular, 590
  using equilateral triangles, 589
  using squares, 89
  using triangles, 589
  vertex arrangement, 589
  vertex figure, 598
Tests for divisibility, 187–91
  by 2, 187
  by 3, 189
  by 4, 188
  by 5, 187
  by 6, 190
  by 8, 188
  by 9, 189
  by 10, 187
  by 11, 189
  prime factor test, 191
Tetrahedron, 602
Tetromino, 11, 573
Theon of Alexandria, 749
Theorem, 126
Theoretical probabilities, 490
Thinking strategies:
  for whole-number addition,
    100–1
  for whole-number
    multiplication, 114–15
Thousand, 63
Thousandths, 265
Three-dimensional effects, 462–64
Three-dimensional shapes,
  597–604
  curved shapes, 603–4
  dihedral angle, 598
  planes, 597–98

polyhedra, 599–603
  skew lines, 598
Ton (English), 627
Tonne (metric), 633
Transformations, 799–811
  clockwise orientation, 806
  congruent polygons, 828
  congruent shapes, 827
  counterclockwise orientation,
    806
  defined, 799
  directed angle, 802
  directed line segment, 800
  equivalent directed line
    segments, 800
  geometric problem solving
    using, 839–42
  glide reflections, 806
  image, 799
  initial side, 802
  isometry, 799–807, 826–27
    distance preserving, 824
    glide reflections, 805–7
    properties of, 824
    reflections, 803–5
    rigid motions, 799
    rotations, 801–3
    translations, 799–801
    triangle congruence,
      822–28
  making Escher-type patterns,
    808–9
  measure of the directed angle,
    802
  similarity using, 828–31
    properties of size
      transformations, 828
    similar polygons, 830
    similar shapes, 830
  similitudes, 811, 829
    properties of, 829
  size, 828
  symmetry, 807–8
    glide reflection, 808
    reflection, 807
    rotation, 807
    translation, 807–8
  terminal side, 802
  triangle congruence using,
    822–28
Transformational geometry,
  797–853
Transitive property, 72
  less than for integers, 340
  less than for rational numbers,
    367
  less than for real numbers,
    376
  less than for whole numbers,
    124–25
Translation, 799–801
Translation symmetry, 807–8
Transposing, 384
Transversal, 579
Trapezoids, 555
  area of, 647–48
  base angles of, 555

height, 647
  isosceles, 555
Traveling Salesman Problem, 883
Traversable
  graph, 877
  Graph Theorem, 878
Tree diagrams:
  approach to multiplication, 111
  and counting techniques,
    500–2
  and the fundamental counting
    property, 502
  one-stage, 510
  probability, 502–9
  two-stage, 510
Triangle congruence, 695–701
  angle-side-angle (ASA)
    congruence, 698
  congruent angles, 695
  congruent line segments, 695
  correspondence, 695
  geometric problem solving
    using, 740–44
  opposite sides and angles of a
    parallelogram, 699
  side-angle-side (SAS)
    congruence, 697–98
  side-side-side (SSS)
    congruence, 700–1
  and similarity, 693–754
  using transformations, 826–27
Triangle inequality, 651
Triangles, 554
  acute, 581
  altitude of, 727
  angle sum in, 580–81
  area of, 647–48
  base, 647
  base angles of an isosceles, 566
  centroid of, 783
  circumcenter, 729
  congruence, 695–701
  congruence and Isometries, 826
  equiangular, 555
  equilateral, 554
  exterior angle, 570, 578
  five-con, 701
  height, 646
  incenter, 729
  inequality, 651
  isosceles, 554
  midsegment, 744
  obtuse, 581
  orthocenter, 731, 785
  Pascal's, 16, 263, 508–9
  properties, 829
  Reuleaux, 846
  right, 581
  scalene, 554
  Sierpinski, 710
  similarity, 706–17
  and similitudes, 829
Triangular numbers, 25
Triangular prism, 601
Trillion, 63
Triple(s):
  prime, 196

Triple(s): *(Continued)*
   primitive Pythagorean, 387
   Pythagorean, 372
Trisecting angles, 724
Troy units, 627
Truncate, 143
Truth table, 858
Turn, 840
Twin prime conjecture, 183
Twin primes, 193
Two-column front-end
     estimation, 142
Two-stage tree diagram, 510

U

Ulam, Stanislaw, 541
Ulam's conjecture, 183
Unbiased standard deviation, 456
Understand the problem, 4
Union of sets, 41
Unitary fractions, 238
Unit distance, 642
Unit fraction exponent, 378
Universal set, 40
Universe, 40
Unknowns, 8
Unlike denominators, 231,
   248–249
Upper quartile, 439
Use Cases strategy, 318
Use Coordinates strategy, 756
Use Dimensional Analysis
   strategy, 622, 635
Use Direct Reasoning strategy,
   94, 861
Use Indirect Reasoning strategy,
   138, 206, 373–74
Use a Model strategy, 548,
   649, 662
Use Properties of Numbers
   strategy, 184
Use Symmetry strategy, 798
Use a Variable strategy, 8–10,
   354, 650

V

Valid argument, 861
Value:
   absolute, 329
   expected, 519
   place, 5, 62, 65–66
Van Hiele, Pierre, 547, 549–51
Van Hiele-Geldorf, Dieke, 547,
   549–51
Van Hiele theory of development
   in geometry, 531–32
   analysis (level 1), 549–50

axiomatics (level 4), 551
deduction (level 3), 551
recognition (level 0), 549
relationships (level 2), 550–51
Variables, 8–10, 354
Variance, 443–44
Venn, John, 40
Venn diagrams, 40
   and conditional probability, 522
Vertex, 554, 577
   angle, 570, 577
   of a graph, 875
   of an angle, 554, 577
   arrangement, 589
   -edge graph, 875
   figure, 592
   of a polyhedron, 601
Vertical angles, 578
Vertical lines:
   equation, 760
   slope, 760
Vertical line test, 398
Vertices, polyhedron, 601
Vieta, Francois, 271
Volume, 672–80
   Cavalieri's principle, 678–80
   cones, 677
   cube, 673
   cylinders, 675–76
   English system of units,
     626–27
   formulas, See inside back cover
   measuring informally, 624
   metric system, 632–33
   prism, 672–75
   pyramid, 676–77
   right rectangular prism, 672–73
   sphere, 678
Von Neumann, John, 128, 132

W

Watt, 640
Weber, W. E., 31
Weight, English system of units,
   627
Weierstrass, Karl, 312
Weight:
   dram, 627
   grain, 627
   ounce, 627
   pound, 627
   ton, 627
Wells, H. G., 413
Whole number(s), 39, 51–53,
   93–132, 133–76
   addend, 96
   "less than" for, 124
   addition, 96, 97–100

additive cancellation, 108
additive identity, 100
algorithms, 149–52, 153–63
associative property for
   addition, 99
associative property of
   multiplication, 112
base of an exponent, 125
base five operations, 171–76
calculator, using, 145–47
Cartesian product approach,
   110
closure property for addition, 97
closure property for
   multiplication, 111
commutative property for
   addition, 97
commutative property for
   multiplication, 111
comparison approach, 103
difference, 103
distributive property of
   multiplication over
   addition, 113
distributive property of
   multiplication over
   subtraction, 114
dividend, 116
division algorithm, 117
division property of zero, 116
division, 115–18
division, 9s for, 155–63
divisor, 116–17, 187
estimation, 141–47
expanded notation, 62, 65–66
exponents, 66, 125–28
factors, 110, 187
four-fact families, 103
"greater than," 52
identity property for addition,
   99
identity property for
   multiplication, 112
measurement division, 115
mental math, 139–41
minuend, 103
missing addend, 103
missing factor, 116
multiples, 187
multiplication, 109–15
multiplication property of zero,
   113
multiplicative cancellation, 121
number line, 53
numbers and numerals, 51–53
ordering, 51–53, 123–25
partitive division, 115
power, 125
product, 110

properties of addition, 95–100
properties of multiplication,
   111–14
quotient, 116–17
reading, 63
rectangular array, 110
remainder, 117
repeated addition, 110
repeated subtraction, 117–18
rounding, 143–44
subtraction, 102–3
subtrahend, 103
summand, 96
take-away approach, 102–3,
   324–25
thinking strategies for addition
   facts, 100–1
thinking strategies for
   multiplication facts, 114
tree diagram approach, 111
writing, 63–64
zero as an exponent, 127
Whole-to-part comparison, 287
Wiles, Andrew, 183
Work Backward strategy, 254,
   380

X

x-axis, 391
x-coordinate, 391

Y

Yard, 625
   cubic, 626
   square, 626
y-axis, 391
y-coordinate, 391
y-intercept, 771
Young, Grace Chisholm, 348
Young, William, 348

Z

Zero:
   addition of, 321
   division by, 116
   division property of, 116
   divisors, 336
   as an exponent, 127
   factorial, 531
   identity for addition, See
     Identity property
   and Mayan numeration system,
     56–57
   multiplication by, 114
   multiplication property of, 113
z-score, 446–51

List of Symbols

Symbol	Meaning	Page
$\{\ldots\}$	set braces	39
$\{x|\ldots\}$	set builder notation	39
$\in$	is an element of	39
$\notin$	is not an element of	39
$\{\}$ or $\varnothing$	empty set	39
$=$	equal to	39
$\neq$	is not equal to	39
$\sim$	is equivalent to (sets)	40
$\subseteq$	is a subset of	40
$\not\subseteq$	is not a subset of	40
$\subset$	is a proper subset of	40
U	universal set	40
$\cup$	union of sets	41
$\cap$	intersection of sets	41
$\overline{A}$	complement of a set	42
$-$	difference of sets	42
(a, b)	ordered pair	44
$\times$	Cartesian product of sets	44
$n(\ldots)$	number of elements in a set	52
$<$	is less than	52
$>$	is greater than	52
$\leq$	less than or equal to	52
$\geq$	greater than or equal to	52
3_{five} (3_5)	three base five	64
a^m	exponent (m)	66, 125
$f(a)$	image of a under the function f	73
$\sim$	is approximately	144
$|$	divides	188
$\nmid$	does not divide	188
$n!$	n factorial	196
GCF	greatest common factor	201
LCM	least common multiple	202
$.\overline{abcd}$	repeating decimal	279
$a:b$	ratio	286
$\%$	percent	297
-3	negative number	319
$-a$	opposite of a number	320
$|a|$	absolute value	329
a^{-n}	negative integer exponent	338
$\sqrt{}$	square root	376
π	pi ($3.14159\ldots$)	376
$\sqrt[n]{}$	nth root	377

Symbol	Meaning	Page
$a^{1/n}$	nth root of a	377
$a^{m/n}$	mth power of the nth root of a	377
$\bar{x}$	mean	438
$P(A)$	probability of event A	488
$P(A|B)$	probability of ABC given B	522
nPr	number of permutations	531
nCr	number of combinations	533
$\overline{AB}$	line segment AB	564
$\angle ABC$	angle ABC	564
$\triangle ABC$	triangle ABC	564
$\overleftrightarrow{AB}$	line AB	576
AB	the length of segment $\overline{AB}$	577
$m\|l$	m is parallel to l	577
$\overrightarrow{AB}$	ray AB	577
$m(\angle ABC)$	measure of angle ABC	578
$l \perp m$	l is perpendicular to m	579
$\leftrightarrow$	correspondence	695
$\cong$	is congruent to	695
$\sim$	is similar to	707
$\overrightarrow{AB}$	directed line segment from A to B	800
T_{AB}	translation determined by $\overrightarrow{AB}$	800
$\measuredangle ABC$	directed angle ABC	802
$R_{O,a}$	rotation around O with directed angle of measure a	803
M_l	reflection in line l	803
M_{AB}	reflection in line AB	803
$S_{O,k}$	size transformation with center O and scale factor k	810
$T_{AB}(P)$	image of P under T_{AB}	822
$R_{O,a}(P)$	image of P under $R_{O,a}$	822
$M_l(P)$	image of P under M_l	822
$M_l(T_{AB}(P))$	image of P under T_{AB} followed by M_l	822
H_O	half-turn with center O	840
$\sim$	negation (logic)	858
$\wedge$	conjunction (and)	859
$\vee$	disjunction (or)	859
$\rightarrow$	implication (if-then)	860
$\leftrightarrow$	biconditional (if and only if)	861
$\oplus, \ominus, \otimes, \oslash$	clock arithmetic operations	869–70
$a \equiv b \bmod m$	a is congruent to b modulo m	871